The American Journey

A History of the United States

FIFTH EDITION
COMBINED VOLUME

DAVID GOLDFIELD
University of North Carolina, Charlotte

CARL ABBOTT
Portland State University

PETER H. ARGERSINGER
Southern Illinois University

VIRGINIA DEJOHN ANDERSON
University of Colorado, Boulder

WILLIAM L. BARNEY
University of North Carolina, Chapel Hill

JO ANN E. ARGERSINGER
Southern Illinois University

ROBERT M. WEIR
University of South Carolina

Upper Saddle River, New Jersey 07458

Library of Congress Cataloging-in-Publication Data

The American journey : a history of the United States / David Goldfield—[et al.]. —5th ed.
    p. cm.
  "Combined volume."
  Includes bibliographical references and index.
    ISBN 0-13-603281-8 (combined) — ISBN 0-13-603255-9 (v. 1) —
  ISBN 0-13-603256-7 (v. 2)
    1. United States–History. 2. United States—History–Software.
  I. Goldfield, David R.
  E178.1.A4925 2009
  973—dc22   2008040113

For our students, who helped us write this book.

Publisher: Charlyce Jones Owen
Executive Marketing Manager: Sue Westmoreland
Editorial Assistant: Maureen Diana
Operations Supervisor: Mary Ann Gloriande
Operations Specialist: Maura Zaldivar
Director of Media and Assessment: Brian Hyland
Media Editor: Sarah Kinney
Senior Art Director/Cover Design: Maria Lange
Interior Design: iDesign
AV Project Manager: Mirella Signoretto

Senior Managing Editor: Ann Marie McCarthy
Project Manager: Denise Brown
Full-Service Production and Composition: Patty Donovan/Pine Tree Composition, Inc.
Manager, Rights and Permissions: Zina Arabia
Manager, Visual Research: Beth Brenzel
Manager, Cover Visual Research and Permissions: Karen Sanatar
Image Permission Coordinator: Craig Jones
Printer/Binder: Courier/Kendallville
Cover Printer: Phoenix Color/Hagerstown

Cover art: "The Last Moments of John Brown": oil on canvas, detail, c. 1884, by Thomas Hovenden (American, 1840–1895). Abolitionist and activist John Brown hugs a black baby which has been handed to him by its mother as he is led from prison by armed soldiers.

Credits and acknowledgments from other sources and reproduced, with permission, in this textbook appear on appropiate page within text (or on page C-1).

Pearson Education LTD.
Pearson Education Singapore, Pte. Ltd
Pearson Education, Canada, Ltd
Pearson Education–Japan
Pearson Education Malaysia, Pte. Ltd

Pearson Educación de Mexico, S.A. de C.V.
Pearson Education North Asia Ltd
Pearson Education Australia PTY, Limited
Pearson Education, Upper Saddle River, NJ

10 9 8 7 6 5 4 3 2 1

Combined Edition
ISBN 13: 978-0-13-603281-6
ISBN 10:   0-13-603281-8

Examination Copy
ISBN 13: 978-0-205-66787-1
ISBN 10:   0-205-66787-2

Brief Contents

CONTENTS

3

A MEETING OF CULTURES   57

4

ENGLISH COLONIES IN AN AGE OF EMPIRE 1660s–1763   85

5

IMPERIAL BREAKDOWN 1763–1774   117

6

THE WAR FOR INDEPENDENCE 1774–1783   141

VOICES FROM THE AMERICAN JOURNEY:
JOHN LAURENS   141

7

THE FIRST REPUBLIC 1776–1789   169

VOICES FROM THE AMERICAN JOURNEY:
WILLIAM SHEPARD   169

8

A NEW REPUBLIC AND THE RISE OF PARTIES 1789–1800   197

VOICES FROM THE AMERICAN JOURNEY:
WILLIAM MACLAY   197

9

THE TRIUMPH AND COLLAPSE OF JEFFERSONIAN REPUBLICANISM 1800–1824   221

VOICES FROM THE AMERICAN JOURNEY:
ROSALIE CALVERT   221

13

THE WAY WEST   373

VOICES FROM THE AMERICAN JOURNEY:
GEORGE CATLIN   373

14

THE POLITICS OF SECTIONALISM
1846–1861   403

VOICES FROM THE AMERICAN JOURNEY:
HARRIET BEECHER STOWE   403

15

BATTLE CRIES AND FREEDOM SONGS THE CIVIL WAR 1861–1865   439

16

RECONSTRUCTION 1865–1877   481

17

A NEW SOUTH: ECONOMIC PROGRESS AND SOCIAL TRADITION 1877–1900   513

18

INDUSTRY, IMMIGRANTS, AND CITIES 1870–1900   547

19

TRANSFORMING THE WEST 1865–1890   583

20

POLITICS AND GOVERNMENT 1877–1900 615

21

THE PROGRESSIVE ERA 1900–1917 643

22

CREATING AN EMPIRE 1865–1917   679

23

AMERICA AND THE GREAT WAR
1914–1920   709

24

TOWARD A MODERN AMERICA: THE 1920S   739

25

THE GREAT DEPRESSION AND THE NEW DEAL 1929–1939   771

26

WORLD WAR II 1939–1945   807

VOICES FROM THE AMERICAN JOURNEY:
ENRICO FERMI   807

27

THE COLD WAR AT HOME AND ABROAD 1946–1952   843

VOICES FROM THE AMERICAN JOURNEY:
BERNADETTE WHEELER   843

28

THE CONFIDENT YEARS
1953–1964   873

VOICES FROM THE AMERICAN JOURNEY:
MELBA PATILLO   873

29

SHAKEN TO THE ROOTS 1965–1980
909

VOICES FROM THE AMERICAN JOURNEY:
BUZZ ALDRIN AND NEIL ARMSTRONG   909

30

THE REAGAN REVOLUTION AND A CHANGING WORLD 1981–1992   945

VOICES FROM THE AMERICAN JOURNEY:
CELIA NOUP   945

31

COMPLACENCY, CRISIS, AND GLOBAL REENGAGEMENT 1993–2007   981

VOICES FROM THE AMERICAN JOURNEY:
JOHN MCNAMARA   981

SPECIAL FEATURES

American Views

Global Perspectives

From Then To Now

Maps

*Denotes a map exploration is available on *myhistorylab* and online.

Figures and Tables

FIGURES

TABLES

Overview Tables

PREFACE

The path that led us to *The American Journey* began in the classroom with our students. Our goal is to make American history accessible to students. The key to that goal—the core of the book—is a strong clear narrative. American history is a compelling story, and we seek to tell it in an engaging, forthright way. But we also provide students with an abundance of tools to help them absorb that story and put it in context. We introduce them to the concerns of the participants in America's history with primary source documents. The voices of contemporaries open each chapter, describing their own personal journeys toward fulfilling their dreams, hopes, and ambitions as part of the broader American journey. These voices provide a personal window on our nation's history, and the themes they express resonate throughout the narrative.

But if we wrote this book to appeal to our students, we also wrote it to engage their minds. We wanted to avoid academic trendiness, particularly the restricting categories that have divided the discipline of history over the last twenty years or so. We believe that the distinctions involved in the debates about multiculturalism and identity, between social and political history, between the history of the common people and the history of the elite, are unnecessarily confusing.

What we seek is integration—to combine political and social history, to fit the experience of particular groups into the broader perspective of the American past, to give voice to minor and major players alike because of their role in the story we have to tell.

Approach

In telling our story, we had some definite ideas about what we might include and emphasize that other texts do not—information we felt that the current and next generations of students will need to know about our past to function best in a new society.

CHRONOLOGICAL ORGANIZATION   A strong chronological backbone supports the book. We have found that the jumping back and forth in time characteristic of some American history textbooks confuses students. They abhor dates but need to know the sequence of events in history. A chronological presentation is the best way to be sure they do.

GEOGRAPHICAL LITERACY   We also want students to be geographically literate. We expect them not only to know what happened in American history, but where it happened as well. Physical locations and spatial relationships were often important in shaping historical events. The abundant maps in *The American Journey*—all numbered and called out in the text—are an integral part of our story.

REGIONAL BALANCE   *The American Journey* presents balanced coverage of all regions of the country. In keeping with this balance, the South and the West receive more coverage in this text than in comparable books.

POINT OF VIEW   *The American Journey* presents a balanced overview of the American past. But "balanced" does not mean bland. We do not shy away from definite positions on controversial issues, such as the nature of early contacts between Native Americans and Europeans, why the political crisis of the 1850s ended in a bloody Civil War, and how Populism and its followers fit into the American political spectrum. If students and instructors disagree, that's great; discussion and dissent are important catalysts for understanding and learning.

RELIGION   This text stresses the importance of religion in American society both as a source of strength and a reflection of some its more troubling aspects.

Historians mostly write for each other. That's too bad. We need to reach out and expand our audience. An American history text is a good place to start. Our students are not only our future historians, but more important, our future. Let their American journey begin.

Features of the Text

The American Journey includes an array of features designed to make American history accessible to students. It provides more learning tools than any other U.S. history text.

- The **Student Tool Kit** that follows this preface helps students get the most out of the text and its features. It introduces students to key conventions of historical writing and it explains how to work with maps, documents, and visuals.

- **Personal Journeys,** brief primary source excerpts, open each chapter. Consisting of letters, diary entries, and other first-hand accounts, these voices highlight the personal dimension of the American journey and show students the wealth and variety of experiences that make up this country's history. From Olaudah Equiano's narrative of his forced journey to Virginia as a slave, to the ultimate journey Sullivan Ballou made during the Civil War defending the Union, to Cambodian refugee Celia Noup's harrowing journey to California where she took her place as one of the thousands of new immigrants who are reshaping the face of our nation, **Personal Journeys** set the stage for the key themes that are explored in each chapter.

- The **American Views** box in each chapter contains a relevant primary source document. Taken from letters, diaries, newspapers, government papers, and other sources, these bring the people of the past and their concerns vividly alive. An introduction and prereading questions relate the documents to the text and direct students' attention to important issues.

- **From Then to Now,** relates important issues and events in each chapter to the issues and events of today, letting students see the relevance of history to their lives. In the fifth edition, this feature has been expanded to a two-page spread with thought-provoking visuals to support and enhance the narrative.

- **Global Perspectives,** included in each chapter, make an appropriate and substantive global connection that links the United States to other nations in the world, thereby enhancing students' understanding of America's development. *Global Perspectives* informs students that globalization is not something new. America was part of global trends long before we were a nation. This feature acknowledges that fact and places the American journey within a broader worldwide context. That journey not only influenced other countries and peoples, but, we in turn have been shaped by global economic, migratory, technological, and political trends.

- **Overview Tables** summarize complex issues.

- **Chapter Chronologies** help students build a framework of key events.

- **Key Terms** are highlighted within each chapter and defined in an alphabetical end of text glossary.

- **Review Questions** at the end of each chapter are organized by key subtopics in each chapter to help students review material and relate it to broader themes.

- A **Recommended Readings** section introduces students to relevant outside reading suggestions that expand on topics within the chapters.

- **Where to Learn More** sections, found at relevant places in the margin, and listed at the end of each chapter, describe important historical sites (both real and virtual) that students can visit to gain a deeper understanding of the events discussed in the chapter.

- Abundant **maps** help students understand the spatial dimension of history. The topographical detail in many of the maps helps students understand the influence of geography on history.

- **Illustrations and photographs**—tied to the text with detailed captions—provide a visual dimension to history.

Changes to the Fifth Edition

Every chapter has been thoroughly revised and improved with new special features as well as updated scholarship.

New to the Fifth Edition

Personal Journeys: References to additional documents from individuals that relate to the content of chapter. These additional voices are included in the *myhistorylab* website.

From Then to Now: This feature is now included in every chapter and includes references to additional documents related to the topic that are available on *myhistorylab*. These online *From Then to Now* activities provide research and writing opportunities for students.

Chapter 1
- **From Then to Now:** *The Disappearance of Cod off the Grand Banks*

Chapter 2
- **American Views:** *Powhatan's Speech to John Smith (1609)*
- **From Then to Now:** *Tobacco and the American Economy*

Chapter 4
- **Global Perspectives:** *Tea and Empire*
- **From Then to Now:** *The Diversity of American Religious Life*

Chapter 5 Imperial Breakdown
- **From Then to Now:** *The Boston Massacre and the Continuing Problem of Peaceful Crowd Control* uses contemporary accounts to examine the problems inherent in confrontations between unruly protestors and tense law-

enforcement officials as exemplified by the Boston Massacre and the recent clash between Los Angeles police and May Day marchers.

- **Global Perspectives:** *A Frenchman Reports on the American Reaction to the Stamp Act* provides perceptive observations by a French spy who reported on the American reaction to the Stamp Act.
- *New section and its accompanying documents:* New documents illustrate that not all was politics in this period. The memoir of a Virginia woman reveals her preoccupation with the health of her children, and a pastor's journal depicts his concern for the welfare of his congregation of Christian Indians in western Pennsylvania.

Chapter 6 The War for Independence

- **From Then to Now:** *Anti-War Churches* examines religiously based opposition to the Revolution and the present war in Iraq.
- **American Views:** *An American Surgeon Reflects on the Winter at Valley Forge, 1777–1778*
- A dramatic new illustration depicting Spanish operations on the Gulf Coast serves to underscore some of the global dimensions of the struggle.

Chapter 7 The First Republic

- **From Then to Now:** *Reshaping the Constitution* includes the debate in the Constitutional Convention over the process of amending the Constitution, the call of Antifederalists for a bill of rights, and the objections of Alexander Hamilton to adding a bill of rights to the Constitution.
- A new opening personal journey on the role of an African American, Moses Sash, in Shays's Rebellion.

Chapter 8 A New Republic and the Rise of Parties

- **From Then to Now:** *Advice for an Empire* includes documents on Washington's Farewell Address, President Wilson's Address to the League to Enforce Peace in 1916, and the main provisions of the NATO Alliance Treaty signed in April, 1949.

Chapter 9 The Triumph and Collapse of Jeffersonian Republicanism

- **American Views:** *Protest of French Settlers in Louisiana* on the protests of French settlers in Louisiana over the curtailment of their liberties when placed under American control following the Louisiana Purchase.

Chapter 10 The Jacksonian Era

- **From Then to Now:** *Voter Turnout* from the Jacksonian period on the role of political parties in stimulating voter participation and a modern assessment on the challenges facing new democracies across the world.

Chapter 11 Slavery and the Old South

- **From Then to Now:** *Overcoming the Economic Legacy of Slavery*

Documents include a travel account from 1857, a New Deal report on economic conditions in the South, and a current effort in a Southern state to adopt to the challenges of globalization.

Chapter 12 The Market Revolution and Social Reform

From Then to Now: *Immigration: An Ambivalent Welcome*

Documents on immigration that cover the fears of a Catholic conspiracy in the 1840s, views of immigrants as a racial threat in the 1920s, and current efforts at immigration reform.

Chapter 13 The Way West

From Then to Now: *Manifest Destiny and American Foreign Policy*

Documents covering a view in the 1840s of America's mission to the world, President Wilson's call in 1920 for the U. S. to defend democracy from global threats, and President George W. Bush's war message to Congress in March, 2003, on Iraq.

Chapter 14 The Politics of Sectionalism

More emphasis on religious sectarian strife as a factor in the political realignment of the 1850s.

Tied "Bleeding Kansas" more closely to the failed European Revolutions of 1848. This also reinforces the "Global Perspectives" feature in the chapter.

Expanded coverage of the Panic of 1857.

New coverage on the similarities between the North and South, and how slavery exacerbated the differences.

Chapter 15 Battle Cries and Freedom Songs: The Civil WAr

Global Perspectives: *Nationalism and Self-Determination in Europe*

Juxtaposes both the destructive and constructive elements of nationalism (as in the American Civil War).

From Then to Now: *Post Traumatic Stress Disorder* Expanded coverage of Clara Barton and women's entrance (North & South) into the nursing profession during the war and the obstacles they confronted.

New discussions of the concept of "Total War," the uprising of the Eastern Sioux in Minnesota in 1862, and creating a national economy.

Expanded discussion of the New York City Draft Riot.

Chapter 16 Reconstruction

New discussion on black gender relations.

Renamed section "Northern Indifference" now makes clear that racism was a national, not merely a southern phenomenon from the beginning of the Reconstruction era and was central to both the growing indifference toward violence against blacks and the willingness to believe southern white propaganda concerning Republican governments in the South.

New subhead called "Economic Transformation." The vast economic transformation of the 1870s affected the lives of millions of Americans, especially in the North where the transformation was most notable. This transformation pushed Reconstruction policy and the South generally to the back burner of public consciousness.

Chapter 17 A New South

Expanded coverage of the growth of evangelical Protestant churches in the South.

New discussion of black women's clubs in the section on Women's Clubs.

Chapter 18 Industry, Immigrants, and Cities

Added discussion on cultural institutions of immigrants.

New section, "The Ideal City," discusses one of the signal events of the late nineteenth century, the World's Columbian Exposition in Chicago and its meaning.

Chapter 19 Transforming the West

New material on the difficulty of settling in the West and on corporate and California aspects of the cattle industry.

Revised treatments of American Indians to direct more attention to Navajos and resistance to Americanization.

Chapter 20 Politics and Government

Added new material dealing with non-electoral politics, including a discussion on lobbying and legal activities of business and labor groups and a discussion of Christian reformers seeking to promote morality through government action.

Expanded discussion on Southern Populism (including a reference to Texas Populists).

Chapter 21 The Progressive Era

New **Global Perspective:** *The New Zealand Way* discusses that country's reform initiatives and their influence in the United States.

Revised discussion of woman suffrage to emphasize its centrality to progressivism.

Revised discussions of muckrakers and of progressive attitudes toward immigration to include new material.

Revised discussion of Wilson's presidency to clarify his attitudes toward government.

Chapter 22 Creating an Empire

Revised discussions of Secretaries of State Seward and Blaine.

Revised discussion of U.S.- Latin American relations.

Chapter 23 America and the Great War, 1914-1920

New opening journey: excerpts from speeches by Woodrow Wilson calling for a declaration of war and from Senator Robert LaFollette opposing U.S. intervention. They suggest different journeys for America's future, point up the opposition to an unpopular war, and correspond to several critical themes in the chapter, including the government's efforts to build support for the war.

The new opening discussion highlights Wilson's ultimate failure at peacemaking in Versailles.

Chapter 24 Toward a Modern America, The 1920s

More information on religion in the cultural conflicts of the 1920s.

New **American Views:** Features Aimee Semple McPherson, the remarkably popular female evangelist who defied traditional roles and embraced modern marketing techniques in broadcasting her religious message.

Chapter 26 World War II

Expanded coverage of World War II homefront.

Deepened coverage of women, Native Americans, and Latinos in the war effort.

Chapter 27 The Cold War at Home and Abroad

Incorporates new discoveries about the character and extent of Cold War esponiage.

Chapter 29 Shaken to the Roots

Rewritten sections on urban violence and minority self-determination in the later 1960s.

Chapter 30 The Reagan Revolution and a Changing World

New tables on U.S. cities compared to world cities and on economic status by ethnicity and race.

Deepened discussion of relations between religious belief and political action.

Chapter 31 Complacency and Crisis

Reduced coverage of domestic politics during Clinton administration

Expanded and updated coverage of Bush administration domestic and foreign policy.

Supplementary Instructional Materials

The American Journey comes with an extensive package of supplementary print and multimedia materials for both instructors and students.

Print Supplements

Instructor's Resource Manual   A time-saver in developing and preparing lecture presentations, the *Instructor's Resource Manual* contains chapter outlines, detailed chapter overviews, lecture outlines, topics for discussion, and information about audiovisual resources.

Test Item File   The test item file contains more than 1,500 multiple-choice, identification, matching, true-false, and essay test questions and 10–15 questions per chapter on the maps found in each chapter.

Prentice Hall Test Generator   Suitable for both Windows and Macintosh environments, this commerical-quality, computerized test-management program allows instructors to select items from the test-item file and design their own exams. Available at www.ivc.com for download.

Transparency Package   Over 100 full-color transparency acetates of all the maps, charts, and graphs in the text are available as transparency acetates for use in the classroom.

American Stories: Biographies in United States History (Volume I and II)   This two-volume collection of sixty-two biographies provides insight into the lives and contributions of key figures as well as ordinary citizens to American history. Introductions, pre-reading questions, and suggested resources helps students connect the relevance of these individuals to historical events.

Retrieving the American Past: A Customized U.S. History Reader   This collection of documents is an on-demand history database written and developed by leading historians and educators. It offers eighty-six compelling modules on topics in American history, such as "Women on the Frontier," "The Salem Witchcraft Scare," "The Age of Industrial Violence," and "Native American Societies, 1870–1995." Approximately thirty-five pages in length, each module includes an introduction, several primary documents and secondary sources, follow-up questions, and recommendations for further reading. Instructor-originated material, including other readings and exercises, can be incorporated. Contact your local Prentice Hall representative for more information about this custom-publishing option.

Prentice Hall and Penguin Bundle Program   Prentice Hall is pleased to provide adopters of *The American Journey* with an opportunity to receive significant discounts when copies of the text are bundled with Penguin titles in American history. Contact your local Prentice Hall representative for details.

Multimedia Supplement

PEARSON
myhistorylab

Myhistorylab   www.myhistorylab.com
MyHistoryLab means access to a wealth of study resources. Organized by major sections within chapters, these resources focus students using an easy-to-use learning system—**Read, Review and Assess, Interact,** and **Research**—that will help them to reinforce and apply what they are learning in class and from the text.

For Students

- Over 300 primary source documents with questions for analysis, classic works from the **History Bookshelf** like Thomas Paine's *Common Sense,* and the e-textbook version of *The American Journey* give students the opportunity to explore historical events in more depth. The e-book online makes the textbook accessible for study and review while students are working with *MyHistoryLab*.
- Chapter review materials include a study guide, learning objectives, PPT review presentations, overview activities, and key term flashcards to help students master the contents of the textbook and prepare for exams. In addition, students have access to **The Tutor Center,** where they can obtain one-on-one assistance with *MyHistorylab* and a **History Toolkit** for guidance on how to read and analyze documents. Each chapter includes pre- and post-tests self-study quizzes with targeted feedback for review and testing of content mastery.
- Hands-on activities and exercises let students explore content in the text in more depth and experience history beyond the textbook. *Exploring America* and other interactive learning activities, map explorations, animations, audio, and videos take students into the key events that have shaped our nation and strengthen geographic literacy and document analysis skills.
- From finding the right articles and journals, to citing sources, drafting and writing effective papers, and completing research assignments, students will turn to Pearson's **Research Navigator**™ for help with the research process.

For Instructors

For instructors using course management, *MyHistoryLab* means access to the student's resources, *and* all of the instructional material available to use in teaching with the text, including the instructor's manual, the test item file, images, maps, charts, and graphs from the text, video and audio clips, and Powerpoint™ lecture presentations and questions for use with CRS technology in the classroom. These are resources are also available to download from the Pearson Instructor Resource Center online at www.irc.com.

ACKNOWLEDGMENTS

We would like to thank the reviewers whose thoughtful and often detailed comments helped shape this fourth edition and the previous editions of *The American Journey:*

Alfred Hunt, SUNY Purchase
Andrew Cayton, Miami University
Andrew Wallace, Northern Arizona University
Armand LaPotin, SUNY Oneonta
Benjamin Newcomb, Texas Technological University
Betsy Powers, Montgomery College
Bill Cecil-Fronsman, Washburn University
Brian Wills, Clinch Valley Community College
Bryan LeBeau, Creighton University
Bufford Satcher, University of Arkansas at Pine Bluff
Caroline Cox, University of the Pacific
Charles Bolton, University of Arkansas at Little Rock
Chris Padgett, Weber State University
Christopher Moss, University of Texas at Arlington
Christopher Phillips, Emporia State University
Colleen O'Connor, San Diego Mesa College
Craig Ferguson, Oklahoma Community College
Dale Carnagey, Blinn College
Dale Schmitt, East Tennessee State University
David Aldstadt, Houston Community College
David Castle, Ohio University, Eastern Campus
David Conrad, Southern Illinois University
David G. Hogan, Heidelberg College
David Hamilton, University of Kentucky
David McFadden, Fairfield University
David Parker, Kennesaw State College
David Sloan, University of Arkansas
Dean Dunlap, Rose State College
Donald Dewey, California State University
Donald Jacobs, Northeastern University
Donald McCoy, University of Kansas
E. Wayne Carp, Pacific Lutheran University
Ed Lukes, Hillsborough Community College
Edward Weller, San Jacinto College, South
Elizabeth Nybakken, Mississippi State University
Emily Teipe, Fullerton College
Eric J. Bolsteri, University of Texas at Arlington

Eugene Berwanger, Colorado State University
Eugene Demody, Cerritos College
Frank Marmolejo, Irvine Valley College
Frank Siltman, U.S. Military Academy
Frank Towers, Clarion University
Fred Blue, Youngstown State University
Frederick Jaher, University of Illinois
Gary Reichard, Florida Atlantic University
Gary Topping, Salt Lake Community College
Gene Kirkpatrick, Tyler Junior College
George Gerdow, Northeastern Illinois University
Gerald Ghelfi, Rancho Santiago College
Gerald MacFarland, University of Massachusetts
Gilbert Cruz, Glendale Community College
Gregory Goodwin, Bakersfield College
Gwendolyn Hall, Rutgers University
Hal Rothman, University of Nevada, Las Vegas
Harland Hagler, University of North Texas
Harmon Mothershead, Northwest Missouri State University
Harry Bralley, Surry Community College
Harry Ward, University of Richmond
Henry Sage, Northern Virginia Community College, Alexandria
Henry William Brands, Texas A&M University
Howard Rock, Florida International University
Ira Gruber, U.S. Military Academy
Iris Engstrand, University of San Diego
J. Edward Lee, Winthrop University
J.B. Smallwood, University of North Texas
James Bradford, Texas A&M University
James Goode, Grand Valley State University
James Matray, New Mexico State University
James Seymour, CY-Fair
James Whittenberg, College of William and Mary
James Woods, Georgia Southern University
Janet Allured, McNeese State University
Jay Fell, University of Colorado
JoAnn Carpenter, Florida Community College
Joe Hapak, Moraine Valley Community College
John Chalberg, Normandale Community College
John Ingham, University of Toronto

John Johnson, University of Northern Iowa
John LaSaine, University of Georgia
John Rector, Western Oregon State University
John Wiseman, Frostburg State University
Jonathan Earle, University of Kansas
Joseph Adams, Saint Louis Community College
Joseph Devine, Stephen F. Austin State University
Joseph E. King, Texas Tech University
Joseph Reidy, Howard University
Juli Jones, St. Charles Community College
Karen Miller, Oakland University
Kay Pulley, Trinity Valley Community College
Ken Weatherbie, Del Mar College
Kenneth Stevens, Texas Christian University
LaShonda Mims, Central Piedmont Community College
Laura Graves, South Plains College
Lawrence Kohl, University of Alabama at Tuscaloosa
Leflett Easley, Campbell University
Leo Lyman, Victor Valley College
Leonard Dinnerstein, University of Arizona
Light T. Cummins, Austin College
Louis Gimelli, Eastern Michigan University
Marilyn Geiger, Washburn University
Mark Grimsley, Ohio State University
Mark Leff, University of Illinois, Urbana-Champaign
Mark Summers, University of Kentucky
Mark Wyman, Illinois State University
Marvin Dulaney, University of Texas at Arlington
Michael Batinski, Southern Illinois University
Michael Bradley, Motlow State Community College
Michael Krenn, University of Miami
Michael Krutz, Southeastern Louisiana University
Michael Schaller, University of Arizona
Michael Weiss, Linn-Benton Community College
Michael Welsh, University of Northern Colorado
Myles Clowers, San Diego City College
Nancy Gabin, Purdue University
Nancy Shoemaker, University of Connecticut
Nancy Smith Midgette, Elon College
Nancy Zen, Central Oregon Community College
Neal Brooks, Essex Community College
Neil York, Brigham Young University
Norman Markowitz, Rutgers University
Norman Raiford, Greenville Technical College
Otis Miller, Belleville Area College
Paul K. Davis, University of Texas at San Antonio
Paula Trekel, Allegheny College
Peggy Pascoe, University of Utah
Peter C. Mancell, University of Kansas
Priscilla Jackson-Evans, Longview Community College
Quintard Taylor, University of Oregon

Ralph Goodwin, East Texas State University
Randolph Campbell, University of North Texas
Rebecca Shoemaker, Indiana State University
Richard Brown, University of Connecticut
Richard Crepeau, University of Central Florida
Richard Lowe, University of North Texas
Richard Sadler, Weber State University
Rick Elder Bay Mills Community College
Robert Cray, Montclair State College
Robert Greene, Morgan State University
Robert Hinkle, Lexington Community College
Robert LaPorte, North Texas University
Robin Fabel, Auburn University
Ronald Hatzenbuchler, Idaho State University
Ronald McArthur, Atlantic Community College
Ronald Reitvald, California State University, Fullerton
Ronald Schultz, University of Wyoming
Samuel Crompton, Holyoke Community College
Sandra Schackel, Boise State University
Scott Garrett, Paducah Community College
Scott Martin, Bowling Green State University
Sheri David, Northern Virginia Community College
Sherry Smith, University of Texas at El Paso
Stanley Underal, San Jose University
Stephen Stein, University of Memphis
Stephen Webre, Louisiana Tech University
Steve Haley, Shelby State Community College
Terry Bilhartz, Sam Houston State University
Thomas C. Reeves, University of Wisconsin, Parkside
Thomas L. Powers, University of South Carolina, Sumter
Thomas McLuen, Spokane Falls Community College
Timothy D. Hall, Central Michigan University
Timothy Morgan, Christopher Newport University
Tom Bryan, Alvin Community College
Tyler Anbinder, George Washington University
Wade Shaffer, West Texas A&M
Wendy St. Jean, Dickinson College
Wilbur Johnson, Rock Valley College
William Allison, Weber State University
William Corbett, Northeastern State University
William Paquette, Tidewater Community College
William Stockton, Johnson County Community College
William Tanner, Humbolt State University
William Young, Johnson County Community College
Worth Robert Miller, Southwest Missouri State University
Yasuhide Kawashima, University of Texas at El Paso
Yvonne Johnson, Central Missouri State University

All of us are grateful to our families, friends, and colleagues for their support and encouragement. Jo Ann and Peter Argersinger would like in particular to thank Anna

Champe, Linda Hatmaker, and John Willits; William Barney thanks Pamela Fesmire and Rosalie Radcliffe; Virginia Anderson thanks Fred Anderson, Kim Gruenwald, Ruth Helm, Eric Hinderaker, and Chidiebere Nwaubani; and David Goldfield thanks Frances Glenn and Jason Moscato, Jim Miller, Sylvia Mallory, and Sally Constable played key roles in the book's inception and initial development.

Finally, we would like to acknowledge the members of our Prentice Hall family. They are not only highly competent professionals but also pleasant people. We regard them with affection and appreciation. None of us would hesitate to work with this fine group again. We would especially like to thank our editorial team: Charlyce Jones Owen, Publisher; Priscilla McGeehon, VP/Publisher; our marketing team: Sue Westmoreland, Executive Marketing Manager, and Brandy Dawson, Director of Marketing; our production team: Anne Marie McCarthy, Patty Donovan, Pine Tree Composition, Denise Brown, Production Liaison, Maura Zaldovar, Manufacturing Manager, and Mary Ann Gloriande, Manufacturing; and Yolanda deRooy, President of Prentice Hall's Humanities and Social Sciences division.

DG
CA
VDJA
JEA
PHA
WLB
RMW

About the Authors

David Goldfield received his Ph.D. in history from the University of Maryland. Since 1982 he has been Robert Lee Bailey Professor of History at the University of North Carolina in Charlotte. He is the author or editor of thirteen books on various aspects of southern and urban history. Two of his works—*Cotton Fields and Skyscrapers: Southern City and Region, 1607–1980* (1982) and *Black, White, and Southern: Race Relations and Southern Culture, 1940 to the Present* (1990)—received the Mayflower Award for nonfiction and were nominated for the Pulitzer Prize in history. His most recent book is *Still Fighting the Civil War: The American South and Southern History* (2002). When he is not writing history, Dr. Goldfield applies his historical craft to history museum exhibits, voting rights cases, and local planning and policy issues.

Carl Abbott is a professor of Urban Studies and planning at Portland State University. He taught previously in the history departments at the University of Denver and Old Dominion University and held visiting appointments at Mesa College in Colorado and George Washington University. He holds degrees in history from Swarthmore College and the University of Chicago. He specializes in the history of cities and the American West and serves as co-editor of the Pacific Historical Review. His books include *The New Urban America: Growth and Politics in Sunbelt Cities* (1981, 1987), *The Metropolitan Frontier: Cities in the Modern American West* (1993), *Planning a New West: The Columbia River Gorge National Scenic Area* (1997), and *Political Terrain: Washington, D.C. from Tidewater Town to Global Metropolis* (1999). He is currently working on a comprehensive history of the role of urbanization and urban culture in the history of western North America.

Virginia DeJohn Anderson is Professor of History at the University of Colorado at Boulder. She received her B.A. from the University of Connecticut. As the recipient of a Marshall Scholarship, she earned an M.A. degree at the University of East Anglia in Norwich, England. Returning to the United States, she received her A.M. and Ph.D. degrees from Harvard University. She is the author of *New England's Generation: The Great Migration and the Formation of Society and Culture in the Seventeenth Century* (1991) and several articles on colonial history, which have appeared in such journals as the *William and Mary Quarterly* and the *New England Quarterly*. Her most recent book is *Creatures of Empire: How Domestic Animals Transformed Early America* (2004).

Jo Ann E. Argersinger received her Ph.D. from George Washington University and is Professor of History at Southern Illinois University. A recipient of fellowships from the Rockefeller Foundation and the National Endowment for the Humanities, she is a historian of social, labor, and business policy. Her publications include *Toward a New Deal in Baltimore: People and Government in the Great Depression* (1988) and *Making the Amalgamated: Gender, Ethnicity, and Class in the Baltimore Clothing Industry* (1999).

Peter H. Argersinger received his Ph.D. from the University of Wisconsin and is Professor of History at Southern Illinois University. He has won several fellowships as well as the Binkley-Stephenson Award from the Organization of American Historians, and he is currently president of the Society for Historians of the Gilded Age and Progressive Era. Among his books on political and rural history are *Populism and Politics* (1974), *Structure, Process, and Party* (1992), and *The Limits of Agrarian Radicalism* (1995). His current research focuses on the political crisis of the 1890s.

William L. Barney is Professor of History at the University of North Carolina at Chapel Hill. A native of Pennsylvania, he received his B.A. from Cornell University and his M.A. and Ph.D. from Columbia University. He has published extensively on nineteenth century U.S. history and has a particular interest in the Old South and the coming of the Civil War. Among his publications are *The Road to Secession* (1972), *The Secessionist Impulse* (1974), *Flawed Victory* (1975), *The Passage of the Republic* (1987), and *Battleground for the Union* (1989). He is currently finishing an edited collection of essays on nineteenth-century America and a book on the Civil War. Most recently, he has edited *A Companion to 19th-Century America* (2001) and finished *The Civil War and Reconstruction: A Student Companion* (2001).

Robert M. Weir is Distinguished Professor of History Emeritus at the University of South Carolina. He received his B.A. from Pennsylvania State University and his Ph.D. from Case Western Reserve University. He has taught at the University of Houston and, as a visiting professor, at the University of Southampton in the United Kingdom. His articles have won prizes from the Southeastern Society for the Study of the Eighteenth Century and the *William and Mary Quarterly*. Among his publications are *Colonial South Carolina: A History, "The Last of American Freemen": Studies in the Political Culture of the Colonial and Revolutionary South,* and, more recently, a chapter on the Carolinas in the new *Oxford History of the British Empire* (1998).

When writing history, historians use maps, tables, graphs, and visuals to help their readers understand the past. What follows is an explanation of how to use the historian's tools that are contained in this book.

TEXT

Whether it is a biography of George Washington, an article on the Civil War, or a survey of American history such as this one, the text is the historian's basic tool for discussing the past. Historians write about the past using narration and analysis. Narration is the story line of history. It describes what happened in the past, who did it, and where and when it occurred. Narration is also used to describe how people in the past lived, how they passed their daily lives and even, when the historical evidence makes it possible for us to know, what they thought, felt, feared, or desired. Using analysis, historians explain why they think events in the past happened the way they did and offer an explanation for the story of history. In this book, narration and analysis are interwoven in each chapter.

MAPS

Maps are important historical tools. They show how geography has affected history and concisely summarize complex relationships and events. Knowing how to read and interpret a map is important to understanding history. Map 5-1 from Chapter 5 shows the British colonies on the eastern seaboard of North America in 1763, about twelve years before the American Revolution. It has three features to help you read it: a caption, a legend, and a scale. The caption explains the historical significance of the map. Here the caption tells us that in 1763 the British government sought to restrict colonial settlement west of the Appalachian Mountains to prevent conflict between colonists and Indians. Colonial frustration with this policy contributed to the outbreak of the American Revolution.

The legend and the scale appear in the lower right corner of the map. The legend provides a key to what the symbols on the map mean. The solid line stretching along the Appalachian Mountains from Maine to Georgia represents the Proclamation Line of 1763. Cities are marked with a dot, capitals with a star, and forts by a black square. Spanish territory west of the Mississippi River is represented in blue; territory settled by Europeans is represented in green. The scale tells us that 7/8ths of an inch on the map represents 300 miles (about 480 kilometers) on the

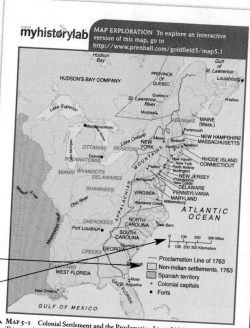

MAP 5-1   Colonial Settlement and the Proclamation Line of 1763
This map depicts the regions claimed and settled by the major groups competing for territory in eastern North America. With the Proclamation Line of 1763, positioned along the crest of the Appalachian Mountains, the British government tried to stop the westward migration of settlers under its jurisdiction and thereby limit conflict with the Indians. The result, however, was frustration and anger on the part of land-hungry settlers.

STUDENT TOOL KIT

ground. With this information, estimates of the distance between points on the map are easily made. Some maps also shows the topography of the region-its mountains, rivers, and lakes. This helps us understand how geography influenced history in this case. For example, the Appalachian Mountains divide the eastern seaboard from the rest of the continent. The mountains obstructed colonial migration to the west for a long time. By running the Proclamation Line along the Appalachians, the British hoped to use this natural barrier to separate Indians and colonists. A critical-thinking question asks for careful considersation of the spatial connections between geography and history.

MAP EXPLORATIONS

Many of the maps in each chapter are provided in a useful interactive version on the text's *Myhistorylab* website. These maps are easily identified by a bar along the top that reads "Map Explorations." An interactive version of Colonial Settlements and the Proclamation Line of 1763 can also be accessed at www.prenhall.com/goldfield5/map5.1. The interactive version of this particular map provides an opportunity to pan over an enlarged version of the territory in question. Cities, forts, settlements, and terrain are shown in detail. By moving the cursor north, south, east, or west one can gain a bird's-eye view of the entire region.

122   Chapter 5   Imperial Breakdown 1763–1774

Cunne Shote, one of three Cherokee chiefs who visited London in 1762, had this portrait painted there by Francis Parsons.

by giving them blankets that smallpox victims had used. Settlers in Paxton township (near modern Harrisburg, Pennsylvania) also committed atrocities. Angered by the Pennsylvania Assembly's lack of aggressive action against the Indians, the settlers lashed out at their peaceful neighbors, the Conestogas. Facing arrest and trial for this outrage, the so-called Paxton Boys marched on Philadelphia, threatening the Pennsylvania Assembly. Benjamin Franklin persuaded them to disperse. Despite the government's efforts, the Paxton Boys were never effectively prosecuted for their acts.

Pontiac's Rebellion and the Cherokee War were costly for both sides. Hoping to prevent such outbreaks, British officials began experimenting with centralized control of Indian affairs during the 1750s. Following the recommendations of the Albany Congress in 1754 (see Chapter 4), they had already created two districts, northern and southern, for the administration of Indian affairs, each with its own superintendent. The Proclamation of 1763, and the line it established restricting further white settlement, gave these officials increased responsibility for protecting the Indians against encroachments by settlers. But land-hungry Americans objected to efforts to keep them off Indian lands, and white traders resented restrictions on their activities. Centralized control of the fur and deerskin trades also proved to be expensive for the British government. British authorities therefore permitted several adjustments in the Indian boundary line and in 1768 returned supervision of the Indian

traders to the individual colonies. But such tacit recognition of local autonomy conflicted with imperial plans to restrict the powers of the colonial assemblies.

Curbing the Assemblies

As early as the 1750s, a dispute over the salaries of Anglican ministers known as the **Parson's Cause** prompted British officials to instruct the governor of Virginia not to sign any legislation that modified existing laws unless it contained a clause making the change inoperative until the king approved it. This restriction, which severely hampered the assembly's ability to respond to emergencies, alarmed Virginians who maintained that their legislators had the "Right to enact ANY Law they shall think necessary for their INTERNAL Government."

British authorities of course disagreed, and in 1764 Parliament bowed to the wishes of British merchants, who suffered from depreciating colonial paper money, by extending an earlier measure to forbid all American legislatures from making such issues legal tender. Because the Currency Act of 1764 came when most colonies were in an economic recession, Americans considered this step especially burdensome or, as one said, "downright Robbery." Worse, however, was yet to come.

The Sugar and Stamp Acts

In 1764, the British Parliament, under Prime Minister George Grenville, passed the American Revenue Act, commonly known as the **Sugar Act**. In order to generate increased revenue, the Sugar Act and accompanying legislation combined new and revised duties on colonial imports with strict enforcement provisions. In particular, Parliament sought to minimize motivation for smuggling by reducing the duty on French West Indian molasses by 50 percent.

The Sugar Act legislation also lengthened the list of enumerated products—goods that could be sent only to England or destinations within the empire—and required that ships carry elaborate new documentation of their cargoes; these requirements were a reasonable attempt to prevent illegal trade with other countries, but unintentional mistakes by a shipper could result in the unreasonable seizure of entire cargoes.

To enforce these cumbersome regulations, the British government continued to use the Royal Navy to seize smugglers' ships, a practice authorized by the Revenue Act of 1762 during the French and Indian War. It also ordered colonial customs collectors to discharge their duties personally. Previously, the collectors had often lived in England, leaving the work of collection in the colonies to poorly paid deputies, who were susceptible to bribes. Finally, Parliament gave responsibility for trying violations of the laws to a new vice-admiralty court in Halifax, Nova Scotia. Vice-admiralty courts had jurisdiction over maritime affairs. Unlike other courts, they normally operated without a jury and were therefore more likely to enforce trade restrictions. For this reason, because of the remote location of the Halifax court—getting to it would be a hardship—Americans immediately opposed this provision of the Sugar Act. In response, Parliament created three other vice-admiralty courts in the more conven-

VISUALS

Visual images embedded thoughout the text can provide as much insight into our nation's history as the written word. Within photographs and pieces of fine art lies emotional and historical meaning. Captions provide valuable information, such as in the example below. When studying the image, consider questions such as: "Who are these people?"; "How were they feeling?"; "What event motivated this photograph or painting?"; and "What can be learned from the backdrop surrounding the focal point?" Such analysis allows for a fuller understanding of the people who lived theAmerican journey.

STUDENT TOOL KIT

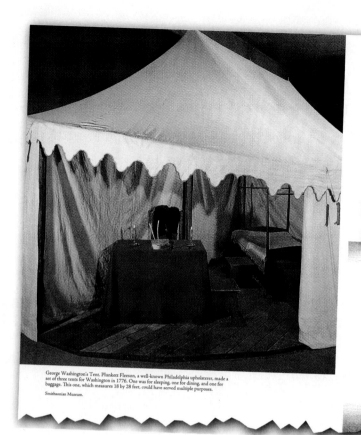

George Washington's Tent. Plunkett Fleeson, a well-known Philadelphia upholsterer, made a set of three tents for Washington in 1776. One was for sleeping, one for dining, and one for baggage. This one, which measures 18 by 28 feet, could have served multiple purposes.
Smithsonian Museum.

STUDY AIDS
Each chapter begins with a stunning visual and a Chapter Outline that provides a road map for study and review.

KEY TERMS/ GLOSSARY
Significant historical terms are called out in heavy type throughout the text and listed at the end of each chapter with appropriate page numbers. All key terms in the text are listed alphabetically and defined in a glossary at the end of the book.

STUDENT TOOL KIT

OVERVIEW

Predominant Colonial Labor Systems, 1750

	Colony	Labor System
New England	Massachusetts	Family farms
	Connecticut	Family farms
	New Hampshire	Family farms
	Rhode Island	Family farms
Middle Colonies	New York	Family farms, tenancy
	Pennsylvania and	Indentured servitude, tenancy, family farms
	Delaware	
	New Jersey	Family farms, tenancy
South	Maryland	Slavery
	Virginia	Slavery
	North Carolina	Family farms, slavery

OVERVIEWS

The Overview Tables in this text are a special feature designed to highlight and summarize important topics within a chapter. The Overview table shown here, for example, shows the predominant colonial labor systems in 1750 by geographic area.

CHRONOLOGY

1861	Tsar Alexander II frees the serfs of Russia.
1863	Lincoln proposes his Ten Percent Plan.
1864	Congress proposes the Wade-Davis Bill.
1865	Sherman issues Field Order No. 15.
	Freedmen's Bureau is established.
	Andrew Johnson succeeds to the presidency, unveils his Reconstruction plan.
	Massachusetts desegregates all public facilities.
	Black citizens in several southern cities organize Union Leagues.
	Former Confederate states begin to pass black codes.
1866	Congress passes Southern Homestead Act, Civil Rights Act of 1866.
	Ku Klux Klan is founded.

CHRONOLOGIES

Each chapter includes a Chronology, a list of the key events discussed in the chapter arranged in chronological order. The chronology for Chapter 16 lists the dates of key events during the Reconstruction era from 1865 to 1877. Chronologies provide a review of important events and their relationship to one another.

STUDENT TOOL KIT

CONCLUSION

The conclusion at the end of each chapter puts the subject of the chapter in the broader perspective of U.S. history.

REVIEW QUESTIONS, RECOMMENDED READING, WHERE TO LEARN MORE

At the end of each chapter there are a number of review and enrichment resources. Review questions reconsider the main topics of each chapter. Annotated Recommended Reading introduce students to interesting books and articles that can expand their knowledge on the topics outlined the chapter. The section called Where to Learn More lists important historical sites and museums around the country and related Websites that provide first-hand exposure to historical artifacts and settings. A new section, Study Resources, notes the availability of materials related to the chapter on the *Myhistorylab* website; this is an excellent resource for additional study aids.

---

136   Chapter 5   *Imperial Breakdown 1763–1774*

to call themselves **Whigs** and condemned their opponents as **Tories**. These traditional English party labels dated from the late seventeenth century, when the Tories had supported the accession of the Catholic King James II, whereas the Whigs had opposed it. By calling themselves Whigs and their opponents Tories (loyalist was a more accurate label), the advocates of colonial rights cast themselves as champions of liberty and their enemies as defenders of religious intolerance and royal absolutism.

Conclusion

All Americans, Whigs and loyalists alike, considered themselves good British subjects. But Americans were a more diverse and more democratic people than the English. A considerably larger percentage of them could participate in government, and for all practical purposes, they had been governing themselves for a long time. British officials recognized the different character of American society and feared it might lead Americans to reject British control. But the steps they took to prevent this outcome had the opposite effect.

Attempts to protect their accustomed autonomy first brought the colonial assemblies into conflict with Parliament. Asserting their rights led to greater cooperation among individual colonies. This development, in turn, led to increasingly widespread resistance, then to rebellion, and finally to revolution. Moving imperceptibly from one stage to the next, Americans grew conscious of their common interests and their differences from the English. They became aware, as Benjamin Franklin would later write, of the need to break "through the bounds, in which a dependent people had been accustomed to think, and act" so that they might "properly comprehend the character they had assumed."

That workingmen and members of the elite dressed as Indians had joined in the dangerous act of defiance known as the Boston Tea Party also foreshadowed coming developments. No one now knows for certain why they adopted that particular disguise, but Indians were a traditional symbol of the New World. And those who were making a new political world were risking much—even, it would shortly turn out, life itself.

Review Questions

1. What do Eliza Farmar's letters tell us about the crisis over duties tea in 1773 and 1774? What does she think has caused the crisis and who was at fault? What makes her think the colonists have any chance of success in resisting British impositions?

2. How did the British victory and French withdrawal from North America after the French and Indian War affect the relations between Native Americans and white settlers? Between British authorities and Americans?

3. What was the relationship between the French and Indian War and changes in British policy toward America? How did the expectations of Americans and Britons differ in 1763? Why were the new policies offensive to Americans?

4. How was stationing British troops in America related to British taxation of the colonists? Why did the colonists consider taxation by Parliament an especially serious threat to their freedom as well as to their pocketbooks?

5. How did Americans oppose the new measures? Who participated in the various forms of resistance? How effective were the different kinds of resistance? What effect did resistance to British measures have on Americans' internal politics and sense of identity as Americans?

6. What led to the meeting of the First Continental Congress? What steps did the Congress take? What did it expect to achieve? What were the differences between Whigs and Tories?

Key Terms

Boston Massacre (p. 129)
Boston Tea Party (p. 131)
British Constitution (p. 123)
Cherokee War (p. 121)
Coercive Acts (p. 131)
Committees of correspondence (p. 129)

First Continental Congress (p. 133)
Intolerable Acts (p. 131)
Nonimportation movement (p. 125)
Parson's Cause (p. 122)
Pontiac's Rebellion (p. 121)
Proclamation of 1763 (p. 120)

Stamp Act (p. 123)
Stamp Act Congress (p. 125)
Sugar Act (p. 122)
Suffolk Resolves (p. 133)
Tea Act of 1773 (p. 129)
Tories (p. 136)

Imperial Breakdown 1763–1774   Chapter 5   137

Recommended Reading

Bailyn, Bernard. *The Ideological Origins of the American Revolution*, 2nd ed. (1992). A clear and illuminating account of how the colonists' ideas about politics prepared them to resist British measures.

Countryman, Edward. *The American Revolution*, 2nd ed. (2003). A brief, readable general history of the Revolutionary period that focuses on the involvement of the common people.

Morison, Samuel Eliot, ed. *Sources and Documents Illustrating the American Revolution, 1764–1788, and the Formation of* the Federal Constitution, 2nd ed. (1965). The most readily available and conveniently used collection of documents (mostly official) from the era of the American Revolution.

Raphael, Ray. *A People's History of the American Revolution: How Common People Shaped the Fight for Independence* (2001). A readable, popular synthesis of much recent scholarship.

Where to Learn More

■ **Charleston, South Carolina.** Many buildings date from the eighteenth century. Officials stored tea in one of them, the Exchange, to prevent a local version of the Boston Tea Party. The website for Historic Charleston, www.cr.nps.gov/nr/travel/charleston, provides a map, a list of buildings, and information about them.

■ **Philadelphia, Pennsylvania.** Numerous buildings and sites date from the eighteenth century. Independence National Historical Park, between Second and Sixth streets on Walnut and Chestnut streets, contains Carpenter's Hall, where the First Continental Congress met, and the Pennsylvania State House (now known as Independence Hall), where the Declaration of Independence was adopted. Philadelphia's Historic Mile, www.ushistory.org/tour/index.html, provides a virtual tour of the great landmarks of the city, including Independence Hall.

■ **Boston, Massachusetts.** Many important buildings and sites in this area date from the seventeenth and eigh-

teenth centuries. They include Faneuil Hall (Dock Square), where many public meetings took place prior to the Revolution, and the Old State House (Washington and State streets), which overlooks the site of the Boston Massacre. The Freedom Trail, www.thefreedomtrail.org/virtual_tour. html, provides a well-illustrated virtual tour of the historic sites.

■ **Fort Michilimackinac National Historic Landmark, Mackinaw City, Michigan.** Near the south end of the Mackinac Bridge, the present structure is a modern restoration of the fort as it was when Pontiac's Rebellion took a heavy toll of its garrison. The Mackinac State Historic Park's website, www.mackinacparks.com/michilimackinac/html, provides a brief description and photographs of the reconstructed colonial village and fort.

Study Resources

PEARSON myhistorylab

For study resources for this chapter, go to www.myhistorylab.com and choose *The American Journey*. You will find a wealth of study and review material for this chapter, including pre-and post-tests, customized study plan, key term review flash cards, interactive map and document activities, and documents for analysis.

STUDENT TOOL KIT

SPECIAL FEATURES

Historians find most of their information in written records and original documents that have survived from the past. These include government publications, letters, diaries, newspapers—whatever people wrote or printed, including many private documents never intended for publication. Several features in the text highlight the written record so important to understanding historical events.

VOICES FROM THE AMERICAN JOURNEY

Each chapter begins with a brief firsthand account from an individual that powerfully recounts the personal journey he or she took in their lives. Each of these "voices" relates to the themes that follow in the chapter. For example, in Chapter 18 is an excerpt from a letter written by Mary Antin, a Russian-Jewish immigrant who came to America at the turn of the last century.

New! Personal Journeys Online
At the end of each document is a list of additional firsthand accounts that are included on the *Myhistorylab* website.

AMERICAN VIEWS

Each chapter contains a selection from a primary source document. The example shown here is the published account of Mary Rowlandson from Lancaster, Massachusetts, who in 1676 was taken captive with two of her children by Indian warriors. Each American Views feature begins with a brief introduction followed by several questions–for discussion or written response–on what the document reveals about key issues and events.

American Views

Mary Rowlandson Among the Indians

In February 1676, in the midst of King Philip's War, Indian warriors attacked the town of Lancaster, Massachusetts. They killed many inhabitants and took 23 colonists captive, including Mary Rowlandson and three of her children. Rowlandson spent the next three months traveling with various groups of Nipmucs, Narragansetts, and Wampanoags. She suffered physically and emotionally, watching her youngest daughter die in her arms and worrying about her other two children, from whom she was frequently sepa-rated. During her captivity, Rowlandson survived by accepting her fate and adapting to the Indians' way of life. Finally, with an English victory imminent, Rowlandson was ransomed and rejoined her husband (who had been away at the time of the attack) and family. In 1682, she published an account of her captivity in which she explored the meaning of her experience. Rowlandson's narrative proved so popular that three editions were printed in the first year.

- How did Rowlandson describe the Indians? How did she characterize her encounter with King Philip?
- In what ways did Rowlandson accommodate herself to the Indians' way of life? How did she employ her skills to fit in? Did her gender make a difference in her experience of captivity?
- How did Rowlandson's Puritan faith shape her narrative?

We travelled on till night; and in the morning, we must go over the River to Philip's crew. When I was in the Cannoo, I could not but be amazed at the numerous crew of Pagans that were on the Bank on the other side. When I came ashore, they gathered all about me, I sitting alone in the midst: I observed they asked one another questions, and laughed, and rejoyced over their Gains and Victories. Then my heart began to fail: and I fell a weeping which was the first time to my remembrance that I wept before them. Although I had met with so much Affliction, and my heart was many times ready to break, yet could I not shed one tear in their sight: but rather had been all this while in a maze, and like one astonished: but now I may say as, Psal. 137.1 *By the rivers of Babylon, there we sat down: yea, we wept when we remembered Zion.* There one of them asked me, why I wept, I could hardly tell what to say: yet I answered, they would kill me: No, said he, none will hurt you. Then came one of them and gave me two spoon-fulls of Meal to comfort me.... Then I went to see King Philip, he bade me come in and sit down, and asked me whether I would smoke (a usual Complement now adayes amongst Saints and Sinners) but this no way suited me. For though I had formerly used Tobacco, yet I had left it ever since I was first taken,

It seems to be a bait, the devil lays to make men loose their precious time....

During my abode in this place, Philip spake to me to make a shirt for his boy, which I did, for which he gave me a shilling: I offered the money to my master, but he bade me keep it: and with it I bought a piece of Horse flesh. Afterwards he asked me to make a Cap for his boy, for which he invited me to Dinner. I went, and he gave me a Pancake, about as big as two fingers; it was made of parched wheat, beaten, and fryed in Bears grease, but I thought I never tasted pleasanter meat in my life. There was a Squaw who spake to me to make a shirt for her *Sannup* [husband], for which she gave me a piece of Bear. Another asked me to knit a pair of Stockins, for which she gave me a quart of Pease.... Hearing that my son was come to this place, I went to see him, and found him lying flat upon the ground: I asked him how he could sleep so? He answered me, *That he was not asleep, but at Prayer;* and lay so, that they might not observe what he was doing. I pray God he may remember these things now he is returned in safety.

Source: Neal Salisbury, ed., *The Sovereignty and Goodness of God, Together with the Faithfulness of His Promises Displayed....* (Boston, 1997), pp. 82–83.

66

GLOBAL PERSPECTIVES

This feature places the American journey within a broader world-wide context. That journey not only influenced other countries and peoples, but we in turn have been shaped by global economic, migratory, technological, and political trends. The example shown here is about a mass exodus of German-speaking people from the Rhineland to various parts of the world, including the United States.

New! Critical thinking questions encourage analysis of the global connections.

Global Perspectives

Early Modern Europe's Biggest Mass Migration

The stream of German immigrants moving to America in the late seventeenth and eighteenth centuries formed only a small part of a much larger flow of emigrants from the Rhineland to many parts of the globe. The Rhineland is not a single political unit, but a region of small states and principalities located along one of Europe's major rivers. Political fragmentation brought religious diversity, with German Reformed or Lutheran churches dominant in some areas and Catholics in others.

Large-scale emigration of Rhineland inhabitants stemmed from many causes, especially warfare. During the Thirty Years' War (1618–1648), much of the Rhineland area was devastated by intense religious conflict and famine. In the 1680s and 1690s, Louis XIV of France invaded the region, sparking more turmoil. Al-most continual warfare from the 1730s to the 1760s made the lives of Rhineland inhabitants even worse.

Economic hardship and political repression also spurred emigration. Harsh winters in 1708–1709 and 1709–1710, for instance, destroyed orchards and vineyards, threatening many farmers with impoverishment and even starvation. Harvests failed in many parts of the Rhineland in the 1740s. In addition, religious minorities suffered from persecution, and everyone bore the burden of increasing taxes and arbitrary rule by local princes. For all of these reasons, over the course of the eighteenth century, hundreds of thousands of Rhinelanders decided to flee their homeland.

Many promoters, land speculators, and even governments sought to direct the flow of emigrants to a favored region. Officials from Russia and Prussia offered cheap land and tax exemptions to lure migrants to their countries. As a result of this promotional campaign, by far the largest number of Rhineland refugees relocated to various parts of Eastern Europe, including Prussia, Russia, Hungary, and Poland. A smaller flow of emigrants, mostly Protestants, made their way to North America, settling principally in Pennsylvania, New York, and the Carolinas. Still others moved to Cayenne (French Guiana) in South America. The exodus of these German-speaking emigrants to destinations in the Old and New Worlds constituted the most significant mass migration in early modern Europe.

- Why might more Rhineland migrants have moved within Europe instead of going to the North American colonies?

equipment, including boats, provisions, and salt (used for preserving fish). Merchants recruited fishermen by advancing credit to coastal villagers so that they could outfit their own boats. To pay off the debt, the fishermen were legally bound to bring their catch to the merchant, who then sold it to Europe and the West Indies. Many fishermen ran up such large debts that the end of the seventeenth century, as the rising population of coastal villages lowered the cost of labor, merchants abandoned the credit system and paid wages to fishermen instead.

In the northern colonies, the same conditions that made men reluctant to become fishermen deterred them from becoming farm laborers, except perhaps for high wages. Paying high wages, however, or the high cost of servants or slaves was difficult for New Englanders with farms that produced no export crops and could not be worked during cold winter months. So northern farmers turned to the cheapest and most dependable workers they could find – their children.

Children as young as 5 or 6 years old began with simple tasks and moved on to more complex work as they grew older. By the time they were in their late teens, girls knew how to run households, and boys knew how to farm. Instead of contracts or outright coercion, fathers used their ownership of property to prolong the time their sons worked for them. Young men could not marry until they could set up their own households and relied on their fathers to provide them with land to do so. Fathers often waited until their sons were in their mid-twenties, compelling them until then to invest their labor in the paternal estate.

Thus New England's labor shortage produced strong ties of dependency between generations. Fathers kept their sons working for them as long as possible; sons accepted this arrangement because they had no other way to become

79

FROM THEN TO NOW

This feature connects events and trends in the past to issues that confront Americans today, illustrating the value a historical perspective can contribute to our understanding of the world we live in. The example here, from Chapter 3, discusses the continuing legacy of slavery in American life.

New! From Then to Now Online
This new section lists additional text and visual primary source documents on the topic that are included on the *Myhistorylab* website.

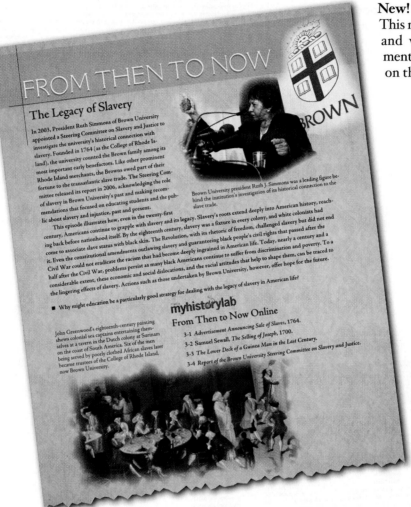

FROM THEN TO NOW

The Legacy of Slavery

In 2003, President Ruth Simmons of Brown University appointed a Steering Committee on Slavery and Justice to investigate the university's historical connection with slavery. Founded in 1764 (as the College of Rhode Island), the university counted the Brown family among its most important early benefactors. Like other prominent Rhode Island merchants, the Browns owed part of their fortune to the transatlantic slave trade. The Steering Committee released its report in 2006, acknowledging the role of slavery in Brown University's past and making recommendations that focused on educating students and the public about slavery and injustice, past and present.

This episode illustrates how, even in the twenty-first century, Americans continue to grapple with slavery and its legacy. Slavery's roots extend deeply into American history, reaching back before nationhood itself. By the eighteenth century, slavery was a fixture in every colony, and white colonists had come to associate slave status with black skin. The Revolution, with its rhetoric of freedom, challenged slavery but did not end it. Even the constitutional amendments outlawing slavery and guaranteeing black people's civil rights that passed after the Civil War could not eradicate the racism that had become deeply ingrained in American life. Today, nearly a century and a half after the Civil War, problems persist as many black Americans continue to suffer from discrimination and poverty. To a considerable extent, these economic and social dislocations, and the racial attitudes that help to shape them, can be traced to the lingering effects of slavery. Actions such as those undertaken by Brown University, however, offer hope for the future.

■ Why might education be a particularly good strategy for dealing with the legacy of slavery in American life?

Brown University president Ruth J. Simmons was a leading figure behind the institution's investigation of its historical connection to the slave trade.

John Greenwood's eighteenth-century painting shows colonial sea captains entertaining themselves at a tavern in the Dutch colony at Surinam on the coast of South America. Six of the men being served by poorly clothed African slaves later became trustees of the College of Rhode Island, now Brown University.

myhistorylab

From Then to Now Online

3-1 *Advertisement Announcing Sale of Slaves*, 1764.

3-2 Samuel Sewall, *The Selling of Joseph*, 1700.

3-3 *The Lower Deck of a Guinea Man in the Last Century*.

3-4 *Report of the Brown University Steering Committee on Slavery and Justice*.

The American Journey

A History of the United States

Mexico: Hernando Cortes is greeted by Montezuma's messenger in 1519: Mexican Indian painting, 16th century.

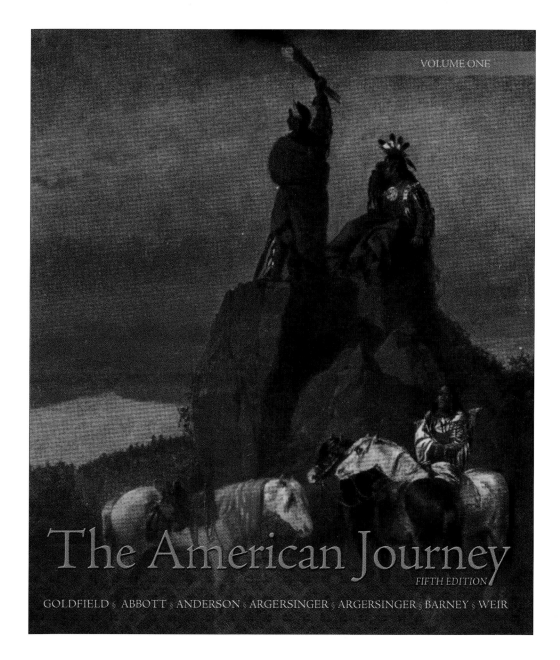

VOLUME ONE

THE AMERICAN JOURNEY

FIFTH EDITION

GOLDFIELD § ABBOTT § ANDERSON § ARGERSINGER § ARGERSINGER § BARNEY § WEIR

VOLUME ONE

CHAPTERS 1–16

To order, please request
ISBN-10: 0-13-603255-9; ISBN-13: 978-0-13-603255-7

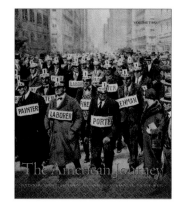

COMBINED EDITION
Chapters 1-31
ISBN-10: 0-13-603281-8
ISBN-13: 978-0-13-603281-6

VOLUME ONE
Chapters 1-16
ISBN-10: 0-13-603255-9
ISBN-13: 978-0-13-603255-7

VOLUME TWO
Chapters 16-31
ISBN-10: 0-13-603256-7
ISBN-13: 978-0-13-603256-4

Worlds Apart 1

After a difficult journey of over two hundred miles, the exhausted man arrived at the royal palace in the grand city of Tenochtitlán. He had hurried all the way from the Gulf Coast with important news for the Aztec leader, Moctezuma.

Our lord and king, forgive my boldness. I am from Mictlancuauhtla. When I went to the shores of the great sea, there was a mountain range or small mountain floating in the midst of the water, and moving here and there without touching the shore. My lord, we have never seen the like of this, although we guard the coast and are always on watch.

[When Moctezuma sent some officials to check on the messenger's story, they confirmed his report.]

Our lord and king, it is true that strange people have come to the shores of the great sea. They were fishing from a small boat, some with rods and others with a net. They fished until late and then they went back to their two great towers and climbed up into them.... They have very light skin, much lighter than ours. They all have long beards, and their hair comes only to their ears.

Miguel Leon–Portilla, *The Broken Spears: The Aztec Account of the Conquest of Mexico* (Boston, 1962).

myhistörylab

Personal Journeys Online

- Christopher Columbus, *Journal of the First Voyage*, October 12, 1492. Account of his first meeting with Caribbean islanders.

- Martin Frobisher, *Account of First Voyage to the New World*, 1576. Description of his arrival in Canada and his encounter with native people.

Moctezuma was filled with foreboding when he received the messenger's initial report. Aztec religion placed great emphasis on omens and prophecies, which were thought to foreshadow coming events. Several unusual omens had recently occurred—blazing lights in the sky, one temple struck by lightning and another that spontaneously burst into flames. Now light-skinned strangers appeared offshore. Aztec spiritual leaders regarded these signs as unfavorable and warned that trouble lay ahead.

The messenger's journey to Tenochtitlán occurred in 1519. The "mountains" he saw were in fact the sails of European ships, and the strange men were Spanish soldiers under the command of Hernán Cortés. Like Columbus's voyage to the Caribbean in 1492, Cortés's arrival in Mexico is considered a key episode in the European discovery of the "New World." But we might just as accurately view the messenger's entry into the Aztec capital as announcing the native Mexicans' discovery of a New World to the east, from which the strangers must have come. Neither the Aztecs nor the Spaniards could have foreseen the far-reaching consequences of these twin discoveries. Before long, a variety of peoples—Native Americans, Africans, and Europeans—who had previously lived worlds apart would come together to create a world that was new to all of them.

This new world reflected the diverse experiences of the many peoples who built it. Improving economic conditions in the fifteenth and early sixteenth centuries propelled Europeans overseas to seek new opportunities for trade and settlement. Spain, Portugal, France, and England competed for political, economic, and religious domination within Europe, and their conflict carried over into the Americas. Native Americans drew upon their familiarity with the land and its resources, patterns of political and religious authority, and systems of trade and warfare to deal with the European newcomers. Africans did not come voluntarily to the Americas but were brought by the Europeans to work as slaves. They too would draw on their cultural heritage to cope with a new land and a new, harsh condition of life.

Native American Societies before 1492

In 1492, the year Columbus landed on a tiny Caribbean island, perhaps 70 million people—nearly equal to the population of Europe at that time—lived on the continents of North and South America, most of them south of the present border between the United States and Mexico. They belonged to hundreds of groups, each with its own language or dialect, history, and way of life. In their own languages, many native groups called themselves "the original people" or "the true men." Europeans called them "Indians," following Columbus's mistaken first impression that he had arrived in the East Indies when his ships reached an island in the Bahamas.

From the start, the original inhabitants of the Americas were peoples in motion. The first migrants may have arrived over forty thousand years ago, traveling from central Siberia and slowly making their way to southern South America. These people, and subsequent migrants from Eurasia, probably traveled across a land bridge that emerged across what is now the Bering Strait. During the last Ice Age, much of the earth's water was frozen in huge glaciers. This process lowered ocean levels, exposing a 600-mile-wide land bridge between Asia and America. Recent research examining genetic and linguistic similarities between Asian and Native American populations suggests that there may have been later migrations as well. Asian seafarers may have crossed the Pacific to settle portions of western North and South America, while as recently as eight thousand years ago, a final migration may have brought Siberians to what is now Alaska and northern Canada.

Paleo-Indians and the Archaic Period

The earliest Americans, called *Paleo-Indians* by archaeologists, traveled in small bands, tracking and killing mammoths, bison, and other large game. These animals were often easy prey, for they had never before encountered human hunters. Archaeologists working near present-day Clovis, New Mexico, have found carefully crafted spear points—some of which may be over thirteen thousand years old. Such efficient tools possibly contributed to overhunting, for by about 9000 B.C.E., mammoths and other large game had become extinct in the Americas. Climatic change also hastened the animals' disappearance. Around twelve thousand years ago, the world's climate began to grow warmer, turning grasslands into deserts and reducing the animals' food supply. Humans too had to find other food sources.

Between roughly 8000 B.C.E. and 1500 B.C.E.—what archaeologists call the **Archaic period**—the Native American population grew and people began living in larger communities. Men and women assumed more specialized roles. Men did most of the hunting and fishing, activities that required travel. Women remained closer to home, gathering and preparing wild plant foods and caring for children.

Across the continent, native communities participated in a complex trade network. Trade was not limited to material goods, but also included exchanges of marriage partners, laborers, ideas, and religious practices. Trade networks sometimes extended over great distances. Valuable goods, such as copper from the Great Lakes area and shells from the Gulf of Mexico, have been discovered at archaeological sites far from their places of origin. Ideas about death and the afterlife also passed between groups. So too did certain burial practices, such as the placing of valued possessions in the grave along with the deceased person's body. In some areas, the increasing complexity of exchange networks, as well as competition for resources, encouraged concentrations of political power. Chiefs might manage trade relations and conduct diplomacy for groups of villages rather than for a single community.

CHRONOLOGY

c. 40,000–8000 B.C.E.	Ancestors of Native Americans cross Bering land bridge.
c. 10,000–9000 B.C.E.	Paleo-Indians expand through the Americas.
c. 9000 B.C.E.	Extinction of large land mammals in North America.
c. 8000–1500 B.C.E.	Archaic Indian era.
c. 8000 B.C.E.	Beginnings of agriculture in the Peruvian Andes and Mesoamerica.
c. 1500 B.C.E.	Earliest mound-building culture begins.
c. 500 B.C.E.–400 C.E.	Adena-Hopewell mound-building culture.
c. 700–1600 C.E.	Rise of West African empires.
c. 900	First mounds built at Cahokia. Ancestral Puebloan expansion.
c. 1000	Spread of Islam in West Africa.
c. 1000–1015	First Viking voyages to North America.
c. 1000–1500	Last mound-building culture, the Mississippian.
c. 1290s	Ancestral Puebloan dispersal into smaller villages.
1400–1600	Renaissance in Europe.
1430s	Beginnings of Portuguese slave trade in West Africa.
1492	End of *reconquista* in Spain. Columbus's first voyage.
1494	Treaty of Tordesillas.
1497	John Cabot visits Nova Scotia and Newfoundland.
1497–1499	Vasco da Gama sails around Africa to reach India.
1517	Protestant Reformation begins in Germany.
1519–1521	Hernán Cortés conquers the Aztec empire.
1532–1533	Francisco Pizarro conquers the Inca empire.
1534–1542	Jacques Cartier explores eastern Canada for France.
1540–1542	Coronado explores southwestern North America.
1542–1543	Roberval's failed colony in Canada.
1558	Elizabeth I becomes queen of England.
1565	Spanish establish outpost at St. Augustine in Florida.
1560s–1580s	English renew attempts to conquer Ireland.
1587	Founding of "Lost Colony" of Roanoke.
1598	Spanish found colony at New Mexico.

The Development of Agriculture

Early in the Archaic period, some Native Americans made a momentous adaptation when they began farming. Scientists working in northern Peru have recently discovered seeds from domesticated squash that are almost ten thousand years old. Inhabitants of central Mexico likewise began growing squash and corn between nine thousand and ten thousand years ago. Agriculture in the Americas may thus have developed as early as it did in the Middle East, Southeast Asia, China, and India. Farming was likely a response to problems generated when population growth threatened to outrun the wild food supply. Women, with their knowledge of wild plants, probably discovered how to save seeds and cultivate them, becoming the world's first farmers.

Farming in the Americas initially supplemented a diet still largely dependent on hunting and gathering, but gradually assumed a greater role. In addition to maize, the main crop in both South and North America, farmers in Mexico, Central America, and the Peruvian Andes cultivated peppers, beans, pumpkins, squash, avocados, sweet and white potatoes (native to the Peruvian highlands), and tomatoes. Mexican farmers also grew cotton. Maize and bean cultivation spread from Mexico in a wide arc to the north and east. Peoples in what is now the southwestern United States began farming between 1500 and 500 B.C.E., and by 200 C.E., farmers were tilling the soil in present-day Georgia and Florida.

Wherever agriculture took hold, important social changes followed. Populations grew, because farming produced a more secure food supply than did hunting and gathering. Permanent villages appeared as farmers settled near their fields. In central Mexico, agriculture eventually sustained the populations of large cities. Trade in agricultural surpluses flowed through networks of exchange. In many Indian societies, women's status improved because of their role as the principal farmers. Even religious beliefs adapted to the increasing importance of farming. In describing the origins of their people, Pueblo Indians of the Southwest compared their emergence from the underworld to a maize plant sprouting from the earth.

The adoption of agriculture further enhanced the diversity of Native American societies that developed over centuries within broad regions, or **culture areas** (see Map 1–1). Within each area, inhabitants shared basic patterns of subsistence and social organization, largely reflecting the natural environment to which they had adapted. Most, but not all of them, eventually relied upon farming.

Nonfarming Societies

In the challenging environment of the Arctic and Subarctic, small nomadic bands of Inuits and Aleuts moved seasonally to fish or hunt whales, seals, and other sea animals, and, in the brief summers, gather wild berries. Farther inland, the Crees and other peoples followed migrating herds of caribou and moose.

Along the Northwest Coast and the Columbia River Plateau, one of the most densely populated areas of North America, native communities prospered from fishing in rivers teeming with salmon and by hunting and gathering in forests full of game and edible plants. Among such groups as the Kwakiutls and Chinooks, extended families lived in large communal houses located in villages of up to several hundred residents. Local rulers displayed their prominence most conspicuously during potlatches, or ceremonies in which wealth was distributed among guests in order to celebrate the power of the hosts.

Farther south, in present-day California, hunter-gatherers once lived in smaller villages, which usually adjoined oak groves where Indians gathered acorns as an important food source. Nomadic hunting bands in the Great Basin, where the climate was warm and dry, learned to survive on the region's limited resources. In what is now Utah and western Colorado, the Utes and other groups fished, hunted large game such as elk, bison, and mountain sheep, and gathered pinyon nuts, seeds, and wild berries.

Mesoamerican Civilizations

Mesoamerica, the birthplace of agriculture in North America, extends from central Mexico into Central America. A series of complex, literate, urban cultures emerged in this region beginning around

Women were the principal farmers in most Native American societies, growing corn, beans, and other crops that made up most of their food supply. This sixteenth-century French engraving shows Indian men preparing the soil for cultivation and Indian women sowing seeds in neat rows.

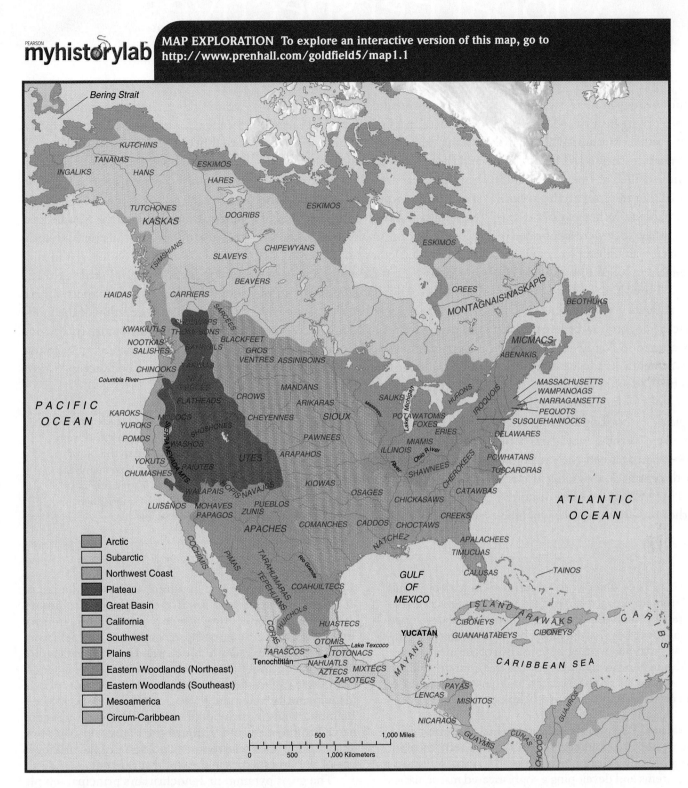

MAP EXPLORATION To explore an interactive version of this map, go to http://www.prenhall.com/goldfield5/map1.1

MAP 1–1   North American Culture Areas, c. 1500
Over the course of centuries, Indian peoples in North America developed distinctive cultures suited to the environments in which they lived. Inhabitants of each culture area shared basic patterns of subsistence, craft work, and social organization. Most, but not all, Indian peoples combined farming with hunting and gathering.

Viking Trade Routes

One summer day in 1957, two archaeologists working near the Maine coast dug up a small coin buried about five inches deep in the soil. There was a small hole drilled at one edge, which suggested that the coin had been worn as an ornament. When experts examined it closely, they were astonished to learn that it was a silver penny that had been minted in Norway in the eleventh century. How had such an ancient penny made its way to Maine?

Archaeologists now believe that the penny arrived in Maine via a massive intercontinental trade network that linked the Old and New Worlds centuries before Columbus's arrival. The key figures in this long-distance commerce were Viking voyagers from Scandinavia. Between the ninth and eleventh centuries, magnificent ships carried the Vikings over vast distances, from the northernmost reaches of Norway to continental Europe, and westward to Iceland, Greenland, and Canada. Viking expeditions to the British Isles and throughout Europe included violent raids that brought widespread destruction to local populations. In the New World, trade and settlement were the Vikings' main goals. Evidence of Viking settlement has been found in various sites in Labrador and Newfoundland. An inhabitant from one of those outposts was the likely source of the penny found in Maine. A Viking settler may have accidentally dropped it, or traded it to one of the local native people. From there the coin made its way as much as a thousand miles southward to Maine, passed along through the Native Americans' own channels of trade.

In the Old World, the geographical extent of Viking trade connections was equally impressive. Archaeologists working at an eighth-century site in Sweden, for instance, have unearthed a small bronze statue of Buddha that was cast in northern India. It made its way to the Scandinavian village via trade networks that traversed vast distances, from Russia to the Middle East to the Indian subcontinent. Exotic items like this one discovered in surprising locations offer striking testimony that global trade connections are by no means an invention of the modern era. A thousand years before our own time, people had already found ways to exchange goods across oceans and continents.

■ How did Viking trade patterns allow the penny to move from the Old World to the New? What does its movement from Labrador to Maine tell us about Native American exchange routes?

1200 B.C.E. The Olmecs, who flourished on Mexico's Gulf Coast from about 1200 to 400 B.C.E., and their successors in the region built cities featuring large pyramids, developed religious practices that included human sacrifice, and devised calendars and writing systems. Two of the most prominent Mesoamerican civilizations that followed the Olmecs were the Mayans in the Yucatán and Guatemala and the Aztecs of Teotihuacán in central Mexico.

The Mayans.   Mayan civilization reached its greatest glory between about 150 and 900 C.E. in the southern Yucatán, creating Mesoamerica's most advanced writing and calendrical systems and developing a sophisticated mathematics that included the concept of zero. The Mayans of the southern Yucatán suffered a decline after 900, but there were still many thriving Mayan centers in the northern Yucatán when Europeans arrived in the Americas. The great city of Teotihuacán dominated central Mexico from the first century to the eighth century C.E. and influenced much of Mesoamerica through trade and conquest.

The Aztecs.   Some two hundred years after the fall of Teotihuacán, the Toltecs, a warrior people, rose to prominence, dominating central Mexico from about 900 to 1100. In the wake of the Toltec collapse, the **Aztecs** migrated from the north into the Valley of Mexico and built a great empire that soon controlled much of Mesoamerica. The magnificent Aztec capital, Tenochtitlán, was a city of great plazas, magnificent temples and palaces, and busy marketplaces. Built on islands in the middle of Lake Texcoco, it was connected to the mainland by four broad causeways. In 1492, Tenochtitlán was home to some 200,000 people, making it one of the largest cities in the world at the time.

The great pyramid in Tenochtitlán's principal temple complex was the center of Aztec religious life. Here Aztec priests sacrificed human victims—by cutting open their chests and removing their still-beating hearts—to offer to the gods. Human sacrifice had been part of Mesoamerican religion since the time of the Olmecs. People believed that such ceremonies pleased the gods and prevented them from destroying the earth. The Aztecs, however, practiced sacrifice on a much larger scale than ever before. Hundreds, even thousands, of victims died in ceremonies that sometimes lasted for days.

The Aztec empire expanded through military conquest, driven by a quest for sacrificial victims and tribute payments of gold, food, and handcrafted goods from hundreds of subject communities. But as the empire grew, it became increasingly vulnerable to internal division. Neighboring peoples submitted to the Aztecs out of fear rather than loyalty.

North America's Diverse Cultures

North of Mexico, the introduction of a drought-resistant type of maize around 400 B.C.E. enabled a series of cultures sharing certain characteristics with Mesoamerica to develop. Beginning about 300 B.C.E., the Hohokams settled in villages in southern Arizona and devised elaborate irrigation systems that allowed them to harvest two crops of corn, beans, and squash each year. Artisans wove cotton cloth and made goods reflecting Mesoamerican artistic styles out of shell, turquoise, and clay. Trade networks linked the Hohokams to people living as far away as California and Mexico. Their culture endured for over a thousand years but mysteriously disappeared by 1450.

Ancestral Puebloans.   Early in the first century C.E., Ancestral Puebloan peoples (sometimes called Anasazis) began to settle in farming communities where the borders of present-day Colorado, Utah, Arizona, and New Mexico meet. Scarce rainfall, routed through dams and hillside terraces, watered the crops. Ancestral Puebloans originally lived in villages, or pueblos (*pueblo* is the Spanish word for "village") built on mesas and canyon floors. In New Mexico's Chaco Canyon, perhaps as many as fifteen thousand people dwelled

in a dozen large towns and hundreds of outlying villages. The largest town, Pueblo Bonito, covered three acres and contained about twelve hundred inhabitants. Its main structure, a four-story-tall complex of over eight-hundred rooms and numerous *kivas,* or ceremonial chambers, served as one of several centers of production and exchange throughout the area. But after about 1200, villagers began carving multistoried stone houses into canyon walls, dwellings that could only be reached by difficult climbs up steep cliffs and along narrow ledges. Warfare and climate change may have worked together to force the Puebloans into these precarious homes.

Around 1200, the climate of the Southwest grew colder, making it more difficult to grow enough to feed the large population. Food scarcity may have set village against village and encouraged attacks by outsiders. Villagers probably resorted to cliff dwellings for protection as violence spread in the region. By 1300, survivors abandoned the cliff dwellings and dispersed into smaller villages along the Rio Grande. Their descendants include the Hopis and Zunis, as well as other Puebloan peoples in the desert Southwest. In many of these villages, men farmed—in contrast to the predominant pattern of women farmers elsewhere in Native America—raising corn, beans, squash, and sunflowers. They established new trade links with nomadic hunting peoples, including the Apaches and Navajos, who exchanged buffalo meat and hides for Pueblo corn, cotton blankets, pottery, and other goods.

Plains Indians.   The Great Plains of the continent's interior were much less densely settled than the desert Southwest. Mandans, Pawnees, and other groups settled along river valleys, where women farmed and men hunted bison. Plains Indians moved frequently, seeking more fertile land or

Acoma Pueblo has perched atop this 300-foot-tall mesa since the twelfth century. Now used mainly for ceremonial purposes, Acoma was once a thriving Ancestral Puebloan village.

better hunting. Wherever they went, they traded skins, food, and obsidian (a volcanic glass used for tools and weapons) with other native peoples.

Mound-building cultures.   As agriculture spread to the Eastern Woodlands, a vast territory extending from the Mississippi Valley to the Atlantic seaboard, several "mound-building" societies—named for the large earthworks their members constructed—developed in the Ohio and Mississippi Valleys. The oldest flourished in Louisiana between 1500 and 700 B.C.E. The members of the Adena-Hopewell culture, which appeared in the Ohio Valley between 500 B.C.E. and 400 C.E., built hundreds of mounds, often in the shapes of humans, birds, and serpents. Most were grave sites, where people were buried with valuable goods, including objects made from materials obtained through long-distance trade.

The last mound-building culture, the Mississippian, emerged between 1000 and 1500 in the Mississippi Valley. Mississippian farmers raised enough food to support sizable populations and major urban centers. The largest city by far was **Cahokia**, located near present-day St. Louis in a fertile floodplain with access to the major river systems of the continent's interior. By 1250, Cahokia had perhaps twenty thousand residents, making it nearly as large as medieval London and the largest American city north of Mexico. Its political leaders collected tribute, redistributed goods, coordinated trade and diplomacy, and mobilized laborers to build large structures and earthworks. Cahokia dominated the Mississippi Valley, linked by trade to dozens of villages in the Midwestern region.

Mississippian culture began to decline in the thirteenth century, perhaps due to an ecological crisis. Cahokia's population may have outstripped its food supply, and a series of hot, dry summers created further hardship. By 1400, most of Cahokia's residents had dispersed into scattered farming villages.

What followed in the Eastern Woodlands region was a century or more of warfare and political instability. In the vacuum left by Cahokia's decline, other groups sought to exert more power. In the northeast, the Iroquois and Hurons moved from dispersed settlements into fortified villages. Both the Hurons and the Iroquois formed confederacies that were intended to diminish internal conflicts and increase their collective spiritual strength. Among the Iroquois, five separate nations—the Mohawks, Oneidas, Onondagas, Cayugas, and Senecas—joined to create the **Great League of Peace and Power** around the year 1450. Similar developments occurred in the southeast, where chronic instability led to regional alliances and shifting centers of trade and political power. One such center at Etowah, in northwestern Georgia, prospered until about 1400, at which point it gave way to a new chiefdom at Coosa.

Eastern Woodlands peoples were the first to encounter English explorers, and later, English settlers, at the start of the seventeenth century. By that point these native peoples relied on a mixture of agriculture and hunting, fishing, and gathering for their subsistence. They lived in villages with a few hundred residents, with greater densities of settlement in the south (where a warmer climate and longer growing season prevailed) than in the north. Although early colonists sometimes described these Indian groups as nomadic, they in fact inhabited semipermanent villages and moved only when declining soil fertility or, in some instances, warfare compelled them to shift location. For the most part, their principal villages were near the coast or along rivers, where the greatest diversity of natural resources could be found.

This artist's rendering, based on archaeological evidence, suggests the size and magnificence of the Mississippian city of Cahokia. By the thirteenth century, it was as populous as medieval London and served as a center of trade for the vast interior of North America.

The Caribbean Islanders

The Caribbean islands were peopled by mainland dwellers who began moving to the islands around 5000 B.C.E. Ancestors of the Tainos probably came from what is now Venezuela. The Guanahatabeys of western Cuba originated in Florida, and the Caribs of the easternmost islands moved from Brazil's Orinoco Valley. Surviving at first by hunting and gathering, island peoples began farming perhaps in the first century C.E. They raised manioc, sweet potatoes, maize, squash, beans, peppers, peanuts, and pineapple on clearings made in the tropical forests. Canoes carried trade goods throughout the Caribbean, as well as to Mesoamerica and coastal South America.

By 1492, as many as 4 million people may have inhabited the Caribbean islands. Powerful chiefs ruled over villages, conducted war and diplomacy, and controlled the distribution of food and other goods obtained as tribute from villagers. Elite islanders were easily recognized by their fine clothing, bright feather headdresses, and golden ear and nose ornaments—items that eventually attracted the attention of European visitors.

Long before Europeans reached North America, the continent's inhabitants had witnessed centuries of dynamic change. Empires rose and fell, and new ones took their place. Large cities flourished and disappeared. Periods of warfare occasionally disrupted the lives of thousands of individuals. The Europeans' arrival, at the end of the fifteenth century, coincided with a period of particular instability, as various Native American groups competed for dominance in the wake of the collapse of the centralized societies at Cahokia and Chaco Canyon. Yet at the same time, Native American societies experienced important continuities. These included an ability to adapt to widely varying environmental conditions, the preservation of religious and ceremonial traditions, and an eagerness to forge relationships of exchange with neighboring peoples. Both continuities with past experience and more recent circumstances of political change would shape the ways native peoples responded to the European newcomers.

West African Societies

In the three centuries after 1492, six out of seven people who crossed the Atlantic to the Americas were not Europeans but Africans. They came from the world's second-largest continent and the one with the longest record of human habitation, where the ancestors of modern humans (*Homo sapiens*) appeared 130,000 or more years ago. Like the Americas, Africa had witnessed the rise of many ancient and diverse cultures (see Map 1–2). They ranged from the sophisticated Egyptian civilization that developed in the Nile Valley over five-thousand years ago to the powerful twelfth-century chiefdoms of Zimbabwe to the West African empires that flourished in the time of Columbus and Cortés. The vast majority of Africans who came to the Americas after 1492 arrived as slaves, transported by Europeans eager to exploit their labor. Although they were involuntary immigrants, Africans could draw upon their ancient cultural heritages to help shape the New World in which they found themselves.

Geographical and Political Differences

Most African immigrants to the Americas came from the continent's western regions. Extending from the southern edge of the Sahara Desert toward the equator and inland for nearly a thousand miles, West Africa was an area of contrasts. On the whole a sparsely settled region, West Africa nevertheless contained numerous densely inhabited communities. Many of these settlements clung to the coast, but several important cities lay well inland. Perhaps the greatest of these metropolises was Timbuktu, which had as many as seventy-thousand residents in the fifteenth century. At that time, Timbuktu served as the seat of the powerful **Songhai empire** and was an important center of trade and government.

The Songhai empire was only the latest in a series of powerful West African states. One of the earliest, Ghana, rose to prominence in the eighth century and dominated the area for nearly three hundred years. Its successor, Mali, emerged around 1200 and lasted another three centuries until a power struggle among its rulers led to its decline. Songhai, larger and wealthier than its predecessors, flourished from around 1450 until it fell to a Moroccan invasion in 1591. Equivalently large empires did not appear in coastal West Africa, although the Asante, Dahomey, Oyo, and Bini kingdoms there grew to be quite powerful.

Geographical as well as political differences marked the inland and coastal regions. In the vast grasslands of the interior, people raised cattle and cultivated millet and sorghum. Rice also served as an important food crop. In the 1500s, Europeans brought an Asian variety to add to indigenous African rice strains. On the coast—where rain falls nearly every day—people grew yams, bananas, and various kinds of beans and peas in forest clearings. They also kept sheep, goats, and poultry.

Craftsmen from the West African kingdom of Benin were renowned for their remarkable bronze sculptures. This intricate bronze plaque depicts four African warriors in full military dress. The two tiny figures in the background may be Portuguese soldiers, who first arrived in Benin in the late fifteenth century.

Benin bronze plaque. National Museum of African Art, Smithsonian Institution, Washington, DC, U.S.A. Aldo Tutino/Art Resource, NY.

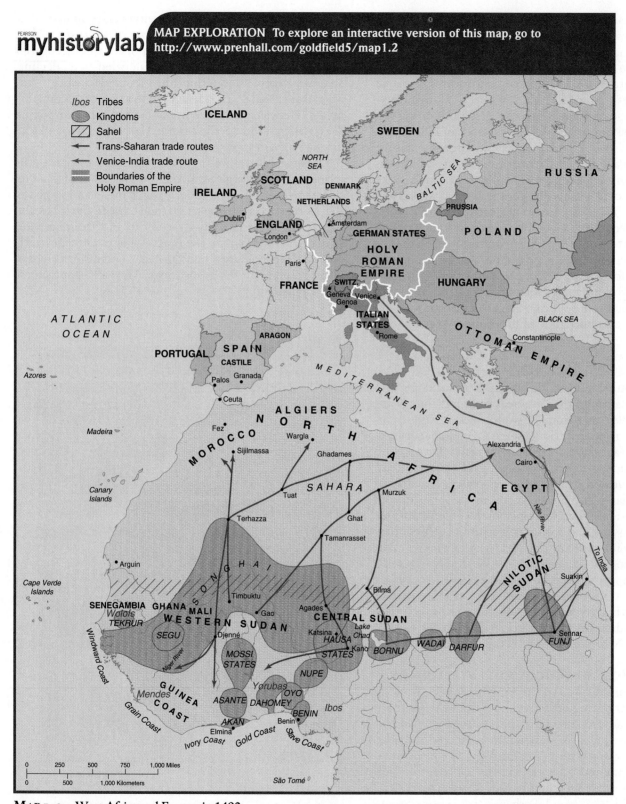

MAP EXPLORATION To explore an interactive version of this map, go to
http://www.prenhall.com/goldfield5/map1.2

Legend:

Ibos Tribes
Kingdoms
Sahel
Trans-Saharan trade routes
Venice-India trade route
Boundaries of the Holy Roman Empire

MAP 1–2   West Africa and Europe in 1492
Before Columbus's voyage, Europeans knew little about the world beyond the Mediterranean basin and the coast of West Africa. Muslim merchants from North Africa largely controlled European traders' access to African gold and other materials.

Artisans and merchants. West Africans excelled as skilled artisans and metalworkers. Smiths in Benin produced intricate bronze sculptures, and Asante craftsmen designed distinctive miniature gold weights. West African smiths also used their skills to forge weapons, attesting to the frequent warfare between West African states.

Trade networks linked inland and coastal states, and long-distance commercial connections tied West Africa to southern Europe and the Middle East. West African merchants exchanged locally mined gold with traders from North Africa for salt, a commodity so rare in West Africa that it was sometimes literally worth its weight in gold. North African merchants also bought West African pepper, leather, and ivory. The wealth generated by this trans-Saharan trade contributed to the rise of the Songhai and earlier empires.

Farming and gender roles. Most West Africans were farmers, whose lives were defined by a daily round of work, family duties, and worship. West African men and women shared agricultural tasks. Men prepared fields for planting, while women cultivated and harvested the crops. Men also hunted and, in the grassland regions, herded cattle. Women in the coastal areas owned and cared for other livestock, including goats and sheep. West African women regularly traded goods, including the crops they grew, in local markets and were thus essential to the vitality of local economies.

Family Structure and Religion

Family connections were exceedingly important to West Africans, helping to define each person's place in society. Children were especially cherished; one Yoruba proverb stated that "Without children you are naked." High rates of infant and child mortality—attributable in good part to a harsh disease environment—made offspring all the more precious, for parents depended on their children for labor and for support in old age. In some regions, men who could afford to do so had more than one wife, thus increasing their chances of having surviving offspring. While ties between parents and children were of central importance, West Africans also emphasized their links with aunts, uncles, cousins, and grandparents. Groups of families formed clans that further extended an individual's kin ties.

Religious beliefs magnified the powerful influence of family on African life. Ideas and practices focused on themes of fertility, prosperity, health, and social harmony. Because many West Africans believed that their ancestors acted as mediators between the worlds of the living and the dead, they held elaborate funerals for deceased members and performed public rituals at their grave sites. Such rituals helped keep the memory of ancestors alive for younger generations.

West Africans believed that spiritual forces suffused the natural world, and they performed ceremonies to ensure the spirits' goodwill. Medicine men and women used rituals to protect people from evil spirits and sorcerers. Religious ceremonies were held in sacred places—often near water—but not in buildings that Europeans recognized as churches. West Africans preserved their faith through oral traditions, not written texts.

Islam began to take root in West Africa around the eleventh century, introduced by Muslim traders and soldiers from North Africa. By the fifteenth century, the cities of Timbuktu and Djenné had become centers of Islamic learning, attracting students from as far away as southern Europe. Urban dwellers, especially merchants, were more likely to convert to the new religion, as were some rulers. Farmers, however, accustomed to religious rituals that focused on agricultural fertility, tended to resist Islamic influence more strongly.

European Merchants in West Africa and the Slave Trade

Before the fifteenth century, Europeans knew little about Africa beyond its Mediterranean coast. Spain, parts of which had been under Islamic rule since the eighth century, had stronger ties to North Africa than did most of Europe. But Christian merchants from other European lands had traded for centuries with Muslims in the North African ports. When stories of West African gold reached European traders, they tried to move deeper into the continent. But they encountered powerful Muslim merchants intent on monopolizing the gold trade.

The kingdom of Portugal sought to circumvent this Muslim monopoly. Portuguese forces conquered Ceuta in Morocco and gained a foothold on the continent in 1415. Because this outpost did not provide direct access to the sources of gold, Portuguese mariners gradually explored the West African coast. They established trading posts along the way, where they exchanged horses, clothing, wine, lead, iron, and steel for African gold, grain, animal skins, cotton, pepper, and camels.

By the 1430s, the Portuguese had discovered perhaps the greatest source of wealth they could extract from Africa—slaves. A vigorous market in African slaves had existed in southern Europe since the middle of the fourteenth century. The expansion of this trade required not only eager buyers of slaves, but also willing suppliers. Chronic underpopulation in many areas had led to the development of slavery within West Africa itself, as a way to maintain control over scarce and valuable laborers. Most slaves within Africa lost their freedom because they were captured in war, but others had been kidnapped or were enslaved as punishment for a crime. African merchants, familiar with the slave trade at home, saw little reason not to sell unfree laborers to European buyers.

European visitors who observed African slaves in their homeland often described them as "slaves in name only" because they were subject to so little coercion. African slaves at work in the fields appeared little different from other farmers. Slaves might also be employed as soldiers or administrators, fulfilling important duties and enjoying considerable freedom in their daily routines. Slavery in Africa was not necessarily a permanent status and did not automatically apply to the slaves' children. African merchants who sold slaves to European purchasers had no reason to suspect that those slaves would be treated any differently by their new owners.

Africans caught in the web of the transatlantic slave trade, however, entered a much harsher world. Separated from the kinfolk who meant so much to them, isolated from a familiar

Elmina Castle, located on the coast of what is now Ghana, was founded by the Portuguese in 1482 as a trading post. In 1637, the Dutch West India Company seized the castle and converted for use in the slave trade.

landscape, and hard-pressed to sustain spiritual and cultural traditions in a wholly new environment, Africans faced daunting challenges as they entered into the history of the New World.

Western Europe on the Eve of Exploration

When Columbus sailed from Spain in 1492, he left a continent recovering from the devastating warfare and disease of the fourteenth century and about to embark on the devastating religious conflicts of the sixteenth. Between 1337 and 1453, England and France had exhausted each other in a series of conflicts known as the Hundred Years' War. And between 1347 and 1351, an epidemic known as the Black Death (bubonic plague, and perhaps in some areas a pneumonic form of the disease as well) wreaked havoc on a European population already suffering from persistent malnutrition. Perhaps a third of all Europeans died, with results that were felt for more than a century.

The plague left Europe with far fewer workers, a result that contributed to southern Europeans' interest in the African slave trade. To help the economy recover, the survivors learned to be more efficient and rely on technological improvements. Farmers tilled their most fertile land, and artisans adopted labor-saving techniques to increase productivity. Metalworkers built larger furnaces with bellows driven by water power. Shipbuilders redesigned vessels with steering mechanisms that could be managed by smaller crews. Innovations in banking, accounting, and insurance also fostered economic recovery. Although prosperity was distributed un-

evenly among social classes, on the whole, Europe had a stronger, more productive economy in 1500 than ever before.

In much of Western Europe, economic improvement encouraged an extraordinary cultural movement known as the Renaissance, a "rebirth" of interest in the classical civilizations of ancient Greece and Rome. The Renaissance originated in the city-states of Italy, where a prosperous and educated urban class promoted learning and artistic expression. Wealthy townspeople joined princes in becoming patrons of the arts, offering financial support to painters, sculptors, architects, writers, and musicians.

The daily lives of most Europeans, however, remained untouched by intellectual and artistic developments. Most Europeans were peasants living in agricultural communities that often differed in important ways from Native American and West African societies. In European societies, men performed most of the heavy work of farming, while women's labors focused on household production of such goods as butter, cheese, and cloth, as well as on caring for the family. Europeans lived in states organized into more rigid hierarchies than could be found in most parts of North America or West Africa, with the population divided into distinct classes. At the top were the monarchs who, along with the next rank of aristocrats, dominated government and owned most of the land, receiving rents and labor services from peasants and rural artisans. Next, in descending order, came prosperous gentry families, independent landowners, and, at the bottom, landless peasants and laborers.

European society was also patriarchal, with men dominating political and economic life. Europe's rulers were, with few exceptions, men, and men controlled the Catholic Church. Only men (or, in rare instances, widows) could own property. According to an ideal not always upheld, Europeans thought that every man should be "as a king in his own house," ruling over his wife, children, and servants.

The Consolidation of Political and Military Authority

By the end of the fifteenth century, a measure of stability returned to the countries about to embark on overseas expansion. Ferdinand and Isabella of Spain, Louis XI of France, and Henry VII of England successfully asserted royal authority over their previously fragmented realms, creating strong state bureaucracies to control political rivals. They gave special trading privileges to merchants to gain their support, creating links that would later prove important in financing overseas expeditions. Spain and Portugal negotiated an end to a long-running dispute about the succession to the throne of Castile, one of Spain's largest kingdoms.

The consolidation of military power went hand in hand with the strengthening of political authority. Portugal developed a strong navy to defend its seaborne merchants. Louis XI of France commanded a standing army, and Ferdinand of Spain created a palace guard to use against potential opponents. Before overseas expansion began, European monarchs exerted military force to extend their authority closer to home. Louis XI and his successors used warfare and intermarriage with the ruling families of nearby provinces to extend French influence. In the early sixteenth century, England's Henry VIII sent soldiers to conquer Ireland. And the Spain of 1492 was forged from the successful conclusion of the *reconquista* ("reconquest") of territory from Muslim control.

Muslim invaders from North Africa first entered Spain in 711 and ruled much of the Iberian peninsula (which includes Spain and Portugal) for centuries. Beginning in the mid-eleventh century, Christian armies embarked on a long effort to reclaim the region. By 1450, only the southern tip of Spain remained under Muslim control. After the marriage of Ferdinand of Aragon and Isabella of Castile in 1469 united Spain's two principal kingdoms, their combined forces completed the *reconquista*. Granada, the last Muslim stronghold, fell in 1492, shortly before Columbus set out on his first voyage.

Religious Conflict and the Protestant Reformation

Even as these rulers sought to unify their realms, religious conflicts began to tear Europe apart. For more than a thousand years, Catholic Christianity had united Western Europeans in one faith. By the sixteenth century, the Catholic Church had accumulated enormous wealth and power. The pope wielded influence not only as the church's spiritual leader but also as the political ruler of parts of Italy. The church owned considerable property throughout Europe. In reaction to this growing influence, many Christians, especially in Northern Europe, began to criticize the popes and the church itself for worldliness and abuse of power.

In 1517, a German monk, Martin Luther, invited open debate on a set of propositions critical of church practices and doctrines. Luther believed that the church had become too insistent on the performance of good works, such as charitable donations or other actions intended to please God. He called for a return to what he understood to be the purer practices and beliefs of the early church, emphasizing that salvation came not by good deeds but only by faith in God. With the help of the newly invented printing press, his ideas spread widely, inspiring a challenge to the Catholic Church that came to be known as the **Reformation**.

When the Catholic Church refused to compromise, Luther and other critics withdrew to form their own religious organizations. Luther urged people to take responsibility for their own spiritual growth by reading the Bible, which he translated for the first time into German. What started as a religious movement, however, quickly acquired an important political dimension.

Sixteenth-century Germany was a fragmented region of small kingdoms and principalities. They were officially part of a larger Catholic political entity known as the Holy Roman Empire, but many German princes were discontented with imperial authority. Many of these princes also supported Luther. When the Holy Roman Empire under Charles V (who was also king of Spain) tried to silence them, the reformist princes protested. From that point on, these princes—and all Europeans who supported religious reform—became known as **Protestants**.

The Protestant movement took a more radical turn under the influence of the French reformer John Calvin, who emphasized the doctrine of **predestination**. Calvin maintained that an all-powerful and all-knowing God chose at the moment of creation which humans would be saved and which would be damned. Nothing a person could do would alter that spiritual destiny. Once the ideas of Luther and Calvin began to spread in Europe, no one could contain the powerful Protestant impulse. In succeeding years, other groups formed, split, and split again, increasing Europe's religious fragmentation.

The Reformation fractured the religious unity of Western Europe and spawned a century of warfare unprecedented in its bloody destructiveness. Protestants fought Catholics

This illustration shows Martin Luther and his Protestant supporters burning the papal decree that announced Luther's excommunication from the Catholic church.

in France and the German states. Popes initiated a "Counter-Reformation" to strengthen the Catholic Church—in part by internal reform and in part by persecuting its opponents and reimposing religious conformity. Europe thus fragmented into warring camps just at the moment when Europeans were coming to terms with their discovery of America. Some of the key participants in exploration, such as Spain and Portugal, rejected Protestantism, while others, including England and the Netherlands, embraced religious reform.

Contact

Religious fervor, political ambition, and the desire for wealth propelled European nations into overseas expansion as well as conflict at home. Portugal, Spain, France, and England competed to establish footholds on other continents in an intense scramble for riches and dominance. The success of these endeavors was a reflection of Europe's prosperity and of a series of technological breakthroughs that enabled its mariners to navigate beyond familiar waters.

By 1600, Spain had emerged as the apparent winner among the European competitors for New World dominance. Its astonishingly wealthy empire included vast territories in Central and South America. The conquerors of this empire attributed their success to their military superiority and God's approval of their imperial ambitions. In reality, it was the result of a complex set of interactions with native peoples as well as an unanticipated demographic catastrophe.

The Lure of Discovery

The potential rewards of overseas exploration captured the imaginations of a small but powerful segment of European society. Most people, busy making a living, cared little about distant lands. But certain princes and merchants anticipated spiritual and material benefits from voyages of discovery. The spiritual advantages included making new Christian converts and blocking Islam's expansion—a Christian goal that dated back to the eleventh-century Crusades against the Muslims in the Middle East and continued with the *reconquista*. On the material side, the voyages would contribute to Europe's prosperity by increasing trade.

Merchants especially sought access to Asian spices like pepper, cinnamon, ginger, and nutmeg that added interest to an otherwise monotonous diet and helped preserve foods. Wealthy Europeans paid handsomely for small quantities of spices, making it worthwhile to transport them great distances. But the overland spice trade—and the trade in other luxury goods such as silk and furs—spanned thousands of miles, involved many middlemen, and was controlled at key points by Muslim merchants. One critical center was Constantinople, the bastion of Christianity in the eastern Mediterranean. When that city fell to the Ottomans—Muslim rulers of Turkey—in 1453, Europeans feared that caravan routes to Asia would be disrupted. This encouraged merchants to turn westward and seek alternative routes.

The reorientation of European trade benefited western Italian cities such as Genoa as well as Portugal and Spain, whose ports gave access to the Mediterranean and the Atlantic Ocean. Mariners ventured farther into ocean waters, seeking direct access to the African gold trade and, eventually, a sea route around Africa to Asia. Had it not been for a set of technological developments that reduced the risks of ocean sailing, such lengthy voyages into unexplored areas would have been impossible.

Advances in navigation and shipbuilding.   Ocean voyages required sturdier ships than those that plied the Mediterranean. Because oceangoing mariners traveled beyond sight of coastal features, they also needed reliable navigational tools. In the early fifteenth century, Prince Henry of Portugal sponsored the efforts of shipbuilders, mapmakers, and other workers to solve these practical problems. By 1500, enterprising artisans had made several important advances. Iberian shipbuilders perfected the caravel, a ship whose narrow shape and steering rudder suited it for ocean travel. Ship designers combined square sails (good for speed) with triangular lateen sails, which increased maneuverability. European mariners adopted two important navigational devices—the magnetic compass (first developed in China) and the astrolabe (introduced to Europe by Muslims from Spain)—that allowed mariners to determine their position in relation to a star's known location in the sky. As sailors acquired practical experience on the high seas, mapmakers recorded their observations of landfalls, wind patterns, and ocean currents. Long-distance voyages remained risky, however, in part because mariners had no accurate way to measure longitude until the eighteenth century.

Portuguese mariners slowly worked their way along Africa's western coast, establishing trading posts where they exchanged European goods for gold, ivory, and slaves (see Map 1–3). Bartolomeu Días reached the southern tip of Africa in 1488. Eleven years later, Vasco da Gama brought a Portuguese fleet around Africa to India, opening a sea route to Asia. These initiatives gave Portugal a virtual monopoly on Far Eastern trade for some time.

The Atlantic islands and the slave trade.   The new Atlantic trade routes gave strategic importance to the islands that lie off the west coast of Africa and Europe. Spain and Portugal vied for control of the Canary Islands, located 800 miles southwest of the Iberian peninsula, with the Spanish eventually prevailing. Portugal acquired Madeira and the Cape Verde Islands, along with a group of tiny islands off Africa's Guinea Coast.

Sugar, like Asian spices, commanded high prices in Europe, so the conquerors of the Atlantic islands began to cultivate sugar cane on them, on large plantations worked by slave labor. In the Canaries, the Spanish first enslaved the native inhabitants. When disease and exhaustion reduced their numbers, the Spanish brought in African slaves, often purchased from Portuguese traders. Elsewhere Europeans

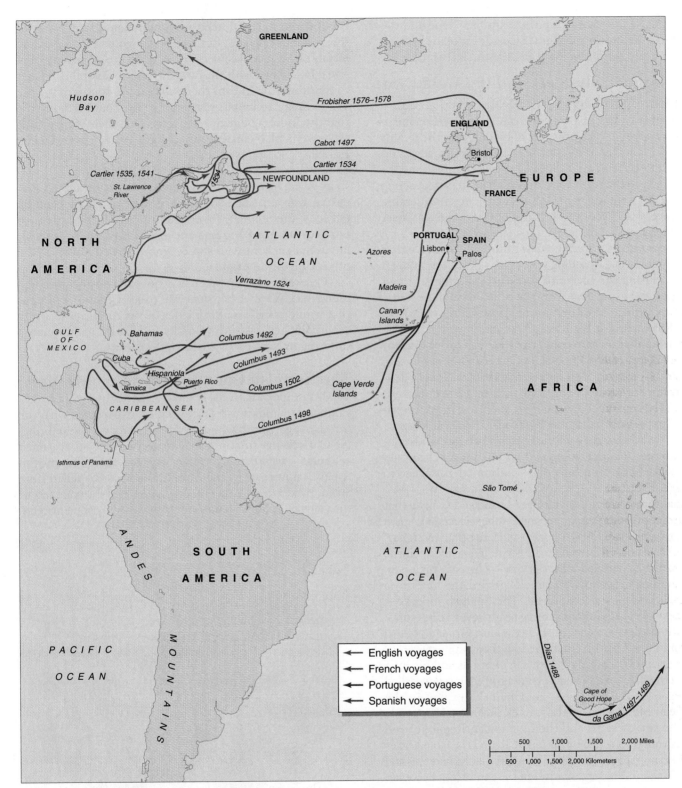

MAP 1-3   European Voyages of Discovery in the Atlantic in the Fifteenth and Sixteenth Centuries
During the fifteenth and sixteenth centuries, Europeans embarked on voyages of discovery that carried them to both Asia and the Americas. Portugal dominated the ocean trade with Asia for most of this period. In the New World, reports of Spain's acquisition of vast wealth soon led France and England to attempt to establish their own territorial claims.

imported African slaves from the start. São Tomé and the other small islands off the Guinea Coast eventually became important waystations in the transatlantic slave trade.

Christopher Columbus and the Westward Route to Asia

Christopher Columbus was but one of many European mariners excited by the prospect of tapping into the wealth of Asia. Born in Genoa in 1451, he later lived in Portugal and Spain, where he read widely in geographical treatises and listened closely to the stories and rumors that circulated among mariners. As a young man, Columbus gained considerable experience with ocean travel, visiting Africa's Guinea Coast and Madeira, and perhaps even voyaging to Iceland.

He was not, however, the first European to believe that he could reach Asia by sailing westward. The idea developed logically during the fifteenth century as mariners gained knowledge and experience from their exploits in the Atlantic and around Africa. Most Europeans knew that the world was round, but scoffed at the idea of a westward voyage to Asia in the belief that no ship could carry enough provisions for such a long trip. Columbus's confidence that he could succeed grew from a mathematical error. He mistakenly calculated the earth's circumference as 18,000 (rather than 24,000) miles and so concluded that Asia lay just 3,500 miles west of the Canary Islands. Columbus first sought financial support for a westward voyage from the king of Portugal, whose advisers disputed his calculations and warned him that he would starve at sea before reaching Asia. Undaunted, he turned to Portugal's rival, Spain.

Columbus tried to convince Ferdinand and Isabella that his plan suited Spain's national goals. If he succeeded, Spain could grow rich from Asian trade, send Christian missionaries to Asia (a goal in keeping with the religious ideals of the *reconquista*), and perhaps enlist the Great Khan of China as an ally in the long struggle with Islam. If he failed, the "enterprise of the Indies" would cost little. The Spanish monarchs nonetheless kept Columbus waiting nearly seven years—until 1492, when the last Muslim stronghold at Granada fell to Spanish forces—before they gave him their support.

After thirty-three days at sea, Columbus and his men reached the Bahamas, probably landing on what is now called Watling Island. They spent four months exploring the Caribbean and visiting several islands, including Hispaniola (now the site of Haiti and the Dominican Republic) and Cuba. Although puzzled by his failure to find the fabled cities of China and Japan, Columbus believed that he had reached Asia. Three more voyages between 1493 and 1504, however, failed to yield clear evidence of an Asian landfall or Asian riches. Columbus reported that the islands he encountered contained "great mines of gold and other metals" and spices in abundance, yet all he brought back to Isabella and Ferdinand were strange plants and animals, some gold ornaments, and several kidnapped Taino Indians.

Frustrated in their search for wealth, Columbus and his men turned violent, sacking native villages and demanding tribute in gold. They forced gangs of Indians to pan rivers for the precious nuggets. But Caribbean gold reserves, found mainly on Hispaniola, Puerto Rico, and Cuba, were not extensive. Dissatisfied with the meager results, Columbus sought to transform the Indians themselves into a source of wealth.

In 1494, Columbus suggested to the Spanish monarchs that the Indies could yield a profit if islanders were sold as slaves. His plan earned him a sharp rebuke from Queen Isabella, who opposed enslaving people she considered to be new Spanish subjects. This royal fastidiousness was short-lived, however. Within a year, the queen agreed that native war captives could be enslaved. In succeeding decades, the Spanish government periodically called for fair treatment of Indians and prohibited their enslavement, but such measures were ignored by colonists on the other side of the Atlantic.

Columbus died in Spain in 1506, still convinced he had found Asia. What he had done was to set in motion a process that would transform both sides of the Atlantic. It would eventually bring wealth to many Europeans and immense suffering to Native Americans and Africans.

The Spanish Conquest and Colonization

Of all European nations, Spain was best suited to take advantage of Columbus's discovery. Its experience with the *reconquista* gave it a religious justification for conquest (bringing Christianity to nonbelievers) and an army of seasoned soldiers—*conquistadores*—eager to seek their fortunes in America now that the last Muslims had been expelled from Spain. In addition, during the *reconquista* and the conquest of the Canary Islands, Spain's rulers developed efficient tech-

A decidedly European view of Columbus's landing appears in this late sixteenth-century print. Columbus and his men, armed with guns and swords, are resplendent in European attire, while nearly naked Indians offer them gifts. To the left, Spaniards erect a cross to claim the land for Christianity. In the upper right, frightened natives flee into the woods.

First published in 1535, this woodcut shows Taino Indians panning for gold. Columbus and his men, desperate for riches to bring back to Spain but unaware that gold reserves on most Caribbean islands were quite small, compelled the Indians to search for the precious metal. After only a few decades of forced labor and harsh treatment, the native populations of the islands had all but disappeared.

niques for controlling newly conquered lands that could be applied to New World colonies.

The Spanish first consolidated their control of the Caribbean, establishing outposts on Cuba, Puerto Rico, and Jamaica (see Map 1–4). The *conquistadores* were more interested in finding gold and slaves than in creating permanent settlements. Leaving a trail of destruction, they attacked native villages and killed or captured the inhabitants. By 1524, the Tainos had all but died out; the Caribs survived on more isolated islands until the eighteenth century. Spanish soldiers then ventured to the mainland. In 1513 Juan Ponce de León led an expedition to Florida looking for the legendary fountain of youth. In that same year, Vasco Núñez de Balboa arrived in Central America, crossing the isthmus of Panama to the Pacific Ocean.

The end of the Aztec Empire.   In 1519, Hernán Cortés and six hundred soldiers—the light-skinned strangers who inspired the Indian messenger to rush to Moctezuma—landed on the coast of Mexico. Their subsequent actions more than fulfilled the Aztec king's belief that the Spaniards' arrival was an evil omen. "I and my companions," Cortés announced, "suffer from a disease of the heart which can be cured only with gold." By 1521, Cortés and his men had conquered the powerful Aztec empire, discovering riches beyond their wildest dreams. They "picked up the gold and fingered it like monkeys," reported one Aztec witness.

The swift, decisive Spanish victory depended on several factors. In part, the Spanish enjoyed certain technological advantages. Their guns and horses often enabled them to overwhelm larger groups of Aztec foot soldiers armed with spears and wooden swords edged with obsidian. But technology alone cannot account for the conquest of a vastly more numerous enemy, capable of absorbing far higher losses in combat.

Cortés benefited from two other factors. First, he exploited divisions within the Aztec empire. The Spanish acquired indispensable allies among subject Indians who resented Aztec domination, tribute demands, and seizure of captives for religious sacrifice. Cortés received invaluable help in communicating with these peoples from Malinche, a captive native woman who served as a translator (and who also bore him a son). He eventually gained 200,000 Indian allies eager to throw off Aztec rule.

A second and more important factor was disease. One of Cortés's men was infected with smallpox, which soon devastated the native population. European diseases had been unknown in the Americas before 1492, and Indians lacked resistance to them. Historians estimate that nearly 40 percent of the inhabitants of central Mexico died of smallpox within a year. Other diseases followed, including typhus, measles, and influenza. By 1600, the population of Mexico may have declined from over 15 million to less than a million people.

Aztec society and culture collapsed in the face of appalling mortality. "The illness was so dreadful," one survivor recalled, "that no one could walk or move. The sick were so utterly helpless that they could only lie on their beds like corpses, unable to move their limbs or even their heads.... If they did move their bodies, they screamed with pain." The epidemic ravaged families, wiped out villages, and destroyed traditional political authority. Early in their bid to gain control of the Aztec empire, the Spanish seized Moctezuma, and eventually put him to death. They did not have to kill his successor, however, for he died of disease not long after gaining the throne.

The fall of the Inca Empire.   In 1532, Francisco Pizarro and 180 men, following rumors of even greater riches than those of Mexico, discovered the Inca empire high in the Peruvian Andes. It was the largest empire in the Americas, stretching more than 2,000 miles from what is now Ecuador to Chile. An excellent network of roads and bridges linked this extensive territory to the imperial capital of Cuzco. Economically prosperous from trade and agriculture based on complex irrigation systems, the empire was also prone to political division. The Spaniards arrived at a moment of weakness for the empire. A few years before, the Inca ruler had died, probably from smallpox, and civil war had broken out between two of his sons. The victor, Atahualpa, was on his way from the empire's northern provinces to claim his throne in Cuzco when Pizarro intercepted him. Pizarro took Atahualpa hostage and despite receiving a colossal ransom—a roomful of gold and silver—had him killed. The Spaniards then captured Cuzco, eventually extended control over the whole empire, and established a new capital at Lima.

By 1550, Spain's New World empire stretched from the Caribbean through Mexico to Peru. It was administered from Spain by the Council of the Indies, which enacted laws for the empire and supervised an elaborate bureaucracy charged with their enforcement. The council aimed to project royal authority into every village in New Spain in order to maintain

MAP 1–4   Spanish, English, and French Settlements in North America in the Sixteenth Century
By the end of the sixteenth century, only Spain had established permanent settlements in North America. French outposts in Canada and at Fort Caroline, as well as the English settlement at Roanoke, failed to thrive. European rivalries for North America, however, would intensify after 1600.

political control and extract as much wealth as possible from the land and its people.

For more than a century, Spanish ships crossed the Atlantic carrying seemingly limitless amounts of treasure from the colonies. To extract this wealth, the colonial rulers subjected the native inhabitants of New Spain to compulsory tribute payments and forced labor. Tens of thousands of Indians toiled in silver mines in Peru and Bolivia and on sugar plantations in the Caribbean. When necessary, Spaniards imported African slaves to supplement a native labor force ravaged by disease and exhaustion.

Spanish incursions to the north.   The desire for gold eventually lured Spaniards farther into North America. In 1528, an expedition to Florida ended in disaster when the Spanish intruders provoked an attack by Apalachee Indians. Most of the Spanish survivors eventually perished, but Álvar Núñez Cabeza de Vaca and three other men (including an African slave) escaped from their captors and managed to reach Mexico after a grueling eight-year journey. In a published account of his ordeal, Cabeza de Vaca insisted that the interior of North America contained a fabulously wealthy empire (see "American Views: Cabeza de Vaca Among the Indians").

In this illustration from a Spanish monk's history of the Aztecs, Moctezuma observes a comet plummeting toward the earth, an omen that he believed presaged disaster for his people. The appearance of the comet coincided with the first reports of white-skinned strangers arriving on the coast of Mexico.

This report inspired other Spaniards to seek the treasures that had eluded its author. In 1539, Hernán de Soto—who tried unsuccessfully to get Cabeza de Vaca to serve as a guide—led an expedition from Florida to the Mississippi River. Along the way, the Spaniards harassed the native peoples, demanding provisions, burning villages, and capturing women to be servants and concubines. De Soto, who reportedly enjoyed "the sport of hunting Indians on horseback," ordered natives who resisted him to be mutilated, thrown to dogs, or burned alive. He and his men also exposed the Indians to deadly European diseases. Although weakened by native resistance, the expedition kept up its rampage for three years, turning toward Mexico only after de Soto died in 1542. In these same years, Francisco Vásquez de Coronado led three hundred troops on an equally destructive expedition through present-day Arizona, New Mexico, and Colorado on a futile search for the mythical Seven Cities of Cíbola, rumored to contain hoards of gold and precious stones.

The failure to find gold and silver halted Spain's attempt to extend its empire to the north. By the end of the sixteenth century, the Spanish maintained just two precarious footholds north of Mexico. One was at St. Augustine, on Florida's Atlantic coast. Founded in 1565, this fortified outpost served as a naval base to defend Spanish treasure fleets from raids by English and French privateers. The other settlement was located far to the west in what is now New Mexico. Juan de Oñate, on a futile search for silver mines, claimed the region for Spain in 1598. He and his men proceeded to antagonize the area's inhabitants. In one surprise attack, the Spaniards destroyed the ancient town of Acoma, killing or enslaving most of the residents. Having earned the enmity of the Pueblo people—astonishing even his own superiors with his brutality—Oñate barely managed to keep his tiny colony together.

Almost from the start of the conquest, the bloody tactics of men such as Oñate aroused protest back in Spain. The Indians' most eloquent advocate was Bartolomé de Las Casas, a Dominican priest shamed by his own role (as a layman) in the conquest of Hispaniola. In 1516, the Spanish king appointed him to the newly created office of Protector of the Indians, but his efforts had little effect. To publicize the horrors he saw, Las Casas wrote *In Defense of the Indians,* including graphic descriptions of native sufferings. Instead of eliciting Spanish reforms, however, his work inspired Protestant Europeans to create the "Black Legend," an exaggerated story according to which a fanatical Catholic Spain sought to spread its control at any cost.

The seeds of economic decline. Meanwhile, the vast riches of Central and South America glutted Spain's treasury. Between 1500 and 1650, an estimated 181 tons of gold and 16,000 tons of silver were shipped from the New World to Spain, making it the richest and most powerful state in Europe (see Figure 1–1). But this influx of American treasure had unforeseen consequences that would soon undermine Spanish predominance.

In 1492, the Spanish crown, determined to impose religious conformity after the *reconquista,* expelled from Spain all Jews who refused to become Christians. The refugees included many leading merchants who had contributed significantly to Spain's economy. The remaining Christian merchants, now awash in American riches, saw little reason to invest in new trade or productive enterprises that might have sustained the economy once the flow of New World treasure diminished. As a result, Spain's economy eventually stagnated.

Compounding the problem, the flood of American gold and silver contributed to what historians have called a "price revolution" in Europe. Beginning in the late fifteenth century, as Europe's population recovered from the Black Death, demographic and economic factors led to a rise in prices. This inflationary cycle was made worse by the influx of New World gold and silver. Workers, whose wages failed to rise as fast as prices, suffered, as did some aristocrats dependent on fixed rents from their estates. At the same time, Spain's monarchs wasted their American wealth fighting expensive wars against their European enemies that ultimately weakened the nation. By 1600, some disillusioned Spaniards were arguing that the conquest had brought more problems than benefits to their country.

The Columbian Exchange

Spain's long-term economic decline was just one of many consequences of the conquest of the New World. In the long run, the biological consequences of contact—what one historian has called the **Columbian exchange**—proved to be the most momentous (see the Overview table, The Columbian Exchange).

The most catastrophic result of the exchange was the exposure of Native Americans to Old World diseases. Europeans and Africans, long exposed to these diseases, had developed some immunity to them. Native Americans, lacking such contact, had not. The Black Death of 1347–1351, Europe's worst epidemic, killed perhaps a third of its population. Epidemics of smallpox, measles, typhus, and influenza struck Native Americans with far greater force, killing half, and sometimes as many as 90 percent, of the people in communities exposed to them. The only American disease that may have infected Old World populations was a sexually transmitted form of syphilis, which appeared in Spain just after Columbus returned from his first voyage.

Another important aspect of the Columbian exchange was the introduction of Old World livestock to the New World, which began when Columbus brought horses, sheep, cattle, pigs, and goats with him on his second voyage in 1493. Native Americans had few domesticated animals of their own (mainly dogs, and, in the Peruvian Andes, llamas and alpacas). The large European beasts created problems as well as opportunities for native peoples. With few natural predators to limit their numbers, livestock populations boomed in the New World, competing with native mammals for grazing. At least at first, the Indians' unfamiliarity with the use of horses in warfare often gave mounted European soldiers a decisive military advantage. But some native groups adopted these animals for their own purposes. Yaquis, Pueblos, and other peoples in the Southwest began to raise cattle and sheep. By the eighteenth century, Plains Indians had reoriented their culture around the use of horses, which had become essential

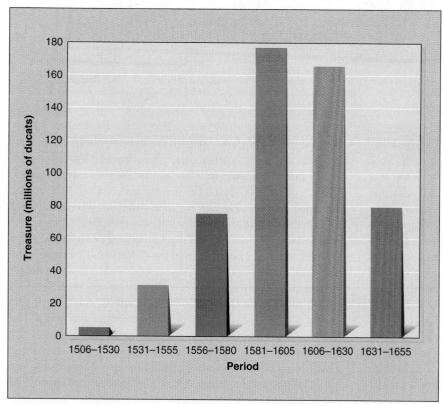

FIGURE 1–1 **Value of New World Treasure Imported into Spain, 1506–1655** During the sixteenth and early seventeenth centuries, Spain was the only European power to reap great wealth from North America. The influx of New World treasure, however, slowed the development of Spain's economy in the long run. [Note: A ducat was a gold coin.]

Data Source: J. H. Elliott, *Imperial Spain, 1469–1716* (1964), p. 175.

for travel and hunting buffalo. Horses also became a primary object for trading and raiding among Plains peoples.

European ships carried unintentional passengers too. The black rat, a carrier of disease, arrived on the first voyages. So did insects, including honeybees, previously unknown in the New World. Ships also brought weeds such as thistles and dandelions, whose seeds were often embedded in hay for animal fodder.

Columbus introduced such European crops as wheat, chickpeas, melons, onions, and fruit trees to the Caribbean. Europeans learned to cultivate native foods, such as corn, tomatoes, squash, beans, cacao, peppers, and potatoes, as well as nonfood plants such as tobacco and cotton, carrying many of these plants back to Europe. New World food crops enriched Old World diets and the nutritional benefits eventually contributed to a sharp rise in Europe's population. Over time, many of these more numerous Europeans chose to leave their overcrowded communities for the New World.

Cultural Perceptions and Misperceptions

As Europeans and Native Americans met one another, curiosity and confusion often marked their early encounters. Even simple transactions produced unexpected results. When Columbus showed swords to Caribbean islanders, for example, "they took them by the edge and through ignorance cut themselves" because they had never touched metal weapons. The first Indians whom Cortés allowed aboard a Spanish ship fainted at the sound of a large cannon being fired. French explorers were similarly taken by surprise when they choked while smoking Iroquois tobacco, which they thought tasted like "powdered pepper." These relatively minor mishaps were soon overshadowed by more substantial interactions that highlighted cultural differences between Indians and Europeans.

Most Indians believed that the universe contained friendly and hostile spiritual forces in human and other-than-human forms (such as plants, animals, and stars). People interacted with the spirit world through ceremonies that often involved exchanging gifts. North of Mexico, Indians (like West Africans) passed on religious beliefs through oral traditions, not in writing. To Europeans accustomed to worshiping one God in an organized church and preserving their beliefs in a written Bible, Indian traditions were incomprehensible. When Columbus noted that the Tainos had no churches, he concluded that they had no religion. Many Europeans went further, assuming that Indians worshiped the Devil. Indians, in turn, often found Christianity confusing and at first rejected European pressure to convert. As some Iroquois explained to colonists, "We do not know that God, we have never seen him, we know not who he is."

Different understandings of gender roles provided another source of confusion. Europeans regarded men as superior to women and thought they were thus the natural rulers of society. They disapproved of the less restrictive gender divisions among Native Americans. Wampanoags and Powhatans sometimes accepted female leaders, for instance, and Huron women helped to select male chiefs. Many Indian societies were matrilineal, tracing descent through the mother's family instead of the father's, as Europeans did. In matrilineal societies, married couples lived with the wife's family, children inherited property from their mother's brother, and rulers succeeded to their positions through their mother's family line. Europeans, accustomed to societies in which men did most agricultural work, objected to Indian women's dominant role in farming and assumed that men's hunting was more for recreation than subsistence. They concluded that Indian women lived "a most slavish life." Indians, in turn, thought that European men failed to make good use of their wives. In Massachusetts, native men ridiculed colonists "for spoiling good working creatures" by not making their women work in the fields.

In order for Indians and Europeans to get along peaceably, each side would have to look past these and other cultural differences and adapt to the new circumstances under which both groups now lived. At first, such harmony seemed possible. But it soon became clear that Europeans intended to dominate the lands they discovered. Only three days after he arrived in America, Columbus announced his intention "not to pass by any island of which I did not take possession." Such claims to dominance sparked vigorous resistance from native peoples everywhere who strove to maintain their autonomy in a changed world.

Competition for A Continent

Spain's New World bonanza attracted the attention of other European states eager to share in the wealth. Portugal soon acquired its own profitable piece of South America. In 1494, the conflicting claims of Portugal and Spain were resolved by the **Treaty of Tordesillas**. The treaty drew a north–south line approximately 1,100 miles west of the Cape Verde Islands. Spain received all lands west of the line, while Portugal held sway to the east. This limited Portugal's New World empire to Brazil, where settlers established sugar plantations worked by slave labor. But the treaty also protected Portugal's claims in Africa and Asia, which lay east of the line.

France and England, of course, rejected the granting of the Western Hemisphere to Spain and Portugal. Their initial challenges to Spanish dominance in the New World, however, proved quite feeble. Domestic troubles—largely sparked by the Protestant Reformation—distracted the two countries from the pursuit of empire. By the close of the sixteenth century, both France and England insisted on their rights to New World lands, but neither had created a permanent settlement to support its claim.

Early French Efforts in North America

France was a relative latecomer to New World exploration. In 1494, French troops invaded Italy, beginning a long and ultimately unsuccessful war with the Holy Roman Empire. Preoccupied with European affairs, France's rulers paid little attention to America. But when news of Cortés's exploits in Mexico arrived in the 1520s, King Francis I wanted his own New World empire to enrich France and block further Spanish expansion. In 1524, Francis sponsored a voyage by Giovanni da Verrazano,

American Views

Cabeza de Vaca among the Indians (1530)

Álvar Núñez Cabeza de Vaca came to the New World in 1527 in search of riches, not suffering. But the Spanish expedition of which he was a member met disaster shortly after it arrived in Florida on a mission to conquer the region north of the Gulf of Mexico. Of an original group of three hundred soldiers, only Cabeza de Vaca and three other men (including one African slave) survived. They did so by walking thousands of miles overland from the Gulf Coast to northern Mexico, an eight-year-long ordeal that tested the men's wits and physical endurance. Instead of entering Indian villages as proud conquistadors,

Cabeza de Vaca and his companions encountered native peoples from a position of weakness. In order to survive, they had to adapt to the ways of the peoples across whose land they passed. After Cabeza de Vaca made it back to Mexico City, he described his experiences in an official report to the king of Spain. This remarkable document offers vivid descriptions of the territory extending from northern Florida to northern Mexico and the many peoples who inhabited it. It is equally interesting, as this extract suggests, for what it reveals about Cabeza de Vaca himself

and the changes he made in the interest of survival.

- While living among the Capoques, what sort of work did Cabeza de Vaca have to do, and why?
- Why did Cabeza de Vaca decide to become a merchant? What advantages did this way of life offer him?
- Why did the Indians welcome Cabeza de Vaca into their communities even though he was a stranger?

[I remained with the Capoques] for more than a year, and because of the great labors they forced me to perform and the bad treatment they gave me, I resolved to flee from them and go to those who live in the forests and on the mainland, who are called those of Charruco, because I was unable to endure the life that I had with these others; because among many other tasks, I had to dig the roots to eat out from under the water and among the rushes where they grew in the ground. And because of this, my fingers were so worn that when a reed touched them it caused them to bleed, and the reeds cut me in many places.... And because of this, I set to the task of going over to the others, and with them things were somewhat better for me. And because I became a merchant, I tried to exercise the vocation as best I knew how. And because of this they gave me food to eat and treated me well, and they importuned me to go from one place to another to obtain the things they needed, because on account of the continual warfare in the land, there is little traffic or communication among them. And with my dealings and wares I entered in-

land as far as I desired, and I went along the coast for forty or fifty leagues. The mainstay of my trade was pieces of snail shell and the hearts of them; and conch shells with which they cut a fruit that is like frijoles [beans], with which they perform cures and do their dances and make celebrations.... And in exchange and as barter for it, I brought forth hides and red ocher with which they smear themselves and dye their faces and hair, flints to make the points of arrows, paste, and stiff canes to make them, and some tassels made from deer hair which they dye red. And this occupation served me well, because practicing it, I had the freedom to go wherever I wanted, and I was not constrained in any way nor enslaved, and wherever I went they treated me well and gave me food out of want for my wares, and most importantly because doing that, I was able to seek out the way by which I would go forward. And among them I was very well known; when they saw me and I brought them the things they needed, they were greatly pleased.

Source: Rolena Adorno and Patrick Charles Pautz, eds., *The Narrative of Cabeza de Vaca* (Lincoln: University of Nebraska Press, 2003), pp. 96–97.

The Columbian Exchange

	From Old World to New World	From New World to Old World
Diseases	Smallpox, measles, plague, typhus, influenza, yellow fever, diphtheria, scarlet fever, whooping cough	Sexually transmitted strain of syphilis
Animals	Horses, cattle, pigs, sheep, goats, donkeys, mules, black rats, honeybees, cockroaches	Turkeys
Plants	Wheat, sugar, barley, apples, pears, peaches, plums, cherries, coffee, rice, dandelions, and other weeds	Maize, beans, peanuts, potatoes, sweet potatoes, manioc, squash, papayas, guavas, tomatoes, avocadoes, pineapple, chili pepper, cacao

an Italian navigator, who mapped the North American coast from present-day South Carolina to Maine. During the 1530s and 1540s, the French mariner Jacques Cartier made three voyages in search of rich mines to rival those of Mexico and Peru. He explored the St. Lawrence River up to what is now Montreal, hoping to discover a water route through the continent to Asia (the so-called Northwest Passage).

On his third voyage, in 1541, Cartier was to serve under the command of a nobleman, Jean-François de la Rocque, Sieur de Roberval, who was commissioned by the king to establish a permanent settlement in Canada. Troubles in recruiting colonists delayed Roberval, who—when he finally set sail in 1542—ended up taking convicts as his settlers. Cartier sailed ahead, gathered samples of what he thought were gold and diamonds, and returned to France.

This first attempt to found a permanent French colony failed miserably. Roberval's expedition was poorly organized, and his cruel treatment of the convicts provoked several uprisings. The Iroquois, suspicious of repeated French intrusions on their lands, saw no reason to help them. A year after they arrived in Canada, Roberval and the surviving colonists were back in France. Their return coincided with news that the gold brought back by Cartier was iron pyrite ("fool's gold"), and the diamonds were worthless quartz crystals.

Disappointed with their Canadian expeditions, the French made a few forays to the south, establishing outposts in what is now South Carolina in 1562 and Florida in 1564. They soon abandoned the Carolina colony, and Spanish forces captured the Florida fort. Then, back in France, a prolonged civil war broke out between Catholics and Protestants. Renewed interest in colonization would have to await the return of peace at home.

English Attempts in the New World

The English were quicker than the French to stake a claim to the New World but no more successful at colonization. In 1497, King Henry VII sent John Cabot, an Italian mariner, to explore eastern Canada on England's behalf. But neither Henry nor any of his wealthy subjects would invest the funds necessary to follow up on Cabot's discoveries. For nearly half a century, English contact with America was limited to the seasonal voyages of fishermen who lived each summer in Newfoundland, fished for cod offshore, and returned in autumn.

The lapse in English activity in the New World stemmed from religious troubles at home. Between 1534 and 1558, England changed its official religion several times. King Henry VIII, who had once defended the Catholic Church against its critics, took up the Protestant cause when the pope refused to annul his marriage to Catherine of Aragon. In 1534, Henry declared himself the head of a separate Church of England and seized the Catholic Church's English property. Because many English people sympathized with the Protestant cause, there was relatively little opposition to Henry's actions. But in 1553, Mary—daughter of the spurned Catherine of Aragon—became queen and tried to bring England back to Catholicism. She had nearly three hundred Protestants burned at the stake for their beliefs (earning her the nickname "Bloody Mary"), and many others went into exile in Europe.

Mary's brief but destructive reign ended in 1558, and her half-sister Elizabeth, a committed Protestant, became queen. Elizabeth ruled for forty-five years (1558–1603), restoring Protestantism as the state religion, bringing stability to the nation, and renewing England's interest in the New World. She and her subjects saw colonization not only as a way to gain wealth and political advantage but also as a Protestant crusade against Catholic domination.

The colonization of Ireland. England's first target for colonization, however, was not America but Ireland. Located less than 60 miles west of England and populated by Catholics, Ireland threatened to become a base from which Spain or another Catholic power might invade England. Henry VIII had tried, with limited success, to bring the island under English control in the 1530s and 1540s. Elizabeth renewed the attempt in the 1560s with a series of brutal expeditions that destroyed Irish villages and slaughtered the inhabitants. Several veterans of these campaigns later took part in New World colonization and drew on their Irish experience for guidance.

Two aspects of that experience were particularly important. First, the English transferred their assumptions about

Irish "savages" to Native Americans. Englishmen in America frequently observed similarities between Indians and the Irish. "When they [the Indians] have their apparel on they look like Irish," noted one Englishman. "The natives of New England," he added, "are accustomed to build their houses much like the wild Irish." Because the English held the "wild Irish" in contempt, these observations encouraged them to scorn the Indians. When Indians resisted their attempts at conquest, the English recalled the Irish example, claiming that native "savagery" required brutal suppression.

Second, the Irish experience influenced English ideas about colonial settlement. English conquerors set up "plantations" surrounded by palisades on seized Irish lands. These plantations were meant to be civilized outposts in a savage land. Their aristocratic owners imported Protestant tenants from England and Scotland to farm the land. Native Irish people, considered too wild to join proper Christian communities, were excluded. English colonists in America followed this precedent when they established plantations that separated English and native peoples.

Expeditions to the New World.   Sir Humphrey Gilbert, a notoriously cruel veteran of the Irish campaigns, became fascinated with the idea of New World colonization. He composed a treatise to persuade Queen Elizabeth to support such an endeavor. The queen, who counted Gilbert among her favorite courtiers, authorized several exploratory voyages, including Martin Frobisher's three trips in 1576–1578 in search of the Northwest Passage to Asia. Frobisher failed to find the elusive passage and sent back shiploads of glittering ore that proved to be fool's gold. Elizabeth had better luck in allowing privateers, such as John Hawkins and Francis Drake, to raid Spanish ships and New World ports for gold and silver. The plunder taken during these raids enriched both the sailors and their investors—one of whom was the queen herself.

Meanwhile, Gilbert continued to promote New World settlement, arguing that it would increase England's trade and provide a place to send unemployed Englishmen. Like many of his contemporaries, Gilbert believed that England's "surplus" population threatened social order. The population was indeed growing, and economic changes often made it difficult for people to support themselves. Many landlords had been converting farmland into sheep pastures in order to profit from the wool trade, but in doing so threw tenant families off the land. Gilbert suggested offering free land in America to English families willing to emigrate.

In 1578, Gilbert received permission to set up a colony along the North American coast. It took him five years to organize an expedition to Newfoundland, which he claimed for England. After sailing southward seeking a more favorable site for a colony, Gilbert headed home, only to be lost at sea during an Atlantic storm. The impetus for English colonization did not die with him, however, for his half-brother, Sir Walter Raleigh (another veteran of the Irish wars), took up the cause.

The Roanoke Colony.   In 1584, Raleigh sent an expedition to find a suitable location for a colony. The Carolina coast seemed promising, so Raleigh sent men in 1585 to build a settlement on Roanoke Island. Most of the colonists were soldiers fresh from Ireland who refused to grow their own food, insisting that the Roanoke Indians should feed them. When the local chief, Wingina, organized native resistance, they killed him. Eventually, the colonists, disappointed not to have found any treasure and exhausted by a harsh winter, returned to England in 1586.

Two members of these early expeditions, however, left a more positive legacy. Thomas Hariot studied the Roanoke and Croatoan Indians and identified plants and animals in the area, hoping that some might prove to be profitable commodities. John White drew maps and painted a series of watercolors depicting the natives and the coastal landscape. When Raleigh tried once more, in 1587, to found a colony, he chose White to be its leader. This attempt also failed. The ship captain dumped the settlers—who, for the first time, included women and children—on Roanoke Island so that he could pursue Spanish treasure ships. White waited until his granddaughter, Virginia Dare (the first English child born in America), was born and then sailed to England for supplies. But the outbreak of war with Spain delayed his return for three years. Spain had gathered an immense fleet to invade England, and all English ships were needed for defense. Although England defeated the Armada in 1588, White could not obtain a relief ship for Roanoke until 1590.

White found the colony deserted. Digging through the ruins of the village, he found "my books torn from the covers, the frames of some of my pictures and Maps rotten and spoiled with rain." He also saw the word CROATOAN carved on a post and assumed that the colonists had moved to nearby Croatoan Island. But bad weather prevented him from searching there. For years, English and Spanish mariners reported seeing white people along the coast of Chesapeake Bay. But no Roanoke colonists were ever found. They may have moved to the mainland and intermarried with local Indians. One historian has speculated that they survived until 1607 when Powhatan Indians, angered by the appearance of more English settlers, killed them. The actual fate of the "Lost Colony" at Roanoke will probably never be known.

At this point, Raleigh gave up on North America and turned his attention to his Irish plantations. But England's interest in colonization did not wane. In 1584, Richard Hakluyt had aroused enthusiasm for America by writing the *Discourse on the Western Planting* for the queen and her advisers. He argued that England would prosper from trade and the sale of New World commodities. Once the Indians were civilized, Hakluyt added, they would eagerly purchase English goods. Equally important, England could plant "sincere religion" (that is, Protestant Christianity) in the New World and block Spanish expansion. Hakluyt's arguments fired the imaginations of many people, and the defeat of the Spanish Armada emboldened England to challenge Spain's New World dominance. The experience of Roanoke should have tempered that enthusiasm, illustrating the difficulty of establishing colonies. Roanoke's fate underscored the need for adequate funding, the unsuitability of soldiers as colonists, and the

The Disappearance of Cod off the Grand Banks

Not long after John Cabot returned from his voyage to America in 1497, rumors circulated that he had found astonishingly rich fishing grounds off the coast of Newfoundland. As it happened, Basque fishermen sailing from ports in northern Spain and southwestern France already knew about this bonanza. But Cabot's discovery spread the news, and by the 1550s, over a hundred ships a year traveled from Europe to fish in the waters of the Grand Banks in the northern Atlantic. By the early sixteenth century, 60 percent of the fish eaten in Europe was cod, and most of it came from the Grand Banks. But now, five hundred years later, cod stocks are at an all-time low due in part to ocean warming but also because of overfishing. Up until the early nineteenth century, most fishermen used handlines—single baited hooks fastened to a weight—dropped in the water from sailing vessels. Now commercial fishermen use enormous nets, harvesting their catch from motorized vessels. Experts differ on whether cod populations can recover. Canadian officials have established a moratorium on fishing in the area in order to see if recovery is possible. The long-term legacy of John Cabot's voyage may well be the disappearance of the resource that drew him and many other European adventurers to North America in the first place.

■ **What does the story of the Grand Banks tell us about the long-run environmental consequences of Europeans' contact with the New World?**

Hand-lining for cod, the fishing method depicted in this eighteenth-century engraving, produced ample catches but did not reduce cod populations to dangerously low levels.

By the twentieth century, commercial fishermen using enormous nets and motorized boats have helped to shrink cod stocks to an all-time low.

PEARSON myhistorylab

From Then to Now Activity

1-1 Raimondo di Soncino to the duke of Milan, December 18, 1497. Letter from Milan's ambassador in London describing John Cabot's discovery of Grand Banks.

1-2 Nicolas Denys, *The Description and Natural History of the Coasts of North America (Acadia)*. Description of Grand Banks fishery and fishing techniques.

1-3 John Smith, *A Description of New England*, 1672. Description of fishing grounds off Cape Cod.

1-4 Map of Newfoundland and Grand Banks, 1977. Shows the 200-mile limit within which foreign boats could not fish.

John White's picture of the village of Pomeiooc offers a rare glimpse of a sixteenth-century Eastern Woodlands Indian community. The village is surrounded by a palisade with two entrances; evidence suggests that White exaggerated the spacing of the poles in order to depict the houses inside. Eighteen dwellings constructed of poles and mats are clustered around the village circumference; inside some of them raised sleeping platforms can be seen. Many of the villagers are clustered around a central fire, while others are working or conversing.

Algonquian Indian village of Pomeiooc, North Carolina: Watercolor, c. 1585 by John White.

need to maintain good relations with the Indians. But the English were slow to learn these lessons; when they resumed colonization efforts in 1607, they repeated Roanoke's mistakes, with disastrous results for the people involved. As it was, the sixteenth century ended with no permanent English settlement in the New World.

Conclusion

Dramatic changes occurred in North America during the century after Moctezuma's messenger spotted the Spanish ships. Europeans, eager for wealth and power, set out to claim a continent that just a hundred years earlier they had not dreamed existed. African slaves were brought to the Caribbean, Mexico, and Brazil, and forced to labor under extremely harsh conditions for white masters. The Aztec and Incan empires collapsed in the wake of the Spanish conquest. In the Caribbean and parts of Mexico and Peru, untold numbers of native peoples succumbed to European diseases they had never before encountered.

And yet conditions in 1600 bore clearer witness to the past than to the future. Despite all that had happened, North America was still Indian country. Only Spain had established North American colonies, and even its soldiers struggled to expand north of Mexico. Spain's outposts in Florida and New Mexico staked claims to territory that it did not really control. Except in Mexico and the Caribbean, Europeans had merely touched the continent's shores. In 1600, despite the virulent epidemics, native peoples (even in Mexico) still greatly outnumbered European and African immigrants. The next century, however, brought many powerful challenges both to native control and to the Spanish monopoly of settlement.

Review Questions

1. How did the Aztecs who first glimpsed Spanish ships off the coast of Mexico describe to Moctezuma what they had seen? What details most captured their attention?

2. Compare men's and women's roles in Native American, West African, and European societies. What were the similarities and differences? How did differences between European and Native American gender roles lead to misunderstandings?

3. Many of the first European colonizers in North America were military veterans. What impact did this have on their relations with Indian peoples?

4. Why did Spain so quickly become the dominant colonial power in North America? What advantages did it enjoy over France and England?

5. What role did religion play in early European efforts at overseas colonization? Did religious factors always encourage colonization, or did they occasionally interfere with European expansion?

6. In what ways were trade networks important in linking different groups of people in the Old and New Worlds?

Key Terms

Archaic Period (p. 3)

Aztecs (p. 6)

Cahokia (p. 8)

Columbian Exchange (p. 20)

Culture areas (p. 4)

Great League of Peace and Power (p. 8)

Predestination (p. 13)

Protestants (p. 13)

Reconquista (p. 13)

Reformation (p. 13)

Songhai Empire (p. 9)

Tordesillas, Treaty of (p. 21)

Recommended Reading

Adorno, Rolena and Patrick Charles Pautz, eds. *The Narrative of Cabeza de Vaca* (2003). A remarkable account of the Spanish explorer's harrowing eight-year-long journey from Florida to Mexico.

Josephy, Alvin M., Jr. *America in 1492: The World of the Indian Peoples before the Arrival of Columbus* (1991). A collection of essays describing the wide variety of Indian cultures in North America prior to contact with Europeans.

Leon-Portillo, Miguel. *The Broken Spears: The Aztec Account of the Conquest of Mexico* (1962; new edition, 1992). Reprints of translated Indian chronicles, providing a moving account of the Aztec experience of the Spanish conquest.

Phillips, William D., Jr., and Carla Rahn Phillips. *The Worlds of Christopher Columbus* (1992). A judicious biography of Columbus that places him firmly in the context of fifteenth-century European culture.

Thornton, John. *Africa and Africans in the Making of the Atlantic World, 1400–1680,* 2nd ed. (1998). A thorough examination of the causes and consequences of the movement of Africans throughout the Atlantic world and the rise of the slave trade.

Townsend, Camilla. *Malintzin's Choices: An Indian Woman in the Conquest of Mexico* (2006). A fascinating account of the native woman whose translating skills helped Cortés in the conquest of the Aztec empire.

Where to Learn More

■ **Cahokia Mounds State Historic Site, Collinsville, Illinois.**   This site, occupied from A.D. 600 to 1500, was the largest Mississippian community in eastern North America. It now includes numerous exhibits, and archaeological excavations continue in the vicinity. The website, www.siue.edu/CAHOKIAMOUNDS, contains information and photos of archaeological excavations, as well as a link to a virtual tour.

■ **Mashantucket Pequot Museum, Mashantucket, Connecticut.**   This tribally owned and operated complex offers a view of eastern Woodlands Indian life, focusing on the Pequots of eastern Connecticut. Exhibits include dioramas, films, interactive programs, and a reconstructed sixteenth-century Pequot village. The homepage for the Mashantucket Pequot Museum and Research Center is www.mashantucket.com.

■ **Mesa Verde National Park, Colorado.**   Occupied by Ancestral Puebloan peoples as early as A.D. 550, the area contains a variety of sites, from early pithouses to spectacular cliff dwellings. The official National Park webpage for Mesa Verde is www.nps.gov/meve. Information on individual houses and sites within the park, plus travel and lodging information can be found at www.mesa.verde.national-park.com.

■ **St. Augustine, Florida.**   Founded in 1565, St. Augustine is the site of the first permanent Spanish settlement in North America. Today the restored community resembles a Spanish colonial town, with narrow, winding streets and seventeenth- and eighteenth-century buildings. The site also contains the restored Castillo de San Marcos, now a national park. The official website for Historic St. Augustine, www.oldcity.com/his2.html, provides considerable information about the origins and development of the Spanish settlement.

Study Resources

PEARSON
myhistorylab

For study resources for this chapter, go to www.myhistorylab.com and choose *The American Journey.* You will find a wealth of study and review material for this chapter, including pre- and post-tests, customized study plan, key term review flash cards, interactive map and document activities, and documents for analysis.

This wooden blockhouse, reconstructed on the basis of archaeological findings, stood at one corner of a fort in Wolstenholme Towne, in Martin's Hundred, Virginia. In 1622, Powhatan Indians attacked this and other Virginia settlements in retaliation for years of English depredations.

Transplantation 2
1600–1685

Martin's Hundred in Virginia, 1623

Loving and kind father and mother:

My most humble duty remembered to you,… This is to let you understand that I your child am in a most heavy case by reason of the nature of the country, [which] is such that it causeth much sickness, as the scurvy and the bloody flux and diverse other diseases, which maketh the body very poor and weak…. [Since] I came out of the ship I never ate anything but peas, and loblollie (that is water gruel)…. A mouthful of bread for a penny loaf must serve for four men which is most pitiful…. [We] live in fear of the enemy every hour…for our plantation is very weak by reason of the death and sickness of our company….

But I am not half a quarter so strong as I was in England, and all is for want of victuals, for I do protest unto you that I have eaten more in [one] day at home than I have allowed me here for a week….

[I] saith that if you love me you will redeem me suddenly, for which I do entreat and beg…. Good father, do not forget me, but have mercy and pity my miserable case. I know if you did but see me, you would weep to see me….

Richard Frethorne

Susan M. Kingsbury, ed., *The Records of the Virginia Company of London*, 4 vols. (Washington, D.C., 1935), 4:58–62.

myhistorylab

Personal Journeys Online

- ■ Rev. Francis Higginson, July 1629. Letter from Massachusetts to His Friends in Leicester, England.

- ■ Father Isaac Jogues, Novum Belgium. 1646. Description of New Amsterdam.

- ■ Hans Sloan, A Voyage to the Islands, 1707. Description of early 18th-century Jamaica.

Richard Frethorne had crossed the Atlantic to seek his fortune in the new colony of Virginia. Like many emigrants, he surely hoped that one day he would become a prosperous landowner, a status beyond his reach in England. He may have read one of several promotional tracts that described Virginia as a healthy and fruitful land. But as his plaintive letter to his parents indicates, life in Virginia was not at all what Frethorne expected it to be. Instead of health and prosperity, Frethorne found sickness and starvation. Fears of an attack by enemy Indians compounded his misery. Not long before Frethorne penned his letter, Powhatan Indians had launched a deadly assault against the colonists in retaliation for English depredations against native villages. Yet the starving young Englishman could not simply board the next ship for England. He was under contract to work for the Virginia Company and could not leave until he had completed his term of service. Hence Frethorne's anguished plea to his father to "redeem" him, or buy out the remainder of his contract so that he could return home sooner.

Frethorne's experience reveals several important aspects of European colonization in the New World. Although his distress was not shared by all colonists, it was sadly typical of many English emigrants to early Virginia. Colonization offered opportunities for advancement, to be sure, but often at the price of sickness, suffering, and danger. Virginia turned out to be England's first permanent colony in the New World, but from Frethorne's perspective in 1623, it was a fragile settlement teetering on the brink of disaster. If he knew about the "Lost Colony" at Roanoke, Frethorne may have wondered if Virginia would share its fate.

Virginia's eventual success, and that of other English colonies, depended upon the willingness of thousands of individuals like Richard Frethorne to face the challenges posed by overseas settlement. Even as their emigration was inspired by hopes of improvement, their quest also reflected England's desire to claim a portion of the New World for itself. Frethorne's journey to Virginia occurred at a time of increased rivalry among European nations eager to replicate Spain's conquest of rich empires. In this scramble for American colonies, England's greatest adversaries were France and the Netherlands. If ordinary colonists were often preoccupied with their own tribulations, their leaders could never forget the high stakes involved in the international race for overseas possessions.

The French in North America

In the mid-sixteenth century, religious warfare between Catholics and Protestants at home had interrupted France's efforts to establish a foothold in North America. So long as this conflict divided the nation, the only French subjects who maintained regular contact with the New World were fishermen making seasonal voyages to the waters off the coast of Newfoundland. But in the early seventeenth century, after King Henry IV restored civil order in France, the situation changed. With the creation of permanent settlements first along the St. Lawrence River and later in the continent's interior, France staked its claim to a New World empire.

The Quest for Furs and Converts

French fishermen who set up frames on the Newfoundland shore to dry their catch frequently encountered Indians interested in trading beaver pelts for European goods. There was a ready market for these furs in Europe, where beaver hats had become very fashionable. Thus furs joined fish as a source of wealth, and a reason for French explorers and entrepreneurs to establish the colony of New France.

In 1608, Samuel de Champlain led an expedition up the St. Lawrence River to found a permanent settlement at Quebec. This village was eventually joined by two others—Trois-Rivières (founded 1634) and Montreal (1642)—located farther up the river (see Map 2–1). For several decades, the colony was managed by the Company of New France, a private

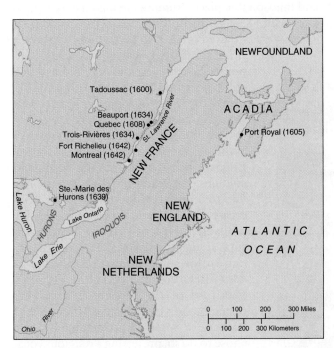

MAP 2–1   New France, c. 1650
By 1650, New France contained a number of thinly populated settlements along the St. Lawrence River Valley and the eastern shore of Lake Huron. Most colonists lived in Quebec and Montreal; other sites served mainly as fur-trading posts and Jesuit missions to the Huron Indians.

CHRONOLOGY

1581	Northern Provinces of Holland declare independence from Spain.
1589	King Henry IV of France signs Edict of Nantes, granting religious toleration to French Protestants and effectively ending civil war over religion.
1602	Founding of Dutch East India Company.
1603–1625	James I reigns as king of England.
1607	Founding of English colonies at Jamestown and Sagadahoc.
1608	Establishment of French colony at Quebec.
1619	First Africans arrive in Jamestown.
	Virginia's House of Burgesses meets for the first time.
1620	Founding of Plymouth Colony in New England.
	Mayflower Compact signed.
1620s	Tobacco boom in Virginia.
1624	Dutch found colony of New Netherland.
1625	Virginia becomes a royal colony.
	Fort Amsterdam founded.
1625–1649	Charles I reigns as king of England.
1627	English colony at Barbados founded.
1630	Massachusetts Bay Colony founded.
1630–1642	Great Migration to New England.
1634	Lord Baltimore (Cecilius Calvert) founds proprietary colony of Maryland.
1635–1636	Roger Williams banished from Massachusetts; founds Providence, Rhode Island.
1637	Anne Hutchinson banished from Massachusetts.
	Pequot War.
1638	New Haven colony founded.
1640s	Sugar cultivation and slavery established in West Indies.
1642–1660	English Civil War and Interregnum.
1649	Maryland's Act for Religious Toleration.
1654	Jewish emigrants from Brazil move to New Amsterdam, creating North America's first permanent Jewish community.
1660	Charles II restored to English throne; reigns until 1685.
1663	Founding of Carolina colony.
1664	New Netherland conquered by the English, becomes New York.
	New Jersey established.
1673	French explorers reach the Mississippi River.
1681	Founding of Pennsylvania.

corporation working on its own behalf as well as in France's imperial interests. New France grew slowly; by the 1660s, there were only 3,200 colonists clustered in and around the three main villages.

The fur trade supporting the colony's development functioned as a partnership between Indians and Europeans. Indians performed most of the work—trapping beavers, preparing skins, carrying pelts from the interior to trading posts along the St. Lawrence—in return for axes, knives, metal pots, and glass beads. At first, some colonists anticipated that economic ties between the two peoples would be supplemented by marital ones as French traders took Indian wives. Intermarriage, however, was never widespread, occurring mainly among **coureurs de bois** ("woods runners"), independent fur traders who ventured into the forests to live and trade among native peoples.

Indian peoples such as the Montagnais and Hurons welcomed the French not only as trading partners, but also as military allies, making sure that the newcomers understood that the two roles had to be linked. As a result, the fur trade entangled the French in rivalries among Indian groups that long predated European contact. Champlain's alliance with the Hurons and other St. Lawrence Valley Indians drew the French into conflict with their Iroquois enemies, forcing colonial authorities for more than a century thereafter to engage in delicate diplomatic maneuvers to ensure New France's security.

For some French colonists, saving Indian souls was even more important than profiting from furs. Beginning in the 1630s, Jesuit missionaries—members of a Catholic religious order founded during the Counter-Reformation—tried to convince Indians to come to the French settlements to hear Christian preaching and learn European ways. When that tactic failed, Jesuits traveled to native villages and learned native languages, bringing Christianity directly to Indian populations.

The Development of New France

After 1663, New France underwent several important changes. King Louis XIV disbanded the Company of New France and assumed direct control of the colony. Political reorganization followed. New France was henceforth ruled by two royal appointees: a governor charged with military and diplomatic affairs, and an *intendant* who oversaw colonial finances and the judicial system. The French government also vastly improved Canada's military defenses, investing money in the construction of forts and sending over professional soldiers. This was a greater investment in defense than English kings would provide for their colonies until the middle of the eighteenth century.

French officials launched a massive campaign to increase migration to the colony. They sent more than 700 orphaned girls and widows—called *filles du roi,* or "king's daughters"—to provide wives in a colony where there were six men of marriageable age for every unmarried French woman. Many male immigrants were *engagés,* or **indentured servants**, who agreed to work for three years in return for food, lodging, a small salary, and a return passage to France.

Despite these efforts, only about 250 French immigrants arrived each year. Several factors discouraged prospective colonists, not least of which was Canada's reputation as a distant and inhospitable place. Rumors circulated about frigid Canadian winters and surprise Indian attacks. In addition, the government required settlers to be Catholic (although Protestants often resided in Canada temporarily), reducing the pool from which colonists could be recruited. In the end, nearly three out of four immigrants who went to Canada returned home.

By 1700, the population had grown to about 15,000 (less than 7 percent of the English population in the mainland colonies that year; see Figure 2–1), mostly due to a remarkable level of natural increase. Because land for farms was readily available, couples faced few obstacles in supporting themselves. It was not unknown for some women to bear ten or even fifteen children. As late as 1666, only one-third of the French settlers were women, and virtually all of them found husbands. Some who remained single chose to do so, preferring a religious vocation with the Ursulines or one of the other orders of nuns, devoting their energies to teaching or administering care to the sick and indigent.

Because Indians expected their trading partners also to be military allies, Europeans were often drawn into native conflicts. This illustration, from Samuel de Champlain's 1613 description of the founding of New France, shows him joining his Huron allies in an attack on the Iroquois.

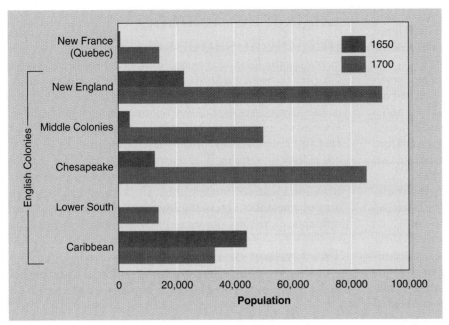

FIGURE 2–1   European Populations of New France (Quebec) and English Colonies in 1650 and 1700
Although New France's population grew rapidly between 1650 and 1700, it remained only a tiny fraction of the population of England's North American colonies. By 1700, English colonists on the mainland outnumbered New France's inhabitants by a factor of about 16 to 1.

Data Source: From John J. McCusker and Russell R. Menard, *The Economy of British America, 1607–1789* (1985). The University of North Carolina Press.

Many families established farms that produced wheat and other provisions mostly for local consumption. Often the land was technically owned by a gentleman, or *seigneur,* who received a rent payment. *Seigneurs* claimed other privileges, including rights to fishing and timber, and collected other fines and taxes. Though powerful, these gentlemen never enjoyed anything comparable to the status of aristocrats back in France.

French officials sought to restrict settlement to the St. Lawrence Valley, fearing that further expansion would render the empire impossible to defend. The impetus to move inland, however, could not be restrained. By the 1670s, French traders and missionaries had reached the Mississippi River. In 1681–1682, Robert, Sieur de La Salle, followed the Mississippi to the Gulf of Mexico, claiming the entire valley (which he named Louisiana in honor of the king) for France. When officials tried to restrict the direct trade between Indians and the *coureurs de bois,* many of these Frenchmen drifted off to settle in what became known as the *pays des Illinois* along the Mississippi. This expansion of French influence alarmed the English, who had founded colonies along the Atlantic seaboard and feared a growing French presence in the west.

Prosperous and expansive, Canada provided France with a secure foothold on the North American mainland. Its successful establishment contributed to an escalating European competition for land and trade in the New World. Soon new rivals entered the scene.

The Dutch Overseas Empire

The Dutch Republic joined the scramble for empire in the early seventeenth century. The Northern Provinces, sometimes known as Holland, had in 1581 declared their independence from Spain (whose kings ruled the region because it was part of the Holy Roman Empire), although sporadic fighting continued for another half-century. The new republic, dominated by Protestants, was intent on challenging Catholic Spain's power in the New World as well as the Old. More than any other factor, however, the desire for profit drove the Dutch quest for colonies.

The Dutch East India Company

By 1600, the Dutch emerged as the leading economic power in Europe. The republic earned considerable wealth from manufacturing such goods as textiles, jewelry, and glass, and Amsterdam soon became Europe's financial capital. The centerpiece of Dutch prosperity, however, was commerce, which expanded dramatically in the early seventeenth century. Thousands of Dutch ships plied the world's oceans, and the republic's earnings from foreign trade may have surpassed those of the rest of Europe combined. This commercial vitality provided the context for overseas expansion.

The instrument of colonial dominance was the Dutch East India Company, founded in 1602 to challenge what had until then been a virtual Portuguese monopoly of Asian trade. Its first success was the capture of the Spice Islands (now Indonesia and East Timor), followed by the takeover of Batavia (Jakarta), Ceylon (Sri Lanka), and Sumatra. The Company established slave-trading posts on the Gold Coast of West Africa, where it competed with the Portuguese, and at the Cape of Good Hope on Africa's southern tip. Its far-flung commercial net eventually encompassed parts of India and Formosa (Taiwan).

The West India Company and New Netherland

The Dutch next set their sights on the Americas, creating the West India Company in 1621. After taking control of West African slave-trading posts and temporarily occupying part of Brazil, the West India Company moved into the Caribbean (acquiring four islands by the 1640s) and North

America. Its claim to the Connecticut, Hudson, and Delaware valleys stemmed from the 1609 voyage of Henry Hudson, an Englishman sailing for the Dutch, who discovered the river that bears his name.

The first permanent Dutch settlers on mainland North America arrived in 1624 to set up a fur-trading post at Fort Orange (now Albany). Two years later, Peter Minuit and a company of Protestant refugees established New Amsterdam on Manhattan Island, which Minuit had purchased from the Indians. The Hudson River corridor between these two settlements became the heart of the New Netherland colony. Like New France, its economic focus was the fur trade. Dutch merchants forged ties with the Iroquois, who exchanged furs for European tools and weapons.

In the 1630s, to help supply colonial traders, the West India Company offered large landed estates (called patroonships) to wealthy Dutchmen who would be responsible for populating them with tenant farmers. The plan never really worked, in part because most would-be patroons disliked the company-imposed limits on their rights, and in part because few Dutch people wanted to emigrate only to live as peasants. At its peak, New Netherland's colonists only numbered about ten thousand.

What they lacked in numbers the colonists made up for in divisiveness. New Netherland became a magnet for religious refugees from Europe, as well as a destination for Africans acquired through the slave trade. (In 1638, about 100 Africans—free and slave—lived in New Amsterdam, constituting nearly a third of that city's population.) Ethnic and religious differences hindered a sense of community. Among the colony's Dutch, German, French, English, Swedish, Portuguese, and African settlers were Calvinists, Lutherans, Quakers, Catholics, Jews, and Muslims.

The West India Company dispatched several inept but aggressive governors who made an unstable situation worse by provoking conflict with Indians. Although the colonists maintained good relations with their Iroquois trading partners on the upper Hudson River, they had far less friendly dealings with the Algonquian peoples around New Amsterdam. In one particularly gruesome incident in 1645, Governor Willem Kieft ordered a massacre at an encampment of Indian refugees who had refused to pay him tribute. A horrified Dutch witness described Indian children being "thrown into the river, and when the fathers and mothers endeavored to save them, the soldiers would not let them come on land, but made both parents and children drown." Ten years later, Governor Peter Stuyvesant antagonized Susquehannock Indians along the Delaware River by seizing a small Swedish colony where the Susquehannocks had traded.

Such actions provoked retaliatory raids by the Indians, further weakening the colony. Though profitable, the fur trade did not generate the riches to be found in other parts of the Dutch empire. By the 1650s, New Netherland increasingly looked like a poor investment to company officials back in Europe.

English Settlement in the Chesapeake

Following the Roanoke colony's disappearance after 1587 (see Chapter 1), twenty years passed before the English again attempted to settle in America. When they did, in 1607, it was in the lower Chesapeake Bay region. The new settlement, Jamestown, at first seemed likely to share Roanoke's dismal fate. But it endured, eventually developing into the prosperous colony of Virginia. The reason for Virginia's success was an American plant—tobacco—that commanded good prices from European consumers. Tobacco also underlay the economy of a neighboring colony, Maryland, and had a profound influence on the development of Chesapeake society.

The Ordeal of Early Virginia

In 1606, several English merchants petitioned King James I for a charter incorporating two companies to attempt New

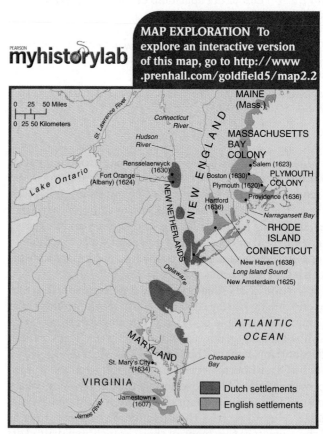

MAP 2–2   English and Dutch Mainland Colonies in North America, c. 1655
Early English colonies clustered in two areas of the Atlantic seaboard—New England and the Chesapeake Bay. Between them lay Dutch New Netherland, with settlements stretching up the Hudson River. The Dutch also acquired territory at the mouth of the Delaware River in 1655 when they seized a short-lived Swedish colony located there.

World settlement. One, the London, or Virginia, Company, included merchants from the city of London; the other, the Plymouth Company, included merchants from England's western ports. James I issued a charter granting the companies two tracts of land along the mid-Atlantic coast. These **joint-stock companies** sold shares to investors (who expected a profit in return) to raise money for colonization.

The Jamestown colony.   Three small ships carried 104 settlers, all men, to the mouth of Chesapeake Bay in May 1607 (see Map 2–2). On a peninsula about 50 miles up a river they named the James in honor of their king, the colonists built a fortified settlement they called Jamestown. Hoping to earn quick profits for Virginia Company investors, they immediately began hunting for gold and searching for the Northwest Passage to Asia. But Jamestown was no Mexico. All they found was disappointment and suffering. The swampy region was a breeding area for malarial mosquitoes and parasites carrying other diseases. Spending all their time searching for riches, the settlers neglected to plant crops, and their food supplies dwindled. By January 1608, only thirty-eight colonists were still alive.

After the disastrous first year, the colony's governing council turned to Captain John Smith for leadership. Just 28 years old, Smith was a seasoned adventurer who had fought against Spain in the Netherlands and the Ottoman Turks in Hungary. He imposed military discipline on Jamestown, organizing settlers into work gangs and decreeing that "he that will not worke shall not eate." His high-handed methods revived the colony but antagonized certain settlers who believed that their social status exempted them from manual labor and who bristled at taking orders from a man of lower social rank. When a gunpowder explosion wounded Smith in 1609 and forced him to return to England, his enemies had him replaced as leader.

Once again, the colony nearly disintegrated. More settlers arrived, only to starve or die of disease. Of the five hundred people in Jamestown in the autumn of 1609, just sixty remained alive by the spring of 1610—some of whom survived only by eating their dead companions. Facing financial ruin, company officials back in England tried to conceal the state of the colony. They reorganized the company twice and sent more settlers, including glassmakers, winegrowers, and silkmakers, in a desperate effort to find a marketable colonial product. They experimented with harsh military discipline, instructing governors to enforce a legal code—the *Lawes Divine, Morall and Martiall*—that prescribed the death penalty for offenses as trivial as swearing or killing a chicken.

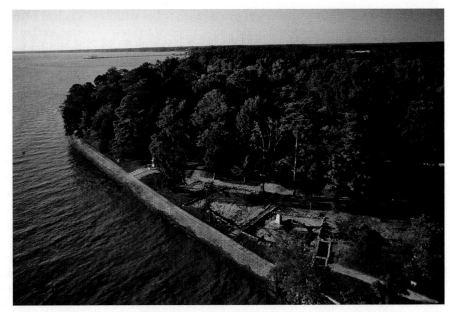

After years of work, archaeologists have excavated the original site of the English fort at Jamestown. This aerial view of the site shows its close proximity to the James River.

When it became clear that such severity discouraged immigration, the company tried more positive inducements.

The first settlers had been expected to work in return for food and other necessities; only company stockholders were to share in the colony's profits. But settlers wanted land, so governors began assigning small plots to those who finished their terms of service to the company. In 1616, the company instituted the **headright system**, giving 50 acres to anyone who paid his own way to Virginia and an additional 50 for each person (or "head") he brought with him.

In 1619, three other important developments occurred. That year, the company began transporting women to become wives for planters and induce them to stay in the colony. It was also the year in which the first Africans arrived in Virginia. In addition, the company created the first legislative body in English America, the **House of Burgesses**, setting a precedent for the establishment of self-government in other English colonies. Landowners elected representatives to the House of Burgesses, which, subject to the approval of the company, made laws for Virginia. In 1621 the *Lawes Divine, Morall and Martiall* gave way to a code based on English common law.

Despite these changes, the settlers were still unable to earn the company a profit. To make matters worse, the headright system expanded English settlement beyond Jamestown. This strained the already tense relations between the English and the Indians onto whose lands they had intruded.

The Powhatan Confederacy and the colonists.   When the English arrived in 1607, they planted their settlement in the heart of territory ruled by the powerful Indian leader

Powhatan. Chief of a confederacy of about thirty tribes with some fourteen thousand people, including 3,200 warriors, Powhatan had little to fear at first from the struggling English outpost. After an initial skirmish with English soldiers, he sent gifts of food, assuming that by accepting the gifts, the colonists acknowledged their dependence on him. Further action against the settlers seemed unnecessary, because they seemed fully capable of destroying themselves.

This conclusion was premature. Armed colonists began seizing corn from Indian villages whenever native people refused to supply it voluntarily. During one raid in 1609, John Smith held a pistol to the chest of Opechancanough, Powhatan's younger brother, until the Indians ransomed him with corn. In retaliation, Powhatan besieged Jamestown and tried to starve the colony to extinction. The colony was saved by the arrival of reinforcements from England, but war with the Indians continued until 1614 (see "American Views: Powhatan's Speech to John Smith").

The marriage of the colonist John Rolfe to Pocahontas, Powhatan's daughter, helped seal the peace in 1614. Pocahon-

This illustration shows John Smith seizing the scalplock of Opechancanough, Chief Powhatan's brother, during an English raid on an Indian village. Smith released his prisoner only after Indians ransomed him with corn. Thirteen years later, Opechancanough led a surprise attack against the colonists.

tas had briefly been held captive by the English during the war and had been instructed in English manners and religion by Rolfe. Sent to negotiate with Powhatan in the spring of 1614, Rolfe asked the chief for his daughter's hand. Powhatan gave his consent, and Pocahontas—baptized in the Church of England and renamed Rebecca—became Rolfe's wife.

Powhatan died in 1618, and Opechancanough succeeded him as chief. Still harboring intense resentment against the English, the new chief made plans for retaliation. Pocahontas had died on a trip to England in 1617, severing the tie between her family and the English. With new settlers arriving each year and the ranks of his warriors depleted by European diseases, Opechancanough could not wait long to act. Early in the morning on March 22, 1622, hundreds of Indian men traveled to the English settlements, as if they meant to visit or trade. Instead, they attacked the unsuspecting colonists, killing 347 by the end of the day—more than one-fourth of the English population.

The surviving colonists almost immediately plotted revenge. Believing that "now we have just cause to destroy them by all meanes possible," English forces struck at native villages, killing the inhabitants and burning cornfields. During the ensuing nine years of war, the English treated the Indians with a ferocity that recalled their earlier subjugation of the Irish.

Although Opechancanough's attack failed to restrain the colonists, it destroyed the Virginia Company. Economic activity ceased as settlers retreated to fortified garrisons. The company went bankrupt, and a royal commission investigating the 1622 attack was shocked to discover that nearly ten times more colonists had died from starvation and disease than at the hands of Indians. King James had little choice but to dissolve the company in 1624, and Virginia became a royal colony the following year. The settlers continued to enjoy self-government through the House of Burgesses, but now the king chose the colony's governor and council, and royal advisers monitored its affairs.

The Importance of Tobacco

Ironically, the demise of the Virginia Company helped the colony succeed. In their search for a marketable product, settlers had begun growing tobacco after 1610. Europeans acquired a taste for tobacco in the late sixteenth century when the Spanish brought samples from the West Indies and Florida. Initially expensive, it became popular among wealthy consumers. The high price appealed to Virginians, but they found that native Virginia leaf was of poor quality. John Rolfe began experimenting with seeds from Trinidad, which did much better. The first cargo of Virginia-grown tobacco arrived in England in 1617 and sold at a profitable 3 shillings per pound.

Settlers planted tobacco everywhere—even in the streets of Jamestown. Company officials, unwilling to base the colony's economy on a single crop, tried to restrict annual production to 100 pounds per person. Colonists ignored

American Views

Powhatan's Speech To John Smith (1609)

In *The Proceedings of the English Colonie in Virginia*, published in 1612, John Smith recorded this speech Powhatan delivered in 1609. After nearly two years of increasingly hostile encounters, Powhatan no longer trusted the English, but tried to dissuade the colonists from embarking on an all-out war. His words offered a mixture of threat and conciliation, addressing Smith as a fellow leader. The speech was to no avail, as mutual suspicion soon led to a deadly conflict that lasted five years.

- According to Powhatan, what benefits would the Indians and colonists enjoy by remaining at peace?
- What provocations had the English inflicted upon the Powhatans?
- How would the Indians respond to the outbreak of war, and what would be the consequences for the English?

Captaine Smith...I knowe the difference of peace and warre, better then any in my Countrie. But now I am old, and ere long must die, my brethren, namely Opichapam, Opechankanough, and Kekataugh, my two sisters, and their two daughters, are distinctly each others successours, I wish their experiences no lesse then mine, and your love to them, no lesse then mine to you; but this brute [rumor] from Nansamund that you are come to destroy my Countrie, so much affrighteth all my people, as they dare not visit you; what will it availe you, to take that perforce, you may quietly have with love, or to destroy them that provide you food? What can you get by war, when we can hide our provision and flie to the woodes, whereby you must famish by wronging us your friends; and whie are you thus jealous of our loves, seeing us unarmed, and both doe, and are willing still to feed you with that you cannot get but by our labours? Think you I am so simple not to knowe, it is better to eate good meate, lie well, and sleepe quietly with my women and children, laugh and be merrie with you, have copper, hatchets, or what I want, being your friend; then bee forced to flie from al, to lie cold in the woods, feed upon acorns, roots, and such trash, and be so hunted by you, that I can neither rest, eat, nor sleepe; but my tired men must watch, and if a twig but breake, everie one crie there comes Captaine Smith, then must I flie I knowe not whether, and thus with miserable fear end my miserable life; leaving my pleasures to such youths as you, which through your rash unadvisednesse, may quickly as miserably ende, for want of that you never knowe how to find? Let this therefore assure you of our loves and everie year our friendly trade shall furnish you with corne, and now also if you would come in friendly manner to see us, and not thus with your gunnes and swords, as to invade your foes.

Philip L. Barbour, ed., *The Complete Works of Captain John Smith (1580-1631)*, 3 vols. (Chapel Hill, 1986), 1: 247-48.

---

these restrictions, and tobacco production really surged after the company dissolved.

Between 1627 and 1669, annual tobacco exports climbed from 250,000 pounds to more than 15 million pounds. As the supply grew, the price per pound plunged from 13 pence in 1624 to a mere penny in the late 1660s, where it remained for the next half-century. What had once been a luxury product thus became affordable for Europeans of average means. Now thoroughly dependent on tobacco for their livelihood, the only way colonists could compensate for falling prices was to grow even more, pushing exports to England to more than 20 million pounds per year by the late 1670s (see Figure 2–2).

Tobacco shaped nearly every aspect of Virginia society, from patterns of settlement to the recruitment of colonists. Planters scrambled to claim lands near navigable rivers so that ships could reach their plantations and carry their crops to market. As a result, the colonists dispersed into plantations located along waterways instead of settling in compact communities. Settlers competed to produce the biggest and best crop and get it to market the fastest, hoping to enjoy even a small price advantage over everyone else.

Tobacco kept workers busy nine months of the year. Planters sowed seeds in the early spring, transplanted seedlings a few weeks later, and spent the summer pinching

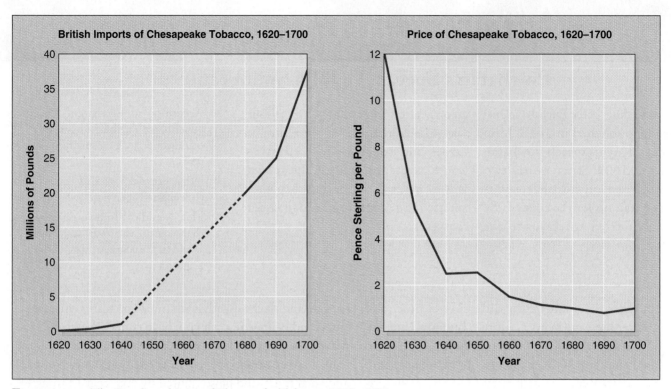

FIGURE 2–2   The Supply and Price of Chesapeake Tobacco, 1620–1700
Tobacco cultivation dominated the economy of the Chesapeake region throughout the seventeenth century. As planters brought more and more land under cultivation, the amount of tobacco exported to Britain shot up and the price plummeted. (As the dashed line indicates, no data on tobacco imports are available for the years 1640–1680.)

Data Source: From Russell R. Menard, "The Tobacco Industry in the Chesapeake Colonies, 1617–1730: An Interpretation," *Research in Economic History*, 5 (1980), app. Jai Press, Inc.

off the tops of the plants (to produce larger leaves) and removing worms. After the harvest, the leaves were "cured"—dried in ventilated sheds—and packed in large barrels. During the winter, planters cleared and fenced more land and made barrels for next year's crop. Working on his own, one planter could tend two thousand plants, which yielded about 500 pounds of cured tobacco. When the price was high, this supplied a comfortable income. But as the price plummeted, planters could keep up only by producing more tobacco, and to do that they needed a large labor force.

The planters turned to England, importing thousands of indentured servants, or contract workers, who (like Richard Frethorne) agreed to a fixed term of labor, usually four to seven years, in exchange for free passage to Virginia. The master provided food, shelter, clothing, and, at the end of the term of service, "freedom dues" paid in corn and clothing. Between 1625 and 1640, one thousand or more indentured servants arrived each year. Some were orphans; others were condemned criminals given a choice between execution and transportation to Virginia. The vast majority, however, came from the ranks of England's unemployed, who emigrated in hopes of "bettering their condition in a Growing Country."

Most found such hopes quickly dashed. Servants died in alarming numbers from disease, and those who survived faced years of backbreaking labor. Masters squeezed as much work out of them as possible with long hours and harsh discipline. Some servants died from mistreatment. One unusually cruel master, Richard Price, punished his servant for pretending to be ill and trying to run away by beating him so severely that the young man died. A jury refused to charge Price with murder, reasoning that the servant deserved punishment and Price had not intended to kill him. Because the courts were administered by masters and thus favored masters' authority over servants' rights, aggrieved servants rarely obtained justice. New obstacles faced servants who managed to survive their terms of indenture. For every ex-servant who became a landholder, dozens died in poverty. To prevent freed servants from becoming economic rivals, established planters avoided selling them good land, particularly after tobacco prices hit bottom in the 1660s. Many ex-servants found land only in places less suitable for tobacco cultivation and more vulnerable to Indian attack. As a result, they became a discontented group. In 1675, their discontent would flare into rebellion (discussed in Chapter 3).

Tobacco and the American Economy

According to a legal settlement reached in 1998, the American tobacco industry agreed to pay $206 billion to forty-six state governments as compensation for the medical costs of treating smoke-related illnesses. Health issues dominated the debates leading to the agreement, but economic questions also influenced the discussion. This was hardly surprising, for tobacco is the oldest commercial crop produced in what is now the United States. The healthfulness of tobacco was debated even in the seventeenth century, but that did not deter Virginia's colonists from growing the crop. The first shipment of Virginia tobacco reached London in 1617, and by the turn of the eighteenth century, colonists exported over 30 million pounds of it annually. High levels of production led to falling prices, but colonists responded by growing even more. After the Revolution, tobacco became a fixture of the agricultural economies in the new states of Kentucky, Tennessee, Missouri, and Ohio. Down to the twentieth century, tobacco remained so vital to the U.S. economy that the federal government subsidized its production—the only non-food crop (besides cotton) to benefit from high price supports. In 2004, however, Congress passed a law ending the price support program. Since many farmers still rely on tobacco to make their livings, it is unclear whether this federal action will substantially reduce production. Thus, four centuries after the founding of Jamestown, economic decisions made by early Virginia colonists continue to affect an American nation they could never have imagined.

This seventeenth-century engraving shows a fashionable European woman indulging in a pipe of tobacco.

■ In what ways have long-term economic issues complicated the task of dealing with tobacco-related health problems?

myhistorylab
PEARSON

From Then to Now

2-1 James I, *King James His Counterblast to Tobacco*. Published version of the King's opposition to tobacco.

2-2 Thomas D'Urfey, "Tobacco's But an Indian Weed." Lyrics to popular 17th-century ballad.

2-3 Thomas Jefferson, *Notes on the State of Virginia*. Discussion of switch from tobacco to wheat farming in Virginia.

Modern-day tobacco fields such as this one in North Carolina testify to the continuing economic importance of the crop.

Maryland: A Refuge for Catholics

The success of tobacco in Virginia encouraged further English colonization in the Chesapeake region. In 1632, King Charles I granted 10 million acres of land north of the bay to the nobleman George Calvert, Lord Baltimore. Unlike Virginia, which was founded by a joint-stock company, Maryland was a **proprietary colony**—the sole possession of Calvert and his heirs. They owned all the land, which they could divide up as they pleased, and had the right to set up the colony's government.

Calvert, who was Catholic, intended Maryland to be a refuge for others of his faith. When Queen Elizabeth's accession made England a Protestant nation, Catholics became a disadvantaged minority. They paid double taxes and could not worship in public or hold political office. In Maryland, Calvert wanted Catholic colonists to enjoy economic and political power. He intended to divide the land into manors—large private estates like those of medieval England—and distribute them to wealthy Catholic friends. These manorial lords would live on rents collected from tenant farmers, hold the most important governmental offices, and run their own law courts.

Calvert died before settlement began, and it was the sad fate of his son, Cecilius, to see his father's plans unravel. The majority of colonists, who began arriving in 1634, were Protestants who despised Catholics. Refusing to live as tenants on Catholic estates, they claimed land of their own—a process that accelerated after 1640, when Maryland adopted a headright system like Virginia's as a way to recruit settlers.

Maryland's problems intensified when civil war broke out in England in 1642. For years, political and religious disputes had divided the nation. Charles I, who became king in 1625, clashed with the **Puritans,** who called for further reform of the Church of England. He also antagonized many government leaders by dissolving Parliament in 1629 and ruling on his own for eleven years. Needing funds to suppress a rebellion in Scotland in 1640, however, Charles was forced to recall Parliament. Its leaders, sympathetic to the Puritan cause, quickly turned against him. Both king and Parliament recruited armies and went to war in 1642. Parliamentary forces triumphed, and in 1649, they executed Charles. For the next decade, England was governed as a protectorate, not a monarchy. Oliver Cromwell, a Puritan general, ruled until his death in 1658. His son, Richard, proved an inept successor, however, and in 1660 a group of army officers invited Charles's exiled son to accept the throne.

During the 1640s and 1650s, Maryland Protestants took advantage of the upheaval in England to contest the Calverts' control of the colony. To pacify them, Cecilius Calvert established a legislature, assuming that Protestants would dominate the elective lower house while he could appoint Catholics to the upper house. In 1649, Calvert also approved the **Act for Religious Toleration,** the first law in America to call for freedom of worship for all Christians, but even this brought no peace. The Protestant majority continued to resist Catholic political influence.

Instead of a peaceful Catholic refuge, Maryland soon resembled neighboring Virginia. Its settlers raised tobacco and imported as many indentured servants as possible. Because Maryland initially provided freed servants with 50 acres of land, more became landholders than in Virginia. As in Virginia, however, economic opportunity diminished after 1660 when the price of tobacco dropped. Maryland's settlers enjoyed more peaceful relations with the Indians than the Virginians had, but they fought intensely among themselves. Throughout the seventeenth century, Protestants kept up their opposition to the proprietor's control and resisted Catholic efforts to govern the colony that was supposed to have been theirs.

Life in the Chesapeake Colonies

Few people could have predicted how much life in the Chesapeake colonies would differ from England. Many differences stemmed from the region's distinctive population. Because of their labor needs, masters preferred to recruit young men in their teens and twenties as indentured servants, importing three or four times as many of them as women. As a result, the populations of Virginia and Maryland were overwhelmingly young and male. Even as late as 1700, Virginia had three English men for every two women.

As a consequence of this gender imbalance, many male ex-servants found that marriage was as remote a possibility as landownership. Very few chose Indian wives: John Rolfe's union with Pocahontas was one of only three English-Indian marriages in seventeenth-century Virginia. One planter suggested that the Chesapeake was a "paradise for women" because their scarcity made them the object of men's competition. While few unmarried women failed to find husbands, and widows usually remarried soon after their spouses' deaths, their lives were hardly easy.

Malaria and other diseases inflicted hardship on nearly everyone. Few colonists lived past 50, and women's susceptibility to disease during pregnancy meant that many of them barely made it to 40. Such high mortality, combined with late marriages (because servants could not wed until their terms were up), limited the size of families and slowed population growth. As many as one out of four children died in their first year, and more died before age 20.

Under such conditions, the only way the populations of the Chesapeake colonies could grow during most of the seventeenth century was through heavy importation of servants. The number of English settlers rose from about 8,000 in 1640 to 24,000 in 1660. Still mostly young and mostly male, the immigrants helped the region's distinctive demographic patterns persist until the end of the century.

These conditions hindered colonists from reproducing customary patterns of family life. The frequency of early death produced unusual households, containing various combinations of step-parents and children from different marriages. There were so many orphans in Maryland that the colony created special courts to protect their property. Many women would be widows at some point in their lives, which gave them temporary control over the family property. Husbands often arranged for their widows to manage their estates until the eldest son reached age 21. Few women received land outright, and if widows remarried, their new spouses usually took control of the estates left by their first husbands. As in England itself, the Chesapeake colonies accorded women little formal authority within society.

The precariousness of life encouraged settlers to invest every penny of profit in land and labor, postponing investment in goods that would bring a more comfortable existence. Early houses were often no larger than 16 by 20 feet, with one or two rooms. Poor settlers slept on the floor on straw mattresses and had few other furnishings, often not even a chair or bench to sit on. Rich planters owned more goods, but often of poor quality. Nearly everyone subsisted on a rude diet of pork and corn. Servants and poor colonists had no choice but to accept crude living conditions. Their more fortunate neighbors tolerated discomfort in order to invest in family estates where their descendants might live in greater luxury.

Rough as these conditions were, they far surpassed the circumstances of most native peoples in the Chesapeake. The English population may have been growing slowly, but it still overwhelmed the Indian population, which suffered high mortality from European diseases. Opechancanough led the Powhatans on another raid against the colonists in 1644, killing nearly five hundred of them, but this had a far less devastating effect than his attack of 1622 because the colonists now outnumbered the Indians. By 1685, there were more than ten colonists for every Indian living in eastern Virginia. By that point, many Native Americans in the Chesapeake had retreated to isolated towns, in hopes of preserving control over dwindling lands and maintaining some independence from English domination.

The Founding of New England
The first English attempt to settle the northeastern coast of North America was a miserable failure. In 1607, the same year that the Virginia Company founded Jamestown, the Plymouth Company sent two ships with 120 Englishmen (and one Indian captive from an earlier raid) to found a colony at the mouth of the Sagadahoc River in present-day Maine. The colonists alienated the Abenaki Indians who lived there, suffered through a harsh winter, and abandoned their settlement the next summer. But explorers and fishermen continued to visit the area, and it was not long before the English renewed their settlement efforts.

Six colonies appeared in the region between 1620 and 1640, settled by thousands of people troubled by religious, political, and economic upheavals in England. Even before permanent colonists arrived, New England's native population felt the effects of European contact. Between 1616 and 1618, a terrible epidemic swept through coastal New England, killing up to 90 percent of the Indians living there. The devastated survivors were struggling to cope with the consequences of this disaster just as the colonists began to arrive.

The Pilgrims and Plymouth Colony
Plymouth Colony, the first of the New England settlements, was founded in 1620. Its origins lay in religious disputes that had plagued England since the late sixteenth century. Most of Queen Elizabeth's subjects approved of her efforts to keep England a Protestant nation, but some reformers believed that she had not rid the Church of England of all Catholic practices. The enemies of these reformers, ridiculing them for wanting to purify the Church of England (or **Anglican** Church) of all corruption, called them Puritans.

Following the doctrine of predestination taught by John Calvin and other Protestant reformers, English Puritans believed in an all-powerful God who, at the moment of Creation, determined which humans would be saved and which would be damned. They held that salvation came through faith alone, not good works, and urged believers to seek a direct, personal relationship with God. The centerpiece of their spiritual life was conversion: the transforming experience that occurred when individuals felt the stirrings of grace in their souls and began to hope that they were among the saved. Those who experienced conversion were considered saints and acquired new strength to live godly lives.

Puritans believed that certain Anglican practices interfered with conversion and the believer's relationship with God. They rejected the Book of Common Prayer, which regulated Anglican worship, insisting that ministers should pray from the heart and preach from the Bible. They objected when Anglican clergy wore vestments that set them apart from ordinary Christians. And they objected to any church organization above the level of the individual congregation, seeing no need for bishops and archbishops. But what they hated most about the Anglican Church was that anyone could be a member. Puritans believed that everyone should attend church services, but they wanted church membership, which conferred the right to partake in the Lord's Supper, or communion, to be limited to saints who had experienced conversion.

Elizabeth and the rulers who followed her—who as monarchs were the "supreme heads" of the Church of England—tried to silence the Puritans. James I viewed their demands as a challenge to his authority and threatened to "harry them out of the land." Some Puritans, known as **separatists,** were convinced that the Church of England would never change and left it to form their own congregations. One such group, mainly artisans and middling farmers from the village of Scrooby, in Nottinghamshire, became the core of Plymouth Colony.

The Scrooby separatists left England in 1607–1608 for Holland, where they stayed for more than a decade. Although they could worship in peace there, many struggled to make a living and feared that their children were being tempted by the worldly pleasures of Dutch city life. Some Scrooby separatists contemplated moving to America and contacted the Plymouth Company, which was eager to make another colonization attempt after the Sagadahoc failure. Called **Pilgrims** because they thought of themselves as spiritual wanderers, they were joined by other separatists and by nonseparatist "strangers" hired to help get the colony started. In all, 102 men, women, and children set sail on the *Mayflower* in September 1620.

After a long and miserable voyage, they landed near Massachusetts Bay. Because this was about 200 miles north of the land their charter permitted them to settle, some of the "strangers" claimed that they were no longer legally bound to obey the expedition's separatist leaders. To prevent the colony from disintegrating into factions before their ship had even landed, the leaders drafted the Mayflower Compact, a document that bound all signers to abide by the decisions of the majority.

The Pilgrims settled at Plymouth, the site of a Wampanoag village recently depopulated by disease. William Bradford, Plymouth's governor for many years, described finding abandoned cornfields, Indian graves, and baskets of corn buried underground. Although it helped feed them for a while, this corn was not enough to prevent the Pilgrims from suffering their first winter through a terrible "starving time" that left nearly half of them dead.

When two English-speaking natives, Squanto and Samoset, emerged from the woods the next spring, the surviving Pilgrims marveled at them as "special instruments sent of God." Samoset had learned English from traders, and Squanto had learned it in England, where he lived for a time after being kidnapped by a sea captain. Squanto was the sole survivor of the Patuxets, who had succumbed to disease while he had been away. The two native men approached the Pilgrims on behalf of Massasoit, the Wampanoag leader. Although suspicious of the newcomers, the Wampanoags thought the Pilgrims might be useful allies against their enemies, the Narragansetts, who had escaped the recent epidemics.

In 1621, the Wampanoags and the Pilgrims signed a treaty of alliance, although each side understood its terms differently. The Pilgrims assumed that Massasoit had submitted to the superior authority of King James, whereas Massasoit assumed that he and the English king were equal partners. Until his death in 1622, Squanto offered advice to each side, hoping to exert influence as a mediator. Economic ties strengthened the alliance. The Indians taught the English how to plant corn and traded corn with them for manufac-

This historical reconstruction of Plymouth Plantation commemorates the founding of the first successful English colony in New England.

tured goods. The Pilgrims also exchanged corn with northern Indians for furs, which they shipped back to England to help pay off their debts to English investors. In the autumn of 1621, Indians and Pilgrims gathered for a feast celebrating the colonists' first harvest—an event Americans still commemorate as the first Thanksgiving.

Plymouth remained small, poor, and weak, never exceeding about seven thousand settlers. Although its families achieved a modest prosperity, the colony as a whole never produced more than small shipments of furs, fish, and timber to sell in England. It took the Pilgrims more than twenty years to repay their English creditors. After 1630, the first New England colony was overshadowed by a new and more powerful neighbor, Massachusetts Bay.

Massachusetts Bay Colony and Its Offshoots

The Puritans who founded Massachusetts shared many beliefs with the Pilgrims of Plymouth Colony—with one important exception. Unlike the Pilgrims, most Massachusetts settlers rejected separatism, insisting that the Anglican Church could be reformed. Their goal was to create godly churches to serve as models for the English church. Charles I, who became king in 1625, opposed the Puritans more forcefully than his father had. England at the time also suffered from economic troubles—including crop failures and a depression in the wool industry—that many Puritans saw as signs of God's displeasure with their country. These ominous events at home encouraged them to move to the New World.

In 1629, a group of Puritan merchants and gentlemen received a royal charter for a joint-stock enterprise, the Massachusetts Bay Company, to set up a colony north of Plymouth. John Winthrop, a prosperous lawyer, was selected as the colony's governor. In the spring of 1630, a fleet of eleven ships carried Winthrop and about a thousand men, women, and children across the Atlantic.

Before Winthrop's ship landed, he preached a lay sermon, called "A Model of Christian Charity," to his fellow passengers, describing his vision of the society they were about to create. The governor reminded them of their goal "to do more service to the Lord" by placing the good of all above private ambitions. Winthrop argued that the Lord had made them his chosen people and that, as a result, "we shall be as a city upon a hill, the eyes of all people are upon us." If they failed to live up to God's expectations, the spectacle of their failure would allow their enemies "to speak evil of the ways of God." With this mingled encouragement and threat ringing in their ears, the emigrants set about establishing their colony. Within a few months of their landing, they founded Boston and six adjoining towns.

Stability, conformity, and intolerance.   Winthrop described the settlers' mission in New England as a **covenant**, or contract, with God, binding them to meet their religious obligations in return for God's favor. The settlers also created covenants to define their duties to one another. When they founded towns, colonists signed covenants agreeing to live to-

John Winthrop (1588–1649) served as the Massachusetts Bay Colony's governor for most of its first two decades. Throughout his life, Winthrop—like many fellow Puritans—struggled to live a godly life in a corrupt world.

Courtesy, American Antiquarian Society.

gether in peace. Worshipers in each town's church likewise wrote covenants binding themselves to live in harmony.

The desire for peace and purity could breed intolerance. Settlers scrutinized their neighbors for signs of unacceptable behavior. Standards for church membership were strict; only those who could prove they were saints by describing their conversion experiences were admitted. But the insistence on covenants and conformity also created a remarkably stable society.

That stability was enhanced by the development of representative government. By 1634, colony leaders had converted the charter of the Massachusetts Bay Company into a plan of government. The General Court, which initially included only the shareholders of the joint-stock company, was transformed into a two-house legislature. Freemen—adult males who held property and were church members—elected representatives to the lower house, as well as eighteen members (called "assistants") to the upper house. They also chose a governor and deputy governor.

The Connecticut Valley and the Pequot War.   At least thirteen thousand settlers came to New England and established dozens of towns between 1630 and 1642, when the outbreak of the English Civil War halted emigration. The progress of settlement was generally untroubled in coastal Massachusetts, but when colonists moved into the Connecticut River Valley, tensions with Indians developed. These erupted in 1637 in the brief, tragic conflict called the **Pequot War.**

English settlers from Massachusetts first arrived in the Connecticut Valley in the mid-1630s. The new arrivals found themselves in a dangerous situation. For several years, the Pequot Indians had used their partnership with nearby Dutch traders to monopolize the trade in European goods and exert dominance over their native neighbors. This political and economic strategy was endangered in 1633 when the Dutch built an outpost near the site of present-day Hartford and invited the Pequots' rivals—including the Narragansetts and Mohegans—to trade. The Pequots, suffering from a recent smallpox epidemic, resented losing their special trading rights and approached Massachusetts Bay as an ally against the Dutch. But when English settlers poured into Connecticut and demanded Pequot submission to English authority, the Pequots turned against them too. A struggle for control over the land and trade of eastern Connecticut began.

The colonists allied with the Pequots' enemies, the Narragansetts and Mohegans. Together they overwhelmed the Pequots in an astonishingly bloody war. In May 1637, English forces surrounded a Pequot village inhabited mainly by women and children, located on the Mystic River. They set it ablaze and shot anyone who tried to escape. Between three hundred and seven hundred Pequots died, a toll that shocked the settlers' Indian allies, who protested that English-style warfare was "too furious, and slays too many men."

The English, for their part, thanked God for giving them "so speedy a victory over so proud and insulting an enemy."

After the surviving Pequots had fled or been sold into slavery, more settlers moved to Connecticut, which soon declared itself a separate colony. In 1639, the settlers adopted the Fundamental Orders, creating a government similar to that of Massachusetts, and the English government granted them a charter in 1662.

Roger Williams and the founding of Rhode Island. Massachusetts spun off other colonies as its population expanded in the 1630s and dissenters ran afoul of its intolerant government. Some dissenting colonists refused to conform. Roger Williams, who founded Rhode Island, was one of them. Williams was a separatist minister who declared that because Massachusetts churches had not rejected the Church of England, they shared its corruption. He opposed government interference in religious affairs—such as laws requiring settlers to attend worship services—and argued for the separation of church and state. Williams even attacked the Massachusetts charter, insisting that the king had no right to grant Indian lands to English settlers.

When Williams refused to be silenced, the General Court banished him, intending to ship him back to England. But in the winter of 1635, Williams slipped away. He and a few followers found refuge among the Narragansett Indians, from whom he purchased land for the village of Providence, founded in 1636. More towns sprang up nearby when a new religious challenge sent additional refugees to Rhode Island from Massachusetts.

Anne Hutchinson's challenge to the Bay Colony.   Anne Hutchinson arrived in Boston from England with her husband and seven children in 1634. Welcomed by the town's women for her talents as a midwife, she began to hold religious meetings in her house. During these meetings, she denounced several ministers, who had taught worshipers that there were spiritual exercises they could perform that might prepare them for sainthood. Hutchinson insisted that there was nothing humans could do to encourage God to make them saints. She implied that any minister who taught otherwise could not be a saint himself, in which case he had no authority over the true saints in his church.

Many people, including prominent Boston merchants, flocked to Hutchinson's meetings. But her critics believed her to be a dangerous antinomian (someone who claimed to be free from obedience to moral law), because she seemed to maintain that saints were accountable only to God and not to any worldly authority. Her opponents also objected to her teaching of mixed groups of men and women. Governor Winthrop complained that such behavior was neither "comely in the sight of God nor fitting for your sex." This suggests that Hutchinson's breach of normal gender roles, which placed women subordinate to men, upset him as much as her religious views did. Colony magistrates arrested her and tried her for sedition—that is, for advocating the overthrow of the government.

During her trial, Hutchinson mounted a lively defense. When asked to explain her views, she reminded her opponents of their objections to her teaching, replying "Why do you call me to teach the court?" In the end, however, the court found her guilty and banished her. With many of her followers, she moved to Rhode Island, where Roger Williams had proclaimed a policy of religious toleration. Other followers returned to England or moved north to what became in 1679 the colony of New Hampshire.

At the height of the Hutchinson controversy, a group of zealous Puritan emigrants led by the Reverend John Davenport arrived in Boston. Appalled by the religious turmoil, they departed for the coast of Long Island Sound, where they founded New Haven in 1638. Davenport's efforts to impose Puritan conformity in his colony made Massachusetts seem easygoing in comparison. But New Haven failed to thrive, and in 1662, the colony was absorbed into Connecticut.

Families, Farms, and Communities in Early New England

"This plantation and that of Virginia went not forth upon the same reasons," declared one of Massachusetts's founders. Virginians came "for profit," whereas New Englanders emigrated to bear witness to their Puritan faith. They believed that economic prosperity would come only if God blessed their efforts to create a godly society. Most New England settlers arrived in the brief span between 1630 and 1642, when the outbreak of the English Civil War convinced many Puritans to stay at home and fight against the king. Unlike the unmarried young men who moved in great numbers to Virginia, most New Englanders settled with their families. This had important implications for the development of New England society.

Even though emigration from England slowed to a trickle after 1642, New England's population continued to grow. By 1660, the number of colonists exceeded thirty-three thousand. This demographic expansion stemmed from the initial emigration of families. With a more balanced sex ratio (about three men to two women) than there was in the early Chesapeake, marriage and childbearing were more common. Families frequently had seven or eight children, compared to the two or three offspring typical of Chesapeake families.

Settling in a region with a healthier climate, New Englanders were largely spared early deaths from malaria and other diseases that ravaged the Chesapeake settlers. Most children survived to reach adulthood and form families of their own. Many New Englanders enjoyed unusually long lives for the seventeenth century, reaching their seventies and even eighties. Long-lived parents exercised considerable control over their children. This was especially true for sons, who could not marry until their fathers provided them with land to support a family. Because fathers depended on their sons for labor, they often postponed granting them the means to economic independence until they were 26 or 27. Daughters, too, contributed their labor to the household economy,

Most New Englanders came in family groups, bringing many children with them. The lace and ribbons on the clothing of the Mason children, depicted in this 1670 portrait, suggest that they came from a well-to-do family. Like many seventeenth-century portraits, this one is rich in symbolism. The cane in David Mason's hand indicates his status as the male heir, while the rose held by his sister Abigail was a symbol of childhood innocence.

Attributed to the Freake-Gibbs Painter, American, active Boston, Mass., c. 1670. The Mason Children: David, Joanna, and Abigail, 1670. Oil on canvas, 39 × 42½ in. The Fine Arts Museum of San Francisco, Gift of Mr. and Mrs. John D. Rockefeller 3rd, 1979.7.3.

but generally married between the ages of 21 and 23. They also depended on the willingness of their fathers to supply them with a dowry (usually livestock and household goods) to bring to their new homes.

Women in early New England.   In New England, as in other colonies and England itself, women were assumed to be legally and economically dependent on the men in their families. Since fewer New England marriages were shortened by the early death of a spouse, fewer New England women experienced widowhood, the one time in their lives when they might enjoy legal independence and exercise control over property. During the seventeenth century, widows occasionally exercised more extensive property rights than the law dictated. By law, they had "dower rights" to possess one-third the value of the husband's personal estate and to use one-third of the land for the remainder of their lives. Many husbands, however, gave their widows control over greater amounts of property, perhaps in recognition of their important contributions to building the family estate.

Women's economic contributions were indeed central to the family's success. In addition to caring for children, cooking, sewing, gardening, and cleaning, most women engaged in household production and traded the fruits of their labor with other families. They sold eggs, made butter and cheese, brewed beer, and spun yarn. Wives of shopkeepers and craftsmen occasionally managed their husbands' businesses when the men had to travel or became ill.

Community and economic life.   New Englanders' lives were shaped not only by their families but also by their towns. Unlike Chesapeake colonists, who tended to disperse into separate plantations, New Englanders clustered into communities that might contain fifty or a hundred families. The Massachusetts government strongly encouraged town formation by granting tracts of land to groups of families who promised to settle together. Once they received a grant, the families divided the land, allotting each family a farm of sufficient size to support its members. Social distinctions were maintained: people who had higher standing in England received larger farms than those of lower status. Land that the families could not yet use was held "in common" to be distributed to their children as they grew up. Once they found a town they liked, families tended to stay in place. Grown children, inheriting parental estates and finding spouses nearby, often settled in the same community as their parents.

At the center of each town stood the meetinghouse, used for religious and secular purposes. Every Sunday, townspeople gathered there to listen to the minister preach God's word. The importance Puritans placed on worship with fellow Christians helped promote communal feeling. At other times, the meetinghouse served as a town hall, where men assembled to discuss matters ranging from local taxes to making sure everyone's fences were mended. Massachusetts law required towns with at least fifty families to support a school (so children could learn to read the Bible), and men often wrangled at town meetings over the choice and salary of a schoolmaster. Townsmen tried, not always successfully, to reach decisions by consensus. To oversee day-to-day local affairs, they chose five to seven trusted neighbors to serve as selectmen. Each town could also elect two men to represent it in the colony legislature.

New England's stony soil and short growing season offered few ways to get rich, but most people achieved a modest prosperity. They grew corn and other foods and raised livestock to feed their families, selling or trading what they could not use. Their goal was to achieve a competency—enough property to ensure the family's economic independence. Without the income generated by a staple crop like tobacco, New England farmers could not hire large numbers of indentured servants and so relied on family labor. Even children as young as five or six could care for younger siblings or fetch water and wood.

New Englanders regularly traded goods and services with their neighbors. A carpenter might erect a house—usually larger and sturdier than the ramshackle Chesapeake dwellings—in return for barrels of salted beef. Men with several teenaged sons sent them to help neighbors whose children were still small. Midwives delivered babies in return for cheese or eggs. Women nursed sick neighbors, whom they might later call on for similar help. These transactions allowed most New Englanders to enjoy a comfortable life, one that many Virginians might have envied.

New England prospered by developing a diversified economy less vulnerable to depression than Virginia's. Farmers sent livestock and meat to merchants to be marketed abroad. Fishermen caught cod and other fish to be sold in Europe. New Englanders became such skilled shipbuilders and seafaring merchants that by the 1670s, London merchants complained about competition from them. England itself had little use for the dried fish, livestock, salted meat, and wood products that New England vessels carried, but enterprising merchants found exactly the market they needed in the West Indies.

Competition in the Caribbean

The Spanish claimed all Caribbean islands by right of Columbus's discovery, but during the seventeenth century, France, the Netherlands, and England acquired their own island colonies. Spain retained Cuba, Hispaniola, Puerto Rico, and Trinidad. The French obtained Guadaloupe, Martinique, St. Lucia, St. Vincent, and smaller outposts in the Leeward and Windward Islands. Aruba, Curaçao, St. Martin, Saba, and St. Eustatius became Dutch possessions. England's share included Antigua, Barbados, Montserrat, Nevis, and St. Christopher; in 1655, the English wrested Jamaica from Spain (see Map 2–3). Although its short-lived Puritan colony on Providence Island off Nicaragua's coast failed, the West Indies soon became the jewel of England's American empire.

Europeans competed for these islands at first in the hope that they would yield precious metals and provide bases for privateering expeditions. It eventually became clear that the islands would produce treasure of another sort—sugar, which was in great demand in Europe. In order to reap the enormous profits that sugar could bring, Caribbean planters of all nationalities imported enormous numbers of African people to work as slaves under the harshest conditions to be found in the New World.

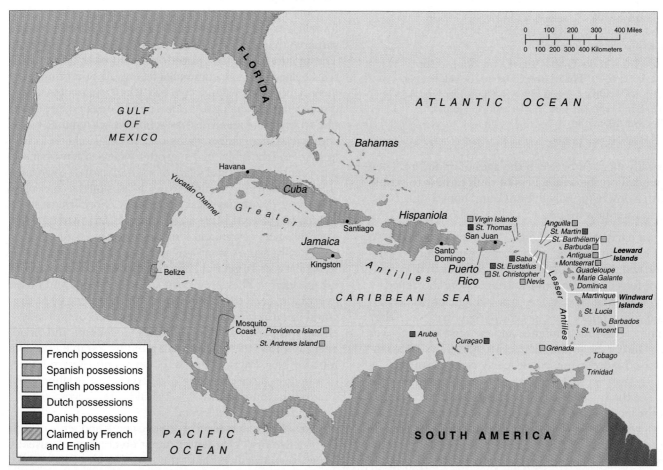

MAP 2–3   Principal European Possessions in the Caribbean in the Seventeenth Century
Europeans scrambled for control of Caribbean islands, where they raised sugar cane with slave labor. On many islands, Africans soon formed the majority of the population. In some cases, colonists from one European country settled on lands claimed by a rival power. For instance, English settlers established bases in Belize and on the Mosquito Coast, both of which were claimed by Spain.

Sugar and Slaves

The Spanish and Portuguese first experimented with sugar production on Atlantic islands such as São Tomé and the Canaries in the fifteenth century. Europeans prized sugar as a sweetener, preservative, decoration—even a medicine—and paid high prices for it. Columbus accordingly brought sugar canes to the New World on his second voyage, in 1493. Soon after the Spanish began growing sugar on Santo Domingo, they began importing African slaves as workers, because Indian slaves were dying in great numbers. The Spanish brought sugar to the South American mainland, as did the Portuguese, who turned Brazil into one of the world's major producers. Everywhere that sugar flourished, first Indian slaves and then enslaved Africans could be found. For the Portuguese and Dutch, who dominated the African slave trade, sugar and slaves provided twin sources of profit. In the early seventeenth century, Portugal alone shipped ten to twenty thousand Africans to the New World every year.

The English in the Caribbean eventually made the same decisions. At first, English colonists who came to the West Indies in the 1620s and 1630s raised tobacco and imported indentured servants to work their fields. By that time, however, tobacco prices were dropping. Moreover, the disease environment of the West Indies proved even harsher than in the Chesapeake, and settlers died in great numbers. That thousands came anyway testifies more to their hopes for prosperity than their actual chances of success. Until the 1660s the islands actually attracted more emigrants than the mainland colonies did.

By the 1640s, a Barbados planter boasted of "a great change on this island of late from the worse to the better, praised be God." That change was a shift from tobacco to sugar cane. Dutch merchants helped finance this transition. The Dutch, who had briefly taken control of Brazil, were being driven out by the Portuguese, and looked to the English islands as a new market for the Dutch slave trade. They taught the English how to grow sugar, supplied them with slaves, and dominated the marketing of the English crop. Before long, English sugar planters grew astonishingly wealthy. On average, a Caribbean sugar plantation was worth four times as much as a prosperous Chesapeake plantation.

Sugar rapidly transformed the West Indies. Planters deforested whole islands to raise sugar cane. They stopped planting food crops and raising livestock—thereby creating a demand for lumber and provisions that boosted New England's economy. In 1647, John Winthrop noted that Barbadians "had rather buy food at very dear rates than produce it by labor, so infinite is the profit of sugar works."

For some years after the transition to sugar, English planters continued to import white indentured servants, including kidnapped English and Irish youths, and supplemented the labor force with African slaves. Due to the islands' unhealthy environment and harsh working conditions, servants died in great numbers. England could barely meet the demand for workers, and English workers, if they survived, often proved rebellious. Given the example of prosperous Spanish and Portuguese plantations using slave labor, and the willingness of the Dutch to supply them with slaves, the English switched to African laborers, whom they considered better suited to agricultural work in a tropical climate. The planters' choice has been called an "unthinking decision," but it had an enormous impact on English colonial life, first in the islands and then on the mainland, where slavery would develop later in the seventeenth century (see Chapter 3).

A Biracial Society

As happened on virtually all the Caribbean islands, the English West Indies developed a biracial plantation society—the first in the English colonial world. By 1700, more than 250,000 slaves had been brought to the English islands, and they soon constituted a majority of the population. In Barbados, black slaves increased from 50 percent to more than 70 percent of the population between 1660 and 1700. Slaves lived in wretched conditions, underfed, poorly dressed, and housed in rough huts. They labored six days a week from sunrise to sunset—except at harvest time, when they toiled seven days a week in round-the-clock shifts. Masters considered

African slaves working at a sugar mill in the West Indies, probably on a Dutch-owned island: line engraving, 17th century.

them property, often branding them like livestock and hunting them with bloodhounds when they ran away.

Laws, sometimes called **slave codes,** declared slavery to be a lifelong condition that passed from slave parents to their children. Slaves had no legal rights and were under the complete control of their masters. Only rarely would masters who killed slaves face prosecution, and those found guilty were subject only to fines. Slaves, in contrast, faced appalling punishments even for minor offenses. They could be whipped, branded, or maimed for stealing food or harboring a runaway compatriot. Serious crimes such as murder or arson brought execution without trial. Slaves who rebelled were burned to death.

Astonishingly, slaves preserved some elements of normal life even under these brutal conditions. When masters began to import African women as well as men—hoping to create a self-reproducing labor force—slaves formed families and preserved at least some African traditions. They gave their children African names (although masters often gave them English names as well). They celebrated and worked to the rhythms of African music. And they drew on their West African heritage to perform elaborate funeral rituals, often burying their dead with food and other goods to accompany them on the journey to the afterlife.

White planters, profiting handsomely from their slaves' toil, lived better than many English gentlemen. They indulged in large houses, fine furnishings, and expensive clothing. Even so, many hated the hot, humid West Indian climate and feared the constant threat of disease. After making their fortunes, planters often fled to England, leaving their estates under the care of hired overseers.

But sugar made relatively few white colonists wealthy. Its production required a heavy investment in land, slaves, mills, and equipment. As great planters took vast amounts of land for themselves, freed servants and small farmers struggled to survive. After 1650, many of these poor men, looking for other places to live, headed for the mainland. They were joined by planters looking for a place to expand their operations.

The Restoration Colonies

The initial burst of English colonization ended in 1640 when England tottered on the brink of civil war. With the restoration of Charles II to the throne in 1660, however, interest in North America revived. Charles II rewarded the supporters who had remained loyal to him during his long exile in France with huge grants of American land. During his reign (1660–1685), four new colonies—Carolina, Pennsylvania, New Jersey, and New York—were created (see Map 2–4). All were proprietary colonies, essentially the private property of the people to whom they had been given. Two of them—Carolina and Pennsylvania—like the earlier proprietary colony of Maryland, provided their owners the chance to test idealistic social visions. The origins of New York and

New Jersey as English colonies, by contrast, lay not in visions of social harmony but in the stern reality of military conquest (see the Overview table, English Colonies in the Seventeenth Century).

Early Carolina: Colonial Aristocracy and Slave Labor

In 1663, Charles II granted a group of supporters an enormous tract of land stretching from southern Virginia to northern Florida. The proprietors, who included several Barbados planters, called their colony Carolina, after *Carolus,* the Latin form of the king's name. They envisioned it as growing from the few English outposts already in the region, established by settlers from New England and the West Indies, into a prosperous, orderly society.

One of the proprietors, Anthony Ashley Cooper, working closely with his secretary, John Locke, devised the **Fundamental Constitutions of Carolina,** a plan to ensure the colony's stability by balancing property ownership and political rights with a hierarchical social order. It called for the creation of a colonial aristocracy, who would own two-fifths of the land and wield extensive political power. Below them, a large class of freeholders would own small farms and elect representatives to an assembly. At the bottom of the social order would be slaves.

This plan never went into effect. People moved in from Virginia and the West Indies and settled where they pleased. They even voted in the assembly to reject the Fundamental Constitutions. They antagonized the local Indians, who had initially welcomed English traders eager to buy deerskins but grew hostile when colonists sold guns to some tribes in exchange for Indian captives. The captives were later sold as slaves, principally to the West Indies. Native resentments deepened as settlers moved onto their lands. The result was a deadly cycle of violence.

The colonists at first raised livestock to be sold to the West Indies. But the introduction of rice in the 1690s transformed the settlers' economy, making it, as one planter noted, "as much their staple Commodity, as Sugar is to Barbados and Jamaica, or Tobacco to Virginia and Maryland." The English had never grown rice, but West Africans had. Rice cultivation in Carolina coincided with an increase in the number of African slaves there, who probably introduced the crop. Ironically, the profits earned from rice persuaded Carolina planters to invest even more heavily in slave labor.

Carolina society soon resembled the sugar islands from which many of its founders had come. By 1708, there were more black slaves than white settlers; two decades after that, black people outnumbered white people by two to one. Rice farming required a substantial investment in land, labor, and equipment, including dikes and dams for flooding fields. Those who could afford such an investment set themselves up as planters in Carolina's coastal rice district, acquiring large estates and forcing poorer settlers to move elsewhere.

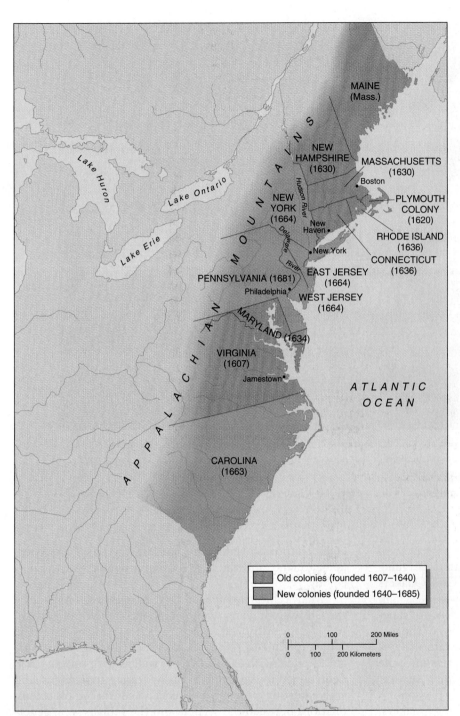

MAP 2–4   English North American Colonies, c. 1685
After the restoration of Charles II in 1660, several large proprietary colonies joined earlier English settlements in New England and the Chesapeake. By 1685, a growing number of English settlers solidified England's claim to the Atlantic coast from Maine (then part of Massachusetts Bay Colony) to the southern edge of Carolina.

forests. So different were the two regions that the colony formally split into two provinces—North and South Carolina—in 1729.

South Carolina rice planters became some of the wealthiest colonists on the mainland. But their luxurious style of life came at a price. As Carolina's slave population grew, planters dreaded the prospect of slave rebellion. To avert this nightmare, they enacted slave codes as harsh as those of the sugar islands.

Although John Locke went on to become one of England's most important philosophers, the visionary plan he and Cooper had devised for Carolina disintegrated on contact with American conditions. Carolina would not be a harmonious colony that balanced wealth and power. It evolved instead into a racially divided society founded on the oppression of a black majority and permeated by fear.

Pennsylvania: The Dream of Toleration and Peace

Even as early Carolina diverged from the plans of its founders, another Englishman dreamed of creating a colonial utopia. William Penn put his plans into action in 1681, when Charles II granted him a huge tract of land north of Maryland. Penn intended his colony to be a model of justice and peace, as well as a refuge for members of the Society of Friends, or **Quakers,** a persecuted religious sect to which Penn belonged.

The Society of Friends was one of many radical religious groups that emerged in England during the civil war. Like the separatists, Quakers abandoned the Church of England as hopelessly corrupt. But they went even further in their beliefs. Rejecting predestination, they maintained that every soul had a spark of grace and that salvation was possible for all who heeded that "Inner Light." They rejected trained clergy and church rituals as unnecessary to salvation. Instead of formal religious services, Quakers held meetings at which silence reigned until someone, inspired by the Inner Light, rose to speak.

Some of these dislocated settlers went to the northern part of Carolina, where the land and climate were unsuited to rice. There they raised tobacco and livestock, and produced pitch, tar, and timber products from the region's pine

Quaker beliefs had disturbing social and political implications. Although they did not advocate complete equality of the sexes, Quakers granted women spiritual equality with

Thomas Coram's oil painting (c. 1770) shows the main residence and slave quarters on the Mulberry Plantation near Charleston, South Carolina. The distinctive steep-roofed design of the slave cabins on the left probably reflects African building styles. Slave quarters may not have been located quite as close to the main house as this picture suggests.

Thomas Coram, "View of Mulberry Street, House and Street." Oil on paper, 10 3 17.6 cm, Gibbes Museum of Art/Carolina Art Association. 68.18.01

men, allowing them to preach, hold separate prayer meetings, and exercise authority over "women's matters." Arguing that social distinctions were not the work of God, Quakers refused to defer to their "betters." People of lower social rank were expected to remove their hats in the presence of superiors, but Quakers would not do so. And instead of the formal *you,* Quakers addressed superiors with the informal *thee* and *thou.* Because their faith required them to renounce the use of force, Quakers refused to perform military service, which their enemies considered tantamount to treason.

When English authorities began harassing Quakers, William Penn, who was himself jailed briefly, conceived his plan for a New World refuge. He aimed to launch a "holy experiment," a harmonious society governed by brotherly love. Knowing that Quakers were unwelcome in the existing colonies—Massachusetts had hanged four of them—Penn looked elsewhere. His aristocratic background gave him advantages that other Quakers, who were mainly of humble origins, lacked. Using his father's connection with the king, he acquired the land that became Pennsylvania ("Penn's Woods") and recruited settlers from among Europe's oppressed peoples and persecuted religious sects. By 1700,

eighteen thousand emigrants had left England, Wales, Scotland, Ireland, and various German provinces for the new colony.

Many came in families and settled in an area occupied by the Delaware Indians, whose numbers, though still substantial, had recently been reduced by disease and warfare. The "holy experiment" required colonists to live "as Neighbours and friends" with the Indians as well as with one another. Penn aimed to accomplish this by paying Indians for land and regulating trade. As long as Penn controlled his colony, relations between the settlers and the Indians were generally peaceful—so much so that refugee Indians from nearby colonies moved into Pennsylvania. Relations between Penn and the settlers, however, were less cordial.

In the **Frame of Government** he devised for Pennsylvania, Penn remained true to his Quaker principles with a provision allowing for religious freedom. But true to his aristocratic origins, he designed a legislature with limited powers and reserved considerable authority for himself. When Penn returned to England after a brief stay in the colony (1682–1684), the settlers began squabbling among themselves. The governor and council, both appointed by Penn, fought

OVERVIEW

English Colonies in the Seventeenth Century

Colony	Date of Founding	Established Religion	Economy	Government
Virginia	1607	Anglican	Tobacco	Royal (after 1625)
Plymouth	1620	Puritan	Mixed farming	Corporate
St. Christopher	1624	Anglican	Sugar	Royal
Barbados	1627	Anglican	Sugar	Royal
Nevis	1628	Anglican	Sugar	Royal
Massachusetts (including present-day Maine)	1630	Puritan	Mixed farming, fishing, shipbuilding	Corporate
New Hampshire	1630 (first settlement, annexed to Massachusetts 1643–1679	Puritan	Mixed farming	Corporate (royal after 1679)
Antigua	1632	Anglican	Sugar	Royal
Montserrat	1632	Anglican	Sugar	Royal
Maryland	1634	None (Anglican after 1692)	Tobacco	Proprietary
Rhode Island	1636	None	Mixed farming	Corporate
Connecticut	1636	Puritan	Mixed farming	Corporate
New Haven	1638	Puritan	Mixed farming	Corporate
Jamaica	1655 (captured from Spanish)	Anglican	Sugar	Royal
Carolina	1663	Anglican	Rice	Proprietary
New York	1664 (captured from Dutch)	None	Mixed farming, furs	Proprietary (royal after 1685)
New Jersey	1664	None	Mixed farming	Proprietary
Pennsylvania	1681	None	Wheat, mixed farming	Proprietary

with elected members of the assembly. Penn's opponents—many of whom were fellow Quakers—objected to his proprietary privileges, including his control of foreign trade and his collection of fees from landholders. Settlers on the lower Delaware River, which the crown had added to Penn's colony to give its port city, Philadelphia, access to the sea, gained autonomy for themselves with their own legislature, in effect creating an unofficial colony that later became Delaware.

A disappointed Penn lamented that the settlers had become "so brutish." He spent his fortune on his beloved colony, only to die in debt with his hopes for a harmonious society dashed. Settlers continued to fight among themselves and with Penn's heirs. A flood of increasingly aggressive immigrants undermined peaceful relations with the Indians, forcing many native people to move west.

By 1720, Pennsylvania's ethnically and religiously diverse colonists numbered more than thirty thousand. The colony, with some of the richest farmland along the Atlantic coast, was widely known as the "best poor man's country in the world." Growing wheat and other crops, the settlers lived mostly on scattered farms rather than in towns. From the busy port of Philadelphia, ships carried much of the harvest to markets in the West Indies and southern Europe. Penn's "holy experiment" in social harmony may have failed, but, as a thriving colony, Pennsylvania succeeded handsomely.

New Netherland Becomes New York

The proprietary colonies of New York and New Jersey were carved out of the Dutch colony of New Netherland. Competition between the English and the Dutch intensified in

In the eighteenth century, Benjamin West painted this scene of William Penn negotiating a treaty with the Delaware Indians. During Penn's lifetime, relations between Pennsylvania colonists and the Indians were relatively peaceful.

the mid-seventeenth century as the two peoples struggled for trade supremacy on the high seas. Their antagonism generated two Anglo-Dutch wars in 1652–1654 and 1665–1667. In the New World, tensions were heightened by the presence of English colonists on Long Island, which the Dutch claimed for themselves.

In 1664, Charles II brought matters to a head by claiming that since the site of New Netherland lay within the bounds of the original charter of Virginia, the land belonged to England. He granted the territory to his brother James, duke of York, who sent ships to back up England's claim. Their arrival provoked a rebellion by Long Island's English colonists, leading the Dutch governor, Peter Stuyvesant—who commanded just 150 soldiers—to surrender without firing a shot.

The duke of York became proprietor of this new English possession, which was renamed New York. James immediately created another colony, New Jersey, which he granted to his supporters. New Jersey's proprietors struggled to control the diverse people already living there. At one point the colony split in two parts, East and West Jersey, which reunited to become a single royal colony in 1702 when the frustrated proprietors surrendered their rights to the king.

New York, which James retained for himself, was the most valuable part of the former Dutch colony. It included the port of New York City (the former New Amsterdam) and the Hudson Valley with its fur trade. James encouraged Dutch colonists to remain and promoted immigration from England to strengthen the colony and gain income from land sales. By 1700, the settlers numbered twenty thousand.

For nearly twenty years after its takeover by the English, New York lacked something all other English colonies had—

a representative assembly. After neighboring New Jersey and Pennsylvania created their own assemblies, however, New Yorkers pressed their proprietor to follow suit. Only in 1683, when it became clear that New York might lose population to Pennsylvania, did James relent and create the assembly that brought New York in line with other English colonies.

Conclusion

During the seventeenth century, France, the Netherlands, and England competed for land and trade in North America. New France's scattered settlements clung to the St. Lawrence River Valley. Profits from the fur trade encouraged the French to maintain friendly relations with their Indian allies and ensured that French kings would closely monitor the colony's affairs. English colonization was a more haphazard process. English kings granted charters—sometimes to joint-stock companies (Virginia, Plymouth, Massachusetts), sometimes to proprietors (Maryland, Carolina, New York, New Jersey, Pennsylvania)—and let the colonies develop more or less on their own. England had no equivalent in the seventeenth century of the imperial bureaucracies Spain and France created to manage their New World holdings.

The result was a highly diverse set of English colonies stretching from the Maine coast to the Caribbean. Settlers adjusted to different environments, developed different economies and labor systems, and worshiped in different churches. In South Carolina, New York, Pennsylvania, and the West Indies, most colonists were not even of English origin. What held these colonies together—besides their establishment under English charters and their enmity toward the Spanish and French—was an overlay of common English institutions of government. By the mid-1680s, all the colonies had legislatures that provided for self-government and laws and judicial institutions based on English models.

The planting of French, Dutch, and English colonies not only ended Spain's monopoly of settlement in North America but also challenged the Indians' hold on the continent. Forced to deal with a rising tide of settlers and often to choose sides between European rivals, native peoples adapted to rapidly changing circumstances. Transplanted Europeans adapted too, not only in their dealings with native peoples but also in finding and controlling the laborers they needed to make their colonies prosper. For English colonists this meant the widespread adoption of slavery, an institution that did not exist in England itself. For millions of Africans, the result was forced migration to the New World.

Global Perspectives

North America's First Jewish Community

In 1654, twenty-three Jews arrived in New Amsterdam after a long voyage from Brazil. The reasons why they ended up in the Dutch colonial town relate to a much larger story of repeated Jewish migrations, undertaken time and again to escape religious persecution. In New Amsterdam these settlers found a home, establishing the first permanent Jewish community in North America.

Many of them could trace their ancestry back to Spain, where there had been a flourishing Jewish community during the Middle Ages. By the fifteenth century, however, the same Christian militancy that inspired the *reconquista* against the Muslims brought trouble for Spain's Jewish population in the form of the Inquisition. Jews who refused to convert to Christianity risked execution as heretics. In 1492, the same year as Columbus's first voyage, Spanish authorities ordered all Jews to leave Spain. Refugee Spanish Jews relocated all over the Mediterranean world, with perhaps a hundred thousand settling in Portugal, Spain's neighbor on the Iberian Peninsula. Many who did so were forced to accept Christian baptism, but continued to follow their own faith in secret. When the authorities threatened to prevent such practices, many Jews chose to leave Portugal. Some sought refuge in the Netherlands, where they found religious toleration and commercial opportunities.

In the early seventeenth century, the same Dutch West India Company that founded New Netherland tried to dislodge the Portuguese from their prosperous sugar-producing colony of Brazil. The company succeeded in capturing the city of Recife in 1630, and for the next twenty four years the Dutch ruled over northeastern Brazil. During that time, more than a thousand Jews moved to the colony from the Netherlands. But when the Portuguese regained control of Brazil in 1654, the Jews were forced to move yet again. Most returned to the Netherlands, but a few decided to take their chances in New Amsterdam. At last they found a place where they could stay. When New Netherland became New York in 1664, English authorities continued the Dutch practice of toleration. Even though Jewish colonists were only supposed to worship in private, there was a synagogue in New York City by 1700. Jews eventually settled in other colonies, such as Rhode Island, Pennsylvania, and South Carolina. Wherever they formed their communities, they contributed to the remarkable religious diversity of England's New World empire.

■ How did religious persecution in early modern Europe affect the lives of its Jewish inhabitants?

Review Questions

1. To what extent was Richard Frethorne's experience typical of that of English colonists in the New World? What were the causes of his distress?

2. Comparing French, Dutch, and English colonies, which ones attracted the most settlers, and which the fewest? In what colonies were women scarce? What impact did these differences in emigration have on the various colonies' development?

3. Which English settlements were proprietary colonies? Did they share any common characteristics? What plans did the various proprietors have for their colonies, and to what extent were those plans put into effect?

4. When Virginia's settlers first arrived, they encountered a numerous and powerful confederation of Powhatan Indians. New England's colonists, in contrast, began their settlements after epidemics had drastically reduced the local native population. In what ways did the presence or absence of substantial Indian populations affect each region's early history?

5. In both Massachusetts and Pennsylvania, religion figured prominently as a motive for settlement. What were the religious beliefs of the settlers in each colony, and how did those beliefs help shape each colony's development?

6. Three colonial regions—the Chesapeake, the West Indies, and Carolina—developed economies dependent on staple crops. What were those crops? In what ways did staple-crop agriculture shape society in each region?

7. In what ways did events in Europe affect the founding of colonies in North America?

Key Terms

Act for Religious Toleration (p. 40)

Anglican (p. 41)

Coureur de bois (p. 32)

Covenant (p. 43)

Frame of Government (p. 50)

Fundamental Constitutions of Carolina (p. 48)

Headright system (p. 35)

House of Burgesses (p. 35)

Indentured servants (p. 32)

Joint-stock company (p. 35)

Pequot War (p. 43)

Pilgrims (p. 42)

Proprietary colony (p. 40)

Puritans (p. 40)

Quakers (p. 49)

Separatists (p. 41)

Slave codes (p. 48)

Recommended Reading

Anderson, Virginia DeJohn. *New England's Generation: The Great Migration and the Formation of Society and Culture in the Seventeenth Century* (1991). Examines the experiences of nearly seven hundred emigrants to New England and explores how they shaped New England society.

Dunn, Richard S. *Sugar and Slaves: The Rise of the Planter Class in the English West Indies, 1624–1713* (1972). The authoritative account of British settlement in the West Indies and the development of the slave labor system.

Greer, Allan. *The People of New France* (1997). A brief and readable overview of the origins and development of New France.

Morgan, Edmund S. *American Slavery, American Freedom: The Ordeal of Colonial Virginia* (1975). A vividly written account of the founding of Virginia and the development of an unfree labor system that remains the best study of an early American colony.

Wood, Peter H. *Black Majority: Negroes in Colonial South Carolina from 1670 through the Stono Rebellion* (1974). A study of the founding of South Carolina that emphasizes the contributions of the black slaves who eventually comprised a majority of the colony's settlers.

Where to Learn More

■ **Jamestown Settlement, near Williamsburg, Virginia.** Site includes replicas of first English passenger ships to Virginia, a reconstructed Powhatan Village, the recreated James Fort, and galleries with Indian and English artifacts. Visitors can also see archaeological excavations of site of the actual James Fort, as well as sample artifacts recovered from the area. For updated information about archaeological excavations at Jamestown, see www.apva.org. At http:jeffersonvillage.virginia.edu, you can take a virtual tour of the Jamestown settlement.

■ **St. Mary's City, Maryland.** Visitors to this site of the first permanent settlement under the Calvert family may tour the area and view exhibits and living history programs that describe life in early Maryland. The website www.somd.com contains information about the historic site of St. Mary's City and has links to a virtual tour of the area.

■ **Plimoth Plantation, Plymouth, Massachusetts.** A living history museum, Plimoth Plantation re-creates colony life in the year 1627. There are reproductions of the English village and a Wampanoag settlement. Visitors may also see a replica of the *Mayflower*. For a virtual tour, go to pilgrims.net/plimothplantation/vtour. Information on Pilgrims and early years of the colony can be found at pilgrims.net/plymouth/history.

■ **Pennsbury Manor, Morrisville, Pennsylvania.** A reconstruction of William Penn's seventeenth-century plantation, this site includes furnished buildings and restored gardens. There are also guided tours and demonstrations of colonial crafts. Both www.bucksnet.com/pennsbury and www.pennsburymanor.org provide information about William Penn, the historic site, and various activities at the manor.

Study Resources

Primary Source: Documents in U.S. History CD-ROM
For primary sources related to this chapter, refer to the document CD-ROM included in the text.

PEARSON
myhistorylab™

For study resources for this chapter, go to www.myhistorylab.com and choose *The American Journey*. You will find a wealth of study and review material for this chapter, including pre- and post-tests, customized study plan, key term review flash cards, interactive map and document activities, and documents for analysis.

As the top portion of this eighteenth-century French engraving suggests, the horrors of slavery began as soon as Africans were torn from their families and marched to ships anchored off the coast. The bottom part of the picture shows how tightly slaves were packed below the decks of these vessels, evidence that merchants' thirst for profit overrode concerns for the slaves' health or welfare.

Archives Charmet, Musee des Arts d'Afrique et d'Oceanie, Paris, France.

A Meeting of Cultures 3

One day [in 1756], when all our people were gone out to their work as usual, and only I and my sister were left to mind the house, two men and a woman got over our walls, and in a moment seized us both; and without giving us time to cry out, or to make any resistance, they stopped our mouths and ran off with us into the nearest wood. Here they tied our hands, and continued to carry us as far as they could…. Thus I continued to travel, both by land and by water, through different countries and various nations, till at the end of six or seven months after I had been kidnapped, I arrived at the sea coast….

The first object that saluted my eyes when I arrived on the coast was the sea, and a slave ship, which was then riding at anchor, and waiting for its cargo. These filled me with astonishment, that was soon converted into terror, which I am yet at a loss to describe…. I was immediately handled and tossed up to see if I was sound, by some of the crew; and I was now persuaded that I had got into a world of bad spirits, and that they were going to kill me. Their complexions too, differing so much from ours, their long hair, and the language they spoke, which was very different from any I had ever heard, united to confirm me in this belief…. I asked…if we were not to be eaten by those white men with horrible looks, red faces, and long hair….

In a little time after, amongst the poor chained men, I found some of my own nation…. They gave me to understand we were to be carried to these white people's country to work for them…. [Many weeks later] we were landed up a river a good way from the sea, about Virginia county, where we saw few of our native Africans, and not one soul who could talk to me.

Olaudah Equiano, *The Interesting Narrative of the Life of Olaudah Equiano, or Gustavus Vassa, The African.*

myhistorylab
Personal Journeys Online

- Pedro Naranjol, *Indian Account of the Pueblo Revolt,* 1680

- Job ben Solomon, *Some Memoirs of the Life of Job,* 1734. Description of Job's capture and sale into slavery.

- Gottlieb Mittelberger, *Journey to Pennsylvania,* 1756. Description of the arrival of German redemptioners to Pennsylvania.

Olaudah Equiano, born in 1745 in the African kingdom of Benin, was only a boy when his terrifying journey to America began. The son of an Igbo chief, he was caught in the web of an expanding transatlantic slave trade that reached from the African interior to nearly every port town in the Americas and the Caribbean. From modest beginnings in the sixteenth century, the slave trade had expanded dramatically, transforming every society it touched. Equiano's Virginia scarcely resembled that of John Smith. Tobacco still reigned supreme, but by the mid-eighteenth century, more workers were black than white. Slavery had spread from England's Caribbean colonies to dominate the Chesapeake settlements as well.

At the same time, in Virginia and elsewhere in North America, Indian peoples faced new challenges as they endeavored to maintain their independence despite a flood of immigrants from Europe and Africa. Indians employed different tactics—adaptation, coexistence, diplomacy, resistance—to assert their claims to land and their right to participate in the events and deliberations that affected their lives. The America to which Olaudah Equiano had been forcibly transported remained a place where Indian voices had to be heeded.

Equiano's journey did not end in Virginia. Over the next quarter-century, he traveled to other mainland colonies, the West Indies, England, Turkey, Portugal, and Spain. He worked as the servant of a naval officer, a barber, a laborer, an overseer, saving money to purchase his freedom. Such an extraordinary career testified to Equiano's resilience and determination. It also bore witness to the emergence of an international market for laborers, which—like slavery and Indian relations—shaped the development of North America. Thousands of people from England, Scotland, Ireland, and Germany attempted to take advantage of that market and seek their fortunes in America, increasing the white population and expanding onto new lands. The interactions of Indians, Africans, and Europeans created not one but many New Worlds.

Indians and Europeans

Although, by 1750, European colonists and African slaves together outnumbered Indians north of the Rio Grande, Native Americans still dominated much of the continent. Colonists remained clustered along the coasts, and some native peoples had scarcely seen any Europeans. Indians living in the Pacific Northwest met their first white men—Russian fur traders—only in the 1740s. By this time, the Pueblos of the Southwest, the Hurons of Canada, and the Algonquians of the Atlantic seaboard had more than a century's experience dealing with Europeans and their American-born descendants.

CHRONOLOGY

1440s	Portuguese enter slave trade in West Africa.
c. 1450	Iroquois form Great League of Peace and Power.
1610–1614	First war between English settlers and Powhatan Indians.
1619	First Africans arrive in Virginia.
1622–1632	Second war between English settlers and Powhatan Indians.
1637	Pequot War in New England.
1640s	Slave labor begins to dominate in the West Indies.
	First phase of the Beaver Wars.
1651	First "praying town" established at Natick, Massachusetts.
1661	Maryland law defines slavery as lifelong, inheritable status.
1670	Virginia law defines status of slaves.
1675–1676	King Philip's War in New England.
1676	Bacon's Rebellion in Virginia.
1680	Pueblo Revolt in New Mexico.
1680s	Second phase of Beaver Wars begins.
1688–1697	England and France fight the War of the League of Augsburg (known in America as King William's War).
1690s	Shift from white indentured servants to black slaves as principal labor force in the Chesapeake.
1701	Iroquois adopt policy of neutrality toward French and English.
1711–1713	Tuscarora War in Carolina.
1713	Beginnings of substantial Scottish, Scots-Irish, and German immigration to colonies.
1715–1716	Yamasee War in Carolina.
1720s	Black population begins to increase naturally in English mainland colonies.
1730	Major slave insurrection in Virginia.
1732	Georgia established.
1739	Stono Rebellion in South Carolina.
1741	Slave conspiracy discovered in New York City.
1750	Slavery legalized in Georgia.
1760–1775	Peak of European and African immigration to English colonies.

The character of the relationship between Indians and Europeans depended on more than relative population size and the length of time they had been in contact. It was also shaped by the intentions of the newcomers—whether they came to extract resources, to trade, to settle, or to gain converts—and by the responses of Native American groups intent on preserving their cultures. The result was a variety of regionally distinctive New World communities.

Indian Workers in the Spanish Borderlands

More than any other European colonists, the Spanish sought direct control over Indian laborers. Their success in doing so depended on two factors: the existence of sizable Indian communities and Spanish military force. North of the Rio Grande, these conditions could be found in New Mexico and, to a lesser extent, in Florida. Native villages provided workers and existing structures of government that the Spanish converted to their own uses. At the same time, Spanish soldiers ensured that the Indians obeyed orders even though they greatly outnumbered the colonists.

One important method of labor control was the *encomienda*. Encomiendas, granted to influential Spaniards in New Mexico, gave these colonists the right to collect tribute from the native peoples living on a specific piece of land. The tribute usually took the form of corn, blankets, and animal hides, which the Spanish could either use or sell. It was not supposed to include forced labor, but often it did.

The Spanish also relied on the *repartimiento,* a mandatory draft of Indian labor for public projects, such as building forts, bridges, and roads. Laws stated that native workers should be paid and limited the length of their service, but the Spanish often ignored these provisions and sometimes compelled Indians to work on private estates.

Spaniards also ransomed captives that Indian groups seized from one another. This practice, called *rescate,* obliged rescued Indians to work for those who had paid their ransom. These "freed" Native Americans usually became servants in Spanish households. Some colonial families welcomed them as foster members, but others mistreated them and even sold them into slavery.

The native peoples strongly resented these Spanish strategies. Spanish demands for labor and tribute remained constant, even when Indian populations declined from disease or crops failed, and workers who resisted were severely punished. Resentments simmered beneath a surface of cooperation until late in the seventeenth century, when long-standing native anger burst forth in rebellion.

The Web of Trade

Not all economic exchanges between Indians and Europeans were directly coercive. Indians sometimes used trade relations to exert influence over Europeans. Native Americans thought of trade not simply as an economic activity but rather as one aspect of a broader alliance between peoples. Europeans who wished to trade with Indians had to prove their friendship by offering gifts such as wampum (shell beads used as a kind of currency) and military aid as well as manufactured goods.

The French readily adapted to the Native American understanding of trade, realizing that good relations were essential to keeping New France's fur trade operating smoothly. The fur trade benefited Indians too. "The Beaver does everything perfectly well," noted one native leader, "it makes kettles, hatchets, swords, knives, bread; and, in short, it makes everything." Initially, Indians used European goods as raw materials to be reshaped as they saw fit. Thus copper kettles might be cut into ornaments instead of used for cooking. As such goods became more readily available, Indians replaced traditional objects with them: metal kettles for ceramic pots, or wool blankets for skins and furs.

The benefits of trade were immediate and obvious; the problems were slower to appear. The one exception was the problem of disease, which followed almost immediately from Indians' contacts with European traders (see Figure 3–1). The Huron population declined by half in just six years between 1634 and 1640. Indians trading with the Dutch in New Netherland in the 1650s reported that their once sizable population "had been melted down" by smallpox.

Although Indian hunters enjoyed considerable autonomy in their work, French merchants began to use economic pressure to control them. By supplying Indians with trade goods in advance, merchants obligated them to bring in furs as payment. One year's hunting thus paid the previous year's debts. Hunters who tried to avoid payment would lose access to more trade goods. Extending credit in this way allowed the French to control native workers without having to subjugate them.

The French could control the Indians through credit because native peoples had grown increasingly dependent on European manufactures. In many communities, Indians abandoned native crafts and instead relied on imported goods. As a result, they had no alternative but to increase their hunting in order to have furs to trade for what they needed. "The Cloaths we wear, we cannot make ourselves," a Carolina Cherokee observed in 1753. "We cannot make our Guns.... Every necessary Thing in Life we must have from the white People." One consequence of this predicament was overhunting; as early as the 1640s, beaver could no longer be found in much of New England, New York, and Pennsylvania.

Trade with Europeans eventually encouraged violence and warfare. Indians had fought one another before European col-

This map illustration depicts an encounter between a French trader and an Indian hunter in the Canadian wilderness. The exchange of European goods for furs was central to the economy of New France.

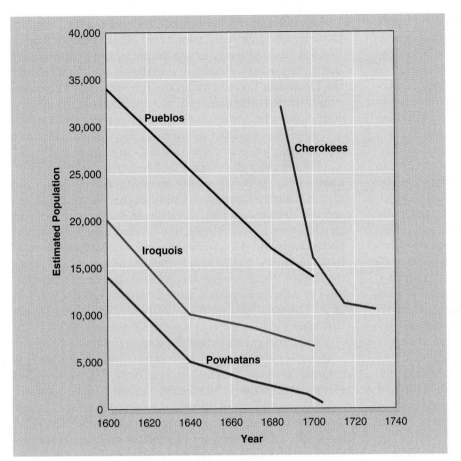

FIGURE 3–1 **Estimated Populations of Selected Indian Peoples, 1600–1730**
Indian populations shrank dramatically due to diseases brought by Europeans from the Old World. By about 1750, native peoples had become a minority of the inhabitants of America north of the Rio Grande.

Data Sources: Daniel Richter, *The Ordeal of the Longhouse* (1992); Helen Rountree, *Pocahontas's People* (1990); David Weber, *The Spanish Frontier in North America* (1992); Peter Wood, et al., eds., *Powhatan's Mantle* (1989).

onization, but these wars were generally limited in scope and destructiveness. In much of eastern North America, "mourning wars" predominated. Warriors conducted raids mainly to seize captives rather than to kill large numbers of their enemies. The captives would either be ritually killed to avenge the deaths of individuals lost in earlier conflicts or adopted into the captors' group to replace the dead. After Europeans arrived, Indians adapted the mourning-war tradition to new circumstances. Warriors raided their enemies to replace family members lost to disease and fought to avenge losses resulting from the fierce competition for a diminishing supply of fur-bearing animals. The proliferation of firearms made the conflicts deadlier, and more casualties led to further mourning wars.

The **Beaver Wars,** a long struggle between the Hurons and the Iroquois that began in the 1640s, illustrated the ferocity of such contests. The Hurons were trading partners and allies with the French, and the Iroquois had forged ties with Dutch merchants in the Hudson River Valley. To satisfy the European demand for furs, the Hurons and Iroquois both hunted beaver at an unsustainable rate. By the 1630s, they had killed nearly all the beavers on their own lands and began to look elsewhere. The Hurons raised more corn in order to trade it for furs with Indians living north of the Great Lakes, where beavers were still abundant. The Iroquois, however, began to raid Huron trading parties and attack Huron villages.

The Iroquois triumphed in this struggle largely because the Dutch supplied them with guns, whereas the French were reluctant to arm the Hurons. In the end, thousands of Hurons were killed or captured, and many others fled westward. The cycle of warfare did not end with the Hurons' destruction. The victorious Iroquois went on to challenge Indian nations near the Great Lakes and in the Ohio Valley. Although trade brought improvements to native life, cemented alliances with Europeans, and strengthened the economic and diplomatic positions of such successful participants as the Iroquois, over the long run its disadvantages—especially Indians' eventual dependence on Europeans and the escalation of violence—overshadowed its benefits.

Displacing Native Americans in the English Colonies
In New France and New Netherland, where the fur trade took precedence over farming, Indians outnumbered Europeans. This numerical superiority and their key role as suppliers of furs allowed native peoples to negotiate with settlers from a position of strength. The situation was different in the English colonies, whose settlers came to farm and thus competed directly with Indians for land. It did not help matters that, as Indian populations declined because of European diseases, colonial populations burgeoned through immigration and natural increase. As early as 1650, colonists outnumbered Native Americans in coastal Massachusetts and eastern Virginia.

English settlers at first assumed that there was enough land for everyone. Colonists thrilled at the sight of what they considered vast unoccupied territory. "The Indians are not able to make use of the one fourth part of the Land," declared one New England settler. Another insisted that the natives "do but run over the grass, as do also the foxes and wild beasts" and therefore that the land was free for the taking.

Land use and property rights.   But the settlers misunderstood how Indians used land. Eastern Algonquian peoples moved frequently to take advantage of the land's diversity. They cleared areas for villages and planting fields, which native women farmed until the soil grew less fertile. Then they moved to a new location, allowing the former village site to return to forest. In ten to twenty years, they or their descendants might return to that site to clear and farm it again. In the winter, village communities broke up into small hunting bands. Thus what the colonists considered "vacant" lands were either being used for nonfarming activities such as hunting or regaining fertility in order to be farmed in years to come. Settlers who built towns on abandoned native village sites deprived the Indians of access to these areas.

Disputes between Europeans and Indians frequently arose from misunderstandings about the definition of land ownership and property rights. Indian villages claimed sovereignty over a certain territory, which their members collectively used for farming, fishing, hunting, and gathering. No Indian claimed individual ownership of a specific tract of land. Europeans, of course, did, and for them ownership conferred on an individual the exclusive right to use or sell a piece of land. These differences created problems whenever Indians transferred land to settlers. The settlers assumed that they had obtained complete rights to the land, whereas the Indians assumed that they had given the settlers not the land itself but only the right to use it. The English understanding of what was meant by a land sale prevailed, however, enforced in the colonists' courts under the colonists' laws.

Colonial agricultural practices also strained relations with the Indians. Cutting down forests destroyed Indian hunting lands. When colonists dammed rivers, they disturbed Indian fishing. When they surrounded their fields with fences, colonists made trespassers of natives who crossed them. Colonial laws prohibited Indians from burning parts of the forest—something they had regularly done to destroy underbrush and make the woods suitable for hunting and travel—because settlers feared that fires might spread to their property. Yet the colonists let their cattle and pigs loose to graze in the woods and meadows, where they could wander into unfenced Indian cornfields and damage the crops.

Colonial land acquisition.   As their numbers grew, the colonists acquired Indian lands and displaced native inhabitants. Some colonial leaders, such as Roger Williams in Rhode Island and William Penn of Pennsylvania, insisted on buying land. But even purchasers who tried to be fair encountered difficulties. Because Indians owned land collectively, only their leaders had the authority to negotiate sales. Settlers, however, sometimes bought land from individual Indians who had no right to sell it. Because land transfers were usually arranged through interpreters and recorded in English, Indians were not always fully informed of the terms of sale. Even Indians who willingly sold land grew resentful as colonists approached them for more. Finally, native peoples could be forced to sell land to settle debts to English creditors.

Settlers occasionally obtained land by fraud. In 1734, for instance, James Logan of Pennsylvania produced what he insisted was a copy of a deed from 1686 by which the Delaware Indians had supposedly transferred a large tract of land to William Penn. Although Logan did not have the original deed and there was no reference to it in the colony's land records, the Delawares had to give up the territory. Some colonists simply settled on Indian lands and appealed to colonial governments for help when the Indians objected. Land speculators amplified this kind of unrest as they sought to acquire land as cheaply as possible and sell it for as much as they could.

Finally, colonists often seized Indian lands in the aftermath of war, as befell, among many others, the Pequots in 1637 in Connecticut and, in Carolina, the Tuscaroras in 1713 and the Yamasees in 1715. In each case, settlers moved onto land left vacant after colonial forces killed, captured, and dispersed native peoples. Sometimes colonial leaders contrived for some Indian groups to help them displace others. During the Pequot War, Narragansetts aided Connecticut settlers' efforts to oust the Pequots. Carolina colonists enlisted the help of the Yamasees against the Tuscaroras and then turned to the Cherokees to help them against the Yamasees.

Some Indians staved off the worst effects of English encroachments by forming new communities just beyond the colonial settlements. The Catawba Nation in the Carolina Piedmont employed this strategy to preserve its independence. Although English colonists continued to covet Catawba lands, the Carolina government recognized the advantages of having friendly native allies in a volatile frontier region and tried to discourage settlers' incursions.

Such small victories helped to sustain Indian autonomy in various parts of the English colonies. But the general trend was hardly encouraging. The colonists' hunger for land generated relentless pressure on native peoples. The pattern of mutual suspicion and territorial competition would be difficult to alter.

Bringing Christianity to Native Peoples

In addition to trade and settlement, religion played a powerful role in shaping relations between Native Americans and Europeans. The three major New World empires of Spain, France, and England competed for Indians' souls as well as their lands and riches.

Catholic missionaries in Spanish colonies.   Franciscan priests were the driving force behind Spain's efforts to control New Mexico and Florida (see Map 3–1). Spain valued both regions for strategic reasons. Its bases in Florida helped protect Spanish ships bearing treasure from Mexico and Peru and discouraged the southward spread of English settlement. New Mexico served as a buffer between the silver mines of northern Mexico and roaming Plains Indians. Neither colony attracted many settlers, however, because neither offered much opportunity for wealth. When Franciscan missionaries proposed to move in, Spanish officials, eager to back up their claims with a more visible Spanish presence, provided financial support.

Franciscans settled near native villages in New Mexico and Florida in order to convert their inhabitants to Catholicism. The priests wore their finest vestments and displayed

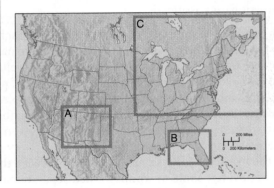

MAP 3–1   Spanish and French Missions in Seventeenth-Century North America
Spanish Franciscans in New Mexico (A) and Florida (B) and French Jesuits in New France (C) devoted considerable effort to converting native peoples to Catholic Christianity.

religious paintings and statues, trying to impress the Indians. They gave away bells, knives, cloth, and food. The natives believed that accepting these gifts obliged them to listen to the priests' Christian message and help the Franciscans build houses and churches.

After brief religious instruction, the missionaries convinced many Indians to accept baptism into the Catholic Church. Many of these conversions were doubtless genuine, but they also had practical motivations. Conversions often followed epidemics that devastated native villages but spared the Spanish, leading Indians to wonder if the Christian God might be more powerful than their own gods. In New Mexico, the Spanish offered Pueblo converts protection against Apache raids and access to Franciscan storehouses in times of famine.

Ironically, the corn in the storehouses often came from the Indians' own fields, collected by the Spanish as tribute.

The Franciscans insisted that converts abandon their former ways of life and adopt Spanish food, clothing, gender relations, and work routines along with Catholicism. Their efforts met with mixed success. Many Indians preferred to supplement native beliefs and practices with the new teachings. They added Jesus, Mary, and the Catholic saints to the list of Indian supernatural beings and saw the missionaries as counterparts of, rather than replacements for, native religious leaders. Because the missionaries reacted to this spiritual mixture with horror, inflicting severe punishments that sometimes led to death, native peoples often practiced their own rituals in secret. By the mid-seventeenth

San Esteban del Rey, built in 1629, is one of the oldest Spanish missions in New Mexico.

century, Spanish missionaries claimed to have made thousands of converts, many of whom were mestizos—people of mixed Spanish and Indian ancestry—occupying a difficult position between two cultures. Christianity had been securely planted in the Spanish borderlands, but not as deeply as the missionaries assumed.

French Jesuits in Canada.   To a certain extent, French Jesuits in Canada followed a similar strategy, moving to native villages and seeking to awe Indians with European technology and Catholic rituals. Priests exhibited the "magical" powers of clocks and magnets and impressed native peoples by predicting eclipses. Missionaries demonstrated their ability to read and write, which fascinated Indian peoples who had no experience with written language.

By the 1650s, the Jesuits claimed to have produced thousands of converts, some of whom formed separate native Christian communities. The priests publicized extraordinary examples of Indian piety, particularly the story of Kateri Tekakwitha. An orphaned Mohawk girl who joined the Christian Indian village of Kahnawake, Tekakwitha sparked a religious revival among female converts and became the first Native American candidate for sainthood.

French missionaries combined economic pressure with preaching. They persuaded merchants to sell guns only to converted Indians and to offer them other trade goods at a discount. Such tactics doubtless brought some success, but as in New Mexico, the crises engendered by epidemics more often than not sparked an upsurge in conversions. Converts in New France also preferred to meld Catholic teachings with native beliefs. Missionaries hardly condoned this response but they resigned themselves, at least in the short run, to a gradual approach to conversion. "One must be careful before condemning a thousand things among their customs," warned one priest, because to do so would "greatly offend minds brought up and

nourished in another world." The Jesuits reduced the potential for confrontation with the Indians by accepting small changes in converts at first in hopes of a wholesale transformation to follow.

Missionaries in English colonies.   The Protestant English were less successful at attracting Native American converts. Puritans frowned on the rituals and religious objects that drew Indians to Catholicism, but Protestant practices, including lengthy sermons and an emphasis on Bible study, held little allure for Indians accustomed to a more ritualistic spiritual life. Even so, Protestant missionaries achieved some success, principally in New England. Beginning in the 1650s and 1660s, Puritan ministers such as John Eliot and Thomas Mayhew, Jr., attracted converts. Eliot helped to establish several "praying towns," where Indians received instruction in Protestant Christianity and English ways. By 1674, about 2,300 Indians resided in these towns.

Elsewhere in the English colonies, missionaries enjoyed little success. Anglican missionaries in the southern colonies did not even begin conversion work until the eighteenth century. In the 1730s and 1740s, German Moravians, a Protestant group that stressed personal piety, converted some Indians in western Pennsylvania. Although individual ministers and some Anglican officials in England showed genuine interest in conversion, the Protestant English never matched the efforts of Spanish or French Catholics.

After the First Hundred Years: Conflict and War

After nearly a century of European settlement, violence between colonists and Indians erupted in all three North American empires. Each deadly encounter—King Philip's War in New England, Bacon's Rebellion in Virginia, the Pueblo Revolt in New Mexico, and the resumption of the Beaver Wars in New France—reflected distinctive features of English, Spanish, and French patterns of colonization.

King Philip's War.   The growing frustration of the Wampanoags, who had befriended the Pilgrims more than a half-century earlier, with the land-hungry settlers whose towns now surrounded them, sparked **King's Philip's War,** which broke out in 1675. Massasoit's younger son, Metacom—called King Philip by the English—led the Wampanoags in the struggle to preserve their independence. He had little reason to trust English settlers.

In the spring of 1675, a colonial court found three Wampanoags guilty of murdering a Christian Indian who had warned the English of Wampanoag preparations for war. Despite Philip's protest that the evidence against the men was tainted, the court sentenced them to be hanged. This act convinced the Wampanoags that they had to strike back against the English before it was too late. Only "a small part of the dominion of my ancestors remains," declared Philip. "I am determined not to live until I have no country." The final blow occurred in June 1675, when colonists killed an Indian they found in an abandoned house and then ignored the Indians' outrage at the murder.

Native warriors attacked outlying villages in Plymouth Colony, moved into the Connecticut River Valley, and then turned eastward to strike towns within 20 miles of Boston. As the Narragansetts and other groups joined the uprising, Philip successfully eluded the combined forces of Massachusetts, Connecticut, and Plymouth (see American Views: Mary Rowlandson Among the Indians). By the summer of 1676, however, the Indians were exhausted, weakened by disease and food shortages. Philip moved into western New England, where his men clashed with the powerful Mohawks, long-standing enemies of the Wampanoags and allies of English fur traders in New York. Philip died in an ambush in August 1676, and the war ended soon after.

At least a thousand colonists and perhaps three thousand Indians died in King Philip's War. One out of every sixteen male colonists of military age was killed, making this the deadliest conflict in American history in terms of the proportion of casualties to total population. The Indians forced back the line of settlement but lost what remained of their independence in New England. The victorious English sold many native survivors, including Philip's wife and young son, into slavery in the West Indies. Others they employed in marginal jobs or confined in one of the few remaining praying towns. Philip's head, impaled on a stake, was left for decades just outside Plymouth as a grisly warning of the price to be paid for resisting colonial expansion.

Bacon's Rebellion.   As King Philip's War raged in New England, **Bacon's Rebellion** erupted in Virginia and had a similarly devastating effect on that colony's native population. Frustrated by shrinking economic opportunities in eastern Virginia, where established planters controlled the good land, many settlers, including new arrivals and recently freed indentured servants, moved to Virginia's western frontier. There they came into conflict with the region's resident Indians. In the summer of 1675, a group of frontier settlers attacked the Susquehannocks to seize their lands. The Indians struck back, prompting Nathaniel Bacon, a wealthy young planter who had only recently arrived in Virginia, to lead a violent campaign against all Indians, even those at peace with the colonial government. Governor William Berkeley ordered Bacon and his men to stop their attacks. They defied him and marched on Jamestown, turning a war between settlers and Indians into a rebellion of settlers against the colonial authorities.

The rebels believed that Berkeley and the colonial government represented the interests of established tobacco planters who wanted to keep men like themselves from emerging as potential competitors. Desperate because of the low price of tobacco, the rebels demanded voting rights, lower taxes and easier access to land—meaning, in effect, the right to take land from the Indians. Berkeley offered to build forts along the frontier, but the rebels were not interested in defensive measures. What they wanted was help in exterminating the Indians. They captured and burned the colonial capital at Jamestown, forcing Berkeley to flee. Directing their aggression against Indians once more, they burned Indian villages and massacred the inhabitants. Trying to appease the rebels, the House of Burgesses allowed them to seize lands belonging to Indians who had left their villages without permission—even though many had fled to escape the rebels. The assembly also legalized the enslavement of Indians.

By the time troops arrived from England to put down the rebellion, Bacon had died of dysentery and most of his men had drifted home. Berkeley hanged twenty-three rebels, but the real victims of the rebellion were Virginia's Indians. The remnants of the once-powerful Powhatans lost their remaining lands and either moved west or lived in poverty on the edges of English settlement. Hatred of Indians became a permanent feature of frontier life in Virginia, and government officials appeared more eager to spend money "for extirpating all Indians" than for maintaining peaceful relations.

The Pueblo Revolt.   In 1680, the **Pueblo Revolt** against the Spanish in New Mexico had a very different outcome

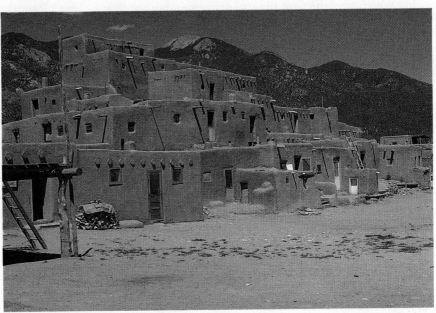

One of the many pueblos scattered along the Rio Grande valley, Taos served as Popé's headquarters at the start of the Pueblo Revolt in August 1680. Within a few weeks, the Indians drove the Spanish from New Mexico and destroyed most of their settlements. The Spanish did not return until 1693.

American Views

Mary Rowlandson Among the Indians

In February 1676, in the midst of King Philip's War, Indian warriors attacked the town of Lancaster, Massachusetts. They killed many inhabitants and took 23 colonists captive, including Mary Rowlandson and three of her children. Rowlandson spent the next three months traveling with various groups of Nipmucs, Narragansetts, and Wampanoags. She suffered physically and emotionally, watching her youngest daughter die in her arms and worrying about her other two children, from whom she was frequently separated. During her captivity, Rowlandson survived by accepting her fate and adapting to the Indians' way of life. Finally, with an English victory imminent, Rowlandson was ransomed and rejoined her husband (who had been away at the time of the attack) and family. In 1682, she published an account of her captivity in which she explored the meaning of her experience. Rowlandson's narrative proved so popular that three editions were printed in the first year.

- How did Rowlandson describe the Indians? How did she characterize her encounter with King Philip?
- In what ways did Rowlandson accommodate herself to the Indians' way of life? How did she employ her skills to fit in? Did her gender make a difference in her experience of captivity?
- How did Rowlandson's Puritan faith shape her narrative?

We travelled on till night; and in the morning, we must go over the River to Philip's crew. When I was in the Cannoo, I could not but be amazed at the numerous crew of Pagans that were on the Bank on the other side. When I came ashore, they gathered all about me, I sitting alone in the midst: I observed they asked one another questions, and laughed, and rejoyced over their Gains and Victories. Then my heart began to fail: and I fell a weeping which was the first time to my remembrance that I wept before them. Although I had met with so much Affliction, and my heart was many times ready to break, yet could I not shed one tear in their sight: but rather had been all this while in a maze, and like one astonished: but now I may say as, Psal. 137.1 *By the rivers of Babylon, there we sat down: yea, we wept when we remembered Zion.* There one of them asked me, why I wept, I could hardly tell what to say: yet I answered, they would kill me: No, said he, none will hurt you. Then came one of them and gave me two spoon-fulls of Meal to comfort me.... Then I went to see King Philip, he bade me come in and sit down, and asked me whether I would smoke (a usual Complement now adayes amongst Saints and Sinners) but this no way suited me. For though I had formerly used Tobacco, yet I had left it ever since I was first taken, *It seems to be a bait, the devil lays to make men loose their precious time....*

During my abode in this place, Philip spake to me to make a shirt for his boy, which I did, for which he gave me a shilling: I offered the money to my master, but he bade me keep it: and with it I bought a piece of Horse flesh. Afterwards he asked me to make a Cap for his boy, for which he invited me to Dinner. I went, and he gave me a Pancake, about as big as two fingers; it was made of parched wheat, beaten, and fryed in Bears grease, but I thought I never tasted pleasanter meat in my life. There was a Squaw who spake to me to make a shirt for her *Sannup* [husband], for which she gave me a piece of Bear. Another asked me to knit a pair of Stockins, for which she gave me a quart of Pease.... Hearing that my son was come to this place, I went to see him, and found him lying flat upon the ground: I asked him how he could sleep so? He answered me, *That he was not asleep, but at Prayer;* and lay so, that they might not observe what he was doing. I pray God he may remember these things now he is returned in safety.

Source: Neal Salisbury, ed., *The Sovereignty and Goodness of God, Together with the Faithfulness of His Promises Displayed....* (Boston, 1997), pp. 82–83.

than did the rebellion in Virginia or the war in New England. Nearly 20,000 Pueblo Indians had grown restless under the harsh rule of only 2,500 Spaniards. Spanish demands for tribute under the *encomienda* system fed native discontent. A prolonged drought increased their distress as corn harvests dwindled and many people starved. The Apaches, who had once traded with the Pueblos for corn, now raided their storehouses instead, and Spanish soldiers could not stop them. The spark that ignited the revolt, however, was an act of religious persecution. Spanish officials unwisely chose this troubled time to stamp out the Pueblo religion. In 1675, the governor arrested forty-seven native religious leaders on charges of sorcery. The court ordered most of them to be publicly whipped and released but sentenced four to death.

Led by Popé, one of the freed leaders, the outraged Pueblos organized for revenge. A growing network of rebels emerged as Spanish soldiers marched into Pueblo villages and destroyed *kivas,* the chambers that Indians used for religious ceremonies. Working from the village of Taos in northern New Mexico, by the summer of 1680, Popé commanded an enormous force of rebels drawn from twenty Pueblo villages. On August 10, they attacked the Spanish settlements. Popé urged them to destroy "everything pertaining to Christianity." Within a few weeks, the rebels had destroyed or damaged every Spanish building and killed more than four hundred Spaniards, including most of the colony's missionaries. By October, all the surviving Spaniards had fled New Mexico.

They did not return for thirteen years. By then, internal rivalries had split the victorious Pueblo coalition, and Popé had been overthrown as leader. Few Pueblo villages offered much resistance to the new Spanish intrusion. Even so, the Spanish now understood the folly of pushing the Indians too far. Officials reduced demands for tribute and ended the *encomienda* system. The Franciscans eased their attacks on Pueblo religion. New Spanish governors, backed by military force, kept the peace as best they could in a place where Indians still outnumbered Europeans.

Resumption of the Beaver Wars.   The Iroquois experience in the last phase of the Beaver Wars threatened to parallel that of the Indians of New England and Virginia. What began as a struggle between the Iroquois and western native peoples for control of the fur trade blossomed into a larger conflict that was absorbed into the imperial rivalry between England and France. Although the Iroquois suffered devastating losses similar to those inflicted on the Indians in the English colonies, they did not lose their independence. The key to Iroquois survival in the war's aftermath was the adoption of a position of neutrality between the European powers.

Looking for new trading partners to replace the Hurons, the French turned in the 1680s to various Indian peoples living near the Great Lakes. But the Iroquois had begun to raid these same peoples for furs and captives, much as they had attacked the Hurons in the first phase of the Beaver Wars in the 1640s. They exchanged the furs for European goods with English traders, who had replaced the Dutch as their partners after the conquest of New Netherland. Many of the captives were adopted into Iroquois families.

The French attacked the Iroquois to prevent them and their English allies from extending their influence in the west. In June 1687, a combined force of French and Christian Indian soldiers invaded the lands of the Senecas, the westernmost of the five nations of the Iroquois League. The Iroquois retaliated by besieging a French garrison at Niagara, where nearly two hundred soldiers starved to death, and killing hundreds of colonists in attacks on French villages along the St. Lawrence River.

The French participated much more directly and suffered greater losses in this renewal of the Beaver Wars than they had in the earlier fighting. In 1688 France and England went to war in Europe, and the struggle between them and their Indian allies for control of the fur trade in North America became part of a larger imperial contest. The European powers made peace in 1697, but calm did not immediately return to the Great Lakes region.

The conflict was even more devastating for the Iroquois. The English, still solidifying their control over their new colony of New York, provided minimal military assistance, and the Iroquois suffered heavy casualties. Perhaps a quarter of their population died from disease and warfare by 1689. The devastation encouraged Iroquois diplomats to find a way to extricate themselves from future English–French conflicts. The result, in 1701, was a pair of treaties, negotiated separately with Albany and Montreal, that recognized Iroquois neutrality and, at least for several decades, prevented either the English or the French from dominating the western lands.

Each of these conflicts grew from a distinctive pattern of contact between colonists and native peoples. English settlers fought with Wampanoags, Powhatans, and Susquehannocks for control of land, and the losers were the outnumbered Indians. Spanish colonists clashed with Pueblos over religion, and the more numerous natives won a temporary victory and permanent accommodation with the Spanish Catholic minority. French soldiers battled with the Iroquois over control of the fur trade until both sides agreed to an uneasy truce. In each case, nearly a century of contact culminated in a struggle that revealed the fragility of Indian autonomy as European populations continued to grow and to seek domination.

Africans and Europeans

The movement of Africans to the Americas was one of the largest forced migrations in world history. By the time New World slavery finally ended, with its abolition in Brazil in 1888, over twelve million Africans had arrived on American shores. From a relatively small stream in the sixteenth century, African migration accelerated to a great flood by the 1700s. Over 350,000 Africans crossed the Atlantic before 1600. More than five times as many, nearly 1.8 million people, arrived in the seventeenth century. In the eighteenth century, another 6.1 million Africans reached American destinations.

Virtually all Africans arrived as slaves, making the history of the African experience in the Americas inseparable from the history of slavery and the slave trade. As one eighteenth-century Englishman noted, Africans were "the strength and sinews of this western world," performing much of the labor of colonization. The vast majority of African slaves ended up in Brazil, the West Indies, or New Spain. Only 1 out of 20 Africans came to the British mainland colonies, but this still amounted to over 300,000 individuals (see Figure 3–2). Their presence transformed English colonial societies everywhere, but particularly in the South. At the same time, Africans were themselves transformed. Out of their diverse African ethnic backgrounds and the experience of slavery itself they forged new identities as African American peoples.

Labor Needs and the Turn to Slavery

Europeans in the New World were thrilled to find that land was abundant and quite cheap by European standards. They were perplexed, however, by the unexpectedly high cost of labor. In Europe, the reverse had been true. There land was expensive but labor cheap, because competition for jobs among large numbers of workers pushed wages down. Colonial workers commanded high wages because there were so few of them compared to the supply of land to be developed. In addition, few settlers wanted to work for others when they could get farms of their own. The scarcity and high cost of labor led some colonial employers to turn to enslaved Africans as a solution.

The development of slavery in the colonies was not inevitable. Europeans had owned slaves (both white and black) long before the beginning of American colonization, but slaves formed a small—and shrinking—minority of European laborers. By the fifteenth century, slavery had all but disappeared in northern Europe except as punishment for serious crimes. English laws in particular protected the personal freedom of the king's subjects.

Slavery persisted longer in southern Europe and the Middle East. In both regions, religion influenced the choice of who was enslaved. Because neither Christians nor Muslims would hold as slaves members of their own faiths, Arab traders turned to sub-Saharan Africa to find slaves. Eventually, the Arabic word for slave—'abd—became a synonym for "black man." By the fifteenth century, a durable link between slave status and black skin had been forged in European minds.

Europeans in the New World, beginning with Columbus, first enslaved Indians as a way of addressing the labor shortage. Spaniards held Indian slaves in all their New World colonies, as did the Portuguese in Brazil. French Canadians enslaved Pawnee Indians captured in wars in the North American interior. English colonists condemned Indian war captives to slavery as punishment for their opposition to English rule. And in early Carolina, English traders saw an opportunity to profit by enslaving thousands of Indians. They encouraged Indians "to make War amongst themselves to get Slaves" whom the traders could buy and then resell to West Indian and local planters.

Native American slaves, however, could not fill the colonists' labor needs. Everywhere disease and harsh working conditions reduced their numbers. English colonists also discovered problems with enslaving Indians. When traders incited Indian wars to gain slaves, bloodshed often spread to English settlements. Enslaved Indian men refused to perform agricultural labor, which they considered women's work. And because they knew the land so well, Indians could easily escape. As a result, although the Indian slave trade persisted in the English colonies through the eighteenth century (and into the nineteenth century), by 1700 it had given way to a much larger traffic in Africans.

The Shock of Enslavement

European traders did not themselves enslave Africans. Instead, they relied on other Africans to capture slaves for them, tapping into and expanding a preexisting internal African slave trade. With the permission of local rulers, Europeans built forts and trading posts on the West African coast and bought slaves from African traders (see Map 3–2). African rulers occasionally enslaved and sold their own people as punishment for crimes, but most slaves were seized in raids on neighboring peoples. Attracted by European cloth, liquor, guns, and other goods, West Africans fought among themselves to secure captives and began kidnapping individuals from the interior.

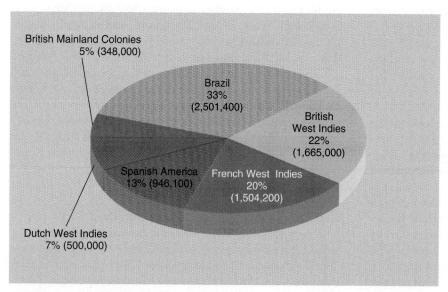

FIGURE 3–2   Destination of Slaves Imported from Africa to the Americas between 1451 and 1810
Approximately 7.5 million Africans were brought as slaves to the Americas before 1810. The vast majority went to the Caribbean, Mexico, and South America, where they toiled in mines and on sugar plantations.

Data Source: Philip Curtin, *The Atlantic Slave Trade: A Census* (1969), p. 268.

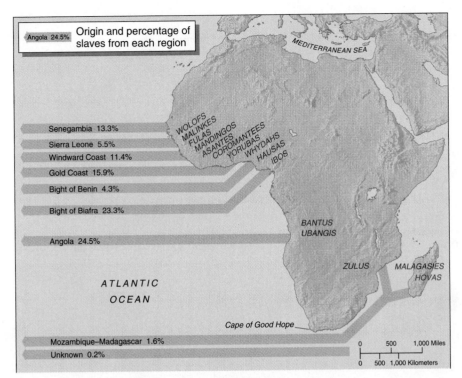

Origin and percentage of slaves from each region

Senegambia	13.3%
Sierra Leone	5.5%
Windward Coast	11.4%
Gold Coast	15.9%
Bight of Benin	4.3%
Bight of Biafra	23.3%
Angola	24.5%
Mozambique–Madagascar	1.6%
Unknown	0.2%

MAP 3–2   African Origins of North American Slaves, 1690–1807
Nearly all slaves in English North America were West Africans. Most had been captured or purchased by African slave traders, who then sold them to European merchants.

People of all social ranks ended up on the slave ships. Some had been slaves in Africa; others had been village leaders or, like Olaudah Equiano, members of chiefs' families and the educated elite. In the end, slavery reduced all Africans, regardless of their social origins, to the same degraded status.

Once captured, slaves marched in chains to the coast, to be confined in cages until there were enough to fill a ship. Captains examined them to ensure their fitness and branded them like cattle with a hot iron. The slaves then boarded canoes to be ferried to the ships. Desperation overwhelmed some of them, who jumped overboard and drowned rather than be carried off to an unknown destination. Even before the ships left African shores, slaves sometimes mutinied, though such rebellions rarely succeeded.

Slaves who could not escape while still in Africa suffered through a horrendous six- to eight-week-long ocean voyage known as the **Middle Passage**. Captains wedged men below decks into spaces about 6 feet long, 16 inches wide, and 30 inches high. Women and children were packed even more tightly. Except for brief excursions on deck for forced exercise, slaves remained below decks, where the air grew foul from the vomit, blood, and excrement in which the terrified victims lay. "The shrieks of the women, and the groans of the dying," recalled Olaudah Equiano, "rendered it a scene of horror almost inconceivable." Some slaves went insane; others refused to eat. On many voyages, between 5 and 20 percent of the slaves perished from disease and other causes, but captains had usually packed the ships tightly enough to make a profit from selling the rest.

Those who survived the dreadful voyage endured the fear and humiliation of sale. Planters generally preferred males and often sought slaves from particular African ethnic groups, in the belief that some Africans would work harder than others. Ship captains sometimes sold slaves at public auctions, where purchasers poked them, looking for signs of disease. Many terrified Africans, like Equiano, thought they were going to be eaten.

African Slaves in the New World

The Spanish and Portuguese first brought Africans to the Americas to replace or supplement the dwindling numbers of Indian slaves toiling in silver mines and on sugar plantations. The Dutch, who scrambled for a share of the lucrative slave trade, quickly followed suit. English colonists, less familiar with slavery, adopted it more slowly. West Indian planters were the first English settlers to do so on a large scale in the 1640s. In most other English colonies, however, different economic conditions either postponed or prevented slavery's widespread adoption.

Slavery in the southern colonies. The first African immigrants arrived in Virginia in 1619. Brought by a Dutch merchant ship, most—if not all—were probably slaves. Yet slavery did not really take hold in Virginia until the end of the seventeenth century, at which point Africans comprised a significant portion of the population (see Figure 3–3). For decades, tobacco planters saw no reason to stop using white indentured servants. Servants (because they worked for masters only for a period of years rather than for life) cost less than slaves, were readily available, and were familiar. For most of the seventeenth century, by contrast, slaves were expensive, difficult to obtain, and exotic. By the 1680s, however, planters in Virginia and Maryland began to shift from servants to slaves.

Two related developments caused this change. First, white indentured servants became harder to find. Fewer English men and women chose to emigrate as servants after 1660 because an improving economy in England provided jobs at home. At the same time, Virginia's white population tripled between 1650 and 1700, increasing the number of planters competing for a shrinking supply of laborers. Planters also faced competition from newer colonies such as Pennsylvania and New Jersey, which had more generous land policies for immigrants.

Second, as white servants grew scarcer, changes in the slave trade made African slaves more available. Before the 1660s, the Dutch and Portuguese merchants who dominated the trade mainly supplied their own colonies and the profitable West Indian market. But beginning in 1674, England's

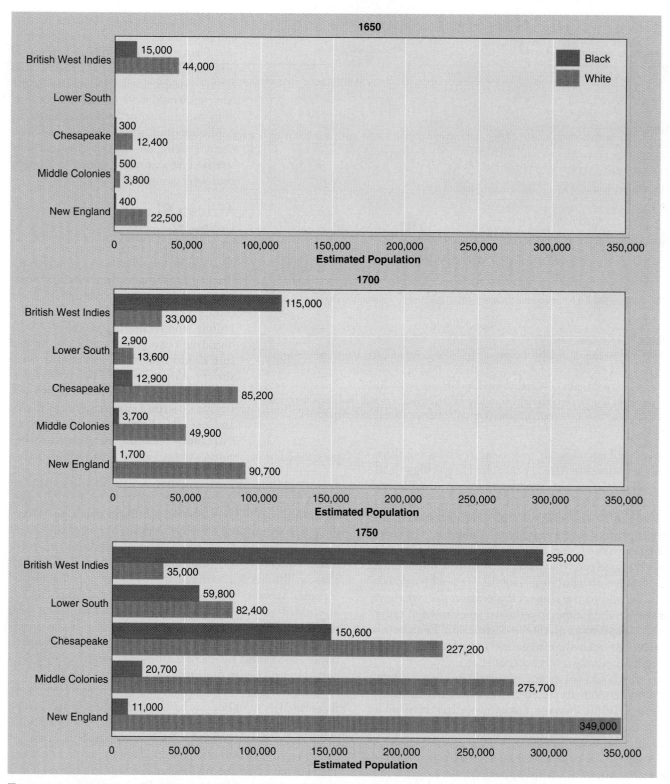

FIGURE 3–3   Estimated Population of Black and White Settlers in British Colonial Regions, 1650–1750
Settler populations increased rapidly in all colonial regions, but the racial composition varied. By 1750, black people overwhelmingly predominated in the West Indies and were quite numerous in the southern colonies; north of Maryland, however, their numbers remained small.

Data Source: John J. McCusker and Russell Menard, *The Economy of British America, 1607–1789* (1985).

The freed slave Olaudah Equiano appears in this 1780 portrait by an unknown artist. After purchasing his freedom, Equiano wrote a vivid account of his capture in Africa and his life in slavery. One of the first such accounts to be published (in 1789), this narrative testified to slavery's injustice and Equiano's own fortitude and talents.

"Portrait of a Negro Man, Olaudah Equiano," 1780s (previously attributed to Joshua Reynolds) by English School (18th c.). Royal Albert Memorial Museum, Exeter, Devon, UK/Bridgeman Art Library, London/New York.

Royal African Company began shipping slaves directly to English buyers. The supply of slaves surged after 1698, when the Royal African Company lost its special trading rights, and many English merchants and New Englanders entered the fiercely competitive trade.

Chesapeake planters eventually found reasons besides availability to prefer slaves to servants. Although more expensive than servants, slaves were a better long-term investment. Because slave status passed from slave mothers to their children, buying both men and women gave planters a self-reproducing labor force. Runaway black slaves were more easily recaptured than escaped servants, who blended into the white population. And unlike indentured servants, slaves were slaves for life. They would never compete as planters with their former masters or, like Nathaniel Bacon's followers, pose a threat to order if they failed to prosper.

Chesapeake planters had already come to see white servants as possessions, people whose labor could be bought and sold like any other commodity. This attitude doubtless eased the transition in the 1680s and 1690s to the much harsher system of slavery. In Carolina, of course, slaves were there from the start, brought in the 1670s by colony founders accustomed to slavery in Barbados. By 1720, slavery was firmly embedded in all the southern colonies except sparsely settled North Carolina. In that year, one-third of Virginia's settler population, and nearly three-quarters of South Carolina's, were black.

Slavery grew rapidly in the southern colonies because it answered the labor needs of planters engaged in the commercial production of tobacco and rice. The demand for slaves became so powerful that it destroyed James Oglethorpe's plan to keep them out of Georgia, the last of England's mainland colonies, founded in 1732. Oglethorpe intended Georgia to be a refuge for English debtors, who normally were jailed until they could repay their creditors. His idea was to send debtors to Georgia to work at producing marketable goods such as silk and wine. Slaves were initially prohibited not only to prevent them from competing with the debtors, but also to make it difficult for fugitive slaves from South Carolina to escape there. With slavery forbidden, any black person seen in Georgia would be immediately recognizable as a runaway. But when Georgia's colonists began to grow rice, they demanded the right to have slaves. In 1750, the colony's founders reluctantly legalized slavery; by 1770, slaves made up nearly half of the colony's population.

Slavery in the northern colonies.   Far fewer slaves lived north of the Chesapeake, although they were present in every British colony. They were too expensive for most northern farmers—who mainly produced food for their families, not staple crops for an international market—to use profitably. This was not true, however, for farmers with larger properties in parts of Long Island, the Hudson Valley, Rhode Island, northern New Jersey, and southeastern Pennsylvania, where commercial wheat farming and livestock raising prevailed. In the eighteenth century, these landowners acquired significant numbers of slaves. By the 1760s, for instance, one-fifth of the farmers in Chester County, Pennsylvania, owned slaves. Some slaves also worked in local industries, such as tanneries and iron foundries, often alongside white servants and hired laborers.

Northern slaves could often be found in cities, especially ports such as Newport, Rhode Island, where newly arrived Africans landed. At the start of the eighteenth century, one out of six Philadelphia residents was a slave; by 1740, slaves made up 15 percent of the city's workingmen. In mid-eighteenth-century New York City, slaves comprised between 12 and 14 percent of the population. Many urban slaves were domestic servants in the homes of rich merchants and professionals. Substantial numbers also labored as artisans.

Changing race relations in the colonies.   Race relations in the mainland colonies were less rigid in the seventeenth century than they would later become. Before 1700, slaves did not form a majority of the population in any colony, a situation that may have made them seem less threatening to white people. Most seventeenth-century Chesapeake planters did not own slaves. Those who did often held only a few slaves along with white servants. In these households, white and

Looking through the iron bars, one can glimpse the enclosure within Elmina Castle where slaves were confined prior to boarding the ships that would carry them into New World slavery.

ican slaves, and his experience reveals how much slavery changed over time. This generation of slaves mainly came from African port towns, where Europeans and Africans had mingled for generations, or by way of the West Indies or New Netherland. Familiar with European ways, often fluent in European languages, they acquired skills and knowledge that enabled them to bargain with their masters in ways their descendants would not be able to replicate. They came in small groups, cultivated their masters as patrons, negotiated for their own property, and often gained their freedom. They enjoyed such advantages because they came to colonies where slavery had not yet become firmly embedded, where the meaning of bondage was still being worked out.

Repressive laws and slave codes.   But Johnson's descendants, and the generations of slaves and free black people who came after them, encountered much harsher conditions. Once slavery became the dominant labor system in the Chesapeake, tobacco planters no longer welcomed free black people, fearing that they might encourage slaves to escape. In 1691, Virginia's legislature prohibited individual masters from freeing their slaves. Lawmakers passed another measure in 1699 requiring newly freed black people to leave the colony altogether. Black families like the Johnsons, who were already free, suffered under increasing discrimination. Laws prohibited them from employing white servants, holding office, bearing arms, and voting. Free black people paid extra taxes and suffered more severe punishments than white people did for the same crimes. Interracial marriages, never common, were prohibited as "shameful Matches."

Bad as the situation of free black people had grown, the condition of slaves was far worse. Slave codes, laws governing slavery, essentially reduced an entire class of human beings to property. In Virginia, from the middle of the seventeenth century on, new laws added to slaves' oppression. A 1662 measure defined slavery as a lifelong and inherited status that passed from slave mothers to their children—even children with white fathers. Masters who might have felt uneasy about holding fellow Christians as slaves were relieved in 1667 when another law stated that baptism would not release slaves from bondage. Two years later, the House of Burgesses gave masters the power of life and death over their slaves, decreeing that masters would not be charged with a felony if their slaves died during punishment. These and other measures were gathered into a comprehensive slave code in Virginia in 1705. Additional restrictions prohibited slaves from testifying in court against white colonists, required them to carry passes whenever they left their masters' estates, and forbade them to gather in groups of more than four people.

Slave codes appeared virtually everywhere, North and South, but were particularly harsh in the southern colonies. White colonists in the Tidewater Chesapeake and South Car-

black people lived and worked in close contact. Black slaves and white servants ran away together and cooperated during Bacon's Rebellion. In some areas, free black people—often slaves who had bought their own freedom—prospered in an atmosphere of racial tolerance that would be unthinkable by the eighteenth century.

The career of an ambitious black Virginian named Anthony Johnson, for example, resembled that of many white settlers—a remarkable achievement, given that he arrived in the colony in 1621 as a slave known only as "Antonio a Negro." Johnson's master allowed him to marry and start a family while he was still a slave and may even have allowed Anthony to purchase his and his family's liberty. Once free, the Johnsons settled in eastern Virginia, where Anthony and his sons eventually acquired substantial plantations. Like white settlers, Johnson occasionally took his neighbors to court and even successfully sued them. He and his sons also owned slaves. Anthony Johnson belonged to the first or what one historian has called the "charter" generation of Amer-

Although this watercolor of a slave ship bound for Brazil dates from the nineteenth century, it depicts a scene common on slavers in the 1700s. The artist's attention to detail suggests both the misery of the slaves' surroundings and the dignity of the individuals forced to live under such conditions.

The Granger Collection, New York.

olina feared the consequences of a growing black population. One South Carolina planter predicted in 1720 that slaves would soon rise up against their masters because black people were "too numerous in proportion to the White Men there."

The changing composition of the slave labor force also created tensions. Unlike the charter generation, the slaves who arrived in the eighteenth century usually came from the African interior and had had less contact with European customs and language. Planters commented on the strange appearance and behavior of these people, with whom they could barely communicate. Their uneasiness, of course, scarcely compared to the Africans' harrowing experience of being torn away from the only world they knew and thrust into the harsh condition of slavery.

African American Families and Communities

The harshness of the slaves' condition could be relieved somewhat by the formation of close ties with others who shared their circumstances. For such ties to be created, however, several developments had to occur. Slaves had to become sufficiently numerous in specific localities so that black people could have regular contact with one another. Ethnic and language barriers carried over from Africa had to erode so that slaves could communicate. And for families to be formed, there had to be enough slave women as well as men. Because these conditions were slow to develop, occurring at different rates in different colonies, the formation of African American families and communities was delayed until well into the eighteenth century.

The situation was perhaps most difficult for slaves in the northern colonies. Many slaves there lived alone or in pairs with their master's family. Only in cities and on substantial commercial farms were slaves numerous enough to create their own communities. The formation of families, however, was slowed by a relative scarcity of women. When slave families did appear, husbands and wives often lived in different households as the property of different masters.

The rise of the creole slave population.   Slaves were far more numerous in the southern colonies, and it was there that African American families and communities emerged with greater success. This was especially true in South Carolina and parts of the Tidewater Chesapeake, where in certain localities slaves formed a majority of the population. Even more significant, these regions witnessed the rise of a creole, or American-born, slave population by about the 1750s. This development distinguished slavery in the mainland British colonies from that in the West Indies, where disease and overwork killed so many slaves that the black population grew only because of the constant importation of Africans.

The rise of a creole slave population in the Chesapeake and in Carolina set off a chain of related events that fostered family and community life. Creoles lived longer than African immigrants, and creole women usually bore twice as many children as African-born mothers. This circumstance allowed the slave population to grow by natural increase and more closely resemble a normal population of men and women, children and elders. At the same time, creole slaves grew up without personal memories of Africa, and thus African ethnic differences receded in importance. Most creoles knew some English and spoke dialects, such as Gullah in parts of South Carolina, that mixed English and African words and speech patterns, so that they were able to communicate with other slaves.

Work and family life.   Most of a slave's life was structured by work. The vast majority of southern slaves were field hands. On tobacco plantations, they toiled in gangs supervised by overseers. In Carolina, rice planters allowed their workers more flexibility, assigning them tasks in the morning and permitting them free time after they finished. On large plantations, masters selected some slave men to be trained as shoemakers, weavers, or tailors and chose others as drivers or leaders of work gangs. With the exception of nurses and cooks, few slave women avoided the drudgery of field labor. If they had families, the end of the day's work in the fields only marked the start of domestic duties back in the slave quarters. But no matter how onerous, work did not absorb every minute of the slaves' lives, and in the intervals around their assigned duties many slaves nurtured ties of family and community that combined African traditions with New World experience.

By the late eighteenth century, more than half of Chesapeake and Carolina slaves lived in family groups. These were fragile units, subject to the whims of masters who did not recognize slave marriages as legal, broke up families by sale, and could take slave women as sexual partners at will. Many slave husbands and wives resided on different plantations, although on larger Carolina estates two-parent slave house-

This English woodcut, dating from about 1700, served as a label on a tobacco package. In the foreground, planters smoke and take their ease, while in the background, slaves toil under the hot sun.

holds grew increasingly common. Over time, dense kinship networks formed, reflecting West African influences. Slaves placed great emphasis on kin connections, even using familiar terms such as "aunt" and "uncle" to address friends. Some slave husbands, as was customary in West Africa, took more than one wife. In naming their children, slaves mingled old and new practices, sometimes giving them the African names of distant kin and sometimes using English names.

Community life and religion.   Community life forged ties between slave families and single slaves on the plantations and offered further opportunities to preserve elements of African heritage. Traces of African religious practices endured in America. Magical charms and amulets have been found buried in slave quarters, indicating that spiritual ceremonies may have been conducted out of sight of white masters. Reflecting their West African background, slaves placed great emphasis on funerals, in the belief that relatives remained members of kin communities even after death.

Christianity offered little competition to African religious practices during most of the colonial period. Few masters showed much interest in converting their slaves. Evangelical ministers, who began to preach to slave audiences around the middle of the eighteenth century, gained some converts, but the widespread adoption of Christianity by slaves did not occur until after the Revolution.

African influences shaped aspects of slaves' recreational activity and material life. Slave musicians used African-style instruments, including drums and banjos, to accompany traditional songs and dances. Where slaves were allowed to build their own houses, they incorporated African elements into the designs—for instance, by using mud walls and roofs thatched with palmetto leaves. Their gardens frequently contained African foods, such as millet, yams, peppers, and sesame seeds, along with European and Native American crops.

Family and community ties gave a sense of belonging and dignity to people whose masters treated them as outcasts. Working and living together, slaves preserved some elements of African culture despite the harrowing conditions of their forced migration. Out of their African past and their American experience, they created new identities as African Americans as they coped with the oppressiveness of slavery.

This eighteenth-century painting from South Carolina records the preservation of certain African traditions in American slave communities. The dance may be Yoruba in origin, while the stringed instrument and drum were probably modeled on African instruments.

Abby Aldrich Rockefeller Folk Art Museum, Colonial Foundation, Williamsburg, VA.

Resistance and Rebellion

Even as family ties made a life in bondage more tolerable, they made it more difficult for slaves to attempt escape or contemplate rebellion. Slaves who resisted their oppression ran the risk of endangering families and friends as well as themselves. But the powerful desire for freedom was not easily suppressed, and slaves found ways to defy the dehumanization that slavery entailed.

Running away from a master was a desperate act, but thousands of slaves did just that. Few runaways shared the mistaken impression of some new arrivals in eighteenth-century Virginia who thought they could "find the Way back to their own Country." But deciding where else to go posed a problem. Escape out of the South did not bring freedom, because slavery was legal in every colony. After 1733, some runaways went to Florida, where Spanish officials promised them freedom. Others tried to survive on their own in the woods or join the Indians—a choice that carried the risk of capture or death. South Carolina planters paid Indians to catch escaped slaves, largely to sow seeds of distrust between the two peoples and prevent them from joining forces against white colonists. For slaves with families, running away carried the high emotional cost of separation from loved ones as well as physical danger. Perilous as it was, escape proved irresistible to some slaves, especially young males. In a few isolated areas on the South Carolina frontier, runaways formed outlaw "maroon" settlements.

Many slaves chose less perilous ways to resist their bondage. Landon Carter, one of Virginia's wealthiest planters, once complained that his slaves "seem to be quite dead hearted and either cannot or will not work." He did not realize that he had become the target of forms of resistance more subtle, but every bit as real, as running away. Slaves worked slowly, broke tools, and pretended to be ill in order to exert some control over their working lives. When provoked, they also took more direct action, damaging crops, stealing goods, and setting fires. Slaves with knowledge of poisonous plants occasionally tried to kill their owners, although the penalty for being caught was to be burned to death.

The most serious, as well as the rarest, form of resistance was organized rebellion. South Carolinians and coastal Virginians, who lived in regions with slave majorities, had a particular dread of slave revolt. But because rebellions required complete secrecy, careful planning, and access to weapons, they were extremely hard to organize. No slave rebellion succeeded in the British colonies. Rumors usually leaked out before any action had been taken, prompting severe reprisals against the alleged conspirators. In Charleston, South Carolina, rumors of a planned uprising in 1740 led to the torture and execution of fifty black suspects. The following year, thirty-five alleged rebels (including four white people) were executed in New York City after a series of fires sparked rumors of a slave conspiracy.

Three major slave revolts did occur and instilled lasting fear in white colonists. In 1712 in New York City, where black people made up 20 percent of the population, about twenty slaves set a building on fire and killed nine white men who came to put it out. The revolt was quickly suppressed, with twenty-four rebels sentenced to death. The largest colonial-era slave insurrection occurred in Virginia in 1730, sparked by a false rumor that local officials had suppressed a royal edict calling for the emancipation of Christian slaves. More than three hundred rebels escaped into the Dismal Swamp along the border with North Carolina, attacking white settlers in the area. Using Indians to hunt down the fugitives, Virginia authorities captured and executed twenty-four of the rebellion's leaders. Another major revolt, the **Stono Rebellion**, struck South Carolina in 1739. About twenty slaves—including several recently arrived Angolans—broke into a store and armed themselves with stolen guns. Marching southward along the Stono River, their ranks grew to perhaps a hundred. Heading for freedom in Spanish Florida, they attacked white settlements along the way. White troops (with Indian help) defeated the rebels within a week, but tensions remained high for months. The death toll, in the end, was about two dozen white people and perhaps twice as many black rebels.

In the wake of these rebellions, colonial assemblies passed laws requiring stricter supervision of slave activities. In South Carolina, other measures encouraged more white immigration to offset the colony's black majority. Planters in the southern colonies in particular considered slavery indispensable to their economic survival, even though this labor system generated so much fear and brutality. Their slaves, in turn, obeyed when necessary, resisted when possible, and kept alive the hope that freedom would one day be theirs.

European Laborers in Early America

Slavery was one of several responses to the scarcity of labor in the New World. It took hold mainly in areas where the profits from export crops such as sugar, rice, and tobacco offset the high purchase price of slaves and where a warm climate permitted year-round work. Elsewhere European masters and employers found various ways to acquire and manage European laborers. Indentured servitude, forced labor, tenancy, and the extension of credit all aimed at limiting the freedom of some people in order to make them work for others.

A Spectrum of Control

Slavery was the most oppressive extreme in a spectrum of practices designed to exert control over workers and relieve the problems caused by the easy availability of land and the high cost of labor. Most colonial laborers were, in some measure, unfree (see the Overview table, "Predominant Colonial Labor Systems, 1750"). One-half to two-thirds of all white immigrants to the English colonies arrived as indentured

OVERVIEW

Predominant Colonial Labor Systems, 1750

	Colony	Labor System
New England	Massachusetts	Family farms
	Connecticut	Family farms
	New Hampshire	Family farms
	Rhode Island	Family farms
Middle Colonies	New York	Family farms, tenancy
	Pennsylvania and Delaware	Indentured servitude, tenancy, family farms
	New Jersey	Family farms, tenancy
South	Maryland	Slavery
	Virginia	Slavery
	North Carolina	Family farms, slavery
	South Carolina	Slavery

servants, bound by contract to serve masters for a period of years. But indentured servants, though less costly than slaves, carried too high a price for farmers who raised crops mainly for subsistence. Servants could be found in every colony, but were most common in the Chesapeake and, to a lesser extent, in Pennsylvania, where they worked for farmers producing export crops.

Slaves replaced white indentured servants in Chesapeake tobacco fields during the eighteenth century. Masters continued to import servants for a while to fill skilled jobs but in time trained slaves to fill those positions. Thus, by the middle of the eighteenth century, white servitude, although it still flourished in some places, was in decline as a dominant labor system.

Eighteenth-century Chesapeake planters also availed themselves of another unfree labor source: transported English convicts. Lawmakers in England saw transportation as a way of getting rid of criminals who might otherwise be executed. Between 1718 and 1775, nearly fifty thousand convicts were sent to the colonies, 80 percent of whom ended up in the Chesapeake. Most were young, lower-class males forced by economic hardship to turn to crime. Although some colonists objected to England's policy of sending its undesirables to America, labor-hungry planters bought them for seven-year terms at relatively low prices and exploited them ruthlessly. A few convicts eventually prospered in America, but most faced lives as miserable as those they had known in England.

An arrangement similar to indentured servitude—the **redemptioner** system—brought many families, especially from German provinces, to the colonies in the eighteenth

century. Instead of negotiating contracts for service before leaving Europe, as indentured servants did, redemptioners promised to redeem, or pay, the costs of passage on arrival in America. They often paid part of the fare before sailing. If they could not raise the rest soon after landing, the ship captain who brought them sold them into servitude. The length of their service depended on how much they still owed. Most Germans went to Pennsylvania, where they hoped to find friends or relatives willing to help them pay off their debt quickly.

Purchasing slaves, servants, or convicts did not make sense for everyone. Colonists who owned undeveloped land faced many tasks—cutting trees, clearing fields, building fences and barns—that brought no immediate profit. Rather than buy expensive laborers to accomplish these ends, landowners rented undeveloped tracts to families without property. Both tenants and landlords benefited from this arrangement. Tenants enjoyed greater independence than servants and could save toward the purchase of their own farms. The landlord secured the labor necessary to transform his property into a working farm, thus increasing the land's value. He also received an annual rent payment and eventually profited from selling the land, often to the tenant family who had rented it. Tenancy worked best in Pennsylvania, New Jersey, and the Hudson and Connecticut River Valleys, where farmers raised wheat and other grains for the market.

Merchants eager to develop New England's fisheries devised other means to fill their labor needs. Because it was fairly easy to get a farm, few New Englanders took on the risky job of fishing. Moreover, few could afford the necessary

The Legacy of Slavery

In 2003, President Ruth Simmons of Brown University appointed a Steering Committee on Slavery and Justice to investigate the university's historical connection with slavery. Founded in 1764 (as the College of Rhode Island), the university counted the Brown family among its most important early benefactors. Like other prominent Rhode Island merchants, the Browns owed part of their fortune to the transatlantic slave trade. The Steering Committee released its report in 2006, acknowledging the role of slavery in Brown University's past and making recommendations that focused on educating students and the public about slavery and injustice, past and present.

Brown University president Ruth J. Simmons was a leading figure behind the institution's investigation of its historical connection to the slave trade.

This episode illustrates how, even in the twenty-first century, Americans continue to grapple with slavery and its legacy. Slavery's roots extend deeply into American history, reaching back before nationhood itself. By the eighteenth century, slavery was a fixture in every colony, and white colonists had come to associate slave status with black skin. The Revolution, with its rhetoric of freedom, challenged slavery but did not end it. Even the constitutional amendments outlawing slavery and guaranteeing black people's civil rights that passed after the Civil War could not eradicate the racism that had become deeply ingrained in American life. Today, nearly a century and a half after the Civil War, problems persist as many black Americans continue to suffer from discrimination and poverty. To a considerable extent, these economic and social dislocations, and the racial attitudes that help to shape them, can be traced to the lingering effects of slavery. Actions such as those undertaken by Brown University, however, offer hope for the future.

■ Why might education be a particularly good strategy for dealing with the legacy of slavery in American life?

John Greenwood's eighteenth-century painting shows colonial sea captains entertaining themselves at a tavern in the Dutch colony at Surinam on the coast of South America. Six of the men being served by poorly clothed African slaves later became trustees of the College of Rhode Island, now Brown University.

PEARSON
myhistorylab

From Then to Now Online

3-1 *Advertisement Announcing Sale of Slaves*, 1764.

3-2 Samuel Sewall, *The Selling of Joseph*, 1700.

3-3 *The Lower Deck of a Guinea Man in the Last Century.*

3-4 *Report of the Brown University Steering Committee on Slavery and Justice.*

Early Modern Europe's Biggest Mass Migration

The stream of German immigrants moving to America in the late seventeenth and eighteenth centuries formed only a small part of a much larger flow of emigrants from the Rhineland to many parts of the globe. The Rhineland was not a single political unit, but a region of small states and principalities located along one of Europe's major rivers. Political fragmentation brought religious diversity, with German Reformed or Lutheran churches dominant in some areas and Catholics in others.

Large-scale emigration of Rhineland inhabitants stemmed from many causes, especially warfare. During the Thirty Years' War (1618–1648), much of the Rhineland area was devastated by intense religious conflict and famine. In the 1680s and 1690s, Louis XIV of France invaded the region, sparking more turmoil. Almost continual warfare from the 1730s to the 1760s made the lives of Rhineland inhabitants even worse.

Economic hardship and political repression also spurred emigration. Harsh winters in 1708–1709 and 1709–1710, for instance, destroyed orchards and vineyards, threatening many farmers with impoverishment and even starvation. Harvests failed in many parts of the Rhineland in the 1740s. In addition, religious minorities suffered from persecution, and everyone bore the burden of increasing taxes and arbitrary rule by local princes. For all of these reasons, over the course of the eighteenth century, hundreds of thousands of Rhinelanders decided to flee their homeland.

Many promoters, land speculators, and even governments sought to direct the flow of emigrants to a favored region. Officials from Russia and Prussia offered cheap land and tax exemptions to lure migrants to their countries. As a result of this promotional campaign, by far the largest number of Rhineland refugees relocated to various parts of Eastern Europe, including Prussia, Russia, Hungary, and Poland. A smaller flow of emigrants, mostly Protestants, made their way to North America, settling principally in Pennsylvania, New York, and the Carolinas. Still others moved to Cayenne (French Guiana) in South America. The exodus of these German-speaking emigrants to destinations in the Old and New Worlds constituted the most significant mass migration in early modern Europe.

■ **Why might more Rhineland migrants have moved within Europe instead of going to the North American colonies?**

equipment, including boats, provisions, and salt (used for preserving fish). Merchants recruited fishermen by advancing credit to coastal villagers so that they could outfit their own boats. To pay off the debt, the fishermen were legally bound to bring their catch to the merchant, who then sold it to Europe and the West Indies. Many fishermen ran up such large debts that they were obliged to continue supplying fish to their creditors, whether they wanted to or not. Toward the end of the seventeenth century, as the rising population of coastal villages lowered the cost of labor, merchants abandoned the credit system and paid wages to fishermen instead.

In the northern colonies, the same conditions that made men reluctant to become fishermen deterred them from becoming farm laborers, except perhaps for high wages. Paying high wages, however, or the high cost of servants or slaves was difficult for New Englanders with farms that produced no export crops and could not be worked during cold winter months. So northern farmers turned to the cheapest and most dependable workers they could find—their children.

Children as young as 5 or 6 years old began with simple tasks and moved on to more complex work as they grew older. By the time they were in their late teens, girls knew how to run households, and boys knew how to farm. Instead of contracts or outright coercion, fathers used their ownership of property to prolong the time their sons worked for them. Young men could not marry until they could set up their own households and relied on their fathers to provide them with land to do so. Fathers often waited until their sons were in their mid-twenties, compelling them until then to invest their labor in the paternal estate.

Thus New England's labor shortage produced strong ties of dependency between generations. Fathers kept their sons working for them as long as possible; sons accepted this arrangement because they had no other way to become

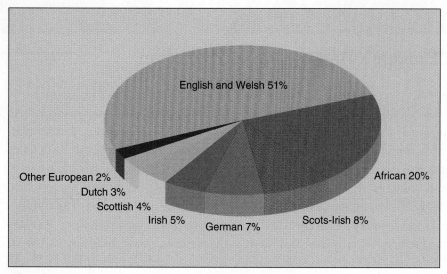

FIGURE 3-4   Ethnic Distribution of Non-Indian Inhabitants of British Mainland Colonies, c. 1770

By the third quarter of the eighteenth century, the colonial population was astonishingly diverse. Only two out of three settlers claimed British ancestry (from England, Wales, Scotland, or northern Ireland), while one out of five was African in origin.

Data Source: Thomas L. Purvis, "The European Ancestry of the United States Population, 1790," *William and Mary Quarterly*, 3d series, 41 (1984), p. 98.

independent farmers. They would eventually employ their own children in the same way.

Property owners in all the English colonies found different ways to control the laborers they so desperately needed. But where property owners saw problems—high wages (often twice what workers in England received) and abundant land (which deterred colonists from working for employers)—others saw opportunities. For tens of thousands of Europeans, the chance to own or rent a farm or to find steady employment made North America an irresistible magnet, promising a prosperity beyond their reach at home.

New European Immigrants

European immigrants flooded into America in the seventeenth and eighteenth centuries (see Figure 3–4). Nearly 250,000 Scots-Irish people—descendants of Protestant Scots who had settled in northern Ireland in the sixteenth and seventeenth centuries—came to the colonies after 1718, when their landlords raised rents to intolerable levels. Tens of thousands of immigrants arrived from Scotland during the same period, some seeking economic improvement and some sent as punishment for rebellions against the king in 1715 and 1745. Thousands of Irish Catholics arrived as servants, redemptioners, and convicts.

Continental Europe contributed another stream of emigrants. Perhaps 100,000 German Protestants left the Rhine Valley, where war, economic hardship, and religious persecution had brought misery. French Protestants

(known as Huguenots) began emigrating after 1685, when their faith was made illegal in France. Swiss Protestants likewise fled religious persecution. Even a few Poles, Greeks, Italians, and Jews reached the colonies in the eighteenth century.

Many emigrants responded to pamphlets and newspaper articles that exaggerated the bright prospects of life in America. Others studied more realistic accounts from friends and relatives who had already emigrated. One Scot who had moved to North Carolina warned his countrymen that at first "poor people will meet with many Difficulties" but they should "take courage and Come to this Country [for] it will be of Benefitt" to their families. Landowners sent agents to port towns to recruit new arrivals to become tenants, often on generous terms. One happy immigrant wrote to his wife back in England that he had signed a lease for a farm in New York that exempted him from paying rent for the first five years and charged him only 7 pence an acre after that.

Streams of emigrants flowed to places where land was cheap and labor most in demand (see Map 3–3). Few went to New England, where descendants of the first settlers occupied the best land. They also avoided areas where slavery predominated—the Chesapeake Tidewater and lowland South Carolina—in favor of the foothills of the Appalachian Mountains, from western Pennsylvania to the Carolinas. There, one emigrant declared, a "poor man that will incline to work may have the value of his labour."

This observation, though partly true, did not tell the whole story. Any person who came as a servant, redemptioner, or tenant learned that his master or landlord received much of "the value of his labour." Not all emigrants realized their dreams of becoming independent landowners. The scarcity of labor in the colonies led as easily to the exploitation of white workers as of slaves and Indians. Even so, for many people facing bleak prospects in Europe, the chance that emigration might bring prosperity was too tempting to ignore.

Conclusion

By the middle of the eighteenth century, America offered a strikingly diverse mosaic of peoples and communities. Along the St. Lawrence River lay Kahnawake, a village of Mohawks and Abenakis who had adopted Catholicism and French ways under Jesuit instruction. In Andover, Massachusetts, New Englanders tilled fields that their Puritan grandparents had cleared. German immigrants seeking spiritual perfection

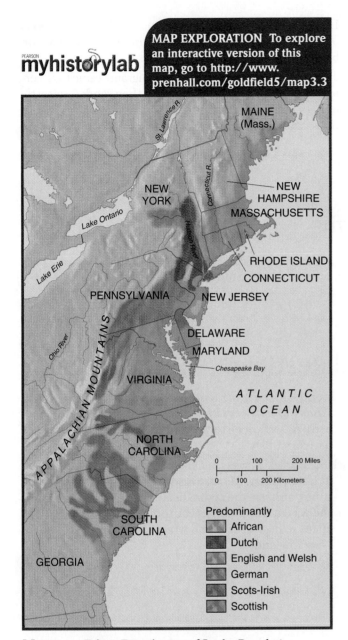

MAP EXPLORATION To explore an interactive version of this map, go to http://www. prenhall.com/goldfield5/map3.3

MAP 3-3 **Ethnic Distribution of Settler Population in British Mainland Colonies, c. 1755**
Settlers of different ethnic backgrounds tended to concentrate in certain areas. Only New Englanders were predominantly English, while Africans dominated in the Chesapeake Tidewater and South Carolina. German, Scottish, and Scots-Irish immigrants often settled in the backcountry.

populated the isolated Pennsylvania settlement of Ephrata. The hundred or so slaves on Robert Carter's Virginia plantation gathered on Sunday evenings to nurture ties of community with songs and dances, while the master cultivated his very different sense of community with the neighboring planters. In North Carolina, Swiss settlers rebuilt the coastal town of New Bern, destroyed during the Tuscarora War, while 100 miles farther west, Scottish emigrants cleared land for farms near present-day Fayetteville. Catawba Indians formed new villages in the South Carolina foothills to distance themselves from white settlers. In Mose, Florida, near St. Augustine, runaway slaves built a town under the protection of Spanish soldiers. Far to the west, the Spanish, mestizo, and Pueblo residents of Santa Fe warily reestablished ties broken during the Pueblo Revolt.

In these and many other communities, peoples from three continents adapted to one another and to American conditions. Indians struggled with the consequences of disease, trade, religious conversion, settlement, and warfare resulting from European immigration. Some native peoples managed to preserve their autonomy, others did not. Millions of African slaves suffered under the most repressive labor regime but fought its grip whenever possible. Slave communities testified to African Americans' assertion of their humanity in the face of a system that sought to deny it. English settlers became landowners in unprecedented numbers and adopted new ways to control laborers, reinventing slavery, unknown in England for centuries. For many, though not all, European immigrants, the colonies offered the chance for economic improvement.

As the eighteenth century wore on, the North American colonies attracted more attention from their home countries. Spain, France, and England recognized the colonies' growing economic power and strove to harness it to block the expansion of their rivals. Everywhere the effort to strengthen imperial ties created ambivalence among colonists. Because the English settlers were by far the most numerous, their responses were the most pronounced. As they saw more clearly the differences between themselves and England itself, some colonists began to defend their distinctive habits, while others tried more insistently than ever to imitate English ways. The tension between new and old had characterized colonial development from the start. What made the eighteenth century distinctive were the many ways in which the tensions worked themselves out.

Review Questions

1. The first phase of Olaudah Equiano's journey into slavery took him from Africa's interior to the coast. What part of this journey most frightened him? Why? How did the development of a transatlantic labor market shape Equiano's experiences in the New World and the Old?

2. English colonists experienced more frequent, and more violent, conflicts with Indians than the settlers of New France did. Why was this so? What factors affected Indian–European relations in the two colonial regions?

3. Why were Catholic missionaries more successful than Protestants in converting Indians to Christianity in early America?

4. When did Chesapeake planters switch from servants to slaves? What factors contributed to their decision to make this change?

5. By about 1750, more slaves in the mainland British colonies were creoles (American-born) than African-born. What effects did this have on the formation of African American communities in America?

6. Different labor systems predominated in various regions of British America. How did the economy of each region help determine its labor system?

7. Tens of thousands of European immigrants came to America in the eighteenth century, but they tended to settle only in certain colonial regions. What destinations did they favor and why?

Key Terms

Bacon's Rebellion (p. 65)

Beaver Wars (p. 61)

Encomienda (p. 59)

King Philip's War (p. 64)

Middle Passage (p. 69)

Pueblo Revolt (p. 65)

Redemptioner (p. 77)

Repartimiento (p. 59)

Rescate (p. 59)

Stono Rebellion (p. 76)

Recommended Reading

Berlin, Ira. *Many Thousands Gone: The First Two Centuries of Slavery in North America* (1998). A magisterial synthesis of the evolution of slavery from its beginnings in America through the Revolution.

Equiano, Olaudah. *The Interesting Narrative of the Life of Olaudah Equiano, or Gustavus Vassa, the African* (numerous editions). A vivid and moving story of an extraordinary individual's passage from Africa to New World slavery and, ultimately, to freedom.

Moore, Brian. *Black Robe* (1985). A powerful novel that explores the experiences of a Jesuit missionary among the Indians in seventeenth-century New France.

Richter, Daniel. *Facing East from Indian Country: A Native History of Early America* (2001). A brilliant synthesis of early American history viewed from the perspective of native peoples.

Vickers, Daniel. *Farmers and Fishermen: Two Centuries of Work in Essex County, Massachusetts, 1630–1830* (1994). A beautifully written and sophisticated analysis that explores the way in which settlers adapted their English experiences to deal with the shortages of labor and capital in New England.

Where to Learn More

- **Ste. Marie among the Hurons, near Midland, Ontario, Canada.** This site contains a reconstructed Jesuit mission from the seventeenth century. There is a museum with information about seventeenth-century France as well as life among the Huron Indians. Further information may be found at www.saintemarieamongthehurons.on.ca.

- **Taos Pueblo, Taos, New Mexico.** Still a residence for Pueblo Indians, portions of this multistoried pueblo date from the fifteenth century. This is the site from which Popé directed the beginnings of the Pueblo Revolt in 1680. Pictures and other information are available at www.cr.nps.gov/worldheritage/taos.htm.

- **Carter's Grove Slave Quarter, near Williamsburg, Virginia.** Site includes reconstructed eighteenth-century slave quarters on the original site where slave cabins once stood. Costumed African American interpreters show visitors around and tell stories about actual slaves who lived on the plantation. Information about the house and plantation can be found at www.williamsburg.com/plant/carter.html. Pictures of the plantation may also be seen at www.wise.virginia.edu.

- **Anacostia Museum and Center for African American History and Culture, Washington, D.C.** Part of the Smithsonian Institution, this museum contains exhibits relating to African American art, culture, and history. Information about current and past exhibitions, as well as online resources, can be found at www.anacostia.si.edu.

Study Resources

For study resources for this chapter, go to www.myhistorylab.com and choose *The American Journey*. You will find a wealth of study and review material for this chapter, including pre- and post-tests, customized study plan, key term review flash cards, interactive map and document activities, and documents for analysis.

Susanna Truax, the subject of this 1730 portrait, was evidently a member of a prosperous colonial family eager to display its imported English wares. Note the tea table at the left of the picture, topped with a teapot, cup and saucer, and sugar bowl—symbols of the Truax family's genteel style of life.

English Colonies in an Age of Empire 1660s–1763

4

Virginia 26th April 1763

Mr. Lawrence

Be pleased to send me a genteel sute of Cloaths made of superfine broad Cloth handsomely chosen; I shou[l]d have Inclosed [for] you my measure but in a general way they are so badly taken here that I am convinced it wou[l]d be of very little service; I wou[l]d have you there-fore take measure of a Gentleman who wears well made Cloaths of the following size—to wit—Six feet high & proportionably made; if any thing rather Slender than thick for a Person of that highth with pretty long arms & thighs—You will take care to make the Breeches longer than those you sent me last, & I wou[l]d have you keep the measure of the Cloaths you now make by you and if any alteration is required, in my next [letter] it shall be

pointed out. Mr Cary will pay your Bill—& I am Sir Yr Very H[um]ble Serv[an]t …

George Washington

W.W. Abbot and Dorothy Twohig, eds., *The Papers of George Washington*, Colonial Series, vol. 7 (Charlottesville, 1990).

myhistorylab

Personal Journeys Online

- Eliza Lucas Pinckney, *Letterbook*, 1742. Description of a South Carolina plantation mistress's day.

- Alexander Hamilton, *Itinerarium*, 1744. Description of sociability in eighteenth-century Philadelphia.

- Nathan Cole, "Spiritual Travels," October 23, 1740. A Connecticut farmer hears George Whitefield preach.

George Washington, along with a few dozen other privileged Virginians, had traveled to Williamsburg for a visit that mixed politics, business, and pleasure. Like Washington, these men had come to the capital to represent their respective counties in the House of Burgesses. When not engaged in government business, they attended to private affairs. They arranged to ship tobacco from their plantations to England, to pay outstanding debts, or to seek credit until the harvest was in. Washington was surely not the only one to take the opportunity to write to his London tailor and order the fashionable clothing that advertised his status as a gentleman. He and his fellow burgesses donned their best coats and breeches to attend dinner parties and theater performances that enlivened days otherwise devoted to debating politics and rendering accounts.

April 1763 marked the fourth time Washington had gone to Williamsburg to take his seat in the legislature. Each journey carried him further away from a youth spent as a surveyor and soldier toward his future as a respected planter and public servant. Just 31 years old in 1763, he had recently married Martha Custis, a wealthy widow, and inherited his older brother's plantation at Mount Vernon. He had served his king during the Seven Years' War; now he was eager to exchange his military uniform for the "genteel" broadcloth suits appropriate to his new station. Washington already owned more land than most English gentlemen. With land and wealth to support his ambitions, he wanted to live, look, and behave like an English country gentleman, not merely like a Virginia planter.

But Washington could not be sure what an English gentleman wore. He had never been to England and trusted neither his own judgment nor Williamsburg tailors to know how a proper English gentleman should dress. So, while he instructed Mr. Lawrence about measurements and fabric quality, Washington said nothing about the color or style of his new suit. He had to trust his tailor to make him clothing as suitable for the drawing rooms of London as for the parlors of Williamsburg.

Throughout British America, colonists who had achieved wealth and power tried, like Washington, to imitate the habits and manners of the English gentry. Their aspirations testified to important developments in the eighteenth century. Prosperity and the demand of a growing population for English products tied the colonies ever more tightly into a trade network centered on the imperial metropolis, London. The flow of goods and information between Britain and America fueled the desires of Washington and other successful colonists for acceptance as transatlantic members of the British elite.

These developments in Great Britain's American colonies brought them to the attention of European statesmen, who increasingly factored North America into their economic, political, diplomatic, and military calculations. Parliament devised legislation to channel colonial products into British ports and away from European competitors. Spain and France viewed the economic growth and geographic expansion of British North America as a threat to their own colonial possessions, and responded by augmenting their own territorial claims. With expansion came conflict, and with conflict, war: a series of four imperial wars, which themselves became powerful engines of change in the New World.

Economic Development and Imperial Trade in the British Colonies

England's greatest assets in its competition with other European nations were a dynamic economy and a sophisticated financial system that put commerce at the service of the state. Its commercial power was further strengthened after 1707, when the Act of Union joined England and Scotland to create the United Kingdom of Great Britain. British leaders came to see colonies as indispensable to the nation's economic welfare. Colonies supplied raw materials unavailable in the mother country, and colonists and Indians provided a healthy market for British manufactured goods.

As the eighteenth century progressed, colonial economies grew in tandem with that of Great Britain. Parliament knitted the colonies into an empire with commercial legislation, while British merchants traded with and extended credit to growing numbers of colonial merchants and planters. Over time, these developments made colonial societies resemble Britain and integrated the economies of the colonies with that of the mother country in a vast transatlantic system.

The Regulation of Trade

To improve its competitive position in transatlantic trade, England adopted a policy of **mercantilism.** The goal was to achieve a favorable balance of trade within the empire as a

CHRONOLOGY

1651–1733	Parliament passes series of Navigation Acts to regulate imperial trade.
1660	Charles II becomes king of England.
1662	Halfway Covenant adopted by Massachusetts clergy.
1685	James II becomes king of England.
1686–1689	Dominion of New England.
1688	Glorious Revolution in England; James II loses the throne.
1689	William and Mary become English monarchs; Leisler's Rebellion begins in New York.
1689–1697	King William's War in America.
1691–1692	Witchcraft trials in Salem, Massachusetts.
1698	First French settlements near mouth of Mississippi River.
1701	Iroquois adopt policy of neutrality toward France and Britain.
1702–1713	Queen Anne's War in America.
1707	Act of Union joins England and Scotland to create Great Britain.
1718	San Antonio, Texas, and New Orleans founded.
1734–1735	Jonathan Edwards leads religious revival in Northampton, Massachusetts.
1739	Great Awakening begins in Middle Colonies with George Whitefield's arrival.
1744–1748	King George's War in America.
1754–1763	Seven Years' War in America.
1760s	Spanish begin establishing missions in California.

whole, with exports exceeding imports. Colonies played a crucial role, since they supplied commodities that British consumers would otherwise have to purchase from foreign competitors. Certain colonial products, such as tobacco or rice, could also be exported to foreign markets, further improving the balance of trade. Between 1651 and 1733, Parliament passed four types of mercantilist regulations to put this policy into action (see the Overview table, British Imperial Trade Regulations, 1651–1733).

The first type of regulation aimed at ending Dutch dominance in overseas trade. Beginning with the Navigation Act of 1651, all trade in the empire had to be conducted in English or colonial ships, with crews of which at least half were Englishmen or colonists. The act stimulated rapid growth in England's merchant marine and New England's shipping industry. Shipbuilding and earnings from what was called the carrying trade soon became the most profitable sector of New England's economy.

The second type of legislation stipulated that certain colonial goods, called **enumerated products**, could be shipped only to England or to another English colony. These goods initially included tobacco, sugar, indigo, and cotton; other products, such as rice, were added later. These laws also required European goods to pass through England before they could be shipped to the colonies. When these goods entered English ports, they were taxed, making them more expensive and encouraging colonists to buy English-made items.

The third and fourth types of regulations further enhanced the advantage of English manufacturers who produced for the colonial market. Parliament subsidized certain goods, including linen and gunpowder, to allow manufacturers to undersell European competitors in the colonies. Other laws protected English manufacturers from colonial competition by prohibiting colonists from manufacturing wool, felt hats, and iron on a large scale.

England's commercial goals were largely achieved. The Dutch eventually lost their preeminence in the Atlantic trade. Colonial trade helped the English economy to grow and contributed to London's emergence as Western Europe's largest city. Colonists enjoyed protected markets for their staple crops and low prices on English imports. Colonial merchants, operating on equal terms with English (and, after 1707, Scottish) traders, took full advantage of commercial opportunities within the empire.

Occasionally, merchants evaded these laws by smuggling. Customs officials, sent over from England beginning

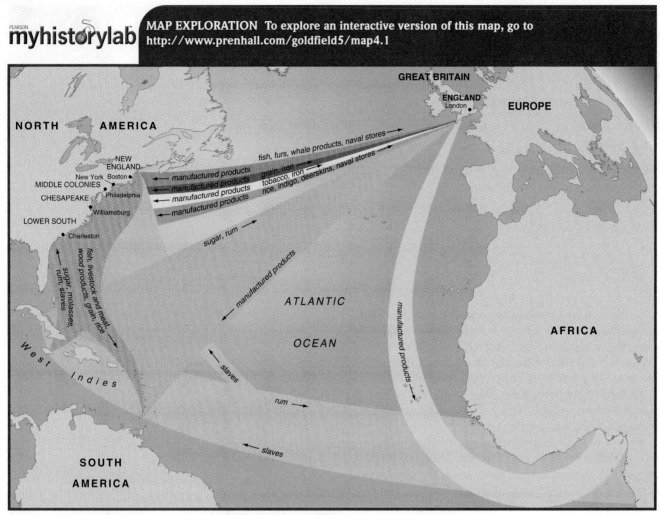

MAP 4–1   Anglo-American Transatlantic Commerce
By the eighteenth century, Great Britain and its colonies were enmeshed in a complex web of trade. Britain exchanged manufactured goods for colonial raw materials, while Africa provided the enslaved laborers who produced the most valuable colonial crops.

in the 1670s, were hard-pressed to stop them. Although they derived much of their income from fines collected from smugglers, officials generally found it easier to accept bribes and look the other way when a ship arrived in port with, say, an illicit cargo of French West Indian sugar. Most colonial trade, however, followed the proper routes. By not pushing for perfect compliance, British officials did not put too much pressure on a system that in fact worked remarkably well.

The Colonial Export Trade and the Spirit of Enterprise

By the mid-eighteenth century, the Atlantic had become a busy thoroughfare of international commerce (see Map 4–1). British and colonial vessels carried goods and people from Great Britain, continental Europe, and West Africa to the colonies and returned tons of raw materials to the Old World. At the heart of Anglo-American trade lay the highly profitable commerce in staple crops, most of which were produced by slave labor.

West Indian sugar far surpassed all other colonial products in importance (see Figure 4–1). By the late 1760s, the value of sugar exports reached almost £4 million per year—nearly 50 percent more than the total value of all other exports from British American colonies. Sugar planters joined with the British merchants who marketed their crop to lobby Parliament for favorable treatment. Parliament responded in 1733 with the Molasses Act, which taxed sugar products from foreign sources, especially the French West Indies. In 1739, Parliament removed sugar from the list of enumerated items, allowing merchants to ship it directly to southern Europe.

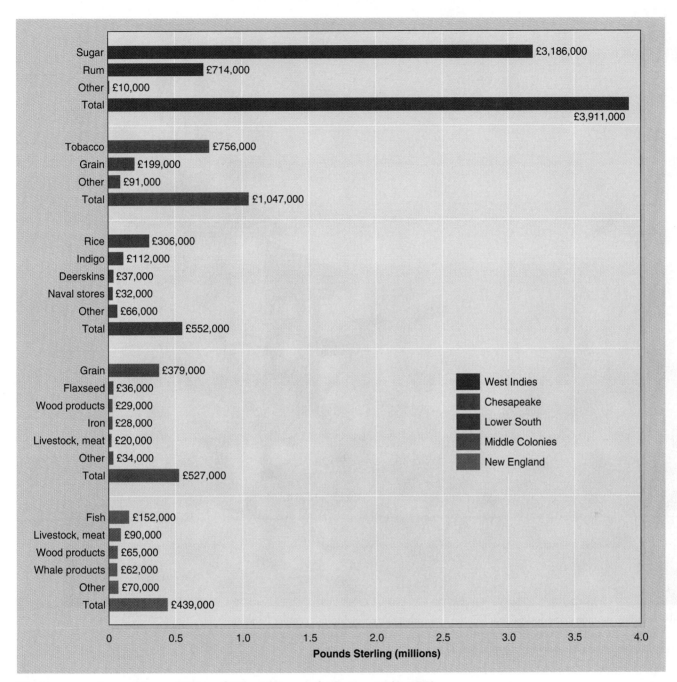

FIGURE 4–1   Average Annual Value of Colonial Exports by Region, 1768–1772
Staple crops—especially sugar—produced by slave labor were the most valuable items exported from Britain's North American colonies.

Data Source: John J. McCusker and Russell R. Menard, *The Economy of British America, 1607–1789*, rev. ed. (1991). University of North Carolina Press.

Tobacco from the Chesapeake colonies was the second most valuable staple crop. Nearly 90 percent of the crop was reexported to continental Europe. Persistent low prices, however, led many tobacco planters to sow some of their land with wheat after about 1750. This change lessened their dependence on tobacco and allowed them to take advantage of the strong demand for flour in southern Europe and the West Indies.

Exports of rice and indigo (a plant that produced a blue dye used in textile manufacture) enriched many South Carolina planters. Most of the rice went to England and the West Indies, although, after 1731, Parliament permitted direct ship-

Scenes like this were common in the dockyards at Deptford and other parts of eighteenth-century London. Boxes and barrels of English goods were loaded aboard sailing ships that returned months later with sugar, tobacco, rice, and other products from every part of England's worldwide empire.

ments to southern Europe. Parliament encouraged indigo production by granting subsidies to growers and placing stiff taxes on foreign indigo. It also subsidized colonial production of naval stores—such as tar, pitch, and turpentine—to reduce England's dependence on Swedish suppliers. The export of these items made up an important part of the North and South Carolina economies.

Wheat exports from the Middle Colonies boomed in the eighteenth century. Since farmers in Great Britain grew enough wheat to supply the domestic market, there was little demand there for colonial flour. But there was a strong market for it in the West Indies and Europe, particularly when a series of poor harvests and warfare disrupted European supplies.

New England had no staple crop and produced little for export except whale products, such as oil used in lamps. The region's merchants nevertheless developed a thriving transatlantic trade by carrying other colonies' goods to market. New England vessels eventually dominated shipping within the empire by transporting these mixed cargoes to England to exchange for manufactured items. By 1770, New England's earnings from shipping fees, freight charges, and insurance exceeded the total value of its own exports.

New England merchants also strengthened trade links to the West Indies that had first been forged in the 1650s. By the mid-eighteenth century, more than half of all New England exports went to the islands: salted meat for planters'

OVERVIEW

British Imperial Trade Regulations, 1651–1733

Name of Act	Key Features
Navigation Act of 1651	Aimed to eliminate Dutch competition in overseas trade Required most goods to be carried in English or colonial ships Required crews to be at least half English
Navigation Act of 1660	Required all colonial trade to be carried in English ships Required master and three-quarters of crew to be English Created list of enumerated goods, such as tobacco and sugar, that could be shipped only to England or another English colony
Staple Act of 1663	Required products from Europe, Asia, and Africa to be landed in England before being shipped to the colonies
Plantation Duty Act of 1673	Attempted to reduce smuggling Required captains of colonial ships to post bond that they would deliver enumerated goods to England or pay the "plantation duty" that would be owed in England
Navigation Act of 1696	Plugged loopholes in earlier laws Created vice-admiralty courts in colonies to enforce trade regulations
Woolens Act of 1699	Forbade export of woolen cloth made in the colonies, to prevent competition with English producers
Hat Act of 1732	Prohibited export of colonial-made hats
Molasses Act of 1733	Placed high tax on French West Indian and other foreign molasses imported into colonies to encourage importation of British West Indian molasses

dinners, salted fish for slaves, wood for sugar barrels and other equipment. Merchants accepted molasses and other sugar by-products in payment, bringing them back to New England to be distilled into cheap rum. Traders then carried rum to Africa to exchange for slaves. Although British merchants dominated the African slave trade, New Englanders also profited. Fewer than 10 percent of New England's population were slaves, but because New Englanders trafficked in human cargo and provisioned the West Indies, their commercial economy nonetheless depended on slavery.

The Import Trade and Ties of Credit

By the late 1760s, over £4 million worth of British manufactured goods flowed into the colonies each year. This import trade satisfied a demand for items that could not be produced—at least not cheaply—in North America. Bales of British cloth and leather, crates of glassware and pottery, casks of nails and lead shot piled onto the wharves of Philadelphia and New York. Dockworkers emptied ships' holds of wrought iron, brass, and copper, barrels of refined sugar, and bundles of beaver hats. Some of these goods—ironware, sugar, hats—were made of raw materials from the colonies.

Certain imported items made their way into Indian villages, including weapons, woolen cloth, knives, and jewelry. Indians were discerning customers and rejected goods not made to their liking. Native consumers, for instance, preferred textiles dyed dark blue, dark red, or gray, and wanted kettles lighter in weight than those made for English purchasers. Native leaders sometimes acquired imported goods for exchange with allies as well as for their own use.

The colonists' even heavier consumption of manufactures was vital to British overseas commerce. In terms of value, colonists imported more goods than they exported. This imbalance was remedied in good part by colonial earnings from shipping fees and payments from the British government for colonial military expenses. The colonial economy ran an annual deficit of £40,000 by the late 1760s, but that was only about 1 percent of a transatlantic trade worth over £4 million a year.

British merchants extended credit to colonists on generous terms so they could buy British products. Major tobacco planters virtually lived on the easy credit that British merchants provided. These merchants marketed the planters' tobacco and supplied them with English goods, charging the costs of purchase and transportation against the profits they expected the next year's crop to bring.

Easy credit let planters indulge themselves with English goods, and many sank into debt. A Virginian noted that in the 1740s, no planter would have dared run up a debt of £1,000 but by the 1760s, "Ten times that sum is...spoke of with Indifference." When trade was brisk and tobacco prices high, no one worried. But when tobacco prices dropped or an international crisis made overseas trading risky, creditors called in the debts owed to them. At such times, colonial debtors realized how much they (like the Indians involved in European trade) depended on goods and credit supplied by distant merchants.

Becoming More Like Britain: The Growth of Cities and Inequality

As colonial commerce grew, so did colonial cities—the connecting points in the economic network tying the colonies to London and other British ports. Boston, New York, Philadelphia, and Charleston were as large as many British provincial towns. By 1770, Philadelphia's population had reached 30,000, New York's 25,000, Boston's 16,000, and Charleston's 12,000. A fifth city, Baltimore, was rapidly developing on Chesapeake Bay. Only about 5 percent of all mainland colonists lived in cities, but the influence of urban centers far outweighed their size.

European visitors marveled at how quickly American cities had developed. One Englishman declared in 1759 that Philadelphia "must certainly be the object of every one's wonder and admiration." Less than eighty years old, it already boasted three thousand houses, impressive public buildings, two libraries, eight or ten churches, and a college (chartered as the College of Philadelphia in 1755, now the University of Pennsylvania). The same visitor judged Boston to be a "most flourishing" place with "much the air of some of our best country towns in England."

All colonial cities (like Britain's major ones) were seaports. Oceangoing ships sailed "right up to the town" of Philadelphia on the Delaware River, according to one European observer. Boston had "a very fine wharf, at least half a mile long" to facilitate shipping. New York, then as now, had one of the world's finest harbors, from which it conducted "a more extensive commerce than any town in the English North American provinces."

Indeed, in their bustle and cosmopolitan atmosphere, colonial cities resembled British provincial cities more than they did the farming villages of the American countryside. Cities provided such amenities as inns, taverns, coffeehouses, theaters, and social clubs. Their populations were diverse in ethnic origin and religion. In addition, the African American population in the northern colonies tended to live in cities. By 1750, slaves made up 20 percent of New York City's population, about 10 percent of Philadelphia's, and nearly 9 percent of Boston's.

Artisans in colonial cities.   Colonial cities had higher proportions of artisans than did rural villages. Many of them labored at trades directly related to overseas commerce, such as shipbuilding or ropemaking. Others produced pottery, furniture, paper, glassware, and iron tools. Colonial products tended to be somewhat cruder and cheaper than British-made goods. Yet talented colonists such as the Boston silversmith Paul Revere fashioned goods that would have been prized possessions in any English gentleman's home.

Colonial manufacturing took place in workshops often attached to artisans' houses. Artisans managed a workforce consisting of their wives and children, along with journeymen or apprentices. Usually teenage boys, apprentices contracted to work for a master for four to seven years in order to learn the "mysteries" of his craft. Like indentured servants, they received no wages but worked for food, clothing, shelter, and a small payment at the end of their service. Once an apprentice finished his training, he became a journeyman, working for a master but now earning wages and saving to set up his own shop.

Many artisans flourished in colonial cities, but prosperity was by no means guaranteed. In Philadelphia, skilled artisans typically earned enough for a modest subsistence. Yet workers at less skilled crafts often made only a bare living, and ordinary laborers faced seasonal unemployment. Silversmiths, tailors, and furniture makers, relying on overseas suppliers of metal, cloth, and exotic woods, suffered when supply ships sank or wars hindered ocean traffic. Makers of luxury goods also feared downturns in the economy, for such trends discouraged nervous customers from purchasing their wares.

Cities like Philadelphia, New York, and Charleston provided opportunities for some women to support themselves with craft work. Mary Wallace and Clementia Ferguson, for instance, stitched fashionable hats and dresses for New York customers. Nonetheless, even in cities, women's options were limited. Most employed women were widows striving to maintain a family business until sons grew old enough to take over. This was true for printers such as Elizabeth Tim-

This view of the Philadelphia waterfront dates from 1720. It shows how the city had developed into one of British America's principal ports just forty years after its founding.

Peter Cooper, "The Southeast Prospect of the City of Philadelphia," ca. 1720. The Library Company of Philadelphia.

John Singleton Copley's portrait of the silversmith Paul Revere, painted about 1769, depicts one of Boston's most prominent artisans. As colonists grew wealthier, some commissioned portraits for their homes to serve as emblems of their rising social aspirations. Even so, Copley despaired that America would ever provide a suitable market for his artistic talents and he eventually moved to England.

Paul Revere, c. 1768–70. Copley, John Singleton, U.S., 1738–1815. Oil on canvas, 35 × 28 1/2 in. (88.9 × 72.3 cm.). Gift of Joseph W., William B., and Edward H. R. Revere. Courtesy, Museum of Fine Arts, Boston. Reproduced with permission. © 1999 Museum of Fine Arts, Boston. All rights reserved.

othy, who ran the *South Carolina Gazette* after her husband's death in 1739. Other widows toiled at less prestigious—and less remunerative—jobs as nurses, laundresses, and boarding-house keepers.

The growing gap between rich and poor.   Wherever colonists engaged heavily in commerce—in cities or on plantations—the gap between rich and poor widened during the eighteenth century. In 1687, the richest 10 percent of Boston's residents owned 46 percent of the taxable property in the town; by 1771, the top tenth held 63 percent of the taxable wealth. Similar changes occurred in Philadelphia. In South Carolina and the Chesapeake, many planters added to the already substantial holdings in land and slaves that they had inherited. It became increasingly

difficult for newcomers to enter their ranks. At the same time, the colonies' growing reliance on slave labor—especially in the South—created a sizable class of impoverished people denied the chance to better their condition. By 1770, slaves, for whom America was anything but a land of opportunity, constituted one out of five residents of the British colonies.

To address the growing problem of poverty among white colonists, cities built workhouses, and towns collected funds for poor relief in greater amounts than ever before. Many poor people were aged or ill, without families to help them. Able-bodied workers forced to accept public relief usually owed their misfortune to temporary downturns in the economy, often the result of wartime dislocations. Such was the case in 1757, for example, when Boston's leaders complained about rising poor relief expenses. Great Britain was then at war with France, and the British commander in chief had halted Boston's overseas trade, a military expedient that hurt the city's economy.

Even in the worst of times, no more than one out of ten white colonists (mainly city dwellers) depended on public assistance. For free black people who were unemployed and denied public relief, conditions were far worse. A Pennsylvania law went so far as to allow them to be enslaved. This was a threat no impoverished white colonist faced. And, bad as it was, the problem of poverty among white colonists had not reached anything like the levels seen in Britain. As much as one-third of England's population regularly received relief, and the numbers swelled during hard times. Eighteenth-century white colonists, on average, enjoyed a higher standard of living than most British residents or other Europeans. So long as land was available—even if one had to move to the edges of settlement to get it—colonists could at least eke out a bare subsistence, and many did much better.

No one would have mistaken Philadelphia for London or Virginia planters for British lords. Even so, colonial society increasingly resembled Great Britain. The growth of cities mirrored British urban development. The widening gap between rich and poor convinced many colonists that their society had at last matured from its crude beginnings. Eighteenth-century Britons on both sides of the Atlantic believed that societies ought to be organized hierarchically, that God intended for people to be arranged in ranks from rich to poor. The more America resembled Britain, many colonists assumed, the more stable and prosperous it would be.

The Transformation of Culture
Despite the convergence of British and colonial society, many influential settlers worried that America remained culturally inferior to Great Britain. Colonial gentlemen tended to see American architecture, manners, and intellectual life as at best poor imitations of superior British models. During

the eighteenth century, some prosperous colonists strove to overcome this provincial sense of inferiority. They built grand houses and filled them with imported goods, cultivated what they took to be the manners of the British gentry, and followed British and European intellectual developments. Some colonial gentlemen even reshaped their religious beliefs to reflect European notions that God played only an indirect role in human affairs.

These elite aspirations, however, were not shared by most settlers. The majority of colonists, although they might purchase a few imported goods, had little interest in copying the manners of the British elite, and few of them altered their spiritual beliefs to fit European patterns. Indeed, familiar religious practices flourished in eighteenth-century America, and when a tremendous revival swept through the colonies beginning in the 1730s, religion occupied center stage in American life.

Goods and Houses

Eighteenth-century Americans imported more manufactured products from England with every passing year. This practice did not simply reflect the growth of the colonial population, for the rate at which Americans bought British goods exceeded the rate of population increase. Colonists owned more goods, often of better quality, than their parents and grandparents had possessed.

In the less secure economic climate of the seventeenth century, colonists had limited their purchases of goods, investing instead in land to pass on to their children. But by the eighteenth century, prosperous colonists felt secure enough to buy goods to make their lives more comfortable. Chairs replaced benches, and carpets covered wooden floors. Colonists hung mirrors and perhaps a portrait on their walls. The dinner table might be covered with a damask cloth and set with individual porcelain plates instead of a common wooden dish. Colonists acquired such goods to advertise their more refined style of life.

By the 1760s, nearly every item that George Washington ordered from his London agent could have been purchased in Philadelphia. But Washington wanted the latest English styles and even worried that his agent might take advantage of him by sending goods that were no longer in fashion in England. Washington's desires were hardly unique. One visitor to Maryland, astonished at the speed with which colonists adopted English styles, declared that he was "almost inclined to believe that a new fashion is adopted earlier by the polished and affluent American than by many opulent persons" in London.

Prosperous colonists built grand houses where they lived in greater comfort than ever before. In the seventeenth century, Virginia's governor lived in the finest house in the colony—a four-room dwelling. His eighteenth-century counterpart, however, resided in Williamsburg in the Governor's Palace, an elegant two-storied mansion. By the 1730s, numerous southern planters had built "great houses" while others transformed older houses into more stylish residences. Washington extensively remodeled Mount Vernon, adding a second story and extra wings to create a home fit for a gentleman. In the northern colonies, merchants built the most impressive houses, often following architectural pattern books imported from England.

These houses were not only larger but also different in design from the homes of less affluent colonists. Most settlers lived in one- or two-room dwellings and thus cooked, ate, and slept in the same chamber. But the owners of great houses could devote rooms to specialized uses, such as kitchens and private bedrooms. The most distinctive feature of these grand homes was the parlor, an elaborately decorated room used for entertaining guests. Parlor doors often opened onto lawns and formal gardens where guests could stroll and engage in polite conversation.

Prosperous colonists did not build such homes merely to advertise their wealth. They wanted to create the proper setting for a refined way of life, emulating the English gentry in their country estates and London townhouses. But they knew that the true measure of their gentility lay not just in where they lived and what they owned but in how they behaved.

Shaping Minds and Manners

Colonists knew that the manners of British gentlefolk set them apart from ordinary people. Many Americans therefore imported "courtesy books" containing the rules of polite behavior. These publications advised would-be gentlemen on how to show regard for social rank, practice personal cleanliness, and respect other people's feelings.

The young George Washington studied such books carefully. At the age of 13, he copied 110 rules from *Youth's Behaviour; or, Decency in Conversation among Men,* including such advice as "In the Presence of Others Sing not to yourself with a humming Noise, nor Drum with your Fingers or Feet" and "In Company of those of Higher Quality than yourself Speak not till you are ask'd a Question then Stand upright put of[f] your Hat and Answer in few words." Many colonists subscribed to English journals such as the *Tatler* and the *Spectator* that printed articles describing good manners.

Women, too, cultivated genteel manners. In Charleston, South Carolina, and other colonial cities, girls' boarding schools advertised instruction in "Polite Education." Female pupils received only the rudiments of intellectual training in reading, writing, and arithmetic, for it was assumed that women had little need of such accomplishments. The private schools' curricula instead focused on French, music, dancing, and fancy needlework. These were skills that advertised girls' genteel status and prepared them for married lives as mistresses of great houses, mothers of future gentlemen and ladies, and hostesses of grand entertainments.

Some people expressed their gentility through more intellectual pursuits, taking advantage of the relatively high literacy rates among white colonists. In New England, where settlers placed great emphasis on Bible study, about 70 percent of men and 45 percent of women could read and write. Only a third of men in the southern colonies, and even fewer women, could read and write, but even these literacy rates were higher than among Britain's general population. Eighteenth-century colonists enjoyed greater access to printed material than ever before. In 1704, the *Boston News-Letter* became the first continuously published newspaper in British America. By the 1760s nearly every colony had a regularly published newspaper, and booksellers opened shops in several cities. Prominent colonists began to participate in a transatlantic world of ideas.

These colonists, however, were consumers of British and European ideas rather than producers of an American intellectual tradition. They imported thousands of books, subscribed to British journals, and established libraries where borrowing privileges could be purchased for a modest fee. Colonists with literary aspirations emulated their favorite writers. In Virginia, William Byrd II, whose father got his start as an Indian trader and tobacco farmer, composed verse in the style of contemporary English poets. Benjamin Franklin honed his writing skills by rewriting essays from the *Spectator* and comparing his versions to the originals.

Educated colonists were especially interested in the new ideas that characterized what has been called the **Age of Enlightenment.** The European thinkers of the Enlightenment drew inspiration from recent advances in science—such as the English scientist Isaac Newton's explanation of the laws of gravity—that suggested that the universe operated according to natural laws that human reason could discover. They also drew on the work of the English philosopher John Locke, who maintained that God did not dictate human knowledge but rather gave us the power to acquire knowledge through experience and understanding. The hallmark of Enlightenment thought was a belief in the power of human reason to improve the human condition.

This optimistic worldview marked a profound intellectual shift. Enlightenment thinkers rejected earlier ideas about God's unknowable will and continued intervention in human and natural events. They instead assigned God a less active role as the creator of the universe, who had set the world running according to predictable laws, and then let nature and humans shape events. Such ideas inspired a growing international community of scholars to try to discover the laws of nature and to work toward human progress.

Colonial intellectuals sought membership in this scholarly community. A few of them—the Reverend Cotton Mather of Massachusetts, William Byrd, Benjamin Franklin—gained election to the Royal Society, the most prestigious learned society in England. Most of their scholarly contributions were unimpressive, but Franklin achieved genuine intellectual prominence. His experiments with a kite proved that lightning was electricity (a natural force whose properties were poorly understood at the time) and gained him an international reputation. He also found practical uses for his scientific knowledge. Franklin invented the lightning rod (which prevented fires in wooden buildings by channeling the electrical charge of a lightning bolt into the ground), bifocal spectacles, the iron "Franklin stove" (in which wood burned more efficiently than in fireplaces), and the glass harmonica, an instrument that made him famous among European musicians and composers.

If Franklin's career embodied the Enlightenment ideal of the rational exploration of nature's laws, it also revealed the

Painted at about the time Franklin retired from his printing business, this portrait depicts the one-time craftsman as an aspiring gentleman. Wearing a wig and a shirt with ruffled cuffs, Franklin would no longer work with his hands but would pursue his scientific experiments and other studies.

Robert Feke (1707–1752), Portrait of Benjamin Franklin (1706–1790), c. 1746. Oil on canvas, 127 × 102 cm. Courtesy of the Harvard University Portrait Collection. Bequest of Dr. John Collins Warren, 1856.

limited impact of Enlightenment thought in colonial America. Only a few prosperous and educated colonists could afford such intellectual pursuits. Franklin came from humble origins—his father was a maker of candles and soap—but his success as a printer allowed him to retire from business at the age of 42. Only then did he purchase the equipment for his electrical discoveries and have the leisure time to begin his scientific work. Franklin's equipment—and leisure—were as much badges of gentlemanly status as George Washington's London-made suit.

Most colonists remained ignorant of scientific advances and Enlightenment ideas, having little leisure to devote to literature and polite conversation. When they found time to read, they picked up not a courtesy book or the *Spectator* but the Bible, which was the best-selling book of the colonial era. Religion principally shaped the way in which they viewed the world and explained human and natural events.

Colonial Religion and the Great Awakening

Church steeples dominated the skylines of colonial cities. By the 1750s, Boston and New York each had eighteen churches, and Philadelphia boasted twenty. Churches and meetinghouses likewise dominated country towns. Often the largest and finest buildings in the community, they bore witness to the diverse and thriving condition of religion in America.

In every New England colony except Rhode Island, the Puritan (or Congregationalist) faith was the established religion. Congregational churches in the region, headed by ministers trained at Harvard College and Yale (founded in 1701), served the majority of colonists, who were required to pay taxes to support them. Though proud of the Puritan tradition that had inspired New England's origins, ministers and believers nonetheless had to adapt to changing social and religious conditions.

The principal adaptation consisted of a move away from strict requirements for church membership. In order to keep their churches pure, New England's founders had required prospective members to give convincing evidence that they had experienced a spiritual conversion before they could receive communion and have their children baptized. By the 1660s, however, fewer colonists sought admission under such strict standards, which left them and their unbaptized children outside the church. To address this problem, the clergy in 1662 adopted the **Halfway Covenant.** This allowed adults who had been baptized (because their parents were church members), but who had not themselves experienced conversion, to have their own children baptized. By the 1680s, some ministers made church admission even easier, requiring members only to demonstrate knowledge of the Christian faith and to live godly lives.

Congregational churches also had to accept a measure of religious toleration in New England. In 1691, Massachusetts received a royal charter granting "liberty of Conscience" to all Protestants, bringing the colony in line with England's religious policy. Anglicans and Baptists eventually won exemptions from paying taxes to support the established Congregational churches. At the same time, some Congregationalist preachers began emphasizing personal piety and good works in their sermons, ideas usually associated with Anglicanism. These changes indicated a shift away from the Puritan exclusiveness of New England's early years.

In the South, the established Church of England consolidated its authority in the early eighteenth century but never exerted effective control over spiritual life. The bishop of London began appointing agents to oversee church matters, and the Society for the Propagation of the Gospel in Foreign Parts, founded in 1701, recruited ministers for colonial parishes. Even so, these parishes often lacked trained clergy, and ministers who did emigrate encountered unexpected obstacles.

Many a parson in England could ride from one side of his parish to the other in an hour, but Anglican clergymen in the southern colonies served parishes that were vast and sparsely settled. One South Carolina parish contained 10,400 square miles and only seven hundred white residents. Ministers also found that influential planters, accustomed to running parishes when preachers were unavailable, resisted their efforts to take control of churches. Aware that the planters' taxes paid their salaries, many ministers found it easiest simply to preach and behave in ways that offered the least offense. Frontier regions often lacked Anglican churches and clergymen altogether. In such places, dissenting religious groups, such as Presbyterians, Quakers, and Baptists, gained followers among people neglected by the Anglican establishment.

No established church dominated in the Middle Colonies of New York, New Jersey, and Pennsylvania. The region's ethnically diverse population and William Penn's policy of religious toleration guaranteed that a multitude of groups would compete for followers. One observer, accustomed to an established church, characterized these conditions as a "soul-destroying whirlpool." Yet religion flourished in the Middle Colonies. By the middle of the eighteenth century, the region had more congregations per capita than even New England.

Groups such as the Quakers and the Mennonites, who did not have specially trained ministers, easily formed new congregations in response to local demand. Lutheran and German Reformed churches, however, required European-educated clergy, who were always scarce. Pious laymen held worship services in their homes even as they sent urgent letters overseas begging for ordained ministers. When more

Lutheran and Reformed clergy arrived in the 1740s and 1750s, they sometimes discovered, as Anglican preachers did in the South, that laymen balked at relinquishing control of the churches. Lutheran and Reformed ministers also learned that their professional training alone could not command respect; their congregations demanded that they be powerful preachers. Because so many other religious alternatives were available, ministers had to compete for their parishioners' allegiance.

Bewildering spiritual diversity, relentless religious competition, and a comparatively weak Anglican Church all distinguished the colonies from Britain. Yet in one important way, religious developments during the middle third of the eighteenth century drew the colonies closer to Britain. A great transatlantic religious revival, originating in Scotland and England, first touched the Middle Colonies in the 1730s. In 1740–1745, it struck the northern colonies with the force of a hurricane, and in the 1760s, the last phase of the revival spread through the South. America had never seen anything like this immense revival, which came to be called the **Great Awakening.**

By 1730, Presbyterians in Pennsylvania had split into factions over such issues as the disciplining of church members and the requirement that licensed ministers have university degrees. One group, led by an immigrant Scottish evangelist, William Tennent, Sr., and his four sons, denounced their opponents as men more interested in regulations than conversion. In the 1730s, Tennent set up the Log College in Neshaminy, Pennsylvania, to train his sons and other young men to be evangelical ministers. What began as a dispute among clergymen eventually blossomed into a broader challenge to religious authority. That challenge gained momentum in late 1739, when one of the most charismatic evangelists of the century, George Whitefield, arrived in the colonies from England.

Whitefield, an Anglican minister, had experienced an intense religious conversion while he was still a university student. Already famous in Britain as a preacher of great emotional fervor, he embarked on a tour of the colonies in the winter of 1739–1740. As soon as Whitefield landed in Delaware, his admirers whipped up local enthusiasm, ensuring that he would preach to huge crowds in Pennsylvania and New Jersey. Whitefield's powerful preaching on the experience of conversion lent support to the Presbyterian faction led by the Tennents and sparked local revivals. Whitefield then moved on to New England, where some communities had already experienced local awakenings. In 1734–1735, for instance, the Congregationalist minis-ter Jonathan Edwards had led a revival in Northampton, Massachusetts, urging his parishioners to recognize their sinfulness and describing hell in such a terrifying way that many despaired of salvation.

Whitefield's tour through the colonies knitted these scattered local revivals into the Great Awakening. Crowds gathered in city squares and open fields to listen to his sermons. Whitefield exhorted his audiences to examine their souls for evidence of the "indwelling of Christ" that would indicate that they were saved. He criticized other ministers for emphasizing good works and "head-knowledge" instead of the emotional side of religion.

Whitefield's open-air sermons scarcely resembled the colonists' accustomed form of worship. Settlers normally gathered with family and neighbors in church for formal, structured services. They sat in pews assigned on the basis of social status, reinforcing standards of order and community hierarchy. But Whitefield's sermons were highly dramatic performances. He preached for hours in a booming voice, gesturing wildly and sometimes even dissolving in tears. Thousands of strangers, jostling in crowds that often outnumbered the populations of several villages put together, wept along with him. When the sermon ended, his listeners dispersed, many never to see each other again.

In the wake of Whitefield's visits, Benjamin Franklin noted, "it seem'd as if all the World were growing Religious." Revivals and mass conversions often followed his appearances, to the happy astonishment of local clergy. But their approval evaporated when more extreme revivalists appeared. Gilbert Tennent, William's son, followed Whitefield to Boston and derided the town's ministers as unconverted "dead Drones." James Davenport—a preacher

During George Whitefield's tour of the American colonies in 1739–1741, the famous revivalist minister often preached to large crowds gathered outdoors to hear one of his powerful sermons.

so erratic that many thought him mad—claimed that God had given him the knowledge of other ministers' spiritual states and routinely denounced by name those he "knew" to be damned. Once, in the midst of a sermon urging his audience to rid itself of worldly finery, Davenport set an example by tearing off his velvet breeches and throwing them into a bonfire. Officials who valued civic order tried to silence such extremists by passing laws that prohibited them from preaching in a town without the local minister's permission.

Disputes between individuals converted in the revivals—called **New Lights**—and those who were not (Old Lights) split churches. New Lights insisted, as the separatist founders of Plymouth once had, that they could not remain in churches with sinful members and unconverted ministers and so left to form new churches. "Formerly the People could bear with each other in Charity when they differ'd in Opinion," lamented one colonist, "but they now break Fellowship and Communion with one another on that Account."

The Awakening came late to the southern colonies, but it was there, in the 1760s, that it produced perhaps its greatest controversy. Many southern converts became Baptists, combining religious criticism of the Anglicans with condemnation of the wealthy planters' way of life. Plainly dressed Baptists criticized the rich clothes, drinking, gambling, and pride of Virginia's gentry. The planters, in turn, viewed the Baptists as dangerous people who could not "meet a man upon the road, but they must ram a text of Scripture down his throat." Most of all, they hated the Baptists for their willingness to preach to slaves.

Although the revivals themselves gradually waned, the Great Awakening had a lasting impact on colonial society. In addition to introducing colonists to a fervent evangelicalism, it forged new links between Great Britain and the colonies. Evangelical ministers on both sides of the Atlantic exchanged correspondence. Periodicals such as the *Christian History* informed British and American subscribers of advances in true religion throughout the empire.

The revivals also brought newcomers into Christian congregations. Chesapeake slaves responded to the evangelists' message and—often contrary to the intent of the white preachers—drew lessons about the equality of humankind. A few black preachers circulated in the slave quarters, spreading the message of salvation and freedom. The impact of revivalism on Indians was less dramatic, but still significant. Evangelicals enjoyed their greatest success in small Native American communities, whose inhabitants were attracted to a less formal style of preaching, particularly in New England. Native converts often urged fellow Indians to heed the Christian message of self-discipline, not to emulate English colonists, but to revitalize villages beset by alcoholism and other problems linked to European domination. Samson Occom, a Mohegan convert, worked as a missionary on Long Island. His experience of poor pay and white prejudice, however, discouraged other native converts from following his example.

The Awakening did not greatly increase women's church membership, since women already constituted majorities in many congregations. But by emphasizing the emotional power of Christianity, revivals accorded greater legitimacy to what was thought to be women's more sensitive temperament. Some women, such as Bathsheba Kingsley, were inspired by their conversions to become traveling preachers. More often, female evangelicals stayed within the bounds of social convention and limited their activities to conducting prayer meetings for other women.

Everywhere, the New Light challenge to established ministers and churches undermined habits of deference to authority. Revivalists urged colonists to think for themselves in choosing which church to join, and not just to conform to what the rest of the community did. As their churches fractured, colonists—particularly New Englanders—faced more choices than ever before in their religious lives.

The exercise of religious choice also influenced political behavior. Voters noticed whether candidates for office were New or Old Lights and cast their ballots for men on their own side. Tactics first used to mobilize religious groups—such as organizing committees and writing petitions and letters—also proved useful for political activities. The Awakening thus fostered greater political awareness and participation among colonists.

The Colonial Political World

The political legacy of the Great Awakening—particularly the emphasis on individual choice and resistance to authority—corresponded to developments in the colonial political world. For most of the seventeenth century, ties within the empire developed from trade rather than governance. But as America grew in wealth and population, king and Parliament sought to manage colonial affairs more directly.

In the late seventeenth century, upheavals on both sides of the Atlantic seemed to confirm for both colonists and Englishmen a common interest in protecting the rights and liberties derived from their shared heritage. The English overthrew King James II, and the people of New England successfully resisted the king's attempt to impose autocratic government in the colonies. But even as colonists and Englishmen asserted their common political culture at the dawn of the eighteenth century, differences in their political practices and ideas began to emerge.

The Dominion of New England and the Limits of British Control

Before 1650, England made little attempt to exert centralized control in North America. Each colony more or less

FROM THEN TO NOW

The Diversity of American Religious Life

In 2001, researchers contacted over 50,000 Americans, asking them to describe themselves in terms of their religious identification. The resulting data revealed the astonishing diversity of the religious environment in the modern United States. While just over three-quarters of the respondents identified themselves as Christians, they claimed affiliation with over twenty-five different denominations. The non-Christians comprised an equally diverse group, including about twenty additional faiths. This data reflects the enduring religious diversity that has characterized American life since colonization began. Religious diversity further increased during the eighteenth century, particularly after the Great Awakening sparked factional splits in churches and creation of new congregations. At the same time, the influx of Irish, Scots, and German immigrants added new faiths to the colonial religious mixture.

By the time of the Revolution, religious diversity had become so firmly entrenched in American life that people feared the establishment of a single state church far more than the consequences of having a multiplicity of faiths within a single nation. This fear helped inspire the First Amendment to the Constitution, with its guarantee of the "free exercise" of religion and its prohibition of any national religious establishment. The First Amendment, in turn, created the conditions under which religious diversity could flourish in America from the founding era to the present day.

This photo of an East Indian family worshiping at a Hindu temple in Pittsburgh offers vivid evidence of America's ongoing experience of religious diversity into the 21st century.

PEARSON myhistorylab

From Then to Now Online

4-1 Peter Kalm, *Travels in North America*, 1770. Kalm describes the religious scene in eighteenth-century Philadelphia.

4-2 Thomas Jefferson, *Bill for Establishing Religious Freedom*, 1777. Draft of a measure to end the Anglican Church's privileged position as a tax-supported established institution.

4-3 *Self-Described Religious Identification Among American Adults*, 1990, 2001. Survey data reveals how Americans have affiliated themselves.

The predominance of church steeples in this engraving of colonial New York's skyline testifies to the religious vitality of the city.

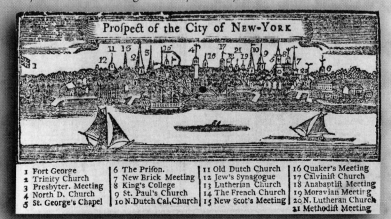

1 Fort George	6 The Prison.	11 Old Dutch Church	16 Quaker's Meeting
2 Trinity Church	7 New Brick Meeting	12 Jew's Synagogue	17 Calvinist Church
3 Presbyter. Meeting	8 King's College	13 Lutherian Church	18 Anabaptist Meeting
4 North D. Church	9 St. Paul's Church	14 The French Church	19 Moravian Meeting
5 St. George's Chapel	10 N.Dutch Cal,Church	15 New Scot's Meeting	20 N. Lutheran Church
			21 Methodist Meeting

governed itself, and most political activity occurred at the town or county level. Busy with the routines of daily life, most colonists devoted little time, and even less interest, to politics.

When Charles II became king in 1660, he initially showed little interest in the colonies except as sources of land and government offices with which he could reward his supporters. The grandest prizes, of course, were the great proprietorships, such as Pennsylvania and Carolina, but the creation of a rudimentary imperial bureaucracy also yielded rewards for the king to distribute. With the passage of mercantilist regulations, for example, Parliament created a number of jobs for customs officers.

Charles's brother James, the duke of York, envisioned a more tightly controlled empire. He encouraged Charles to appoint military officers with strong ties of loyalty to him as royal governors. In 1675, James convinced Charles to create the Lords of Trade, a committee of the Privy Council (the group of nobles who served as royal advisers), to oversee colonial affairs.

When James II became king in 1685, the whole character of the empire abruptly changed. Seeking to transform it into something much more susceptible to England's control, James set out to reorganize it along the lines of Spain's empire, combining the colonies into three or four large provinces. He appointed powerful governors to carry out policies that he himself would formulate.

James began in the north, creating the **Dominion of New England** out of eight previously separate colonies stretching from Maine (then part of Massachusetts) to New Jersey. He chose Sir Edmund Andros, a former army officer, to govern the vast region with an appointive council but no elective assembly. Andros moved to Boston and initially gained some support from merchants excluded from politics by Massachusetts's insistence that only church members could vote. But he eventually antagonized them and other New Englanders by rigidly enforcing the Navigation Acts, limiting towns to just one annual meeting, remodeling the law courts, challenging property titles, and levying taxes without the colonists' consent. He even compelled Boston Puritans to share a meetinghouse with Anglicans.

Events in England ultimately sealed the fate of the Dominion. For years, English Protestants had worried about James's absolutist governing style and his conversion to Catholicism. Their fears increased in 1688, when the queen bore a son to carry on a Catholic line of succession. Parliament's leaders invited James's Protestant daughter, Mary, and her husband, William of Orange, the stadtholder of the Netherlands, to take over the throne. In November 1688, William landed in England and gained the support of most of the English army. In December, James fled to France, ending a bloodless coup known as the **Glorious Revolution.**

Sir Edmund Andros was appointed by King James II to serve as governor of the ill-fated Dominion of New England. Sent back to England by rebellious New Englanders during the Glorious Revolution, Andros later returned to the colonies as governor of Virginia from 1692 to 1698.

Bostonians overthrew Andros the following April and shipped him back to England. Massachusetts colonists hoped that their original charter of 1629 would be reinstated, but a new one was issued in 1691. It made several important changes. Massachusetts now included the formerly separate Plymouth Colony as well as Maine. Its colonists no longer elected their governor, who would instead be appointed by the monarch. Voters no longer had to be church members, and religious toleration was extended to all Protestants.

The new charter ended exclusive Puritan control in Massachusetts but also restored political stability. During the three years between Andros's overthrow and the arrival of a royal governor in 1692, the colony lacked a legally established government. In this atmosphere of uncertainty, an outbreak of accusations of witchcraft in Salem grew to unprecedented proportions. Colonists, like most Europeans of the time, believed in the existence of witches — humans who acted as Satan's agents and used supernatural powers to hurt their enemies. Over the years, New Englanders had executed a dozen or so accused witches, usually older women. But in the winter of 1691–1692, when several young girls of Salem experienced fits and other strange behavior, hundreds of settlers were accused of witchcraft, and nineteen were hanged. Salem's crisis occurred against a backdrop of local economic change, but it gathered momentum because the Dominion crisis had generated uncertainty about political and legal authority. Special courts had to be created to deal with the witchcraft outbreak. The judges' unusual methods, including the acceptance of "spectral evidence," or accusers' uncorroborated testimony that they had seen apparitions, later aroused considerable criticism.

The impact of the Glorious Revolution in other colonies likewise reflected local conditions. In New York, after Andros's deputy left, Jacob Leisler, a rich merchant and militia captain, gained power and ruled in a dictatorial fashion, persecuting men against whom he held personal grievances. Too slow in relinquishing command to the newly arrived royal governor in 1691, Leisler was arrested for treason and executed. In Maryland, Protestants used the occasion of William and Mary's accession to the throne to lobby for the end of the Catholic proprietorship. They were partly successful. The Calvert family lost its governing powers but retained rights to vast quantities of land. The Anglican Church became the established faith, and Catholics were barred from public office.

The colonists rejected James II, not English authority in general. Their motives largely reflected powerful anti-Catholic sentiment. William's firm Protestantism reassured them, and most colonists assumed that life would return to normal. But the Glorious Revolution in England and the demise of the Dominion had long-lasting effects that shaped political life in England and America for years to come.

The Legacy of the Glorious Revolution

In England, the Glorious Revolution signaled a return to political stability after years of upheaval. English people celebrated the preservation of their rights from the threat of a tyrannical king. In 1689, Parliament passed the Bill of Rights, which justified James's ouster and bound future monarchs to abide by the rule of law. They could not suspend statutes, collect taxes, or engage in foreign wars without Parliament's consent, or maintain a standing army in peacetime. Parliamentary elections and meetings would follow a regular schedule, without royal interference. In sum, Parliament claimed to be the crown's equal partner in governing England.

Colonists, too, celebrated the vindication of their rights as Englishmen. They believed that their successful resistance to Andros confirmed that their membership in the empire was founded on voluntary allegiance, not forced submission to the mother country. Observing the similarity between Parliament and the colonial assemblies, they concluded that their own legislatures had a critical role in governance and in the protection of their rights and liberties.

On both sides of the Atlantic, representative government had triumphed.

In fact, Parliament claimed full authority over the colonies and did not recognize their assemblies as its equal. For more than a half-century, however, it did not vigorously assert that authority. In addition, William and his immediate successors lacked James's compulsion to control the colonies. William did make a few changes to the imperial administration. In 1696, he replaced the Lords of Trade with a new committee, the Board of Trade. This advisory body gathered information from the colonies and recommended policy changes but itself had no executive role. William also approved the Navigation Act of 1696, which closed loopholes in earlier laws and created vice-admiralty courts in the colonies similar to those in England. Admiralty judges settled maritime disputes and smuggling cases without using juries.

During the early eighteenth century, Parliament and royal ministers confined their attention to matters of trade and military defense and otherwise left the colonies on their own. This mild imperial rule, later called the era of "salutary neglect," allowed the colonies to grow in wealth, population, and self-government. It also encouraged colonists to assume equality with the English as members of the empire.

Diverging Politics in the Colonies and Great Britain

British people on both sides of the Atlantic believed that politics ought to reflect social organization. They often compared the state to a family. Just as fathers naturally headed families, adult men led societies. In particular, adult male property holders, who enjoyed economic independence, claimed the right to vote and hold office. Women (who generally could not own property), propertyless men, and slaves had no political role because they, like children, were subordinate to the authority of others. Their dependence on husbands, fathers, masters, or employers—who could influence their political decisions—rendered them incapable of exercising freedom of choice.

States, like families, worked best when all members fulfilled their responsibilities. Rulers ought to govern with the same fairness and benevolence that fathers should exercise within their families. In return for protection, the people owed their rulers the same obedience that children accorded their parents. Although rulers and their subjects agreed on these principles, differences could still arise when one group believed that the other failed to perform its obligations.

Eighteenth-century people also believed that government should reflect society's hierarchical organization. In Britain, this idea was embodied in the monarchy and Parliament. The crown, of course, represented the interests of the royal family. Parliament represented society's two main divisions: the aristocracy in the House of Lords and the common people in the House of Commons. Americans shared the view that government should mirror social hierarchies but found it much more difficult to put the idea into practice.

American society grew closer to the British model during the eighteenth century but was never identical to it. Thus, its political structure would never fully mirror that of Britain. One obvious difference was that America lacked an aristocracy. In Britain, the members of this tiny privileged minority were easily recognizable by their great wealth, prestigious family lines, leisured lives, and official titles of nobility. British America had elites but no titled aristocracy. Elite colonists were often just two or three generations removed from humble beginnings. Hence the acute anxiety that inspired George Washington and other colonial gentlemen to seek refinement, to gain the automatic recognition that Britain's elites enjoyed.

In both Britain and America, land ownership was the prerequisite for political participation, because it freed people from dependence on others and gave them a stake in society. In Britain, this requirement sharply limited participation. By the mid-eighteenth century, one-tenth of all English heads of households owned all the country's land, and thus only a correspondingly tiny proportion of men could vote. Landholding in America, however, was much more widespread. A majority of white male farmers eventually owned the land they tilled, and in most colonies, 50 to 75 percent of white men were eligible to vote.

Distinctive social conditions in Britain and America also gave rise to different notions of political representation. Electoral districts for Parliament came in a confusing mixture of shapes, reflecting their status in past centuries. Once-important towns sent representatives on the basis of their former prominence. Dunwich even retained its right to elect a parliamentary representative long after the city itself had washed into the North Sea. At the same time, rapidly growing cities, such as Manchester, lacked any representative at all. Some English radicals protested this inequity. Most of their countrymen, however, accepted the idea of **virtual representation,** which held that representatives served the interests of the nation as a whole, not just the locality from which they came. They maintained that since the colonists held interests in common with British people at home, they were virtually represented in Parliament, just like Manchester's residents.

Since the founding of their colonies, however, Americans had experienced **actual representation** and believed that elected representatives should be directly responsive to local interests. They were accustomed to sending written instructions to their legislators, informing them how to vote on important issues. Colonial representatives, unlike members of Parliament, resided in their districts. The Americans' experience with actual representation made them extremely skeptical of Parliament's claims to virtual representation. For the first half of the eighteenth century, however, Parliament did not press this claim, and the tensions between the two ideas remained latent.

The most direct political confrontations between Britain and the colonies instead focused on the role of colonial governors. In every colony except Connecticut and Rhode Island (where voters chose the executive), either the king or the proprietor appointed the governor. The governors' interests thus lay with their British patrons and not the colonies. More important, governors exercised great power over the colonial assemblies. Governors could veto laws enacted by the assemblies and initiate legislation in consultation with councilors whom they appointed. They could delay legislative sessions and dissolve the assemblies at will. Governors could also nominate and dismiss colonial judges.

In practice, several conditions hampered governors' efforts to exercise their legal authority. Many arrived with detailed instructions on how to govern, which limited their ability to negotiate with colonists over sensitive issues. Governors controlled few offices or other prizes to use as patronage to buy the allegiance of their opponents. They struggled to dominate assemblies that grew in size as the colonial population expanded. And in several colonies, including Massachusetts and New York, governors relied on the assemblies to appropriate the money for their salaries—a financial dependence that restrained even the most autocratic executive.

In response to the perceived, if not always realized, threat of powerful governors, colonial assemblies asserted themselves as the guarantors of colonists' liberties. They sent agents to London to lobby on behalf of colonial interests. Local factions fought for election to the legislature, leading to some of the most contentious politics in the British empire. Governors often stood on the sidelines, either frustrated with their inability to govern or, at times, enlisted on the side of one faction or another.

Despite concerns about the power of governors, most colonists accepted the loose and sometimes contradictory political ties of empire. They saw their connections to Britain as voluntary, based on common identity and rights. So long as Parliament treated them as partners in empire and refrained from ruling by coercion, colonists could celebrate British government as "the most perfect combination of human powers in society...for the preservation of liberty and the production of happiness."

By the middle of the eighteenth century, the blessings of British government extended to more colonists than ever before. The population of British America grew rapidly and spread out over vast amounts of land. The expansion of British settlement, in turn, alarmed other European powers. Both Spain and France launched new settlements as the competition for the continent entered a new and volatile phase.

Expanding Empires

During the first half of the eighteenth century, England, Spain, and France enlarged their North American holdings according to patterns established during the previous cen-

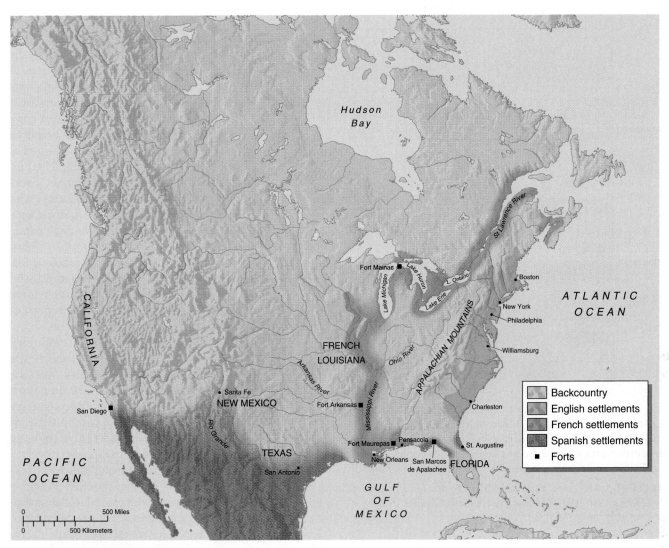

MAP 4–2 **Expanding Settlement, c. 1750**
Imperial rivalries drove Spain, France, and England to expand their North American empires in the mid-eighteenth century. Once again, this sparked conflict with native peoples as well as with European competitors.

tury. England's empire expanded in tandem with the unrelenting growth of its colonial population. Spain and France still relied on missionaries, soldiers, and traders to stake their claims to American territory. In the eighteenth century, as in the seventeenth, English settlement displaced native peoples. Newly established Spanish and French colonies, however, contained small numbers of Europeans amid much larger populations of Indians. Over time, these empires came into closer contact with one another, intensifying the competition for land, trade, resources, and Indian allies (see Map 4–2).

British Colonists in the Backcountry

Population growth in eighteenth-century British North America was truly astonishing. The non-Indian population in the mainland colonies numbered about 260,000 in 1700; by 1760, it had increased to over 1.5 million (see Figure 4–2).

Much of this growth stemmed from natural increase. Many white families, particularly in the northern colonies, had between five and ten children, most of whom survived to produce more offspring. The descendants of a single couple, after three or four generations, could people small towns. When 80-year-old Judith Coffin, the matriarch of an unusually large Massachusetts family, died in 1705, she had a total of 177 children and grandchildren. By the mid-eighteenth century, even the slave population, first in the Chesapeake and later in the Lower South, began slowly to reproduce itself.

Immigration also boosted the population. Thousands of Scots-Irish and German settlers, in addition to thousands of African slaves, helped the population of the Lower South increase at nearly twice the rate of New England, which attracted few immigrants (and therefore remained the most thoroughly English of all colonial regions). By

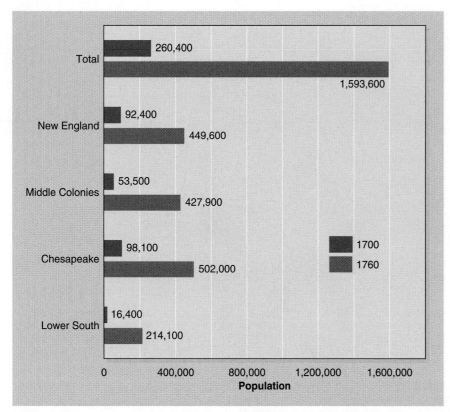

FIGURE 4–2   Population Growth in British Mainland Colonies, 1700–1760
Both natural increase and immigration contributed to a staggering rate of population growth in British North America. Some colonists predicted that Americans would soon outnumber Britain's inhabitants—a possibility that greatly concerned British officials.

Data Source: John J. McCusker and Russell R. Menard, *The Economy of British America, 1607–1789,* rev. ed. (1991). University of North Carolina Press.

1770, Pennsylvania had 240,000 settlers, ten times the number it had in 1710. Indeed, extensive German immigration worried Pennsylvania leaders like Benjamin Franklin, who feared that the newcomers would "never adopt our Language or Customs."

Most of the coast from Maine to Georgia was settled by 1760, forcing new immigrants to move inland. Descendants of earlier settlers often joined them, seeking farms that could no longer be had in the more crowded towns of their birth. New Englanders pushed up the Connecticut River Valley and into the hills of western Massachusetts. Settlement in New York followed the Hudson, Mohawk, and Schoharie rivers into the interior. But the most dramatic expansion occurred in the foothills and valleys of the Appalachian Mountains from Pennsylvania to Georgia, a region known as the backcountry.

Between 1730 and 1770, nearly a quarter of a million German, Scots-Irish, and English colonists entered the backcountry. They mainly raised crops and livestock for subsistence on small, isolated farms. Community life developed slowly, because many backcountry settlers moved frequently and a surplus of men among the first settlers delayed the formation of families.

Contemporary observers, especially eastern elites, derided the crudeness of frontier life. Their disparaging comments reflected emerging tensions between backcountry settlements and older seacoast communities. Many eastern planters acquired vast tracts of western land with the intent of selling it to these "crude" settlers. Their interests collided with those of many backcountry settlers, including squatters who occupied the land without acquiring legal title in the hope that their labor in clearing farms would establish their property rights.

Backcountry settlers often complained that the rich eastern planters who dominated the colonial legislatures ignored western demands for adequate representation. They also argued that the crudeness of frontier life was only temporary. Perhaps the best measure of their desire to resemble eastern planters was the spread of slaveholding in the backcountry. In one western Virginia county in 1750, only one-fifth of the household heads owned slaves. Just nineteen years later, more than half of them did.

Tensions grew throughout the backcountry as colonists encroached on Indian lands. Colonists who moved to Pennsylvania's Susquehanna Valley displaced Delawares, Shawnees, and other native peoples who had sought refuge there from earlier white migrations. In South Carolina, the Catawbas moved to ever more remote sites. Indians moving to avoid friction with whites, however, frequently encroached on lands claimed by other tribes—particularly those of the Iroquois Confederacy—leading to conflict among native peoples.

Even where British settlers had not yet appeared, English and Scottish traders could often be found, aggressively pursuing trade with the Indians. Spanish and French observers feared this commercial expansion even more than the movement of settlers. Knowing that the Indians viewed trade as a counterpart to military alliance, they worried that the British, with cheaper and better trade goods, would lure away their native allies. In response, the Spanish and French expanded their own territorial claims and tried to strengthen relations with Indian peoples.

The Spanish in Texas and California

Spanish Florida had become the target of English raiders from South Carolina, who attacked Spanish missions with the help of local Indians. Years of religious persecution and forced labor encouraged Florida's Indians to oppose the Spanish, but the natives also wanted English trade goods, such as guns, which Spanish traders were officially prohibited from selling. Spain maintained a precarious hold on coastal bases at St. Augustine, San Marcos de Apalachee, and Pensacola. By the mid-eighteenth century, however, control of Florida's interior effectively passed to Indian bands allied with English (and, in the west, French) traders.

In New Mexico, Spanish farmers and missionaries slowly moved back up the Rio Grande Valley. Fearful of sparking another uprising like the Pueblo Revolt, Franciscan priests eased their labor demands and avoided outright religious persecution, allowing the Pueblos to retain many of their customs and religious practices. New Mexican officials worried about news brought by Apache hunters that Frenchmen had been seen on the plains. Persistent rumors of their approach fueled Spanish fears that New Mexico would fall into French hands.

To create a buffer zone around their existing colonies, the Spanish moved into Texas and California. Franciscan priests established several missions in east Texas between 1690 and 1720. San Antonio was founded in 1718 as a waystation between the Rio Grande and the east Texas missions; its fortified chapel, San Antonio de Valero, later became famous as the Alamo. The Spanish advance into Texas, however, met with resistance from the French (who also had outposts on the Gulf Coast) and from the Caddos and other Indians armed with French guns. Efforts to fill east Texas with settlers from Spain, Cuba, and the Canary Islands failed when Spanish officials could not guarantee their safety. With only 1,800 settlers there as late as 1742, Spain exerted a weak hold on Texas.

Sixteenth-century Spaniards had considered building outposts in California to supply ships traveling between Mexico and the Philippines but were deterred by the region's remoteness. Spanish interest revived in the 1760s, when it seemed that Russia, which had built fur-trading posts in Alaska, might occupy California. Largely through the efforts of two men—José de Gálvez, a royal official, and Junípero Serra, a Franciscan priest—the Spanish constructed a string of forts and missions from San Diego north to San Francisco between 1769 and 1776.

They initially encountered little opposition from California's Indians, who lived in small, scattered villages. With no European rivals nearby, the Spanish erected an extensive mission system de-signed to convert and educate Indians and set them to work. Thousands of native laborers farmed irrigated fields and tended livestock. They did so under extremely harsh conditions.

According to one observer, Christian Indians who settled at the missions endured a fate "worse than that of slaves." The Spanish worked them hard and maintained them in overcrowded, unsanitary dwellings. Native women suffered from sexual exploitation by Spanish soldiers. Epidemics of European diseases swept through the Indian population, reducing it from 300,000 in 1769 to about 200,000 fifty years later. Signs of native resistance met with quick and cruel punishment so that the Indians would not (as one official later wrote) "come to know their power" over the vastly outnumbered Spanish. (As late as 1790, California had only 990 Spanish residents.) Indians staged several revolts during the eighteenth century, but Spanish soldiers usually suppressed them quickly.

Spain's empire grew, even as it weakened, during the eighteenth century. Its scattered holdings north of the Rio Grande functioned as colonies of another colony—Mexico—shielding it from foreign incursions. The scarcity of Spanish settlers, especially women, encouraged racial intermixture in the borderlands and ensured that racial distinctions would never be drawn as sharply there as in the English colonies. From the beginning, Spain's vision of empire had rested not on extensive settlement but on subjugation of native peoples in order to control their labor. After 1700, the limitations of this coercive approach to empire became apparent. As their experiences in Florida

An idealized depiction of a California mission, this engraving shows pious Indian converts kneeling before a procession of Spanish clergy. Conditions for native peoples living in the missions were often much harsher than this image suggests.

American Views

An English Minister Visits the Backcountry

In 1766, Charles Woodmason, a newly ordained Anglican minister, embarked on a six-year-long tour to bring religion to backcountry settlers. Born in England, he came to the colonies around 1752, settling first in Charleston, South Carolina. He lived in the area as a planter and merchant for more than a decade before deciding on a career in the ministry. Assigned to work in the backcountry, he was shocked to find crude living conditions and ethnically diverse settlers with little or no knowledge of religion. As the following excerpt shows, the journal Woodmason kept during these years contains a fascinating mix of his observations and prejudices.

- How does Woodmason characterize the behavior of backcountry settlers?
- What is Woodmason's opinion of the settlers' religious beliefs?
- How accurately do you think Woodmason's account reflects backcountry society? To what extent did his identity as an English-born gentleman shape his impressions of the region?

In this Circuit of a fortnight I've eaten Meat but thrice, and drank nought but Water—Subsisting on my Bisket and Rice Water and Musk Melons, Cucumbers, Green Apples and Peaches and such Trash. By which am reduc'd very thin. It is impossible that any Gentleman not season'd to the Clime, could sustain this…. Nor is this a Country, or place where I would wish any Gentleman to travel, or settle…. [The settlers'] Ignorance and Impudence is so very high, as to be past bearing—Very few can read—fewer write…. They are very Poor—owing to their extreme Indolence for they possess the finest Country in America, and could raise but ev'ry thing. They delight in their present low, lazy, sluttish, heathenish, hellish Life, and seem not desirous of changing it. Both Men and Women will do any thing to come at Liquor, Cloaths, furniture, &c. &c. rather than work for it….

It is very few families whom I can bring to join in Prayer, because most of them are of various Opinions the Husband a Churchman, Wife, a Dissenter, Children nothing at all…. Few or no Books are to be found in all this vast Country…. Nor do they delight in Historical Books or in having them read to them, as do our Vulgar in England for these People despise Knowledge, and instead of honouring a Learned Person, or any one of Wit or Knowledge be it in the Arts, Sciences, or Languages, they despise and Ill treat them—And this Spirit prevails even among the Principals of this Province…. [At Flatt Creek] I found a vast Body of People assembled—Such a Medley! such a mixed Multitude of all Classes and Complexions I never saw. I baptized about 20 Children and Married 4 Couple—Most of these People had never before seen a Minister, or heard the Lords Prayer, Service, or Sermon in their Days. I was a Great Curiosity to them—And they were as great Oddities to me. After Service they went to Revelling Drinking Singing Dancing and Whoring—and most of the Company were drunk before I quitted the Spot—They were as rude in their Manners as the Common Savages, and hardly a degree removed from them.

Source: Richard J. Hooker, ed., *The Carolina Backcountry on the Eve of the Revolution: The Journal and Other Writings of Charles Woodmason, Anglican Itinerant* (Chapel Hill, 1953), pp. 52–56.

and Texas demonstrated, the Spanish simply could not compete with the vigorous commercial empires of France and England.

The French along the Mississippi and in Louisiana

French expansion followed the major waterways of the St. Lawrence River, the Great Lakes, and the Mississippi into the heart of North America. Explorers reached the Mississippi Valley in the 1670s. Within twenty years, French outposts appeared along the Gulf Coast. New Orleans, the main port of French Louisiana, was founded in 1718. Soon forts, trading posts, and villages sprang up in the continent's interior and formed a chain of way stations between Canada and the Gulf of Mexico. Concerned about defending scattered settlements, French officials forbade colonists to move into the interior. But colonists went anyway, building six villages along the Mississippi in a place they called the *pays des Illinois.*

The first Illinois settlers were independent fur traders (*coureurs de bois,* or "woods runners") unwilling to return to Canada after the French government tried to prohibit their direct trade with Indians. Many found Christian Indian wives and farmed the rich lands along the river. The settlers, using the labor of their families and of black and Indian slaves, produced surpluses of wheat, corn, and livestock to feed the growing population of New Orleans and the lower Mississippi Valley.

French Louisiana contained a remarkably diverse population of Indian peoples, French soldiers and settlers, and German immigrants, as well as African slaves, who by the 1730s outnumbered the European colonists. Settlers and slaves raised some tobacco and indigo as cash crops, but Louisiana's economy depended mainly on food crops, herding, fishing, and the deerskin trade. Discouraged by the lack of profits, French officials and merchants neglected Louisiana, and even Catholic missionaries failed to establish a strong presence. Significant European emigration to Louisiana essentially ceased after the 1720s.

But the French approach to empire in Louisiana as in Canada depended more on Indian alliances than on settlement. Louisiana's principal allies were the Choctaws, whom one military official called "the bulwark of the colony." The Choctaws and other native allies offered trade and military assistance in return for guns, trade goods, French help in fighting British raiders seeking Indian slaves, and occasional French mediation of Indian disputes.

French expansion along the Mississippi Valley drove a wedge between Florida and Spain's other mainland colonies; it also blocked the westward movement of English settlers. But France's enlarged empire was only as strong as the Indian alliances on which it rested. Preserving good relations was expensive, however, requiring the constant exchange of diplomatic gifts and trade goods. When France ordered Louisiana officials to limit expenses and reduce Indian gifts in 1745, the officials objected that the Choctaws "would ask for nothing better than to have such pretexts in order to resort to the English."

The fear of losing Indian favor preoccupied officials in 1745 because at that moment France's empire in America consisted of two disconnected pieces: New France, centered in the St. Lawrence Valley and the Great Lakes basin, and Louisiana, stretching from New Orleans to the *pays des Illinois.* Between them lay a thousand miles of wilderness, through which only one thoroughfare passed—the Ohio River. For decades, communication between the two parts of France's North American empire had posed no problem because Indians in the Ohio Valley allowed the French free passage through their lands. If that policy ended, however, France's New World empire would be dangerously divided.

A Century of Warfare

The expansion of empires in North America reflected the policies of European states locked in a relentless competition for power and wealth. From the time of the Glorious Revolution, English foreign policy aimed at limiting the expansion of French influence. This, in turn, resulted in a series of four wars. As the eighteenth century wore on, the conflicts between the two countries increasingly involved their American colonies as well as Spain and its colonies. The outcome of each of the wars in America depended no less on the participation of colonists and Indians than on the policies and strategies of the European powers. The conclusion of the final conflict signaled a dramatic shift in North American history (see the Overview table, The Colonial Wars, 1689–1763).

Imperial Conflict and the Establishment of an American Balance of Power, 1689–1738

When he became king of England in 1688, the Dutch Protestant William of Orange was already fighting the War of the League of Augsburg against France's Catholic king, Louis XIV. Almost immediately, William brought England into the conflict. The war lasted until 1697 and ended, as most European wars of this period did, in a negotiated peace that reestablished the balance of power. Little territory changed hands, either in this war or in the War of the Spanish Succession (1702–1713), which followed it.

In America, these two imperial wars—known to British colonists as **King William's War** and **Queen Anne's War,** after the monarchs on the throne at the time—ended with equal indecisiveness. New France's Indian allies attacked New England's northern frontier, destroying the Massachusetts town of Deerfield in 1704. New Englanders struck back at the exposed settlements of Acadia, which ultimately entered the British Empire as Nova Scotia, and tried unsuccessfully to seize Quebec. Neither war caused more than marginal changes for the colonies in North America. Both had profound effects, however, on the English state and the Iroquois League.

All European states of the eighteenth century financed their wars by borrowing. But the English were the first to realize that wartime debts did not necessarily have to be repaid during the following peace. The government instead created a funded debt. Having borrowed heavily from large joint-stock corporations, the government used tax revenues to pay the interest on the loans but not to pay off the loans themselves. The corporations accepted this because the interest payments amounted to a steady income that over the long run could amount to more than the original loans. In this way, England became the first European country to harness its national economy efficiently to military ends.

As the debt grew larger, more taxes were necessary to pay interest on it. Taxes also rose to pay for a powerful navy

OVERVIEW

The Colonial Wars, 1689–1763

Name in the Colonies	European Name and Dates	Dates in America	Results for Britain
King William's War	War of the League of Augsburg, 1688–1697	1689–1697	Reestablished balance of power between England and France
Queen Anne's War	War of the Spanish Succession, 1702–1714	1702–1713	Britain acquired Nova Scotia
King George's War	War of the Austrian Succession, 1739–1748	1744–1748	Britain returned Louisbourg to France British settlers began moving westward Weakening of Iroquois neutrality
French and Indian War	Seven Years' War, 1756–1763	1754–1763	Britain acquired Canada and all French territory east of Mississippi Britain gained Florida from Spain

and a standing army. When the treasury created a larger bureaucracy to collect taxes, many Englishmen grew nervous. Their anxiety emerged as a strain of thought known as **Country**, or **"Real Whig," ideology**. Country ideology stressed the threats that a standing army and a powerful state posed to personal liberty. It also emphasized the dangers of taxation to property rights and the need for property holders to retain their right to consent to taxation. Real Whig politicians publicized their fears but could not stop the growth of the state. In every successive war, the claims of national interest and patriotism—and the prospect of profit for parties rich enough to lend money to the government—overrode the objections of those who feared the expansion of state power.

In America, the first two imperial wars transformed the role of the Iroquois League. During King William's War, the Iroquois allied with the English, but received little help from them when the French and their Indian allies attacked Iroquois villages. By 1700, the Iroquois League had suffered such horrendous losses—perhaps a quarter of the population had died from causes related to the war—that its leaders sought an alternative to direct alliance with the English.

With the **Grand Settlement of 1701**, the Iroquois adopted a policy of neutrality with regard to the French and British empires. Their goal was to refrain from alliances with either European power and instead maneuver between them. The Iroquois's strategic location between New France and the English colonies allowed them to serve as a geographical and diplomatic buffer. Neutral Iroquois diplomats could play the English against the French, gaining favors from one side

in return for promises not to ally with the other. This neutralist policy ensured that for nearly fifty years neither Britain nor France could gain ascendancy in North America.

Iroquois neutrality offered benefits to the Europeans as well as the Indians. The British began to negotiate with them for land. The Iroquois claimed sovereignty over much of the country west of the Middle and Chesapeake colonies. To smooth relations with the British, the Iroquois sold them land formerly occupied by Delawares and Susquehannocks. These transactions helped to satisfy the colonists' land hunger and to enrich the Iroquois League.

Meanwhile a neutral Iroquois League claiming control over the Ohio Valley and blocking British access across the Appalachian Mountains helped the French protect the strategic corridor that linked Canada and Louisiana. If the British ever established a permanent presence in the Ohio Valley, however, the Iroquois would cease to be of use to the French. The Iroquois remained reasonably effective at keeping the British out of the valley until the late 1740s. The next European war, however, altered these circumstances.

King George's War Shifts the Balance, 1739–1754

The third confrontation between Britain and France in Europe, the War of the Austrian Succession—**King George's War** to the British colonists—began as a small war between Britain and Spain in 1739. Its immediate cause was British attempts to poach on trade to Spain's Caribbean colonies. But in 1744, France joined in the war against Britain and conflict once again erupted in North America.

New Englanders saw yet another chance to attack Canada. This time their target was the great fortress of Louisbourg on Cape Breton Island, a naval base that dominated the Gulf of St. Lawrence. An expedition from Massachusetts and Connecticut, supported by a squadron of Royal Navy warships, captured Louisbourg in 1745. This success cut Canada off from French reinforcement. English forces should now have been able to conquer New France.

Instead, politically influential merchants in Albany, New York, chose to continue their profitable trade with the enemy across Lake Champlain, enabling Canada to hold out until the end of the war. When the peace treaty was signed in 1748, Britain, which had fared badly in the European fighting, returned Louisbourg to France. This diplomatic adjustment, routine by European standards, shocked New Englanders. At the same time, New York's illegal trade with the enemy appalled British administrators. They began thinking of ways to prevent such independent behavior in any future war.

King George's War furnished an equal share of shocks for New France, which had suffered more than in any previous conflict. Even before the war's end, traders from Pennsylvania began moving west to buy furs from Indians who had once traded with the French. The movements of these traders, along with the appearance of Virginians in the Ohio Valley after 1748, gravely concerned the French.

In 1749, the governor general of New France set out to assert direct control over the region by building a series of forts from Lake Erie to the Forks of the Ohio (where the Monongahela and Allegheny Rivers meet to form the Ohio River). This decision signaled the end of France's commitment to Iroquois neutrality. The Iroquois now found themselves trapped between empires edging closer to confrontation in the Ohio Valley.

The Iroquois, in fact, had never exerted direct power in the Ohio Country. Their control instead depended on their ability to dominate the peoples who actually lived there—western Senecas, as well as Delawares and Shawnees, in theory Iroquois dependents. The appearance of English traders in the valley offering goods on better terms than the French or the Iroquois had ever provided undermined Iroquois dominance.

The Ohio Valley Indians increasingly pursued their own independent course. One spur to their disaffection from the Iroquois was the 1744 **Treaty of Lancaster,** by which Iroquois chiefs had sold the rights to trade at the Forks of the Ohio to Virginia land speculators. The Virginians assumed that these trading rights included the right to acquire land for eventual sale to settlers. The Ohio Valley Indians found this situation intolerable, as did the French. When, in 1754, the government of Virginia sent out a small body of soldiers under Lieutenant Colonel George Washington to protect Virginia's claim to the Forks of the Ohio, the French struck back.

The French and Indian War, 1754–1760: A Decisive Victory

In April 1754, French soldiers overwhelmed a group of Virginians who had been building a small fort at the Forks of the Ohio. They erected a much larger fort of their own, Fort Duquesne, on the spot. The French intended to follow up by similarly ousting Washington's weak, untrained troops, who had encamped farther up the Monongahela River. However, at the end of May, Washington's men killed or captured all but one member of a small French reconnaissance party. The French decided to teach the Virginians a lesson. On July 3, they attacked Washington at Fort Necessity, forcing him to surrender.

Even before this news reached Britain, imperial officials worried that the Iroquois might ally with the French. Britain ordered New York's governor to convene an intercolonial meeting in Albany—known as the Albany Congress—

Sauvage Iroquois

The Iroquois policy of neutrality prevented either Britain or France from dominating the Ohio Valley for the first half of the eighteenth century. The outbreak of the French and Indian War destroyed that delicate diplomatic balance. During the war, which led to France's loss of its North American empire, Iroquois warriors such as the man depicted here generally fought on Britain's side.

to discuss matters with the Iroquois. Several prominent colonists, including Governor William Shirley of Massachusetts and Benjamin Franklin, took advantage of the occasion to put forward the **Albany Plan of Union,** which called for an intercolonial union to coordinate defense, levy taxes, and regulate Indian affairs. But the colonies, too suspicious of one another to see their common interests, rejected the Albany Plan, which British officials also disliked. Meanwhile, events in the west took a turn for the worse.

The French expulsion of the Virginians left the Indians of the region, Delawares and Shawnees, with no choice but to ally with the French in what came to be called the French and Indian War (see Map 4–3). Soon French and Indian attacks fell like hammer blows on backcountry settlements from Pennsylvania to the Carolinas. The Iroquois tried to remain neutral, but their neutrality no longer mattered. Europeans were at last contending directly for control of the Ohio Country.

The **French and Indian War** blazed in America for two years before it erupted as a fourth Anglo-French war in Europe in 1756. Known in Europe as the Seven Years' War (1756–1763), it involved fighting in the Caribbean, Africa, India, and the Philippine Islands as well as in Europe and North America. It was unlike any other eighteenth-century conflict, not only in its immense scope and expense but also in its decisive outcome.

The war had two phases in North America—1754 to 1758 and 1758 through 1760. During the first phase, the French enjoyed a string of successes as they followed their proven strategy—guerrilla war. Relying on Indian allies acting with Canadian soldiers, the French raided British frontier settlements, killing and capturing hundreds of civilians and forcing tens of thousands more to flee. Then they attacked fortified outposts whenever possible. This style of warfare allowed the Canadians' Indian allies to act independently in choosing targets and tactics.

The first full campaign of the war, in 1755, saw not only the British colonial frontiers collapsing in terror but also a notable defeat inflicted on the troops Britain had dispatched to attack Fort Duquesne. The British commander in chief, Major General Edward Braddock, with immense self-confidence and no real knowledge of the countryside or his enemy, marched to within 10 miles of Fort

Duquesne, only to have his 1,450-man force surrounded and destroyed by Indians and Canadian militiamen. Braddock's defeat set the tone for virtually every military engagement of the next three years and opened a period of demoralization and internal conflict in the British colonies.

Britain responded to Braddock's defeat by sending a new commander in chief with more trained British soldiers. The new commander, Lord Loudoun, insisted on managing every aspect of the war effort, not only directing the campaigns but also dictating the amount of support, in men and money, that each colony would provide. Colonial soldiers, who had volunteered to serve under their own officers, objected to Loudoun's command. By the end of 1757, a year of disastrous military campaigns, colonial assemblies were also refusing to cooperate.

Britain's aim had been to "rationalize" the war by making it conform to European professional military standards. This approach required soldiers to advance in formation in

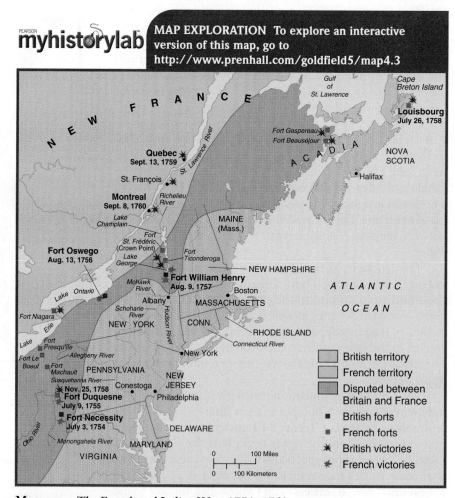

MAP 4–3   The French and Indian War, 1754–1763
Most of the battles of the French and Indian War occurred in the frontier regions of northern and western New York and the Ohio Valley. The influx of settlers into these areas created tensions that eventually developed into war.

Global Perspectives

Tea and Empire

We went ashore [near Greenwich, New York] to fill water near a small log cottage on the west side of the river inhabited by one Stanespring and his family.... This cottage was very clean and neat but poorly furnished. Yet Mr. Milne observed severall superfluous things which showed an inclination to finery in these poor people, such as a looking glass with a painted frame, half a dozen pewter spoons and as many plates,... a set of stone tea dishes, and a tea pot. These, Mr. Milne said, were superfluous and too splendid for such a cottage.... As for the tea equipage it was quite unnecessary....

Source: Wendy Martin, ed., *Colonial American Travel Narratives* (New York, 1994), p. 216.

Alexander Hamilton, a Scottish physician, made this observation while traveling from Maryland to New Hampshire in 1744. Few colonists would have agreed that the family's teapot and dishes were "quite unnecessary." By the eighteenth century, many colonists—even residents of Philadelphia's poorhouse—regarded tea as an essential part of their diet. How had a beverage from a native Chinese plant become commonplace in towns and villages located thousands of miles away? The answer lies in the expanding network of British commerce. By the start of the eighteenth century, Britain's East India Company had established a thriving trade in tea and silks with Chinese merchants in Canton. Large ships, specially designed to withstand the rigors of lengthy voyages around Africa's Cape of Good Hope, carried more tea every year. Imports rose from 50 tons in 1700 to 15,000 tons by 1800. Increased supplies meant that tea became affordable for all classes of British subjects and colonists. Poorer folk relied on the mild stimulant to help them endure hard days at work. For wealthier people, drinking tea became a marker of sociability. This was especially true for women, whose elegant tea parties offered opportunities to display fine porcelain tea pots and cups, silver or pewter spoons, sugar tongs, and other equipment. Until factories began producing porcelain in Britain itself, British and colonial consumers sipped their tea from cups that arrived as ballast aboard the East India Company ships. Only with the onset of the Revolutionary movement, when British taxes on tea discouraged colonial purchases, did American consumers reject the beverage that had previously linked them with Great Britain and, by extension, a commercial empire that virtually circled the globe.

- ■ **Why might Alexander Hamilton have thought it unsuitable for a poor family to drink tea?**

---

the face of massed musket fire without breaking rank. It needed iron discipline, which was enforced—as in the British army—by savage punishments, including hundreds of lashes at the whipping post. Few colonial volunteers met professional standards, and few colonists thought them necessary, especially when British soldiers suffered defeat after defeat at the hands of French and Indian guerrillas. British officers assumed that colonial soldiers were simply lazy cowards. But colonial volunteers saw British officers as brutal taskmasters. They resisted all efforts to impose such discipline on their own units, even to the point of desertion and mutiny.

Despite the astonishing success of their guerrilla tactics, the French, too, began moving toward a more European style of warfare. In the process, they destroyed their strategic and tactical advantages. In 1756, the Marquis de Montcalm assumed command of French forces. In his first battle, the successful siege of Fort Oswego, New York, Montcalm was horrified by the behavior of his Indian allies, who killed wounded prisoners, took personal captives, and collected scalps as trophies. He came to regard the Indians—so essential to the defense of New France—as mere savages.

Following his next victory, the capture of Fort William Henry, New York, Montcalm conformed to European practice by allowing the defeated garrison to go home in return for the promise not to fight again. Montcalm's Indian allies, a thousand or more strong, were not to take prisoners, trophies, or plunder. The tragic result came to be known as the Massacre of Fort William Henry. Feeling betrayed by their French allies, the Indians took captives and trophies anyway. This action not only outraged the New England colonies (most of the victims were New Englanders) but also alienated the Indians on whom the defense of Canada depended. Ironically, Montcalm's efforts to limit the war's violence—to impose European standards of conduct—prepared the way for the British army and its colonial auxiliaries to win.

For at the same time that the Europeanization of the war was weakening the French, the British moderated their policies and reached accommodation with the colonists. A remarkable politician came to power in London as England's chief war minister. William Pitt, who as secretary of state directed the British war effort from late 1757 through 1761, realized that friction arose from the colonists' sense that they were bearing all the financial burdens of the war without having any say in how the war was fought. Pitt's ingenious solution was to promise reimbursements to the colonies in proportion to their contribution to the war effort, reduce the power of the commander in chief, and replace the arrogant Loudoun with a less objectionable officer.

Pitt's money and measures restored colonial morale and launched the second phase of the war. He sent thousands of British soldiers to America to fight alongside colonial troops. As the Anglo-American forces grew stronger, they operated more successfully, seizing Louisbourg again in 1758. Once more, Canada experienced crippling shortages of supplies. But this time, the Anglo-Americans were united and able to take advantage of the situation. British emissaries persuaded the Delawares and Shawnees to abandon their French alliance, and late in 1758, an Anglo-American force again marched on Fort Duquesne. In command of its lead battalion was Colonel George Washington. The French defenders, abandoned by their native allies and confronted by overwhelming force, blew up the fort and retreated to the Great Lakes.

From this point on, the Anglo-Americans suffered no setbacks, and the French won no victories. The war became a contest in which the larger, better-supplied army would triumph. Montcalm, forced back to Quebec, decided to risk everything in a European-style, open-field battle against a British force led by General James Wolfe. At the Battle of Quebec (September 13, 1759), Montcalm lost the gamble—and his life (as did the victorious General Wolfe).

The French had not yet lost the war. If they could revive their Indian alliances, they still had a chance. What finally decided the outcome of the war in America was not the Battle of Quebec but two other developments: the Battle of Quiberon Bay in France (November 20, 1759) and the Iroquois's decision to join the Anglo-American side in 1760. The sea battle cost the French navy its ability to operate in the Atlantic, preventing it from reinforcing Canada. Montcalm's successor could not rebuild the Indian alliances he so desperately needed. At the same time, the Iroquois decision to enter the war on the Anglo-

American side tipped the balance irrevocably against the French. The last defenders of Canada surrendered on September 8, 1760.

The Triumph of the British Empire, 1763

The war pitting Britain against France and Spain (which had entered the fighting as a French ally in 1762) concluded with an uninterrupted series of British victories. In the Caribbean, where every valuable sugar island the French owned came under British control, the culminating event was the surrender of Havana on August 13, 1762. Even more spectacular was Britain's capture of the Philippine capital of Manila on October 5—a victory that literally carried British power around the world.

These conquests created the unshakable conviction that British arms were invincible. An immense surge of British patriotism spread throughout the American colonies. When news of the conquest of Havana reached Massachusetts, bells rang, cannons fired salutes, and bonfires blazed. General John Winslow of Plymouth, a portly man, rejoiced by be-

This, the earliest known portrait of George Washington, was painted by Charles Willson Peale in 1772. It depicts him in his military uniform from the French and Indian War. Military service helped to strengthen Washington's ties with the British Empire.

Washington/Custis/Lee Collection, Washington and Lee University, Lexington, VA.

MAP 4–4   **European Empires in North America, 1750–1763**
Great Britain's victory in the French and Indian War transformed the map of North America. France lost its mainland colonies, England claimed all lands east of the Mississippi, and Spain gained nominal control over the Trans-Mississippi West.

coming "so intoxicated as to jump on the table, and break a great number of bowls."

Hostilities ended formally on February 10, 1763, with the conclusion of the **Treaty of Paris.** France regained its West Indian sugar islands—its most valuable colonial possessions—but lost the rest of its North American empire. France ceded to Britain all its claims to lands east of the Mississippi River (except the city of New Orleans) and compensated Spain for the losses it had sustained as an ally by handing over all claims to the Trans-Mississippi West and the port of New Orleans (see Map 4–4). Britain returned Cuba and the Philippines to Spain and in compensation received Florida. Now Great Britain owned everything east of the Mississippi, from the Gulf of Mexico to Hudson's Bay. With France and Spain both humbled and on the verge of financial collapse, Britain seemed preeminent in Europe and ready to dominate in the New World. Never before had Americans felt more pride in being British, members of the greatest empire on earth.

Conclusion

The George Washington who ordered a suit from England in 1763 longed to be part of the elite of the great British empire. If he feared any threat to his position in that elite, it was not Parliament and the king but the uncomfortably large debts he owed to his London agents or perhaps the unruly Baptists who challenged the superiority of the great planters. But such worries, though real, were merely small, nagging doubts, shared by most of his fellow planters.

What was more real to Washington was the great victory that the British had just gained over France, a victory that he had helped to achieve. For Washington, as for virtually all other colonial leaders, 1763 was a moment of great promise and patriotic devotion to the British empire. It was a time to rejoice in the fundamental British identity and liberty and rights that seemed to ensure that life in the colonies would be better and more prosperous than ever.

In his most famous painting, American artist Benjamin West depicted the death of the British general James Wolfe at the Battle of Quebec. He portrays Wolfe as a glorious martyr to the cause of British victory. In the left foreground, West added the figure of an Indian, a "noble savage" who contemplates the meaning of Wolfe's selfless sacrifice of his life.

Benjamin West (1738–1820), "The Death of General Wolfe," 1770, Oil on canvas, 152.6 × 214.5 cm. Transfer from the Canadian War Memorials, 1921 (Gift of the 2nd Duke of Westminster, Eaton Hall, Cheshire, 1918). National Gallery of Canada, Ottawa, Ontario.

Review Questions

1. Why did George Washington prefer to order a suit from London rather than trust a Virginia tailor to make him one? How does his decision reflect elite colonists' attitudes about American society and culture in the eighteenth century?

2. In what ways did economic ties between Britain and the colonies grow closer in the century after 1660?

3. What was the Great Awakening, and what impact did it have? How did it affect different groups in colonial society?

4. In what ways were colonial and British political ideas and practices similar? In what ways were they different?

5. Why did England, Spain, and France renew their competition for North America in the eighteenth century?

6. What role did warfare play in North America in the eighteenth century? What role did the Iroquois play?

Key Terms

Actual representation (p. 102)

Age of Enlightenment (p. 95)

Albany Plan of Union (p. 110)

Country, or "Real Whig," ideology (p. 108)

Dominion of New England (p. 100)

Enumerated products (p. 87)

French and Indian War (p. 110)

Glorious Revolution (p. 100)

Grand Settlement of 1701 (p. 108)

Recommended Reading

Anderson, Fred. *Crucible of War: The Seven Years' War and the Fate of Empire in British North America, 1754–1766* (2000). A vivid narrative of the last great imperial war.

Bushman, Richard L. *The Refinement of America: Persons, Houses, Cities* (1992). A sophisticated exploration of the quest for gentility in early America.

Franklin, Benjamin. *Autobiography* (numerous editions). The classic account of Franklin's rise from poor beginnings to prominence in colonial Philadelphia.

McCusker, John J., and Russell R. Menard. *The Economy of British America, 1607–1789,* rev. ed. (1991). The most comprehensive study of the economies of each colonial region.

Stout, Harry S. *The Divine Dramatist: George Whitefield and the Rise of Modern Evangelicalism* (1991). A thorough account of Whitefield's career and the religious context in which it occurred.

Where to Learn More

■ **Colonial Williamsburg, Williamsburg, Virginia.** A reconstruction of the capital of eighteenth-century Virginia, this site covers 173 acres and contains many restored and rebuilt structures, including houses, churches, the House of Burgesses, and the Governor's Palace. Many educational and cultural programs are available. Historical interpreters, dressed in period costume, provide information about eighteenth-century Chesapeake life. The website www.colonialwilliamsburg.com/history/index.cfm has a variety of links that include biographical information on eighteenth-century residents of Williamsburg, aspects of colonial life, and material culture. The link to "Electronic Field Trips" has information on how to arrange for an interactive television program and special Internet activities.

■ **Mount Vernon, Virginia.** Site of George Washington's much-refurbished home. There is also a reconstructed gristmill and barn, as well as various outbuildings. Exhibits include information on Washington's agricultural experiments. The website www.mountvernon.org offers virtual tours of the house and grounds, as well as information on "George Washington, Pioneer Farmer."

■ **Johnson Hall, Johnstown, New York.** Eighteenth-century home of William Johnson, who served as superintendent of Indian affairs and directed much of Britain's diplomacy with the Iroquois. Biographical information and pictures can be found at the website www.johnstown.com/city/johnson.html.

■ **Berkeley and Westover Plantations, Charles City, Virginia.** These two eighteenth-century James River plantations suggest the elegance of elite planters' lives. The house and grounds at Berkeley are open to the public, the grounds only at Westover, the home of William Byrd. Pictures, descriptions of the sites, and background on their owners can be found at www.jamesriverplantations.org, which has links to each plantation.

Study Resources

For study resources for this chapter, go to www.myhistorylab.com and choose *The American Journey.* You will find a wealth of study and review material for this chapter, including pre- and post-tests, customized study plan, key term review flash cards, interactive map and document activities, and documents for analysis.

Having apparently originated in a May Day–like celebration of the repeal of the Stamp Act in the spring of 1766, liberty poles were particularly characteristic of New York City, where citizens of all social classes supported their erection (as in the picture). However, British soldiers repeatedly destroyed them, thereby prompting serious rioting. Elsewhere, liberty trees served similar symbolic functions. John C. McRae of New York published this print in 1875.

Imperial Breakdown 5
1763–1774

Philadelphia, January 1774

My Dear Jack,

Your Uncle wrote the 27 Dec. by Capt. Ayres who brought the Tea. His ship came within four miles of this City on Sunday the 26th where she was stopped, not being suffered to come any farther. ... The inhabitants sent a Supply of fresh provisions & a Pilot on board [who put them on course for England]. I believe they were glad they came off so well, for at Boston they threw it all into the River, and it would have gone near to have shared the same fate here, but the Capt. had more prudence than to endeavour to force a landing by which means he prevented a great deal of Mischief & Confusion, for they were all determined to oppose it. They think now that the India Company will get the Act which imposes a duty of 3d per pound repealed and then send more over.

Kensington, September 19, 1774

Dear Jack,

The Congress [The First Continental Congress] are now Setting here & have been a fortnight but nothing Transpires. All is kept a profound Secret. There was a [false] report the other day of the Town of Boston being Bombarded by the Men of War lying off the Town ... which Occasioned a general consternation along the Continent, and in some parts of the Country they Armed and Marched to the Number of 15,000 & more were getting ready. ... In Short the Provinces are determined one and all to stand by each other. What the Consequences will be we don't know.

Kensington, Nov 1, 1774

My Dear Jack,

Our Congress are broke up and are come to a great Spirited Resolves ... together with a petition to his Majestie. ... It is to be published and they have bound themselves to abide by those resolves ... and if Necessitated to repel force with force. All Importation ceases after the first of December next.

Kensington, June 28, 1775

My Dear Jack,

All the Provinces [are] arming and Training in the same Manner, for they are all determined to die or be Free. ... God knows how it will end but I fear it will be very bad on both sides, and if your drivalish minestry and parliament dont make some concessions and Repeal the Acts, England will lose America for as I said before they are determined to be free.

Eliza Farmar

Pennsylvania Magazine of History and Biography, vol. 40 (1916): 199–207.

myhistorylab
PEARSON

Personal Journeys Online

- Mary Ambler, *Diary of M. Ambler*, 1770. This memoir records Ambler's trip to Baltimore to have her two young children inoculated for smallpox.

- Reverend John Ettwein, *Notes of Travel from the North Branch of the Susquehanna to the Beaver River, Pennsylvania*, 1772. This journal recorded the journey of about one hundred Christianized Indians through western Pennsylvania to their new homes at the village of Friedenstadt.

- Nicholas Cresswell, *The Journal of Nicholas Cresswell, 1774–1777*. A prospective immigrant sails, having decided to go to America, but the Revolution changes his mind.

Eliza Farmar and her family had recently moved to Kensington, a suburb of Philadelphia, when she wrote these letters, and her ties to relatives in England remained strong. Jack, the recipient of these letters, was her nephew and a clerk in the London office of the East India Company, whose shipment of tea precipitated the Boston Tea Party. Although she hoped that he might come to America, she minced no words in emphasizing the determination of Americans to resist British measures that appeared to infringe upon their freedoms. These letters accordingly chronicle a psychological counterpart to her move to Kens-

ington. She began both journeys as an English subject; she ended them as an American citizen. Her initial reports of political developments, though sympathetic to the colonial point of view, were fairly objective, but by the eve of the Revolution she had disowned the British government.

Like most colonists, she started out proud to be a British subject and part of Britain's increasingly powerful empire. Americans had fought the king's enemies as well as their own in a series of imperial wars and had gloried in British successes. But over the course of the eighteenth century, they had also developed a sense of their identity as Americans. Largely governing themselves through their own legislatures, they believed that they enjoyed all the rights of British subjects anywhere.

But in the wake of the French and Indian War, British officials found themselves with a burdensome debt and vastly increased territory to administer. In response, they attempted to change the way they governed the colonies and, for the first time, imposed direct taxes on the colonists. Most Americans saw these measures as violations of their rights and opposed them, although they disagreed over how far to carry their resistance.

Imperial Reorganization

At the close of the French and Indian War, British officials adopted a new and ultimately disastrous course in dealing with America. Lacking experience and led by the young and somewhat naive new monarch, George III, they took measures that worked mostly to the disadvantage of the colonies. As one contemporary critic observed, "A great Empire and little minds go ill together."

British Problems

Britain's empire in 1763 was immense, and the problems its rulers faced were correspondingly large. Its territories in North America stretched from Hudson's Bay to the Caribbean Sea and from the Atlantic Ocean to the Mississippi River. Britain also had possessions in the Mediterranean region, Africa, and India. It still faced threats, if diminished ones, from its traditional European enemies. French territory on the North American mainland had been reduced to two tiny islands in the Gulf of St. Lawrence. But France would be eager for revenge, and French inhabitants in the recently acquired territories might prove disloyal to their new rulers in any future war between the two countries.

Spain was less powerful militarily than France but a more significant presence on the North American mainland. At the end of the French and Indian War, it surrendered East

CHRONOLOGY

1759–1761	Cherokee War takes place.
1760	George III becomes king.
1761–1762	Writs of Assistance case in Massachusetts.
1761–1769	British, French, German, Russian, and American astronomers observe transit of Venus across the sun.
1763	Peace of Paris ends French and Indian War.
	Spanish accelerate imperial reforms.
	British troops remain in America.
	Proclamation Line of 1763 limits western expansion of colonial settlement.
	Pontiac's Rebellion begins.
	Paxton Boys murder peaceful Indians.
	Virginia Court decides Parson's Cause.
1764	Sugar Act passed.
	Currency Act passed.
1765	Quartering Act passed.
	Stamp Act passed.
	Stamp Act Congress meets in New York.
1766	Stamp Act repealed; Declaratory Act passed.
	New York Assembly refuses to comply with Quartering Act.
1767	Townshend duties imposed.
	Regulator movements begin in North and South Carolina.
1769	James Watt, a British inventor, patents a steam engine.
1769–1770	Famine kills one-third of the population in Bengal, India.
1770	Boston Massacre takes place.
	Tea duty retained, other Townshend duties repealed.
1771	North Carolina Regulator movement defeated.
1772	*Gaspee* burned.
	Committees of Correspondence formed.
	First Partition of Poland gives large parts of its territory and population to Russia, Austria, and Prussia.
1773	Boston Tea Party takes place.
1774	Coercive Acts passed.
	Quebec Act passed.
	First Continental Congress meets and agrees to boycott British imports.

and West Florida to Britain but got back its possessions in Cuba and the Philippines that the British had captured. Spain acquired Louisiana from its French ally as compensation for the loss of the Floridas. Shocked by their inability to defend Cuba and the Philippines, Spanish officials accelerated ongoing reforms: Like the French, they appointed *intendants* to ensure better collection of taxes, and because Jesuit priests were too independent of royal control, the crown expelled them from its dominions. Spain also strengthened its military forces in much of the empire, including Mexico, which then encompassed Texas, New Mexico, and California as well as present-day Mexico, and began to establish settlements in California in 1769 (see Chapter 4).

Because these outposts were weak and remote, British officials were not much concerned about them, and the same was true of Louisiana, though it was closer and more populated. Florida was under British control after 1763, and the Spanish evacuated it completely, taking with them not only the free black population of Mose (a settlement of former slaves who had escaped from Georgia and South Carolina) but even the bones of a dead royal governor.

Protecting and controlling the old and new territories in North America as inexpensively as possible presented British officials with difficult questions. How should they administer the new territories? How should they deal with Indians likely to resist further encroachments on their lands? And perhaps most vexing, how could they rein in the seemingly out-of-control colonists in the old territories?

Permitting most of the new areas to have their own assemblies seemed inadvisable but was unavoidable if these areas were to attract settlers. Believing that the increasing power of the legislatures had long since "unhinged" the government of the older colonies, British authorities hoped to avoid similar unruliness in the new territories. In fact, they had long wanted to roll back the power of the old colonial assemblies. But Britain had needed the cooperation of these assemblies during the years of war with France. Now, with France vanquished, imperial officials felt that they could crack down on the local governments. Some British statesmen, however, recognized that this new approach was risky. With France gone from the continent, Americans would be less dependent on Britain for protection and therefore more inclined to resist unpopular restrictions.

Resentment against American conduct during the war also colored British thinking. Some of the colonies had failed to enlist their quota of recruits. Worse yet, illicit trade was so common in New England that it cost Britain more to operate the customs service in America than it collected in duties.

England emerged from the war with what was then an immense national debt of approximately £146 million, nearly double the amount at the beginning of the conflict. Alarmed by the unprecedented debt, many Britons concluded that Americans should bear more of the financial burden of running the empire. The colonists certainly looked both prosperous and undertaxed to British soldiers who had served in America. Many Americans normally paid no more than 5 per-

cent of their income in taxes; in comparison, the English averaged 33 percent. An economic recession—triggered by the reduction in spending that followed the war—put further pressure on British officials to reduce taxes in England.

Dealing with the New Territories

In 1763, the British government took several important steps to deal with the new territories, protect the old colonies, and maintain peace with the Indians. One was to keep a substantial body of troops stationed in America even in peacetime—10,000 were initially planned. Another, announced in the royal **Proclamation of 1763**, was to establish civilian governments in East and West Florida (Canada remained under military rule). A third, in the same proclamation, was to temporarily forbid white settlement west of the Appalachian Mountains. The purpose of the Proclamation Line restricting white settlement was presumably twofold: to keep white settlers and Indians apart, preventing fighting between them, and to hold the colonists closer to the coast, where they would be easier to control (see Map 5–1). Permanent arrangements for the Mississippi Valley could come later, after British officials had time to ponder matters.

Neither the Proclamation Line nor the stationing of troops in America was particularly wise. The Proclamation Line provoked resentment because it threatened to deprive settlers and speculators in the rapidly developing colonies of the land they coveted. Some who had moved into the Ohio area were removed by force. Other Americans merely ignored the restriction. Moreover, someone had to pay for the troops, forcing the British government to take additional measures that further provoked American resentment. These measures included the imposition of direct taxes and the passage of **Quartering Acts** that required colonial assemblies to provide barracks and certain supplies for the soldiers.

The presence of troops in peacetime alarmed Americans. Sharing the traditional English distrust of standing armies, they wondered whether the soldiers were there to coerce rather than protect them. And the military presence may, in fact, have made imperial authorities less cautious in dealing with the colonies. Given their wariness, Americans would doubtless have objected to the troops and to the taxes necessary to support them even if the troops had done an exemplary job of protecting the frontier. But conflicts with Indians cast doubt on their ability to do even that.

The Status of Native Americans

If Britain confronted complex problems in North America, Native Americans faced even more difficult ones in dealing with the British. Colonial settlers and their livestock were displacing Indians from their ancient lands, while liquor and rampant cheating by white traders were debasing the fur trade. Each of the colonies tried to regulate its Indian traders, but lack of coordination made most of these efforts ineffective.

Meanwhile the British victory over the French and the westward expansion of British territory undermined the Indians' traditional strategies and alignments. British officials

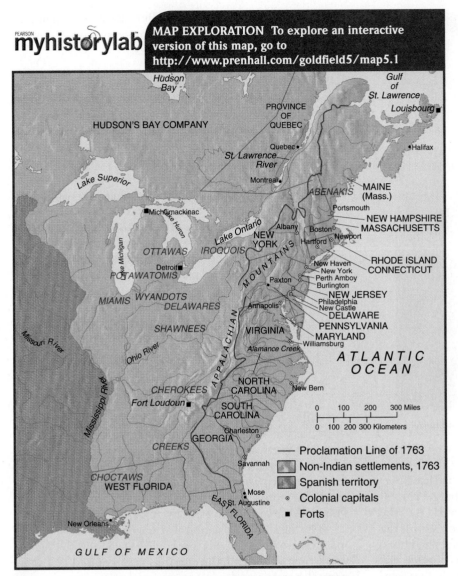

MAP EXPLORATION To explore an interactive version of this map, go to http://www.prenhall.com/goldfield5/map5.1

MAP 5-1 Colonial Settlement and the Proclamation Line of 1763
This map depicts the regions claimed and settled by the major groups competing for territory in eastern North America. With the Proclamation Line of 1763, positioned along the crest of the Appalachian Mountains, the British government tried to stop the westward migration of settlers under its jurisdiction and thereby limit conflict with the Indians. The result, however, was frustration and anger on the part of land-hungry settlers.

Cherokee War, took place in the southern Appalachian highlands. Though increasingly alarmed at the abuses and encroachments of their white neighbors, the Cherokees had long remained allies of the British. But in 1759, Cherokee warriors (who were returning home from a campaign with the British against the French and their Indian allies in western Pennsylvania) may have stolen horses belonging to Virginia colonists. The colonists attacked the Cherokees, killing some of them. The Cherokees retaliated with attacks on western settlements in all of the southern colonies. In 1760, they captured Fort Loudoun in eastern Tennessee, stuffing the commander's mouth full of dirt and telling him, "Dog, since you are so hungry for land, eat your fill." Three expeditions, manned by British as well as colonial troops, eventually forced the Cherokees to agree, in a 1761 treaty, to surrender land in the Carolinas and Virginia to the colonists.

The second major conflict, **Pontiac's Rebellion**, broke out in 1763 among Indians in the Great Lakes and Ohio Valley regions formerly claimed by France. Many Native American groups feared that the British planned to exterminate them and take their lands now that the French could no longer help them. They also resented the contempt and increased stinginess of British traders and officials, who were no longer forced to compete commercially with the French to secure Indian allegiance. These concerns helped to inspire a united effort to resist the British and revitalize Indian cultures. Neolin, also known as the Delaware Prophet, urged Native Americans to reject European goods and ways. Pontiac, an Ottawa chief, was the most respected leader of at least eight major groups of Native Americans that attacked British forces and American settlers from the Great Lakes to Virginia in 1763.

no longer found Native American neutrality or military help as important as they once had. Increasingly superfluous as allies and unable to play the European powers off against each other, Native Americans therefore lost much of their former ability to protect themselves by any means short of military resistance. Arrogant British officials took advantage of this increasing vulnerability; traders exploited the Indians, and settlers encroached on their lands.

Two major Indian wars—one breaking out in the late 1750s, during the closing years of the French and Indian War, and the other erupting in its aftermath in the early 1760s—tested British policy toward Native Americans. The first conflict, the

Pontiac's Rebellion raged until 1766. During intermittent negotiations, Pontiac insisted that British possession of the old French forts in western Pennsylvania and Ohio did not give Great Britain title to the area, which, he believed, God intended for the Indians. The French, he maintained, had been there merely as tenants of the Indians, not owners of the land. But the British eventually forced the Indians to give up portions of their territory in return for compensation and guarantees that traditional hunting grounds in the Ohio Valley would remain theirs.

During the war, British commanders sanctioned what would now be regarded as germ warfare against the Indians

Cunne Shote, one of three Cherokee chiefs who visited London in 1762, had this portrait painted there by Francis Parsons.

by giving them blankets that smallpox victims had used. Settlers in Paxton township (near modern Harrisburg, Pennsylvania) also committed atrocities. Angered by the Pennsylvania Assembly's lack of aggressive action against the Indians, the settlers lashed out at their peaceful neighbors, the Conestogas. Facing arrest and trial for this outrage, the so-called Paxton Boys marched on Philadelphia, threatening the Pennsylvania Assembly. Benjamin Franklin persuaded them to disperse. Despite the government's efforts, the Paxton Boys were never effectively prosecuted for their acts.

Pontiac's Rebellion and the Cherokee War were costly for both sides. Hoping to prevent such outbreaks, British officials began experimenting with centralized control of Indian affairs during the 1750s. Following the recommendations of the Albany Congress in 1754 (see Chapter 4), they had already created two districts, northern and southern, for the administration of Indian affairs, each with its own superintendent. The Proclamation of 1763, and the line it established restricting further white settlement, gave these officials increased responsibility for protecting the Indians against encroachments by settlers. But land-hungry Americans objected to efforts to keep them off Indian lands, and white traders resented restrictions on their activities. Centralized control of the fur and deerskin trades also proved to be expensive for the British government. British authorities therefore permitted several adjustments in the Indian boundary line and in 1768 returned supervision of the Indian

traders to the individual colonies. But such tacit recognition of local autonomy conflicted with imperial plans to restrict the powers of the colonial assemblies.

Curbing the Assemblies

As early as the 1750s, a dispute over the salaries of Anglican ministers known as the **Parson's Cause** prompted British officials to instruct the governor of Virginia not to sign any legislation that modified existing laws unless it contained a clause making the change inoperative until the king approved it. This restriction, which severely hampered the assembly's ability to respond to emergencies, alarmed Virginians who maintained that their legislators had the "Right to enact ANY Law they shall think necessary for their INTERNAL Government."

British authorities of course disagreed, and in 1764 Parliament bowed to the wishes of British merchants, who suffered from depreciating colonial paper money, by extending an earlier measure to forbid all American legislatures from making such issues legal tender. Because the Currency Act of 1764 came when most colonies were in an economic recession, Americans considered this step especially burdensome or, as one said, "downright Robbery." Worse, however, was yet to come.

The Sugar and Stamp Acts

In 1764, the British Parliament, under Prime Minister George Grenville, passed the American Revenue Act, commonly known as the **Sugar Act**. In order to generate increased revenue, the Sugar Act and accompanying legislation combined new and revised duties on colonial imports with strict enforcement provisions. In particular, Parliament sought to minimize motivation for smuggling by reducing the duty on French West Indian molasses by 50 percent.

The Sugar Act legislation also lengthened the list of enumerated products—goods that could be sent only to England or destinations within the empire—and required that ships carry elaborate new documentation of their cargoes; these requirements were a reasonable attempt to prevent illegal trade with other countries, but unintentional mistakes by a shipper could result in the unreasonable seizure of entire cargoes.

To enforce these cumbersome regulations, the British government continued to use the Royal Navy to seize smugglers' ships, a practice authorized by the Revenue Act of 1762 during the French and Indian War. It also ordered colonial customs collectors to discharge their duties personally. Previously, the collectors had often lived in England, leaving the work of collection in the colonies to poorly paid deputies, who were susceptible to bribes. Finally, Parliament gave responsibility for trying violations of the laws to a new vice-admiralty court in Halifax, Nova Scotia. Vice-admiralty courts had jurisdiction over maritime affairs. Unlike other courts, they normally operated without a jury and were therefore more likely to enforce trade restrictions. For this reason, and because of the remote location of the Halifax court—getting to it would be a hardship—Americans immediately opposed this provision of the Sugar Act. In response, Parliament created three other vice-admiralty courts in the more convenient localities of Boston, Philadelphia, and Charleston, a decision that was not exactly what the colonists had had in mind.

In the spring of 1765, Parliament enacted another tax on Americans, the **Stamp Act**. This legislation required all valid legal documents, as well as newspapers, playing cards, and various other papers, to bear a government-issued stamp, for which there was a charge. The Sugar Act, though intended to raise revenue, appeared to fall within Britain's accepted authority to regulate commerce; the Stamp Act, by contrast, was the first internal tax (as opposed to an external trade duty) that Parliament had imposed on the colonies. Grenville, a lawyer, realized that it raised a constitutional issue: Did Parliament have the right to impose direct taxes on Americans when Americans had no elected representatives in Parliament? Following the principle of virtual representation—that members of Parliament served the interests of the nation as a whole, not just the locality from which they came—Grenville maintained that it did. Americans, he would find, vigorously disagreed, and so did some members of Parliament. One, Colonel Isaac Barré, who had served in the colonies, opposed the Stamp Act and referred to Americans as "Sons of Liberty"—a label Americans would soon adopt for themselves.

American Reactions

The measures Britain took to solve its financial and administrative problems first puzzled, then shocked, and eventually outraged Americans. The colonists had emerged from the French and Indian War believing that they had done their fair share and more toward making Great Britain ruler of the greatest empire the world had yet seen. They expected to be rewarded for their efforts and treated with respect. They were certain that as British Americans they shared in the glory and enjoyed all the rights of Englishmen in England. The new restrictions and taxes accordingly hit them like a slap in the face, made worse by a postwar economic recession in many of the colonies.

Constitutional Issues

To Americans, it was self-evident that the British measures were unfair. It was difficult to contend, however, that the British authorities had no right to impose them. The king and Parliament were considered the sovereign, or highest, authority in the empire. Then as now, the **British Constitution** was not a single written document. It consisted, rather, of the accumulated body of English law and custom, including acts of Parliament. How, then, could the colonists claim that an act of Parliament was unconstitutional?

Constitutional conflict surfaced early in Massachusetts over the issue of **writs of assistance**. These general search warrants, which gave customs officials in America the power to inspect virtually any building suspected of holding smuggled goods, had to be formally renewed at the accession of a new monarch. When George III became king in 1760, Massachusetts merchants—perhaps out of a fondness for smuggling as well as for liberty—sought to block the reissuance of the writs. Their attorney, James Otis, Jr., called the writs "instruments of

slavery." Parliament, he maintained, lacked the authority to empower colonial courts to issue them. Otis lost, but "then and there," a future president of the United States, John Adams, would later write, "the child independence was born."

Taxation and the Political Culture

The constitutional issue that most strained the bond between the colonies and the empire was taxation. British measures on other issues annoyed and disturbed Americans, and their cumulative effect helped to alienate the colonists from England. But it was outrage over taxation that would be the midwife of American independence. Because Parliament had customarily refrained from taxing them, Americans assumed that it could not, and because their own assemblies had taxed them, they believed that those legislatures were in fact their parliaments.

Most Americans, including many who would later side with the British, believed that to deprive them of the right to be taxed only by their own elected representatives was to deny them one of the most basic rights of Englishmen. British subjects everywhere believed that Parliament's exclusive authority to impose taxes on its constituents made Britain the freest country in the world. British officials, who believed in parliamentary sovereignty, counted the colonists among those constituents. Americans thought otherwise. Given the selfishness of human nature, they believed that to have governing officials who could do unto them without doing the same to themselves was to risk disaster.

American views on taxation and the role of government reflected the influence of country ideology. As mentioned in Chapter 4, this opposition political philosophy emerged in England in the late seventeenth and early eighteenth centuries partly in response to the development of Britain's powerful standing army and navy. It viewed these forces, and the financial measures needed to support them, as threats to personal liberty. Country ideology proceeded from two basic assumptions: that human beings are selfish and that they need governments to protect them from one another. But country ideology also held that government power, no matter how necessary or to whom entrusted, is inherently aggressive and expansive. According to the English political philosopher John Locke, rulers have the authority to enforce law "only for the public good." When government exceeds this proper function, the people have the right to change it. Only in the last resort does this right justify revolution; the preferable alternative is a system with less-disruptive ways of protecting the freedom of the people.

Country ideology stressed that in the English system of government, it was the duty of Parliament, in particular the House of Commons (which represented the people as a whole), to check the executive power of the crown. The House of Commons's control of taxation enabled it to curb tyrannical rulers. When the crown did its job properly, the Commons appropriated the necessary funds; when rulers infringed on the liberty of the people, the Commons restrained them by withholding taxes.

A Frenchman Reports on the American Reaction to the Stamp Act

Britain emerged from the Great War for Empire as the victor, but France had no intention of quietly giving up the struggle. French officials therefore took a keen interest in what was happening in the British North American colonies. The Duc de Choiseul, who was in charge of foreign affairs in the 1760s, was in fact remarkably prescient in believing that the British acquisition of Canada would prompt the thirteen mainland colonies to revolt since they no longer needed protection from the French next door. Choiseul and his successor in office, the Comte de Vergennes, accordingly sent agents to take the temperature of affairs in America and report on items of interest such as fortifications, navigable rivers, and the like.

An anonymous traveler whose journal wound up in the French naval archives may have been such a spy, and his findings doubtless pleased French officials. After landing in North Carolina in early 1765, he went north through Williamsburg, Virginia, Annapolis, Maryland, Philadelphia, Pennsylvania, and New York, New York. On May 30 he was visiting the Virginia House of Burgesses when Patrick Henry gave an historic speech against the Stamp Act, and the traveler's account remains one of our best sources for what was actually said that day (see below). But at all of his major stops, he found Americans condemning the Stamp Act and claiming that they "would fight to the last Drop of their blood before they would Consent to any such slavery." He was sure that this act "had made a great alteration in the Americans Disposition towards great britain" and turned them toward manufacturing goods for themselves. If the trend continued, he predicted that it would be a "fatal stroke to England, for their Chief Dependance is on their manufactures to which these colonys were a Considerable suport."

British officials, he believed, had encouraged religious and other differences among the colonists to keep them dependent on the mother country. But, he concluded, "great is their mistake in this, for the Inhabitants of north America Can lay aside their religion, when their Interest requires it as well as the English Can, and always have done."

■ **Do you think the Frenchman was right in his assessment of the American reaction to the Stamp Act and the value of the colonies to Great Britain?**

Such important responsibilities required the people's representatives to be men of sufficient property and judgment to make independent decisions. A representative should be "virtuous" (meaning public-spirited), and he should avoid political partisanship, because divisions within the House of Commons could undermine its ability to resist or curb the executive. A representative of the appropriate social status who exhibited the proper behavior deserved the deference of his constituents. They should assume, in other words, that he was more qualified to understand and manage public affairs than they were, and they should accordingly follow his lead. But if he did not measure up, the people should be able to vote him out.

Country ideology appealed to Americans for a number of reasons. In part, colonists were drawn to it as they were to other English ideas and trends. More important, country ideology's suspicion of those in power suited American politics on the local level, where rivalries and factionalism fostered distrust between those with and without power. And it emboldened the many Americans who feared they had no voice in the decisions of the government in London on matters of vital importance to them. Finally, with its insistence on the important political role of the propertied elite, country ideology appealed to America's local gentry. It suggested that it was their duty, as elected political officials, to safeguard the freedom of their constituents.

These ideas have had an enduring influence on American politics, surfacing even today in the suspicion of Washington and "big government." During the eighteenth century, they predisposed Americans to value local control and to expect the worst from remote governments. In so doing, they helped inspire the American Revolution. Many Americans were ready to attribute any new imperial regulations or taxes to a conspiracy of corrupt British officials to tyrannize them.

Protesting the Taxes

Given this ideological background, the initial American response to the Sugar Act was surprisingly mild. This was because the new taxes it imposed took the form of duties on trade and thus appeared consistent with the earlier Navigation Acts. The actual reaction varied from colony to colony in ways that reflected regional self-interest. The speaker of the legislature in one southern colony commented that it was "much divided" over the effects of the act and would probably not petition against it. In New England, by contrast, the Sugar Act threatened to cut into the profits of the lucrative smuggling trade with the French West Indies. As a result, people there were quicker to recognize the act's implications. But as one alarmed colonist elsewhere noted, if his fellow Americans anywhere submitted to any tax imposed by Parliament, they were dumb and docile donkeys; "more Sacks, more Sacks," or burdens, were coming.

The size of the burden was less important than the principle involved. To Americans steeped in country ideology, direct taxation by London threatened to undercut the elected representatives' power of the purse and thereby remove the traditional first line of defense against a tyrannical executive. Thus all the assemblies eventually passed resolutions flatly maintaining that any parliamentary tax on America, including the Sugar Act, was unconstitutional. Colonists in New York, their assembly stated, claimed to be exempt from taxation by anyone but their own representatives not "as a Privilege" but "as their Right." By the end of 1764, New York merchants had joined the artisans and merchants of Boston in a **nonimportation movement**, an organized boycott of British manufactured goods. The goal was to cut into the profits of British employers, inducing them and the workers laid off as a result to pressure the government to back down.

Unlike the Sugar Act, the Stamp Act had an equal impact throughout the colonies, and the response to it was swift and vociferous. Newspapers and pamphlets were filled with denunciations of the supposedly unconstitutional measure, and in taverns everywhere outraged patrons roundly condemned it. "The minds of the freeholders," wrote one observer, "were inflamed...by many a hearty damn of the Stamp Act over bottles, bowls and glasses." The colonial legislatures were also quick to condemn the new measure. Virginia's lower house was the first to act, approving Patrick Henry's strong resolutions against the Stamp Act. These were then reprinted in newspapers throughout the colonies, and other legislatures passed similar formal objections.

Popular protests also expressed widespread outrage at the Stamp Act. Men and women had long gathered in the colonies for public purposes, such as closing houses of prostitution or rolling back exorbitant price increases. With a postwar economic slump in some of the colonies, many people now turned to direct action. The **Sons of Liberty**, a collection of loosely organized activists, put pressure on stamp distributors and British authorities. In August 1765, a Boston group led by Ebenezer MacIntosh, a volunteer fireman and shoemaker, demolished property belonging to a revenue agent, and another mob sacked Lieutenant Governor Thomas Hutchinson's house. About a month later, rioters roamed the streets of New York, smashing windows and telling the governor, "[Y]ou'll die a Martyr to your own villany...and every man, that assists you, shall be, surely, put to Death." The Sons of Liberty organized demonstrations in other cities but kept most of them more peaceful with tighter discipline.

The Sons of Liberty included people from all ranks of society. The leaders, however, came mostly from the middle and upper classes. Often pushed by more radical common people, some of the elite doubtless joined in the hope of protecting their own positions and interests. How threatened these might be was seen most dramatically in Charleston, where slaves paraded through the streets crying, "Liberty!" Movement leaders were also concerned that violence could discredit the American cause. Even the fiery Samuel Adams, one of the leading organizers of the protest in Boston, would later claim, "I am no friend to Riots." Still, he added, "when the People are oppressed," they will be "discontented, and they are not to be blamed."

Partly as a result of the growing unrest, leaders throughout the colonies determined to meet and agree on a unified response to Britain. As Christopher Gadsden of South Carolina, an ardent advocate of American rights and opponent of taxation, observed at the time, "There ought to be no New England men, no New Yorker, etc. known on the Continent, but all of us Americans." Nine colonies eventually sent delegates, Gadsden among them, to the **Stamp Act Congress**, which met in New York City in October 1765. A humorist in the Carolina legislature, who had opposed sending anyone, observed that the

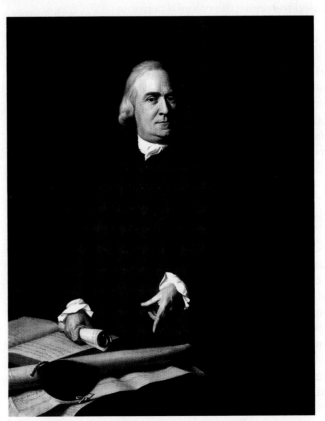

Samuel Adams, the leader of the Boston radicals, as he appeared to John Singleton Copley in the early 1770s. In this famous picture, thought to have been commissioned by another revolutionary leader, John Hancock, Adams points to legal documents guaranteeing American rights.

Samuel Adams, about 1772 John Singleton Copley, American, 1738–1815 Oil on canvas 125.73 × 100.33 cm 49 1/2 × 39 1/2 in.) Deposited by the City of Boston L-R 30.76c.

gathering would produce a most unpalatable combination: New England would throw in fish and onions; the middle provinces, flaxseed and flour; Virginia and Maryland, tobacco; North Carolina, pitch, turpentine, and tar; South Carolina, indigo and rice — and Georgia would sprinkle the whole with sawdust. "Such an absurd jumble will you make if you attempt to form [a] union among such discordant materials as the thirteen British provinces," he concluded. A quick-witted member of the assembly shot back that he would not choose his colleague for a cook, but that the congress would prepare a dish fit for any king.

It did indeed. The congress adopted the **Declaration of Rights and Grievances**, which denied Parliament's right to tax the colonies, and petitioned both king and Parliament to repeal the Stamp and Sugar acts. Parliament, unwilling to acknowledge this challenge to its authority, refused to receive the colonial petitions.

As protests spread, the stamp distributors resigned "for the welfare of the people." In some areas, Americans went about their business as usual without using stamped paper. In other places, they avoided activities that required taxed items. They also stepped up the boycott of British goods that had begun in response to the Sugar Act. British merchants, hurt by this economic pressure, petitioned Parliament for repeal of the Stamp Act, and a new ministry obliged them by rescinding it in March 1766. Modifications in the provisions of the Sugar Act came later in the year.

The Aftermath of the Stamp Act Crisis

During the Stamp Act crisis, Benjamin Franklin appeared before Parliament to present American objections to the Stamp and Sugar acts. Some members apparently concluded from his remarks that the colonists would accept port duties but would oppose direct taxes. They were wrong. At this point, Americans were in no mood to accept any tax imposed by Parliament.

Americans in turn misunderstood the **Declaratory Act** that accompanied the repeal of the Stamp Act. Intended to make Parliament's retreat more acceptable to its members, this act stated that Parliament had the right to "legislate for the colonies in all cases whatsoever." Did *legislate* mean *tax?* Not necessarily, for taxes were traditionally deemed to be a voluntary gift to the king from the people acting through their own representatives. (This is why money bills, as distinct from other acts, had to originate in the House of Commons.) Americans therefore tended to consider the Declaratory Act a mere face-saving gesture. Unfortunately, it was more than that.

A satirical British engraving from 1766 showing English politicians burying the Stamp Act, "born 1765 died 1766." The warehouses in the background symbolize the revival of trade with America.

A Strained Relationship

Most members of Parliament continued to believe that they represented everyone in the empire and that they could therefore tax people in the colonies as well as in England. Americans believed just as strongly that "in taxing ourselves and making Laws for our own internal government … we can by no means allow our Provincial legislatures to be subordinate to any legislative power on earth."

Relations were never quite the same between England and America after the Stamp Act crisis. Each side became ever more suspicious of the other. Americans were convinced that they had forced the British to back down and that, if need be, they could do it again. March 18, the anniversary of the repeal of the Stamp Act, became an occasion for celebration, giving Americans a national holiday before they had a nation. In the process Americans also began developing a new conception of their special role in history. Because freedom seemed to be under widespread attack in Europe as well as in the British empire, they increasingly saw themselves as champions in "ONE COMMON CAUSE" that had global dimensions.

Events in America also revealed continuing tensions between Great Britain and the colonies. When British officials required Massachusetts to compensate those who had suffered losses in the Stamp Act rioting, the legislature complied but pardoned the rioters. In 1767, an irritated Parliament then passed an act suspending the New York legislature because it had not complied with the Quartering Act of 1765. This law required colonial assemblies to provide facilities and certain supplies for royal troops. The New York legislature finally obeyed before the suspending act went into effect and thus remained in business. But such incidents boded ill for the hopes of some colonists that a British government that had repealed the Stamp Act would prove cooperative in other ways.

Regulator Movements

In 1766, a committee of the South Carolina legislature appointed to consider "the State of the Province" recommended that it establish courts in the rapidly growing backcountry and petition Parliament for repeal of the Currency Act. These suggestions were prompted by mounting unrest in the southern backcountry. Vigilante groups calling themselves **Regulators** had emerged in North Carolina in response to official corruption and in South Carolina in response to lawlessness. High taxes and high court costs in North Carolina oppressed the colony's western farmers. Because the Currency Act reduced the amount of money in circulation, it compounded people's problems, leaving them "crouched beneath their sufferings" and unable to pay their debts and taxes. In South Carolina, the devastation and disruptions of the Cherokee War left a legacy of violence. Outlaws roamed the backcountry, stealing livestock and raiding isolated houses. In both colonies, because representation in the assemblies failed to reflect the rapidly growing backcountry populations, legislatures were slow to respond to their needs. As a result, the Regulators did by extralegal action what they could not do through legal channels. In North Carolina, they closed courts and intimidated tax officials. In South Carolina, they pursued outlaws and whipped people suspected of harboring them.

These activities brought the Regulators into conflict with the local elites of both North and South Carolina. The British government, however, only made matters worse. Instead of encouraging the assemblies to increase western representation, the crown sought to curb their power by limiting their size. Americans termed this instruction "perhaps [as] peculiar as any that have been given on the continent." As for the shortage of currency, Lord Hillsborough, the secretary of state for the colonies, callously informed North Carolinians that "no Consideration of a possible local inconvenience" would prompt Britain to modify the "sound Principles" of the Currency Act. And instead of approving legislation to establish courts in the South Carolina backcountry, British officials disallowed it because it specified that judges would hold their positions contingent on good behavior rather than at the pleasure of the crown.

Thanks to such help from London as well as to their own mistakes, a crisis confronted local officials by 1767. In South Carolina, the assembly belatedly reapportioned itself, giving the backcountry some representation, and permitted the crown

This depiction of Governor William Tryon's confrontation with the North Carolina Regulators during May 1771 was produced at Philadelphia in 1876 by F.O.C. Darley (1822–1888).

to dictate the terms of judicial appointments. These and other concessions to western residents narrowly averted bloodshed. But in North Carolina, fighting broke out in 1771. Governor William Tryon led the local militia against the Regulators, who had gathered near Alamance Creek. There, he ordered the Regulators to disperse or his men would fire. "Fire and be damned," someone replied, and gunfire erupted, killing 29 men and wounding more than 150 on both sides. During the next several weeks, seven Regulators were hanged and 6,000 pardoned.

The confrontation in North Carolina was the most serious of its kind, but similar social tensions were apparent in other colonies. To deal with them, colonial leaders had to understand local conditions and be able to act on their knowledge. But British attempts to reform colonial governments threatened to hamstring them.

The Townshend Crisis

Britain had not given up the idea of taxing the colonies with the repeal of the Stamp Act in 1766. Little over a year later, Parliament passed a new set of taxes, the Townshend duties. Another crisis ensued, lasting until an American boycott of British goods forced repeal of most of the new duties. The relatively quiet period that followed ended when Britain made a serious attempt to enforce compliance with the one Townshend duty still on the books, the duty on tea.

Townshend's Plan

Charles Townshend became the leading figure in Britain's government in 1767. A former member of the Board of Trade, he thought he understood the colonies, and he knew that many members of Parliament still wanted to tax Americans. The legislation that bears his name, the **Townshend Duty**

Act, was intended to help pay the cost of government in America. It imposed new duties, or external taxes, which Townshend believed the colonists were willing to accept, but no direct, or internal, taxes like the Stamp Tax. The duties covered a number of items the colonists regularly imported—tea, paper, paint, lead, and glass. To make sure that the duties were collected, the British added a new board of customs commissioners for America and located its headquarters in Boston, the presumed home port of many smugglers.

Coming on top of the threatened suspension of the New York legislature, the Townshend Duty Act seemed to fore-shadow greater British interference in colonial affairs. And the new customs officials were, in fact, far more diligent than their predecessors, harassing among others the wealthy Boston merchant John Hancock, perhaps because he was openly contemp-tuous of them. Seizing his appropriately named vessel *Liberty,* they accused him of smuggling. Hancock may indeed have vi-olated the acts of trade at times, but in this case the accusations were apparently false. The incident sparked a riot in Boston during which a crowd on the waterfront roughed up members of the customs service. Britain responded in 1768 by sending troops to Boston. The soldiers would remain there amid mounting hostility for the next year and a half.

American Boycott

The Townshend duties, like the stamp tax, provoked resist-ance throughout the colonies. Rejecting the argument that duties were somehow different from taxes, John Dickin-son, a wealthy lawyer who wrote under the pen name "A Farmer" in Pennsylvania, asserted that a tax was a tax, what-ever its form. The purpose of the taxes—to help pay the costs of government in the colonies, including the salaries of governors and judges—also seemed dangerous. Ameri-cans believed it was the role of their own assemblies to raise revenues for these costs. By bypassing the assemblies, the Townshend Act threatened to undermine their authority.

There was no equivalent to the Stamp Act Congress in response to the Townshend Act, because British officials (acting through the colonial governors) barred the assem-blies from sending delegates to such a meeting. Even so, Americans gradually organized an effective nonimporta-tion movement. When, for example, the governor of Vir-ginia dissolved the House of Burgesses for passing resolutions opposing British measures, the members met on their own in the Raleigh Tavern at Williamsburg and adopted a nonimportation agreement. Once again, vigilant laborers and artisans threatened violators of the general boycott with physical violence, but few disturbances oc-curred. Many Americans signed subscription lists binding themselves, with the other signers, to buy only goods made in the colonies and nothing made in Great Britain. Hand-bills, like one urging "the Sons and Daughters of LIB-ERTY" to shun a particular Boston merchant, brought pressure on uncooperative importers. To avoid imported English textiles, American women spun more thread and wove more cloth at home. Wearing homespun became a

moral virtue, a sign of self-reliance, personal independence, and the rejection of "corrupting" English luxuries (see American Views: Social Status and the Enforcement of the Nonimportation Movement).

The nonimportation movement forged a sense of com-mon purpose and trust among all who participated in it—men and women, southern planters and northern artisans alike—giving them the sense of belonging to a larger commu-nity of fellow Americans. Although it was at this point more an imagined community than a political community, it was real enough and large enough to mobilize many ordinary Americans and sharply reduce imports from Britain.

Because Britain had increased its exports to Europe since the Stamp Act crisis, it took longer than before for the nonimportation movement to produce a reaction in Lon-don (see Figure 5–1). Still, the troubles in America con-tributed to the king's decision to appoint a new prime

Mr. and Mrs. Thomas Mifflin of Philadelphia. Mifflin was a promi-nent merchant and radical opponent of British policy toward the colonies. He and his wife were visiting Boston in 1773, when John Singleton Copley painted them. Working at a small loom, Sarah Morris Mifflin weaves a decorative fringe. She no doubt did the same during the nonimportation movement against the Townshend duties, thereby helping to make importation of such goods from Eng-land unnecessary.

John Singleton Copley, Portrait of Mr. and Mrs. Thomas Mif-flin. PMA of Art: Beq. of Mrs. Esther B. Wistar to the HS, Pa. in 1900 and acquired by the PMA # EW 1999–45–1, Photograph © Museum of Fine Arts, Boston.

minister, Lord North. Thinking—and even looking—remarkably alike, George III and North complemented each other. At the king's insistence, North would remain prime minister until 1782. In 1770, he was prepared to concede that the Townshend duties had been counterproductive because they interfered with British trade. But when Parliament repealed most of them, it left the duty on tea. This symbolic equivalent of the Declaratory Act served to assert Parliament's continuing right to tax the colonies.

The Boston Massacre

Ironically, on the same day that North proposed that Parliament rescind most of the Townshend duties—March 5, 1770—British troops fired on American civilians in Boston. This incident, which came to be known to Americans everywhere as the **Boston Massacre,** resulted from months of increasing friction between townspeople and the British troops stationed in the city. The townspeople complained that the soldiers insulted them, leered at women, and competed for scarce jobs. The hostility was so great, complained a British officer, that "twenty" soldiers could be "knocked down in the Streets" and nothing be heard of it, but if a soldier merely kicked a resident, "the Town is immediately in an Alarm."

The Boston Massacre occurred when angry and frightened British soldiers fired on a crowd that was pelting them with sticks and stones. Five men died, including Crispus Attucks— subsequently described as "that half Indian, half negro and altogether rowdy"—who has since become the most celebrated casualty of the incident. To preserve order, the troops withdrew from the city. Later, two prominent local lawyers successfully defended the soldiers accused of murder.

The "Quiet Period"

In the so-called Quiet Period that followed, no general grievance united all Americans. But in almost every colony, issues continued to simmer. In Massachusetts and South Carolina, for example, the royal governors temporarily moved the meeting places of the legislatures to small towns miles away from the capital, "for the sole Purpose," as the Declaration of Independence would later charge, "of fatiguing them into compliance" with British measures.

Local circumstances produced a more spectacular confrontation in Rhode Island where a British revenue schooner, the *Gaspee,* ran aground. Because its crew had been allegedly harassing local residents, Rhode Islanders got even. Led by John Brown, a local merchant, they boarded and burned the ship. The British government appointed a commission of inquiry with in-

structions to arrest the culprits and send them to England for trial. Despite its offer of a reward for information about the incident, the commission learned nothing. The British attempt to stamp out smuggling in the colonies was so heavy-handed that it offended the innocent more than it frightened the guilty. Such incidents, and in particular the British threat to send Americans to England for trial, led American leaders to resolve to keep one another informed about British actions. Twelve colonies established **committees of correspondence** for this purpose. Leaders in Boston established similar committees in Massachusetts. There would soon be plenty for these organizations to do, for Boston was about to become the scene of a showdown between imperial authority and colonial resistance.

The Boston Tea Party

During the Quiet Period, Americans drank smuggled (and therefore untaxed) Dutch tea. Partly as a result, the British East India Company, which had the exclusive right to distribute tea in the British empire, nearly went bankrupt. Lord North tried to rescue it with the **Tea Act of 1773,** which exempted it from the duty normally collected as the tea was transshipped through Britain. Being cheaper, British authorities assumed the tea would appeal to Americans who would now pay the old Townshend duty.

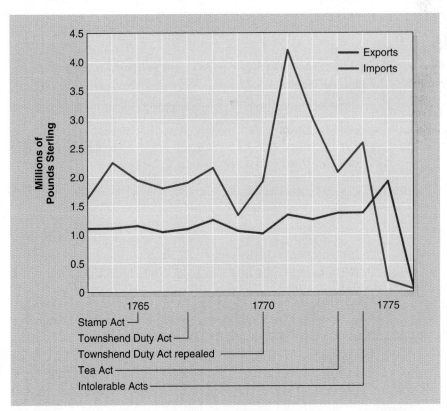

FIGURE 5-1   Value of American Exports to and Imports from England, 1763–1776
This figure depicts the value of American exports to and imports from England. The decrease of imports in 1765–1766 and the even sharper drop in 1769 illustrate the effect of American boycotts in response to the Stamp Act and Townshend duties.

Data Source: U.S. Bureau of the Census, *Historical Statistics of the United States, Colonial Times to 1970,* Bicentennial Edition, Part 1 (1975).

FROM THEN TO NOW

The Boston Massacre and the Continuing Problem of Peaceful Crowd Control

Rowdy crowds and armed law-enforcement personnel make a volatile mixture. On the night of March 5, 1770, British troops fired into a Boston mob in what has become the most famous explosion to result from this combination, but similar incidents have occurred sporadically throughout American history. The turbulent 1960s and 1970s, in particular, produced a number of bloody encounters such as the Orangeburg Massacre (February 8, 1968) in which South Carolina police killed three African-American students who had been trying to integrate a local bowling alley, as well as the more widely publicized Kent State University shootings (see *American Journey*, chapter 29). Most recently (in 2007), when a few provocateurs threw rocks at them, Los Angeles police fired rubber bullets at a largely Hispanic group who had been holding a peaceful May Day rally in favor of immigrant rights. No one was killed, but at least fifteen civilians were injured. As the police chief later admitted, "Command and control" broke down so that no one knew who was in charge and "things were done that shouldn't have been done."

These policemen in riot gear were part of the 500 to 600 law enforcement officers deployed in or near MacArthur Park in Los Angeles who clashed with demonstrators at an immigrants' rights rally on May 1, 2007.

■ Why do confrontations between law enforcement personnel and crowds occasionally turn violent? What can be done to improve the situation?

The Boston Massacre, March 5, 1770, in an engraving by Paul Revere. Copied from an earlier print, Revere's widely circulated version shows—somewhat inaccurately—well-organized soldiers firing on helpless civilians; the names of the dead, including Crispus Attucks, appear below.

PEARSON
myhistorylab

From Then to Now Online

5-1 Thomas Hutchinson, *The History of the Province of Massachusetts Bay.* Lt. Governor Hutchinson describes the Boston Massacre.

5-2 "Action by Police at Rally Troubles Los Angeles Chief," 2007. An early account of the events at the May Day rally.

5-3 "Los Angeles Police Chief Notes Failures of Command at Rally," 2007. A later, fuller account of the events.

This plan angered Americans. Some may have been jealous of the merchants chosen as exclusive agents of the company. Most, however, were outraged at the attempt to trick them into paying the tax on tea. Men and women by the thousands decided not to touch the stuff. Newspapers discussed its dangers to the body as well as to the body politic and offered recipes for substitutes.

Thomas Hutchinson, who had been lieutenant governor of Massachusetts during the Stamp Act riots, was now the colony's royal governor, and two of his sons were agents for the East India Company. In most other cities, threats from the Sons of Liberty convinced the captains of the tea ships to return to England without landing their cargo. Hutchinson, however, was determined to have the tea unloaded in Boston, and he barred the tea ships there from leaving. As a result, violence once again erupted in the city.

When the Sons of Liberty realized that they could not force the ships to leave, they decided to take decisive action. On December 16, 1773, Samuel Adams reportedly told a large gathering at Old South Meeting House that it "could do nothing more to preserve the liberties of America." This remark was apparently a prearranged signal for what came to be known as the **Boston Tea Party**. War whoops immediately answered him from the street outside, and a well-organized band of men disguised as Indians raced aboard the *Dartmouth* and two other tea ships, broke open 342 chests of tea, and heaved the contents into the harbor. In a similar action in 1774, residents of Annapolis, Maryland, forced some merchants to burn their own ship when it arrived with dutied tea.

The Intolerable Acts

The destruction of property in the Boston Tea Party shocked many Americans. Surprised and angry, Britain reacted even more strongly. Parliament passed a series of repressive measures known as the **Coercive Acts**. The first of these, effective June 1, 1774, was the Boston Port Act, which closed the port of Boston until the East India Company and the crown were paid for the tea and uncollected duties. The Administration of Justice Act, which followed, declared that an official who, while performing his duties, killed a colonist could be tried in England (where he would almost certainly receive sympathetic treatment) rather than in Massachusetts. The third measure, the Massachusetts Government Act, drastically modified that colony's charter of 1691. Henceforth, members of the governor's council and sheriffs would be appointed rather than elected. In addition, the Massachusetts Government Act limited the number of town meetings that could be held without the governor's prior approval. In another measure, the British government made its commander in chief in America, General Thomas Gage, the governor of Massachusetts and, in the Quartering Act of 1774, declared that the troops under his command could be lodged in virtually any uninhabited building.

On the same day that Parliament enacted these measures, it also passed the **Quebec Act**. This statute enlarged Quebec's boundaries south to the Ohio River and stipulated that the colony was to be governed by an appointed governor and council but no elected assembly (see Map 5–2). The act also provided for the trial of civil cases without a jury and gave the Catholic Church the same privileges that it had enjoyed under the French. The colonists linked the Quebec Act with the Coercive Acts and labeled them the **Intolerable Acts**.

The Road to Revolution

Americans throughout the colonies considered the Intolerable Acts so threatening that they organized the First Continental Congress to respond to them. Congress renewed the nonimportation movement and took measures to enforce it strictly. These measures widened the gap between those who supported the British and those who opposed them.

Protestantism and the American Response to the Intolerable Acts

Americans found the territorial, administrative, and religious provisions of the Quebec Act deeply disturbing. As one royal governor observed, "The securing of lands for the rising Generation is a matter of great importance to a poor and provident Man with a large family." The Quebec Act, however, gave Canada jurisdiction over lands north of the Ohio River claimed by Connecticut, Pennsylvania, and Virginia. This deprived settlers of their hoped-for homesteads and land speculators of their hoped-for profits, angering both. The administrative provisions of the act—appointed government, no assemblies, no jury for civil cases—also suggested to Americans what Britain might have in store for them.

Americans had similar fears about the religious provisions of the Quebec Act. During the 1760s, some Anglican clergymen had sought to have a bishop appointed for America. But most Americans, including Anglicans, opposed this proposal. They were convinced that the creation of such an office would strengthen the Anglican Church at the expense of other denominations, weaken local control of religious affairs, and require the payment of additional taxes. Many Americans believed that the British had scrapped the idea. The Quebec Act's concessions to Canadian Catholics, however, seemed to resurrect it in more ominous form. As one Virginian observed, the hierarchical organization of the Anglican Church was "a Relick of the Papal Incroachments" on English law. The Quebec Act accordingly "gave a General Alarm to all Protestants," whose ministers throughout the continent warned their congregations that they might be "bound by Popish chains."

American reactions to the religious provisions of the Quebec Act may have been exaggerated, but some features of the Coercive Acts were cause for real concern. The Boston Port Act arbitrarily punished innocent and guilty Bostonians alike. The Administration of Justice Act—which some with vivid imaginations dubbed the Murder Act—seemed to declare open season on colonists, allowing crown officials to kill them without fear of punishment. The Massachusetts Government Act raised the more realistic fear that no colonial charter was safe. A Parliament that had stripped the Massachusetts legislature of an important power might equally decide to abolish the lower houses of all the colonies.

American Views

Social Status and the Enforcement of the Nonimportation Movement

Many Americans enthusiastically supported the nonimportation movement called in response to the Townshend Duty Act crisis of the late 1760s. A few, however, openly opposed it. Among these was the aristocratic William Henry Drayton of South Carolina, who objected to the composition of the committee chosen to enforce the nonimportation agreement in his region. The committee included artisans and shopkeepers, men who, Drayton claimed, should have no role in public affairs. Their education prepared them only "to cut up a beast in the market to the best advantage, to cobble an old shoe in the neatest manner, or to build a necessary house [privy]," not to make public policy. As the following document makes clear, deference had its limits, and the committeemen emphatically disagreed with him. Drayton was later to reverse himself and actively support the Continental Association's ban on importing British goods in 1775. "The people" wanted it, he would later explain, and "it was our duty, to satisfy our constituents; as we were only servants of the public [at large]."

- Who makes policy in the United States today?
- What qualifications do you think they should have?
- How do your answers to these questions differ from Drayton's? From the "Mechanicks's"?
- How would you explain Drayton's later switch?

The Mechanicks of the General Committee to William Henry Drayton

The gracious Giver of all good things, has been pleased to bestow a certain principle on mankind, which properly may be called common sense: But, though every man hath a natural right to a determined portion of this ineffable ray of the Divinity, yet, to the misfortune of society, many persons fall short of this most necessary gift of God....

The Mechanicks pretend to nothing more, than having a claim from nature, to their share in this inestimable favour, in common with Emperors and Kings, and, were it safe to carry the comparison still higher, they would say with William-Henry Drayton himself; who, in his great condescention, has been pleased to allow us a place amongst human beings: But whether it might have happened from an ill construction of his sensory, or his upper works being damaged by some rough treatment of the person who conducted his birth, we know not; however so it is, that, to us, he seems highly defective in this point, whatever exalted notions he may entertain of his own abilities.

By attending to the dictates of common sense, the Mechanicks have been able to distinguish between RIGHT and WRONG; in doing which indeed no great merit is claimed, because every man's own feelings will direct him thereto, unless he obstinately, or from a pertinacious opinion of his own superior knowledge, shuts his eyes, and stoickally submits to all the illegal encroachments that may be made on his property, by an ill-designing and badly-informed ministry.

Mr. Drayton may value himself as much as he pleases, on his having had a liberal education bestowed on him, tho' the good fruits thereof have not hitherto been conspicuous either in his public or private life: He ought however to know, that this is not so absolutely necessary to these, who move in the low sphere of mechanical employments. But still, though he pretends to view them with so contemptuous and oblique an eye, these men hope, that they are in some degree useful to society, without presuming to make any comparisons between themselves and him, except with regard to love for their country; for he has amply shewn, that an attachment of this sort is not one of his ruling passions. Nor does he appear in the least to have regarded the peace and good order of that community of which he is a member; otherwise he would not wilfully, and without any cause, have knocked his head against ninety-nine out of every hundred of the people, not only in this province, but of all North-America....

Mr. Drayton may be assured, that so far from being ashamed of our trades, we are in the highest degree thankful to our friends, who put us in the way of being instructed in them; and that we bless God for giving us strength and judgment to pursue them, in order to maintain our families, with a decency suitable to their stations in life. Every man is not so lucky as to have a fortune ready provided to his hand, either by his own or his wife's parents, as has been his lot; nor ought it to be so with all men; and Providence accordingly hath wisely ordained otherwise, by appointing the greatest part of mankind, to provide for their support by manual labour; and we will

be bold to say, that such are the most useful people in a community....

 We are, Yours, &c.
MECHANICKS of the COMMITTEE.
October 3d, 1769.

Source: *South Carolina Gazette,* October 5, 1769; reprinted in *The Letters of Freeman, etc.: Essays on the Nonimportation Movement in South Carolina* by William Henry Drayton, ed. Robert M. Weir (1977), University of South Carolina Press, pp. 111–114.

Die Einwohner von Boston werfen den englisch-ostindischen Thee ins Meer am 18. December 1773.

"The inhabitants of Boston throwing English-East India tea into the sea," December 16, 1773, as depicted by German engraver D. Berger in 1784. By this time Germans, who were increasingly knowledgeable about the American Revolution, commonly considered the Boston Tea Party to have been the triggering event.

Nightmarish scenarios filled the colonial newspapers. One clergyman observed that the terms of the Coercive Acts were such that if someone were to "make water" on the door of the royal customs house, an entire colonial city "might be laid in Ashes." He undoubtedly knew that he was exaggerating, but his words embodied real fear and anger, and many other Americans shared his feelings. Trying to make an example of Boston,

the British government had taken steps that united Americans as nothing had ever done before (see the Overview table, New Restraints and Burdens on Americans, 1759–1774).

The First Continental Congress

Massachusetts wanted to respond to the Intolerable Acts with an immediate renewal of the nonimportation movement. Leaders in other colonies wanted to organize a more coordinated response and called for another meeting like the Stamp Act Congress. The colonies accordingly agreed to send delegates to a meeting in Philadelphia that came to be called the **First Continental Congress**. Because royal governors attempted to prevent the meeting by barring the legislatures from naming delegates, the colonies called extralegal public meetings for the purpose. In the end, all the colonies except Georgia were represented.

 The First Continental Congress met at Carpenter's Hall in Philadelphia from September 5 to October 26, 1774, with fifty-five delegates present at one time or another. All were leading figures in their home colonies, but only a few knew members from elsewhere. Each colony had one vote, irrespective of the size of its delegation. Some of the more conservative participants favored a compromise with Britain. The speaker of the Pennsylvania Assembly, Joseph Galloway, introduced a measure reminiscent of the Albany Plan of Union. It called for creation of an American "grand council" that would have veto power over parliamentary legislation dealing with America. His plan failed in the Congress by one vote. Instead, those who favored stronger measures—such as Samuel Adams and his cousin John, Patrick Henry, and Christopher Gadsden—prevailed. They persuaded most of their colleagues to endorse the **Suffolk Resolves**, which had been passed at a meeting held in Suffolk County (the site of Boston). These strongly worded resolutions denounced the Coercive Acts as unconstitutional, advised the people to arm, and called for general economic sanctions against Britain.

The Continental Association

The Congress created the **Continental Association** to organize and enforce sanctions against the British. As a first step, the Association pledged Americans to cut off imports

MAP EXPLORATION To explore an interactive version of this map, go to http://www .prenhall.com/goldfield5/map5.2

MAP 5–2   The Quebec Act of 1774
The Quebec Act enlarged the boundaries of the Canadian province southward to the Ohio River and westward to the Mississippi, thereby depriving several colonies of claims to the area granted them by their original charters.

of America, to the inhabitants of Great Britain, and to the king. The address to the king asked him to use his "royal authority and interposition" to protect his loyal subjects in America. The words were significant, for protection and allegiance were considered the reciprocal duties of a sovereign and his people. After agreeing to convene again on May 10, 1775, if its grievances had not been redressed by then, the First Continental Congress adjourned.

The proceedings of the First Continental Congress revealed division as well as agreement. All the delegates believed that the Coercive Acts were unconstitutional, but they differed on methods to resist them. Only a minority was prepared to take up arms against Britain. Most representatives tried to protect the interests of their own colonies. Those from Virginia and Maryland, for example, insisted that the embargo on exports not begin until planters had finished shipping the current tobacco crop. Even more alarming, some South Carolina delegates, in an early example of the sectional stubbornness that would culminate nearly a century later in the Civil War, threatened to walk out of the meeting unless the nonexportation agreement omitted rice, most of which went to northern Europe by way of Britain. To placate the Carolinians, northerners agreed to the exemption. Gadsden, the most radical of the South Carolina delegates, was disgusted with his colleagues. Their actions, he felt, betrayed the spirit of united purpose Patrick Henry had spoken of so stirringly earlier in the Congress: "The distinctions between Virginians, Pennsylvanians, New Yorkers and New Englanders are no more. I am not a Virginian, but an American."

Political Divisions

In the wake of the First Continental Congress, Americans were forced to take sides for and against the Continental Association. At this point, not even such well-known radicals as Samuel Adams and Gadsden were advocating independence. Throughout the pre-Revolutionary period, most colonists hoped and expected that the imperial government would change its policy toward America.

What Americans were divided over was the extent of Parliament's authority and the degree to which they could legitimately question it. As British officials failed, with the passing of time, to accommodate American views of their rights, Americans began in increasing numbers to challenge London's control. The experience of James Wilson, a Pennsylvania lawyer, illustrates this shift. In *Considerations on the Nature and Extent of the Legislative Authority of the British Parliament* (published in 1774), Wilson wrote that he had set out to find a reasonable dividing line between those areas in which Parliament had legitimate authority over the colonies and those in which it did not. But the more he thought, the more he became convinced "that such a line does not exist" and that there can be "no medium between acknowledging and denying that power in all cases." Wilson therefore concluded that Parliament had no authority at all over the colonies, that the colonies' only legal governing bodies were

from Britain after December 1, 1774. If the dispute with Britain was not resolved by September 1775, the Association called for barring most exports to Britain and the West Indies. Voters in every district throughout the colonies were to choose committeemen to enforce the terms of the Association. All who violated them were to be considered "enemies of American liberty." Their names were to be published, and associators (people agreeing to the Association) would "break off all dealings" with them.

Congress also issued a declaration of rights and grievances summarizing its position. This declaration condemned most of the steps taken by Britain since 1763, but "cheerfully" consented to trade regulations for the good of the whole empire. In addition, the Congress sent addresses to the people

OVERVIEW

New Restraints and Burdens on Americans, 1759–1774

	Limits on Legislative Action	Curbs on Territorial Expansion	Burdens on Colonial Trade	Imposition of New Taxes
1759	Royal instructions restrict ability of Virginia assembly to pass timely legislation.			
1762			Writs of assistance issued.	
			Revenue Act authorizes navy to help enforce customs regulation.	
1763		Proclamation Line keeps white settlement east of the Appalachians.	Peacetime use of navy and new customs officials to enforce Navigation Acts.	
1764	Currency Act limits the colonial legislatures' ability to issue paper money.		Vice-admiralty courts strengthened for Sugar Act.	Sugar Act imposes taxes for revenue (modified 1766).
1765				Quartering Act requires assemblies to provide facilities for royal troops.
				Stamp Act imposes internal taxes on various items (repealed 1766).
	Declaratory Act proclaims Parliament's right to legislate for colonies in all cases whatsoever.			
1767	Royal instructions limit size of colonial assemblies.		Vice-admiralty courts strengthened for Townshend duties.	Townshend duties imposed on some imported goods in order to pay colonial officials. (All but tax on tea repealed 1770.)
			American Customs Service established in Boston.	
1773				Tea Act reduces duty and prompts Boston Tea Party.
1774 (Intolerable Acts)	Massachusetts Government Act limits town meetings, changes legislature, and violates Massachusetts charter.	Quebec Act enlarges Quebec at expense of colonies with claims in the Ohio River Valley.	Boston Port Act closes harbor until East India Company's tea is paid for.	Quartering Act of 1774 declares that troops could be lodged in virtually any uninhabited building in Boston.

their own assemblies, and that their only link to the British empire was through the king, to whom colonists owed allegiance. British officials and their American supporters strongly disagreed, insisting that Parliament had complete authority over the colonies.

During 1774 and early 1775, as the British–American confrontation grew more heated, lively debates raged in newspapers and pamphlets, and the colonists became increasingly polarized. In the last months before the outbreak of the American Revolution, the advocates of colonial rights began to call themselves **Whigs** and condemned their opponents as **Tories**. These traditional English party labels dated from the late seventeenth century, when the Tories had supported the accession of the Catholic King James II, whereas the Whigs had opposed it. By calling themselves Whigs and their opponents Tories (loyalist was a more accurate label), the advocates of colonial rights cast themselves as champions of liberty and their enemies as defenders of religious intolerance and royal absolutism.

Conclusion

All Americans, Whigs and loyalists alike, considered themselves good British subjects. But Americans were a more diverse and more democratic people than the English. A considerably larger percentage of them could participate in government, and for all practical purposes, they had been governing themselves for a long time. British officials recognized the different character of American society and feared it might lead Americans to reject British control. But the steps they took to prevent this outcome had the opposite effect.

Attempts to protect their accustomed autonomy first brought the colonial assemblies into conflict with Parliament. Asserting their rights led to greater cooperation among individual colonies. This development, in turn, led to increasingly widespread resistance, then to rebellion, and finally to revolution. Moving imperceptibly from one stage to the next, Americans grew conscious of their common interests and their differences from the English. They became aware, as Benjamin Franklin would later write, of the need to break "through the bounds, in which a dependent people had been accustomed to think, and act" so that they might "properly comprehend the character they had assumed."

That workingmen and members of the elite dressed as Indians had joined in the dangerous act of defiance known as the Boston Tea Party also foreshadowed coming developments. No one now knows for certain why they adopted that particular disguise, but Indians were a traditional symbol of the New World. And those who were making a new political world were risking much—even, it would shortly turn out, life itself.

Review Questions

1. What do Eliza Farmar's letters tell us about the crisis over dutied tea in 1773 and 1774? What does she think has caused the crisis and who was at fault? What makes her think the colonists have any chance of success in resisting British impositions?

2. How did the British victory and French withdrawal from North America after the French and Indian War affect the relations between Native Americans and white settlers? Between British authorities and Americans?

3. What was the relationship between the French and Indian War and changes in British policy toward America? How did the expectations of Americans and Britons differ in 1763? Why were the new policies offensive to Americans?

4. How was stationing British troops in America related to British taxation of the colonists? Why did the colonists consider taxation by Parliament an especially serious threat to their freedom as well as to their pocketbooks?

5. How did Americans oppose the new measures? Who participated in the various forms of resistance? How effective were the different kinds of resistance? What effect did resistance to British measures have on Americans' internal politics and sense of identity as Americans?

6. What led to the meeting of the First Continental Congress? What steps did the Congress take? What did it expect to achieve? What were the differences between Whigs and Tories?

Key Terms

Boston Massacre (p. 129)
Boston Tea Party (p. 131)
British Constitution (p. 123)
Cherokee War (p. 121)
Coercive Acts (p. 131)
Committees of correspondence (p. 129)
Continental Association (p. 133)
Declaration of Rights and Grievances (p. 126)
Declaratory Act (p. 126)

First Continental Congress (p. 133)
Intolerable Acts (p. 131)
Nonimportation movement (p. 125)
Parson's Cause (p. 122)
Pontiac's Rebellion (p. 121)
Proclamation of 1763 (p. 120)
Quartering Acts (p. 120)
Quebec Act (p. 131)
Regulators (p. 127)
Sons of Liberty (p. 125)

Stamp Act (p. 123)
Stamp Act Congress (p. 125)
Sugar Act (p. 122)
Suffolk Resolves (p. 133)
Tea Act of 1773 (p. 129)
Tories (p. 136)
Townshend Duty Act (p. 127)
Whigs (p. 136)
Writs of assistance (p. 123)

Recommended Reading

Bailyn, Bernard. *The Ideological Origins of the American Revolution,* 2nd ed. (1992). A clear and illuminating account of how the colonists' ideas about politics prepared them to resist British measures.

Countryman, Edward. *The American Revolution,* 2nd ed. (2003). A brief, readable general history of the Revolutionary period that focuses on the involvement of the common people.

Morison, Samuel Eliot, ed. *Sources and Documents Illustrating the American Revolution, 1764–1788, and the Formation of the Federal Constitution,* 2nd ed. (1965). The most readily available and conveniently used collection of documents (mostly official) from the era of the American Revolution.

Raphael, Ray. *A People's History of the American Revolution: How Common People Shaped the Fight for Independence* (2001). A readable, popular synthesis of much recent scholarship.

Where to Learn More

- **Charleston, South Carolina.** Many buildings date from the eighteenth century. Officials stored tea in one of them, the Exchange, to prevent a local version of the Boston Tea Party. The website for Historic Charleston, www.cr.nps.gov/nr/travel/charleston, provides a map, a list of buildings, and information about them.

- **Philadelphia, Pennsylvania.** Numerous buildings and sites date from the eighteenth century. Independence National Historical Park, between Second and Sixth streets on Walnut and Chestnut streets, contains Carpenter's Hall, where the First Continental Congress met, and the Pennsylvania State House (now known as Independence Hall), where the Declaration of Independence was adopted. Philadelphia's Historic Mile, www.ushistory.org/tour/index.html, provides a virtual tour of the great landmarks of the city, including Independence Hall.

- **Boston, Massachusetts.** Many important buildings and sites in this area date from the seventeenth and eigh-teenth centuries. They include Faneuil Hall (Dock Square), where many public meetings took place prior to the Revolution, and the Old State House (Washington and State streets), which overlooks the site of the Boston Massacre. The Freedom Trail, www.thefreedomtrail.org/virtual_tour.html, provides a well-illustrated virtual tour of the historic sites.

- **Fort Michilimackinac National Historic Landmark, Mackinaw City, Michigan.** Near the south end of the Mackinac Bridge, the present structure is a modern restoration of the fort as it was when Pontiac's Rebellion took a heavy toll of its garrison. The Mackinac State Historic Park's website, www.mackinacparks.com/michilimackinac/html, provides a brief description and photographs of the reconstructed colonial village and fort.

Study Resources

PEARSON
myhistorylab™

For study resources for this chapter, go to www.myhistorylab.com and choose *The American Journey.* You will find a wealth of study and review material for this chapter, including pre- and post-tests, customized study plan, key term review flash cards, interactive map and document activities, and documents for analysis.

George Washington's Tent. Plunkett Fleeson, a well-known Philadelphia upholsterer, made a set of three tents for Washington in 1776. One was for sleeping, one for dining, and one for baggage. This one, which measures 18 by 28 feet, could have served multiple purposes.

Smithsonian Museum.

The War for Independence
1774–1783

6

Headquarters, Valley Forge
January 14, 1778

I barely hinted to you my dearest Father my desire to augment the Continental Forces from an untried Source.... I would solicit you to cede me a number of your able bodied men Slaves, instead of leaving me a fortune. I would bring about a twofold good, first I would advance those who are unjustly deprived of the Rights of Mankind to a State which would be a proper Gradation between abject Slavery and perfect Liberty and besides I would reinforce the Defenders of Liberty with a number of gallant Soldiers....

Headquarters, Valley Forge
February 2, 1778

My dear Father,

The more I reflect upon the difficulties and delays which are likely to attend the completing our Continental Regiments, the more anxiously is my mind bent upon the Scheme which I lately communicated to you....

You seem to think my dear Father, that men reconciled by long habit to the miseries of their Condition would prefer their ignominious bonds to the untasted Sweets of Liberty, especially when offer'd upon the terms which I propose.... I am tempted to believe that this trampled people have so much human left in them, as to be capable of aspiring to the rights of men by noble exertions, if some friend to mankind would point the Road, and give them prospect of Success.

I have long deplored the wretched State of these men and considered in their history, the bloody wars excited in Africa to furnish America with Slaves. The Groans of despairing multitudes toiling for the Luxuries of Merciless Tyrants. I have had the pleasure of conversing with you sometimes upon the means of restoring them to their rights. When can it be better done than when their enfranchisement may be made conducive to the Public Good.

John Laurens

Henry Laurens Papers, vol. 12, pp. 305, 390–392.

myhistorylab

Personal Journeys Online

- Baikia Harvey, *Baikia Harvey to Thomas Baikie, Snowhill, South Carolina, December 30, 1775*. A new immigrant describes conditions in Georgia in 1775.

- Joseph Martin, *The Revolutionary Adventures of Joseph Plumb Martin, 1776–1783*. A Continental soldier remembers the Revolution.

John Laurens wrote these letters to his father, Henry, at one of the low points of the American Revolution, when victory seemed most remote. The letters reveal much, not only about the course of the war but also about the aspirations and limitations of the Revolutionary generation. Henry, a wealthy slaveholder from South Carolina, was president of the Continental Congress; his son John was an aide to General George Washington.

John, 23 years old in 1778, had been born in South Carolina but educated for the most part in Geneva and London, where he had been exposed to some of the most progressive currents of the Enlightenment. Among these were compassion for the oppressed and the conviction that slavery should be abolished. As the controversy between Britain and its colonies grew into war, John became increasingly impatient to enlist in a cause that appealed deeply to him.

The American version of republicanism combined a New Whig distrust of central authority with a belief in a government rooted in the public spirit of a virtuous citizenry. Clinging fervently to this ideology, Americans at first expected to defeat the British Army with a zealous citizens' militia. But as the war intensified, they learned that they could prevail only by developing a professional fighting force. With vital French assistance, the new American army eventually overcame the enemy, but the Continental Army was often critically short of soldiers. During the summer of 1776, for example, Britain had 30,000 troops in New York City alone; at Valley Forge in 1777–1778, Washington had 8,200 men fit for duty.

Aware of this discrepancy in manpower, Laurens saw an opportunity to solve two problems at once when he returned to America in 1777. Enlisting slaves in the army would provide blacks with a stepping stone to freedom and American forces with desperately needed troops. His father, however, was a conditional emancipationist—though he detested slavery—and conditions were never quite right for him. John, however, tried and failed repeatedly to convince legislatures in the deep south to enroll black troops in exchange for their freedom.

CHRONOLOGY

1775	April 19: Battles of Lexington and Concord.
	May 10: Second Continental Congress meets.
	June 17: Battle of Bunker Hill.
	December 31: American attack on Quebec.
1776	January 9: Thomas Paine's *Common Sense* published.
	July 4: Declaration of Independence.
	September 15: British take New York City.
	December 26: Battle of Trenton.
1777	January 3: Battle of Princeton.
	September 11: Battle of Brandywine Creek.
	October 17: American victory at Saratoga.
	Runaway inflation begins.
	Continental Army winters at Valley Forge.
1778	February 6: France and the United States sign an alliance.
	June 17: Congress refuses to negotiate with British peace commissioners.
	July 4: George Rogers Clark captures British post in the Mississippi Valley.
	December 29: British capture Savannah.
	Death of the great French Enlightenment writer, François-Marie Arouet Voltaire.
1779	June 21: Spain declares war on Britain.
	Americans devastate the Iroquois country.
	September 23: John Paul Jones captures the British ship *Serapis*.
1780	May 12: Fall of Charleston, South Carolina.
	October 7: Americans win Battle of Kings Mountain.
	December 3: Nathanael Greene takes command in the South.
1781	January 17: Americans defeat British at Battle of Cowpens.
	March 15: Battle of Guilford Court House.
	October 19: Cornwallis surrenders at Yorktown.
	Influential German philosopher Immanuel Kant publishes his first major work, *The Critique of Pure Reason*.
1783	March 15: Washington quells the Newburgh "Conspiracy."
	September 3: Peace of Paris signed.
	November 21: British begin evacuating New York.
	First manned balloon flight, in France.
	Quakers present first anti-slavery petition to the British parliament.
1784	United States vessel opens trade with Canton, China.
1788	Britain transports convicts to Australia.

John's idealistic quest for social justice ended on the banks of the Combahee River in South Carolina, where he died in one of the last skirmishes of the war. "Where liberty is," he once wrote, "there is my country." Americans won their independence, but eight long years of warfare strained and in some ways profoundly altered the fabric of American society, though not as much as Laurens had wished.

The Outbreak of War and The Declaration of Independence, 1774–1776

After the Boston Tea Party, both the British and the Americans knew that they were approaching a crisis. A British officer in Massachusetts commented in late 1774 that "it is thought by every body here" that British forces would soon have "to take the field." "The people in general are very enraged," he explained, and some would "defend what they call their Liberties" to the death. Many Americans also expected a military confrontation but continued to hope that the king would not "reason with us only by the roar of his Cannon."

Mounting Tensions

In May 1774, General Thomas Gage, the commander in chief of the British army in America, replaced Thomas Hutchinson as governor of Massachusetts. After Gage dissolved the Massachusetts legislature, the General Court, it defied him by assembling anyway. Calling itself the Provincial Congress, the legislature in October 1774 appointed an emergency executive body, the **Committee of Safety**, headed by John Hancock, which began stockpiling weapons and organizing militia volunteers. Some localities had already provided for the formation of special companies of **Minute Men**, who were to be ready at "a minute's warning in Case of an alarm."

Enforcing the Continental Association's boycott of British goods, local committees sometimes assaulted suspected loyalists and destroyed their property. The increasingly polarized atmosphere, combined with the drift toward military confrontation, drove a growing wedge between American loyalists and the patriot anti-British American Whigs.

The Loyalists' Dilemma

Loyalists and Whigs began to part company in earnest during the fall and winter of 1774–1775 as the threat of war mounted. Like other Americans, the loyalists were a mixed group. Most were farmers, though officeholders and professionals were overrepresented. Recent immigrants to the colonies, as well as locally unpopular minorities (Scots in the South, Anglicans in New England), often remained loyal because they believed the crown offered protection against more established Americans. Most loyalists thought, in short, that they had something to lose—including their honor—if America broke with Britain. During the War for Independence, about 19,000 American men would join British provincial units and fight to restore royal authority. (This compares with the perhaps 200,000 who served in some military capacity on the rebel side.) The loyalists numbered close to half a million men and women—some 20 percent of the colonies' free population. Of these, up to 100,000 would leave with the British forces at the end of the war.

British Coercion and Conciliation

Britain held parliamentary elections in the fall of 1774, but if Americans hoped that the outcome would change the government's policy toward them, they were disappointed. North's supporters won easily. Angry and alarmed at the colonists' challenge to Parliament's sovereignty, they took a hard line. Under North's direction, in February 1775, Parliament resolved that Massachusetts was in rebellion and prohibited the New England colonies from trading outside the British Empire or sending their ships to the North Atlantic fishing grounds. Similar restrictions on most of the other colonies soon followed.

Meanwhile, in a gesture of appeasement, Parliament endorsed Lord North's **Conciliatory Proposition**, which pledged not to tax the colonies if they would voluntarily contribute to the defense of the empire. British officials, however, would decide what was a sufficient contribution. Parliament, as a result, would remain sovereign and the colonial legislatures strictly subordinate to it.

Had the Conciliatory Proposition specified a maximum colonial contribution, and had it been offered ten years earlier, the colonists might have found it acceptable. Now it was too late. North's government, in any case, had already sent orders to General Gage to take decisive action against the Massachusetts rebels. These orders triggered the first clash between British and American forces.

The Battles of Lexington and Concord

Gage received his orders on April 14, 1775. On the night of April 18, he assembled 700 men on the Boston Common and marched them toward the little towns of Lexington and Concord, some 20 miles away (see Map 6–1). Their mission was to arrest rebel leaders Samuel Adams and John Hancock (then staying in Lexington) and to destroy the military supplies the Committee of Safety had assembled at Concord. Learning of the troop movements, patriots sent riders—one of them the silversmith Paul Revere—to spread the alarm. Adams and Hancock escaped.

When the British soldiers reached Lexington at dawn, they found about seventy armed militiamen drawn up in formation on the village green. Their precise intentions are not clear. Outnumbered ten to one, they probably did not plan to begin a fight. More likely, they were there in a show of defiance, to demonstrate that Americans would not run at the sight of a superior British force.

A British major ordered the militia to disperse. They were starting to obey when a shot from an unknown source shattered the stillness. The British responded with a volley that killed or wounded 18 Americans.

The British troops pressed on to Concord and burned what few supplies the Americans had not been able to hide. But when their rear guard came under fire at Concord's North Bridge, the British panicked. As they retreated to Boston, patriot Minute Men and other militia harried them from both sides of the road. By the time the column reached safety, 273 British soldiers were dead, wounded, or missing. The 4,000 Americans who had shot at them along the way suffered nearly 100 casualties.

News of the fighting at the **Battles of Lexington and Concord** spread quickly. Patriots in Providence, Rhode

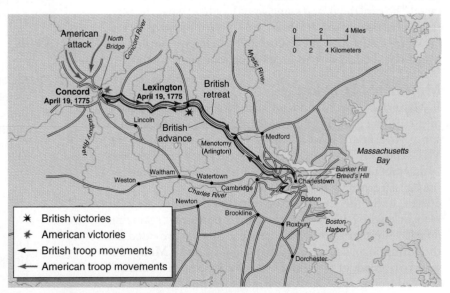

MAP 6–1   The Battles of Lexington and Concord, April 19, 1775
This map shows the area around Boston, where in April 1775 British and American forces fought the first military engagements of the Revolution.

Island, knew of it by evening of the Wednesday on which it occurred. Rumors of the fighting had already reached New York by the time an express rider confirmed the stories at noon the following Sunday. The Philadelphia newspaper *Pennsylvania Packet* carried the story the next Monday. Williamsburg's *Virginia Gazette* printed an account on May 4, only two weeks after the event. South Carolinians knew by May 9, and Georgians probably soon after. The speed with which distant colonies heard about the outbreak of fighting suggests both the importance Americans attached to it and the extraordinary efforts patriots made to spread word of it. Everywhere, news of Lexington and Concord spurred Whigs into action.

The shots fired that April morning would, in the words of the nineteenth-century Concord philosopher and poet Ralph Waldo Emerson, be "heard round the world." They signaled the start of the American Revolution, which would help to inspire many revolutions elsewhere.

The Second Continental Congress, 1775–1776

By the time the **Second Continental Congress** convened in Philadelphia on May 10, 1775, Gage's troops had limped back into Boston from Lexington and Concord, and patriot militia had surrounded the city. American forces from Vermont and Massachusetts under, respectively, Ethan Allen and Benedict Arnold overwhelmed the British garrison at Fort Ticonderoga at the southern end of Lake Champlain on the very day Congress met. Rebel forces elsewhere seized arms and ammunition from royal storehouses.

Assuming leadership of the rebellion, the Congress in the succeeding months became, in effect, a national government. It called for the patchwork of local forces to be organized into the **Continental Army**, authorized the formation of a navy, established a post office, and printed paper continental dollars to meet its expenses. Denying Parliament's claim to govern the colonies but not yet ready to declare themselves independent, the delegates sought to preserve their ties to Britain by expressing loyalty to the crown. In the **Olive Branch Petition**, addressed to George III on July 5, they asked the king to protect his American subjects from the military actions ordered by Parliament. The following day, Congress approved the **Declaration of the Causes and Necessity of Taking Up Arms**, asserting the resolve of American patriots "to die freemen, rather than to live slaves." And at the end of the month, it formally rejected North's Conciliatory Proposition.

Commander-in-Chief George Washington

To take command of the patriot forces around Boston—the newly named Continental Army—Congress turned to George Washington who had been suggested by John Adams, a Whig leader from Massachusetts. Selecting the Virginian, Adams and others realized, would help transform a local quarrel in New England into a continental conflict involving all of British North America and—they hoped—attract recruits from Virginia, the most populous colony. Despite (or per-haps because of) his experience in the French and Indian War, Washington claimed to feel inadequate to the task, but by attending the Congress in military uniform, he seemed to be volunteering for it.

He was the ideal person for the job. Some of his contemporaries had quicker minds and broader educations; Washington, however, was blessed with good judgment, a profound understanding of both the uses and the limitations of power, and the gift of command. He soon realized that the fate of the patriot cause depended on the survival of the army. Early in the war, he almost suffered catastrophic military defeat at least twice, but he learned from his mistakes and thereafter did not risk lives unnecessarily. The troops in turn revered him.

Early Fighting: Massachusetts, Virginia, the Carolinas, and Canada

General Gage, finding himself besieged in Boston after the fighting at Lexington and Concord, decided to seize and fortify territory south of Boston, where his cannons could command the harbor. But the Americans seized the high ground first, entrenching themselves on Breed's Hill north of town. On June 17, 1775, Gage sent 2,200 well-trained soldiers to drive the 1,700 patriot men and boys from their new position. The British succeeded, but at the cost of more than 1,000 casualties. One despondent British officer observed afterward that another such victory "would have ruined us." Misnamed for another hill nearby, this encounter has gone down in history as the Battle of Bunker Hill (see Map 6–2).

Washington, who arrived in Boston after the battle, took command of the American forces there in early July. Months of standoff followed, with neither side able to dislodge the other. During the winter of 1775–1776, however, the Americans dragged some sixty cannons—the largest weighing as much as a ton—300 miles through snow and over mountains from Fort Ticonderoga to Boston. In March 1776, Washington mounted the newly arrived guns to overlook Boston harbor, putting the British in an indefensible position. The British then evacuated Boston—which really had no strategic value for them—and moved their troops to Halifax, Nova Scotia. New England was for the moment secure for the patriots.

Fighting in the South also went well for the patriots. Virginia's last royal governor, Lord Dunmore, fled the capital, Williamsburg, and set up a base in nearby Norfolk. Promising freedom to slaves who joined him, he succeeded in raising a small force of black and white loyalists and British marines. On December 9, 1775, most of these men died when they attacked a much larger force of 900 Virginia and North Carolina patriots at Great Bridge, near Norfolk. On February 27, a force of loyalist Scots suffered a similar defeat at Moore's Creek Bridge in North Carolina. And in June 1776, patriot forces successfully repulsed a large British expedition sent to attack Charleston, South Carolina.

In contrast, an American attempt against Canada in 1775 failed, though one expedition quickly captured Montreal. Another, under Benedict Arnold, advanced through the

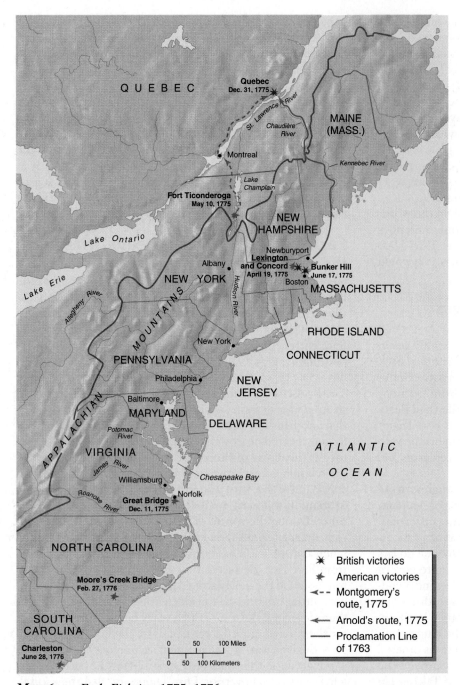

MAP 6–2   Early Fighting, 1775–1776
As this map clearly reveals, even the earliest fighting occurred in widely scattered areas, thereby complicating Britain's efforts to subdue the Americans.

gress's Olive Branch Petition, proclaimed the colonies to be in rebellion, and denied them his protection. In December, Parliament barred all exports from the American colonies. These actions prompted many Whigs to think seriously of declaring full independence from Britain.

At this critical moment, Thomas Paine, a ne'er-do-well Englishman, recently arrived on American soil, made a historic contribution. A corsetmaker—and twice a fired tax collector—he was a man of radical ideas and forceful writing who used the everyday English of ordinary people. His pamphlet *Common Sense,* published in Philadelphia in January 1776, denounced King George and made the case for independence. Ridiculing the absurdity of "supposing a continent to be perpetually governed by an island," Paine argued that America would be better off on every count if it were independent. The king, he said bluntly, was "the Royal Brute" whose tyranny should be thrown off. This assertion, which not long before would have shocked even Whigs, seemed self-evident now in light of the king's rejection of the Olive Branch Petition. Simple common sense, Paine concluded, dictated that "'TIS TIME TO PART."

Common Sense, which sold more than 100,000 copies throughout the colonies, helped predispose Americans toward independence. Tactical considerations also influenced patriot leaders. Formal separation from Great Britain would make it easier for them to gain desperately needed aid from England's rival France and other foreign countries. Declaring independence would also provide a better legal basis for American leaders' newly claimed authority. Accordingly, most of the states (as the rebellious colonies now called themselves) either instructed or permitted their delegates in the Congress to vote for independence.

On June 7, 1776, Virginian Richard Henry Lee introduced in the Congress a resolution stating that the united colonies "are, and of right ought to be, free and independent States." Postponing a vote on the issue, the Congress appointed a committee to draw up a declaration of independence. "You can write ten times better than I," John Adams is supposed to have told Thomas Jefferson; so the Virginian wrote the first draft. On June 28, after making revisions in Jefferson's proposed text, the committee presented the document to Congress. In the debate that fol-

Maine wilderness in the face of great hardships. They joined forces outside of Quebec and mounted a hasty attack on December 31 that failed. Canada accordingly remained a British province.

Independence

The American forces' stunning early successes bolstered the patriots' confidence as attempts to promote reconciliation failed. In August 1775, King George III rejected the Con-

This fine portrait of George Washington appears in multiple versions depicting the victorious general against different backgrounds, including the battles of Princeton and Yorktown. The painter, Charles Willson Peale, served under Washington at Princeton, and the French commander at Yorktown, the Count de Rochambeau, took an appropriate version home with him in 1783.

lowed, the South Carolina, Pennsylvania, and New York delegations initially opposed independence. As it became clear that the majority favored it, the Pennsylvania and South Carolina delegations switched sides, and the New York delegation decided to abstain. A few delegates—including the notable patriot leaders John Dickinson and Robert Morris of Pennsylvania—clung to the hope of remaining loyal to the crown. But when the Congress voted on the resolution for independence on July 2, 1776, all voting delegations approved it. After further tinkering with the wording, the Congress officially adopted the **Declaration of Independence** on July 4, 1776.

Congress intended the declaration to be a justification for America's secession from the British Empire and an invitation to potential allies. Jefferson later maintained that what he wrote was only what everyone was thinking. But his prose

transformed a version of the **contract theory of government** into one of history's great statements of human rights. Developed by the late-seventeenth-century English philosopher John Locke and others, the contract theory maintains that legitimate government rests on an agreement between the people and their rulers. The people are bound to obey their rulers only so long as the rulers offer them protection.

The Declaration of Independence consists of a magnificently stated opening assumption, two premises, and a powerful conclusion. The opening assumption is that all men are created equal, that they therefore have equal rights, and that they can neither give up these rights nor allow them to be taken away. The first premise—that people establish governments to protect their fundamental rights to life, liberty, and property—is a restatement of contract theory. (With a wonderful flourish reflecting the Enlightenment's optimism about human potential, Jefferson changed "property" to "the pursuit of happiness.") The second premise is a long list of charges meant to prove that George III had failed to defend his American subjects' rights. This indictment, the heart of the declaration, justified the Americans' rejection of their hitherto legitimate ruler. Then followed the dramatic conclusion: that Americans could rightfully overthrow King George's rule and replace it with something more satisfactory to them.

Historians have spilled oceans of ink debating Jefferson's use of the expression "all men." In practice, of course, many people were excluded from full participation in eighteenth-century American society. Women had no formal political rights and limited legal rights. Property-less white and free black men had similarly restricted rights, and slaves enjoyed no rights at all. (Although himself a slaveowner, Jefferson was deeply troubled by American slavery. He had wanted to include a denunciation of the slave trade among the charges against George III in the Declaration of Independence, but the Congress took it out, believing that to blame the king for this inhumane business would appear hypocritical.) But if the words "all men are created equal" had limited practical meaning in 1776, they have ever since confronted Americans with a moral challenge to make good on them.

Religion, Virtue, and Republicanism

Americans reacted to news of the Declaration of Independence with mixed emotions. There was rejoicing as orators read the declaration to large crowds. Soldiers fired salutes, and candles illuminated the windows of public buildings. But even many who favored independence worried about how Americans would govern themselves. Most Whigs, animated by the political ideology known as **republicanism**, thought a republican government was best suited to American society.

John Adams once complained that republicanism was too shadowy a concept to define, and indeed it was a complex, changing body of ideas, values, and assumptions. Closely related to country (New Whig) ideology, republicanism was

In this painting of the Battle of Bunker Hill, the artist John Trumbull highlighted the death of Major General Joseph Warren of the Massachusetts militia. Like Trumbull, historians have traditionally emphasized prominent historical figures. More recently, however, they have focused on the common people, such as the militiamen, black and white, who appear at the margins of this picture but who composed the majority of the American forces fighting that day.

seventeenth century, English Puritans had for a time replaced the monarchy with a republican "Commonwealth," dedicated to advancing the "common weal," or common good. Most eighteenth-century Americans thought of the Puritan Commonwealth as a misguided product of fanaticism that had ended in a military dictatorship. However, some New Englanders, spiritual descendants of the Puritans, considered the Commonwealth to have been a noble experiment. To them, the American Revolution offered another chance to establish a republic of the godly.

"When the mere Politician weighs the Danger or Safety of his Country," warned one clergyman, "he computes them in Proportion to its Fortresses, Arms, Money, Provisions, Numbers of Fighting Men, and its Enemies." But, he continued, the "Christian Patriot" calculates them "by its Numbers of Sinful or praying People, and its Degrees of Holiness or Vice." Such language recalled the Great Awakening; it reached beyond the upper classes who had been directing the resistance to the British and mobilized ordinary people for what their ministers repeatedly assured them was a just war against sin and despotism. Out of this fusion of republican theory (with which only the educated were familiar) and the religious heritage that all Americans understood, a common belief developed that God was on their side and that Americans must have "resolution enough to forgo Self gratification" and be willing to stake their all "upon the prospect of Securing freedom and happiness to future Generations."

derived from the political ideas of classical antiquity, Renaissance Europe, and early modern England. It held that self-government—either directly by the citizens of a country or indirectly by their elected representatives—provided a more reliable foundation for the good society and individual freedom than did rule by kings. Thus, drawing on contract theory, as in the Declaration of Independence, republicanism called for government by consent of the governed. Drawing on country ideology, it was suspicious of excessively centralized government and insistent on the need for a virtuous, public-spirited citizenry. Republicanism therefore helped to give the American Revolution a moral dimension.

But other than a state that was not ruled by a hereditary king, what was a republic? And what were the chances that one would survive? Every educated person knew, of course, that ancient Rome and Athens had been republics. Classical political theory, beginning with the ancient Greek thinkers Plato and Aristotle, had insisted that republics could endure only as long as their citizens remained virtuous and self-sacrificing. Once individual citizens, greedy for wealth and power, began fighting among themselves, a republic would certainly collapse. Europe's three surviving republics in the eighteenth century—the Netherlands, Switzerland, and Venice—seemed to bear out this dismal picture: All were rather corrupt and uninspiring societies, and none of them was democratic.

But Americans had at hand a more recent example of a republic than ancient Athens or Rome, one more closely linked to their own history than the republics of eighteenth-century Europe. During the English Civil War of the mid-

The Combatants

At the outset of the American Revolution, republican fervor produced a spontaneous eruption of patriotism that to skeptical foreign observers looked like religious fanaticism. But this enthusiastic flocking to the colors eventually waned, and in any case, its results were often unsatisfactory.

Republican theory mistrusted professional armies as the instruments of tyrants. A free people, republicans insisted, relied for defense on their own patriotism. But militiamen, as one American general observed, had trouble coping with "the shocking scenes of war" because they were not "steeled by habit or fortified by military pride." In real battles, they often proved unreliable. Americans therefore faced a hard choice: Develop a professional army or lose the war. In the end, they did what they had to do. While state militias continued to offer support, it was the disciplined forces of the Continental Army that won the crucial battles.

Global Perspectives

American Independence Abroad

The main purpose of the Declaration of Independence was to announce to other nations that the United States had assumed a place among them and was therefore available as a trading partner and military ally. Most countries, however, at first took a wait-and-see approach. As one historian has observed, a "deafening diplomatic silence" greeted the American debut on the world stage.

Unofficial admiration and emulation were quicker and more widespread. As early as 1777, a German newspaper noted that American success would give "new life to the spirit of liberty," and by 1790 at least 26 works on America had been published in three or more European languages. Elsewhere, slaves took direct action. In the West Indies, they celebrated Americans for meriting "Immortal Honour" for "encountering death in every form rather than submit to slavery." Jamaican bondsmen unsuccessfully revolted in 1776, and on islands off the southeastern coast of Africa, rebelling slaves explained their actions by observing that "America is free. Could not we be?"

The success of the American Revolution also had profound repercussions in the two most powerful nations of Europe. In France the American example and the depletion of the treasury during the war contributed to a revolution that overthrew the monarchy. In Britain the results were less dramatic but important. The loss of the North American colonies accelerated an eastward shift in British attention that would make India the crown jewel in the nineteenth-century empire. Whites also began settling Australia in 1788 when Britain started sending convicts there because, unlike the colonies, an independent United States could—and did—refuse to accept them.

Even the abolition of slavery in the British Empire occurred when it did partly as a result of American independence. By tarnishing England's reputation as the model of freedom, the American Revolution prompted a reaction in Britain that helped to stimulate a popular antislavery movement. In addition, the independence of the United States weakened the political influence of the West Indian planters by dividing them from their fellow slaveholders on the mainland. Thus, ironically, Great Britain was able to emancipate its slaves during the 1830s—a full generation before the United States took the same step in a bloody civil war.

Professional Soldiers

Drawing on their colonial experience and on republican theory, the new state governments first tried to meet their military needs by relying on the militia and by creating new units based on short-term enlistments. Officers, particularly in the North, were often elected, and their positions depended on personal popularity. As a result, their orders sometimes sounded more like requests than commands, and rules were lax. Discipline became a major problem in both the militia and the new state units, and often volunteers had barely received basic training before their term of duty ended and they returned home.

Washington tightened things up in the new Continental Army. Eventually, he prevailed on Congress to adopt stricter regulations and to require enlistments for three years or the duration of the war. Although he used militia effectively, his consistent aim was to turn the Continental Army into a disciplined force that could defeat the British in the large engagements of massed troops characteristic of eighteenth-century European warfare, for only such victories could impress the other European powers and establish the legitimacy of the United States.

Many soldiers of fortune, as well as a few idealists, offered their services. Both Washington and Congress soon learned to regard most of them as nuisances, but several proved especially valuable in helping Washington forge a professional army. France's 19-year-old Marquis de Lafayette was one of the youngest, wealthiest, and most idealistic. Two Poles, Tadeusz Kosciuszko, an engineer, and Kazimierz Pulaski, a cavalry commander who would be mortally wounded at the Battle of Savannah in 1779, also rendered good service. Johann Kalb, a bogus baron from Germany, became a general and died heroically at Camden, South Carolina, in 1780. Most useful of all, probably, was Baron von Steuben. His title,

FROM THEN TO NOW

Anti-War Churches

One of the thornier problems that confronts nations when they are at war is how to deal with people whose conscience tells them that a particular war—or any war—is wrong; and such persons often have a difficult time deciding what duties they owe to the state. During the Revolution, the Methodists, Moravians, Mennonites, and Quakers were among the peace churches; that is, in the words of one Quaker meeting, they generally believed "that the Setting up and Putting down Kings and Government is God's Peculiar Prerogative [sic]... and that it is not our work or Business to have any hand or Contrivance therein. ..." Many of their members therefore refused to swear oaths of allegiance or join the militia. The states often responded by imposing stiff fines or extra taxes.

Since then, most of the wars in which the United States has been engaged—including the Vietnam War and the present war in Iraq—have prompted significant opposition at home. One recent example involved a church in Pasadena, California, whose former minister preached a sermon during the 2004 presidential campaign in which he imagined Jesus saying, "Mr. President, your doctrine of preemptive [sic] war is a failed doctrine." The United States Internal Revenue Service responded by preparing to revoke the church's tax exempt status on the grounds that exempt organizations such as churches and charities are not supposed to engage in political campaigns. "There's much more at stake" here, the church's current minister said. "I think it's a defining moment about religious freedom in the United States."

As Mark Twain is supposed to have observed, "history doesn't repeat, but it does Rhyme."

Benezet instructing colored children.

Anthony Benezet (1713–1784), a noted Pennsylvania Quaker, educator, and abolitionist, identified himself in his will, as in this picture, as "a leader of the Free School for the Black People in Philadelphia."

■ How much dissent or criticism should a nation permit when it is at war? How should it decide where to draw the line between the permissible and the impermissible?

George F. Regas' controversial sermon before the 2004 presidential election prompted the Internal Revenue Service to question the tax-exempt status of one of the largest Episcopal churches in the country. All Saints Church in Pasadena, California. He had been rector for twenty-eight years.

myhistorylab
From Then to Now Online

6-1 George F. Regas, *Extracts from sermon*, delivered October 31, 2004.

6-2 Anthony Benezet, *A Short Account of the People Called Quakers, Their Rise, Religious Principles and Settlement in America .... Philadelphia, Joseph Crukshank, 1780.*

6-3 North Carolina, *An Act for Ascertaining what Property in this State shall be deemed Taxable Property...,* 1778.

Thomas Jefferson, author of the Declaration of Independence and future president of the United States. Mather Brown, an American artist living in England, painted this picture of Jefferson for John Adams while the two men were in London on diplomatic missions in 1786. A companion portrait of Adams that Jefferson ordered for himself also survives. Brown's sensitive portrait of a thoughtful Jefferson is the earliest known likeness of him.

too, was new, but he had experience in the Prussian army, Europe's best. He became the Continental Army's drillmaster, and thanks partly to him, Washington's troops increasingly resembled their disciplined European counterparts.

The enemy British soldiers—and the nearly 30,000 German mercenaries (Americans called them "Hessians") whom the British government employed—offered Americans the clearest model of a professional army. British regulars were not (as Americans, then and later, assumed) the "dregs of society." Although most of the enlisted men came from the lower classes and from economically depressed areas, many also had skills. British officers usually came from wealthy families and had simply purchased their commissions. Only rarely could a man rise from the enlisted ranks to commissioned-officer status.

Most British troops carried the "Brown Bess" musket. With bayonet attached, it was almost 6 feet long and weighed over 16 pounds. It fired a lead ball slightly more than 1/2 inch in diameter, which might hit its target at up to 100 yards. Skilled troops could get off more than two rounds per minute under combat conditions. In battle, soldiers usually stood close together in lines three deep. They were expected to withstand bombardment without flinching, fire on command in volleys, and charge with the bayonet.

Military life was tough. On the march, seasoned troops carrying 60-pound packs normally covered about 15 miles a day but could go 30 miles in a "forced" march. In most weather conditions, they wore heavy woolen uniforms dyed bright red for visibility on smoke-filled battlefields (hence their nickname "Redcoats"). In their barracks, British soldiers doubled up in a bed slightly over 4 feet wide; in the field, they were often wet, crawling with lice, and hungry. Under the best conditions, they ate mainly beef or salt pork and bread. They were frequently undernourished, and many more died of disease than of injury in battle. Medical care was, by modern standards, primitive.

Severe discipline held soldiers in line. Striking an officer or deserting could bring death; lesser offenses usually incurred a beating. Several hundred lashes, "well laid on" with the notorious cat-o'-nine-tails (a whip with multiple cords, each ending in a nasty little knot or a metal ball), were not uncommon.

Soldiers amused themselves with gambling (despite regulations against it) and drinking. As one officer lamented, America was a terrible country where one drank "to get warm, or to get cool, or … because you get no letters." Perhaps two-thirds of the Redcoats were illiterate, and all suffered from loneliness and boredom. Camaraderie and a legendary loyalty to their regiments sustained them.

After the winter of 1777–1778, conditions in the Continental Army came to resemble those in the British army. Like British regulars, American recruits tended to be low on the social scale. They included young men without land, indentured servants, some criminals and vagrants—in short, men who lacked better prospects. The chances for talented enlisted men to win an officer's commission were greater than in the British army. But Continental soldiers frequently had little more than "their ragged shirt flaps to cover their nakedness," and their bare marching feet occasionally left bloody tracks in the snow.

The British and the Americans both had trouble supplying their troops. The British had plenty of sound money, which many American merchants and farmers were happy to take in payment for supplies. But they had to rely mostly on supplies shipped to them from the British Isles. The Continental Army, by contrast, had to pay for supplies in depreciating paper money. After 1780, the burden of provisioning the Continental Army fell on the states, which did little better than Congress had done. Unable to obtain sufficient supplies, the army sometimes threatened to seize them by force. This, in turn, increased the public's republican distrust of its own professional army.

Feeling themselves outcasts from an uncaring society, the professional soldiers of the Continental Army developed a community of their own. The soldiers were "as strict a band of brotherhood as Masons," one later wrote, and their spirit kept

An American Surgeon Reflects on the Winter at Valley Forge, 1777–1778

Dr. Albigence Waldo was a surgeon in the First Connecticut Infantry Regiment of the Continental Army while it was encamped at Valley Forge, Pennsylvania. His diary, from which the following excerpts are taken, reveals much about the attitudes of the soldiers as well as the conditions they faced. Waldo resigned from the service in 1779 because of illness but lived until 1794.

- How serious was Waldo in describing the reasons for the location of the soldiers' winter quarters?
- Did his griping reflect a serious morale problem?
- What do his remarks about the Indian soldier's death reveal about Waldo's values?

[December 13, 1777.—] It cannot be that our Superiors are about to hold consultation with Spirits infinitely beneath their Order, by bringing us into these [remote] regions. ... No, it is, upon consideration for many good purposes since we are to Winter here—1st There is plenty of Wood & Water. 2dly There are but few families for the soldiery to Steal from—tho' far be it from a Soldier to Steal. 4ly [sic] There are warm sides of Hills to erect huts on. 5ly They will be heavenly Minded like Jonah when in the Belly of a Great Fish. 6ly They will not become home Sick as is sometimes the case when Men live in the Open World—since the reflections which will naturally arise from their present habitation, will lead them to the more noble thoughts of employing their leisure hours in filling their knapsacks with such materials as may be necessary on the Journey to another Home.

December 14.—Prisoners & Deserters are continually coming in. The Army which has been surprisingly healthy hitherto, now begins to grow sickly from the continued fatigues they have suffered this Campaign. Yet they still show a spirit of Alacrity & Contentment not to be expected from so young Troops. I am Sick—discontented—and out of humour. Poor food—hard lodging—Cold Weather—fatigue—Nasty Cloaths—nasty Cookery—Vomit half my time—smoak'd out of my senses—the Devil's in't—I can't Endure it—Why are we sent here to starve and Freeze—What sweet Felicities have I left at home; A charming Wife—pretty Children—Good Beds—good food—good Cookery—all agreeable—all harmonious. Here all Confusion—smoke & Cold—hunger &

filthyness—A pox on my bad luck. There comes a bowl of beef soup—full of burnt leaves and dirt, sickish enough to make a Hector spue—away with it Boys—I'll live like the Chameleon upon Air. Poh! Poh! Crys Patience within me—you talk like a fool. Your being sick Covers your mind with a Melanchollic Gloom, which makes everything about you appear gloomy. See the poor Soldier, when in health—with what cheerfulness he meets his foes and encounters every hardship—if barefoot, he labours thro' the Mud & Cold with a Song in his mouth extolling War & Washington—if his food be bad, he eats it notwithstanding with seeming content—blesses God for a good Stomach and Whistles it into digestion. But harkee Patience, a moment—There comes a Soldier, his bare feet are seen thro' his worn out Shoes, his legs nearly naked from the tatter'd remains of an only pair of stockings, his Breeches not sufficient to cover his nakedness, his Shirt hanging in Strings, his hair dishevell'd, his face meager; his whole appearance pictures a person forsaken & discouraged. He comes, and crys with an air of wretchedness & despair, I am Sick, my feet lame, my legs are sore, my body cover'd with this tormenting Itch—my Cloaths are worn out, my Constitution is broken, my former Activity is exhausted by fatigue, hunger & Cold, I fail fast. I shall soon be no more! And all the reward I shall get will be—"Poor Will is dead."

December 21.—[Valley Forge.] Heartily wish myself at home, my Skin & eyes are almost spoil'd with continual smoke. A general cry thro' the Camp this evening among the Soldiers, "No Meat! No Meat!"—the Distant vales Echo'd back the melancholy sound—"No

Meat! No Meat!" Immitating the noise of Crows & Owls, also, made a part of the confused Musick.

What have you for your Dinners Boys? "Nothing but Fire Cake & Water, Sir." At night, "Gentlemen the Supper is ready." What is your Supper Lads? "Fire Cake & Water, Sir."

December 30.—Eleven Deserters came in to-day—some Hessians & some English—one of the Hesns took an Ax in his hand & cut away the Ice of the Schuylkill which was 1 1/2 inches thick & 40 Rod wide and waded through to our Camp—he was 1/2 hour in the Water. They had a promise when they engag'd that the war would be ended in one year—they were now tired of the Service.

[January 3, 1778.—] I was call'd to relieve a Soldier tho't to be dying—he expir'd before I Reach'd the Hutt. He was an Indian—an excellent Soldier—and an obedient good natur'd fellow. He engaged for money doubtless as others do;—but he has serv'd his country faithfully—he has fought for those very people who disinherited his forefathers—having finished his pilgrimage, he was discharged from the War of Life & Death. His memory ought to be respected, more than those rich ones who supply the world with nothing better than Money and Vice.

Source: "Valley Forge, 1777–1778. Diary of Surgeon Albigence Waldo, of the Connecticut Line," *Pennsylvania Magazine of History and Biography,* 21 (1897): 306–07, 309, 315–16, 319.

them together in the face of misery. They groused, to be sure—sometimes alarmingly. In May 1780, Connecticut troops at Washington's camp in Morristown, New Jersey, staged a brief mutiny. On January 1, 1781, armed units from Pennsylvania stationed in New Jersey marched to Philadelphia demanding their back pay. The Pennsylvania Executive Council met part of the soldiers' demands, but some of the men left the service. Washington ordered subsequent mutinies by New Jersey and Pennsylvania troops suppressed by force.

Occasionally, American officers let their disgruntlement get out of hand. The most notorious such case was that of Benedict Arnold, a general who compiled a distinguished record during the first three years of the war but then came to feel himself shabbily treated by Congress and his superiors. Seeking better rewards for his abilities, he offered to surrender the strategic fort at West Point (which he commanded) to the enemy. Before he could act, however, his plot was discovered, and he fled to the British, serving with them until the end of the war. Among Americans, his name became a synonym for traitor.

What was perhaps the most serious expression of army discontent—one that might have threatened the future of republican institutions and civilian government in the United States—occurred in March 1783, after the fighting was over. Washington's troops were then stationed near Newburgh, New York, waiting for their pay before disbanding. During the war, the Congress had promised officers a pension of half-pay for life (the custom in Great

Britain), but many veterans now demanded instead full pay for six years. When the Congress failed to grant real assurances that any pay would be forthcoming, hotheaded young officers called a meeting that could have led to an armed coup. General Washington, who had scrupulously deferred to civilian authority throughout the war, asked permission to address the gathering and, in a dramatic speech, subtly warned the men of all that they might lose by insubordination. A military coup

George Washington viewing troops at Valley Forge during the winter of 1777–78. This modern depiction is somewhat romanticized. While making a similar tour on foot, Washington once saw a soldier who was literally clothed in nothing but a blanket.

would "open the flood Gates of Civil discord" and "deluge" the nation in blood; loyalty now, he said, would be "one more distinguished proof" of their patriotism. With the fate of the Revolution apparently hanging in the balance, the movement collapsed. The officers and politicians behind the "conspiracy" were probably only bluffing, using the threat of a discontented army to frighten the states into granting the Congress the power (which it then lacked) to levy taxes so that it could pay the army. In any case, the Continental Army disbanded without further serious incidents.

Women in the Contending Armies

Women accompanied many units on both sides, as was common in eighteenth-century warfare. A few were prostitutes. Some were officers' wives or mistresses, but most were the married or common-law consorts of ordinary soldiers. These "camp followers" cooked and washed for the troops, occasionally helped load artillery, and provided most of the nursing care. A certain number in a company were subject to military orders and were authorized to draw rations and pay.

The role of these women found its way into American folklore in the legend of Molly Pitcher (perhaps Mary Ludwig Hays, the wife of a Continental artillery sergeant), who in 1778 heroically carried water to cool overheated men and guns at the Battle of Monmouth Court House. Other women also found themselves under fire. A British officer in New York, for example, reported discovering the bodies of three Americans—one a woman with cartridges in her hands. And a few women disguised as men even managed to serve in the Continental Army's ranks.

African American Participation in the War

Early in the war, as we have seen, some royal officials like Lord Dunmore recruited slaves with promises of freedom. But these efforts often proved counterproductive, frightening potentially loyalist slaveowners and driving them to the Whig side. Thus it was not until June 30, 1779, that the British commander in chief, Sir Henry Clinton, promised to allow slaves who fled from rebel owners to join the royal troops to "follow … any Occupation" they wished. Hedged as this promise of freedom was, news of it spread quickly among the slave communities, and late in the war, African Americans flocked to the British army in South Carolina and Georgia.

Sharing prevailing racial prejudices, the British were often reluctant to arm blacks. Instead, they put most of the ex-slaves to work as agricultural or construction workers (many of the free and enslaved blacks accompanying American troops were similarly employed). However, a few relatively well-equipped black British dragoons (mounted troops) did see combat in South Carolina.

On the other hand, approximately 5,000 African Americans fought against the British and for American independence, hundreds of them in the Continental Army. Many were freemen from Massachusetts and Rhode Island. Several free black men served among the defenders at Bunker Hill, and at least one distinguished himself sufficiently for his commander to commend him as "an experienced officer as well as an excellent soldier."

But farther south, as discussed above, John Laurens, a young Carolina patriot, repeatedly but vainly tried to convince the South Carolina assembly to raise and arm black troops. (Instead, the legislature eventually voted to give slaves confiscated from loyalists to white volunteers as a reward for their service.) It is therefore scarcely surprising that, as one Whig put it, many African Americans were "a little Toryfied," especially in the South.

Native Americans and the War

At first, most of the approximately 200,000 Native Americans east of the Mississippi River would probably have preferred to remain neutral, and both sides initially took them at their word. But Indians' skills and manpower were valuable, and by 1776 both the British and Americans sought their assistance. Forced to choose, many Native Americans favored the British, hoping thereby to safeguard their lands. "Remember," as a Cherokee chief once observed, the crucial "difference is about our land."

Prewar experience convinced Native Americans that British officials would be more apt to protect them against white settlers, and the British could provide more trade goods and arms. Many Indians, including the Cherokees, Creeks, Choctaws, and Chickasaws, therefore decided to back the British, and Cherokee warriors accordingly raided the southern frontier starting in 1776. Virginians, North and South Carolinians, and ultimately Tennesseans countered with expeditions that repeatedly devastated Cherokee towns. But when older chiefs sought peace, Dragging Canoe (Tsi'yugunsi'ny) and the more militant younger men established new communities on the Chickamauga River in northern Georgia and continued to fight.

Pushed and pulled by the British and the Americans, other Indian groups also split. Among these was the powerful Iroquois Confederation in upstate New York. Under the leadership of Thayendanegea—known to whites as Joseph Brant—the Mohawks and some of the other Iroquois nations supported the British, while most of the Oneidas and Tuscaroras joined the Americans. Thus, after some Iroquois attacked the northern frontiers of New York and Pennsylvania in 1777 and 1778, another Iroquois guided the American expedition that retaliated in 1779. Brother, sometimes quite literally, killed brother.

In other cases, though, the war promoted greater unity among Native Americans. Despite factionalism, the Shawnees, Delawares, Miamis, Wyandots, and others in the Ohio Valley eventually forged an alliance to preserve their control of the area with British support. And a few Native American nations aided the Americans. Most of these were small groups, like the Catawbas of South Carolina, who lived in the midst of white settlements.

John Laurens, who hoped to raise black troops in South Carolina as a prelude to the general abolition of slavery, was the only member of George Washington's staff to be killed in battle. This commemorative portrait by Charles Willson Peale bears the Latin inscription "Sweet and proper it is to die for one's country."

In sum, the British had more Indian allies, but they seldom made unrestricted use of them. Because Native Americans pursued their own purposes, British control of them was frequently tenuous, and the result could sometimes be counterproductive. In one such incident, an Indian attack in the Hudson River Valley resulted in the mistaken scalping of Jane McCrae, the fiancée of a British officer. Whig propagandists exploited this tragedy to the fullest. Neither side, however, had a monopoly on atrocities; both the Americans and the British committed more than their share.

The War in the North, 1776–1777

The Revolutionary War can be divided into three phases. In the first, from the outbreak of fighting in 1775 through 1777, most of the important battles took place in New England, New York, New Jersey, and Pennsylvania, while the Americans faced the British alone. But in 1778, France entered the war on the American side, opening the second phase of the war

in which fighting would rage from 1778 to 1781, mainly in the South, at sea, and on the western frontier. The third phase of the war, from late 1781 to 1783, saw little actual fighting. With American victory assured, attention shifted to the diplomatic maneuvering leading up to the Peace of Paris (1783).

Britain Hesitates: Crucial Battles in New York and New Jersey

During the first phase of the war, the British concentrated on subduing New England, the hotbed, they believed, of "rebellious principles." Replacing General Gage, the government appointed Sir William Howe as commander in chief of British forces and his brother, Richard Howe, as admiral of the naval forces in North American waters. New York City had been the headquarters of the British army during the late colonial period, and the Howes made it their base of operations. To counter this move, Washington moved his forces to New York in the spring of 1776. In August 1776, the Howes landed troops on Long Island and, in the Battle of Brooklyn Heights, quickly drove the American forces deployed there back to Manhattan Island (see Map 6–3).

Following instructions to negotiate peace as well as wage war, Richard Howe then met with three envoys from Congress on Staten Island on September 11, 1776. The British commanders were prepared to offer fairly generous terms but could not grant independence. The Americans would accept nothing less. So the meeting produced no substantive negotiations.

In the ensuing weeks, British forces overwhelmed Washington's troops, driving them out of Manhattan and then, moving north, clearing them from the area around the city at the Battle of White Plains. But the Howes were hesitant to deal a crushing blow, and the Americans were able to retreat across New Jersey into Pennsylvania. The American cause seemed lost, however, and the Continental Army almost melted away. Realizing that without a success he would soon be without troops, Washington led his forces back across the icy Delaware and launched a successful surprise attack on a garrison of Hessian mercenaries at Trenton, New Jersey, on the morning of December 26. A week later, Washington overwhelmed a British force at Princeton, New Jersey. Thereafter, both sides suspended operations until the spring.

"These are the times that try men's souls," Tom Paine wrote. "The summer soldier and the sunshine patriot will, in this crisis, shrink from the service of his country; but he that stands it NOW, deserves the love and thanks of man and woman."

By raising morale, the victories at Trenton and Princeton probably saved the American cause, but why the Howes failed to annihilate the Continental Army while they had the chance is a bit more puzzling. Perhaps, as a favorite Whig ditty had it, it was because Sir William Howe was "snug" abed with his mistress in New York. More to the point, the Howes were seeking to restore peace as well as end the rebellion;

MAP 6-3   The War in the North, 1776–1777
Most of the fighting between the British and Americans during the first part of the war occurred in the North, partly because the British commanders assumed that the New England colonies were the most rebellious.

they wanted to regain loyal subjects, not alienate them. And a crushing defeat might have made the Americans permanent enemies of British rule. By the time it became apparent that this cautious strategy was not working, Britain had lost its best chance to win the war.

The Year of the Hangman: Victory at Saratoga and Winter at Valley Forge

Contemporaries called 1777 the Year of the Hangman because the triple sevens suggested a row of gallows; and it was in fact a critical year for the American cause.

Mounting a major effort to end the rebellion, the British planned to send an army down the Hudson River from Canada. It would then link up with the Howes in New York City, isolate New England, and defeat the rebellion there. But there was little effort to coordinate strategy between the forces advancing from Canada and those in New York. Thus, the poorly planned and poorly executed campaign ended in disaster for the British.

Some 5,000 Redcoats and 3,000 German mercenaries assembled in Canada during the winter of 1776–1777. Ravaged by disease, the troops were unable to bury their dead until the frozen ground thawed in the spring. Under the command of the high-living and popular "Gentleman Johnny" Burgoyne, the army finally set off in June with 1,500 horses hauling its heavy artillery and ponderous supply train. A second, smaller column, supported by an Indian force under Thayendanegea (Joseph Brant) moved to the west to capture an American fort near Oriskany, New York, and then join up with Burgoyne's main force. Crossing Lake Champlain, Burgoyne's army made a splendid spectacle. Indians in canoes led the way, followed by row after row of boats filled with uniformed regulars. On July 5, Burgoyne's army recaptured Fort Ticonderoga, but success eluded him after that.

Trouble began as the troops started overland through the woods at the southern end of the lake. Huge trees felled by American axmen blocked their way, and the army crawled along at only two or three miles a day. Early in August, the column sent to capture the American fort near Oriskany turned back to Canada. Burgoyne's Indian allies under Joseph Brant likewise went home. Promised reinforcements never arrived. Ten days later, a Whig militia force wiped out a force of 800 men trying to gather supplies in Vermont.

By October 1777, Burgoyne's army was down to less than 6,000 men and facing disaster. Nearly 3,000 Continentals and 9,000 American militia, commanded by General Horatio Gates, exerted relentless pressure on the increasingly dispirited invaders. Unable to break through the American lines, Burgoyne surrendered to Gates following the Battle of Saratoga on October 17, 1777.

Burgoyne's defeat was a stunning reversal for the British. It would prove an important factor in convincing the French, eager for a way to strike back at their old enemy, the British, to join the fighting on the American side.

Meanwhile, General William Howe, rather than moving north to support Burgoyne, made plans to destroy Washington's army and capture Philadelphia. In July 1777, Howe's troops sailed from New York to Chesapeake Bay and from there marched on Philadelphia from the south. They met Washington's army on the banks of Brandywine Creek, near the Pennsylvania–Delaware border. The Americans put up a good fight before giving way with a loss of 1,200 killed or captured (twice as many as the British).

Howe occupied Philadelphia, and his men settled down in comfortable winter quarters. The Congress fled to York, Pennsylvania, and the Continental Army established its own winter camp outside Philadelphia at Valley Forge. Here Washington was joined by his wife, Martha, in a small stone farmhouse, surrounded by the log huts that his men built for themselves.

The Continental Army's miserable winter at **Valley Forge** has become famous for its hardships. Suffering from cold, disease, and starvation, as many as 2,500 soldiers died. Meanwhile, some congressmen and a few unhappy officers plotted unsuccessfully to replace Washington with Gates as commander in chief. Yet despite the difficulties, the Continental Army completed its transformation into a disciplined professional force. Under the watchful eye of General von Steuben, the soldiers drilled endlessly. And by spring, pleased observers felt that Washington at last had an army capable of meeting the British on equal terms.

The War Widens, 1778–1781

Since late 1776, Benjamin Franklin and a team of American diplomats had been in Paris negotiating French support for the patriot cause. In the winter of 1777–1778, aware that a Franco-American alliance was close, Parliament belatedly tried to end the rebellion by giving the Americans everything they wanted except independence itself. A peace commission sailed to America with authorization to grant the former colonies full autonomy, including the exclusive right to tax themselves, in return for a resumption of allegiance to the crown. But France and the United States concluded an alliance on February 6, 1778, and Congress refused to negotiate with the British.

Foreign intervention transformed the American Revolution into a virtual world war, engaging British forces in heavy fighting not only in North America but also in the West Indies and India. In the end, had it not been for French assistance, the American side probably would not have won the clear-cut victory it did.

The United States Gains an Ally

If the American victory at Saratoga had persuaded the French that the United States had a viable future, Washington's defeat at Brandywine Creek suggested it was a fragile one. Hoping to get even with their old enemy, Britain, the French had already been secretly supplying some aid to the United States. They now became convinced that they needed to act quickly lest further reverses force the Americans to agree to reconciliation with Britain. France accordingly signed a commercial treaty and a military alliance with the United States. Both sides promised to fight together until Britain recognized the independence of the United States, and France pledged not to seek the return of lands in North America.

French entry into the war was the first step in the consolidation of a formidable alliance of European powers eager to see Britain humbled and to gain trading rights in the former British colonies. France then persuaded Spain to declare war on Britain in June 1779. Unlike France, Spain never recognized the independence of the United States and gave only minimal financial aid, though it did contribute important logistical support. Much of the salt used to preserve American soldiers' provisions came from Spanish territories, and New Orleans became a base for American privateers. More important, the Spanish fleet increased the naval power of the countries arrayed against Great Britain.

Meanwhile, Catherine the Great of Russia suggested that the European powers form a League of Armed Neutrality to protect their trade with the United States and other warring countries against British interference. Denmark and Sweden soon joined; Austria, Portugal, Prussia, and Sicily eventually followed. Britain, which wanted to cut off Dutch trade with the United States, used a pretext to declare war on the Netherlands before it could join. Great Britain thus found itself isolated and even, briefly, threatened with invasion. In the spring of 1779, a joint Franco-Spanish fleet tried to ferry thousands of French troops across the English Channel but abandoned the effort after weeks at sea. These threats did not frighten the British leaders into suing for peace, but they forced them to make important changes in strategy.

Accordingly, in the spring of 1778, the British replaced the Howes with a new commander, Sir Henry Clinton, and instructed him to send troops to attack the French West Indies. To replace these troops, Clinton sought closer cooperation with Britain's Indian and loyalist allies. Knowing that he now faced a serious French threat, Clinton began consolidating his forces by evacuating Philadelphia and pulling his troops slowly back across New Jersey to New York.

On June 28, 1778, Washington caught up with the British at Monmouth Court House. For a while, it looked as if the now well-trained Americans might win the resulting battle, but a mix-up in orders cost Washington the victory. This inconclusive battle proved to be the last major engagement in the North. Clinton withdrew to New York, and Continental troops occupied the hills along the Hudson Valley north of the city. The war shifted to other fronts.

Fighting on the Frontier and at Sea

Known as "a dark and bloody ground" to Native Americans, Kentucky became even bloodier after the British instructed their Indian allies to raid the area in 1777. Because the British post at Detroit coordinated these attacks, the Americans tried to take it in 1778. Three expeditions failed for various reasons, but the last, under a Virginian, George Rogers Clark, did capture three key British settlements in the Mississippi Valley: Kaskaskia, Cahokia, and Vincennes (see Map 6–4). These successes may have strengthened American claims to the West at the end of the war.

In 1778 bloody fighting also occurred on the eastern frontiers. During the summer, a British force of 100 loyalists and 500 Indians struck the Wyoming Valley of Pennsylvania. After Americans at Forty Fort surrendered on July 4, raiders killed its wounded and fleeing defenders. Four months later, a similar group of attackers burned farmsteads and slaughtered civilians at Cherry Valley, New York. Both raids became the stuff of legend and stimulated equally savage reprisals against the Indians. Congress authorized an expedition against the Iroquois, and during the late summer of 1779 more than 4,000 Continental soldiers and state militia swept through the Finger Lakes region of New York, destroying 41 Indian villages and the crops that supported them. As a result, some 5,000 Iroquois sought refuge with the British at Fort Niagara.

The Americans and British also clashed at sea throughout the war. Great Britain was the preeminent sea power of the age, and the United States never came close to matching it. But in 1775 Congress authorized the construction of 13 frigates—medium-sized, relatively fast ships, mounting 32 guns—as well as the purchase of several merchant vessels for conversion to warships. By contrast, the Royal Navy in 1779 had more than a hundred large, heavily armed "ships of the line." The Americans therefore engaged in what was essentially a guerrilla war at sea. Their naval flag, appropriately, pictured a rattlesnake and bore the motto "Don't Tread on Me."

The country's first naval hero, Scottish-born John Paul Jones, was primarily a hit-and-run raider. Having gone to sea at age 12, he was originally known only as John Paul, but he took the name Jones as an alias after he killed another sailor during a mutiny. Offering his services to the Congress, he became the commander of the new vessel *Ranger,* and as such took news of the American victory at Saratoga to France in late 1777.

With Benjamin Franklin's help, Jones then obtained an old French merchant ship, which he armed and renamed the *Bon Homme Richard* in honor of Franklin's famous *Poor Richard's Almanac.* After a successful cruise, he encountered the formidable *H.M.S. Serapis* in the North Sea on September 23, 1779. Completely outgunned, Jones brought his ship close enough to make his small-arms fire more effective. Asked by the British if he were surrendering, Jones reportedly replied, "I have not yet begun to fight." Four hours later, the *Serapis* surrendered and Jones's crew took possession of the British vessel leaving the crippled *Bon Homme Richard* to sink.

The Congress and the individual states also supplemented America's naval forces by commissioning privateers. In effect legalized pirates, privateers preyed on British shipping. Captured goods were divided among the crew according to rank; captured sailors became prisoners of war. Some 2,000 American privateers took more than 600 British ships and forced the British navy to spread itself thin doing convoy duty.

The Land War Moves South

During the first three years of the war, the British made little effort to mobilize what they believed to be considerable loyalist strength in the South. But in 1778, the enlarged threat from France prompted a change in strategy: Redcoats would sweep through a large area and then leave behind a Tory militia to reestablish loyalty to the crown and suppress local Whigs. The British hoped thereby to recapture everything from Georgia to Virginia; they would deal with New England later.

The British southern strategy began to unfold in November 1778, when General Clinton dispatched 3,500 troops to take control of Georgia (see Map 6–5). Meeting only light resistance, they quickly seized Savannah and Augusta and restored the old colonial government under civilian control.

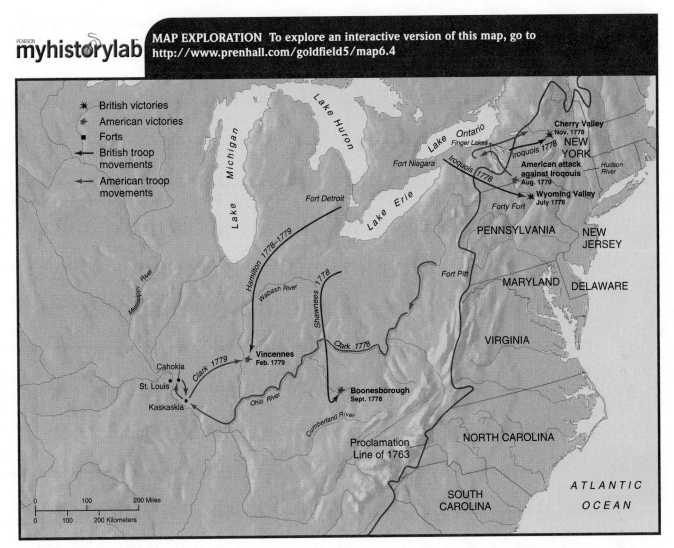

MAP EXPLORATION To explore an interactive version of this map, go to http://www.prenhall.com/goldfield5/map6.4

MAP 6–4   The War on the Frontier, 1778–1779
Significant battles in the Mississippi Valley and the frontiers of the seaboard states added to the ferocity of the fighting and strengthened some American claims to western lands.

After their initial success, however, the British suffered some serious setbacks. Spain entered the war and seized British outposts on the Mississippi and Mobile rivers while Whig militia decimated a loyalist militia at Kettle Creek, Georgia.

But the Americans could not beat the British army. In late September and early October 1779, a combined force of 5,500 American and French troops, supported by French warships, laid siege to Savannah. Moving too slowly to encircle the city, they allowed British reinforcements to get through. Then, impatient to get their ships away from the hurricane-prone coast, the French forced the Americans to launch a premature assault on the city on October 9. The assault failed, and the French sailed off.

The way was now open for the British to attack Charleston, the military key to the Lower South. In December 1779, Clinton sailed through stormy seas from New York to the Carolina coast with about 9,000 troops. In the Battle of Charleston, he

encircled the city, trapping the patriot forces inside. On May 12, 1780, more than 5,000 Continentals and militia laid down their arms in the worst American defeat of the war.

The British were now poised to sweep the entire South. Most local Whigs, thinking the Revolution over, at first offered little resistance to the Redcoats striking into the Carolina backcountry. At the South Carolina–North Carolina border, British troops under Colonel Banastre Tarleton overtook 350 retreating Virginia Continentals. When they tried to surrender, Tarleton's men slaughtered most of them. The British success seemed so complete that Clinton tried to force American prisoners to resume their duties as British subjects and join the loyalist militia. Thinking that matters were now well in hand, Clinton sailed back to New York, leaving the southern troops under the command of Lord Cornwallis.

Clinton's confidence that the South had returned securely to the loyalist camp was premature. Atrocities like Tarleton's

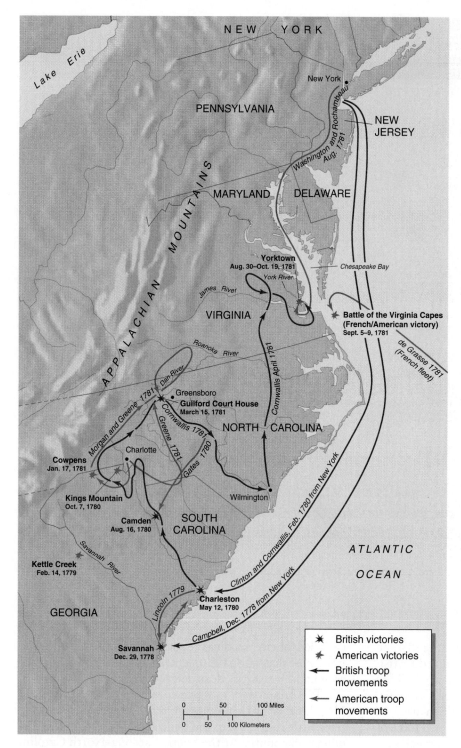

MAP 6–5   The War in the South, 1778–1781
During the latter part of the war, most of the major engagements occurred in the South. British forces won most of the early ones but could not control the immense territory involved and eventually surrendered at Yorktown.

thority. "Tarleton's Quarter" and "a Georgia parole" (a bullet in the back) became Whig euphemisms for "take no prisoners."

American Counterattacks

In the summer of 1780, Congress dispatched a substantial Continental force to the South under General Horatio Gates, the hero of Saratoga. Local patriots flocked to join him. But Gates was reckless. Pushing through North Carolina, his men tried to subsist on green corn. Weakened by diarrhea, they blundered into Cornwallis's British army near Camden, South Carolina, on August 16, and suffered a complete rout. More than 1,000 Americans were killed or wounded and many captured. Gates—transformed from the hero of Saratoga into the goat of Camden—fled to Hillsborough, North Carolina.

American morale revived on October 7, 1780, when "over mountain men" (militia) from Virginia, western North Carolina, and South Carolina defeated the British at Kings Mountain, South Carolina. And in December 1780, Nathanael Greene replaced the discredited Gates, bringing competent leadership to the Continentals in the South.

Ever resourceful, Greene divided his small forces, keeping roughly half with him in northeastern South Carolina and sending the other half westward under General Daniel Morgan. Cornwallis ordered Tarleton to pursue Morgan, who retreated northward until he reached Cowpens, South Carolina. There, on January 17, 1781, Morgan cleverly posted his least reliable troops, the militia, in the front line and ordered them to retreat after firing two volleys. When they did as told, the British thought the Americans were fleeing and charged after them—straight into devastating fire from Morgan's Continentals. Tarleton escaped, but his reputation for invincibility had been destroyed.

Cornwallis now badly needed a battlefield victory. Burning his army's excess baggage, he set off in hot pursuit of Greene and Morgan, whose rejoined forces retreated northward ahead of the British. On February 13, 1781, Greene's tired men crossed the Dan River into Virginia, and Cornwallis gave up the chase, marching his equally exhausted Redcoats southward. To his surprise, Cornwallis now found himself pursued—though cautiously—by Greene. On March 15, the opposing forces met at Guilford Court House, North Carolina, in one of the war's bloodiest battles. Although the British held the field at the end of the

"massacre" of the Virginians inflamed anti-British feeling. And Clinton's decision to force former rebels into the loyalist militia backfired, infuriating real loyalists—who saw their enemies getting off lightly—as well as Whigs. Atrocities and reprisals mounted on both sides as Whigs continued to defy British au-

This wash drawing, which was published in Paris by Nicholas Ponce in 1784, depicts the explosion of a British powder magazine at Pensacola on the morning of May 8, 1781. That afternoon the British defenders surrendered to Spanish troops under Bernardo de Gálvez.

had orders to support an attack on the British in North America. Faking preparations for an assault on British-occupied New York, the Continentals (commanded by Washington) and the French headed for the Chesapeake. Cornwallis and his 6,000 Redcoats soon found themselves besieged behind their fortifications at Yorktown by 8,800 Americans and 7,800 French. A French naval victory gave the allies temporary command of the waters around Yorktown. Cornwallis had nowhere to go, and Clinton—still in New York—could not reinforce him quickly enough. On October 19, 1781, the British army surrendered. When he learned the news in London, the British prime minister, Lord North, took it like "a ball in his breast." "It is all over," he groaned.

day, an Englishman accurately observed, "another such victory would destroy the British Army." Cornwallis retreated to the coastal town of Wilmington, North Carolina, to rest and regroup.

By the late summer of 1781, British fortunes were waning in the Lower South. The Redcoats held only the larger towns and the immediately surrounding countryside. With their superior staying power, they won most major engagements, but these victories brought them no lasting gain. As General Greene observed, "We fight, get beat, and rise and fight again." When the enemy pressed him too hard, Greene retreated out of reach, advancing again as the British withdrew.

Meanwhile patriot guerrilla forces, led by such colorful figures as "Gamecock" Thomas Sumter and "Swamp Fox" Francis Marion, disrupted British communications between their Charleston headquarters and outlying garrisons. Equally important, the loyalist militias that the British had hoped would pacify the countryside proved unequal to the task. Thus, although Greene never defeated the Redcoats outright, his campaign was a strategic success.

Disappointed and frustrated, Cornwallis decided to conquer Virginia to cut off Greene's supplies and destroy Whig resolve. British forces, including units commanded by turncoat Benedict Arnold, were already raiding the state. Cornwallis marched north to join them, reaching Yorktown, Virginia, during the summer of 1781.

The final military showdown of the war was at hand. By now, French soldiers were in America ready to fight alongside the Continentals, and a large French fleet in the West Indies

The American Victory, 1782–1783

The British surrender at Yorktown marked the end of major fighting in North America, though skirmishes continued for another year. In April 1782, the Royal Navy defeated the French fleet in the Caribbean, strengthening the British bargaining position. Although George III insisted on continuing the war because he feared that defeat would threaten British rule in Canada and the West Indies, the majority in Parliament now felt that enough men and money had been wasted trying to keep the Americans within the empire. In March 1782, the king accepted Lord North's resignation and appointed a new prime minister, with a mandate to make peace.

The Peace of Paris

The peace negotiations, which took place in Paris, were lengthy. The Americans demanded independence, handsome territorial concessions, and access to the rich British-controlled fishing grounds in the North Atlantic. The current British prime minister, Lord Shelburne, was inclined to be conciliatory to help British merchants recover their lost colonial trade. The French had achieved their objective of weakening the British and now wanted out of an increasingly costly worldwide war. Spain had not won its most important goal, the recovery of British-held Gibraltar, and thus gave the Americans no support at all.

The American negotiators, Benjamin Franklin, John Adams, and John Jay, skillfully threaded their way among these conflicting interests. With good reason, they feared that the French and Spanish might strike a bargain with the British at the expense of the United States. As a result, the Americans disregarded Congress's instructions to avoid making peace unilaterally and secretly worked out their

Ki-On-Twog-Ky, also known as Corn Planter (1732/40–1836), was a Seneca Indian Chief who raided American settlements for the British, while he observed that "war is war, death is death, a fight is hard business." He later presided over the surrender of much land to the United States.

own arrangements with the British. On November 30, 1782, the negotiators signed a preliminary Anglo-American treaty of peace whose terms were embodied in the final **Peace of Paris**, signed by all the belligerents on September 3, 1783.

The Peace of Paris gave the United States nearly everything it sought. Great Britain acknowledged that the United States was "free, sovereign and independent." The northern boundary of the new nation extended west from the St. Croix River (which separated Maine from Nova Scotia) past the Great Lakes to what were thought to be the headwaters of the Mississippi River (see Map 6–6). The Mississippi itself—down to just north of New Orleans—formed the western border. Spain acquired the provinces of East and West Florida from Britain. This territory included parts of present-day Louisiana, Mississippi, Alabama, and Georgia. The treaty did not, however, provide the United States with access to the Gulf of Mexico, a situation that would be a source of diplomatic friction for years.

Several provisions of the treaty addressed important economic issues. Adams, on behalf of New Englanders, insisted on a provision granting American fishermen access to the waters off eastern Canada. The treaty also required that British forces, on quitting American soil, were to leave behind all American-owned property, including slaves. Another provision declared existing debts between citizens of Britain and the United States still valid, giving British merchants hope of collecting on their American accounts. Congress was to "recommend" that the states restore rights

and property taken from loyalists during the war. Nothing was said about the slave trade, which Jay had hoped to ban.

The Components of Success

The War for Independence was over. In December 1783, the last British troops left New York. Despite the provisions of the peace treaty and the objections of southern planters, about 3,000 African Americans went with them. General Guy Carleton, who had replaced Clinton as commander in chief after Yorktown, refused to renege on British promises of freedom for slaves who fled rebel owners.

The Continental Army had already disbanded during the summer of 1783 (but not, as we have seen, before the incident at Newburg). On December 4, Washington said farewell to his officers at New York City's Fraunces Tavern and later that month resigned his commission to the Congress. Like the legendary citizen-soldier Cincinnatus, who after defending the ancient Roman Republic gave up his power as dictator and went back to plowing his land, Washington went home to Mount Vernon. By now he had won the respect of friend and foe alike. Only a natural genius, even the British said, could have accomplished what he did. How else could one explain the victory of ragtag provincials over the world's greatest military and naval power?

Washington's leadership was just one of the reasons why the Americans won the Revolutionary War. French assistance played a crucial role. Indeed, some historians contend that without the massive infusion of French men and money in 1781, the Revolution would have failed. The British also contributed heavily to their own downfall with mistakes that included bureaucratic inefficiency, hesitant command, and overconfidence. British authorities consistently underestimated the enormous difficulty of waging war 3,000 miles from home in an era of slow and uncertain communications, against a people who were sparsely distributed over more than 1,500 miles from Maine to Georgia. British forces occupied, at one time or another, most of the important seaports and state capitals—Boston, New York, Philadelphia, Charleston, and Savannah—but patriot forces driven from these centers could simply regroup elsewhere. Finally, Great Britain had tried to solve a political problem by military means, but an occupying army is far more likely to alienate people than to secure their goodwill.

Yet it took 175,000 to 200,000 soldiers—Continentals and militia troops—to prevent Great Britain from recovering the colonies. Of these, some 7,000 died in battle. Perhaps 10,000 more succumbed to disease while on active duty, another 8,500 died while prisoners of war, and nearly 1,500 were reported missing in action. More than 8,000 were wounded and survived. Those who served in the Continental Army, probably more than half of all who fought, served the longest and saw the most action. Their casualty rate—30 to 40 percent—may have been the highest of any war in which the United States has been engaged. In proportion to the population, these losses would be the equivalent of more than 2 million people in the United States today.

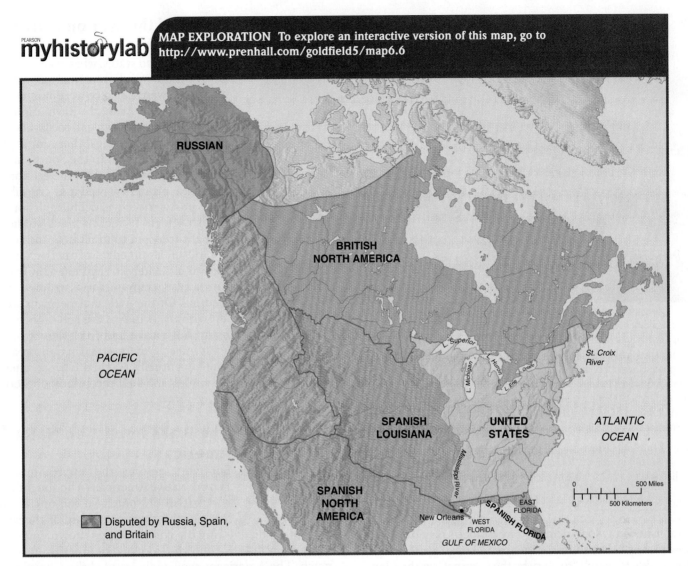

PEARSON
myhistorylab   MAP EXPLORATION To explore an interactive version of this map, go to
http://www.prenhall.com/goldfield5/map6.6

MAP 6–6   North America after the Peace of Paris, 1783
The results of the American Revolution redrew the map of North America, confining Britain to Canada and giving the United
States most of the area east of the Mississippi River, though Spain controlled its mouth for most of the next 20 years.

War and Society, 1775–1783

Regular combatants were not the only ones to suffer during
the struggle for independence. Eight years of warfare also
produced profound dislocations throughout American society. Military service wrenched families apart, sporadic raids
brought the war home to vast numbers of people, and everyone endured economic disruptions. As a forge of nationhood, the Revolution tested all Americans, whatever their
standing as citizens.

The Women's War

Women everywhere had to see their loved ones go off to
fight and die. Like Mary Silliman in Connecticut, they
waited, trying to stay calm until they knew "what tidings
God" had for them. At first, with spirits still running high,
Mary's letters to her husband, Selleck, reveal an affectionate lightheartedness. "These cold nights make me shudder

for you," she wrote, adding "Oh, King George, what hardships does thy tyranny put thy late subjects to!" Selleck responded with similarly suggestive banter. Later, the couple's
letters grew less playful. Then her husband was captured.
The daily round of domestic duties helped to keep her going,
but his extended absence increased her burdens and enlarged her responsibilities.

Such circumstances elevated women's domestic status.
Couples began referring to "our"—not "my" or "your"—property. Wives frequently became more knowledgeable about
the family's financial condition than their long-absent husbands. "What shall I do my Dearest? I wish I had Your Advice," Selleck Silliman asked his wife after he had been
released from captivity.

Women also assumed new public roles during the conflict. Some nursed the wounded. More wove cloth for uniforms. The Ladies' Association of Philadelphia was

The surrender of Lord Cornwallis at Yorktown on October 19, 1781, led to the British decision to withdraw from the war. Cornwallis, who claimed to be ill, absented himself from the ceremony and is not in the picture. Washington, who is astride the horse under the American flag, designated General Benjamin Lincoln (on the white horse in the center) as the one to accept the submission of a subordinate British officer. John Trumbull, who painted *The Battle of Bunker Hill* and some 300 other scenes from the Revolutionary War, finished this painting while he was in London about 15 years after the events depicted. A large copy of the work now hangs in the rotunda of the United States Capitol in Washington, D.C.

John Trumbull (American 1756–1843), *Surrender of Lord Cornwallis at Yorktown, October 1781*, oil on canvas, 20 7/8 × 30 5/8 inches. Yale University Art Gallery, Trumbull Collection.

established in 1780 to demonstrate women's patriotism and raise money to buy shirts for the army. Though women might not be able to march "to glory by the same path as the Men," wrote the association's founder, "we should at least equal and sometimes surpass them in our love for the public good." Similar associations formed in other states.

Despite their increasing private responsibilities and new public activities, it did not occur to most women to encroach on traditional male prerogatives. When John Adams's wife, Abigail, urged him and the Second Continental Congress to "Remember the Ladies," she was not expecting equal political rights. What she wanted, rather, was some legal protections for women and recognition of their value and need for autonomy in the domestic sphere. "Remember," she cautioned, "all Men would be Tyrants if they could." Why not, then, make it impossible for "the vicious and lawless" to abuse women with impunity? "I will never consent to have our sex considered in an inferior point of light," she wrote.

Republican ideology, responding to the changing status of women, assigned them a role that was at once exalted and subordinate. Their job was to nurture wise, virtuous, and public-spirited men. It was this view of women that would prevail in the post-Revolutionary era.

Effect of the War on African Americans

In the northern states, where slavery was already economically marginal and where black men were welcome as volunteers in the Continental Army, the Revolutionary War helped to bring an end to slavery, although it remained legal there for some time (see Chapter 7). In the South, however, slavery was integral to the economy, and white planters viewed it as crucial to their postwar recovery. Thus, although British efforts to recruit black soldiers brought freedom to thousands and temporarily undermined slavery in the South, the war ultimately strengthened the institution, especially in the Carolinas and Georgia. Of the African Americans who left with the British at the end of the war, many, both slave and free, went to the West Indies. Others settled in Canada, and some eventually reached Africa, where Britain established the colony of Sierra Leone for them.

The War's Impact on Native Americans

Survivors among the approximately 13,000 Native Americans who fought for the British did not have the option of leaving with them at the end of the war. How many died during the conflict is not known, but certainly many did. Not only the Iroquois but other groups lost much. The Americans repeatedly invaded the Cherokees' homeland in the southern Appalachian Mountains. "There was no withstanding them," recalled a Cherokee chief of the many frontiersmen who assaulted his people. "They dyed their hands in the blood of many of our Women and children, burnt seventeen towns, destroyed all our provisions," and spread famine across the land. Americans also attacked the Shawnees of Ohio. In one notorious incident, militiamen massacred peaceful Christian Indians at Gnadenhutten, Ohio.

In the peace treaty of 1783, Britain surrendered its territory east of the Mississippi, shocking and infuriating the Native Americans living there. They had not surrendered, and none of them had been at the negotiations in Paris. The Iroquois accordingly told a British commander that if the English really "had basely betrayed them by pretending to give up their Country to the Americans without their Consent, or Consulting them, it was an Act of Cruelty and injustice that Christians only were capable of doing." Because it enabled Americans to claim Indian territory by conquest, the Revolutionary War was a disaster for many Native Americans that opened the floodgates to a torrent of white settlers. During

Benjamin West's painting of the American commissioners who negotiated the Peace of Paris includes, from left to right, John Jay, John Adams, Benjamin Franklin, and Franklin's grandson, who served as the commissioners' secretary. A fourth American commissioner who arrived only at the end of the negotiations, Henry Laurens, stands in the background. The British commissioners, who would have occupied the blank space on the right, did not sit for their portraits. Chagrin at the outcome of the war probably contributed to their absence, but an apocryphal story attributed it to the reluctance of Richard Oswald, who was blind in one eye, to have his portrait painted.

Benjamin West, 1783, *American Commissioners of Preliminary Negotiations*. Courtesy Winterthur Museum.

immediately raising taxes to pay for the war, the states printed paper money supposedly redeemable through future tax revenues. But because the quantity of this paper money rose faster than the supply of goods and services, prices skyrocketed, and the value of the money plunged. By April 1779, as Washington commented, "a wagon load of money will scarcely purchase a wagon load of provisions." Those who had paper money tried to spend it before its value could drop further; whereas those who had salable commodities such as grain tended to hoard them in the hope that the price would go even higher. Prices also climbed faster than wages, leaving many working people impoverished.

The rampant inflation was demoralizing and divisive. Lucky speculators and unscrupulous profiteers could grow rich, while ordinary and patriotic people suffered. These conditions sparked more than thirty protest demonstrations. In October 1779, frustrated Philadelphia militiamen marched on the house of a local Whig leader, demanding better price controls. The confrontation left six people dead and achieved little. Freebooters—rovers in search of plunder—sailed Long Island Sound in boats with names such as *Retrieve My Losses*, ostensibly to harry the British but all too often to trade with them. As usual, war and its deprivations brought out both the best and the worst in human nature.

Nevertheless, the successful outcome of the war and the stable peace that followed suggest that most Americans somehow managed to cope. But during the last years of the conflict, their economic and psychological reserves ran low. The total real wealth of private individuals declined by an average of 0.5 percent annually from 1774 to 1805, even with the returning prosperity of the 1790s. Such statistics suggest the true economic cost of the War for Independence. And the atrocities committed on both sides provide a comparable measure of the conflict's psychological cost.

1779 and 1780 alone, approximately 20,000 settlers streamed into Kentucky. Five years later, there were reportedly 2,200 squatter families in parts of Ohio where the United States government forbade settlement.

Economic Disruption

The British and American armies both needed enormous quantities of supplies. This heavy demand disrupted the normal distribution of goods and drove up real prices seven- or eightfold; in addition, widespread use of depreciating paper money by the American side amplified the rise in prices and triggered severe inflation.

When the British did not simply seize what they needed, they paid for it in hard currency—gold and silver. American commanders, by contrast, had to rely on paper money because the Congress and the states had almost no hard currency at their disposal. The Continental dollar, however, steadily declined in value, and by March 1780, the Congress was forced to admit officially that it was worthless. (Not surprisingly, American farmers and merchants, whatever their political opinions, sometimes sold food to the British while their own forces went hungry.)

Necessity, not folly, drove Congress and the states to rely on the printing press. Rather than alienate citizens by

The Price of Victory

Most American and British commanders tried to keep hostilities "civilized"—if such a characterization can ever be applied to a war—but discipline sometimes broke down among regular troops. Controlling militias or civilians acting on their own was even more difficult. Residents of contested areas near British-occupied cities, such as New York and Charleston, were often in peril, as the following incident reveals. Sometime during 1779, roving Tories knocked on the door of a Whig militiaman in New Jersey. Entering his house, they announced that he was a dead man. While drinking his

OVERVIEW

Important Battles of the Revolutionary War

	Battle	Date	Outcome
Early Fighting	Lexington and Concord, Massachusetts	April 19, 1775	Contested
	Fort Ticonderoga, New York	May 10, 1775	American victory
	Breed's Hill ("Bunker Hill"), Boston, Massachusetts	June 17, 1775	Contested
	Great Bridge, Virginia	December 9, 1775	American victory
	Quebec, Canada	December 31, 1775	British repulsed American assault
	Moore's Creek Bridge, North Carolina	February 27, 1776	American victory
The War in the North	Brooklyn Heights, New York	August 27, 1776	British victory
	White Plains, New York	October 28, 1776	British victory
	Trenton, New Jersey	December 26, 1776	American victory
	Princeton, New Jersey	January 3, 1777	American victory
	Brandywine Creek, Pennsylvania	September 11, 1777	British victory (opened way for British to take Philadelphia)
	Saratoga, New York	September 19 and October 17, 1777	American victory (helped persuade France to form an alliance with United States)
	Monmouth Court House, New Jersey	June 28, 1778	Contested
The War on the Frontier	Wyoming Valley, Pennsylvania	June and July 1778	British victory
	Kaskaskia and Cahokia, Illinois; Vincennes, Indiana	July 4, 1778– February 23, 1779	American victories strengthen claims to Mississippi Valley
	Cherry Valley, New York	November 11, 1778	British victory
The War in the South	Savannah, Georgia	December 29, 1778	British victory (took control of Georgia)
	Kettle Creek, Georgia	February 14, 1779	American victory
	Savannah, Georgia	September 3–October 28, 1779	British victory (opened way for British to take Charleston)
	Charleston, South Carolina	February 11–May 12, 1780	British victory
	Camden, South Carolina	August 16, 1780	British victory
	Kings Mountain, South Carolina	Oct. 7, 1780	American victory
	Cowpens, South Carolina	January 17, 1781	American victory
	Guilford Court House, North Carolina	March 15, 1781	Contested
	Yorktown, Virginia	August 30–October 19, 1781	American victory (persuaded Britain to end war)

American soldiers at Yorktown in 1781 as drawn by a young officer in the French army, Jean-Baptiste-Antoine de Verger. The African American on the left is an infantryman of the First Rhode Island Regiment; the next, a musketeer; the third, with the fringed jacket, a rifleman. The man on the right is a Continental artilleryman, holding a lighted match used to fire cannons.

liquor and terrorizing his wife, they argued about how to execute him until one of the intruders abruptly resolved the dispute by shooting him. Whigs could be equally brutal. Late in the war, British sympathizers in the Lower South compiled a list of more than 300 loyalists who had been massacred by Whigs—some, the survivors claimed, while they slept.

Although the British were probably the worse offenders, both sides burned, plundered, and murdered. One can see the results in a returning refugee's description of the area around Beaufort, South Carolina, in the early 1780s: "All was desolation. ... Robberies and murders are often committed on the public roads. The people that remain have been peeled, pillaged, and plundered. Poverty, want, and hardship appear in almost every countenance ..., and the morals of the people are almost entirely extirpated."

Conclusion

Despite the devastation and divisiveness of the war, many people in Europe and the United States were convinced that it represented something momentous. The *Annual Register,* a popular and influential British magazine, commented accurately in 1783 that the American Revolution "has already overturned those favourite systems of policy and commerce, both in the old and in the new world, which the wisdom of the ages, and the power of the greatest nations, had in vain endeavored to render permanent; and it seems to have laid the seeds of still greater revolutions in the history and mutual relations of mankind."

Americans, indeed, had fired a shot heard round the world. Thanks in part to its heavy investment in the American Revolution, France suffered a financial crisis in the late 1780s. This, in turn, ushered in the political crisis that culminated in the French Revolution of 1789. The American Revolution helped to inspire among French people (including soldiers returning from service in America) an intense yearning for an end to arbitrary government and undeserved social inequalities. Liberty also proved infectious to thousands of German troops who had come to America as mercenaries but stayed as free citizens after the war was over. Once prosperous but distant provinces of a far-flung empire, the North American states had become an independent confederation, a grand experiment in republicanism whose fate mattered to enlightened men and women throughout the Western world. In his written farewell to the rank and file of his troops at the end of October 1783, Washington maintained that "the enlarged prospects of happiness, opened by the confirmation of our independence and sovereignty, almost exceed the power of description." He urged those who had fought with him to maintain their "strong attachments to the union" and "prove themselves not less virtuous and useful as citizens, than they have been persevering and victorious as soldiers." The work of securing the promise of the American Revolution, Washington knew, would now shift from the battlefield to the political arena.

Review Questions

1. Who were the loyalists, and how many of them were there? What attempts did the British and Americans make in 1775 to avert war? Why did these steps fail?

2. What actions did the Second Continental Congress take in 1775 and 1776? Why did it choose George Washington as the commander of its army? Why was he a good choice?

3. Why did Congress declare independence in July 1776? How did Americans justify their claim to independence?

4. What was republicanism, and why was the enthusiasm that it inspired insufficient to win the war?

5. Why were most of the early battles fought in the northern states? What effect did French entry into the war have on British strategy?

6. Why did the initial British victories in the South not win the war for them? Why did the United States ultimately win? What did it obtain by winning?

7. What were the effects of the war on Native Americans, African Americans, women, and American society in general?

8. What were some of the global effects of American independence?

Key Terms

Battles of Lexington and Concord (p. 142)

Committee of Safety (p. 141)

Conciliatory Proposition (p. 142)

Continental Army (p. 143)

Contract theory of government (p. 145)

Declaration of Independence (p. 145)

Declaration of the Causes and Necessity of Taking Up Arms (p. 143)

Minute Men (p. 141)

Olive Branch Petition (p. 143)

Peace of Paris (p. 160)

Republicanism (p. 145)

Second Continental Congress (p. 143)

Valley Forge (p. 155)

Recommended Reading

Armitage, David. *The Declaration of Independence: A Global History* (2007). A wide-ranging account of the initial worldwide reception and later counterparts of the Declaration of Independence, with significant documents.

Buel, Joy D., and Richard Buel, Jr. *The Way of Duty: A Woman and Her Family in Revolutionary America* (1984). A readable and unusually full biography of Mary Fish of Connecticut, who lived from 1736 to 1818. Her experiences during the Revolutionary War while her husband, Selleck Silliman, was a prisoner of the British have become the subject of a good movie, *Mary Silliman's War* (1993).

Dann, John C. ed. *The Revolution Remembered: Eyewitness Accounts of the War for Independence* (1980). A collection of 79 narratives by veterans seeking pensions for their Revolutionary War service; sometimes poignant and frequently illuminating.

Ferling, John E. *Almost a Miracle: The American Victory in the War of Independence* (2007). A very readable account of the war.

Gross, Robert A. *The Minutemen and Their World* (1976). An example of "history from the bottom up" that provides a close look at the Minute Men of Concord from the late colonial period through the Revolution.

Shy, John. *A People Numerous and Armed: Reflections on the Military Struggle for American Independence* (1990). A collection of essays on various aspects of the American Revolution by a perceptive military historian; full of interesting ideas.

Where to Learn More

■ **Independence National Historical Park, Philadelphia, Pennsylvania.**   Independence Hall, where Congress adopted the Declaration of Independence, is the most historic building in Philadelphia. The informative website can be accessed through Links to the Past: National Park Service Cultural Resources' comprehensive listing of historic sites in the National Park system, www.cr.nps.gov.

■ **Kings Mountain National Military Park and Cowpens National Battlefield, South Carolina.**   Situated approximately 20 miles apart, these were the sites of two battles in October 1780 and January 1781 that turned the tide of the war in the South. Both have museums and exhibits. The official site is accessible through Links to the Past: National Park Service Cultural Resources, www.cr.nps.gov. But see also Battles of the American Revolutionary War, www.ilt.columbia.edu/k12/history/aha/battles.html, for a brief description of the battles and their contexts.

■ **Minute Man National Historical Park, Lexington and Concord, Massachusetts.**   There are visitors' centers at both Lexington and Concord with explanatory displays. Visitors may also follow the self-guided Battle Road Automobile Tour. The official website is accessible through Links to the Past: National Park Service Cultural Resources, www.cr.nps.gov.

■ **Yorktown Battlefield, Colonial National Historical Park, Yorktown, Virginia.**   The park commemorates the great American victory here. Innovative exhibits enable visitors to follow the course of the war from a multicultural perspective. The official website is accessible through Links to the Past: National Park Service Cultural Resources, www.cr.nps.gov.

Study Resources

For study resources for this chapter, go to www.myhistorylab.com and choose *The American Journey*. You will find a wealth of study and review material for this chapter, including pre- and post-tests, customized study plan, key term review flash cards, interactive map and document activities, and documents for analysis.

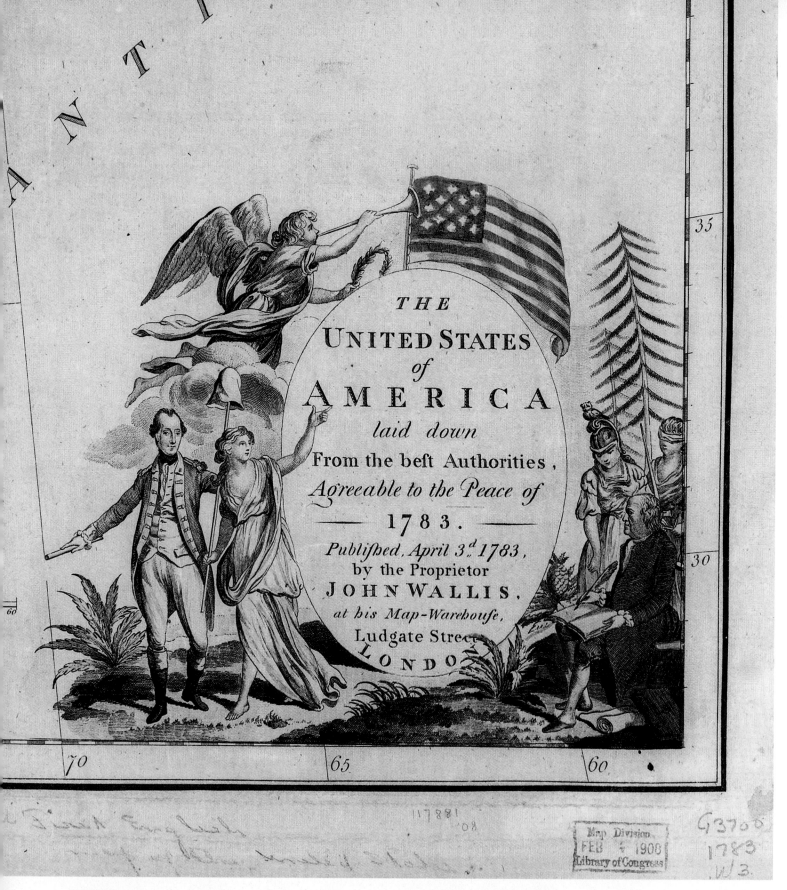

The illustration on this 1783 map of the United States pairs George Washington on the left with Liberty and Benjamin Franklin on the right with Justice in a symbolic identification of the new republic with the values of equality and individual dignity.

The First Republic 7
1776–1789

The jurors of the Commonwealth of Massachusetts upon their oath present that Moses Sash of Worthington…a negro man & Labourer being a disorderly, riotous & seditious person & minding & contriving as much as in him lay unlawfully by force of arms to stir up promote incite & maintain riots mobs tumults insurrections in this Commonwealth & to disturb impede & prevent the Government of the same & the due administration of justice in the same, & to prevent the Courts of justice from sitting as by Law appointed for that purpose & to promote disquiets, uneasiness, jealousies, animosities & seditions in the minds of the Citizens of this Commonwealth on the twentieth day of January in the year of our Lord Seventeen hundred & eighty seven & on divers other days & times as well before as since that time at Worthington…unlawfully & seditiously with force & arms did advise persuade invite incourage & procure divers persons…of this Commonwealth by force of arms to oppose this Commonwealth & the Government thereof & riotously to join themselves to a great number of riotous seditious persons with force & arms thus opposing this Commonwealth & the Government thereof…and in pursuance of his wicked seditious purposes…did procure guns, bayonets, pistols, swords, gunpowder, bullets, blankets & provisions & other warlike instruments offensive

& defensive…& did cause & procure them to be carried & conveyed to the riotous & seditious persons as aforesaid in evil example to others to offend in like manner against the peace of the Commonwealth aforesaid & dignity of the same.

Source: Indictment of Moses Sash by the Supreme Judicial Court of Massachusetts for Suffolk County, April 9, 1787, cited in Sidney Kaplan and Emma Nogrady Kaplan, *The Black Presence in the Era of the American Revolution* (Amherst: University of Massachusetts Press, 1989), p. 259.

myhistorylab
Personal Journeys Online

- William Shepard, *Letter to Governor Bowdoin, Jan. 26, 1787.* A militia captain describes the routing of the Shaysites at Springfield Arsenal.

- Henry Lee, *Letter to George Washington, Oct. 1, 1786.* One of Washington's former generals expresses his fears over the outbreak of agrarian insurgencies.

Thus, in the dry, legalistic language

of the highest court in Massachusetts was Moses Sash, a twenty-eight-year-old African American veteran of the Revolutionary War, indicted by a grand jury for his role in Shays's Rebellion. Named after its leader, Daniel Shays, another Revolutionary veteran, this armed insurgency pitted debt-ridden farmers in the western half of Massachusetts against conservative interests in the east. Farmers and laborers in western Massachusetts faced hard times in the 1780s. A combination of falling farm prices, a shortage of money, heavy taxes, and mounting debts produced an economic crisis that threatened imprisonment of debtors and, worse yet, the loss of their farms, the basis of their independence as free men. Faced with an unresponsive state legislature controlled by eastern merchants and creditors, angry farmers reacted much as they had during the revolutionary agitation against the British a decade earlier: They organized, protested, and shut down the county courts.

Most of the state's small black population lived in the eastern port cities, and some of them followed the lead of Prince Hall, the founder of the world's first lodge of black Freemasonry, in supporting the call of Governor James Bowdoin to restore law and order. A few black farmers did join the insurgency, but Sash, identified as a farmer and laborer, was the only black man to be indicted. Routed in a battle at Springfield Arsenal in January 1787 by an army raised by Governor Bowdoin, the Shaysites fled into the hills. Nearly all of them, including Sash, were pardoned by the new administration of Governor John Hancock. Sash moved to Connecticut and died in poverty.

More than any other domestic disturbance in the 1780s, Shays's Rebellion dramatized the fragile nature and conflicting values of America's first republic under the Articles of Confederation. Providing for little more than a loose union of otherwise independent states, the Articles were ratified in 1781. The years that followed were a period of trial and error marked by a running debate over the meaning of liberty and the extent of power to be entrusted to a national government. Americans favoring a stronger, more centralized government repeatedly cited Shays's Rebellion as an example of the impending chaos that would destroy the republic unless fundamental changes were made. Those changes came with the writing of the United States Constitution in 1787 and its ratification in 1788.

CHRONOLOGY

1776	States begin writing the first constitutions.
1777	Articles of Confederation proposed.
1780s	English textile production begins to surge with new technological advances.
1781	Articles ratified.
1783	Americans celebrate independence and the peace treaty with Britain.
	British West Indies closed to U.S. traders.
1784	Onset of the postwar depression.
	Opening of China trade by the United States.
	Spain closes the Mississippi.
	Separatist plots in the West.
	Treaty of Fort Stanwix.
1785	Land Ordinance of 1785.
	States begin to issue more paper money.
	Treaty of Fort McIntosh.
1786	Shays's Rebellion breaks out.
	Jay-Gardoqui Treaty defeated.
	Annapolis Convention.
1787	Constitutional Convention at Philadelphia.
	Northwest Ordinance.
1788	Constitution ratified and goes into effect.
	Publication of *The Federalist*.

The New Order of Republicanism

As royal authority collapsed during the Revolution, provincial congresses and committees assumed power in each of the former colonies. The Continental Congress, seeking to build support for the war effort, was concerned that these new institutions should have a firm legal and popular foundation. In May 1776, the Congress called on the colonies to form new state governments "under the authority of the people."

This call reflected the political philosophy of republicanism that animated the Revolution (see Chapter 6). To Americans, republicanism meant, first and foremost, that legitimate political authority derives from the people. It is they who are sovereign, not the king or the aristocracy. The people should elect the officials who govern them, and those officials should represent the interests of the people who elected them. Another key aspect of republicanism was the revolutionary idea that the people could define and limit governmental power through written constitutions. These core republican principles held that governmental authority should flow from the people, but it was not always clear just who was included in "the people."

Defining the People

When news of the peace treaty with Britain reached New Bern, North Carolina, in June 1783, the citizens held a grand celebration. As reported by Francisco de Miranda, a visiting Spanish officer, "There was a barbecue [a roast pig] and a barrel of rum, from which the leading officials and citizens of the region promiscuously drank with the meanest and lowest kind of people, holding hands and drinking from the same cup. It is impossible to imagine, without seeing it, a more purely democratic gathering."

For Miranda, this boisterous mingling of all citizens as seeming equals confirmed the central tenet of republicanism, the belief that the people were sovereign. But republicanism also taught that political rights should be limited to those who owned private property, because the independent will required for informed political judgment required economic self-sufficiency. This, in effect, restricted political participation to propertied white men. Virtually everyone else, property-less white men, servants legally bound to others, women, slaves, and most free black people, were denied political rights. As for Native Americans, they were outside the U.S. body politic and exercised political rights within their own nations.

Because the ownership of property was relatively widespread among white men, some 60 to 85 percent of adult white men could participate in politics, a far higher proportion than elsewhere in the world of the eighteenth century. The greatest concentration of the remaining 25 percent or so shut out of the political process were unskilled laborers and mariners living in port cities. The working poor in the cities still included indentured servants, bound by contract to give personal service for a

With the exception of New Jersey, where women meeting the property qualifications were eligible to vote, the state constitutions of the Revolutionary era prohibited women from voting.

white men," explicitly barred women from voting in almost all state constitutions of the 1770s. Only the New Jersey constitution of 1776 defined **suffrage,** the right to vote, in gender-free terms, extending it to all adults "worth fifty pounds." As a result, until 1807, when the state legislature changed the constitution, propertied women, including widows and single women, enjoyed the right to vote in New Jersey.

The Revolution otherwise did bring women a few limited gains. They benefited from slightly less restrictive divorce laws and gained somewhat greater access to educational and business opportunities, changes that reflected the relative autonomy of many women during the war when their men were off fighting. The perception of women's moral status also rose. As the Philadelphia physician Benjamin Rush argued in his *Thoughts upon Female Education* (1787), educated and morally informed women were needed to instruct "their sons in the principles of liberty and government." Often called republican motherhood, this more positive view of women's influence entrusted mothers with the responsibility of passing on republican virtues from one generation to the next.

fixed time. The walking poor—vagrants and transients—might be jailed by local authorities, confined to work-houses, or hired out in public auctions for fixed terms of labor. Those who incurred debts they were unable to pay faced imprisonment.

Women and the Revolution

The Revolution did little to change the traditional patriarchal assumption that politics and public life should be the exclusive domain of men. Women, according to republican beliefs, were part of the dependent class and belonged under the control of propertied men, their husbands and fathers. Under common law (the customary, largely unwritten, law that Americans had inherited from Britain), women surrendered their property rights at marriage unless they made special arrangements to the contrary. Legally and economically, husbands had complete control over their wives. As a result, argued Theophilus Parsons of Massachusetts in 1778, women were, as a matter of course, "so situated as to have no wills of their own."

To be sure, some women saw in the political and social enthusiasm of the Revolution an opportunity to protest the most oppressive features of their subordination. "I won't have it thought that because we are the weaker sex as to bodily strength we are capable of nothing more than domestic concerns," wrote Eliza Wilkinson of South Carolina. Men, she lamented, "won't even allow us liberty of thought and that is all I want." Such protests, however, had little enduring effect. Most women were socialized to accept that their proper place was in the home with their families.

Gender-specific language, including such terms as "men," "Freemen," "white male inhabitants," and "free

The Revolution and African Americans in the South. The Revolution had a more immediate impact on the lives of many African Americans, triggering the growth of free black communities and the development of an African American culture. Changes begun by the Revolution were the main factor in the tremendous increase of free blacks from a few thousand at mid-century to more than 100,000 by 1800 (see Figure 7–1). One key to this increase was a shift in the religious and intellectual climate. Revolutionary principles of liberty and equality and evangelical notions of human fellowship convinced many whites for the first time to challenge black slavery. In 1784, Virginia Methodists condemned slavery as "contrary to the Golden Law of God on which hang all the Laws and Prophets, and the unalienable Rights of Mankind, as well as every Principle of Revolution." As many whites grew more hostile to slavery, slaves in the North submitted petitions for freedom to the new state legislatures and blacks everywhere began to seize opportunities for freedom.

Upwards of 50,000 slaves, or one in ten of those in bondage, gained their freedom as a result of the war. One route was through military service, which generally carried a promise of freedom. When the British began raising black troops, the Americans followed suit. All the states except Georgia and South Carolina recruited black

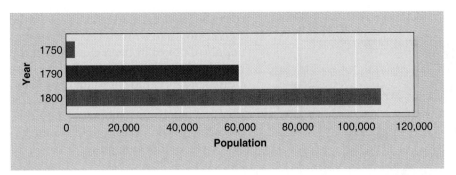

FIGURE 7-1   Growth of the Free Black Population between 1750 and 1800 Gradual emancipation in the North, the freeing of many slaves by their owners in the South, and the opportunities for freedom offered by the Revolution, all contributed to an explosive growth in the free population of African Americans in the second half of the eighteenth century.

Source: *A Century of Population Growth in the United States, 1790–1900 (1909). p. 80. Data for 1750 estimated.*

regiments. Some 5,000 blacks served in the Continental Army, and they, like their counterparts in British units, were mostly slaves. Most of the slaves who gained freedom during the war, however, had fled their owners and made their way to the port cities of the North.

By making slave property generally less secure, the Revolution encouraged many masters to free their slaves. Once freed, blacks tried to break all the bonds of their former servitude. "Negro Soloman," his former owner griped, "now free, prefers to mould bricks rather than serve me." A Delaware mistress felt rejected when a slave she had freed spurned her offer of employment with a friend and found her own job. "I cannot help think," she noted sourly, that "it is too generally the case with all those of colour to be ungrateful." As the number of free blacks increased, those still enslaved grew bolder in their efforts to gain freedom. "Henny," warned a Maryland slaveowner in 1783, "will try to pass for a free woman as several have lately been set free in this neighbourhood."

Northern Blacks and the Revolution.   If the control mechanisms of slavery experienced some strain in the South during the Revolution, in the North, where slaves were only a small percentage of the population, they crumbled. Most northern states ended slavery between 1777 and 1784. New York followed in 1799, and New Jersey in 1804. Nonetheless, although a majority of northern whites now agreed that slavery was incompatible with the Revolution's commitment to **natural rights** (the inherent human rights to life and liberty) and human freedom, they refused to sanction a sudden emancipation. The laws ending slavery in most of the northern states called for only the children of slaves to be freed, and only when they reached adulthood.

Northern blacks had to struggle to overcome white prejudice. Although black males were allowed to vote if they met the property qualifications, most were poor and held little property. Facing discrimination in jobs and housing, barred from juries, and denied a fair share of funds for schools, urban blacks had to rely on their own resources. With the help of the small class of property holders among them, they began establishing their own churches and self-help associations.

The Revolution's impact on Native Americans.   Most Indian peoples had stayed neutral during the war or fought for the British (see Chapter 6). Just as the Americans sought to shake off British control, so the Indians, especially the western tribes and most of the Iroquois Confederation, sought to free themselves from American dominance. The British defeat was thus a double blow, depriving the Indians of a valuable ally and exposing them to the wrath of the victorious patriots. Late in the war a British officer observed of the pro-British southern Indians, "The minds of these people appear as much agitated as those of the unhappy Loyalists, they have very seriously proposed to abandon their country and accompany us [in an evacuation], having made all the world their enemies by their attachment to us."

The state governments, as well as the Confederation Congress, treated Indian lands as a prize of war to be distributed to white settlers. Territorial demands on the Indians escalated, and even the few tribes that had furnished troops for the American side struggled to maintain control

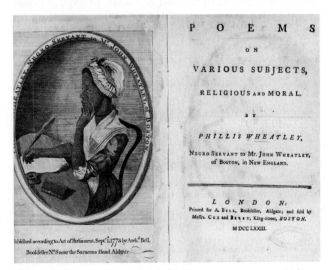

Phillis Wheatley was an acclaimed African American poet. Kidnapped into slavery as a child in Africa, she was a domestic slave to the Wheatley family of Boston when her first poems were published in 1773.

BETHEL AFRICAN METHODIST EPISCOPAL CHURCH, PHILAD⁵

The Mother Bethel Church in Philadelphia, dedicated in 1794, was home to the first independent black congregation in America and the founding establishment of the African Methodist Episcopal denomination. Churches were central to the communal life of black northerners and provided leadership in the struggle for racial justice.

The Library Company of Philadelphia.

over their homelands. As they did so, it was clear that white Americans did not consider Native Americans to be part of their republican society. With the exception of Massachusetts, the states denied voting and legal rights to the Indians within their borders.

Most Native Americans did not want or expect equal rights within the new American republic. They viewed themselves as belonging to their own nations, composed of distinct villages and settlements, with a common culture and interests. They wanted political rights and control over the land within their nations. Above all, they wanted independence. As George Rogers Clark wrote in 1783 of the Indians he had fought during the Revolution, "They have no notion of being dependent on Either the brittish or americans, But would make war on both if Equally Insulted."

In seeking to defend their independence against the growing pressure of white Americans on their lands, Native Americans forged new confederacies in the 1780s that temporarily united them against a common enemy. They were encouraged in these efforts by the imperial powers of England and Spain, both of which sought to curb the westward expansion of the United States. Thus, the immediate impact of the Revolution on Native Americans was a mixed one. On the one hand, the Revolution had created a new expansionist power in the United States that was intent on settling lands already occupied by Indians. On the other hand, American victory in the Revolution had broken the British monopoly of power in the region west of the Appalachian Mountains. Before the United States could consolidate its claim over the region, new imperial rivalries sprang up that allowed Native Americans to stake out a political middle ground between the competing powers. Throughout the 1780s, Native Americans continued to act as independent political agents in playing off outside powers against each other.

The State Constitutions

"Oppose everything that leans to aristocracy, of power in the hands of the rich and chief men exercised to the oppression of the poor." So the voters of Mecklenburg County, North Carolina, instructed their delegates to the state's constitutional convention in 1776. These instructions reflect a basic premise embodied in the new state constitutions of the Revolutionary period: Power had to be checked to ensure individual liberty and safeguard against tyranny.

Ten new state constitutions were in place by the end of 1777. All these constitutions were written documents, a striking departure from the English practice of treating a constitution as a collection of customary rights and practices that had evolved over time. In the American view, a constitution was a formal expression of the people's sovereignty, a codification of the powers of government and the rights of citizenship that functioned as a fundamental law to which all public authority was held accountable.

Because Americans had come to associate tyranny with the privileges of royal governors, all the new state constitutions cut back sharply on executive power. Most important, for it struck at what patriots felt was the main source of executive domination and corruption, governors lost control over patronage, the power to appoint executive and judicial officials. As the new constitutions curbed the power of governors, they increased that of the legislatures, making them the focal point of government. Colonial assemblies had been in the forefront of the popular opposition to British authority, and the state legislatures were now seen as the most trustworthy defenders of individual liberty. The new constitutions expanded the power of the legislatures to appoint officials and to oversee military and financial matters.

To make the legislatures more expressive of the popular will, the new constitutions included provisions that lowered property requirements for voting and officeholding, mandated annual elections, increased the number of seats in the legislatures, and made representation more proportional to the geographical distribution of population. Upper houses were made independent of the executive office and opened to popular election, as opposed to the colonial practice of having their members appointed by the governor.

Americans knew that legislatures, too, could act tyrannically, as they believed Britain's Parliament had done. So in a final check on arbitrary power, each state constitution eventually included some form of a **bill of rights** that set explicit limits on the power of government to interfere in the lives of citizens. The Virginia Declaration of Rights, written by the planter George Mason and adopted in June 1776, set the precedent for this notable republican feature. By 1784, the constitutions of all thirteen states had provisions guaranteeing religious liberty, freedom of the press, and a citizen's right to such fair legal practices as trial by jury.

Toward religious pluralism.   The new constitutions weakened but did not always sever the traditional tie between church and state. Many Americans held, as the Massachusetts Constitution of 1780 put it, that "the happiness of a people, and the good order and preservation of civil government, essentially depend upon piety, religion, and morality." Reflecting this belief, many states, notably in New England, levied taxes for the support of religion. The states of New England also continued to maintain Congregationalism as the established, or state-supported, religion, while allowing dissenting Baptists and Methodists to use funds from the compulsory religious taxes to support their ministers. The "common people," explained the Baptist leader Isaac Backus, insisted that they had "as good a right to judge and act for themselves in matter of religion as civil rulers or the learned clergy."

The mid-Atlantic states lacked the religious uniformity of New England. The region supported several prominent denominations—Quaker, Episcopalian, Presbyterian, Dutch Reformed, and Lutheran—and none was able to dominate the others. This pluralism checked legislative efforts to impose religious taxes or designate any denomination as the established church. In the South, where many Anglican (or Episcopalian) clergymen had been Tories, the Anglican Church lost its former established status. Thomas Jefferson, in Virginia's religious freedom law of 1786, went so far as to assert that "our civil rights have no dependence on our religious opinions any more than on opinions in physics or geometry."

Conflicting visions of republicanism.   Although in general the executive lost power and the legislature gained power under the new state constitutions, the actual structure of each state government reflected the outcome of political struggles between radical and conservative visions of republicanism. The democratically inclined radicals wanted to open government to all male citizens. The conservatives, fearing "mob rule," wanted to limit government to an educated elite of substantial property holders. Although they agreed that government had to be derived from the people, most conservatives, like Jeremy Belknap of New Hampshire, thought that the people had to be "taught...that they are not able to govern themselves."

In South Carolina, where conservative planters gained the upper hand, the constitution mandated property qualifications that barred 90 percent of the state's white males from holding elective public office. By contrast, Pennsylvania had the most democratic and controversial constitution. Many of Pennsylvania's conservatives had discredited themselves during the Revolution by remaining neutral or loyal to the crown. The Scots-Irish farmers and Philadelphia artisans who stepped into the resulting political vacuum held an egalitarian view of republicanism. The constitution they pushed through in 1776 gave the vote to all free males who paid taxes, regardless of wealth, and eliminated property qualifications for office-holding. In addition, the constitution concentrated power in a unicameral (single-house) legislature, eliminating both the office of governor and the more elite upper legislative house. To prevent the formation of an entrenched class of officeholders, the constitution's framers also required legislators to stand for election annually and barred them from serving more than four years out of seven.

The constitutions of the other states, although not as bold in their democratic reforms as Pennsylvania's, typically enhanced the political influence of ordinary citizens more than the constitution of South Carolina did. Unlike the colonial assemblies, the new bicameral (two-house) legislatures included substantially more artisans and small farmers and were not controlled by men of wealth. The proportion of legislators who came from a common background—those with property valued under £200—more than tripled to 62 percent in the North and more than doubled in the South from the 1770s to the 1780s.

Summing up the prevailing view among Americans about the proper basis for government, William Hooper of North Carolina wrote in 1776, "Rulers must be conceived as the creatures of the people, made for their use, accountable to them, and subject to removal as soon as they act inconsistent with the purposes for which they were formed."

The Articles of Confederation

Once the Continental Congress decided on independence in 1776, it needed to create a legal basis for a permanent union of the states. John Dickinson of Pennsylvania, a reluctant supporter of independence, presented a draft plan for such a union as early as the summer of 1776. Dickinson favored a strong central government, but Congress fundamentally altered his original plan to recognize the sovereign power of the individual states. According to the key provision of the

American Views

A French Observer Describes A New Society

In 1782, J. Hector St. John Crevecoeur, a Frenchman who had lived and traveled in British North America, published his impressions of America. The following selection from his *Letters from an American Farmer* captures the striking optimism and sense of newness that he found. More so than any other literary work, the *Letters* stamped the new American republic, especially in the minds of Europeans, as the home of the world's freest and most equal people.

- What is Crevecoeur's image of America? Do you believe it was overly optimistic?
- Why does Crevecoeur put such emphasis on the absence of titles and great disparities of wealth?
- Just what was so new about America to Crevecoeur?
- Why did Crevecoeur ignore African slaves in his definition of the American?
- What happened to Native Americans in his account of the making of the American?

I wish I could be acquainted with the feelings and thoughts which must agitate the heart and present themselves to the mind of an enlightened Englishman when he first lands on this continent.... He is arrived on a new continent; a modern society offers itself to his contemplation, different from what he had hitherto seen. It is not composed, as in Europe, of great lords who possess everything and of a herd of people who have nothing. Here are no aristocratical families, no courts, no kings, no bishops, no ecclesiastical dominion, no invisible power giving to a few a very visible one, no great manufactures employing thousands, no great refinements of luxury. The rich and the poor are not so far removed from each other as they are in Europe. Some few towns excepted, we are all tillers of the earth, from Nova Scotia to West Florida. We are a people of cultivators scattered over an immense territory, communicating with each other by means of good roads and navigable rivers, united by the silken bands of mild government, all respecting the laws without dreading their power, because they are equitable. We are all animated with the spirit of an industry which is unfettered and unrestrained, because each person works for himself.... A pleasing uniformity of decent competence appears throughout our habitations. The meanest of our log-houses is a dry and comfortable habitation. Lawyer and merchant are the fairest titles our towns afford; that of a farmer is the only appellation of the rural inhabitants of our country. It must take some time ere he can reconcile himself to our dictionary, which is but short in words of dignity and names of honour.... We have no princes for whom we toil, starve, and bleed; we are the most perfect society now existing in the world. Here man is free as he ought to be, nor is this pleasing equality so transitory as many others are. Many ages will not see the shores of our great lakes replenished with inland nations, nor the unknown bounds of North America entirely peopled....

The next wish of this traveller will be to know whence came all these people. They are a mixture of English, Scotch, Irish, French, Dutch, Germans, and Swedes. From this promiscuous breed, that race now called Americans have arisen.... What, then, is the American, this new man? He is either an European or the descendant of an European; hence that strange mixture of blood, which you will find in no other country.... He is an American, who, leaving behind him all his ancient prejudices and manners, receives new ones from the new mode of life he has embraced, the new government he obeys, and the new rank he holds. He becomes an American by being received in the broad lap of our Alma Mater. Here individuals of all nations are melted into a new race of men, whose labours and posterity will one day cause great changes in the world.

Source: J. Hector St. John Crevecoeur, *Letters from an American Farmer and Sketches of Eighteenth-Century America*, ed. Albert E. Stone (1986), pp. 66–70.

Articles of Confederation that the Congress finally submitted to the states more than a year later, in November 1777, "Each State retains its sovereignty, freedom and independence, and every power, jurisdiction and right, which is not by this confederation expressly delegated to the United States, in Congress assembled." The effect was to create a loose confederation of autonomous states.

The powers the Articles of Confederation delegated to the central government were extremely limited, in effect little more than those already exercised by the Continental Congress. There were no provisions for a national judiciary or a separate executive branch of government. The Articles made Congress the sole instrument of national authority but restricted it with a series of constitutional safeguards that kept it from threatening the interests of the states. Each state had only one vote in Congress, making it politically equal to the others regardless of its size or population. State legislatures were to choose their congressional delegations in annual elections, and delegates could serve only three years out of six. Delegates were expected to follow the instructions of their state legislatures and could be recalled at any time. Important measures, such as finances or war and peace, required approval from a majority of nine state delegations voting in the Congress. Amendments to the Articles of Confederation, including the levying of national taxes, required the unanimous consent of the states.

The Congress had authority primarily in the areas of foreign policy and national defense. It could declare war, make peace, conduct foreign affairs, negotiate with Native Americans, and settle disputes between the states. It had no authority, however, to raise troops or impose taxes; it could only ask the states to supply troops and money and hope that they would comply.

The central principle behind the Articles was the fear of oppressive, centralized power encroaching on the freedoms for which the Revolution had been fought. "It is freedom, Gentlemen, it is freedom, & not a choice of the forms of servitude for which we contend," resolved the residents of West Springfield, Massachusetts, in their instructions to their congressional representatives in 1778.

Most states quickly ratified the Articles of Confederation, but Maryland stubbornly held out until March 1781. Because they needed the approval of all thirteen states, only then did the Articles officially take effect. Surprisingly, given the prevailing deep suspicion of central power, what caused the delay was the demand of some states to give the Congress a power not included in the Articles submitted for ratification in 1777.

The issue here concerned the unsettled lands in the West between the Appalachian Mountains and the Mississippi River (see Map 7–1). Some states claimed these lands

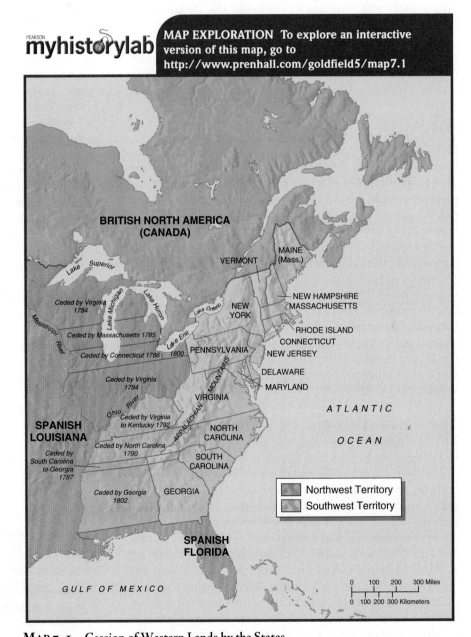

MAP 7–1   Cession of Western Lands by the States
Eight states had claims to lands in the West after the Revolution, and their willingness to cede them to the national government was an essential step in the creation of a public domain administered by Congress.

by virtue of their colonial charter rights, and led by Virginia and Massachusetts, they insisted on maintaining control over these territories. The so-called landless states—those with no claim to the West—insisted that the territories should be set aside as a national domain, a reserve of public land controlled by Congress for the benefit of all the states. Land speculators who had purchased huge tracts of land from the Indians before the Revolution sided with the landless states. Many of them leading politicians, they expected that the Congress would be more likely to honor their land titles than would the individual states.

Threatened by the British presence in the Chesapeake area in early 1781, Virginia finally broke the impasse over the Articles. Though it retained control of Kentucky, Virginia gave up its claim in the West to a vast area extending north of the Ohio River. In turn, Maryland, the last holdout among the landless states and now desperate for military aid from the Congress, agreed to ratify the Articles.

Problems at Home

Neither prosperity nor political stability accompanied the return of peace in 1783. The national government struggled to avoid bankruptcy, and in 1784, an economic depression struck. As fiscal problems deepened, creditor and debtor groups clashed angrily in state legislatures. When legislatures passed measures that provided relief to debtors at the expense of creditors, the creditors decried what they saw as the interference of ignorant majorities with the rights of private property. Raising the cry of "legislative despotism," the abuse of power by tyrannical lawmakers, the creditors joined their voices to those who early on had wanted the power of the states curbed by a stronger central government. The only solid accomplishment of the Confederation Congress during this troubled period was to formulate an orderly and democratic plan for the settlement of the West.

The Fiscal Crisis

The Continental Congress and the states had incurred heavy debts to finance the Revolutionary War. Unable to impose and collect sufficient taxes to cover the debts and without reserves of gold or silver, they had little choice but to borrow funds and issue certificates, or bonds, pledging repayment. The Congress had the largest responsibility for meeting the war's costs, and to do so, it printed close to $250 million in paper notes backed only by its good faith. By the end of the war in 1781, these Continental dollars were nearly worthless, and the national debt—primarily certificates issued by the Continental Loan Office—stood at $11 million. As Congress issued new securities to settle claims by soldiers and civilians, the debt rose to $28 million within just a few years.

The Congress never did put its tottering finances on a sound footing, and its fiscal problems ultimately discredited the Articles of Confederation in the eyes of the **nationalists,** a loose bloc of congressmen, army officers, and public creditors who wanted to strengthen the Confederation at the expense of the states. The nationalists first began to organize in the dark days of 1780 and 1781, when inflation was rampant, the army was going unpaid, the Congress had ceased paying interest on the public debt, and the war effort itself seemed in danger of collapsing. Galvanized by this crisis, the nationalists rallied behind Robert Morris, a Philadelphia merchant appointed as superintendent of finance for the Confederation government.

Morris sought to enhance national authority through a bold program of financial and political reform. He began by securing a charter from Congress in 1781 for the Bank of North America, the nation's first commercial bank, which was located in Philadelphia. Morris wanted it to serve as a national institution, and he used it to hold government funds, make loans to the government, and issue bank notes—paper money that could be used to settle debts and pay taxes owed to the United States. Morris was able to resume some specie payments, and he temporarily brought order and economy to the nation's finances. Nonetheless, he was blocked in his efforts to gain the taxing power that was essential for restoring the shattered credit of the Confederation government.

In 1781, Morris proposed a national impost, or tariff, of 5 percent on imported goods. Because this was a national tax, it required an amendment to the Articles of Confederation and the consent of all thirteen states. Twelve of the states quickly ratified the impost amendment, but Rhode Island—critically dependent on its own import duties to finance its war debt—rejected it, sending it down to defeat. When a revised impost plan was considered two years later, New York blocked its passage. These failures doomed Morris's financial reforms. He left office in 1784, and in the same year, the Bank of North America severed its ties to the national government and became a private corporation in Pennsylvania.

BANK

IT appearing to be the disposition of the Gentlemen in this City to establish a BANK on liberal principles, the stock to consist of specie only; they are therefore hereby invited to meet To-Morrow Evening at Six o'Clock, at the Merchants Coffee House where a plan will be submitted to their consideration.

from New York Packet
February 23, 1784

This invitation in 1784 to discuss plans for a new bank led to the founding of the Bank of New York by Alexander Hamilton.

The failure of the impost tax was one of many setbacks that put the nationalists temporarily on the defensive. With the conclusion of peace in 1783, confidence in state government returned, taking the edge off calls to vest the central government with greater authority. The states continued to balk at supplying the money requisitioned by Congress and denied the Congress even limited authority to regulate foreign commerce. Most ominously for the nationalist cause, the states began to assume responsibility for part of the national debt. By 1786, New Jersey, Pennsylvania, Maryland, and New York had absorbed one-third of the debt by issuing state bonds to their citizens in exchange for national securities. As Morris had warned in 1781, such a policy entailed "a principle of disunion...which must be ruinous." Without the power to tax, the Congress was a hostage to the sovereignty of the individual states with no real authority over the nation's economic affairs. When the economy plunged into a severe depression in 1784, Congress could only look on helplessly.

Economic Depression

During the Revolutionary War, Britain closed its markets to American goods. After the war, the British continued this policy, hoping to keep the United States weak and dependent. In the summer of 1783, they excluded Americans from the lucrative trade with the British West Indies. Before the Revolution, this trade in foodstuffs and timber with the sugar islands had been the primary means by which the colonists had built up the credit they needed to offset their imports from Britain.

Meanwhile, British merchants were happy to satisfy America's pent-up demand for consumer goods after the war. Cheap British imports inundated the American market, and coastal merchants made them available to inland traders and shopkeepers by extending easy credit terms. In turn, these local businessmen sold the goods to farmers and artisans in the interior. Ultimately, however, the British merchants required payment in hard currency, gold and silver coins. Without access to its former export markets, America's only source of hard currency was foreign loans obtained by Congress and what money the French army had spent during the war. This was soon exhausted, and America's trade deficit with Britain—the excess of imports over exports—ballooned in the early 1780s (see Figure 7–2).

The result was an immense bubble of credit that finally burst in 1784, triggering a depression that would

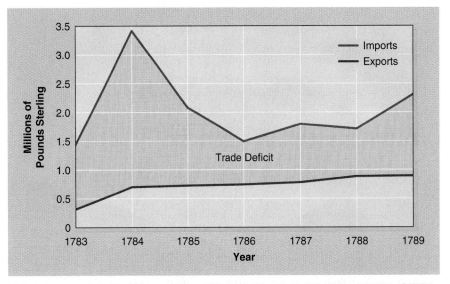

FIGURE 7–2   American Exports to and Imports from Britain between 1783 and 1789 During the 1780s, the United States imported far more from Britain than it exported there. The resulting huge trade deficit drained the country of gold and silver and was a major factor in the credit crisis that triggered an economic depression in the middle of the decade.

Source: U.S. Bureau of the Census, *Historical Statistics of the United States: Colonial Times to 1970*, pt. 2 (1975) p. 1176.

linger for most of the decade. As merchants began to press debtors for immediate payment, prices collapsed (they fell more than 25 percent between 1784 and 1786), and debtors were unable to pay. The best most could hope for was to avoid bankruptcy.

Small farmers everywhere had trouble paying their taxes. In 1786, James Swan of Massachusetts wrote of farmers in his state: "There is no family that does not want [i.e., need] some money for some purposes, and the little which the farmer carries home from market, must be applied to other uses, besides paying off the [tax] collector's bills." Rural shopkeepers often could not move goods unless they agreed to barter them for farm produce.

In the cities, wages fell 25 percent between 1785 and 1789, and workers began to organize. They called for tariffs to protect them from cheap British imports and for legislative measures to promote American manufacturers. In the countryside, farmers faced lawsuits for the collection of debts and the dread possibility of losing their land. "To be tenants to landlords, we know not who," protested the farmers of Conway, Massachusetts, "and pay rent for lands, purchased with our money, and converted from howling wilderness, into fruitful fields, by the sweat of our brows, seems...truly shocking."

With insufficient money in circulation to raise prices and reverse the downturn, the depression fed on itself. Congress was powerless to raise cash and was unable to pay off its old debts, including what it owed to the Revolutionary soldiers. Many state governments made things worse by imposing

Depicted here in a folding fan, the *Empress of China* was the first American ship to undertake an extensive trading voyage to China. Sailing from New York in February 1784, the *Empress of China* returned on May 11, 1785, and netted a profit of $37,000 for the investors who had financed the voyage. Building trading contacts with new markets in Asia and Europe helped the United States break its economic dependence on England.

Courtesy of The Historical Society of Pennsylvania Collection, Atwater Kent Museum of Philadelphia.

slaves and repair their plantations and dikes. Burdened by new British duties on American rice, planters saw their rice exports fall by 50 percent. Small farmers in the pine barrens of North Carolina likewise had to adjust to the loss of their formerly protected British market for naval stores—tar, pitch, and turpentine.

By the late 1780s, the worst of the depression was over and an upturn was under way in the mid-Atlantic states. Food exports to continental Europe were on the rise, and American merchants were developing new trading ties with India and China. Commercial treaties with the Dutch, Swedes, and Prussians also opened up markets that had been closed to the colonists. Nonetheless, a full recovery had to await the 1790s.

As the economy stagnated in the 1780s, the population was growing rapidly. There were 50 percent more Americans in 1787 that there had been in 1775. As a result, living standards fell and economic conflict dominated the politics of the states during the Confederation period.

heavy taxes payable in the paper money they had issued during the Revolution. The result was to further reduce the amount of money in circulation, thus increasing deflationary pressures and forcing prices still lower.

Britain's trade policies caused particular suffering among New England merchants. No longer protected under the old Navigation Acts as British vessels, American ships were now barred from most ports in the British trading empire. Incoming cargoes from the West Indies to New England fell off sharply, and the market for whale oil and fish, two of New England's major exports, dried up. The economy of the mid-Atlantic region held up somewhat better, but even there the loss of the provisioning trade to the British West Indies in grains, livestock, and dairy products cut into the income of merchants and farmers and forced layoffs among artisans who serviced the shipping trade.

In the southern states, British policies compounded the problem of recovering from the physical damage and labor disruptions inflicted by the war. Some 10 percent of the region's slaves had fled during the war, and production levels on plantations fell in the 1780s. Chesapeake planters needed a full decade to restore the prewar output of tobacco, and a collapse in tobacco prices in 1785 left most of them in the same chronic state of indebtedness that had plagued them on the eve of the Revolution.

Farther south, in the Carolina lowcountry, the plantation economy was crippled. War damage had been extensive, and planters piled up debts to purchase additional

The Economic Policies of the States

The depression had political repercussions in all the states. Britain was an obvious target of popular anger, and merchants poorly positioned to adjust to the postwar dislocations of trade led a campaign to slap retaliatory duties on British ships and special taxes on British goods. Likewise artisans and workers, especially in the North, pushed for tariff barriers against cheap British goods as a way to encourage domestic manufacturing and protect their jobs and wages. Most northern states imposed anti-British measures, but these varied from state to state, limiting their impact and producing squabbles when goods imported in one state were shipped to another.

State legislatures in the North responded to the protests of artisans by passing tariffs, but the lack of a uniform national policy doomed their efforts. Shippers evaded high tariffs by bringing their cargoes in through states with no tariffs or less restrictive ones. States without ports, such as New Jersey and North Carolina, complained of economic discrimination. When they purchased foreign goods from a neighboring shipping state, they were forced to pay part of the tariff cost, but all the revenue from the tariff accrued to the importing state. James Madison neatly summarized the plight of these states when he noted that "New Jersey, placed between Philadelphia and New York, was likened to a cask tapped at both ends; and North Carolina, between Virginia and South Carolina, to a patient bleeding at both Arms."

Tariff policies also fed sectional tensions between northern and southern states that undermined efforts to confer on the Congress the power to regulate commerce. The agrarian states of the South, which had little in the way of mercantile or artisan interests to protect, generally favored free trade policies that encouraged British imports. Southern planters were also happy to take advantage of the low rates charged by British ships for transporting their crops to Europe; by doing so, they put pressure on northern shippers to reduce their rates.

The most bitter divisions exposed by the depression of the 1780s, however, were not between states but between debtors and creditors within states. As the value of debt securities the states had issued to raise money dropped during the Revolutionary War, speculators bought them up for a fraction of their face value from farmers and soldiers desperate for cash. The speculators then pressured the states to raise taxes and repay the debts in full in hard currency. Wealthy landowners and merchants likewise supported higher taxes and the rapid repayment of debts in hard currency.

Arrayed against these creditor groups by the mid-1780s was a broad coalition of debtors: middling farmers, small shopkeepers, artisans, laborers, and people who had overextended themselves speculating in western land. The debtors wanted the states to issue paper money that they could use instead of hard money—gold and silver—to pay their debts. The paper money would have an inflationary effect, raising wages and the prices of farm commodities and reducing the value of debts contracted in hard currency. The townspeople of Atkinson, New Hampshire, expressing the feelings of many hard-pressed rural areas, put the issue this way: "For want of a suitable medium of trade the Citizens of this State are altogether unable to pay their public taxes, or private debts, or even to support the train of needless and expensive lawsuits, which alone would be an insupportable burden."

Shays's Rebellion.   This was the economic context in which **Shays's Rebellion** exploded in the fall of 1786. Farm foreclosures and imprisonments for failure to pay debts had skyrocketed in western Massachusetts. When the creditor and seaboard interests in the legislature refused to pass any relief measures, some 2,000 farmers took up arms against the state government in Shays's Rebellion.

Outside of western Massachusetts, discontented debtors generally stopped short of armed resistance because of their success in changing the monetary policy of their states. In 1785 and 1786, seven states enacted laws for new paper money issues. In most cases, the result was a qualified success. Controls on the supply of the new money kept it from depreciating rapidly, so that its inflationary effect was mild. It was used chiefly to provide loans to farmers so that they could meet their tax or mortgage payments. Combined with laws that prevented or delayed creditors

This clash between Shays's rebels and government troops at the Springfield arsenal marked the violent climax of the agrarian protests of the 1780s.

from seizing property from debtors to satisfy debts, the currency issues helped keep a lid on popular discontent.

The most notorious exception to this pattern of fiscal responsibility was in Rhode Island, already nicknamed "Rogue's Island" for the sharp trading practices of its merchants. A rural party that gained control of the Rhode Island legislature in 1786 pushed through a currency law that flooded the state with paper money that could be used to pay all debts. Creditors who balked at accepting the new money at face value were subject to heavy penalties. Shocked, they went into hiding or left the state entirely, and merchants denounced the law as outright fraud.

Debtors vs. conservatives.   The actions of the debtor party in Rhode Island alarmed conservatives everywhere, confirming their fears that legislative bodies dominated by common farmers and artisans rather than, as before the Revolution, by men of wealth and social distinction, were dangerous. One South Carolina conservative declared that he could see nothing but an "open and outrageous…violation of every principle of justice" in paper money and debt relief laws. Conservatives, creditors, and nationalists alike now spoke of a democratic tyranny that would have to be checked if the republic were to survive and protect its property holders.

Congress and the West

The Peace of Paris and the surrender of charter claims by the states gave the Congress control of a magnificent expanse of land between the Appalachian Mountains and the Mississippi River. This was the first American West. In what would prove the most enduring accomplishment of the Confederation government, the Congress set forth a series of effective provisions for its settlement, governance, and eventual absorption into the Union.

Asserting for the national government the right to formulate Indian policy, the Congress negotiated a series of treaties with the Indians beginning in 1784 for the abandonment of their land claims in the West. By threatening to use military force, congressional commissioners in 1784 coerced the Iroquois Confederation of New York to cede half of its territory to the United States in the Treaty of Fort Stanwix. Similar tactics in 1785 resulted in the Treaty of Fort McIntosh, in which the Wyandots, Chippewas, Delawares, and Ottawas ceded much of their land in Ohio. Against the opposition of states intent on grabbing Indian lands for themselves, Congress resolved in 1787 that its treaties were binding on all the states. And anxious for revenue, Congress insisted on payment from squatters who had filtered into the West before provisions had been made for land sales.

The most pressing political challenge was to secure the loyalty of the West to the new and fragile Union. To satisfy the demands of settlers for self-government, the Congress resolved as early as 1779 that new states would be carved out of the western domain with all the rights of the original states. An early plan for organizing the territories, the Ordinance of 1784, was largely the work of Thomas Jefferson. In it, he proposed to create ten districts, or territories, each of which could apply for admission as a state when its population equaled that of the free inhabitants in the least populous of the existing states. Jefferson also proposed that settlers be permitted to choose their own officials, and he called for the prohibition of slavery in the West after 1800. Shorn of its no-slavery features, the ordinance passed Congress but was never put into practice.

As settlers and speculators began pouring into the West in 1784, however, the Congress was forced to move quickly to formulate a policy for conveying its public land into private hands. If it could not regulate land sales and pass on clear titles, Congress would, in effect, have surrendered its claim to govern. One way or another, settlers were going to get their land, but a pell-mell process of private acquisitions in widely scattered settlements threatened to touch off costly Indian wars, deprive the national government of vitally needed revenue, and encourage separatist movements. The members of Congress had to act on national land policy, warned a western Pennsylvanian, or else "lose the only opportunity they ever will have of extending their power and influence over this new region."

The Congress responded with the **Land Ordinance of 1785.** The crucial feature of this seminal legislation was its stipulation that public lands be surveyed in a rectangular grid pattern before being offered for sale (see Figure 7–3). By requiring that land first be platted into townships of 36 uniform sections of 640 acres each, the ordinance adopted the New England system of land settlement, an approach that promoted compact settlements and produced undisputed land titles. In sharp contrast was the typical southern pattern, whereby settlers picked out a piece of land in a large tract ahead of a precise survey and then fought each other in the courts to secure legal title. In an effort to avoid endless litigation, Congress opted for a policy geared to order and regularity.

Congress also attempted to attract a certain type of settler to the West by offering the plots of 640 acres at the then hefty sum of no less than $640, or $1 per acre, payable in hard currency or its equivalent. The goal here was to keep out the shiftless poor and reserve the West for enterprising and presumably law-abiding farm families who could afford the entry cost. Concerned about westerners' reputation for lawlessness and afraid that the primitive living conditions might cause them to lapse into savagery, Congress also set aside the income from the sale of the sixteenth section in each township for the support of public schools. Support for education, as a congressional report of 1783 put it, would help provide for "security against the increase of feeble, disorderly and dispersed settlements in those remote and extended territories [and] against the depravity of manners which they have a tendency to produce."

Before any land sales occurred under the Ordinance of 1785, impatient settlers continued to push north of the Ohio River and claim homesteads as squatters. They clashed both with local Indian tribes and with the troops sent by the Congress to evict them. Impatient with the slow process of surveying, the Congress sold off 1.5 million acres to a group of New England speculators organized as the Ohio Company. The speculators bought the land with greatly depreciated loan-office certificates that had been issued to Revolutionary War veterans, and their cost per acre averaged less than 10 cents in hard money. They now pressed their allies in Congress to establish a governmental structure for the West that would protect their investment by bringing the unruly elements in the West under control.

Both the Congress and speculators wanted political stability and economic development in the West and a degree of supervision for settlers commonly viewed in the East as "but little less savage than the Indians." What was needed, wrote James Monroe of Virginia, were temporary controls—made acceptable by the promise of eventual statehood—that "in effect" would place the western territories under "a colonial government similar to that which

GRAPHIC EXPLORATION To explore an interactive version of this graph, go to
http://www.prenhall.com/goldfield5/fig7.3

FIGURE 7-3   Land Ordinance of 1785
The precise uniformity of the surveying system initiated in the Land Ordinance of 1785 created a rectangular grid pattern that was the model for all future land surveyed in the public domain.

prevail'd in these States previous to the revolution." The **Northwest Ordinance of 1787,** the most significant legislative act of the Confederation Congress, filled this need, creating a phased process for achieving statehood that neatly blended public and private interests.

According to the ordinance, controls on a new territory were to be strictest in the early stage of settlement, when Congress would appoint a territorial government consisting of a governor, a secretary, and three judges. When a territory reached a population of 5,000 adult males, those with 50 acres of land or more could elect a legislature. The actions of the legislature, however, were subject to an absolute veto by the governor. Once a territory had a population of 60,000, the settlers could draft a constitution and apply for statehood "on an equal footing with the original states in all respects whatsoever."

Unlike Jefferson's Ordinance of 1784, which called for ten states, the Northwest Ordinance of 1787 stipulated that only three to five states were to be formed out of the Northwest. This change was because the admission of new states would weaken the control over Congress that the original thirteen states wanted to maintain for themselves as long as possible. Although less democratic in many respects than Jefferson's plan in that it mandated a period of outside control by Congress, the 1787 ordinance provided greater protection for property rights as well as a bill of rights guaranteeing individual freedoms.

Most significant, it prohibited slavery. Southern congressmen agreed to the ban, in part because they saw little future for slavery in the region. More important, they expected slavery to be permitted in the region south of the Ohio River that was still under the administrative authority of Virginia, North Carolina, and Georgia in the 1780s. Indeed, slavery was allowed in this region when the **Southwest Ordinance of 1790** brought it under national control, a decision that would have grave consequences in the future sectionalization of the United States.

Although the Northwest Ordinance applied only to the national domain north of the Ohio River, it provided the organizational blueprint by which all future territory was brought into the Union. It went into effect immediately and set the original Union on a course of dynamic expansion through the addition of new states.

Diplomatic Weaknesses

In the international arena of the 1780s, the United States was a weak and often ridiculed nation. Under the Articles of Confederation, the Congress had the authority to negotiate foreign treaties but no economic or military power to enforce their terms. Unable to regulate commerce or set tariffs, Congress had no leverage with which to pry open the restricted trading empires of France, Spain, and most important, Britain.

France and the United States, allies during the Revolutionary War, remained on friendly terms after it. The United States even had a favorable trade balance with France, selling more there than it bought. Britain, however, treated its former colonies with contempt, and Spain was also openly antagonistic. Both of these powers sought to block American expansion into the trans-Appalachian West. And a dispute with Spain over the West produced the most serious diplomatic crisis of the period, one that spilled over into domestic politics, increasing sectional tensions between northern and southern states and leading many to question the country's chances of survival.

Impasse with Britain

The Confederation Congress was unable to resolve any of the major issues that poisoned Anglo-American relations in the 1780s. Key among those issues were provisions in the peace treaty of 1783 that concerned prewar American debts to the British and the treatment of Loyalists by the patriots. Britain used what it claimed to be America's failure to satisfy these provisions to justify its own violations of the treaty. The result was a diplomatic deadlock that hurt American interests in the West and in foreign trade.

Article 4 of the peace treaty called for the payment of all prewar debts at their "full value in sterling money"—that is, in gold or silver coin. Among the most numerous of those with outstanding debts to British creditors were tobacco planters in the Chesapeake region of Virginia and Maryland. During the Revolution, the British army had carried off and freed many of the region's slaves without compensating the planters. Still angry, the planters were in no mood to repay their debts. Working out a scheme with their respective legislatures, they agreed only to pay the face value of their debts to their state treasuries in state or Continental paper money. Since this money was practically worthless, the planters in effect repudiated their debts.

During the Revolution, all the states had passed anti-Loyalist legislation, and many state governments had seized Loyalists' lands and goods, selling them to raise revenue for the war effort. Upwards of 100,000 Loyalists fled to Canada and England, and their property losses ran into millions of dollars. Articles 5 and 6 of the peace treaty pledged the Congress to "recommend" to the states that they stop persecuting Loyalists and restore confiscated Loyalist property. But wartime animosities remained high, ebbing only gradually during the 1780s. Despite the pleadings of John Jay, the secretary for foreign affairs in the Confederation government, the states were slow to rescind their punitive legislation or allow the recovery of confiscated property.

Combined with the matter of the unpaid debts, the continued failure of the states to make restitution to the Loyalists gave the British a convenient pretext to hold on to the forts in the West that they had promised to relinquish in the Treaty of Paris. Their refusal to abandon the forts, which extended from Lake Champlain in upstate New York westward along the Great Lakes, was part of an overall strategy to keep the United States weak, divided, and small. The continued British presence in the region effectively shut Americans out of the fur trade with the Indians. It also insulted the sovereignty of the United States and threatened the security of its northern frontier. In 1784, exasperated New Yorkers warned the Congress that unless the British were forced to leave, New York would "be compelled to consider herself as left to pursue her own Councils, destitute of the Protection of the United States." Elsewhere, the British, spurred on by Canadian officials, encouraged secessionist movements in the Northwest and sought out Indian allies to fight for a possible buffer state south of the Great Lakes that would keep Americans hemmed in along the Atlantic seaboard.

Throughout the 1780s, the British also explored the possibility of entering into an economic alliance with Vermont. Created in 1777 out of land claimed by both New York and New Hampshire, Vermont proclaimed itself an independent republic, free from the control of the British Parliament and the American Congress. Ethan Allen and his brothers Ira and Levi held the power in Vermont politics, and their ambitious schemes for profiting from the sale of such raw materials as lumber and naval stores depended on a favorable treaty with Britain. The Allen brothers initiated a series of negotiations with the British in the 1780s in which they offered a treaty of friendship in exchange for recognition of Vermont's independence and trading privileges within the British Empire. The British were tempted but held back for fear of unduly antagonizing the United States. (Most Vermonters were strongly pro-American in their loyalties, and in 1791, after settlement of the disputed land claims, Vermont joined the Union as the fourteenth state.)

For all of the British provocations in the West, American officials viewed Britain's retaliatory trade policies as the gravest threat to American security and prosperity. John Adams, the American minister to London, concluded that the British would never lift their trading and shipping restrictions until forced to do so by a uniform American system of discriminatory duties on British goods. Retaliatory navigation acts by individual states did little good because they left the British free to play one state off against another. Adams could denounce Parliament as a "parcel of sots" for restricting American trade, but only with a strong, centralized government could Americans fashion a navigation system that would command Britain's respect.

Spain and the Mississippi River

At the close of the Revolutionary War, Spain reimposed barriers on American commerce within its empire. Anxious to maintain as large a buffer zone as possible between its Louisiana and Florida possessions and the restless Americans, Spain also refused to recognize the southern and western boundaries of the United States as specified in the treaty with Britain in 1783, holding out instead for a more northerly border (see Map 7–2). And of greatest consequence, it denied the claim of the United States to free navigation of the entire length of the Mississippi River.

The Mississippi question was explosive because on its resolution hinged American settlement and control of the entire western region south of the Ohio River. Only with access to the Mississippi and the commercial right of deposit at New Orleans—that is, the right to transfer cargoes to oceangoing vessels—could the region's farmers, then mostly in what would become Tennessee and Kentucky, profitably reach national and international markets.

In the wake of the Revolution, the settlers of Kentucky, which was still part of Virginia, and Tennessee, which was still part of North Carolina, flirted with the idea of secession. According to a 1785 report, settlers in Kentucky felt that they did "not at present enjoy a greater portion of liberty [under Virginia] than an American colony might have done a few years ago had she been allowed a Representation in the British Parliament." Impatient to secure both political independence and the economic benefits that would come with access to the Mississippi, the separatists were not particular about whom they dealt with. They became entangled in a web of diplomatic intrigue that included the Spanish, the Indians, and American officials east of the mountains.

Spain sought to use the divided loyalties of American speculators and frontier settlers to its advantage, employing

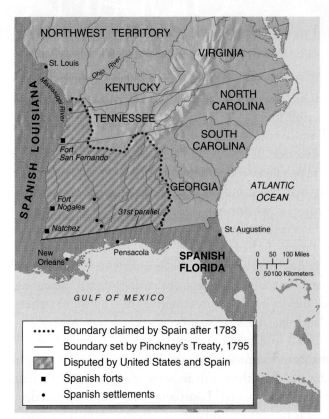

MAP 7–2   **Disputed Territory in the West after the Treaty of Paris**
Throughout the 1780s, Spain asserted title to a large area in the West south of the Ohio River.

some of them as spies and informers. Led by General James Wilkinson in Kentucky, these agents encouraged separatist plots and talk of a western confederation under Spanish protection. Spain likewise sought to exploit divisions among Indian groups. In a bewildering variety of treaties negotiated by the Congress, individual southern states, and land speculators, white Americans laid claim to much of the ancestral land of the major Indian nations in the Southeast—the Cherokee, Chickasaw, Choctaw, and Creek. Fraud was rampant, and many Native Americans believed, with good reason, that they had never been consulted in the dispossession of their land. The Spanish responded by recruiting disaffected Indians into an alliance system of their own. Their staunchest allies came from a faction of the Creeks led by Alexander McGillivray, the son of a trader father and a half-French, half-Creek mother. Supplied with arms by the Spanish, these Creeks succeeded in forcing white settlers off their tribal land in Georgia.

Spain stepped up pressure on the West in the summer of 1784, when it closed the Mississippi River within Spanish territory to American trade. Hoping now to benefit from American weakness, Spain also opened negotiations for a long-term settlement with the United States. The Spanish negotiator, Don Diego de Gardoqui, offered a deal that cleverly played the interests of the North against those of the South and West.

Foreign Threats

"I think I have done all possible to make it possible for the Government of New Orleans to reap benefit from the present situation of the United States.... These people intend to live on friendly terms with Spain and we no longer hear the threats we formerly heard...we must not neglect them. I think time will bring them to the King."

In this letter of 1788 to the Spanish secretary of state, Don Diego de Gardoqui, the Spanish representative in Philadelphia, outlined Spain's efforts in the 1780s to detach the American settlements in Kentucky from the United States and draw them into an economic alliance with Spanish Louisiana. The goal was to protect Louisiana by both weakening the United States and expanding trading opportunities for the American goods and services desired by the Spanish subjects of Louisiana. Westward expansion by Americans was inevitable, but Spain hoped to control it

and turn it to its advantage by offering trading rights on the Mississippi River that would lead to a partnership with the Spanish colony in New Orleans.

The efforts of Spain to draw Kentuckians into its empire, combined with the presence of the British in Canada and the willingness of both of these foreign powers to subsidize Native Americans as they fought to protect their tribal lands against encroachments by white settlers, threatened any effective American control of the trans-Appalachian territory. Meanwhile, British trading restrictions had largely succeeded in reducing the United States to a colonial dependency that furnished British factories with cheap raw materials and purchased British-made goods delivered in British ships. In struggling to establish its sovereign rights in a world of hostile imperial powers, the United States under the Articles of Confederation suffered the crippling disadvan-

tage of lacking any means of formulating or implementing a uniform policy for its defense. More so than any of the other delegates at the Constitutional Conventions, Alexander Hamilton drew the obvious conclusion. "You have to protect your rights against Canada in the north, Spain in the south, and your western frontier against the savages.... No Government could give us tranquility and happiness at home, which did not possess sufficient strength and stability to make us respectable abroad." Like any new nation confronted with threats to its security, the United States could not afford the luxury or indulge in the utopian hope of dispensing with power politics.

■ **How could Spain try to control the westward expansion of America and use that expansion to its advantage?**

In exchange for an American agreement to surrender claims to navigate the Mississippi for the next thirty years, Gardoqui proposed to grant the United States significant trading concessions in the Spanish Empire that would open new markets and new sources of hard money to the financially pressed merchants of the northeastern states. John Jay, his American negotiating partner, reluctantly accepted the offer.

When Jay released the terms of the proposed treaty with Spain in 1786, Congress erupted in angry debate. Southerners, who had taken the lead in the settlement of the West, accused Jay of selling out their interests. The treaty threatened the agrarian alliance they hoped to forge with the West, increasing the odds that the West would break from the East and go its own way. Vowing that they would not surrender the West, southern congressmen united to defeat the treaty. Nine states' votes were required for ratification under the Articles, and Jay's treaty gained only seven—all in the North.

The regional antagonisms exposed by the Jay–Gardoqui talks heightened the alarm over the future of the republic provoked by Shays's Rebellion earlier in 1786. As the sense of crisis deepened in 1786, the nationalists grew in influence and numbers. Led by Alexander Hamilton of New York and James Madison of Virginia, they now argued that only a radical political change could preserve the republic and fulfill the promise of its greatness.

Toward A New Union

In June 1786, a worried John Jay wrote to General George Washington that he was "uneasy and apprehensive; more so than during the war. Then we had a fixed object. ... The case is now altered; we are going and doing wrong, and therefore I look forward to evils and calamities, but without being able to guess at the instrument, nature, or measure of them."

This portrait, sketched in about 1790 by John Trumbull, is the only known likeness of Alexander McGillivray, a Creek leader who effectively played off Spanish and American interests in the Southeast to gain a measure of independence for the Creeks in the 1780s.

Other nationalists fully shared Jay's forebodings. Everywhere they saw unsolved problems and portents of disaster: unpaid debts, social unrest, squabbling states, sectional hostilities, the uncertain status of the West, blocked channels of trade, foreign intrigues, and a paralyzing lack of centralized authority and purpose. They feared that the republic's very survival was now at stake.

In September 1786, delegates from several states met at the **Annapolis Convention,** in Annapolis, Maryland, seeking to devise a uniform system of commercial regulation for the country. While there, a group of nationalist leaders issued a call for a convention at Philadelphia "to devise such further provisions as shall appear to them necessary to render the constitution of the Federal Government adequate to the exigencies of the Union." The leaders who met at the **Constitutional Convention** in Philadelphia forged an entirely new framework of governance, the **Constitution of the United States,** which called for a federal republic with a powerful and effective national government. In 1788, after a close struggle in state ratifying conventions, the Constitution was adopted.

The Road to Philadelphia

The road to Philadelphia began at Mount Vernon, George Washington's estate in Virginia. Commissioners from

Maryland and Virginia met there in March 1785 to resolve jurisdictional and navigational disputes over the Potomac River and Chesapeake Bay, waters shared by the two states. Washington had a personal stake in hosting the conference, for he was president of the Potomac Company, a newly formed group of investors hoping to build canals linking the Potomac River with the Shenandoah and Ohio valleys. The meeting went so well that the participants invited representatives from Delaware and Pennsylvania to join them at a conference in Annapolis the following year to formulate policies for interstate commerce on the waterways that linked the Chesapeake region and the Ohio Valley. James Madison then broadened the scope of the Annapolis Conference to include representatives from all thirteen states for a general discussion of how best to promote and regulate interstate trade.

Only nine states sent delegates to the Annapolis Convention, and only those from five states had actually arrived when the nationalists, at the prompting of Madison and Hamilton, abruptly adjourned the meeting. They then called on the states and the Congress to approve a full-scale constitutional convention for Philadelphia in May 1787.

The timing of the call for the Philadelphia Convention could not have been better. During the fall and winter of 1786, the agrarian protests unleashed by Shays's Rebellion in Massachusetts spilled over into other states. Coupled with talk of a dismemberment of the Union in the wake of the Jay–Gardoqui negotiations, the agrarian unrest strengthened the case of the nationalists for more centralized authority.

All the states except Rhode Island, which wanted to retain exclusive control over its own trade, sent delegates to Philadelphia. The fifty-five men who attended the convention represented an extraordinary array of talent and experience. Chiefly lawyers by training or profession, most had served in the Confederation Congress, and more than one-third had fought in the Revolution. Extremely well educated by the standards of the day, the delegates were members of the intellectual as well as the political and economic elite. As a group, they were far wealthier than the average American. Most had investments in land and the public securities of the United States. At least nineteen owned slaves. Their greatest asset as a working body was their common commitment to a nationalist solution to the crisis of confidence they saw gripping the republic. Most of the strong supporters of the Articles of Confederation refused to attend, perhaps because, as Patrick Henry of Virginia remarked, they "smelt a rat."

The Convention at Work

When it agreed to the Philadelphia Convention, the Congress authorized only a revision of the Articles of Confederation. Almost from the start, however, the delegates set about replacing the Articles altogether. Their first action was to elect George Washington unanimously as the convention's presiding officer, gaining credibility for their deliberations from his prestige. The most ardent nationalists then immediately seized the initiative by presenting the **Virginia Plan.** Drafted by James Madison, this plan replaced the Confederation Congress with a truly national government, organized like most of the state governments with a bicameral legislature, an executive, and a judiciary.

Two features of the Virginia Plan stood out. First, it granted the national Congress power to legislate "in all cases in which the separate states are incompetent" and to nullify any state laws that in its judgment were contrary to the "articles of Union." Second, it made representation in both houses of the Congress proportional to population. This meant that the most populous states would have more votes in Congress than the less populous states, giving them effective control of the government. In short, Madison sought to all but eliminate the independent authority of the states while also forcing the smaller states to defer to the more populous ones in national affairs.

Delegates from the small states countered with the **New Jersey Plan,** introduced on June 15 by William Paterson. This plan kept intact the basic structure of the Confederation Congress—one state, one vote—but otherwise amended the Articles by giving the national government the explicit power to tax and to regulate domestic and foreign commerce. In addition, it gave acts of Congress precedence over state legislation, making them "the supreme law of the respective states."

The Great Compromise.   The New Jersey Plan was quickly voted down, and the convention remained deadlocked for another month over how to apportion state representation in the national government. The issue was finally resolved on July 16 with the so-called **Great Compromise.** Based on a proposal by Roger Sherman of Connecticut, the compromise split the difference between the small and large states. Small states were given equal footing with large states in the Senate, or upper house, where each would have two votes. In the lower house, the House of Representatives, the number of seats was made proportional to population, giving larger states the advantage. The Great Compromise also settled a sectional dispute over representation between the free (or about to be free) states and the slave states. The southern states wanted slaves counted for apportioning representation in the House but excluded from direct tax assessments. The northern states wanted slaves counted for tax assessments but excluded for apportioning representation. To settle the issue, the Great Compromise settled on an expedient, if morally troubling, formula: Free residents were to be counted precisely; to that count would be added, "excluding Indians not taxed, three-fifths of all other persons (meaning enslaved blacks)." Thus the slave states gained additional political representation, while the states in the North received assurance that the owners of nonvoting slaves would have to bear part of the cost of any direct taxes levied by the new government.

The Great Compromise ended the first phase of the convention, which had focused on the general framework of a stronger national government. In its next phase, the convention debated the specific powers to be delegated to the new government. It was at this point that the sectional cleavage between North and South over slavery and other issues came most prominently to the fore. As Madison had warned in late June, "the great division of interests" in the United States would arise from the effect of states "having or not having slaves."

Regulation of commerce and the issue of slavery.   The sectional clash first erupted over the power of Congress to regulate commerce. At issue was whether Congress could regulate trade and set tariffs by a simple majority vote. Southerners worried that a northern majority would pass navigation acts favoring northern shippers and drive up the cost of sending southern commodities to Europe. To counter this threat, delegates from the Lower South demanded that a two-thirds majority be required to enact trade legislation. Suddenly, the central plank in the nationalists' program—the unified power to force trading concessions from Britain—was endangered. A frustrated Madison urged his fellow southerners to remember that "as we are laying the foundation of a great empire, we ought to take a permanent view of the subject."

In the end, Madison had his way; the delegates agreed that enacting trade legislation would require only a simple majority. In return, however, southerners exacted concessions on the slavery issue. When planters from South Carolina and Georgia made it clear that they would agree to join a new Union only if they could continue to import slaves, the convention abandoned a proposal to ban the foreign slave trade. Instead, following the lead of Roger Sherman of Connecticut, who argued that emancipation sentiment would eventually lead to abolition of slavery anyway, antislavery New Englanders reached a compromise with the delegates from the Lower South: Congress would be barred from acting against the slave trade for twenty years. In addition, bowing to the fears of planters that Congress could use its taxing power to undermine slavery, the convention denied Congress the right to tax exports from any state. And to alleviate southern concerns that slaves might escape to freedom in the North, the new Constitution included an explicit provision calling on the states to return "persons held to Service or Labour" in any other state.

After settling the slavery question in late August, the convention had one last significant hurdle to clear: the question of the national executive. For months the delegates had gone around in circles debating how presidents should be elected, how long they should serve, and what their powers should be. But in early September, eager to wrap matters up and close to exhaustion after working through a long, hot summer, they resolved these issues.

The office of the chief executive.   In large part because of their confidence in George Washington, whom nearly everyone expected to be the first president, the delegates fashioned a chief executive office with broad discretionary powers. The prerogatives of the president included the rank of commander-in-chief of the armed forces, the authority to conduct foreign affairs and negotiate treaties, the right to appoint diplomatic and judicial officers, and the power to veto congressional legislation. The president's term of office was set at four years, with no limits on how often an individual could be reelected.

Determining how to elect the president proved a thorny problem. The delegates envisioned a forceful, energetic, and independent executive, insulated from the whims of an uninformed public and the intrigues of the legislature. As a result, they rejected both popular election and election by Congress. The solution they hit upon was the convoluted system of an "electoral college." Each state was left free to determine how it would choose presidential electors equal to the number of its representatives and senators. These electors would then vote by ballot for two persons. The person receiving a majority of all the electoral votes would become president and the second highest vote-getter the vice president. If no candidate received a majority of the electoral votes, the election would be turned over to the House of Representatives, where each state would have one vote.

After a style committee polished the wording in the final draft of the Constitution, thirty-nine of the forty-two delegates still in attendance signed the document on September 17. The Preamble, which originally began with a list of the states, was reworded at the last minute to begin simply: "We the people of the United States, in order to form a more perfect Union...." This subtle change had significant implications. By identifying the people, and not a collection of states, as the source of authority, it emphasized the national vision of the framers and their desire to create a government quite different from a confederation of states.

Overview of the Constitution

Although not as strong as the most committed nationalists would have liked, the central government outlined in the Constitution was to have far more powers than were entrusted to Congress under the Articles of Confederation (see the Overview table, The Articles of Confederation and the Constitution Compared). The Constitution's provision for a strong, single-person executive had no precedent in the Articles. Nor did the provision for a Supreme Court. The Constitution vested this court, as well as the lower courts that Congress was empowered to

establish, with the judicial power of the United States. In addition, the Constitution specifically delegated to Congress the powers to tax, borrow and coin money, regulate commerce, and raise armed forces, all of which the Confederation government had lacked.

Most of the economic powers of Congress came at the expense of the states, which were prohibited from passing tariffs, issuing money, or—in an obvious reference to the debtor relief legislation of the 1780s—enacting any law that infringed on the contractual rights of creditors to collect money from debtors. Further curbing the sovereignty of the states was a clause stipulating that the Constitution and all national legislation and treaties were to be "the supreme law of the land." This clause has subsequently been interpreted as giving the central government the power to declare state laws unconstitutional.

A no-nonsense realism, as well as a nationalist outlook, infused the Constitution. Its underlying political philosophy was that, in Madison's wonderful phrase, "ambition must be made to counter ambition." Madison and the other members of the national elite who met at Philadelphia were convinced that self-interest, not disinterested virtue, motivated political behavior. As proof, they cited what to them was the sorry record of the state governments in protecting property rights and promoting social order. In their view, these governments were failures because they had been captured by unrestrained majorities corrupted by the selfishness of competing interest groups. Accepting interest-group politics as inevitable and seeking to prevent a tyrannical majority from forming at the national level, the architects of the Constitution designed a central government in which competing blocs of power counterbalanced one another.

The Constitution placed both internal and external restraints on the powers granted to the central government. The functional division of the government into executive, legislative, and judicial branches, each with ways to keep the others from exercising excessive power, created an internal system of checks and balances. For example, the Senate's authority to approve or reject presidential appointments and to ratify or reject treaties was a curb on the powers of the executive. The president commanded the armed forces, but only Congress could declare war. The president could veto congressional legislation, but Congress could override that veto with a two-thirds vote. To pass in the first place, legislation had to be approved by both the House of Representatives, which, with its membership proportional to population, represented the interests of the people at large, and the Senate, which represented the interests of the states. And as an ultimate check against executive abuse of power, Congress could impeach, convict, and remove from office a president who tried to set himself above the law.

Although the Constitution did not explicitly grant it, the Supreme Court soon claimed the right to invalidate

OVERVIEW

The Articles of Confederation and the Constitution Compared

	Articles	Constitution
Sovereign power of central government	No power to tax or raise armies	Power granted on taxes and armed forces
Source of power	Individual states	Shared through federalism between states and national government
Representation in Congress	Equal representation of states in unicameral Congress	Bicameral legislature with equal representation of states in Senate and proportional representation in House
Amendment process	Unanimous consent of states	Consent of three-fourths of states
Executive	None provided for	Office of president
National judiciary	None provided for	Supreme Court

acts of Congress and the president that it found to be unconstitutional. This power of **judicial review** provided another check against legislative and executive authority (see Chapter 9). To guard against an arbitrary federal judiciary, the Constitution empowered Congress to determine the size of the Supreme Court and to impeach and remove federal judges appointed by the president.

The external restraints on the central government were to be found in the nature of its relationship to the state governments. This relationship was based on **federalism,** the division of power between local and central authorities. By listing specific powers for Congress, the Constitution implied that all other powers were to be retained by the states. Thus, while strengthening the national government, the Constitution did not obliterate the sovereign rights of the states, leaving them free to curb the potential power of the national government in the ambiguous areas between national and state sovereignty.

This ambiguity in the federalism of the Constitution was both its greatest strength and its greatest weakness. It allowed both nationalists and advocates of states' rights to support the Constitution. But the issue of slavery, left unresolved in the gray area between state and national sovereignty, would continue to fester, sparking sectional conflict over the extent of national sovereignty that would plunge the republic into civil war three-quarters of a century later.

The Struggle over Ratification

The realism the Philadelphia delegates displayed in the drafting of the Constitution extended to the procedure they devised for implementing it. Knowing that they had exceeded their instructions by proposing an entirely new government, and aware that the Articles' requirement of unanimous consent by the state legislatures to any amendment would result in certain defeat, they boldly bypassed both Congress and the state legislatures.

The last article of the Constitution stipulated that it would go into effect when it had been ratified by at least nine of the states acting through specially elected popular conventions. Congress, influenced by the nationalist sentiments of many of its members, one-third of whom had attended the Philadelphia Convention, and perhaps weary of its own impotence, accepted this drastic and not clearly legal procedure, submitting the Constitution to the states in late September 1787.

The delegates in Philadelphia had excluded the public from their proceedings. The publication of the Constitution lifted the veil of secrecy and touched off a great political debate. Although those who favored the Constitution could most accurately have been defined as nationalists, they referred to themselves as **Federalists,** a term that helped deflect charges that they favored an excessive centralization of political authority. By default, the opponents of the Constitution were known as **Antifederalists,** a negative-sounding label that obscured their support of the state-centered sovereignty that most Americans associated with federalism. Initially outmaneuvered in this way, the Antifederalists never did mount an effective campaign to counter the Federalists' pamphlets, speeches, and newspaper editorials (see the Overview table, Federalists versus Antifederalists). The Antifederalists did attract some men of wealth and social standing. Two of them—Elbridge Gerry of Massachusetts and George Mason of Virginia—had been delegates at Philadelphia but refused to sign the Constitution. They feared that the new national government would swallow up the state governments. Most Antifederalists, however, were backcountry farmers, men with mud on their boots who lived far from centers of communication and market outlets for their produce. They distrusted the social and commercial elite, and many Antifederalists saw in the Constitution a sinister plot by this elite "to lord it over the rest of their fellow citizens, to trample the poorer part of the people under their feet that they may be rendered their servants and slaves." The

FROM THEN TO NOW

Reshaping the Constitution

The U.S. Constitution remains the world's longest continuously applied written charter of government. Key to its remarkable durability has been the power of the American people to reshape it as public expectations, needs, and values have changed. The twenty-seven amendments added to the Constitution since its inception have maintained it as a responsive, living document.

The most far-reaching of these amendments have protected individual rights and extended the democratic promise of America to all its inhabitants. Added to the Constitution in 1791 and known collectively as the Bill of Rights, the first ten amendments, enumerated individual liberties not to be abridged by the federal government. The three great Civil War amendments wrote Union victory into the Constitution by abolishing slavery and extending citizenship and the vote to African Americans. By nationalizing princi-

President Johnson signs the 24th Amendment barring the poll tax in Federal elections.

ples of freedom and equal rights, these amendments laid the basis for a new conception of American identity in the twentieth century. The four amendments ratified between 1913 and 1920—which permitted the imposition of a national income tax, required the popular election of U.S. senators, prohibited the sale of alcoholic beverages (repealed in 1933), and extended the vote to women—reflected the attempts of reformers to curb corporate power, broaden democratic governance, and enforce civic virtue. The egalitarian movements of the 1960s produced three amendments that in turn allowed residents of the District of Columbia to vote in presidential elections, outlawed the poll tax, a device segregationists had used to deny the vote to poor African Americans, and lowered the voting age to 18. Far more so than when it was ratified, the Constitution of today speaks to themes of universal liberties.

- Which amendment or group of amendments discussed above had the greatest impact in altering the original intent and purpose of the Constitution?

Washington presides over the Constitutional Convention.

myhistorylab

From Then to Now Online

7-1 *Amending the Constitution, Sept. 15, 1787.* The amendment process and debate in Constitutional Convention.

7-2 *Pennsylvania Antifederalist, 1788.* "Centinel," the case for a Bill of Rights.

7-3 Alexander Hamilton, *Federalist No. 84, 1788.* The case against a Bill of Rights.

Lesy Watchington

exfelene georg general Washington

This c1790 folk art depiction of Washington and his wife reveals how quickly Washington's fame became part of the public consciousness and made him the obvious choice to preside over the Constitutional Convention.

Antifederalists clung to the belief that only a small republic, one composed of relatively homogeneous social interests, could secure the voluntary attachment of the people necessary for a free government. They argued that a large republic, such as the one framed by the Constitution, would inevitably become tyrannical because it was too distant and removed from the interests of common citizen-farmers.

However much the Antifederalists attacked the Constitution as a danger to the individual liberties and local independence that they believed the Revolution had been fought to safeguard, they were no political match for the Federalists. They lacked the wealth, social connections, access to newspapers, and self-confidence of the more cosmopolitan and better-educated Federalists. In addition, the Federalists could more easily mobilize their supporters, who were concentrated in the port cities and commercial farming areas along the coast.

With talent, intellect, and political savvy on their side, the Federalists skillfully built on the momentum for change that had developed out of the crisis atmosphere of 1786. They successfully portrayed the Constitution as the best opportunity to erect a governing structure capable of preserving and extending the gains of the Revolution.

Conservatives shaken by Shays's Rebellion lined up behind the Constitution. So, too, did groups—creditors, merchants, manufacturers, urban artisans, commercial farmers—whose interests would be promoted by economic development. The enhanced powers of the national government held out the promise of protecting the home market from British imports, enlarging foreign markets for American exports, promoting a stable and uniform currency, and raising revenues to pay off the Revolutionary War debt.

In the early stages, the Federalists scored a string of easy victories (see Map 7–3). Delaware ratified the Constitution on December 7, 1787, and within a month, so, too, had Pennsylvania, New Jersey, Georgia, and Connecticut. Except for Pennsylvania, these were small, sparsely populated states that stood to benefit economically or militarily from a stronger central government. The Constitution carried in the larger state of Pennsylvania because of the Federalists' strength in the commercial center of Philadelphia.

The Federalists faced their toughest challenge in the large states that had generally been more successful in going it alone during the 1780s. One of the most telling arguments of the Antifederalists in these and other states was the absence of a bill of rights in the Constitution. The framers had felt it unnecessary to include such an explicit protection of individual rights in a document intended to specify the powers of a national government and had barely discussed a bill of rights in Philadelphia. Realizing the importance of the issue, and citing Article 5 of the Constitution, which provided for an amendment process, the Federalists promised to recommend amending the Constitution with a bill of rights once it was ratified. By doing so, they split the ranks of the Antifederalists in Massachusetts.

After the Federalists gained the support of two venerable heroes of the Revolution, John Hancock and Sam Adams, the Massachusetts convention approved the Constitution by a close vote in February 1788. To win over Hancock, the Federalists had played on his vanity, suggesting that they would back him for a top national post. Adams was persuaded to back the Federalists by demonstrations of Boston artisans in favor of national tariff protection.

The major hurdles remaining for the Federalists were Virginia, the most populous state, and strategically located New York. Technically, the Constitution could have gone into effect without them once Maryland, South Carolina, and New Hampshire had ratified it, bringing the total number of states to nine. But without Virginia, which ratified on June 25, and New York, which followed a month later, the new Union would have been weak and the Federalist victory far from assured.

To eke out victory in these crucial states, the Federalists drew on their pragmatism and persuasiveness. As in Massachusetts, they were helped by their promise of a bill of rights. And for the New York campaign, Madison, Jay, and Hamil-

Federalists versus Antifederalists

	Federalists	Antifederalists
Position on Constitution	Favored Constitution	Opposed Constitution
Position on Articles of Confederation	Felt Articles had to be abandoned	Felt Articles needed only to be amended
Position on power of the states	Sought to curb power of states with new central government	Felt power of states should be paramount
Position on need for bill of rights	Initially saw no need for bill of rights in Constitution	Saw absence of bill of rights in proposed Constitution as threat to individual liberties
Position on optimum size of republic	Believed large republic could best safeguard personal freedoms	Believed only a small republic formed on common interests could protect individual rights
Source of support	Commercial farmers, merchants, shippers, artisans, holders of national debt	State-centered politicians, most backcountry farmers

ton wrote an eloquent series of eighty-five essays known collectively as *The Federalist* to allay fears that the Constitution would so consolidate national power as to menace individual liberties. In the two most original and brilliant essays in *The Federalist,* essays 10 and 51, Madison turned traditional republican doctrine on its head. A large, diverse republic like the one envisaged by the Constitution, he reasoned, not a small and homogeneous one, offered the best hope for safeguarding the rights of all citizens. This was because a large republic would include a multitude of contending interest groups, making it difficult for any combination of them to coalesce into a tyrannical majority that could oppress minority rights. With this argument, Madison had developed a political rationale by which Americans could have both an empire and personal freedom.

North Carolina and Rhode Island did not ratify until after the new government was functioning. North Carolina joined the Union in 1789 once Congress submitted the amendments that constituted the Bill of Rights. The obstinate Rhode Islanders stayed out until 1790, when Congress forced them in with a threat of commercial reprisal.

Conclusion

In freeing themselves from British rule, Americans embarked on an unprecedented wave of constitution-making that sought to put into practice abstract principles of republicanism that held that political power should derive from the people. Between 1776 and 1780, Americans developed a unique system of constitutionalism that went far beyond the British model of an unwritten constitution. They proclaimed the supremacy of constitutions over ordinary legislation, detailed the powers of government in a written document, provided protection for individual freedoms in bills of rights, and fashioned a process for framing governments through the election of delegates to a special constitutional convention and the popular ratification of the work of that convention. In all of these areas, Americans were pioneers in demonstrating to the rest of the world how common citizens could create their own governments.

The curbs on centralized power that characterized the state constitutions also applied to what amounted to the first national constitution, the Articles of Confederation. Indeed, the inability of the Confederation Congress to exercise effective power in the areas of taxation and foreign trade was a crippling flaw that thoroughly discredited the Articles in the eyes of the nationalist-minded leaders who had emerged during the Revolution. These leaders overthrew the Articles at the Constitutional Convention in 1787 and engineered a peaceful revolution in securing the ratification of the Constitution. Their victory in creating a new central government with real national powers was built on the foundation of constitutional concepts and mechanisms that Americans had laid down in their state constitutions. The new Constitution rested on the consent of the governed, and it endured because it could be amended to reflect shifts in popular will and to widen the circle of Americans granted the rights of political citizenship.

Accepting as a given that self-interest drove political action, the framers of the Constitution designed the new national government to turn ambition against itself. They created rival centers of power that forced selfish factions to compete in a constant struggle to form a workable majority. The struggle occurred both within the national government and between that government and the states in the American system of federalism. The Constitution thus set the stage for an entirely new kind of national politics.

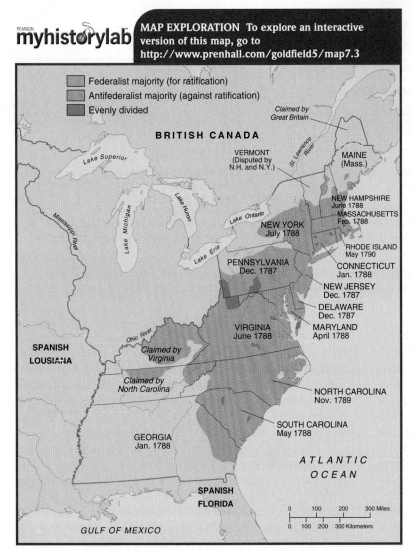

MAP EXPLORATION To explore an interactive version of this map, go to http://www.prenhall.com/goldfield5/map7.3

Federalist majority (for ratification)
Antifederalist majority (against ratification)
Evenly divided

Map 7–3   The Ratification Vote on the Constitution
Aside from some frontier districts exposed to possible foreign attack, the strongest support for the Constitution came from coastal and interior areas tied into a developing commercial economy.

Review Questions

1. How did the Shaysites justify their taking up arms against the government of Massachusetts? Can you imagine any way in which the crisis could have been resolved short of violence?

2. Why do you think that the U.S. Constitution does not cite God or mention religion in any direct way?

3. What was so unprecedented about the new state constitutions, and what principles of government did they embody?

4. What were the problems of the economy in the 1780s, and why did clashes between debtors and creditors become so divisive? Do you think that an economic recovery could have been achieved under the Articles of Confederation?

5. Do you feel that the diplomatic weaknesses of the United States under the Articles were as serious as its internal

problems? What were the sources of those weaknesses, and what threat did they pose for national unity?

6. What sorts of men drafted the Constitution in 1787, and how representative were they of all Americans? What explains the differences between the Federalists and the Antifederalists? Do you think they shared the same vision of what they wanted America to become? How widespread was the popular backing for the Constitution, and what accounts for its ratification?

7. Compare and contrast the options open to the United States in the 1780s in developing its economy with those of the new nations that have also emerged out of former colonial empires since World War II.

Key Terms

Annapolis Convention (p. 187)

Antifederalists (p. 190)

Articles of Confederation (p. 177)

Bill of rights (p. 175)

Constitutional Convention (p. 187)

Constitution of the United States (p. 187)

Federalism (p. 190)

Federalists (p. 190)

Great Compromise (p. 188)

Judicial review (p. 190)

Land Ordinance of 1785 (p. 182)

Nationalists (p. 178)

Natural rights (p. 173)

New Jersey Plan (p. 188)

Northwest Ordinance of 1787 (p. 183)

Shays's Rebellion (p. 181)

Southwest Ordinance of 1790 (p. 184)

Suffrage (p. 172)

Virginia Plan (p. 188)

Recommended Readings

Beeman, Richard, Stephen Botein, and Edward C. Carter III, eds., *Beyond Confederation: Origins of the Constitution and American National Identity* (1987). These twelve essays offer a fine overview of the competing ideologies and issues that shaped the history of the 1780s and pushed the republic toward a new framework of government in the Constitution.

Crevecoeur, J. Hector St. John. *Letters from an American Farmer and Sketches of Eighteenth-Century America,* ed. Albert E. Stone (1986). This modern reprint of Crevecoeur's work provides an accessible account of Americans and their living conditions in the late eighteenth century.

Jensen, Merrill. *The New Nation: A History of the United States during the Confederation, 1781–1787* (1948). This work

makes the strongest case for the Articles as a tentative success that was overturned in a conservative reaction that exaggerated the threats to social order.

Morris, Richard B. *The Forging of the Union, 1781–1789* (1987). The best-balanced synthesis of the 1780s, this book documents the creative statesmanship of the leaders of the Constitutional Convention.

Wood, Gordon. *The Creation of the American Republic, 1776–1787* (1969). This masterful study is indispensable for understanding the transformation of American republicanism between the winning of independence and the ratification of the Constitution.

Where to Learn More

■ **South Street Seaport Museum, New York City, New York.** Maritime commerce was the lifeblood of the postrevolutionary economy. The artifacts and exhibits here offer a fine introduction to the seafaring world of the port city that became the nation's first capital in the new federal Union. See www.southstseaport.org for more on the impact of trade on the development of New York and information on preservation projects underway in the city.

■ **Independence National Historical Park, Philadelphia, Pennsylvania.** Walks and guided tours through this historic district enable one to grasp much of the physical setting in which the delegates to the Constitutional

Convention met. The website www.nps.gov/inde/home.htm includes a virtual tour of many of the collections at the park, a portrait gallery of leading figures in the Revolution, and a look at the archaeological projects underway in the park.

■ **Northern Indiana Center for History, South Bend, Indiana.** The permanent exhibition on the St. Joseph River valley of northern Indiana and southern Michigan explains the material world of this region and how it changed as first Europeans and then Americans mingled and clashed with the Native American population. At www.centerforhistory.org one can learn more about the center and the variety of programs it offers.

Study Resources

For study resources for this chapter, go to www.myhistorylab.com and choose *The American Journey*. You will find a wealth of study and review material for this chapter, including pre- and post-tests, customized study plan, key term review flash cards, interactive map and document activities, and documents for analysis.

The text within the engraving reads:

DEC 26. 1776

THE DEFENDER OF THE MOTHERS, WILL BE THE PROTECTOR OF THE DAUGHTERS.

This engraving shows respectful crowds greeting Washington as he passes through Trenton on the way to New York City for his inauguration as president.

A New Republic and the Rise of Parties 1789–1800

8

April 30, 1789

New York City

This is the great important day. Goddess of Etiquette assist me while I describe it…. The President was conducted out of the middle window into the Gallery [of Federal Hall] and the Oath administered by the Chancellor [Robert R. Livingston, Chancellor of New York]. Notice that the Business was done, was communicated to the Croud by Proclamation…who gave three Cheers…. As the Company returned into the Senate Chamber, the president took the Chair, and the Senate and representatives their Seats. He rose & all arose also and [he] addressed them [in his inaugural address]. This great Man was agitated and embarrassed more than ever he was by the levelled Cannon or pointed Musket. He trembled and several times could scarce make out to read, tho it must be supposed he had often read it before. He put part of the fingers of his left hand, into the side, of what I think the Taylors call the fall, of his Breetches. Changing the paper into his left hand, after some time, he then did the same with some of the fingers of his right hand. When he came to the Words *all the World*, he made a flourish with his right hand, which left rather an ungainly impression…. He was dressed in deep brown, with Metal buttons, with an Eagle on them, White Stockings a Bag and Sword—from the Hall there was a grand Procession to St. Pauls Church where prayers were said by the Bishop. The Procession was well conducted and without accident, as far as I have heard. The Militias were all under Arms. [They] lined the Street near the Church, made a good figure and behaved well. The Senate returned to their Chamber after Service, formed & took up the Address....In the Evening there were grand fire Works...and after this the People went to bed.

[William Maclay]

Kenneth R. Bowling and Helen E. Veit, eds., *The Diary of William Maclay and Other Notes on Senate Debates,* March 4, 1789– March 3, 1791 (Baltimore: Johns Hopkins University Press, 1988), pp. 11–13.

myhistorylab

Personal Journeys Online

- New York *Daily Advertiser,* April 24, 1789. Newspaper description of Washington's arrival in New York.

- Tobias Lear, *Diary,* April 30, 1789. Account of presidential procession for Washington's inauguration.

- George Washington, *Excerpts from the First Inaugural Address,* April 30, 1789.

Senator William Maclay of Pennsylvania wrote this account in his personal journal of the inauguration of George Washington as the first president of the United States at Federal Hall in New York City on April 30, 1789. Born in Pennsylvania in 1737 of Scotch-Irish parents, Maclay had amassed substantial wealth as a surveyor and lawyer by the eve of the Revolution. He held a number of popularly elected offices in the 1780s before his selection by the Pennsylvania legislature in September 1788 as one of the state's first two U.S. senators. A Presbyterian with a strong sense of rectitude that often made him overly critical of others, he quickly broke with the Washington administration over its fiscal and diplomatic policies. Before his death in 1804, he switched his political allegiance to the opposition party led by Thomas Jefferson.

Washington's shakiness at his inaugural reflected the shaky start of the country's new government. Two states, North Carolina and Rhode Island, had not yet ratified the Constitution. The newly elected members of Congress had been scheduled to meet in New York on March 4, 1789, to count the ballots of the Electoral College and officially confirm Washington's election, but only one-quarter of them

arrived by then. A month would go by before the minimum needed to count the ballots could be mustered. Washington, his dignity ruffled by this show of congressional disinterest, dallied at Mount Vernon until formally notified of his election.

He had every reason to dread taking on the burden of the presidency. As head of the new national government, he would put at risk the legendary status he had achieved during the Revolution. Most Americans intensely feared centralized authority, which is why the framers deliberately left the word *national* out of the Constitution. Washington somehow had to establish loyalty to a new government whose main virtue in the eyes of many was the very vagueness of its defined powers.

The Constitution had created the framework for a national government, but pressing problems demanded the fleshing out of that framework. The government urgently needed revenue to begin paying off the immense debt incurred during the Revolution. It also had to address the unstable conditions in the West, where the settlers wavered in their loyalties. Ultimately, the key to solving these and other problems was to inspire popular backing for the government's authority.

CHRONOLOGY

1789	Inauguration of Washington.
	Congress establishes the first federal departments.
	French Revolution begins.
1790	Hamilton submits the first of his financial reports to Congress.
1791	Bill of Rights ratified.
	Congress charters the Bank of the United States.
	Slave revolt breaks out in saint-Domingue (Haiti).
1792	St. Clair's defeat along the Wabash.
	Reelection of Washington.
	Austria and Prussia invade France.
	Execution of King Louis XVI.
1793	France goes to war against Britain, Spain, and Holland.
	Genêt Mission.
	Washington issues Proclamation of Neutrality.
1794	Ohio is opened with the victory of General Anthony Wayne at the Battle of Fallen Timbers.
	Suppression of the Whiskey Rebellion in western Pennsylvania.
1795	Jay's Treaty with Britain ratified.
	Treaty of Greenville with Ohio Indians.
1796	Pinckney's Treaty with Spain ratified.
	Washington's Farewell Address.
	John Adams elected president.
1797	Beginning of the Quasi-War with France.
1798	XYZ Affair.
	Alien and Sedition Acts.
	Provisional army and direct tax.
	Virginia and Kentucky Resolutions.
1799	Fries's Rebellion in Pennsylvania.
	Napoleon assumes power in France.
1800	Franco-American Accord.
	Thomas Jefferson elected president.

The realities of governing would soon shatter the nonpartisan ideal that had prevailed when the Constitution was ratified. By the end of Washington's first term, two political parties had begun to form. The Federalist party (the name came from that used by the original backers of the Constitution), which included Washington and his successor, John Adams, favored a strong central government. The opposition party, the Jeffersonian Republicans, took shape as a result of differences over financial policy and the American response to the French Revolution. Led by Thomas Jefferson, the Republicans were distrustful of excessive central power.

The Federalists, who governed through 1800, succeeded in showing a doubting world ruled by kings and queens that the American experiment in republican government could work. But as inheritors of a political tradition that equated parties with factions—temporary coalitions of selfish private interests—the Federalists doubted the loyalty of the Republicans. When the Federalists under President John Adams attempted to suppress the Republicans, the stage was set for the critical election of 1800. Jefferson's victory in that election ended both Federalist rule and the republic's first major internal crisis.

Washington's America

The Americans whom Washington was called on to lead were hardly one unified people. They identified and grouped themselves according to many factors, including race, sex, class, ethnicity, religion, and degree of personal freedom. Geographical factors, including climate and access to markets, further divided them into regions and sections. The resulting hodgepodge sorely tested the assumption—and it was never more than an assumption in 1789—that a single national government could govern Americans as a whole (see Figure 8–1).

The Uniformity of New England

The national census of 1790 counted nearly 4 million Americans, one in four of whom lived in New England. Although often viewed as the most typically "American" part of the young nation, New England in fact was rather atypical. It alone of the nation's formative regions had largely shut itself off from outsiders. The Puritan notions of religious liberty that prevailed in the region extended only to those who subscribed to the Calvinist orthodoxy of the dominant Congregationalist Church. Geography conspired with this religious exclusiveness to limit population diversity. New England's

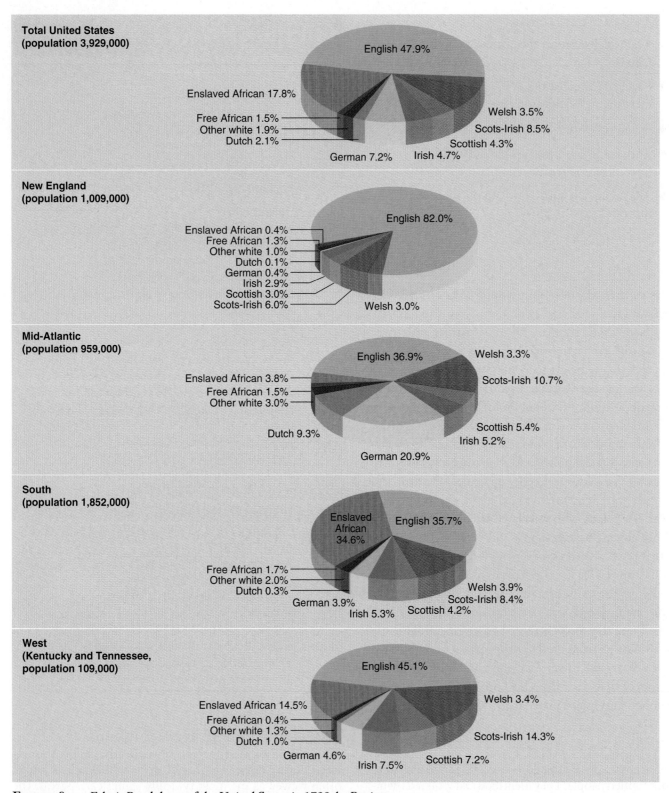

Total United States
(population 3,929,000)

English 47.9%
Enslaved African 17.8%
Free African 1.5%
Other white 1.9%
Dutch 2.1%
German 7.2%
Irish 4.7%
Scottish 4.3%
Scots-Irish 8.5%
Welsh 3.5%

New England
(population 1,009,000)

English 82.0%
Enslaved African 0.4%
Free African 1.3%
Other white 1.0%
Dutch 0.1%
German 0.4%
Irish 2.9%
Scottish 3.0%
Scots-Irish 6.0%
Welsh 3.0%

Mid-Atlantic
(population 959,000)

English 36.9%
Welsh 3.3%
Scots-Irish 10.7%
Enslaved African 3.8%
Free African 1.5%
Other white 3.0%
Scottish 5.4%
Irish 5.2%
Dutch 9.3%
German 20.9%

South
(population 1,852,000)

Enslaved African 34.6%
English 35.7%
Free African 1.7%
Other white 2.0%
Dutch 0.3%
Welsh 3.9%
Scots-Irish 8.4%
German 3.9%
Scottish 4.2%
Irish 5.3%

West
(Kentucky and Tennessee,
population 109,000)

English 45.1%
Welsh 3.4%
Enslaved African 14.5%
Free African 0.4%
Other white 1.3%
Dutch 1.0%
Scots-Irish 14.3%
German 4.6%
Scottish 7.2%
Irish 7.5%

FIGURE 8–1   Ethnic Breakdown of the United States in 1790, by Region
Unique racial and ethnic patterns shaped each of the nation's four major regions in 1790. New England was most atypical in its lack of racial or ethnic diversity.

Source: *The Statistics of the Population of the United States*, comp. Francis A. Walker (1872), pp. 3–7; Thomas L. Purvis, "The European Ancestry of the United States Population, 1790," *William and Mary Quarterly*, 41(1984), p. 98.

poor soils and long, cold winters made it an impractical place to cultivate cash crops like the tobacco and rice of the South. As a result, New England farmers had little need of imported white indentured servants or black slaves. Family members, helped by neighbors and the occasional hired hand, provided the labor on New England farms.

Puritan values and a harsh environment thus combined to make New England the most religiously and ethnically uniform region in the United States. Most of the people living there were descended from English immigrants who had arrived in the seventeenth century. Small pockets of Quakers, Baptists, and Catholics had gained the legal right of worship by the 1720s, but Congregationalism remained the official, state-supported religion in Connecticut and Massachusetts. Blacks and Indians together barely constituted 3 percent of New England's population. The few remaining Indians lived on reservations of inferior land, which they usually left only to find work as servants or day laborers.

New Englanders found slavery incompatible with the natural-rights philosophy that had emerged during the Revolution and gradually began to abolish it in the 1780s (though they remained profitably tied to slavery through shipping plantation crops). Slavery had, in any case, always been marginal in New England's economy. Owning slaves as domestic servants or artisans had been a status symbol for wealthy urban whites in Boston, Portsmouth, and Newport. As a result, about 20 percent of New England's small African American population lived in cities, where jobs were relatively easy to find, in contrast to the white population, only 10 percent of which lived in cities.

Women outnumbered men in parts of New England in 1789. This pattern—not found in other parts of the country—was the result of the pressure of an expanding population and the practice of dividing family farms among male heirs. As farms in the older, more densely settled parts of New England were divided into ever-smaller lots, many young men migrated west in search of cheap, arable land. They first pushed into the hilly regions of northern New England and then, by the 1790s, through the Mohawk River Valley into New York. Thus by 1789, women formed a slight majority in Connecticut, Massachusetts, and Rhode Island.

Despite their superior numbers, women in New England, as elsewhere, remained subordinate to men. Even so, the general testing of traditional authority that accompanied the Revolution led some New England women to question male power. The Massachusetts poet Judith Sargeant Murray, for example, published essays asserting that women were the intellectual equals of men. Murray was the first woman to argue publicly in favor of equal educational opportunities for young women, and she boldly asserted that women should learn how to become economically independent. Republican ideology, emphasizing the need for women to be intellectually prepared to raise virtuous, public-spirited children, led reformers in New England to seek equal access for women to education. In 1789, Massachusetts became the first state to allocate funds specifically for girls' elementary education. And beginning in the 1780s, wealthy residents of eastern cities set up private academies for women that would later provide the foundation for women's higher education. Liberalized divorce laws in New England also allowed a woman to seek legal separation from an abusive or unfaithful spouse.

In other respects, political and social life in New England remained rooted in the Puritan past. Age, property, and reputation determined one's standing in a culture that valued a clearly defined social order. The moral code that governed town life promoted curbs on individual behavior for the benefit of the community as a whole. With their notions of collective liberty, New Englanders subscribed to a version of republicanism that favored strong government, setting themselves apart from most other Americans, who embraced a more individualistic idea of liberty and a suspicion of government power. New Englanders perceived government as a divine institution with a moral responsibility to intervene in people's lives. Acting through town meetings, they taxed themselves for public services at rates two to four times higher than in the rest of the country. Their courts were also far more likely than those elsewhere to punish individuals for crimes against public order (like failing to observe the Sabbath properly) and sexual misconduct.

The Pluralism of the Mid-Atlantic Region

The states of the mid-Atlantic region—New York, New Jersey, and Pennsylvania—were the most ethnically and religiously diverse in the nation. People of English descent constituted somewhat less than 40 percent of the population. Other major ethnic groups included the Dutch and Scots-Irish in New York and Germans and Scots-Irish in New Jersey and Pennsylvania. With ethnic diversity came religious diversity. Transplanted New Englanders made up about 40 percent of New York's ethnic English population. Among others of English descent, Anglicans predominated in New York, and Quakers in New Jersey and Pennsylvania. The Dutch, concentrated in the lower Hudson Valley, had their own Dutch Reformed Church, and most Germans were either Lutherans or **pietists**, such as the Mennonites and the Moravians, who stressed personal piety over theological doctrine. The Presbyterian Scots-Irish settled heavily in the backcountry.

This mosaic-like pattern of ethnic and religious groupings was no accident. In contrast to Puritan New England, the Middle Colonies had offered freedom of worship to attract settlers. In addition, economic opportunities for newcomers were much greater than in New England. The soil was better, the climate was milder, and market outlets for agricultural products were more abundant. These conditions made the mid-Atlantic region the nation's first breadbasket. The region produced surpluses of wheat, flour, and corn that were shipped out of New York and Philadelphia, the two largest cities in North America by 1790. Commercial agriculture fed urban growth and created a greater demand for labor in both rural and urban areas than in New England. The influx of Germans and Scots-Irish into the region in the eighteenth century occurred in response to this demand.

The demand for labor had also been met by importing African slaves. Blacks, both free and enslaved, made up

Idealized classical images of women—white, chaste, and pure—were popular emblems in the early republic to portray national ideals of liberty and republican motherhood.

5 percent of the mid-Atlantic population in 1790, and, as in New England, they were more likely than whites to live in the maritime cities. New York had more slaveholders in 1790 than any other American city except Charleston, South Carolina. About 40 percent of the white families in the city's nearby rural outposts of Queens County, Brooklyn, and Staten Island owned slaves, a rate as high as in Maryland and South Carolina.

Despite its considerable strength in the port cities and adjacent rural areas, slavery was never an economically vital institution in most of the mid-Atlantic region. The region's major cash crop, wheat, required seasonal labor, which did not warrant tying up capital in slaves. Commercial agriculture did not rest on a slave base, nor did it produce a politically powerful class of planters. As a result, slavery in the mid-Atlantic region gave way to the demands for emancipation inspired by the natural-rights philosophy of the Revolution.

Pennsylvania in 1780, New York in 1799, and New Jersey in 1804 all passed laws of gradual emancipation. These laws did not free adult slaves but provided that children born of a slave mother were to be freed at ages ranging between 18 and 28. Soon after the laws were passed, however, adult slaves began hastening their own freedom. They ran away, set fires, and pressured their owners to accept cash payments in return for a short, fixed term of labor service. But even as they gained their freedom, African Americans had to confront enduring white racism. The comments of one white New Yorker suggest what they were up against. "We may sincerely advocate the freedom of black men," he wrote, "and yet assert their moral and physical inferiority."

The diversity of the mid-Atlantic region created a complex political environment. Competing cultural and economic interests prevented the kind of broad consensus on the meaning of republicanism that had emerged in New England. Some mid-Atlantic groups favored a strong central government to foster economic development and maintain traditional authority. Others wanted to keep government weak to foster a republican equality that would promote individual freedom.

Those who supported strong government included mercantile and financial leaders in the cities and commercial farmers in the countryside. These people tended to be Anglicans, Quakers, and Congregationalists of English descent. Those opposing them and favoring a more egalitarian republicanism tended to come from the middle and lower classes. They included subsistence farmers in the backcountry and artisans and day laborers in the cities. Most were Scots-Irish Presbyterians, but their number also included Dutch Calvinists and German Lutherans. Fiercely independent and proud of their liberties, they resented the claims of the wealthy to political authority. They resisted government aid to business as a form of political corruption that unfairly enriched those who were already economically powerful.

The Slave South and Its Backcountry

In the South—the region from Maryland and Delaware to Georgia—climate and soil conditions favored the production of cash staples for world markets. Cultivating these crops required backbreaking labor that white immigrants preferred to avoid. As Thomas Jefferson put it, "In a warm climate no man will work for himself, who can make another labor for him." Southern planters relied on the coerced labor of African slaves, whose numbers made the South the most populous region in the country.

Just under 40 percent of all southerners were slaves, but their concentration varied within the region. They were a majority in the Chesapeake Tidewater region, where slave ownership was widely distributed among white tobacco planters, including small and middling growers as well as the few great plantation owners. Farther south, in the tidal swamps of the South Carolina and Georgia lowcountry, where draining and clearing the land required huge inputs of labor, blacks outnumbered whites five to one. In the lowcountry, large planters, the richest men in the country, worked hundreds of slaves in the production of rice, indigo, and sea-island cotton. Because yellow fever and malaria plagued the lowcountry, whites avoided the area, and the death rate among slaves was very high.

Slaves were less numerous in the Piedmont, or foothills, region of the South that lies between the coastal plain and the Appalachian highlands. Although sons of Tidewater planters had expanded tobacco production with slave labor into the Piedmont of Virginia and South Carolina, this was predominantly an area of nonslaveholding farmers. They relied on family labor to raise livestock, corn, and wheat. In the southern mountains, sloping to the southwest from the Blue Ridge in Virginia, the general absence of marketable crops diminished the demand for slave labor.

The free black population in the South had grown rapidly during the 1780s. Thousands of slaves fled behind British lines to win their freedom, and patriots freed others as a reward for enlisting in their forces. The Revolutionary values of liberty and equality also led many slave owners to question the morality of slavery. Legislatures in the Upper South passed laws making it financially easier than before for masters to manumit (free) their slaves. In Virginia alone, 10,000 slaves were manumitted in the 1780s. Slavery remained the foundation of the southern economy, however, and whites feared competition from freed blacks. As a result, no southern state embarked on a general program of emancipation, and slavery in the region survived the turbulence of the Revolutionary era.

Economic conditions in the South, where the raw poverty of the backcountry offset the great wealth of the lowcountry, stamped the region's politics and culture. Tidewater planters were predominantly Anglican and of English descent. Piedmont farmers were more likely to be Scots-Irish Presbyterians and Baptists. More evangelical in their religion, and with simpler habits and tastes, the backcountry Baptists denounced the lowcountry planters for their luxury and arrogance. The planters retaliated by trying unsuccessfully to suppress the backcountry evangelicals.

The planters were indeed proud, domineering, and given to ostentatious displays of wealth. An English traveler observed that Virginia planters "are haughty and jealous of their liberties, impatient of restraint, and can scarcely bear the thought of being controlled by any superior power." Planters understood liberty to mean the power of white males, unchecked by any outside authority, to rule over others. The only acknowledged check on this power was the planter's sense of duty, his obligation to adhere to an idealized code of conduct befitting a gentleman and a man of honor.

Backcountry farmers also jealously guarded their liberties. "They are," noted a late eighteenth-century traveler, "extremely tenacious of the rights and liberties of republicanism. They consider themselves on an equal footing with the best educated people of the country, and upon the principles of equality they intrude themselves into every company." Backcountry farmers shared with the planters a disdain for government and restraints on the individual. But they opposed the planters' belief in a social hierarchy based on wealth and birth that left both poor whites and black slaves in a subordinate position.

Many German Lutherans settled in southeastern Pennsylvania. Hung above the gallery in this interior view of a Lutheran church in York are paintings of the 12 apostles and of figures drawn from the Old Testament.

Collection of the New York Historical Society, Negative number 28824c.

The Growing West

Between the Appalachian Mountains and the Mississippi River stretched the most rapidly growing region of the new nation, the West. Land-hungry settlers poured across the mountains once the British recognized the American claim to the region in the Treaty of Paris. During the 1780s, the white population of the West exploded from less than 10,000 to 200,000. The region's Native American population was about 150,000.

Indians strongly resisted white claims on their lands. A confederation of tribes in the Ohio Valley, led by the Miamis and supplied with firearms by the British in exchange for furs, kept whites out of the Old Northwest territory, the area north of the Ohio River. South of the Ohio, white settlements were largely limited to Kentucky and Tennessee. In what is today Alabama and Mississippi, the Creeks and their allies blocked American expansion.

Most white migrants in Kentucky and Tennessee were the young rural poor from the seaboard slave states. The West offered them the opportunity to claim their own farms and gain economic independence, free from the dominance of planters and the economic competition of slave labor. But planters also saw the West as a land of opportunity. The planters of Tidewater Virginia were especially likely to speculate in vast tracts of western land. And many planters' sons migrated to the West with a share of the family's slaves to become planters in their own right. This process laid the foundation for the extension of slavery into new regions. As early as 1790, slaves made up more than 10 percent of the population of Tennessee and Kentucky.

Life in the western settlements was harsh and often cruel. Mortality was high, especially among infants. Travelers from the East described settlers living in crudely built log cabins with squalid, filthy interiors infested with fleas and lice. Easterners also found an appallingly casual acceptance of violence. Men commonly settled disputes in knife-slashing, eye-gouging brawls.

Isolation and uncertainty haunted frontier life. The Appalachians posed a formidable barrier to social and economic intercourse with the East. Few settlers had the labor resources, which chiefly meant slaves, to produce an agricultural surplus for shipment to market down the Ohio and Mississippi rivers. Most farmers lived at a semisubsistence level. Many of them, mostly Scots-Irish, did not own the land they cultivated. These squatters, as they were called, occupied the land hoping someday to obtain clear title to it.

In Kentucky, squatters, aligned with a small class of middling landowners, spearheaded the movement for political separation from Virginia that gained statehood for the territory in 1792. (In similar fashion, white settlers in Vermont established their independence from New York and New Hampshire and gained statehood in 1791.) The settlers wanted to break the control that Tidewater planters had gained over most of the land and lucrative government offices in Kentucky. In their minds, planters, officeholders, land speculators, and gentlemen of leisure were all part of an aristocracy tied to the distant government in Richmond and intent on robbing them of their liberty. As one proponent of statehood proudly announced, "I never was a frend to larned men for I see it is those sort of fokes who always no how to butter thare own bred and care not for others."

Despite the movement in Kentucky for statehood, the ultimate political allegiance of the West was uncertain. Westerners wanted the freedom to control their own affairs and outlets for their crops. Apparently, they were willing to strike a deal with any outside power offering to meet these needs. Aware of the threat to the region posed by the British and Spanish, Washington had warned in 1784 that the political loyalties of the West wavered "on a pivot." The future of the region loomed as a major test for his administration.

Forging A New Government

The Congress that assembled in New York (the temporary capital) from 1789 to 1791 faced a challenge scarcely less daunting than that of the Constitutional Convention of 1787. It had to give form and substance to the framework of the new national government outlined in the Constitution. Executive departments had to be established, a federal judiciary organized, sources of revenue found, terms of international trade and foreign policy worked out, and the commitment to add a bill of rights to the Constitution honored.

Staunch supporters of the new government had easily carried the first national elections in 1788 and enjoyed large majorities in both houses of Congress. These men brought superb administrative talents to the task of governing. Many, however, were clumsy politicians and unsympathetic to the egalitarian sensibilities of the electorate. By 1792, they faced growing political opposition.

"Mr. President" and the Bill of Rights

The first problem for Washington and Congress was to decide just how the chief executive of the new republic should be addressed. Vice President John Adams of Massachusetts and his like-minded colleagues in the Senate wanted a title that imparted proper respect both for the office and for national political authority. They preferred "His Highness." In a debate that tied up Congress for a month, the more democratically inclined members of the House argued that such a title smacked of a longing for monarchical rule. Adams and the others grudgingly agreed to accept "Mr. President."

Whatever his title, Washington was intent on surrounding the presidency with an aura of respectability. He set down strict rules for his interactions with the public. He met with visitors twice a week for an hour and bowed with republican deference to the people but refused to shake hands. He traveled outside New York in a luxurious coach pulled by six horses, and at all times he carried himself with stern reserve. After a dinner with the president, one senator remarked that "as usual the company was as grave as at a funeral."

Meanwhile, Congress got down to business. James Madison, now a representative from Virginia, early emerged as the most forceful leader in the House. He pushed for speedy action on the bill of rights, which the Federalists had promised to add to the Constitution during the ratification debate. To allay the fears of Antifederalists that the Constitution granted too much power to the national government, the Federalists had promised to consider amendments that protected both individual rights and liberties and the rights of states. But Madison astutely kept the focus of the amendments on personal liberties. He submitted nineteen amendments, and Congress soon settled on twelve. Ten of these, known collectively as the **Bill of Rights**, were ratified by the states and became part of the Constitution as of December 15, 1791.

The Bill of Rights is one of the most enduring legacies of the first Congress. Most of the first eight amendments are concerned with individual rights. They guarantee religious freedom, freedom of expression, and the safeguarding of individuals and their property against arbitrary legal proceedings. Only three amendments speak of state interests. Citing the necessity of a "well regulated Militia" for "the security of a free State," the Second Amendment guarantees "the right of the people to keep and bear Arms." This assured the states that they could rely on their militias for protection against federal tyranny. The Ninth and Tenth Amendments stipulate that the powers not granted to the national government in the Constitution are retained by the people and the states.

The Bill of Rights broadened the government's base of popular support. Once Congress submitted the amendments to the states for ratification, North Carolina (1789) and Rhode Island (1790) overcame their lingering objections and joined the Union. The Bill of Rights also assured Americans that the central government would not try to impose a uniform national culture.

Departments and Courts

In the summer of 1789, Congress authorized the first executive departments: the State Department for foreign affairs, the Treasury for finances, and the War Department for the nation's defense. These departments already existed under the Articles of Confederation, and the only debate about them concerned the extent of presidential control over the officials who would head them. The Constitution gave the president the right to nominate public officials but required the consent of the Senate to confirm their appointments. The Constitution was silent, however, on whether the president could dismiss an official without the Senate's consent. Congress decided that the president could do so, setting an important precedent that bolstered presidential power. Department heads would now be closely bound to the president. As a group, they would evolve into the cabinet, the president's chief advisory body.

Greater controversy attended the creation of the federal judiciary. The Constitution called for "one Supreme Court" but left it up to Congress to authorize lower federal courts. The framers were deliberately vague about the federal judiciary, because Antifederalists and proponents of states' rights did not want national courts enforcing a uniform judicial system. National courts, they argued, would be far removed from the people and would act as engines of oppression.

The **Judiciary Act of 1789** represented an artful compromise that balanced the concerns of the Antifederalists and states' rights advocates with the concerns of nationalists who strongly opposed leaving matters of national law up to state courts. It created a hierarchical national judiciary based on thirteen federal district courts, one for each state. Appeals from these courts were to be heard in one of three circuit courts, and the Supreme Court was to have the final say in contested cases. In a major concession to the Antifederalists, however, the act limited jurisdiction in federal courts to legal issues stemming from the Constitution and the laws and treaties of the national government. The distinctive legal systems and customs of the states remained intact. State courts would continue to hear and rule on the vast majority of civil and criminal cases.

Revenue and Trade

The government's most pressing need was for revenue. Aware that Congress under the Articles of Confederation had been crippled by its inability to secure a reliable source of income, Madison acted to put the finances of the new federal government on a firm footing. Nearly everyone agreed that the government's chief source of income should be a tariff on imported goods and tonnage duties (fees based on cargo capacity) on ships entering American ports. The United States imported most of its manufactured goods, as well as many raw materials, and foreign-owned ships accounted for nearly half of entering tonnage.

The **Tariff Act of 1789** was designed primarily to raise revenue, not to protect American manufacturers by keeping out foreign goods with high duties. It levied a duty of 5 percent on most imported goods but imposed tariffs as high as 50 percent on a limited number of items, such as steel, salt, cloth, and tobacco. The debate on the Tariff Act provoked some sectional sparring. Manufacturers, who were concentrated in the North, wanted high tariffs for protection against foreign competition. In contrast, farmers and southern planters wanted low tariffs to keep down the cost of the manufactured goods they purchased.

Madison originally hoped to use tonnage duties not only to raise revenue but also to strike at foreign nations that had not signed a commercial treaty with the United States. He had in mind specifically Great Britain. He proposed a duty of 60 cents per ton on British ships entering American ports, twice the proposed duty on French ships. His aim was to dislodge the British from their dominant position in American markets and to open up overseas trade for American and French shippers.

An unlikely coalition of sectional interests defeated Madison's duties. Southerners voted against them because they feared their result would be to give New England merchants a monopoly on the carrying trade and raise the cost of shipping tobacco to Europe. But northern merchants, presumably the beneficiaries of the duties, also opposed them. They were leery of disrupting their profitable trade with Britain, especially with the economic slump of the 1780s abating. The Tonnage Act of 1789, as finally passed, treated all foreign ships equally.

Hamilton and the Public Credit

The Treasury was the largest and most important new department. To its head, Alexander Hamilton of New York, fell the task of bringing order to the nation's ramshackle finances. The basic problem was the huge debt left over from the Revolution. With interest going unpaid, the debt was growing, and by

Waterborne commerce was the key in the early emergence of New York City as a trading center. Shown here is the Manhattan end of the Brooklyn Ferry in 1790.

1789, it had reached $52 million. Most of this—about $40 million—was held by Americans in the form of securities and certificates issued during the Revolution. Foreigners, mostly French and Dutch, held another $12 million. In addition, state governments had debts totaling close to $25 million. Until the government set up and honored a regular schedule for paying interest, the nation's public credit would be worthless. Unable to borrow, the government would collapse.

More than any other individual, Hamilton imparted energy and purpose to the Washington administration. He was ambitious, egotistical, and overbearing. When he spoke of the people, he usually did so with a sneer. But he also had a brilliant financial mind and a sweeping vision of national greatness. He was convinced that the economic self-interests of the wealthy and well-born offered the only sound foundation for the success of the new government.

Born illegitimate in the West Indies in 1755 and orphaned at the age of 13, Hamilton craved power and social connections. Friends impressed with his potential sent him to New York City as a teenager for an education at Kings College (now Columbia University). An eager patriot, he served as Washington's personal aide during the Revolution. Washington's backing enabled him to marry into a wealthy New York family. He now had entrée into the social and economic elite, and he parlayed it into a flourishing legal practice and a rising political career. With no ancestral loyalties to any individual state, he brought an unabashed nationalism to Washington's cabinet. And with a conviction, born of his own rise, that wealth and power were synonymous, he made no apologies for trying to link the interests of the government with those of the wealthy.

At the request of Congress, Hamilton prepared a series of reports on the nation's finances and economic condition. In the first, issued in January 1790, Hamilton proposed a bold plan to address the Revolutionary War debt. The federal government, he maintained, should fund the national debt at full face value. To do this, he proposed exchanging the old debt, including accrued interest, for new government bonds bearing interest at about 4 percent. In addition, Hamilton maintained that the federal government should assume the remaining war debt of the state governments. The intent of this plan was to give the nation's creditors an economic stake in the stability of the new nation and to subordinate state financial interests to those of the central government.

In his second report, issued in December 1790, Hamilton called for an excise tax (a tax on the production, sale, or consumption of a commodity) on distilled whiskey produced within the United States. The purpose of the tax was to raise additional revenue for interest payments on the national debt and establish the government's authority to levy internal taxes on its citizens.

The third report recommended the chartering of a national bank, the Bank of the United States. Hamilton patterned his proposed bank after the Bank of England and intended it to meet a variety of needs. Jointly owned by the federal government and private investors, it would serve as the fiscal (financial) and depository agent of the government and make loans to businesses. Through a provision that permitted up to three-fourths of the value of bank stock to be purchased with government bonds, the bank would create a market for public securities and hence raise their value. Most important, the bank would provide the nation with a stable currency. At the time, the country had only three private banks, and specie—hard currency in the form of gold and silver coins—was scarce. The government needed a reliable source of money, as did the economy as a whole. Hamilton proposed to allow the Bank of the United States to issue money in the form of paper banknotes that would be backed by a small reserve of specie and the security of government bonds. His goal was both to strengthen the economy and to consolidate the power of the national government.

Hamilton's final report, issued in December 1791, recommended government actions to promote industry. Looking, as always, to the British model of economic development, he argued that the United States would never become a great power until it diversified its largely agrarian economy. As long as the nation imported most of its manufactured goods, Hamilton warned, it would be no more than a second-rate power. Moreover, American manufacturers, saddled with both high labor costs and primitive technology, would remain at a severe competitive disadvantage unless they received government assistance. Hamilton advocated aid in the form of protective tariffs (high tariffs meant to make imported goods more expensive than domestic goods) for such industries as iron, steel, and shoemaking—which had already begun to establish themselves—and direct subsidies to assist with start-up costs for other industries. Hamilton believed that such "patronage," as he called it, would ultimately foster interregional economic dependence. An industrializing Northeast, for example, would depend on the South and West for foodstuffs for its workers and raw materials for its factories. In turn, farmers and planters would buy manufactured goods from the Northeast. Thus, in Hamilton's vision, manufacturing, like a national currency, would be a great national unifier.

Reaction and Opposition

The breadth and boldness of Hamilton's program invited opposition. About half the members of Congress owned some of the nation's debt, and nearly all of them agreed with Hamilton that it should be paid off. Some opponents, however, were concerned that Hamilton's plan was unfair. Hard times had forced most of the original holders of the debt—by and large, ordinary citizens—to sell their certificates to speculators at a fraction of their face value. Should the government, asked Madison, reward speculators with a windfall profit when the debt was paid back in full and forget about the true patriots who had sustained the Revolution in its darkest hours?

Others objected, on republican grounds, that Hamilton had no intention of actually eliminating the government's debt. He envisioned instead a permanent debt, with the government making regular interest payments as they came due. The debt, in the form of government securities, would serve as a vital prop for the support of moneyed groups. One congressman saw this as a violation of "that great principle which alone was the cause of the war with Great Britain …that taxation and representation should go hand in hand." Future generations, he argued, would be unfairly taxed for a debt incurred by the present generation.

Opposition to Hamilton's proposal to have the federal government assume state debts reflected sectional differences. With the exception of South Carolina, the southern states had already paid back a good share of their war debts. Thus Hamilton's plan stood to benefit the northern states disproportionately. Because Hamilton had linked the funding of the national debt with the assumption of state debts, southern opposition threatened funding as well. Tensions mounted as the deadlock continued into the summer of 1790. Frustrated over southern intransigence, New Englanders muttered about seceding. Southerners responded in kind. A Virginia senator charged that disunion would be a small price to pay to escape "the rule of a fixed insolent northern majority."

Tempers cooled when a compromise was reached in July. Southerners agreed to accept funding in its original form because, as Hamilton correctly noted, it would be impractical, if not impossible, to distinguish between the original and current holders of the national debt. Assumption passed after Hamilton cut a deal with Virginians James Madison and Thomas Jefferson. In exchange for southern support of assumption, Hamilton agreed to line up northern votes for locating the nation's permanent capital on the banks of the Potomac River, where it would be surrounded by the slave states of Maryland and Virginia. The package was sweetened by extra grants of federal money to states with small debts.

Hamilton's alliance with Madison and Jefferson proved short-lived, dissolving when Madison led the congressional opposition to Hamilton's proposed bank. Madison and most other southerners viewed the bank as evidence of a willingness to sacrifice the interests of the agrarian South in favor of the financial and industrial interests of the North. They feared that the bank, with its power to dispense economic favors, would re-create in the United States the kind of government corruption and privilege they associated with Great Britain. They argued that the Constitution did not explicitly authorize Congress to charter a bank or any other corporation.

The bank bill passed Congress on a vote that divided along sectional lines. Madison's objections, however, left Washington concerned that the bank might not be constitutional. He sought the cabinet's opinion, provoking the first great debate over how the Constitution should be interpreted. Thomas Jefferson, the secretary of state, sided with Madison and for the first time openly clashed with Hamilton. Taking a strict-constructionist position, he argued that all powers the Constitution had not expressly delegated to the national government were reserved to the states under the Tenth Amendment. Hamilton, in a brilliant rejoinder, argued that Article 1, Section 8, of the Constitution, which declares that Congress has the right "to make all laws which shall be necessary and proper" to exercise its powers and those of the federal government, gives Congress implicit authority beyond its explicitly enumerated powers. With this broad-constructionist position, he won Washington to his side.

With Washington's signature on the bill, Hamilton's bank was chartered for twenty years. Congress also passed a hefty 25 percent excise tax on distilled liquor. Little, however, of Hamilton's plan to promote manufacturing survived the scrutiny of the agrarian opposition. Tariff duties were raised moderately in 1792, but no funds were forthcoming to accelerate industrial development.

The Emergence of Parties

By the end of Washington's first term, Americans were dividing into two camps. On one side stood those who still called themselves **Federalists**. These were the supporters of Hamilton's program—speculators, creditors, merchants, manufacturers, and commercial farmers. They were the Americans most fully integrated into the market economy and in control of it. Concentrated in the North, they included New England Congregationalists and mid-Atlantic Episcopalians (former Anglicans), members of the more socially prestigious churches. In both economic and cultural terms, the Federalists were drawn from the more privileged segments of society. Jefferson and Madison shrewdly gave the name **Republican** to the party that formed in opposition to the Federalists, thus identifying it with individual liberties and the heritage of the Revolution. The Republicans accused Hamilton and the Federalists of attempting to impose a British system of economic privilege and social exploitation. The initial core of the party consisted of southern planters and backcountry Scots-Irish farmers, Americans outside the market economy or skeptical of its benefits. They feared that the commercial groups favored by Hamilton would corrupt politics in their pursuit of power and foster commerce and manufacturing at the expense of agriculture. The Republicans were committed to an agrarian America in which power remained in the hands of farmers and planters.

In 1792, parties were still in a formative stage. The political divisions that had appeared first in Congress and then spread to Washington's cabinet did not yet extend very deeply into the electorate. Washington remained aloof from the political infighting and was still seen as a great unifier. Unopposed, he was reelected in 1792. However, a series of crises in his second term deepened and broadened the incipient party divisions. By 1796, rival parties were contesting the presidency and vying for the support of an increasingly politically organized electorate.

The French Revolution

The French Revolution began in 1789, and in its early phase, most Americans applauded it. France had been an ally of the United States during the Revolutionary War and now seemed to be following the example of its American friends in shaking off monarchical rule. By 1792, however, as threats against it mounted, the French Revolution turned violent and radical. Its supporters confiscated the property of aristocrats and the church, slaughtered suspected enemies, and executed the king, Louis XVI. In early 1793, republican France was at war against Britain and the European powers.

The excesses of the French Revolution and the European war that erupted in its wake touched off a bitter debate in America. Federalists drew back in horror from France's new regime. They insisted that the terror unleashed by the French was far removed from the reasoned republicanism of the American Revolution. As the Federalist *Gazette of the United States* argued: "The American Revolution, it ought to be repeated, was not accomplished as the French has been, by massacres, assassinations, or proscriptions." For the Republicans, however, the French remained the standard-bearers of the cause of liberty for common people everywhere. Jefferson admitted that the French Revolution was tarnished by the loss of innocent lives, "but rather than it should have failed, I would have seen half the earth desolated." He was convinced that "the liberty of the whole earth was depending on the issue in the contest."

Franco-American relations.   When the new French ambassador, Edmond Genêt, arrived in the United States in April 1793—just as the debate in America over the French Revolution was heating up—Franco-American relations reached a turning point. The two countries were still bound to one another by the Franco-American Alliance of 1778. The alliance required the United States to assist France in the defense of its West Indian colonies and to open U.S. ports to French privateers if France were attacked. Genêt, it soon became clear, hoped to embroil the United States in the French war against the British. He commissioned U.S. privateers to attack British shipping and tried to enlist an army of frontiersmen to attack Spanish possessions in Louisiana and Florida.

Genêt's actions, as well as the enthusiastic reception that greeted him as he traveled from Charleston to Philadelphia (chosen in 1790 as the temporary national capital), forced Washington to call a special cabinet meeting. The president feared that Genêt would stampede Americans into the European war, with disastrous results for the nation's finances. The bulk of U.S. foreign trade was with the British, and tariff duties on British imports were by far the main source of revenue to pay for Hamilton's assumption and funding programs. Hamilton urged Washington to declare U.S. neutrality in the European war, maintaining that the president could commit the nation to neutrality on his own authority when Congress, as was then the case, was not in session. Disputing Washington's power to act on his own, Jefferson maintained that the warmaking powers of Congress reserved for it alone the right to issue a declaration of neutrality. Washington accepted Hamilton's argument on his authority to declare neutrality and issued a proclamation on April 22, 1793, stating that the United States would be "friendly and impartial toward the belligerent powers."

Despite this proclamation, Genêt continued to meddle. Washington was on the verge of forcing his recall to France when news arrived that a new and more radical French government had decided to bring Genêt back as a political pris-

oner. The president graciously permitted Genêt to remain in the United States as a private citizen. Had he returned to France, he would have faced almost certain execution.

The growth of Democratic–Republican societies. Genêt quickly faded from public view, but U.S. politics became more open and aggressive in the wake of his visit. Pro-French enthusiasm lived on in a host of grassroots political organizations known as the Democratic–Republican societies. Nearly forty of these societies formed in 1793 and 1794. As their name suggests, these societies reflected a belief that democracy and republicanism were one and the same. This was a new concept in U.S. politics. Democracy had traditionally been equated with anarchy and mob rule. The members of the new societies argued, to the contrary, that only democracy—meaning popular participation in politics and direct appeals by politicians to the people—could maintain the revolutionary spirit of 1776, because the people were the only true guardians of that spirit. As a letter writer to the *Newark Gazette* put it: "It must be the mechanics and farmers, or the poorer class of people (as they are generally called), that must support the freedom which they and their fathers purchased with their blood—the nobility will never do it—they will be always striving to get the reins of government into their own hands, and then they can ride the people at pleasure."

The Democratic-Republican societies attacked the Washington administration for failing to assist France, and they expressed the popular feeling that Hamilton's program favored the rich over the poor. For the first time, Washington himself was personally assailed in the press.

The core members of the societies were urban artisans whose egalitarian views shocked the Federalists, who expected deference, not criticism and political activism, from the people. In their view, the Democratic-Republicans were rabble-rousers trying to dictate policy to the nation's natural leaders. The Federalists harshly condemned the emergence of organized political dissent from below, but in so doing they only enhanced the popular appeal of the growing Republican opposition.

Securing the Frontier

Control of the West remained an elusive goal throughout Washington's first term. Indian resistance in the Northwest Territory initially prevented whites from pushing north of the Ohio River. The powerful Miami Confederacy, led by Little Turtle, routed two ill-trained American armies in 1790 and 1791. The 1791 encounter, which took place on the banks of the Wabash River in western Ohio, was the worst defeat an American army ever suffered in frontier fighting. More than 900 soldiers were killed or wounded, and the commander, General Arthur St. Clair, was lucky to survive. The southern frontier was quieter, but the Spanish continued to use the Creeks and Cherokees as a buffer against American penetration south of the Tennessee River.

By 1793, many western settlers felt abandoned by the national government. They believed that the government had broken a promise to protect them against Indians and

OVERVIEW

Federalist Party versus Republican Party

Federalists	Republicans
Favored strong central government	Wanted to limit role of national government
Supported Hamilton's economic program	Opposed Hamilton's economic program
Opposed French Revolution	Generally supported French Revolution
Supported Jay's Treaty and closer ties to Britain	Opposed Jay's Treaty and favored closer ties to France
In response to threat of war with France, proposed and passed Direct Tax of 1798, Alien and Sedition Acts, and legislation to enlarge army	Opposed Alien and Sedition Acts and enlarged army as threats to individual liberties
Drew strongest support from New England; lost support in mid-Atlantic region after 1798	Drew strongest support from South and West

foreigners. Much of the popularity of the Democratic-Republican societies in the West fed off these frustrations. Westerners saw the French, who were at war with Britain and Spain, as allies against the foreign threat on the frontier, and they forwarded resolutions to Congress embracing the French cause. These resolutions also demanded free and open navigation on the Mississippi River. This, in the minds of Westerners, was their natural right. Without it, they would be forever impoverished. "If the interest of Eastern America requires that we should be kept in poverty," argued the Mingo Creek society of western Pennsylvania, "it is unreasonable from such poverty to exact contributions. The first, if we cannot emerge from, we must learn to bear, but the latter, we never can be taught to submit to."

Submission to national authority, however, was precisely what the Federalists wanted from both the Indians and the western settlers. St. Clair's humiliating defeat in 1791 prompted a reorganization of the War Department. By the summer of 1794, Washington's administration felt prepared to move against the Indians. This time, it sent into the Ohio region not the usual ragtag crew of militia and unemployed city dwellers but a force built around veterans from the professional army. The commander, General Anthony Wayne, was a savvy, battle-hardened war hero.

Wayne's victory on August 4, 1794, at the Battle of Fallen Timbers, near present-day Toledo, broke the back of Indian military resistance in Ohio. In the resulting **Treaty of Greenville**, signed in August 1795, twelve tribes ceded most of the present state of Ohio to the U.S. government in return for an annual payment of $9,500. The Ohio country was now open to white settlement (see Map 8–1 and American Views, Little Turtle Defends the Miami Lands).

The Whiskey Rebellion

Within a few months of Wayne's victory at Fallen Timbers, another American army was on the move. Its target was the so-called whiskey rebels of western Pennsylvania, who were openly resisting Hamilton's excise tax on whiskey. This tax had always

been unpopular among western farmers. The high cost of transport across the mountains made it unprofitable for them to sell their grain in the East. But by distilling corn or rye into whiskey, they reduced it enough in bulk to lower transportation costs and earn a profit. Hamilton's excise tax wiped out this profit.

Hamilton was determined to enforce the tax and assert the supremacy of national laws. Although resistance to the tax was widespread, he singled out the Pennsylvania rebels. It was easier to send an army into the Pittsburgh area than into the Carolina mountains. Washington, moreover, was convinced that the Democratic-Republican societies of western Pennsylvania were behind the defiance of federal authority there. He welcomed the opportunity to chastise these organizations, which he identified with the dangerous doctrines of the French Revolution.

Washington called on the governors of the mid-Atlantic states to supply militia forces to crush the **Whiskey Rebellion**. The 13,000-man army that assembled at Harrisburg and marched into western Pennsylvania in October 1794 was larger than any Washington had commanded during the Revolution. But the rebellion, as Jefferson sardonically noted, "could never be found." The army met no resistance and expended considerable effort rounding up 20 prisoners. Two men were found guilty of treason, but Washington pardoned both. Still, at Hamilton's insistence, the Federalists had made their point: When its authority was openly challenged, the national government would use military force to compel obedience.

The Whiskey Rebellion starkly revealed the conflicting visions of local liberty and national order that divided Americans of the early republic. The non-English majority on the Pennsylvania frontier, Irish, Scots-Irish, German, and Welsh, justified resistance to the whiskey tax with the same republican ideology that had fueled the American Revolution. Mostly poor farmers, artisans, and laborers, they appealed to notions of liberty, equality, and freedom from oppressive taxation that were deeply rooted in backcountry settlements from Maine to Georgia. In putting down the Pennsylvania rebels, Washington and Hamilton acted on behalf of more English and cosmopolitan groups in the East who valued central power

Global Perspectives

Neutrality in an Age of Revolution

Whereas it appears that a state of war exists between Austria, Prussia, Sardinia, Great Britain, and the United Netherlands on the one part and France on the other, and the duty and interest of the United States require that they should with sincerity and good faith adopt and pursue a conduct friendly and impartial toward the belligerent powers:

I have therefore thought fit ... to exhort and warn the citizens of the United States carefully to avoid all acts and proceeding whatsoever which may in any manner tend to contravene such disposition.

In these words President Washington proclaimed the neutrality of the United States in the European war spawned by the French Revolution. He realized, as did most Americans, that the new and still weak nation had far more to lose than gain by embroiling itself in the European war. Still, before the French Rev-

olution turned to regicide and the Reign of Terror in 1793–1794, Americans basked in pride for having first raised the revolutionary banner of liberty and equality that their former ally was now spreading over Europe. But by the mid-1790s exultation had turned into disillusionment and fears of social upheaval. By the time that Napoleon assumed what amounted to dictatorial powers in 1799, most Americans had reverted to their earlier belief in the uniqueness of the American Revolution. As Madison observed when reflecting on the French experience, America remained as "the only Theatre in which true liberty can have a fair trial."

Despite believing that the French had discredited the cause of liberty, Americans clung to the hope that the contagion of liberty they had first unleashed in their Revolution would topple autocratic regimes across the world. And spread it did in a wide arc of revolutionary movements that stretched across the Western world. The French

colony of Saint-Domingue (Haiti) exploded in unrest in 1791 once the French Revolution had outlawed slavery. Touissant L'Ouverture, the slave grandson of an African king, led black armies in a ten-year war of liberation that resulted in the independence of Haiti in 1804. Napoleon's invasion of the Iberian Peninsula in 1809 created a power vacuum in Spain's American empire. A host of revolutions broke out to fill the vacuum, and Mexico, Argentina, Bolivia, Chile, Colombia, Ecuador, Peru, and Venezuela all gained their freedom from Spanish rule. None of these revolutions closely followed the American or French model. All, however, were united by a common political language of liberty, popular self-rule, and constitutionalism that the Americans and the French had bequeathed to global politics.

■ **In what ways did the American Revolution soon serve as a liberating example for revolutionary change elsewhere?**

as a check on any local resistance movement that might begin unraveling the still fragile republic.

Treaties with Britain and Spain

Much of the unrest in the West stemmed from the menacing presence of the British and Spanish on the nation's borders. Washington's government had the resources to suppress Indians and frontier dissidents but lacked sufficient armed might to push Spain and especially Britain out of the West.

The British, embroiled in what they saw as a life-or-death struggle against revolutionary France, clamped a naval blockade on France and its Caribbean colonies in the fall of 1793. They also supported a slave uprising on the French island of Saint-Domingue (present-day Haiti), enraging southern planters who feared that slave rebellions might spread to the United States. The French countered by opening their colonial

trade, which had been closed to outsiders during peacetime, to neutral shippers. American merchants stepped in and reaped profits by supplying France. The British retaliated by seizing American ships involved in the French trade. They further claimed the right to search American ships and impress, or forcibly remove, sailors they suspected of having deserted from the British navy. News of these provocations reached America in early 1794 and touched off a major war scare. Desperate to avert a war, Washington sent John Jay, the chief justice of the United States, to London to negotiate an accord.

Jay brought a weak hand to the negotiating table. Britain had enormous military resources, the United States only a small army and navy. What is more, tariffs on British trade were the main source of revenue for the United States government. But the British, too, benefited from their trade with the United States, and they wanted to keep the United States neutral.

MAP EXPLORATION To explore an interactive version of this map, go to
http://www.prenhall.com/goldfield5/map8.1

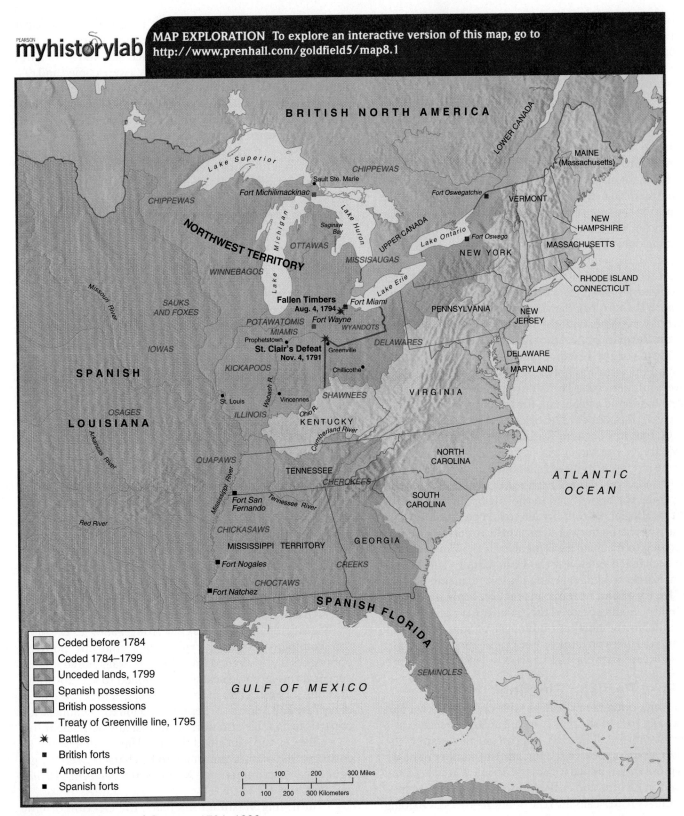

MAP 8–1 Indian Land Cessions, 1784–1800
The persistent pressure of white settlers and the military forces of the new national government forced Native Americans to cede huge tracts of their western lands.

From the American point of view, the resulting agreement, known as **Jay's Treaty**, was flawed but acceptable. Jay had to abandon the American insistence on the right of neutrals to ship goods to nations at war without interference (meaning in this case the right of the United States to continue trading with France without British harassment). He also had to grant Britain "most favored nation" status, giving up the American right to discriminate against British shipping and merchandise. And he had to reconfirm the American commitment to repay in full pre-Revolutionary debts owed to the British. In return for these major concessions, Britain pledged to compensate American merchants for the ships and cargoes it had seized in 1793 and 1794, to abandon the six forts it still held in the American Northwest, and to grant the United States limited trading rights in India and the British West Indies.

Signed in November 1794, Jay's Treaty caused an uproar in the United States when its terms became known in March 1795. Southerners saw in it another sellout of their interests. It required them to pay their prewar debts to British merchants but was silent about the slaves Britain had carried off during the Revolution. And the concessions Britain did make seemed to favor the North, especially New England merchants and shippers. Republicans, joined now by urban artisans, were infuriated that Jay had stripped them of their chief weapon, economic retaliation, for breaking free of British commercial dominance. The Senate ratified the treaty in June 1795, but only because Washington backed it.

Jay's Treaty, combined with a string of French victories in Europe in 1795, convinced Spain to adopt a more conciliatory attitude toward the United States. With France apparently gaining the upper hand in the war, Spain was anxious to shift its allegiance from Britain to France. But it saw the Jay treaty as the beginning of an Anglo-American alliance and decided to reach an agreement with the United States before it changed sides, lest the United States and Britain combine forces to challenge Spain's American possessions. In the **Treaty of San Lorenzo** in 1795 (also known as Pinckney's Treaty), Spain accepted the American position on the 31st parallel as the northern boundary of Spanish Florida and granted American farmers free transit through the port of New Orleans with the right of renewal after three years.

The First Partisan Election

Partisanship, open identification with one of the two parties, steadily rose in the 1790s, fueled in large measure by a new print culture. The first opposition newspaper, the *National Gazette,* appeared in 1791, and the number of newspapers more than doubled within the decade. Circulated and discussed in taverns and coffeehouses, newspapers helped draw ordinary Americans into the political process. Ongoing involvement in the raucous, celebratory political culture that Americans fashioned also politicized them. Through festivals on July 4 honoring the nation's independence, street parades and demonstrations favoring or opposing such events as the French Revolution or Jay's Treaty, and an endless stream of toasts, speeches, banquets, and broadsides, various groups

publicly proclaimed and acted out their version of what it meant to be an American. No single version held sway. National self-identity varied by class, race, sex, and region, but as newspaper reports of local activities were copied and disseminated across the country, Americans could feel that they were joined in a collective effort to define what the nation meant to them. As a national identity was being forged and contested, lines of partisanship were marked and deepened.

Women also participated in this public arena of political activism. Although denied formal political rights, they wrote and attended plays with explicit political messages, joined in patriotic rituals, and organized their own demonstrations. To show their support for the French Revolution, women in Menetomy, Massachusetts, wore liberty caps and cockades, the symbols of the French cause. Two widows in Charleston, South Carolina, one American, the other French, went further in July 1793, when they staged a clever form of street theater in front of a large crowd. As reported by a Charleston newspaper, "after having repudiated their husbands on account of their ill-treatment, [they] conceived the design of living together in the strictest union and friendship in order to give a pledge of their fidelity [and] requested that their striped gowns should be penned together, that their children should be looked upon as one family, while their mothers showed them an equal affection." Here was a double-edged message. Just as a union of the French and the Americans could dispense with the need for Britain, so, it appeared, two women could enjoy domestic bliss without the need for husbands. Shocked by such pro-French sympathies and declarations of women's independence, the Federalists moved quickly to find a safe outlet for women's political activism. They invited women to join Federalist-sponsored events that denounced the French Revolution as a threat to all civilized order. By the late 1790s, both parties were seeking to broaden their popular appeal by including women in their partisan rallies.

As partisanship spread, no symbol of traditional authority, Washington included, was safe from challenge. Washington complained bitterly to friends that his political opponents had maligned him "in such exaggerated and indecent terms as could scarcely be applied to a...notorious defaulter, or even a common pickpocket." He devoted most of his Farewell Address of September 1796 to a denunciation of partisanship. He also warned against any permanent foreign alliances and cautioned that the Union itself would be endangered if parties continued to be characterized "by geographical discriminations, *Northern* and *Southern, Atlantic* and *Western.*"

Confirming Washington's fears, the election of 1796 was the first openly partisan election in American history. John Adams was the Federalist candidate, and Thomas Jefferson, the Republican candidate. Each was selected by a party caucus, a meeting of party leaders. As a result of disunity in the Federalist ranks, the election produced the anomaly of a Federalist president (Adams) and a

American Views

Little Turtle Defends the Miami Lands

The climax of what had become a thirty-year war between Native Americans and white settlers for control of the Ohio country came in 1794 with the American victory at the Battle of Fallen Timbers. The most innovative and successful of the Indian leaders who had emerged in the conflict was the Miami war chief Mishikinakwa, or Little Turtle, as he was known by whites. The following is from one of Little Turtle's speeches during the peace negotiations with the victorious Americans at Greenville, Ohio, in July, 1795.

- How would you characterize Little Turtle's stance during the negotiations and his attitude toward Wayne?
- On what basis did Little Turtle justify the land claims of the Miamis in the Ohio country? How would this differ from the way in which whites staked their claim to the land?
- How did Little Turtle explain his leadership of the Miamis, and how did this differ from white notions of leadership?
- What might account for the divisions among the Indians that were cited by Little Turtle?

General Wayne: I hope you will pay attention to what I now say to you. I wish to inform you where your younger brothers, the Miamies, live, and, also, the Pottawatamies of St. Joseph's, together with the Wabash Indians. You have pointed out to us the boundary line between the Indians and the United States, but I now take the liberty to inform you, that the line cuts off from the Indians a large portion of country, which has been enjoyed by my forefathers time immemorial, without molestation or dispute. The print of my ancestors' houses are every where to be seen in this portion....It is well known by all my brothers present, that my forefathers kindled the first fire at Detroit; from thence, he extended his lines to the head waters of Scioto; from thence, down the Ohio, to the mouth of the Wabash, and from thence to Chicago, on Lake Michigan....I have now informed you of the boundaries of the Miami nation, where the Great Spirit placed my forefathers a long time ago, and charged him not to sell or part with his lands, but to preserve them

for his posterity. This charge has been handed down to me....I was much surprised to find that my other brothers differed so much from me on this subject: for their conduct would lead one to suppose, that the Great Spirit, and their forefathers, had not given them the same charge that was give[n] to me, but, on the contrary, had directed them to sell their lands to any white man who wore a hat, as soon as he should ask it of them. Now, elder brother, your younger brothers, the Miamies, have pointed out to you their country, and also to our brothers present. When I hear your remarks and proposals on this subject [of Miami lands], I will be ready to give you an answer; I came with an expectation of hearing you say good things, but I have not heard what I have expected.

Source: *Documents, Legislative and Executive, of the Congress of the United States, From the First Session of the First to the Third Session of the Thirteenth Congress, Inclusive: commencing March 3, 1789, and ending March 3, 1815*, vol. IV (Washington, DC: Gales and Seaton, 1832), pp. 570–571.

Republican vice president (Jefferson). Written with no thought of organized partisan competition for the presidency, the Constitution simply stated that the presidential candidate with the second-highest number of electoral votes would become vice president. In this case, that candidate was Jefferson.

Despite the election's confused outcome, the sectional pattern in the voting was unmistakable. Only the solid support of regional elites in New England and the mid-Atlantic states enabled the Federalists to retain the presidency. Adams received all the northern electoral votes, with the exception of Pennsylvania's. Jefferson was the overwhelming favorite in the South.

The Last Federalist Administration

The Adams administration got off to a rocky start from which it never recovered. The vice president was the leader of the opposition party; key members of the cabinet, which Adams had inherited from Washington, owed their primary loyalty to Hamilton; and the French, who saw Adams as a dupe of the British, instigated a major crisis that left the threat of war hanging over the entire Adams presidency. Adams had been a lawyer before the Revolution; he was a veteran of both Continental Congresses, had been a diplomat in Europe for a decade, and had served as Washington's vice president for eight years. But despite this extraordinarily rich background in public affairs, he was politically naive. Scrupulously honest but quick to take offense, he lacked the politician's touch for inspiring personal loyalty and crafting compromises based on a realistic recognition of mutual self-interest. But putting the interests of the country before those of his party, he almost single-handedly prevented a nearly certain war with France and a possible civil war at home. The price he paid was a badly split Federalist Party that refused to unite behind him when he sought reelection in 1800.

The French Crisis and the XYZ Affair

An aggressive coalition known as the Directory gained control of revolutionary France in 1795 and denounced the Jay treaty as evidence of an Anglo-American alliance against France. When Jefferson and the pro-French Republicans lost the election of 1796, the Directory turned openly hostile. In short order, the French annulled the commercial treaty of 1778 with the United States, ordered the seizure of American ships carrying goods to the British, and declared that any American sailors found on British ships, including those forcibly pressed into service, would be summarily executed. By the time Adams had been in office three months, the French had confiscated more than 300 American ships.

In the fall of 1797, Adams sent three commissioners to Paris in an effort to avoid war. The French treated the three with contempt. Having just conquered the Netherlands and detached Spain from its British alliance, France was in no mood to compromise. Through three intermediaries, identified by Adams only as X, Y, and Z when he informed Congress of the negotiations, the French foreign minister demanded a large bribe to initiate talks and an American loan of $12 million.

In April 1798, the Senate published a full account of the insulting behavior of the French in what came to be called the **XYZ Affair**. The public was indignant, and war fever swept the country. The Federalists, who had always warned against the French, enjoyed greater popularity than they ever had or ever would again. Congress acted to upgrade the navy, and responsibility for naval affairs, formerly divided between the Treasury and War departments, was consolidated in a new Department of the Navy. By the fall of 1798, American ships were waging an undeclared war against the French in Caribbean waters, a conflict that came to be known as the **Quasi-War**.

With the horrors of the French Revolution forming a backdrop, this cartoon depicts France as a five-headed monster demanding a bribe from the three Americans sent by Adams. The Federalists hoped that such anti-French sentiments would lead to an open war.

The Federalists in Congress, dismissing Republican objections, also voted to create a vastly expanded army. They tripled the size of the regular army to 10,000 men and authorized a special provisional army of 50,000. Congress put the provisional army under Washington's command, but he declined to come out of retirement except for a national emergency. In the meantime, he insisted that Hamilton be appointed second in command and given charge of the provisional army's field operations. To pay for both the expanded army and the naval rearmament, the Federalists pushed through the Direct Tax of 1798, a levy on the value of land, slaves, and dwellings.

Crisis at Home

The thought of Hamilton in charge of a huge army convinced many Republicans that their worst nightmares were about to materialize. One congressman shuddered that "the monarchy-loving Hamilton is now so fixed, as to be able, with one-step, to fill the place of our present commander in chief." Adams shared such fears. He was furious that Hamilton had been forced on him as commander of the provisional army. Years later, he wrote that "the British faction was determined to have a war with France, and Alexander Hamilton at the head of the army and then Pres. of U.S. Peace with France was therefore treason against their fundamental maxims and reasons of State." As Adams came to realize, Hamilton's supporters, known as the High Federalists, saw the war scare with France as an opportunity to stamp out dissent, cement an alliance with the British, and strengthen and consolidate the powers of the national government.

The Federalists passed four laws in the summer of 1798, known collectively as the **Alien and Sedition Acts**, that confirmed the Republicans' fears. Three of these acts were aimed at immigrants, especially French and Irish refugees who voted for the Republicans. The president was empowered to deport foreigners who came from countries at war with the United States and to expel any alien resident he suspected

FROM THEN TO NOW

Advice for an Empire

Although devoted primarily to domestic concerns, Washington's Farewell Address became a seminal document in the formulation of U. S. foreign policy. In his vision for American greatness he called not for a policy of isolation, for the United States has never been isolated from the rest of the world, especially in economic matters. Instead, he advised Americans "to steer clear of permanent alliances with any portion of the foreign world so far…as we now at liberty to do it." Here was hardheaded advice grounded in the reality of America's still shaky independence and its threatened security in a world of hostile foreign powers. Rather than risk becoming the pawn of such powers or being dragged into a war in exchange for a temporary advantage, he counseled that the wisest course for the nation was to maintain its freedom of action, consolidate its strength, expand its commercial ties, and bide its time until American power could set its own terms.

U.S. soldiers were needed for the pacification of Iraqi cities.

The American empire that Washington saw in the future gradually took shape through territorial expansion in the nineteenth century and the emergence of the United States as first a world power in the twentieth century and then as the world power after the collapse of the Soviet Union in the late 1980s. U. S. entry into World War I marked the first sharp departure from the tradition spawned by the Farewell Address of avoiding political and military involvement with the affairs of Europe and the challenges of the Cold War replaced a policy of non-entangling alliances with unilateral military commitments across the globe. However, as Washington well understood, unilateral commitments undertaken without a judicious assessment of the nation's best interests and the limits of its power have a way of feeding upon themselves and becoming self-defeating.

■ How would Washington have responded to those who wanted the United States to enter into a formal alliance with Britain, its major trading partner, against revolutionary France?

General Anthony Wayne wins a decisive victory over the Miami Confederation at the battle of Fallen Timbers in 1794.

PEARSON myhistorylab
From Then to Now Online

8-1 George Washington, *Farewell Address*, Sept. 1796. Washington's advice on foreign policy.

8-2 Woodrow Wilson, *Address to the League to Enforce Peace*, May 1916. Wilson announces willingness to commit the United States to an international body to enforce peace.

8-3 *NATO Treaty*, April 1949. United States commits to a political and military alliance with Europe.

of subversive activities. The Naturalization Act extended the residency requirement for U.S. citizenship (and hence the right to vote) from five to fourteen years. Worst of all in the minds of Republicans was the Sedition Act, a measure that made it a federal crime to engage in any conspiracy against the government or to utter or print anything "false, scandalous and malicious" against the government. Federalist judges were blatantly partisan in their enforcement of the Sedition Act. Twenty-five individuals, mostly Republican editors, were indicted under the act, and ten were convicted.

Outraged at this threat to the freedom of speech, Jefferson and Madison turned to the safely Republican legislatures of Kentucky and Virginia for a forum from which to attack the constitutionality of the Alien and Sedition Acts. Taking care to keep their authorship secret, they each drafted a set of resolutions—Jefferson for the Kentucky legislature, and Madison for the Virginia legislature—that challenged the entire centralizing program of the Federalists. In doing so, they produced the first significant articulation of the southern stand on **states' rights**.

The resolutions—adopted in the fall of 1798—proposed a compact theory of the Constitution. They asserted that the states had delegated specific powers to the national government for their common benefit. It followed that the states reserved the right to decide whether the national government had unconstitutionally assumed a power not granted to it. If a state decided that the national government had exceeded its powers, it could "interpose" its authority to shield its citizens from a tyrannical law. In a second set of resolutions, the Kentucky legislature introduced the doctrine of **nullification**, the right of a state to render null and void a national law it deemed unconstitutional.

Jefferson and Madison hoped that these resolutions would rally voters to the Republican Party as the defender of threatened U.S. liberties. Yet not a single additional state seconded them. In the end, what aroused popular rage against the Federalists was not legislation directed against aliens and subversives but the high cost of Federalist taxes.

The Direct Tax of 1798 fell on all owners of land, dwellings, or slaves and provoked widespread resentment. Enforcing it required an army of bureaucrats—more than 500 for the state of Pennsylvania alone. In February 1799, in the heavily German southeastern counties of Pennsylvania, a group of men led by an auctioneer named John Fries released tax evaders from prison in Bethlehem. President Adams responded to Fries's Rebellion with a show of force, but the fiercest resistance the soldiers he sent to Pennsylvania encountered was from irate farm wives, who doused them with hot water and the contents of chamber pots. Fries and two other men were arrested, convicted of treason, and sentenced to be executed. (Adams later pardoned them.) But the Federalists had now lost much of their support in Pennsylvania.

The End of the Federalists

The events in Pennsylvania reflected the air of menace that gripped the country as the campaign of 1800 approached. The army was chasing private citizens whose only crime was resisting hateful taxes—in the eyes of many, a continuation of an honorable Revolutionary ideal. Federal soldiers also roughed up Republican voters at polling places. No wonder Adams later wrote that "the army was as unpopular as if it had been a ferocious wild beast let loose upon the nation to devour it." Southern Republicans talked in private of the possible need to resist Federalist tyranny by force and, failing in that, to secede from the Union. Hamilton and the High Federalists saw in the Kentucky and Virginia resolutions "a regular conspiracy to overturn the government." Reports that Virginia intended to strengthen its militia heightened their anxieties, and they proposed to meet force with force. Speaking of Virginia, Hamilton said that "the government must not merely defend itself, it must attack and arraign its enemies."

No one did more to defuse the charged atmosphere than President Adams. The Federalists depended for their popular support on the expectation of a war with France, which as late as 1798 had swept them to victory in the congressional elections. Still, Adams refrained from asking for a declaration of war. The United States had been successful in the Quasi-War against France. By early 1799, French ships had been forced out of the Caribbean and American coastal waters. And in Europe, the tide of war had turned against the French. As a result, Adams believed that the French would now be more open to conciliation. Of greater importance, Adams recognized that war with France could trigger a civil war at home. Hamilton and the High Federalists, he realized, would use war as an excuse to crush the Republican opposition in Virginia. Fearful of Hamilton's intentions and unwilling to run the risk of militarizing the government and saddling it with a huge war debt, Adams broke with his party and decided to reopen negotiations with France in February 1799.

The **Franco-American Accord of 1800** that resulted from Adams's initiative released the United States from its 1778 alliance with France. It also obligated the United States

This contemporary cartoon shows Republican Matthew Lyon, in the center with the fire tongs, fighting against Roger Griswold, a Connecticut Federalist. This brawl in Congress on February 15, 1798, revealed the depth of the feeling that now divided the Republicans and Federalists.

Congressional Pugilists, caricature 1798. Neg. #33995. Collection of The New-York Historical Society.

to surrender all claims against the French for damages done to U.S. shipping during the Quasi-War. Once peace with France seemed likely, the Hamiltonian Federalists lost their trump card in the election of 1800. The Republicans could no longer be branded as the traitorous friends of an enemy state. The enlarged army, with no foe to fight, became a political embarrassment, and the Federalists dismantled it. Although rumors of possible violence continued to circulate, the Republicans grew increasingly confident that they could peacefully gain control of the government.

The Federalists nonetheless ran a competitive race in 1800. Adams's peace policy bolstered his popularity. And because U.S. merchants had profited from supplying both sides in the European war, the country was enjoying a period of prosperity that benefited the president and his party. But the party wounds opened by Adams's decision to broker a peace with France continued to fester. Hamilton wrote a scathing attack on the president in a letter that fell into the hands of Aaron Burr, a crafty politician from New York whom the Republicans had teamed up with Jefferson for the presidential election. Burr published the letter, airing the Federalists' squabbling in public.

The Federalists, hampered by party disunity, could not counter the Republicans' aggressive organizational tactics. They found it distasteful to appeal to common people. One party member lamented that the Republicans sent spokesmen "to every class of men, and even to every individual man, that can be gained. Every threshing floor, every husting, every party at work on a house-frame or raising a building, the very funerals are infected with bawlers or whisperers against government."

Wherever they organized, the Republicans attacked the Federalists as monarchists plotting to undo the gains of the Revolution. The Federalists responded with emotional appeals that depicted Jefferson as a godless revolutionary whose election would usher in a reign of terror. "The effect," intoned the Reverend William Linn, "would be to destroy religion, introduce immorality, and loosen all bonds of society."

Attacks like Linn's reflected the fears of Calvinist preachers that a tide of disbelief was about to submerge Christianity in the United States. Church attendance had declined in the 1790s, particularly among men, and perhaps no more than one in twenty Americans was a member of any church. **Deism**, an Enlightenment religious philosophy popular among the leaders of the Revolutionary era, was now beginning to make inroads among ordinary citizens. Deists viewed God as a kind of master clockmaker who created the laws by which the universe runs but otherwise leaves it alone. They rejected revelation for reason, maintaining that the workings of nature alone reveal God's design. In 1794, the famed pamphleteer Thomas Paine, in *The Age of Reason,* denounced churches as "human inventions set up to terrify and enslave mankind, and monopolize power and profit."

These developments convinced Calvinist ministers, nearly all of them Federalists, that the atheism of the French Revolution was infecting U.S. republicanism. They lashed out at the Republicans, the friends of the French Revolution, as perverters of religious and social order. Jefferson, a deist known for his freethinking in religion, bore the brunt of their attack in 1800.

The Republicans won the election by mobilizing voters through strong party organizations. Voter turnout in 1800 was twice what it had been in the early 1790s, and most of the new voters were Republicans. The Direct Tax of 1798 cost the Federalists the support of commercial farmers in the mid-Atlantic states. Artisans in port cities had already switched to the Republicans in protest over Jay's Treaty, which they feared left them exposed to a flood of cheap British imports. Adams carried New England and had a smattering of support elsewhere. With New York added to their solid base in the South and the backcountry, the Jeffersonians gained an electoral majority (see Map 8–2).

Party unity among Republican electors was so strong that Jefferson and Burr each received 73 electoral votes. Consequently, the election was thrown into the House of Representatives, which, until the newly elected Congress was seated, was still dominated by Federalists. Hoping to deny Jefferson the presidency, the Federalists in the House backed Burr. They believed that he was untainted by the Revolutionary virus that made Jefferson seem so dangerous, even though Hamilton, who faced Burr as a political rival in New York, sought to convince them otherwise. The result was a deadlock that persisted into the early months of 1801. Pennsylvania and Virginia mobilized their state militias, a clear message that the Republicans were prepared to use force against what Jefferson termed any "legislative usurpation" of the people's will as expressed in the election. On February 16, 1801, the Federalists yielded. Informed through intermediaries that Jefferson would not dismantle Hamilton's fiscal system, enough Federalists cast blank ballots to give Jefferson the majority he needed for election. The Twelfth Amendment to the Constitution, ratified in 1804, prevented a similar impasse from arising again by requiring electors to cast separate ballots for president and vice president.

REPUBLICANS

Turn out, turn out and save your Country from ruin !

From an *Emperor*—from a *King*—from the iron grasp of a *British Tory Faction*—an unprincipled banditti of British speculators. The hireling tools and emissaries of his majesty king George the 3d have thronged our city and diffused the poison of principles among us.

DOWN WITH THE TORIES, DOWN WITH THE BRITISH FACTION,

Before they have it in their power to enslave you, and reduce your families to distress by heavy taxation. Republicans want no Tribute-liars—they want no ship Ocean-liars—they want no Rufus King's for Lords —they want no Varick to lord it over them—they want no Jones for senator, who fought with the British against the Americans in time of the war.—But they want in their places such men as

Jefferson & Clinton,

who fought their Country's Battles in the year '76

By associating their Federalist opponents with the hated Tories of the American Revolution, the Republicans appealed to the voters as the true defenders of American liberation.

Collection of the New York Historical Society, Negative # 35609.

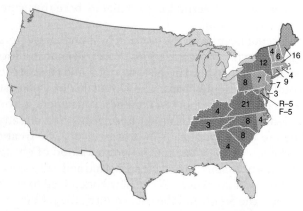

	Electoral Vote (%)
THOMAS JEFFERSON **(Republican)**	**73** **(53)**
John Adams (Federalist)	65 (47)

MAP 8–2 **The Election of 1800**
The sharp erosion of Federalist strength in New York and Pennsylvania after 1798 swung the election of 1800 to the Republicans.

Conclusion

In 1789, the U.S. republic was little more than an experiment in self-government. The Federalists provided a firm foundation for that experiment. Hamilton's financial program, neutrality in the wars of the French Revolution, and the diplomatic settlement with Britain in Jay's Treaty bequeathed the young nation a decade of peace and prosperity.

Federalist policies, however, provoked strong opposition rooted in conflicting economic interests and contrasting regional views over the meaning of liberty and government in the new republic. Federalist leadership initially depended on a coalition of regional elites in New England, the mid-Atlantic region, and the slave districts of the South. Each of these elites favored the establishment of effective national power, though often for

different reasons. Merchants in Congregationalist New England were concerned mainly with reviving their British trading connections and reversing what they saw as the social and moral decline of the 1780s. Quaker and Episcopal businessmen and commercial farmers in the mid-Atlantic states wanted a central government to promote economic development at home and expand markets aboard. Southern slaveholders, hoping to expand into the West, needed a national government strong enough to secure the trans-Appalachian region.

The Federalist coalition split during Washington's second term when southern planters joined urban artisans and back-country Scots-Irish farmers in opposing Jay's Treaty and the commercially oriented program of the Federalists. During John Adams's administration, Quaker and German farmers in the mid-Atlantic states defected from the Federalists over the tax legislation of 1798, and three of the four regions of the country lined up behind the Republicans. The new Republican majority was united by the belief that the actions of the New England Federalists—the expansion of the army, the imposition of new taxes, and the passage of the Alien and Sedition Acts—threatened individual liberty and regional autonomy. Non-English groups and farmers south of New England turned to the Republicans as the upholders of these threatened freedoms.

The openly partisan politics of the 1790s surprised the country's founders, who equated parties with the evils of factionalism. They had not foreseen that parties would forge a necessary link between the rulers and the ruled and create a mechanism by which group values and regional interests could be given a political voice. Party formation climaxed in the election of 1800, when the Republicans ended the Federalists' rule. The Republicans won by embracing the popular demand for a more egalitarian social and political order.

To the credit of the Federalists, they relinquished control of the national government peacefully. The importance of this precedent can scarcely be exaggerated. It marked the first time in modern political history that a party in power handed over the government to its opposition. It now remained to be seen what the Republicans would do with their newfound power

Review Questions

1. What role did the "people" play in Washington's inauguration in 1789? What was the purpose of the grand procession, and why were the militia present?

2. What was distinctive about the four regions of the United States in 1790? What were the common values and goals that brought white Americans together?

3. What were the major problems confronting the Washington administration, and how effectively were they resolved? Why was Washington so cautious when confronted with the outbreak of war in Europe?

4. Who were the Federalists and the Republicans, and how did they differ over the meaning of liberty and the power

of the national government? What were the major steps in the formation of two distinct parties in the early United States?

5. Why did regional differences tend to pit the North against the South by the late 1790s?

6. How did the XYZ Affair lead to a political crisis in the United States? Why did the Federalists believe that they would benefit from a war against France?

7. Jefferson called his election in 1800 the "revolution of 1800." What do you think he meant? Would you agree with him?

Key Terms

Alien and Sedition Acts (p. 214)

Bill of Rights (p. 204)

Deism (p. 217)

Federalists (p. 207)

Franco-American Accord of 1800 (p. 216)

Jay's Treaty (p. 212)

Judiciary Act of 1789 (p. 205)

Nullification (p. 216)

Pietists (p. 201)

Quasi-War (p. 214)

Republican (Jeffersonian) (p. 207)

States' rights (p. 216)

Tariff Act of 1789 (p. 205)

Treaty of Greenville (p. 209)

Treaty of San Lorenzo (p. 212)

Whiskey Rebellion (p. 209)

XYZ Affair (p. 214)

Recommended Reading

Elkins, Stanley, and Eric McKitrick. *The Age of Federalism* (1993). A magisterial work of narrative history that includes brilliant sketches of the major political actors in the 1790s.

Ellis, Joseph J. *His Excellency: George Washington* (2004). A fresh and insightful rereading of the qualities of leadership that Washington brought to the presidency.

Freeman, Joanne B. *Affairs of Honor: National Politics in the New Republic* (2001). By showing how politicians in the early republic based their behavior on codes of male honor, this study offers a fresh way of understanding the often bitter political divisions of the 1790s.

Lipset, Seymour. *The First New Nation: The United States in Historical and Comparative Perspective* (1963). This work draws on insights from political sociology to show what was unique and enduring in America's pioneering role as a new nation with a written constitution.

Palmer, R. R. *The Age of the Democratic Revolutions: A Political History of Europe and America, 1760–1800*, 2 vols. (1959–64). A comparative work that places the French and American revolutions in a global context.

Waldstreicher, David. *In the Midst of Perpetual Fetes: The Making of American Nationalism, 1776–1820* (1997). An imaginatively conceived work that reveals how Americans in the early republic created their own sense of nationalism through popular festivals, street parades, and other forms of political celebration at the local level.

Where to Learn More

■ **Cincinnati Historical Society, Cincinnati, Ohio.** Collections include written and visual materials on the history of the Old Northwest Territory. Visit its website, www.cincymuseum.org, for information on its programs and the accessibility of its printed and audiovisual collections.

■ **Federal Hall National Memorial, New York, New York.** This museum and historic site holds artifacts relating to President Washington's inauguration. Its website, www.nps.gov/feha, includes a printable travel guide to various sites in Manhattan administered by the National Parks Service.

■ **Hamilton Grange National Memorial, New York, New York.** The home of Alexander Hamilton contains materials on his life. A brief history of the home and Hamilton's life can be found at its website, www.nps/gov/hagr.

■ **Adams National Historic Site, Quincy, Massachusetts.** This site preserves buildings and manuscripts associated with four generations of the Adams family. See its website, www.nps.gov/adam, for information on guided tours and the various homes that are part of the site.

■ **Alexander Hamilton Exhibition.** On tour through 2009, this exhibition mounted by the New-York Historical Society offers a wonderful introduction to Hamilton's financial legacy. For more information, see its website: www.alexanderhamiltonexhibition.org.

Study Resources

The low point in what many Americans viewed as a second War of Independence, the War of 1812, came when British troops seized and burned Washington, D.C., on August 24, 1814.

The Triumph and Collapse of Jeffersonian Republicanism 9

1800–1824

Riversdale, 30 August 1814

My dear Sister,

Since I started this letter [on Aug. 9] we have been in a state of continual alarm, and now I have time to write only two or three lines to ask you to tell Papa that we are alive, in good health, and I hope safe from danger. I am sure that you have heard the news of the battle of Bladensburg where the English defeated the American troops with Madison 'not at their head, but at their rear.'

From there they went to Washington where they burned the Capitol, the President's House, all the public offices, etc. During the battle I saw several cannonballs with my own eyes, and I will write all the details to your husband. At the moment the English ships are at Alexandria which is also in their possession.

I don't know how all this will end, but I fear very badly for us. It is probable that it will also bring about a dissolution of the union of the states, and in that case, farewell to the public debt. You know I have predicted this outcome for a long time. Wouldn't it be wise to send your husband here without delay, in order to plan with me the best course to pursue for Papa's interests as well as yours?

This letter will go, I think, by a Dutch ship. If I have time with the confusion we are in, I will write again in a few days, perhaps by the same vessel. At present my house is full of people every day and at night my bedroom is full of rifles, pistols, sabers, etc. Many thanks to your husband for the information in his letter of 27 April, and tell him that I invested all his money in the May loan [of the U.S. Treasury]. Please give many greetings to my dear Father and to Charles [her brother]. Embrace your children for me and believe me,

> Your affectionate sister,
>
> Rosalie E. Calvert

Margaret Law Callcott, ed., *Mistress of Riversdale: The Plantation Letters of Rosalie Stier Calvert, 1795–1821* (Baltimore: Johns Hopkins University Press, 1991), pp. 271–272.

myhistorylab

Personal Journeys Online

- George Robert Gleig, *Burning of Washington*, August 23, 1814. A British soldier describes the destruction in Washington.
- Dolley Madison, *Letter to her sister*, August 23, 1814. Dolley Madison describes the abandonment of the White House.
- Lt. Col. R. E. Parker, *Letter to the governor*, June 11, 1814. A Virginia soldier relates how the slaves plotted to escape behind British lines.

Rosalie Calvert, from her plantation home in nearby Bladensburg, Maryland, wrote to her sister in Europe with news of the British attack on Washington, DC, in August 1814, the low point of the American cause in the War of 1812. The youngest of the three children of a wealthy Belgian family that had fled the advancing armies of revolutionary France, Rosalie was 16 when her family arrived in Philadelphia in the summer of 1794. Her father, Henri J. Stier, had planned in advance for his family's departure and brought with him a sizable fortune in gold, U.S. currency, and paintings. The family lived off the income from Henri's investments in U.S. securities and, unsurprisingly, was strongly Federalist in its political leanings. After resettling in Annapolis, most of the Stiers returned to Europe in 1803 when political conditions had stabilized. Left behind was Rosalie, entrusted with the management of the family's financial holdings. In 1799, Rosalie had married George Calvert, a descendant of the proprietors of the Maryland colony and a kinsman of the Washingtons.

The Calverts lived at Riversdale, a home built by her father, and shared in the responsibilities of managing three plantations worked by slave labor. Rosalie's wealth and elite social standing deepened her political conservatism. Moreover, the coming to power of the Jeffersonian Republicans in 1801 triggered bitter memories of the revolutionary turmoil she had experienced as a young woman in Belgium. In her eyes, Jefferson and his followers were demagogues who catered to the poor and threatened to infect the United States with the political radicalism of the French Revolution. She blamed the War of 1812 on ignorant, ill-conceived Republican policies and feared that the war would unleash massive unrest. Particularly alarming was the news that a mob in Baltimore had brutally beaten twelve prominent Federalists for their antiwar stand. Thus the sense of "continual alarm" that runs through her letter in August 1814, at a time when the war had spilled over into her home.

Her fears were overblown. The United States weathered the War of 1812, and the Calverts were spared property damage. Rosalie, however, survived the war by only six years. The strain of ten pregnancies in twenty-one years of marriage likely contributed to her death at the age of 43 from congestive heart failure. Despite her denunciations of the Republicans, Jefferson's party succeeded in promoting the growth and independence of the United States in the first quarter of the nineteenth century. Expansionist policies to the south and west more than doubled the size of the republic and fueled the westward spread of slavery. The war against Britain from 1812 to 1815, if less than a

CHRONOLOGY

1801	Thomas Jefferson is inaugurated, the first Republican president.
	John Marshall becomes chief justice.
1802	Congress repeals the Judiciary Act of 1801.
1803	*Marbury v. Madison* sets the precedent of judicial review by the Supreme Court.
	Louisiana Purchase.
	Lewis and Clark expedition begins.
	Britain and France resume their war after a brief peace.
1804	Vice President Aaron Burr kills Alexander Hamilton in a duel.
	Judges John Pickering and Samuel Chase impeached by Republicans.
1806	Britain and France issue orders restricting neutral shipping.
	Betrayal of the Burr conspiracy.
1807	*Chesapeake* affair.
	Congress passes the Embargo Act.
	Congress prohibits the African slave trade.
1808	James Madison elected president.
1809	Repeal of the Embargo Act.
	Passage of the Nonintercourse Act.
1810–1825	Revolutions and independence movements in Latin America.
1810	Macon's Bill No. 2 reopens trade with Britain and France.
	United States annexes part of West Florida.
	Georgia state law invalidated by the Supreme Court in *Fletcher v. Peck*.
1811	Battle of Tippecanoe and defeat of the Indian confederation.
	Charter of the Bank of the United States expires.
1812	Congress declares war on Britain.
	American loss of Detroit.
	Napoleon invades Russia.

1813	Perry's victory at Battle of Put-in-Bay.
	Battle of the Thames and death of Tecumseh.
1814	Jackson crushes the Creeks at the Battle of Horseshoe Bend.
	British burn Washington, DC, and attack Baltimore.
	Macdonough's naval victory on Lake Champlain turns back a British invasion.
	Hartford Convention meets.
	Treaty of Ghent signed.
1815	Jackson routs British at the Battle of New Orleans.
	Congress of Vienna arranges a peace settlement for Europe after Napoleon's defeat at Waterloo.
1816	Congress charters the Second Bank of the United States and passes a protective tariff.
	James Monroe elected president.
1817	Rush-Bagot Treaty demilitarizes the Great Lakes.
1818	Anglo-American Accords on trade and boundaries.
	Jackson's border campaign in Spanish East Florida.
1819	Trans-Continental Treaty between United States and Spain.
	Beginning of the Missouri controversy.
	Financial panic sends economy into a depression.
	McCulloch v. Maryland upholds constitutionality of the Bank of the United States.
1820	Missouri Compromise on slavery in the Louisiana Purchase.
	Monroe reelected.
1821	Greek revolt against the Turks.
1822	The United States extends diplomatic recognition to the new nations of Latin America.
1823	Monroe Doctrine proclaims Western Hemisphere closed to further European colonization.
1825	John Quincy Adams elected president by the House of Representatives.

military triumph, nonetheless freed Americans to look inward for economic development.

At the height of Republican success just after the War of 1812, the Federalist party collapsed. Without an organized opposition to enforce party discipline, the Republicans soon followed the Federalists into political oblivion. The nation's expansion produced two crises—a financial panic and a battle over slavery in Missouri—that shattered the facade of republican unity. By the mid-1820s, a new party system was emerging.

Jefferson's Presidency

Thomas Jefferson believed that a true revolution had occurred in 1800, a peaceful overthrow of the Federalist party and its hated principles of government consolidation and military force. In his eyes, the defeat of the monarchical Federalists reconfirmed the true political legacy of the Revolution by restoring the republican majority to its rightful control of the government.

Unlike the Hamiltonian Federalists, whose commercial vision of the United States accepted social and economic inequalities as inevitable, the Jeffersonians wanted a predominantly agrarian republic based on widespread economic equality for white yeomen families to counter any threat posed by the privileged few to the people's liberties. Thus, they favored territorial expansion as a means of adding enough land to maintain self-reliant farmers as the guardians of republican freedoms. They also favored the spread of slavery. As long as racial slavery promoted a sense of unity among free white men, they were confident that a populist democracy could coexist with elite rule.

Jefferson's first administration was a solid success. A unified Republican party reduced the size and scope of the federal government, allowed the Alien and Sedition Acts to lapse, and celebrated the Louisiana Purchase. An enfeebled Federalist party weakly opposed Jefferson's reelection in 1804. His second term, however, was a bitter disappointment, marked by the massive unpopularity of Jefferson's embargo on U.S. foreign trade. As a result, Jefferson left his successor, James Madison, a divided party, a revived Federalism, and an unresolved crisis in foreign affairs.

Reform at Home

Jefferson was the first president to be inaugurated in Washington, DC, and his inauguration was as unpretentious as the raw and primitive capital city itself. Then little more than a scraggly collection of huts, a few boardinghouses, and unfinished public buildings, Washington lacked, one senator ruefully noted, "only houses, wine cellars, learned men, amiable women, and other trifles to make our city perfect." Jefferson walked from his lodgings to the Capitol building to be sworn in. His dress was neat but shorn of such gentlemanly refinements as a wig. He emphasized in his inaugural

address the overwhelming commitment of Americans to the "republican form" of government.

Believing that the Federalists had promoted aristocratic pretensions and courtly intrigue through such practices as weekly levees (formal receptions) for presidential guests, Jefferson replaced the levees with small, men-only dinners, where he aired his political views. This effort to achieve republican purity in governance, one that denied women any political role, created a void in the capital's social life that was filled by the wives of cabinet members and women drawn from the social elite. It was their dinner parties and receptions that enabled politically minded women and men to come together, lobby on behalf of friends and relatives, and build the networks that influenced how political offices and favors were distributed. These occasions provided a setting in which politicking could occur in a capital where the formal institutions of power—the executive, legislative, and judicial branches of government—were cut off from each other, not only by the distance between their physical locations, but also by the constitutional doctrine of separation of powers. Influential Washington hostesses such as Dolley Madison soon wielded a good deal of informal political power as they helped make possible a national political culture.

The cornerstone of Republican domestic policy was retrenchment, a return to the frugal, simple federal establishment the Jeffersonians believed to be the original intent of the Constitution. Determined to root out what they viewed as Federalist corruption and patronage, the Republicans began by reforming fiscal policy. Jefferson's secretary of the treasury was Albert Gallatin, a native of Switzerland who emerged in the 1790s as the best financial mind in the Republican party. He convinced Jefferson that the Bank of the United States was essential for financial stability and blocked efforts to dismantle it. Unlike Hamilton, however, Gallatin thought that a large public debt was a curse, a drag on productive capital, and an unfair burden on future generations. He succeeded in reducing the national debt from $83 million in 1800 to $57 million by 1809.

Gallatin's conservative fiscal policies shrank both the spending and taxes of the national government. The Republicans eliminated all internal taxes, including the despised tax on whiskey. Slashes in the military budget kept government expenditures below the level of 1800. The army was cut back to 3,000 men, and the navy was nearly eliminated. Jefferson's defense strategy called for gunboats and coastal fortifications. If the country were invaded, he would rely on the militia, citizen soldiers commanded by professional officers to be trained at the newly established (1802) military academy at West Point. The cuts in military spending, combined with soaring revenues from customs collections, left Gallatin with a surplus in the budget that he could devote to debt repayment.

Jeffersonian reform targeted the political character, as well as the size, of the national government. He moved to break the Federalist stranglehold on federal offices by appointing officials with sound Republican principles. Arch-

The classical design and bucolic setting of Monticello, Jefferson's home outside Charlottesville, Virginia, visually expressed both his aristocratic tastes and his vision of a harmonious agrarian republic.

Jane Braddick Petticolas (1791–1852), View of the West Front of Monticello and Garden, 1825, watercolor on paper, 13 5/8 × 18 1/18 inches. Edward Owen/Monticello/Thomas Jefferson Foundation, Inc.

Federalists, those Jefferson deemed guilty of misusing their offices for openly political reasons, were immediately replaced, and Republicans filled other posts opened up by attrition. By the time Jefferson left the presidency in 1809, Republicans held nearly all the appointive offices.

Jefferson moved most aggressively against the Federalists in the judiciary. Just days before they relinquished power, the Federalists passed the Judiciary Act of 1801, legislation that both enlarged the judiciary and packed it with more Federalists appointed by Adams, the outgoing president.

The Republicans fought back. Now dominant in Congress, they quickly repealed the Judiciary Act of 1801. Frustrated Federalists now turned to John Marshall, a staunch Federalist appointed chief justice of the United States by President Adams in 1801, hoping that he would rule that Congress had acted unconstitutionally in removing the recently appointed federal judges. Marshall moved carefully to avoid an open confrontation. He was aware that the Republicans contended that Congress and the president had at least a coequal right with the Supreme Court to decide constitutional questions.

The issue came to a head in the case of **Marbury v. Madison** (1803), which centered on Secretary of State James Madison's refusal to deliver a commission to William Mar-

bury, one of Adams's "midnight appointments" (so-called because Adams made them on his next-to-last day in office) as a justice of the peace for the District of Columbia. Marshall held that although Marbury had a legal right to his commission, the Court had no jurisdiction in the case. The Court ruled that the section of the Judiciary Act of 1789 granting it the power to order the delivery of Marbury's commission was unconstitutional because it conferred on the Court a power not specified in the Constitution. Stating that it was "emphatically the province and duty of the judicial department to say what the law is," Marshall created the precedent of judicial review, the power of the Supreme Court to rule on the constitutionality of federal law. This doctrine rejected the Republican view expressed in the Virginia and Kentucky Resolutions that the states could decide on the constitutionality of federal laws and was of pivotal importance for the future of the Court.

Raising the charge of judicial tyranny, congressional Republicans brought formal charges against two notorious Federalist judges. One of them, John Pickering, a district judge from New Hampshire and a mentally unstable alcoholic, was convicted and removed from office. The other was bigger game: Justice Samuel Chase of the Supreme Court, the most

Masterful hunters, the Plains Indians encountered by Lewis and Clark depended on the buffalo for their economic survival.

obnoxious Federalist still in a position of national power. For all his blatant partisanship, however, Chase was clearly sane, and he escaped conviction in the Senate in early 1805, when the Republicans failed to show that he was guilty of "high crimes and misdemeanors," the constitutionally defined grounds for removal from office. His acquittal ended the Republican offensive against the judiciary.

The Louisiana Purchase

In foreign affairs, fortune smiled on Jefferson during his first term. The European war that had almost sucked in the United States in the 1790s subsided. Britain and France agreed on a truce in 1802. Meanwhile, Jefferson, despite his distaste for a strong navy, ordered a show of force in the Mediterranean to punish the Barbary pirates who were preying on U.S. shipping and taking U.S. sailors hostage. For years, the North African states of Morocco, Algeria, Tunis, and Tripoli had demanded cash tribute from foreigners trading in the Mediterranean. Jefferson stopped the payments in 1801, and when attacks on U.S. shipping resumed, he retaliated by sending warships and marines to the Mediterranean. The tribute system continued until 1815, but thanks to the success of U.S. forces in Tripoli, Jefferson got much better terms.

The Anglo-French peace allowed Spain and France to reclaim their colonial trade in the Western Hemisphere. The new ruler of France, Napoleon Bonaparte, was also now free to develop his plans for reviving the French empire in America. In a secret treaty with Spain in 1800, Napoleon reacquired for France the Louisiana Territory, a vast, vaguely defined area stretching between the Mississippi River and the Rocky Mountains.

Sketchy, unconfirmed reports of the treaty reached Jefferson in the spring of 1801, and he was immediately alarmed. He had long believed that Spain, proud but militarily impotent, would be powerless to stem the spread of the expanding American population into its territories in western North America. France, by contrast, was a formidable opponent. French control of the Mississippi Valley, combined with the British presence in Canada, threatened to hem in the United States and deprive Jefferson's farmers of their empire of liberty.

Jefferson was prepared to reverse his party's traditional foreign policy to eliminate this threat. He opened exploratory talks with the British on an Anglo-American alliance to drive the French out of Louisiana. He also strengthened U.S. forces in the Mississippi Valley and secured congressional approval for the Lewis and Clark expedition through upper Louisiana. Although best known for its scientific discoveries, this expedition was designed initially as a military mission. Jefferson applied diplomatic and military pressure to induce Napoleon to sell New Orleans and a small slice of coastal territory to its east to the United States. This was his main objective: to possess New Orleans and control the mouth of the Mississippi River, outlet to world markets. To his surprise, Napoleon suddenly decided in early 1803 to sell all of the immense Louisiana Territory to the United States (see Map 9–1).

Napoleon's failure to reconquer Saint-Domingue (modern-day Haiti) was instrumental in his about-face on plans for a revived French empire in America. He had envisioned this rich sugar island as the jewel of his new empire and intended to use the Louisiana Territory as a granary to supply the island. During the upheavals of the French Revolution, the slaves on the island, led by Touissant L'Ouverture, rebelled in a bloody and successful bid for independence. Napoleon sent a large army to reassert French control, but it succumbed to disease and the islanders' fierce resistance. Without firm French control of Saint-Domingue, Louisiana was of little use to Napoleon. And when the U.S. Congress passed resolutions threatening a U.S. attack on New Orleans, he realized that he was likely to have to fight to keep it. With a renewed war against Britain looming, he had better use for his troops in Europe and wanted to keep Americans neutral. For $15 million (including about $4 million in French debts owed to American citizens), he offered to part with the whole of Louisiana. The cost to the United States was about 3.5 cents per acre.

Jefferson, the strict-constructionist, now turned pragmatist. Despite the lack of any specific authorization in the Constitution for the acquisition of foreign territory or the incorporation as U.S. citizens of the 50,000 French

MAP EXPLORATION To explore an interactive version of this map, go to
http://www.prenhall.com/goldfield5/map9.1

MAP 9–1   The Louisiana Purchase and the Lewis and Clark Expedition
The vast expanse of the Louisiana Purchase was virtually unknown territory to Americans before the Lewis and Clark expedition gathered a mass of scientific information about it.

and Spanish descendants then living in Louisiana, he accepted Napoleon's deal. The Louisiana Purchase doubled the size of the United States and offered seemingly endless space to be settled by yeoman farmers. It also opened up another frontier for slaveholders in the lower Mississippi Valley.

Jefferson was willing, as the Federalists had been when they were in power, to stretch the Constitution to support his definition of the national good. Conversely, it was now the Federalists, fearful of a further decline in their political power, who relied on a narrow reading of the Constitution in a futile attempt to block the Louisiana acquisition.

Florida and Western Schemes

The magnificent prize of Louisiana did not satisfy Republican territorial ambitions. Still to be gained were river outlets on the Gulf Coast essential for the development of

plantation agriculture in Alabama and Mississippi. The boundaries of the Louisiana Purchase were so vague that Jefferson felt justified in claiming Spanish-held Texas and the Gulf Coast eastward from New Orleans to Mobile Bay, including the Spanish province of West Florida. Against stiff Spanish opposition, he pushed ahead with his plans to acquire West Florida. This provoked the first challenge to his leadership of the party.

Once it was clear that Spain did not want to sell West Florida to the United States, Jefferson accepted Napoleon's offer to act as a middleman in the acquisition. Napoleon's price was $2 million. He soon lost interest in the project, however, and Jefferson lost prestige in 1806, when he pushed an appropriations bill through Congress to pay for Napoleon's services. Former Republican stalwarts in Congress denounced the bill as bribe money and staged a party revolt against the president's devious tactics.

American Views

Protest of French Settlers in Louisiana

In the Louisiana Ordinance of 1804, Congress divided the Louisiana Purchase territory into northern and southern parts along a line that later separated the future state of Louisiana (originally designated the Territory of Orleans) from the territory to the north. No rights of self-government were extended to the settlers in Louisiana. Instead, a territorial government was established for which the president appointed both the governor and his advisory council. Congress also prohibited the inhabitants from engaging in the foreign slave trade and restricted the admission of future slaves to the bona-fide property of the actual settlers. A bill limiting the bondage of incoming slaves to one year passed the House but was rejected in the Senate. The following memorial to Congress registers the grievances of the French settlers over their treatment.

- What feature of congressional policy did the settlers single out as a major grievance?
- Why were the settlers so insistent that slavery was essential to their economic progress?
- Why do you think that Congress quickly abandoned its initial effort to restrict the growth of slavery in the Territory of Orleans?

We the subscribers, Planters, Merchants and other inhabitants of Louisiana respectfully approach the Legislature of the United States with a memorial of our rights, [and] a remonstrance against certain laws which contravene them....

Without any agency in the events which have annexed our country to the United States, we yet considered them as fortunate, and thought our liberties secured even before we knew the terms of the cession. Persuaded that a free people would acquire territory only to extend the blessings of freedom, that an enlightened nation would never destroy those principles on which its government was founded, and that their Representatives would disdain to become the instruments of oppression, we calculated with certainty that their first act of sovereignty would be a communication of all the blessings they enjoyed....

We pray leave to examine the law for erecting Louisiana.... This act does not "incorporate us into the Union," that it vests us with none of the "Rights," gives us no advances and deprives us of all the "immunities" of American citizens....

A Governor is to be placed over us, whom we have not chosen, whom we do not even know, who may be ignorant of our language, uninformed of our institutions, and who may have no connections with our Country or interest in its welfare....

We know not with what view the territory North of the 33d degree has been severed from us.... If this division should operate as to prolong our state of political tutelage, on account of any supposed deficiency of numbers, we cannot but consider it as injurious to our rights, and therefore enumerate it among those points of which we have reason to complain....

There is one subject however extremely interesting to us, in which great care has been taken to prevent any interference even by the Governor and Council, selected by the President himself. The African trade is absolutely prohibited, and severe penalties imposed on a traffic free to all the Atlantic states, who choose to engage in it, and as far as it relates to procuring the subjects of it from other states [the domestic slave trade], permitted even in the territory of the Mississippi.

It is not our intention to enter into arguments that have become familiar to every reasoner on this question. We only ask the right of deciding it for ourselves, and of being placed in this aspect on an equal footing with other states. To the necessity of employing African labourers, which arises from climate, and the species of cultivation [sugar], pursued in warm latitudes, is added reason in this country peculiar to itself. The banks raised to restrain the waters of the Mississippi can only be kept in repair by those whose natural constitution and habits of labour enable them to resist the combined effects of a deleterious moisture, and a degree of heat intolerable to whites; this labour is great, it requires many hands and it is all important to the very existence of our country....

strong position to force a southward adjustment of the Canadian-U.S. boundary and to claim the Louisiana Purchase territory.

The British attacks could hardly have come at a worse time for the Madison administration. The Treasury was nearly bankrupt. Against the wishes of Treasury Secretary Gallatin, Congress had refused to preserve the Bank of the United States when its charter expired in 1811. Lacking both a centralized means of directing wartime finances and any significant increase in taxes, the Treasury was forced to rely on makeshift loans. These loans were poorly subscribed, largely because the cash-rich New England banks refused to buy them. Inflation also became a problem when state banks, no longer restrained by the control of a national bank, overissued paper money in the form of bank notes.

In celebration of the defeat of the British warship *Boxer* by the U.S. frigate *Enterprise* in September 1813, the artist depicts Madison bloodying the nose and blackening the eye of a humbled George III.

As the country's finances tottered toward collapse, political dissent in New England was reaching a climax. In 1814, the British extended their blockade of U.S. commerce northward to include New England. Federalist merchants and shippers, who had earlier profited from their illegal trade with the British, now felt the economic pinch of the war. Cries for resistance against "Mr. Madison's war" culminated in a call issued by the Massachusetts legislature for a convention to consider "a radical reform of the national compact." The convention was scheduled for December in Hartford, Connecticut.

The darkest hour came in August 1814. A British amphibious force occupied and torched Washington, DC, in retaliation for a U.S. raid on York (now Toronto), the capital of Upper Canada. The defense of Washington was slipshod at best, and a local inhabitant can be excused for scribbling on a wall: "The capital and the Union lost by cowardice." Still, the British actions stiffened U.S. resistance, and the failure of a follow-up attack on Baltimore deprived the British of any strategic gain. Baltimore's defenses held, stirring Francis Scott Key, a young lawyer who viewed the bombardment from a British prisoner-of-war ship, to write "The Star-Spangled Banner." Fittingly in this strange war, the future national anthem was set to the tune of a British drinking song.

The Chesapeake raids were designed to divert U.S. attention from the major offensive General George Prevost was leading down the shores of Lake Champlain. Prevost commanded the largest and best-equipped army the British had yet assembled, but he was forced to turn back when Commodore Thomas McDonough defeated a British fleet on September 11 at the **Battle of Plattsburgh.**

The tide had turned. When news of the setbacks at Baltimore and Plattsburgh reached England, the Foreign Office scaled back the demands it had been making on U.S. negotiators at peace talks in the city of Ghent, in present-day Belgium. The British were ready for peace, but one of their trump cards had yet to be played—the southern offensive against New Orleans. The outcome of that campaign could still upset whatever was decided at Ghent.

The Treaty of Ghent and the Battle of New Orleans

By the fall of 1814, the British were eager to redraw the map of post-Napoleonic Europe, restore profitable relations with America, and reduce their huge war debt. The British negotiators at Ghent agreed to a peace treaty on terms the Americans were delighted to accept. The **Treaty of Ghent,** signed on Christmas Eve, 1814, simply restored relations to their status at the start of the war. No territory changed hands, and nothing was said about impressment or the rights of neutrals. The ink had barely dried on the Treaty of Ghent when the British government sent reinforcements to General Edward Pakenham, the commander of the Louisiana invasion force. By this action, the British indicated that they were not irrevocably committed to the peace settlement, which, though signed, could not be formally ratified until weeks later, when it was sent across the Atlantic. The British had always held that the Louisiana Purchase was fraudulent (they insisted that Louisiana was never Napoleon's to sell), and they were prepared to install a new government in Louisiana if Pakenham succeeded. Far from being an anticlimax to a war that was already over, the showdown between British and U.S. forces at the **Battle of New Orleans** in January 1815 had immense strategic significance for the United States.

The hero of New Orleans, in song and legend, was Andrew Jackson. A planter-politician from Tennessee, Jackson rose to prominence during the war as a ferocious Indian fighter. The Creeks of Alabama and Georgia, much like the Shawnees farther north, had undergone a religious revival that culminated in a military effort to drive U.S. settlers out of their tribal homelands. As a general in the Tennessee militia, Jackson crushed Indian resistance in the Old Southwest at the Battle of Horseshoe Bend in March 1814. Supported by 600 Indian allies, Jackson's militia virtually slaughtered some 1,000 Creek warriors. The number of Indians who fought and died in this battle was the largest in the history of American-Indian warfare. Jackson then forced the vanquished Creeks to cede two-thirds of their territory to the United States. On the southern frontier as well as the northern, Native Americans emerged as the major losers of the war.

After his Indian conquests, Jackson was promoted to general in the regular army and given command of the defense of the Gulf Coast. In November 1814, he seized Pensacola in Spanish Florida to deny the British its use as a supply depot and then hurried to defend New Orleans. The overconfident British frontally attacked Jackson's lines on January 8, 1815. The result was a massacre. Artillery fire laid down by French-speaking cannoneers from New Orleans accounted for most of the carnage. More than 2,000 British soldiers were killed or wounded. U.S. casualties totaled 21.

Strategically, Jackson's smashing victory at New Orleans ended any possibility of a British sphere of influence in Louisiana. Politically, it was a deathblow to Federalism. At the Hartford Convention in December 1814, party moderates had forestalled talk of secession with a series of proposed constitutional amendments designed to limit southern power in national affairs. At the top of their list was a demand for eliminating the three-fifths clause by which slaves were counted for purposes of congressional representation. They also wanted to require a two-thirds majority in Congress for the admission of new states, declarations of war, and the imposition of embargoes. These demands became public as Americans were rejoicing over the Treaty of Ghent and Jackson's rout of the British. Set against the revived nationalism that marked the end of the war, the Federalists now seemed to be parochial sulkers who put regional interests above the national good. Worse yet, they struck many Americans as quasi-traitors who had been prepared to desert the country in the face of the enemy. As a significant political force, Federalism was dead.

The Era of Good Feelings

In 1817, on the occasion of a presidential visit by James Monroe, a Boston newspaper proclaimed the **Era of Good Feelings,** an expression that nicely captured the spirit of political harmony and sectional unity that washed over the republic in the immediate postwar years. National pride surged with the humbling of the British at New Orleans, the demise of the Federalists lessened political tensions, and the economy was booming. The Republicans had been vindicated, and for a short time they enjoyed de facto status as the only governing party.

At the end of Madison's presidency, and in the first administration of his successor, James Monroe of Virginia, the Republicans embarked on a program of economic nationalism that would have pleased Alexander Hamilton. In foreign policy, they moved aggressively to stake out U.S. leadership in the Western Hemisphere. A series of decisions handed down by the Supreme Court reinforced the postwar nationalism. In 1819, however, an economic depression and a bitter controversy over slavery shattered the harmony. The nationalist tide set in motion by the end of the war had run its course, and the Republicans divided on sectional and economic issues.

Economic Nationalism

The War of 1812 had taught the Republicans to appreciate the old Federalist doctrines on centralized national power. In his annual message of December 1815, Madison outlined a

Fittingly placing President James Monroe next to a globe, this painting depicts one of the cabinet meetings that led to the formulation of the Monroe Doctrine.

program of economic nationalism that was pushed through Congress by Henry Clay and John C. Calhoun, the most prominent of the new generation of young, nationalist-minded Republicans.

The first order of business was to create a new national bank. Reliance on state banks for wartime financing had proved a major mistake. The banks lacked sufficient capital reserves or, as occurred in New England, held them back. The demand for credit was met by a flood of state bank notes that fell in value because there was insufficient gold and silver to back them. Many banks suspended specie payments for their notes, and inflation was a persistent problem. After the British burned Washington, the Treasury was temporarily bankrupt, and throughout the war it could borrow only at high interest rates. Fiscal stability required the monetary coordination and restraint that only a new Bank of the United States could provide. Introduced by Calhoun, the bank bill passed Congress in 1816. Modeled after Hamilton's original bank and also headquartered in Philadelphia, the **Second Bank of the United States** was capitalized at $35 million, making it by far the nation's largest bank. Its size and official status as the depository and dispenser of the government's funds gave the bank tremendous economic power. It also enjoyed the exclusive privilege of being able to establish branches in any state.

After moving to repair the fiscal damage of the war, the Republicans then acted to protect what the war had fostered. Embargoes followed by three years of war had forced U.S. businessmen to manufacture goods they previously had imported. This was especially the case with iron and textile goods long supplied by the British. In 1815 and again in 1816, the British inundated the U.S. market with cheap imports to strangle U.S. industry in its infancy. Responding to this challenge to the nation's economic independence, the Republicans passed the Tariff of 1816, the first protective tariff in U.S. history. The act levied duties of 20 to 25 percent on imported goods that could be produced in the United States.

Congress earmarked revenue from the tariff and $1.5 million from the Bank of the United States (a cash payment in return for its charter) for transportation projects. The lack of a road system in the trans-Appalachian region had severely hampered troop movements during the war. Also, as settlers after the war moved onto lands seized from the pro-British Indians, western congressmen demanded improved outlets to eastern markets.

In early 1817, an internal-improvements bill sponsored by Calhoun passed Congress. Though in agreement with the bill's objectives, President Madison was convinced that the Constitution did not permit federal financing of primarily local projects. He vetoed the bill just before he left office.

Congressional passage of Calhoun's internal-improvements bill marked the pinnacle of the Republicans' economic nationalism. Frightened by the sectional disunity of the war years, a new generation of Republicans jettisoned many of the ideological trappings of Jefferson's original agrarian party.

Their program was a call for economic, and therefore political, unity. Such unity was to be achieved through a generous program of national subsidies consisting of tariffs for manufacturers in the Northeast and transportation funds for planters and farmers in the South and West. The new national bank would provide a uniform currency and credit facilities for the internal exchange of raw materials and manufactured goods. Support for this program was strongest in the mid-Atlantic and western states, the regions that stood to gain the most economically. Opposition centered in the Southeast, notably among die-hard proponents of states' rights in the old tobacco belt of Virginia and North Carolina and in New England, a region not only well served already by banks and a road network but also anxious not to be politically overshadowed by the rising West. This opposition took on an increasingly hard edge in the South as the Supreme Court outlined an ever more nationalist interpretation of the Constitution.

Judicial Nationalism

Under Chief Justice John Marshall, the Supreme Court had long supported the nationalist perspective Republicans began to champion after the war. A Virginia Federalist whose nationalism was forged during his service in the Revolutionary War, Marshall dominated the Court throughout his tenure (1801–1835) by his forceful personality and the logical power of his nationalist convictions. Two principles defined Marshall's jurisprudence: the primacy of the Supreme Court in all matters of constitutional interpretation and the sanctity of contractual property rights. In *Fletcher v. Peck* (1810), for example, the Court ruled that a Georgia law voiding a land grant made by an earlier legislature—on the grounds that it had involved massive fraud—violated the constitutional provision barring any state from "impairing the obligation of contracts." Marshall held that despite the fraud, the original land grant constituted an unbreakable legal contract.

Out of the political limelight since the Burr trial in 1807, the Court was thrust back into it by two controversial decisions in 1819. The first involved Dartmouth College and the attempt by the New Hampshire legislature to amend its charter in the direction of greater public control over this private institution. In *Dartmouth College v. Woodward,* the Court ruled that Dartmouth's original royal charter of 1769 was a contract protected by the Constitution. Therefore, the state of New Hampshire could not alter the charter without the prior consent of the college. By sanctifying charters, or acts of incorporation, as contracts, the Court prohibited states from interfering with the rights and privileges they had bestowed on private corporations.

The second important decision in 1819, *McCulloch v. Maryland,* rested on a positive assertion of national power over the states. The case involved the Bank of the United States. Many state bankers were jealous of the privileges of the national bank, a feeling shared by legislators who viewed the bank's branches as an infringement on the states' economic sovereignty. In 1818, the Maryland legislature placed a heavy tax on the branch of the Bank of the United States established in Baltimore (and on all other banks in the state established without legislative authority). James McCulloch, the cashier of the Baltimore branch, refused to pay the tax. This set up a test case that involved two fundamental legal issues: Was the bank itself constitutional? And could a state tax federal property within its borders?

A unanimous Court, in language similar to but even more sweeping than that used by Alexander Hamilton in the 1790s, upheld the constitutional authority of Congress to charter a national bank and thereby regulate the nation's currency and finances. As long as the end was legitimate "within the scope of the Constitution," Congress had full power to use any means not expressly forbidden by the Constitution to achieve that end. As for Maryland's claim of a constitutional right to tax a federal agency, Marshall stressed that "the power to tax involves the power to destroy." Surely, he reasoned, when the people of the United States ratified the Constitution, they did not intend the federal government to be controlled by the states or rendered powerless by state action. Here was the boldest statement to date of the loose, or "implied powers," interpretation of the Constitution.

Toward a Continental Empire

Marshall's legal nationalism paralleled the diplomatic nationalism of John Quincy Adams, secretary of state from 1817 to 1825. A former Federalist and the son of the second president, Adams broke with the party over its refusal to support an expansionist policy and held several diplomatic posts under the Madison administration. Convinced in his Puritan soul that God and nature had ordained that America stretch from the Atlantic to the Pacific as a beacon of liberty to the world, Adams used whatever tactics were necessary to realize that vision. Adams shrewdly exploited Britain's desire for friendly and profitable relations after the War of 1812. The British wanted access to U.S. cotton and foodstuffs in exchange for manufactured goods and investment capital. The United States wanted more trading opportunities in the British Empire and a free hand to deal with Spain's disintegrating empire in the Americas.

The **Rush-Bagot Agreement** of 1817 signaled the new pattern of Anglo-American cooperation. The agreement strictly limited naval armaments on the Great Lakes, thus effectively demilitarizing the border with Canada. The **Anglo-American Accords** of the following year resolved several issues left hanging after the war. The British once again recognized U.S. fishing rights off Labrador and Newfoundland, a concession that was of great importance to New England. The boundary of the Louisiana Territory abutting Canada was set at the 49th parallel, and both nations agreed to the joint occupation of Oregon, the territory in the Pacific Northwest that lay west of the Rocky Mountains.

Having secured the northern flank of the United States, Adams was now free to deal with the South and West. Adams

As Secretary of State, John Quincy Adams was unrelenting in his pursuit of a continental empire for the United States.

wanted all of Florida and an undisputed American window on the Pacific. The adversary here was Spain. Much weaker than it had been in the eighteenth century and struggling to suppress independence movements in its South American possessions, Spain resorted to delaying tactics in trying to hold off the tenacious Adams. Negotiations remained deadlocked until Andrew Jackson gave Adams the leverage he needed.

In March 1818, Jackson led his troops across the border into Spanish Florida. He destroyed encampments of the Seminole Indians, seized two Spanish forts, and executed two British subjects on the grounds that they were selling arms to the Seminoles for raids on the Alabama-Georgia frontier. Despite later protestations to the contrary, Jackson had probably exceeded his orders. He might well have been censured by the Monroe administration had not Adams supported him, telling Spain that Jackson was defending U.S. interests and warning that he might be unleashed again.

Spain yielded to the U.S. threat in the **Trans-Continental Treaty of 1819.** The United States annexed East Florida, and Spain recognized the prior U.S. seizures of West Florida in 1810 and 1813. Adams secured a U.S. hold on the Pacific

Coast by drawing a boundary between the Louisiana Purchase and the Spanish Southwest that ran stepwise up the Sabine, Red, and Arkansas rivers to the Continental Divide and then due west along the 42nd parallel to the Pacific (see Map 9–3). Spain renounced any claim to the Pacific Northwest; the United States in turn renounced its shaky claim to Texas under the Louisiana Purchase and assumed $5 million in Spanish debts to American citizens.

Adams's success in the Spanish negotiations turned on the British refusal to threaten war or assist Spain in the wake of Jackson's high-handed actions in Florida. Spanish possessions and the lives of two British subjects were worth little

when weighed against the economic advantages of retaining close trading ties with the United States. Moreover, Britain, like the United States, had a vested interest in developing trade with the newly independent Latin American countries. Recognizing this common interest, George Canning, the British foreign minister, proposed in August 1823 that the United States and Britain issue a joint declaration opposing any European attempt to recolonize South America or to assist Spain in regaining its colonies.

President Monroe rejected the British overture, but only at the insistence of Adams. Canning's offer had a string attached to it: a mutual pledge by the British and Americans not

MAP EXPLORATION   To explore an interactive version of this map, go to
http://www.prenhall.com/goldfield5/map9.3

MAP 9–3   The Missouri Compromise of 1820 and Territorial Treaties with Britain and Spain, 1818–1819
Treaties with Britain and Spain in 1818 and 1819 clarified and expanded the nation's boundaries. Britain accepted the 49th parallel as the boundary between Canada and the United States and agreed Trans-Mississippi West to the Oregon Country; Spain ceded Florida to the United States and agreed to a boundary stretching to the Pacific between the Louisiana Purchase territory and Spanish possessions in the Southwest. Sectional disputes over slavery led to the drawing of the Missouri Compromise line of 1820 that prohibited slavery in the Louisiana Territory north of 36° 30′.

to annex former Spanish territory. But Adams was confident that within a generation, the United States would acquire California, Texas, and perhaps Cuba as well. He wanted to maintain the maximum freedom of action for future U.S. policy and avoid any impression that America was beholden to Britain. He also wanted to cement relations with the new nations of Latin America that he had refused to recognize formally until 1822. Thus originated the most famous diplomatic statement in early American history, the **Monroe Doctrine.**

In his annual message to Congress in December 1823, Monroe declared that the Americas "are henceforth not to be considered as subjects for future colonization by any European power." In turn, Monroe pledged that the United States would not interfere in the internal affairs of European states. With its continental empire rapidly taking shape and new Latin American republics to be courted, the United States was more than willing to proclaim a special position for itself as the guardian of New World liberties.

The Breakdown of Unity

For all the intensity with which he pursued his continental vision, John Quincy Adams worried in early 1819 that "the greatest danger of this union was in the overgrown extent of its territory, combining with the slavery question." His words were prophetic. A sectional crisis flared in 1819 over slavery and its expansion when the territory of Missouri sought admission to the Union as a slave state. Simultaneously, a financial panic ended postwar prosperity and crystallized regional discontent over banking and tariff policies. Party unity cracked under these pressures, and each region backed its own presidential candidate in the wide-open election of 1824.

The Panic of 1819

From 1815 to 1818, Americans enjoyed a wave of postwar prosperity. European markets were starved for U.S. goods after a generation of war and trade restrictions, so farmers and planters expanded production and brought new land into cultivation. The availability of public land in the West on easy terms of credit sparked a speculative frenzy, and land sales soared. State banks and, worse yet, the Bank of the United States fed the speculation by making loans in the form of bank notes far in excess of their hard-currency reserves. Before the bubble burst, cotton prices doubled to 30 cents a pound, real-estate values became wildly inflated, and the money Westerners owed the federal government for the purchase of public lands rose to $21 million, an amount greater than the value of all western farm goods.

European markets for U.S. cotton and food supplies returned to normal by late 1818. In January 1819, cotton prices sank in England, and the Panic of 1819 was on. Cotton was the most valuable U.S. export, and expected returns from the staple were the basis for an intricate credit network anchored in Britain. The fall in cotton prices triggered a credit contraction that soon engulfed the overextended U.S. economy. Commodity prices fell across the board, and real-estate values collapsed, especially in and around western cities.

A sudden shift in policy by the Bank of the United States virtually guaranteed that the economic downturn would settle into a depression. The Bank stopped all loans, called in all debts, and refused to honor drafts drawn on its branches in the South and West. Hardest hit by these policies were farmers and businessmen in the West, who had mortgaged their economic futures. Bankruptcies mushroomed as creditors forced the liquidation of farms and real estate. For westerners, the Bank of the United States now became "the Monster," a ruthless institution controlled by eastern aristocrats who callously destroyed the hopes of farmers.

Southern resentment over the hard times brought on by low cotton prices focused on the tariff. Planters charged that the Tariff of 1816 unfairly raised their costs and amounted to an unconstitutional tax levied for the sole benefit of northern manufacturers. Unreconstructed Jeffersonians, now known as the Old Republicans, spearheaded a sharp reaction against the South's flirtation with nationalist policies in the postwar period by demanding a return to strict states'-rights doctrines.

The Missouri Compromise

Until 1819, slavery was not a major divisive issue in U.S. politics. The Northwest Ordinance of 1787, which banned slavery in federal territories north of the Ohio River, and the Southwest Ordinance of 1790, which permitted slavery south of the Ohio, represented a compromise that had allowed slavery in areas where climate and soil conditions favored slave-based agriculture. What was unforeseen in the 1780s, however, was the explosive demand for slave-produced cotton generated by the English textile industry in the early nineteenth century (see Chapter 11). At the republic's founding in 1787, slavery was identified with the declining tobacco economy of the South Atlantic states, and many Americans felt, perhaps wishfully, that the institution would gradually wither away.

Despite the prohibition of the African slave trade in 1807 (under the sectional compromise of 1787 this was the first year in which Congress could exercise this power), all hopes for the natural death of slavery were gone by 1819. Kentucky, Tennessee, Louisiana, Mississippi, and Alabama had all been added to the Union as slave states since 1787. Florida had just been annexed and surely would be another slave state. A thriving cotton market was underwriting slavery's expansion across the South, and even Missouri, a portion of the Louisiana Purchase that northerners initially assumed would be inhospitable to slavery, had fallen under the political control of slaveholders.

The Missouri issue increased long-simmering northern resentment over the spread of slavery and the southern dominance of national affairs under the Virginia presidents. In February 1819, James Tallmadge, a Republican congressman from New York, introduced an amendment in the House mandating a ban on future slave imports and a program of gradual emancipation as preconditions for the admission of Missouri as a state. Missourians, as well as southerners in general, rejected the Tallmadge Amendment. The states, they argued, had absolute sovereignty in the drafting of their constitutions, and any attempt by Congress to set conditions for statehood was unconstitutional. Nonetheless, a solid phalanx of northern congressmen supported the amendment.

Without a two-party system in which each party had to compromise to protect its interests, voting followed sectional lines. The amendment passed in the northern-controlled House, but it was repeatedly blocked in the Senate, which was evenly divided between free and slave states. The debates were heated, and southerners spoke openly of secession if Missouri were denied admission as a slave state.

The stalemate over Missouri persisted into the next session of Congress. Finally, Speaker of the House Henry Clay engineered a compromise in March 1820. Congress put no restrictions on slavery in Missouri, and the admission of Missouri as a slave state was balanced by the admission of Maine (formerly part of Massachusetts) as a free state. In return for their concession on Missouri, northern congressmen demanded a prohibition on slavery in the remainder of the Louisiana Purchase north of the 36°30′ parallel, the southern boundary of Missouri (see Map 9–3). With the **Missouri Compromise,** the Louisiana Purchase was closed to slavery in the future, except for the Arkansas Territory and what would become the Indian Territory of Oklahoma. The compromise almost unraveled when Missouri submitted a constitution the following November that required the state legislature to bar the entry of free black people. This mandate violated the guarantee in the U.S. Constitution that "the citizens of each State shall be entitled to all privileges and immunities of citizens in the several States." Missouri's restrictionist policy obviously denied African American citizens the constitutional right to move from one state to any other state. Southerners were quick to point out, however, that free states as well as slave states already restricted the right of free black people to vote or to serve in the militia.

The nearly universal acceptance by white Americans of second-class citizenship for free black Americans permitted Clay to dodge the issue. Missouri's constitution was accepted with the proviso that it "shall never be construed" to discriminate against citizens in other states. With these meaningless words, the Missouri Compromise was salvaged. By sacrificing the claims of free black citizens for equal treatment, the Union survived its first great sectional crisis over slavery.

The Missouri crisis made white southerners aware that they were now a political minority within the Union. More rapid population growth in the North had reduced south-

ern representation in the House to just over 40 percent. Of greater concern was the crystallization in Congress of a northern majority array against the expansion of slavery. Southern threats of secession died out in the aftermath of the Missouri Compromise, but it was an open question whether the sectional settlement really solved the intertwined issues of slavery and expansion or merely sidestepped them for a day of final reckoning.

The Election of 1824

The election of 1820 made Monroe, like both his Republican predecessors, a two-term president. The Federalists were too weak to run a candidate, and although Monroe won all but one of the electoral votes, Republican unity was more apparent than real. Voters had no choice in 1820, and without two-party competition, no outlets existed for expressing popular dissatisfaction with the Republicans. Instead, the Republicans split into factions as they began jockeying almost immediately for the election of 1824 (see Map 9–4).

Monroe had no obvious successor, and five candidates competed to replace him. All of them were nominal Republicans, and three were members of his cabinet. Secretary of War John C. Calhoun soon dropped out. He

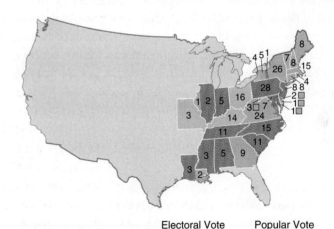

	Electoral Vote (%)	Popular Vote (%)
Andrew Jackson (Republican)	99 (38)	153,544 (43)
JOHN QUINCY ADAMS (Republican)	**84 (32)**	**108,740 (31)**
William H. Crawford (Republican)	41 (16)	46,618 (13)
Henry Clay (Republican)	37 (14)	47,136 (13)

MAP 9–4   The Election of 1824
The regional appeal of each of the four presidential candidates in the election of 1824 prevented any candidate from receiving a majority of the electoral vote. Consequently, and as set forth in the Constitution, the House of Representatives now had to choose the president from the three leading candidates. Its choice was John Quincy Adams.

FROM THEN TO NOW

The Lewis and Clark Expedition in Their World and Ours

In its day the Lewis and Clark expedition was as daring a venture as space exploration is today. The expedition, which began in 1803 and ended in 1806, brought Americans their first knowledge of the vast territory they had secured in the Louisiana Purchase. The West described by Lewis and Clark was a land of change, diversity, and abundance. They catalogued 122 animals and 178 plants that were new to American science. Traveling through present-day South Dakota in September 1804, Lewis observed "Vast herds of Buffaloe deer elk and Antilopes…feeding in every direction as far as the eye of the observer could reach." Clark wrote that the numbers of salmon in the Columbia River were "almost inconceivable." Before the end of the nineteenth century, the great herds of grazing animals in the West and the carnivores that stalked them had nearly been wiped out by government-sponsored extermination programs. Most of the vast prairie landscape that Lewis and Clark crossed has disappeared, replaced by uniform fields of row-to-row crops. The prairie grasslands were once the largest ecosystem in North America, a patchwork of native grasses and herbs that supported a wide diversity of habitats.

Corn fields now stretch across the plains crossed by Lewis and Clark.

The journals of Lewis and Clark provide a baseline from which to gauge how much the West has changed, putting Americans in a better position to preserve what is left and even restore some of what has been lost.

■ What successful restoration programs have been undertaken in the modern trans-Mississippi West?

The Amerindian Sacajawea was an indispensable guide for Lewis and Clark on their famed expedition.

PEARSON myhistorylab

From Then to Now Online

9-1 Lewis and Clark, *Journals of Expedition*, 1805. Descriptions of what they saw.

9-2 Arrapooish, *Statement to fur trader*, 19th century. Impressions of a Crow chief.

9-3 Drs. Deborah E. and Frank J. Popper, *The Buffalo Commons*, 2005. Call for a National Grasslands preserve.

Global Perspectives

The U.S. Response to Independence Movements

"America...proclaimed to mankind the inextinguishable rights of human nature, and the only lawful foundations of government.... Wherever the standard of freedom and Independence has been or shall be unfurled, there will her heart, her benedictions and her prayers be. But she goes not abroad, in search of monsters to destroy.... She well knows that by once enlisting under other banners than her own, were they even the banners of foreign independence, she would involve herself beyond the power of extrication, in all the wars of interest and intrigue, of individual avarice, envy, and ambition, which assume the colors and usurp the standards of freedom. The fundamental maxims of her policy would insensibly change from *liberty to force*.... She might become the dictatress of the world. She would no longer be the ruler of her spirit.... [America's] glory is not *dominion*, but *liberty*. Her march is the march of the mind."

Drawn from the Independence Day speech of Secretary of State John Quincy Adams in 1821, these words gave classic expression to an enduring tension in America's relations with the outside world: Should the United States promote liberty and independence by the force of its example or the force of its arms? Adams was responding to political opponents who were demanding that the United States involve itself in the independence movements in Latin America and Greece. Adams refused to do so. The United States had no vital interests at stake in Greece, and aid to the rebels or premature recognition of the government they were struggling to form carried the risk of embroiling the United States in a conflict with their enemies, the Turks and Russians. Moreover, direct involvement in a European affair would set a dangerous precedent that Europeans could cite to intervene in the Western Hemisphere, where Adams wanted the United States to have a free hand.

As for the Latin American revolutionaries, Adams noted their disregard of the civil rights for which Americans had contended during the Revolution. He had no doubt that the independence movements to the south would eventually succeed, but he believed that the United States could best support them and the cause of liberty by championing and vindicating its own freedom and independence. To intervene abroad in an effort to transform foreign societies was to endanger liberty at home.

At the insistence of President Monroe, Adams extended diplomatic recognition to the new Latin American nations in 1822. In so doing, he insisted that the United States would recognize only governments that promised to adhere to all of their international obligations. Recognition, he stressed, carried no moral approval. This was the recognition policy followed by the U.S. government for ninety years, until President Woodrow Wilson committed it to a policy of liberal interventionism abroad.

■ What is your position on the stand taken by Adams against the involvement of the United States in wars of liberty and independence?

---

preferred to accept a nomination as vice president, confident that his turn would come in 1828. The other candidates, Secretary of the Treasury William Crawford from Georgia, Secretary of State John Quincy Adams from Massachusetts, Henry Clay from Kentucky, and Andrew Jackson from Tennessee, each had a strong regional following. As the Republican party fragmented, sectional loyalties were replacing partisan allegiances.

The early favorite was Crawford. He was the "official" party nominee in the sense that he had received the support of the congressional caucus, but most Republicans had boycotted the caucus, by now a useless relic of past party unity. Clay, Jackson, and Adams were nominated by their state legislatures. None of the candidates ran on a platform, but Crawford was identified with states' rights, and Clay and Adams with centralized government. Clay in particular was associated with the national bank, protective tariffs, and federally funded internal improvements, a package of federal subsidies he called the **American System.** Jackson took no stand on any of the issues.

Jackson's noncommittal stance turned out to be a great asset. It helped him to project the image of a military hero, fresh from the people, who was unsullied by any connection with Washington politicians, whom the public associated with hard times and sectional controversies. He was the highest vote-getter (43 percent of the popular vote), but none of the four candidates had a majority in the electoral college.

As in 1800, the election was thrown into the House of Representatives. Each state had one vote. Clay, who had received the fewest electoral votes, was eliminated. Crawford had suffered a debilitating stroke and was no longer a viable candidate. Thus it came down to Adams or Jackson. Anxious to undercut Jackson, his chief rival in the West, Clay used his influence as speaker of the House to line up support for Adams, a fellow advocate of a strong centralized government. Adams won the election, and he immediately named Clay as his secretary of state, the office traditionally viewed as a stepping-stone to the presidency. Jackson and his followers were outraged. They smelled a "corrupt bargain" in which Clay had bargained away the presidency to the highest bidder. Vowing revenge, they began building a new party that would usher in a more democratic era of mass-based politics.

Conclusion

In 1800, the Republicans were an untested party whose rise to power frightened many Federalists into predicting the end of the Union and constitutional government. The Federalists were correct in sensing that their days of power had passed, but they underestimated the ideological flexibility the Republicans would reveal once in office and the imaginative ways in which Jefferson and his successors would wield executive power to expand the size of the original Union. Far from being anarchists and demagogues, the Republicans were shrewd empire builders astute enough to add to their base of political support in the South and West. They also paved the way for the nation to evolve as a democratic republic rather than the more aristocratic republic preferred by the Federalists.

Although foreign-policy issues leading up to the War of 1812 kept the Federalists alive and even briefly revived the party, the British posed the greatest test of Republican leadership. The Republicans chose war rather than surrender their claims of U.S. rights. Jackson's victory at the Battle of New Orleans ended the war in a burst of U.S. glory, and the Federalists were swept aside by the postwar surge of nationalism.

By the mid-1820s, the Republicans were about to join the Federalists as political dinosaurs. With no Federalist threat to enforce party discipline, the Republicans lost their organizational strength. Embracing economic nationalism after the war made the party's original focus on states' rights all but meaningless. Ideologically and organizationally adrift, the party split into regional coalitions in the wake of the Missouri controversy and the panic of 1819. But before it dissolved, the party left as its most enduring legacy the foundations of a continental empire.

Review Questions

1. What changes did the Republicans bring to the federal government? How did their policies differ from those of their Federalist predecessors?

2. Why were the Republicans so intent on expanding the boundaries of the United States, and why did the Federalists oppose an expansionist program?

3. What factors accounted for the Federalists' inability to regain national power after they lost the election of 1800?

4. What external and internal factors drew the United States into war against Britain? Could the war have been avoided?

5. What accounted for the difficulties of the United States in waging the War of 1812, and why was the war widely viewed as a great U.S. victory? How did the war lead to an increasing pattern of diplomatic cooperation between the United States and Britain?

6. Why was Rosalie Calvert so critical of the Republican party and U.S. entry into the War of 1812? To what extent would New England Federalists have shared her views?

7. What explains the upsurge of nationalism that underlay the Era of Good Feelings? Why were the Republicans unable to maintain their party unity after 1819?

8. What accounted for the noninvolvement of the United States in the revolutionary movements in Latin America and the long delay in extending formal recognition to the new governments established there?

Key Terms

American System (p. 243)

Anglo-American Accords (p. 238)

Chesapeake Incident (p. 229)

Dartmouth College v. Woodward (p. 237)

Embargo Act of 1807 (p. 230)

Era of Good Feelings (p. 236)

Fletcher v. Peck (p. 237)

Ghent, Treaty of (p. 235)

Impressment (p. 229)

Marbury v. Madison (p. 225)

McCulloch v. Maryland (p. 237)

Missouri Compromise (p. 241)

Monroe Doctrine (p. 240)

New Orleans, Battle of (p. 236)

Pan-Indian resistance movement (p. 230)

Recommended Reading

Allgor, Catherine. *Parlor Politics: In Which the Ladies of Washington Help Build a City and a Government* (1999). A witty and engagingly written work that describes how women exercised political power in the early republic.

Hickey, Donald R. *The War of 1812: A Forgotten Conflict* (1989). Breaks no new ground, but presents a complete and very readable account of all aspects of the war.

McCoy, Drew R. *The Elusive Republic: Political Economy in Jeffersonian America* (1980). A gracefully written study that examines how attitudes on economic development influenced Jeffersonian notions of republicanism and were central to the Republicans' stand on free trade.

Onuf, Peter S., ed. *Jeffersonian Legacies* (1993). A collection of essays that presents the latest thinking on the extraordinary range of Jefferson's activities.

Vidal, Gore. *Burr* (1973). A superbly entertaining novel that satirically brings to life the leading personalities of Jefferson's America.

Weeks, William Earl. *John Quincy Adams and American Global Empire* (1992). Presents Adams as a cynical, tough-minded negotiator utterly driven by his vision of an American continental empire. Though questioning his tactics, confirms Adams's reputation as America's greatest secretary of state.

Where to Learn More

■ **Fort McHenry National Monument, Baltimore, Maryland.** This historic site preserves the fort that was the focal point of the British attack on Baltimore and contains a museum with materials on the battle and the writing of the Star-Spangled Banner. For the military history of the fort and the archaeological work at the site, see www.nps.gov/fomc/archeology/overview.html

■ **Tallgrass Prairie National Preserve, Cottonwood Falls, Kansas.** This site preserves one of the last significant expanses of the once vast tallgrass ecosystem that Lewis and Clark entered at the beginning of their expedition. For information on visits and schedule of events, see http://nps.gov/archive/tapr/home.htm

■ **Tippecanoe Battlefield Museum, Battle Ground, Indiana.** This museum includes artifacts from the Indian and white settlement of Indiana and visual materials on the Battle of Tippecanoe of 1811. The museum's website at www.tcha.mus.in.us/battlefield.htm includes an account of the battle and its aftermath.

■ **Monticello, Charlottesville, Virginia.** The architecturally unique home of Thomas Jefferson and the headquarters for his plantation serves as a museum that provides insights into Jefferson's varied interests. Information on educational programs and upcoming events at Monticello, as well as the new Jefferson Library in Charlottesville, can be found at www.monticello.org

■ **Perry's Victory and International Peace Memorial, Put-in-Bay, Ohio.** At the site of Perry's decisive victory on Lake Erie in 1813 now stands a museum that depicts the role of the Old Northwest in the War of 1812. For a printable travel guide and information on the new visitor center, see www.nps.gov/pevi

Study Resources

For study resources for this chapter, go to www.myhistorylab.com and choose *The American Journey*. You will find a wealth of study and review material for this chapter, including pre- and post-tests, customized study plan, key term review flash cards, interactive map and document activities, and documents for analysis.

This early nineteenth-century painting of a polling place in Philadelphia illustrates the growing involvement of ordinary Americans in politics. As suffrage broadened and more Americans came out to vote, elections became more heated and emotional.

John L. Krimmel, Painting (1786–1821), Oil on Canvas, H. 16 3/8″ × W. 25 5/8″. (AN: 59.131) Courtesy, Winterthur Museum, *Election Day in Philadelphia* (1815) - DETAIL.

The Jacksonian Era 10
1824–1845

Newport, New Hampshire

September, 1828

Wherever a person may chance to be in company, he will hear nothing but politicks discussed. In the ballroom, or at the dinner table, in the Stagecoach & in the tavern; even the social chitchat of the tea table must yield up to the everlasting subject.

How many friendships are broken up! With what rancor the political war is carried on between the editorial corps! To what meanness[,] vulgarity & abuse is that champion of liberty, in proper hands, the press prostituted! With what lies and scandal does the columns of almost every political paper abound! I blush for my country when I see such things, & I often tremble with apprehension that our Constitution will not long withstand the current which threatens to overwhelm it. Our government is so based that an honest difference between American citizens must always exist. But the rancorous excitement which now threatens our civil liberties and a dissolution of this Union does not emanate from an honest difference of opinion, but from a determination of an unholy league to trample down an Administration, be it ever so pure, & be its acts ever so just. It must not be. There is a kind Providence that overlooks the destinies of this Nation and will not suffer it to be overthrown by a party of aspiring office seekers & political demagogues.

Benjamin B. French

Donald B. Cole and John J. McDonough, eds., *Witness to the Young Republic: A Yankee's Journal, 1828–1870* (Hanover, NH: University Press of New England, 1989), pp. 15–16.

Benjamin Brown French, a young editor and county clerk in Newport, New Hampshire, penned these words in his journal in September 1828. Like most other Americans, he was amazed, indeed, shocked, by the intense, seemingly all-pervasive partisanship stirred up in the presidential election of 1828 between Andrew Jackson and John Quincy Adams. Whether measured by the vulgar personal attacks launched by a partisan press, the amount of whiskey and beef consumed at political barbecues, or the huge increase in voter turnout, this election marked the entrance of ordinary Americans onto the political stage.

The sense of shock soon wore off for French. The son of a wealthy Federalist lawyer with whom he was always at odds, French broke with his father at the age of 25, when he married without his permission. With no income, job, or family support, he now began to make a business out of law, politics, and journalism. In so doing he was part of the first generation of professional politicians, young men who compensated for their lack of social connections and family wealth by turning to politics. The partisanship that French found so disturbing in 1828 quickly became the basis of his livelihood. After rejecting his father's politics by joining the Democrats in 1831, he spent most of his subsequent years as a political officeholder in Washington, holding a variety of appointive jobs until his death in 1870.

What made French's career possible was the ongoing democratization of U.S. politics in the early decades of the nineteenth century. The number and potential power of the voters expanded, and professional politicians realized that party success now depended on reaching and organizing this enlarged electorate. Men like French, working for the party, could help them do this. The **Jacksonian Democrats,** named for their leader, Andrew Jackson, were the first party to learn this fundamental lesson. Trumpeting Andrew Jackson as the friend of the common man and the foe of aristocratic privilege, they won a landslide victory in 1828 and held national power through the 1830s. The Jacksonians promised to protect farmers and workers from the monied elite, whom they portrayed as the enemies of equality and the corruptors of public morality.

By the mid-1830s, the Whig party had formed in opposition to the Jacksonians. The Whigs offered an ordered vision of American progress and liberty, anchored in the use of governmental power to expand economic opportunities and promote morality. By embracing electoral techniques of popular appeal first used by the Democrats, the Whigs captured the presidency in 1840. Their triumph heralded a new party system, one based on massive voter turnouts and two-party competition in every state.

The luckless Whigs failed to capitalize on their victory, however. Their newly elected president, William Henry Harrison, died shortly after entering office, and Vice President John Tyler, his successor, blocked the Whigs' economic program. Spurned by the Whigs as a traitor, Tyler then reopened the explosive question of slavery and territorial expansion by pushing to annex the independent republic of Texas, where slavery was legal.

The Democrats regained power in 1844 by skillfully exploiting the Texas issue, but they set an ominous prece-

CHRONOLOGY

1826	Disappearance of William Morgan.
1827	Emergence of the Anti-Masons, the first third party.
1828	Andrew Jackson elected president.
	John C. Calhoun writes *The South Carolina Exposition and Protest*.
1830	Congress passes the Indian Removal Act.
	Greek independence established.
	July Revolution in France.
	Revolutions break out in Belgium, Poland, and Italian states.
1831	William Lloyd Garrison starts publication of the *Liberator*.
	Nat Turner leads a slave uprising in Virginia.
1832	Jackson vetoes bill for rechartering the Second Bank of the United States; Bank War begins.
	South Carolina nullifies the Tariffs of 1828 and 1832.
	Jackson reelected.
	Election reform bill passes in Britain.
1833	Congress passes the Force Act and the Compromise Tariff.
	American Anti-Slavery Society established.
1834	Whig party begins to organize.
1836	Texas War of Independence and establishment of the Republic of Texas.
	Congress passes first gag rule on abolitionist petitions.
	Van Buren elected president.
1837	Panic of 1837 sets off a depression.
1840	Independent Treasury Act passes.
	William Henry Harrison elected first Whig president.
1841	John Tyler succeeds to presidency on death of Harrison.
1842	United States and Britain sign the Webster-Ashburton Treaty.
1844	James K. Polk elected president.
	Gag rule repealed.
1845	Texas admitted to the Union.

dent. The debate over the expansion of slavery became embedded in the political system, and the greatest strength of the mass-based parties, their ability to tap and unleash popular emotions, now became their greatest weakness. The slavery issue began to take on a life of its own beyond the control of party leaders. The seeds of the Civil War were being sown.

The Egalitarian Impulse

Political democracy, defined as the majority rule of white males, was far from complete in early nineteenth-century America. Acting on the belief that only property owners with a stake in society should have a voice in governing it, the landed and commercial elites of the Revolutionary era erected legal barriers against the full expression of majority sentiments. These barriers, property requirements for voting and officeholding, the prevalence of appointed over elected offices, and the overrepresentation of older and wealthier regions in state legislatures, came under increasing attack after 1800 and were all but eliminated by the 1820s.

As politics opened to mass participation, popular styles of religious leadership and worship emerged in a broad reaction to the formalism and elitism of the dominant Protestant churches. The same egalitarian impulse drove these twin democratic revolutions, and both represented an empowerment of the common man. Popular movements now spoke his language and appealed to his quest for republican equality. (Women would have to wait longer.)

The Extension of White Male Democracy

In 1789, Congress set the pay of representatives and senators at $6 a day plus travel expenses. By 1816, inflation had so eroded this salary that many government clerks earned more than members of Congress. Thus Congress thought itself prudent and justified when it voted itself a hefty raise to $1,500 a year. The public thought otherwise. In a resolution typical of the popular response, the citizens of Saratoga, New York, accused Congress of "wanton extravagance" and "a daring and profligate trespass against...the *morals* of the *Republic*."

So sharp was the reaction against the Salary Act of 1816 that 70 percent of the members of Congress were turned out of office at the next election. Chastised congressmen quickly repealed the salary increase. As Richard M. Johnson of Kentucky noted, "The presumption is, that the people are always right."

The uproar over the Salary Act marked a turning point in the transition from the deferential politics of the Federalist–Republican period to the egalitarianism of the coming Jacksonian era. The public would no longer passively accept decisions handed down by local elites or established national figures. Individual states, not the federal government, defined who could vote. Six states, Indiana, Mississippi, Illinois, Alabama, Missouri, and Maine, entered the Union between 1816 and 1821, and none of them required voters to own property. Meanwhile, proponents of suffrage liberalization won major victories in the older states. Constitutional conventions in Connecticut in 1818 and Massachusetts and New York in 1821 eliminated property requirements for voting. By the end of the 1820s, near universal white male suffrage was the norm everywhere except Rhode Island, Virginia, and Louisiana.

Extending the suffrage and democratic reform.

Broadening the suffrage was part of a general democratization of political structures and procedures in the state governments. Representation in most state legislatures was made more equal by giving more seats to newer, rapidly growing regions. States removed or reduced property qualifications for officeholding. The selection of local officials and, in many cases, judges was taken out of the hands of governors and executive councils and given to the voters. With the end of oral, or "stand-up," voting, the act of casting a ballot became private and freer from the intimidation of influential neighbors. Written ballots were the norm by the 1820s. Most significant for national politics, voters acquired the power to choose presidential electors. In 1800, only two states had provided for a statewide popular vote in presidential elections. By 1824, most did so, and by 1832 only South Carolina still clung to the practice of having the state legislature choose the electors (see Map 10–1).

Several currents swelled the movement for democratic reform. Limiting voting rights to those who owned landed property seemed increasingly elitist when economic changes were producing new classes—workers, clerks, and small tradesmen—whose livelihoods were not tied directly to the land. At the same time, the middling and lower ranks of society demanded the ballot and access to offices to protect themselves from the commercial and manufacturing interests that benefited most from economic change. Propertyless laborers in Richmond argued in an 1829 petition that "virtue [and] intelligence are not among the products of the soil. Attachment to property, often a sordid sentiment, is not to be confounded with the sacred flame of patriotism."

Of greatest importance, however, was the incessant demand that all white men be treated equally. Seth Luther, an advocate for workers' rights, insisted that "we wish nothing, but those equal rights, which were designed for us all." The logical extension of the ideology of the American Revolution, with its leveling attacks against kings and aristocrats, this demand for equality made republicanism by the 1820s synonymous with simple majority rule. If any white male was the equal of any other, regardless of wealth or property holdings, then only the will of the majority could be the measure of a republican government.

The disfranchisement of free blacks and women.

As political opportunities expanded for white males, they shrank for women and free black people. In the state constitutions of the Revolutionary era, free black males who met the minimum property requirements usually had the same voting rights as white males. New Jersey's constitution of 1776 was exceptional in also granting the suffrage to single women and widows who owned property. By the early 1800s, race and gender began to replace wealth and status as the basis for defining the limits of political participation. Thus, in 1807 New Jersey's new constitution broadened suffrage by requiring only a simple taxpaying qualification to vote, but it also denied the ballot to women and free black men. In state after state, the same constitutional conventions that embraced universal suffrage for white men deprived black men of the vote or burdened them with special property qualifications. Moreover, none of the ten states that entered the Union from 1821 to 1861 allowed black suffrage. African Americans protested in vain. "Foreigners and aliens to the government and laws," complained black New Yorkers in 1837, "strangers to our institutions, are permitted to flock to this land and in a few years are endowed with all the privileges of citizens; but we native born Americans…are most of us shut out." By the 1850s, black males could vote only in certain New England states.

Advocates of greater democratization explicitly argued that only white males had the intelligence and love of liberty to be entrusted with political rights. Women, they said, were too weak and emotional, black people too lazy and lascivious. In denouncing distinctions drawn on property as artificial and demeaning, the white egalitarians simultaneously erected new distinctions based on race and sex that were supposedly natural and hence immutable. Thus personal liberties were now to be guarded not by propertied gentlemen but by all white men, whose equality ultimately rested on assumptions of their shared natural superiority over women and nonwhite people.

The Popular Religious Revolt

In religion as well as politics, ordinary Americans demanded a greater voice in the early nineteenth century. Insurgent religious movements rejected the formalism and traditional Calvinism of the Congregational and Presbyterian churches, the dominant Protestant denominations in Washington's America. In a blaze of fervor known as the **Second Great Awakening** (recalling the Great Awakening of colonial America), evangelical sects led by the Methodists and Baptists radically transformed the religious landscape between 1800 and 1840. A more popularly rooted Christianity moved outward and downward as it spread across frontier areas and converted marginalized and common folk. By 1850, one in three Americans was a regular churchgoer, a dramatic increase since 1800.

The Baptists and Methodists, both spinning off numerous splinter groups, grew spectacularly and were the largest religious denominations by the 1820s. The key to their success was their ability to give religious expression to the popular impulse behind democratic reform. Especially in the

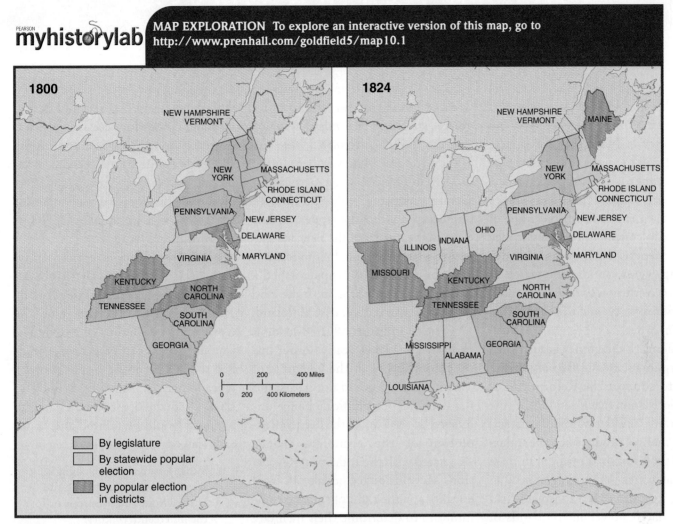

myhistorylab   MAP EXPLORATION To explore an interactive version of this map, go to
http://www.prenhall.com/goldfield5/map10.1

MAP 10–1   Methods of Electing Presidential Electors, 1800 and 1824
The Constitution permits each state legislature to choose the method of electing presidential electors for its state. In 1800 the legislatures in most states appointed the electors. By 1824 most states had adopted more democratic systems in which electors pledged to specific presidential candidates were selected by popular vote in statewide elections.

Data Source: U.S. Bureau of the Census, *Historical Statistics of the United States, Colonial Times to 1957* (1960), p. 681.

backcountry of the South and West, where the first revivals occurred, itinerant preachers reshaped religion to fit the needs and values of ordinary Americans.

Evangelical Christianity emphasized personal, heartfelt experience that would produce a spiritual rebirth. Preaching became a form of theater, as preacher and audience acted out scenes of damnation and salvation. The emotional force unleashed at the mass revivals known as camp meetings astounded observers. "The scene that then presented itself to my mind was indescribable," recalled James Finley of the camp meeting at Cane Ridge, Kentucky, in 1801. "At one time I saw at least five hundred swept down in a moment, as if a battery of a thousand guns had been opened upon them, and then immediately followed shrieks and shouts that rent the very heavens."

The evangelical religion of the traveling preachers was democratic in its populist rejection of traditional religious canons and its encouragement of organizational forms that gave a voice to popular culture. Salvation was no longer simply bestowed by an implacable God, as taught by the Calvinist doctrine of individual predestination (see Chapter 1). Ordinary people could now actively choose salvation, and this possibility was exhilarating. "Why, then, I can be saved!" exclaimed Jesse Lee upon hearing a Methodist preacher in Massachusetts. "I have been taught that only a part of the race could be saved, but if this man's singing be true, all may be saved." Evangelical churches bound the faithful into tightly knit communities that expressed and enforced local values and standards of conduct. Their hymns borrowed melodies from popular music and were accompanied by fiddles and other folk instruments.

Evangelicalism and minority rights.   Evangelicalism was a religion of the common people, and it appealed especially to

An Age of Reform

"Turn where we may—within, around—the voice of great events is proclaiming to us, 'Reform, that you may preserve.' Now, therefore…take counsel…of the signs of this most portentous time…. The danger is terrible. The time is short. If this Bill should be rejected, I pray to God that none of those who concur in rejecting it may ever remember their votes with unavailing regret, amidst the wreck of laws, the confusion of ranks, the spoliation of property, and the dissolution of social order."

Thomas Babington Macaulay used this argument in the British Parliament to support the Reform Bill of 1832, legislation that extended the vote to Britain's industrial middle classes. Social changes produced by the Industrial Revolution had resulted in massive inequities and corruption in an electoral system that traditionally had consolidated power in the hands of wealthy conservative landowners. Events on the European continent gave greater weight to Macaulay's warning that England must reform or face revolution at home. The July Revolution of 1830 in France had deposed a conservative king and replaced him with one acceptable to the upper middle class. In the same year the Belgians succeeded in establishing their independence, but Austrian troops crushed a nationalist revolution in Italy, and Russian troops did likewise in Poland.

The revolutions of 1830 made it clear that the conservative order imposed on Europe at the Congress of Vienna in 1815 could not withstand the demands for political change unleashed by the wars of the French Revolution or the economic change associated with the Industrial Revolution. Revolutionary ideals of legal equality and the right of cultural communities to determine their own fate as independent nations intersected with demands by the new middle and working classes for access to political power. The result was a continuing challenge to the status quo that periodically erupted into uprisings and revolutions. The next great wave of unrest that spilled over Europe after 1830 was the revolutions of 1848.

With the glaring exception of slavery, the United States by the 1830s was already a reformed society by the standards of Europe and the rest of the world. Liberal notions of individualism and self-improvement were wedded to mass democratic politics and a vibrant nationalism. But as long as slavery remained, America's national purpose would be tainted and tragically flawed.

■ **What lessons in establishing a republican government did the United States offer Europe in the nineteenth century?**

---

women and African Americans. The revivals converted about twice as many women as men. Excluded from most areas of public life, women found strength and comfort in the evangelical message of Christian love and equality. As the wife of a Connecticut minister explained, church membership offered women a welcome release from "being treated like beasts of burden [and] drudges of domineering masters." In the first flush of evangelical excitement, female itinerant preachers spread the gospel up and down the East Coast. By thus defying social convention, these women offered a model of independent action. Other women organized their own institutions within denominations still formally controlled by men. Women activists founded and largely directed hundreds of church-affiliated charitable societies and missionary associations.

Evangelicalism also empowered black Americans. African American Christianity experienced its first sustained growth in the generation after the Revolutionary War. As a result of their uncompromising commitment to convert slaves, the Baptists and Methodists led the way. They welcomed slaves at their revivals, encouraged black preachers, and above all else, advocated secular and spiritual equality. Many of the early Baptist and Methodist preachers directly challenged slavery. In converting to Methodism, one slave stated that "from the sermon I heard, I felt that God had made all men free and equal, and that I ought not be a slave." Perceiving in it the promise of liberty and deliverance, the slaves received the evangelical gospel in loud, joyous, and highly emotional revivals. They made it part of their own culture, fusing Christianity with folk beliefs from their African heritage.

The limits of equality. But for all its liberating appeal to women and African Americans, evangelicalism was eventually limited by race and gender in much the same way as the democratic reform movement. Denied positions of authority in white-dominated churches and resentful of white op-

The Second Great Awakening originated on the frontier. Preachers were adept at arousing emotional fervor, and women in particular responded to the evangelical message of spiritual equality open to all who would accept Christ into their lives.

Collection of the New York Historical Society, Negative # 26275.

position to integrated worship, free black northerners founded their own independent churches.

As increasing numbers of planters embraced evangelicalism after the 1820s, southern evangelicals first muted their attacks on slavery and then developed a full-blown religious defense of it based on the biblical sanctioning of human bondage. They similarly cited the Old Testament patriarchs to defend the unquestioned authority of fathers over their households, the masters of slaves, women, and children. Many popular religious sects in the North also used a particularist reading of the Bible to exalt the independence of white males at the expense of everyone else.

Whether in religion or politics, white men retained the power in Jacksonian America. Still, the Second Great Awakening removed a major intellectual barrier to political democracy. Traditional Protestant theology, whether Calvinist, Anglican, or Lutheran, viewed the mass of humanity as sinners predestined to damnation and hence was loath to accept the idea that those same sinners, by majority vote, should make crucial political decisions. In rejecting this theology, ordinary Americans made a fundamental intellectual breakthrough. "Salvation open to all" powerfully reinforced the legitimacy of "one man, one vote."

The Rise of the Jacksonians

The Jacksonian Democrats were the first party to mold and organize the democratizing impulse in popular culture. At the core of the Jacksonian appeal was the same rejection of established authority that marked the secular and religious populists. Much like the revivalists and the democratic reformers, the Jacksonians fashioned communications techniques that tapped into the hopes and fears of ordinary Americans. In so doing, they built the first mass-based party in U.S. history.

In Andrew Jackson the new **Democratic party** that formed between 1824 and 1828 had the perfect candidate for the increasingly democratic temperament of the 1820s. Born of Scots-Irish ancestry on the Carolina frontier in 1767, Jackson was a self-made product of the southern backcountry. Lacking any formal education, family connections, or inherited wealth to ease his way, he relied on his own wits and raw courage to carve out a career as a frontier lawyer and planter in Tennessee. He won fame as the military savior of the republic with his victory at the Battle of New Orleans. Conqueror of the British, the Spanish, and the Indians, all of whom had blocked frontier expansion, he achieved incredible popularity in his native South. His strengths and prejudices were those most valued by the restless, mobile Americans to whom he became a folk hero.

As a presidential candidate, Jackson's image was that of the antielitist champion of the people. "Take for your President a man from your own body, untainted by the corruption of a court and uninitiated in Cabinet secrets," urged a New Jersey Jackson convention in 1824. Jackson lost the election of 1824, but his defeat turned out to be a blessing in disguise. The wheeling and dealing in Congress that gave the presidency to John Quincy Adams enveloped his administration in a cloud of suspicion from the start. It also enhanced Jackson's appeal as the honest tribune of the people whose rightful claim to the presidency had been spurned by intriguing politicians in Washington by the "corrupt bargain" between Adams and Clay (see page 249). Moreover, the ill-fated Adams presidency virtually destroyed itself. Adams seemed frozen in an eighteenth-century past. Uncomfortable with the give and take of politics or the idea of building a coalition to support himself, Adams was out of touch with the political realities of the 1820s.

Just how out of touch was revealed when Adams delivered his first annual message to Congress in 1825. He presented a bold vision of an activist federal government promoting economic growth, social advancement, and scientific progress. Such a vision might have received a fair hearing in 1815, when postwar nationalism was in full stride. By 1825, postwar nationalism had dissolved into sectional bickering and burning resentments against banks, tariffs, and the

political establishment, which were blamed for the hard times after the Panic of 1819. The Jacksonians charged that an administration born in corruption now wanted to waste the people's money by promoting more corruption and greed. And when Adams urged Americans not "to proclaim to the world that we are palsied by the will of our constituents," the Jacksonians attacked him as an arrogant aristocrat contemptuous of the common man.

Little of Adams's program passed Congress, and his nationalist vision drove his opponents into the Jackson camp. Southern planters jumped onto the Jackson bandwagon out of fear that Adams might use federal power against slavery; westerners joined because Adams revived their suspicions of the East. The most important addition came from New York, where Martin Van Buren had built the **Albany Regency**, a tightly disciplined state political machine.

Van Buren belonged to a new breed of professional politicians. The son of a tavern keeper, he quickly grasped, as a young lawyer, how politics could open up career opportunities. The discipline and regularity of strict party organization gave him and others from the middling ranks a winning edge in competition against their social betters. In battling against the system of family-centered wealth and prestige on which politics had previously been based, Van Buren redefined parties as something good in and of themselves. Indeed, he and his followers argued that parties were indispensable instruments for the successful expression of the popular will against the dominance of elites.

State leaders such as Van Buren organized the first national campaign that relied extensively on new techniques of mass mobilization. In rallying support for Jackson against Adams in 1828, these state leaders put together chains of party-subsidized newspapers and coordinated a frantic schedule of meetings and rallies. Grassroots Jackson committees reached out to voters by knocking on their doors, pressing party literature into their hands, dispensing mass-produced medals and buttons with a likeness of Jackson, and lavishly entertaining all who would give them a hearing. Politics became a folk spectacle as torchlight parades awakened sleepy towns and political barbecues doled out whiskey and food to farmers from the surrounding countryside.

The election of 1828 centered on personalities, not issues. This in itself was a victory for Jackson's campaign managers, who proved far more skillful in the new presidential game of image making than did their Adams counterparts, now known as the National Republicans. Although each side tried to depict the other's candidate as morally unfit, the Jackson men were more in tune with public sentiment, which identified Adams's call for a strong government

To the opponents of the Jacksonians, elections had become a degrading spectacle in which conniving Democratic politicians, such as the one shown above handing a voting ticket to the stereotypical Irishman in the light coat, were corrupting the republic's political culture.

First State Election in Detroit, Michigan, 1837, c. 1837. Thomas Mickell Burnham. Gift of Mrs. Samuel T. Carson. Photograph 1991 The Detroit Institute of Arts.

This bust portrait of Jackson in uniform, issued as print during the 1832 presidential race, invokes his military image and especially his victory at New Orleans in 1815.

with special privileges for the favored few. Thus for many voters, Adams personified a discredited elite and Jackson the voice of the people.

Jackson carried every state south and west of Pennsylvania in 1828 and polled 56 percent of the popular vote (see Map 10–2). Voter turnout shot up to 55 percent from the apathetic 25 percent of 1824. Adams ran well only in New England and in commercialized areas producing goods for outside markets. Aside from the South, where he was virtually untouchable, Jackson's appeal was strongest among ordinary Americans who valued their local independence and felt threatened by outside centers of power beyond their control. He rolled up heavy majorities from Scots-Irish farmers in the Baptist–Methodist evangelical belt of the backcountry and from unskilled workers with an Irish Catholic background. To these voters, Jackson was a double hero, for he had defeated their hated British enemy and promised to do the same to the Yankee capitalists of the Northeast and all the elitist politicians. Democracy, they were convinced, had at last come to presidential politics.

Jackson's Presidency

Once in office, Jackson proved to be the most forceful and energetic president since Jefferson. Like a military chieftain tolerating no interference from his subordinates, Jackson dominated his presidency with the sheer force of his personality.

The Jacksonians had no particular program in 1828. Apart from removing Indians to areas west of the Mississippi River, Jackson's first term was notable primarily for its political infighting. Two political struggles that came to a head in 1832–1833, the Bank War and the nullification crisis, stamped the Jacksonians with a lasting party identity. By destroying the Second Bank of the United States and rejecting the attempt of South Carolina to nullify (or annul) a national tariff, Jackson firmly established the Democrats as the enemy of special privilege, the friend of the common man, and the defender of the Union. Consequently, even when Jackson stepped down in 1837, the Democrats were so identified with the interests of the people that they were able to elect Martin Van Buren, who had none of Jackson's personal magnetism or broad appeal.

Jackson's Appeal

Jackson's inauguration struck many conservatives as ushering in a vulgar new order in national affairs. A vast crowd poured into Washington to applaud the people's hero. They cheered loudly when Jackson took his oath of office and then rushed to the White House for a postinauguration reception, where they pressed in on waiters trying to serve refreshments. Bowls of liquor-laced punch went flying, and glass and china crashed to the floor as a seeming mob surged through the White House. "But it was the People's day," reported one conservative onlooker, "and the People's President and the People would

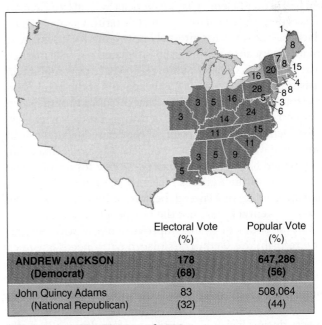

	Electoral Vote (%)	Popular Vote (%)
ANDREW JACKSON (Democrat)	**178** **(68)**	**647,286** **(56)**
John Quincy Adams (National Republican)	83 (32)	508,064 (44)

MAP 10–2   The Election of 1828
Andrew Jackson won a decisive victory in 1828 by sweeping the South and West and making major inroads in the Northeast.

rule. God grant that one day or other, the People do not put down all rule and rulers."

Although they were led by wealthy planters and entrepreneurs—hardly average Americans—the Jacksonians skillfully depicted themselves as the champions of the common man against aristocratic interests that had enriched themselves through special privileges granted by the government. Jackson proclaimed his task as one of restoring the federal government to the ideal of Jeffersonian republicanism, in which farmers and artisans could pursue their individual liberty free of any government intervention that favored the rich and powerful.

Jackson began his assault on special privilege by proclaiming a reform of the appointment process for federal officeholders. Accusing his predecessors, especially Adams, of having created a social elite of self-serving bureaucrats, he vowed to make government service more responsive to the popular will. He insisted that federal jobs required no special expertise or training and proposed to rotate honest, hardworking citizens in and out of the civil service.

Jackson's reform of the federal bureaucracy had more style than substance. He removed only about one-fifth of the officeholders he inherited, and most of his appointees came from the same relatively high-status groups as the Adams people. But by providing a democratic rationale for government service, he opened the way for future presidents to move more aggressively against incumbents. Thus emerged the **spoils system,** in which the victorious party gave government jobs to its supporters and removed the appointees of the defeated party. This parceling out of jobs was a powerful technique for building party strength, because it tied party loyalty to the reward of a federal appointment.

When Jackson railed against economic privilege, he most often had in mind Henry Clay's American System (see Chapter 9). Clay's program called for a protective tariff, a national bank, and federal subsidies for internal improvements; his goal was to bind Americans together in an integrated national market. To the Democrats, Clay's system represented government favoritism at its worst, a set of costly benefits at the public's expense for special-interest groups that corrupted politicians in their quest for economic power. In 1830, Jackson struck a blow for the Democratic conception of the limited federal role in economic development. He vetoed the Maysville Road Bill, which would have provided federal money for a road to be built entirely within Kentucky, Clay's home state. The bill was unconstitutional, he claimed, because it benefited only the citizens of Kentucky and not the U.S. people as a whole.

On the issue of internal improvements, as with bureaucratic reform, the Democrats placed party needs ahead of ideology. Jackson's Maysville veto did not rule out congressional appropriations for projects deemed beneficial to the general public. This pragmatic loophole gave Democrats all the room they needed to pass more internal-improvement projects during Jackson's presidency than during all of the previous administrations together. Having built a mass party, the Democrats soon discovered that they had to funnel federal funds to their constituents back home.

Even at a Washington ball in his home in 1824, Adams, shown on the left, had to share the spotlight with his arch rival Jackson, the striking figure in the middle of the painting.

Any support Jackson might have lost among market-minded entrepreneurs and farmers in the West by his Maysville veto was more than made up by the popularity of his Indian removal policy. Jackson's strongest base of support was in the West and South, and by driving Native Americans from these regions, he more than lived up to his billing as the friend of the common (white) man.

Indian Removal

Some 125,000 Indians lived east of the Mississippi when Jackson became president. The largest concentration was in the South, where five Indian nations, the Cherokees, Creeks, Choctaws, Chickasaws, and Seminoles, controlled millions of acres of land in what soon would become the great cotton frontiers of southwestern Georgia and central Alabama and Mississippi. That, of course, was the problem: Native Americans held land that white farmers coveted for their own economic gain.

Pressure from the states to remove the Indians had been building since the end of the War of 1812. It was most intense in Georgia. In early 1825, Georgia authorities finalized a fraudulent treaty that ceded most of the Creek Indians' land to the state. When Adams tried to obtain fairer terms for the Creeks in a new treaty, he was brazenly denounced in Georgia, which based its case for grabbing Indian territory on the inviolability of states' rights. Georgia dared Adams to do something about it; not willing to risk an armed confrontation between federal and state authorities, Adams backed down.

In 1828, Georgia moved against the Cherokees, the best-organized and most advanced (by white standards) of the Indian nations. The Cherokees in particular had adopted many white practices, including the ownership of some 1,500 slaves. By now a prosperous society of small farmers with their own newspaper and schools for their children, the Cherokees wanted to avoid the fate of their Creek neighbors. In 1827, they adopted a constitution declaring themselves an independent nation with complete sovereignty over their land. The Georgia legislature reacted by placing the Cherokees directly under state law, annulling Cherokee laws and even the right of the Cherokees to make laws, and legally defining the Cherokees as tenants on land belonging to the state of Georgia. By also prohibiting Indian testimony in cases against white people, the legislature stripped the Cherokees of any legal rights. They were now easy prey for white settlers, who scrambled onto Cherokee land after gold was discovered in northern Georgia in 1829. Alabama and Mississippi followed Georgia's lead in denying Indians legal rights.

Thus the stage was set for what Jackson always considered the most important measure of the early days of his administration, the **Indian Removal Act.** Jackson had long considered the federal policy of negotiating with the Indians as sovereign entities a farce. But it was awkward politically for the president to declare that he had no intention of enforcing treaty obligations of the U.S. government. The way out of this dilemma was to remove Native Americans from the center of the dispute. In his first annual message, Jackson sided with state officials in the South and advised the Indians "to emigrate beyond the Mississippi or submit to the laws of those States." This advice enabled Jackson to pose as the friend of the Indians, the wise father who would lead them out of harm's way and save them from rapacious white people.

Congress acted on Jackson's recommendation in the Indian Removal Act of 1830. The act appropriated $500,000 for the negotiation of new treaties under which the southern Indians would surrender their territory and be removed to land in the trans-Mississippi area (primarily present-day Oklahoma). Although force was not authorized and Jackson stressed that removal should be voluntary, no federal protection was provided for Indians harassed into leaving by land-hungry settlers. Ultimately, Jackson did deploy the U.S. Army, but only to round up and push out Indians who refused to comply with the new removal treaties.

And so most of the Indians left the eastern United States, the Choctaws in 1830, the Creeks and Chickasaws in 1832, and the Cherokees in 1838 (see Map 10–3). The government was ill prepared to supervise the removal. The private groups that won the federal contracts for transporting and provisioning the Indians were the ones that had entered the lowest bids; they were a shady lot, interested only in a quick profit. Thousands of Indians, perhaps as many as one-fourth of those who started the trek, died on the way to Oklahoma,

SE - QUO - YAH

Sequoyah, a Cherokee scholar, developed a written table of syllables for the Cherokee language that enabled his people to publish a tribal newspaper in both Cherokee and English.

the victims of cold, hunger, disease, and the general callousness of the white people they met along the way. "It is impossible to conceive the frightful sufferings that attend these forced migrations," noted a Frenchman who observed the Choctaw removal. It was indeed, as recalled in the collective memory of the Cherokees, a **Trail of Tears.**

Tribes that resisted removal were attacked by white armies. Federal troops joined local militias in 1832 in suppressing the Sauk and Fox Indians of Illinois and Wisconsin in what was called **Black Hawk's War.** More a frantic attempt by the Indians to reach safety on the west bank of the Mississippi than an actual war, this affair ended in the slaughter of 500 Indian men, women, and children by white troops and their Sioux allies. The Seminoles, many of whose leaders were runaway slaves adopted into the tribe, fought the army to a standstill in the swamps of Florida in what became the longest Indian war in U.S. history. Not even the loss of their leader Osceola, who was captured while negotiating under a flag of truce, broke their will to resist.

Jackson forged ahead with his removal policy despite the opposition of eastern reformers and Protestant missionaries.

Aligned with conservatives concerned by Jackson's cavalier disregard of federal treaty obligations, they came within three votes of defeating the removal bill in the House of Representatives. Jackson ignored their protests (see American Views: Native Americans Speak Out) as well as the legal rulings of the Supreme Court. In *Cherokee Nation v. Georgia* (1831) and *Worcester v. Georgia* (1832), the Court ruled that Georgia had violated the U.S. Constitution in extending its jurisdiction over the Cherokees. Chief Justice John Marshall defined Indian tribes as "dependent domestic nations" subject only to the authority of the federal government. Marshall may have won the legal argument, but he was powerless to enforce his decisions without Jackson's cooperation. Aware that southerners and westerners were on his side, Jackson ignored the Supreme Court rulings and pushed Indian removal to its tragic conclusion.

The Nullification Crisis

Jackson's stand on Indian removal confirmed the impression of many of his followers that when state and national power conflicted, he could be trusted to side with the states. But when states'-rights forces in South Carolina precipitated the **nullification crisis** by directly challenging Jackson in the early 1830s over tariff policy, Jackson revealed himself to be an ardent nationalist on the issue of majority rule in the Union.

After the first protective tariff in 1816, rates increased further in 1824 and then jumped to 50 percent in 1828 in what was denounced as the "Tariff of Abominations," a measure contrived by northern Democrats to win additional northern support for Jackson in the upcoming presidential campaign. The outcry was loudest in South Carolina, an old cotton state losing population to the West in the 1820s as cotton prices remained low after the Panic of 1819. For all of the economic protests that high tariffs worsened the agricultural depression by raising the cost of manufactured goods purchased by farmers and planters and lowering the foreign demand for agricultural exports, the tariff issue was a stalking-horse for the more fundamental issue of setting limits on national power so that the federal government could never move against slavery.

South Carolina was the only state where African Americans made up the majority of the population. Slaves were heavily concentrated in the marshes and tidal flats south of Charleston, the lowcountry district of huge rice plantations. Here black people outnumbered white people ten to one in the summer months. Ever fearful that growing antislavery agitation in the North and in England was feeding slave unrest, state leaders such as James Hamilton, Jr. warned that the time had come to "stand manfully at the Safety Valve of Nullification."

With the lowcountry planters in charge, the antitariff forces in South Carolina controlled state politics by 1832. They called themselves the nullifiers, a name derived from the constitutional theory developed by John C. Calhoun in an anonymous tract of 1828 titled *The South Carolina Exposition and Protest*. Pushing to its logical extreme the states'-rights doctrine first outlined in the Kentucky and Virginia Resolutions of 1798, Calhoun argued that a state, acting through a popularly elected convention, had the sovereign power to declare an act of the national government null and inoperative. Once a state nullified a law, it was to remain unenforceable within that state's borders unless three-fourths of all the states approved a constitutional amendment delegating to the national government the power that was challenged. If such an amendment passed, the nullifying state had the right to leave the Union.

Calhoun, who had been elected vice president in 1828, openly embraced nullification after he broke with Jackson in 1830. Just as the president learned that Calhoun, while secretary of war in 1818, had wanted to censure Jackson for his raid into Spanish Florida, a curious episode known as the Eaton Affair was reaching a climax. When the wives of Jackson's cabinet members, led by Floride Calhoun, pointedly snubbed Peggy Eaton, the wife of Jackson's secretary of war, on the grounds that she

MAP 10–3   Indian Removals
The fixed policy of the Jackson administration and pressure from the states forced Native Americans in the 1830s to migrate from their eastern homelands to a special Indian reserve west of the Mississippi River.

For the Cherokees, the Trail of Tears stretched 1,200 miles from the homeland in the East to what became the Indian Territory in Oklahoma.

was a "loose woman" who had driven her first husband to suicide, Jackson was convinced that Calhoun was plotting to discredit his administration. The political consequences of the Eaton Affair included not only Calhoun's fall from Jackson's favor but also the resignation of the entire cabinet. Much of the rancor stemmed from the belief of elite Washington women that Peggy Eaton had violated the rules of women's political behavior. Rather than exerting influence indirectly by using social gatherings to lobby on behalf of male friends, she seemingly sought power in her own right by appealing directly to Jackson for his support. Moreover, Eaton, the daughter of a tavern keeper, was overstepping her bounds by claiming political influence that Washington society felt belonged only to women of the social elite.

With Calhoun's approval, a South Carolina convention in November 1832 nullified the tariffs of 1828 and 1832 (a compromise tariff that did not reduce rates to a low enough level to satisfy the nullifiers). The convention decreed that customs duties were not to be collected in South Carolina after February 1, 1833.

Although Calhoun defended his doctrine as a constitutional means of protecting minority rights within a Union dominated by a tyrannical national majority, Jackson rejected such reasoning as the talk of a scheming disunionist. He considered nullification a dangerous and nonsensical perversion of the Constitution, and he vowed to crush any attempt to block the enforcement of federal laws. He told a congressman

from South Carolina that "if a single drop of blood shall be shed there in opposition to the laws of the United States, I will hang the first man I can lay my hand on engaged in such treasonable conduct, upon the first tree I can reach."

In January 1833, Jackson, in the Force Bill, asked for and received from Congress full authorization to put down nullification by military force. Meanwhile, a compromise tariff in 1833 provided for the lowering of tariff duties to 20 percent over a 10-year period. Up against this combination of the carrot and the stick, the nullifiers backed down, but not before they scornfully nullified the Force Bill.

Jackson's stand established the principle of national supremacy grounded in the will of the majority. Despite his victory, however, states'-rights doctrines remained popular both in the South and among many northern Democrats. South Carolina had been isolated in its stand on nullification, but many southerners, and especially slaveholders, agreed that the powers of the national government had to be strictly limited. By dramatically affirming his right to use force against a state in defense of the Union, Jackson drove many planters out of the Democratic party. In the shock waves set off by the nullification crisis, a new anti-Jackson coalition began to form in the South.

The Bank War

What amounted to a war against the Bank of the United States became the centerpiece of Jackson's presidency and a defining event for the Democratic Party. The **Bank War** erupted in 1832, when Jackson vetoed draft legislation for the early rechartering of the national bank.

Like most westerners, Jackson distrusted banks. Because gold and silver coins were scarce and the national government did not issue or regulate paper currency, money consisted primarily of notes issued as loans by private and state banks. These bank notes fluctuated in value according to the reputation and creditworthiness of the issuing banks. In the credit-starved West, banks were particularly unreliable. Many bankers made quick profits by issuing notes without the gold or silver reserves to redeem them and then skipping town when they were on the verge of being found out. Even when issued by honest bankers, notes often could not be redeemed at face value because of market conditions. All of this struck many Americans, and especially farmers and workers, as inherently dishonest. They wanted to be paid in "real" money, gold or silver coin, and they viewed bankers as parasites who did nothing but fatten their own pockets by manipulating paper money. The largest and most powerful bank was the Bank of the United States, and citizens who were wiped out or forced to retrench drastically by the Panic of 1819 never forgave the Bank for saving itself at the expense of its debtors. Still, under the astute leadership of a new president, Nicholas Biddle of Philadelphia, the Bank performed well in the 1820s. Prosperous times had returned, and the Bank underwrote the economic expansion with its healthy credit reserves, stable bank notes, and policing of the state banks through its policy of returning their notes for redemption in specie. By 1832, the Bank was as popular as it ever would be.

Searching for an issue to use against Jackson in the presidential campaign of 1832, Clay forced Jackson's hand on the Bank. Clay convinced Biddle to apply to Congress for a new charter, even though the current charter would not expire until 1836. Confident of congressional approval, Clay reasoned that he had Jackson trapped. If Jackson went along with the new charter, Clay could take credit for the measure. If he vetoed it, Clay could attack Jackson as the enemy of a sound banking system.

Clay's clever strategy backfired. Jackson turned on him and the Bank with a vengeance. As he told his heir apparent, "The bank, Mr. Van Buren, is trying to kill me, but *I will kill it!*" Jackson and his advisers realized that the Bank was vulnerable as a symbol of privileged monopoly, a monstrous institution that deprived common Americans of their right to compete equally for economic advantage. Moreover, many of these advisers were also state bankers and local developers, who backed Jackson precisely because they wanted to be free of federal restraints on their business activities. On July 10, 1832, Jackson vetoed the rechartering bill for the Bank in a message that appealed both to state bankers and to foes of all banks. He took a ringing "stand against all new grants of monopolies and exclusive privileges, against any prostitution of our Government to the advancement of the few at the expense of the many."

The business community and eastern elites lashed out at Jackson's veto as the demagogic ravings of an economic fool. For Biddle, the veto message had "all the fury of a chained panther, biting the bars of his cage." In rejecting Jackson's claims that the Bank had fostered speculative and corrupt financial practices, the pro-Bank forces had the better of the economic argument. But Jackson won the political battle, and he went to the people in the election of 1832 as their champion against the banking aristocracy. Although his support was no stronger than it had been in 1828, he easily defeated Clay, the candidate of the short-lived National Republican party, which had also backed Adams in 1828.

After Congress failed to override his veto, Jackson then set out to destroy the Bank. He claimed that the people had given him a mandate to do so by reelecting him in 1832. In Roger B. Taney he finally found a secretary of the treasury (his first two choices refused) who agreed to sign the order removing federal deposits from the Bank in 1833. Drained of its lifeblood, the deposits, the Bank was reduced by 1836 to seeking a charter as a private corporation in the state of Pennsylvania. In the meantime, the government's moneys were deposited in "pet banks," state banks controlled by loyal Democrats.

Jackson won the Bank War, but he left the impression that the Democrats had played fast and loose with the nation's credit system. The economy overheated in his second term. High commodity prices and abundant credit, both at home and abroad, propelled a buying frenzy of western lands. Prices soared, and inevitably the speculative bubble had to burst. When it did, the Democrats would be open to the charge of squandering the people's money by shifting deposits to reckless state bankers who were part of a corrupt new alliance between the government and private economic interests. Jackson was out of office when the Panic of 1837 hit; Van Buren, his successor, paid the political price for Jackson's economic policies.

Van Buren and Hard Times

Like John Adams and James Madison, Martin Van Buren followed a forceful president who commanded a strong popular following. Fairly or not, he would come out, as they did, second-best compared to his predecessor.

Facing a sharp economic downturn, Van Buren appeared indecisive and unwilling to advance a bold program. When the rise of a radical **abolitionist movement** in the North revived sectional tensions over slavery, he awkwardly straddled the divisive issue. In the end, he undermined himself by failing to offer a compelling vision of his presidency.

The Panic of 1837

Van Buren was barely settled into the White House when the nation was rocked by a financial panic. For over a decade, the economy had benefited from a favorable business cycle. Easy credit and the availability of territories opened up by Jackson's Indian removal policy generated a stampede to buy land in the West. Government land sales ballooned from

American Views

Native Americans Speak Out

Memorial and Protests of the Cherokee Nation, 1836

Of the major tribes in the Southeast, the Cherokees fought longest and hardest against the Jacksonian policy of Indian removal. Led by their principal chief, John Ross, the son of a Scot and a mixed-blood Cherokee woman, they submitted the following protest to Congress against the fraudulent 1835 Treaty of New Echota forced on them by the state of Georgia. Although clearly opposed by an overwhelming majority of the Cherokees, this treaty provided the legal basis for the forced removal of the Cherokee people from Georgia to the Indian Territory.

- On what legal grounds did the Cherokees base their protest? What pledges had been made to them by the U.S. government?
- What did the Cherokees mean when they said they had been "taught to think and feel as the American citizen"? If the Cherokees had become "civilized" by white standards, why did most whites still insist on their removal?
- Why would President Jackson have allowed white intruders to remain on land reserved by treaties for the Cherokees?
- Do you feel that the Cherokees were justified in believing that they had been betrayed by the U.S. government?

The undersigned representatives of the Cherokee nation, east of the river Mississippi, impelled by duty, would respectfully submit…the following statement of facts: It will be seen, from the numerous treaties between the Cherokee nation and the United States, that from the earliest existence of this government, the United States, in Congress assembled, received the Cherokees and their nation into favor and protection; and that the chiefs and warriors, for themselves and all parts of the Cherokee nation, acknowledged themselves and the said Cherokee nation to be under the protection of the United States of America, and of no other sovereign whatsoever: they also stipulated, that the said Cherokee nation will not hold any treaty with any foreign power, individual State, or with individuals of any State: that for, and in consideration of, valuable concessions made by the Cherokee nation, the United States solemnly guaranteed to said nation all their lands not ceded, and pledged the faith of the government, that "all white people who have intruded, or may hereafter intrude, on the lands reserved for the Cherokees, shall be removed by the United States, and proceeded against, according to the provisions of the act, passed 30th March, 1802," entitled "An act to regulate trade and intercourse with the Indian tribes, and to preserve peace on the frontiers." It would be useless to recapitulate the numerous provisions for the security and protection of the rights of the Cherokees, to be found in the various treaties between their nation and the United States. The Cherokees were happy and prosperous under a scrupulous observance of treaty stipulations by the government of the United States, and from the fostering hand extended over them, they made rapid advances in civilization, morals, and in the arts and sciences. Little did they anticipate, that when taught to think and feel as the American citizen, and to have with him a common interest, they were to be despoiled by their guardian, to become strangers and wanderers in the land of their fathers, forced to return to the savage life, and to seek a new home in the wilds of the far west, and that without their consent. An instrument purporting to be a treaty with the Cherokee people, has recently been made public by the President of the United States, that will have such an operation, if carried into effect. This instrument, the delegation aver before the civilized world, and in the presence of Almighty God, is fraudulent, false upon its face, made by unauthorized individuals, without the sanction, and against the wishes, of the great body of the Cherokee people. Upwards of fifteen thousand of those people have protested against it, solemnly declaring they will never acquiesce.

Source: U.S. Congress, *Executive Documents* (1836)

The Militant Consciousness of William Apess

Although virtually erased in the historical record, the Native Americans of New England had not vanished by the nineteenth century. They persisted, both as individuals and as a culture. Numbering no more than a few thousand, most lived impoverished on reservations where they were denied the local self-governance extended to whites. The young left early, searching for whatever paying jobs they could find. One of these marginalized, transient Indians, the Pequot William Apess, produced a remarkable collection of autobiographical and protest writings that he began publishing in pamphlet form in 1829. The following excerpts reveal the anger, passion, and eloquence he brought to his indictment of white injustices to his people in Massachusetts.

- Why does Apess link the plight of Indians in Massachusetts with that of Indians in Georgia?
- How does he use the military contributions of Indians on the patriot side in the American Revolution to stake a claim for himself and his people to the liberties of republicanism?
- In what way does does his condemnation of the dispossession of Indian lands by whites change or complicate the traditional approach to American history as an unfolding story of freedom and opportunity?

Perhaps you have heard of the oppression of the Cherokees and lamented over them much, and thought the Georgians were hard and cruel creatures; but did you ever hear of the poor, oppressed and degraded Marshpee Indians in Massachusetts and lament over them? ... And we do not know why the people of this Commonwealth want to cruelize us any longer, for we are sure that our fathers *fought, bled, and died for the liberties* of their now weeping and suffering children. ... *Oh, white man! white man!* The blood of our fathers, spilt in the Revolutionary War, cries from the ground of our native soil, to break the chains of oppression, and let our children *go free!"* ...

No doubt there are many good people in the United States who would not trample upon the rights of the poor, but there are many others who are willing to roll in their coaches upon the tears and blood of the poor and unoffending natives—those who are ready at all times to speculate on the Indians and defraud them out of their rightful possessions. Let the poor Indian attempt to resist the encroachments of his white neighbors, what a hue and cry is instantly raised against him. It has been considered as a trifling thing for the whites to make war on the Indians for the purpose of driving them from their country and taking possession thereof. This was, in their estimation, all right, as it helped to extend the territory and enriched some individuals. But let the thing be changed. Suppose an overwhelming army should march into the United States for the purpose of subduing it and enslaving the citizens; how quick would they fly to arms, gather in multitudes around the tree of liberty, and contend for their rights with the last drop of their blood. And should the enemy succeed, would they not eventually rise and endeavor to regain their liberty? And who would blame them for it?

Source: Barry O'Connell, ed., *On Our Own Ground: The Complete Writings of Willaim Apess, a Pequot* (University of Massachusetts Press, 1992).

under 4 million acres in 1833 to 20 million acres in 1836. As in 1817 and 1818, Americans piled up debt on the assumption that the good times would never end. A banking crisis in 1837 painfully reintroduced economic reality.

Even as it expanded, the U.S. economy had remained vulnerable to disruptions in the supply of foreign capital and the sale of agricultural exports that underpinned prosperity. The key foreign nation was Britain, a major source of credit and demand for exports. In late 1836, the Bank of England tightened its credit policies. Concerned about the large outflow of specie to the United States, it raised interest rates and reduced the credit lines of British merchants heavily involved in U.S. trade. Consequently, the British demand for cotton fell and with it the price of cotton (see Figure 10–1). Because cotton, as the leading export, was the main security for most loans issued by U.S. banks and mercantile firms, its drop in value set off a chain reaction of contracting credit and falling prices. When panic-stricken investors rushed to the banks to redeem their notes in specie, the hard-pressed banks suspended specie payments.

The shock waves hit New Orleans in March 1837 and spread to the major New York banks by May. What began as a bank panic soon dragged down the entire economy. Bankruptcies multiplied, investment capital dried up, and business stagnated. State governments, which had borrowed lavishly during the boom years to finance canals and other internal improvements, slashed their budgets and halted all construction projects. Nine states in the South and West defaulted (stopped making payments) on their bonds. Workers in the shoe, textile, mining, and construction industries suddenly found themselves without jobs. As unemployment mounted and workers mobilized mass protest meetings in eastern cities, conservatives feared the worst. "Workmen thrown out of employ by the hundred daily," nervously noted a wealthy merchant in New York City in May 1837. He half expected that "we shall have a revolution here."

After a brief recovery in 1838, another round of credit contraction drove the economy into a depression that did not bottom out until 1843. In the manufacturing and commercial centers of the Northeast, unemployment reached an unheard-of 20 percent. The persistence of depressed agricultural prices meant that farmers and planters who had incurred debts in the 1830s faced the constant threat of losing their land or their slaves. Many fled west to avoid their creditors.

The Independent Treasury

Although the Democrats bore no direct responsibility for the economic downturn, they could not avoid being blamed for it. Their political opponents, now coalescing as the **Whig party,** claimed that Jackson's destruction of the Bank of the United States had undermined business confidence. In their view, Jackson had then compounded his error by trying to force a hard-money policy on the state banks that had received federal deposits. The "pet banks" were required to replace small-denomination bank notes with coins or hard money. This measure, it was hoped, would protect the farmers and workers from being paid in depreciated bank notes.

Jackson had taken his boldest step against paper money when he issued the **Specie Circular** of 1836, which stipulated that large tracts of public land could be bought only with specie. Aimed at breaking the speculative spiral in land purchases, the Specie Circular contributed to the Panic of 1837 by requiring the transfer of specie to the West for land transactions just when eastern banks were strapped for specie reserves. Bankers and speculators denounced Jackson for interfering with the natural workings of the economy and blundering into a monetary disaster.

Conservative charges of Democratic irresponsibility were overblown, but the Democrats were caught in a dilemma. By dramatically politicizing the banking issue and removing federal moneys from the national bank, the Democrats had in effect assumed the burden of protecting the people from the banking and business community. Once they shifted treasury receipts to selected state banks, they had to try to regulate these banks. Otherwise they would be accused of creating a series of little "monsters" and feeding the paper speculation they so decried. But any regulatory policy contradicted the Democratic commitment to limit governmental power. A restrictive policy, especially one aimed at replacing bank notes with specie, was bound to upset business interests and drive them out of the Democratic Party. Worse yet, even the "pet banks" joined in the general suspension of specie payments when the Panic of 1837 hit. Thus the banks favored by the Democrats proved themselves unworthy of the people's trust.

The only way out of the dilemma was to make a clean break between the government and banking. Van Buren reestablished the Democrats' tarnished image as the party of limited government when he came out for the **Independent Treasury System.** Under this plan, the government would dispense with banks entirely. The Treasury would conduct its business only in gold and silver coin and would store its specie in regional vaults or subtreasuries. First proposed in 1837, the Independent Treasury System finally passed Congress in 1840 on the heels of a second wave of bank failures.

The Independent Treasury System made more political than economic sense. It restored the ideological purity of the Democrats as the friends of honest money, but it prolonged the depression. Specie locked up in government vaults was unavailable for loans in the private banking system that could have expanded the credit needed to revive the economy. The end result was to reduce the money supply and further depress prices.

Uproar over Slavery

In 1831, William Lloyd Garrison of Boston inaugurated a radical new phase in northern attacks on slavery with the publication of his abolitionist paper the *Liberator.*

Broken families and demoralized workers were among the litany of evils blamed on the Panic of 1837.

The abolitionists embraced the doctrine of immediatism, an immediate moral commitment to begin the work of emancipation. Inspired by the wave of religious revivals sweeping the North in the late 1820s, they seized on slavery as the greatest sin of all. With the righteous wrath of evangelical ministers, they called on all Americans to recognize their Christian duty to end a system of human bondage that deprived the enslaved of their God-given right to be free moral beings. (For more on the abolitionists, see Chapter 12.)

The abolitionists touched off a political uproar when they launched a propaganda offensive in 1835. Taking advantage of technological improvements in the printing industry, they produced over a million pieces of antislavery literature, much of which was sent to the South through the U.S. mail. Alarmed white southerners vilified the abolitionists as fanatics intent on enticing the slaves to revolt. Abolitionist tracts were burned, and, with the open approval of Jackson, southern postmasters violated federal law by censoring the mail to keep out antislavery materials.

Unable to receive an open hearing in the South, the abolitionists now focused on Congress. Beginning in 1836 and continuing through Van Buren's presidency, hundreds of thousands of antislavery petitions, some with thousands of signatures, flooded into Congress. Most called for the abolition of slavery in the District of Columbia. Southern congressmen responded by demanding that free speech be repressed in the name of southern white security. The enemy, they were convinced, was fanaticism, and nearly all agreed with Francis Pickens of South Carolina that they must "meet it and strangle it in its infancy." The strangling took the form of the **gag rule,** a procedural device whereby antislavery petitions were automatically tabled with no discussion.

The gag rule first passed in 1836 and was renewed in a series of raucous debates through 1844. Only the votes of some three-fourths of the northern Democrats enabled the southern minority to have its way. With Van Buren's reluctant support, the gag rule became a Democratic party measure, and it identified the Democrats as a prosouthern party in the minds of many northerners. Ironically, while Van Buren was attacked in the North as a lackey of the slave interests, he was damned in the South, if only because he was a nonslaveholder from the North, as being unsafe on the slavery issue. In short, tensions over slavery and the economy doomed Van Buren to be cast as a vacillating president fully trusted by neither section.

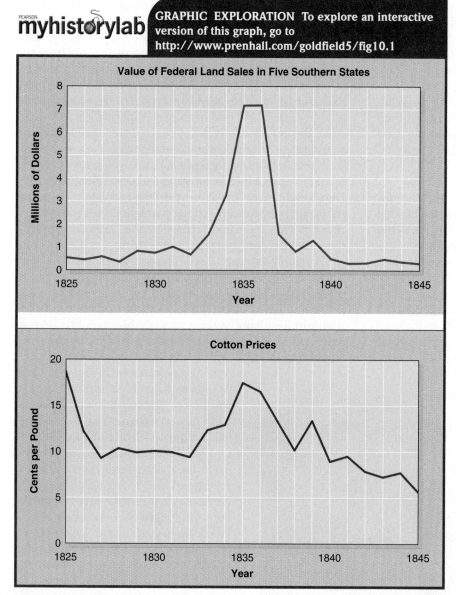

GRAPHIC EXPLORATION To explore an interactive version of this graph, go to http://www.prenhall.com/goldfield5/fig10.1

FIGURE 10–1   Cotton Prices and the Value of Federal Land Sales in Five Southern States, 1825–1845

Because the U.S. economy was heavily dependent on cotton exports as a source of credit, the collapse of cotton prices, and a corresponding plunge in the sales of federal land after a speculative runup in the newer cotton regions of the South, triggered a financial panic in the late 1830s.

Data source: Douglas C. North, *The Economic Growth of the United States, 1790–1860* (1966), tab. A-X, p. 257.

The Rise of the Whig Party

The early opponents of the Democrats were known as the National Republicans, a label that captured the nationalist vision of former Jeffersonian Republicans who adhered to the economic program of Henry Clay and John Quincy Adams. The Bank War and Jackson's reaction to nullification shook loose pro-Bank Democrats and many southern states' righters from the original Jacksonian coalition, and these groups joined the opposition to Jackson. By 1834, the anti-Jacksonians started to call themselves Whigs, a name associated with eighteenth-century American and British opponents of monarchical tyranny. The name stuck because of the party's constant depiction of Jackson as King Andrew, a tyrant who ran roughshod over congressional prerogatives and constitutional liberties.

By 1840, the Whigs had mastered the techniques of political organization and mobilization pioneered by the Democrats in the late 1820s. They ran William Henry Harrison, their own version of a military hero, and swept to victory. The **second party system** of intense national competition between Whigs and Democrats was now in place (see the Overview table, The Second Party System). It would dominate politics until the rise of the antislavery Republican Party in the 1850s.

The Party Taking Shape

The Whig party was born in the congressional reaction to Jackson's Bank veto and his subsequent attacks on the national bank. What upset the congressional opposition, apart from the specific content of Jackson's policies, was how he enforced his will. Jackson wielded his executive power like a bludgeon. Whereas all earlier presidents together had used the veto only ten times, Jackson did so a dozen times. He openly defied the Supreme Court and Congress, and unlike his predecessors, he took each case directly to the people. It seemed to his opponents that Jackson was threatening to undermine the constitutional system of checks and balances and bypass the established leadership of public-spirited gentlemen who had hitherto ruled on behalf of the people.

Local and state Whig coalitions sent an anti-Jackson majority to the House of Representatives in 1835. The most powerful of these coalitions was in New York, where a third party, the **Anti-Masons,** joined the Whigs. The party had originated in western New York in the late 1820s as a grassroots response to the sudden disappearance and presumed murder of William Morgan, an itinerant artisan who threatened to expose the secrets of the Order of Freemasons. An all-male order steeped in ritual and ceremony, the Masons united urban and small-town elites into a tightly knit brotherhood through personal contacts and mutual aid. When efforts to investigate Morgan's disappearance ran into a legal dead end, rumors spread that the exclusivist Masons constituted a vast conspiracy that conferred special privileges and legal protection on its members. To combat this "monster," farmers and townspeople flocked to the new Anti-Masonic party. They sought, in the words of an 1831 Anti-Masonic address, "equal rights and equal privileges among the freemen of the country."

Western New York, an area of religious fervor and rapid economic change after the opening of the Erie Canal in 1825, provided fertile ground for the growth of the new party. With close ties to rural landlords and town creditors, the Masons were vulnerable to the charge of economic favoritism. In addition, evangelicals accused the Masons of desecrating the Christian faith with their secret rituals. The Anti-Masons were thus the first party to combine demands for equal opportunity with calls for the moral reform of a sinful society. They were also the first party to select their presidential ticket in a national nominating convention, a precedent immediately followed by the Whigs and Democrats.

Although it spread into New England and the neighboring mid-Atlantic states, the Anti-Mason party was unable to sustain itself. Its presidential candidate in 1832, William Wirt of Maryland, won only Vermont. Recognizing that the opponents of the Anti-Masons were usually the entrenched local interests of the Democratic Party, shrewd politicians, led by Thurlow Weed and William Seward of New York, took up the movement and absorbed most of it into the anti-Jackson coalition. They did so by calling for equal opportunity and for such evangelical reforms as a ban on the sale of alcohol. The Whigs thus broadened their popular base and added an egalitarian message to their appeal.

By 1836, the Whigs were strong enough to mount a serious challenge for the presidency. However, they still lacked an effective national organization that could unite their regional coalitions behind one candidate. They ran four sectional candidates, and some Whigs hoped that the regional popularity of these candidates would siphon off enough votes from Van Buren to throw the election into the House of Representatives. The strategy, if such it can be called, failed. Van Buren won an electoral majority by holding on to the populous mid-Atlantic states and improving on Jackson's showing in New England. Still, the Whigs were encouraged by the results. Compared to Jackson, Van Buren did poorly in what had been the overwhelmingly Democratic South, which was now open to further Whig inroads.

Whig Persuasion

The Whigs, like the Democrats, based their mass appeal on the claim that they could best defend the republican liberties of the people. Whereas the Democrats attributed the threat to those liberties to privileged monopolies of government-granted power, the Whigs found it in the expansive powers of the presidency as wielded by Jackson and in the party organization that put Jackson and Van Buren into office. In 1836, the Whigs called for the election of "a president of the nation, not a president of party." Underlying this call was the persistent Whig belief that parties undermined individual liberties and the public good by fostering and rewarding the selfish interests of the party faithful. Although the Whigs dropped much of this ideology when they matured as a party, they never lost their fear of the presidency as an office of unchecked, demagogic power. They always insisted that Congress should be the locus of power in the federal system.

Most Whigs viewed governmental power as a positive force to promote economic development. They favored the spread of banking and paper money, chartering corporations, passing protective tariffs to support U.S. manufacturers, and

OVERVIEW

The Second Party System

	Democrats	Whigs
Ideology	Favor limited role of federal government in economic affairs and matters of individual conscience; support territorial expansion	Favor government support for economic development and controls over individual morality; opposed to expansion
Voter support	Mainly subsistence farmers, unskilled workers, and Catholic immigrants	Mainly manufacturers, commercial farmers, skilled workers, and northern evangelicals
Regional strength	South and West	New England and Upper Midwest

opening up new markets for farmers through government-subsidized transportation projects. Such policies, they held, would widen economic opportunities for Americans and provide incentives for material self-improvement.

The Whigs' economic program appealed mostly to Americans who were benefiting from economic change or expecting to do so. They drew heavily from commercial and planting interests in the South. They were also the party of bankers, manufacturers, small-town entrepreneurs, farmers prospering from the market outlets of canals and railroads, and skilled workers who valued a high tariff as protection from the competition of goods produced by cheap foreign labor. These Whig groups also tended to be native-born Protestants of New England or Yankee ancestry, particularly those caught up in the religious revivals of the 1820s and 1830s. The strongest Whig constituencies comprised an arc of Yankee settlements stretching from rural New England through central New York and around the southern shores of the Great Lakes.

Whether as economic promoters or evangelical reformers, Whigs believed in promoting social progress and harmony through an interventionist government. The Whigs favored such social reforms as prohibiting the consumption of alcohol, preserving the sanctity of the Protestant Sabbath through bans on business activities on Sundays, caring for orphans, the physically handicapped, and the mentally ill in state-run asylums and hospitals, and teaching virtuous behavior and basic knowledge through a centralized system of public education. Whig ideology blended economic, social, and spiritual reform into a unified message of uplift. An activist government would provide economic opportunities and moral guidance for a harmonious, progressive society of freely competing individuals whose behavior would be shaped by the evangelical norms of thrift, sobriety, and self-discipline. Much of the Whigs' reform impulse was directed against non-English and Catholic immigrants, those Americans who the Whigs believed most needed to be taught the virtues of self-control and disciplined work habits. Not coincidentally, these groups, the Scots-Irish in the backcountry, the Reformed Dutch, and Irish and German Catholics, were the most loyal Democrats. They resented the Whigs' aggressive moralism and legislative attempts to interfere with their drinking habits and Sunday amusements. These Democrats were typically subsistence farmers on the periph-

ery of market change and unskilled workers forced by industrial change to abandon their hopes of ever opening their own shops. They equated an activist government with special privileges for the economically and culturally powerful and identified with the Democrats' desire to keep the government out of the economy and individual religious practices.

The Election of 1840

One of the signs of the Whigs' maturing as a party was their decision in 1840 to place victory above principle. Because of the lingering economic depression, Democratic rule had been discredited for many voters. Aside from the Independent Treasury Act and legislation establishing a 10-hour workday for federal employees, the Van Buren administration had no program to combat the Whig charge of helplessness in the face of economic adversity. Henry Clay, who promised that his American System would revive the economy with government aid, appeared the most likely Whig candidate for president against Van Buren in 1840. Yet Whig power brokers dumped Clay, who represented the party's ideological heart, for a popular military hero, William Henry Harrison of Ohio.

Harrison had run surprisingly well as one of the Whigs' regional candidates in 1836 and had revealed a common touch with the voters. Unlike Clay, he was untainted by any association with the Bank of the United States, the Masonic Order, or slaveholding. As the victor at the Battle of Tippecanoe and a military hero in the War of 1812, he enabled Whig image-makers to cast him, like Jackson, as the honest, patriotic soldier worthy of the people's trust. In a decision that came back to haunt them, the Whigs geographically balanced their ticket by selecting John Tyler, a planter from Virginia, as Harrison's running mate. Tyler was an advocate of states' rights and a former Democrat who had broken with Jackson over the Force Bill.

The Democrats inadvertently gave the Whig campaign a tremendous boost. A Democratic editor wisecracked that "Old Granny" Harrison (he was 67) was such a simpleton that he would like nothing better than to retire to a log cabin with a government pension and a barrel of hard cider. Pouncing on this sneer, the Whigs created a Harrison who never was, a yeoman farmer of humble origins and homespun tastes, whose rise to prominence was a democratic model of success for other Americans to follow. Thus Harrison, who was descended from the Virginia slaveholding aristocracy, became a symbol of the common man, and the Whigs were finally able to shed their aristocratic image. Indeed, they pinned the label of the dandified and elitist aristocrat on Van Buren. "Martin Van Ruin," as effectively portrayed by the Whigs, squandered public revenue on effete luxuries and was concerned only with the spoils of office.

The Whigs beat the Democrats at their own game of mass politics in 1840. They reversed the roles and symbolism of the Jackson–Adams election of 1828 and seized the high ground as the party of the people. In a further adaptation of earlier Democratic initiatives, the Whigs put together a frolicking campaign of slogans, parades, and pageantry. Politics became a carnival in which voters were shamelessly wooed with food, drink, and music in huge rallies complete with live animals and gigantic buckskin balls that were triumphantly rolled from one rally to another.

The Whigs gained control of both Congress and the presidency in 1840. Harrison won 53 percent of the popular vote, and for the first time the Whigs carried the South (see Map 10–4). With the arrival of politics as mass spectacle, the turnout surged to an unprecedented 78 percent of eligible voters, a whopping increase over the average of 55 percent in the three preceding presidential elections (see Figure 10–2). The Whigs claimed most of the new voters and were now fully competitive with the Democrats in all parts of the nation. As the new majority party, they finally had the opportunity, or so they thought, to implement their economic program.

The Whigs in Power

Although the Whigs had been noncommittal on their plans during the campaign of 1840, it was common knowledge that Clay would move quickly on Whig economic policies by marshaling his forces in Congress and trying to dominate a pliant Harrison. But Harrison died from pneumonia in April 1841, barely a month after his inauguration, ruining Clay's plans. Tyler, Harrison's successor, was a particularly rigid states'-rights ideologue who betrayed party expectations by blocking key pieces of Clay's program. The Whigs reacted by reading Tyler out of the party.

In 1843, Tyler latched on to the annexation of the slaveholding Republic of Texas as an issue that might get him back into the good graces of the Democratic party and establish his own successful record as president. At the end of his administration, Tyler did succeed in securing the annexation of Texas, but his main accomplishment was to shift the focus of national politics from economic issues to sectional ones of territorial expansion. Running on an expansionist platform, the Democrats regained the presidency in 1844.

Harrison and Tyler

Harrison had pledged to follow the dictates of party leaders in Congress and defer to the judgment of his cabinet. Bowing to Clay's demands, he agreed to call Congress into special session to act on Whig party measures. Precisely because he was the type of president the Whigs needed and wanted, his death

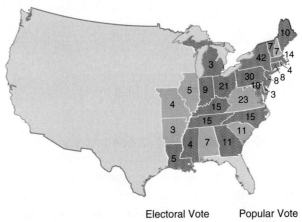

	Electoral Vote (%)	Popular Vote (%)
WILLIAM HENRY HARRISON (Whig)	**234 (80)**	**1,274,624 (53)**
Martin Van Buren (Democrat)	60 (20)	1,127,781 (47)

MAP 10–4   The Election of 1840
Building upon their strength in the commercializing North, the Whigs attracted enough rural voters in the South and West to win the election of 1840.

was a real blow to Whig hopes of establishing the credibility of their party as an effective agent for positive change.

Just how serious that blow was soon became apparent when Tyler became president, the first vice president to succeed on the death of a president. Tyler was cut from quite different cloth from Harrison. This stiff, unbending planter subscribed to a states'-rights agrarian philosophy that put him at odds with the urban and commercial elements of the Whig party even in his home state of Virginia. Clay's economic nationalism struck him as a program of rank corruption that surrendered the constitutional rights of the South to power-hungry politicians and manufacturers in the North. Clay refused to cultivate Tyler's prickly pride with soothing gestures, and he forged ahead with the party agenda, the repeal of the Independent Treasury System and its replacement by a new national bank, a protective tariff, and the distribution of the proceeds of the government's public land sales to the states as funds for internal improvements.

Tyler used the negative power of presidential vetoes to stymie the Whig program. He twice vetoed bills to reestablish a national bank. The second veto led to the resignation of the cabinet he had inherited from Harrison, save for Secretary of State Daniel Webster, who was in the midst of negotiations with the British. Enraged congressional Whigs then expelled Tyler from the party.

A now desperate Clay sought to salvage what was left of his American System. He lined up southern votes for the distribution of federal funds to the states by agreeing to a ceiling of 20 percent on tariff rates. Westerners were won over by Clay's support for the Preemption Act of 1841, a measure that allowed squatters to purchase up to 160 acres of public land at the minimum government price of $1.25 per acre. This act

FROM THEN TO NOW

Voter Turnout

The political innovations of the Jacksonian era invented mass-based political parties and turned elections into democratic theater that left Americans excited about politics. After the first record turnout in the election of 1840, voter participation in presidential elections remained between 70 and 80 percent for the rest of the nineteenth century. These consistently high turnouts began to fall in the early twentieth century, and by the 1920s only 52 percent of eligible voters were casting a ballot in presidential elections. The onset of the New Deal sparked a partial upturn that raised turnouts to about 60 percent down to the election of 1960, but since then a long decline has brought turnouts back to the trough of the 1920s.

The factors behind this decline, a disengagement from politics that has characterized most democratic societies in the past forty years, are complex, but one that stands out for the United States has been the transformation of the popular politics pioneered by the Democrats and Whigs. What made politics popular, apart from elaborately staged campaigns that mobilized common Americans in huge rallies and street parades, was the voting link provided by openly partisan parties between individual political beliefs and action. That link has been blurred, if not broken, by the rise of the modern administrative state in the twentieth century that took over most of the functions of governance that were once performed by the parties. At the same time a new electoral style replaced partisanship with personalities and treated potential voters as passive recipients of information in media campaigns conducted by television and the internet. As emotional partisanship waned, so also did voter turnout.

Kerry-Bush presidential debate in 2004

■ What do you think are the major reasons behind the chronically low voter turnouts in modern U.S. elections?

Whig political rally in 1840

From Then to Now Online

10-1 Enos Throop, *Message of the Governor*, 1829. Message on the value of political parties.

10-2 James Buchanan, *Letter to a fellow Democrat*, 1840. Excitement generated in 1840 campaign.

10-3 Dieter Nohlen, *Internet article*, 2007. The challenges facing new democracies.

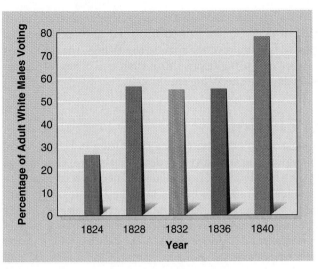

FIGURE 10–2   Voter Turnout in Presidential Elections, 1824–1840

The creation of mass-based political parties dramatically increased voter turnout in presidential elections. Voting surged in 1828 with the emergence of the Jacksonian Democratic party and again in 1840 when the Whig party learned to appeal to the mass electorate.

Date Source: Richard P. McCormick, "New Perspectives on Jacksonian Politics," in *The Nature of Jacksonian America*, ed. Douglas T. Miller (1972), p. 103.

was popular in the West because squatters no longer had to match the bids of speculators at government land sales.

Clay's legislative wizardry got him nowhere. When the Whigs passed a higher tariff in 1842 with a provision for distribution, Tyler vetoed it and forced them to settle for a protective tariff with no distribution. In the end, Clay had no national bank, no funds for internal improvements, and only a slightly higher tariff. Although Clay's leadership of the Whigs was strengthened, Tyler had deprived that leadership of meaning by denying the Whigs the legislative fruits of their victory in 1840.

The Texas Issue

Constrained by his states'-rights view to a largely negative role in domestic policy, Tyler was a much more forceful president in foreign policy, an area in which the Constitution gives the chief executive considerable latitude. In 1842, Tyler's secretary of state, Daniel Webster, wrapped up his negotiations with the British over a long-standing boundary dispute. The **Webster-Ashburton Treaty** of that year established the boundary between British Canada and Maine and parts of the Upper Midwest. An agreement was also reached to cooperate in suppressing the African slave trade. Webster now resigned from the cabinet to join his fellow Whigs, allowing Tyler to follow a pro-southern policy of expansion that he hoped would gain him the Democratic nomination for the presidency in 1844. His goal was the annexation of Texas.

Texas had been a slaveholding republic since 1836, when rebellious Americans, joined by some *tejanos* (Texans of Mexican descent), declared their independence from Mexico. Jack-

son extended diplomatic recognition before leaving office, but he refused the new nation's request to be annexed to the United States out of fear of provoking a war with Mexico, which did not recognize Texan independence. But he was also aware that the addition of Texas, a potentially huge area for the expansion of plantation slavery, would inflame sectional tensions and endanger Van Buren's chances in the upcoming presidential election. In private, however, he urged Texans to seize harbors on the Pacific Coast from Mexican control and thus make annexation more attractive to the commercial interests of the Northeast.

For the sake of sectional harmony, party leaders sidestepped the Texas issue after 1836. Tyler renewed the issue in 1843 to curry favor among southern and western Democrats. He replaced Webster as secretary of state with a proannexationist Virginian, Abel P. Upshur, and secretly opened negotiations with the Texans. After Upshur's death in an accidental explosion on the battleship *Princeton,* John C. Calhoun, his successor, completed the negotiations and dramatically politicized the slavery issue. In the spring of 1844, Calhoun and Tyler submitted to the Senate a secretly drawn up treaty annexing Texas to the United States. Calhoun also made public his correspondence with Richard Pakenham, the British minister in Washington. In his letter, Calhoun accused the British of seeking to force emancipation on Texas in return for economic aid and a British-brokered Mexican recognition of Texan independence. These British efforts, warned Calhoun, were just the opening wedge in a master plan to block U.S. expansion and destroy slavery in the South. After pointedly defending slavery as a benign institution, Calhoun concluded that the security and preservation of the Union demanded the annexation of Texas. The Pakenham letter hit the Senate like a bombshell, convincing antislavery Northerners that the annexation of Texas was a slaveholders' conspiracy to extend slavery and swell the political power of the South. In June 1844, the Senate rejected Calhoun's treaty of annexation by a two-to-one margin. All but one Whig senator voted against it. Still, the issue was hardly dead. Thanks to Tyler and Calhoun, Texas dominated the election of 1844.

The Election of 1844

The Whig and Democratic National Conventions met in the spring of 1844 in the midst of the uproar over Texas. Both Clay, who had the Whig nomination locked up, and Van Buren, who was the strong favorite for the Democratic one, came out against immediate annexation. Clay's stand was consistent with Whig fears that territorial expansion would disrupt the party's plans for ordered economic development. But Van Buren's anti-Texas stand cost him his party's nomination. In a carefully devised strategy, western and southern Democrats united to deny him the necessary two-thirds vote of convention delegates. A deadlocked convention turned to James K. Polk of Tennessee, a confirmed expansionist who had the blessing of Jackson, the party's patriarch.

To counter the charge that they were a prosouthern party, the Democrats ran in 1844 on a platform that linked Oregon to Texas as a territorial objective. Oregon had first attracted public attention during the Tyler presidency. Glowing reports from Protestant missionaries of the boundless fertility of Oregon's Willamette Valley triggered a migration to the new promised land on the shores of the Pacific by midwestern farm families still reeling from the Panic of 1837. At the same time, the report of a naval expedition sent to explore the Pacific aroused the interest of New England merchants in using Oregon as a jumping-off point for expanded trade with China.

Some 6,000 Americans were in Oregon by the mid-1840s, and demands mounted, especially from northern Democrats, that the United States abandon its 1818 agreement of joint occupation with the British and lay exclusive claim to Oregon as far north as the 54°40' parallel, the border with Russian-owned Alaska. These were bold, even reckless, demands, because the actual area of U.S. settlement in Oregon was south of the Columbia River, itself well south of even the 49th parallel. Nonetheless, the Polk Democrats seemed to endorse them when they asserted a U.S. claim "to the whole of the Territory of Oregon."

Polk's expansionist program united the Democrats and enabled them to campaign with much more enthusiasm than in 1840. Acquiring Texas and Oregon not only held out the hope of cheap, abundant land to debt-burdened farmers in the North and planters in the South but also played on the anti-British sentiments of many voters. In contrast, the Whig campaign was out of focus. Clay sensed that his opposition to the immediate annexation of Texas was hurting him in the South, and he started to hedge by saying that he would accept Texas if the conditions were right. This wavering, however, failed to stem the defection of proslavery southern Whigs to the Democrats and cut into his support among antislavery Whigs in the North. Clay lost to Polk by less than 2 percent of the popular vote.

Tyler claimed Polk's victory as a mandate for the immediate annexation of Texas. He knew that it would still be impossible to gain the two-thirds majority in the Senate necessary for the approval of a treaty. Thus, he resorted to the constitutionally unprecedented expedient of a joint resolution in Congress inviting Texas to join the Union. By the narrow margin of 27 to 25, the Senate concurred with the House in favor of annexation. Tyler signed the joint resolution on March 1, 1845.

Although Tyler had failed to secure the Democratic nomination in 1844, he had gained Texas. He also had the satisfaction of getting revenge against the Whigs, the party that had disowned him. Texas, more than any other issue, defeated Clay and the Whigs in 1844.

Conclusion

The Jacksonian era ushered in a revolution in U.S. political life. Responding to a surge of democratization that was in full swing by the 1820s, politicians learned how to appeal to a mass electorate and to build disciplined parties that channeled popular desires into distinctive party positions. In the two decades after 1824, voter participation in national elections tripled, and Democrats and Whigs competed on nearly equal terms in every region.

Although the origins of a national political culture can be traced back to the Federalists and the Jeffersonian Republicans, politics did not fully enter the mainstream of U.S. life until the rise of the second party system of Democrats and Whigs. The election of 1824 revived interest in presidential politics, and Jackson's forceful style of leadership highlighted the presidency as the focal point of U.S. politics. Professional politicians soon mastered the art of tailoring issues and images to reach the widest popular audience. Voters in favor of government aid for economic development and a social order based on Protestant moral controls turned to the Whigs. Conversely, those who saw an activist government as a threat to their economic and cultural equality turned to the Democrats.

The national issues around which the Democrats and Whigs organized and battled down to 1844 were primarily economic. As long as this was the case, party competition tended to diffuse sectional tensions and strengthen a national political culture. Slavery, in the form of the Texas question, replaced the economy as the decisive issue in the election of 1844. With this shift, party appeals began to focus on the place of slavery in U.S. society, creating an escalating politics of sectionalism. Within a decade, the slavery issue would rip apart the second party system.

Review Questions

1. Explain the democratic movements of the early nineteenth century. What role did race and gender play in these movements? What evidence is there for the existence of similar democratic sentiments in Europe?

2. What distinguished Jackson's presidency from those of his predecessors? How did he redefine the role of the president?

3. How was the Bank War central to the development of the Democratic and Whig parties? Why did the political debates of the 1830s focus on financial issues?

4. In terms of ideology and voter appeal, how did the Democrats and Whigs differ? How did each party represent a distinctive response to economic and social change?

5. How would you describe the changes in U.S. politics between 1824 and 1840? What accounted for these changes?

6. How did the annexation of Texas emerge as a political issue in the early 1840s? Why were the Democrats more in favor of territorial expansion than the Whigs?

7. What do you think accounted for the sense of shock, even outrage, with which Benjamin Brown French reacted to the partisanship of the election of 1828?

Key Terms

Abolitionist movement (p. 260)

Albany Regency (p. 254)

Anti-Masons (p. 265)

Bank War (p. 260)

Black Hawk's War (p. 257)

Democratic Party (p. 253)

Gag rule (p. 264)

Independent Treasury System (p. 263)

Indian Removal Act (p. 257)

Jacksonian Democrats (p. 248)

Nullification crisis (p. 258)

Second Great Awakening (p. 250)

Second party system (p. 265)

Specie Circular (p. 263)

Spoils system (p. 256)

Trail of Tears (p. 257)

Webster-Ashburton Treaty (p. 269)

Whig party (p. 263)

Recommended Reading

Howe, Daniel Walker. *What Hath God Wrought: The Transformation of America, 1815–1848* (2007). A balanced and gracefully written synthesis of the key changes that transformed the U.S. in the generation after the War of 1812.

Remini, Robert V. *The Life of Andrew Jackson* (1988). A lively account of Jackson's career, written by his most noted biographer.

Sellers, Charles. *The Market Revolution: Jacksonian America, 1815–1846* (1991). A boldly conceived work that places responses to market change at the center of the era's political development.

Varon, Elizabeth R. *We Mean to Be Counted: White Women and Politics in Antebellum Virginia* (1998). A recent work that reveals the surprising extent to which elite white women in Virginia engaged in partisan politics.

Watson, Harry. *Liberty and Power: The Politics of Jacksonian America* (1990). A very readable and concise synthesis of Jacksonian politics.

Wilentz, Sean. *The Rise of American Democracy: Jefferson to Lincoln* (2005). A sweeping narrative history that reveals the extent of democratic change in the antebellum United States.

Where to Learn More

■ **Rice Museum, Georgetown, South Carolina.** Rice planters were the leaders of the nullification movement, and the interpretive materials here on the history of rice cultivation help one understand how slave labor was employed to produce their great wealth. Maps to the museum and news of special events can be found at www.ricemuseum.com.

■ **The Hermitage, Hermitage, Tennessee.** This site, the plantation home of Andrew Jackson, includes a museum with artifacts of Jackson's life. Its website, www.thehermitage.com, lists events and programs and examines the archaeological projects undertaken at the Hermitage.

■ **Martin Van Buren National Historic Site, Kinderhook, New York.** The site preserves Lindenwald, Van Buren's home after he left the presidency, and includes a

library with materials on Van Buren and his political era. Its recently expanded website, www.nps.gov/mava/home.htm, discusses the history of Lindenwald and includes a virtual tour of its art collection.

■ **Cherokee Trail of Tears Commemorative Park, Hopkinsville, Kentucky.** Used as an encampment by the Cherokees in 1838 and 1839, this historic park is a documented site of part of the actual trail followed by the Cherokees during their forced removal. www.trailoftear.org

■ **Trail of Tears National Historic Trail.** For access and information on the land and water routes followed by the Cherokees as they were forced out of the East, see www.nps.gov/trte

Study Resources

For study resources for this chapter, go to www.myhistorylab.com and choose *The American Journey*. You will find a wealth of study and review material for this chapter, including pre- and post-tests, customized study plan, key term review flash cards, interactive map and document activities, and documents for analysis.

The spectacle of the slave market was commonplace in the cities of the antebellum South. The above scene is of a slave auction in Richmond, Virginia.

Slavery and the Old South 11
1800–1860

Had Mrs Wheeler condemned me to the severest corporal punish, or exposed me to be sold in the public slave market in Wilmington [New Carolina] I should probably have resigned myself with apparent composure to her cruel behests. But when she sought to force me into a compulsory union with a man whom I could only hate and despise it seemed that rebellion would be a virtue, that duty to myself and my God actually required it, and that whatever accidents or misfortunes might attend my flight nothing could be worse than what threatened my stay.

Marriage like many other blessings I considered to be especially designed for the free, and something that all the victims of slavery should avoid as tending essentially to perpetuate that system. Hence to all overtures of that kind from whatever quarter they might come I had invariably turned a deaf ear. I had spurned domestic ties not because my heart was hard, but because it was my unalterable resolution never to entail slavery on any human being. And now when I had voluntarily renounced the society of those I might have learned to love should I be compelled to accept one, whose person, and speech, and manner could not fail to be ever regarded by me with loathing and disgust. Then to be driven in to the fields beneath the eye and lash of the brutal overseer, and those miserable huts, with their promiscuous crowds of dirty, obscene and degraded objects, for my home I could not, I would not bear it.

Hannah Crafts

Henry Louis Gates, Jr., ed., *The Bondwoman's Narrative* (New York: Warner Books, 2002), pp. 206–207.

myhistorylab

Personal Journeys Online

- Marie Perkins, *Letter*, 1852. A slave writes her husband informing him of the sale of their son.

- Lucy Skipwith, *Letter*, 1855. A slave writes her master in Virginia from his plantation in Alabama.

- Stephen Pembroke, *Speech by a slave*, 1854. A former slave describes his life under slavery.

Hannah Crafts was the name an African American woman adopted after she escaped from slavery in the late 1850s. This passage is from *The Bondwoman's Narrative*, a recently discovered manuscript that stands as the only known novel written by a female black slave. Although the precise identity of Crafts remains uncertain, the evidence strongly suggests that she was a house slave of John Hill Wheeler of North Carolina who fled north in the spring of 1857, married a Methodist clergyman, and merged into the black middle class of southern New Jersey. As a fugitive slave in the North, Crafts risked recapture at any time prior to the outbreak of the Civil War. Her decision not to publish her autobiographical slave narrative might well have been based on the fear that its detailed portrayal of the Wheeler family would reveal her whereabouts to an owner intent on reclaiming her. The novel contains searingly candid observations on the brutalized living conditions that field slaves were forced to endure.

Knowing from firsthand experience that masters frequently violated the sanctity of slave marriages and, under the law, could keep any resulting children as slaves, she believed that all slaves should remain celibate: "plain, practical common sense must teach every observer that any situation involving such responsibilities as marriage can only be filled with profit, and honor, and advantage by the free." Triggering her decision to flee was Mrs. Wheeler's demand that she "marry" the field hand Bill, that is, submit to being raped by a man she despised and to living in the squalor of the huts in the slave quarters.

Only the system of slavery that Crafts described with revulsion makes it possible to speak of the antebellum South as a single region despite its geographical and cultural diversity. It was black slavery that created a bond among white Southerners and cast them in a common mold.

Not only did slavery make the South distinctive, it was also the source of the region's immense agricultural wealth, the foundation on which planters built their fortunes, the basis for white upward mobility, and the means by which white people controlled a large black minority. Slavery also frightened white southerners with a vision of what might happen to them should they not protect their own personal liberties, including, paradoxically, the liberty to enslave African Americans. Southern white men were thus quick to take offense at any challenge to their honor or independence. The code of honor for planters demanded an apology or vindication in a duel for any insult, whether real or perceived. Precisely because slavery was so deeply embedded in southern life and customs, white leadership reacted to the mounting attacks on slavery after 1830 with an ever more defiant defense of the institution. That defense, in turn, reinforced a growing sense of sectionalism among white southerners, the belief that their values divided them from their fellow citizens in the Union.

CHRONOLOGY

1790s	Large-scale conversions of slaves to Christianity begin.
1793	Eli Whitney patents the cotton gin.
1800	Gabriel Prosser leads a rebellion in Richmond, Virginia.
1807	Britain abolishes the slave trade.
1808	Congress prohibits the African slave trade.
1811	Slaves rebel in Louisiana.
1816–1819	First cotton boom in the South.
1822	Denmark Vesey's Conspiracy fails in Charleston, South Carolina.
1823	Spain outlaws slavery.
1831	Nat Turner leads a rebellion in Southampton County, Virginia.
1831–1832	Virginia legislature debates and rejects gradual emancipation.
1832	Thomas R. Dew publishes the first full-scale defense of slavery.
1837–1845	Slavery issue divides Presbyterians, Methodists, and Baptists into separate sectional churches.
1845	Florida and Texas, the last two slave states, are admitted to the Union.
1848	France outlaws slavery.
1850s	Cotton production doubles.
1857	Hinton R. Helper publishes *The Impending Crisis of the South*.

Economically and intellectually, the Old South developed in stages. The South of 1860 was geographically much larger and more diverse than it had been in 1800. It was also more uniformly committed to a single cash crop, cotton. Demand for cotton had exploded as the industrial revolution made the mass production of textiles possible. New England mill owners were now as dependent on slavery as southern planters. Cotton became king, as contemporaries put it, and it provided the economic basis for southern sectionalism. During the reign of King Cotton, however, regional differences emerged between the Lower South, where the linkage between cotton and slavery was strong, and the Upper South, where slavery was relatively less important and the economy was more diversified.

The Lower South

South and west of South Carolina stretched some of the best cotton land in the world. A long growing season, adequate rainfall, navigable rivers, and untapped fertility gave the Lower South—consisting, in 1850, of South Carolina, Georgia, Florida, Alabama, Mississippi, Louisiana, and Texas—incomparable natural advantages for growing cotton. Ambitious white southerners exploited these advantages by extending slavery to the newer cotton lands that opened up in the Lower South after 1800 (see Map 11–1). Cotton production and slavery thus went hand in hand.

Cotton and Slaves

Before 1800, slavery was associated with the cash crops of tobacco, rice, and sea island (or long-staple) cotton. Tobacco, the mainstay of the colonial Chesapeake economy, severely depleted the soil. Its production stagnated after the Revolutionary War, when it lost its formerly protected markets in Britain. Rice and long-staple cotton, named for its long, silky fibers, were profitable but geographically limited to the humid sea islands and tidal flats off the coast of South Carolina and Georgia. Like sugar cane, introduced into Louisiana in the 1790s, they required a huge capital investment in special machinery, dikes, and labor. Upland, or short-staple, cotton faced none of these constraints, once the cotton gin removed the technical barrier to its commercial production (see Chapter 13). It could be planted far inland, and small farmers could grow it profitably because it required no additional costs for machinery or drainage systems.

As a result, after the 1790s, the production of short-staple cotton boomed. Moreover, like the South's other cash crops, upland cotton was well suited for slave labor because it required fairly continuous tending throughout the year. Once the harvest was in, a time when northern agricultural workers were laid off, the slaves cleared land, cut wood, and made repairs. The long work year maximized the return on capital invested in slave labor.

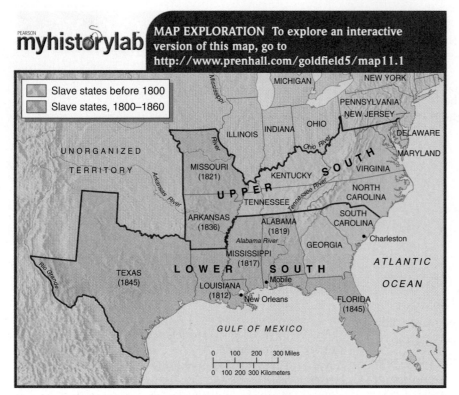

MAP EXPLORATION To explore an interactive version of this map, go to http://www.prenhall.com/goldfield5/map11.1

MAP 11–1 The Spread of Slavery: New Slave States Entering the Union, 1800–1850. Seven slave states entered the Union after 1800 as cotton production shifted westward.

Despite the care required, the cultivation of cotton left time for slaves to grow food. The major grain in the southern diet was corn, which nicely complemented the labor cycle of cotton. Corn needed little attention while cotton was being harvested and could be planted earlier or later than cotton during the long growing season. Surplus corn could be fed to hogs and converted into pork. Because almost all cotton farms and plantations also raised corn and hogs, the South virtually fed itself.

The linkage of cotton and slaves was at the heart of the plantation system that spread westward after the War of 1812. From its original base in South Carolina and Georgia, the cotton kingdom moved into the Old Southwest and then into Texas and Arkansas. As wasteful agricultural practices exhausted new lands, planters moved to the next cotton frontier farther west. Cotton output exploded from 73,000 bales (a bale weighed close to 500 pounds) in 1800 to more than 2 million bales by midcentury, thanks to the fertility of virgin land and to technological changes, such as improved seed varieties and steam-powered cotton gins (see Figure 11–1). Slave labor accounted for more than 90 percent of cotton production.

Plantations, large productive units specializing in a cash crop and employing at least 20 slaves, were the leading economic institution in the Lower South. Planters were the most prestigious social group, and, although less than 5 percent of white families were in the planter class, they controlled more than 40 percent of the slaves, cotton output, and total agricultural wealth. Most had inherited or married into their wealth, but they could stay at the top of the South's class structure only by continuing to profit from slave labor.

Plantations were generally more efficient producers of cotton than small farms. Planters had the best land because only they commanded the labor resources to exploit the wet bottomlands, drain the swamps, or clear the raw jungle in the Mississippi Delta. They were also more likely than farmers to belong to agricultural reform societies and to learn about superior seed varieties and progressive growing techniques. Most important, the ownership of 20 or more slaves enabled planters to use gangs to do both routine and specialized agricultural work. This **gang system**, a crude version of the division of labor that was being introduced in northern factories, permitted a regimented work pace. Teams of field hands, made up of women as well as men, had to work at a steady pace or else feel the lash. They were supervised by white overseers and black drivers, slaves selected for their managerial skills and agricultural knowledge.

By 1850, the plantations of the Lower South were larger and more specialized than those elsewhere in the South, and the wealth of their owners was more ostentatiously displayed. More clusters of slave cabins, overseers' quarters, and cotton gins dotted the countryside. The few towns were little more than haphazard collections of plain wooden houses scattered around a tavern, country store, and blacksmith's shop.

The plantation districts of the Lower South stifled the growth of towns and economic enterprise. Planters, as well as ordinary farmers, strove to be self-sufficient. The most significant economic exchange, exporting cotton, took place in international markets and was handled by specialized commission merchants in Charleston, Mobile, and New Orleans. The Lower South had amassed great wealth, but most outsiders saw no signs of progress there.

The Profits of Slavery

Slavery was profitable on an individual basis. Most modern studies indicate that the average rate of return on capital invested in a slave was about 10 percent a year, a rate that at least equaled that of alternative investments in the South or the North. Not surprisingly, the newer regions of the cotton kingdom in the Lower South, with the most productive land and the greatest commitment to plantation agriculture, consistently led the nation in per capita income.

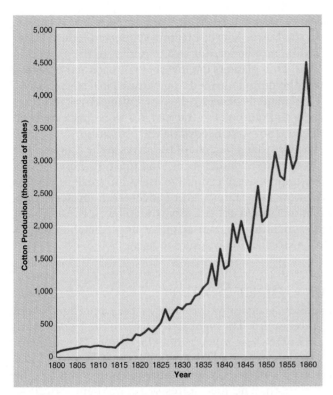

FIGURE 11–1   U.S. Cotton Production, 1800–1860
Cotton production spiraled upward after 1800, and the South
became the world's leading supplier.

Data Source: U.S. Bureau of the Census, *Historical Statistics of
the United States* (1960).

The profitability of slavery ultimately rested on the enormous demand for cotton outside the South. This demand
grew at about 5 percent a year during the first half of the
nineteenth century. Demand was so strong that prices held
steady at around 10 cents a pound in the 1850s, even as southern production of cotton doubled. Textile mills in Britain
were always the largest market, but demand in continental
Europe and the United States grew even faster after 1840.

The slave trade.   Southern law defined slaves as chattel,
the personal property of their owners, and their market value
increased along with the profitability of slavery. Prices for a
male field hand rose from $250 in 1815 to $900 by 1860.
Prices at any given time varied according to the age, sex, and
skills of the slave, as well as overall market conditions, but
the steady rise in prices meant that slave owners could sell
their human chattel and realize a profit over and above what
they had already earned from the slaves' labor. This was especially the case with slave mothers; the children they bore
increased the capital assets of their owners. Slave women of
childbearing age were therefore valued nearly as much as
male field hands.

The domestic slave trade brought buyers and sellers of
slaves together. Slaves flowed from the older areas of the

Upper South to the newer plantation districts in the Lower
South. Despite some smuggling of African slaves, planters
in the Deep South had to rely on the internal trade for the
bulk of their labor supply once Congress closed off the
African slave trade in 1808. This trade was extensive: More
than 800,000 slaves were moved between regions in the
South from 1790 to 1860, and professional slave traders transported at least 60 percent of them. Drawing on lines of credit
from banks, the traders paid cash for slaves, most of whom
they bought from plantations in the Upper South. By selling these slaves in regional markets where demand had driven
up the price, they turned a tidy profit.

The sheer size of the internal slave trade indicates just
how profit-driven slave owners were. Few of them hesitated
to break up slave families for sale when market conditions
were right. About half of all slave sales separated family members. Slave children born in the Upper South after 1820 stood
a one-in-three chance of being sold during their lifetime.
Most of the profits from slave labor and sales went into buying more land and slaves. As long as slaves employed in growing cash staples returned 10 percent a year, slave owners had
little economic incentive to shift their capital resources into
manufacturing or urban development. The predictable result was that industrialization and urbanization fell far behind
the levels in the free states, creating what outsiders came to
decry as southern "backwardness." The South had one-third
of the nation's population in 1860 but produced by value only
10 percent of the nation's manufacturing output. Fewer than
one in ten Southerners lived in a city, compared to more than
one in three northeasterners and one in seven midwesterners.

Nowhere was the indifference of planters to economic
diversification more evident than in the Lower South, which

Like most slave traders, Thomas Griggs of Charleston offered cash for ill
slaves he purchased.

had the smallest urban population and the fewest factories. Planters here were not opposed to economic innovations that promised greater profits, but they feared social changes that might undermine the stability of slavery. Urbanization and industrialization both entailed such risks. Most planters suspected that the urban environment weakened slavery. An editorial in the *New Orleans Crescent* charged that slaves in the city were "demoralized to a deplorable extent, all owing to the indiscriminate license and indulgence extended them by masters, mistresses, and guardians, and to the practice of forging passes, which has now become a regular business in New Orleans." For a white person, a "demoralized" slave was one who behaved as if free. Urban slaves, though scarcely free, enjoyed a degree of personal and economic independence that blurred the line between freedom and servitude.

Urban slavery.   Urban slaves were artisans, semiskilled laborers, and domestics, and, unlike their rural counterparts, they usually lived apart from their owners. They had much more freedom than field hands to move around, interact with white people and other black people, and experiment with various social roles. Many of them, especially if they had a marketable skill, such as carpentry or tailoring, could hire out their labor and retain some of their wages for themselves after reimbursing their owners. In short, the direct authority of the slave owner was less clear-cut in the town than in the country.

Urban slavery declined from 1820 to 1860 as slaves decreased from 22 percent to 10 percent of the urban population. This decline reflected both doubts about the stability of slavery in an urban setting and the large profits that slave labor earned for slave owners in the rural cotton economy.

Industrial slavery.   The ambivalence of planters toward urban slavery also characterized their attitudes toward industrial slavery and, indeed, to industrialization itself. If based on free labor, industrialization risked promoting an antislavery class consciousness among manufacturing laborers that would challenge the property rights of slave owners. William Gregg, the owner of a large cotton mill in upcountry South Carolina, showed that these fears were overblown when he built a company town in the 1840s that kept his white workers under tight, paternalistic controls. Still, many planters considered free workers potential abolitionists. But the use of slaves as factory operatives threatened slave discipline because an efficient level of production required special incentives. "Whenever a slave is made a mechanic, he is more than half freed," complained James Hammond, a South Carolina planter. Elaborating on Hammond's fears, a Virginian noted of slaves that he had hired out for industrial work, "They were worked hard, and had too much liberty, and were acquiring bad habits. They earned money by overwork, and spent it for whisky, and got a habit of roaming about and *taking care of themselves;* because, when they were not at work in the furnace, nobody looked out for them."

The anxieties of planters over industrialization and their refusal to shift capital from plantation agriculture to factories

ensured that manufacturing played only a minor economic role in the Lower South. Planters supported industrialization only as an adjunct, not an alternative, to the plantation economy. Thus planters did invest in railroads and factories, but their holdings remained concentrated in land and slaves. They augmented their incomes by renting slaves to manufacturers and railroad contractors but were quick to recall them when they were needed on the plantation.

No more than 5 percent of the slaves in the Lower South ever worked in manufacturing, and most of these were in rural enterprises serving local markets too small to interest northern manufacturers. Ever concerned to preserve slavery, planters would not risk slave discipline or the profits of cotton agriculture by embracing the unpredictable changes that industrialization was sure to bring.

The Upper South

Climate and geography distinguished the Upper South from the Lower South. The eight slave states of the Upper South lay north of the best growing zones for cotton. The northernmost of these states—Delaware, Maryland, Kentucky, and Missouri—bordered on free states and were known as the Border South. The four states south of them—Virginia, North Carolina, Tennessee, and Arkansas—constituted a middle zone. Slavery was entrenched in all these states, but it was less dominant than in the cotton South.

The key difference between the Upper and Lower South was the suitability of the Lower South for growing cotton with gangs of slave laborers. Except for prime cotton districts in middle Tennessee, eastern Arkansas, and parts of North Carolina, the Upper South lacked the fertile soil and long growing season necessary for the commercial production of cotton, rice, or sugar (see Map 11–2). Consequently, the demand for slaves was smaller than in the Lower South. Two-thirds of white southerners lived in the Upper South in 1860, but they held only 45 percent of all slaves. Percentages of slave ownership and of slaves in the overall population were roughly half those in the cotton South. While the Lower South was undergoing a cotton boom after the War of 1812, the Upper South was mired in a long economic slump, from which it did not emerge until the 1850s. The improved economy of the Upper South in the late antebellum period increasingly relied on free labor, a development that many cotton planters feared would diminish southern unity in defense of slavery.

A Period of Economic Adjustment

To inhabitants and visitors alike, vast stretches of the Upper South presented a dreary spectacle of exhausted fields and depopulation in the 1820s and 1830s. The soil was most depleted where tobacco had been cultivated extensively. Even where the land was still fertile, farmers could not compete against the fresher lands of the Old Southwest. Land values fell as farmers dumped their property and headed west.

FROM THEN TO NOW

Overcoming the Economic Legacy of Slavery

Slavery generated immense wealth for the planter elite and consistent profits from the production and export sale of cash staples such as cotton. As long as plantation agriculture remained profitable, planters had little incentive to diversify the Southern economy along the path of manufacturing and transportation improvements followed by the antebellum North. At the same time, the vast bulk of Southerners—black slaves to be sure as well as most nonslaveholding whites—lacked the cash income and educational skills needed to create a sectional demand for consumer goods or improvements in their standard of living. Defeat in the Civil War and the revolutionary changes that emancipation brought to Southern agriculture wiped out capital reserves and left in its wake persistent poverty and underdevelopment. From near parity in 1860, the region's per capita income fell to but half that of the nation as a whole by 1880 and remained at that trough until well into the twentieth century. It is no wonder that by the 1930s the South was labeled as the nation's number one economic problem.

BMW employees on an assembly line in Greer, South Carolina.

Massive federal spending programs associated with the New Deal initiated a tentative upswing in the Southern economy. Then, during World War II, abundant, well-paying jobs accelerated the outflow of the South's low-skill workers and federal money poured into the South for new defense plants and war-related projects. By the 1950s, the Southern economy had turned the corner. Southern politicians became adept at attracting new sources of capital and large federal subsidies, and the white business elite, at first reluctantly and then with increasing speed, backed the formal end of segregation in order to improve the South's image. Today, well over a century after slavery had placed it on a separate path of economic development, the Southern economy has entered the national mainstream and enjoys one of the highest rates of economic growth in the nation.

■ How would you explain the role that the sudden end of slavery played in the chronic poverty that plagued the South for so long after the Civil War?

African-American field hands return from a cotton field in the 1860s

PEARSON
myhistorylab

From Then to Now Online

11-1 Robert Russell, travel account. 1857. Describes lack of economic development in a slave state.

11-2 The Report on Economic Conditions of the South, 1938. Findings of the National Emergency Council on the economic conditions and needs of the South.

11-3 Darla Moore, Chairman, Palmetto Institute, a report of South Carolina's Council on Competitiveness, 2007. Challenges confronting the economic future of South Carolina.

MAP EXPLORATION To explore an interactive version of this map, go to http://www.prenhall.com/goldfield5/map11.2

MAP 11–2   Cotton and Other Crops in the South, 1860
Most of the Upper South was outside the cotton belt, where the demand for slave labor was greatest.

"Emigration is here raging with all the strength of fanaticism," wrote a Virginian in 1837, "and nothing else can be talked of but selling estates, at a great sacrifice, and '*packing off*' for the '*far west.*'"

Agricultural reform emerged in the 1830s as one proposed solution to this economic crisis. Its leading advocate was Edmund Ruffin, a Virginia planter who tirelessly promoted the use of marl (calcium-rich seashell deposits) to neutralize the overly acidic and worn-out soils of the Upper South. He also called for deeper plowing, systematic rotation of crops, and upgrading the breeding stock for animal husbandry.

Ruffin's efforts, and those of the agricultural societies and fairs spawned by the reform movement, met with some success, especially in the 1840s, when the prices of all cash staples fell. Still, only a minority of farmers ever embraced reform. These were generally the well-educated planters who read the agricultural press and could afford to change their farming practices. The landscape of Ruffin's beloved Virginia Tidewater still provoked travelers to remark, as one did in the early 1850s, "I've heard 'em say out West that old Virginny was the mother of statesmen, reckon she must be about done, eh? This 'ere's about the barrenest look for a mother ever I see."

Although soil exhaustion and wasteful farming persisted, agriculture in the Upper South had revived by the 1850s. A rebound in the tobacco market accounted for part of this revival, but the growing profitability of general farming was responsible for most of it.

Particularly in the Border South, the trend was toward agricultural diversification. Farmers and planters lessened their dependence on slave labor or on a single cash crop and practiced a thrifty, efficient agriculture geared to producing grain and livestock for urban markets. Western Maryland and the Shenandoah Valley and northern sections of Virginia grew wheat, and in the former tobacco districts of the Virginia and North Carolina Tidewater, wheat, corn, and garden vegetables became major cash crops.

Expanding urban markets and a network of internal improvements facilitated the transition to general farming. Both these developments were outgrowths of the movement for industrial diversification launched in the 1820s in response to the heavy outflow of population from the Upper South.

Growing urbanization.   Although not far advanced by northern standards, urbanization and industrialization in the Upper South were considerably greater than in the Lower South. The region had twice the percentage of urban residents of the cotton South, and it contained the leading manufacturing cities in the slave states, St. Louis, Baltimore, and Louisville. By 1860, the Upper South accounted for three-fourths of the South's manufacturing capital and output and nearly all of its heavy industry. Canals and railroads linked cities and countryside in a denser transportation grid than in the Lower South.

With an economy more balanced among agriculture, manufacturing, and trade than a generation earlier, the Upper South at midcentury was gradually becoming less tied to plantation agriculture and slave labor. The rural majority increasingly prospered by growing foodstuffs for city-dwellers and factory workers. The labor market for railroad construction and manufacturing work attracted northern immigrants, helping to compensate for the loss of the native-born population through migration to other states.

The economic adjustment in the Upper South converted the labor surplus of the 1820s into a labor scarcity by the 1850s. "It is a fact," noted Edmund Ruffin in 1859, "that labor is greatly deficient in all Virginia, and especially in the rich western counties, which, for want of labor, scarcely yet yield

The internal slave trade was the primary means by which the slaves of the Upper South were brought into the plantation markets of the Old Southwest. This illustration shows professional slave traders driving a chained group of slaves, known as a coffle, to prospective buyers in the Lower South.

Collection of The New-York Historical Society

in the proportion of one tenth of their capacity." Ruffin's commitment to agricultural reform was exceeded only by his devotion to slavery. He now feared that free labor was about to replace scarce and expensive slave labor in Virginia and much of the Upper South.

The Decline of Slavery

Slave owners tended to exaggerate all threats to slavery, and Ruffin was no exception. But slavery was clearly growing weaker in the Upper South by the 1850s (see Figure 11–2). The decline was most evident along the northern tier of the Upper South, where the proportion of slaves to the overall population fell steadily after 1830. By 1860, slaves in the Border South had dropped to 2 percent of the population in Delaware, 13 percent in Maryland, 19 percent in Kentucky, and 10 percent in Missouri. In Virginia, from 1830 to 1860, slaves fell from 39 to 31 percent of the population.

Elsewhere in the Upper South, slavery was holding its own by the 1850s. Tobacco and cotton planters in North Carolina and Tennessee continued to rely heavily on slave labor, but most small farmers were indifferent, if not opposed, to the institution. Only in Arkansas, whose alluvial lands along the Mississippi River offered a new frontier for plantation agriculture, was slavery growing rapidly. Slaves, however, still made up only 25 percent of the population of Arkansas in 1860 and were confined mainly to the southeastern corner of the state. Geographically dominated by the Ozark Highlands, Arkansas was best suited to general farming.

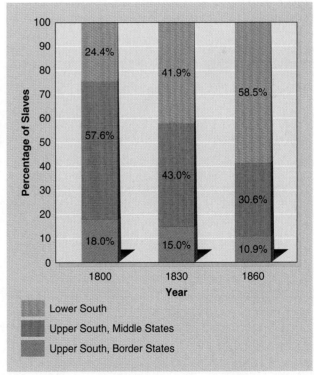

FIGURE 11–2 The Changing Regional Pattern of Slavery in the South, 1800–1860
As the nineteenth century progressed, slavery increasingly became identified with the cotton-growing Lower South.

The region's role as a slave exporter to the Lower South hastened the decline of slavery in the Upper South. In every decade after 1820, the internal slave trade drained off about 10 percent of the slaves in the Upper South, virtually the entire natural increase. Slave traders initially made most of their purchases in Virginia and Maryland, but by the 1850s, they were also active in the Carolinas, Kentucky, and Missouri. New Orleans, Memphis, and Natchez, Mississippi, were the major western distribution points for the slaves, who were sent west both by sea and by land.

Selling slaves to the Lower South reinforced the Upper South's economic stake in slavery at a time when the institution was otherwise barely profitable there. The sale of surplus slaves was a windfall for planters whose slaves had become an economic burden. This same windfall gave planters the capital to embark on agricultural reform and shift out of tobacco production. Investment capital in the Upper South was not flowing into slave property but into economic diversification that expanded urban manufacturing. Both of these structural changes increasingly put slavery at a competitive disadvantage against free labor.

The wheat, corn, oats, and fodder crops that replaced tobacco in much of the Upper South did not require continuous attention. Unlike tobacco, wheat needed intensive labor only at planting and harvest. Thus, as planters abandoned tobacco, they kept fewer slaves and relied on cheap seasonal workers to meet peak labor demand.

The cheapness and flexibility of free labor made it better suited than slave labor for general farming. Urban manufacturers likewise wanted workers who could be hired and fired at a moment's notice. Despite the successful use of slaves in tobacco manufacturing and at the large Tredegar Iron Works in Richmond, immigrant workers displaced slaves in most of the factories in the Border South. By 1860, slaves made up just 1 percent of the population in St. Louis and Baltimore, the South's major industrial cities.

Slavery was in economic retreat across the Upper South after 1830. There were still plantation districts with large concentrations of slaves, and slave owners retained enough political power to defeat all challenges to their property interests. Nevertheless, the gradual turn to free labor was unmistakable. As Alfred Iveson, a Georgia planter, noted with alarm in 1860, "Those border States can get along without slavery. Their soil and climate are appropriate to white labor; they can live and flourish without African slavery; but the cotton States cannot."

Slave Life and Culture

Nearly 4 million slaves lived in the South by 1860, a more than fivefold increase since the ratification of the Constitution. This population gain was overwhelmingly due to an excess of births over deaths. The British-led effort to suppress the foreign slave trade was successful in closing off fresh supplies from Africa after 1807.

Almost all southern slaves were thus native-born by the mid-nineteenth century. They were not Africans but African Americans, and they shared the common fate of bondage. By resisting an enslavement they could not prevent, they shaped a culture of their own that eased their pain and raised their hopes of someday being free. They retained their dignity in the face of continual humiliation and relied on their family life and religious beliefs as sources of strength under nearly intolerable circumstances.

Work Routines and Living Conditions

Being treated as a piece of property to be worked for profit and bought and sold when financially advantageous to one's owners, this was the legal and economic reality that all slaves confronted. Each southern state had its own **slave code,** laws defining the status of slaves and the rights of masters; the codes gave slave owners near-absolute power over their human property.

On June 8, 1857, the slaves on the Stirrup Branch plantation in Bishopville, South Carolina, had their picture taken in the rear of their owner's house. The occasion was the seventy-fifth birthday of Captain James Rembert.

The Suppression of the African Slave Trade

"Who durst have hoped that when we abolished the Slave Trade last spring we should be so soon in a situation to compel all other Powers to renounce it too? & that merely by the use of a maritime system, which are own interest & self-preservation prescribe to us, which every party in the country is prepared to acquiesce in, if not loudly applaud, & which even the British West Indies will be the first to rejoice in & commend…"

James Stephen, a British abolitionist who played a key role in the passage of legislation that prohibited slave-trading within the British empire beginning in 1808, deftly combined idealism and national self-interest in the above argument calling on the British navy to put an end to the Atlantic slave trade. He was writing against the backdrop of the Napoleonic Wars in the early nineteenth century when the British were deploying their naval power to interdict all neutral shipping to Napoleonic Europe. By seizing ships trading with the French, Dutch, Spanish, and Portuguese colonies, the British were also choking off supplies of slaves and provisions to these colonies. For Stephen, the British now had a providentially ordained opportunity to liberate Africa from the curse of the slave trade while simultaneously furthering their strategic objectives in the war against Napoleon. As he emphasized, a British decision to abolish the slave trade during peacetime would only have benefited rival nations willing to continue the trade and reap its profits.

With the British taking the lead (and the United State following in 1808), most of the countries of Europe had prohibited the slave trade by 1815. The major exceptions were Spain and Portugal, which were intent on maintaining a flow of African slaves into Spanish Cuba and Portuguese Brazil. Only unrelenting British pressure that forced Spain, Portugal, and, Brazil, following its independence in the 1820s, to sign treaties suppressing the slave trade finally brought an end to the legal shipment of slaves out of Africa to the Western Hemisphere. The smuggling of slaves, especially into Cuba and Brazil, continued until the 1860s, but by the end of the U.S. Civil War, the trade had finally been closed off. Long before it had, slaveholders in the American South relied on the natural increase of their slaves and the sale of slaves from the Upper to the Lower South to meet their labor needs. And now, once they had to rely exclusively on native-born slaves, many slaveholders convinced themselves that they had transformed slavery into a progressive, paternalistic institution.

- **What combination of factors explains why Great Britain, and not the United States, took the lead in suppressing the African slave trade?**

"The right of personal liberty in the slave is utterly inconsistent with the idea of slavery," wrote Thomas R. R. Cobb of Georgia in a legal treatise on slavery. The slave codes, accordingly, severely restricted the lives of slaves. Slaves could not own property, make contracts, possess guns or alcohol, legally marry (except in Louisiana), leave plantations without the owner's written permission, or testify against their masters or any other white person in a court of law. Many states also prohibited teaching a slave to read or write. The law assumed that the economic self-interest of masters in their slave property gave slaves adequate legal protection against injury. The murder of a slave by a master was illegal, but in practice, the law and community standards looked the other way if a disobedient slave was killed while being disciplined.

The slave codes penalized any challenge to a master's authority or any infraction of plantation rules. Whippings were the most commonly authorized punishment: 20 lashes on the bare back for leaving a plantation without a pass, 100 lashes for writing a pass for another slave, and so on. Striking a master, committing arson, or conspiring to rebel were punishable by death. The owner, as expressed in the Alabama Slave Code of 1852, had "the right to the time, labor and services of the slave." This, of course, was the whole purpose of owning a slave. Most masters recognized that it made good business sense to feed, clothe, and house their slaves well enough to ensure productive labor and to encourage a family life that would enable the slave population to reproduce itself. Thus planters' self-interest probably improved the living standards for slaves in the first half of the nineteenth century, and the slave population grew at a rate only slightly below that of white southerners.

Diet and housing.   Planters rarely provided their slaves with more than the bare necessities. The slaves lived mainly on rations of cornmeal and salt pork, supplemented with vegetables they grew on the small garden plots that many planters permitted and with occasional catches of game and fish. This diet provided ample calories but often insufficient vitamins and nutrients to protect slaves (as well as the many poor whites who ate the same diet) against such diseases as beriberi and pellagra. Intestinal disorders were chronic, and dysentery and cholera were common. About 20 percent of the slaves on a typical plantation were sick at any given time. Infant mortality was twice as high among slaves as among white southerners in 1850; so was mortality among slave children up to age 14. According to one study, the life expectancy for slaves at birth was 21 to 22 years, roughly half the white life expectancy.

Planters furnished slaves with two sets of coarse clothing, one for summer and one for winter. Their housing, typically a 15-by-15-foot one-room cabin for five or six occupants, provided little more than basic shelter against the elements. Small and unadorned, slave cabins showed the planters' desire to minimize housing costs and their determination to treat slaves as a regimented collective population. Large planters placed these cabins in a row, an arrangement that projected precision and undifferentiated order. Slaves expressed their individuality by furnishing their cabins with handmade beds and benches and by pushing for the right to put in gardens.

Working conditions.   The diet and housing of most slaves may have been no worse than that of the poorest whites in both the North and the South, but their workload was undoubtedly heavier. Just over half of the slave population at midcentury was concentrated on plantation units with 20 or more slaves, and most of these slaves worked as field hands in gang labor. Overseers freely admitted that they relied on whippings to make slaves in the gangs keep at their work.

Most plantation slaves toiled at hard physical labor from sunup to sundown. The work was more intense and sustained than that of white farmers or white factory hands. The fear of the whip on a bare back set the pace. At daybreak, recalled Solomon Northrup of his enslavement on a Louisiana plantation, "the fears and labors of another day begin; and until its close there is no such thing as rest. [The slave] fears he will be caught lagging through the day; he fears to approach the gin-house with his basket-load of cotton at night; he fears, when he lies down, that he will oversleep himself in the morning."

Some 15 to 20 percent of plantation slaves were house servants or skilled artisans who had lighter and less regimented workloads than field hands. Some planters used the prospect of transfer to these relatively privileged positions as an incentive to field hands to work harder. Extra rations, time off on weekends, passes to visit a spouse on a nearby

Especially on large plantations, slave nursemaids cared for the young children in the white planter's family.

From the Collection of the Louisiana State Museum

plantation, and the right to have a garden plot were among the other incentives planters used to keep labor productivity high. However, what a planter viewed as privileges, benevolently bestowed, slaves quickly came to see as customary rights. Despite the power of the whip, if planters failed to respect these "rights," slave morale would decline, and the work routine would be interrupted.

Nearly three-fourths of the slaves worked on plantations and medium-sized farms. Most of the remainder, those in units with fewer than 10 slaves, worked on small farms in close contact with the master's family. Their workloads were more varied and sometimes less taxing than those of plantation hands, but these slaves were also more directly exposed to the whims of their owners and less likely to live in complete family units. Slave couples on small holdings were more likely to live on separate farms. Owners with only a few slaves were also more vulnerable than planters to market downturns that could force them to sell slaves and further divide families.

Of all slaves, 10 percent were not attached to the land, laboring instead at jobs that most white workers shunned. Every southern industry, but most particularly extractive industries such as mining and lumbering, relied heavily on slaves. The Tredegar Iron Company in Richmond, the largest iron foundry in the South, used slaves as its main workforce after 1847, partly to curb strikes by its white workers. Racial tensions often flared in southern industry, and when the races worked together, skilled white laborers typically insisted on being placed in supervisory positions.

Digging coal as miners or shoveling it as stokers for boilers on steamboats, laying down iron for the railroads or shaping hot slabs of it in a foundry, industrial slaves worked at least as hard as field hands. Compared to plantation slaves, however, they had more independence off the job and greater opportunities to earn money of their own. Because many of them had to house and feed themselves, they could also enjoy more time free from direct white scrutiny. By undertaking extra factory work, known as "overwork," industrial slaves could earn $50 or more a month, money they could use to buy goods for their families or, in rare cases, to purchase their freedom.

Families and Religion

The core institution of slave life was the family. Except in Louisiana, southern law did not recognize slave marriages, but masters permitted, even encouraged, marital unions in order to raise the morale of their labor force and increase its value by having it produce marketable children. Slaves embraced their families as a source of loving warmth and strength in a system that treated them as commodities.

Despite all the obstacles arrayed against them, many slave marriages produced enduring commitments and a supportive moral code for family members. Most slave unions remained intact until the death or, frequently, the sale of one spouse. Close to one-third of slave marriages were broken up by sales or forced removals. A slave bitterly recalled that "the separation of slaves in this way is little thought of. A few masters regard their union as sacred, but where one does, a hundred care nothing about it."

Both parents were present in about two-thirds of slave families, the same ratio as in contemporary peasant families in western Europe. Although the father's role as protector of and provider for his wife and children had no standing under slavery, most slave fathers struggled to help feed their families by hunting and fishing, and they risked beating and death to defend their wives against sexual abuse by the overseer or master. Besides their field labors, slave mothers had all the burdens of pregnancy, child care, laundry, and cooking. Many of them still found the time to patch quilts, the patterns of which incor-porated family histories and encoded messages of escape routes to the North.

No anguish under slavery was more heartrending than that of a mother whose child was sold away from her. "Oh, my heart was too full!" recalled Charity Bowery on being told that her boy Richard had been sold. "[My mistress] had sent me away on an errand, because she didn't want to be troubled with our cries. I hadn't any chance to see my poor boy. I shall never see my poor boy. I shall never see him again in this world. My heart felt as if it was under a great load."

Charity Bowery's experience was hardly unique. Slave parents had to suppress the rage they felt at their powerlessness to protect their children from the cruelties of slavery. Slave accounts are full of stories of children running in vain to their parents to save them from a whipping. Most parents could only teach their children the skills of survival in a world in which white people had a legal monopoly on violence. The most valuable of these skills was the art of hiding one's true feelings from white people and telling them what they wanted to hear. As a perceptive traveler noted: "When therefore a white man approaches [the slaves] with inquiries concerning their condition, they are at once put upon their guard, and either make indefinite and vague replies, or directly contradict their real sentiments."

Extensive kinship ties provided a support network for the vulnerable slave family. Thickest on the older and larger plantations, these networks included both blood relatives and other significant people. Children were taught to address elders as "Aunt" and "Uncle" and fellow slaves as "sister" and

Satirically entitled *Virginian Luxuries,* this antislavery painting sought to expose how the unchecked power of slaveowners resulted in the physical beating and sexual abuse of their slaves.

"brother." If separated from a parent, a child could turn to relatives or the larger slave community for care and assistance.

Slaves followed West African customs by prohibiting marriage between cousins and by often naming their children after departed grandparents. They also drew on an African heritage kept alive through folklore and oral histories to create a religion that fit their needs. The ancestors of nineteenth-century slaves brought no common religion with them when they were taken to the New World. However, beliefs common to a variety of African religions survived. Once slaves began to embrace Christianity in the late eighteenth century, they blended these beliefs into an African Christianity.

In keeping with African traditions, the religion of the slaves fused the natural and spiritual worlds, accepted the power of ghosts over the living, and relied on an expressive form of worship in which the participants shouted and swayed in rhythm with the beat of drums and other instruments. Associated with reverence for ancestors, dance was sacred in Africa. Spirituals, the religious songs of the slaves, accompanied a dance known in America as the ring shout. Moving counterclockwise and stamping their feet to establish a beat, slaves blended dance and song in a religious ceremony that helped them to endure oppression and sustain their self-confidence.

By most estimates, no more than 30 percent of slaves ever converted to Christianity. Those who did found in Christianity a message of deliverance rooted in the liberation of Moses's people from bondage in Egypt. The Jesus of the New Testament spoke to them as a compassionate God who had shared their burden of suffering, so that all peoples could hope to find the Promised Land of love and justice. By blending biblical imagery into their spirituals, the slaves expressed their yearning for freedom: "Didn't my Lord deliver Daniel/Then why not every man?"

The initial exposure of slaves to Christianity usually came from evangelical revivalists, and slaves always favored the Baptists and Methodists over other denominations. The evangelical message of universal spiritual equality confirmed the slaves' sense of personal worth. Less formal in both their doctrines and organization than the Presbyterians and Episcopalians, the evangelical sects allowed the slaves more leeway to choose their own preachers and engage in their physical call-and-response pattern of worship. Perhaps because they baptized by total immersion, which evoked the purifying power of water so common in African religions, the Baptists gained the most slave converts.

Most planters were pragmatic about encouraging Christianity among their slaves. They wished to control religion, as they did other aspects of slaves' lives. Thus, while many planters allowed black preachers at religious services on their plantations, they usually insisted that white observers be present. Worried that abolitionist propaganda might attract the slaves to Christianity as a religion of secular liberation, some planters in the late antebellum period tried to convert their slaves to their own version of Christianity. They invited white ministers to their plantations to preach a gospel of passivity and obedience, centered on Paul's call for servants to "obey in all things your Masters."

Although most slaves viewed the religion of their owners as hypocritical and the sermons of white ministers as propaganda, they feigned acceptance of the religious wishes of their masters. They attended the special slave chapels some masters built and sat in segregated galleries in white churches on Sunday mornings. But in the evening, out of sight of the master or overseer, they held their own services in the woods and listened to their own preachers. As much as they could, the slaves hid their religious life from white people. Many slaves experienced religion as a spiritual rebirth that gave them the inner strength to endure their bondage. As one recalled, "I was born a slave and lived through some hard times. If it had not been for my God, I don't know what I would have done."

Resistance

Open resistance to slavery was futile. The persistently disobedient slave would be sold "down river" to a harsher master or, in extreme cases, killed. The fate of Richard, Charity Bowery's son who was sold away from her, typified that of the openly defiant slave. He resisted the efforts of his new owner in Alabama to break his will. When the owner threatened to shoot him if he did not consent to being whipped, Richard replied, "Shoot away, I won't come to be flogged." The master shot and killed him.

Although the odds of succeeding were infinitesimal, slaves as desperate as Richard did plot rebellion in the nineteenth century. The first major uprising, **Gabriel Prosser's Rebellion** in 1800, involved about 50 armed slaves around Richmond, though perhaps as many as 1,000 slaves knew about Prosser's plans. The rebels' failure to seize a key road to Richmond and a slave informer's warning to white authorities doomed the rebellion before it got under way. State authorities executed Prosser and 25 of his followers.

A decade later, in what seems to have been a spontaneous bid for freedom, several hundred slaves in the river parishes (counties) above New Orleans marched on the city. Poorly armed, they were no match for the U.S. Army troops and militiamen who stopped them. More than 60 slaves died, and the heads of the leading rebels were posted on poles along the Mississippi River to warn others of the fate that awaited rebellious slaves.

The most carefully planned slave revolt (at least in the minds of whites who resorted to torture to gain "confessions"), **Denmark Vesey's Conspiracy,** like Prosser's, failed before it got started. Vesey, a literate carpenter and lay preacher in Charleston who had purchased his freedom, allegedly planned the revolt in the summer of 1822. Fearful whites believed that he had assigned teams of rebels specific targets, such as the municipal guardhouse and arsenal, and that once Charleston was secured, the rebels planned to flee

to Haiti. The plot collapsed when two domestic servants betrayed it. White authorities responded swiftly and savagely. They
hanged 35 conspirators, including Vesey,
and banished 37 others from the state.
After destroying the African Methodist
Episcopal church where Vesey had
preached and the purported conspirators
had met, they tried to seal off the city from
subversive outsiders by passing the Negro
Seamen's Act, which mandated the imprisonment of black sailors while their ships
were berthed in Charleston.

One slave revolt, **Nat Turner's Rebellion,** in Southampton County, Virginia, did
erupt before it could be suppressed. Turner
was a literate field hand driven by
prophetic visions of black vengeance
against white oppressors. Convinced by
what he called "signs in heaven" that he
should "arise and prepare myself and slay
my enemies with their own weapons," he
led a small band of followers on a murder-
ous rampage in late August 1831. The first
white man to be killed was Joseph Travis,

This contemporary woodcut of Nat Turner's Rebellion depicts the fervency of both the actions
of the slaves and the response of the whites.

Turner's owner. In the next two days, the rebels killed 60
other white people. An enraged posse, aided by slaves, captured or killed most of Turner's party. Turner hid for two
months before being apprehended. He and more than 30
other slaves were executed, and panicky white people killed
more than 100 others.

Slaves well understood that the odds against a successful
rebellion were insurmountable. They could see who had all
the guns. White people were also more numerous. In contrast to the large black majorities in the slave societies of the
West Indies and Brazil, majorities made possible only by the
continuous heavy importation of Africans, slaves made up
only one-third of the population of the antebellum U.S. South.
They lacked the numbers to overwhelm the white population and could not escape to mountain hideaways or large
tracts of jungle. Surveillance by mounted white patrols, part
of the police apparatus of slavery, limited organized rebellion
by slaves to small, local affairs that were quickly suppressed.

Nor could many slaves escape to freedom. Few runaways
made it to Canada or to a free state. White people could stop
black people and demand to see papers documenting their
freedom or right to travel without a master. The
Underground Railroad, a secret network of stations and
safe houses organized by Quakers and other black and white
antislavery activists, provided some assistance. However, fellow slaves or free black people, especially in the cities of the
Border South, provided the only help most runaways could
count on. Out of more than 3 million slaves in the 1850s, only
about 1,000 a year permanently escaped. (See American
Views: A Letter from an Escaped Slave to His Former Master.)

The few who made it to the North did so by running at
night and hiding during the day. The most ingenious resorted
to clever stratagems. Henry "Box" Brown arranged to have
himself shipped in a box from Richmond to Philadelphia. Ellen
Craft, a light-skinned slave who could pass as white, disguised
herself as a male slaveholder accompanied by his dark-skinned
servant (her husband, William). What could have been a fatal
flaw in their plan, their inability to write and hence sign their
names or document their assumed identities, was overcome by
having Ellen pose as a sickly, rheumatic master whose right
hand had to be kept bandaged. Running away was common,
but most runaways fled no farther than to nearby swamps and
woods. Most voluntarily returned or were tracked down by
bloodhounds within a week. Aside from those who were
protesting a special grievance or trying to avoid punishment,
slaves who ran away usually did so to visit a spouse or loved
one. Occasionally, runaways could bargain for lenient treatment in return for faithful service in the future. Most were severely punished. Such temporary flights from the master's
control siphoned off some of the anger that might otherwise
have erupted in violent, self-destructive attacks on slave owners. All planters had heard about the field hand who took an ax
to an overseer, the cook who poisoned her master's family, or
the house servant who killed a sleeping master or mistress.

Slaves resisted complete domination by their masters
in less overt ways. They mocked white people in folktales
like those about B'rer Rabbit, for example, in which weak
but wily animals cunningly outsmart their stronger enemies.
Slave owners routinely complained of slaves malingering at
work, abusing farm animals, losing tools, stealing food, and

American Views

A Letter from an Escaped Slave to His Former Master

In 1859, Jackson Whitney was one of 6,000 fugitive slaves living in Canada, a sanctuary of freedom beyond the reach of the Fugitive Slave Act of 1850. Like most fugitives, he was male, and he had been forced to leave his family behind in Kentucky. His letter, as well as other direct testimony by African Americans about their experiences and feelings while enslaved, gives us information about slavery that only the slaves could provide.

- How would you characterize the tone of Whitney's letter? How did he express his joy at being a free man?
- How did Whitney feel that Riley, his former owner, had betrayed him?
- What did Whitney mean by the phrase "a slave talking to 'massa'"? How did he indicate that he had been hiding his true feelings as a slave?

- How did Whitney contrast his religious beliefs and those of Riley? How did he expect Riley to be punished?
- What pained Whitney about his freedom in Canada, and what did he ask of Riley?

March 18, 1859

Mr. Wm. Riley, Springfield, Ky.,
Sir:

I take this opportunity to dictate a few lines to you, supposing you might be curious to know my whereabouts. I am happy to inform you that I am in Canada, in good health, and have been here several days. Perhaps, by this time, you have concluded that robbing a woman of her husband, and children of their father does not pay, at least in your case; and I thought, while lying in jail by your direction, that if you had no remorse or conscience that would make you feel for a poor, broken-hearted man, and his worse-than-murdered wife and child,…and could not by any entreaty or permission be induced to do as you promised you would, which was to let me go with my family for $800, but contended for $1,000, when you had promised to take the same you gave for me (which was $660.) at the time you bought me, and let me go with my dear wife and children! but instead would render me miserable, and lie to me, and to your neighbors…and when you was at Louisville trying to sell me! then I thought it was time for me to make my feet feel for Canada, and let your conscience feel in your pocket. Now you cannot say but that I did all that was honorable and right while I was with you, although I was a slave. I pretended all the time that I thought you, or some one else had a better right to me than I had to myself, which you know is rather hard thinking.

You know, too, that you proved a traitor to me in the time of need, and when in the most bitter distress that the human soul is capable of experiencing; and could you have carried out your purposes there would have been no relief. But I rejoice to say that an unseen, kind spirit appeared for the oppressed, and bade me take up my bed and walk, the result of which is that I am victorious and you are defeated. I am comfortably situated in Canada, working for George Harris [another fugitive slave from Kentucky who had bought a farm in Canada]…

There is only one thing to prevent me being entirely happy here, and that is the want of my dear wife and children, and you to see us enjoying ourselves together here. I wish you could realize the contrast between Freedom and slavery; but it is not likely that we shall ever meet again on this earth.

But if you want to go to the next world and meet a God of love, mercy, and justice, in peace; who says, "Inasmuch as you did it to the least of them my little ones, you did it unto me", making the professions that you do, pretending to be a follower of Christ, and tormenting me and my little ones as you have done, [you] had better repair the breaches you have made among us in this world, by sending my wife and children to me; thus preparing to meet your God in peace; for, if God don't punish you for inflicting such distress on the poorest of His poor, then there is no use of having any God, or talking about one…

I hope you will consider candidly, and see if the case does not justify every word I have said, and ten times as much. You must not consider that it is a slave talking to 'massa' now, but one as free as yourself.

I subscribe myself one of the abused of America, but one of the justified and honored of Canada.

Jackson Whitney

Source: John W. Blassingame, ed., *Slave Testimony: Two Centuries of Letters, Speeches, Interviews, and Autobiographies* (Louisiana State University Press, 1977).

committing arson. These subversive acts of protest never challenged the system of slavery itself, but they did help slaves to maintain a sense of dignity and self-respect.

Free Society

The abolitionists and the antislavery Republican party of the 1850s portrayed the social order of the slave South as little more than haughty planters lording it over shiftless poor white people. The reality was considerably more complex. Planters, who set the social tone for the South as a whole, did act superior, but they were a tiny minority and had to contend with an ambitious middle class of small slaveholders and a majority of nonslaveholding farmers. Some landless white people on the margins of rural society fit the stereotype of "poor whites," but they were easily outnumbered by self-reliant farmers who worked their own land. Southern cities, though small by northern standards, provided jobs for a growing class of free workers who increasingly clashed with planters over the use of slave labor. These same cities, notably in the Upper South, were also home to the na-

tion's largest concentration of free black people. Their freedom, though restricted, contradicted the racial justification of slavery. They competed with white workers for jobs, and by the 1850s pressure was mounting on them to leave the South or be enslaved. The free society in the South was surely more diverse than its antislavery critics charged, but overriding racism bonded most white people together to defend the prerogatives of white supremacy.

The Slaveholding Minority

The white-columned plantation estate approached from a stately avenue of shade trees and framed by luxuriant gardens remains the most popular image of the slave South. In fact, such manorial estates were utterly unrepresentative of the lifestyle of the typical slaveholder. Only the wealthiest planters could live in such splendor, and they constituted less than 1 percent of southern white families in 1860. Yet their wealth and status were so imposing that they created an idealized image of grace and grandeur that has obscured the cruder realities of the slave regime.

Large planters.   Only in the rice districts of the South Carolina lowcountry and in the rich sugar- and cotton-growing areas of the Mississippi Delta were large planters more than a small minority of the slaveholding class, let alone the general white population. Families of the planter class, those who held a minimum of 20 slaves, constituted only around 3 percent of all southern families in 1860. Fewer than one out of five planter families, less than 1 percent of all families, owned more than 50 slaves. Far from conspicuously exhibiting their wealth, most planters lived in drab log cabins. "The planter's home is generally a rude ungainly structure, made of logs, rough hewn from the forest; rail fences and rickety gates guard its enclosures," complained a speaker to the Alabama horticultural society in 1851. "We murder our soil with wasteful culture because there is plenty of

After fleeing from slavery in Maryland in 1849, Harriet "Moses" Tubman, standing on the left, risked reenslavement by returning to the South on several occasions to assist in the escapes of other slaves. She is photographed here with some of those she helped free.

Smith College, Sophia Smith Collection, Northampton, Massachusetts.

OVERVIEW

Structure of Free Society in the South, c. 1860

Group	Size	Characteristics
Large planters	Less than 1 percent of white families	Owned 50 or more slaves and plantations in excess of 1,000 acres; the wealthiest class in United States
Planters	About 3 percent of white families	Owned 20 to 49 slaves and plantations in excess of 100 acres; controlled bulk of southern wealth and provided most of the political leaders
Small slaveholders	About 20 percent of white families	Owned fewer than 20 slaves and most often fewer than five; primarily farmers, though some were part of a small middle class in towns and cities
Nonslaveholding whites	About 75 percent of white families	Mostly yeomen farmers who owned their own land and stressed production for family use; one in five owned neither slaves nor land and squatted on the least desirable land where they planted some corn and grazed some livestock; in cities they worked as artisans or, more typically, day laborers
Free blacks	About 3 percent of all free families	Concentrated in the Upper South; hemmed in by legal and social restrictions; mostly tenants or farm laborers; about one-third lived in cities and generally were limited to lowest paying jobs

fresh land West, and we live in tents and huts when we might live in rural palaces." Most planters wanted to acquire wealth, not display it. They were restlessly eager to move on and abandon their homes when the allure of profits from a new cotton frontier promised to relieve them of the debts they had incurred to purchase their slaves.

Planters' wives. Most planters expected their wives to help supervise the slaves and run the plantation. Besides raising her children, the plantation mistress managed the household staff, oversaw the cooking and cleaning, gardened, dispensed medicine and clothing to the slaves, and often assisted in their religious instruction. When guests or relatives came for an extended visit, the wife had to make all the special arrangements that such occasions entailed. When the master was called off on a business or political trip, she kept the plantation accounts. In many respects, she worked harder than her husband.

Planters' wives often complained in their journals and letters of their isolation from other white women and the physical and mental toil of managing slaves. Still, they enjoyed a wealth and status unknown to most southern women and only rarely questioned the institution of slavery. Their deepest anger stemmed from their humiliation by husbands who kept slave mistresses or sexually abused slave women. Bound by their duties as wives not to express this anger publicly, and unwilling to renounce the institution that both victimized and benefited them, white women tended to vent their frustrations on black women whose alleged promis-

cuity they blamed for the sexual transgressions of white males. "Sometimes white mistresses will surmise that there is an intimacy between a slave woman & the master," recalled a former slave, "and perhaps she will make a great fuss & have her whipped, & perhaps there will be no peace until she is sold."

Small slaveholders. Despite the tensions and sexual jealousies it aroused, owning slaves was the surest means of social and economic advancement for most white families. Most slave owners, however, never attained planter status. Nine out of 10 slave owners in 1860 owned fewer than 20 slaves, and fully half of them had fewer than five. Many white people also rented a few slaves on a seasonal basis.

Generally younger than the planters, small slaveholders were a diverse lot. About 10 percent were women, and another 20 percent or so were merchants, businessmen, artisans, and urban professionals. Most were farmers trying to acquire enough land and slaves to become planters. To keep costs down, they often began by purchasing children, the cheapest slaves available, or a young slave family, so that they could add to their slaveholdings as the slave mother bore more children. Other slaveholding farmers had inherited their slaves and were trying to regain their fathers' planter status. Partible inheritance, the equal division of property among children, was the norm in the nineteenth-century South. Except among the richest planter families, this division reduced the sons to modest slaveholders who had to struggle to build their own plantations.

290

Colonel James A. Whiteside and his family were among the small elite of white southerners who enjoyed the wealth and ease of life on a large plantation. Reflecting the ideal of patriarchy, this portrait, c. 1858, projects the colonel as a figure of power and authority.

James Cameron (1817–1882), *Colonel and Mrs. James A. Whiteside, son Charles and servants.* Oil on canvas; c. 1858–1859. Hunter Museum of Art, Chattanooga, Tennessee, Gift of Mr. and Mrs. Thomas Whiteside.

Small slaveholders had scant economic security. A deadly outbreak of disease among their slaves or a single bad crop could destroy their credit and force them to sell their slaves to clear their debts. Owners of fewer than ten slaves stood a fifty-fifty chance within a decade of dropping out of the slaveholding class. Nor could small holders hope to compete directly with the planters. In any given area suitable for plantations, they were gradually pushed out as planters bought up land to raise livestock or more crops. In general, only slave owners who had established themselves in business or the professions had the capital reserves to rise into the planter elite.

Especially in the Lower South, owning slaves was a necessary precondition for upward mobility, but it was hardly a sufficient one. Slaveholders who failed to advance had nonetheless acquired a badge of social respectability. As a Baptist opponent of slavery put it, "Without slaves a man's children stand but poor chance to marry in reputation." Aside from conferring status, owning a few slaves could relieve a white household of much hard domestic labor. "I wish to God every head of a family in the United States had one [slave] to take the drudgery and menial service off his family," proclaimed Andrew Johnson of Tennessee in the U.S. Senate. (Johnson succeeded Abraham Lincoln as president in 1865.)

The White Majority

Three-fourths of southern white families owned no slaves in 1860. Although most numerous in the Upper South, non-slaveholders predominated wherever the soil and climate were not suitable for plantation agriculture. Most were yeoman farmers who worked their own land with family labor.

These farmers were quick to move when times were bad and their land was used up, but once settled in an area, they formed intensely localized societies in which fathers and husbands held sway over their families. The community extended 5 to 10 miles around the nearest country store or county courthouse. Networks of kin and friends provided labor services when needed, fellowship in evangelical churches, and staple goods that an individual farm could not produce. Social travel and international markets, so central to the lives of planters, had little relevance in the farmers' community-centered existence. The yeomanry aimed to be self-sufficient and limited their market involvement to the sale of livestock and an occasional cotton crop that could bring in needed cash.

Yeoman farmers jealously guarded their independence, and in their tight little worlds of face-to-face relationships, they demanded that planters treat them as social equals. Ever fearful of being reduced to dependence, they avoided debt and sought to limit government authority. Rather than risk financial ruin by buying slaves on credit to grow cotton, they grew food crops and depended on their sons and, when needed, their wives and daughters to work the fields. Far longer than most northern farmers, and in part because poor transportation raised the cost of manufactured goods, they continued to rely on their wives and daughters to make their own clothes, shoes, soap, and other consumer items.

Nonslaveholding farmers from the mountains and planters on the bottomlands rarely mixed, and their societies developed in isolation from each other. In areas where there were both small farms and scattered plantations, the interests of the yeomen and the planters were often complementary. Planters provided local markets for the surplus grain and livestock of nonslaveholders and, for a small fee, access to gristmills and gins for grinding corn and cleaning cotton. They lent small sums to poorer neighbors in emergencies or to pay taxes. The yeomen staffed the slave patrols and became overseers on the plantations. Both groups sought to protect property rights from outside interference and to maintain a system of racial control in which white liberties rested on black degradation.

When yeomen and planters clashed, it was usually over economic issues. Large slaveholders needing better credit and marketing facilities gravitated toward the Whig Party, which called for banks and internal improvements. Nonslaveholding farmers, especially in the Lower South, tended to be Democrats who opposed banks and state-funded economic projects. They viewed bankers as grasping outsiders who wanted to rob them of their economic independence, and they suspected that state involvement in the economy led only to higher taxes and increased public debt. These partisan battles, however, rarely involved a debate about the merits of slavery. As long as planters deferred to the egalitarian sensibilities of the yeomen by courting them at election time and promising to safeguard their liberties, the planters were able to maintain broad support for slavery across class lines.

Around 15 percent of rural white families owned neither land nor slaves. These were the so-called poor whites, stigmatized by both abolitionists and planters as lazy and shiftless. The abolitionists considered them a kind of underclass who proved that slavery so degraded the dignity of labor that it led people to shun work and lapse into wretched poverty. To the planters, they were a constant nuisance and a threat to slave discipline. Planters habitually complained that poor whites demoralized their slaves by showing that a person could survive without steady labor. Planters also accused them of trading guns and alcohol with slaves for stolen plantation property. Despite the efforts of slave owners to crack down on this illicit trade, poor whites and slaves continued to swap goods and socially intermingle on the fringes of the plantations.

Some landless white people did live down to their negative stereotype. Still, the "poor white trash" label with which they were stigmatized is misleading. Most were resourceful and enterprising enough to supply themselves with all the material comforts they wanted. Back in the swamps and pine barrens, shunned by planters and yeomen alike, they squatted on a few acres of land, put up crude cabins for shelter, planted some corn, and grazed livestock in the surrounding woods. Aided by the mild southern climate, they had all the corn and pork they could eat. Not having to do steady work for survival, they hunted, fished, and took orders from no one. Although poor by most standards, they were also defiantly self-reliant.

Nonslaveholders were a growing majority in southern cities, especially among the working classes. These urban workers shared no agricultural interests or ties with the planters. Nor were most of them, especially in the unskilled ranks, southern-born. Northerners and immigrants dominated the urban work force. Free workers, especially Irish and German immigrants, increasingly replaced slaves in urban labor markets. These white workers bitterly resented competition from black slaves, and their demands to exclude slaves from the urban workplace reinforced planters' belief that cities bred abolitionism. When urban laborers protested against slave competition in the 1850s, planters singled them out as the nonslaveholders most likely to attack slavery.

Free Black People

A small minority of southern black people, 6 percent of the total in 1860, were "free persons of color." They constituted 3 percent of the free population in the South (see Figure 11–3). These free black people occupied a precarious and vulnerable position between degraded enslavement and meaningful freedom. White intimidation and special legal provisions known as **black codes** (found throughout the North as well) denied them nearly all the rights of citizenship. Because of the legal presumption in the South that all black people were slaves, they had to carry freedom papers, official certificates of their freedom. They were shut out of the political process and could not testify against white people in court. Many occupations, especially those involved in the communication of ideas, such as the printing trades, were closed to them.

Every slave state forbade the entry of free black people, and every municipality had rules and regulations that forced them to live as an inferior caste. In Charleston, for example, a free black person could not smoke a cigar or carry a cane in public. Any sign of upward mobility or intimation of equal standing was ruthlessly suppressed. White people had the right of way, and a free black person who bumped into a white person on the street was likely to be flogged. More than four-fifths of the southern free black population lived in the Upper South. Most were the offspring of slaves freed by private manumissions between 1780 and 1800, when slavery temporarily loosened in the Chesapeake region in the wake of the Revolutionary War. Manumissions dropped sharply after 1810, the result of heightened white anxieties after Prosser's Rebellion and the rising demand for slaves in the Lower South.

As in the North, legal barriers and white prejudice generally confined free black people to the poorest paying and most menial work. In rural areas, a handful became independent farmers, but most worked as farm laborers or tenants. The best economic opportunities were in the cities, where some found factory jobs and positions in the skilled trades. Because the South had a general shortage of skilled labor, free black artisans—carpenters, barbers, shoemakers, tailors, and plasterers—could earn a respectable income. Indeed, the percentage of black people in the skilled trades was generally higher in the South than in the North. Talented artisans, such as Thomas Day, widely recognized as the finest cabinetmaker in North Carolina, could command a premium in wages from white employers.

One-third of the free black people in the Upper South lived in cities, a much higher proportion than among white people. Cities offered black people not only jobs but also enough social space to found their own churches and mutual-aid associations. Especially after 1840, urban African American churches became the center of black community life. Church Sunday schools and day schools provided black people practically their only access to education, which they persisted in pursuing despite white opposition. A "good education," declared a black schoolmaster in Baltimore, "is the *sine qua non* as regards the elevation of our people."

Less than 2 percent of the black people in the Lower South were free in 1860. Given the greater profitability of slavery there, manumissions were rare. Most of the Lower

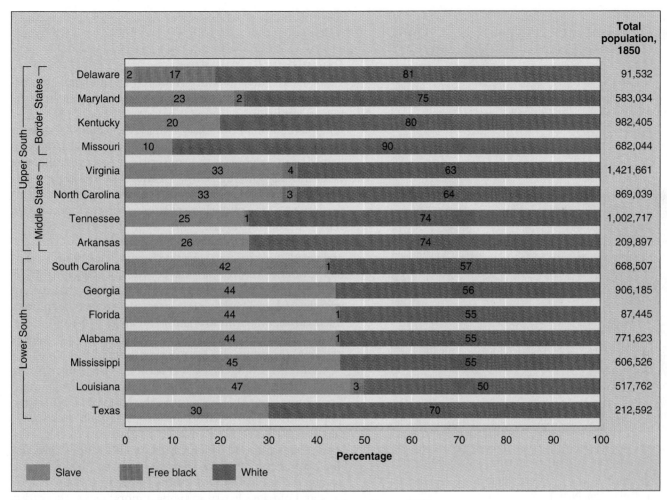

FIGURE 11–3   Slave, Free Black, and White Population in Southern States, 1850
Except for Texas, slaves by 1850 comprised over 40 percent of the population in every state of the Lower South. The small population of free black people was concentrated in the Upper South.

South's free black population descended from black emigrants who fled the revolutionary unrest in Haiti in the 1790s. These refugees were artisans, shopkeepers, and farmers who settled primarily in Charleston and New Orleans. Able to secure a solid economic footing, they left their descendants wealthier than any other free black people in the United States. Free black people in the Lower South were more likely than those in the Upper South to have a marketable skill, and two-thirds of them lived in cities.

A light skin enhanced the social standing of free black people among color-conscious whites in the Lower South. Nearly 70 percent of free black people in 1860 were mulattoes, and from their ranks came nearly all of the very small number of black planters. Mulattoes could count on greater white patronage, and they monopolized the best jobs available to free black people. A mulatto elite emerged in Charleston, Mobile, and New Orleans that carefully distanced itself from most black people, slave or free. In New Orleans, where a tradition of racially mixed unions dated

back to French and Spanish rule, mulattoes put on lavish "octoroon balls," attended by freewomen of color and by white men. Even here, however, the mulatto elite remained suspended between black and white worlds, never fully accepted by either.

Despite the emergence of a three-tiered racial hierarchy in the port cities of the Lower South, white officialdom insisted on maintaining a white and black racial dichotomy. As the racial defense of slavery intensified in the 1850s, more calls were made for laws to banish or enslave free black people. Arkansas passed such a law in 1859, and similar bills were proposed in Florida, Tennessee, Mississippi, and Missouri. Even Maryland held a referendum in 1859 on whether to reenslave its free black population, among the largest in the South. Only the opposition of nonslaveholders heavily dependent on cheap free black labor defeated the referendum.

Despised and feared by white people as a subversive element in a slave society, free black Southerners were daily reminded that their freedom rested on the whims of the

Barbering was one of the skilled trades open to black men during the antebellum years. Several wealthy African Americans began their careers as barbers.

The Granger Collection, New York.

white majority. As white attitudes turned uglier in the late antebellum period, that freedom became ever less secure.

The Proslavery Argument

In the early nineteenth century, white Southerners made no particular effort to defend slavery, because the institution was not under heavy outside attack. If pressed, most white people would have called slavery a necessary evil, an unfortunate legacy from earlier generations that was needed to maintain racial peace.

The 1830s marked a turning point. After the twin shocks of Nat Turner's Rebellion and the onset of the abolitionist crusade (for more on this crusade, see Chapter 12), white mobs emerged to stifle any open criticism of slavery in the Lower South. White Southerners also began to develop a defense of slavery. By the 1850s, politicians, intellectuals, and evangelical ministers were arguing that slavery was a positive good, an institution ordained by God as the foundation of southern prosperity, white democracy, and Christian instruction for heathen Africans. Slavery, they insisted, was a mild, paternalistic, and even caring institution. This de-

fense obviously portrayed slavery as the defenders imagined it, not as it was.

Religious Arguments

Evangelical Protestantism dominated southern religious expression by the 1830s, and its ministers took the lead in combating abolitionist charges that slavery was a moral and religious abomination. Except for a radical minority of antislavery evangelicals in the Upper South, a group largely silenced or driven out by the conservative reaction following Nat Turner's uprising, southern churches had always supported slavery. This support grew more pronounced and articulate once the abolitionists stepped up their attacks on slavery in the mid-1830s.

Southern evangelicals accepted the Bible as God's literal word, and through selective reading they found abundant evidence to proclaim slavery fully in accord with His moral dictates. They pointed out, for example, that the patriarchs of Israel had owned slaves. Slavery had been practiced throughout the Roman world at the time of Christ, they noted, and the apostles had urged obedience to all secular laws, including those governing slavery.

Southern evangelicals also turned to the Bible to support their argument that patriarchal authority, the unquestioned power of the father, was the basis of all Christian communities. Part of that authority extended over slaves, and slavery thus became a matter of family governance, a domestic institution in which Christian masters of slaves, unlike capitalist masters of free "wage slaves" in the North, accepted responsibility for caring for their workers in sickness and old age. Far from being a moral curse, therefore, slavery was part of God's plan to Christianize an inferior race and teach its people how to produce raw materials that benefited the world's masses.

The growing commitment of southern evangelicals to slavery as a positive good clashed with the antislavery position and the generally more liberal theology of northern evangelicals. In 1837, the Presbyterians split along sectional lines in part because of differences over slavery. In 1844, as a direct result of the slavery issue, the Methodist Episcopal Church, the nation's largest, divided into northern and southern churches. The Baptists did the same a year later. These religious schisms foreshadowed the sectionalized political divisions of the 1850s; they also severed one of the main emotional bonds between whites in the North and the South. The religious defense of slavery was central to the slaveholding ethic of paternalism that developed after 1830. By the 1850s, planters commonly described slaves as members of an extended family who were treated better than free workers in the North. This language often reflected the planters' psychological need to feel appreciated, even loved, as caring parents by their slave dependents. Some evangelical masters tried to act as moral stewards to their slaves and to curb the worst features of their bondage. Led by Charles Colcock Jones, a minister and planter in the

As this printed label from the 1850s for a box of cigars reveals, antebellum manufacturers of consumer goods produced by slave labor had every incentive to present an idealized picture of slave life in the South.

Georgia lowcountry, they founded religious missions to the slaves and sought legal reforms that would prevent the separation of slave families. Such slaveholders, however, were a minority, and efforts to reform slavery failed largely because masters would accept no limits on their power to control and work their slaves as they saw fit.

The crusade to sanctify slavery won few converts outside the South. Most northern churches did not endorse abolitionism but did have moral qualms about slavery. In a particularly stinging rebuke to southern church leaders in the 1850s, black abolitionists succeeded in having slaveholders barred from international religious conventions.

Racial Arguments

More common than the biblical defense of slavery was the racial argument that black people were unfit for freedom. Drawing in part on the scientific wisdom of the day, the racial defense alleged that black people were naturally lazy and inherently inferior to white people. If freed, so went the argument, they would turn to crime and sexually assault white women. Only the controls of slavery enabled the races to co-exist in the South. Slavery as necessary racial control was a central theme in Thomas R. Dew's *Review of the Debates in the Virginia Legislature of 1831 and 1832,* the first major justification of slavery by a southerner. Dew, a Tidewater planter, was responding to a proposal for gradual emancipation that had been introduced in the Virginia legislature. Although the plan was defeated (largely because the eastern plantation counties were over-represented in the legislature), upper-class conservatives such as Dew were alarmed by the potentially dangerous class division it had revealed between slaveholders and nonslaveholders. He tried to unite white people on the issue of race.

The racial argument resonated powerfully among white people because nearly all of them, including those otherwise opposed to slavery, dreaded emancipation. The attitude of a Tennessee farmer, as recorded by a northern traveler in the 1850s, was typical: "He said he'd always wished there hadn't been any niggers here…, but he wouldn't like to have them free." Unable to conceive of living in a society with many free black people, most white people could see no middle ground between slavery and the presumed social chaos of emancipation.

The existence of *black* slavery also had egalitarian implications for the nonslaveholding majority of whites. Slavery supposedly spared white southerners from the menial, degrading labor that white northerners had to perform. Moreover, because slaves lacked political rights, champions of slavery argued that black bondage buttressed the political liberties of all white males by removing from politics the leveling demands of the poor and propertyless for a redistribution of wealth.

Despite its apparent success in forging white solidarity, the racial argument could be turned on its head and used to weaken slavery. Most white northerners were about as racist as their southern counterparts, but they were increasingly willing to end slavery on the grounds that the stronger white race should help black people improve themselves as free persons. In short, nothing in the internal logic of racist doctrines required enslaving black people. The same logic also encouraged some white southerners to challenge the economic prerogatives of slaveholders. Why, for example, should any white people, as members of the master race, be forced into economic competition against skilled slave artisans? Why should not all nonagricultural jobs be legally reserved for white people? Doctrines of black inferiority could not prevent white unity from cracking when the economic interests of nonslaveholders clashed with those of planters.

Conclusion

Slavery and a biracial social order defined the South as a distinctive region. The spread of plantation agriculture across the Lower South after 1830 deepened the involvement of white southerners in cotton and slavery. At the same time, the abolitionist movement in the North attacked slavery on moral grounds and demanded that it be abolished. As southern interests became more enmeshed in an institution that outsiders condemned, religious and intellectual leaders portrayed slavery as a Christian institution and a positive good necessary for white democracy and harmonious race relations. Proslavery ideologues stridently insisted that the South was separate from and superior to the rest of the nation.

The proslavery argument depicted a nearly ideal society blessed by class and racial harmony. In reality, social conditions in the slave South were contradictory and conflict-ridden. Slaves were not content in their bondage. They dreamed of freedom and sustained that dream through their own forms of Christianity and the support of family and kin. Relations between masters and their slaves were antagonistic, not affectionate, and wherever the system of control slackened, slaves resisted their owners.

Nor did all white southerners, who confronted increasing economic inequality after 1830, accept racial slavery as in their best interests. It divided as well as united them. The publication in 1857 of Hinton Rowan Helper's *The Impending Crisis of the South,* a scathing indictment by a white North Carolinian of slavery's harmful effect on economic opportunities for average white people, vividly showed that not all were convinced by the proslavery argument.

During the 1850s, the size of the slaveholding class fell from 31 percent of southern white families to 25 percent. Slave owners were a shrinking minority, and slavery was in decline throughout the Upper South. In the Border South, free labor was replacing slavery as the dominant means of organizing economic production. In these states, slavery was a vulnerable institution. Planters were not fooled by the public rhetoric of white unity. They knew that slavery was increasingly confined to the Lower South, and that elsewhere in the South white support for it was gradually eroding. Planters feared the double-edged challenge to their privileged position posed by outside interference with slavery and internal white disloyalty. By the 1850s, many of them were concluding that the only way to resolve their dilemma was to make the South a separate nation.

Review Questions

1. What factors accounted for the tremendous expansion of cotton production in the South? How was this expansion linked to slavery and westward movement?

2. What differentiated the Upper South from the Lower South? What role did slavery play in each region after 1815?

3. How would you characterize the life of a plantation slave? What insights does Hannah Crafts's opening account provide into the special vulnerability of slave women? Why were religion and family such key features of the world that slaves built for themselves? What evidence is there of resistance and rebellion among the slaves?

4. How did most nonslaveholding white southerners live? What values did they prize most highly? Why did most non-slaveholders accept slavery or at least not attack it directly?

5. What was the position of free black southerners in southern society? How were their freedoms restricted?

6. How did white southerners attempt to defend slavery and reconcile it with Christianity?

7. How was the development of the Old South linked to the international cotton market?

Key Terms

Black codes (p. 292)

Denmark Vesey's Conspiracy (p. 286)

Gabriel Prosser's Rebellion (p. 286)

Gang system (p. 276)

Nat Turner's Rebellion (p. 287)

Slave codes (p. 282)

Underground Railroad (p. 287)

Recommended Reading

Berlin, Ira. *Generations of Captivity: A History of African-American Slaves* (2003). A splendid overview of slavery in North America that stresses how slavery evolved over time for successive generations of the enslaved.

Freehling, William W. *The Road to Disunion: Secessionists at Bay, 1776–1854* (1990). A fine introduction to the social diversity of the Old South, especially strong in exploring the tensions over slavery between the Upper South and the Lower South.

Genovese, Eugene D. *Roll, Jordan, Roll: The World the Slaves Made* (1974). A richly textured study of slavery that is an excellent source on the interaction between masters and slaves. Argues that paternalistic relations of dependent rights and obligations characterized slavery.

Johnson, Walter. *Soul by Soul: Life Inside the Antebellum Slave Market* (1999). An innovative study that takes the reader inside the daily life of the slave market and lays bare its multiple meanings for slave, slave trader, and slaveholder.

Stampp, Kenneth M. *The Peculiar Institution* (1956). A work that has aged well and is still the best one-volume his-tory of southern slavery; it leaves no doubt that slavery was both brutal and profitable.

Wyatt-Brown, Bertram. *Southern Honor: Ethics and Behavior in the Old South* (1982). Valuable for its insights into the culture of the planter class and the notions of honor that structured social relations among all white people.

Where to Learn More

■ **Aboard the Underground Railroad.**   For a National Travel Itinerary that provides maps and descriptions and photographs of sixty historic places associated with the Underground Railroad, go to www.cr.nps.gov/nr/travel/underground

■ **The Anacostia Museum Center for African American History.**   This museum of the Smithsonian Institution explores American history and cultures from an African American perspective. Go to www.si.edu/anacostia for information on its exhibits and a calendar of events.

■ **Appalachian Museum of Berea College, Berea, Kentucky.**   This museum is an excellent source for under-standing the lifestyle and material culture of the nonslave-holding farmers in the Appalachian highlands. For an overview of its exhibits, see www.museum.appstate.edu/exhibits/exhibits.shtml

■ **Cottonlandia Museum, Greenwood, Mississippi.** The library and museum depict the history of cotton in the Mississippi Delta. Special collections include some Native American artifacts. Information on its displays can be found at www.gcvg.com/CL.html

Study Resources

For study resources for this chapter, go to www.myhistorylab.com and choose *The American Journey*. You will find a wealth of study and review material for this chapter, including pre- and post-tests, customized study plan, key term review flash cards, interactive map and document activities, and documents for analysis.

Whether at home or on the road, the contributions of women were indispensable to the success of ante-bellum reform movements.

North Wind Picture Archives

The Market Revolution and Social Reform 1815–1850 12

East Boylston, Mass. 10th mo. 2d, 1837

Dear Friend:...

The investigation of the rights of the slave has led me to a better understanding of my own. I have found the Anti-Slavery cause to be the high school of morals in our land—the school in which *human rights* are more fully investigated, and better understood and taught, than in any other. Here a great fundamental principle is uplifted and illuminated, and from this central light, rays innumerable stream all around. Human beings have *rights*, because they are *moral* beings: the rights of *all* men grow out of their moral nature; and as all men have the same moral nature, they have essentially the same rights. These rights may be wrested from the slave, but they cannot be alienated: his title to himself is as perfect *now*, as is that of

Lyman Beecher [a prominent minister]: it is stamped on his moral being, and is, like it, imperishable. Now if rights are founded on the nature of our moral being, then the *mere circumstance of sex* does not give to man higher rights and responsibilities, than to woman. To suppose that it does, would be to deny the self-evident truth, that the "physical constitution is the mere instrument of the moral nature." To suppose that it does, would be to break up utterly the relations, of the two natures, and to reverse their functions, exalting the animal nature into a monarch, and humbling the moral into a slave; making the former a proprietor, and the latter its property. When human beings are regarded as *moral* beings, *sex*, instead of being enthroned upon the summit,...sinks into insignificance and nothingness. My doctrine then is, that whatever it is morally right for man to do, it is morally right for woman to do. Our duties originate, not from difference of sex, but from the diversity of our relations in life, the various gifts and talents committed to our care, and the different eras in which we live.

Angelina Emily Grimké

Aileen S. Kraditor, ed., *Up From the Pedestal: Selected Writings in the History of American Feminism* (New York: Quadrangle, 1968), pp. 62–63.

PEARSON
myhistorylab

Personal Journeys Online

■ Margaret Fuller, *Excerpt from book,* 1845. Arguments for women's rights.

■ Lydia Maria Child, *Letter,* 1839. Issue of women's rights in the antislavery movement.

Angelina Grimké wrote the above as part of a public letter to Catherine Beecher, a pioneer in women's education and the daughter of the evangelical preacher Lyman Beecher mentioned in the letter. In 1837, on an abolitionist lecture tour in New England with her sister Sarah, Angelina had become the first U.S. woman to defy the social taboo against women speaking in public to a mixed audience of men and women.

Born in 1805 to a wealthy slaveholding family in Charleston, Angelina was the daughter of a prominent jurist. Despite all the social and economic benefits that membership in the planter class conferred upon her, she passionately rejected slavery when she became a young adult. As was also true for her sister, this rejection was part of a religious conversion to Quakerism. Angelina left her home in Charleston in 1829 and joined Sarah in Philadelphia. The sisters joined the abolitionist movement in 1835, and within two years had become the crusade's most celebrated (and notorious) platform lecturers.

Soon after her marriage in 1838 to the abolitionist Theodore Weld, Angelina compiled much of the first-hand documentation on slavery for his *American Slavery as It Is*, a popular antislavery tract that appeared in 1839.

Although she worked for the emancipation of the slaves during the Civil War, she only rarely spoke in public after her marriage. Before her death in 1879, Angelina learned that her brother Henry, who had become the family patriarch after the death of her father in 1819, had fathered three slave children and had retained them as slaves. Her worst fears about the corrupting influence of slavery were confirmed.

Although Angelina, in her commitment to radical reform, was hardly typical of antebellum U.S. women, let alone women of the planter class, her journey from a privileged life in Charleston to one of social activism in the North speaks to the radicalizing potential of the reform impulse that swept over the nation after the War of 1812.

This reform impulse was strongest in the North, where traditional social and economic relations were undergoing wrenching changes as a market revolution accelerated the spread of cities, factories, and commercialized farms. Cities grew at the fastest rate in U.S. history. Urbanization also brought new production patterns and increasingly separated one's home from one's place of work. New middle and working classes evolved in response to such changes, which were

◆ The increasing industrialization of the U.S. economy between 1815 and 1850

◆ The growth of cities and the emergence of a new middle-class society and a lower class of working poor

◆ New wealth and the increasing inequalities among the rich, the middle class, and the working classes

◆ The rise of the reform movement after the War of 1812

◆ The growth of abolitionist agitation and sentiment in the North

◆ Women's crucial role in the reform movements and the rise of an organized women's rights movement

the most pronounced in the Northeast. The North was also the area where the emotional fires of evangelical revivals burned the hottest.

The religious message of the Second Great Awakening, which began in the early 1800s, provided a framework for responding to the changes that accompanied the market revolution. New in mainstream Protestantism was the belief that anyone who sought salvation could attain it, not just those whom God had predestined to be saved. Evangelicalism taught that in both the spiritual and secular realms, individuals were accountable for their own actions. Through Christian activism, individuals could strive toward moral perfectibility. Social evils, and the sinful consequences of economic and social changes, could be cleansed only if good Christians helped others find the path of righteousness.

The first wave of reform after the War of 1812 focused on individual behavior, targeting drinking, gambling, sexual misconduct, and Sabbath-breaking. By the 1830s, a second phase of reform turned to institutional solutions for crime, poverty, and social delinquency, largely untouched by voluntary moral suasion. The third phase of the reform cycle rejected the social beliefs and practices that prescribed fixed and subordinate positions to certain Americans based on race and also

on sex. This radical phase culminated in the abolitionist and women's rights movement.

Industrial Change and Urbanization

In 1820, 80 percent of the free labor force worked in agriculture, and manufacturing played a minor role in overall economic activity. Over the next three decades, however, the United States joined England as a world leader in industrialization. By 1850, manufacturing accounted for one-third of total commodity output, and 45 percent of the labor force were nonfarm workers.

The most direct cause of this rapid and sustained surge in manufacturing was increased consumption within the United States of the goods the country was producing. The **transportation revolution** dramatically reduced transportation costs and shipping times, opened up new markets for farmers and manufacturers alike, and provided an incentive for expanding production (see Table 12–1). As agricultural and manufactured goods were exchanged more efficiently, a growing home market continually stimulated the development of U.S. manufacturing.

The Transportation Revolution

Aside from some 4,000 miles of toll roads in the Northeast, the nation had nothing approaching a system of transportation in 1815. The cost of moving goods by land transportation was prohibitively high. It cost just as much to haul heavy goods by horsedrawn wagons 30 miles into the interior as to ship them 3,000 miles across the Atlantic Ocean. Water transportation was much cheaper, but it was limited to the coast or navigable rivers. Thus, only farmers located near a city or a river could grow surplus crops for sale in an outside market. Western farm surpluses followed the southerly flow of the Ohio and Mississippi river systems to market outlets in New Orleans.

Steamboats and canals.   Steamboats provided the first transportation breakthrough. In 1807, Robert Fulton demonstrated their commercial practicality when he sent the *Clermont* 150 miles up the Hudson River from New York City to Albany. By the 1820s, steamboats had reduced the cost

Table 12–1			
Impact of the Transportation Revolution on Traveling Time			
Route	**1800**	**1830**	**1860**
New York to Philadelphia	2 days	1 day	Less than 1 day
New York to Charleston	More than 1 week	5 days	2 days
New York to Chicago	6 weeks	3 weeks	2 days
New York to New Orleans	4 weeks	2 weeks	6 days

CHRONOLOGY

1790	Samuel Slater opens the first permanent cotton mill in Rhode Island.
1793	Eli Whitney patents the first cotton gin.
1807	Robert Fulton's steamboat, the *Clermont*, makes its pioneering voyage up the Hudson River.
1814	The Boston Associates opens its Waltham mill, the first textile factory to mechanize all phases of production.
1817	Construction of the Erie Canal begins. American Colonization Society is founded.
1819–1823	Economic depression.
1820s	The new nations of Latin America commit themselves to policies of gradual emancipation.
1824	In *Gibbons v. Ogden,* the Supreme Court strikes down a state monopoly over steamboat navigation.
1825	Erie Canal is completed. Opening of the Stockton and Darlington Railroad in England.
1826	American Temperance Society launches its crusade.
1828	The Baltimore and Ohio, the most important of the early railroads, is chartered.
1829	David Walker publishes *Appeal to the Colored Citizens of the World.*
1830	Joseph Smith founds the Church of Jesus Christ of Latter-Day Saints.
1830–1831	Evangelical revivals are held in northern cities.
1831	William Lloyd Garrison begins publishing the *Liberator.*
1833	Slaves in the British Empire are emancipated. American Anti-Slavery Society is organized.

1834	New York Female Reform Society is founded. Female workers at the Lowell Mills stage their first strike.
1836	Congress passes gag rule.
1837	Horace Mann begins campaign for school reform in Massachusetts. Antiabolitionist mob kills Elijah P. Lovejoy. In *Charles River Bridge v. Warren Bridge,* the Supreme Court encourages economic competition by ruling that presumed rights of monopolistic privileges could not be used to block new economic enterprises.
1839–1843	Economic depression.
1840	Abolitionists split into Garrisonian and anti-Garrisonian societies. Political abolitionists launch the Liberty party.
1841	Brook Farm is established. Dorothea Dix begins her work to improve conditions for the mentally ill.
1842	Massachusetts Supreme Court in *Commonwealth v. Hunt* strengthens the legal right of workers to organize trade unions.
1845	Potato famine in Ireland sets off a mass migration of Irish to the United States.
1846–1848	Mormons migrate to the West.
1847	John Humphrey Noyes establishes the Oneida Community.
1848	Seneca Falls Convention outlines a program for women's rights.

and the time of upriver shipments by 90 percent. As steamboats spread to western waters, more and more farmers could reap the economic benefits of exporting corn, pork, and other foodstuffs.

Western trade did not start to flow eastward until the completion of the Erie Canal in 1825, the first and most successful of the artificial waterways designed to link eastern seaboard cities with western markets (see Map 12–1). Funded by the New York legislature, the Erie Canal stretched 364 miles from Albany to Buffalo, a small port on Lake Erie. Its construction by Irish immigrants was the greatest engineering feat of its era. An immediate success, the Erie Canal reduced the cost of sending freight from Buffalo to New York City by more than 90 percent, and by the 1840s, it was pulling

in more western trade than was being sent to New Orleans on the Mississippi River.

Anxious to match the Erie's success, other states launched plans for competing canals to the West. More than 3,000 miles of canal were in place by 1840, but no other canal could overcome the tremendous advantage of the Erie's head start in fixing trading patterns along its route. Before the Panic of 1837 abruptly ended the canal boom by drying up financing, three broad networks of canals had been built. One set linked seaboard cities on the Atlantic with their agricultural hinterlands, another connected the Mid-Atlantic states with the Ohio River Valley, and a third funneled western grain to ports on the Great Lakes.

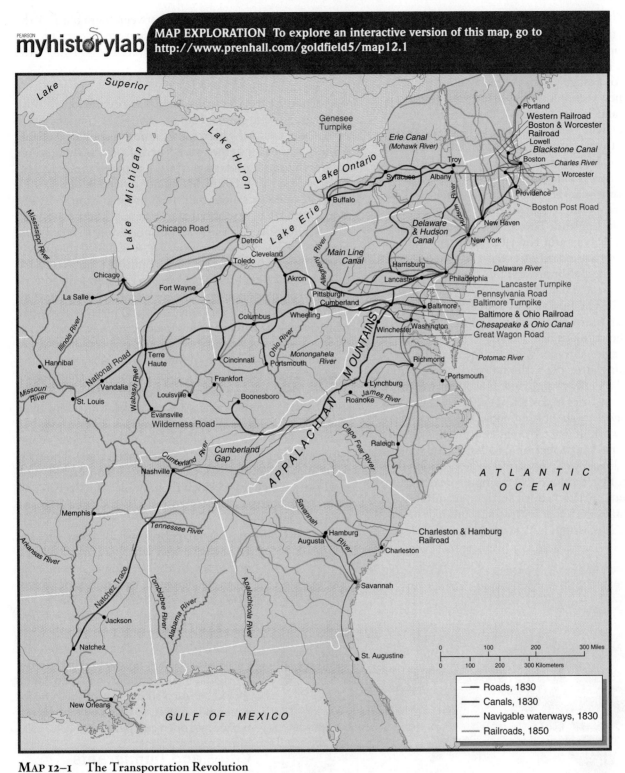

MAP EXPLORATION To explore an interactive version of this map, go to
http://www.prenhall.com/goldfield5/map12.1

MAP 12–1   The Transportation Revolution
By 1830, a network of roads, canals, and navigable rivers was spurring economic growth in the first phase of the transportation revolution. By 1850, railroads, the key development in the second phase of the transportation revolution, were opening up additional areas to commercial activity.

Railroads.   Railroads were the last and ultimately the most important of the transportation improvements that spurred economic development in Jacksonian America. Moving at 15 to 20 miles per hour, four times as fast as a canal boat and twice the speed of a stagecoach, the railroads of the 1830s were a radically new technology that overturned traditional notions of time and space. "I cannot describe the strange sensation produced on seeing the train of cars come up. And when I started in them … it seemed like a dream," exclaimed Christopher Columbus Baldwin of Massachusetts when he saw his first railroad car in 1835.

In 1825, the same year the Erie Canal was completed, the world's first general-purpose railroad, the Stockton and Darlington, opened in England. The construction of the first American railroads began in the late 1820s, and they all pushed outward from seaboard cities eager to connect to the western market. The Baltimore and Ohio crossed the Appalachians and connected Baltimore with Wheeling, Virginia, on the Ohio River. The Boston and Worcester linked New England and the eastern terminus of the Erie Canal at Albany. By 1840, the railroads had become the most dynamic booster of interregional trade. Whereas the canal network stopped expanding after 1840, the railroads tripled their mileage in the 1840s. By 1849, trunk lines built westward from Atlantic Coast cities had reached the Great Lakes and the Ohio Valley and were about to enter the Mississippi Valley.

The rail network in place by mid-century was already altering the North-South sectional balance. The bulk of western trade no longer went downriver to New Orleans but was shipped east by rail. Moving in the opposite direction, to the West, were northern-born settlers, manufactured goods, and cultural values that increasingly unified the free states east of the Mississippi into a common economic and cultural unit. As the distinctions between them blurred, the Northeast and the Old Northwest were becoming just the North. Significantly, no direct rail connection linked the North and the South.

Government and the transportation revolution.   Both national and state government promoted the transportation revolution. Given the high construction costs and uncertain profits, private investors were leery of risking their scarce capital in long-term transportation projects. State legislatures stepped in and furnished some 70 percent of the funding for canals and about half of all railroad capital. By the 1830s, the states were also making it easier for private businesses, and especially those in transportation, to receive the legal privileges of incorporation. These included the protection of limited liability, that is, the limiting of investors' liability to their direct financial stake in the company, and the power of eminent domain, the legal right to purchase whatever land was needed for rights-of-way. The federal government provided engineers for railroad surveys, lowered tariffs on iron used in rail construction, and granted subsidies to the railroads in the form of public land. Most important, however, were two Supreme Court decisions that helped open up the economy to competition. In *Gibbons v. Ogden* (1824), the Court overturned a New York law that had given Aaron Ogden a monopoly on steamboat service between New York and New Jersey. Thomas Gibbons, Ogden's competitor, had a federal license for the coastal trade. The right to compete under the national license, the Court ruled, took legal precedence over Ogden's monopoly. The decision affirmed the supremacy of the national government to regulate interstate commerce.

A new Court, presided over by Roger B. Taney, who became chief justice when John Marshall died in 1835, struck a bolder blow against monopoly in the landmark case of *Charles River Bridge v. Warren Bridge* in 1837. Taney ruled that the older Charles River Bridge Company had not received a monopoly from Massachusetts to collect tolls across the Charles River. Any uncertainties in the charter rights of corporations, reasoned Taney, should be resolved in favor of the broader community interests that would be served by free and open competition.

Cities and Immigrants

Barely one in 20 Americans in the 1790s lived in an urban area (defined by the federal census as a place with a population of 2,500 or more), and Philadelphia, with a population just over 40,000, was the nation's largest city. By 1850, more than one in seven Americans was a city-dweller, and the nation had 10 cities whose population exceeded 50,000

Canal boats below a lock at the Junction of the Erie with the Northern (Champlain) Canal. Aquatint by John Hill.

Collection of the New York Historical Society, Negative #34684.

(see Map 12–2). The transportation revolution triggered this surge in urban growth. The cities that prospered were those with access to the expanding network of cheap transport on steamboats, canals, and railroads. This network opened up the rural interior for the purchase of farm commodities by city merchants and the sale of finished goods by urban importers and manufacturers. A huge influx of immigrants after the mid-1840s and simultaneous advances in steam engines provided the cheap labor and sources of power that increasingly made cities focal points of manufacturing production.

The port cities. America's largest cities in the early nineteenth century were its Atlantic ports: New York, Philadelphia, Baltimore, and Boston. All these cities grew as a result of transportation improvements, but only New York experienced phenomenal growth. By 1810, New York had become the largest U.S. city, and by the 1850s its population exceeded 800,000. Between 1820 and 1860 one-third of the nation's exports and more than three-fifths of its imports passed through New York. No wonder the poet Walt Whitman trumpeted this metropolis as "the heart, the brain, the focus, the main spring, the pinnacle, the extremity, the no more beyond of the new world."

New York's harbor gave oceangoing ships direct, protected access to Manhattan Island, and from there, the Hudson River provided a navigable highway flowing 150 miles north to Albany, deep in the state's agricultural interior. No other port was so ideally situated for trade. And no other had the advantage of access to the Erie Canal. New York City benefited, not only from the increased volume of western foodstuffs sent east across the Erie and then down the Hudson River for export to Europe, but also from the swelling flow of finished goods shipped out of New York for sale to western farmers. New Yorkers plowed the profits of this commerce into local real estate, which soared in value fifty-fold between 1823 and 1836, and into financial institutions such as the New York Stock Exchange, founded in 1817. The city's banks brought together the capital that made New York the country's chief financial center.

As they grew, the Atlantic ports pioneered new forms of city transportation. Omnibuses, horsedrawn coaches carrying up to 20 passengers, and steam ferries were in common use by the 1820s. The first commuter railroad, the Boston and Worcester, began service in 1838. At mid-century, horsedrawn street railway lines moved at speeds of about 6 miles an hour, overcoming some of the limitations of the "walking cities" of the early nineteenth century.

Accompanying this growth were the first slums, the most notorious of which was the Five Points district of New York City. Small, flimsy wooden structures, often crammed into back alleys, housed the working poor in cramped, fetid conditions. Backyard privies, supplemented by chamber pots, were the standard means of disposing of human waste. These outhouses overflowed in heavy rain and often contaminated private wells, the source of drinking water. Garbage and animal wastes simply accumulated on streets, scavenged by roving packs of hogs.

Inland cities. The fastest growing cities were in the interior. Rochester, New York, was a village that the opening of the Erie Canal transformed into a major flour-milling center. Pittsburgh, at the head of the Ohio River, was the first western city to develop a manufacturing sector to complement its exchange function. With access to the extensive coalfields of western Pennsylvania, Pittsburgh had a cheap fuel that provided the high heat needed to manufacture iron and glass. It emerged as America's best-known and most polluted manufacturing city. Cincinnati, downstream on the Ohio, soon became famous for its hogs. "Porkopolis," as it was called, was the West's first meatpacking center. St. Louis, just below the merger of the Missouri and Mississippi rivers, prospered by servicing American trade with the trans-Mississippi West.

New York City's busy harbor was the entry to the largest metropolitan center that emerged in the nineteenth-century United States.

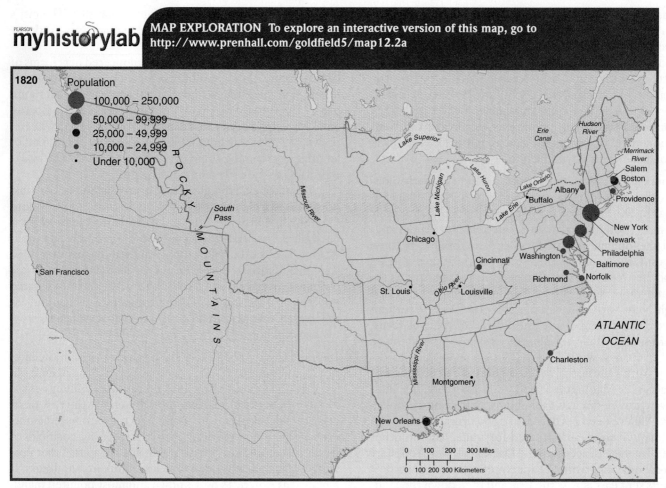

MAP EXPLORATION To explore an interactive version of this map, go to
http://www.prenhall.com/goldfield5/map12.2a

MAP 12–2   The Growth of Cities, 1820–1860
In 1820, most cities were clustered along the Atlantic seaboard. By 1860, new transportation outlets—canals and railroads—had fostered the rapid growth of cities in the interior, especially at trading locations with access to navigable rivers or to the Great Lakes. Much of this growth occurred in the 1850s.

Data Source: *Statistical Abstract of the United States.*

By the 1840s, the Great Lake ports of Cleveland, Detroit, Milwaukee, and Chicago were the dynamic centers of western urbanization. Their combined population increased twenty-five-fold between 1830 and 1850. The Great Lakes served as an extension of the Erie Canal, and cities on the lakes where incoming and outgoing goods had to be unloaded for transshipment benefited enormously. They attracted settlers and soon evolved into regional economic centers. They also aggressively promoted themselves into major rail hubs and thus reaped the economic advantages of being at the junctions of both water and rail transport.

New industrial cities.   The only other cities growing as fast as the Great Lakes ports were the new industrial towns. The densest cluster of these was in rural New England along the fall line of rivers, where the rapidly falling water provided cheap power to drive the industrial machinery of factories and machine shops. Each town was tied to a transportation network that brought in raw cotton for the textile mills from the mercantile centers of Boston and Providence and shipped out the finished goods.

Lowell, Massachusetts, was America's first large-scale planned manufacturing city. Founded in 1822 by Boston businessmen, Lowell was built around the falls of the Merrimack River. Within a decade, rural fields had been transformed into a city of 18,000 people. Multistoried brick factories surrounded by detached housing for the supervisory staff and large boardinghouses for the workers dominated the landscape and defined the city's industrial functions. Lowell's success became a model for others to follow, and by 1840, New England led the North in both urbanization and industrialization.

Immigration.   Swelling the size of nearly all the cities was a surge of immigrants after the 1830s. The number of immigrants from 1840 to 1860, 4.2 million, represented a tenfold increase over the number that had come in the two preceding decades. At mid-century, most of the population

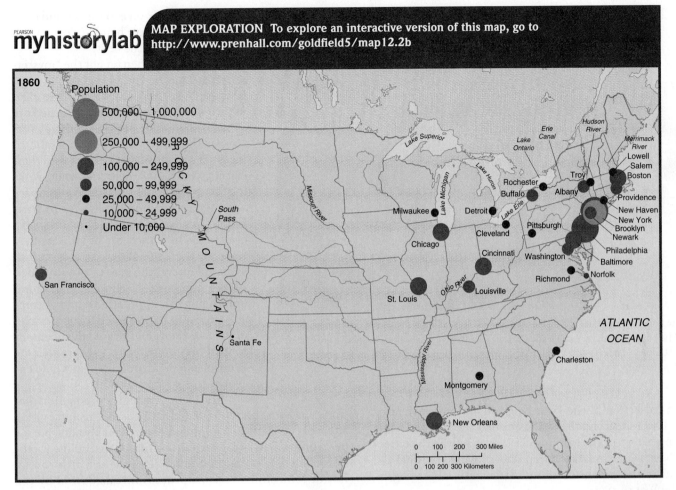

MAP EXPLORATION To explore an interactive version of this map, go to http://www.prenhall.com/goldfield5/map12.2b

MAP 12–2 (CONTINUED)

of New York was foreign-born, and in all the port cities of the Northeast, immigrants dominated the manufacturing work force. Most of these immigrants were Irish and German (see Figure 12-1).

In the 1840s, economic and political upheavals in Europe spurred mass migration, mostly to the United States. Catholic peasants in Ireland, dominated by their Protestant English landlords, eked out a subsistence as tenants on tiny plots of land. A potato blight wiped out the crop in 1845 and 1846, and in the next five years about 1 million Irish died of malnutrition and disease. Another 1.5 million fled, many to the United States.

The Irish had no money to buy land or move west unless they joined construction gangs for canals and railroads. Without marketable skills, they had to take the worst and lowest paying jobs: rag pickers, porters, day laborers, unskilled factory hands. Wives and daughters became laundresses and maids for the urban middle class. Packed into dark cellars, unventilated attics, and rank tenements, the Irish suffered from very high mortality rates. Still, cash wages and access to food made the U.S. city preferable to the prospect of starvation in Ireland. Urging her parents to join her, Margaret McCarthy,

an Irish domestic servant, wrote in 1850 that New York was a place "where no man or woman ever Hungered or ever will and where you will not be Seen Naked ...where you would never want or be at a loss for a good Breakfast and Dinner."

German immigrants were second in number only to the Irish by the 1850s. They came to America to escape poor harvests and political turmoil. Far more Germans than Irish had owned property as farmers, artisans, and shopkeepers and had the capital to purchase land in the West and the skills to join the ranks of small businessmen in the cities. They were also more likely than the Irish to have entered the country through Baltimore or New Orleans, southern ports engaged in the tobacco and cotton trade with continental Europe. From there they fanned out into the Mississippi and Ohio valleys. With the Irish, they made up over half of the population of St. Louis by the 1850s and were close to a majority in the other large cities of the Midwest and Northeast. With their diversified skills, they found ample economic opportunities in the fast-growing cities of the West and a setting in which to build tightly knit communities with German-speaking shops, churches, schools, and benevolent societies. About four in five of all the immigrants arriving

Lowell was the nation's leading textile center and the second-largest city in Massachusetts by 1850. The building with the cupola and the structure with dormers and chimneys were part of the mill complex. The two detached buildings were boardinghouses for the young women who worked in the mills.

came from hands-on experience and craft traditions that were handed down from one generation to the next.

Master craftsmen taught the "mysteries of the craft" to the journeymen and apprentices who lived with them and worked in their shops. Journeymen had learned the skills of their craft but lacked the capital to open their own shops. Before establishing their own businesses, they saved their earnings and honed their skills while working for a wage under a master. Apprentices were adolescent boys legally sent by their fathers to live with and obey a master craftsman in return for being taught a trade. By the terms of the contract, known as an indenture, the master also provided for the apprentice's schooling and moral upbringing. An apprentice could reasonably expect to be promoted to journeyman in his late teens and begin advancement toward his competency, a secure income from an independent trade that would enable him to support a family.

The factory system of production that would undercut both household and artisanal manufacturing after 1815 could produce goods far more quickly and cheaply per worker than could artisans or rural households. Factories subdivided the specialized skills of the artisan into a series of semiskilled tasks, a process foreshadowed by the putting-out system. Factories also put workers under systematic controls. And in the final stage of industrialization, they boosted workers' productivity through the use of power-driven machinery.

Britain pioneered the technological advances that drove early industrialization. The secrets of this technology, especially the designs for the machines that mechanized textile production, were closely guarded by the British government. Despite attempts to prohibit the emigration of artisans who knew how the machinery worked, some British mechanics made it to the United States. Samuel Slater was one of them, and he took over the operation of a fledging mill in Providence, Rhode Island. With his knowledge of how to build the water-powered spinning machinery, he converted the mill into the nation's first permanent cotton factory in 1790.

Slater's factory, and those modeled on it, manufactured yarn that was put out to rural housewives to be woven into cloth. The first factory to mechanize the operations of spinning and weaving and turn out finished cloth was incorporated in Waltham, Massachusetts, in 1813 by the Boston Associates, a group of wealthy merchants. The Waltham factory was heavily capitalized, relied on the latest technology, and recruited its work force from rural farm families.

The first real spurt of factory building came with the closing off of British imports during the Embargo and the

after 1840 settled in the New England and mid-Atlantic states. Their sheer numbers transformed the size and ethnic composition of the working class, especially in the cities of the Northeast. And their cheap labor provided the final ingredient in the expansion of industrialization that began after the War of 1812.

The Industrial Revolution

The Northeast led America's industrial revolution. In 1815, this region had the largest cities, the most developed capital markets, the readiest access to the technological skills of artisans, and the greatest supply of available labor. The first large-scale factories, the textile mills, were erected in New England in the 1820s. For the next 30 years, the United States had the most rapidly developing industrial economy in the world.

The household and the small workshop were the sites of manufacturing in Jefferson's America. Wider markets for household manufactures began to develop in the late eighteenth century with the coming of the **putting-out system.** Local merchants furnished ("put out") raw materials to rural households and paid at a piece rate for the labor that converted the raw materials into manufactured products. The supplying merchant then marketed and sold these goods.

In the cities and larger towns, most manufacturing was done by artisans, skilled craftsmen known as mechanics. Working in their own shops and with their own tools, they produced small batches of finished goods. Each artisan had a specific skill that set him above common laborers— shoemaking, furniture making, silver smithing. These skills

FIGURE 12–1   **Immigration to the United States, 1820–1860**
The potato famine in Ireland and economic and political unrest on the continent led to a surge in immigration in the 1840s. The pace slackened in the mid-1850s, when economic conditions in Europe improved.

Data Source: U.S. Bureau of the Census, *Historical Statistics of the United States, Colonial Times to 1957* (1960), p. 57.

War of 1812. Hundreds of new cotton and woolen mills were established from 1808 to 1815. But the great test of U.S. manufacturing came after 1815, when peace with Britain brought a flood of cheap British manufactured goods. If factories were to continue to grow, U.S. manufacturers had to reach more consumers in their home market and overcome the British advantage of lower labor costs.

Sources of labor.   Industrial labor was more expensive in America than in England, where the high cost of land forced the rural poor into the cities to find work. In contrast, land was cheap and plentiful in the United States, and Americans preferred the independence of farm work to the dependence of factory labor. Consequently, the first mill workers were predominantly children. The owners set up the father on a plot of company-owned land, provided piecework for the mother, and put the children to work in the mills.

Although this so-called **Rhode Island system** of family employment sufficed for small mills, it was inadequate for the larger, more mechanized factories that were built in New England after the War of 1812. The owners of these mills recruited unmarried adolescent daughters of farmers from across New England as their laborers in the **Waltham system.** Jemima Sanborn, one of these young farm daughters, explained that she had left home for the mills because of "the hard times to get a living off the farm for so large a family." Although factory wages were low (a little over a dollar per week,

after deductions for room and board), they were more than these young women could earn doing piecework in the home or as domestics. The wages also brought a liberating degree of financial independence. "When they felt the jingle of silver in their pockets," recalled Harriet Hanson Robinson of her fellow workers at Lowell in the 1830s, "there for the first time, their heads became erect and they walked as if on air."

To overcome parental fears that their daughters might be exposed to morally corrupting conditions in the mills and mill towns, New England manufacturers set up paternalistic moral controls. Single female workers had to live in company-owned boardinghouses that imposed curfews, screened visitors, and mandated church attendance. The mill women worked six days a week from dawn to dusk for low wages. They tended clattering, fast-moving machinery in a work environment kept humid to minimize the snapping of threads in the machines. There were limits to what the women would endure, and in 1834 and 1836 the female hands at Lowell "turned out" to protest wage reductions in demonstrations that were the largest strikes in American history up to that time.

After the economic downturn of the late 1830s, conditions in the mills grew worse. By the mid-1840s, however, the Irish, desperate for work, sent their children into the mills at an earlier age than Yankee families. These workers did

At mid-century most industrial work was still done by hand. Shown here are two foundry workers holding floor rammers used for packing sand against molds.

not leave after two or three years of building up a small dowry for marriage, as many New Englanders did. By the early 1850s, more than half the textile operatives were Irish women.

In the mid-Atlantic region, where the farm population was more prosperous than in New England and fewer young women were available for factory work, immigrants were an important source of manufacturing workers as early as the 1820s. They played an especially crucial role in urban manufacturing. The port cities lacked usable waterpower, but by drawing on a growing pool of cheap, immigrant labor, manufacturers could expand production while driving down the cost. Particularly in finished consumer goods, such as the clothing and leather industries, where low-paid workers could stitch cloth or sole a shoe, urban manufacturing became labor-intensive, depending more heavily on workers than on investment in machines and other capital.

Except in New England textile factories and the smaller factories and shops in the seaboard cities, native-born males were the largest group of early manufacturing workers. They came from poor rural families that lacked enough land to pass on to male heirs. As late as 1840, women, including those working at home, made up about half of the manufacturing work force and one-quarter of the factory hands. Regardless of their sex, few of these workers brought any specific skills to their jobs, and thus they had little bargaining power. Economic necessity forced them to accept low wages and harsh working conditions. The sheer increase in their numbers, as opposed to any productivity gains from technological innovations, accounted by 1850 for two-thirds of the gains in manufacturing output.

Technological gains.   After 1815, U.S. manufacturers began to close the technological gap with Britain by drawing on the versatile skills of U.S. mechanics. The Dominy family of Easthampton, Long Island, for example, worked with wood and iron, built gristmills, and made clocks and watches. Mechanics experimented with new designs, improved old ones, and patented inventions that found industrial applications outside their own crafts.

The most famous early American invention was the cotton gin. Eli Whitney, a Massachusetts Yankee who, as a teenager, had turned out knives and blades at a forge on his father's farm, built the prototype of the gin in 1793 while working as a tutor on a Georgia plantation. By cheaply and quickly removing the seeds from cotton fibers, the cotton gin spurred the cultivation of cotton across the South.

Whitney also pushed the idea of basing production on interchangeable parts. After receiving a federal contract to manufacture muskets, he designed new milling machines and turret lathes that trans-

formed the technology of machine tool production. The federal arsenal at Harpers Ferry, Virginia, developed machine tools that could manufacture standardized, interchangeable parts. The new techniques were first applied in 1815 to the manufacture of wooden clocks and by the 1840s to sewing machines, farm machinery, and watch parts. The **American system of manufacturing,** low-cost, standardized mass production, built around interchangeable parts stamped out by machines, was America's unique contribution to the industrial revolution.

As the pace of technological innovation accelerated after 1840, so did the growth of manufacturing. Indeed, the 1840s registered the highest rate of expansion in the manufacturing sector of the economy in the nineteenth century. The adoption of the stationary steam engine in urban manufacturing fueled much of this expansion. High-pressure steam engines enabled power-driven industry to locate in the port cities of the Northeast and the booming cities on the Great Lakes. With limited access to waterpower, early manufacturing in the West was confined to the processing of farm goods. By turning to steam power and new machine tools, western manufacturers after 1840 enlarged their region's industrial base and created a new industry, the mass production of agricultural implements. The West was the center of the farm-machinery industry, and the region produced 20 percent of the nation's manufacturing output by the 1850s.

A greater control over natural resources, as well as new technologies, drove industrial growth. To provide their mills with a steady, reliable source of water, one that would not be affected by the whims of nature, the Boston Associates constructed a series of dams and canals that extended to the headwaters of the Merrimack River in northern New Hampshire. Inevitably, the ecology of the region changed. The level of the lakes was altered, the flow of rivers interrupted, the upward migration of spawning fish blocked, and the foraging terrain of wild game flooded. Farmers protested when their

Shown here working at power looms under the supervision of a male overseer, young single women constituted the bulk of the labor force in the first textile factories of New England.

fields and pastures were submerged, but lawyers for the Boston Associates successful argued that water, like other natural resources, should be treated as a commodity that could contribute to economic progress. Increasingly, the law treated nature as an economic resource to be engineered and bought and sold.

Growing Inequality and New Classes

In the first half of the nineteenth century, the economy grew three times faster than in the eighteenth century, and per capita income doubled. Living standards for most Americans improved. Houses, for those who could afford them, became larger, better furnished, and better heated. There was a price to be paid, however, for the benefits of economic growth. Half of the adult white males were propertyless at mid-century. Wealth had become more concentrated, and extremes of wealth and poverty eroded the Jeffersonian ideal of a republic of independent proprietors who valued liberty because they were economically free.

The gap between the rich and the poor widened considerably in the early phases of industrialization (see Figure 12–2). In 1800, the richest 10 percent of Americans owned 40 to 50 percent of the national wealth. By the 1850s, their share was about 70 percent. The most glaring discrepancies in wealth appeared in the large cities. In all cities by the 1840s, the top 10 percent of the population owned 80 percent of urban wealth. Most of the urban rich had been born wealthy,

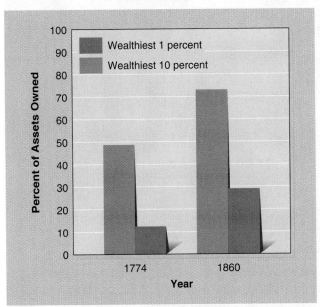

FIGURE 12–2   Growth in Wealth Inequality, 1774–1860
The two benchmark years for the gathering of data on the nationwide distribution of wealth are 1774 and 1860. Specialized studies on regions and subregions indicate that wealth inequality increased most sharply from the 1820s to 1850, the period that coincides with early industrialization.

Data Source: Jeffrey G. Williamson and Peter H. Lindert, *American Inequality: A Macroeconomic History* (1980), p. 38.

the offspring of old-money families who had married and invested wisely. They belonged to exclusive clubs, attended lavish balls and dinners, were waited on by a retinue of servants in their mansions, and generally recoiled from what they considered the "mob government" ushered in by the Jacksonian Democrats. As one of the urban elite noted, it was a society "characterized by a spirit of exclusiveness and persecution unknown in any other country. Its gradations not being regulated according to rank and titles, selfishness and conceit are its principal elements; and its arbitrary distinctions the more offensive, as they principally refer to fortune."

The new middle class.   The faster pace of economic growth that enabled the urban rich to increase their wealth also created opportunities for a rapidly expanding new middle class. This class grew as the number of nonmanual jobs increased. Most of these jobs were in northern cities and bustling market towns, where the need was greatest for office and store clerks, managerial personnel, sales agents, and independent retailers. The result by mid-century was a new middle class superimposed on the older one of independent farmers, artisans, shopkeepers, and professionals. The separation of work and home constituted the first step in an evolving sense of class consciousness. As the market revolution advanced, the workplace increasingly became a specialized location of production or selling. Middle-class fathers now left for work in the morning, while mothers governed households that were primarily residential units and places of material comfort, where growing quantities of consumer goods—pianos, carpets, draperies, mirrors, oil lamps, and ornate furniture—were on display. Having servants, domestic service being the single largest field of employment in the cities, became a status symbol. Shunned as degrading by most native-born white women, these low-paying jobs were filled by African American and young immigrant (especially Irish) women. Work had not left the middle-class home; instead, it was disguised as the "domestic duties" of middle-class wives who supervised the servants.

Besides turning to etiquette books for advice on proper manners in public and in the home, the middle class also tried to shape its behavior by the tenets of evangelical religion. Revivals swept northern cities in the late 1820s. Charles G. Finney led the most dramatic and successful ones in the cities along the Erie Canal in upstate New York. Finney preached that salvation was available to those who willed it. He also stressed that both economic and moral success depended on the virtues of sobriety, self-restraint, and hard work. Aggressiveness and ambition at work were not necessarily sinful so long as businessmen reformed their own moral lives and helped others do the same. This message was immensely reassuring to employers and entrepreneurs, for it confirmed and sanctified their own pursuit of economic self-interest. It also provided them with a religious inspiration for attempting to exert moral control over their communities and employees. **Temperance,** the prohibition of alcoholic beverages, was the greatest of the evangelically inspired reforms, and abstinence from alcohol became the most telling evidence of middle-class respectability.

Women and the cult of domesticity.   In a reversal of traditional Calvinist doctrine, the evangelical ministers of the northern middle class enshrined women as the moral superiors of men. Though considered weak and passive, women were also held to be uniquely pure and pious. Women, who easily outnumbered men at Sunday services and weeknight prayer meetings, were now responsible for converting their homes into loving, prayerful centers of domesticity, and the primary task of motherhood became the Christian nurturing of souls entrusted to a mother's care. "There is a ministry that is older and deeper and more potent than ours," wrote a liberal Presbyterian clergyman; "it is the ministry that presides over the crib and impresses the first gospel influence on the infant soul."

This sanctified notion of motherhood reflected and reinforced shifting patterns of family life. Families became smaller as the birthrate fell by 25 percent in the first half of the nineteenth century. The decline was greatest in the urban middle class after 1820. Children were no longer an economic asset as they had been on a family farm. Middle-class couples consciously limited the size of their families, and women stopped having children at an earlier age. As a result, parents devoted more care and financial resources to child rearing. Middle-class children lived at home longer than children had in the past and received more schooling than working-class children.

Beginning in the 1820s, ministers and female writers elevated the family role of middle-class women into a **cult of domesticity.** This idealized conception of womanhood insisted that the biological differences of God's natural order determined separate social roles for men and women. Characterized as strong, aggressive, and ambitious, men naturally belonged in the competitive world of business and politics. Women's providential task was to preserve religion and morality in the home and family. Held to be innately weak, nurturing, and selfless, only they possessed the moral purity necessary for rearing virtuous children and preserving the home as a refuge from the outside world.

The working classes.   The economic changes that produced a new middle class also fundamentally transformed the working class. In the preindustrial United States, the working class was predominantly native-born and of artisan origins. By mid-century, most urban workers were immigrants or the children of immigrants and had never been artisans in a skilled craft.

Job skills, sex, race, and ethnicity all divided workers after 1840. Master craftsmen were the most highly skilled and best-paid workers. As industrialization proceeded, the unity of the old artisan class splintered. Ambitious master craftsmen with access to capital rose into the ranks of small businessmen and manufacturers. They expanded output and

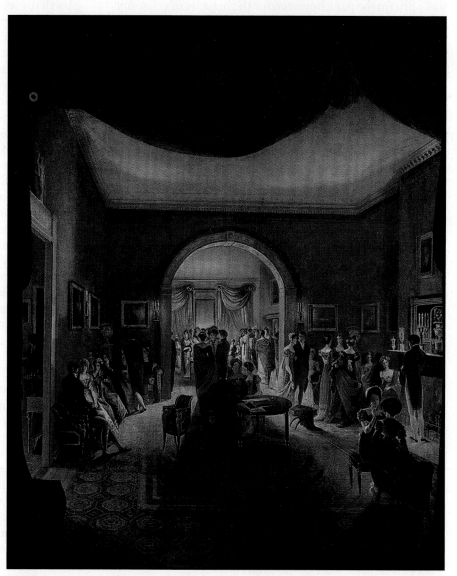

This scene, entitled The Tea Room, by Henry Sargent in his 1821 painting, depicts how the wealthy elite in Boston used their social gatherings to set themselves apart as an elegantly cultured class.

The Tea Party, about 1824 Henry Sargent, American, 1770–1845 Oil on canvas 163.51 × 133.03 cm (64 3/8 × 52 3/8 in.) Museum of Fine Arts, Boston Gift of Mrs. Horatio A. Lamb in memory of Mr. and Mrs. Winthrop Sargent 19.12(c) 2003 Museum of Fine Arts.

This pen-and-watercolor drawing of a middle-class family in 1832 illustrates how the home, as it lost its productive functions, became idealized as a center of domestic refinement and material comfort.

Family Group, Joseph H. Davis, American, 1811–1865, Graphite pencil and watercolor on paper, Sheet: 24.8 × 41 cm (9 3/4 × 16 1/8 in.), Museum of Fine Arts, Boston, Gift of Maxim Karolik for the proposed M. and M. Karolik Collection of American Watercolors, - 2003 Museum of Fine Arts, Boston.

drove down the cost of production by contracting out work at piece wages and hiring the cheapest workers they could find. The result was to transform the apprentice system into a system of exploited child labor.

By the 1830s, journeymen were becoming permanent wage earners with little prospect of opening their own shops. This new wage-earning class denounced the new industrial relations as a "system of mental and physical slavery." To protect their liberties from what they considered a new aristocracy of manufacturers, they organized workingmen's parties in the 1830s, centered in the eastern cities. At the top of these parties' lists of reforms were free public education, the abolition of imprisonment for debt, and a 10-hour workday. But the depression of 1839–1843 forced mechanics to concentrate on their economic survival, and the Democrats siphoned off many of their political leaders.

Early trade unions. Journeymen also turned to trade union activity in the 1820s and 1830s to gain better wages, shorter hours, and enhanced job security. Benefiting from a strong demand for their skills, workers in the building trades organized the first unions. They were soon followed by shoemakers, printers, and weavers, workers in trades where pres-

sure on urban journeymen was the most intense. Locals from various trades formed the National Trades Union, the first national union, in 1834. The new labor movement launched more than 150 strikes in the mid-1830s.

Although the Panic of 1837 decimated union membership, the early labor movement did achieve two notable victories. First, by the late 1830s, it had forced employers to accept the 10-hour day as the standard for most skilled workers. Second, in a landmark decision handed down in 1842, the Massachusetts Supreme Court ruled in *Commonwealth* v. *Hunt* that a trade union was not necessarily subject to laws against criminal conspiracies and that a strike could be used to force employers to hire only union members.

The unions defended artisanal rights and virtues, and they ignored workers whose jobs had never had craft status. As massive immigration merged with industrialization after 1840, this basic division between workers widened. On one side was the male, Protestant, and native-born class of skilled artisans. On the other side was the working-class majority of factory laborers and unskilled workers, predominantly immigrants and women who worked for a wage as domestics or factory hands. On average, they earned less than $500 a year, about half what skilled workers earned. Their financial survival rested on a family economy in which all members contributed whatever they could earn.

Increasingly fearing these workers as a threat to their job security and Protestant values, in the 1840s U.S.-born artisans joined **nativist** organizations that sought to curb mass immigration from Europe and limit the political rights of Catholic immigrants. Whereas immigrants viewed temperance as business-class meddling in their lives, nativist workers tended to embrace the evangelical, middle-class ideology of temperance and self-help. One of the few issues that brought immigrants and nativists together was the nearly universal demand of white workers that black workers be confined to the most menial jobs.

Gender also divided workers. Working-class men shared the dominant ideology of female dependence. They measured their own status as husbands by their ability to support their wives and daughters. Beginning in the 1830s, male workers argued that their wages would be higher if women were barred from the labor force. A report of the National Trades Union in 1836 insisted that a woman's "efforts to sustain herself and her family are actually the same as tying a stone around the neck of her natural protector, Man, and destroying him with the weight she has brought to his assistance."

With these views, male workers helped lock wage-earning women into the lowest paying and most exploited jobs. "If we do not come forth in our defence, what will become of us?" asked Sarah Monroe of New York City in the midst of a strike by seamstresses in 1831. Women workers tried to organize, but the male labor movement refused to lend much support. The men tried to channel the discontent of women workers into "proper female behavior" and generally restricted their assistance to pushing for legislation that would limit the hours worked by women and children, a stand that enhanced their male image as protectors of the family.

Reform and Moral Order

The rapidity and extent of the social and economic changes that accompanied the market revolution were disorienting, even frightening, to many Americans, particularly religious leaders and wealthy businessmen in the East. They saw signs of moral wickedness and disorder all around them in the more fluid, materialistic society that was emerging. In their eyes, licentiousness was rampant in the cities, and the evils of drink were causing workers to forsake God and their families. Alarmed by what they perceived as a breakdown in moral authority, they sought to impose moral discipline on Americans.

These eastern elites, with the indispensable support of their wives and daughters, created a network of voluntary church-affiliated reform organizations known collectively as the **benevolent empire**. Revivals in the 1820s and 1830s broadened the base of reform to include the newly evangelicalized middle class in northern cities and towns.

The Benevolent Empire

For the Reverend Lyman Beecher, the United States in 1814 presented "a scene of destitution and wretchedness." From his Presbyterian pulpit in Litchfield, Connecticut, and then in Boston, he became the leader of a clerical drive to restore morality to America.

Evangelical businessmen in the seaboard cities backed the call to restore moral order. Worried by the increasing number of urban poor, wealthy merchants contributed vital financial support for a network of reform associations, which grew to include the American Board of Commissioners for Foreign Missions (1810), the American Bible Society (1816), the American Sunday School Union (1824), the American Tract Society (1825), and the American Home Missionary Society (1826).

The reform societies built on the Second Great Awakening's techniques of organization and communication. The Protestant reformers sent out speakers on regular schedules along prescribed routes. They developed organizations that maintained a constant pressure for reform. National and local boards of directors supervised the work of salaried managers, who inspired volunteers to combat sin among the unconverted. When steam presses and stereotype plates halved the cost of printing and dramatically increased its speed, the American Bible Society was the first organization to exploit this revolution in the print media. Between 1790 and 1830, the number of religious newspapers grew from 14 to more than 600. By then, religious presses were churning out more than 1 million Bibles and 6 million tracts a year.

A host of local societies targeted individual vices. Their purpose, as summed up by a Massachusetts group, the Andover South Parish Society for the Reformation of Morals, was "to discountenance [discourage] immorality, particularly Sabbath-breaking, intemperance, and profanity, and to promote industry, order, piety, and good morals." These goals linked social and moral discipline, appealing both to churchgoers concerned about godlessness and profit-oriented businessmen eager to curb their workers' unruly behavior.

With volunteers drawn largely from the teenage daughters of evangelical businessmen, Sunday interdenominational schools combined elementary education with the teaching of the Bible and Protestant principles. The American Sunday School Union coordinated local efforts and published books and periodicals. By 1832, nearly 10 percent of all U.S. children aged 5 to 14 were attending Sunday schools.

The boldest expression of the drive to enhance Protestant Christian power was the **Sabbatarian movement**. In 1828, evangelicals led by Lyman Beecher formed the General Union for Promoting the Observance of the Christian Sabbath. Their immediate goal was the repeal of a law passed by Congress in 1810 directing post offices to deliver mail on Sunday. This law symbolized to Protestant reformers the moral degeneracy into which the republic had fallen. Their broader mission was to enforce local statutes that shut down business and leisure activities on Sundays. The Sabbatarians

OVERVIEW

Changes Promoting Growth in the Transformed Economy

Sector	1815	1850
Travel and transportation	By foot and horsedrawn wagon	Cheaper and faster with canals, steamboats, and railroads opening up new markets
Population	Overwhelmingly native-born, rural, and concentrated east of Appalachian Mountains	Four times larger as a result of natural increase and surge of immigration after 1840; settlement of West and growth of cities
Wage labor	Native-born, primarily women and children in manufacturing	Expanding as rural poor and immigrants enter manufacturing work force
Power	Water-driven mills	Steam-driven engines
Farming	Subsistence-oriented; surplus sold in localized markets	Commercialized agriculture spreading in response to improvements in transportation
Manufacturing	Small-scale production in household units and artisan shops	Large-scale production in eastern cities and factories

considered such statutes no less "necessary to the welfare of the state" than "laws against murder and polygamy."

In 1829, insisting on the separation of church and state, the Democratic Congress upheld the postal law of 1810. The Sabbatarians had outraged canal operators, hotelkeepers, tavern owners and other businesses threatened with the loss of their Sunday trade. Businessmen, workingmen, southern evangelicals, and religious conservatives all felt that the Sabbath purists had gone too far in a movement now seen as a threat to civil liberties and the rights of private property.

The General Union disbanded in 1832, but it left an important legacy for future reform movements. On the one hand, it developed techniques that converted the reform impulse into direct political action. In raising funds, training speakers, holding rallies, disseminating literature, lobbying for local Sunday regulations, and coordinating a petition to Congress, the Sabbatarians created an organizational model for other reformers to follow in mobilizing public opinion and influencing politicians. On the other hand, the failure of the Sabbatarians revealed that a new approach was needed that encouraged individuals to reform themselves without coercive controls. It soon emerged in the temperance movement.

The Temperance Movement

Temperance, the drive against the consumption of alcohol, had the greatest impact on the most people of any reform movement. Its success rested on what Lyman Beecher called "a new moral power." Dismayed by popular resistance to the coercive moralism of the first wave of Protestant reform, evangelicals concluded that reform had to rest on persuasion, and it had to begin with the voluntary decision of individuals to free themselves from sin. For these evangelicals, the self-control to renounce alcohol became the key to creating a harmonious Christian society of self-regulating citizens.

In 1826, evangelicals founded the **American Temperance Society.** Their goal was to bring about a radical change in U.S. attitudes toward alcohol and its role in social life. By 1830, U.S. consumption of alcohol had reached an all-time high of 7.1 gallons of pure alcohol per year for every American

Temperance Cartoon

aged 14 and over (about three times present-day levels). "Liquor at that time," recalled a carpenter, "was used as commonly as the food we ate." Taverns easily outnumbered churches as gathering places. Alcohol was used to pay common laborers and itinerant preachers on the early Methodist circuit. Masters and journeymen shared a drink as a customary way of taking a break from work, and no wedding, funeral, or meeting of friends was complete without alcohol.

For the temperance crusade to succeed, the reformers had to finance a massive propaganda campaign and link it to an organization that could mobilize and energize thousands of people. They built such a mass movement by merging temperance into the network of churches and lay volunteers that the benevolent empire had developed and by adopting the techniques of revivals to win converts.

Evangelical reformers denounced intemperance as the greatest sin of the land. In the words of the Reverend Herman Humphrey, it deprived "its victims of the means of grace.... If there is any evil which hardens the heart faster, ... or quickens hatred [of] God and man into a more rapid and frightful maturity, I know not what it is." Alcohol represented all that was wrong in America, crime, poverty, insanity, broken families, boisterous politicking, Sabbath-breaking.

This message thundered from the pulpit and the public lectern. Thanks to the generous financial subsidies of wealthy benefactors, it was also broadcast in millions of tracts printed on the latest high-speed presses. Like revivals, temperance rallies combined emotionally charged sermons with large, tearful prayer meetings to evoke guilt among sinners, who would then seek release by taking the pledge of abstinence.

Within a decade, the American Temperance Society had more than 5,000 local chapters and statewide affiliates, most in the Northeast. A million members had pledged abstinence by 1833. Women constituted one-third to more than one-half of the members in local temperance societies. Lacking legal protections against abusive husbands who drank away the family resources, women had a compelling reason to join the crusade. As the moral protectors of the family, they pressured their husbands to take the teetotaler's pledge and stick by it, raised sons to shun alcohol, and banished liquor from their homes. By the 1840s, temperance and middle-class domesticity had become synonymous.

The first wave of temperance converts came from the upper and middle classes. Businessmen welcomed temperance as a model of self-discipline in their efforts to regiment factory work. Young, upwardly mobile professionals and petty entrepreneurs learned in temperance how to be thrifty, self-controlled, respectable, and creditworthy. Many of them presumably agreed with the *Temperance Recorder* that "the enterprise of this country is so great, and competition so eager in every branch of business…, that profit can only result from …*temperance.*" Temperance made its first significant inroads among the working classes during the economic depression of 1839–1843. Joining together in what they called Washington Temperance Societies, small businessmen and artisans, many of them reformed drunkards, carried temperance into working-class districts. The Washingtonians insisted that workers could survive the depression only if they stopped drinking and adopted the temperance ethic of frugality and self-help. Their wives organized auxiliary societies and pledged to enforce sobriety and economic restraint at home.

In a telling measure of the temperance movement's success, per capita alcohol consumption fell to less than 2 gallons per year by 1845. In 1851, Maine passed the first statewide prohibition law. Other northern states followed suit, but anti-temperance coalitions soon overturned most of these laws outside New England. Nonetheless, alcohol consumption remained at the low level set in the 1840s.

Women's Role in Reform

The first phase of women's reform activities represented an extension of the domestic ideal promoted in the cult of domesticity. Assumptions about women's unique moral qualities permitted, and even encouraged, them to assume the role of "social mother" by organizing on behalf of the orphaned and the widowed. Founded in 1797, the Society for the Relief of Poor Widows with Small Children in New York typified these early approaches to reform. The women in the society came from socially prominent families. Motivated by religious charity and social duty, they visited poor women and children, dispensed funds, and set up work programs. However, they limited their benevolence to the "deserving poor," socially weak but morally strong people who had suffered personal misfortune, and screened out all who were thought to be unworthy.

The revivalist call in the 1820s for moral action inspired middle-class women to join voluntary female groups. They founded maternal associations, where they prayed and fasted for the moral strength to save the souls of their children. Other associations sponsored revivals, visited the poor, established Sunday schools, and distributed Bibles and religious tracts. These reformers widened the public role of women, but their efforts also reinforced cultural stereotypes of women as nurturing helpmates who deferred to males.

A second phase in the reform efforts by women developed in the 1830s. Unlike their benevolent counterparts, the reformers now began to challenge male prerogatives and move beyond moral suasion. The crusade against prostitution exemplified the new militancy. Women seized leadership of the movement in 1834 with the founding of the New York Female Moral Reform Society. In the pages of their journal, *Advocate for Moral Reform,* members identified male greed and licentiousness as the causes for the fallen state of women. Identified, too, were the male patrons of the city's brothels. The society blamed businessmen for the low wages that forced some women to resort to prostitution and denounced lustful men for engaging in "a regular crusade against [our] sex."

In 1839, this attack on the sexual double standard became a national movement with the establishment of the **American Female Moral Reform Society.** With 555 affiliates throughout the evangelical heartland of the North, female activists mounted a lobbying campaign that, unlike earlier efforts, bypassed prominent men and reached out to a mass audience. By the 1840s, such unprecedented political involvement enabled women to secure the first state laws criminalizing seduction and adultery.

Other women's groups developed a more radical critique of U.S. society and its male leadership. The Boston Seamen's Aid Society, founded in 1833 by Sarah Josepha Hale, a widow with five children, soon rejected the benevolent tradition of distinguishing between "respectable" and "unworthy" poor. Hale discovered that her efforts to guide poor women toward self-sufficiency flew in the face of the low wages and substandard housing that trapped her clients in poverty. She concluded in 1838 that "it is hardly possible for the hopeless poor to avoid being vicious." Hale attacked male employers for exploiting the poor. "Combinations of selfish men are formed to beat down the price of female labor," she wrote in her 1836 annual report, "and then they call the diminished rate the market price."

Backlash Against Benevolence

Some of the benevolent empire's harshest critics came out of the populist revivals of the early 1800s. They considered the Protestant reformers' program a conspiracy of orthodox Calvinists from old-line denominations to impose social and moral control on behalf of a religious and economic elite. The goal of the "orthodox party," warned the Universalist *Christian Intelligencer,* was the power of "governing the nation."

These criticisms revealed a profound mistrust of the emerging market society. In contrast to the evangelical reformers, drawn from the well-educated business and middle classes who were benefiting from economic change, most evangelical members of the grassroots sects and followers of the itinerant preachers were unschooled, poor, and hurt by market fluctuations that they could not control. Often they were farmers forced by debt to move west or artisans and tradesmen displaced by new forms of factory production and new commercial outlets. Socially uprooted and economically stranded, they found a sense of community in their local churches and resisted control by wealthier, better-educated outsiders. Above all, they clung to beliefs that shored up the threatened authority of the father over his household.

With the elevation of women to the status of moral guardians of the family and agents of benevolent reform outside the household, middle-class evangelicalism in the Northeast was becoming feminized. This new social role for women was especially threatening, indeed, galling, for men who were the casualties of the more competitive economy. Raised on farms where the father had been the unquestioned lawgiver and provider, these men attacked feminized evangelicalism for undermining their paternal authority. They found in Scripture an affirmation of patriarchal power for any man, no matter how poor or economically dependent.

The **Church of Jesus Christ of Latter-Day Saints** (also known as the **Mormon Church**) represented the most enduring religious backlash of economically struggling men against the aggressive efforts of reforming middle-class evangelicals. Joseph Smith, who established the church in upstate New York in 1830, came from a New England farm family uprooted and impoverished by market speculations gone sour. He and his followers were alienated not only from the new market economy but also from what they saw as the religious and social anarchy around them.

Based on Smith's divine revelations as set forth in the Book of Mormon (1830), their new faith offered converts both a sanctuary as a biblical people and a release from social and religious uncertainties. They believed that the mainstream evangelical churches had corrupted Christ's original gospel. "This generation abounds in ignorance, superstition, selfishness, and priestcraft," charged the Mormon John Whitmer; "for this generation is truly led by … hireling priests whose God is the substance of the world's goods."

Mormonism provided a defense of communal beliefs centered on male authority. It assigned complete spiritual and secular authority to men. Only through subordination and obedience to their husbands could women hope to gain salvation. To be a Mormon was to join a large extended family that was part of a shared enterprise. Men bonded their labor in a communal economy to benefit all the faithful. A law of tithing, instituted in 1841, required Mormons to give 10 percent of their property to the church upon conversion and 10 percent of their annual income thereafter. Driven by a strong sense of social obligation, the Mormons forged the most successful alternative vision in antebellum America to the individualistic Protestant republic of the benevolent reformers. (For the Mormons' role in the westward movement, see Chapter 13.)

Institutions and Social Improvement

Although evangelical Protestantism was its mainspring, antebellum reform also had its roots in the European Enlightenment. Like the evangelicals inspired by religious optimism, reformers drawing on Enlightenment doctrines of progress had unbounded faith in social improvement. They saw in the United States an unlimited potential to fashion a model republic of virtuous, intelligent citizens.

Studies published in the 1820s that documented increasing urban poverty, crime, and teenage delinquency created a sense of urgency for many reformers. Guided by the Enlightenment belief that environmental conditions shaped human character, reformers created a new system of public schooling in the North. They also prodded state legislatures to fund penitentiaries for criminals, asylums for the mentally ill, reformatories for the delinquent, and almshouses for the poor.

As reformers were implementing new institutions for shaping individual character after 1820, a host of utopian communities also tapped into an impulse for human betterment. They typically rejected either private property or family life based on monogamous marriage and offered a communitarian life designed to help people reach perfection. Most of these communities were short-lived because the new forms of social and economic organization they promoted were far too radical for all but a handful of Americans.

School Reform

Before the 1820s, schooling in America was an informal, haphazard affair that nonetheless met the basic needs for reading, writing, and arithmetic skills of an overwhelmingly rural population. Private tutors and academies for the wealthy, a few charitable schools for the urban poor, and rural one-room schoolhouses open for a few months each year constituted formal education at the primary level.

The first political demands for free tax-supported schools originated with the **Workingmen's movement** in eastern cities in the 1820s. In pushing for "equal republican education," workers sought to guarantee that all citizens, no matter how poor, could achieve meaningful liberty and equality. Their proposals, however, met stiff resistance from wealthier property holders, who refused to pay taxes to support the education of working-class children.

The breakthrough in public education came in New England, where the disruptive forces of industrialization and urbanization were felt the earliest. Increased economic inequality, growing numbers of impoverished Irish Catholic immigrants, and the emergence of a mass democracy based on nearly universal white male suffrage convinced reformers of the need for state-supported schools.

In 1837, the Massachusetts legislature established the nation's first state board of education. The head of the board for the next twelve years was Horace Mann, a former Whig politician and temperance advocate who now tirelessly championed educational reform. Mann demanded that the state government assume centralized control over Massachusetts schools. All schools should have the same standards of compulsory attendance, strict discipline, common textbooks, professionally trained teachers, and graded, competitive classes of age-segregated students.

Once this system was in place, Mann promised, the schools would become "the great equalizer of the conditions of men, the balance-wheel of the social machinery." Poverty would no longer threaten social disruption because the ignorant would have the knowledge to acquire property and wealth. Education, Mann stated, "does better than disarm the poor of their hostility against the rich; it prevents being poor." Trained in self-control and punctuality, youths would be able to take advantage of economic opportunities and become intelligent voters concerned with the rights of property.

Democrats in the Massachusetts legislature denounced Mann's program as "a system of centralization and of mo-nopoly of power in a few hands, contrary in every respect, to the true spirit of our democratical institutions." The laboring poor, who depended for economic survival on the wages their children could earn, resisted compulsory-attendance laws and a longer school year. Farmers fought to maintain local control over schooling and to block the higher taxes needed for a more comprehensive and professionalized system. The Catholic Church protested the thinly veiled attempts of the reformers to indoctrinate all students in the moral strictures of middle-class Protestantism. Catholics began, at great expense, to build their own parochial schools.

Mann and his allies nonetheless prevailed in most of the industrializing states, with strong support from the professional and business constituencies of the Whig party. Manufacturers hoped that the schools would turn out a more obedient and punctual labor force, and the more skilled and prosperous workers saw in public education a key to upward mobility for their children.

Most important for its political success, school reform appealed to the growing northern middle class. Schools would instill the moral and economic discipline that the middle class deemed essential for a progressive and ordered society. Teaching morality and national pride was central to the educational curriculum, and from the popular McGuffey Readers used as a classroom text, students learned such lessons as "God gives a great deal of money to some persons, in order that they may assist those [who] are poor."

Out of the northern middle class also came the young female teachers who increasingly staffed elementary schools. Presumed by their nature to be more nurturing than men, women now had an entry into teaching, the first profession open to them. Besides, women could also be paid far less than men; school boards assumed that they would accept low wages while waiting to be married.

Just over 50 percent of the white children between 5 and 19 years of age in the United States were enrolled in school in 1850, the highest percentage in the world at the time. Working-class parents pulled their children out of school at an earlier age than higher-income middle-class parents. Planters continued to rely on private tutors or academies, and southern farmers saw little need for public education. The slave states, especially in the Lower South, lagged behind the rest of the nation in public education.

Prisons, Workhouses, and Asylums

Up to this time, Americans had depended on voluntary efforts to cope with crime, poverty, and social deviance. Convinced that these efforts were inadequate, reformers turned to public authorities to establish a host of new institutions to deal with social problems.

All these public institutions reflected a new attitude toward conditions that until then had been regarded as inevitable and irreversible. For example, eighteenth-century Americans never thought of rehabilitating criminals. Prisons were simple structures used to hold criminals before

LESSON XI.

Boys at Play.

Can you fly a kite ? See how the boy flies his kite. He holds the string fast, and the wind blows it up.

Now it is high in the air, and looks like a bird. When the wind blows hard, you must hold fast, or your kite will get away.

Boys love to run and play.

But they must not be rude. Good boys do not play in a rude way, but take care not to hurt any one.

Moral lessons, such as this one for boys at play, filled the pages of the McGuffey's readers.

they were fined, whipped, mutilated, or executed. But the institutional reformers of the Jacksonian era believed that criminals, as well as the poor and other deviants, could be morally redeemed.

The reformers held that people's environments shaped their character for good or evil. The Boston Children's Friend Society was devoted to the young, "whose plastic natures may be molded into images of perfect beauty, or …perfect repulsiveness." Samuel Gridley Howe, a prison reformer, proclaimed: "Thousands of convicts are made so in consequence of a faulty organization of society…." In the properly ordered environment of new institutions, discipline and moral character would be instilled in criminals and other deviants who lacked the self-control to resist the society's corrupting vices and temptations.

Reformers had particularly high expectations for the penitentiary systems pioneered in Pennsylvania and New York in the 1820s. As two French observers noted in the early 1830s, "The penitentiary system …to them seems the remedy for all the evils of society." Unlike earlier prisons, the penitentiaries were huge, imposing structures that isolated the prisoners from each other and the outside world. No longer were criminals to be brutally punished or thrown together under inhumane conditions that perpetuated a cycle of moral depravity. Now, cut off from all corrupting influences, forced to learn that hard work teaches moral discipline, and uplifted by religious literature, criminals would be guided toward becoming law-abiding, productive citizens.

Workhouses. The same philosophy of reform provided the rationale for asylums to house the poor and the insane. The number of transient poor and the size of urban slums increased as commercial capitalism uprooted farmers from the land and undercut the security of craft trades. Believing that the poor, much like criminals, had only themselves to blame, public officials and their evangelical allies prescribed a therapeutic regimen of discipline and physical labor to cure the poor of their moral defects. The structured setting for the regimen was the workhouse.

The custodians of the workhouses banished drinking, gambling, and idleness. Their prime responsibility was to supervise the inmates in a tightly scheduled daily routine built around manual labor. Once purged of their laziness and filled with self-esteem as the result of work discipline, the poor would be released to become useful members of society.

Asylums for the mentally ill. Public insane asylums offered a similar order for the mentally ill. Reformers believed that too many choices in a highly mobile, materialistic, and competitive society drove some people insane. Following the lead of New York and Massachusetts in the 1830s, 28 states had established mental hospitals by 1860. These facilities set rigid rules and work assignments to teach patients how to order their lives.

In the early 1840s Dorothea Dix, a Massachusetts schoolteacher, discovered that the insane in her home state were dumped into jails and almshouses, where they suffered filthy, inhumane treatment. She found the insane "confined …in cages, closets, cellars, stalls, pens! Chained, naked, beaten with rods, and lashed into obedience." Horrified, Dix lobbied state legislatures across the nation for the next twenty years to improve treatment for the mentally ill.

While the reformers did provide social deviants with cleaner, safer living conditions, their penitentiaries and asylums succeeded more in classifying and segregating inmates than in reforming them. Submission to routine turned out not to be the best builder of character. Penitentiaries, reformatories, and workhouses failed to eliminate or noticeably check poverty, crime, and vice. Refusing to question their basic premise that repressive institutions could promote individual responsibility, reformers abandoned their environmental explanations for deviance. By mid-century, they were defining deviants and dependents as permanent misfits with ingrained character defects. The asylums remained; but, stripped of their earlier optimism, they became little more than holding pens for the outcasts of society.

Utopian Alternatives

Unlike the reformers, who aimed to improve the existing order by guiding individuals to greater self-discipline, the utopians sought perfection by withdrawing from society and its confining institutions. A radically new social order, not an improved old one, was their goal.

Though following different religious and secular philosophies of communitarian living, all the utopians wanted to fashion a more rational and personally satisfying alternative to the competitive materialism of antebellum America. Nearly all the communities sought to transform the organization and rewards of work, thus challenging the prevailing dogmas about private property.

The most successful utopian communities were religious sects whose reordering of both sexual and economic relations departed sharply from middle-class norms. The **Shakers,** at their height in the 1830s, attracted some 6,000 followers. Named for the convulsive dancing that was part of their religious ceremonies, the Shakers traced their origins to the teachings of Ann Lee ("Mother Lee"). An illiterate factory laborer in mid-eighteenth-century England, Lee had a revelation in 1770 that the Second Coming of Christ was to be fulfilled in her own womanly form, the embodiment of the female side of God. Fired by another vision in 1774, Lee led eight of her followers to America, where, after her death in 1784, her disciples established the first Shaker community in New Lebanon, New York. Organized around doctrines of celibate **communism,** Shaker communities held all property in common. The sexes worked and lived apart from each other. Dancing during religious worship brought men and women together and provided an emotional release from enforced sexual denial. As an early Shaker leader explained, "There is no labor which so fully absorbs all the faculties of soul and body, as real spiritual devotion and energetic exercise in sacred worship." In worldly as well as spiritual terms, women enjoyed an equality in Shaker life that the outside world denied them. For this reason, twice as many women as men joined the Shakers.

The Shakers gradually dwindled. Their rule of celibacy meant, of course, that they could propagate themselves only by recruiting new members, and few new converts joined the movement after 1850. Viewed as eccentric outsiders by contemporaries, the Shakers today are best remembered for the beautiful simplicity of the furniture and other household objects they made in their workshops.

John Humphrey Noyes, a graduate of Dartmouth who studied for the ministry at Yale, established the **Oneida Community** in upstate New York in 1847. He attracted over 200 followers with his perfectionist vision of plural marriage, community nurseries, group discipline, and common ownership of property. Charged with adultery, Noyes fled to Canada in 1879, but the Oneida Community, reorganized in 1881 as a joint-stock company in the United States and committed thereafter to conventional sexual mores, survived into the twentieth century.

In the concern etched in her face, this photograph captures the compassion that Dorothea Dix brought to her crusade for mental health reform.

Secular utopians aspired to perfect social relations through rationally designed planned communities. Bitter critics of the social evils of industrialization, they tried to construct models for a social order free from poverty, unemployment, and inequality. They envisioned cooperative communities that balanced agricultural and industrial pursuits in a mixed economy that recycled earnings to the laborers who actually produced the wealth.

Despite their high expectations, nearly all the planned communities ran into financial difficulties and soon collapsed. The pattern was set by the first of the controversial socialist experiments, **New Harmony** in Indiana, the brainchild of the wealthy Scottish industrialist and philanthropist Robert Owen. A proponent of utopian **socialism,** Owen promised to create a new order where "the degrading and pernicious practices in which we are now well trained, of buying cheap and selling dear, will be rendered unnecessary" and "union and co-operation will supersede individual interest." But within two years of its founding in 1825, New Harmony fell victim to inadequate financing and internal bickering.

The economic misery of the depression of the 1840s revived interest in utopian ventures and helped popularize the ideas of Charles Fourier, a French utopian who proposed to restore dignity to labor and end poverty by dividing society into phalanxes, cooperative units of workers who lived communally. Scores of **Fourierist communities** were set up, but few survived into the 1850s.

About the only secular cooperative that gained lasting fame was **Brook Farm** in West Roxbury, Massachusetts (today part of Boston). Established in 1841, Brook Farm was a showcase for the transcendentalist philosophy of Ralph Waldo Emerson. A former Unitarian minister in Boston, Emerson taught that intuition and emotion could grasp a truer ("transcendent") reality than could the senses alone. The Boston intellectuals drawn to Brook Farm in the 1840s saw it as a refuge from the pressures and coarseness of commercial society, a place where they could realize the Emersonian ideal of spontaneous creativity. Although disbanded after six years as an economic failure, Brook Farm inspired intellectuals such as Nathaniel Hawthorne, who briefly lived there. In turn, his writings and those of other writers influenced by **transcendentalism** flowed into the great renaissance of American literature in the mid-nineteenth century, an outpouring of work that grappled with Emersonian themes of individualism and the reshaping of the American character.

A distinctly national literature.   In an 1837 address at Harvard titled "The American Scholar," Emerson called for a distinctly national literature devoted to the democratic possibilities of American life. "The literature of the poor, the feelings of the child, the philosophy of the street, the meaning of household life, are the topics of the time," he proclaimed. Writers soon responded to Emerson's call.

Walt Whitman, whose *Leaves of Grass* (1855) foreshadowed modern poetry in its use of free verse, shared Emerson's faith in the possibilities of individual fulfillment, and his poems celebrated the democratic variety of the American people. Henry David Thoreau, Emerson's friend and neighbor, embodied the transcendentalist fascination with nature and self-discovery by living in relative isolation for 16 months at Walden Pond, near Concord, Massachusetts. His *Walden; or, Life in the Woods* (1854) became an American classic. "I went to the woods," he wrote, "because I wished to ...confront only the essential facts of life, and see if I could not learn what it had to teach, and not, when I came to die, discover that I had not lived."

Nathaniel Hawthorne and Herman Melville, the greatest novelists of the American renaissance, focused on the existence of evil and the human need for community. In *The Scarlet Letter* (1850) and *The House of the Seven Gables* (1851), Hawthorne probed themes of egoism and pride to reveal the underside of the human soul. Melville's *Moby Dick* (1851) depicted the consequences of a competitive individualism unchecked by a social conscience. In his relentless pursuit of the great white whale, Captain Ahab destroys himself and his crew.

Much of the appeal of the utopian communities flowed from the same concern about the splintering and selfishness of antebellum society that animated Hawthorne and Melville.

The works of these novelists have endured, but the utopian experiments quickly collapsed. Promising economic security and social harmony to buttress a threatened sense of community, the utopians failed to lure all but a few Americans from the acquisitiveness and competitive demands of the larger society.

Abolitionism and Women's Rights

Abolitionism emerged from the same religious impulse that energized reform throughout the North. Like other reformers, the abolitionists came predominantly from evangelical, middle-class families, particularly those of New England stock. What distinguished the abolitionists was their insistence that slavery was *the* great national sin, an evil that mocked American ideals of liberty and Christian morality. Under the early leadership of William Lloyd Garrison, the abolitionists uncompromisingly attacked not only slaveholders but also all others whose moral apathy helped support slavery. After provoking a storm of protest in both the North and the South, the abolitionist movement split in 1840. Crucial in this division was Garrison's support of women's rights. Most abolitionists broke with him and founded their own antislavery organization. Female abolitionists took the lead in organizing a separate women's rights movement.

Rejecting Colonization

In the early nineteenth century, when slavery was expanding westward, almost all white Americans regardless of class or region were convinced that emancipation would lead either to a race war or the debasement of their superior status through racial interbreeding. This paralyzing fear of general emancipation, rooted in pervasive racism, long shielded slavery from sustained attack.

In 1817, antislavery reformers from the North and the South founded the **American Colonization Society.** Slaveholding politicians from the Upper South, notably Henry Clay, James Madison, and President James Monroe, were the leading organizers of the society. Gradual emancipation accompanied by the removal of black people from America to Africa was the only solution these white reformers could imagine for ridding the nation of slavery and avoiding a racial bloodbath. Their goal was to make America all free *and* all white.

The American Colonization Society had no real chance of success. No form of emancipation, no matter how gradual, could appeal to slaveowners who could profit from the labor of their slaves. Moreover, the society could never afford to purchase the freedom of any significant number of slaves. Almost all the African Americans it transported to Liberia, the West African colony it helped found, were already free. At the height of its popularity in the 1820s, the society sent only 1,400 colonists to Africa. During that same decade, the U.S. slave population increased by more than 450,000.

Free African Americans bitterly attacked the colonizers' central assumption that free black people were unfit to live as citizens in America. Typical of the colonizers' racist thinking was the claim by Henry Clay in 1827 that the "free coloured" were the "most vicious" of all Americans. "Contaminated themselves, they extend their vices to all around them, to the slaves and to the whites." The annual report of the American Colonization Society in 1824 approvingly quoted a New England minister who said of the free African American: "You cannot raise him from the abyss of his degradation."

Most free African Americans were native-born, and they considered themselves Americans with every right to enjoy the blessings of republican liberty. As a black petition in 1817 stated, banishment from America "would not only be cruel, but in direct violation of the principles, which have been the boast of this republic."

Organizing through their own churches in northern cities, free African Americans founded some fifty abolitionist societies, offered refuge to fugitive slaves, and launched the first African American newspaper in 1827, *Freedom's Journal*. David Walker, a free black man who had moved from North Carolina to Massachusetts, published his **Appeal to the Colored Citizens of the World** in 1829. In a searing indictment of white greed and hypocrisy, he rejected colonization and insisted that "America is more our country, than it is the whites', we have enriched it with our *blood and tears*." He warned white America that "wo, wo, will be to you if we have to obtain our freedom by fighting."

As if in response to this call for revolutionary resistance by the enslaved, Nat Turner's Rebellion exploded in the summer of 1831 (see Chapter 11). Both alarmed and inspired by the increased tempo of black militancy, a small group of antislavery white people abandoned all illusions about colonization and embarked on a radically new approach for eradicating slavery.

Abolitionism

William Lloyd Garrison, a Massachusetts printer and the leading figure in early abolitionism, became coeditor of an antislavery newspaper in Baltimore in 1829. Before the year was out, Garrison was arrested and convicted of criminal libel for his editorials against a Massachusetts merchant engaged in the domestic slave trade, and he spent seven weeks in jail before a New York City philanthropist paid his $100 fine. Recognizing that his lack of freedom in jail paled against that of the slave, Garrison emerged with an unquenchable hatred of slavery. Returning to Boston, he launched his own antislavery newspaper, the *Liberator,* in 1831. A year later, he was instrumental in founding the New England Anti-Slavery Society.

As militant as the free African Americans who comprised the bulk of the early subscribers to the *Liberator,* Garrison thundered, "If we would not see our land deluged in blood, we must instantly burst asunder the shackles of the slaves." He committed abolitionism to the twin goals of immediatism, an immediate moral commitment to end slavery, and racial equality. Only by striving toward these goals, he insisted, could white America ever hope to end slavery without massive violence.

The abolitionists' demand for the legal equality of black people was as unsettling to public opinion as their call for immediate, uncompensated emancipation. Discriminatory laws, aptly characterized by the abolitionist Lydia Maria Child as "this legalized contempt of color," restricted the political and civil liberties of free African Americans in every state. Denied the vote outside New England, segregated in all public facilities, prohibited from moving into several western states, and excluded from most jobs save menial labor, free black people everywhere were walled off as an inferior caste.

Garrison, harsh and uncompromising in denouncing slavery and advocating black rights, instilled the antislavery movement with moral urgency. But without the organizational and financial resources of a national society, the message of the early Garrisonians rarely extended beyond free black communities in the North. The success of British abolitionists in 1833, when gradual, compensated emancipation was enacted for Britain's West Indian colonies, inspired white and black abolitionists to gather at Philadelphia in December 1833 and form the **American Anti-Slavery Society.**

Arthur and Lewis Tappan, two wealthy merchants who dominated the abolitionist movement in New York City, provided financial backing for the Anti-Slavery Society. The young evangelical minister Theodore Dwight Weld, fusing abolitionism with the moral passion of religious revivalism,

The illustration on the masthead of this 1831 issue of the *Liberator* condemns the relegation of slaves to the legal status of chattel, mere livestock to be bought and sold, no different from cattle or horses. Revulsion at the treatment of human beings as property was central to the abolitionist indictment of slavery.

The Library Company of Philadelphia

OVERVIEW

Types of Antislavery Reform

Type	Definition	Example
Gradualist	Accepts notions of black inferiority and attempts to end slavery gradually by purchasing the freedom of slaves and colonizing them in Africa	American Colonization Society
Immediatist	Calls for immediate steps to end slavery and denounces slavery and racial prejudice as moral sins	Abolitionists
Political Antislavery	Recognizes slavery in states where it exists but insists on keeping slavery out of the territories	Free-Soilers

brought the antislavery message of the eastern radicals to the West in 1834 with the revivals he preached at Lane Theological Seminary in Cincinnati. The "Lane rebels," students gathered by Weld, fanned out as itinerant agents to seek converts for abolitionism throughout the Yankee districts of the rural North. Weld's *American Slavery as It Is: Testimony of a Thousand Witnesses,* a massively documented indictment of slavery, became a bestseller in 1839.

Revivalist exhortations were just one of the techniques the abolitionists exploited to mobilize public opinion against slavery. They spread their message through rallies, paid lecturers, children's games and toys, and the printed word. Drawing on the experience of reformers in Bible and tract societies, the abolitionists harnessed steam power to the cause of moral suasion. They distributed millions of antislavery tracts, and by the late 1830s, abolitionist sayings appeared on posters, emblems, song sheets, and even candy wrappers.

Women were essential in all of these activities. From the very beginning of the movement, they established their own antislavery societies as auxiliaries to the national organizations run and dominated by men. As Christian wives and mothers, they identified with the plight of the black family under slavery. Initially, their role was limited to raising funds, circulating petitions, and visiting homes to gain converts. Often operating out of local churches, women were grassroots organizers of a massive petition campaign launched in the mid-1830s. Women signed more than half of the antislavery memorials sent to Congress. "There would be but a few abolition petitions if the ladies ... would let us alone," complained a Mississippi congressman.

The abolitionists focused their energies on mass propaganda because they saw their role as social agitators who had to break through white apathy and change public opinion. By 1840 they had succeeded in enlisting nearly 200,000 northerners in 2,000 local affiliates of the American Anti-Slavery Society. Most whites, however, remained unmoved, and some violently opposed the abolitionists.

Antiabolitionist mobs in the North went on a rampage in the mid-1830s (see Figure 12-3). They disrupted antislavery meetings, beat and stoned speakers, destroyed printing presses, burned the homes of the wealthy benefactors of the movement, and vandalized free black neighborhoods in a wave of terror that drove many black people from several northern cities. Elijah P. Lovejoy, an abolitionist editor in Illinois, was killed by a mob in 1837. Local elites, especially those with profitable ties to the slave economy of the South, often incited the mobs, whose fury expressed the anxiety of semiskilled and common laborers that they might lose their jobs if freed slaves moved north.

In the South, the hostility to abolitionism took the form of burning and censoring antislavery literature, offering rewards for the capture of leading abolitionists to stand trial for allegedly inciting slave revolts, and tightening up slave codes and the surveillance of free black people. Meanwhile,

FIGURE 12-3 **Mob Violence and the Abolitionists**
Civil disturbances resulting in attacks on individuals or property increased sharply in the 1830s. The abolitionist campaign to flood the country with antislavery literature triggered much of this surge. Nearly half of the mob activity in the 1830s was directed against abolitionists.

Data Source: Leonard L. Richards, *"Gentlemen of Property and Standing": Anti-Abolitionist Mobs in Jacksonian America* (1970).

American Views

Appeal of A Female Abolitionist

Lydia Maria Child's *Appeal*, published in Boston in 1833, was a landmark in abolitionist literature for both the thoroughness of its attack on slavery and its refutation of racist ideology and discrimination. This condemnation of racial prejudice was the most radical feature of abolitionist ideology. It directly challenged the deeply held beliefs and assumptions of nearly all white Americans, in the North as well as the South. Racism and slavery, as Child shows in this excerpt from her Appeal, fed off one another in the national curse of slavery.

- How does Child argue that northern white people must bear some of the responsibility for perpetuating slavery?

- What arguments does Child make against racial discrimination in northern society?

- What did Child mean when she wrote that "the Americans are peculiarly responsible for the example they give"? Do you agree with her?

- How does Child deal with the charge that the abolitionists threatened the preservation of the Union?

While we bestow our earnest disapprobation on the system of slavery, let us not flatter ourselves that we are in reality any better than our brethren of the South. Thanks to our soil and climate, and the early exhortations of the Quakers, the form of slavery does not exist among us; but the very spirit of the hateful and mischievous thing is here in all its strength....Our prejudice against colored people is even more inveterate than it is at the South. The planter is often attached to his negroes, and lavishes caresses and kind words upon them, as he would on a favorite hound: but our cold-hearted, ignoble prejudice admits of no exception, no intermission.

The Southerners have long continued habit, apparent interest and dreaded danger, to palliate the wrong they do; but we stand without excuse....If the free States wished to cherish the system of slavery forever, they could not take a more direct course than they now do. Those who are kind and liberal on all other subjects, unite with the selfish and the proud in their unrelenting efforts to keep the colored population in the lowest state of degradation; and the influence they unconsciously exert over children early infuses into their innocent minds the same strong feelings of contempt....

The state of public feeling not only makes it difficult for the Africans to obtain information, but it prevents them from making profitable use of what knowledge they have. A colored man, however intelligent, is not allowed to pursue any business more lucrative than that of a bar-

ber, a shoeblack, or waiter. These, and all other employments, are truly respectable, whenever the duties connected with them are faithfully performed; but it is unjust that a man should, on account of his complexion, be prevented from performing more elevated uses in society. Every citizen ought to have a fair chance to try his fortune in any line of business, which he thinks he has ability to transact. Why should not colored men be employed in the manufactories of various kinds? If their ignorance is an objection, let them be enlightened, as speedily as possible. If their moral character is not sufficiently pure, remove the pressure of public scorn, and thus supply them with motives for being respectable. All this can be done. It merely requires an earnest wish to overcome a prejudice, which ...is in fact opposed to the spirit of our religion, and contrary to the instinctive good feelings of our nature....When the majority heartily desire a change, it is effected, be the difficulties what they may. The Americans are peculiarly responsible for the example they give; for in no other country does the unchecked voice of the people constitute the whole of government....

The strongest and best reason that can be given for our supineness on the subject of slavery, is the fear of dissolving the Union. The Constitution of the United States demands our highest reverence....But we must not forget that the Constitution provides for any change that may be required for the general good. The great machine is constructed with a safety valve, by which any rapidly increasing evil may be expelled whenever the people desire it.

If the Southern politicians are determined to make a Siamese question of this also, if they insist that the Union shall not exist without slavery, it can only be said that they join two things, which have no affinity with each other, and which cannot permanently exist together. They chain the living and vigorous to the diseased and dying; and the former will assuredly perish in the infected neighborhood.

The universal introduction of free labor is the surest way to consolidate the Union, and enable us to live together in harmony and peace. If a history is ever written entitled "The Decay and Dissolution of the North American Republic," its author will distinctly trace our downfall to the existence of slavery among us.

Source: Lydia Maria Child, *An Appeal in Favor of That Class of Americans Called Africans* (originally published 1833), ed. Carolyn L. Karcher (University of Massachusetts Press, 1996).

Democrats in Congress yielded to slaveholding interests in 1836 by passing a gag rule that automatically tabled antislavery petitions with no debate.

The hostility and violence abolitionism provoked convinced Garrison and some of his followers that U.S. institutions and values were fundamentally flawed. In 1838, Garrison helped found the New England Non-Resistant Society, dedicated to the belief that a complete moral regeneration, based on renouncing force in all human relationships, was necessary if the United States were ever to live up to its Christian and republican ideals. The Garrisonian nonresistants rejected all coercive authority, whether expressed in capital punishment, human bondage, clerical support of slavery, male dominance in the patriarchal family, the racial oppression of back people, or the police power of government. The logic of their stand as Christian **anarchists** drove them to denounce all formal political activities and even the legitimacy of the Union, based as it was on a pact with slaveholders.

Garrison's opponents within the abolitionist movement accused him of alienating the public by identifying the antislavery cause with radical attacks on traditional authority. His support for the growing demand of antislavery women to be treated as equals in the movement brought the factional bickering to a head and split the American Anti-Slavery Society. In turn, the opposition of most male abolitionists to the public activities of their female counterparts provoked a militant faction of these women into founding their own movement to achieve equality in U.S. society.

The Women's Rights Movement

Feminism grew out of abolitionism because of the parallels many women drew between the exploited lives of the slaves and their own subordinate status in northern society. Considered biologically inferior to men, women were denied the vote, deprived of property or control of any wages after marriage, and barred from most occupations and advanced education. "In striving to cut [the slave's] irons off, we found most surely that we were manacled *ourselves*," argued Abby Kelley, a Quaker abolitionist.

In 1837, Angelina and Sarah Grimké, the South Carolina–born abolitionists, attracted large crowds of men and women to their antislavery lectures in New England. By publicly lecturing to a "promiscuous" (mixed) audience of men and women, they defied restrictions on women's proper role and enraged the Congregational clergy of Massachusetts. Harshly criticized for their unwomanly behavior, the Grimkés publicly responded with an indictment of the male patriarchy and the shocking assertion that "men and women are *created equal!* They are both moral and accountable beings and whatever is right for man to do is right for woman."

Now more sensitive than ever to the injustice of their assigned role as men's submissive followers, antislavery women demanded an equal voice in the abolitionist movement. Despite strong opposition from many of his fellow male abolitionists, Garrison helped Abby Kelley win a seat on the business committee of the American Anti-Slavery Society at its convention in 1840. The anti-Garrisonians walked out of the convention and formed a separate organization, the American and Foreign Anti-Slavery Society.

What was rapidly becoming known as the "woman question" also disrupted the 1840 World Anti-Slavery Convention in London. The refusal of the convention to seat the U.S. female delegates was the final indignity that transformed the discontent of women into a self-conscious movement for women's equality. Two of the excluded delegates, Lucretia Mott and Elizabeth Cady Stanton, vowed to build an organization to "speak out for *oppressed* women."

Their work went slowly. Early feminists were dependent on the abolitionists for most of their followers, and they were unable to do more than hold local meetings and sponsor occasional speaking tours. Many women sympathetic to the feminist movement hung back lest they be shunned in their communities. A minister's wife in Portsmouth, New Hampshire, wrote to a feminist friend, "There are but few here who think of women as anything more than slave or plaything, and they think I am different from most women."

In 1848, Stanton and Mott were finally able to call the first national convention ever devoted to women's rights at Seneca

The International Dimensions of Abolition

"The trumpet has sounded through all the colonial dependencies of our country, which proclaims 'liberty to the captives.' O! what heart is there so cold, so seared, so dead, as to feel no thrill of exulting emotion at the thought, that on the morning of this day, eight hundred thousand fellow-men and fellow-subjects, who, during the past night, slept bondmen, awoke freemen! [British emancipation will be] but the first day of a Jubilee year,—of a period of successive triumphs ...of continuous and rapidly progressive prosperity, to the cause of freedom. [Once America joins Britain in the work of emancipation] the world will be shamed into imitation:—and in no long period, there will not be found on a earth a remnant of it."

On August 1, 1834, the day that the British Emancipation Act of 1833 took effect, the Reverend Ralph Wardlaw of Glasgow, Scotland, spoke these words of millennial joy and hope for the future.

It was a day of exultation for reformers on both sides of the Atlantic. The spark of freedom was first struck in Britain by the creation in 1787 of the Quaker-inspired Society for the Abolition of the Slave Trade. It exploded into a revolutionary conflagration when the slaves in Saint-Domingue rose up in rebellion in 1791 and unleashed the greatest slave revolt in the Western Hemisphere. By 1808, reformers in Britain and the United States had prohibited the African slave trade. When the Spanish Empire in Latin America began to break up after 1810, the independence movements in Spain's former colonies committed themselves to emancipation. In a startling reversal from the situation in 1800, only Brazil and Cuba remained as major slave areas in Latin America by the 1820s. Then, as the result of a massive grassroots campaign that inundated Parliament with 5,000 petitions and half a million signers, Britain passed the Emancipation Act of 1833, which emancipated the slaves in its colonies as of August 1, 1834.

British emancipation buoyed the abolitionist cause in the United States and was a major factor in emboldening the abolitionists to organize a national society in 1833. It also convinced them, as the Reverend Wardlaw had argued, that Protestant Christianity was poised to take the lead in an epic struggle for human betterment. That was the vision that inspired the abolitionists as they set out to redeem America's revolutionary heritage by cleansing the nation of slavery.

■ How does placing the American antislavery movement in a transatlantic context broaden our understanding of the antislavery cause and its place in the intellectual history of the nineteenth century?

Falls, in upstate New York. The **Seneca Falls Convention** issued the **Declaration of Sentiments,** a call for full female equality. Modeled directly on the Declaration of Independence, it identified male patriarchy as the source of women's oppression and demanded the vote for women as a sacred and inalienable right of republican citizenship. This call for suffrage raised the prospect of women's self-determination as independent citizens. The Seneca Falls agenda defined the goals of the women's movement for the rest of the century. The call for the vote met the stiffest opposition, and male legislators refused to budge. The feminists' few successes before the Civil War came in economic rights. By 1860, 14 states had granted women greater control over their property and wages, most significantly under New York's Married Women's Property Act of 1860. Largely the result of the intense lobbying of Susan B. Anthony, the act established women's legal right to control their own wage income and to sue fathers and husbands who tried to deprive them of their wages.

Despite such successes, the feminist movement did not attract broad support. Most women found in the doctrine of separate spheres a reassuring feminine identity that they could express either at home or in benevolent and reform societies. Within the reform movement as a whole, women's rights were always a minor concern. Abolitionists focused on emancipation.

Political Antislavery

Most of the abolitionists who had broken with Garrison in 1840 believed that emancipation could best be achieved by moving abolitionism into the mainstream of U.S. politics. Political abolitionism had its roots in the petition campaign of the late 1830s. Congressional efforts to suppress the discussion of slavery backfired when John Quincy Adams, the former president who had become a Massachusetts congressman, resorted to an unending series of parliamentary ploys to get around the gag rule (see Chapter 10). Adams became a champion of the constitutional right to petition Congress for redress of grievances. White northerners who had shown no interest in abolitionism as a moral crusade for black people now began to take a stand against slavery when the issue involved the civil liberties of whites and the dominant political power of the South. By the hundreds of thousands, they signed abolitionist petitions in 1837 and 1838 to protest the gag rule and the admission of Texas as a slave state.

In 1840, anti-Garrisonian abolitionists tried to turn this new antislavery constituency into an independent political party. They formed the **Liberty Party** and ran James G. Birney, a former slaveholder converted by Weld to abolitionism, as their candidate for the presidency. He failed to draw even 1 percent of the popular vote, but antislavery districts dominated by evangelical New Englanders elected several antislavery congressmen.

The Liberty Party opposed any expansion of slavery in the territories, condemned racial discrimination in the North as well as slavery in the South, and won the support of most black abolitionists. "To it," recalled Samuel Ward of New York, "I devoted my political activities; with it I lived my political life." In 1843, a national African American convention in Buffalo endorsed the Liberty party.

This political activism was part of a concerted effort by African Americans to assert leadership in an antislavery movement that rarely treated them as equals. Frederick Douglass was their most dynamic spokesman. After escaping from slavery in 1838, Douglass became a spellbinding lecturer for abolitionism and in 1845 published his classic autobiography, *Narrative of the Life of Frederick Douglass, an American Slave*. Increasingly dissatisfied with Garrison's Christian pacifism and his stand against political action, Douglass broke with Garrison in 1847 and founded a black abolitionist newspaper, the *North Star*. The break became irreparable in 1851 when Douglass publicly denied the Garrisonian position that the Constitution was a proslavery document. If properly interpreted, Douglass insisted, "the Constitution is a *glorious liberty document*," and he called for a political war against slavery.

That war had started in the 1840s with the Liberty Party. Although the party elected only one of its candidates to Congress (Gerrit Smith of New York), it kept slavery in the forefront of national politics. Led by Joshua R. Giddings, a small but vocal bloc of antislavery politicians began to popularize the frightening concept of "the Slave Power," a vast conspiracy of planters and their northern lackeys that controlled the federal government and was plotting to spread slavery and subvert any free institutions that opposed it. As proof, they cited the gag rule, which had shut off debate on slavery, and the campaign of the Tyler administration to annex slaveholding Texas. The Michigan Liberty Party in 1843 claimed that slavery was "not only a monstrous legalized system of wickedness ... but an overwhelming political monopoly ... which has thus tyrannically subverted the constitutional liberties of more than 12,000,000 of nomi-

William Whipper, an African-American businessman, was active in temperance and other reform movements

nal American freemen." The Liberty Party blamed the depression of 1839–1843 on the "withering and impoverishing effect of slavery on the free States." Planters, it charged, had reneged on their debts to northern creditors and manipulated federal policies on banking and tariffs to the advantage of the South.

The specter of the Slave Power made white liberties, and not black bondage, central to northern concerns about slavery. This shift redefined the evil of slavery to appeal to the self-interest of white northerners who had rejected the moral appeals of the Garrisonians. White people who had earlier been apathetic now began to view slavery as a threat to their rights of free speech and self-improvement.

Birney again headed the Liberty Party ticket in 1844, but he ran only marginally stronger than in 1840. Nonetheless, the image of the Slave Power predisposed many northerners to see the expansionist program of the incoming Polk administration as part of a southern plot to secure more territory for slaveholders at the expense of northern farmers. Northern fears that free labor would be shut out of the new territories won in the Mexican War provided the rallying cry for the Free-Soil Party of 1848, which foreshadowed the more powerful Republican Party of the late 1850s.

FROM THEN TO NOW

Immigration: An Ambivalent Welcome

Americans have long extended an ambivalent welcome to newcomers. Yet the United States, whose founding ideals promise equality and opportunity to all, is a nation settled and built by immigrants. And for much of its history it has offered asylum for the world's oppressed.

The first sustained attack against newcomers emerged as a result of the surge in immigration during the 1840s and 1850s. It was directed by established immigrant groups, the descendants of settlers from Britain and northwestern Europe, at unfamiliar newcomers, particularly the Irish. These nativists especially feared religious contamination, claiming that the Catholicism of the Irish was alien to the Protestant values held to be indispensable to the preservation of American liberties. In the late nineteenth century a massive new immigrant surge dominated by people from southern and eastern Europe seeking economic opportunity and fleeing religious oppression transformed U.S. society and renewed nativist fears. This time, race replaced religion as the basis for drawing invidious comparisons between established residents and the newcomers. Pseudoscientific theories relegated Jews, Slavs, and Mediterranean peoples, together with Africans, to an inferior status below people of northern European. The newcomers, it was claimed, were unfit for democratic government and would endanger American civilization. Strict anti-immigrant legislation in the 1920s sharply curtailed immigration from outside the Western Hemisphere, banning Asians entirely and setting quotas based on national origin for others.

These Italian children on board an immigrant ship were part of the huge influx of southern and eastern Europeans after 1880.

Recent concerns about immigration result from the unforeseen consequences of a 1965 reform of the immigration law that abolished quotas. Since then, immigration has risen sharply, and the vast majority of the immigrants come from areas outside of Europe. As cries are again raised that alien newcomers are threatening the cohesiveness of the nation's institutions and values, Americans would do well to recall the words of Abraham Lincoln: "What held the nation together was an idea of equality that every newcomer could claim and defend by free choice."

Their nativist critics depicted the Irish as drunken brawlers with the derogatory racial characteristics that native-born whites assigned to African Americans.

THE USUAL IRISH WAY OF DOING THINGS.

■ **What recurring patterns occur in the ambivalence with which resident Americans have viewed the acceptance of newcomers?**

From Then to Now Online myhistorylab

12-1 Samuel F. B. Morse, *Nativist pamphlet*, 1844. Charges a Catholic conspiracy against American liberties.

12-2 Lothrop Stoddard, *Immigrants as a Racial Threat*, 1920. Depicts immigrants from southern and eastern Europe as racially inferior.

12-3 New York Times, *Efforts at Immigration Reform*, June 28, 2007. Summarizes the difficulties in achieving immigration reform.

Mobs of angry men often broke up meetings organized by women seeking the right to vote. Shown here is a male escort offering protection to Lucretia Mott and another suffragette at one such meeting.

The Fugitive Song
Library of Congress: Digital ID: cph 3a10460;
LC-USZ62-7823.
The abolitionists used all media outlets to promote the antislavery cause. Shown here on a sheet music cover is Frederick Douglass, the escaped slave who became the most prominent black abolitionist.

Conclusion

With surprising speed after 1815, transportation improvements, technological innovations, and expanding markets drove the economy toward industrialization. Wealth inequality increased, old classes were reshaped, and new ones formed. These changes were most evident in the Northeast, where capital, labor, and growing urban markets spurred the acceleration of manufacturing. The reform impulse that both reflected and shaped these changes was also strongest in the Northeast. The new evangelical Protestantism promised that human perfectibility was possible if individuals strove to free themselves from sin. Influenced by this promise, the northern middle class embraced reform causes that sought to improve human character. Temperance changed U.S. drinking habits and established sobriety as the cultural standard for respectable male behavior. Middle-class reform also emphasized institutional solutions for what were now defined as the social problems of ignorance, crime, and poverty.

The most radical of the reform movements focused on women's equality and the elimination of slavery. The women's rights movement emerged out of women's involvement in reform, especially in abolitionism. Feminism and abolitionism triggered a backlash from the more conservative majority. This backlash prevented women from gaining legal and political equality, the major demand of the feminists, and convinced most abolitionists that they had to switch from moral agitation to political persuasion. The political abolitionists soon found that the most effective approach in widening the antislavery appeal was their charge that a Slave Power conspiracy threatened the freedoms of white northerners.

Review Questions

1. Why were improvements in transportation so essential to the growth of the economy after 1815? What were the nature and scope of these improvements?

2. What is an industrial revolution? How can we explain the surge in manufacturing in the United States from 1815 to 1850?

3. What was the religious impulse behind the first wave of reform? What innovations in reaching a mass audience did the benevolent reformers pioneer?

4. What drew women into reform? Why did many of them feel a special affinity for abolitionism?

5. Why was abolitionism the most radical reform of all? How was it linked to an international movement calling for the end of slavery?

6. Why do you think so few Southern women of the plantation class followed Angelina Grimké on her journey from social privilege to social activism?

Key Terms

American Anti-Slavery Society (p. 322)

American Colonization Society (p. 321)

American Female Reform Society (p. 317)

American system of manufacturing (p. 310)

American Temperance Society (p. 315)

Anarchists (p. 325)

Appeal to the Colored Citizens of the World (p. 322)

Benevolent empire (p. 314)

Brook Farm (p. 321)

Charles River Bridge v. Warren Bridge (p. 304)

Church of Jesus Christ of Latter-Day Saints (Mormon Church) (p. 317)

Communism (p. 320)

Cult of domesticity (p. 312)

Declaration of Sentiments (p. 326)

Fourierist communities (p. 321)

Gibbons v. Ogden (p. 304)

Liberty Party (p. 327)

Mormon Church (p. 317)

Nativist (p. 314)

New Harmony (p. 320)

Oneida Community (p. 320)

Putting-out system (p. 308)

Rhode Island system (p. 309)

Sabbatarian movement (p. 314)

Seneca Falls Convention (p. 326)

Shakers (p. 320)

Socialism (p. 320)

Temperance (p. 311)

Transcendentalism (p. 321)

Transportation revolution (p. 301)

Waltham system (p. 309)

Workingmen's movement (p. 318)

Recommended Reading

Abzug, Robert H. *Cosmos Crumbling: American Reform and the Religious Imagination* (1994). Provides a fresh look at antebellum reform by using the lives of individual reformers to show how Protestant Christianity inspired a rethinking of U.S. values in a period of rapid economic change.

Boydston, Jeanne. *Home and Work: Housework, Wages, and the Ideology of Labor in the Early Republic* (1990). Shows how issues of gender shaped the emergence of a market for labor and influenced the very notion of work.

Larkin, Jack. *The Reshaping of Everyday Life, 1790–1840* (1988). A very readable depiction of how social and economic changes were reflected in the rhythms and customs of daily life in the first half of the nineteenth century.

Meyer, David R. *The Roots of American Industrialization* (2003). A boldly argued interpretation of early industrialization that links it to the prosperity of northern farmers.

Mintz, Steven. *Moralists and Modernizers: America's Pre–Civil War Reformers* (1995). A recent survey that demonstrates how both the fears and possibilities of change influenced the impulse of reform.

Stewart, James Brewer. *Holy Warriors: The Abolitionists and American Society* (1978). Provides the best brief overview of abolitionism and what distinguished it from the mainstream of the reform tradition.

Where to Learn More

■ **Lowell National Historical Park.**   The park is a wonderful resource for visualizing the early stages of America's industrial revolution. For hours and a schedule of events, see www.nps.gov/lowe

■ **Slater Hill Historic Site, Pawtucket, Rhode Island.** The Sylvanus Brown House of 1758, the Slaren Mill of 1793, and the Wilkinson Mill of 1810 are on the site. An extensive library and holdings provide insight into the social and economic world of the early industrial revolution. Information on hours, collections, and exhibits can be found at www.artcom.com/museums/vs/sz/02862-06.htm

■ **Erie Canal Museum, Syracuse, New York.**   The museum houses extensive collections on the building and maintenance of the Erie Canal, and its photo holdings visually record much of the history of the canal. In addition to information on exhibits, tours, and school programs,

its website, www.eriecanalmuseum.org, includes pictures of a replica of an Erie Canal line boat.

■ **Historic New Harmony, New Harmony, Indiana.** The tours and museum holdings at this preserved site offer a glimpse into the communal living that Robert Owen tried to promote in his utopian plan. For a brief history of New Harmony and links to special events and programs at the site, go to www.newharmony.org

■ **Women's Rights Historical Park, Seneca Falls, New York.**   The park provides an interpretive overview of the first women's rights convention and includes among its historical sites the restored home of Elizabeth Cady Stanton. Go to www.nps.gov/wori/wrnhp.htm for links to the museum's summer calendar of events and information on programs.

Study Resources

For study resources for this chapter, go to www.myhistorylab.com and choose *The American Journey*. You will find a wealth of study and review material for this chapter, including pre- and post-tests, customized study plan, key term review flash cards, interactive map and document activities, and documents for analysis.

As depicted in this painting by George Catlin, Native Americans were still the dominant power on the Great Plains when this Comanche war party met up with a scouting expedition of the U.S. Army in the 1830s. Within a decade, a wave of white settlement challenged the power in a series of clashes for control of the trans-Mississippi West.

The Way West 13
1815–1850

On an occasion when I had interrogated a Sioux chief, on the upper Missouri, about their Government, their punishments and tortures of prisoners, for which I had freely condemned them for the cruelty of the practice, he took occasion, when I had got through, to ask *me* some questions relative to modes in the *civilized world,* which, with his comments upon them, were nearly as follows: and struck me, as I think they must every one, with great force.

He...told me he had often heard that white people hung their criminals by the neck, and choked them to death like dogs, and those their own people; to which I answered, "yes." He then told me he had learned that they shut each other up in prisons, where they keep them a great part of their lives *because they can't pay money!* I

replied in the affirmative to this, which occasioned great surprise and excessive laughter, even among the women. ... He said...that he had been along the Frontier, and a good deal amongst the white people, and he had seen them whip their little children, a thing that is very cruel, he had heard also, from several white *medicine-men,* that the Great Spirit of the white people was the child of a white woman, and that he was at the last put to death by the white people! This seemed to be a thing that he had not been able to comprehend, and he concluded by saying, "the Indians' Great Spirit got no mother—the Indians no kill him, he never die." He put me a chapter of other questions as to the trespasses of the white people on their lands, their continual corruption of the morals of their women, and digging open the Indians' graves to get

333

their bones, &c. To all of which I was compelled to reply in the affirmative, and quite glad to close my note-book, and quietly to escape from the throng that had collected around me, and saying (though to myself and silently), that these and an hundred other vices belong to the civilized world, and are practiced upon (but certainly, in no instance, reciprocated by) the "cruel and relentless savage."

George Catlin

—————

Virgil J. Vogel, ed., *A Documentary History of the American Indian* (New York: Harper & Row, 1972), pp. 138–139.

myhistorylab

Personal Journeys Online

■ Edward Harris, *Journal excerpt*, 1843. Account by a naturalist of the smallpox epidemic of 1837 on the Upper Missouri.

■ Pierre Jean de Smet, S. J., *Letter from a Catholic priest*, 1841. Impressions of the character and intelligence of Indians in the Rocky Mountains

George Catlin, one of the great illustrators of the American Indians, recorded these words in the 1830s when he traveled over the trans-Mississippi West painting and sketching, in his words, "the looks and customs of the vanishing races of native man in America." Unlike most whites of his generation, he approached Indian cultures with respect, and he realized that native peoples had a valid critique of the culture and values of white America. Born in 1796 in the Wyoming Valley of northeastern Pennsylvania, an area wracked by Indian raids during the Revolutionary War, including one in which his mother was held captive, he was raised among memories of Indians and their warfare. After attending law school in Litchfield, Connecticut, and briefly practicing law, he turned to painting and portraiture as a career in the 1820s. He was so taken with the physical grace and dignity of a group of Indians visiting Philadelphia in 1824 that he committed his life's work to a visual recording of Indian history and customs.

From his first contact with the tribes along the upper Missouri River in the early 1830s, Catlin sensed that he was witness to a way of life that was about to vanish. He worked at a feverish pace to create a pictorial record of what he saw in a collection of art he called "Catlin's Indian Gallery." The proceeds from exhibiting his work in Europe enabled him to live quite comfortably in the 1840s, but he suffered a severe setback in 1852 when a financial speculation went sour. He had to pledge his art collection as security to obtain a large loan, and he never succeeded in redeeming it. A failure as an entrepreneur, he nonetheless succeeded brilliantly as an artist in depicting the Native American peoples of the trans-Mississippi West just as they were about to be engulfed by a surging tide of white settlement.

Some 300,000 Americans traveled the Oregon Trail in the 1840s and 1850s in a trek that eventually made the United States a nation that spanned the continent. These overlanders, as they came to be known, were part of a restless tide of white migration that eventually saw more than 50,000 Americans a year migrate west of the Appalachians after the War of 1812.

After settling the area between the Appalachian Mountains and the Mississippi River, the American West of the early nineteenth century, migrants headed beyond

◆ Westward migration spurred by economic and demographic pressures in the East after the War of 1812

◆ The development of free commercial agriculture tied to eastern markets and increased industrialization and urbanization of the Old Northwest

◆ The development of a plantation economy based on cotton and slavery in the Old Southwest

◆ Manifest Destiny and westward expansion, relegating Native Americans and Mexican Americans to subjugated status

◆ U.S. annexation of Texas and the wresting of the Southwest and California from Mexico

CHRONOLOGY

1803–1806	Lewis and Clark travel up the Missouri River in search of a water route to the Pacific.
1816	Settlers surge into the trans-Appalachian region.
1821	Mexico gains its independence from Spain.
	Santa Fe Trail opens.
	Stephen F. Austin establishes the first American colony in Texas.
1824	Rocky Mountain Fur Company begins the rendezvous system.
1830	Congress creates the Indian Territory.
1834	Protestant missions are established in Oregon.
	Santa Anna seizes power in Mexico.
1836	Texas wins its independence from Mexico.
1837	Smallpox epidemic hits the Plains Indians.
1842	First large parties of migrants set out on the Oregon Trail.
1845	United States annexes Texas.
	Democrats embrace Manifest Destiny.
	The Great Irish Famine begins.
1846	Mexican War breaks out.
	United States and Britain reach an agreement in Oregon.
1847	Mormons begin settlement of Utah.
1848	Oregon Territory is organized.
	Treaty of Guadalupe Hidalgo ends the Mexican War.
	Revolutions sweep across Europe.
1851	Fort Laramie Treaty with the Plains Indians is signed.

the Mississippi River in the 1840s. The edge of settlement pushed into the Louisiana Purchase territory and across a huge area of plains, desert, mountains, and ocean coast that had seen few American settlers before 1840. The broad expanse of the trans-Mississippi region (stretching from the Mississippi Valley to the Pacific Coast) had become the new American West by mid-century. The West became a meeting ground of people from diverse cultures as Anglo-Americans came into contact and conflict with the Indians of the Plains and the Mexicans of the Southwest. Convinced of the superiority of their political and cultural values, Anglo-Americans asserted a God-given right to spread across the continent and impose their notions of liberty and democracy on peoples whose land they coveted. In the process, they defeated and subjugated those who stood in their way.

Manifest Destiny was the label for this presumed providential right, and it provided a justification for the aggressively expansionist Democratic administration of James K. Polk, which came to power in 1845. The most dramatic result of these policies was the Mexican War of 1846–1848, which made California and the present-day Southwest part of the U.S. continental empire.

The Agricultural Frontier

The U.S. population ballooned from 5.3 million in 1800 to more than 23 million by 1850. The population grew about 33 percent per decade, and four-fifths of this extraordinary gain was from natural increase, the surplus of births over deaths. As the population expanded, it shifted westward. Fewer than one in ten Americans lived west of the Appalachians in 1800; by 1850, about half did (see Map 13–1).

The tremendous amount of land available for settlement accounted for both phenomena. Through purchase and conquest, the land area of the United States more than tripled in the first half of the nineteenth century. Here was space where Americans could raise the large families of a rural society in which, on average, six to eight children survived to adolescence.

Declining soil fertility and rising population pressure in the rural East propelled these migrations. A common desire for greater economic opportunity, however, resulted in two distinct western societies by the 1840s. North of the Ohio River, in the Old Northwest, free labor and family farms defined the social order. South of the Ohio was the Old Southwest, a society dominated by slave labor and the plantation.

MAP EXPLORATION To explore an interactive version of this map, go to
http://www.prenhall.com/goldfield5/map13.1

MAP 13-1   The Westward Shift of the United States Population, 1790–1850
With a speed that was unimaginable in 1790, the United States quickly became a continental nation that stretched from the Atlantic to the Pacific by 1850. Particularly dramatic was the population growth in what became the Midwest.

The Crowded East

Looking back at his rural youth, Omar H. Morse recalled, "My Parents were in very limited circumstances financially yet blessed with a large family of children which is a poor man's capital though capital of this kind is not considered very available in case of financial Depression." Born in 1824 in the upstate New York village of Hastings, Morse was typical of the hard-pressed eastern youth who moved west after the War of 1812. With no prospect of inheriting land from his father, he moved in the 1840s to Wisconsin. Even after this fresh start, bad luck and too many debts prevented Morse from ever achieving landed independence. He lost three farms and eventually settled in Minnesota, where he worked at odd jobs and built houses. Heading west did not guarantee economic success, but it was the best option open to land-starved easterners who dreamed of leaving a productive farm to their children.

By the early nineteenth century, land was scarce in the East, especially in New England. After generations of population growth and subdivisions of landholdings to male heirs, most New England communities no longer had enough arable land to satisfy all the young men who wanted their own farms. Even such recently opened areas as Vermont felt the pressure of rural overpopulation.

Land was more productive and expensive farther south, in the Mid-Atlantic States. Keyed to the major export crop of wheat, agriculture was more commercialized than in New England, and economic inequality was thus higher. Successful farmers became wealthy by specializing in wheat and hiring the rural poor to work their fields. One-third to one-half of the young men in the commercialized agricultural districts of New Jersey and Pennsylvania were landless by the end of the eighteenth century. These men and their families, many of whom were recently arrived Scots-Irish and German immigrants, led the western migration from Pennsylvania. The pressure to move west was greatest in the slave states along the eastern seaboard. Although population density here was just two-thirds of that in New England, landholdings were more concentrated and the soil more exhausted than in the Northeast. Repeated plantings of tobacco in Virginia and Maryland and of cotton farther south had depleted the soil. In the Chesapeake states, established planters with extensive capital and labor resources shifted to wheat production or bought out their nonslaveholding neighbors. Tenants who wanted their own land and small farmers tired of competing against slave labor were forced west across the mountains. They were joined by the sons of planters. Despite marriages arranged to keep land within the wealthy families, there was no longer enough good land left to carve out plantations for all the younger sons.

By the early 1800s, the young and the poor in the rural East had every incentive to head west, where fertile land was abundant, accessible, and, at $2 to $3 per acre, far cheaper than in the East. Land was the basis of wealth and social standing, and its ownership separated the independent from the dependent, the rooted from the rootless. According to the principles of Jeffersonian democracy, the independent farmer was the backbone of the republic, the virtuous citizen who made republican government possible.

The western settler, observed a traveler on the Missouri frontier in the 1820s, wanted "to be a freeholder, to have plenty of rich land, and to be able to settle his children around him." Government policy under the Jeffersonian Republicans and Jacksonian Democrats attempted to promote these goals. Central to the land policy of the federal government after 1800 was the conviction that political liberties rested on the broadest possible base of land ownership. Thus, public policy and private aspirations merged in the belief that access to land was the key to preserving U.S. freedom.

When Jefferson took office in 1801, the minimum price for public land was $2 per acre, and a block of 320 acres had to be purchased at one time. By the 1830s, the price was down to $1.25 per acre, and the minimum purchase was only 80 acres. Congress also protected squatters, who had settled on public land before it was surveyed, from being outbid by speculators at land sales. The Preemption Act of 1841 guaranteed the right to purchase up to 160 acres at the minimum price of $1.25 when the public auction was held.

The Old Northwest

The number of Americans who settled in the heartland of the Old Northwest, Ohio, Indiana, and Illinois, rose tenfold from 1810 to 1840. Ohio had already entered the Union in 1803; Indiana joined in 1816, Illinois in 1818. The end of the War of 1812 and the abandonment by the British of their former Indian allies opened the region to a flood of migrants.

Travelers passing through the Ohio Valley just after the war were astonished by the number of Americans trekking west. Wagonloads of migrants bounced along turnpikes to disembark on the Ohio River at Pittsburgh and Wheeling, where they bought flatboats to carry them down to the interior river valleys. Moving north across the Ohio were families from the hill country of Virginia and Kentucky. These two streams of migrants, one predominantly northern and the other southern, met in the lower Midwest and viewed each other as strangers. Lucy Maynard, a New Englander living in south-central Illinois, noted that her neighbors were "principally from Indiana and Kentucky, some from Virginia, all friendly but very different from our people in their manners and language and every other way."

A mosaic of settlements.   The Old Northwest was less a melting pot in which regional cultures merged than a mosaic of settlements in which the different values and folkways of regional cultures from throughout the East took root and expanded. Belts of migration generally ran along a line from east to west as settlers sought out soil types and ecological conditions similar to those they had left behind. Thus, the same North-South cultural differences that existed along the Atlantic seaboard in 1800 were to be found half a century later in the Mississippi Valley.

A transplanted Yankee culture from New England and upstate New York spread over the upper Midwest, northern Ohio, Indiana, and Illinois, as well as Michigan and Wisconsin. These westerners were Whiggish in their politics, tended to be antislavery, and valued a communal sense of responsibility that regulated moral behavior and promoted self-improvement. The highland southerners who settled the lower Midwest, southern Ohio, Indiana, and Illinois, as well as Kentucky, were Democrats: They fiercely distrusted any centralized authority, political or moral, and considered Yankees intolerant do-gooders. Holding the balance of cultural and political power were the migrants from Pennsylvania and New Jersey, who were accustomed to ethnic diversity and the politics of competing economic groups. They settled principally in central Ohio, Indiana, and Illinois. By emphasizing economic growth and downplaying the cultural politics that pitted Yankees against southerners, they built a consensus around community development.

Much as they had done in the East, the early settlers practiced a diversified agriculture. The first task was to clear the land and sow a crop of corn, a hardy grain that required little care. Wild game and livestock left to forage in the woods supplemented the corn-based diet.

It took about ten years of backbreaking labor to create an 80-acre farm in heavily wooded sections. The work of women was essential for the success of the farm and the production of any salable surplus. Wives and daughters helped to tend the field crops, milked cows, and churned butter, and they produced the homespun cloth that, along with their dairy goods, found a market in the first country stores on the frontier. Charlotte Webb Jacobs, from the Sugar Creek community on the Illinois prairie, proudly recalled, "I made everything that we wore; I even made my towels and table cloths, sheets and everything in the clothing line."

Because outside labor was scarce and expensive, communities pooled their efforts for such tasks as raising a cabin. Groups of settlers also acted as cooperative units at public land auctions. Local associations known as **claims clubs** enforced the extralegal right of squatters to enter noncompetitive bids on land they had settled and improved. Members of the clubs physically intimidated speculators and refused to step aside until local settlers had acquired the land they wanted. The high cost of hauling goods to outside markets kept the early frontier economy barely above self-sufficiency. Any surplus was sold to newcomers moving into the area or bartered with local storekeepers for such

essentials as salt, sugar, and metalware. This initial economy, however, soon gave way to a more commercially oriented agriculture when steamboats, canals, and railroads opened up vast new markets (see Chapter 12). Western lands were at least twice as fertile as those in the East, and farmers could now profit from their bountiful yields.

The first large market was in the South, down the corridor of the Ohio and Mississippi rivers, and its major staples were corn and hogs. By the 1830s, the Erie Canal and its feeder waterways in the upper Midwest began to reorient much of the western farm trade to the Northeast. Wheat, because of its ready marketability for milling into flour, became the major cash crop for the northern market.

Wheat production skyrocketed when settlers overcame their initial reluctance to farm in a treeless terrain and moved into the prairies of Indiana and Illinois in the 1840s. New plows, a cast-iron one patented by Jethro Wood in 1819 and a steel version developed by John Deere in 1837, helped break the thick prairie sod. The plows were followed in the 1840s by horsedrawn mechanical harvesters. Traditional harvesting methods that relied on a worker using a scythe with a cradle frame were slow and relatively expensive. An experienced worker could cut no more than 2 acres a day. The same worker with the new machinery could harvest 12 acres a day, and the per-acre cost of labor fell dramatically. Once railroads provided direct access to eastern markets, the Midwest became the nation's breadbasket.

Although southern cotton was the raw material that fueled New England textile factories in the first stages of industrialization, the commercialization of agriculture in the West also contributed to the growth of eastern manufacturing. Western farms supplied eastern manufacturers with inexpensive raw materials for processing into finished goods. By

Cyrus McCormick pioneered the development of horse-drawn mechanical reapers. Shown here demonstrating his reaper to potential customers, McCormick helped revolutionize American agriculture with labor-saving machinery that made possible far larger harvests of grain crops.

flooding national markets with corn and wheat, western produce not only supplied eastern workers with cheap food but also forced noncompetitive eastern farmers either to move west or to work in factories in eastern cities. In turn, the West itself became an ever-growing market for eastern factory goods. For example, nearly half of the nation's iron production in the 1830s was fashioned into farm implements.

In the 1820s, the Old Northwest was just emerging from semisubsistence and depended on the southern trade. Thirty years later it had become part of a larger Midwest whose economy was increasingly integrated with that of the Northeast. Settlers continued to pour into the region, and three additional states, Michigan (1837), Iowa (1846), and Wisconsin (1848), joined the Union.

The combination of favorable farm prices and steadily decreasing transportation costs generated a rise in disposable income that was spent on outside goods or invested in internal economic development. A network of canals and railroads was laid down, and manufacturing cities grew from towns favorably situated by water or rail transport. There was still room for subsistence farming, but the West north of the Ohio was now economically specialized and socially diverse.

The Old Southwest

"The *Alabama Feaver* rages here with great violence and has carried off vast numbers of our Citizens," wrote a North Carolina planter in 1817 about the westward migration from his state. About as many people migrated from the old slave states in the East to the Old Southwest as those states gained by natural increase in the 1820s and 1830s. By 1850, more than 600,000 white settlers from Maryland, Virginia, and the Carolinas lived in slave states to the south and west, and many of them had brought their slaves with them. Indeed, from 1790 to 1860, more than 800,000 slaves were moved or sold from the South Atlantic region into the Old Southwest.

Soaring cotton prices after the War of 1812 and the smashing of Indian confederations during the war, which opened new lands to white settlement, propelled the first surge of migration into the Old Southwest (see Map 13-1). Before cotton prices plunged in the Panic of 1819, planters flooded into western Tennessee and the Black Belt, a crescent-shaped band of rich, black loamy soil arcing westward from Georgia through central Alabama and Mississippi. Migration surged anew in the 1830s when cotton prices were again high and the Chickasaws and Choctaws had been forced out of the incredibly fertile Delta country between the Yazoo and Mississippi rivers (see Chapter 10). The 1840s brought Texas fever to replace the Alabama fever of the 1810s, and a steady movement to the Southwest rounded out the contours of the cotton South. In less than thirty years, six new slave states—Mississippi (1817), Alabama (1819), Missouri (1821), Arkansas (1836), Florida (1845), and Texas (1845)—joined the Union (see the Overview table, Westward Expansion and the Growth of the Union, 1815–1850).

The southwestern frontier attracted both slaveholding planters and small independent farmers. The planters, though a minority, had the capital or the credit to acquire the best lands and the slave labor to make those lands productive. The slaveholders were responding both to the need for fresh land and to the extraordinary demand for short-staple cotton. As one North Carolina planter put it, Alabama would be a "garden of plenty" compared to the "old-fields and empty corn-house" of his native state.

Short-staple cotton could be grown anywhere with a minimum of 210 consecutive frost-free days. The crop, however, was of minor commercial importance before the 1790s, when Eli Whitney's gin eliminated the problem of removing the sticky, green seeds from cotton fiber, an essential step in preparing it to be spun and woven into cloth. Meanwhile, the mechanization of the British textile industry had created a seemingly unquenchable demand for raw cotton. No place in the world was better positioned to meet that demand than the U.S. South. Most important, a slave labor force was available to work the land. Led by the booming output of the new plantations in the Old Southwest, the South increased its share of world cotton production from 9 percent in 1800 to 68 percent in 1850.

The most typical settlers on the southern frontier were the small independent yeomen farmers who generally owned no slaves. Usually settling in the valleys, on the ridges, and in the hill country, they often soon sold out to neighboring planters and headed west again.

The yeomanry moved onto the frontier in two waves. The first consisted of stockmen-hunters, a restless, transient group that spread from the pine barrens in the Carolina backcountry to the coastal plain of eastern Texas. These pioneers prized unfettered independence and measured their wealth in the livestock left to roam and fatten on the sweet grasses of uncleared forests. They were quick to move on when farmers, the second wave, started to clear the land for crops.

The yeoman farmers practiced a diversified agriculture aimed at feeding their families. Corn and pork were the mainstays of their diet, and both could readily be produced as long as there was room for the open-range herding of swine and for patches of corn. The more ambitious farmers, usually those who owned one or two slaves, grew some cotton, but most preferred to avoid the economic risks of cotton production. The yeoman's chief source of labor was his immediate family, and to expand that labor force to produce cotton meant going into debt to purchase slaves. The debt could easily cost the yeoman his farm if the price of cotton fell.

Measured by per capita income, and as a direct result of the profits from slave-produced cotton on virgin soils, the Old Southwest was a wealthier society than the Old Northwest in 1850. In the short term, the settlement of the Old Southwest was also more significant for national economic development. Cotton accounted for more than half the value of all U.S. exports after the mid-1830s. More than any other commodity, cotton paid for U.S. imports and underpinned

OVERVIEW

Westward Expansion and the Growth of the Union, 1815–1850

New Free States	New Slave States	Territories (1850)
Indiana, 1816	Mississippi, 1817	Minnesota
Illinois, 1818	Alabama, 1819	Oregon
Maine, 1820	Missouri, 1821	New Mexico
Michigan, 1837	Arkansas, 1836	Utah
Iowa, 1846	Florida, 1845	
Wisconsin, 1848	Texas, 1845	

national credit. But southern prosperity was not accompanied by the same economic development and social change as in the Old Northwest. Compared to the slave West in 1860, the free-labor West was twice as urbanized, and far more of its workforce was engaged in nonagricultural pursuits.

The Southwest Ordinance, enacted by Congress in 1790, opened all territories south of the Ohio River to slavery. Slaves, land, and cotton were the keys to wealth on the southern frontier, and agricultural profits were continually plowed back into more land and slaves to produce more cotton. In contrast, prosperous farmers in the Old Northwest had no slaves to work additional acres. Hence, they were much more likely to invest their earnings in promotional schemes designed to attract settlers whose presence would raise land values and increase business for local merchants and entrepreneurs. As early as the 1840s, rural communities in the Old Northwest were supporting bustling towns that offered jobs in trade and manufacturing on a scale far surpassing anything in the slave West. By the 1850s, the Midwest was almost as urbanized as the Northeast had been in 1830, and nearly half its labor force no longer worked on farms.

The Old Southwest remained overwhelmingly agricultural. Once the land was settled, the children of the first generation of slaveholders and yeomen moved west to the next frontier rather than compete for the good land that was left. Relatively few newcomers took their place. By the 1850s, Kentucky, Tennessee, Alabama, and Mississippi, the core states of the Old Southwest, were all losing more migrants than they were gaining.

The Frontier of the Plains Indians

Few white Americans had ventured west of the Mississippi by 1840. What scanty knowledge there was of this huge inland expanse was the result of government-sponsored expeditions. Reports of explorations of the southern plains by Zebulon Pike in 1806 and Stephen Long in 1819 dismissed the area as the Great American Desert, an arid, treeless landscape with little agricultural potential. The vast plains and plateaus climbing westward to the foothills of the Rocky Mountains in a seemingly endless ocean of grass were unfamiliar and intimidating to farmers accustomed to the wooded, well-watered East.

Moreover, Americans had no legal claim to much of the trans-Mississippi West, or merely the paper title of the Louisiana Purchase, to which none of the native inhabitants had acquiesced. Beyond Texas and the boundary line drawn by the Trans-Continental Treaty of 1819 lay the northern possessions of Mexico. Horse-mounted Indian tribes dominated by the Sioux were a formidable power throughout the central Plains.

Before the 1840s, only fur trappers and traders, who worked with and not against the powerful Sioux, had pushed across the Great Plains and into the Rockies. The 1840s brought a sudden change, a large migration westward that radically altered the ecology of the Great Plains. Farm families trapped in an agricultural depression and enticed by Oregon's bounty turned the trails blazed by the fur traders into ruts on the **Oregon Trail,** the route that led to the first large settlement of Americans on the Pacific Coast.

Tribal Lands

At least 350,000 Native Americans lived in the plains and mountains of the trans-Mississippi West in 1840. They were loosely organized into tribal groups, each with its own territory and way of life. Most inhabited the Great Plains region, which lay north and west of the Indian Territory reserved for eastern tribes in the present state of Oklahoma. The point where the prairies of the Midwest gave way to the higher, drier plains marked a rough division between predominantly agricultural tribes to the east and nomadic, hunting tribes to the west. The Kansas, Osages, and Omahas in what is now Kansas and Iowa and the Arikaras, Mandans, and Hidatsas along the upper Missouri River grew corn, beans, and squash and lived in semipermanent villages, much as woodland Indians had in the East. On the open plains were hunting and raiding peoples, such as the western Sioux, Crows, Cheyennes, and Arapahos.

In the 1830s, the U.S. government set aside a broad stretch of country between the Platte River to the north and the Red River to the south (most of what is now Oklahoma and eastern Kansas) exclusively for tribes resettled from the East under

Shown here is a Lakota shirt, c. 1850, that was specially woven for Sioux warriors who had distinguished themselves in battle. The blue and yellow dyes symbolize sky and earth, and the strands of human hair represent acts of bravery performed in defense of the Lakota people.

Shirt, about 1860s, unknown Sioux artist. Deer skin, hair, quills, feathers, paint, 1947.235. Denver Art Museum Collection, Native Arts Acquisitions Funds. (c) Photo by Denver Art Museum. All Rights Reserved.

the Indian Removal Act of 1830 and for village-living groups native to the area. Many government officials envisioned this territory as a permanent sanctuary that would separate Indians from white people and allow them to live in peace on allotments of land granted as compensation for the territory they had ceded to the federal government. However, even as Congress was debating the idea of a permanent Indian reserve, the pressure on native peoples in the Mississippi Valley both from raiding parties of Plains Indians and the incessant demands of white farmers and speculators for land was rendering a stable Indian-white boundary meaningless.

On the eve of Indian removal in the East, the Sauks, Foxes, Potawatomis, and other Indian peoples inhabited Iowa. The defeat of the Sauks and Foxes in what white Americans called Black Hawk's War in 1832 opened Iowa to white settlement and forced tribes to cede land (see Chapter 10). In 1838, Congress created the Territory of Iowa, which encompassed all the land between the Mississippi and Missouri rivers north of the state of Missouri. The remaining Indians were now on the verge of being pushed completely out of the region. Throughout the upper Mississippi Valley in the 1830s, other groups suffered a similar fate, and the number of displaced Indians swelled.

The first to be displaced were farming peoples whose villages straddled the woodlands to the east and the open plains to the west. These border tribes were caught in a vise between the loss of their land to advancing white people and the seizure of their horses and agricultural provisions by Indian raiders from the plains. The Pawnees were among the hardest hit.

By the 1830s, the Pawnees were primarily an agricultural people who embarked on seasonal hunts for game in the Platte River Valley. In 1833, they signed a treaty with the U.S. government in which they agreed to withdraw north of the Platte in return for subsidies and military protection from the hostile Indians on the plains. Once the Pawnees moved north of the Platte, Sioux attacked them and seized control of the prime hunting grounds. Sioux raiders seeking provisions and horses also harassed Pawnee agricultural villages. When the Pawnees in desperation filtered back south of the Platte, in violation of the treaty of 1833, they encountered constant harassment from white settlers. In vain the Pawnee leaders cited the provisions of the treaty that promised them protection from the Sioux. Forced back north of the Platte by the U.S. government, the Pawnees were eventually driven out of their homeland by the Sioux.

The Sioux were the dominant power on the northern and central Great Plains, more than able to hold their own against white Americans in the first half of the nineteenth century. The Tetons, Yanktons, and Yanktonais constituted the main divisions of the western Sioux. In the eighteenth century, these western Sioux had separated from their woodland kin (known as the Santee Sioux), left their homeland along the headwaters of the Mississippi River, and pushed onto the Minnesota prairies. Armed with guns they had acquired from the French, the western Sioux dominated the prairies east of the Missouri River by 1800.

The Sioux learned to use the horse from the Plains Indians. Introduced to the New World by the Spanish, horses had revolutionized the lives of native peoples on the Great Plains. As they acquired more horses through trading and raids, the Plains Indians evolved a distinctly new nomadic culture. Horses made buffalo hunting vastly more productive, they made it easier to transport bulky possessions, and they made possible an aggressive, highly mobile form of warfare. The Sioux were the most successful of all the tribes in melding two facets of white culture, the gun and the horse, into an Indian culture of warrior-hunters.

Although the Sioux frequently fought other tribes, casualties from these encounters were light. The Sioux and other Plains Indians fought not to kill the greatest number of the enemy, but rather to dominate hunting grounds and to win individual honor by "counting coup" (touching a live foe). When an Army officer in 1819 urged the Sioux to make peace with the Chippewas, Little Crow, a Santee Sioux, explained why war was preferable: "Why, then, should we give up such an extensive country to save the life of a man or two annually?"

When the United States acquired title to the Great Plains in the Louisiana Purchase of 1803, the western Sioux economy was based on two seasonally restricted systems of hunting. In summer, the Sioux hunted buffalo on horseback on the plains. In winter, on foot, they trapped beaver. In great spring trading fairs, the western Sioux exchanged their buffalo robes and beaver pelts for goods acquired by the Santee Sioux from European traders.

As the supply of beaver dwindled and the demand for buffalo hides from American and European traders increased in the early 1800s, the Sioux extended their buffalo hunts. In a loose alliance with the Cheyennes and Arapahos, Sioux war parties pushed aside or subjugated weaker tribes to the south and west of the Missouri River basin. The Sioux gained access to new sources for buffalo and raided the village tribes for horses and provisions. Reduced to a dependent status, these tribes were forced to rely on the Sioux for meat and trading goods.

Epidemic diseases brought to the plains by white traders helped Sioux expansion. Because they lived in small wandering bands, the Sioux were less susceptible to these epidemics than the more sedentary village peoples. The Sioux were also one of the first tribes to be vaccinated against smallpox by doctors sent up the Missouri River by the Bureau of Indian Affairs in the early 1830s. Smallpox reached the plains in the 1780s, and a major epidemic in 1837 probably halved the region's Indian population. Particularly hard hit were tribes attempting to resist the Sioux advance. Sioux losses were relatively light and, unlike the other tribes, their population grew.

Some 25,000 strong by 1850, the western Sioux had increased in power and numbers since they first encountered American officials during the Lewis and Clark Expedition in 1804 and 1805. Even then, Jefferson had cautioned Lewis to cultivate good relations with the Sioux "because of their immense power." "These are the vilest miscreants of the savage race," Lewis and Clark wrote of the Sioux, "and must ever remain the pirates of the Missouri, until such measures are pursued by our government as will make them feel a dependence on its will for their supply of merchandise."

Words were one thing, gaining power over the Sioux another. Americans could vilify the Sioux, but they could not force them into dependence in the first half of the nineteenth century. The Sioux continued to extend their influence, and they were shrewd enough to align themselves with the Americans whenever their interests dictated conciliation.

The Fur Traders

"Curiosity, a love of wild adventure, and perhaps also a hope of profit, for times are hard, and my best coat has a sort of sheepish hang-dog hesitation to encounter fashionable folk, combined to make me look upon the project with an eye of favour." As best he could recollect, these were the motives that induced Warren A. Ferris, a New York civil engineer, to join the American Fur Company in 1829 at the age of 19 and go west as a fur trapper and mountain man. During their golden age in the 1820s and 1830s, the trappers blazed the trails that far greater numbers of white settlers would follow in the 1840s.

The western fur trade originated in the rivalry between British and U.S. companies for profitable furs, especially beaver pelts. Until the early 1820s, the Hudson's Bay Company, a well-capitalized British concern, dominated the trans-Mississippi fur trade. A breakthrough for U.S. interests came in 1824 when two St. Louis businessmen, William Henry Ashley and Andrew Henry of the Rocky Mountain Fur Company, developed the rendezvous system, which eliminated the need for permanent and costly posts deep in Indian territory. In keeping with Indian traditions of periodic intertribal meetings, the rendezvous system brought together trappers, Indians, and traders in a grand annual fair at a designated site in the high mountain country of Wyoming. White trappers and Indians exchanged the animal skins they had gathered in the seasonal hunt for guns, traps, tobacco, whiskey, textiles, and other trading goods with agents of the fur companies in St. Louis. The mountain men signed up for two- or three-year stints with the fur companies. Except for the annual fairs, they lived isolated, hard lives in the wilderness. Their closest relations were with Indians, and about 40 percent of the trappers married Indian women, unions that often linked them economically and diplomatically to their bride's tribe.

Living conditions in the wilderness were primitive, even brutal. Mortality rates among trappers ran as high as 80 per-

The annual rendezvous in Wyoming of fur trappers and traders was a multinational affair in which Anglo Americans, French Canadians, Mexican Americans, and Native Americans gathered to trade, drink, and swap stories.

The Denver Public Library, Western History Department.

cent a year. Death could result from an accidental gunshot wound, an encounter with a grizzly, or an arrow from an Indian whose hunting grounds a trapper had transgressed.

For all its dangers, the life of a trapper appealed to unattached young men like Warren Ferris. They were fleeing the confinements, as well as the comforts, of white civilization and were as free as they could be. When on a hunt with the Indians, they were part of a spectacle unknown to other white Americans, one that was already passing into history. "Fancy to yourself," Ferris asked readers of his published journals, "three thousand horses of every variety of size and colour, with trappings almost as varied as their appearance... ridden by a thousand souls...their persons fantastically ornamented.... Listen to the rattle of numberless lodgepoles [trailed] by packhorses.... Yonder see a hundred horsemen pursuing a herd of antelopes." He was describing the color, bustle, and motion of a hunt with the Salish Indians of Montana in the 1830s, played out on "a beautiful level prairie, with dark blue snow-capped mountains in the distance for the locale."

Such spectacles were increasingly rare after 1840, the year of the last mountain men's rendezvous on the Green River in Wyoming. The most exploitative phase of the fur trade in the 1830s had ravaged the fur-bearing animals and accelerated the spread of smallpox among the tribes. Whiskey, the most profitable item among the white man's trading goods, had corrupted countless Indians and undermined the vitality of tribal cultures.

The mountain men were about to pass into legend, but before they did, they explored every trail and path from the front (or eastern) range of the Rockies to the Pacific. The main trading corridor of the fur trade, up the lower Missouri to the North Platte and across the plains to the South Pass, a wide plateau crossing the Continental Divide, and into the Wyoming basin, became the main overland route to the West in the 1840s. The mountain men had removed the mystery of western geography, and in so doing they hastened the end of the frontier conditions that had made their unique way of life possible.

The Oregon Trail

The ruts are still there. One can follow them to the horizon in the Platte River Valley of Nebraska and the dry tablelands of Wyoming, Idaho, and Nevada. They were put there by the wheels of wagons hauled by oxen on a jolting 2,000-mile journey across plains, mountains, and deserts from Missouri to Oregon, Utah, and California (see Map 13–2). Some 150,000 Americans made this overland trek in the heyday of the Oregon Trail in the 1840s and early 1850s (see Figure 13–1). Most of them walked alongside their wagons. They covered up to 15 miles a day on a journey that lasted close to six months.

Before the 1830s, few Americans had heard of Oregon, and practically none lived there. Under an agreement reached in 1818, the Oregon Country was still jointly administered by the United States and Great Britain. Furs, whether beaver

MAP 13–2   Western Overland Trails
The great overland trails to the West began at the Missouri River. The Oregon Trail crossed South Pass in Wyoming and then branched off to Oregon, California, or Utah. The Santa Fe Trail carried American goods and traders to the Mexican Southwest.

pelts or the skins of the Pacific sea otter, had attracted a few U.S. trappers and merchants, but the British-controlled Hudson's Bay Company dominated the region. Protestant missionaries established the first permanent white settlements in the 1830s. Under the leadership of Jason Lee, they set up their missions in the fertile Willamette Valley, south of the

A bit of luck and a cooperative effort from everyone were necessary for a successful crossing of the Oregon Trail.

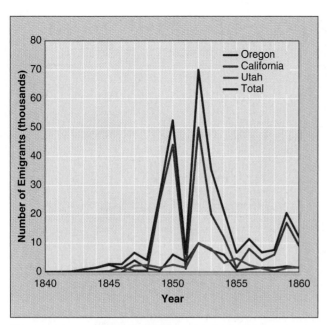

FIGURE 13–1   Overland Emigration to the West, 1840–1860 Immigration to the trans-Mississippi West steadily increased in the 1840s as farm families moved to Oregon or Utah. After the discovery of gold in California in 1849, California attracted the bulk of the emigrants, many of whom were single men hopeful of striking it rich.

Data Source: John D. Unruh, Jr., *The Plains Across: The Overland Emigrants and the Trans-Mississippi West, 1840–60* (1982), pp. 84–85.

Columbia River. Reports of Oregon's fertility that the missionaries sent east sparked the first popular interest in the region, especially among Midwestern farmers stuck in the agricultural depression that followed the Panic of 1837.

The missionaries repeatedly failed in their efforts to convert the Indians of the region to Christianity. Unlike the trappers, the missionaries sought to change the entire structure of Indian life and beliefs. But with their numbers already thinned by the diseases brought in by the trappers, Oregon tribes such as the Cayuses refused to abandon their traditional culture based on hunting and fishing to work for white farmers. During a measles epidemic in 1847, the Cayuses killed two of the most prominent missionaries, Marcus and Narcissa Whitman. In retaliation, white Americans, who now numbered more than 5,000, virtually exterminated the Cayuses.

The first large party of overlanders on the Oregon Trail left Independence, Missouri, for the Willamette Valley in 1842. Independence and St. Joseph in Missouri and, by the 1850s, Council Bluffs in Iowa were the jumping-off points for the Oregon Trail. Merchants profited from supplying, usually at inflated prices, wagons, mules, oxen, guns, ammunition, and staples like flour, bacon, and sugar.

Most overlanders were young farm families from the Midwest, who had moved at least once before in their restless search for the perfect farm that would keep them out of

debt. Indeed, Medorum Crawford said of one family that made the journey to Oregon with him in 1842 and then quickly left for California, "They had practically lived in the wagon for more than twenty years, only remaining in one locality long enough to make a crop, which they had done in every State and Territory in the Mississippi Valley."

Usually the male head of a household made the decision to move. Women often regretted giving up ties with kin and friends. They were well aware of the dangers of childbirth on a long, hard journey. Besides their usual work of minding the children and cooking and cleaning, they would now have to help drive wagons and tend livestock. Still, many women were also optimistic about the journey. "Ho—for California, at last we are on the way," exclaimed Helen Carpenter in 1857, "and with good luck may some day reach the 'promised land.'" A study of 159 women's trail diaries indicates that about one-third of the women strongly favored the move. Margaret Frink, for example, recalled that she "never had occasion to regret the prolonged hardships of the toilsome journey." By adapting to the new conditions of trail life, pitching tents, yoking oxen, cooking over open fires, and gathering buffalo chips (dried dung used for fuel), women learned skills that would help them start a new life in the West.

The journey was long and dangerous. In the 1840s, some 5,000 of the 90,000 men, women, and children who set out on the Oregon Trail died along the way. But although the overlanders were terrified of encountering Indians, who they assumed would be hostile, few died from Indian attacks. As long as the wagon trains were just passing through, the Plains Indians left the white people alone. At first they watched with bemused curiosity, and then, as the white migrants kept coming, they traded game for clothing and ammunition. Indians killed only 115 migrants in the 1840s, and trigger-happy white migrants provoked most of the clashes. Disease, especially cholera, was the great killer. Second to disease were accidents, especially drownings that resulted when drivers tried to force overloaded wagons across swollen rivers.

Cooperation between families was the key to a successful overland crossing. The men in a party often drew up a formal, written constitution at the start of a trip spelling out the assignments and work responsibilities of each wagon. Before the trail was well marked, former mountain men hired on as captains to lead wagon trains. Timing was crucial. A wagon train had to leave late enough in the spring to get good grass in Nebraska for the oxen and mules. Too early a departure, and the wagon train risked getting bogged down in spring mud; too late, and it risked being trapped in the snows of the Pacific coastal ranges.

Before "Oregon fever" had run its course, the flow of white settlers across the continent radically changed the economy and ecology of the Great Plains. Pressure mounted on plants and animals, reducing the land's ability to support all the tribes accustomed to living off it. Intertribal warfare intensified as the supply of buffalo and other game dwindled. Far from being separated from white people by a per-

This painting by Alfred James Miller depicts the busy interior of Fort Laramie in 1837.

Alfred Jacob Miller, The Interior of Fort Laramie, 1858–60. The Walters Art Museum, Baltimore.

manent line of division, the Plains Indians now stood astride the main path of white migration to the Pacific.

In response, officials in the Bureau of Indian Affairs organized a great gathering of the tribes in 1851. At this conference they pushed through the Fort Laramie Treaty, the first U.S. government attempt to draw boundaries within which to contain the Plains Indians. In exchange for accepting limitations on their movements and for the loss of game, the tribes were to receive annual compensation of $50,000 a year for fifty years (later reduced by the U.S. Senate to ten years).

Most of the Indians at the Fort Laramie conference were Sioux and their allies. The Sioux viewed the treaty as confirming their dominance on the Great Plains. When U.S. negotiators tried to restrict Sioux hunting to north of the Platte, the Sioux demanded and received treaty rights to lands south of the Platte as well. "These lands once belonged to the Kiowas and the Crows," argued a western Sioux, "but we whipped those nations out of them, and in this we did what the white men do when they want the lands of the Indians." This was an argument white Americans could understand, and they conceded the point.

The Fort Laramie Treaty represented a standoff between the Sioux and the U.S. government, the two great powers on the Plains. If neither yielded its claim to the region, war between them would be inevitable.

The Mexican Borderlands

By the mid-1840s, parties of emigrant Americans were beginning to branch off the main Oregon Trail on their way to Utah and California, which were then part of Mexico's northern borderlands (see Map 13-2). Mostly a semiarid and thinly populated land of high plateaus, dry basins, and desert bisected north to south by mountain ranges, the borderlands had been part of the Spanish Empire in North America. Mexico inherited this territory when it won independence from Spain in 1821. Mexico's hold on the region was always weak. It lost Texas in 1837, and, in the next decade, the U.S. penetration of Utah and California set the stage for the U.S. seizure of most of the rest in the Mexican War.

The Peoples of the Southwest

Diverse peoples lived in the Southwest. Imperial Spain had divided them into four main groupings: Indians, full-blooded Native Americans who retained their own languages and customs; *mestizos,* people of racially mixed ancestry, usually Spanish and Indian; *criollos,* U.S.-born whites of Spanish ancestry; and Spaniards. By far the smallest group was the Spaniards. Compared to the English, few Spaniards emigrated to the New World, and most who did were men. Consequently, Spanish males married or lived with native women, creating a large class of *mestizos.* Despite their small numbers, the Spanish, along with the *criollos,* monopolized economic and political power. This wealthy elite controlled the labor of the *mestizos* in the predominantly ranching economy of the borderlands.

The largest single group in the borderlands were the Indians, about half the population in the 1820s. Most had not come under direct Spanish or Mexican control. Those who had were part of the mission system. This instrument of Spanish imperial policy forced Indians to live in a fixed area, convert to Catholicism, and work as agricultural laborers.

Spanish missions, most of them established by the Franciscan order, aimed both to Christianize and "civilize" the Indians, making them loyal imperial subjects. Mission Indians were forced to abandon their native economies and culture and settle in agricultural communities under the tight supervision of the friars (see Chapter 1). Spanish soldiers and royal officials, who lived in military garrisons known as *presidios,* accompanied the friars.

The largest concentration of Indians, some 300,000 when the Spanish friars arrived in the 1760s, was in California. Most of these, the Paiutes, Chumashes, Pomos, Shastas, and a host of smaller tribes, occupied their own distinct ecological zones where they gathered and processed what the rivers, forests, and grasslands provided. Fish and game were abundant, and wild plants and nuts, especially acorns, provided grain and flour. The Paiutes in the Owens Valley perfected an intricate system for irrigating wild grasses, but only the Yumans along the Colorado River in southeastern California practiced full-scale agriculture. The Spanish marveled at their lush fields of wheat, maize, beans, tobacco, and melons. The Yumans also had an elaborate religion based on an oral tradition of dream songs. (Dream songs remain a distinctive feature of Native American culture.)

The major farming Indians east of California were the Pueblo peoples of Arizona and New Mexico. Named after

The paintings by George Catlin are among the best visual sources for understanding the material culture of the Plains Indians. This painting, c. 1834, shows how central was the buffalo in the life of the Comanches, the most powerful tribe on the Southern Plains.

the adobe or stone communal dwellings in which they lived atop mesas or on terraces carved into cliffs, the Pueblo Indians were a peaceful people closely bound to small, tightly knit communities. (*Pueblo* is Spanish for "village.") Indeed, some of their dwellings, such as those of the Hopis in Arizona or the Acomas in New Mexico, have been continuously occupied for more than 500 years. Corn and beans were the staples of their irrigation-based agriculture. Formally a part of the Spanish mission system, they had incorporated the Catholic God and Catholic rituals into their own polytheistic religion, which stressed the harmony of all living things with the forces of nature. They continued to worship in their underground sanctuaries known as *kivas*.

Once the Pueblos made their peace with the Spaniards after their great revolt in 1680 (see Chapter 3), their major enemies were the nomadic tribes that lived by hunting and raiding. These tribes outnumbered the Pueblos four to one and controlled most of the Southwest until the 1850s. The horse, which many of the tribes acquired during Spain's temporary retreat from the region during the late seventeenth century in the wake of the Pueblo Revolt, was the basis of their way of life. As the horse frontier spread, the peoples of the southern Plains gained enormous mobility and the means of ranging far and wide for the economic resources that sustained their transformation into societies of mounted warriors.

West of the pueblos around Taos was the land of the Navajos, who herded sheep, raised some crops, and raided other tribes from their mountain fastnesses. Spilling over onto Navajo lands, the Southern Utes ranged up and down the canyon lands of Utah. The Gila Apaches were the dominant tribe south of Albuquerque and westward into Arizona. To the east in the Pecos River Valley roamed bands of Mescalero and Jicarillo Apaches. On the broad plains rolling northward

from the Texas panhandle and southward into northern Mexico were war parties of Comanches and Kiowas.

The Comanches, a branch of the mountain Shoshonis who moved to the plains when horses became available, were the most feared of the nomadic peoples. Utterly fearless, confident, and masterful horsemen, they gained a reputation of mythic proportions for their prowess as mounted warriors. For food and clothing, they relied on the immense buffalo herds of the southern plains. For guns, horses, and other trading goods, they lived off their predatory raids. When the Santa Fe Trail opened in the early 1820s, their shrewdness as traders gave them a new source of firearms that strengthened their raiding prowess.

The three focal points of white settlement in the northern borderlands of Mexico, Texas, New Mexico, and Alta California (as distinguished from Lower, or Baja, California), were never linked by an effective network of communications or transportation. Navigable rivers were few, and travel was limited to tortuous journeys along Indian and Spanish trails that barely indented the dry and largely barren landscape. Each of these settlements was an isolated offshoot of Hispanic culture with a semiautonomous economy based on ranching and a mostly illegal trade with French, British, and U.S. merchants that brought in a trickle of needed goods.

Neither Spain, which tried to seal off its northern outposts from economic contact with foreigners, nor Mexico, which opened up the borderlands to outsiders, had integrated this vast region into a unified economic or political whole. Indeed, Mexico's most pressing problem in the 1820s was protecting its northern states from the Comanches. To serve as a buffer against the Comanches, the Mexican government in 1821 invited Americans into Texas, opening the way to the eventual U.S. takeover of the territory.

The Americanization of Texas

The Mexicans faced the same problems governing Texas that the Spanish had. Mexico City was about a thousand miles from San Antonio, the center of Hispanic settlement in Texas, and communications were slow and cumbersome. The ranching elite of *Tejanos* (Spanish-speaking Mexicans born in Texas) had closer economic ties to American Louisiana than they did to Coahuila, the Mexican state to which Texas was formally attached. These large ranchers had long been smuggling horses and cattle into Louisiana in exchange for manufactured items and tobacco. Markets for farm crops were limited, and the ranchers and scattered tenant farmers produced little surplus food. The low agricultural productivity, combined with the low birthrate among mission Indians, outbreaks of disease, and the generally hostile frontier environment, sharply restricted population growth. Only some 5,000 Mexicans lived in Texas in the 1820s.

Sparsely populated and economically struggling, Mexican Texas shared a border with the United States along the Sabine River in Louisiana and the Red River in the Arkansas

THE MEXICAN RULERS,
migrating from Matamoras, with their Treasures.

This anti-Catholic lithograph sarcastically depicts the "rulers" of Mexico as lecherous Catholic clerics who were quick to desert the Mexican town of Matamoras when U.S. troops arrived in May 1846. The priest and monk ride out of Matamoras accompanied by young women, bottles of wine, and other booty.

As early as 1830, eastern and south-central Texas was becoming an extension of the plantation economy of the Gulf coastal plain. More than 25,000 white settlers, with around 1,000 slaves, had poured into the region (see American Views, A Mexican View of the Texans in 1828).

More Americans moved into Texas with slaves than the Mexicans had anticipated. Many settlers simply ignored Mexican laws, especially the Emancipation Proclamation of 1829, which forbade slavery in the Republic of Mexico. In 1830, the Mexican government attempted to assert its authority. It levied the first taxes on the Americans, prohibited the further importation of slaves, and closed the international border to additional immigration. Still, another 10,000 Americans spilled across the border in the early 1830s, and they continued to bring in slaves.

Unlike the *empresarios,* many of whom became Catholic and married into elite *Tejano* families, these newcomers lived apart from Mexicans and rejected Mexican citizenship. Cultural tensions escalated. Believing that they belonged to a superior race of liberty-loving white Anglo-Saxons, most of these new arrivals sneered at the Mexicans as a mongrelized race of black people, Indians, and Spaniards and resented having to submit to their rule. They considered Catholicism a despotic, superstitious religion and ignored legal requirements that they convert to it. A clash became inevitable in 1835 when General Santa Anna, elected president of Mexico in 1833, overturned the liberal Mexican constitution of 1824. He established himself as a dictator in 1834, and his centralist rule ended any hope of the Americans *empresarios* and their *Tejano* allies that Texas might become an autonomous state within a federated Mexico. Skirmishing between Mexican troops and rebellious Texans began in the fall of 1835.

At first, the Anglo-*Tejano* leadership sought to overthrow Santa Anna, restore the constitution of 1824, and win separate statehood for Texas within a liberal Mexican republic. Santa Anna, however, refused to compromise. When he raised a large army to crush the uprising, he radicalized the rebellion and pushed its leaders to declare complete independence on March 2, 1836. Four days later, a Mexican army of 4,000 annihilated the 187 defenders of the **Alamo,** an abandoned mission in San Antonio. A few weeks later at Goliad, another 300 Texans were killed after they had agreed to surrender (see Map 13–3).

"Remember the Alamo!" and "Remember Goliad!" were powerful rallying cries for the beleaguered Texans. Volunteers from the U.S. South rushed to the aid of the main Texan army, commanded by Sam Houston. A product of the Tennessee frontier and a close friend of Andrew Jackson's, Houston did Jackson proud by catching the overconfident Santa

Territory (see Map 13-2). The threat that the nearby Americans posed to Mexico's security was obvious to Mexican officials. As one of them early noted with alarm: "If we do not take the present opportunity to people Texas, day by day the strength of the United States will grow until it will annex Texas, Coahuila, Saltillo, and Nuevo León like the Goths, Visigoths, and the other tribes that assailed the Roman Empire." However, attempts to promote Mexican immigration into Texas failed. Reasoning that the Americans were going to come in any event and anxious to build up the population of Texas against Indian attacks, the Mexican government encouraged Americans to settle in Texas by offering huge grants of land in return for promises to accept Mexican citizenship, convert to Catholicism, and obey the authorities in Mexico City.

The first American *empresario,* the recipient of a large grant in return for a promise to bring in settlers, was Stephen F. Austin. He inherited a huge Spanish grant from his father, Moses Austin, a Missourian who had had business dealings with the Spanish since 1797. After having the grant confirmed by the new Mexican government in 1821, Stephen Austin founded the first American colony in Texas. The Austin grant encompassed 18,000 square miles. Other grants were smaller but still lavish. The *empresarios* stood to grow wealthy by leasing out land, selling parcels to settlers, and organizing the rest into large-scale farms that produced cotton with slave labor in the bottomlands of the Sabine, Colorado, and Brazos rivers. For the Americans who followed in their wake, Texas offered good land that was so cheap it was almost free.

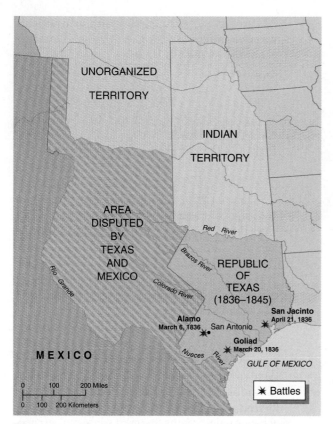

MAP 13–3   Texas and Mexico after the Texas Revolt
The Battle of San Jacinto was the decisive American victory
that gained the independence of Texas, but the border dispute
between Texas and Mexico would not be resolved until the
Mexican War a decade later.

Anna off guard in eastern Texas. Houston's victory in April
1836 at the Battle of San Jacinto established the independence
of Texas. Captured while trying to flee, Santa Anna signed a
treaty in May 1836, recognizing Texas as an independent republic with a boundary on the south and west at the Rio
Grande. However, the Nueces River to the north of the Rio
Grande had been the administrative border of Texas under
Mexican rule. The Mexican Congress rejected the treaty, and
the boundary remained in dispute.

Soon forgotten during the ensuing eight years of Texas
independence was the support that many *Tejanos* had given
to the successful revolt against Mexican rule. In part because
Mexico refused to recognize the Texas Republic, Anglos
feared *Tejanos* as a subversive element. Pressure mounted on
them to leave, especially after Santa Anna launched a major
counterattack in 1842, capturing San Antonio. Those who
stayed lost much of their land and economic power as Anglos used their knowledge of U.S. law or just plain chicanery
to reduce the *Tejanos* to second-class citizens.

More difficult to subordinate were the Comanches.
While president of Texas, Houston tried to fix a permanent
boundary between the Comanches and white settlers, but
Texas pride and ongoing white encroachments on Indian

land undercut his efforts. By the early 1840s, Texans and Comanches were in a state of nearly permanent war. Only the
force of the federal army after the Civil War ended the Comanches' long reign over the high, dry plains of northern
and western Texas.

The Push into California and the Southwest

California.   Mexican rule in California was always weak.
The Sonoran desert and the resistance of the Yuman Indians
in southeastern California cut off Mexico from any direct
land contact with Alta California. Only irregular communications were maintained over a long sea route. For
Californios, Californians of Spanish descent, Mexico was literally *la otra banda,* "the other shore." In trying to strengthen
its hold on this remote and thinly populated region, the Mexican government relied on a program of economic development. As in Texas, however, Mexican policy had unintended
consequences.

The centerpiece of the Mexican program was the secularization of the missions, opening up the landholdings of
the Catholic Church to private ownership and releasing the
mission Indians from paternalistic bondage. Small allotments
of land were set aside for the Indians, but most returned to
their homelands. Those who remained became a source of
cheap labor for the *rancheros* who carved up the mission lands
into huge cattle ranches. Thus, by the 1830s, California had
entered what is called the *rancho* era. The main beneficiaries
of this process, however, were not the Mexican authorities
who had initiated it but the American traders who responded
to the economic opportunities presented by the privatiza-
tion of the California economy.

New England merchants had been trading in California since the 1780s. What first attracted them were the seal
fisheries off the California coast, a source of otter pelts
highly prized in the China trade. After the seals had been all
but exterminated by the 1820s, Yankee merchants shipped
out hides and tallow to New England for processing into
shoes and candles. Ships from New England and New York
sailed around Cape Horn to California ports, where they
unloaded trading goods. Servicing this trade in California
was a resident colony of American agents, some 300 strong
by the mid-1840s.

Whereas Yankees dominated the American colonies in
coastal California, it was mostly midwestern farm families
who filtered into the inner valleys of California from the
Oregon Trail in the 1830s and 1840s. About one in ten of the
overland parties took a cutoff on the Trail near Fort Hall on
the Snake River that led them across the desert to a passage
across the Sierra Nevada (see Map 13–2). At the end of the
journey, they dropped down into the fertile Sacramento River
Valley. Nearly a thousand Americans had arrived by 1846.

California belonged to Mexico in name only by the
early 1840s. The program of economic development had
strengthened California's ties to the outside world at the

American Views

Mexican Views of the U.S. Expansion

A Mexican View of the Texans, 1828

By the late 1820s, Mexico was reassessing its policy of encouraging American immigration to Texas. Concerned over the large numbers and uncertain loyalties of the American settlers, the government appointed a commission in 1827 ostensibly to survey the boundary between Louisiana and the province of Texas. The real purpose of the commission was to recommend policy changes that would strengthen Mexico's hold on Texas. The following excerpt is from a journal kept by José María Sánchez, the draftsman of the boundary commission.

- Why was the Mexican government so ineffective in maintaining control over Texas?
- What was the appeal of Texas for Americans? How did most of them enter Texas and take up land?
- Why did Sánchez have such a low opinion of the Americans in the Austin colony? What did he think of Stephen Austin?
- Why did the Mexicans fear that they would lose Texas?

The Americans from the north have taken possession of practically all the eastern part of Texas, in most cases without the permission of the authorities. They immigrate constantly, finding no one to prevent them, and take possession of the *sitio* [location] that best suits them without either asking leave or going through any formality other than that of building their homes. Thus the majority of inhabitants in the Department are North Americans, the Mexican population being reduced to only Bejar, Nacogdoches, and La Bahía del Espíritu Santo, wretched settlements that between them do not number three thousand inhabitants, and the new village of Guadalupe Victoria that has scarcely more than seventy settlers. The government of the state, with its seat at Saltillo, that should watch over the preservation of its most precious and interesting department, taking measures to prevent its being stolen by foreign hands, is the one that knows the least not only about actual conditions, but even about its territory.... Repeated and urgent appeals have been made to the Supreme Government of the Federation regarding the imminent danger in which this interesting Department is of becoming the prize of the ambitious North Americans, but never has it taken any measures that may be called conclusive....

[Sánchez goes on to describe the village of Austin and the American colony founded by Stephen Austin.]

Its population is nearly two hundred persons, of which only ten are Mexicans, for the balance are all Americans from the North with an occasional European. Two wretched little stores supply the inhabitants of the colony: one sells only whiskey, rum, sugar, and coffee; the other, rice, flour, lard, and cheap cloth.... The Americans from the North, at least the great part of those I have seen, eat only salted meat, bread made by themselves out of corn meal, coffee, and home-made cheese. To these the greater part of those who live in the village add strong liquor, for they are in general, in my opinion, lazy people of vicious character. Some of them cultivate their small farms by planting corn; but this task they usually entrust to their negro slaves, whom they treat with considerable harshness. Beyond the village in an immense stretch of land formed by rolling hills are scattered the families brought by Stephen Austin, which today number more than two thousand persons. The diplomatic policy of this empresario, evident in all his actions, has, as one may say, lulled the authorities into a sense of security, while he works diligently for his own ends. In my judgment, the spark that will start the conflagration that will deprive us of Texas, will start from this colony. All because the government does not take vigorous measures to prevent it. Perhaps it does not realize the value of what it is about to lose.

Source: José María Sánchez, excerpted from "A Trip to Texas in 1828," trans. Carlos E. Castaneda from *Southwestern Historical Quarterly*, vol. 29 Copyright 1926. Reprinted courtesy of Texas State Historical Association, Austin, Texas. All rights reserved.

A Mexican Rebel in 1859

The U.S. victory in the Mexican War intensified cultural conflict along the now expanded Hispanic frontier. The Anglos (as Mexicans called white Americans) quickly assumed positions of political and economic dominance. They broke treaties designed to protect the property rights and land titles of Mexican Americans and under the cover of legality bullied peoples of Mexican descent. The resulting anger and resentment flared up in a brief revolt in 1859 in the lower Rio Grande valley led by Juan Cortina, a ranch owner who had fought for Mexico in the Mexican War. The following is from one of the proclamations issued by Cortina.

■ What was Cortina's opinion of the Anglos?

■ What reasons did he cite for the uprising?

■ How did he attempt to rally support for his cause?

Mexicans! When the State of Texas [became] an integrant part of the Union, flocks of vampires, in the guise of men, came and scattered themselves in the settlements, without any capital except the corrupt heart and the most perverse intentions. Some, brimful of laws, pledged to us their protection against the attacks of the rest; others assembled in shadowy councils, attempted and excited the robbery and burning of our relatives on the other side of the river Bravo; while others, to the abusing of our unlimited confidence, when we entrusted them with our titles [to land], which secured the future of our families, refused to return them under false and frivolous pretexts. … Many of you have been robbed of your property, incarcerated, chased, murdered, and hunted like wild beasts, because your labor was fruitful, and because your industry excited the vile avarice which led them.

Mexicans! Is there no remedy for you?…Mexicans! My part is taken; the voice of revelation whispers to me that to me is entrusted the work of breaking the chains of your slavery, and that the Lord will enable me, with powerful arm, to fight against our enemies, in compliance with the requirements of that Sovereign Majesty [God], who, from this day forward, will hold us under His protection. On my part, I am ready to offer myself as a sacrifice for your happiness; and counting upon the means necessary for the discharge of my ministry, you may count upon my cooperation, should no cowardly attempt put an end to my days.

Source: House Executive Documents, No. 52, 36th Congress, 1st session, 1860, pp. 80–82.

---

expense of Mexico. American merchants and California *rancheros* ran the economy, and both groups had joined separatist movements against Mexican rule. Unlike the *Californios,* who were ambivalent about their future political allegiance, the Americans wanted to be part of the United States and assumed that California would shortly be annexed. With the outbreak of the Mexican War in 1846, their wish became reality.

New Mexico.   Except for Utah, the American push into the interior of the Mexican Southwest followed the California pattern of trade preceding settlement. When Mexico liberalized the formerly restrictive trading policies of Spain, American merchants opened up the 900-mile-long **Santa Fe Trail** from Independence, Missouri, to Santa Fe, New Mexico. Starved for mercantile goods, the New Mexicans were a small but highly profitable market. They paid for their American imports with gold, silver, and furs.

Bent's Old Fort, an impregnable adobe structure built on the Arkansas River at the point where the Santa Fe Trail turned to the southwest, was the fulcrum for the growing economic influence of Americans over New Mexican affairs. Completed in 1832, the fort enabled the Bent brothers from Missouri to control a flourishing and almost monopolistic trade with Indians, trappers, caravans on the Santa Fe Trail, and the large landowners and merchants of New Mexico. This trade pulled New Mexico into the cultural and economic orbit of the United States and undermined what little sovereign power Mexico held in the region.

Although only a few hundred Americans were permanent residents of New Mexico in the 1840s, they had married into the Spanish-speaking landholding elite and were themselves beginning to receive large grants of land. Ties of blood and common economic interests linked this small group of American businessmen with the local elite. American merchants and New Mexican landlords were further united by their growing disdain for the instability of Mexican rule, Santa Anna's dictatorship, and sporadic attempts by Mexico to levy heavy taxes on the Santa Fe trade. Another bond was their concern over the aggressive efforts of the Texans to seize eastern New Mexico. After thwarting an 1841 Texan attempt to occupy Santa Fe, the leaders of New Mexico increasingly looked to the United States to protect their local autonomy. They quickly decided to cooperate with the U.S. army of invasion when the Mexican War got under way. Over the opposition of the clergy and ranchers still loyal to Mexico, this group was instrumental in the U.S. takeover of New Mexico.

Utah.   At the extreme northern and inner reaches of the Mexican borderlands lay Utah. Dominated by an intermountain depression called the Great Basin, Utah was a starkly beautiful but dry region of alkaline flats, broken tablelands, cottonwood canyons, and mountain ranges. Here, and along the flat expanse of the Colorado Plateau to the southeast, lived the Bannocks, Utes, Navajos, Hopis, and small bands of other Indians. Aside from trade with the Utes, Spain and Mexico had largely ignored this remote region. Its isolation and lack of white settlers, however, were precisely what made Utah so appealing to the Mormons, the Church of Jesus Christ of Latter-Day Saints. For the Mormons in the 1840s, Utah became the promised land in which to build a new Zion.

Founded by Joseph Smith in upstate New York in the 1820s, Mormonism grew rapidly within a communitarian framework that stressed hard work and economic cooperation under the leadership of patriarchal leaders (see Chapter 12). The economic success of close-knit Mormon communities, combined with the righteous zeal of their members, aroused the fears and hostility of non-Mormons. Harassed out of New York, Ohio, and Missouri, the Mormons thought they had found a permanent home by the late 1830s in Nauvoo, Illinois. But the murder of Joseph Smith and his brother by a mob in 1844 convinced the beleaguered Mormons that they had to leave the settled East for a refuge in the West. In 1846 a group of Mormons migrated to the Great Basin in Utah. Under the leadership of Brigham Young, they established a new community in 1847 at the Great Salt Lake on the western slopes of the Wasatch Mountains. An annual influx of about 2,000 converts enabled the initial settlement to grow rapidly.

The Mormons succeeded by concentrating their farms along the fertile and relatively well-watered Wasatch Front. They dispensed land and organized an irrigation system that coordinated water rights with the amount of land under production. To their dismay, however, they learned in 1848 that they had not left the United States after all. The Union acquired Utah, along with the rest of the northern borderlands of Mexico, as a result of the Mexican War.

Politics, Expansion, and War

The Democrats viewed their victory in the election of 1844 (see Chapter 10) as a popular mandate for expansion. They had campaigned on a platform that boldly demanded both Texas and the "reoccupation" of Oregon up to 54°40′.

James K. Polk, the new Democratic president, fully shared this expansionist vision. The greatest prize in his eyes was California. When he was stymied in his efforts to purchase California and New Mexico, he tried to force concessions from the Mexican government by ordering American troops to the mouth of the Rio Grande, far within the territory claimed by Mexico. When the virtually inevitable clash of arms occurred in late April 1846, war broke out between the United States and Mexico.

Victory resulted in the **Mexican Cession of 1848,** which added a half-million square miles to the United States. Polk's administration also finalized the acquisition of Texas and reached a compromise with the British on the Oregon Territory that recognized U.S. sovereignty in the Pacific Northwest up to the 49th parallel. The United States was now a nation that spanned a continent.

Manifest Destiny

With a phrase that soon entered the nation's vocabulary, John L. O'Sullivan, editor and Democratic politician, proclaimed in 1845 America's "manifest destiny to overspread and to possess the whole of the continent which Providence has given us for the development of the great experiment of Liberty and federated self-government entrusted to us." Central to Manifest Destiny was the assumption that white Americans were a special people, a view that dated back to the Puritans' belief that God had appointed them to establish a New Israel cleansed of the corruption of the Old World. Evangelical revivals in the early nineteenth century then added an aggressive sense of urgency to America's presumed mission to spread the benefits of Protestantism and Christian civilization. Protestant missionaries, as in Oregon, were often in the vanguard of U.S. expansion.

What distinguished the special U.S. mission as enunciated by Manifest Destiny was its explicitly racial component. Between 1815 and 1850, the term Anglo-Saxon, originally loosely applied to English-speaking peoples, acquired racial overtones, in keeping with the then-current interest of European and American scientists in defining, classifying, and ranking human races (with themselves, of course, at the top). Caucasian Anglo-Saxon Americans, as the descendants of ancient Germanic tribes that had purportedly brought the seeds of free institutions to England, were now said to be the foremost race in the world. The superior racial pedigree they claimed for themselves gave white Americans the natural right to expand westward, a chosen people carrying the blessings of democracy and progress. Only they, it was argued, had the energy, industriousness, and innate love of liberty to establish a successful free government.

FROM THEN TO NOW

Manifest Destiny and American Foreign Policy

U.S. troops faced far more hazardous conditions in Iraq than had been predicted.

From the birth of the nation in 1776 to the U.S. war on terrorism in the wake of the attacks on September 11, 2001, a sense of mission has often imbued U.S. foreign policy. Manifest Destiny was one expression of that sense of mission. According to its lofty rhetoric, the United States would fulfill its divinely ordained mission by absorbing all the peoples of North America, at least those deemed capable of self-government, into the republic. Manifest Destiny helped inspire the U.S. surge to the Pacific and justify the Mexican War. But the war also provoked a contrary fear: Was the United States guilty of an imperial conquest that threatened the liberty of others rather than promoting it?

Expansionists in the late nineteenth century invoked Manifest Destiny to justify U.S. acquisition of an overseas empire following the Spanish-American War, but the new empire did not really fit the model. The advocates of Manifest Destiny had envisioned neighboring peoples in North America voluntarily joining the republic, not being forced into it as dependent possessions. Critics of that war insisted that America's true mission must be to serve as the "model republic" for others to follow. This is the theme that characterized at least the public face of U.S. diplomacy in the twentieth century. President Woodrow Wilson justified U.S. intervention in World War I as a moral duty to save democracy in Europe, and Wilsonian idealism infused the foreign policy of President Franklin D. Roosevelt during World War II. Throughout the Cold War, the United States identified itself as the protector of democratic freedoms from the threat of international communism. In the post–Cold War world, Presidents George H.W. Bush and Bill Clinton cited the need to uphold human rights as grounds for U.S. military intervention abroad. President George W. Bush has gone further by claiming that the United States has the right to use preemptive force against any "evil power" deemed a threat to world peace and the future security of the United States.

■ What do you believe explains the long-held view of many Americans that the United States has been entrusted with a unique mission to redeem the rest of the world?

In this late-1872 evocation of the spirit of Manifest Destiny, Indians retreat westward as white settlers, guided by a diaphanously clad America, spread the benefits of American civilization.

PEARSON myhistorylab

From Then to Now Online

13-1 Albert Gallatin, *The Mission of the United States,* 1847. Calls on U.S. to lead by its moral example.

13-2 Woodrow Wilson, *On Defending Democracy,* 1920. Urges the U.S. to set the highest democratic standards in its international relations.

13-3 George W. Bush, *War Message,* March 19, 2003. Defends U.S. mission in military terms.

Global Perspectives

The Nineteenth-Century Frontier

"If I was to till you of our own township how it is growing as if it were by m[a]gic and also our market town Castlemaine you would not feel much interest in them. But realy they astonish me. As to our digging there is little new but likely I will send you a newspaper which will give you all the information of these Things.... Our great railroad is now all the talk but is not begun yet.... There is a great many goldmining compenys starting up about this place I believe five or six some of them so large as 2000 shares. It is causing work to get more plenty for those who is willing to work for wages and if our great railway was started I think there need not be many idle. But I think that wages will never be high again as there is still a goodly number waiting in hops of the same perhaps more Than will work when they get the chance."

In this letter, with words and details that we might expect from an American prospecting for gold in California, John McCance, an Irish emigrant to Australia, wrote back home describing the conditions he faced in the goldfields in the province of Victoria. Settling a frontier, and displacing and subjugating native peoples in the process, was not a unique American experience in the nineteenth century. It was part of a worldwide process replicated by migrants, especially of European origin, in such areas as Latin America, Canada, South Africa, Australia, and New Zealand. Population growth on a global scale, combined with improved and cheap forms of international travel, fed a stream of migrants into the frontier regions of the Southern Hemisphere and the North American West. In a radical environmental adaptation that made possible a tremendous increase in global supplies of food, vast, open expanses of grasslands, increasingly accessible by railroads, were transformed for the commercial production of grain and livestock. As newcomers poured in, indigenous foraging and pastoral peoples were wiped out, displaced, herded onto reservations, or forced to fundamentally change their ways of living, the victims of disease and superior military force and technology. The advance of global frontiers and the growing dominance of European-based societies went hand-in-hand in the nineteenth century.

- How would you define a frontier?
- To what extent would you argue that the U.S. frontier experience has been unique?

Advocates of Manifest Destiny insisted that U.S. expansion would be irresistible and peaceful. They were not warmongers calling for conquest. Still, the doctrine was undeniably a self-serving justification for what other peoples would see as territorial aggrandizement. Certainly, that was true of the Mexican Americans and Native Americans who lost land and cultural independence as they were brought under American control. Manifest Destiny and popular stereotypes lumped Indians and Mexicans together as inferior peoples. An emigrant guide of 1845 spoke of the Mexican Californians as "scarcely a visible grade in the scale of intelligence, above the barbarous tribes by whom they are surrounded." For Waddy Thompson, a U.S. diplomat minister in Mexico in the early 1840s, the Mexicans in general were "lazy, ignorant, and, of course, vicious and dishonest." This alleged Mexican inferiority was attributed to racial intermixture with the Indians, who, it was said, were hopelessly unfit for civilization.

Manifest Destiny was closely associated with the Democratic party. For Democrats, expansionism would counterbalance the debilitating effects of industrialization and urbanization. As good Jeffersonians, they stressed the need for more land to realize the ideal of a democratic republic rooted in the virtues and rough equality of independent farmers. For their working-class Irish constituency, the Democrats touted the broad expanses of the West as the surest means to escape the misery of wage slavery.

Manifest Destiny captured the popular imagination when the country was still mired in depression after the Panic of 1837. The way out of the depression, according to many Democrats, was to revive the export trade to soak up the agricultural surplus. Thomas Hart Benton, a Democratic senator from Missouri, was the leading spokesman for the vast potential of U.S. trade with India and China, a trade to be secured by U.S. possession of the harbors on the Pacific Coast.

The Mexican War

Once in office, Polk proved far more conciliatory with the British than with the Mexicans. Despite a stridently anti-British tone in his annual message to Congress in December

1845, Polk was willing to compromise on Oregon because he dreaded the possibility of a two-front war against both the Mexicans and the British. Mexico had severed diplomatic ties with the United States over the annexation of Texas (see Chapter 10), and a war could break out at any time.

In the spring of 1846, after Polk had abrogated the agreement on the joint occupation of Oregon, the British offered a compromise that they had earlier rejected. They agreed to a boundary at the 49th parallel if they were allowed to retain Vancouver Island in Puget Sound. Polk sent the offer to the Senate, which quickly approved it in June 1846. British-American trade continued to flourish, Mexico lost a potential ally, and, most important, Polk could now concentrate on the Mexican War, which had erupted a month earlier.

Unlike Oregon, where he backed off from extravagant territorial claims, Polk refused to budge on the U.S. claim (inherited from the Texans when the United States annexed Texas in 1845) that the Rio Grande was the border between Texas and Mexico. The Mexicans insisted that the Nueces River, 100 miles north of the Rio Grande, was the border, as it had been when Texas was part of Mexico. An immense territory was at stake, for the headwaters of the Rio Grande were in northern New Mexico, and a boundary on the Rio Grande would more than double the size of Texas.

Citing rumors of a Mexican invasion, Polk sent 3,500 troops under General Zachary Taylor to the Nueces River in the summer of 1845. Polk also stepped up his efforts to acquire California. He instructed Thomas Larkin, the U.S. consul in Monterey, California, to inform the *Californios* and Americans that the United States would support them if they revolted against Mexican rule. Polk also secretly ordered the U.S. Pacific naval squadron to seize California ports if war broke out with Mexico. Polk's final effort at peaceful expansion was the Slidell mission in November 1845. He sent John L. Slidell to Mexico City to offer $30 million to purchase California and New Mexico and to secure the Rio Grande boundary.

When Polk learned that the Mexican government had refused to receive Slidell, he set out to draw Mexico into a war that would result in the U.S. acquisition of California. In early 1846, he ordered General Taylor to advance to the Rio Grande, deep in the disputed border region. Taylor blockaded the mouth of the Rio Grande (an aggressive act even if the river had been an international boundary) and built a fort on the northern bank across from the Mexican town of Matamoros. The Mexicans attacked and were repulsed on April 24.

Even before the news reached Washington, Polk had decided on war, on the grounds that the Mexican government had unjustifiably refused to sell territory to the United States and had fallen behind on debt payments owed to American citizens. Informed of the clash between Mexican and American troops in early May (it took ten days for the news to reach Washington), he sent a redrafted war message to Congress on May 9 asserting that Mexico "has invaded our territory, and shed American blood on American soil." Congress declared war on May 13, 1846.

The war was a stunning military success for the United States (see Map 13–4). The Mexicans fought bravely, but they lacked the leadership, modern artillery, and naval capacity to check the U.S. advances. By the end of 1846, Polk had gained his objectives in the Mexican borderlands. An army sent west under Colonel Stephen W. Kearny occupied New Mexico. The conquest was relatively bloodless, because most of the local elite cooperated with the U.S. forces. Sporadic resistance was largely confined to poorer Mexicans and the Pueblo Indians, who feared that their land would be confiscated. The largest uprising, ruthlessly suppressed, was the **Taos Revolt** in January 1847, led by Jesús Trujillo and Tomasito, a Pueblo chieftain. A sympathetic observer described the rebels as "those who defend to the last their country and their homes."

Kearny's army then moved to Tucson and eventually linked up in southern California with pro-American rebels and U.S. forces sent ashore by the Pacific squadron. As in New Mexico, the stiffest resistance came from ordinary Mexicans and the Spanish-speaking Indians.

Despite the loss of its northern provinces, Mexico refused to concede defeat. After Taylor had established a secure defensive line in northeastern Mexico with a victory at Monterrey in September 1846 and repulsed a Mexican counterattack at Buena Vista in February 1847, Polk directed General Winfield Scott to invade central Mexico. Following an amphibious assault on Vera Cruz in March 1847, Scott captured Mexico City in September.

After a frustrating delay while Mexico reorganized its government, peace talks finally got under way and concluded in the Treaty of Guadalupe Hidalgo, signed on February 2, 1848. Mexico surrendered its claim to Texas north of the Rio Grande and ceded Alta California and New Mexico (including present-day Arizona, Utah, and Nevada). The United States paid $15 million, assumed over $3 million in claims of American citizens against Mexico, and agreed to grant U.S. citizenship to Mexican residents in its new territories.

Polk had gained his strategic goals, but the cost was 13,000 American lives (most from diseases such as measles and dysentery), 50,000 Mexican lives, and the poisoning of Mexican American relations for generations. The war also, as will be seen in Chapter 14, heightened sectional tensions over slavery and weakened the political structure that was vital to preserving the Union.

Conclusion

Americans were an expansionist people. Their surge across the continent between 1815 and 1850 was fully in keeping with their restless desire for personal independence on a plot

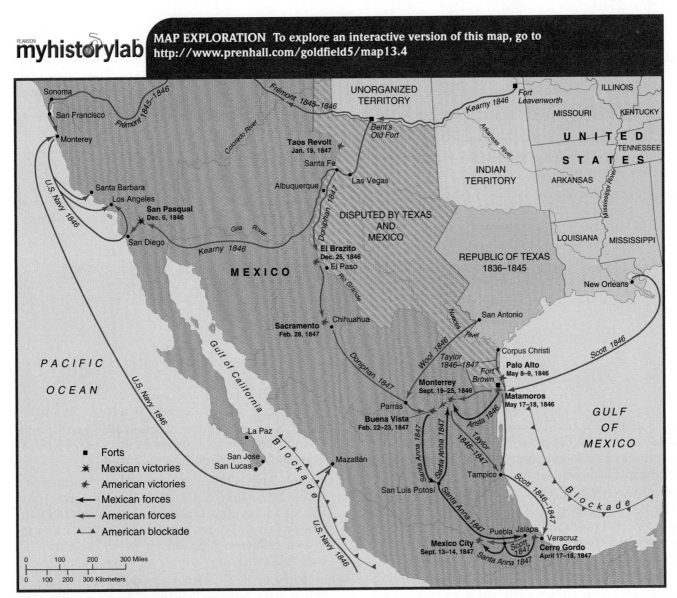

MAP 13–4   **The Mexican War**
Victories by General Zachary Taylor in northern Mexico secured the Rio Grande as the boundary between Texas and Mexico. Colonel Stephen Kearny's expedition won control of New Mexico, and reinforcements from Kearny assured the success of American troops landed by the Pacific Squadron in gaining Alta California for the United States. The success of General Winfield Scott's amphibious invasion at Vera Cruz and his occupation of Mexico City brought the war to an end.

of land. Population pressure on overworked farms in the East impelled much of this westward migration, but by the 1840s, expansion had seemingly acquired a momentum all its own, one that increasingly rejected the claims of other peoples to the land. Far from being a process of peaceful, evolutionary, and democratic change, expansion involved the spread of slavery, violent confrontations, and the uprooting and displacement of native peoples. By 1850, the earlier notion of reserving the trans-Mississippi West as a permanent Indian country had been abandoned. The Sioux and Comanches were still feared by white settlers, but their final subjugation

was not far off. The derogatory stereotypes of Mexican Americans that were a staple of both popular thought and expansionist ideology showed clearly that U.S. control after the Mexican War would relegate Spanish-speaking people to second-class status. However misleading and false much of it was, the rhetoric of Manifest Destiny did highlight a central truth. Broad, popular support existed for expanding across the continent. As the Mexican War made clear, the United States was now unquestionably the dominant power in North America. The only serious threat to its dominance in the near future would come from inside, not outside, its domain.

Review Questions

1. What accounted for the westward movement of Americans? How did the presence or absence of slavery affect developmental patterns in the new settlements?

2. How was the West of the Plains Indians transformed after 1830 as peoples migrated both within the region and into it from various directions? Why were the Sioux so powerful? How did they interact with other Native Americans and the U.S. government?

3. Who lived in the Mexican borderlands of the Southwest? Why was it so difficult for the Mexican government to maintain effective control of the region? What role did trade play in the American penetration of the Southwest?

4. What did Americans mean by Manifest Destiny? Why was territorial expansion so identified with the Democratic Party?

5. Who was responsible for the outbreak of the Mexican War? Were Mexicans the victims of American aggression? Why did the British make no effort to intervene?

6. How valid was the Sioux chief's indictment of the pretensions of white civilization as related to George Catlin?

Key Terms

Alamo (p. 347)

Californios (p. 348)

Claims clubs (p. 338)

Empresarios (p. 347)

Manifest Destiny (p. 335)

Mexican Cession of 1848 (p. 351)

Oregon Trail (p. 340)

Santa Fe Trail (p. 350)

Taos Revolt (p. 354)

Tejanos (p. 346)

Recommended Reading

Brandon, Richard. *The Last Americans: The Indian in American Culture* (1974). A beautifully written, panoramic account that looks at Indian cultures and their interactions with the spread of white settlement.

Limerick, Patricia Nelson. *The Legacy of Conquest: The Unbroken Past of the American West* (1987). A forcefully argued work that overturns many stereotypes and places the federal government and cultural antagonisms at the center of western history.

Meinig, D. W. *The Shaping of America*, vol. 2: *Continental America, 1800–1867* (1993). A comprehensive work that offers a distinctive interpretation of continental expansion from the perspective of historical geography.

Milner, Clyde A., II, Carol A. O'Connor, and Martha A. Sandweiss, eds. *The Oxford History of the American West* (1994). A comprehensive collection of essays that summarize much of the best work in the modern rethinking of the history of the American West.

Stephanson, Anders. *Manifest Destiny: American Expansionism and the Empire of Right* (1995). A tightly argued study that traces Manifest Destiny back to its roots in Puritan ideology and shows how, in revised form, it continued to influence U.S. foreign policy well into the twentieth century.

White, Richard. *"It's Your Misfortune and None of My Own": A History of the American West* (1991). An outstanding work that draws on cultural and environmental approaches to show how complex and often unequal relationships among a host of peoples shaped the history of the West.

Where to Learn More

■ **Indian Pueblo Cultural Center, Albuquerque, New Mexico.**   This center provides an excellent orientation to the culture, crafts, and community life of the Pueblo and southwestern Indians. It also includes much material on archaeological findings. Visit www.indianpueblo.org for a calendar of events and an introduction to the history of the nineteen pueblos.

■ **Indian Museum of North America, Crazy Horse, South Dakota.**   This is one of the best sources for learning about the culture of the Teton Sioux and other American and Canadian tribes on the Great Plains. Holdings include outstanding examples of Indian art and artifacts. For information on exhibits, educational and cultural programs, and special collections of Native American art, go to www.crazyhorse.org/museum.shtml.

■ **Scotts Bluff National Monument, Gering, Nebraska.**   Scotts Bluff was a prominent landmark on the Oregon Trail, and the museum exhibits here have interpretive material on the trail and the western phase of expansion. Go to www.nps.gov/scbl to print a park travel guide and to access a website devoted to the frontier photographer and artist William Henry Jackson.

■ **Conner Prairie, Noblesville, Indiana.**   The museum and historic area re-create a sense of life on the Indiana frontier during the period of the Old Northwest. www.connerprairie.org.

■ **Fort Union National Monument, Watrous, New Mexico.**   Fort Union was a nineteenth-century military post, and the holdings and exhibits in the museum relate to frontier military life and the Santa Fe Trail. For a printable travel guide and a history of the park that includes bibliographical aids, go to www.nps.gov/foun

Study Resources

For study resources for this chapter, go to www.myhistorylab.com and choose *The American Journey*. You will find a wealth of study and review material for this chapter, including pre- and post-tests, customized study plan, key term review flash cards, interactive map and document activities, and documents for analysis.

Vivid illustrations accompanied the numerous editions of *Uncle Tom's Cabin* depicting the brutal realities of slavery and the unmerited suffering of the slave. These images sharpened the tragedy of Harriet Beecher Stowe's story. Here, Tom dies following a savage beating.

The Politics of Sectionalism 1846–1861 14

December 16, 1852

My Dear Madam,

So you want to know what sort of woman I am! Well, if this is any object, you shall have statistics free of charge. To begin, then, I am a little bit of a woman, somewhat more than forty, about as thin and dry as a pinch of snuff, never very much to look at in my best days and looking like a used up article now.

I was married when I was twenty-five years old to a man rich in Greek and Hebrew and Latin and Arabic, and alas, rich in nothing else....But then I was abundantly furnished with wealth of another sort. I had two little curly headed twin daughters to begin with and my stock in this line has gradually increased, till I have been the mother of seven children, the most beautiful and the most loved of whom lies buried near my Cincinnati residence. It was at his dying bed and at his grave that I learned what a poor slave mother may feel when her child is torn away from her. In those depths of sorrow which seemed to me immeasurable, it was my only prayer to God that such anguish might not be suffered in vain. There were circumstances about his death of such peculiar bitterness, of what seemed almost cruel suffering that I felt that I could never be consoled for it unless this crushing of my own heart might enable me to work out some great good to others.

I allude to this here because I have often felt that much that is in that book had its root in the awful scenes and bitter sorrow of that summer. It has left now, I trust, no trace on my mind except a deep compassion for the

359

sorrowful, especially for mothers who are separated from their children....

This horror, this nightmare abomination! Can it be in my country! It lies like lead on my heart, it shadows my life with sorrow; the more so that I feel, as for my own brothers, for the South, and am pained by every horror I am obliged to write, as one who is forced by some awful oath to disclose in court some family disgrace....

Yours affectionately,

H. B. Stowe

Harriet Beecher Stowe to Eliza Cabot Follen, December 16, 1852; from Jeanne Boydston, Mary Kelley, and Anne Margolis, *The Limits of Sisterhood* (Chapel Hill: University of North Carolina Press, 1988), pp. 178–180.

myhistorylab

Personal Journeys Online

■ Carl Schurz, *Reminiscences*, 1908. Account of his participation in Germany's failed Revolution of 1848 and his subsequent journey to freedom in the United States.

■ Frederick Douglass, three excerpts: "What of the Night?" May 5, 1848; "A Letter to American Slaves," September 5, 1850; "Letter to James Redpath, June 29, 1860." These excerpts chart the famous black abolitionist's journey from a belief in moral suasion and political action as the best strategy to liberate the nation's slaves to an embrace of direct action and violence as the only remedy for bondage.

Harriet Beecher Stowe, in her letter to the poet and fellow abolitionist Eliza Cabot Follen in the year that *Uncle Tom's Cabin* became an international best seller, revealed how being a wife and a mother had influenced her perception of slavery and inspired her writing. The deep piety and self-effacement expressed in the letter, as well as her transparent grief over the loss of her son, typified mid-nineteenth-century correspondence between women. Her beloved son had died of cholera in 1849; that wrenching event, coupled with the passage of the Fugitive Slave Act a year later, galvanized Stowe to pour her grief and indignation into a novel about plantation slavery.

Slavery was an abstract concept to most white northerners at the time. Stowe personalized it in a way that made them see it as an institution that did not just oppress black people but also destroyed families and debased well-meaning Christian masters. The deep piety expressed in the letter permeated the book and changed people's moral perceptions about slavery.

Stowe had grown up in a family of evangelical Protestant ministers and abolitionists. Her father, Lyman Beecher, was a prominent evangelical reformer. He had moved his large family from New England to Cincinnati in 1832 to assume the presidency of Lane Theological Seminary, where he used his office to promote the abolition of slavery. All six of his sons became ministers. Two of his three daughters, Catharine and Harriet, became accomplished writers. In Beecher's view, evangelical Christianity erased the line between public and private. Personal and societal salvation were closely connected, a principle that is apparent in Harriet's letter. Stowe went on to write ten novels, became a popular children's-book author, and wrote extensively on family and travel matters. She died in 1896, in Hartford, Connecticut, at the age of 85.

As slavery took on a personal and tragic meaning for Stowe, so it would move from being just another political issue to a moral crusade. Stowe's personal journey transformed it into a political passion; for the millions who read her book, the political became personal. Yet the anguish she expressed in her writing and the outrage it generated among her readers was hardly prefigured when a relatively obscure congressman from Pennsylvania stepped forward in 1846 with a modest proposal that not only placed slavery front and center as a national political issue, a position that only strengthened over the next fifteen years, but would shake the Union to its very core.

CHRONOLOGY

1846	Wilmot Proviso is submitted to Congress but is defeated.
1848	Gold is discovered in California.
	Whig Party candidate Zachary Taylor defeats Democrat Lewis Cass and Free-Soiler Martin Van Buren for the presidency.
	Revolutions in Europe; publication of Karl Marx and Friedrich Engels's *Communist Manifesto*.
1850	California applies for statehood.
	President Taylor dies; Vice President Millard Fillmore succeeds him.
	Compromise of 1850 is passed.
1851	Harriet Beecher Stowe publishes *Uncle Tom's Cabin*.
1852	Democrat Franklin Pierce is elected president in a landslide over Whig candidate Winfield Scott.
	Whig Party disintegrates.
1853	National Black Convention convened in Rochester, New York, to demand repeal of the Fugitive Slave Act.
	Crimean War erupts between Russia and Turkey over Russian demand to protect Christian shrines in Palestine; soon engulfs Britain and France; eventually leads to the unification of Germany and Italy.
1854	Ostend Manifesto is issued.
	Kansas-Nebraska Act repeals the Missouri Compromise.
	Know-Nothing and Republican parties are formed.
1855	Civil war erupts in "Bleeding Kansas."
	William Walker attempts a takeover of Nicaragua.

1856	"Sack of Lawrence" occurs in Kansas; John Brown makes a retaliatory raid at Pottawatomie Creek.
	Democratic congressman Preston Brooks of South Carolina canes Massachusetts senator Charles Sumner in the U.S. Senate.
	Democrat James Buchanan is elected president over Republican John C. Frémont and American (Know-Nothing) candidate Millard Fillmore.
1857	Supreme Court issues *Dred Scott* decision.
	Kansas territorial legislature passes the proslavery Lecompton Constitution.
	Panic of 1857 begins.
1858	Senatorial candidates Abraham Lincoln and Stephen A. Douglas hold series of debates in Illinois.
1859	John Brown's Raid fails at Harpers Ferry, Virginia.
1860	Constitutional Union Party forms.
	Democratic Party divides into northern and southern factions.
	Republican candidate Abraham Lincoln is elected president over southern Democratic candidate John C. Breckinridge, northern Democratic candidate Stephen A. Douglas, and Constitutional Unionist candidate John Bell.
	South Carolina secedes from the Union.
1861	The rest of the Lower South secedes from the Union.
	Crittenden Plan and Tyler's Washington peace conference fail.
	Jefferson Davis assumes presidency of the Confederate States of America.
	Lincoln is inaugurated.
	Fort Sumter is bombarded; Civil War begins.
	Several Upper South states secede.
	Tsar Alexander II of Russia frees the serfs.

Slavery was not, of course, a new political issue: The debate over the Missouri Compromise, the nullification controversy, and the battles in Congress over abolitionist mailings and petitions had roiled the political waters for nearly a generation prior to 1846. But after 1846, the clashes between northern and southern congressmen over issues relating to slavery became more frequent and more difficult to resolve. In the coming years, several developments, including white southerners' growing consciousness of themselves as a minority, the mixture of political issues with religious questions, and the rise of the Republican Party, would aggravate sectional antagonism. But the flash point that first brought it to the fore was the issue of slavery in the territories acquired from Mexico.

Slavery in the Territories

Whatever its boundaries over the years, the West symbolized the hopes and dreams of white Americans. It was the region of fresh starts, of possibilities. To exclude slavery from the western territories was to exclude white southerners from pursuing their vision of the American dream. Exclusion, an Alabamian declared, meant "that a free citizen of Massachusetts was a better man and entitled to more privileges than a free citizen of Alabama." Northern politicians disagreed. They argued that exclusion preserved equality, the equality of all white men and women to live and work without competition from slave labor or rule by despotic slaveholders. The issue of slavery in the territories became an issue of freedom for both sides. From the late 1840s until 1861, northern and southern leaders attempted to fashion a solution to the problem of slavery in the territories. Four proposals dominated the debate:

- Outright exclusion
- Extension of the Missouri Compromise line to the Pacific
- Popular sovereignty, allowing the residents of a territory to decide the issue
- Protection of the property of slaveholders (meaning their right to own slaves) even if few lived in the territory

The first major debate on these proposals occurred during the early days of the Mexican War and culminated in the Compromise of 1850.

The Wilmot Proviso

In August 1846, David Wilmot, a Pennsylvania Democrat, offered an amendment to an appropriations bill for the Mexican War. The language of the **Wilmot Proviso** stipulated that "as an express and fundamental condition to the acquisition of any territory from the Republic of Mexico…neither slavery nor involuntary servitude shall ever exist in any part of said territory." This language deliberately reflected Thomas Jefferson's Northwest Ordinance of 1787, which prohibited

slavery in the Old Northwest. The proviso did not apply to Texas, which had become a state before the war began.

Wilmot explained that he wanted only to preserve the territories for "the sons of toil, of my own race and own color." By thus linking the exclusion of slavery in the territories to freedom for white people, he hoped to generate support across the North, regardless of party, and even in some areas of the Upper South. Linking freedom for white people to the exclusion of slaves infuriated southerners. It implied that the mere proximity of slavery was degrading and that white southerners were therefore a degraded people, unfit to join other Americans in the territories.

Northern lawmakers, a majority in the House of Representatives (because the northern states had a larger population than the southern states), passed more than 50 versions of the proviso between 1846 and 1850. In the Senate, however, where each state had equal representation, the proviso was consistently rejected and never became law.

The proviso debate sowed distrust and suspicion between northerners and southerners. Congress had divided along sectional lines before, but seldom had the divisions become so personal.

Religious differences also sharpened the sectional conflict over the proviso. The leading evangelical Protestant denominations—Methodists, Baptists, and Presbyterians—split along sectional lines by the mid-1840s. Growing numbers of northern evangelicals advocated political action. During the debate on the Wilmot Proviso, a Boston minister wrote, "The great problem for the Christian world now to accomplish is to effect a closer union between religion and politics.…We must make men to do good and be good." Southern evangelicals recoiled from such mixing of church and state, charging northerners with abandoning the basic tenets of evangelical Christianity: the importance of individual salvation above all, and the Bible as the unerring word of God. The leaders of the Democratic and Whig parties, disturbed that the issue of slavery in the territories could so monopolize Congress and poison sectional relations, sought to defuse the issue as the presidential election of 1848 approached.

The Election of 1848

Both Democrats and Whigs wanted to avoid identification with either side of the Wilmot Proviso controversy, and they selected their 1848 presidential candidates accordingly. The Democrats nominated Michigan senator Lewis Cass, a party stalwart, whose public career stretched back to the War of 1812. Cass understood the destructive potential of the slavery issue. In 1847, he suggested that territorial residents, not Congress, should decide slavery's fate. This solution, **popular sovereignty,** had a do-it-yourself charm: Keep the politicians out of it, and let the people decide. Cass was deliberately ambiguous, however, on when the people should decide. The timing was important. If residents could decide only when applying for statehood, slavery would be legal up to that point. The ambiguity aroused more fears than it allayed.

Global Perspectives

The Revolutions of 1848

New Yorkers greeted the "Magnificent Magyar," Hungarian patriot Louis Kossuth, as a conquering hero in December 1851. Supporters rushed the stage from which he was to deliver a speech, and one female admirer tore off a section of his coat as a prized souvenir. To New Yorkers, Kossuth embodied the democratic ideals of their nation founded on the principles of liberty and equality.

Fueled by rapid industrial and urban transformation, democratic sentiment spread over the European continent among the new working and middle classes in the 1840s. France showed the way. When the government of King Louis-Philippe failed to respond to demands for economic and political reforms, these groups banded together to overthrow the monarchy in February 1848. But the resulting government and new constitution under Charles Louis Napoleon Bonaparte, the nephew of the famous ruler, offered only superficial change, as reformers squandered their advantage with internal bickering between radicals and moderates.

When students at the University of Bonn heard the news of Louis-Philippe's downfall, they rushed into the town square to demand civil and religious liberties and the formation of a German national state. "We were dominated by a vague feeling," one student recalled, "as if a great outbreak of elemental forces had begun, as if an earthquake was impending of which we had felt the first shock." But the authoritarian rulers of the nine German states, while they allowed the formation of an all-German parliament and the drafting of a republican constitution, ignored both and the revolution failed.

A similar scenario played out in the Austrian Empire, a conglomeration of eleven different ethnic peoples, including Kossuth's Hungary. The ruling Hapsburg monarchy initially accepted some of the reformers' demands but then ruthlessly suppressed uprisings in Prague, Vienna, and Buda (Hungary). The Austrians also reestablished their control over portions of Italy, successfully overcoming a movement for Italian unity and reform.

These setbacks troubled Americans. Their initial enthusiasm for the revolutionary movements of 1848 was rooted in the belief that mankind naturally prefers liberty and equality and that the American experiment was exportable to other peoples. President James K. Polk hailed developments in Europe in 1848: "The great principles of popular sovereignty which were proclaimed in 1776 by the immortal author of our Declaration of Independence, seem now to be in the course of rapid development throughout the world."

The failure of these revolutionary movements made the American experiment that much more precious, and it also highlighted some contradictions in American democratic life. Frederick Douglass wondered how Americans could lionize a Hungarian freedom fighter, but hunt down Americans with the same aspirations. Events of the 1850s would sorely test that experiment.

- How did Americans come to view their own ideals in the aftermath of the revolutions of 1848 in Europe?

The Whigs were silent on the slavery issue. Reverting to their winning 1840 formula of nominating a war hero, they selected General Zachary Taylor of Mexican War fame. If the Whigs were looking for someone with no political record, they found him in the squat and craggy-faced Taylor. Taylor belonged to no party and had never voted. He was also inarticulate to the point of unintended humor. In one address, he intoned: "We are at peace with all of the world, and seek to maintain...amity with the rest of mankind." If one had to guess his views, his background provided some clues. He owned a hundred-slave plantation in Louisiana, and his now-deceased daughter had been married to Jefferson Davis, Mississippi's staunch proslavery senator.

Taylor's background disturbed many antislavery northern Whigs. These Conscience Whigs, along with remnants of the old Liberty Party and a scattering of northern Democrats, bolted their parties and formed the Free-Soil Party. The name reflected the party's vow to keep the territories free. Its slogan, "Free soil, free speech, free labor, free men," was a catalog of white liberties that the South had allegedly threatened over the previous decade.

The Free-Soilers' appeal centered on their opposition to slave labor in the territories. Free labor, they believed, could not compete with bonded labor. Slavery condemned the white worker to unemployment, poverty, and eventually a condition little better than slavery itself. The party nominated former president Martin Van Buren. The old New Yorker, who had remained active in state politics, had little hope of winning. But he wielded some influence because of the possibility that his candidacy might prevent one of the major party candidates from winning a majority of electoral votes, thereby throwing the election into the House of Representatives.

Chalking up one out of seven northern votes, Van Buren ran strongly enough in 11 of the 15 northern states to deny the winning candidate in those states a majority of the votes cast. But he could not overcome Taylor's strength in the South. Taylor was elected, giving the nation its first president from the Lower South.

The Gold Rush

Events in distant California, recently acquired from Mexico, would leave Taylor little time to savor his victory. By the time he took office in March 1849, a gold rush was underway there. John Sutter, a Swiss immigrant, contracted with James Marshall in late 1847 to build a sawmill on his property at the junction of the American and Sacramento rivers in central California. In January 1848, Marshall was nearly finished with his project when something caught his eye: "I reached my hand down and picked it up; it made my heart thump, for I was certain it was gold. The piece was about half the size and shape of a pea. Then I saw another." Few believed the story at first, but Sam Brannan, a San Francisco merchant, witnessed Marshall's finds and literally ran through the streets of the sparsely settled town shouting about the new discovery. Brannan would become the wealthiest man in California, provisioning miners and staking claims.

Through 1849 and 1850, more than 100,000 hopefuls flooded into California. Anarchy and geology combined to form a volatile mixture in appropriately named settlements like Hangtown, Gouge Eye, and Whiskeytown. One unfortunate miner wrote back east to his family in 1850: "I take this opportunity of writing these few lines to you hoping to find you in good health. Me and Charley is sentenced to be hung at five o/clock for robbery. Give my best to Frank and Sam." Though the trek to California took months, whether overland or by the sea route, and travelers battled disease, weather, and each other, the lure of gold, easy to get at with just simple tools, was a powerful motivator.

Huge fortunes accrued, not only from the gold, but from supplying the miners. Young Levi Strauss experimented with trousers made out of canvas that miners particularly favored; two brothers, Henry Wells and William Fargo, offered banking, transportation, and mail services for the newcomers.

The California Gold Rush attracted a multi-national population. Here, Chinese miners relax at their camp. The placid scene masks the occasionally violent confrontations between different racial and ethnic groups drawn to the gold fields.

The rush also attracted migrants from around the world. California soon became a polyglot empire of Chinese, Chileans, Mexicans, Irish, Germans, and Turks. Blacks, mostly slaves brought by southern masters, also roamed the gold fields.

By 1853 gold-mining operations had undergone structural and technological changes that made many miners superfluous. The new hydraulic extraction techniques also severely damaged the pristine rivers of central California. Almost overnight, San Francisco was transformed from a modest port to a cosmopolitan metropolis. In 1847, a typical lot in the town cost $16; by 1849, the same lot sold for $45,000. During these two years, the town burned to the ground no less than six times, and six times the residents rebuilt on an ever-grander scale. By the mid-1850s, a half-billion dollars in gold money had passed through the city, and a good bit of it stayed. The city by then boasted a fine theater, an opera house, and more newspapers than any other city in the world save London. The image of California, and of the West in general, as wild or golden, dates from this era. But the romance of California and the wealth it generated loomed more troubling back east as the territory filled up with people in 1849. For the western dream would soon become ensnared in the conflict over slavery.

The Compromise of 1850

When the California territory's new residents began asking for statehood and drafted a state constitution, the document contained no provision for slavery. The constitution reflected antiblack rather than antislavery sentiment. Keeping California white would shield residents against social and economic interaction with black people. In the context of territorial politics, "free" became a synonym for "whites only." If Congress accepted the residents' request for statehood, California would enter the Union as a free state. The Union at the time consisted of 15 free states and 15 slave states. The admission of California would tip the balance and give free states a majority in the Senate. California, with its rapidly growing population, would also add to the 61-vote majority the North enjoyed in the House of Representatives. New Mexico (which then included most of present-day New Mexico, Arizona, small parts of Nevada, and Colorado) appeared poised to follow suit and enter the Union as the seventeenth free state. Southerners saw their political power slipping away. Northern leaders saw an opportunity to stop the extension of slavery and reduce southern influence in the federal government.

When Congress confronted the issue of California statehood in December 1849, partisans on both sides began marshaling forces for what promised to be a long and bitter struggle. Because nine Free-Soil candidates had won seats in the House of Representatives, neither Whigs nor Democrats held a majority there. South Carolina senator John C. Calhoun understood that only a politically unified South could protect its interests. He urged southern congressmen to ignore party ties and unite behind a plan he proposed to gain federal protection for slavery in the territories. Most southern Whigs ignored Calhoun and waited to hear from President Taylor before abandoning him and their party.

No one, at first, knew where Taylor stood. Although a political novice, the president was not stupid. Recognizing his lack of political experience, he selected Whig senator William H. Seward of New York as his advisor. Seward, a committed antislavery man, was one of the most hated politicians in the South; Taylor, a slaveholder from Louisiana, was distrusted by many northern members of his party. This odd match provided the first insight into the president's thinking on California.

He supported, it turned out, a version of popular sovereignty and favored allowing California and the other territories acquired from Mexico to decide the slavery issue for themselves. Under normal circumstances, the residents of a new territory organized a territorial government under the direction of Congress. When the territory's population approached 30,000 or so, residents could draft a constitution and petition Congress for statehood. California already easily exceeded the population threshold. Taylor proposed bypassing the territorial stage, and congressional involvement in it, and having California and New Mexico admitted as states directly. (Before his inauguration in March 1849, he had already privately encouraged people in both territories to write state constitutions and to request admission.) The result would be to bring both into the Union as free states.

Although Seward no doubt encouraged him, Taylor's position was his own. The president was a nationalist and a strong believer in Manifest Destiny. He did not oppose slavery, but he abhorred the slavery issue because it threatened his vision of a continental empire. Thus he was willing to forgo the extension of slavery into the territories. Southerners were certain to object strongly. But the president had a chilling message for them: "Whatever dangers may threaten [the Union] I shall stand by it and maintain it in its integrity."

Southerners resisted Taylor's plan, and Congress deadlocked on the territorial issue. Henry Clay then stepped forward with his last great compromise. To break the impasse, Clay urged that Congress should take five steps:

- Admit California as a free state, as its residents clearly preferred.
- Allow the residents of the New Mexico and Utah territories to decide the slavery issue for themselves.
- End the slave trade in the District of Columbia.
- Pass a new fugitive slave law to enforce the constitutional provision stating that a person "held to Service or Labor in one state...escaping into another...shall be delivered upon Claim of the party to whom such Service or Labor may be due."
- Set the boundary between Texas and New Mexico and pay Texas $10 million for the territory given up to New Mexico. (Texas, incidentally, would use this payment to retire its state debt and fund a public school system.)

Clay's proposal provoked a historic Senate debate that began in February 1850, featuring America's three most prominent statesmen, Clay, Calhoun, and Daniel Webster, together for the last time. The emaciated Calhoun, who would be dead in two months, had to be carried into the Senate chamber. Too weak to read his remarks, he passed them to Virginia senator James M. Mason. Calhoun argued that the compromise did not resolve the slavery issue to the South's satisfaction, and he proposed to give southerners in Congress the right to veto legislation as a way to safeguard their minority rights. Webster stood up to support the compromise, at deep political peril to himself. His Massachusetts constituents detested the fugitive slave provision, which gave southern slaveholders the right to "invade" northern states to reclaim escaped slaves. Webster declared that he came to the debate "not as a Massachusetts man, nor as a Northern man, but as an American." He would swallow the fugitive slave law to save the Union.

After tumultuous deliberation that lasted into the summer of 1850, the Senate rejected the compromise. Calhoun had died at the end of March 1850, before the debate ended. The 73-year-old Clay, exhausted, left Washington to recover his health. He would die less than two years later. Webster, estranged from fellow northern Whigs, left the Senate and went to his grave a few months after Clay. President Taylor, who had vowed to veto any compromise, died unexpectedly of a stomach ailment after overindulging in cherries and milk in the hot sun at a July 4 celebration in Washington. Vice President Millard Fillmore, a pro-Clay New Yorker, assumed the presidency after Taylor's death. Compared with Taylor, who had stormed around the White House daring southerners to attempt secession, Fillmore was a back-room man, quiet, at home with the cigar-and-brandy crowd, and effective with the deal. Fillmore let it be known that he favored Clay's package and would sign it if passed.

Although the Senate had rejected the compromise, Illinois senator Stephen A. Douglas kept it alive. A small man with a large head that gave him a mushroom-like appearance, Douglas epitomized the promise of American life for men of his generation. A native Vermonter, he migrated first to New York, then to Illinois as a teenager, became a lawyer, and developed a voracious appetite for politics. By the age of 28, he had already served as state legislator, chairman of the state Democratic Party, and judge of the state supreme court. He envisioned an urban, industrial West linked to the East by a vast railroad network eventually extending to the Pacific. Above all, Douglas professed an unbending nationalism. To him, according to a biographer, "the Union was sacred, the symbol of all human progress." After his election to Congress in 1842, the Little Giant, as his constituents affectionately called him, developed a reputation as an astute parliamentarian and a tenacious debater.

Like Webster, Douglas feared for the Union if the compromise failed. Realizing that it would never pass as a package, he proposed to break it up into its components and hold a separate vote on each. With a handful of senators voting for all parts, and with different sectional blocs supporting one provision or another, Douglas engineered a majority for the compromise, and Fillmore signed it.

The **Compromise of 1850** (see Map 14–1) was not a compromise in the sense of each opposing side consenting to certain terms desired by the other. The North gained California but would have done so in any case. Southern leaders looked to the West and saw no slave territories awaiting statehood. Their future in the Union appeared to be one of numerical and economic decline, and the survival of their institutions seemed doubtful. They gained the **Fugitive Slave Act,** which reinforced their right to seize and return to bondage slaves who had fled to free territory, but it was slight consolation. One Lower South senator termed it "useless." Since most slaves who escaped to the North did so from neighboring slave states, the law affected mainly the states of the Upper South. Few slave owners from the Lower South would bear the expense and uncertainty of chasing an escaped slave into free territory. And the North's hostile reception to the law made southerners doubt its commitment to the compromise.

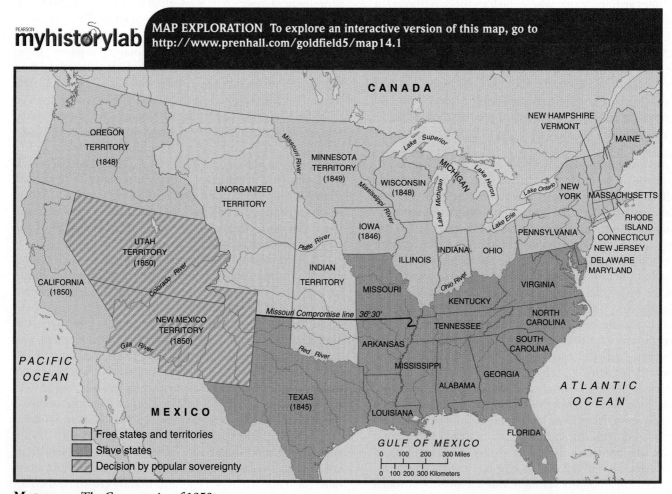

MAP 14–1   The Compromise of 1850
Given the unlikely prospect that any of the western territories would opt for slavery, the compromise sealed the South's minority status in the Union.

Response to the Fugitive Slave Act

The Fugitive Slave Act was ready-made for abolitionist propaganda mills and heartrending stories. A few months after Congress passed it, a Kentucky slaveholder visited Madison, Indiana, and snatched a black man from his wife and children, claiming that the man had escaped nineteen years earlier. Black people living in northern communities feared capture, and some fled across the Canadian border. Several northern cities and states vowed resistance, but except for a few publicized cases, northern authorities typically cooperated with southern slave owners to help them retrieve their runaway property. The effect of the act on public opinion, however, was to polarize North and South even further.

The strongest reaction to the act was in the black communities of the urban North. Previously, black abolitionists in the North had focused on freeing slaves in the South. The Fugitive Slave Act brought the danger of slavery much closer to home. No black person was safe under the new law. Mistaken identity, the support of federal courts for slaveholders' claims, and the presence of informants made reenslavement a real possibility. The lives that 400,000 black northerners had constructed, often with great difficulty, appeared suddenly uncertain.

Black northerners formed associations to protect each other and repel, violently if necessary, any attempt to capture and reenslave them. Boston's black leaders created the League of Freedom. Black Chicagoans organized the Liberty Association, with teams assigned to "patrol the city, spying for possible slave-hunters." Similar associations appeared in Cleveland and Cincinnati. Frederick Douglass, an escaped slave himself, explained the need for such organizations: "We must be prepared...see the streets...running with blood... should this law be put into operation." Some black people left the United States. In October 1850, 200 left Pittsburgh for Ontario, Canada, vowing that "they would die before being taken back into slavery." As many as 20,000 African Americans may have found their way across the border during the 1850s in response to fears over capture and reenslavement. Another solution was proposed by Martin Delany, a prominent black abolitionist. He argued for the establishment of a black homeland at several potential sites in Central or South America or on the west coast of Africa. "Go we must," he wrote in 1852. "To remain here in North America and be crushed to the earth in vassalage and degradation, we never will."

On several occasions, black northerners fought to defend their rights. In September 1851, Edward Gorsuch, a Maryland slaveholder, went to Christiana, Pennsylvania, where two of his escaped slaves were living. A fugitive slave named William Parker had organized the town's black community to defend against such an incident. Gorsuch located the two fugitives in a house occupied by Parker and a dozen other armed black men. Another 50 black people and some white people arrived and surrounded Gorsuch, his son, two other relatives, two neighbors, and a federal marshal. Gun-

CAUTION!!

COLORED PEOPLE OF BOSTON, ONE & ALL,

You are hereby respectfully CAUTIONED and advised, to avoid conversing with the Watchmen and Police Officers of Boston,

For since the recent ORDER OF THE MAYOR & ALDERMEN, they are empowered to act as

KIDNAPPERS AND Slave Catchers,

And they have already been actually employed in KIDNAPPING, CATCHING, AND KEEPING SLAVES. Therefore, if you value your LIBERTY, and the *Welfare of the Fugitives* among you, *Shun* them in every possible manner, as so many *HOUNDS* on the track of the most unfortunate of your race.

Keep a Sharp Look Out for KIDNAPPERS, and have TOP EYE open.

APRIL 24, 1851.

The Fugitive Slave Act threatened the freedom of escaped slaves living in the North, and even of free black northerners. This notice, typical of warnings posted in northern cities, urged Boston's African-American population to take precautions.

fire erupted, wounding both Gorsuch and his son. As the elder Gorsuch lay on the ground, a group of black women "rushed from the house with corn cutters and scythe blades [and] hacked the bleeding and lifeless body."

How much of this militancy filtered down to slaves in the South is difficult to say. Slaveholders detected an increase in black resistance during the early 1850s, a white Virginian noting in 1852 "it is useless to disguise the fact, its truth is undeniable, that a greater degree of insubordination has been manifested by the negro population within the last few months, than at any previous period in our history as a state."

Uncle Tom's Cabin

Sectional controversy over the Fugitive Slave Act was relatively modest compared to the firestorm ignited by abolitionist writer Harriet Beecher Stowe with the publication of a novel about southern slavery. *Uncle Tom's Cabin,* which first appeared in serial form in 1851, moved many northern white people from the sidelines of the sectional conflict to more active participation.

At the beginning of *Uncle Tom's Cabin,* a Kentucky slave owner is reluctantly forced by financial ruin to sell some of his slaves. Among them are the son of two mulatto slaves, George and Eliza Harris, and an older slave, Tom. Eliza escapes across the ice-choked Ohio River, clutching her son to her breast as slave catchers and their bloodhounds pursue them. Tom submits to sale to a New Orleans master. When that master dies, Tom is sold to Simon Legree, who owns a plantation on the Red River in Louisiana. Legree is vicious and sadistic, the only major slaveholding character in the book whom Stowe portrays in this manner. Tom, a devout Christian, remains loyal and obedient until Legree asks him to whip another slave. When Tom refuses, Legree beats him to death. Legree, incidentally, is from Vermont. Aiming to evoke strong emotions in the reader, Stowe offered not abstractions but characters that seemed real. The broken family, the denial of freedom, and the Christian martyr were emotional themes. The presence of mulattoes in the book testified to widespread interracial and extramarital sex, which northerners, then in the midst of a religious revival, viewed as an abhorrent sin destructive to family life. And the depiction of southern masters struggling unsuccessfully with their consciences focused public attention on how slavery subverted Christianity.

Uncle Tom's Cabin created a sensation in the United States and abroad. The book sold 10,000 copies in its first week and 300,000 within a year. By the time of the Civil War, it had sold an unprecedented 3 million copies in the United States and tens of thousands more in Europe. Stowe's book gave slavery a face; it changed people's moral perceptions about the institution in an era of deep Protestant piety; it was a Sermon on the Mount for a generation of northerners seeking witness for their Christianity and a crusade on behalf of their faith. It transformed abolitionism, bringing the movement, whose extreme rhetoric many northerners had previously viewed with disapproval, to the edge of respectability.

For southerners, *Uncle Tom's Cabin* was a damnable lie, a political tract disguised as literature. One southerner denounced the book as a "criminal prostitution of the high functions of the imagination to the pernicious intrigues of sectional animosity." Some southerners retaliated with crude plays and books of their own. In these versions of slavery, no slave families were broken up, no slaves were killed, and all masters were models of Christian behavior. Few northerners, however, read these southern responses. The writers penned them more to convince fellow southerners that slavery was necessary and good than to change opinions in the North.

Black northerners embraced *Uncle Tom's Cabin.* Frederick Douglass's National Black Convention resolved that the book was "a work plainly marked by the finger of God" on behalf of black people. Some black people hoped that the book's popularity would highlight the hypocrisy of white northerners who were quick to perceive evil in the South but were often blind to discrimination against African Americans in the North. Despite reactions to Stowe's book, how-ever, black northerners continued to face voting restrictions, segregation, and official harassment.

The Election of 1852

While the nation was reading and reacting to *Uncle Tom's Cabin,* a presidential election campaign took place. The Compromise of 1850 had divided the Whigs deeply. Northern Whigs perceived it as a capitulation to southern slaveholding interests and refused to support the renomination of President Millard Fillmore. Many southern Whigs, angered by the suspicions and insults of their erstwhile northern colleagues, abandoned the party. Although the Whigs nominated Mexican War hero and Virginian Winfield Scott for president, few southern Whigs viewed the nonslaveholding general as a friend of their region.

The Democratic Party entered the campaign more united. Despite reservations, the northern and southern wings of the party both announced their support for the Compromise of 1850. Southern Democrats viewed the party's nominee, Franklin Pierce of New Hampshire, as safe on the slavery issue despite his New England heritage. Pierce satisfied northerners as a nationalist devoted to the idea of Manifest Destiny. He belonged to Young America, a mostly Democratic group that advocated extending American influence into Central and South America and the Caribbean

An advertisement for *Uncle Tom's Cabin.* The book became a worldwide best-seller illuminating the tragedy of slavery in its corruption of family, human dignity, and Christianity.

with an aggressive foreign policy. His service in the Mexican War and his good looks and charm won over doubters from both sections.

Given the disarray of the Whigs and the relative unity of the Democrats, the election results were predictable. Pierce won overwhelmingly with 254 electoral votes to Scott's 42. But Pierce's landslide victory could not obscure the deep fissures in the American party system. The Whigs, although they would continue to run local candidates through the rest of the 1850s, were finished as a national party. And the Democrats, despite their electoral success, emerged frayed from the election. In the Lower South, conflicts within the party between supporters and opponents of the Compromise of 1850 had overshadowed the contests between Democrats and Whigs. Southern Democrats had wielded great influence at the party's nominating convention and dominated party policy, clouding its prospects in the North. During the election, much of the party's support in the North had come from the first-time votes of mainly Catholic immigrants. But the growing political influence of Catholics alarmed evangelical Protestants of both parties, thus adding religious bigotry to the divisive issues undermining the structure of the national parties.

Political Realignment

The conflicts over slavery and religion wrecked the Second American Party system. The Whigs disintegrated, though remnants persisted in several states and localities, and the Democrats became more Southern and more closely identified with immigrants, especially Roman Catholics. The Republicans, a new party, combined the growing anti-slavery and anti-southern sentiment in the North with religious nativism. Whether America would dissolve into warring factions over slavery or sectarian strife was anyone's guess in the mid-1850s. Eventually, the issue of slavery overwhelmed ethnic and religious concerns.

Franklin Pierce hoped to duck the slavery issue by focusing on Young America's dreams of empire. But his attempts to forge national sentiment around an aggressive foreign policy failed. And his administration's inept handling of a new territorial controversy in Kansas forced him to confront the slavery debate.

As Missouri senator Thomas Hart Benton, a Democrat, had realized during the debates over the Wilmot Proviso in 1848, no matter what policies a president pursued, Congress and the American people would interpret them in the light of their impact, real or potential, on slavery. The issue, said Benton, was like the plague of frogs that God had inflicted on the Egyptians to convince them to release the Hebrews from bondage. "You could not look upon the table but there were frogs, you could not sit down at the banquet but there were frogs, you could not go to the bridal couch and lift the sheets but there were frogs!" So it was with "this black question, forever on the table, on the nuptial couch, everywhere!"

Franklin Pierce lacked the skilled leadership the times demanded. Troubled by alcoholism, worried about his chronically ill wife, and grief-stricken over the death of three young sons, Pierce presided weakly over the nation and increasingly deferred to proslavery interests.

Young America's Foreign Misadventures

Pierce's first missteps occurred in pursuit of Young America's foreign ambitions. The administration turned a greedy eye toward Spanish-ruled Cuba, just 90 miles off the coast of Florida. Spanish authorities were harassing American merchants exporting sugar from Cuba and the American naval vessels protecting the merchants' ships. Southerners supported an aggressive Cuba policy, seeing the island as a possible new slave state. And nationalists saw great virtue in replacing what they perceived as a despotic colonial regime with a democratic government under the guidance of the United States.

In October 1854, three American diplomats met in Ostend, Belgium, to discuss Cuba. It is not clear whether Pierce approved or even knew of their meeting, but the diplomats believed that they had the administration's blessing. One of them, the American minister to Spain, Pierre Soulé of Louisiana, was especially eager for the United States to acquire Cuba. The group composed a document on Cuba called the **Ostend Manifesto** that claimed that the island belonged "naturally to the great family of states of which the Union is the Providential Nursery." The implication was that Spain's control of Cuba was unnatural. The United States would offer to buy Cuba from Spain, but if Spain refused to sell, the authors warned, "by every law, human and Divine, we shall be justified in wresting it from Spain."

The Ostend Manifesto caused an uproar and embarrassed the Pierce administration when it became public. In the polite world of nineteenth-century diplomacy, it was a significant breach of etiquette. Other nations quickly denounced it as a "buccaneering document" and a "highwayman's plea." It provoked a similar reaction in the United States, raising suspicions in the North that the South was willing to provoke a war with Spain to expand the number of slaveholding states.

While Pierce fumbled in the area of foreign policy, Senator Stephen A. Douglas of Illinois was developing a national project that also promised to draw the country together, the construction of a transcontinental railroad and the settling of the land it traversed. The result was worse conflict and the first outbreak of sustained sectional violence.

Stephen Douglas's Railroad Proposal

Douglas, like many westerners, wanted a transcontinental railroad. He himself had a personal stake in railroad building in that he owned some Chicago real estate and speculated in western lands. Railroads and the people and business they carried drove up property values. But beyond personal gain, Douglas, the supreme nationalist, understood that a transcontinental railroad would tie the nation together. Not only would it physically link East and West, it would also help spread American democracy. In short, a transcontinental railroad made good economic and political sense.

Douglas had in mind a transcontinental route extending westward from Chicago through the Nebraska Territory. Unfortunately for his plans, Indians already occupied this region, many of them on land the U.S. government had set aside as Indian Territory and barred to white settlement. "How," Douglas complained, "are we to develop, cherish, and protect our immense interests and possessions on the Pacific with a vast wilderness 1,500 miles in breadth, filled with hostile savages, and cutting off all direct communication?" Removing the "Indian barrier" and establishing white government were "first steps," in the senator's view, toward a "tide of emigration and civilization."

Once again, and not for the last time, the federal government responded by reneging on earlier promises and forcing Indians to move. In 1853, President Pierce sent agents to convince the Indians in the northern part of the Indian Territory to cede land for the railroad.

With the Indian "obstacle" removed, Douglas sought congressional approval to establish a government for the Nebraska Territory. But southern senators defeated his proposal. They objected to it not only because it called for a northern rather than southern route for the transcontinental railroad but also because the new territory lay above the Missouri Compromise line and would enter the Union as yet another free state. Bowing to southern pressure, Douglas rewrote his bill and resubmitted it in January 1854. He predicted that the new bill would "raise a hell of a storm." He was right.

The Kansas-Nebraska Act

Douglas's Kansas-Nebraska Bill split the Nebraska Territory into two territories, Kansas and Nebraska, with the implicit understanding that Kansas would become a slave state and Nebraska a free state. Consistent with Douglas's belief in popular sovereignty, it left the actual decision on slavery to the residents of the territories. But because it allowed southerners to bring slaves into an area formerly closed to slavery, it repealed the Missouri Compromise (see Map 14–2).

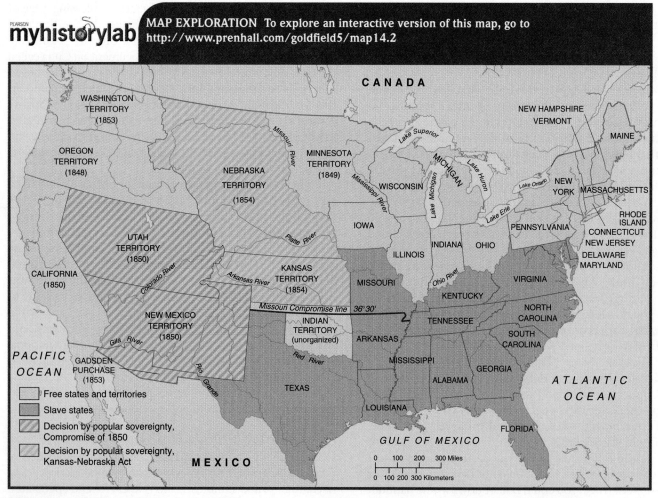

PEARSON
myhistorylab   MAP EXPLORATION To explore an interactive version of this map, go to
http://www.prenhall.com/goldfield5/map14.2

MAP 14–2   The Kansas Nebraska Act, 1854.
The Kansas-Nebraska Act of 1854, which divided the Nebraska Territory in two and repealed the Missouri Compromise, reopened the incendiary issue of slavery in the territories.

Northerners of all parties were outraged. The Missouri Compromise had endured for thirty-four years as a basis for sectional accord on slavery. Now it was threatened, northern leaders charged, by the South's unquenchable desire to spread slavery and expand its political power. In defense of the bill, Douglas claimed that it was unlikely that a majority in either territory would vote for slavery. But a group of northern leaders of Douglas's own Democratic Party countered vehemently that repealing the Missouri Compromise was more than a political maneuver. Using language indicative of the way religious and conspiratorial imagery had infected political debate, transforming it into a contest of good against evil, of liberty against oppression, they said it was "a gross violation of a sacred pledge," "a criminal betrayal of precious rights," and "part and parcel of an atrocious plot" to make a free territory a "dreary region of despotism, inhabited by masters and slaves." President Pierce, however, backed the bill, assuring the support of enough northern Democrats to secure it a narrow victory. The **Kansas-Nebraska Act** was law.

In August 1854, shortly after Congress adjourned, Douglas left Washington for his home in Chicago, to rest and mend political fences. He did not enjoy a pleasant journey home. "I could travel," he later recalled, "... by the light of my own effigy on every tree we passed." Arriving in Chicago, he addressed a large hostile crowd outside his hotel balcony. As he departed, he lost his temper and blurted, "It is now Sunday morning. I'll go to church; you can go to hell."

"Bleeding Kansas"

Because of its fertile soil, favorable climate, and location adjacent to the slave state of Missouri, Kansas was the most likely of the new territories to support slavery. As a result, both southerners and antislavery northerners began an intensive drive to recruit settlers and establish a majority there. Speaking for the antislavery forces, William H. Seward said in the Senate, "We will engage in competition for the virgin soil of Kansas, and God give this victory to the side which is strong in numbers as it is in right." South Carolina editor Robert Barnwell Rhett accepted the challenge, urging fellow southerners to "send men to Kansas, ready to cast in their lot with the proslavery part there and able to meet Abolitionism on its own issue, and with its own weapons."

As proslavery residents of Missouri poured into Kansas, antislavery organizations funded and armed their own migrants. In March 1855, proslavery forces, relying on the ineligible votes of Missouri residents, fraudulently elected a territorial legislature. This legislature promptly passed a series of harsh measures, including a law mandating the death penalty for aiding a fugitive slave and another making it a felony to question slaveholding in Kansas. For good measure, the proslavery majority expelled the few free-staters elected to the assembly. In response, free-staters established their own government in Topeka and vowed to make Kansas white.

A sporadic civil war erupted in Kansas in November 1855 and reached a climax in the spring of 1856. Journalists dubbed the conflict **"Bleeding Kansas."** On May 21, a group of proslavery officials attacked the free-state stronghold of Lawrence, subjecting it to a heavy artillery barrage. No one was killed, but the town suffered substantial damage. Eastern newspapers, exaggerating the incident, called it "the sack of Lawrence." Three days later, antislavery agitator John Brown, originally from Connecticut, went with several sympathizers to Pottawatomie Creek south of Lawrence in search of proslavery settlers. Armed with razor-sharp broadswords, they split the skulls and hacked the bodies of five men.

The memory of the failed revolutions in Europe remained fresh in the minds of Americans concerned about their own fragile democratic institutions. The disintegration of law and order on the Plains brought a foreboding recognition to many Americans. Indiana Congressman Schuyler Colfax compared the Kansas territorial legislature's proslavery statutes, "dictated and enacted by usurpers and tyrants," to Louis Napoleon's wresting of democracy from the French people and confirming his office with a fraudulent plebiscite: "the mockery of the pretended freedom of elections...the shackles upon the freedom of speech; all...emanate from an autocrat who...governs France with a strong arm and an iron rule." For increasing numbers of Northerners, the double outrage of a fraudulent election followed by severe legislation resembled more the despotism of restored regimes in Europe than the extension of American democracy.

Kansans were not the only Americans bleeding over slavery. Five days before the "sack of Lawrence," Massachusetts senator Charles Sumner delivered a longwinded diatribe, "The Crime Against Kansas," full of personal insults against several southerners, especially elderly South Carolina senator Andrew P. Butler. Two days after Sumner's outburst, and a day after the story of the sack of Lawrence appeared in the newspapers, Butler's cousin, South Carolina congressman Preston Brooks, entered the mostly vacant Senate chamber, where Sumner sat working on a speech. Seeking to defend his cousin's honor, Brooks raised his walking cane and beat Sumner over the head. Bloody and unconscious, the senator slumped to the floor. He recovered but did not return to the Senate for over three years. His empty chair offered northerners' mute confirmation of their growing conviction that southerners were despotic. Southerners showered Brooks with new walking canes.

Know-Nothings and Republicans: Religion and Politics

The Sumner incident, along with the Kansas-Nebraska Bill and the civil war in Kansas, further polarized North and South, widening sectional divisions within the political parties. Some northern Democrats distanced themselves from their party and looked for political alternatives; northern Whigs seized on changing public opinion to form new coalitions; and free-soil advocates gained new adherents. From 1854 to 1856, northerners moved into new political parties that altered the national political landscape and sharpened sectional conflict.

Although the slavery issue was mainly responsible for the party realignment in the North, other factors played a role as well. Nearly 3.5 million immigrants entered the United States between 1848 and 1860, the greatest influx in American history in proportion to the total population. Some of these newcomers, especially the Germans, were escaping failed democratic revolutions in Europe. They were predominantly middle-class Protestants who, along with the smaller number of German Catholics and Jews, settled mostly in the cities, where they established shops and other businesses. More than 1 million of the immigrants, however, were poor Irish Roman Catholics, fleeing their homeland to avoid starvation.

The Irish immigrants made their homes in northern cities, which were in the midst of Protestant revivals and reform. They also competed for jobs with native-born Protestant workers. Because the Irish would work for lower wages, the job competition bred animosity and sometimes violence. Culturally, the Irish held different views on keeping the Sabbath, and they preferred to send their children to separate sectarian schools. But it was their Roman Catholic religion that most concerned some urban Protestants, who associated Catholicism with despotism and immorality, the same evils they attributed to southerners. For their part, the Irish made it clear that they had little use for Protestant reform, especially temperance and abolitionism. The clash of cultures would soon further disturb a political environment increasingly in flux over the slavery issue.

New parties emerged from this cauldron of religious, ethnic, and sectional strife. Anti-immigrant, anti-Catholic sentiment gave rise to the **Know-Nothing Party,** which began as a secret organization in July 1854. Its name derived from the reply that members gave when asked about the party: "I know nothing." Although strongest in the North, Know-Nothing chapters blossomed in several southern cities that had experienced some immigration since 1848, among them Richmond, Louisville, New Orleans, and Savannah. The party's members in both North and South were mostly former Whigs. In addition to their biases against Catholics and foreigners, the Know-Nothings shared a fear that the slavery issue could destroy the Union. But because attempts to solve the issue seemed only to increase sectional tensions, the Know-Nothings hoped to ignore it.

Know-Nothing candidates fared surprisingly well in local and congressional elections during the fall of 1854, carrying 63 percent of the statewide vote in Massachusetts and making strong showings in New York and Pennsylvania. In office, Know-Nothings achieved some notable reforms. In Massachusetts, where they pursued an agenda similar to that of the Whigs in earlier years, they secured administrative reforms and supported public health and public education programs.

The Know-Nothings' anti-Catholicism, however, overshadowed their reform agenda. In several states and cities, they passed legislation barring Catholics from public office and unsuccessfully sought to increase the time required for an immigrant to become a citizen from one year to 21 years. The Know-Nothings also fostered anti-Catholic violence, such as the bloody election day riot that erupted in Louisville, Kentucky, in 1855. A few Know-Nothings called for drastic measures to restore order and preserve the integrity of the ballot box. William Brownlow, a Philadelphia editor, declared, "We can have no peace in this country until the CATHOLICS ARE EXTERMINATED."

Ethnic and religious bigotry were weak links to hold together a national party. Southern and northern Know-Nothings soon fell to quarreling over slavery despite their vow to avoid it, and the party split. Many northern Know-Nothings soon found a congenial home in the new **Republican Party.** The Republican Party formed in the summer of 1854 from a coalition of antislavery Conscience Whigs and Democrats disgusted with the Pierce administration's Kansas policy. Like the Know-Nothings, the Republicans advocated strong state and federal governments to promote economic and social reforms. But the new party did not espouse the Know-Nothings' anti-Catholic and anti-immigrant positions. The overriding bond among Republicans was their opposition to the extension of slavery in the territories.

Reflecting its opposition to slavery, the Republican Party was an antisouthern sectional party. Northern Whig merchants and entrepreneurs who joined the party were impatient with southern obstruction in Congress of federal programs for economic development, such as a transcontinental railroad, harbor and river improvements, and high tariffs to protect American industries (located mostly in the North) from foreign competition. In a bid to keep slavery out of the territories, the Republicans favored limiting homesteads in the West to 160 acres. Not incidentally, populating the territories with northern whites would ensure a western base for the new party.

Heightened sectional animosity laced with religious and ethnic prejudice fueled the emergence of new parties and the weakening of old political affiliations in the early 1850s. Accompanying the political realignment were diverging views on the proper role of government. As the nation prepared for the presidential election of 1856, the Democrats had become a party top-heavy with southerners; the Know-Nothings splintered along sectional lines; some Whigs remained active under the old party name, mainly on the state and local levels in North and South; and the Republican Party was becoming an important political force in the North and, to southerners, the embodiment of evil.

The Election of 1856

The presidential election of 1856 proved to be one of the strangest in American history. The Know-Nothings and the Republicans faced a national electorate for the first time while the Democrats were deeply divided over the Kansas issue.

The upstart Republicans held their convention in Philadelphia in mid-July. The platform condemned the "twin relics of barbarism"—slavery and polygamy. There was no epidemic, current or pending, of men and women seeking multiple partners. But, as everyone understood at the time, the Mormons in Utah Territory espoused, though did not require, polygamy. Memories of Mormon settlements in the Midwest and the turmoil they generated remained fresh in the minds of residents in a region where Republicans hoped to pick up significant support. While anti-southern sentiment varied, few voters were sympathetic to the Mormons.

Polygamy was also a code word to mid-nineteenth-century Americans, especially to northerners and especially when paired with slavery. Polygamy attacked traditional family relations, as did slavery. The pairing of slavery and polygamy also highlighted the threat of both to a modern America, a nation devoted to progress, technology, and self-improvement. These "relics of barbarism" harked back to a dark past when superstition and dependence limited mankind's achievements. They were, in a word, un-American, at least the America envisioned by the new party and its followers.

The Republicans passed over their most likely candidate, the New York senator and former Whig William H. Seward. Instead, they followed a tried-and-true Whig precedent and nominated a military hero, John C. Frémont, a handsome, dark-haired soldier of medium height and medium intelligence. His wife, Jessie Benton, the daughter of Missouri senator Thomas Hart Benton, was his greatest asset. In effect, she ran the campaign and wisely encouraged her husband to remain silent. The Know-Nothings split into "South Americans" and "North Americans." The South Americans nominated Millard Fillmore, although he was not a Know-Nothing. The North Americans eventually and reluctantly embraced Frémont, despite the widespread but mistaken belief that he was a Roman Catholic.

The Democrats, facing a Northern revolt and Southern opposition to any candidate who did not support the extension of slavery, turned to Pennsylvania's James Buchanan whose greatest virtue was that he had been out of the country the previous four years as Ambassador to Great Britain. Southerners accepted him as electable and sensitive to slavery. Northern Democrats hoped for the best. Tall and white-haired, he exuded the air of experience, though he looked like a "well-preserved mummy." Whether he would preside over the nation as a competent veteran or as a cadaver well beyond his time remained to be seen.

Democratic Party strategy in the North focused on shoring up their immigrant base by connecting the Republicans to the Know-Nothings and simultaneously appealing to evangelical Protestants by intimating that Frémont had received a Catholic education, had studied for the priesthood, or was himself a Roman Catholic secretly attending mass and "going through all the crosses and gyrations, and eating wafers," take your pick. Democratic papers cried out that Frémont was "*the instrument of vice, and the foe of God and of Freedom.*" They edited the Republicans slogan, "Free Soil and Frémont," to "Free Love and Frémont." The Democrats played both sides of the religious divide because the sectional crisis had energized Northern Protestant churches.

The importance of evangelical imagery in the political campaigns of the major parties was especially evident among the Republicans. A participant in the party convention likened the party platform to "God's revealed Word," and a minister supporting the Republican ticket saw the election as "as a decisive struggle…between freedom and Slavery, truth and falsehood, justice and oppression, God and the devil."

Away from the pulpit, Republican campaigners sometimes found tough going in the North, indicating how much the slavery extension debate had overtaken sectarian issues. A portion of the Northern electorate viewed the Republican Party as a gilded version of the radical anti-slavery parties of the 1840s, promoting racial equality and emancipation to the detriment of whites.

James Buchanan emerged victorious. The only national party had won a national election. The Democrats did it by holding the lower North as Pennsylvania, New Jersey, Illinois, Indiana, and California voted for Buchanan, and sweeping the Lower South. But "Old Buck's" victory was narrow in these Northern states; the Republicans performed remarkably well considering it was the first time they had fielded a presidential candidate. They had achieved a "victorious defeat," making Buchanan the first candidate to win without carrying the North since 1828. Republicans eagerly looked forward to the next presidential contest and the good prospects of prying at least Pennsylvania, Indiana, and Illinois from the Democratic column. For the first time ever, an avowedly antislavery party had carried eleven free states.

The South had not yet lapsed into one-party politics. Millard Fillmore garnered 40 percent of the popular vote in the South, but won only the state of Maryland. He fared poorly in the Lower South. The states that had the greatest stake in the slave economy voted solidly Democratic.

Buchanan, who brought more than a generation of political experience to the presidency, would need every bit and more. He had scarcely settled into office when two major crises confronted him: a Supreme Court decision that challenged the right of Congress to regulate slavery in the territories and renewed conflict over Kansas.

The Dred Scott Case

Dred Scott was a slave owned by an army surgeon based in Missouri. In the 1830s and early 1840s, he had traveled with his master to the state of Illinois and the Wisconsin Territory before returning to Missouri. In 1846, Scott sued his master's widow for freedom on the grounds that the laws of Illinois and the Wisconsin Territory barred slavery. After a series of appeals, the case reached the Supreme Court. Chief

Justice Roger Taney of Maryland, joined by five other justices of the nine-member Supreme Court (five of whom came from slave states), dismissed Scott's suit two days after Buchanan's inauguration in March 1857.

Taney's opinion contained two bombshells. First, using dubious logic and failing to take into account the status of African Americans in several northern states, he argued that black people were not citizens of the United States. Because Scott was not a citizen, he could not sue. In reaching this conclusion, Taney noted that the framers of the Constitution had never intended citizenship for slaves. The framers, according to Taney, respected a long-standing view that slaves were "beings of an inferior order…so far inferior that they had no rights which the white man was bound to respect."

Second, Taney held that even if Scott had standing in court, his residence in the Wisconsin Territory did not make

Dred Scott and his wife, Harriet, are portrayed here with their children as an average middle-class family, an image that fueled northern opposition to the Supreme Court's 1857 decision that denied Scott's freedom and citizenship.

him a free man. This was because the Missouri Compromise, which was still in effect in the 1840s, was, in Taney's view, unconstitutional. (The Wisconsin Territory lay above the compromise line.) The compromise, the chief justice explained, deprived citizens of their property (slaves) without the due process of law granted by the Fifth Amendment to the U.S. Constitution. In effect, Taney ruled that Congress could not bar slavery from the territories.

The **Dred Scott Decision** was especially unsettling to the tens of thousands of free blacks throughout the country, especially in the South. The Court, in stripping their citizenship, made them vulnerable to re-enslavement or expulsion. Southern states feared the collaboration of the mostly urban free black population with slaves, and white workers disliked competing with them for jobs. Virginia, North Carolina, and Missouri in 1858 debated offering free blacks the "choice" of expulsion or enslavement. Nothing came of these proposals, but their debate caused many free blacks to leave the South for Canada. The case also accelerated restrictions on the Southern free black population as its legal recourse vanished with the decision. Several cities, including Charleston, experimented with requirements that free blacks purchase and wear badges identifying them as free.

For African Americans, the enemy was no longer the slaveholder, but the very government from which they had hoped for redress. As the State Convention of Ohio Colored Men concluded in 1858, "that if the Dred Scott dictum be the true exposition of the law of the land, then are the founders of the American Republic convicted by their descendants of base hypocrisy, and colored men absolved from all allegiance to a government which withdraws all protection."

The decision also shocked Republicans. The right of Congress to ban slavery from the territories, which Taney had apparently voided, was one of the party's central tenets. Republicans responded by ignoring the implications of the decision for the territories while promising to abide by it so far as it affected Dred Scott himself. Once in office, Republicans vowed, they would seek a reversal. This position allowed them to attack the decision without appearing to defy the law.

The Dred Scott decision boosted Republican fortunes in the North even as it seemed to undercut the party. Fears of a southern Slave Power conspiracy now seemed ever more justified. If Congress could not ban slavery from the territories, Republicans asked, how secure was the right of states to ban slavery within their borders? A small group of slaveholders, they charged, was holding nonslaveholding white people hostage to the institution of slavery.

A few addenda to the case: John Sandford, the executor of Dred Scott's deceased master's estate, died in an insane asylum shortly after the decision. His master's widow, who had refused to allow Dred Scott to purchase his freedom, moved to Massachusetts, married an anti-slavery Congressman, and transferred ownership of Scott to the son of his original owner who promptly manumitted both Scott and his wife on May 26, 1857. Dred Scott died one year later.

The Lecompton Constitution

Establishing a legitimate government in Kansas was the second major issue to bedevil the Buchanan administration. The president made a good start, sending his friend and fellow Pennsylvanian Robert Walker (then a resident of Mississippi) to Kansas as territorial governor to oversee the election of a constitutional convention in June 1857. Walker, though sickly, was a man of integrity.

The violence had subsided in Kansas, and prospects had grown for a peaceful settlement. But free-staters, fearing that the slavery forces planned to stuff the ballot box with fraudulent votes, announced a boycott of the June election. As a result, proslavery forces dominated the constitutional convention, which was held in Lecompton. And Walker, although a slaveholder, let it be known that he thought Kansas would never be a slave state. He thus put himself at odds with proslavery residents from the outset.

Walker persuaded the free-staters to vote in October to elect a new territorial legislature. The returns gave the proslavery forces a narrow victory, but Walker discovered irregularities. In McGee, Kansas, 20 voters somehow had cast 1,200 votes for proslavery candidates. And in Oxford, a community of a mere six houses, 1,601 names appeared on the voting rolls, all in the same handwriting and all copied from the Cincinnati city directory. Walker threw out these returns, and the free-staters took control of the territorial legislature for the first time.

Undeterred, the proslavery forces drafted a proslavery constitution at the constitutional convention in Lecompton. Buchanan, who had promised southerners a proslavery government in Kansas, dismissed Walker before he could rule on the **Lecompton Constitution,** then ignored the recommendation of Walker's successor that he reject it. He submitted the Lecompton Constitution to the Senate for approval even though it clearly sidestepped the popular sovereignty requirement of the Kansas-Nebraska Act.

Like the Kansas-Nebraska Act, the Lecompton Constitution outraged many northerners. The proslavery Kansans behind the constitution had a record of fraud, and Buchanan's own appointee had advised him against it. Northern Democrats facing reelection refused to support a president of their own party, and, though the constitution passed in the Senate, Democratic opposition killed it in the House. Among Lecompton's opponents was Stephen A. Douglas, who justified his vote with an impassioned defense of popular sovereignty, which the president and proslavery Kansans had openly defied. Congress admitted Kansas to the Union as a free state in January 1861.

Douglas knew that the Dred Scott decision and Buchanan's support of the Lecompton Constitution would help the Republicans and hurt him and his fellow northern

Democrats in the 1858 congressional elections. The **Panic of 1857,** a severe economic recession that lingered into 1858, also worked to the advantage of the Republicans. Wild speculation in western lands and railroads had infested the centers of financial power. Was not progress unending? Was not gold flowing from California? Never mind that railroad stock existed on paper, with the railroads themselves present only in the dreams of promoters. A ship sank carrying millions in gold bullion from California. A bank failed. Then others began to call in loans, and the call fell on deaf ears. British banks withdrew their funds from New York banks. Manufacturers could not find credit as lenders closed their books, and then their doors. Workers were dismissed and the misery mounted.

The economic downturn not only cost jobs and deepened urban poverty, it shattered the confidence of the flamboyant fifties, when progress seemed limitless and when God appeared on the streets, within men, and across the American continent ratifying the deeds of His chosen people; an era when steam engines conquered time and space, and when the Western rivers and rocks offered up untold treasures, and when a few dollars down today yielded a fortune tomorrow. America was transcendent, transcending the Western tribes, the prideful slaveholder, the culture-bound Catholic. But the rising misery of the winter of 1857–1858 crashed the party and sent stocks and confidence tumbling one after the other. As sometimes happens, one bad event highlights other bad events generating a collective accounting that eventually transforms reality into something different from what existed just yesterday.

The political system apparently was as diseased as the economy. Allegations of widespread corruption, incompetence, and collusion saturated the press. Poet Walt Whitman was furious that the political process had served up "swarms of cringers, suckers, doughfaces, lice, ..." Add another concern to the general feeling that American political institutions were indeed fragile. And just as the Panic of 1857 eroded the confidence of Americans in the inevitability of their progress and prosperity, the political events of that year shook many Americans' trust in their government. Political leaders seemed to compromise two basic principles of American democracy: an independent judiciary and the sanctity of majority rule.

The Democratic administration did nothing as unemployment rose; starvation stalked the streets of northern cities, and homeless women and children begged for food and shelter. Republicans claimed that government intervention, specifically, Republican-sponsored legislation to raise certain tariffs, give western land to homesteaders, and fund transportation projects, if passed by Congress, could have prevented the panic. The Democrats' inaction, they said, reflected the southern Slave Power's insensitivity to northern workers.

Southerners disagreed. The panic had scarcely touched them. Cotton prices were high, and few southern banks failed. Cotton seemed indeed to be king. The financial crisis in the North reinforced the southern belief that northern society was corrupt and greedy. The Republicans' proposed legislative remedies, in their view, would enrich the North and beggar the South.

The Religious Revival of 1857–1858

In the midst of economic depression and sectional controversy, a religious revival swept across the nation's cities in the winter of 1857–1858. Beginning with lunchtime prayer meetings among businessmen in New York City, the phenomenon spread throughout the country, though concentrating in the larger urban centers of the Northeast. The sectional crisis and the economic downturn had a part in bringing urban middle-class men into churches and meeting halls at the noon hour, but the gatherings emphasized prayer and personal reflection, avoiding political discussion and focusing on individual redemption. Sectional strife had diverted attention from personal salvation, and the financial panic served as a reminder that wealth and possessions could be fleeting, but the soul was everlasting. Ministers and lay leaders of the movement encouraged men to turn away from the reform "isms" of the era—feminism, abolitionism, and socialism among them. Men, they suggested, should not worship secular ideologies, but should make the Bible the foundation of their behavior and thought. And they should reestablish their leadership both in spiritual and family matters.

Although the revival peaked by the spring of 1858, its long-range impact was significant. The event marked the first major national forum for the Young Men's Christian Association (YMCA), an organization dedicated to improving the spiritual life of urban men. The "Y" would play a significant role in organizing religious services and distributing sacred literature to Union troops during the Civil War. The revival also provided an early opportunity for a young Chicago minister, D. L. Moody, to hone his evangelical skills. After the Civil War, Moody became the nation's first prominent evangelist, preaching to immense crowds and offering a message that transcended individual Protestant denominations.

Finally, the revival highlighted the growing importance of the urban middle class in the cultural and religious life of the nation. The outpouring of religious sentiment would leave a lasting impression on the men, especially the young men who had now found a soul in the city and a group of likeminded fellows as friends. The scripted prayer meetings fell away, but the spiritual rebirth did not. Religion provided not only solace but also explanations for a time beset by increasing uncertainty. The revival did not change society dramatically any more than it pulled the nation out of the economic doldrums. But now with each turn in the political arena many more people, not only the fervent evangelicals, came to understand that these mere events held transcendent meaning.

Some feared that the growing integration of religion and politics could harm the nation's religious life and burden the political process with sharper divisions than were necessary. But by 1858, it became increasingly difficult to distinguish the political from the spiritual. The Illinois senatorial contest between Democrat Stephan A. Douglas and Abraham Lincoln of the Republican Party proved a case in point. Their debates underscored the moral dimensions of political questions and the resulting difficulties of effecting compromises.

The Lincoln-Douglas Debates

Douglas faced a forceful opponent in his 1858 reelection campaign. The Republicans had nominated Abraham Lincoln, a 49-year-old lawyer and former Whig congressman. The Kentucky-born Lincoln had risen from modest circumstances to become a prosperous lawyer in the Illinois state capital of Springfield. His marriage to wealthy and well-connected Mary Todd helped both his law practice and his pocketbook. After one term in Congress from 1847 to 1849, he returned to his law practice but maintained his interest in politics. Strongly opposed to the extension of slavery into the territories, he considered joining the Republican Party after the passage of the Kansas-Nebraska Act. Lincoln had developed a reputation as an excellent stump speaker with a homespun sense of humor, a quick wit, and a self-deprecating style that fit well with the small-town residents and farmers who composed the majority of the Illinois electorate.

But substance counted more than style with Illinois voters. Most of them opposed the extension of slavery into the territories, although generally not out of concern for the slaves. Illinois residents, like most northerners, wanted to keep the territories free for white people. Few voters would support dissolving the Union over the slavery issue. Douglas, who knew his constituents well, branded Lincoln a dangerous radical for warning, in a biblical paraphrase, that the United States, like "a house divided against itself," could not "endure permanently half slave and half free."

Lincoln could not allow the charge of radicalism to go unanswered. Little known beyond the Springfield area, he had to find a way to gain greater exposure. So, in July 1858, he challenged Douglas to a series of debates across the state. Douglas was reluctant to provide exposure for his lesser-known opponent, but he could not reject Lincoln's offer outright, lest voters think he was dodging his challenger. He agreed to debates in seven of the state's nine congressional districts.

The **Lincoln-Douglas debates** were a defining event in American politics. Farmers rode into such market towns as Ottawa, Galesburg, Alton, and Freeport, bringing their families and picnic baskets. They settled in their wagons or on the ground under trees to hear the two great debaters confront each other on the most troubling issue of the day. What a sight it must have been, the stubby-legged, animated, barrel-chested Little Giant engaging the gangly, deliberate former rail-splitter, Abe Lincoln.

For Douglas, slavery was not a moral issue. What mattered was what white people wanted. If they wanted slavery,

Abraham Lincoln making a point at Coles County (Illinois) Fairgrounds, 1858. His U.S. Senate opponent, Stephen A. Douglas, sitting at Lincoln's right, waits his turn. The Lincoln-Douglas debates captivated Illinois voters, who turned out in great numbers to witness the rhetorical fireworks.

fine; if they did not, fine also. Lincoln and many Republicans had a very different view. For them, slavery was a moral issue. As such, it was independent of what the residents of a territory wanted. In the final Lincoln-Douglas debate, Lincoln turned to his rival and explained: "The real issue in this controversy... is the sentiment on the part of one class that looks upon the institution of slavery *as a wrong,* and of another class that does not look upon it as a wrong.... The Republican party...look[s] upon it as being a moral, social and political wrong...and one of the methods of treating it as a wrong is to make provision that it shall grow no larger....That is the real issue....It is the eternal struggle between these two principles, right and wrong, throughout the world."

Lincoln not only identified the cause of the Republican Party with the forces of liberty and freedom all over the world, but also framed the debate as a contest between good and evil. Evangelical rhetoric had pervaded political discourse for nearly two decades. But coming on the heels of a national religious revival, Lincoln's assertion reinforced the perception that the nation was approaching a crossroads, not only a secular divide, but a battle that could determine the future of mankind for eternity: "As I view the contest, it is not less than a contest for the advancement of the kingdom of Heaven or the kingdom of Satan." The difficulty with raising the stakes of an election so high is that it threatened to polarize the electorate so that one side or the other could find the results of a democratic election totally unacceptable. For how do you compromise with the devil?

Lincoln tempered his moralism with practical politics. He took care to distance himself from the abolitionists, asserting that he abided by the Constitution and did not seek to interfere in places where slavery existed. At Charleston, Illinois, the site of the fourth debate, Lincoln stated, "I am not, nor ever have been, in favor of bringing about in any way the social and political equality of the white and black race, that I am not nor ever have been in favor of making voters or jurors of negroes, nor of qualifying them to hold office, nor to intermarry with white people; and I will say in addition to this that there is a physical difference between the white and black races which I believe will forever forbid the two races living together on terms of social and political equality." Historians have pondered over the seeming contradictions between these remarks and the statements he made during other debates and would make in the coming years on slavery and African Americans generally.

Lincoln, like most Republicans, hated the institution of slavery, but held ambivalent views about African Americans. These views would change in time, sometimes prodded by events, other times by thought and prayer. About slavery, there was little ambiguity in his position, even if he tried to project a moderate image on the campaign trail. Privately, he prayed for its demise. To Lincoln, slavery was immoral, but inequality was not. The Republican Party was antislavery, but it did not advocate racial equality.

Illinois voters retained a narrow Democratic majority in the state legislature, which reelected Douglas to the U.S. Senate. (State legislatures elected senators until 1913, when the Seventeenth Amendment provided for direct election by the people.) But Douglas alienated southern Democrats with his strong defense of popular sovereignty and lost whatever hope he had of becoming the standard-bearer of a united Democratic Party in 1860. Lincoln lost the senatorial contest but won national respect and recognition.

Despite Lincoln's defeat in Illinois, the Republicans made a strong showing in the 1858 congressional elections across the North. The increased Republican presence and the sharpening sectional divisions among Democrats portended a bitter debate over slavery in the new Congress. Americans, more than ever before, were viewing issues and each other in sectional terms. *Northern* and *southern* took on meanings that expressed a great deal more than geography.

The Road to Disunion

The unsatisfying Compromise of 1850, "Bleeding Kansas" and "Bleeding Sumner," the *Dred Scott* case, and Lecompton convinced many northerners that southerners were conspiring with the federal government to restrict their political and economic liberties. Southerners saw these same events as evidence of a northern conspiracy to reduce the South's political and economic influence. There were no conspiracies, but with so little goodwill on either side, hostility predominated. Slavery, above all, accounted for the growing divide.

In 1859 abolitionist John Brown, who had avenged the "sack of Lawrence" in 1856, led a raid against a federal arsenal at Harpers Ferry, Virginia, in the vain hope of sparking a slave revolt. This event brought the frustrations of both sides of the sectional conflict to a head. The presidential election campaign of 1860 began before the uproar over the raid had subsided. In the course of that contest, one of the last nationally unifying institutions, the Democratic Party, broke apart. The election of Abraham Lincoln, a sectional candidate, triggered a crisis that defied peaceful resolution.

Although the crisis spiraled into a civil war, this outcome did not signal the triumph of sectionalism over nationalism. Ironically, in defending their stands, both sides appealed to time-honored nationalist and democratic sentiments. Southern secessionists believed they were the true keepers of the ideals that had inspired the American Revolution. They were merely re-creating a more perfect Union. It was not they, but the Republicans, who had sundered the old Union by subverting the Constitution's guarantee of liberty. Lincoln similarly appealed to nationalist themes, telling northerners that the United States was "the last best hope on earth."

Objectively, northerners and southerners shared many things. They both believed in the American dream that hard work brought financial well-being and independence. Both regions harbored aspiring urban middle classes that looked to investments in their families and communities as down payments on a rosy future. Northerners and southerners chased after railroads, canals, harbor improvements, and real estate with the hope of something better. For all the urban hubbub, the hiss of steam engines, and the click-click of the telegraph, the family farm and the small shop occupied a majority of Americans, regardless of section.

Americans prayed in similar ways; theirs was a personal God, and they reached for heaven with the same fervor that they sought out the main chance of financial success. Northerners and southerners interpreted the world around them through their evangelical theology, that God had a purpose for them and their country, and that events, seemingly unconnected and sometimes obscure, all fit into a larger divine plan.

North and South shared a revolutionary heritage, what Abraham Lincoln would call the "mystic chords of memory." Northerners and southerners both prized the West, not only as the newest land, but also as the American dreamscape, a place of renewal and redemption. The expansionist, fever, manifest destiny, flared especially hot in the South, and if more sober Yankees scoffed at southern boasts of Mexican and Caribbean empires, southerners were merely perpetuating the tradition that had carried New Englanders westward across the Plains.

Northerners and southerners both appealed to nationalism and democracy but applied different meanings to these concepts. The differences underscored how far apart the sections had grown. When southerners and northerners looked at each other, they no longer saw fellow Americans; they saw enemies.

North-South Differences

Economic differences.   Behind the ideological divide that separated North and South lay real and growing social and economic differences (see the Overview Table, South and North Compared in 1860). As the North became increasingly urban and industrial, the South remained primarily rural and agricultural. The urban population of the free states increased from 10 to 26 percent between 1820 and 1860. In the South, in the same period, it increased only from 5 to 10 percent. Likewise the proportion of the northern workforce in agriculture declined from 68 percent to 40 percent between 1800 and 1860, whereas in the South it increased from 82 percent to 84 percent. Northern farmers made up for the decline in farm workers by relying on machinery. In 1860, the free states had twice the value of farm machinery per worker as the slave states.

The demand for farm machinery in the North reflected the growing demand for manufactured products in general. The need of city-dwellers for ready-to-wear shoes and clothing, household iron products, processed foods, homes, workplaces, and public amenities boosted industrial production in the North. In contrast, in the South, the slower rate of urbanization, the lower proportion of immigrants, and the region's labor-intensive agriculture kept industrial development modest. The proportion of U.S. manufacturing capital invested in the South declined from 31 to 16 percent between 1810 and 1860. In 1810, per capita investment in industrial enterprises was 2.5 times greater in the North than in the South; in 1860, it was 3.5 times greater.

The rate of urban and industrial growth in the North was greater than anywhere else in the world in the early nineteenth century. As a result, the South inevitably suffers by comparison. Even when compared to the West, however, the South was falling behind. The South and West had about the same levels of manufacturing investment and urban population in the 1850s, but the rate of growth was even greater in the West than in the North. What is more, a vast railroad network linked the West to the Northeast rather than to the South (see Map 14–3).

These economic developments generated communities of innovation in the North, especially in the rapidly expanding cities, where people traded ideas and technical information and skills. One of the most important innovations of the era was the telegraph, pioneered by Samuel F. B. Morse, who convinced the government to subsidize a line from Washington, DC, to Baltimore, Maryland, in 1843 and then electrified his patrons with instantaneous reports from the political party conventions of 1844. As information became a valuable currency for a new age, such improvements in communications and transportation tended to reinforce the economic dominance of the Northeast.

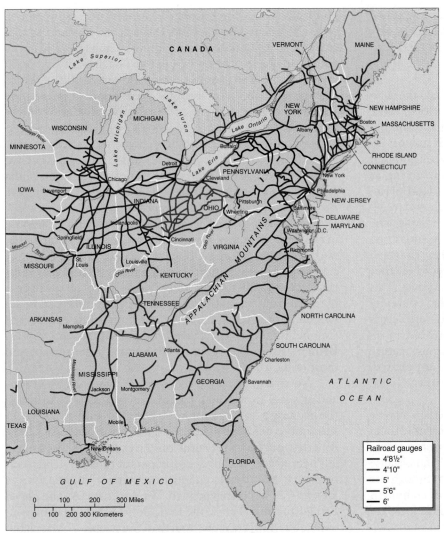

MAP 14–3   Railroads in the United States, 1860
A vast network of railroads honeycombed the North and West by 1860. While the South made considerable progress in railroad construction during the 1850s, its lines had many different gauges, and it lacked suitable connections to the West.

Social and religious differences.   More subtle distinctions between North and South became evident as well by midcentury. The South had a high illiteracy rate, nearly three times greater than the North, eight times greater if black southerners are included. The "ideology of literacy," as one historian called it, was not as widespread in the South as in the North. Northerners, for example, supported far more public schools and libraries than southerners. In the South, education was barred by law to slaves and limited for most white people. Many white leaders viewed education more as a privilege for the well-to-do than a right for every citizen. A South Carolinian wrote in the 1850s that "it is better that a part should be fully and highly educated and the rest utterly ignorant."

Evangelical Protestantism attracted increasing numbers in both North and South, but its character differed in the two regions. In the North, evangelical Protestants viewed so-

cial reform as a prerequisite for the Second Coming of Christ. As a result, they were in the forefront of most reform movements. Southern evangelicals generally defended slavery.

The effects of slavery.   Slavery accounted for many of the differences between the North and the South. Investment in land and slaves limited investment in manufacturing and railroads. The availability of a large slave labor force reduced the need for farm machinery and limited the demand for manufactured products. Slaves were relatively immobile. They did not migrate to cities in massive numbers as did northern farmers. Nor could they quickly fill the labor demands of an expanding urban economy. Agriculture usually took precedence.

Slavery also divided northern from southern churches. And it accounted for the contrast between the inward, otherworldly emphasis of southern theology and the reformist theology of northern evangelicals. Southerners associated black slavery with white freedom; northerners associated it with white degradation.

Slavery contributed to the South's martial tradition and its lukewarm attitude toward public education. Fully 95 percent of the nation's black population lived in the South in 1860, and 90 percent of these were slaves. As a result, the South was often a region on edge. Fearful of revolt, especially in the 1850s, when rumors of slave discontent ran rampant, white people felt compelled to maintain patrols and militias in constant readiness. The South was also determined to keep slaves as ignorant as possible. Educated slaves would be susceptible to abolitionist propaganda and more inclined to revolt.

The South's defense of slavery and the North's attack on it fostered an array of stereotypes that exaggerated the real differences between the sections. Like all stereotypes, these reduced individuals to dehumanized categories. They encouraged the people of each section to view those of the other less as fellow Americans than as aliens in their midst.

Southerners saw northerners as crass and materialistic but themselves as generous and compassionate. Northerners saw southerners as brutal and backward, themselves as progressive and temperate. Southerners perceived themselves as honorable and chaste and saw northerners as corrupt and loose living. Northerners saw southerners as perverse and lazy, themselves as righteous and hardworking. The South, according to southerners, was the land of moonlight and magnolias (an image that actually originated in the North), while the North was the region of muggings and mudslinging. Northerners saw southerners as lords of the lash and themselves as angels of mercy.

Ironically, although slavery increasingly defined the character of the South in the 1850s, a growing majority of white southerners did not own slaves. Slavery nonetheless implicated nonslaveholders in ways that ensured their support for it. By satisfying the demand for labor on large plantations, it relieved many rural white southerners from serving as farmhands and enabled them to work their own land. Slaveholders also recruited nonslaveholders to suppress slave violence or rebellion. It was nonslaveholders, for example, who often manned patrols and militia companies. Some nonslaveholders hoped to purchase slaves someday. Many dreamed of migrating westward to the next cotton frontier where they might find greater opportunity to own land and slaves. This dream not only bound white southerners together on slavery but also prompted their strong support for southern access to the western territories. Finally, regardless of a white man's social or economic status, he shared an important feature with the largest slaveholder: As long as racial slavery existed, the color of his skin made him a member of a privileged class that could never be enslaved.

While white southerners were more united on slavery than on other issues, their defense of slavery presented them with a major dilemma. By the 1850s, most Western nations had condemned and abolished the institution. And because northerners controlled the flow of information through the popular newspapers and the national network of communications, credit, and commerce, southerners were likely to find themselves increasingly isolated. A minority in their own country and a lonely voice for a despised institution that was for them a significant source of wealth, southerners were understandably jittery.

John Brown's Raid

Shortly after he completed his mayhem at Pottawatomie Creek, John Brown left Kansas and approached several New England abolitionists for funds to continue his private war in the territory. By 1857, Brown had become a rustic celebrity in New England. He had dined at Ralph Waldo Emerson's home, had tea with Henry David Thoreau, and discussed theology with the abolitionist minister Theodore Dwight Weld. Brown's frontier dress, rigid posture, reticent manner, and piercing eyes gave him the appearance of a biblical prophet. After several failed businesses, more than twenty lawsuits for nonpayment of debts, and a brush with horse rustling, he had at last found his life's calling: He had become a moderately successful fundraiser for his own violent frontier exploits.

But when Brown returned to Kansas in late 1857, he discovered that peace had settled over that troubled territory. Residents now cared more about making money than about

making war. Leaving Kansas for the last time, he went east with a new plan. He proposed to attack and capture the federal arsenal at Harpers Ferry, Virginia, a small town near the Maryland border. The assault, Brown imagined, would spark a slave uprising that would eventually spread to the rest of the state. With funds from his New England friends, he equipped a few dozen men and hired an English army officer to train them.

When Brown outlined his scheme to Frederick Douglass, the noted black abolitionist warned him against it. But his white New England friends were less cautious, and a group of six prominent abolitionists (the "Secret Six") gave Brown additional funds for his project.

Brown and his "army" moved to a Maryland farmhouse in the summer of 1859 to train and complete planning for the raid. On the night of October 16, 1859, he and 22 followers captured the federal arsenal at Harpers Ferry and waited for the slaves to rally to his banner. Meanwhile, the townspeople alerted outside authorities. The Virginia militia and a detachment of United States Marines under the command of Colonel Robert E. Lee arrived and put a quick end to **John Brown's Raid.** They wounded Brown and killed or captured most of his force.

Brown had launched the operation without provisions and at a site from which escape was impossible. Although the primary goal of the attack had been to inspire a slave insurrection, no one had bothered to inform the local slaves. And despite the secret nature of the expedition, Brown had left behind a mountain of documents at the Maryland farmhouse. He had tried to conquer the state of Virginia with 22 men and an ill-conceived plan. Was he crazy? As the *Boston Post* editorialized after the raid, "John Brown may be a lunatic, [but if so] then one-fourth of the people of Massachusetts are madmen."

Although the *Post* may have exaggerated, the editorial reflected an article of faith among many abolitionists that, given the signal, slaves would immediately throw off their chains, slaughter their masters, and join a rebellion. But even those slaves in the area who knew of the raid understood the odds against Brown and had the good sense not to join him. As Abraham Lincoln observed, "It was not a slave insurrection. It was an attempt by white men to get up a revolt among slaves, in which the slaves refused to participate."

The raid, though foolish and unsuccessful, played on southerners' worst fears of slave rebellion, adding a new dimension: Here was an attack engineered not from within the South but from the North. Some southern white people may have dismissed the ability or even the desire of slaves to mount revolts on their own, but they less easily dismissed the potential impact of outside white agitators. The state of Virginia tried Brown on the charge of treason to the state. Brown, recovering from his wounds, attended most of the trial on a stretcher. The trial was swift but fair. The jury sentenced Brown to hang. Throughout his brief imprisonment and trial, Brown maintained a quiet dignity that impressed

OVERVIEW

South and North Compared in 1860

	South	North
Population	Biracial; 35 percent African American	Overwhelmingly white; less than 2 percent African American
Economy	Growing, though relatively undiversified; 84 percent of workforce in agriculture	Developing through industrialization and urbanization; 40 percent of workforce in agriculture
Labor	Heavily dependent on slave labor, especially in Lower South	Free wage labor
Factories	15 percent of national total	85 percent of national total; concentrated in the Northeast
Railroads	Approximately 10,000 miles of track; primarily shorter lines, with fewer links to trunk lines	Approximately 20,000 miles of track; more effectively linked in trunk lines connecting east and west
Literacy	17 percent illiteracy rate for free population	6 percent illiteracy rate

even his jailers. The governor of Virginia spoke admiringly of him as "a man of clear head, of courage, fortitude, and simple ingenuousness." Speaking to the court after his sentencing, Brown suggested that he was God's agent in a holy war: "I believe that to have interfered as I have done…in behalf of [God's] despised poor, is no wrong, but right. Now, if it is deemed necessary that I should forfeit my life for the furtherance of the ends of justice, and mingle my blood further with the blood of my children and with the blood of millions in this slave country whose rights are disregarded by wicked, cruel, and unjust enactments, I say, let it be done."

The outpouring of northern grief over Brown's death convinced white southerners that the threat to their security was not over. The discovery of Brown's correspondence at his Maryland farmhouse further fueled southern rancor, and southerners increasingly ceased to believe northern disclaimers about the raid. Several members of the Secret Six had ties to the Republican Party, and southerners targeted them for special censure. Mississippi senator Jefferson Davis remarked that the Republican Party "was organized on the basis of making war" against the South. John Brown's Raid significantly changed southern public opinion. However much they defended slavery, most southerners were for the Union. The northern reaction to John Brown's trial and death, however, troubled them. The *Richmond Whig,* a newspaper that reflected moderate Upper South opinion, observed in early 1860 "recent events have wrought almost a complete revolution in the sentiments, the thoughts, the hopes, of the oldest and steadiest conservatives in all the southern states.… There are thousands upon…thousands of men in our midst who, a month ago, scoffed at the idea of a dissolution of the Union as a madman's dream, but who now hold the opinion that its days are numbered, its glory perished."

It was one thing to condemn slavery in the territories but another to attack it violently where it was long established. Southerners now saw in the Republican Party the em-

bodiment of John Brown's ideals and actions. So, in their view, the election of a Republican president would be a death sentence for the South.

The impact of this shifting sentiment was immediately apparent in Congress. South Carolina Senator James H. Hammond captured the mood well when he remarked of his colleagues on the Senate floor that "the only persons who do not have a revolver and a knife are those who have two revolvers." The southern and northern wings of the Democratic Party were now almost totally estranged. Southern Democrats seemed concerned only to promote an extreme proslavery agenda rather than to initiate real legislation.

The Election of 1860

An atmosphere of mutual sectional distrust and animosity characterized the campaign for the presidential election of 1860. In April, the Democratic Party, the sole surviving national political organization, held its convention in Charleston, South Carolina. The location was not conducive to sectional reconciliation. The city had been a hotbed of nullification sentiment during the 1830s, and talk of disunion had surfaced periodically ever since. At the convention, Charlestonians packed the galleries and cheered for their favorite extremists.

Northern Democrats arrived in Charleston united behind Stephen A. Douglas. Although they constituted a majority of the delegates, they could not muster the two-thirds majority necessary to nominate their candidate. Other issues, however, were decided on a simple majority vote, permitting northern Democrats to defeat a platform proposal for a federal slave code in the territories.

Southern extremists who favored secession hoped to disrupt the convention and divide the party. They reasoned that the Republicans would then win the presidency, providing the South with the justification to secede. The platform vote gave them the opportunity they were seeking. Accompanied by spectators' cheers, delegates from five Lower South states, South Carolina, Florida, Mississippi, Louisiana, and Texas, walked out. The Arkansas and Georgia delegations joined them the following day.

Still without a nominee, the Democrats agreed to reconvene in Baltimore in June. This time, the Upper South delegations marched out when Douglas Democrats, in a commanding majority, refused to seat the Lower South delegations that had walked out in Charleston. The remaining delegates nominated Douglas for president. The bolters, who included almost all the southern delegates plus a few northerners loyal to President Buchanan, met in another hall and nominated John C. Breckinridge of Kentucky.

The disintegration of the national Democratic Party alarmed those southerners who understood that it would ensure the election of a Republican president in November. The *Memphis Appeal* warned that "the odium of the Black-Republican party has been that it is *Sectional*." Should southerners now allow a group of "restless and reckless or misguided men to destroy the national Democratic party?" the *Appeal* asked. Its emphatic answer was "No!"

The *Appeal* reflected the sentiment of many former Whigs, mainly from the Upper South, who would not support Breckinridge and could not support Douglas. Together with Whig allies in the North who had not defected to the Republican Party, they met in Baltimore in May 1860 to form the **Constitutional Union Party** and nominated John Bell of Tennessee for president.

Sensing victory, the Republicans convened in Chicago. If they could hold the states won by Frémont in 1856, add Minnesota (a new Republican-leaning state), and win Pennsylvania and one of three other Lower North states, Illinois, Indiana, or New Jersey, their candidate would win. These calculations dictated a platform and a candidate who could appeal to the four Lower North swing states, where antislavery sentiment was not so strong.

The issue of slavery in the territories had dominated the Republicans' 1856 platform. Now they embraced other issues as well, presenting themselves as the party of sound economy, business, and industry. Delegates enthusiastically cheered a tariff plank calling for the protection of American industry.

In selecting an appropriate presidential nominee, the Republicans faced a dilemma. Senator William H. Seward came to Chicago as the leading candidate. But his immoderate condemnation of southerners and slavery worried moderate northern voters—precisely the voters the party needed for victory.

Reservations about Seward benefited Abraham Lincoln. Lincoln's lieutenants at the convention stressed their candidate's moderation and morality, distancing him from both the abolitionists and Seward. Moreover, Chicago was Lincoln's home turf, and he had many friends working for him at the convention. When Seward faltered, Lincoln rose and won the Republican nomination.

True to their Whig heritage, the Republicans staged a colorful campaign, featuring drill teams as well as organized groups of young men called the **Wide Awakes,** outfitted in flowing black oil-cloth capes. Douglas supporters countered by enrolling teams of "Little Giants." Breckinridge and Bell followed suit, and soon large groups of young men were marching all over the country in support of one candidate or another. The theme was political, but the atmosphere was an odd mix of military parade and religious revival.

The presidential campaign of 1860 actually comprised two campaigns. In the South, the contest was between Breckinridge and Bell; in the North, it was Lincoln against Douglas. Breckinridge and Bell had scattered support in the North, as did Douglas in the South, but in the main this was a sectional election. Lincoln did not even appear on the ballot in most southern states.

In those days, states did not hold gubernatorial elections on the same day, or even in the same month, as the national presidential election. When, in mid-October, Republicans swept the statehouses

"Dividing the National Map": Reflecting the sectional nature of the campaign, three of the four candidates in the 1860 Presidential election tear the fabric of national unity. Lincoln and Douglas yank at the North and West and Breckinridge pulls at the South, while the fourth candidate, John Bell of the Constitutional Union Party makes a futile attempt to glue the pieces back together.

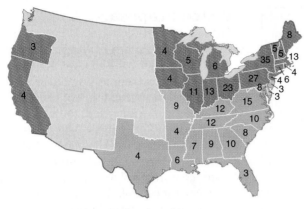

	Electoral Vote (%)	Popular Vote (%)
ABRAHAM LINCOLN **(Republican)**	**180** **(59)**	**1,865,593** **(40)**
John C. Breckinridge (Southern Democrat)	72 (24)	848,356 (18)
John Bell (Constitutional Union)	39 (13)	592,906 (13)
Stephen A. Douglas (Northern Democrat)	12 (4)	1,382,713 (29)

MAP 14–4   The Election of 1860
The election returns from 1860 vividly illustrate the geography of sectionalism.

in two crucial states, Pennsylvania and Indiana, Douglas made an extraordinary decision, but one consistent with his ardent nationalism. He abandoned his campaign and headed south at great personal peril to urge southerners to remain in the Union now that Lincoln's election was inevitable.

Lincoln became the nation's sixteenth president, with 40 percent of the popular vote (see Map 14–4). Douglas, though second after Lincoln in the popular balloting, won the undivided electoral vote of only one state, Missouri.

Lincoln took most northern states by significant margins and won all the region's electoral votes except three in New Jersey. This gave him a substantial majority of 180 electoral votes. Breckinridge won eleven southern states but received a majority of the popular vote in just four. In the South as a whole, his opponents, Bell and Douglas, together reaped 55 percent of the popular vote, confirming Republicans' skepticism about southern determination to secede.

Secession Begins

The events following Lincoln's election demonstrated how wildly mistaken were those who dismissed southern threats of secession. Four days after Lincoln's victory, the South Carolina legislature called on the state's citizens to elect delegates to a convention to consider secession. Meeting on December 20, the delegates voted unanimously to leave

the Union. By February 1, six other states had all held similar conventions and decided to leave the Union (see Map 14–5). Representatives from the seven seceding states met to form a separate country, the **Confederate States of America.** On February 18, Jefferson Davis was sworn in as its president.

Curiously, for a people trumpeting the virtues of democratic government, only Texas of all the seceding states submitted its secession ordinance for popular referendum. Further, though subsequent generations of white southerners would dwell on states' rights as the precipitating cause of secession, leaders of the new Confederate nation emphasized slavery as the state right most valued. A month after the formation of the Confederacy, Alexander H. Stephens of Georgia, vice president of the new government, praised the just-framed Confederate Constitution in the following words: "[T]he new Constitution has put at rest forever all the agitating questions relating to our peculiar institution, African slavery as it exists amongst us, the proper status of the negro in our form of civilization. This was the immediate cause of the late rupture and present revolution.... Our new Government'[s]...foundations are laid, its cornerstone rests, upon the great truth that the negro is not equal to the white man; that slavery, subordination to the superior race, is his natural and normal condition."

The swiftness of secession in the Lower South obscured the divisions in most southern states over the issue. Secessionists barely secured a majority in the Georgia and Louisiana conventions. In Mississippi, Florida, and Alabama, the secessionist majority was more comfortable, but pro-Union candidates polled a significant minority of votes. With Lincoln headed for the White House, the greatest support for secession came from large landowners in counties in which slaves comprised a majority of the population. Support for secession was weakest among small, nonslaveholding farmers.

The secessionists mounted an effective propaganda campaign, deftly using the press to persuade voters to elect their delegates to the state conventions. Framing the issue as a personal challenge to every southern citizen, they argued that it would be cowardly to remain in the Union, a submission to despotism and enslavement. Southerners, they maintained, were the true heirs to the spirit of 1776. Lincoln and the Republicans meant to deny southerners the right to life, liberty, and the pursuit of happiness.

Presidential Inaction

Because Lincoln would not take office until March 4, 1861, the Buchanan administration had to cope with the secession crisis during the critical months of December and January. The president's failure to work out a solution with Congress as secession fever swept the Lower South undermined Unionist forces in the seceding states.

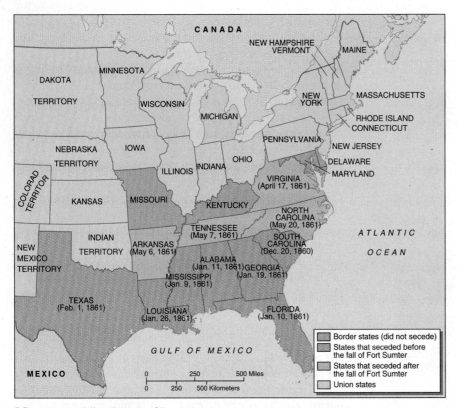

MAP 14–5   The Course of Secession
Before the firing on Fort Sumter in April 1861, the Confederacy consisted primarily of states in the Lower South. After Sumter, and after President Lincoln called upon them for troops, the Upper South states of Virginia, North Carolina, Tennessee, and Arkansas seceded.

When Buchanan lost the support of northern Democrats over the Lecompton Constitution, he turned to the South for support and filled his cabinet with southerners. Now, facing the secession crisis, he proposed holding a constitutional convention to amend the Constitution in ways that would satisfy the South's demands on slavery. This outright surrender to southern demands, however, had no chance of passing in Congress.

Buchanan's administration quickly fell apart. As the Lower South states left the Union, their representatives and senators left Washington, and with them went Buchanan's closest advisers and key cabinet officials. Commenting on the emotionally charged atmosphere in the Senate as prominent southerners gave their farewells and departed, one observer wrote, "There was everywhere a feeling of suspense, as if, visibly, the pillars of the temple were being withdrawn and the great Government structure was tottering."

Buchanan, a lame duck, bereft of friends and advisers, did little more than condemn secession. He was reluctant to take action that would limit the options of the incoming administration or, worse, tip the balance in the Upper South toward secession. He hoped that waiting might bring an isolated Lower South to its senses and give efforts to mediate the sectional rift a chance to succeed.

Peace Proposals

Previous sectional conflicts, dating from the Missouri Compromise of 1820, had brought forth the ingenuity and goodwill of political leaders to effect compromise and draw the Union back from the brink of disintegration. Both ingenuity and goodwill were scarce commodities in the gray secession winter of 1860–1861. The two conflicting sides had little trust in each other, and the word "compromise" was viewed as more a synonym for capitulation than salvation.

Kentucky senator John J. Crittenden chaired a Senate committee that proposed a package of constitutional amendments in December 1860 designed to solve the sectional crisis. The central feature of the Crittenden Plan was the extension of the Missouri Compromise line through the territories all the way to California. The plan was of marginal interest to the South, because it was unlikely to result in any new slave states. And Republicans opposed it because it contradicted one of their basic principles, the exclusion of slavery from the territories. Despite a flood of letters supporting the Crittenden Plan, including a petition from 38,000 citizens of New York City, Republicans bottled it up in Congress and prevented action on it.

Meanwhile, ex-president John Tyler emerged from retirement to lead an effort by the Border States, the Upper South and the Lower North, to forge a peace. Delegates from these states met in February 1861, but their plan differed little from Crittenden's, and it, too, got nowhere in Congress.

Lincoln's Views on Secession

President-elect Lincoln monitored the secession of the Lower South states and the attempts to reach a compromise from his home in Springfield. Although he said nothing publicly, he made it known that he did not favor compromises like those proposed by Crittenden and Tyler. As he put it to a friend, "We have just carried an election on principles fairly stated to the people. Now we are told in advance, the government shall be broken up, unless we surrender to those we have beaten, before we take the offices.... If we surrender, it is the end of us, and of the government."

Lincoln counted on Unionist sentiment to keep the Upper South from seceding. Like Buchanan, he felt that the longer the Lower South states remained isolated, the more likely they would be to return to the fold. For a while, events seemed to bear him out. In North Carolina, the *Wilmington Herald* responded to South Carolina's secession by asking readers, "Will you suffer yourself to be spit upon in this way? Are you submissionists to the dictation of South Carolina...are you to be called cowards because you do not follow the crazy lead of that crazy state?"

One by one, Upper South states registered their support for the Union. North Carolinians went to the polls in February and turned down the call for a secession convention. Also in February, Virginians elected Unionists to their convention by a five-to-one margin. In Missouri, not one secessionist won election to the state convention. In Kentucky, the legislature adjourned without taking action on a convention or a statewide referendum on secession. And the Maryland legislature, already out of session, showed no inclination to reconvene.

A closer look, however, reveals that there were limits to the Upper South's Unionism. Most voters in the region went to the polls assuming that Congress would eventually reach a compromise based on the Crittenden proposals, Tyler's peace conference, or some other remedy. Leaders in the Upper South saw themselves as peacemakers. As one Virginian explained, "Without submission to the North or desertion of the South, Virginia has that moral position within the Union which will give her power to arbitrate between the sections." But what if arbitration failed? Or what if the Lower South states precipitated a crisis that forced the Upper South to choose sides? It was unlikely that the Upper South would abide the use of federal force against its southern neighbors.

Lincoln believed that the slavery issue had to come to a crisis before the nation could solve it. Although he said in public that he would never interfere with slavery in the slave states, the deep moral revulsion he felt toward the institution left him more ambivalent in private. As he confided to a colleague in 1860, "The tug has to come, and better now, than any time hereafter" (see American Views, Lincoln on Slavery).

Fort Sumter: The Tug Comes

In his inaugural address on March 4, 1861, Abraham Lincoln denounced secession and vowed to uphold federal law but tempered his firmness with a conciliatory conclusion. Addressing southerners specifically, he assured them, "We are not enemies but friends.... Though passion may have strained, it must not break our bonds of affection. The mystic chords of memory, stretching from every battlefield, and patriot grave, to every living heart and hearthstone, all over this broad land, will yet swell the chorus of the Union, when again touched, as surely they will be, by the better angels of our nature."

Southerners wanted concessions, not conciliation, however. The new president said nothing about slavery in the territories, nothing about the constitutional amendments proposed by Crittenden and Tyler, and nothing about the release of federal property in the South to the Confederacy. Even some northerners hoping for an olive branch were disappointed. But Lincoln was hoping for time—time to get the Lower South states quarreling with one another, time to allow Union sentiment to build in the Upper South, and time to convince northerners that the Union needed preserving. He did not get that time.

One day after Lincoln's inauguration, Major Robert Anderson (like Lincoln, a native Kentuckian), the commander of **Fort Sumter** in Charleston harbor, informed the administration that he had only four to six weeks' worth of provisions left. Sumter was one of three southern forts still under federal control. Confederate batteries had ringed the fort, and Anderson estimated that only a force of at least 20,000 troops could provision and defend the fort. Anderson assumed that Lincoln would understand the hopeless arithmetic and order him to evacuate Fort Sumter. The commanding General of the Army, Winfield Scott, advised the president accordingly, as did many members of his cabinet. Lincoln stalled.

The issue was simple, though the alternatives were difficult: Do not provision Fort Sumter and the garrison would fall to the Confederate government; provision the fort and risk a military confrontation as the Confederate authorities would perceive such action as an act of war. Lincoln had vowed in his inaugural address to uphold the Constitution and "to protect and defend" the country's interests; yet, he had also promised that he would not make any aggressive movements against the South.

News of Anderson's plight changed the mood in the North. The Slave Power, some said, was holding him and his men hostage. Frustration grew over Lincoln's silence and inaction. The Confederacy's bold resolve seemed to contrast sharply with the federal government's confusion and inertia. "The bird of our country," cracked New York diarist George Templeton Strong, "is a debilitated chicken, disguised in eagle feathers.... We are a weak, divided, disgraced people unable to maintain our institutional existence."

By the end of March, nearly a month after Anderson had informed Lincoln of the situation at Fort Sumter, the president finally moved. By this time, northern public opinion and Lincoln's cabinet (with Secretary of State Seward a notable exception) favored an effort to provision Major Anderson.

Seward made a last, desperate attempt to avert armed conflict by drawing on the reservoir of common American nationalism. He suggested that Lincoln trump up charges of Spanish and French aggression in the Caribbean and convene Congress to declare war. Seward hoped that his absurd plan would draw seceding states back into the Union to make common cause against Spain and France. Lincoln politely rejected the advice and ordered an expedition to provision Fort Sumter.

Hoping to avoid a confrontation, the president did not send the troops that Anderson had requested. Instead, he ordered unarmed ships to proceed to the fort, deliver the provisions, and leave. Only if the Confederates fired on them were they to force their way into the fort with the help of armed reinforcements. Lincoln notified South Carolina authorities that he intended to do nothing more than "feed the hungry."

At Charleston, Confederate general P. G. T. Beauregard had standing orders to turn back any relief expedition. But President Davis wanted to take Sumter before the provisions arrived to avoid fighting Anderson and the

American Views

Lincoln on Slavery

In the weeks after the 1860 election, northern and southern leaders sought out President-elect Abraham Lincoln for his views on slavery. But Lincoln had spoken often on the institution in the years immediately preceding the election. His speech two years earlier, excerpted here, offered an unequivocal statement of his moral and philosophical opposition to slavery. Implied in the speech was the belief that the contradiction between American ideals and slavery could not be brokered, compromised, or ignored.

- How do Lincoln's actions from his election in November 1860 to the firing on Fort Sumter in April 1861 reflect the principles enunciated in his Springfield address?

- The two letters, one to fellow Illinois Republican Lyman Trumbull and the other to Virginia Democrat John A. Gilmer, indicate Lincoln's firm opposition to the extension of slavery into the territories. Are they consistent with the views expressed in Springfield two years earlier?

- Despite the difference in tone, do you think the letters both say essentially the same thing?

Speech of Hon. Abraham Lincoln

Springfield, Illinois, June 17, 1858

We are now far into the fifth year since policy was initiated with the avowed object and confident promise of putting an end to slavery agitation. Under the operation of that policy, that agitation has not only not ceased, but has constantly augmented. In my opinion, it will not cease until a crisis shall have been reached and passed. "A house divided against itself cannot stand." I believe this government cannot endure permanently half slave and half free. I do not expect the Union to be dissolved; I do not expect the house to fall; but I do expect it will cease to be divided. It will become all one thing, or the other.…So I say in relation to the principle that all men are created equal, let it be as nearly reached as we can. If we cannot give freedom to every creature, let us do nothing that will impose slavery upon any other creature.…I leave you, hoping that the lamp of liberty will burn in your bosoms until there shall no longer be a doubt that all men are created free and equal.

Springfield, Ills. Dec. 10, 1860

Hon. L. Trumbull

My dear Sir: Let there be no compromise on the question of extending slavery. If there be, all our labor is lost, and ere long, must be done again. The dangerous ground, that into which some of our friends have a hankering to run, is Pop[ular] Sov[ereignty]. Have none of it. Stand firm. The tug has to come, & better now, than any time hereafter. Yours as ever,

A. Lincoln

Springfield, Ill. Dec. 15, 1860

Hon. John A. Gilmer:

My dear Sir:…I have no thought of recommending the abolition of slavery in the District of Columbia, nor the slave trade among the slave states…and if I were to make such recommendation, it is quite clear Congress would not follow it. As to the use of patronage in the slave states, where there are few or no Republicans, I do not expect to inquire for the politics of the appointee, or whether he does or not own slaves.…In one word, I never have been, am not now, and probably never shall be, in a mood of harassing the people, either North or South. On the territorial question, I am inflexible.…On that, there is a difference between you and us; and it is the only substantial difference. You think slavery is right and ought to be extended; we think it is wrong and ought to be restricted. For this, neither has any just occasion to be angry with the other.

Your obt. Servt.

A. Lincoln

Source: John G. Nicolay and John Hay, eds., *Works of Abraham Lincoln*, vol. 6 (New York: Century Co., 1905).

FROM THEN TO NOW

Religion and Politics

When evangelical Protestantism first emerged in the late eighteenth century, its adherents advocated the separation of church and state. By the 1850s, however, the social landscape of America had changed. A wave of immigrants, many of them Roman Catholic, threatened Protestant dominance. Growing cities and rapid technological and economic change strained the traditional moral and social order. Alarmed by these changes, evangelicals entered the political arena. Their convictions, as we saw in Chapter 12, helped drive the antebellum reform movement.

The give-and-take of politics, however, posed a challenge to the evangelical belief in an absolute truth grounded in the Bible. Eventually, the two great evangelical crusades of the 1850s, anti-Catholicism and abolitionism, were subsumed within the Republican Party. And after the Civil War, the Republican Party gradually lost its radical fervor.

Activists display a representation of the Ten Commandments October 2003 during a rally at the West Lawn of the U.S. Capitol in Washington, DC. Christian activists gathered on Capitol Hill as the last stop of a five-state rally tour.

By the twentieth century, the evangelical movement had begun to turn away from politics and revert to its traditional focus on saving souls. But then came the upheavals of the 1960s and 1970s that challenged traditional morality and authority, including the Supreme Court's decision in *Roe v. Wade* to legalize abortion. Once again, a changing social landscape compelled evangelicals to enter the political arena, this time to defend themselves against what they perceived as an encroaching government. Organizations emerged to mobilize evangelical voters, including Jerry Falwell's Moral Majority in the late 1970s and Pat Robertson's Christian Coalition in 1989.

Most Americans today, as in the 1850s, recoil from the overt intrusion of religion into politics, and groups like the Christian Coalition have had only limited success in electing their favored candidates. Today, some evangelical strategists call for a "popular front" approach, allying themselves with candidates not openly associated with the evangelical agenda. Abolitionists in the 1850s faced the same quandary between ideological purity and political pragmatism. Their support of Abraham Lincoln in 1860 reflected a bow toward pragmatism, a course that ultimately proved successful for their cause, but not without a bloody civil war.

■ Evangelicals in the 1850s eventually achieved their goal of abolishing slavery. What accounted for their success and the difficulties of twenty-first century evangelical Christians to translate their social agenda to public policy?

One of Thomas Nast's vitriolic comments on the separation between Church (i.e., the Roman Catholic church) and State

From Then to Now Online   PEARSON myhistorylab

14-1 Rev. George B. Cheever, D.D., *God Against Slavery and the Freedom and Duty of the Pulpit To Rebuke It, As a Sin against God, 1857*. In this excerpt from a sermon delivered in response to "Bleeding Kansas" and the assault on Senator Charles Sumner, Cheever argues that separating Church and State does not require ministers to lose their moral compass.

14-2 Archbishop Donald W. Wuerl, *Red Mass Homily*, October 1, 2006. In his homily (sermon), delivered on the Sunday before the start of the Supreme Court session, Wuerl asserts that the Church should not abdicate its moral responsibilities in the public sphere.

14-3 Rev. Caroline M. Kelly, "Death and Taxes," October 16, 2005. Kelly, Presbyterian minister, takes a less dogmatic view of the separation issue, focusing on the ambiguous relationship between Church and State and the dangers of both too little and too much engagement with political issues.

OVERVIEW

The Emerging Sectional Crisis

Event	Year	Effect
Wilmot Proviso	1846	Congressman David Wilmot's proposal to ban slavery from territories acquired from Mexico touched off a bitter sectional dispute in Congress.
Compromise of 1850	1850	Law admitted California as a free state, granted the population of Utah and New Mexico Territories the right to decide on slavery, and established a new and stronger Fugitive Slave Act, all of which "solved" the territorial issue raised by the Wilmot Proviso but satisfied neither North nor South and planted the seeds of future conflict.
Election of 1852	1852	Results confirmed demise of the Whig Party, initiating a period of political realignment.
Kansas-Nebraska Act	1854	Law created the Kansas and Nebraska Territories and repealed the Missouri Compromise of 1820 by leaving the question of slavery to the territories' residents. Its passage enraged many northerners, prompting some to form the new Republican Party.
"Bleeding Kansas"	1855–1856	Sometimes violent conflict between pro- and antislavery forces in Kansas further polarized the sectional debate.
Election of 1856	1856	Presidency was won by Democrat James Buchanan of Pennsylvania, but a surprisingly strong showing by the recently formed Republican Party in the North set the stage for the 1860 election.
Dred Scott Case	1857	The Supreme Court ruling that slaves were not citizens and that Congress had no authority to ban slavery from the territories boosted Republican prospects in the North.
Lecompton Constitution	1857	Proslavery document, framed by a fraudulently elected constitutional convention in Kansas and supported by President Buchanan, further convinced northerners that the South was subverting their rights.
John Brown's Raid	1859	Unsuccessful attempt to free the South's slaves, this attack on a federal arsenal in Harpers Ferry, Virginia, increased sectional tension.
Election of 1860	1860	Republican Abraham Lincoln won a four-way race for the presidency. The last major national party, the Democrats, disintegrated. Lower South states seceded.
Fort Sumter	1861	Confederate forces attacked the fort in April 1861, Lincoln called for troops, and several Upper South states seceded. The Civil War was underway.

reinforcements at the same time. He also realized that the outbreak of fighting could compel the Upper South to join the Confederacy. But his impatience to force the issue placed the Confederacy in the position of firing, unprovoked, on the American flag and at Major Anderson, who had become a national hero.

On April 10, Davis ordered Beauregard to demand the immediate evacuation of Fort Sumter. Anderson refused but wondered what the hurry was, considering that his provisions would run out in a few days. The remark gave Beauregard pause and prompted additional negotiations. Anderson did not yield, and before dawn on April 12, 1861, the first Confederate shell whistled down on the fort. After more than a day of shelling, during which more than 5,000 artillery rounds struck Fort Sumter, Anderson surrendered. Remark-

ably, neither side suffered any casualties, a deceptive beginning to an exceptionally bloody war.

When the verdict of Fort Sumter reached President Lincoln, he called on the southern states still in the Union to send troops to put down the rebellion. Refusing to make war on South Carolina, the Upper South states of Virginia, North Carolina, Tennessee, and Arkansas seceded, and the Confederacy expanded to eleven states.

Conclusion

When David Wilmot submitted his amendment to ban slavery from the territories gained from Mexico, he could not have foreseen that the debate he unleashed would end in civil war just fifteen years later. Northerners and southerners had lived together in one nation for nearly eighty years. During that time, they had reached accommodations on slavery at the Constitutional Convention of 1787, in the Compromises of 1820 and 1850, and on numerous lesser occasions. But by the 1850s the slavery issue had become weighted with so much moral and political freight that it defied easy resolution. Throughout the Western world, attitudes toward slavery were changing. Northern evangelical Protestants in the 1840s and 1850s branded slavery a sin and slaveholders sinners. The overwhelming popularity of *Uncle Tom's Cabin* both tapped and fed this sentiment.

The political conflict over slavery coalesced around northern efforts to curtail southern expansion and power and southern attempts to maintain power and influence in the federal government by planting the institution in the western territories. This conflict eventually helped undo the Compromise of 1850 and turned Stephen A. Douglas's railroad bill into a battle royal over Kansas. Unable to resolve sectional differences over slavery, the Whigs disintegrated, and the Democrats divided into northern and southern factions. The Republican Party was formed from the political debris. Ethnic and religious conflicts further disturbed the political landscape and contributed to party realignment.

Northerners and southerners eventually interpreted any incident or piece of legislation as an attempt by one side to gain moral and political advantage at the other's expense. Northerners viewed the *Dred Scott* decision, the Lecompton Constitution, and the southern reaction to John Brown's Raid as evidence of a Slave Power conspiracy to deny white northerners their constitutional rights. Southerners interpreted the northern reaction to these same events as evidence of a conspiracy to rob them of security and equality within the Union.

By 1861, the national political parties that had muted sectional animosities were gone, and so were national church organizations and fraternal associations. The ideals that had inspired the American Revolution remained in place, especially the importance of securing individual liberty against encroachment by government. But with each side interpreting them differently, these ideals served more to divide than to unite. Southerners viewed the North and the Republican Party as threats to their individual liberties. Northerners believed that the South was conspiring to rob them of their individual rights, and that only the federal government stood between their freedom and the despotism of the Slave Power. Both sides claimed for themselves the role of guardian of the Revolutionary tradition. Lincoln's election left northerners feeling vindicated and southerners feeling vulnerable.

Ironically, as Americans in both sections talked of freedom and self-determination, the black men and women in their midst had little of either. Lincoln went to war to preserve the Union; Davis, to defend a new nation. Slavery was the spark that ignited the conflict, but white America seemed more comfortable embracing abstract ideals than real people. Northerners and southerners would confront this irony during the bloodiest war in American history, but they would not resolve it.

Review Questions

1. How do you account for the great success of Harriet Beecher Stowe's *Uncle Tom's Cabin?*

2. How did the failure of democratic revolutions in Europe affect Americans' perspectives on their own system of government?

3. Discuss the role of evangelical religion in sharpening the sectional conflict between North and South.

4. Between the time he was elected president in November and his inauguration in March, what options did Abraham Lincoln have for resolving the sectional crisis?

5. Northerners and southerners appealed to the same American ideals in support of their respective positions. Could they both have been correct?

Key Terms

"Bleeding Kansas" (p. 371)
Compromise of 1850 (p. 366)
Confederate States of America (p. 383)
Constitutional Union Party (p. 382)
Dred Scott Decision (p. 374)
Fort Sumter (p. 385)

Fugitive Slave Act (p. 366)
John Brown's Raid (p. 380)
Kansas-Nebraska Act (p. 371)
Know-Nothing Party (p. 372)
Lecompton Constitution (p. 375)
Lincoln-Douglas debates (p. 376)

Ostend Manifesto (p. 369)
Panic of 1857 (p. 375)
Popular Sovereignty (p. 362)
Republican Party (p. 372)
Wide Awakes (p. 382)
Wilmot Proviso (p. 362)

Recommended Reading

Freehling, William W. *The Road to Disunion,* Vol. 1: *Secessionists at Bay, 1776–1854* (1990). A detailed and lively treatment of events and personalities in the years leading up to passage of the Kansas-Nebraska Act.

Potter, David M. *The Impending Crisis, 1848–1861* (1976). The most comprehensive analysis of the coming of the war; a balanced account that is especially strong on political events.

Stowe, Harriet Beecher. *Uncle Tom's Cabin* (1852; reprint edition 1982, with notes by Kathryn Kish Sklar). Reading this book is essential for understanding why and how it generated so much controversy and intensified sectional antagonisms in the early 1850s.

Where to Learn More

- **The Underground Railroad Freedom Center, Cincinnati, Ohio.**   The Center provides information on the Northern response to the Fugitive Slave Act. See its website at www.undergroundrailroad.org

- **Adair Cabin and John Brown Museum, John Brown Memorial Park, Osawatomie, Kansas.**   Maintained by the Kansas Historical Society, the cabin (which once belonged to John Brown's sister) and the museum are located on the site of the Battle of Osawatomie, one of the critical events of "Bleeding Kansas." Its website is www.kshs.org/places/adair.htm

- **Harpers Ferry National Historical Park, West Virginia.**   Exhibits interpret John Brown's Raid and re-create some of the atmosphere and structures of the 1850s village and the federal arsenal. Its website is www.nps.gov/hafe

- **Fort Sumter National Monument, Charleston, South Carolina.**   This historic site interprets the bombardment of the fort and the events that immediately preceded the Civil War. Go to www.nps.gov/fosu

Study Resources

For study resources for this chapter, go to www.myhistorylab.com and choose *The American Journey*. You will find a wealth of study and review material for this chapter, including pre- and post-tests, customized study plan, key term review flash cards, interactive map and document activities, and documents for analysis.

Awaiting combat, 1861: Union Soldiers from New York relax at camp awaiting orders to move to the front. The young men show great confidence and determination for their coming engagements, though one fellow to the left of the tent, perhaps a teenager far from home, seems to long for something as he stares beyond the camera. At this early stage of the war, a combination of romance and apprehension enveloped these hopeful recruits. Note the young African American with a broom sitting apart from the soldiers.

Battle Cries and Freedom Songs the Civil War 1861–1865 15

July 14, 1861

Camp Clark, Washington, DC

My very dear Sarah:

The indications are very strong that we shall move in a few days, perhaps tomorrow. And lest I should not be able to write you again I feel impelled to write a few lines that may fall under your eye when I am no more. Our movement may be one of a few days' duration and be full of pleasure. And it may be one of severe conflict and death to me. "Not my will but thine O God be done." If it is necessary that I should fall on the battle-field for my Country I am ready. I have no misgivings about, or lack of confidence in the cause in which I am engaged, and my courage does not halt or falter. I know how American Civilization now leans upon the triumph of the government and how great a debt we owe to those who went before us through the blood and suffering of the Revolution. And I am willing, perfectly willing, to lay down all my joys in this life, to help maintain this government, and to pay that debt. But my dear wife, when I know that with my own joys I lay down nearly all of yours,…is it weak or dishonorable that while the banner of my purpose floats calmly and proudly in the breeze, underneath, my unbounded love for you my darling wife and children should struggle in fierce though useless contest with my love of country? ...

Sarah, my love for you is deathless, it seems to bind me with mighty cables that nothing but omnipotence can break; and yet my love of Country comes over me like a strong wind and bears me irresistibly with all those chains to the battle-field.

The memories of the blissful moments I have enjoyed with you come crowding over me, and I feel most deeply grateful to God and you, that I have enjoyed them for so long. And how hard it is for me to give them up and burn to ashes the hopes and future years, when, God willing, we might still have lived and loved together, and see our boys grown up to honorable manhood around us....If I do not [return], my dear Sarah, never forget how much I loved you, nor that when my last breath escapes me on the battle-field, it will whisper your name.

Forgive my many faults, and the many pains I have caused you. How thoughtless, how foolish I have sometimes been! ...

But, O Sarah, if the dead can come back to this earth and flit unseen around those they love, I shall be with you, in the gladdest days and the darkest nights...always, always, and if there be a soft breeze upon your cheek, it shall be my breath[;] as the cool air fans your throbbing temple, it shall be my spirit passing by. Sarah do not mourn me dead; think I am gone and wait for thee, for we shall meet again....

Sullivan

Sullivan Ballou to Sarah Ballou, July 14, 1861. Geoffrey C. Ward, et al., *The Civil War: An Illustrated History* (New York: Alfred A. Knopf, 1990), 82–83.

myhistorylab

Personal Journeys Online

- Sam R. Watkins, Co. *"Aytch": A Confederate Memoir of the Civil War*, 1882. A Confederate soldier recounts the horrors of war he witnessed in a southern hospital and on the battlefield.

- Ambrose Bierce, "What I saw of Shiloh," *Civil War Stories*, 1909. Account of a Union soldier's experiences at the Battle of Shiloh.

Sullivan Ballou's letter to his wife on the eve of the First Battle of Bull Run typified the sentiments of the civilian armies raised by both North and South: a clear purpose of the importance of their mission, a sense of foreboding, an appeal and acknowledgment of the guiding hand of God, and, most of all, words of love for family. Such romantic expressions were common in mid-nineteenth-century American correspondence between husband and wife, lover and loved.

Yet the Civil War lent urgency to such expressions. Most of the soldiers had no combat experience and, aside from some perfunctory training, knew little about military life before going into battle. Just a few months earlier, Major Sullivan Ballou of the Second Regiment, Rhode Island Volunteers, was a 32-year-old attorney. He led a quiet life in Providence with his wife and two young sons. But the events of the 1850s stoked Ballou's interest in politics, and he became a dedicated Republican and devoted supporter of Abraham Lincoln. When the war came, he volunteered and was sent to Washington, DC, to await further orders. He wrote this letter from his camp. A few days later, his company marched to Manassas, Virginia, where they engaged Confederate troops on July 21 at the First Battle of Bull Run. Sullivan Ballou was killed in the battle.

Sullivan Ballou took the ultimate journey for his beliefs and his love. The Civil War preserved the Union, abolished slavery, and killed at least 620,000 soldiers, more than in all the other wars the country fought from the Revolution to the Korean conflict combined. To come to terms with this is to try to reconcile the war's great accomplishments with its awful consequences. When the war began, only a small minority of northerners linked the preservation of the Union with the abolition of slavery. By 1863, Union and freedom had become inseparable federal objectives. The Confederacy fought for independence and the preservation of slavery. The Confederate objectives dictated a defensive military strategy; the Union objectives dictated an offensive strategy.

During the war's early years, both sides faced similar problems, raising an army, financing the war effort, mobilizing the civilian population, and marshaling resources. The Confederates confronted the added burden of starting a government from scratch with relatively fewer resources than the federals.

At the end of the war's first year, the Confederacy's strong military position east of the Appalachians belied

CHRONOLOGY

1861	January	Benito Juarez becomes president of Mexico, dedicated to restoring national unity.
	March	Tsar Alexander II emancipates Russia's serfs. Kingdom of Italy proclaimed.
	April	Confederates fire on Fort Sumter; Civil War begins.
	July	First Battle of Bull Run.
1862	February	Forts Henry and Donelson fall to Union forces.
	March	Peninsula Campaign begins. Battle of Glorieta Pass, New Mexico.
	April	Battle of Shiloh. New Orleans falls to Federal forces.
	May	Union captures Corinth, Mississippi.
	July	Seven Days' Battles end. Congress passes the Confiscation Act
	August	Second Battle of Bull Run.
	September	Battle of Antietam.
	December	Battle of Fredericksburg.
1863	January	Emancipation Proclamation takes effect.
	May	Battle of Chancellorsville; Stonewall Jackson is mortally wounded.
	June	French forces capture Mexico City
	July	Battle of Gettysburg. Vicksburg falls to Union forces. New York Draft Riot occurs. Black troops of the 54th Massachusetts Volunteer Infantry Regiment Assault Fort Wagner outside Charleston.
	September	Battle of Chickamauga.
	November	Battle of Chattanooga.
1864	May	Battle of the Wilderness.
	June	Battle of Cold Harbor. Ferdinand Maximilian Joseph, archduke of Austria, crowned emperor of Mexico with support of French troops.
	September	Sherman captures Atlanta.
	November	President Lincoln is reelected. Sherman begins his march to the sea.
1865	January	Congress passes Thirteenth Amendment to the Constitution, outlawing slavery (ratified December 1865).
	February	Charleston surrenders.
	March	Confederate Congress authorizes enlistment of black soldiers.
	April	Federal troops enter Richmond. Lee surrenders to Grant at Appomattox Court House. Lincoln is assassinated.

its numerical and economic inferiority. By the end of 1862, Union officers had begun to expose southern military shortcomings, and federal officials had expanded the North's war aims to include the abolition of slavery. Within a year, the trans-Mississippi portion of the Confederacy capitulated. A slim victory at Gettysburg, Sherman's destructive and demoralizing march through Georgia, and the relentless assaults of the new Union commander, Ulysses S. Grant, overwhelmed Confederate resistance. The North, too, suffered social and political disruption, but the marvelous elixir of battlefield victory did wonders to allay these ills.

Black southerners seized the initiative in the war against slavery, especially in the months after the Emancipation Proclamation, eventually joining Union forces in combat against their former masters. Soon, another war to secure the fruits of freedom would begin.

Mobilization, North and South

Neither side was prepared for a major war. The Confederacy lacked a national army. Each southern state had a militia, but by the 1850s, these companies had become more social clubs than fighting units. Aside from privately owned ships and some captured Federal vessels, the Confederacy also lacked a navy. The Union had a regular army of only 16,000 men, most of whom were stationed west of the Mississippi River. Their major responsibility had been to intervene between white settlers and Indians.

Each government augmented these meager military reserves with thousands of new recruits and developed a bureaucracy to mount a war effort. At the same time, the administrations of Presidents Lincoln and Davis secured the loyalty of their civilian populations and devised military strategies for a war of indeterminate duration. How North and South went about these tasks reflected both the different objectives of the two sides and the distinctive personalities of their leaders, Abraham Lincoln and Jefferson Davis.

War Fever

The day after Major Robert Anderson surrendered Fort Sumter, President Lincoln moved to enlarge his small, scattered army by mobilizing state militias for 90 days. Four states—Virginia, Arkansas, North Carolina, and Tennessee—refused the call and seceded from the Union. About one-third of the officer corps of the regular army, including some of the highest ranking officers, resigned their commissions to join the Confederacy. Still, Lincoln seemed likely to meet his target of 75,000 troops.

Lincoln's modest 90-day call-up reflected the general belief, North and South, that the war would end quickly. The *New York Times* predicted that the "local commotion" in the

South would be put down "in thirty days." Some southerners believed that the Yankees would quit after the first battle. "Just throw three or four shells among those blue-bellied Yankees," a North Carolinian blustered, "and they'll scatter like sheep." Not everyone thought the war would be brief. William T. Sherman, who had recently headed a Louisiana military academy and would become one of the Union's few great commanders, wrote in April 1861, "I think it is to be a long war, very long, much longer than any politician thinks."

Northerners closed ranks behind the president after the Confederacy's attack on Fort Sumter. Stephen A. Douglas, a leading Democrat, called on the Republican Lincoln to offer his and his party's support. "There can be no neutrals in this war," Douglas said, "only patriots, or traitors." Residents of New York City, where sympathy for the South had probably been greater than anywhere else in the North, now sponsored huge public demonstrations in support of the war effort.

Southerners were equally eager to support their new nation. A *London Times* correspondent traveling in the South witnessed large crowds with "flushed faces, wild eyes, screaming mouths." They punctuated stirring renditions of "Dixie" with the high-pitched piercing sounds that would later be known as the "rebel yell." Enlistment rallies, wild send-offs at train stations, and auctions and balls to raise money for the troops were staged throughout the Confederacy. As in the North, war fever fired hatred of the enemy.

Appeals to God were commonplace on both sides. The feeling that a holy war was unfolding energized recruits. A Union soldier expressed his feelings in a letter home at the beginning of the war: "I believe our cause to be the cause of liberty and light ... the cause of God, and holy and justifiable in His sight, and for this reason, I fear not to die in it if need be." Equally convinced of the righteousness of his cause, a Confederate soldier wrote: "Our Cause is Just and God is Just and we shall finally be successful whether I live to see the time or not."

As war fever gripped North and South, volunteers on both sides rushed to join, quickly filling the quotas of both armies. Most soldiers were motivated by patriotism, a desire to defend their homes and loved ones, and a craving for glory and adventure. A recruiting poster in one Massachusetts town promised "travel and promotion" as well as good pay. Some men succumbed to the pressure of companions and sweethearts. A young Alabamian received a package from his fiancée with a skirt, a petticoat, and a note demanding "wear these or volunteer!" The initial enthusiasm, however, wore off quickly. After four months of war, a young Confederate soldier admitted, "I have seen quite enough of a soldier's life to satisfy me that it is not what it is cracked up to be."

The South in particular faced a contradiction between its ideology and the demands of full-scale war. Southerners were loyal to their localities, counties, and states. Southern leaders had been fighting for decades to defend states' rights against national authority. Now these same leaders had to forge the states of the Confederacy into a nation. By early spring of 1862, the Confederate government was compelled to order the first general draft in American history. It required three years service for men between 18 and 35 (a range later expanded from 17 to 50). In 1864, the Confederate Congress added a compulsory reenlistment provision. At that point, the only way a recruit could get out of the army was to die or desert.

The Confederate draft law allowed several occupational exemptions. Among them was an infamous provision that allowed one white man on any plantation with more than 20 slaves to be excused from service. The reason for the exemption was to ensure the security and productivity of large plantations, not to protect the privileged, but it led some southerners to conclude that the struggle had become "a rich man's war but a poor man's fight."

The initial flush of enthusiasm faded in the North as well. Responding to a call for additional troops, some northern states initiated a draft during the summer of 1862. In March 1863, Congress passed the Enrollment Act, a draft law that, like the Confederate draft, allowed for occupational exemptions. A provision that allowed a draftee to hire a substitute aroused resentment among working-class northerners. Anger at the draft, as well as poor working conditions, sparked several riots during 1863. But the North was less dependent on conscription than was the South. Only 8 percent of the Union's soldiers were drafted, compared to 20 percent for the Confederacy.

The complaints of many rank-and-file soldiers may give the impression that only people of lesser or modest means fought, but in fact the armies of both sides included men from all walks of life, from common laborers to clerks to bankers. An undetermined number of women, typically disguised as men, also served in both armies. Perhaps as many as 300 women joined the Union ranks, and about half that number enlisted in the Confederate army. They joined for the same reasons as men: adventure, patriotism, and glory.

The North's Advantage in Resources

The resources of the North, including its population, industrial and agricultural capacity, and transportation network, greatly exceeded those of the South (see Figure 15–1). The 2.1 million men who fought for the Union represented roughly half the men of military age in the North. The 900,000 men who fought for the Confederacy, by contrast, represented fully 90 percent of its eligible population. Irish and German immigrants continued to flow into the North during the war, although at a slower rate than before, and thousands of them enlisted, often as substitutes for native-born northerners. Nearly 200,000 African Americans, most of them ex-slaves from the South, took up arms for the Union. Not until the last month of the war did the Confederacy consider arming slaves.

The Confederacy compensated somewhat for its numerical disadvantage by requiring long tours of duty, which meant that its forces tended to be more experienced than those of the Union. But the Union's greater numbers left the South vulnerable to a war of attrition.

At the beginning of the war, the North controlled 90 percent of the nation's industrial capacity. It produced 17 times more cotton and woolen cloth than the South, 30 times more boots and shoes, and 32 times more firearms. The North had dozens of facilities for producing war matériel; the South had only one munitions plant, the Tredegar Iron Works in Richmond. Northern farms, more mechanized than their southern counterparts, produced record harvests of meat, grain, and vegetables. Southern farms were also productive, but the South lacked the North's capacity to transport and distribute food efficiently. The railroad system in the North was more than twice the size of the South's.

Thanks to the North's abundance of resources, no soldier in any previous American army had ever been outfitted as well as the blue-uniformed Union trooper. The official color of the Confederate uniform was gray, although a dusty brown shade was more common. Most southern soldiers, however, did not wear distinguishable uniforms, especially toward the end of the war. They also often lacked proper shoes or any footwear at all. In winter and on certain road surfaces, this shortage was a severe handicap. When the Confederate general Robert E. Lee invaded Maryland in 1862, he left behind several thousand barefoot soldiers because they could not march on gravel roads. Still, the South never lost a battle because of insufficient supplies or inadequate weaponry. New foundries opened, and manufacturing enterprises in Augusta, Georgia; Selma, Alabama; and elsewhere joined the Tredegar Iron Works in keeping the Confederate armies equipped.

Unstable finances proved more of a handicap for the Confederacy than its relatively low industrial capacity. The Confederate economy, and its treasury, depended heavily on cotton exports. But a Union naval blockade and the ability of textile manufacturers in Europe to find new sources of supply restricted this crucial source of revenue. The imposition of taxes would have improved the Confederacy's finances, but southerners resisted taxation. The government sold interest-bearing bonds to raise money, but as Confederate fortunes declined, so did bond sales. With few other options, the Confederacy financed more than 60 percent of the $1.5 billion it spent on the war with printing-press money. Inflation spiraled out of control, demoralizing civilians.

The Union had more abundant financial resources than the Confederacy, and the federal government was more successful than the Confederate government at developing innovative ways to meet the great cost of the war. Its first recourse was to borrow money by selling long-term interest-bearing bonds and shorter-term interest-bearing treasury notes. Together these bonds accounted for 66 percent of the $4 billion that the Union raised to wage the war. Like the Confederacy, the Federal government issued paper money, bills derisively known as "greenbacks," that was not backed by gold or silver. But the Federal government also offset its expenses with the country's first income tax, which citizens

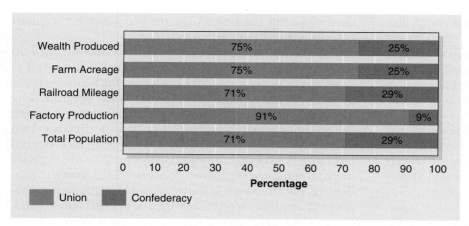

FIGURE 15–1   A Comparison of the Union and Confederate Control of Key Resources at the Outset of the Civil War

could pay in greenbacks, a move that bolstered the value and credibility of the paper currency. These financial measures eliminated the need for wage and price controls and rationing and warded off ruinous inflation in the North.

Leaders, Governments, and Strategies

Leadership ability, like resources, played an important role in the war. It was up to the leaders of the two sides to determine and administer civilian and military policy, to define war objectives, and to inspire a willingness to sacrifice in both citizens and soldiers.

Jefferson Davis and the South.   The Confederate president, Jefferson Davis, had to build a government from scratch during a war. Abraham Lincoln at least had the benefit of an established governmental structure, a standing army, healthy financial resources, and established diplomatic relations with the nations of Europe.

Davis and Lincoln were both born in Kentucky within a year and 100 miles of each other. Davis, like Lincoln, was born into modest circumstances. He attended the military academy at West Point, where he was a mediocre student. He abandoned his military career after seven years of service and married the 16-year-old daughter of General Zachary Taylor. Davis and his bride moved to a plantation in Mississippi, where she soon died of yellow fever. Immersing himself in books and cotton farming, Davis had emerged as a gentleman planter by the 1840s and married Varina Howell in 1845. He returned to military service during the Mexican War, fought well, and used his success to become a senator from Mississippi in 1847. He served as secretary of war under President Franklin Pierce and returned to the Senate in 1857.

Although Davis's career qualified him for the prodigious task of running the Confederacy, aspects of his character compromised his effectiveness. He had a sharp intellect but related awkwardly to people. Colleagues found him aloof. He was inclined to equate compromise with weakness and in-terpreted any opposition as a personal attack. His wife commented, "[I]f anyone disagrees with Mr. Davis he resents it and ascribes the difference to the perversity of his opponent." Davis was also fatalistic. According to his wife, when he heard that the Confederate Congress had selected him as president, he spoke of it "as a man might speak of a sentence of death."

Southerners viewed themselves as the genuine heirs of the American Revolution and the true defenders of the United States Constitution. If the South were to establish itself as a separate country, however, southerners had to renounce their American identity and develop one of their own. But on what distinctive aspects of southern life could the Confederacy build such an identity? Slavery was distinctively southern, but most white southerners, even if they believed that slavery served their interests, did not own slaves. Southerners had forcefully advanced the ideology of states' rights, but, with its emphasis on the primacy of state sovereignty over central authority, states' rights, too, was a weak foundation on which to build a national consciousness.

Although southerners fought for a variety of reasons, protecting their homes and families remained paramount. When these were threatened or destroyed, where would loyalty lie? Did Davis, or anyone else for that matter, possess the skill to hold together a new nation that was more like the nation it had renounced than anything that could replace it?

Abraham Lincoln and the North.   Northerners, like southerners, needed a convincing reason to endure the prolonged sacrifice of the Civil War. For them, the struggle was a distant one, fought mostly on southern soil. Lincoln and other northern leaders secured support by convincing their compatriots of the importance of preserving the Union. Lincoln eloquently articulated this view, framing the war as more than a military conquest. In a message to Congress on July 4, 1861, he explained that the struggle to preserve the Union was "not altogether for today; it is for a vast future." The president viewed the conflict in global terms, its results affecting the hopes for democratic government around the world. He concluded that the war "presents to the whole family of man, the question, whether a constitutional republic . . . can or cannot maintain its territorial integrity, against its own domestic foes."

Lincoln handled disagreement better than Davis did. He defused tense situations with folksy humor, and his simple eloquence captured the imagination of ordinary people, even if it did not persuade his political enemies. Lincoln viewed himself as a man of the people. He was not aloof, like Davis. Friends and critics alike agreed that Lincoln made himself available to them. Lincoln generated the type of affection among rank-and-file soldiers that eluded Davis. The president's occasional visit to the front generated both amusement and gratitude from the troops, owing to his ungainly appearance on a horse, and his easy way of conversing with the men. They serenaded "Old Abe," as they called him affectionately, with the popular tune "We Are Coming, Father Abraham." There is no record of Confederate tunesmiths composing similar ditties for their leaders.

Lincoln's fight for the border states.   The secession of Virginia, Arkansas, North Carolina, and Tennessee left four border slave states, Maryland, Delaware, Kentucky, and Missouri, hanging in the balance. Were Maryland and Delaware to secede, the federal capital at Washington, DC, would be surrounded by Confederate territory. The loss of Kentucky and Missouri would threaten the borders of Iowa, Illinois, Indiana, and Ohio and remove the Deep South from the threat of imminent invasion. Kentucky's manpower, livestock, and waterways were important to both sides. The state also had special symbolic significance as the birthplace of the two rival presidents. Lincoln viewed Kentucky as the key to retaining the three other border states: "I think to lose Kentucky is nearly to lose the whole game. Kentucky gone, we cannot hold Missouri, nor, as I think, Maryland.... We would as well consent to separation at once, including the surrender of this capital."

Lincoln adopted a "soft" strategy to secure the border states, stressing the restoration of the Union as the sole objective of Federal military operations and assuring border residents that his government would not interfere with slavery. Union commanders barred fugitive slaves from their camps during the first year of the war, promising "to keep the war a lily-white crusade," as one officer put it. But early reports from the four states were troubling. The four governors displayed polite indifference or overt hostility to the federal government.

Maryland's strategic location north of Washington, DC, rendered its loyalty to the Union vital. Although a majority of its citizens opposed secession, a mob attack on Union troops passing through Baltimore in April 1861 indicated strong pro-southern sentiment. Lincoln dispatched Federal troops to monitor the fall elections in the state, placed its legislature under military surveillance, and arrested officials who opposed the Union cause, including the mayor of Baltimore. This show of force guaranteed the pro-Union candidate for governor an overwhelming victory and saved Maryland for the Union. Delaware, although nominally a slave state, remained staunchly for the Union.

Missourians settled their indecision by combat. The fighting culminated with a Union victory in March 1862 at the Battle of Pea Ridge, Arkansas. Pro-Confederate Missourians refused to concede defeat and waged an unsuccessful guerrilla war over the next two years.

Kentucky never seceded but attempted to remain neutral at the outset of the war. The legislature was pro-Union,

the governor pro-southern. Both sides actively recruited soldiers in the state. In September 1861, when Confederate forces invaded Kentucky and Union forces moved to expel them, the state became one of the war's battlegrounds.

Although Virginia went with the Confederacy, some counties in the western part of the state opposed secession and, as early as the summer of 1861, took steps to establish a pro-Union state. In June 1863, West Virginia became the nation's thirty-fifth state.

Strategies and tactics.   To a great extent, the political objectives of each side determined its military strategy. Southerners wanted independence and protection of their institutions; Northerners fought to preserve the Union. The North's goal required conquest. Federal forces had to invade the South, destroy its armies, and rout its government. The Confederacy, for its part, did not need to conquer the North. Fighting a defensive battle in its own territory, the South had only to hang on until growing northern opposition to the war or some decisive northern military mistake convinced the Union to stop fighting.

But the South's strategy had two weaknesses. First, it demanded more patience than the South had shown in impulsively attacking Fort Sumter. Second, the South might not have sufficient resources to draw out the war long enough to swing northern public opinion behind peace. The question was: What would break first, northern support for the war or southern ability to wage it?

The Early War, 1861–1862

The North's offensive strategy dictated the course of the war for the first two years. In the West, the federal army's objectives were to hold Missouri, Kentucky, and Tennessee, to control the Mississippi River, and eventually to detach the area west of the Appalachians from the rest of the Confederacy. In the East, Union forces sought to capture Richmond, the Confederate capital. The U.S. Navy imposed a blockade along the Confederate coast and pushed into inland waterways to capture southern ports.

The Confederates defended strategic locations throughout their territory or abandoned them when prudence required. Occasionally, taking advantage of surprise or terrain, southern forces ventured out to engage Union armies. Between engagements, each side sniped at, bushwhacked, and trapped the other.

By the end of 1862, the result remained in the balance. Although Union forces had attained some success in the West, the southern armies there remained intact. In the East, where resourceful Confederate leaders several times stopped superior Union forces, the southerners clearly had the best of it.

First Bull Run

By July 1861, when the border states appeared more secure for the Union, President Lincoln shifted his attention southward

Global Perspectives

Nationalism and Self-Determination in Europe

The resurgence of nationalism in Europe coincided with the disintegration of the United States. In one sense, however, the American Civil War paralleled developments in Europe. White southerners claimed they were exercising the right of self-determination by seceding and forming the Confederate States of America. Similarly, peoples in Europe who shared the same language, culture, and sense of identity, chafed under the domination of Austrian or Russian imperial rule. Even within countries, such as Spain and France, ethnic minorities expressed their nationalism during this era as well. Castilians, Catalans, Basques, and Galicians, for example, identified more with their ethnic groups than with the national entity, Spain.

The twofold danger of surging nationalism, however, was that minorities within new nation states could find themselves vulnerable, as occurred with Jews when the Austro-Hungarian Empire collapsed after World War I, and, second, that the desire for a nation state could invariably lead to bloody conflicts and long-term misery. As the foreign minister of the Ottoman Empire, an entity with a shaky hold on various peoples in southeast Europe, noted in 1862, "Judge what would happen if free scope were given to all the different national aspirations.... It would need a century and torrents of blood to establish even a fairly stable state of affairs." Romanians, Serbs, and Bulgarians, still under Turkish rule at the time had different ideas, as did residents of the southern United States.

And in Italy as well, where parts of the country lay under the dominance of the Austrian Empire, the spirit of nationalism coursed through the kingdom of Piedmont-Sardinia in the modernizing north of Italy. The kingdom's prime minister, Camillo di Cavour, provoked the Austrian invasion of northern Italy in 1859 and employed newly built railroads to speed troops to the front. Cavour achieved two lightning victories against the Austrians that electrified the rest of Italy. In May 1860, Giuseppe Garibaldi along with nearly a thousand teenaged boys in red shirts liberated Sicily. A year later, King Victor Emmanual of Piedmont-Sardinia proclaimed the new kingdom of Italy. For Italians, their new nation culminated the *Risorgimento*—literally "rebirth" — much as Abraham Lincoln hoped that the U.S. Civil War would lead to "a new birth of freedom" across a united country.

- **Was Confederate nationalism comparable to the nationalist movements in Europe occurring at the same time?**

---

and ordered General Irvin McDowell to move his forces into Virginia to take Richmond (see Map 15–1). Confronting McDowell 20 miles southwest of Washington at Manassas, an important junction on the railroad that supplied the Confederate capital, was a Confederate army under General P. G. T. Beauregard. The two armies clashed on July 21 at the First Battle of Bull Run (known to the Confederacy as the First Battle of Manassas). The Union troops seemed at first on the verge of winning. But Beauregard's forces, along with General Joseph E. Johnston's reinforcements, repulsed the assault, scattering not only the Union army but also hundreds of picnickers who had come out from Washington to watch the fight. At the height of the battle, General Barnard Bee of South Carolina called out to Colonel Thomas J. Jackson for assistance. Jackson, a Virginia college professor turned officer, either did not hear Bee or chose to ignore him. In exasperation, Bee shouted, "There stands Jackson, like a damned stone wall!" The rebuke became, in the curious alchemy of battlefield gossip, a shorthand for courage and steadfastness. Jackson's men henceforth called him "Stonewall."

Bull Run dispelled some illusions and reinforced others. It boosted southerners' confidence and seemed to confirm their boast that one Confederate could whip ten Yankees, even though the opposing armies were of relatively equal strength when the fighting began. The Union rout planted the suspicion in northern minds that perhaps the Confederates were invincible and destroyed the widespread belief in the North that the war would be over quickly.

The War in the West

Federal forces may have retreated in Virginia, but they advanced in the west. Two Confederate forts on the Tennessee-Kentucky border, Fort Henry on the Tennessee River and Fort Donelson on the Cumberland River, guarded the strategic waterways that linked Tennessee and Kentucky to the Mississippi Valley. The forts also defended Nashville, the

MAP 15–1   From First Bull Run to Antietam: The War in the East, 1861–1862
The early stages of the war demonstrated the strategies of the Confederacy and the Union. Federal troops stormed into Virginia hoping to capture Richmond and bring a quick end to the war. Through a combination of poor generalship and Confederate tenacity, they failed. Confederate troops hoped to defend their territory, prolong the war, and eventually win their independence as northern patience evaporated. They proved successful initially, but, with the abandonment of the defensive strategy and the invasion of Maryland in the fall of 1862, the Confederates suffered a political and morale setback at Antietam.

Tennessee state capital (see Map 15–2). In February 1862, Union general Ulysses S. Grant coordinated a land and river campaign against the forts, with Flag Officer Andrew H. Foote commanding a force of ironclad Union gunboats.

Grant, recently promoted to brigadier general, had resigned from the army in the 1850s after a mediocre career marked by bouts of excessive drinking. Before rejoining the army, he had worked in his family's struggling leather business

in Illinois. A plain-looking man, with dark-brown hair and a beard streaked with gray, he often looked as if he had slept in his uniform. Behind the rumpled appearance lay a flexible military mind that would eventually grasp how the Civil War must be won.

Grant appreciated the strategic importance of river systems in the conquest of the western Confederacy. His combined river and land campaign caught the southerners unprepared and outflanked. By February 16, both forts had fallen. The Union victory drove a wedge into southern territory and closed the Confederacy's quickest path to the west from Virginia and the Carolinas. The Confederacy's only safe link across the Appalachians was now through Georgia. The Confederacy never recovered its strategic advantage in the West after the loss of Forts Henry and Donelson.

Grant next moved his main army south to Pittsburgh Landing on the Tennessee River, to prepare for an assault on the key Mississippi River port and rail center of Vicksburg. After blunting a surprise Confederate attack at Shiloh Church near Pittsburgh Landing, Grant pushed the southerners back to Corinth, Mississippi.

Federal forces complemented their victories at Shiloh and Corinth with another important success at New Orleans. Admiral David G. Farragut, who remained a Unionist even though born in Tennessee, blasted the Confederate river defenses protecting New Orleans and sailed a federal fleet to the city in April 1862. The result was to open 200 miles of the Mississippi River, the nation's most vital commercial waterway, to Union traffic. With the fall of Memphis to Union forces in June, Vicksburg remained the only major river town still in Confederate hands. The western losses exposed a major problem in the Confederates' defensive strategy: Their military resources were stretched too thin to defend their vast territory.

Reassessing the War: The Human Toll
The fierce fighting at Shiloh wrought unprecedented carnage. More American soldiers were lost at Shiloh than in all of the nation's wars combined up to that time. Each side suffered more than 10,000 casualties. By the time the smoke had cleared, the soldiers' initial enthusiasm and bravado were replaced by the sober realization that death or capture was a likely outcome, and that heroism, courage, and piety did not guarantee survival. "Too shocking, too horrible," a Confederate survivor of Shiloh wrote. "God grant that I may never be the partaker in such scenes again...when released from this I shall ever be an advocate of peace." A Union soldier wrote of "the dead and dying lying in masses, some with arms, legs, and even their jaws shot off, bleeding to death, and no one to wait upon them to dress their wounds."

Landing in a hospital scarcely improved a wounded or ill soldier's chances of survival. Kate Cumming, a nurse at a Confederate hospital in Corinth, wrote of soldiers brought from the battle "mutilated in every imaginable way." The wounded lay packed together on the floor, and Cumming negotiated

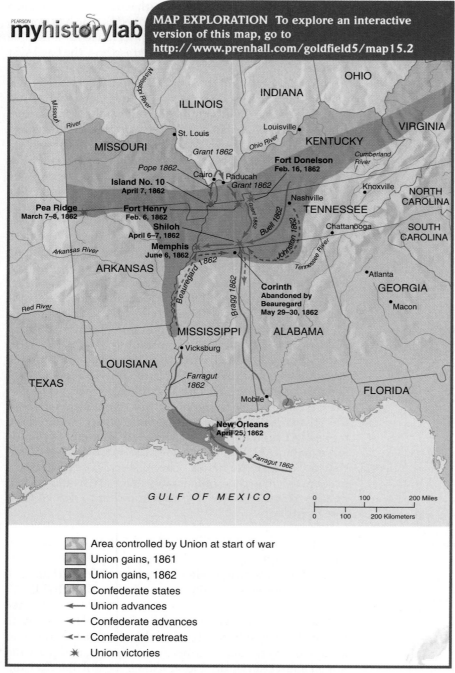

MAP EXPLORATION To explore an interactive version of this map, go to http://www.prenhall.com/goldfield5/map15.2

Area controlled by Union at start of war
Union gains, 1861
Union gains, 1862
Confederate states
Union advances
Confederate advances
Confederate retreats
Union victories

MAP 15–2   The War in the West, 1861–1862
Because of the early Union emphasis on capturing Richmond, the war in the West seemed less important to northerners. But from a strategic standpoint, the victories at Forts Henry and Donelson, which drove a wedge into southern territory and closed the Confederacy's quickest path to the West from Virginia and the Carolinas, and the capture of New Orleans and its Mississippi River port were crucial and set the stage for greater federal success in the West in 1863.

the rooms with great difficulty to avoid stepping on the dead and dying. Piercing the air were the screams of men undergoing amputations, often with little or no anesthetic. Some pleaded with physicians to kill them and end their misery. Others bore the pain stoically and entrusted last words and letters to nurses, dying with the word "Mother" or the name of their wife or sweetheart on their lips.

Women on both sides played a major role in caring for the wounded and sick. In the North, members of the U.S. Sanitary Commission attempted to upgrade hospital and medical care. This voluntary organization, founded in April 1861, was staffed mainly by women volunteers who collected and distributed medical supplies and clothing and advised on cleaning hospitals and camps. The commission made some headway during the first year of the war, but in the months after Shiloh and with the resumption of fighting in the east, the extent of casualties often overwhelmed the dedicated volunteers. And the bloodiest fighting lay ahead.

Along with the U.S. Christian Commission, the "Sanitarians" also looked after soldiers' spiritual needs regardless of whether they wanted such ministrations. Nurses who operated independently, such as Clara Barton, had little use for the Sanitarians. She chafed at the bureaucratic red tape that she claimed had replaced nursing as the primary objective of caring for the wounded. Barton resented the care with spiritual strings attached. She never gave the soldiers lectures or handed out religious tracts. She mostly just sat and listened, dressed their wounds, and offered them food.

Barton considered the Sanitarians amateurs and unfeeling, but the dark-haired New Englander set a very high standard. She would go out to battlefields, horrific as they were, and tend to the wounded even before the smoke had cleared. When the Confederates launched an artillery attack at Antietam, every male surgical assistant abandoned the field, but Barton and the surgeon stayed behind to save the lives of maimed soldiers. After the Union debacle at Fredericksburg in December 1862, she commandeered the homes of the townspeople, few of whom took kindly to

Several hundred women, disguised as men, made their contribution to the war effort by enlisting. Frances Clalin served with Federal forces in Missouri. Many were found out after suffering wounds or illness.

the invading federal army, so the wounded would have shelter, an action her male superiors were reluctant to take. As she noted with sarcasm, the city's elegant homes "were opened to the 'dirty, lousy soldiers' of the Union Army." Little wonder that a Union surgeon remarked, "I thought that night, if heaven ever sent out a homely angel, she must be one; her assistance was so timely."

Yet, it was a struggle for these women. It was a milestone when the federal government appointed Dorothea Dix as Superintendent of Female Nurses of the Army, but the recruiting restrictions she operated under gave numerous potential volunteers pause: "No women under thirty years of age need apply to serve in government hospitals. All nurses are required to be very plain looking women. Their dresses must be brown or black, with no bows, no curls, no jewelry." Barton's heated clashes with surgeons and military officials who wanted to limit her access or who devalued her advice and work probably accounted for her foolhardy heroism in braving enemy fire to tend the wounded.

Southern female nurses confronted similar male opposition. Kate Cumming, a Scottish immigrant who had settled in Alabama, constantly fought Confederate authorities and male medical personnel for her right to tend the wounded soldiers, plan their meals, and even suggest treatment. Cumming spilled out her frustration in her diary concerning the "opposition of surgeons [to] all of the ladies who have desired to go into hospitals. I can not see what else we can do, as the war is certainly ours as well as that of the men. We can not fight, so must take care of those who do." Worse, for a southern woman, their presence in the hospitals seemed to remove the responsibility of men to act chivalrous toward them. As Cumming demanded, "I ask but one thing from any surgeon, and that is, to be treated with the same respect due to men in their own sphere of life. I waive all claim for that due me as a lady, but think I have a right to expect the other."

Advanced weaponry combined with outdated military tactics to increase the death toll. The rifle, a relatively new innovation, was the weapon of choice for both sides. Unlike the smooth-bore musket, a rifled bore spun the bullets it fired, thereby increasing the killing range from 50 to 400 yards, although soldiers rarely began firing before the enemy came within 100 yards. Tactics, however, did not change accordingly. Soldiers still lined up close together and attacked in a line as they approached the entrenched enemy forces. Only late in the war did these wasteful tactics change, but even then, the problems of communication and the inability to precisely coordinate attacks led officers to continue the practice of ordering packed ranks of men to advance forward at a trot, often in the face of withering fire.

Even if a soldier escaped death on the battlefield and survived a hospital stay, he still faced the possibility of death from disease. Roughly twice as many men died from disease as on the battlefield during the Civil War. Heaps of garbage, contaminated food and water, and swarming mosquitoes, flies, and lice created unhealthy camp conditions. Typhoid, commonly and appropriately known as "camp fever," claimed the most lives.

Many soldiers turned to religion for consolation in response to the growing carnage. The frequency of camp prayer meetings and revivals increased after Shiloh. Many a recruit carried books with such titles as *Satan's Bait* and *A Mother's Parting Words to Her Soldier Boy* in his knapsack. Soldiers often gathered with their comrades to sing hymns before retiring for the night. Stories circulated of a Bible carried in a pocket that stopped a bullet whistling toward a soldier's heart. But veterans knew that a deck of cards did just as well, and they understood that neither Bibles nor cards offered protection against artillery.

The harsh conditions of camp life often strained relations between officers and enlisted men. Soldiers also suffered from boredom. Battles rarely lasted more than a day or two. In camp between engagements, a recruit faced seemingly incessant drilling (loading and firing a rifle required nine separate steps) and heavy chores such as chopping wood and hauling water. Typically, he spent what little time remained resting, writing, reading, and eating. To relieve their anxieties, soldiers talked about home and loved ones, upcoming or recent battles, and food. Soldiers also fought the boredom and harsh physical conditions of camp life by singing, playing cards, and competing in sports like foot racing and makeshift forms of football and baseball.

Women camp followers cooked, did laundry, and provided sexual services for a price. The two capitals, Washington and Richmond, had notorious vice districts. A Confederate recruit lamented that "almost half of the women in the vicinity of the army, married and unmarried, are lost to all virtue." Both armies experienced soaring rates of venereal disease.

By 1862, the war's carnage and brutality had dispelled any lingering notions of war as a chivalrous enterprise. At a battle in Virginia that year, Stonewall Jackson reprimanded a Confederate general who had ordered his men not to shoot at a Union officer riding before his own men, rallying them on. "This is no ordinary war," Jackson said, "and the brave and gallant Federal officers are the very kind that must be killed. Shoot the brave officers and the cowards will run away and take the men with them." The reluctance of some commanders to pursue retreating armies or to initiate campaigns resulted in part from their recognition of how awful the war really was.

There is no doubt, though, that the war became more brutal after Shiloh. Civilian populations became fair game, and when Confederate marksmen used severely wounded Union combatants for target practice as they lay below them at Fredericksburg that winter, it was clear that the war was entering a new, more brutal phase. Total war? As far back as the Peloponnesian War, officers had targeted civilians. But the Civil War was the first industrialized war and the impact on combat was devastating. Union General William T. Sherman understood the terrible nature of this war early on: "war is cruelty, and you cannot refine it." And Sherman did not attempt to refine it. The length of the war contributed to its brutality. Time to dehumanize the enemy and rationalize the killing. The North became more desperate to end the struggle, and the South to prolong it in order to exhaust the patience of northerners. Both objectives were prescriptions for tragedy.

The War in the East

With Grant and Farragut squeezing the Confederacy in the West, Lincoln ordered a new offensive against Richmond in the East that he believed would end the war. Following the defeat at Bull Run, he had shaken up the Union high command and appointed General George B. McClellan to lead what was now called the Army of the Potomac. A West Point graduate, McClellan had served with distinction in the Mexican War. He was now called back into active duty to assume command of the Army of the Potomac, which was no more than a collection of raw recruits and disgruntled veterans. McClellan succeeded in transforming it into a disciplined fighting force. He was well liked by his soldiers, who referred to him affectionately as "Little Mac." McClellan returned their affection, perhaps too much. A superb organizer, he would prove overly cautious on the field of battle.

In March 1862, at the outset of the Peninsula Campaign, McClellan moved his 112,000-man army out of Washington and maneuvered his forces by boat down the Potomac River and Chesapeake Bay to the peninsula between the York and James rivers southeast of the Confederate capital (see Map 15–1). Union forces took Yorktown, Williamsburg, and Norfolk. Confederate general Joseph E. Johnston withdrew his forces up the peninsula toward Richmond, preparing for what most felt would be the decisive battle of the war. McClellan, moving ponderously up the peninsula, clashed with Johnston's army inconclusively at Seven Pines in late May 1862. Johnston was badly wounded in the clash, and President Davis replaced him with General Robert E. Lee, who renamed the forces under his command the Army of Northern Virginia.

Lee was from a prominent Virginia family long accustomed to power and command. His father, "Light-Horse Harry" Lee, had been a Revolutionary War hero. Lee attended West Point, served with distinction in the Mexican War, and commanded the federal force that captured John Brown at Harpers Ferry in 1859. In 1831, he married Mary Custis, the daughter of George Washington's adopted son. Their gracious home in Arlington, Virginia, had a commanding view of the Potomac and Washington, DC. Before the war, it had seemed as if Lee would live out his days as a soldier-farmer, much like his wife's grandfather.

In 1860, the army posted Lee to Texas, where he watched the secession drama unfold. He opposed secession but was unwilling to take up arms against his native Virginia. Refusing an offer from Winfield Scott to take command of the federal forces, he resigned from the U.S. Army and went with Virginia after it left the Union. Lee's reserved and aristocratic bearing masked a gambler's disposition. A fellow officer noted, "his name might be Audacity. He will take more chances, and take them quicker than any other general in this country." Under his daring leadership, the Confederacy's defensive strategy underwent an important shift.

Lee seized the initiative on June 25, 1862, attacking McClellan's right flank. Although inconclusive, the attack pushed the nervous McClellan into a defensive position. For a week, the armies sparred in a series of fierce engagements known collectively as the Seven Days' Battles. More than 30,000 men were killed or wounded on both sides, the deadliest week of the war so far. Although McClellan prevailed in these contests,

The Soldiers' War

The Civil War was a conflict where military tactics had not yet caught up with weapons technology. The result was unprecedented carnage experienced by a mainly civilian army on both sides. Military doctors at the time reported soldiers who suffered from extreme "exhaustion," so severe that it was difficult to rouse them from sleep in the morning. They also noted "disordered actions of the heart," a type of arrhythmia traumatized soldiers experienced after combat. When the soldiers returned home after the war, the symptoms persisted. The first professional paper diagnosing what we now term Post Traumatic Stress Disorder (PTSD) appeared in 1876. During World War I, physicians termed the trauma "shell shock," but, as after the Civil War, treatment, other than a rest cure, remained elusive. At the outset of World War II, military recruiters attempted to screen inductees for psychological problems, assuming a connection between shell shock and a previously existing mental illness, a correlation that remained unproved.

PTSD was first termed in 1980 in response to chronic physical and emotional problems suffered by returning Vietnam veterans, especially a relatively high suicide rate. The recognition of exhaustion, flashbacks, hypervigilance, heart arrhythmia, and the inability to relax or relate as a specific mental illness aided in treatment. The illness has been especially widespread among soldiers who have served in Iraq. By 2007, of the nearly 250,000 veterans discharged from duty in Iraq and Afghanistan, more than 12,000 have sought counseling for PTSD. The Veterans Administration now has a specific program that addresses the psychological needs of returning veterans.

Although technology has improved the survival rate, the care of trained nurses (usually women) remain indispensable for both the physical and mental recovery of the wounded.

■ If medical recognition of the psychological trauma of war existed during and after the Civil War, why did not the medical profession and the government address the problem until more than a century later?

Nurse Ann Bell tends a fallen Union Soldier. The war helped open nursing as a respectable occupation for women.

PEARSON myhistorylab
From Then to Now Online

15-1 Ambrose Bierce, "What I Saw at Shiloh," in Bierrce, *Civil War Stories* (New York: Dover, 1994): p. 17.

15-2 Walt Whitman, from *With Walt Whitman in Camden.*

15-3 "Hearing on Mental Health Problems Confronting Soldiers Returning from Iraq, Afghanistan," U.S. House of Representatives, Committee on Oversight and Government Reform, May 24, 2007.

the carnage so shocked him that he withdrew to Harrison's Landing on the James River. An exasperated Lincoln replaced McClellan with John Pope. Although Lee had saved Richmond, his troops had suffered frightfully. He had lost one-fourth of his 80,000-man army, but he remained convinced of the wisdom of his offensive-defensive strategy.

Lee went to work to vindicate these tactics. A series of inconclusive skirmishes brought Union and Confederate armies together once more near Manassas Junction. The Second Battle of Bull Run was as much a disaster for the Union as the first had been. Lee's generalship befuddled Pope and again saved Richmond. Lee and the Army of Northern Virginia were developing a reputation for invincibility.

Turning Points, 1862–1863

The impressive Confederate victories in the East masked the delicate condition of southern fortunes. Lee's offensive-defensive strategy seemed to be working, but it raised the possibility that the Confederacy could exhaust its men and resources before it sealed its independence.

The waning summer months of 1862 brought other concerns to the Davis administration in Richmond. The Union navy was choking the South's commercial link with Europe. Davis looked to the nations of Europe for diplomatic recognition as well as for trade.

Having stymied the Union war machine, Lee contemplated a bold move, a thrust into northern territory to bring the conflict to the North and stoke northerners' rising hostility to the war. President Lincoln also harbored a bold plan. Gradually, during the spring and summer of 1862, the president had concluded that emancipation of the Confederacy's slaves was essential for preserving the Union. Emancipation would provide federal forces with both moral and strategic advantages over their foes. But Lincoln was reluctant to take this step before the Union's fortunes on the battlefield improved. Without a significant victory, emancipation would appear to be an act of desperation. As the fall of 1862 approached, the Union and Confederate governments both prepared for the most significant conflicts of the war to date.

The Naval and the Diplomatic War

The Union's naval strategy was to blockade the southern coast and capture its key seaports and river towns. The intention was to prevent arms, clothing, and food from reaching the Confederacy and keep cotton and tobacco from leaving. Destroying the South's ability to carry on trade would prevent the Confederacy from raising money to purchase the goods it needed to wage war. This vital trade brought the Confederacy into contact with European nations, a connection its leaders hoped to reinforce on the diplomatic front.

The Naval War.   Neither side had much of a navy at the outset of the war. With more than 3,000 miles of Confederate coastline to cover, the Union blockade was weak at first.

As time passed and the number of ships in the Union navy grew, the blockade tightened. The skyrocketing prices of southern staples on world markets by 1862 attested to the effectiveness of the Union strategy.

Understandably, the Confederate naval strategy was to break the blockade and defend the South's vital rivers and seaports. The Confederacy built several warships to serve as blockade runners and as privateers to attack Union merchant ships, and they briefly disrupted federal operations before Union vessels regained the advantage. Historians disagree about the effectiveness of the Union naval blockade, but with limited resources and capital, the Confederacy was heavily dependent on the flow of trade. Any restriction in the flow hurt the southern cause.

The diplomatic front.   Southerners were convinced that their cotton was so important to the world economy that they could use it as a diplomatic bargaining chip. "You dare not to make war on cotton.... Cotton is king." So declared South Carolina senator James H. Hammond in a warning to the North in 1858. But the British had large cotton reserves and an alternative source of supply in Egypt, and thus King Cotton was no more successful at coercing them into granting recognition to the Confederacy than it was at stopping the North from going to war.

The Davis administration did chalk up some minor diplomatic victories early in the war. Great Britain declared itself neutral and allowed British merchants to sell arms and supplies to both the Confederacy and the Union. This policy especially benefited the Confederacy because of its limited arsenal. France followed with a similar concession.

In the end, the Confederacy's hopes for diplomatic recognition depended on its ability to show that it could secure its independence on the battlefield. After Lee's victories in Virginia in the spring of 1862 and his subsequent decision to invade the North, British intervention in the war grew more likely. The British government had more or less decided that if Lee emerged victorious from his planned invasion, it would press for mediation. William Gladstone, England's future prime minister, believed that Lee would achieve his goal.

Antietam

The alarming arithmetic of the offensive-defensive strategy convinced Lee that the South could not sustain a prolonged conflict. He knew that his army must keep up the pressure on the Union forces and, if possible, destroy them quickly. Union success in the Mississippi Valley threatened to cut the Confederacy in two and deprive it of the resources of a vast chunk of territory. Within a year, the Confederacy might cease to exist west of the Appalachians. He desperately needed a dramatic victory.

In September 1862, Lee crossed the Potomac into Maryland (see Map 15–1). He was on his way to cut the Pennsylvania Railroad at Harrisburg. Lee established camp at Frederick, scattering his army at various sites, convinced that McClellan and the Army of the Potomac would not attack him.

Luck intervened for the North. At an abandoned Confederate encampment, a Union corporal found three wrapped cigars on the ground, evidently tossed away by a careless Confederate officer. To the corporal's amazement, the wrapping was a copy of Lee's orders for the disposition of his army. But even with this information, "Little Mac" moved so cautiously that Lee had time to retreat to defensive positions at Sharpsburg, Maryland, along Antietam Creek. There Lee's army of 39,000 men came to blows with McClellan's army of 75,000.

The Battle of Antietam saw the bloodiest single day of fighting in American history. About 2,100 Union soldiers and 2,700 Confederates died, and another 18,500, equally divided, were wounded. McClellan squandered his numerical superiority with uncoordinated and timid attacks. Although the armies had fought to a tactical draw, the battle was a strategic defeat for the Confederacy. In the battle's aftermath, Lee's troops limped back across the Potomac into Virginia and McClellan did not pursue them.

Antietam marked a major turning point in the war. It kept Lee from directly threatening northern industry and financial institutions. It prompted Britain and France to abandon plans to grant recognition to the Confederacy. And it provided Lincoln with the victory he needed to announce the abolition of slavery.

Emancipation

President Lincoln despised slavery, but he had always maintained that preserving the Union was his primary war goal. "If I could save the Union without freeing any slave I would do it," he wrote to the newspaper editor Horace Greeley in August 1862, "and if I could save it by freeing all the slaves I would do it; and if I could save it by freeing some and leaving others alone, I would also do that." An astute politician, Lincoln realized that he had to stress Union and equivocate on slavery to keep the northern public united in support of the war. But from the war's outset, the possibility of emancipation as a war objective was considered in the Republican Congress, in the Union army, and among citizens throughout the Northern states. Northern soldiers, as they moved South, saw slaves building trenches, earthworks, bridges, and roads for the Confederate army as well as working southern farms. As a result, pressure grew within the Union army to declare emancipation as a way of depriving the South and the Confederate army of their labor force.

Lincoln had said in his inaugural address that he had "no purpose, directly or indirectly, to interfere with the institution of slavery in the states where it exists." By March 1862, however, his moral repugnance for slavery, and the military arguments for abolition, led him to propose a resolution, which Congress adopted, supporting the compensated emancipation of slaves. The measure died, however, when Congress failed to appropriate funds for it and slaveholders in the border states expressed no interest in the plan.

Pressure from northern civilians, Union soldiers, and Congress for some form of emancipation mounted in the spring of 1862. In response, the Republican Congress prohibited slavery in the territories and abolished slavery in the District of Columbia. The act emancipating the district's slaves called for compensating slave owners and colonizing the freed slaves in black republics, such as Haiti and Liberia. Then, in July 1862, Congress passed the **Confiscation Act,** which ordered the seizure of land from disloyal southerners and the emancipation of their slaves.

Although support for emancipation had grown both in the army and among civilians, Lincoln still faced political considerations that dictated against it. Emancipation was still not favored by a majority in the North, especially not in the border states. The thousands of Irish Catholic immigrants who entered the Union army and who had competed with black workers for jobs in northern cities during the 1850s were especially opposed to emancipation, fearing a loss of economic security. They also resented the abolitionists' Protestant moralizing. The Roman Catholic archbishop of New York, John Hughes, declared that "We Catholics, and a vast majority of our brave troops in the field, have not the slightest idea of carrying on a war that costs so much blood and treasure just to gratify a clique of abolitionists in the North." But other considerations favored emancipation. Freeing the slaves would appeal to the strong antislavery sentiment in Britain and gain support for the Union cause abroad. And it would weaken the Confederacy's ability to wage war by removing a crucial source of labor.

The Emancipation Proclamation. By mid-1862, the president had resolved to act on his moral convictions and proclaim emancipation. Taking the advice of Secretary of State Seward, however, he decided to wait for a battlefield victory so that the measure would not appear an act of desperation. Antietam gave the president his opening, narrow though it was, and on September 22, 1862, he announced his intention to issue the **Emancipation Proclamation,** to take effect January 1, 1863, in all states still in rebellion. The proclamation exempted slaves in the border states loyal to the Union and in areas under Federal occupation. By raising the stakes of the war, President Lincoln hoped to shorten it. And, by leaving slaves in the border states untouched, he maintained their loyalty, or at least their neutrality.

But it would be a mistake to attribute Lincoln's motives primarily to military necessity. Like most Americans of the time, he believed that God intervened directly in the affairs of men. Secretary of the Navy Gideon Welles took notes on the cabinet meeting that followed the victory at Antietam. According to Welles's account, Lincoln made little reference to political or military strategy at the meeting. Instead, the president explained that he "had made a vow, a covenant, that if God gave us the victory in the approaching battle, he would consider it an indication of Divine will, and that it was his duty to move forward in the cause of emancipation."

Even before the Emancipation Proclamation, slaves throughout the South "stole" their freedom. After the Proclamation, the trickle of black slaves abandoning their masters became a flood as they sought freedom behind Union lines.

Theodore Kaufman (American, b. 1814), *On to Liberty*, 1867, oil on canvas, 36″ × 56″ (91.4 × 142.2 cm). The Metropolitan Museum of Art. Gift of Irving and Joyce Wolf, 1982 (1982.443.3). Photograph 1982 The Metropolitan Museum of Art.

Southerners reacted to the Emancipation Proclamation with outrage. Some viewed it as an invitation to race war and conjured up fears of freed slaves slaying white women and children while their men were at the battlefront. Jefferson Davis, taking a positive view, thought that the proclamation would invigorate the southern war effort. Some observers abroad were skeptical. One London newspaper, noting that emancipation did not apply to all slaves, stated, "the principle is not that a human being cannot justly own another, but that he cannot own him unless he is loyal to the United States."

Northerners generally approved of the Emancipation Proclamation. Although abolitionists comprised a minority of the northern population, most civilians and soldiers recognized the military advantages of emancipation. A private in the Army of the Potomac wrote home his support for "putting away any institution if by so doing it will help put down the rebellion."

The Emancipation Proclamation represented far more than its qualified words and phrases expressed. "A mighty act," Massachusetts governor John Andrew called it. Lincoln had freed the slaves. He and the Union war effort were now tied to the cause of freedom. What had begun as a war to save the Union was now a holy war of deliverance. Freedom and Union entwined in the public consciousness of the North. As Lincoln noted in his December 1862 message to Congress, "[I]n giving freedom to the slave, we assure freedom to the free." Emancipation also unified the Republican Party and strengthened the president's hand in conducting the war.

"Stealing" freedom.   As word of the Emancipation Proclamation raced through the slave grapevine, slaves rejoiced. But the proclamation only continued a process that had begun when the first Union armies invaded the South. In the months before freedom came, many slaves had run away to Union camps, dug Union trenches, and scouted for Federal troops.

Southern masters fought to deter their slaves by severely punishing the families of black men who fled to the Union lines. They used the courts and slave catchers to reclaim runaways. Some Confederate masters protected their investments by removing slaves to Texas or to areas far from federal forces. And a few slave owners whipped, sold, and even killed their slaves to prevent them from joining the Union troops.

But in the end, slaveholders could not stem the tide of slaves fleeing toward the Union lines and freedom. The 1862 Confiscation Act included slaves with other Confederate property as "contraband" of war and subject to confiscation. As they helped the Union cause, contrabands also sought to help fellow slaves "steal" their freedom. When Union forces occupied part of the Georgia coast in April 1862, for example, March Haynes, a slave who had worked as a river pilot in Savannah, began smuggling slaves to the Union lines. Federal general Quincy Adams Gilmore provided a fast boat for Haynes's missions. In return, Haynes supplied Gilmore with "exact and valuable information" on the strength and location of Confederate defenses.

The former slaves who arrived at federal camps after emancipation often encountered poor conditions but relished their freedom nonetheless. A northern missionary in occupied Louisiana wrote in 1863 that he was surrounded by "negroes in uniform, negroes in rags, negroes in frame houses, negroes living in tents, negroes living in rail pens covered with brush, and negroes living under brush piles without any rails, negroes living on the bare ground with the sky for their covering; all hopeful... every one pleading to be taught, willing to do anything for learning."

The Emancipation Proclamation accelerated the slaves' flight from bondage. After 1863, ex-slaves served in increasing numbers in the Union army.

however, public opinion was changing. One reason was that white northerners realized that the enlistment of African Americans relieved them from military service. President Lincoln strongly advocated enlisting former slaves. In March 1863, he wrote, with exaggerated enthusiasm, that "the bare sight of 50,000 armed and drilled black soldiers on the banks of the Mississippi would end the rebellion at once." On the contrary, the appearance of black Union troops infuriated the Confederates. After a battle at Milliken's Bend, Louisiana, in 1863, for example, observers found dead Confederate and black Union soldiers entangled in each other's arms and impaled on one another's bayonets.

The Confederate government formally labeled white officers leading black troops as instigators of slave rebellion and punished them accordingly, presumably by hanging. Black soldiers, when captured, were returned to slavery. The Lincoln administration retaliated by suspending prisoner exchanges, which resulted in horrible conditions in Confederate and Union prisons. Roughly 56,000 prisoners died in captivity, a toll that would have been much lower had Confederate authorities treated black prisoners of war the same as whites.

On some occasions, Confederate treatment of African American prisoners of war was worse than a return to bondage. In April 1864, General Nathan Bedford Forrest, a slave-trader prior to the war and a founder of the Ku Klux Klan after the war, overran federal positions at Fort Pillow, Tennessee. Although the black Union defenders surrendered, Forrest's men shouted, "Kill the damn niggers, shoot them down!" More than 100 surrendered black soldiers were murdered, along with some white officers. The same month, a Confederate regiment of Choctaw Indians scalped and mutilated an even larger number of surrendered black troops at Poison Spring, Arkansas.

But for black volunteers, the promise of freedom and redemption outweighed the dangers of combat. Black abo-

Black troops in the Union Army. More than 80 percent of the roughly 180,000 black soldiers and 20,000 black sailors who fought for the Union were slaves and free black men from the South. For the typical black southerner who joined the army, the passage from bondage to freedom came quickly. Making his escape from his master, he perhaps "stole" his family as well. He typically experienced his first days of freedom behind Union lines, where he may have learned to read and write. Finally, he put on the federal uniform, experiencing, as one black southern volunteer commented, "the biggest thing that ever happened in my life."

Initially, the enlistment of black soldiers in South Carolina encountered opposition in the North. By early 1863,

Black Union troops—former slaves—repelling Confederates at New Bern, NC, February 1864; African Americans, both free and slave, fought valiantly and often fiercely for their freedom; the alternative was sometimes execution on the spot or re-enslavement.

litionists campaigned tirelessly for the enlistment of free black men and fugitive slaves in the Union army. Frederick Douglass, whose son Lewis distinguished himself in the all-black 54th Massachusetts Volunteer Infantry Regiment, explained in early 1863, "Once let the black man get upon his person the brass letters, 'U.S.,' let him get an eagle on his buttons and a musket on his shoulder and bullets in his pockets, and there is no power on earth which can deny that he has earned the right to citizenship in the United States." Other black abolitionists took up the refrain. Sojourner Truth, a former slave who saw many of her thirteen children sold into slavery, canvassed northern cities to rally public opinion for the deployment of black troops.

Although black soldiers were eager to engage the enemy and fought as ably as their white comrades, they received lower pay and performed the most menial duties in camp. Abolitionists and black leaders pressured President Lincoln for more equitable treatment of African American recruits. When Frederick Douglass complained to Lincoln about the lower pay for black troops, the president defended the practice, noting that "their enlistment was a serious offense to popular prejudice" and the fact "that they were not to receive the same pay as white soldiers seemed a necessary concession to smooth the way to their employment at all as soldiers."

Despite discrimination, black soldiers fought valiantly at Port Hudson, Louisiana; near Charleston; and, late in the war, at the siege of Petersburg, Virginia. The most celebrated black encounter with Confederate troops occurred in July 1863, during a futile assault by the 54th Massachusetts Regiment on Fort Wagner outside Charleston. The northern press, previously lukewarm toward black troops, heaped praise on the effort. "Through the cannon smoke of that dark night," intoned a writer in the *Atlantic Monthly,* "the manhood of the colored race shines before many eyes that would not see."

If only President Lincoln could find such gallantry among his generals! George McClellan had failed to follow his advantage at Antietam in September 1862, allowing Lee's army to escape to Virginia and remain a formidable fighting force. And despite Union successes in the West, the Confederate forces massed there remained largely intact.

From Fredericksburg to Gettysburg

In late 1862, after Antietam, the president replaced McClellan with General Ambrose E. Burnside. The new chief of the Army of the Potomac, an imposing physical presence, sported bushy whiskers on his cheeks that came to be known as "sideburns," a

transposition of the two parts of his name. Despite his commanding stature, Burnside was shy and insecure. Claiming incompetence, he had twice refused the command. His judgment proved better than Lincoln's.

Fredericksburg.   Moving swiftly against Lee's dispersed army in northern Virginia, Burnside reached the Rappahannock River opposite Fredericksburg in November 1862 (see Map 15–3). But the pontoon bridges to ford his 120,000 soldiers across the river arrived three weeks late, giving Lee an opportunity to gather his 78,000 men. On December 13, the Union forces launched a poorly coordinated and foolish frontal assault that the Confederates repelled, inflicting heavy federal casualties. Burnside, having performed to his own expectations, was relieved of command, and Major General Joseph Hooker was installed in his place.

Chancellorsville.   The hard-drinking Hooker lacked Burnside's humility but not his incompetence. Resuming the offensive in the spring of 1863, Hooker hoped to outflank Lee. But the Confederate commander surprised Hooker by sending Stonewall Jackson to outflank the Union right. Between May 1 and May 4, Lee's army delivered a series of crushing attacks on Hooker's forces at Chancellorsville. Outnumbered two to one, Lee had pulled off another stunning victory, but at a high cost. Lee lost some 13,000 men, fewer than Hooker's 17,000, but more than the Confederacy could afford.

Lee also lost Stonewall Jackson at Chancellorsville. Nervous Confederate sentries mistakenly shot and wounded him as he returned from a reconnoitering mission, and he died a

The goddess "Columbia" (a popular depiction of America in contemporary cartoons) rebukes President Lincoln for the slaughter of Federal troops at Fredericksburg in December 1862: "Where are my 15,000 sons—murdered at Fredericksburg?" The President, as he often did to defuse tense situations, makes a weak attempt at humor: "This reminds me of a little joke." An incensed Columbia cuts him off: "Go tell your joke at Springfield [Illinois]." This was typical of the searing criticism Lincoln received in the press and the erosion of public support in the North after this military debacle.

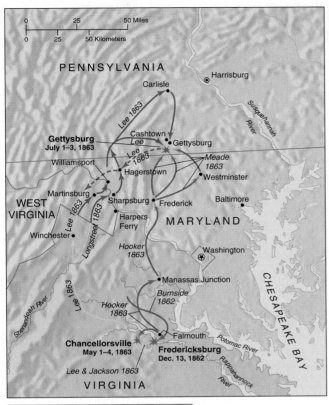

MAP 15–3   From Fredericksburg to Gettysburg: The War in the East, December 1862–July 1863
By all logic, the increasingly outgunned and outfinanced Confederacy should have been showing signs of faltering by 1863. But bungling by Union generals at Fredericksburg and Chancellorsville sustained southern fortunes and encouraged Robert E. Lee to attempt another invasion of the North.

few days later. Known for his lightning strikes at the enemy and his brilliant understanding of the tactics of modern warfare, Jackson had helped Lee win some of the Confederacy's most stunning victories in 1862. Lee recognized the tragedy of Jackson's loss for himself and his country. "Any victory," the Confederate commander wrote, "would be dear at such a price. I know not how to replace him."

Still, Lee appeared invincible. Chancellorsville thrust Lincoln into another bout of despair. "My God!" he exclaimed in agony, "What will the country say! What will the country say!" Meanwhile, Lee, to take advantage of the Confederacy's momentum and the Union's gloom, planned another bold move. On June 3, 1863, the 75,000-man Army of

Northern Virginia broke camp and headed north once again (see American Views, Why They Fought On).

Gettysburg.   President Lincoln sent the Union Army of the Potomac after Lee. But General Hooker dallied, requested more troops, and allowed the Confederates to march from Maryland into Pennsylvania. An infuriated Lincoln replaced Hooker with George Gordon Meade.

Lee and Meade were personal friends, they had served together during the Mexican War, and the change in command worried the Confederate general. He had counted on the bungling Hooker as his opponent. "General Meade," he commented prophetically, "will commit no blunder in my front."

Lee's Army of Northern Virginia occupied a wide swath of Pennsylvania territory from Chambersburg to Wrightsville along the Susquehanna River, across from the state capital at Harrisburg. When Lee learned of Meade's movements, he ordered his troops to consolidate in a defensive position at Cashtown, 45 miles from Harrisburg. That the greatest battle of the war erupted at nearby Gettysburg was pure chance. A Confederate brigade left Cashtown to confiscate much-needed shoes from a factory in Gettysburg. Meeting federal cavalry resistance near the town, the brigade withdrew. On July 1, 1863, a larger Confederate force advanced toward Gettysburg to disperse the cavalry and seize the shoes. What the Confederates did not realize was that the entire Army of the Potomac was coming up behind the cavalry (see Map 15–4).

During the first day of battle, July 1, the Confederates appeared to gain the upper hand, forcing Union forces back from the town to a new position on Cemetery Hill. On the second day, the entire Union army was in place, but the Confederates took several key locations along Cemetery Ridge before federal forces pushed them back to the previous day's positions. Although the opposing sides had suffered heavy casualties, both armies were intact; and, if anything, Lee had the advantage. On July 3, the third day of the battle, Lee made a fateful error. Believing that the center of Meade's line was weak, he ordered an all-out assault against it. The night before, Meade had remarked to his colleague, Brigadier General John Gibbon, "If Lee attacks tomorrow, it will be in your front. He has made attacks on both our flanks and failed and if he concludes to try it again, it will be on our center." Thus Meade was prepared for Lee's assault.

The next morning, a bright, hot summer day, the Confederates launched an assault on Culp's Hill, only to fall back by noon. The key battle of the day occurred at three in the afternoon at Cemetery Ridge, preceded by a fierce artillery duel. When the Union guns suddenly went silent, the Confederates, thinking they had knocked them out, began a charge led by General George Pickett. As the Confederate infantry marched out with battle colors flying, the Union artillery opened up again and tore apart the charging southerners. Some managed to reach their objective, a low stone wall at the crest of the hill, but the federals who held the wall outnumbered them and pushed them back. The Confederates retreated down the gentle slope strewn with their fallen

American Views

Why They Fought On

As the bloody war dragged on, fatigue and homesickness mounted among the soldiers of both sides, while morale faltered. Still, their letters and diary entries typically indicated a determination to fight on. This was true even for Confederate soldiers after the losses at Gettysburg and Vicksburg in July 1863.

- Soldiers from both sides appealed to the nation's Revolutionary heritage, but in different ways. What are the differences?
- Religion played a major role in motivating troops from both sides. How is this evident in the excerpts presented here?

- How do the writers balance feelings for family with their sense of duty as soldiers?
- Is there irony in the Confederate soldier's fighting "for the sake of liberty"? Would Union soldiers have found it ironic at this stage of the war?

A Pennsylvania officer writing to his wife in 1864: "[A]s sick as I am of this war and bloodshed, as much oh how much I want to be at home with my dear wife and children…every day I have a more religious feeling, that this war is a crusade for the good of mankind….I [cannot] bear to think of what my children would be if we were to permit this Hellbegotten conspiracy to destroy this country."

Alfred Lacey Hough to Mary Hough, March 13, 1864, in *Soldier in the West: The Civil War Letters of Alfred Lacey Hough*, ed. Robert G. Athearn (Philadelphia: University of Pennsylvania Press 1957), 178.

An Ohio officer writing to his 10-year-old son in 1864: "It tells me that while I am absent from home, fighting the battles of our country, trying to restore law and order, to our once peaceful & prosperous nation, and endeavoring to secure for each and every American citizen of every race, the rights garenteed to us in the Declaration of Independence…I have children growing up that will be worthy of the rights that I trust will be left for them."

Ephraim S. Holloway to John W. Holloway, August 7, 1864, Holloway Papers, Ohio Historical Society, Columbus, Ohio.

A Texas officer writing to his wife in 1863: "I am sick of war [and] no gratification could exceed that of my being safe at home with you….[W]ere the contest just commenced I would willingly undergo it again for the sake of…our country's independence [so I can]…point with pride your children to their father as one who fought for their liberty & freedom."

Edward W. Cade to his wife, January 30, July 9, and November 19, 1863, in *A Texas Surgeon in the C.S.A.*, ed. John Q. Anderon (Tuscaloosa: University of Alabama Press, 1957): 33, 67–68, 81.

A Georgia captain writing to his wife in 1863: "What a calamity! [the losses of Gettysburg and Vicksburg] But let us not despair….We just put forth even greater energy—resolve more fully to conquer or die. Our forefathers were whipped in nearly every battle & lost their capital & yet after seven years of trials and hardships achieved their independence."

William O. Fleming to Georgia Fleming, July 13, 1863, in Fleming Papers, Southern Historical Collection, University of North Carolina, Chapel Hill.

An Alabama lieutenant confiding to his diary in 1864: "We should be proud of [that] noble name [Rebel]. George Washington…Thomas Jefferson, Patrick Henry, and 'Light Horse' Harry Lee…were all Rebels….Our martyred Saviour was called *seditious*, and I may be pardoned if I rejoice that I am a Rebel."

"War Diary of Captain Robert Emory Park, Twelfth Alabama Regiment," *Southern Historical Society Papers*, II (1876), December 24, 1864, p. 237.

comrades, the hopes of a Southern victory dashed. Half of Pickett's 13,000-man division lay dead or wounded.

After the battle, Lee explained his disastrous frontal assault: "I believed my men were invincible." After Pickett's charge, Lee rode among his troops and urged them to brace for a final Union assault. The attack never came. Meade allowed Lee to withdraw into Maryland and cross the Potomac to Virginia. Gettysburg was the bloodiest battle of the war. The Union suffered 23,000 casualties; the Confederacy, 28,000. The battle's outcome boosted morale in the North and drained Lee's army of men and matériel. Yet Lincoln blasted Meade for failing to follow up on his victory. "I do

MAP 15–4   The Battle of Gettysburg, July 1–3, 1863
In a war that lasted four years, it is difficult to point to the decisive battle. But clearly, the outcome during those hot July days at Gettysburg set the tone for the rest of the war. The result was unclear until the final day of battle, and even then it might have gone either way. Winning by a whisker was enough to propel Union armies to a string of victories over the next year and to throw Confederate forces back on their defenses among an increasingly despairing population. Gettysburg marked the last major southern invasion of the North.

not believe you appreciate the magnitude of the misfortune involved in Lee's escape," he wrote to his general. "He was within your easy grasp, and to have closed upon him would, in connection with our other late successes, have ended the war. As it is, the war will be prolonged indefinitely.... Your golden opportunity is gone, and I am distressed immeasur-

ably because of it." Convinced by his aides that Meade would resign when he read the letter, Lincoln never sent it.

Despite Lincoln's perturbation, the Union victory at Gettysburg lifted the veil of gloom in the North. People exhaled collectively when Union troops foiled the Confederate invasion. A New Yorker exulted, "The results of this victory are priceless. Philadelphia, Baltimore, and Washington are safe.... The rebels are hunted out of the North, their best army is routed, and the charm of Robert E. Lee's invincibility broken." For northern evangelicals, the battle marked a prophecy. A Baptist minister in Philadelphia expressed the sentiment that the victory at Gettysburg would bring a time that the Founders "pictured and dreamed about, and prayed for. It will come with blessings, and be greeted with Hallelujahs, it will be the Millennium of political glory, the Sabbath of Liberty, the Jubilee of humanity." President Lincoln, in his address dedicating the cemetery at Gettysburg in November of that year, used the evangelical metaphor of rebirth to comment on the importance of the sacrifice on that battlefield. On this consecrated ground, he declared, from the "honored dead," will come "a new birth of freedom."

While the battle changed the mood in the North, it did not mark the beginning of the end of the Confederacy. But coupled with the loss of Vicksburg on July 4 (see below), it dealt a serious blow to Rebel fortunes. Many Confederate troops considered the Gettysburg campaign a draw or a temporary setback at worst; but there was no doubting the implications of the Vicksburg surrender on the nation's birthday.

Vicksburg, Chattanooga, and the West

As Union forces thwarted Confederate dreams in Pennsylvania, other federal troops bore down on strategic Rebel strongholds in the Western theater of the war. Union military success in the West would seriously compromise the South's ability to move goods and men across rail lines and over waterways and leave vulnerable the ultimate western prize, the Confederate bread basket, Georgia.

Vicksburg.   When Lincoln mentioned "our other late successes" in his letter to Meade, he was referring to another crucial Union victory. On July 4, one day after Pickett's charge at Gettysburg, the city of Vicksburg, the last major Confederate stronghold on the Mississippi, surrendered to Ulysses S. Grant.

Grant had demonstrated an ability to use his forces creatively, swiftly, and with a minimum loss of life in his campaigns in the western Confederacy, but Vicksburg presented him with several strategic obstacles (see Map 15–5). In 1862, the formidable defenses on the city's western edge, which overlooked and controlled the Mississippi, had thwarted a Union naval assault, and the labyrinth of swamps, creeks, and woods protecting the city from the north had foiled General Sherman. The only feasible approaches appeared to be from the south and east.

By March 1863, Grant had devised a brilliant plan to take Vicksburg that called for rapid maneuvering and expert

MAP 15–5   Vicksburg and Chattanooga: The War in the West, 1863
Devising a brilliant strategy, Union General Ulysses S. Grant took the last major Mississippi River stronghold from Confederate hands on July 4, 1863, dealing a significant economic and morale blow to the South. Coupled with the defeat at Gettysburg a day earlier, the fall of Vicksburg portended a bitter finale to hopes for southern independence. Grant completed his domination of the West by joining forces with several Union generals to capture Chattanooga and push Confederate forces into Georgia, setting the stage for the capture of that key southern state in 1864.

Timothy H. O'Sullivan's photograph of dead Union soldiers at the southern end of the Gettysburg battlefield, July 2, 1863. O'Sullivan titled the work "The Harvest of Death." Note the bodies bloodied and blackened by the July heat. Such photographs brought home the carnage of the war in vivid detail to northern civilians.

coordination. Grant had his 20,000 Union troops ferried across the Mississippi from the Louisiana side at a point south of Vicksburg. Then he marched them quickly into the interior of Mississippi. They moved northeastward, captured the Mississippi state capital at Jackson, and turned west toward Vicksburg. On May 22, 1863, Grant settled down in front of the city, less than 600 yards from Confederate positions. Grant's tight siege and the Union navy's bombardment from the river cut the city off completely. As food stores dwindled, residents were forced to eat mules and rats to survive. Their situation hopeless, General John Pemberton and his 30,000-man garrison surrendered on July 4.

Chattanooga.

As Grant was besieging Vicksburg in June 1863, Union general William S. Rosecrans, commanding the Army of the Cumberland, advanced against Confederate general Braxton Bragg, whose Army of the Tennessee held Chattanooga, a "doorway" on the railroad that linked Richmond to the lower South. The capture of the city would complete the uncoupling of the West from the eastern Confederacy.

Bragg lacked confidence in his men and consistently overestimated the force and cunning of his enemy. At Rosecrans's approach, he abandoned Chattanooga and took up positions at nearby Chickamauga Creek. When the two armies clashed at Chickamauga on September 19, Bragg pushed Rosecrans back to Chattanooga. Bragg seized the railroad leading into Chattanooga and bottled up Rosecrans there, much as Grant had confined Pemberton at Vicksburg. Both sides had suffered heavily. Suddenly, the Union's careful strategy for the conquest of the western Confederacy seemed in jeopardy.

The Confederate position on the heights overlooking Chattanooga appeared impregnable. But the Confederate camp was plagued by dissension, with some officers openly questioning Bragg's ability. President Davis considered replacing him but had no one else available with Bragg's experience. Instead, Davis ordered General James Longstreet (along with one-third of Bragg's army) on a futile expedition against Union forces at Knoxville, Tennessee. Converging on Chattanooga with reinforcements, Union generals Grant, Sherman, and Hooker took advantage of the divided Confederate army to break the siege and force Bragg's army to retreat into Georgia. The Union now dominated most of the West and faced an open road to the East.

The war in the Trans-Mississippi West.

The Confederacy's reverses at Vicksburg and Chattanooga mirrored its misfortunes farther west of the Mississippi River. Although a relatively minor theater of war, the territory west of the Mississippi provided supplies and strategic advantages for the Confederate West. Success in the trans-Mississippi West could divert Federal troops and relieve the pressure on other parts of the Confederacy while allowing food and munitions to reach desperate southern armies.

Native American tribes in the trans-Mississippi West, such as the Navajos, Dakotas, and Lakotas, spent a good deal of the Civil War battling Federal troops for territory and resources, quite apart from the sectional conflict. The Civil War drew federal troops from the frontier affording Indians an opportunity to press their concerns about tardy and incomplete delivery of food and supplies and the loss of lands granted to them by treaty. The Eastern Sioux in Minnesota confronted both starvation and the migration of whites onto their lands during the fall of 1862. About 200 warriors rampaged across southern Minnesota to call attention to their plight and feed their families. With the white man's war raging in the East, the Sioux struck in the fall of 1862. About 200 Eastern Sioux struck at white settlements and killed between 350 and 800 men, women, and children. The Minnesota militia quelled the uprising. More than three hundred Sioux were tried and condemned to death, though President Lincoln pardoned all but thirty-eight. Federal authorities removed the remainder of the Eastern Sioux to a desolate area in the Dakota Territory and extinguished all of their remaining land rights in Minnesota.

Other tribes cast their lot with the Confederacy in the hope of securing a better deal. Three regiments of Cherokee Indians led by Colonel (later Brigadier General) Stand Watie, fought for the South at the Battle of Pea Ridge in 1862. The Union won the battle and, with it, control of Missouri and northern Arkansas. Most of the battles between pro-Union and pro-Confederate Native American forces occurred in the Indian Territory (now Oklahoma).

Lincoln's second inaugural. When Abraham Lincoln took the oath of office for a second time on March 4, 1865, the result of the war was a foregone conclusion even if the precise date of its end was not. In a brief but inspirational address, the president provided the spiritual blueprint for reconciliation, though it disappointed some in the crowd who hoped for a declaration of victory, a promise of retribution against the rebel traitors, or at least an acknowledgment that God was clearly on the side of the Union. Instead, Lincoln declared that God had cursed both sides and had visited a destructive war on the nation because of the sin of slavery, a sin, he stressed, that was national, not regional: "If we shall suppose that American Slavery is one of those offences which, in the providence of God, must needs come, but which, having continued through His appointed time, He now wills to remove, and that He gives to both North and South, this terrible war, as the woe due to those by whom the offence came, shall we discern therein any departure from those divine attributes which the believers in a Living God always ascribe to Him?"

Nor was the president prepared to proclaim victory, despite its inevitability. In fact, the war could continue for some indeterminate time: "Fondly do we hope—fervently do we pray—that this mighty scourge of war may speedily pass away. Yet, if God wills that it continue, until all the wealth piled by the bond-man's two hundred and fifty years of unrequited toil shall be sunk, and until every drop of blood drawn with the lash, shall be paid by another drawn with the sword, as was said three thousand years ago, so still it must be said 'the judgments of the Lord, are true and righteous altogether.'"

And once the bloody conflict ends, Lincoln intoned, let reconciliation rather than retribution inform the national policy: "With malice toward none; with charity for all; with firmness in the right, as God gives us to see the right, let us strive on to finish the work we are in; to bind up the nation's wounds; to care for him who shall have borne the battle, and for his widow, and his orphan—to do all which may achieve and cherish a just, and a lasting peace, among ourselves, and with all nations." In the meantime, the bitter struggle would continue.

Arming the Confederacy's slaves. In March 1865, in a move reflecting their desperation, Confederate leaders revived a proposal that they had previously rejected: to arm and free slaves. President Davis hoped this action would gain the Confederacy not only a military benefit but also diplomatic recognition from countries that had balked because of slavery.

The issue divided Confederate leaders. General Howell Cobb argued that "if slaves will make good soldiers, our whole theory of slavery is wrong." Others thought that it was preferable to abandon slavery than to lose independence. A Confederate congressman from Georgia wrote to a friend in October 1864 that if the South lost the war, slavery was over anyway, and "we and our children will be slaves, while our freed Negroes will lord it over us." But if the Confederacy

enlisted slaves, it could "win our independence, and have liberty and homes for ourselves and our children."

Not surprisingly, slaves themselves greeted the proposal with little enthusiasm. They might have found service in the Confederate army an acceptable alternative to bondage earlier in the war, but not now, with Union victory imminent. Mary Chesnut recalled in March 1865 that early in the war, when her husband "spoke to his Negroes about it, his head men were keen to go in the army, to be free and get a bounty after the war. Now they say coolly that they don't want freedom if they have to fight for it. That means they are pretty sure of having it anyway."

On March 13, 1865, a reluctant Confederate Congress passed a bill to enlist black soldiers, but without offering them freedom. Ten days later, President Davis and the War Office issued a general order that promised immediate freedom to slaves who enlisted. The war ended before the order could have any effect. The irony was that in the summer of 1864, a majority of northerners probably would have accepted reunion without emancipation had the Confederacy abandoned its fight.

The Road to Appomattox and the Death of Lincoln

With Sherman's triumph in Georgia and the Carolinas and Sheridan's rout of the Confederates in the Shenandoah Valley, Lee's army remained the last obstacle to Union victory. On April 1, Sheridan's cavalry seized a vital railroad junction on Lee's right flank, forcing Lee to abandon Petersburg and the defense of Richmond. Lee tried a daring run westward toward Lynchburg, hoping to secure much-needed supplies and to join Johnston's Army of Tennessee in North Carolina to continue the fight.

President Davis fled Richmond with his cabinet and headed toward North Carolina. Richard Gill Forrester, a 17-year-old black youth, awoke to find the evacuation underway. He reached under his bed and pulled out an American flag. Maneuvering through the chaotic streets, young Forrester reached the state capitol building, climbed to the top, and affixed the banner to the flagpole. Union troops occupied the Confederate capital on April 3, and two days later, President Lincoln walked through its streets to the cheers of his army and an emotional reception from thousands of black people. "I know I am free," shouted one black spectator, "for I have seen Father Abraham and felt him."

The surrender at Appomattox. Grant's army of 60,000 outran Lee's diminishing force of 35,000 and cut off his escape at Appomattox Court House, Virginia, on April 7. Convinced that further resistance was futile, the Confederate commander met Grant on April 9, 1865, in the McLean house at Appomattox to sign the documents of surrender. The Union general offered generous terms, allowing Lee's men to go home unmolested and to take with them horses or mules "to put in a crop." Grant reported feeling "sad and depressed" at "the downfall of a foe who had fought so long and valiantly, and had suffered so much for a cause, though that cause was,

I believe, one of the worst for which a people ever fought." Lee rode through the thinned ranks of his troops, who crowded around him in silent tribute, brushing the general's boots and the withers of his horse with their hats.

Though some southerners entertained fleetingly the idea of launching a guerilla campaign against Union forces, most were sick of the war. One Confederate leader, traveling through the stricken South in April 1865, reported that soldiers and civilians alike considered any continuation of the conflict "madness." Joseph E. Johnston surrendered to Sherman near Durham, North Carolina, on April 26. On May 10, Union cavalry captured President Davis in southern Georgia. On May 26, Texas general Kirby Smith surrendered his trans-Mississippi army, and the Civil War came to an end.

The death of Lincoln.   Washington greeted the Confederate surrender at Appomattox with predictable and raucous rejoicing, torchlight parades, cannon salutes, and crowds

General Robert E. Lee at Appomattox after his surrender to Union General U. S. Grant on April 9, 1865. His men followed the defeated leader, poignantly brushing their hats against the withers of his horse, Traveler. Many wept openly. The war was over as the sun set on the dream of southern independence.

spontaneously bellowing "The Star-Spangled Banner." On April 11, President Lincoln addressed a large crowd from the White House balcony and spoke briefly of his plans to reconstruct the South with the help of persons loyal to the Union, including recently freed slaves. At least one listener found the speech disappointing. A sometime actor and full-time Confederate patriot, John Wilkes Booth, muttered to a friend in the throng, "That means nigger citizenship. Now, by God, I'll put him through. That is the last speech he will ever make."

On the evening of April 14, Good Friday, the president went to Ford's Theatre in Washington to view a comedy, *Our American Cousin*. During the performance, Booth shot the president, wounding him mortally, then jumped from Lincoln's box to the stage shouting "*Sic semper tyrannis*" ("Thus ever to tyrants") and fled the theater. Union troops tracked him down to a barn in northern Virginia and killed him. Investigators arrested eight accomplices who had conspired with Booth to murder other high officials in addition to Lincoln. Four of the accomplices were hanged. Besides the president, however, the only other official attacked was Secretary of State Seward, who received serious but not fatal knife wounds.

Southerners reacted to Lincoln's assassination with surprisingly mixed emotions. Many saw some slight hope of relief for the South's otherwise bleak prospects. But General Johnston and others like him were aware of Lincoln's moderating influence on the radical elements in the Republican Party that were pressing for harsh terms against the South. The president's death, Johnston wrote, was "the greatest possible calamity to the South."

Conclusion

Just before the war, William Sherman had warned a friend from Virginia, "You people of the South don't know what you are doing. This country will be drenched in blood.... [W]ar is a terrible thing." He was right. More than 365,000 Union soldiers died during the war, 110,000 in battle, and more than 256,000 Confederate soldiers, 94,000 in battle. Total casualties on both sides, including wounded, were more than 1 million.

The southern armies suffered disproportionately higher casualties than the northern armies. One in four Confederate soldiers died or endured debilitating wounds, compared to one in ten federal soldiers. During the first year after the war, Mississippi allocated one-fifth of its budget to artificial limbs. Compounding the suffering of the individuals behind these gruesome statistics was the incalculable suffering, in terms of grief, fatherless children, women who never married, families never made whole, of the people close to them.

The war devastated the South. The region lost one-fourth of its white male population between the ages of 20 and 40. It also lost two-fifths of its livestock and half its farm machinery. Union armies destroyed many of the South's railroads and shattered its industry. Between 1860 and 1870, the

Major Battles of the Civil War, 1861–1865

Battle or Campaign Date		Outcome and Consequences
First Bull Run	July 21, 1861	Confederate victory, destroyed the widespread belief in the North that the war would end quickly, fueled Confederate sense of superiority
Forts Henry and Donelson	February 6–16, 1862	Union victory, gave the North control of strategic river systems in the western Confederacy and closed an important link between the eastern and western Confederacy
Shiloh Church	April 6–7, 1862	Union victory, high casualties transformed attitudes about the war on both sides
Seven Days' Battles	June 25–July 1, 1862	Stand-off, halted McClellan's advance on Richmond in the Peninsula Campaign
Second Bull Run	August 29–30, 1862	Confederate victory, reinforced Robert E. Lee's reputation for invincibility
Antietam	September 17, 1862	Stand-off, halted Lee's advance into the North, eliminated Confederacy's chance for diplomatic recognition, encouraged Lincoln to issue the Emancipation Proclamation
Fredericksburg	December 13, 1862	Confederate victory, revived morale of Lee's army
Chancellorsville	May 2–6, 1863	Confederate victory, Stonewall Jackson killed, encouraged Lee to again invade North
Gettysburg	July 1–3, 1863	Union victory, halted Confederate advance in the North, major psychological blow to Confederacy
Vicksburg	November 1862–July 1863	Union victory; closed the key Confederate port on the Mississippi, also dealt a severe blow to Confederate cause
Chattanooga	August–November 1863	Union victory, solidified Union dominance in the West
Wilderness and Cold Harbor	May and June 1864	Two Confederate victories, inflicted huge losses on Grant's army; turned public opinion against Grant but failed to force him to withdraw
Atlanta	May–September 1864	Union victory; Confederacy lost key rail depot and industrial center
Sherman's March	November 1864–March 1865	Nearly unopposed, Sherman's army cut a path of destruction through Georgia and South Carolina, breaking southern morale
Battles of Franklin and Nashville	November and December 1864	Union victories in Tennessee; effectively destroyed Army of Tennessee
Siege of Petersburg	June 1864–April 1865	Long stalemate ended in Union victory; led to fall of Richmond and surrender of Lee's army at Appomattox Court House

wealth of the South declined by 60 percent, and its share of the nation's total wealth dropped from more than 30 percent to 12 percent. The wealth of the North, in contrast, increased by half in the same period.

The Union victory solved the constitutional question about the right of secession and sealed the fate of slavery. The issue that dominated the prewar sectional debate had vanished. Now, when politicians intoned Independence Day orations or campaign speeches about the ideals of democracy and freedom, the glaring reality of human bondage would no longer mock their rhetoric.

The Civil War stimulated societal changes that grew more significant over time. It did not make the Union an industrial nation, but it taught the effectiveness of centralized management, new financial techniques, and the coordination of production, marketing, and distribution. Entrepreneurs would apply these lessons to create the expanding corporations of the postwar American economy. Likewise, the war did not revolutionize gender relations in American society, but by opening new opportunities to women in fields such as nursing and teaching, it helped lay the foundation for the woman's suffrage movement of the 1870s and 1880s.

For many Americans, especially black and white southerners, the war was the most important event in their lives, but it was not responsible for every postwar change in American society, and it left many features of American life intact. The experience of pulling together in a massive war effort, for example, did not soften class antagonisms. Capitalism, not labor, triumphed during the war. And it was industrialists and entrepreneurs, not working people, who most benefited from the war's bonanza. Lincoln brutally suppressed strikes at defense plants and threw labor leaders into military prisons.

For black southerners, emancipation was the war's most significant achievement. The war to end slavery changed some American racial attitudes, especially in the North. When Lincoln broadened the war's objectives to include the abolition of slavery, he connected the success of the Union to freedom for the slave. At the outset of the Civil War, only a small minority of northerners considered themselves abolitionists. After the Emancipation Proclamation, every northern soldier became a liberator. By the end of the war, perhaps a majority of northerners supported granting freedmen the right to vote and to equal protection under the law, even if they believed (as many did) that black people were inferior to white people. The courage of black troops and the efforts of African American leaders to link the causes of reunion and freedom were influential in bringing about this shift.

Most white southerners did not experience a similar enlightenment. Some were relieved by the end of slavery, but most greeted it with fear, anger, and regret. For them, the freed slaves would be living reminders of the South's defeat and the end of a way of life grounded in white supremacy.

If the Civil War resolved the sectional dispute of the 1850s by ending slavery and denying the right of the southern states to secede, it created two new equally troubling problems: how to reunite South and North and how to deal with the legacy of slavery. At his last cabinet meeting on April 14, Lincoln seemed inclined to be conciliatory, cautioning against reprisals on Confederate leaders and noting the courage of General Lee and his officers. The president said nothing about the rights of freedmen, although earlier statements indicated that he favored suffrage, but not social equality, for African Americans.

America's greatest crisis had closed. In its wake, former slaves tested their new freedom, and the nation groped for reconciliation. The struggle to preserve the Union and abolish slavery had renewed and vindicated the nation's ideals. It was time to savor the hard-fought victories before plunging into the uncertainties of Reconstruction.

In November 1863, President Lincoln was asked to say a few words at the dedication of the federal cemetery at Gettysburg. There, surrounded by a somber scene of fresh graves, Lincoln bound the cause of the Union to that of the country's founders: "Fourscore and seven years ago our fathers brought forth upon this continent a new nation, conceived in liberty and dedicated to the proposition that all men are created equal. Now we are engaged in a great civil war, testing whether that nation, or any nation so conceived and so dedicated can long endure." A Union victory, Lincoln hoped, would not only honor the past but also call forth a new nation, cleansed of its sins, to serve as an inspiration to oppressed peoples around the world. He called on the nation to resolve "that the nation shall, under God, have a new birth of freedom; and that government of the people, by the people, for the people, shall not perish from the earth." The two-minute Gettysburg Address captured what Union supporters were fighting for and connected their sacrifices to the noble causes of freedom and democratic government. That would be both the hope and the challenge of the peace that followed a hard war.

Review Questions

1. How did the Union and the Confederacy compare in terms of resources, leadership, and military strategies in the period 1861–1863? What impact did these factors have on the course of the war?

2. What was the significance of the battles of Antietam and Gettysburg? In what ways were they turning points in the Civil War?

3. Given that the federal government was fighting a civil war, why did not European powers, other than France, take advantage of that distraction and meddle in Latin American affairs?

4. What effects did the Emancipation Proclamation have on the Union and Confederate causes?

5. Compare and contrast the roles played by women, in the North and in the South, during the Civil War, and explain how their actions and activities aided or hindered the war effort of their respective nations.

6. Sullivan Ballou made the ultimate sacrifice for his cause. Why did he fight?

Key Terms*

Confiscation Act (p. 407)

Copperheads (p. 416)

Emancipation Proclamation (p. 407)

Homestead Act (p. 417)

Land Grant College Act (p. 417)

New York Draft Riot (p. 417)

Radical Republicans (p. 416)

Thirteenth Amendment (p. 424)

*See the Overview table, on p. 428 for important battles of the Civil War.

Recommended Reading

Crane, Stephen. *The Red Badge of Courage* (Originally published 1895; reprinted various dates). The Civil War did not inspire great American novels. This notable exception depicts, not only the horrors of combat, but also its impact on the soldiers who fought.

McPherson, James M. *Battle Cry of Freedom: The Civil War Era* (1982). Probably the best account of the war in print. The author draws a number of interesting conclusions on several controversial topics, from military strategy to the home front.

Where to Learn More

■ **Museum of the Confederacy, Richmond, Virginia.** This museum has rotating exhibits on various aspects of the Confederate effort during the Civil War, both on the home front and on the battlefield. The Confederate White House, which is open to the public, is next door to the museum. Visit its website at www.moc.org

■ **Gettysburg National Military Park, Gettysburg, Pennsylvania.** An excellent and balanced interpretation awaits the visitor at this national park. See its website, www.nps.gov/gett

■ **Ford's Theatre National Historical Site, Washington, DC.** The place where John Wilkes Booth assassinated President Abraham Lincoln not only depicts those events, including artifacts from the assassination, but also presents period plays. Its website is www.nps.gov/foth/index2.htm

■ **Appomattox Court House, Appomattox, Virginia.** What historian Bruce Catton termed "a stillness at Appomattox" can be felt at the McLean house in this south-central Virginia town. The house is much as it was when General Robert E. Lee surrendered his forces to General Ulysses S. Grant on April 9, 1865. An almost reverential solitude covers the house and the well-maintained grounds today. Its website is at www.nps.gov/apco

Study Resources

For study resources for this chapter, go to www.myhistorylab.com and choose *The American Journey*. You will find a wealth of study and review material for this chapter, including pre- and post-tests, customized study plan, key term review flash cards, interactive map and document activities, and documents for analysis.

"A Hunger to Learn." This 1863 watercolor by Henry L. Stephens depicts an elderly African American, probably a former slave, learning to read. The newspaper's headline states, "Presidential Proclamation, Slavery." Learning transcended age among freed blacks in the South.

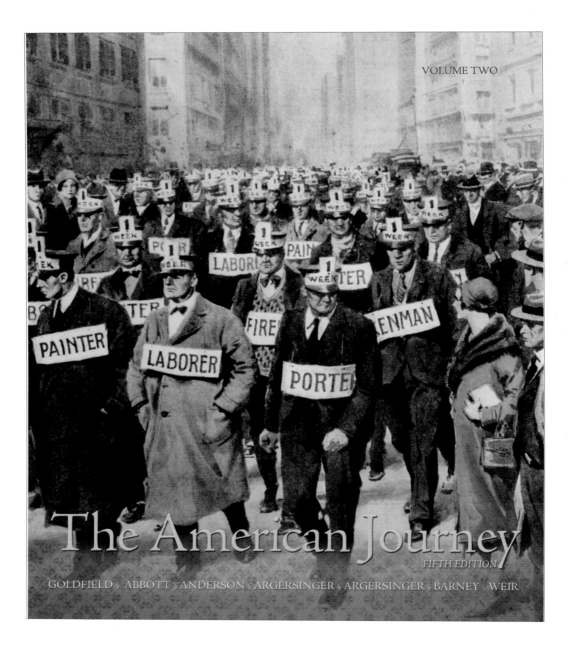

VOLUME TWO

CHAPTERS 16–31

To order, please request
ISBN-10: 0-13-603256-7; ISBN-13: 978-0-13-603256-4

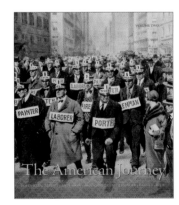

COMBINED EDITION
Chapters 1-31
ISBN-10: 0-13-603281-8
ISBN-13: 978-0-13-603281-6

VOLUME ONE
Chapters 1-16
ISBN-10: 0-13-603255-9
ISBN-13: 978-0-13-603255-7

VOLUME TWO
Chapters 16-31
ISBN-10: 0-13-603256-7
ISBN-13: 978-0-13-603256-4

Reconstruction 1865–1877 16

Marianna, Florida 1866

The white academy opened about the same time the church opened the school for the Negro children. As the colored children had to pass the academy to reach the church it was easy for the white children to annoy them with taunts and jeers. The war passed from words to stones which the white children began to hurl at the colored. Several colored children were hurt and, as they had not resented the rock-throwing in kind because they were timid about going that far, the white children became more aggressive and abusive.

One morning the colored children armed themselves with stones and determined to fight their way past the academy to their school. [They] approached the academy in formation whereas in the past they had been going in pairs or small groups. When they reached hailing distance, a half dozen white boys rushed out and hurled their missiles. Instead of scampering away, the colored children not only stood their ground and hurled their missiles but maintained a solemn silence. The white children, seeing there was no backing down as they expected, came rushing out of the academy and charged the colored children.

During some fifteen minutes it was a real tug of war. In the close fighting the colored children got the advantage gradually and began to shove the white children back. As they pressed the advantage the white children broke away and ran for the academy. The colored fighters did not follow them but made it hot for the laggards until they also took to their heels. There were many bruises on both sides, but it taught the white youngsters to leave the colored ones alone thereafter.

T. Thomas Fortune, *Norfolk Journal and Guide*

T. Thomas Fortune, "Norfolk Journal and Guide," August 20, 1927, reprinted in Dorothy Sterling, ed., *The Trouble They Seen: Black People Tell the Story of Reconstruction* (Garden City, NY: Doubleday, 1976): 22–24.

myhistorylab

Personal Journeys Online

■ N. J. Bell, *Southern Railroad Man*, 1865. A railroad conductor recalls the aftermath of the Civil War and its impact on a white family in Wilmington, NC.

■ Adelbert Ames, *Letter from the Republican Governor of Mississippi*, 1875. Letter to his wife expressing frustration at the violence against black voters in his state and his hope for federal intervention.

T. Thomas Fortune, a New York newspaper editor, recalled this battle between black and white schoolchildren sixty years after it occurred at the beginning of the Reconstruction era. In the scheme of things, it did not amount to much. However, for 10-year-old Thomas, born a slave in Marianna, the incident encapsulated the dilemma of Reconstruction. In the journey from slavery to freedom, education emerged as an important element of full citizenship for African Americans. The eagerness with which black children (and adults) flooded schools, often spaces converted in churches and staffed initially by white missionaries from the North, was matched by the hostility of the white community, which resented any social advance or pretense of equality in the former bondsmen.

Reconstruction was not merely a series of white aggressions against African American aspirations, followed by black retreats. The former slaves did not shy away from asserting their rights. The violence and disorder that punctuated southern society after the Civil War was due in part to the refusal of blacks to relinquish their dreams of equal citizenship, including the right to a decent education.

Young Thomas did not back down, although by 1878 he understood that the promise of his schoolboy days could not be realized in the South. The journey from slavery to freedom, he felt, would always be incomplete in the South. Together with his young bride, Carrie Smiley of Jacksonville, Florida, Thomas left for New York City, where he obtained a job as a printer for the *New York Sun*. Shaped by his early years in Florida, and the difficulties involved in obtaining a decent education, Fortune used the pages of the *Sun* to promote equality of education for all races and integrated public schools in New York State. He died there in 1928. New York's gain was the South's loss, a process repeated many times over in the decades after the Civil War as talented young black men and women migrated north. It was a double tragedy for the South: losing people who could have rebuilt a shattered region and missing the opportunity to create a society based on racial equality.

The position of African Americans in American society was one of the two great issues of the Reconstruction era. Americans of both sections disagreed about how much freedom to grant the former slaves, almost all of whom lived in the South. The other great issue was how and under what terms to readmit the former Confederate states. The Constitution was silent on the subject. As with the issue of black equality, opinions in both sections varied widely.

The formation of a national consensus on freedom and reunification began with the demands and hopes of three broad groups. One was the Republican Party, which controlled the federal government. Most Republicans were unwilling to accept the seceding states back in the Union without an expression of loyalty and a commitment to protect the rights of freedmen. A second group, the more than 4 million former slaves, demanded voting rights, access to education, and the opportunity to seek economic self-sufficiency. Few black northerners yet enjoyed all these benefits, and few white southerners could conceive of former slaves possessing them. The third group, white southerners, hoped to restore their shattered lives, fortunes, and dignity. In their vision of a renewed South, black people remained subservient, and the federal government stopped interfering in southern affairs.

Between 1865 and 1867, under President Andrew Johnson's Reconstruction plan, white southerners pretty much had their way with the former slaves and with their own state governments. Congressional action between 1867 and 1870 attempted to balance black rights and home rule, with mixed results. After 1870, white southerners gradually regained control of their states and localities, often through violence and intimidation, denying black southerners their political gains while Republicans in Washington and white northerners lost interest in policing their former enemies.

By the time the last federal troops left the South in 1877, the white southerners had prevailed. The Confederate states had returned to the Union with all of their rights and many of their leaders restored. And the freed slaves remained in mostly subservient positions with few of the rights and privileges enjoyed by other Americans.

CHRONOLOGY

1861	Tsar Alexander II frees the serfs of Russia.
1863	Lincoln proposes his Ten Percent Plan.
1864	Congress proposes the Wade-Davis Bill.
1865	Sherman issues Field Order No. 15.
	Freedmen's Bureau is established.
	Andrew Johnson succeeds to the presidency, unveils his Reconstruction plan.
	Massachusetts desegregates all public facilities.
	Black citizens in several southern cities organize Union Leagues.
	Former Confederate states begin to pass black codes.
1866	Congress passes Southern Homestead Act, Civil Rights Act of 1866.
	Ku Klux Klan is founded.
	Fourteenth Amendment to the Constitution is passed (ratified in 1868).
1867	Congress passes Military Reconstruction Acts, Tenure of Office Act.
1868	President Johnson is impeached and tried in the Senate for defying the Tenure of Office Act.
	Republican Ulysses S. Grant is elected president.
1869	Fifteenth Amendment passed (ratified 1870).
1870	Congress passes Enforcement Act.
	Republican regimes topple in North Carolina and Georgia.
1871	Congress passes Ku Klux Klan Act.
1872	Freedmen's Bureau closes down.
	Liberal Republicans emerge as a separate party.
	Ulysses S. Grant is reelected.
1873	Severe depression begins.
	Colfax Massacre occurs.
	U.S. Supreme Court's decision in the *Slaughterhouse* cases weakens the intent of the Fourteenth Amendment.
	Texas falls to the Democrats in the fall elections.
1874	White Leaguers attempt a coup against the Republican government of New Orleans.
	Democrats win off-year elections across the South amid widespread fraud and violence.
1875	Congress passes Civil Rights Act of 1875.
1876	Supreme Court's decision in *United States v. Cruikshank* nullifies Enforcement Act of 1870.
	Outcome of the presidential election between Republican Rutherford B. Hayes and Democrat Samuel J. Tilden is contested.
1877	Compromise of 1877 makes Hayes president and ends Reconstruction.

White Southerners and the Ghosts of the Confederacy, 1865

Confederate soldiers, generals and troops alike, returned to devastated homes. General Braxton Bragg returned to his "once prosperous" Alabama home to find "all, all was lost, except my debts." Bragg and his wife found temporary shelter in a slave cabin. Yeomen farmers, the backbone of the Confederacy, found uprooted fences, farm animals dead or gone, and buildings destroyed. They and their families wandered about in a living nightmare, seeking shelter where they could. They lived in morbid fear of vengeful former slaves or the hated Yankee soldiers wreaking more damage.

Nathaniel Bell, a former Confederate soldier, was lucky enough to get a job on the North Carolina Railroad in 1865. Every two weeks, Bell enjoyed a two-day layover in the coastal city of Wilmington. "On one of these occasions," he wrote, "a small boy and little girl, both pretty children, came to me and asked me for something to eat. I gave them all the meat, bread, potatoes, and syrup that they could carry away. They were very proud of this. They said their father was killed in the war, and that their mother and grandmother were both sick. Some months afterwards I was passing by the same place where I saw the children, and a man got on my train.... I asked him about the two children.... He said the little boy and girl starved to death."

The casualties of war in the South continued long after the hostilities ceased. These were hardly the only cases of starvation that stalked the defeated region in the months after the surrender. Although soldiers of both sides would experience difficulty in reentering civilian life, the southerner's case was the more difficult because of the economic devastation, the psychological burdens of defeat, and the break-up of families through death, migration, or poverty. Cities such as Richmond, Atlanta, Savannah, Charleston, and Columbia lay in ruins; farmsteads were stripped of everything but the soil; infrastructure, especially railroads, was damaged or destroyed; factories and machinery were demolished; and at least 5 million bales of cotton, the major cash crop, had gone up in smoke. Add a worthless currency, and the loss was staggering, climbing into hundreds of billions of dollars in today's currency.

Law and order, when not closely supervised by federal troops, often broke down. Deserters, guerilla fighters, and just plain hungry people stole and fought to survive. As a Georgia woman explained, "We have no currency, no law, save the primitive code that might makes right."

Their cause lost and their society destroyed, white southerners lived through the summer and fall of 1865 surrounded by ghosts, the ghosts of lost loved ones, joyful times, bountiful harvests, self-assurance, and slavery. Defeat shook the basic tenets of their religious beliefs. A North Carolinian cried, "Oh, our God! What sins we must have been guilty of that we should be so humiliated by Thee now!" Some praised God for delivering the South from the sin of slavery. A Virginia woman expressed thanks that "we white people are no longer permitted to go on in such wickedness, heaping up more and more wrath of God upon our devoted heads." But many other white southerners refused to accept their defeat as a divine judgment. How could they, as a devout people, believe that God had abandoned them? Instead, they insisted, God had spared the South for a greater purpose. They came to view the war as the **Lost Cause** and interpreted it, not as a lesson in humility, but as an episode in the South's journey to salvation. Robert E. Lee became the patron saint of this cause, his poignant nobility a contrast to the crassness of the Yankee warlords. White southerners transformed the bloody struggle into a symbol of courage against great odds and piety against sin. Eventually, they believed, redemption would come.

The southern white view of the Civil War (and of Reconstruction) was not a deliberate attempt to falsify history, but rather a need to justify and rationalize the devastation that accompanied defeat. This view, in which the war became the Lost Cause, and Reconstruction became the Redemption, also served to forge a community among white southerners at a time of great unrest. A common religion solidified the bond and sanctified it. The Lost Cause also enabled white southerners to move on with their lives and concentrate on rebuilding their shattered region. The Lost Cause was a historical rationalization that enabled believers to hope for a better future. The regrettable feature of elevating the Civil War to a noble, holy enterprise was that it implied a stainless Old South, a civilization worth fighting and dying for. This new history required the return of the freedmen, if not to the status of slaves, then at least to a lowly place in society. This new history also ignored the savagery of the war by romanticizing the conflict.

The Lost Cause would not merely exist as a memory, but also as a three-dimensional depiction of southern history, in rituals and celebrations, and as the educational foundation for future generations. The statues of the Confederate common soldier erected typically on the most important site in a town, the courthouse square; the commemorations of Confederate Memorial Day, the birthdays of prominent Confederate leaders, and the reunions of veterans, all marked with flourishing oratory, brass bands, parades, and related spectacles; and the textbooks implanting the white history of the South in young minds and carrying the legacy down through the generations—all of these ensured that the Lost Cause would not only be an interpretation of the past, but also the basic reality of the present and the foundation for the future.

Fifteen years after the war, Mark Twain traveled the length of the East Coast. After visiting a gentlemen's club in Boston, he recalled that the conversation had covered a va-

This engraving shows Southerners decorating the graves of rebel soldiers at Hollywood Memorial Cemetery in Virginia in 1867. Northerners and southerners alike honored their war dead. But in the South, the practice of commemorating fallen soldiers became an important element in maintaining the myth of the Lost Cause that colored white southerners' view of the war.

riety of topics, none of which included the Civil War. Northerners had relegated the conflict to history books and moved on. Such was not the case in the South. There, Twain reported, gentlemen's talk inevitably wandered to the war and to heroism and sacrifice. "In the South," Twain wrote, "the war is what A.D. is elsewhere: they date from it." White southerners would not accept the changes implied by defeat. They would fight to preserve as much of their past as the victors allowed. For the past was both their present and their future.

Most white southerners approached the great issues of freedom and reunification with unyielding views. They saw African Americans as adversaries whose attempts at self-improvement were a direct challenge to white people's belief in their own racial superiority. White southerners saw outside assistance to black southerners as another invasion. The Yankees might have destroyed their families, their farms, and their fortunes, but they would not destroy the racial order. The war may have ended slavery, but white southerners were determined to preserve strict racial boundaries.

More Than Freedom: African American Aspirations in 1865

Black southerners had a quite different perspective on the Civil War and Reconstruction, seeing the former as a great victory for freedom and the latter as a time of great possibility. But their view did not matter; it was invisible or,

worse, distorted, in books, monuments, and official accounts. If, as the British writer George Orwell later argued, "who controls the present controls the past, and who controls the past controls the future," then the vanishing black perspective is not surprising. The ferocity with which white southerners attempted to take back their governments and their social structure was not only about nostalgia; it was about power and the legitimacy that power conferred.

And, of course, the black perspective was decidedly different from that of whites. To black southerners the Civil War was a war of liberation, not a Lost Cause. At an emancipation parade in Norfolk in 1863, black women took joy in stomping on Confederate flags and burning an effigy of Jefferson Davis. Less raucous displays followed the war, especially on July 4, which in the South, until well into the 1880s, was primarily a black holiday. The response of southern whites to black aspirations still stunned African Americans, who believed, naively perhaps, that what they sought—education, land, access to employment, and equality in law and politics—were basic rights and modest objectives. The former slaves did not initially even dream of social equality; far less did they plot murder and mayhem, as white people feared. They did harbor two potentially contradictory aspirations. The first was to be left alone, free of white supervision. But the former slaves also wanted land, voting and civil rights, and education. To secure these, they needed the intervention and support of the white power structure.

In 1865, African Americans had reason to hope that their dreams of full citizenship might be realized. They enjoyed a reservoir of support for their aspirations among some Republican leaders. The views of James A. Garfield, Union veteran, U.S. congressman, and future president, were typical of these Republicans. Commenting on the ratification of the Thirteenth Amendment, Garfield asked, "What is freedom? Is it the bare privilege of not being chained?... If this is all, then freedom is a bitter mockery, a cruel delusion."

The first step Congress took beyond emancipation was to establish the Bureau of Refugees, Freedmen, and Abandoned Lands in March 1865. Congress envisioned the **Freedmen's Bureau,** as it came to be called, as a multipurpose agency to provide social, educational, and economic services, advice, and protection to former slaves and destitute white southerners. The Bureau marked the federal government's first foray into social welfare legislation. Congress also authorized the bureau to rent confiscated and abandoned farmland to freedmen in 40-acre plots, with an option to buy. This auspicious beginning belied the great disappointments that lay ahead.

Education

The greatest success of the Freedmen's Bureau was in education. The bureau coordinated more than fifty northern philanthropic and religious groups, which, in turn, established 3,000 freedmen's schools in the South, serving 150,000 men, women, and children.

Initially, single young women from the Northeast comprised much of the teaching force. One of them, 26-year-old Martha Schofield, came to Aiken, South Carolina, from rural Pennsylvania in 1865. Like many of her colleagues, she had joined the abolitionist movement as a teenager and decided to make teaching her life's work. Her strong Quaker beliefs reflected the importance of Protestant Christianity in motivating the young missionaries. When her sponsoring agency, the Pennsylvania Freedmen's Relief Association, folded in 1871, her school closed. Undaunted, she opened another school on her own, and, despite chronic financial problems and the hostility of Aiken's white citizens, she and the school endured. (Since 1953, her school has been part of the Aiken public school system.)

By the time Schofield opened her school in 1871, black teachers outnumbered white teachers in the "colored" schools. The financial troubles of northern missionary societies and white northerners' declining interest in the freedmen's condition opened opportunities for black teachers. Support for them came from black churches, especially the African Methodist Episcopal (AME) Church.

The former slaves crowded into basements, shacks, and churches to attend school. "The children...hurry to school as soon as their work is over," wrote a teacher in Norfolk, Virginia, in 1867. "The plowmen hurry from the field at night to get their hour of study. Old men and women strain their dim sight with the book two and a half feet distant from the eye, to catch the shape of the letter. I call this heaven-inspired interest."

At the end of the Civil War, only about 10 percent of black southerners were literate, compared with more than 70 percent of white southerners. Within a decade, black literacy had risen above 30 percent. Joseph Wilson, a former slave, attributed the rise to "this longing of ours for freedom of the mind as well as the body."

The Freedmen's Bureau, northern churches, and missionary societies established more than 3,000 schools, attended by some 150,000 men, women, and children in the years after the Civil War. At first, mostly young white women from the Northeast staffed these schools.

Some black southerners went on to one of the thirteen colleges established by the American Missionary Association and black and white churches. Between 1860 and 1880 more than 1,000 black southerners earned college degrees at institutions still serving students today, such as Howard University in Washington, DC, Fisk University in Nashville, Hampton Institute (now University), Tuskegee Institute, and Biddle Institute (now Johnson C. Smith University) in Charlotte.

Pursuing freedom of the mind involved challenges beyond those of learning to read and write. Many white southerners condemned efforts at "Negro improvement." They viewed the time spent on education as wasted, forcing the former slaves to catch their lessons in bits and pieces between work, often by candlelight or on Sundays. White southerners also harassed white female teachers, questioning their morals and threatening people who rented rooms to them. After the Freedmen's Bureau folded in 1872 and many of the northern societies that supported freedmen's education collapsed or cut back their involvement, education for black southerners became more haphazard.

"Forty Acres and a Mule"

Although education was important to the freed slaves in their quest for civic equality, land ownership offered them the promise of economic independence. For generations, black people had worked southern farms and had received nothing for their labor.

An overwhelmingly agricultural people, freedmen looked to farm ownership as a key element in their transition from slavery to freedom. "Gib us our own land and we take care of ourselves," a Charleston freedman asserted to a northern visitor in 1865. "But without land, de ole massas can hire or starve us, as dey please." Even before the war's end, rumors circulated through black communities in the South that the government would provide each black family with 40 acres and a mule. These rumors were fueled by General William T. Sherman's **Field Order No. 15** in January 1865, which set aside a vast swath of abandoned land along the South Atlantic coast from the Charleston area to northern Florida for grants of up to 40 acres. The Freedmen's Bureau likewise raised expectations when it was initially authorized to rent 40-acre plots of confiscated or abandoned land to freedmen.

By June 1865, about 40,000 former slaves had settled on Sherman land along the southeastern coast. In 1866, Congress passed the **Southern Homestead Act,** giving black people preferential access to public lands in five southern states. Two years later, the Republican government of South Carolina initiated a land-redistribution program financed by the sale of state bonds. The state used proceeds from the bond sales to purchase farmland, which it then resold to freedmen, who paid for it with state-funded long-term low-interest loans. By the late 1870s, more than 14,000 African American families had taken advantage of this program.

The highest concentration of black land ownership was in the Upper South and in areas of the Lower South with better economic conditions and less white hostility toward black people. By 1890, one out of three black farmers in the Upper South owned his land, compared to one out of five for the South as a whole. In Virginia, 43 percent of black farmers owned the land they farmed.

Land ownership did not ensure financial success. Most black-owned farms were small and on marginal land. The value of these farms in 1880 was roughly half that of white-owned farms. Black farmers also had trouble obtaining credit to purchase or expand their holdings. A lifetime of fieldwork left some freedmen without the managerial skills to operate a farm. The hostility of white neighbors also played a role in thwarting black aspirations. Black farmers often had the most success when groups of families settled together, as in the farm community of Promise Land in upcountry South Carolina.

The vast majority of former slaves, however, especially those in the Lower South, never fulfilled their dreams of land ownership. Rumors to the contrary, the federal government never intended to implement a land-redistribution program in the South. General Sherman viewed his field order as a temporary measure to support freedmen for the remainder of the war. President Andrew Johnson nullified the order in September 1865, returning confiscated land to its former owners. Even Republican supporters of black land ownership questioned the constitutionality of seizing privately owned real estate. Most of the land-redistribution programs that emerged after the war, including government-sponsored programs, required black farmers to have capital. But in the impoverished postwar economy of the South, it was difficult for them to acquire it.

Republican Party rhetoric of the 1850s extolled the virtues and dignity of free labor over the degradation of slave labor. Free labor usually meant working for a wage or under some other contractual arrangement. But unlike slaves, according to the then prevailing view, free laborers could enjoy the fruits of their work and might someday become owners or entrepreneurs themselves. It was self-help, not government assistance, that guaranteed individual success. After the war, many white northerners envisioned former slaves assuming the status of free laborers, not necessarily of independent landowners.

Most of the officials of the Freedmen's Bureau shared these views and therefore saw reviving the southern economy as a higher priority than helping former slaves acquire farms. They wanted both to get the crop in the field and start the South on the road to a free labor system. Thus, they encouraged freedmen to work for their former masters under contract and to postpone their quest for land. Bureau and military officials lectured former slaves on the virtues of staying home and working "faithfully" in the fields.

Freed women washing laundry along a creek near Circleville, Texas, circa 1866. Other than farming, domestic service was the only work open to freed women after the Civil War.

At first, agents of the Freedmen's Bureau supervised labor contracts between former slaves and masters. But after 1867, bureau surveillance declined. Agents assumed that both black laborers and white landowners had become accustomed to the mutual obligations of contracts. The bureau, however, underestimated the power of white landowners to coerce favorable terms or to ignore those they did not like. Contracts implied a mutuality that most planters could not accept in their relations with former slaves. As the northern journalist Whitelaw Reid noted in 1865, planters "have no sort of conception of free labor. They do not comprehend any law for controlling laborers, save the law of force."

By the late 1870s, most former slaves in the rural South had been drawn into a subservient position in a new labor system called **sharecropping.** The premise of this system was relatively simple: The landlord furnished the sharecroppers with a house, a plot of land to work, seed, some farm animals, and farm implements and advanced them credit at a store the landlord typically owned. In exchange, the sharecroppers promised the landlord a share of their crop, usually one-half. The croppers kept the proceeds from the sale of the other half to pay off their debts at the store and save or spend as they and their families saw fit. In theory, a sharecropper could save enough to secure economic independence.

But white landlords perceived black independence as both contradictory and subversive. With landlords keeping the accounts at the store, black sharecroppers found that the proceeds from their share of the crop never left them very far ahead. In exchange for extending credit to sharecroppers, storeowners felt justified in requiring collateral, but sharecroppers had no assets other than the cotton they grew. So southern states passed crop-lien laws, which gave the storeowner the right to the following year's crop in exchange for the current year's credit. If the following year's harvest could not pay off the debt, the sharecropper sank deeper into dependence. Some found themselves in perpetual debt and worked as virtual slaves. They could not simply abandon their debts and go to another farm, because the new landlord would check their references. Those found to have jumped their debts could end up on a prison chain gang. Not all white landlords cheated their tenants, but given the sharecroppers' innocence regarding accounting methods and crop pricing, the temptation to do so was great. Thus weak cotton prices conspired with white chicanery to keep black people economically dependent.

Migration to Cities

Even before the hope of land ownership faded, African Americans looked for alternatives to secure their personal and economic independence. Before the war, the city had offered slaves and free black people a measure of freedom unknown in the rural South. After the war, African Americans moved to cities to find families, seek work, escape the tedium and supervision of farm life, or simply to test their right to move about.

For the same reasons, white people disapproved of black migration to the city. It reduced the labor pool for farms. It also gave black people more opportunities to associate with white people of similar social status, to compete for jobs, and to establish schools, churches, and social organizations, fueling their hopes for racial equality. Between 1860 and 1870, the African American population in every major southern city rose significantly. In Atlanta, for example, black people accounted for one in five residents in 1860 and nearly one in two by 1870. Some freedmen came to cities initially to reunite with their families. Every city newspaper after the war carried advertisements from former slaves seeking their mates and children. In 1865, the Nashville *Colored Tennessean* carried this poignant plea: "During the year 1849, Thomas Sample carried away from this city, as his slaves, our daughter, Polly, and son....We will give $100 each for them to any person who will assist them ... to get to Nashville, or get word to us of their whereabouts."

Once in the city, freedmen had to find a home and a job. They usually settled on the outskirts of town, where building codes did not apply. Rather than developing one large ghetto, as happened in many northern cities, black southerners lived in small concentrations in and around cities. Sometimes armed with a letter of reference from their former masters, black people went door to door to seek employment. Many found work serving white families, as guards, laundresses, or maids, for very low wages. Both skilled and unskilled laborers found work rebuilding war-torn cities like Atlanta. Frederick Ayer, a Freedmen's Bureau agent in Atlanta, reported to a colleague in 1866 that "many of the whites are making most vigorous efforts to retrieve their broken fortunes and ... rebuild their dwellings and shops....This furnished employment to a large number of colored people as Masons, Carpenters, Teamsters, and Common Workmen."

Most rural black southerners, however, worked as unskilled laborers. The paltry wages men earned, when they could find work, pushed black women into the work force. They often had an easier time securing a job in cities as domestics and laundresses. Black men had hoped to assert their patriarchal prerogatives, like white men, by keeping wives and daughters out of the labor market, but necessity dictated otherwise. In both Atlanta and Nashville, black people comprised more than 75 percent of the unskilled workforce in 1870. Their wages were at or below subsistence level. A black laborer in Richmond admitted to a journalist in 1870 that he had difficulty making ends meet on $1.50 a day. "It's right hard," he reported. "I have to pay $15 a month rent, and only two little rooms." His family survived because his wife took in laundry, while her mother watched the children. Considering the laborer's struggle, the journalist wondered, "Were not your people better off in slavery?" The man replied, "Oh, no sir! We're a heap better off now.... We're men now, but when our masters had us we was only change in their pockets."

The black church was the center of African-American life in the postwar urban South. Most black churches were founded after the Civil War, but some, such as the first African Baptist Church in Richmond, shown here in an 1874 engraving, traced their origins to before 1861.

Global Perspectives

Emancipation and Freedom in the United States and Russia

Tsar Alexander II (1855–1881) freed Russia's serfs in 1861, two years before Abraham Lincoln's Emancipation Proclamation. Although Russian serfs had more rights than American slaves, both were tied to the land and to their landlords/masters. The liberation of the serfs was part of a broader reform plan designed to help modernize Russia.

On becoming tsar in 1855, Alexander II had relaxed the speech, travel, and press restrictions imposed by his predecessors, resulting in an influx of Western ideas into Russia. These ideas helped create widespread public support for the liberation of the serfs. The tsar couched his emancipation proclamation in the ideals of God and country, but its origin lay primarily in Russia's economic aspirations and the tsar's political strategy. While most Americans perceived their liberated slaves as forming an agricultural working class, Alexander made land ownership one of the major attractions of emancipation. The government divided farms equally between the landlords and the former serfs, compensating the owners for the divided property.

In theory at least, Russian serfs seemed in a better position than the southern freedmen to secure economic independence, given the land they received. One Russian official exulted, "The people are erect and transformed; the look, the walk, the speech, everything is changed." But the Russian serfs found their economic situation little improved. The land chosen for redistribution was marginal, and redistribution came with a major catch: The former serfs were required to repay the state on the installment plan. Given the quality of the land, the relatively high interest rates attached to the loans, and the vast numbers of serfs and their families, repayment was unrealistic even in the long term. To ensure that the former serfs would pay up, the tsar allowed local governments to keep the peasants on their land until they fulfilled their financial obligations. In other words, they were as much tied to the land after emancipation as before. And, as a method to improve the quality of agricultural cultivation, the multiplicity of small plots and impoverished peasants was also a failure.

As in the United States, violence marred the transition from bondage to freedom. Rebellions flared in several parts of Russia, but the tsar's armies put these uprisings down quickly. Some of the former serfs managed to escape to towns and cities and become part of the growing laboring class, much as freedmen went to southern cities. In the cities, both former serfs and slaves came closer to the free-labor ideal posited but not supported by their respective governments. In rural areas, reform broke down through a lack of planning and a failure of will.

■ After emancipation, did the Russian serf or the American slave have a better opportunity to establish economic independence?

Faith and Freedom

Religious faith framed and inspired the efforts of African Americans to test their freedom on the farm and in the city. White southerners used religion to transform the Lost Cause from a shattering defeat to a premonition of a greater destiny. Black southerners, in contrast, saw emancipation in biblical terms as the beginning of an exodus from bondage to the Promised Land.

Some black churches in the postwar South had originated during the slavery era, but most split from white-dominated congregations after the war. White churchgoers deplored the expressive style of black worship, and black churchgoers were uncomfortable in congregations that treated them as inferiors. A separate church also reduced white surveillance.

The church became a primary focus of African American life. It gave black people the opportunity to hone skills in self-government and administration that white-dominated society denied them. Within the supportive confines of the congregation, they could assume leadership positions, render important decisions, deal with financial matters, and engage in politics. The church also operated as an educational institution. Local governments, especially in rural areas, rarely constructed public schools for black people; churches often served that function.

The desire to read the Bible inspired thousands of former slaves to attend the church school. The church also spawned other organizations that served the black community, such as burial societies, Masonic lodges, temperance groups, trade unions, and drama clubs. African Americans took great pride in their churches, which became visible measures of their progress. In Charleston, the first building erected after the war was a black church. The First Colored Baptist Church in Nashville became a landmark for its imposing brick and stone façade. Black people donated a greater proportion of their earnings to their churches than white people. The church and the congregation were a cohesive force in black communities. They supported families under stress from discrimination and poverty. Husbands and wives joined church-affiliated societies together. Their children joined organizations such as the Young Rising Sons and Daughters of the New Testament. The church enforced family and religious values, punishing violators guilty of such infractions as adultery. Black churchwomen, both working-class and middle-class, were especially prominent in the family-oriented organizations.

Most black churches looked inward to strengthen their members against the harsh realities of postwar southern society. Few ministers dared to engage in or even support protest activities. Some, especially those in the Colored Methodist Episcopal Church, counseled congregants to abide by the rules of second-class citizenship and to trust in God's will to right the wrongs of racism. Northern-based denominations, however, notably the AME Church, were more aggressive advocates of black rights. AME ministers stressed the responsibility of individual black people to realize God's will of racial equality.

The efforts of former slaves in the classroom, on the farm, in cities, and in the churches reflect the enthusiasm and expectations with which black southerners greeted freedom. But the majority of white southerners were unwilling to see those expectations fulfilled. For this reason, African Americans could not secure the fruits of their emancipation without the support and protection of the federal government. The issue of freedom was therefore inextricably linked to the other great issue of the era, the rejoining of the Confederacy to the Union, as expressed in federal Reconstruction policy.

Federal Reconstruction, 1865–1870

When the Civil War ended in 1865, no acceptable blueprint existed for reconstituting the Union. President Lincoln believed that a majority of white southerners were Unionists at heart, and that they could and should undertake the task of reconstruction. He favored a conciliatory policy toward the South in order, as he put it in one of his last letters, "to restore the Union, so as to make it ... a Union of hearts and hands as well as of States." He counted on the loyalists to be fair with respect to the rights of the former slaves.

As early as 1863, Lincoln had proposed to readmit a seceding state if 10 percent of its prewar voters took an oath of loyalty to the Union, and it prohibited slavery in a new state constitution. But this Ten Percent Plan did not require states to grant equal civil and political rights to former slaves, and many Republicans in Congress thought it was not stringent enough. In 1864, a group of them responded with the Wade-Davis Bill, which required a majority of a state's prewar voters to pledge their loyalty to the Union and demanded guarantees of black equality before the law. The bill was passed at the end of a congressional session, but Lincoln kept it from becoming law by refusing to sign it (an action known as a "pocket veto").

Lincoln, of course, died before he could implement a Reconstruction plan. His views on reconstructing the Union during the war did not necessarily prefigure how his views would have unfolded after the war. Given his commitment in the Gettysburg Address to promote "a new birth of freedom," it is likely that had white southerners resisted black civil rights, Lincoln would have responded with harsher terms. Above all, Lincoln was a savvy politician: He would not have allowed a stalemate to develop between himself and the Congress, and, if necessary, he would have moved closer to the radical camp. On April 11, 1865, in one of his last pronouncements on Reconstruction, Lincoln stated that he favored a limited suffrage for the freedmen, though he admitted that each state had enough peculiarities that a blanket policy might not work. In a cabinet meeting on April 14, he dismissed an idea for military occupation, though he acknowledged that allowing the states to reconstruct themselves might not work either. In any case, his successor, Andrew Johnson, lacked his flexibility and political acumen.

The controversy over the plans introduced during the war reflected two obstacles to Reconstruction that would continue to plague the ruling Republicans after the war. First, neither the Constitution nor legal precedent offered any guidance on whether the president or Congress should take the lead on Reconstruction policy. Second, there was no agreement on what that policy should be. Proposals requiring various preconditions for readmitting a state, loyalty oaths, new constitutions with certain specific provisions, guarantees of freedmen's rights, all provoked vigorous debate.

President Andrew Johnson, some conservative Republicans, and most Democrats believed that because the Constitution made no mention of secession, the southern states had been in rebellion but had never left the Union, and therefore that there was no need for a formal process to readmit them. Moderate and radical Republicans disagreed, arguing that the defeated states had forfeited their rights. Moderates and radicals parted company, however, on the conditions necessary for readmission to the Union. The radicals wanted to treat the former Confederate states as territories, or "conquered provinces," subject to congressional legislation. Moderates wanted to grant the seceding states more autonomy and limit federal intervention in their affairs while they satisfied the conditions of readmission. Neither group held a majority in Congress, and legislators sometimes changed their positions (see the Overview table, Contrasting Views of Reconstruction).

Presidential Reconstruction, 1865–1867

When the Civil War ended in April 1865, Congress was not in session and would not reconvene until December. Thus, the responsibility for developing a Reconstruction policy initially fell on Andrew Johnson, who succeeded to the presidency upon Lincoln's assassination. Johnson seemed well suited to the difficult task. He was born in humble circumstances in North Carolina in 1808. He learned the tailoring trade and struck out for Tennessee as a teenager to open a tailor shop in the eastern Tennessee town of Greenville. Obtaining his education informally, he prospered modestly, purchased a few slaves, and began to pursue politics. He was elected alderman, mayor, state legislator, congressman, governor, and then, in 1856, U.S. senator. Johnson was the only southern senator to remain in the U.S. Senate after secession. This defiant Unionism won him acclaim in the North and credibility among Republican leaders, who welcomed him into their party. During the war, as military governor of Tennessee, he solidified his Republican credentials by advocating the abolition of slavery in Tennessee and severe punishment of Confederate leaders. His views landed him on the Republican ticket as the candidate for vice president in 1864. Indiana Republican congressman George W. Julian, who advocated harsh terms for the South and broad rights for black people, viewed Johnson's accession to the presidency in 1865 as "a godsend."

Most northerners and many Republicans approved Johnson's Reconstruction plan when he unveiled it in May 1865. Johnson extended pardons and restored property rights, except in slaves, to southerners who swore an oath of allegiance to the Union and the Constitution. Southerners who had held prominent posts in the Confederacy, however, and those with more than $20,000 in taxable property, had to petition the president directly for a pardon, a reflection of Johnson's disdain for wealthy whites. The plan said nothing about the voting rights or civil rights of former slaves.

Northern Democrats applauded the plan's silence on these issues and its promise of a quick restoration of the southern states to the Union. They expected the southern states to favor their party and expand its political power. Republicans approved the plan because it restored property rights to white southerners, although some wanted it to provide for black suffrage. Republicans also hoped that Johnson's conciliatory terms might attract some white southerners to the Republican Party.

On the two great issues of freedom and reunion, white southerners quickly demonstrated their eagerness to reverse the results of the Civil War. Although most states accepted President Johnson's modest requirements, several objected to one or more of them. Mississippi and Texas refused to ratify the Thirteenth Amendment, which abolished slavery. Alabama accepted only parts of the amendment. South Carolina declined to nullify its secession ordinance. No southern state authorized black voting. When Johnson ordered special congressional elections in the South in the fall of 1865, the all-white electorate returned many prominent Confederate leaders to office.

In late 1865, the newly elected southern state legislatures revised their antebellum slave codes. The updated **black codes** allowed local officials to arrest black people who could not document employment and residence or who were "disorderly" and sentence them to forced labor on farms or road crews. The codes also restricted black people to certain occupations, barred them from jury duty, and forbade them to possess firearms. Apprenticeship laws permitted judges to take black children from parents who could not, in the judges' view, adequately support them. Given the widespread poverty in the South in 1865, the law could apply to almost any freed black family. Northerners looking for contrition in the South found no sign of it. Worse, President Johnson did not seem perturbed about this turn of events.

The Republican-dominated Congress reconvened in December 1865 in a belligerent mood. A few radical Republicans pushed for swift retribution. George W. Julian thundered that he would "indict, convict and hang Jefferson Davis in the name of God; as for Robert E. Lee, unmolested in Virginia, hang him too." His colleague, Benjamin F. Wade, suggested that "if the negroes by insurrection would contrive to slay one-half of the White Southerners, the remaining half would then hold them in respect and treat them with justice." Few in Congress took such statements seriously. Nonetheless, a consensus formed among radical Republicans, who comprised nearly half of the party's strength in Congress, that to gain readmission, a state would have to extend suffrage to black citizens, protect freedmen's civil rights, and have its white citizens officially acknowledge these rights. Some radicals also supported the redistribution of land to former slaves, but few pressed for social equality. They envisioned a new South of modest farms, some owned by former slaves, and a Republican Party built on an alliance between black people and white loyalists.

But the radicals could not unite behind a program, and it fell to their moderate colleagues to take the first step toward a congressional Reconstruction plan. The moderates shared the radicals' desire to protect the former slaves' civil rights. But they would not support land-redistribution schemes or punitive measures against prominent Confederates, and disagreed on extending voting rights to the freedmen. The moderates' first measure, passed in early 1866, extended the life of the Freedmen's Bureau and authorized it to punish state officials who failed to extend equal civil rights to black citizens. But President Johnson vetoed the legislation.

Undeterred, Congress passed the Civil Rights Act of 1866 in direct response to the black codes. The act specified the civil rights to which all U.S. citizens were entitled. In creating a category of national citizenship with rights that su-

Selling a Freeman to Pay his Fine at Monticello, Florida. This 1867 engraving shows how the black codes of the early Reconstruction era reduced former slaves to virtually their pre–Civil War status. Scenes like this convinced northerners that the white South was unrepentant and prompted congressional Republicans to devise their own Reconstruction plans.

perseded state laws, the act changed federal-state relations (and in the process overturned the *Dred Scott* decision). President Johnson vetoed the act, but it became law when Congress mustered a two-thirds majority to override his veto, the first time in American history that Congress passed major legislation over a president's veto.

Andrew Johnson's position reflected both his view of government and his racial attitudes. The Republican president remained a Democrat in spirit. Republicans had expanded federal power during the Civil War. Johnson, however, like most Democrats, favored more of a balance between federal and state power. He also shared with many whites a belief in black inferiority. In supporting abolition, Johnson had assumed that black people, once free, would emigrate to Africa.

Given the president's views and his inflexible temperament, a clash between him and Congress became inevitable.

To keep freedmen's rights safe from presidential vetoes, state legislatures, and federal courts, the Republican-dominated Congress moved to incorporate some of the provisions of the 1866 Civil Rights Act into the Constitution. The **Fourteenth Amendment,** which Congress passed in June 1866, addressed the issues of civil and voting rights. It guaranteed every citizen equality before the law. The two key sections of the amendment prohibited states from violating the civil rights of their citizens, thus outlawing the black codes, and gave states the choice of enfranchising black people or losing representation in Congress. Some radical Republicans expressed disappointment that the amendment, in a reflec-

American Views

Mississippi's 1865 Black Codes

White southerners, especially landowners and business owners, feared that emancipation would produce a labor crisis; freedmen, they expected, would either refuse to work or strike hard bargains with their former masters. White southerners also recoiled from the prospect of having to treat their former slaves as full social equals. Thus, beginning in late 1865, several southern states, including Mississippi, enacted laws designed to control black labor, mobility, and social status. Northerners responded to the codes as a provocation, a bold move to deny the result of the war and its consequences.

- How did the black codes fit into President Andrew Johnson's Reconstruction program?
- Some northerners charged that the black codes were a backdoor attempt at reestablishing slavery. Do you agree?
- If southern states enacted black codes to stabilize labor relations, how did the provisions below effect that objective?

From An Act to Confer Civil Rights on Freedmen, and for other Purposes

Section 1. All freedmen, free negroes and mulattoes may sue and be sued, implead and be impleaded, in all the courts of law and equity of this State, and may acquire personal property, and choose in action, by descent or purchase, and may dispose of the same in the same manner and to the same extent that white persons may: Provided, That the provisions of this section shall not be so construed as to allow any freedman, free negro or mulatto to rent or lease any lands or tenements except in incorporated cities or towns, in which places the corporate authorities shall control the same.

Section 7. Every civil officer shall, and every person may, arrest and carry back to his or her legal employer any freedman, free negro, or mulatto who shall have quit the service of his or her employer before the expiration of his or her term of service without good cause; and said officer and person shall be entitled to receive for arresting and carrying back every deserting employee aforesaid the sum of five dollars, and ten cents per mile from the place of arrest to the place of delivery; and the same shall be paid by the employer, and held as a set off for so much against the wages of said deserting employee: Provided, that said arrested party, after being so returned, may appeal to the justice of the peace or member of the board of police of the county, who, on notice to the alleged employer, shall try summarily whether said appellant is legally employed by the alleged employer, and has good cause to quit said employer. Either party shall have the right of appeal to the county court, pending which the alleged deserter shall be remanded to the alleged employer or otherwise disposed of, as shall be right and just; and the decision of the county court shall be final.

From An Act to Amend the Vagrant Laws of the State

Section 2. All freedmen, free negroes and mulattoes in this State, over the age of eighteen years, found on the second Monday in January, 1866, or thereafter, with no lawful employment or business, or found unlawfully assembling themselves together, either in the day or night time, and all white persons assembling themselves with freedmen, Free negroes or mulattoes, or usually associating with freedmen, free negroes or mulattoes, on terms of equality, or living in adultery or fornication with a freed woman, freed negro or mulatto, shall be deemed vagrants, and on conviction thereof shall be fined in a sum not exceeding, in the case of a freedman, free negro or mulatto, fifty dollars, and a white man two hundred dollars, and imprisonment at the discretion of the court, the free negro not exceeding ten days, and the white man not exceeding six months.

Source: "Laws in Relation to Freedmen," 39 Congress, 2 Session, Senate Executive Document 6, Freedmen's Affairs, 182–86.

tion of northern ambivalence, failed to give the vote to black people outright.

The amendment also disappointed advocates of woman suffrage, for the first time using the word *male* in the Constitution to define who could vote. Wendell Phillips, a prominent abolitionist, counseled women, "One question at a time. This hour belongs to the Negro." Susan B. Anthony, who had campaigned for the abolition of slavery before the war and helped mount a petition drive that collected 400,000 signatures for the Thirteenth Amendment, founded the American Equal Rights Association in 1866 with her colleagues to push for woman suffrage at the state level.

The Fourteenth Amendment had little immediate impact on the South. Although enforcement of black codes diminished, white violence against black people increased. In the 1870s, several decisions by the U.S. Supreme Court weakened the amendment's provisions. Eventually, however, it would play a major role in securing the civil rights of African Americans.

President Johnson encouraged southern white intransigence by openly denouncing the Fourteenth Amendment. In August 1866, at the start of the congressional election campaign, he undertook an unprecedented tour of key northern states to sell his message of sectional reconciliation to the public. Although listeners appreciated Johnson's desire for peace, they questioned his claims of southern white loyalty to the Union. The president's diatribes against the Republican Congress won him followers in those northern states with a reservoir of opposition to black suffrage. But the tone and manner of his campaign offended many as undignified. In the November elections, the Democrats suffered embarrassing defeats in the North as Republicans managed better than two-thirds majorities in both the House and Senate, sufficient to override presidential vetoes. Radical Republicans, joined by moderate colleagues buoyed by the election results and revolted by the president's and the South's intransigence, seized the initiative when Congress reconvened.

Congressional Reconstruction, 1867–1870

The radicals' first salvo in their attempt to take control of Reconstruction occurred with the passing over President Johnson's veto of the Military Reconstruction Acts. The measures, passed in March 1867, inaugurated a period known as **Congressional Reconstruction** or Radical Reconstruction. With the exception of Tennessee, the only southern state that had ratified the Fourteenth Amendment and been readmitted to the Union, Congress divided the former Confederate states into five military districts, each headed by a general (see Map 16–1). The commanders' first order of business was to conduct voter-registration campaigns to enroll black people and bar white people who had held office before the Civil War and supported

the Confederacy. The eligible voters would then elect delegates to a state convention to write a new constitution that guaranteed universal manhood suffrage. Once a majority of eligible voters ratified the new constitution and the Fourteenth Amendment, their state would be eligible for readmission to the Union.

The Reconstruction Acts fulfilled the radicals' three major objectives. First, they secured the freedmen's right to vote. Second, they made it likely that southern states would be run by Republican regimes that would enforce the new constitutions, protect former slaves' rights, and maintain the Republican majority in Congress. Finally, they set standards for readmission that required the South to accept the preeminence of the federal government and the end of slavery.

To limit presidential interference with their policies, Republicans passed the **Tenure of Office Act,** prohibiting the president from removing certain officeholders without the Senate's consent. Johnson, angered at what he believed was an unconstitutional attack on presidential authority, deliberately violated the act by firing Secretary of War Edwin M. Stanton, a leading radical, in February 1868. The House responded by approving articles of impeachment against a president for the first time in American history. That set the stage for the next step prescribed by the Constitution: a Senate trial to determine whether the president should be removed from office.

MAP 16–1 Congressional Reconstruction, 1865–1877
When Congress wrested control of Reconstruction policy from President Andrew Johnson, it divided the South into the five military districts depicted here. The commanding generals for each district held the authority both to hold elections and to decide who could vote.

Johnson had indeed violated the Tenure of Office Act, a measure of dubious constitutionality even to some Republicans, but enough Republicans felt that his actions fell short of the "high crimes and misdemeanors" standard set by the Constitution for dismissal from office. Seven Republicans deserted their party, and Johnson was acquitted. Defiant to the end, he continued to issue pardons to leading Confederates, even to Robert E. Lee and Jefferson Davis, and he refused to follow the traditional courtesy of accompanying and welcoming his successor, Ulysses S. Grant, into office. The seven Republi-

cans who voted against their party did so not out of respect for Johnson but because they feared that a conviction would damage the office of the presidency and violate the constitutional separation of powers. The outcome weakened the radicals and eased the way for Grant, a moderate Republican, to gain the party's nomination for president in 1868.

The Republicans viewed the 1868 presidential election as a referendum on Congressional Reconstruction. They supported black suffrage in the South but equivocated on allowing African Americans to vote in the North. Black northerners could vote in only eight of the twenty-two northern states, and between 1865 and 1869, white northerners rejected equal suffrage referendums in eight of eleven states. Republicans "waved the bloody shirt," reminding voters of Democratic disloyalty, the sacrifices of war, and the peace only Republicans could redeem. Democrats denounced Congressional Reconstruction as federal tyranny and, in openly racist appeals, warned white voters that a Republican victory would mean black rule. Grant won the election, but his margin of victory was uncomfortably narrow. Reflecting growing ambivalence in the North over issues of race and federal authority, New York's Horatio Seymour, the Democratic presidential nominee, probably carried a majority of the nation's white vote. Black voters' overwhelming support for Grant probably provided his margin of victory.

The Republicans retained a strong majority in both houses of Congress and managed to pass another major piece of Reconstruction legislation, the **Fifteenth Amendment,** in February 1869. In response to growing concerns about voter fraud and violence against freedmen, the amendment guaranteed the right of American men to vote, regardless of race. Although the amendment provided a loophole allowing states to restrict the right to vote based on literacy or property qualifications, it was nonetheless a milestone. It made the right to vote perhaps the most distinguishing characteristic of U.S. citizenship.

The Fifteenth Amendment allowed states to keep the franchise a male prerogative, angering many in the woman-suffrage movement more than had the Fourteenth Amendment. The resulting controversy severed the ties between the movement and Republican politics. Susan B. Anthony broke with her abolitionist colleagues and opposed the amendment. A fellow abolitionist and woman suffragist, Elizabeth Cady Stanton, charged that the amendment created an "aristocracy of sex." In an appeal brimming with ethnic and racial animosity, Stanton warned that "if you do not wish the lower orders of Chinese, African, Germans and Irish, with their low ideas of womanhood to make laws for you and your daughters...awake to the danger...and demand that woman, too, shall be represented in the government!" Such language created a major rift in the nascent women's movement.

The Democratic Party ran an openly racist presidential campaign in 1868. This pro-Republican drawing by noted cartoonist Thomas Nast includes three Democratic constituencies: former Confederate soldiers (note the "CSA: on the belt buckle); the Irish or immigrant vote (note the almost Simian depiction of the Irishman), and the well-dressed man sporting a "5th Avenue" button and waving a wallet full of bills, a reference to the corrupt Democratic politics in New York City. The three have their feet on an African American soldier. In the background note the "colored orphan asylum" and southern school" ablaze, and the lynching of black children. *Courtesy of the Library of Congress.*

African American Voting Rights in the South

Official photograph Congressional Black Caucus, 106th Congress.

Right from the end of the Civil War, white southerners resisted African American voting rights. Black people, with equal determination, used the franchise to assert their equal right to participate in the political process. Black voting rights proved so contentious that Congress sought to secure them with the Fourteenth and Fifteenth Amendments to the U.S. Constitution. But U.S. Supreme Court decisions in *United States v. Cruikshank* (1876) and in the Civil Rights Cases (1883) undermined federal authority to protect the rights of freedmen, including voting rights. A combination of violence, intimidation, and legislation effectively disfranchised black southerners by the early twentieth century.

During the 1960s, Congress passed legislation designed to override state prohibitions and earlier court decisions limiting African American voting rights. The key measure, the 1965 Voting Rights Act, not only guaranteed black southerners (and later, other minorities) the right to register and vote but also protected them from procedural subterfuges. These protections proved necessary because of the extreme racial polarization of southern elections.

To ensure African American candidates an opportunity to win elections, the federal government after 1965 insisted that states and localities establish procedures to increase the likelihood of such a result. By the early 1990s, states were being directed to draw districts with majority-black voting populations to ensure African American representation in the U.S. Congress and in state legislatures. The federal government cited the South's history of racial discrimination and racially polarized voting to justify these districts. But white southerners challenged such claims, as they had more than a century earlier, and their challenges proved partially successful in federal court.

As with the First Reconstruction, the U.S. Supreme Court has narrowed the scope of black voting rights in several decisions since the early 1990s. Despite the history of racial discrimination with respect to voting rights, the Court has often championed the standard of "colorblindness," which justices insist was codified in the Fourteenth Amendment. The principle of colorblindness, however wonderful in the abstract, ignores the history of black voting rights from the Reconstruction era to the present. The framers of the Reconstruction Amendments had the protection of the rights of the freedmen in mind (including and especially voting rights) when they wrote those measures. The issue of African American voting rights in the South and the degree to which the federal goverment may or may not intercede to protect those rights remains as much at issue as it was more than a century ago.

■ There is considerable debate as to whether the U.S. Constitution is colorblind with respect to voting rights. Should it be?

Southern black men during Reconstruction went to great lengths to vote and to protect themselves on election day as these voters fording a stream with rifles aloft attest.

PEARSON myhistorylab
From Then to Now Online

Additional Documents and Brief Descriptions

16–1 "An Eloquent Appeal," *Harper's Weekly*, September 26, 1868.

16–2 U.S. Supreme Court Justice Sandra Day O'Connor strikes down a North Carolina Congressional district, in *Shaw v. Reno*, 509 U.S. 360 (1993).

OVERVIEW

Contrasting Views of Reconstruction: President and Congress

Politician or Group	Policy on Former Slaves	Policy on Readmission of Former Confederate States
President Johnson	Opposed to black suffrage	Maintained that rebellious states were already readmitted
	Silent on protection of black civil rights	Granted pardons and restoration of property to all who swore allegiance to the United States
	Opposed to land redistribution	
Radical Republicans	Favored black suffrage	Favored treating rebellious states as territories and establishing military districts*
	Favored protection of black civil rights	Favored limiting franchise to black people and loyal white people
	Favored land redistribution	
Moderate Republicans	Favored black suffrage*	Favored some restrictions on white suffrage**
	Favored protection of civil rights	Favored requiring states to meet various requirements before being readmitted*
	Opposed land redistribution	Split on military rule

*After 1866.

**True of most but not all members of the group.

Southern Republican Governments, 1867–1870

Away from Washington, the first order of business for the former Confederacy was to draft state constitutions. The documents embodied progressive principles new to theSouth. They mandated the election of numerous local and state offices. Self-perpetuating local elites could no longer appoint themselves or cronies to powerful positions. The constitutions committed southern states, many for the first time, to public education. Lawmakers enacted a variety of reforms, including social welfare, penal reform, legislative reapportionment, and universal manhood suffrage.

The Republican regimes that gained control in southern states promoted vigorous state government and the protection of civil and voting rights. Three Republican constituencies supported these governments: native whites, native blacks, and northern transplants. The native white group was mostly made up of yeomen farmers. Residing mainly in the upland regions of the South and long ignored by lowland planters and merchants in state government, they were left devastated by the war. They struggled to keep their land and hoped for an easing of credit and for debt-stay laws to help them escape foreclosure. They wanted public schools for their children and good roads to get their crops to market. Some urban merchants and large planters also called themselves Republicans. They were attracted to the party's emphasis on economic development, especially railroad construction, and would become prominent in Republican leadership after 1867, forming a majority of the party's elected officials.

Collectively, opponents called these native white southerners **scalawags.** Although their opponents perceived them as a unified group, scalawags held a variety of views. Planters and merchants opposed easy debt and credit arrangements and the use of their taxes to support programs other than railroads or port improvements. Yeomen farmers desperately needed the debt and credit legislation to retain their land. And even though they supported public schools and road building, which would require increased state revenues, they opposed higher taxes.

Northern transplants, or **carpetbaggers,** as many southern whites called them, constituted a second group of southern Republicans. Cartoonists depicted carpetbaggers as shoddily dressed and poorly groomed, their worldly possessions in a ratty cloth satchel, slinking into a town and swindling the locals before departing with their ill-gotten gains. The reality was far different from the caricature. Thousands of northerners came south during and after the war. Many were Union soldiers who simply enjoyed the climate and perhaps married a local woman. Most were drawn by economic opportunity. Land was cheap and the price of cotton high. Although most carpetbaggers had supported the Republican Party before they moved south, few became politically active until the cotton economy nosedived in 1866. Financial

"Time Works Wonders." This Thomas Nast cartoon has Jefferson Davis, former President of the Confederacy, dressed as Iago in William Shakespeare's play *Othello*, declaring with considerable anguish, "For that I suspect the lusty moor [Othello] hath leap'd into my seat: the thought where of doth like a poisonous mineral gnaw my inwards," Indeed, Hiram Revels occupies Davis's old seat in the U.S. Senate representing the state of Mississippi in 1870.

concerns were not all that motivated carpetbaggers to enter politics; some hoped to aid the freedmen.

Carpetbaggers never comprised more than 2 percent of any state's population. Most white southerners viewed them as an alien presence, instruments of a hated occupying force. They estranged themselves from their neighbors by supporting and participating in the Republican state governments that most white people despised. In Alabama, local editors organized a boycott of northern-owned shops. Because many of them tended to support extending political and civil rights to black southerners, carpetbaggers were also often at odds with their fellow white Republicans, the scalawags.

African Americans constituted the Republican Party's largest southern constituency. In three states, South Carolina, Mississippi, and Louisiana, they also constituted the majority of eligible voters. They viewed the franchise as the key to civic equality and economic opportunity and demanded an active role in party and government affairs.

Black people began to take part in southern politics even before the end of the Civil War, especially in cities occupied by Union forces. In February 1865, black people in Norfolk,

Virginia, gathered to demand a say in the new government that Union supporters were forming in that portion of the state. In April, they created the Colored Monitor Union club, modeled after regular Republican Party organizations in northern cities, called **Union Leagues.** They demanded "the right of universal suffrage" for "all loyal men, without distinction of color." Black people in other southern cities held similar meetings, seeking inclusion in the democratic process to protect their freedom. White southerners viewed these developments with alarm but could not at first counter them. Despite white threats, black southerners thronged to Union League meetings in 1867, even forging interracial alliances in states such as North Carolina and Alabama. Focusing on political education and recruitment, the leagues successfully mobilized black voters. In 1867, more than 90 percent of eligible black voters across the South turned out for elections. Black women, even though they could not vote, also played a role. During the 1868 presidential campaign, for example, black maids and cooks in the South wore buttons touting the candidacy of the Republican presidential nominee, Ulysses S. Grant.

Black southerners were not content just to vote; they also demanded political office. White Republican leaders in the South often took the black vote for granted. But on several occasions after 1867, black people threatened to run independent candidates, support rival Democrats, or simply stay home unless they were represented among Republican nominees. These demands brought them some success. The number of southern black congressmen in the U.S. House of Representatives increased from two in 1869 to seven in 1873, and more than 600 African Americans, most of them former slaves from plantation counties, were elected to southern state legislatures between 1867 and 1877.

White fears that black officeholders would enact vengeful legislation proved unfounded. African Americans generally did not promote race-specific legislation. Rather, they supported measures such as debt relief and state funding for education that benefited all poor and working-class people. Like all politicians, however, black officials in southern cities sought to enact measures beneficial to their constituents, such as roads and sidewalks. And they succeeded in having a black police commissioner appointed in Jacksonville, Florida. Gains like these underscored the advantages of suffrage for the African American community.

During the first few years of Congressional Reconstruction, Republican governments walked a tightrope, attempting to lure moderate Democrats and unaffiliated white voters into the party without slighting the black vote. They used the lure of patronage power and the attractive salaries that accompanied public office. In 1868, for example, Louisiana's Republican governor, Henry C. Warmoth, appointed white conservatives to state and local offices, which he divided equally between Confederate veterans and black people, and repealed a constitutional provision disfranchising former Confederate officials.

Republicans also gained support by expanding the role of state government to a degree unprecedented in the South. Southern Republican administrations appealed to hard-pressed upland white constituents by prohibiting foreclosure and passing stay laws that allowed farm owners additional time to repay debts. They undertook building programs that benefited black and white citizens, erecting hospitals, schools, and orphanages. Stepping further into social policy than most northern states at the time, Republican governments in the South expanded women's property rights, enacted legislation against child abuse, and required child support from fathers of mulatto children. In South Carolina, the Republican government provided medical care for the poor; in Alabama, it provided free legal aid for needy defendants.

Despite these impressive policies, southern Republicans were unable to hold their diverse constituency together. Although the party had some success among white yeoman farmers, the liberal use of patronage failed to attract white conservatives. At the same time, it alienated the party's core supporters, who resented seeing their former enemies rewarded with lucrative offices.

The high costs of their activist policies further undermined the Republicans by forcing them to raise state taxes. In Mississippi, where the Republican governor built a public school system for both black and white students, founded a black university, reorganized the state judiciary, built new courthouses and two state hospitals, and pushed through legislation giving black people equal access to public facilities, the state debt soared to $1.5 million between 1869 and 1873. This was in an era in which state budgets rarely exceeded $1 million.

Unprecedented expenditures and the liberal use of patronage sometimes resulted in waste and corruption. Officials charged with selecting railroad routes, appointing lesser officials, and erecting public buildings were well positioned to benefit from their power. Their high salaries offended many in an otherwise impoverished region. Problems like these were not limited to the South, but the perception of dishonesty was nonetheless damaging to governments struggling to build legitimacy among a skeptical white electorate.

The excesses of some state governments, high taxes, contests over patronage, and conflicts over the relative roles of white and black party members opened rifts in Republican ranks. Patronage triggered intraparty warfare. Every office secured by a Democrat created a disappointed Republican. Class tensions erupted in the party as economic development policies sometimes superseded relief and social service legislation supported by small farmers. The failure of Alabama Republicans to deliver on promises of debt relief and land redistribution eroded the party's support among upcountry white voters. There were differences among black voters too. In the Lower South, divisions that had developed in the prewar era between urban, lighter-skinned free black people and darker, rural slaves persisted into the Reconstruction era. In many southern states, black clergy, because of their independence from white support and their important spiritual and educational role, became leaders. But most preached salvation in the next world rather than equality in this one, conceding more to white people than their rank-and-file constituents.

Counter-Reconstruction, 1870–1874

Republicans might have survived battles over patronage, policy, expenditures, and taxes. But they could not overcome racism and the violence it generated. Racism killed Republican rule in the South because it deepened divisions within the party, encouraged white violence, and eroded support in the North. Southern Democrats discovered that they could use race baiting and racial violence to create solidarity among white people that overrode their economic and class differences. Unity translated into election victories.

Northerners responded to the persistent violence in the South, not with outrage, but with a growing sense of tedium. They came to accept the arguments of white southerners that it was folly to allow black people to vote and hold office. Racism became respectable. Noted intellectuals and journalists espoused "scientific" theories that claimed to demonstrate the natural superiority of white people over black people. These theories influenced the Liberal Republicans, followers of a new political movement that splintered the Republican Party, further weakening its will to pursue Reconstruction policy.

By 1874, Americans were concerned with an array of domestic problems that overshadowed Reconstruction. An economic depression left them more preoccupied with survival than racial justice. Corruption convinced many that politics was part of the nation's problems, not a solution to them. With the rest of the nation thus distracted and weary, white southerners reclaimed control of the South.

The Klan directed violence at African Americans primarily for engaging in political activity. Here, a black man, John Campbell, vainly begs for mercy in Moore County, North Carolina, in August 1871.

odic violence against black residents, such as during the New York draft riots of 1863. Northerners' views were bolstered by prevailing scientific theories of race that "proved" blacks' limited capacities and, therefore, unfitness for either the ballot or skilled occupations.

Northerners also grew increasingly wary of federal power. The emerging scandals of the Grant administration, fueled, it seemed, by government subsidies to railroads and other private businesses, demanded a scaling back of federal power and discretion. The Civil War had grown government bureaucracy without corresponding checks on power. Intervening in southern elections, taking sides with a particular faction, ordering troops to put down local disturbances now seemed less an exercise in establishing law and order and protecting civil rights than bullying citizens to comply with the whims of Republicans in Washington, DC. When white southerners complained about federal meddling, again, they found resonance in the North.

The excesses and alleged abuses of federal power inspired a reform movement among a group of northern Republicans and some Democrats. In addition, business leaders decried the ability of wealthy lobbyists to influence economic decisions. An influential group of intellectuals and opinion makers lamented the inability of politicians to understand "natural" laws, particularly those related to race. And some Republicans joined the reform movement out of fear that Democrats would capitalize on the turmoil in the South and the political scandals in the North to reap huge electoral victories in 1872.

Liberal Republicans and the Election of 1872

Liberal Republicans, as the reformers called themselves, put forward an array of suggestions to improve government and save the Republican Party. They advocated civil service reform to reduce reliance on patronage and the abuses that accompanied office seeking. To limit government and reduce artificial economic stimuli, the reformers called for tariff reduction and an end to federal land grants to railroads. For the South, they recommended a general amnesty for white people and a return to "local self-government" by men of "property and enterprise."

When the Liberals failed to convince other Republicans to adopt their program, they broke with the party. Taking advantage of this split, the Democrats forged an alliance with the Liberals. Together, they nominated journalist Horace Greeley to challenge Ulysses S. Grant for the presidency in the election of 1872. Grant won resoundingly, helped by high turnout among black voters in the South. He carried every southern state except Georgia, Tennessee, and Texas. Elsewhere, Republicans again used the tactic of waving the bloody shirt to good effect. It was the Republicans, they declared, who had saved the Union, the Democrats who had

almost destroyed it. Greeley had been a staunch Republican during the Civil War and had spent most of his career attacking Democrats. Republicans used his own words against him. Many Democratic voters stayed home.

The election suggested that the Grant administration had not yet exhausted public tolerance and that the Republican experiment in the South retained some public support. But Greeley had helped the Republicans by running an inept campaign. Within a year, an economic depression, continued violence in the South, and the persistent corruption of the Grant administration would erode the last remnants of support for Reconstruction and black rights in the South.

Economic Transformation

After 1873, the Republican Party in the South became a liability for the national party, especially as Americans fastened on economic issues. The major story of the decade would not be equal rights for African Americans—a long-shot even in the heady days following freedom—but the changing nature of the American economy. An overextended banking and credit system generated the Panic of 1873 and caused extended suffering, particularly among working-class Americans. But the depression masked a remarkable economic transformation as the nation moved toward a national industrial economy.

During the 1870s, the economy grew annually between 4.5 and 6 percent, among the fastest decadal growth rates on record. Consumption grew even faster; Americans purchased more food, more fuel, and more manufactured products than at any other previous time in the nation's history. While unemployment was severe, overall, employment grew by 40 percent between 1870 and 1880 and productivity increased at least as fast. This seeming contradiction is explained by the rapid expansion of new industries such as oil refining and meatpacking, and the application of technology in iron and steel production. Technology also eliminated jobs, and those that remained were primarily low-skilled, low-paying positions—painful, to be sure, for those caught in the change, but liberating for those with education and ability who populated a burgeoning middle-management sector of the growing urban middle class.

The depression and the economic transformation occupied center stage in the American mentality of the mid-1870s, at least in the North. Most Americans had mentally forsaken Reconstruction long before the Compromise of 1877 made its abandonment a political fact. The sporadic violence against black and white Republicans in the South, and the cries of help from freedmen as their rights and persons were abused by white Democrats, became distant echoes from another era, the era of the Civil War, now commemorated and memorialized, but no longer an active part of the nation's present and future. Of course, for white southerners, the past was not yet past. There was still work to do.

Redemption, 1874–1877

For southern Democrats, the Republican victory in 1872 underscored the importance of turning out larger numbers of white voters and restricting the black vote. They accomplished these goals over the next four years with a surge in political violence, secure in the knowledge that federal authorities would rarely intervene against them. Preoccupied with corruption and economic crisis and increasingly indifferent, if not hostile, to African American aspirations, most Americans looked the other way. The elections of 1876 confirmed the triumph of white southerners.

In a religious metaphor that matched their view of the Civil War as a lost crusade, southern Democrats called their victory "Redemption" and depicted themselves as **Redeemers**, holy warriors who had saved the South from the hell of black Republican rule. Generations of American boys and girls would learn this interpretation of the Reconstruction era, and it would affect race relations for nearly a century.

The Democrats' Violent Resurgence

The violence between 1874 and 1876 differed in several respects from earlier attempts to restore white government by force. Attackers operated more openly and more closely identified themselves with the Democratic Party. Mounted, gray-clad ex-Confederate soldiers flanked Democratic candidates at campaign rallies and "visited" black neighborhoods afterward to discourage black men from voting. With black people intimidated and white people already prepared to vote, election days were typically quiet.

Democrats swept to victory across the South in the 1874 elections. "A perfect reign of terror" redeemed Alabama for the Democrats. The successful appeal to white supremacy inspired a massive white turnout to unseat Republicans in Virginia, Florida (legislature only), and Arkansas. Texas had fallen to the Democrats in 1873. Only South Carolina, Mississippi, and Louisiana, states with large black populations, survived the debacle. But the relentless tide of terror would soon overwhelm them as well.

As this Thomas Nast cartoon makes clear, the paramilitary violence against black southerners in the early 1870s threatened not only the voting rights of freedmen, but their dreams of education, prosperity, and family life. In this context, the slogan "The Union As It Was" is highly ironic.

In Louisiana, a group of elite Democrats in New Orleans organized a military organization, known as the White League, in 1874 to challenge the state's Republican government. In September 1874, more than 8,000 White Leaguers staged a coup to overthrow the Republican government of New Orleans. The city's police, commanded by the former Confederate general, James Longstreet, and the intervention of nearby federal troops saved the government and prevented a wholesale slaughter. But the incident only inspired White Leaguers to redouble their efforts.

The Weak Federal Response

Unrest like the events in Louisiana also plagued Mississippi and South Carolina. When Governor Daniel H. Chamberlain could no longer contain the violence in South Carolina in 1876, he asked the president for help. Grant acknowledged the gravity of Chamberlain's situation but would offer him only the lame hope that South Carolinians would exercise "better judgment and cooperation" and assist the governor in bringing offenders to justice "without aid from the federal Government."

Congress responded to blacks' deteriorating status in the South with the Civil Rights Act of 1875. The act prohibited discrimination against black people in public accommodations, such as theaters, parks, and trains, and guaranteed freedmen's rights to serve on juries. It had no provision for voting rights, which Congress presumed the Fifteenth Amendment protected. A Texas judge fined a Galveston theater $500 for refusing to allow black people to sit wherever they wanted, but most judges either interpreted the law narrowly or declared it unconstitutional. In 1883, the U.S. Supreme Court agreed and overturned the act, declaring that only the states, not Congress, could redress "a private wrong, or a crime of the individual."

The Election of 1876 and the Compromise of 1877

Reconstruction officially ended with the presidential election of 1876, in which the Democrat Samuel J. Tilden ran against the Republican Rutherford B. Hayes. Republicans again waved the bloody shirt, touting their role in preserving the Union during the Civil War, but they ignored Reconstruction. The Democrats hoped that their resurgent strength in the South and a respectable showing in the North would bring them the White House. The scandals of the Grant administration, northern weariness with southern Republican governments, and the persisting economic depression worked in the Democrats' favor.

When the ballots were counted, it appeared that Tilden, a conservative New Yorker respectable enough for northern voters and Democratic enough for white southerners, had won. But despite a majority in the popular vote, disputed returns in three southern states left him with only 184 of the 185 electoral votes needed to win (see Map 16–2). The three

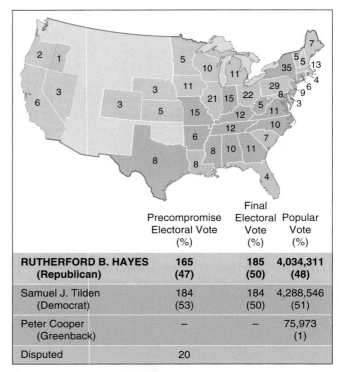

	Precompromise Electoral Vote (%)	Final Electoral Vote (%)	Popular Vote (%)
RUTHERFORD B. HAYES (Republican)	**165 (47)**	**185 (50)**	**4,034,311 (48)**
Samuel J. Tilden (Democrat)	184 (53)	184 (50)	4,288,546 (51)
Peter Cooper (Greenback)	–	–	75,973 (1)
Disputed	20		

MAP 16–2   The Election of 1876
The Democrat Samuel F. Tilden won a majority of the popular vote but eventually fell short of an electoral vote majority when the contested electoral votes of Florida, Louisiana, and South Carolina went to his Republican opponent, Rutherford B. Hayes. The map also indicates the Republicans' failure to build a base in the South after more than a decade of Reconstruction.

states—Florida, South Carolina, and Louisiana—were the last in the South still to have Republican administrations.

Both camps maneuvered intensively in the following months to claim the disputed votes. Congress appointed a 15-member commission to settle the issue. Because the Republicans controlled Congress, they held a one-vote majority on the commission.

Southern Democrats wanted Tilden to win, but they wanted control of their states more. They were willing to deal. As one South Carolina newspaper editorialized in February 1877, "It matters little to us who rules in Washington, if South Carolina is allowed to have [Democratic governor Wade] Hampton and Home Rule." Hayes intended to remove federal support from the remaining southern Republican governments anyway. It thus cost him nothing to promise to do so in exchange for the contested electoral votes. Republicans also made vague promises to invest in the southern economy and support a southern transcontinental railroad, but these were secondary. What the South wanted most was to be left alone, and that is what it got. The so-called **Compromise of 1877** installed Hayes in the

White House and gave Democrats control of every state government in the South. Congress never carried through on the economic promises, and southern Democrats never pressed it to. Southern Democrats emerged the major winners from the Compromise of 1877. President Hayes and his successors into the next century left the South alone. In practical terms, the Compromise signaled the revocation of civil rights and voting rights for black southerners. The Fourteenth and Fifteenth Amendments would be dead letters in the South until well into the twentieth century. On the two great issues confronting the nation at the end of the Civil War, reunion and freedom, the white South had won. It reentered the Union largely on its own terms with the freedom to pursue a racial agenda consistent with its political, economic, and social interests.

The Memory of Reconstruction

Southern Democrats used the memory of Reconstruction to help maintain themselves in power. Reconstruction joined the Lost Cause as part of the glorious fight to preserve the civilization of the Old South. As white southerners elevated Civil War heroes into saints and battles into holy struggles, they equated Reconstruction with Redemption. For white southerners, white Democrats in particular, had rescued the South from a purgatory of black rule and federal oppression. Whenever southern Democrats felt threatened over the next century, they reminded their white constituents of the sacrifices and heroism of the war, the "horrors of Reconstruction," the menace of black rule, and the cruelty of the Yankee occupiers. The southern view of Reconstruction permeated textbooks, films, and standard accounts of the period. By the early 1900s, professional historians at the nation's finest institutions concurred in this view, ignoring contrary evidence and rendering the story of African Americans invisible. By that time, therefore, most Americans believed that the policies of Reconstruction had been misguided and had brought great suffering to the white South. The widespread acceptance of this view allowed the South to maintain its system of racial segregation and exclusion without interference from the federal government.

Not all memories of Reconstruction conformed to this thesis. In 1913, John R. Lynch, a former black Republican congressman from Mississippi, published *The Facts of Reconstruction* to "present the other side." He hoped that his book would "bring to public notice those things that were commendable and meritorious, to prevent the publication of which seems to have been the primary purpose of nearly all who have thus far written upon that important subject." But most Americans ignored his book. Two decades later, a more forceful defense, W. E. B. Du Bois's *Black Reconstruction* (1935), met a similar fate. An angry Du Bois attacked the prevailing view of Reconstruction as "one of the most stupendous efforts the world ever saw to discredit human beings, an effort involving universities, history, science, social life and religion."

The national historical consensus grew out of a growing national reconciliation concerning the war, a mutual agreement that both sides had fought courageously and that it was time to move on. Immediately after the Civil War, a number of prominent white southerners urged their neighbors to work on rebuilding the South rather than hating the Yankees. But general reconciliation remained on hold until the end of Reconstruction, when white southerners reclaimed both their governments and their dominance over African Americans. Once that recovery occurred, joint battlefield commemorations stressed mutual bravery and shared sacrifice. Hidden in all the goodwill was the tacit agreement between southern and northern whites that the South was now free to work out its own resolution to race relations. Reconstruction rested on a national consensus of African American inferiority.

There is much to be said in favor of sectional reconciliation as opposed to persistent animosity. There are enough examples in the world today of antagonists in the same country never forgetting or never forgiving their bloody histories. Ideally, Americans could have had *both* healing and justice, but instead they settled for the former. Frederick Douglass, prescient as ever, worried about the peace that followed the Civil War and what it would mean for race relations: "If war among the whites brought peace and liberty to the blacks, what will peace among the whites bring?"

The Failed Promise of Reconstruction

If the demise of Reconstruction elicited a resounding indifference from most white Americans, black southerners greeted it with frustration. Their dreams of land ownership faded as a new labor system relegated them to a lowly position in southern agriculture. Redemption reversed their economic and political gains and deprived them of most of the civil rights they had enjoyed under Congressional Reconstruction. Although they continued to vote into the 1890s, they had by 1877 lost most of the voting strength and political offices they held. Rather than becoming part of southern society, they were increasingly set apart from it, valued only for their labor.

Still, the former slaves were better off in 1877 than in 1865. They were free, however limited their freedom. Some owned land; some held jobs in cities. They raised their families in relative peace and experienced the spiritual joys of a full religious life. They socialized freely with relatives and friends, and they moved about. The Reconstruction amendments to the Constitution guaranteed an array of civil and political rights, and eventually these guarantees would form the basis of the civil rights revolution after World War II. But that outcome was long, too long, in the future. By 1877, the "golden moment," an unprecedented opportunity for the na-

OVERVIEW

Constitutional Amendments and Federal Legislation of the Reconstruction Era

Amendment or Legislation	Purpose	Significance
Thirteenth Amendment (passed and ratified in 1865)	Prevented southern states from reestablishing slavery after the war	Final step toward full emancipation of slaves
Freedmen's Bureau Act (1865)	Oversight of resettlement, labor for former slaves	Involved the federal government directly in relief, education, and assisting the transition from slavery to freedom; worked fitfully to achieve this objective during its seven-year career
Southern Homestead Act (1866)	Provided black people preferential access to public lands in five southern states	Lack of capital and poor quality of federal land thwarted the purpose of the act
Civil Rights Act of 1866	Defined rights of national citizenship	Marked an important change in federal-state relations, tilting balance of power to national government
Fourteenth Amendment (passed 1866; ratified 1868)	Prohibited states from violating the rights of their citizens	Strengthened the Civil Rights Act of 1866 and guaranteed all citizens equality before the law
Military Reconstruction Acts (1867)	Set new rules for the readmission of former Confederate states into the Union and secured black voting rights	Initiated Congressional Reconstruction
Tenure of Office Act (1867)	Required congressional approval for the removal of any official whose appointment had required Senate confirmation	A congressional challenge to the president's right to dismiss cabinet members; led to President Andrew Johnson's impeachment trial
Fifteenth Amendment (passed 1869; ratified 1870)	Guaranteed the right of all American male citizens to vote regardless of race	The basis for black voting rights
Civil Rights Act of 1875	Prohibited racial discrimination in jury selection, public transportation, and public accommodations	Rarely enforced; Supreme Court declared it Unconstitutional in 1883

tion to live up to its ideals by extending equal rights to all its citizens, black and white alike, had passed.

Modest Gains and Future Victories

Black southerners experienced some advances in the decade after the Civil War, but these owed little to Reconstruction. Black families functioned as economic and psychological buffers against unemployment and prejudice. Black churches played crucial roles in their communities. Self-help and labor organizations offered mutual friendship and financial assistance. All of these institutions had existed in the slavery era, although on a smaller scale. And some of them, such as black labor groups, schools, and social welfare associations, endured because comparable white institutions excluded black people.

Black people also scored some modest economic successes during the Reconstruction era, mainly from their own pluck. In the Lower South, black per capita income increased 46 percent between 1857 and 1879, compared with a 35 percent decline in white per capita income. Sharecropping, oppressive as it was, represented an advance over forced and gang labor. Collectively, black people owned more than $68 million worth of property in 1870, a 240 percent increase over 1860, but the average worth of each was only $408. Those who had been free before the war sometimes fared worse after it, especially property-owning free black people in the Lower South. Black city dwellers, especially in the Upper South, fared somewhat better. The overwhelming majority of black people, however, were landless agricultural laborers eking out a meager income that merchants and landlords often snatched to cover debts.

The Fourteenth and Fifteenth Amendments to the Constitution are among the few bright spots in Reconstruction's otherwise dismal legacy. The Fourteenth Amendment guaranteed former slaves equality before the law; the Fifteenth Amendment protected their right to vote. Both amendments elevated the federal government over the states by protecting freedmen from state attempts to deny them their rights. But the benefits of these two landmark amendments did not accrue to African Americans until well into the twentieth century. White southerners effectively nullified the Reconstruction amendments, and the U.S. Supreme Court virtually interpreted them, and other Reconstruction legislation, out of existence.

In the *Slaughterhouse* cases (1873), the Supreme Court contradicted the intent of the Fourteenth Amendment by decreeing that most citizenship rights remained under state, not federal, control. In *United States v. Cruikshank* (1876), the Court overturned the convictions of some of those responsible for the Colfax Massacre, ruling that the Enforcement Act applied only to violations of black rights by states, not individuals. Within the next two decades, the Supreme Court would uphold the legality of racial segregation and black disfranchisement, in effect declaring that the Fourteenth and Fifteenth Amendments did not apply to African Americans. The Civil War had killed secession forever, but states' rights enjoyed a remarkable revival.

As the historian John Hope Franklin accurately concluded, Reconstruction "had no significant or permanent effect on the status of the black in American life.... [Black people] made no meaningful steps toward economic independence or even stability."

Conclusion

Formerly enslaved black southerners had entered freedom with many hopes, among the most prominent of which was to be left alone. White southerners, after four bloody years of unwanted attention from the federal government, also longed to be left alone. But they did not include their ex-slaves as equals in their vision of solitude. Northerners, too, began to seek escape from the issues and consequences of the war abandoning their weak commitment to secure civil and voting rights for black southerners.

White southerners robbed black southerners of their gains and sought to reduce them again to servitude and dependence, if not to slavery. But in the process, the majority of white southerners lost as well. Yeoman farmers missed an opportunity to break cleanly from the Old South and establish a more equitable society. Instead, they allowed the old elites to regain power and gradually ignore their needs. They preserved the social benefit of a white skin at the cost of almost everything else. Many lost their farms and sank into tenancy. Few had a voice in state legislatures or the U.S. Congress. A new South, rid of slavery and sectional antagonism, had indeed emerged—redeemed, regenerated, and disenthralled. But the old South lingered on.

As federal troops left the South, an era of possibility for American society ended, and a new era began. "The southern question is dead," a Charleston newspaper proclaimed in 1877. "The question of labor and capital, work and wages" had moved to the forefront. The chance to redeem the sacrifice of a bloody civil war with a society that fulfilled the promise of the Declaration of Independence and the Constitution for all citizens slipped away. It would take a new generation of African Americans a long century later to revive it.

Review Questions

1. Both Russia and America hoped to develop a free-labor agricultural class after their respective emancipations. Why didn't these governments follow through on their own objectives?

2. Given the different perspectives on the Civil War's outcome and what the social structure of a postwar South should be, was there any common ground between southern white and southern black on which to forge a Reconstruction policy?

3. Black people did achieve some notable gains during Reconstruction, despite its overall failure. What were those gains?

4. In T. Thomas Fortune's recollection of a boyhood incident, why was it important for him and his friends to fight back?

Key Terms

Black codes (p. 444)

Carpetbaggers (p. 450)

Compromise of 1877 (p. 458)

Congressional Reconstruction (p. 447)

Field Order No. 15 (p. 439)

Fifteenth Amendment (p. 448)

Fourteenth Amendment (p. 445)

Freedmen's Bureau (p. 437)

Ku Klux Klan (p. 454)

Lost Cause (p. 436)

Redeemers (p. 457)

Scalawags (p. 450)

Sharecropping (p. 440)

Slaughterhouse cases (p. 461)

Southern Homestead Act (p. 439)

Tenure of Office Act (p. 447)

Union Leagues (p. 452)

United States v. Cruikshank (p. 461)

Recommended Reading

Du Bois, W. E. B. *Black Reconstruction in America, 1860–1880* (1935). An early and long-ignored study by the foremost black scholar of his time that refuted the contemporary historical wisdom that Reconstruction was a horror visited on the South by an overbearing federal government and ignorant, willful black people.

Foner, Eric. *Reconstruction: America's Unfinished Revolution, 1863–1877* (1988). The standard work on Reconstruction, notable for its emphasis on the experience and aspirations of black southerners.

Foster, Gaines M. *Ghosts of the Confederacy: Defeat, the Lost Cause, and the Emergence of the New South, 1865 to 1913* (1987). A fine picture of how the memory of the Civil War affected white southerners and their views on Reconstruction policy.

Litwack, Leon. *Been in the Storm So Long: The Aftermath of Slavery* (1979). An eloquent account of the early days of freedom from the freedmen's perspective, up to 1867.

Tourgée, Albion W. *A Fool's Errand* (1879). A novel written by an Ohioan who migrated to North Carolina in 1865 to take advantage of economic opportunities in the state and eventually became involved in politics; his frustrations with Reconstruction and his keen analysis of racism are important themes.

Where to Learn More

- **Penn Center Historic District, St. Helena Island, South Carolina.** The Penn School was a sea-island experiment in the education of free black people established by northern missionaries Laura Towne and Ellen Murray in 1862. They operated it until their deaths in the early 1900s. The Penn School became Penn Community Services in 1948, serving as an educational institution, health clinic, and a social service agency. See its website at www.penncenter.com

- **Hampton University Museum, Hampton, Virginia.** Hampton University was founded by the Freedmen's Bureau in 1868 to provide "practical" training in the agricultural and mechanical fields for former slaves. In addition to a history of the institution, the museum includes one of the oldest collections of African art in the United States. Its website is at www.hamptonu.edu/museum

- **Beauvoir, Biloxi, Mississippi.** The exhibits at Beauvoir, the home of Jefferson Davis, evoke the importance of the Lost Cause for the white survivors of the Confederacy. Especially interesting is the Jefferson Davis Soldiers Home on the premises and the Confederate Veterans Cemetery. Davis spent his retirement in Beauvoir. Go to www.beauvoir.org

- **Levi Jordan Plantation, Brazoria County, Texas.** This site provides an excellent depiction and interpretation of the lives of sharecroppers and tenants during and immediately after the Reconstruction era. The site is especially valuable for demonstrating the transition from slavery to sharecropping. Go to www.webarchaeology.com

Study Resources

For study resources for this chapter, go to www.myhistorylab.com and choose *The American Journey*. You will find a wealth of study and review material for this chapter, including pre- and post-tests, customized study plan, key term review flash cards, interactive map and document activities, and documents for analysis.

Booker T. Washington at his desk, Tuskegee Institute, 1902.

then, in 1881, founded the Tuskegee Institute for black students in rural Alabama. Washington thought that his students would be best served if they learned a trade and workplace discipline. By learning industrial skills, he maintained, black people could acquire self-respect and economic independence. As a result, Tuskegee emphasized vocational training over the liberal arts.

Washington argued that African Americans should accommodate themselves to segregation and disfranchisement until they could prove their economic worth to American society. In exchange for this accommodation, however, white people should help provide black people with the education and job training they would need to gain their independence. Washington articulated this position, known as the **Atlanta Compromise**, in a speech at the Atlanta Cotton States and International Exposition in 1895. Despite his conciliatory public stance, Washington secretly helped to finance legal challenges to segregation and disfranchisement. The social and economic realities of the South, meanwhile, frustrated his educational mission. Increasingly, black people were shut out of the kinds of jobs for which Washington hoped to train them. Facing a depressed rural economy and growing racial violence, they had little prospect of advancement.

W. E. B. Du Bois attacks the Atlanta Compromise.
Another prominent African American leader, W. E. B. Du Bois, challenged Washington's acceptance of black social inequality. Born in Massachusetts in 1868, Du Bois was the first African American to earn a doctorate at Harvard.

Du Bois promoted self-help, education, and black pride. A gifted teacher and writer, he taught at Atlanta University and wrote 18 books on various aspects of black life in America. In *The Souls of Black Folk,* published in 1903, he described the strengths of black culture and attacked Washington's Atlanta Compromise. Du Bois was a cofounder, in 1910, of the **National Association for the Advancement of Colored People (NAACP),** an interracial organization dedicated to restoring African American political and social rights.

Despite their differences, which reflected their divergent backgrounds, Washington and Du Bois agreed on many issues. Both had reservations about allowing illiterate black people to vote, and both believed that black success in the South required some white assistance. As Du Bois wrote in *The Souls of Black Folk,* "Any movement for the elevation of the Southern Negro needs the cooperation, the sympathy, and the support of the best white people in order to succeed." But it became apparent to Du Bois that "the best white people" did not care to elevate black southerners. In 1906, after a bloody race riot in Atlanta, Du Bois left the South, a decision millions of black southerners would make over the next two decades.

A curtain had descended between black and white, in both the North and the South, on the issue of race. Northerners did not care to look behind that curtain to acknowledge the injustice of southern treatment of black people. As long as it provided the raw materials for the North's new urban industrial economy and maintained the peace, the South could count on the rest of the country not to interfere in its solution to race relations. Indeed, to the extent that most white Americans concerned themselves with race, they agreed with the southern solution.

Conclusion

In many respects, the South was more like the rest of the nation in 1900 than at any other time since 1860. Southern cities hummed with activity, and industries from textiles to steel dotted the southern interior. Young men and women migrated to southern cities to pursue opportunities unavailable to their parents. Advances in the production and marketing of cigarettes and soft drinks would soon make southern entrepreneurs and their products household names. Southerners ordered fashions from Sears, Roebuck catalogs and enjoyed electric lights, electric trolleys, and indoor plumbing as much as other urban Americans.

Americans idealized the South—not the urban industrial South, but a mythical South of rural grace and hospitality. National magazines and publishers rushed to print stories about this land of moonlight and magnolias, offering it as a counterpoint to the crowded, immigrant-infested, factory-fouled, money-grubbing North. It was this fantasy South that white people in both the North and the South imagined as they came to a common view on race and reconciled their differences. Northern journalists offered admiring portraits of such southern heroes as Robert E. Lee, of whom one declared in 1906, "the nation has a hero to place beside her greatest." The Republican-dominated Congress agreed to care for the graves of the Confederate dead and ordered the return to the South of captured Confederate flags. White southerners cultivated national reconciliation but remained fiercely dedicated to preserving the peculiarities of their region: a one-party political system, disfranchisement of African Americans, and segregation by law. The region's urban and industrial growth, impressive from the vantage of 1865, paled before that of the North. The South remained a colonial economy characterized more by deep rural poverty than urban prosperity.

How one viewed the New South depended on one's vantage point. White northerners accepted at face value the picture southerners painted for them of a chastened and prosperous, yet still attractive, region. Middle-class white people in the urban South enjoyed the benefits of a national economy and a secure social position. Middle-class white women enjoyed increased influence in the public realm, but not to the extent of their northern sisters. And the institutionalization of white supremacy gave even poor white farmers and factory workers a place in the social hierarchy a rung or two above the bottom.

For black people, the New South proved a crueler ruse than Reconstruction. No one now stepped forward to support their cause and stem the erosion of their economic independence, political freedom, and civil rights. Yet they did not give up the American dream, nor did they give up the South for the most part. They built communities and worked as best they could to challenge restrictions on their freedom.

The New South was thus both American and southern. It shared with the rest of the country a period of rapid urban and industrial growth. But the legacy of war and slavery still lay heavily on the South, manifesting itself in rural poverty, segregation, and black disfranchisement. The burdens of this legacy would limit the attainments of both black and white southerners for another half-century, until Americans finally rejected racial inequality as an affront to their national ideals.

Review Questions

1. In what ways did the growing activism of white middle-class women, the increasing assertiveness of young urban black people, and the persistence of the agricultural depression affect the politics of the South in the late 1880s and early 1890s?

2. We associate segregation and disfranchisement with reactionary political and social views. Yet many white people who promoted both seriously believed them to be reforms. How could white people hold such a view?

3. What strategies did black southerners employ in response to the narrowing of economic and political opportunities in the New South?

4. What accounted for Anna J. Cooper's optimism for African American women in the South at a time when southern whites were beginning an extensive legal and physical assault on black civil rights?

5. Why did racial "problems" emerge as a major issue in Europe and the United States in the late nineteenth century?

Key Terms

Atlanta Compromise (p. 488)
Colored Farmer's Alliance (p. 475)
Disfranchisement (p. 480)
Grandfather clause (p. 482)
Grange (p. 474)
Jim Crow laws (p. 481)
Lynching (p. 479)

National Association for the Advancement of Colored People (NAACP) (p. 488)
Plessy v. Ferguson (p. 481)
Poll taxes (p. 482)
Populist party (p. 475)
Segregation (p. 480)
Settlement house (p. 476)

Solid South (p. 468)
Southern Farmers' Alliance (p. 474)
Subtreasury plan (p. 475)
Women's Christian Temperance Union (WCTU) (p. 476)

Recommended Reading

Gaston, Paul M. *The New South Creed: A Study in Southern Mythmaking* (1970). An important assessment of how New South booster rhetoric matched up against the economic reality; especially good at examining how New South spokesmen turned images of the Old South and other southern traditions to the ends of urban and industrial development.

Rabinowitz, Howard N. *Race Relations in the Urban South, 1865–1890* (1978). A fine survey of how African Americans built communities in the urban South despite the worsening racial situation after Reconstruction.

Williamson, Joel. *The Crucible of Race: Black-White Relations in the American South since Emancipation* (1984). An innovative work that details the racial attitudes of white southerners and reveals how elites in particular used race to further political and social objectives.

Woodward, C. Vann. *Origins of the New South, 1877–1913* (1951). A classic interpretation of the New South era that stresses the discontinuities between Old South and New.

Where to Learn More

- **Levine Museum of the New South, Charlotte, North Carolina.** The museum has exhibits on various New South themes and a permanent exhibit on the history of Charlotte and the Carolina Piedmont. www .museumofthenewsouth.org

- **Atlanta History Center, Atlanta, Georgia.** The major exhibit, "Metropolitan Frontiers, 1835– 2000," includes a strong segment on the New South era, including the development of separate black and white economies in At-

lanta. The Herndon home, on the grounds of the center, has an exhibit on black upper-class life in Atlanta from 1880 to 1930. www.atlhist.org/exhibitions/html/metropolitan_ frontiers.htm

- **Sloss Furnaces National Historical Landmark, Birmingham, Alabama.** The site recalls the time when Birmingham challenged Pittsburgh as the nation's primary steel-producing center. www.slossfurnaces.com

Study Resources

For study resources for this chapter, go to www.myhistorylab.com and choose *The American Journey*. You will find a wealth of study and review material for this chapter, including pre- and post-tests, customized study plan, key term review flash cards, interactive map and document activities, and documents for analysis.

Photographer Lewis Hine's portrait of a young Jewish woman arriving from Russia at Ellis Island in 1905. Like hundreds of thousands of other immigrants who passed through the portals of New York harbor, this young woman's expression carries the hope, fear, and remembrance that touched her fellow wanderers as they embarked on their new life in America.

Industry, Immigrants and Cities 1870–1900 18

We were homeless, houseless, and friendless in a strange place. We had hardly money enough to last us through the voyage for which we had hoped and waited for three long years. We had suffered much that the reunion we longed for might come about; we had prepared ourselves to suffer more in order to bring it about, and had parted with those we loved, with places that were dear to us in spite of what we passed through in them, never again to see them, as we were convinced, all for the same dear end. With strong hopes and high spirits that hid the sad parting, we had started on our long journey. And now we were checked so unexpectedly but surely.... When my mother had recovered enough to speak, she began to argue with the *gendarme,* telling him our story and begging him to be kind. The children were

frightened and all but I cried. I was only wondering what would happen.... Here we had been taken to a lonely place;...our things were taken away, our friends separated from us; a man came to inspect us, as if to ascertain our full value; strange-looking people driving us about like dumb animals, helpless and unresisting; children we could not see crying in a way that suggested terrible things; ourselves driven into a little room where a great kettle was boiling on a little stove; our clothes taken off, our bodies rubbed with a slippery substance that might be any bad thing; a shower of warm water let down on us without warning.... We are forced to pick out our clothes from among all the others, with the steam blinding us; we choke, cough, entreat the women to give us time; they persist, "Quick! Quick!, or you'll miss the train!", Oh, so

493

we really won't be murdered! They are only making us ready for the continuing of our journey, cleaning us of all suspicions of dangerous sickness. Thank God! ...

Oh, what solemn thoughts I had! How deeply I felt the greatness, the power of the scene! The immeasurable distance from horizon to horizon; ...the absence of any object besides the one ship; ...I was conscious only of sea and sky and something I did not understand. And as I listened to its solemn voice, I felt as if I had found a friend, and knew that I loved the ocean.

Mary Antin

Mary Antin, *The Promised Land* (Boston: Houghton Mifflin Co., 1912), chap. VIII.

myhistorylab

Personal Journeys Online

■ *Young Chinese immigrant memoir,* 1882. A Chinese immigrant recalls his migration to America and his early days in San Francisco.

■ *Letters of Negro Migrants,* 1917. Letters from southern black migrants to the North back home.

Mary Antin, a 13-year-old Jewish girl from Russia, describes her family's perilous journey from persecution in tsarist Russia to the ship that would take her from Hamburg, Germany, to faraway America. In 1894, Mary and her mother and sisters set out from their village to join her father in Boston.

Millions of European immigrants made similar journeys across the Atlantic (as did Chinese and Japanese immigrants, across the Pacific), a trip fraught with danger, unpredictable detours, occasional heartbreak, the sundering of family ties, and the fear of the unknown. So powerful was the promise of American life for the migrants that they willingly risked these obstacles to come to the United States. Mary wrote this extended letter to her uncle, who remained behind, during the first few months after her arrival in Boston. The letter was a way both of conveying the details of her family's exodus and of maintaining contact with a world and a family she had left behind.

Mary recalls the fear and frustration of being removed from the train at the Russian-German border by Russian police because of improper documents. Once her mother had settled the issue with the help of a local Jewish family, they reboarded the train to Berlin. Outside that city, they were once again removed from the train and, although they did not immediately understand what was happening, German authorities had arranged for a thorough cleansing and health inspection, since a cholera epidemic was raging in Russia. As the excerpt ends, you can sense Mary's exultation of joy and freedom as the ship leaves Hamburg for the open ocean and the place that lay beyond the horizon.

For Mary, America did indeed prove to be *The Promised Land*, as she titled her emigration memoir, published in 1912. At the age of 15, she published her first poem in the *Boston Herald* and, after attending Barnard College in New York City, she wrote on immigrant issues, lectured widely, and worked for Theodore Roosevelt's Progressive Party. She fought against immigration-restriction legislation and promoted public education as the main channel of upward mobility for immigrants. Although some have viewed her work as a bit too optimistic and perhaps naive, her own life is a strong testament of how a teenage girl moved from a medieval life in tsarist Russia to a career as a respected writer in the United States.

Mary and her family were part of a major demographic and economic transformation in the United States between 1870 and 1900. Rapid industrial development changed the nature of the workforce and the workplace.

CHRONOLOGY

1869	The Knights of Labor is founded in Philadelphia.
1870	John D. Rockefeller organizes the Standard Oil Company.
	Congress passes the Naturalization Act barring Asians from citizenship.
1871	Unification of Germany in the wake of rising nationalism following the Franco-Prussian War.
1876	The Centennial Exposition opens in Philadelphia.
	Beginning of the rule of dictator Porfirio Diaz in Mexico, whose regime is ended by the Mexican Revolution.
1877	Execution of ten Molly Maguires in Pennsylvania.
	The Great Uprising railroad strike, the first nationwide work stoppage in the United States, provokes violent clashes between workers and federal troops.
1879	Thomas Edison unveils the electric light bulb.
1880	Founding of the League of American Wheelmen helps establish bicycling as one of urban America's favorite recreational activities.
1881	Assassination of Tsar Alexander II begins a series of pogroms that triggers a wave of Russian Jewish immigration to the United States.
1882	Congress passes the Chinese Exclusion Act.
	First country club in the United States founded in Brookline, Massachusetts.
1883	National League merges with the American Association and opens baseball to working-class fans.
1884	Berlin Conference on Africa to set rules for competing European powers annexing African territory.

1886	The Neighborhood Guild, the nation's first settlement house, opens in New York City.
	Riot in Chicago's Haymarket Square breaks the Knights of Labor.
	American Federation of Labor is formed.
1887	Anti-Catholic American Protective Association is formed.
1888	Wanamaker's department store introduces a "bargain room," and competitors follow suit.
1889	Jane Addams opens Hull House, the nation's most celebrated settlement house, in Chicago.
1890	Jacob A. Riis publishes *How the Other Half Lives*.
1891	African American Chicago physician Daniel Hale Williams establishes Provident Hospital, the nation's first interracially staffed hospital.
1892	General Electric opens the first corporate research and development division in the United States.
	Strike at Andrew Carnegie's Homestead steelworks fails.
1894	Pullman Sleeping Car Company strike fails.
	Immigration Restriction League is formed.
1895	American-born Chinese in California form the Native Sons of the Golden State to counter nativism.
1897	George C. Tilyou opens Steeplechase Park on Coney Island in Brooklyn, New York.
	First Zionist Congress meets in Switzerland proclaiming its aim to create a home in Palestine for the Jewish people.
1898	Congress passes the Erdman Act to provide for voluntary mediation of railroad labor disputes.

"pleasant, cultured people whose society we could enjoy" and a cure for Russell's rheumatism. Russell owned and managed a small metal brokerage in New York and enjoyed gardening, reading, and socializing with his new neighbors. Ella Russell cared for their six children with the help of a servant and also found time for several clubs and charities.

The design of the Russell home reflected the principles Catharine Beecher and Harriet Beecher Stowe outlined in their suburban home bible, *American Woman's Home* (1869). The kitchen, according to Beecher and Stowe, should be organized for expedience and hygiene. The home's utilities should be confined to a central core, freeing wall areas for other functions. The new technology of central heating made it unnecessary to divide a house into many small rooms, each with its own fireplace or stove. Taking advantage of this change, Beecher and Stowe recommended that a home's ground floor have fewer but larger rooms, to encourage the family to pursue their individual activities in a common space. Parlors and reception rooms disappeared, along with such former standards as the children's wing, the male "smoking room," and the female parlor.

The once-prevailing view that women were too frail for vigorous exercise was changing. Thus, the entire Russell family was to be found enjoying the tennis, swimming, and skating facilities at the Short Hills Athletic Club. Because the community bordered on undeveloped woodland traversed by trails, "wheel clubs" appeared in the 1880s to organize families for bicycle outings. The emphasis on family togetherness also reflected the changing role of men in late-nineteenth-century society. Women's roles also broadened, as Ella Russell's club work attested.

Suburbs differed, not only from the city, but also from one another. With the growth after 1890 of the electric trolley, elevated rail lines, and other relatively inexpensive forms of commuter travel, suburbs became accessible to a broader spectrum of the middle class. The social structure, architecture, and amenities of suburbs varied, depending on the rail service and distance from the city. The commuter railroad remained popular among people like the Russells who could afford the time and expense of commuting to and from the city center.

The suburb underscored the growing fragmentation of life in and around American cities in the late nineteenth century. Residence, consumer habits, and leisure activities reflected growing social and class divisions. Yet, at the same time, the growing materialism of American society promised a common ground for its disparate ethnic, racial, and social groups.

The New Middle Class

From the colonial era, America's urban middle class had included professionals, physicians, lawyers, ministers, educators, editors, as well as merchants, shopkeepers, and skilled artisans (until they dropped from the middle class in the late nineteenth century). In the late nineteenth century, industrial technology and urban growth expanded the urban middle class to include salespeople, factory supervisors, managers, civil servants, technicians, and a broad range of "white-collar" office workers, such as insurance agents, bank tellers, and legal assistants. This newer middle class set national trends in residential patterns, consumption, and leisure.

The more affluent members of the new middle class, like the Russells, repaired to new subdivisions within and outside the city limits. Simple row houses sheltered the growing numbers of clerks and civil servants who remained in the city. These dwellings contrasted sharply with the crowded one- or two-room apartments that confined the working class. Rents for these apartments ran as much as $3 a week, at a time when few workers made more than $9 or $10.

A Consumer Society

The new middle class transformed America into a consumer society. In earlier times, land had been a symbol of prestige. Now it was consumer goods. And the new industries obliged with a dazzling array of merchandise and technologies. By 1910, the new middle class lived in all-electric homes with indoor plumbing. A typical kitchen might include an electric coffeepot, a hot plate, a chafing dish, and a toaster. The modern city dweller worked by the clock, not by the sun. Eating patterns changed: Cold packaged cereals replaced hot meats at breakfast; fast lunches of Campbell's soup, "a meal in itself," or canned stews weaned Americans from the heavy lunch. Jell-O appeared in the 1890s, touted as America's "most quick and easy" dessert. In Nashville at the same time, Joel Cheek ground and blended coffee beans in his store for customers' convenience. He convinced the city's Maxwell House Hotel to serve his new concoction, and in 1907, when President Theodore Roosevelt visited the hotel and drained his cup, he turned to Cheek and declared that the coffee was "good to the very last drop." A slogan and Maxwell House coffee were born.

Advertising played an important role in the consumer society. Advertisers created demand and developed loyalty for brand-name products. In early-twentieth-century New York, a six-story-high Heinz electric sign was a sensation, especially the 40-foot-long pickle at its top.

The middle class liked anything that saved time: trolleys, trains, electric razors, vacuum cleaners. The telephone replaced the letter for everyday communication; it was quicker and less formal. By 1900, some 1.4 million phones were in service, and many middle-class homes had one.

The middle class liked its news in an easy-to-read form. Urban tabloids multiplied after 1880, led by Joseph Pulitzer's *New York World* and William Randolph Hearst's *New York Journal*. The newspapers organized the news into topical sections, used bold headlines and graphics to catch the eye, ran human interest stories to capture the imagination, inaugurated sports pages to attract male readers, and offered advice columns for women. And they opened their pages to a wide range of attractive advertising, much of it directed to women, who did about 90 percent of the shopping in American cities by 1900.

As the visual crowded out the printed in advertising, newspapers, and magazines, these materials became accessible to a wider urban audience. Although mainly middle class in orientation, the tabloid press drew urban society together with new features such as the comic strip, which first appeared in the 1890s, and heart-rending personal sagas drawn from real life. Immigrants, who might have had difficulty reading small-type newspapers, received their initiation into the mainstream of American society through the tabloids.

In a similar manner, the department store, essentially a middle-class retail establishment, became one of the city's most democratic forums and the focus of the urban downtown after 1890. Originating in the 1850s and 1860s with the construction of retail palaces such as Boston's Jordan Marsh, Philadelphia's Wanamaker & Brown, New York's Lord & Taylor, and Chicago's Marshall Field, the department store came to epitomize the bounty of the new industrial capitalism. At the time of the Philadelphia Exposition in 1876, only 30 or so department stores existed; by 1920, there were thousands. They exuded limitless abundance with their extensive inventories, items for every budget, sumptuous surroundings, and efficient, trained personnel.

At first, most department-store customers were middle-class married women. Not expected to work and with disposable income and flexible schedules, these women had the means and time to wander department store aisles. The stores catered to their tastes, and the current emphasis on home and domesticity, with such items as prefabricated household furnishings, ready-made clothing, toys, and stationery. Industry churned out uniform, high-quality products in abundance, and middle-class salaries absorbed them. Department stores maintained consumers' interest with advertising campaigns arranged around holidays like Easter and Christmas, the seasons, and the school calendar. Each event required new clothing and accessories, and the ready-made clothing industry changed fashions accordingly.

Soon the spectacle and merchandise of the department store attracted shoppers from all social strata, not just the middle class. "The principal cause of the stores' success," one shopper explained in 1892, "is the fact that their founders have understood the necessity of offering a new democracy whose needs and habits" are satisfied "in the cheapest possible way," providing "a taste for elegance and comfort unknown to previous generations." Although many less affluent women came merely to "window-shop" (a new expression inspired by the large plate-glass display windows retailers installed in their stores to attract customers), some came to buy. After 1890, department stores increasingly hired young immigrant women to cater to their growing foreign-born clientele.

The department store, the turn-of-the-century shopping mall, provided inexpensive amusement for young working-class people, especially immigrants. Mary Antin recalled how she and her teenage friends and sister would spend their Saturday nights patrolling "a dazzlingly beautiful palace called a 'department store.'" It was there that Mary and her sister "exchanged our hateful homemade European costumes...for real American machine-made garments, and issued forth glorified in each other's eyes."

By 1900, department stores had added sporting goods and hardware sections and were attracting customers from a wide social spectrum. When Wanamaker's introduced a "bargain room" in 1888, other retail stores, including Filene's famous "Automatic Bargain Basement" in Boston, followed suit.

The Growth of Leisure Activities

The expanding floor space devoted to sporting goods reflected the growth of leisure in urban society. And like other aspects of that society, leisure and recreation both separated and cut across social classes. The leisure activities of the wealthy increasingly removed them from the rest of urban society. For them, the good life required such prerequisites as a mansion on Fifth Avenue, carriages and horses for transportation, a pony for the younger children, a saddle horse for the older ones, and a yacht. As such sports as football became important extracurricular activities at Harvard, Yale, and other elite universities, intercollegiate games became popular occasions for the upper class to congregate and, not incidentally, to discuss business. The elite also gathered at the athletic clubs and country clubs that emerged as open spaces disappeared in the city. High fees and strict membership criteria kept these clubs exclusive. The first country club in the United States was founded in Brookline, Massachusetts, a Boston suburb, in 1882. Country clubs built golf courses for men and tennis courts primarily for women. The clubs offered a suburban retreat, away from the diverse middle- and working-class populations, where the elite could play in privacy.

Middle-class urban residents could not afford country clubs, but they rode electric trolleys to the end of the line to enjoy suburban parks and bicycle and skating clubs. Reflecting the emphasis on family togetherness in late-nineteenth-century America, both men and women participated in these sports. Bicycling in particular became immensely popular. New bikes cost at least $50, putting them beyond the reach of the working class.

If college football was the rage among the elite, baseball was the leading middle-class spectator sport. Organized baseball originated among the urban elite before the Civil War. The middle class took over the sport after the war. Baseball epitomized the nation's transition from a rural to an urban industrial society. Reflecting rural tradition, it was played on an expanse of green, usually on the outskirts of the city. It was leisurely; unlike other games, it had no time limit. Reflecting industrial society, however, it had clearly defined rules and was organized into leagues. Professional leagues were profit-making enterprises, and, like other enterprises, they frequently merged. Initially, most professional baseball games were played on weekday afternoons, making it hard for

Amusement for the masses. Better transportation, more leisure time, and disposable income fueled escapes such as Luna Park in Coney Island, Brooklyn, a place where people could come together and have fun in a relatively controlled environment.

working-class spectators to attend. After merging with the American Association in 1883, the National League adopted some of its innovations to attract more fans, including beer sales, cheap admission, and, despite the objections of Protestant churches, Sunday games.

The tavern, or saloon, was the workingman's club. Typically an all-male preserve, the saloon provided drink, cheap food, and a place to read a newspaper, socialize, and learn about job opportunities. Advances in refrigeration in the 1870s allowed large breweries such as Anheuser-Busch and Pabst to distribute their product nationwide. Alcoholism was a severe problem in cities, especially, though not exclusively, among working-class men, fueling the prohibition movement of the late nineteenth century.

Amusement parks, with their mechanical wonders, were another hallmark of the industrial city. Declining trolley fares made these parks accessible to the working class around 1900. Unlike taverns, they provided a place for working-class men and women to meet and date.

The most renowned of these parks was Brooklyn's Coney Island. In 1897, George C. Tilyou opened Steeplechase Park

on Coney Island. He brought an invention by George Washington Ferris, a giant rotating vertical wheel, equipped with swinging carriages, to the park from Chicago, and the Ferris Wheel quickly became a Coney Island signature. Together with such attractions as mechanical horses and 250,000 of Thomas Edison's light bulbs, Steeplechase dazzled patrons with its technological wonders. It was quickly followed by Luna Park and Dreamland, and the Coney Island attractions became collectively known as "the poor man's paradise." Immigrant entrepreneurs, seeing a good thing, flocked to Coney Island to set up sideshows, pool halls, taverns, and restaurants. One German immigrant opened a small café serving sausages that he named "frankfurters" after his native Frankfurt. Locals called them "Coney Island hots" or "hot dogs" because they resembled the dachshund, a German-bred dog.

After 1900, the wonders of Coney Island began to lure people from all segments of an increasingly diverse city. Sightseers came from around the world. Notables such as Herman Melville, Mark Twain, and even Sigmund Freud (what did he think of Dreamland?) rubbed shoulders with factory workers, domestics, and department store clerks. In much the same manner, baseball was becoming a national pastime as games attracted a disparate crowd of people with little in common but their devotion to the home team.

Increasing materialism had revealed great fissures in American urban society by 1900. Yet places like department stores, baseball parks, and amusement parks provided democratic spaces for some interaction. Newspapers and schools also offered diverse groups the vicarious opportunity to share similar experiences.

The Ideal City

For all its problems, the American city was undeniably the locus of the nation's energy; in some ways, with the passing of the frontier, it had replaced the West in the national imagination as the environment where possibility was boundless. This sense of limitless energy and innovation appeared most notably in urban skylines where skyscrapers reached heavenward as graceful cathedrals of commerce. The tall buildings bespoke a confidence that declared even the sky was not the limit. The profile of the city center reflected what contemporary architect Louis Sullivan asserted: "what the people are within, the buildings express without; and inversely what the buildings are objectively is a sure index of what the people are subjectively."

Few landscapes expressed this ideal better than the 1893 World's Columbian Exposition in Chicago, a World's Fair to celebrate the 400th anniversary of the European discovery of America (though delays caused the Fair to open one year later). But timing was the only aspect of the Fair that was not a smashing success. The Fair demonstrated how with foresight, planning, and copious funds, it was possible to create a safe and esthetic urban environment, quite different from the gritty industrial city just beyond its borders. Dubbed the White City, the exposition epitomized cleanliness, grandeur, beauty, and order in its architecture. A writer for *Harper's* could barely contain himself: "The fair! The fair! Never had the name such significance before. Fairest of all the World's present sights it is. A city of palaces set in spaces of emerald, reflected in shining lengths of water which stretch in undulating lines under flat arches of marble bridges and along banks planted with consummate skill." That it was sheer fantasy, a temporary respite from the reality beyond the gates, did not faze the millions who attended. The White City represented the possibility, and in America, anything was possible.

Conclusion

The new industrial order, the changing nature of work, the massive migrations of populations from the countryside and abroad, and the rise of great cities changed the American landscape in the late nineteenth century. By 1900, the factory worker and the department store clerk were more representative of the new America than the farmer and small shopkeeper. Industry and technology had created thousands of new jobs, but they also eliminated the autonomy many workers had enjoyed and limited their opportunities to advance.

Immigrants thronged to the United States to realize their dreams of economic and religious freedom. They found both to varying degrees but also discovered a darker side to the promise of American life. The great cities thrilled newcomers with their possibilities and their abundance of goods and activities. But the cities also bore witness to the growing divisions in American society. As the new century dawned, the prospects for urban industrial America seemed limitless, yet the stark contrasts that had appeared so vividly inside and outside the Centennial Exposition persisted and deepened.

Still, it would be wrong to depict the nation in 1900 as merely a larger and more divided version of what it had been in 1876. Although sharp ethnic, racial, and class differences persisted, the nation seemed better poised to address them in 1900 than it had a quarter-century earlier. Labor unions, ethnic organizations, government legislation, and new urban institutions promised ways to remedy the worst abuses of the new urban, industrial economy.

Review Questions

1. Were there ways to achieve the benefits of industrialization without its social costs, or did the nation's political and economic systems make that impossible?

2. How did working-class women respond to the new economy? How did their participation and responses differ from that of working-class men?

3. What factors accounted for immigration becoming a global phenomenon during the late nineteenth century?

4. The growing fragmentation of urban life reflected deep divisions in modern urban industrial society. At the same time, there were forces that tended to overcome these divisions. What were these forces, and were they sufficient to bridge the divisions?

5. How did Old World conditions influence Mary Antin's adjustment to American life? Would individuals from other immigrant groups have expressed similar sentiments, or was Mary's reaction specific to her Jewish background?

Key Terms

American Federation of Labor (p. 505)

Chain migration (p. 509)

Collective bargaining (p. 505)

Gilded Age (p. 496)

Gospel of Wealth (p. 503)

Great Migration (p. 515)

Great Uprising (p. 505)

Horatio Alger Stories (p. 504)

Horizontal integration (p. 499)

Hull House (p. 503)

Knights of Labor (p. 505)

Molly Maguires (p. 504)

Nativism (p. 511)

Pogroms (p. 506)

Social Darwinism (p. 504)

Sweatshops (p. 501)

Tenements (p. 503)

Trusts (p. 499)

Vertical integration (p. 499)

Recommended Reading

Blumin, Stuart M. *The Emergence of the Middle Class: Social Experience in the American City, 1760–1900* (1989). Analyzes the key factors in the emergence of the urban middle class, especially in the late nineteenth century, and its impact on urban society and culture.

Bodnar, John. *The Transplanted: A History of Immigrants in Urban America* (1985). An excellent starting point for learning about the diverse immigrant experience in the United States that is also sensitive to conditions in the countries of origin.

Daniels, Roger. *Coming to America: A History of Immigration and Ethnicity in American Life* (1990). Preferred by some to Bodnar's survey. Has the great virtue of covering all immigrant groups; the discussion of Asian immigrants is especially good.

Dreiser, Theodore. *Sister Carrie* (1900). One of the best novels to capture life in late-nineteenth-century Chicago and New York. Few detail so clearly the moral and economic dilemmas newcomers faced in the fast-evolving American urban environment.

Higham, John. *Strangers in the Land: Patterns of American Nativism, 1860–1925* (1965). Despite its age, an excellent overview of and introduction to the subject of nativism; especially good in setting the context of nativism in American society and politics.

Where to Learn More

■ **Edison National Historic Site, West Orange, New Jersey.**   The site contains the Edison archives, including photographs, sound recordings, and industrial and scientific machinery. Its 20 historic structures dating from the 1880–1887 period include Edison's home and laboratory. www.nps.gov/edis

■ **Pasa al Norte.**   This museum, located in El Paso, Texas, serves as the Mexico–United States International Immigration History Center. Its exhibits focus on the importance of El Paso ("the Southwest Ellis Island") as a port-of-entry between the United States and Mexico from the late sixteenth century to the present. Utminers.utep.edu/panihm/default.htm

■ **Missouri Historical Society, St. Louis, Missouri.** The Society displays a long-term exhibition accompanied by public programs called "St. Louis in the Gilded Age," which focuses on the changes generated by industrialization and urban development in St. Louis from 1865 to 1900. www.mohistory.org

■ **Angel Island State Park, San Francisco Bay.**   Angel Island served as a detention center from 1910 to 1940 for Asian immigrants who were kept there for days, months, and, in some cases, years while immigration officials attempted to ferret out illegal entries. Exhibits depict the era through pictures and artifacts. www.Angelisland.org

■ **Statue of Liberty National Monument and Ellis Island, New York, New York.**   More than 12 million immigrants were processed at Ellis Island between 1892 and 1954. The exhibits provide a fine overview of American immigration history during this period. There is an ongoing oral history program as well. www.nps.gov/stli

Study Resources

For study resources for this chapter, go to www.myhistorylab.com and choose *The American Journey*. You will find a wealth of study and review material for this chapter, including pre- and posttests, customized study plan, key term review flash cards, interactive map and document activities, and documents for analysis.

new system, an integrated economy directed by forces beyond their control. And it was a system that did not work well. "There is," one of them charged, "something radically wrong in our industrial system. There is a screw loose."

Conclusion

In a few decades, millions of people had migrated westward in search of new opportunities. With determination, ingenuity, and hard work they had settled vast areas, made farms and ranches, built villages and cities, brought forth mineral wealth, and imposed their values on the land. These were remarkable achievements, though tempered by the shameful treatment of Indians and the often destructive exploitation of natural resources. But if most westerners took pride in their accomplishments, and a few enjoyed wealth and power, many also grew discontented with the new conditions they encountered as the "Wild" West receded.

The farmers' complaints indicted the major processes by which the West was developed and exploited in the late nineteenth century. Railroad expansion, population movements, eastern investment, corporate control, technological innovations, and government policies had incorporated the region fully into the larger society. Indians experienced this incorporation most thoroughly and most tragically, losing their lands, their traditions, and often their lives; the survivors were dependent on the decisions and actions of interlopers determined to impose "Americanization," the name itself implying the adoption of national patterns.

Cowboys and miners also learned that the frontier merely marked the cutting edge of eastern industrial society. Both groups were wageworkers, often for corporations controlled by eastern capital, and if industrial technology directly affected miners more than cowhands, neither could escape integration into the national economy by managerial decisions, transportation links, and market forces. Most settlers in the West were farmers, but they too learned that their distinctive environment did not insulate them from assimilation into larger productive, financial, and marketing structures.

Western developments, in short, reflected and interacted with those of eastern industrial society. The processes of incorporation drained away westerners' hopes along with their products, and many of the discontented would demand a serious reorganization of relationships and power. Led by angry farmers, they turned their attention to politics and government, where they encountered new obstacles and opportunities.

Review Questions

1. Why was the completion of the first transcontinental railroad, described by Andrew J. Russell, celebrated from Boston to San Francisco? How did western railroads shape the settlement and development of the West and affect the East as well?

2. What factors were most influential in the subjugation of American Indians?

3. What were the major goals of federal Indian policy, and how did they change?

4. How did technological developments affect Indians, miners, and farmers in the West?

5. How did the federal government help transform the West?

6. In what ways did European investors, markets, and migrants influence the development of the American West?

Key Terms

Chisholm Trail (p. 538)

Dawes Act (p. 534)

Homestead Act (p. 541)

Little Bighorn, Battle of the (p. 531)

Sand Creek Massacre (p. 529)

Second Treaty of Fort Laramie (p. 531)

Wounded Knee Massacre (p. 532)

Recommended Reading

Ball, Eve. *Indeh: An Apache Odyssey* (1980). An absorbing collection of the Apaches' own memories of the "Indian wars."

Paul, Rodman W. *The Far West and the Great Plains in Transition* (1988). A valuable survey of regional development that devotes particular attention to mining.

Riley, Glenda. *The Female Frontier: A Comparative View of Women on the Prairie and the Plains* (1988). A useful guide to women's experiences in the West.

Weeks, Philip. *Farewell, My Nation: The American Indian and the United States, 1820–1890,* 2nd ed. (2001). Modern discussion of Indian policy that provides insights into the perspectives of the Indians.

White, Richard. *"It's Your Misfortune and None of My Own": A New History of the American West* (1991). An important and original analysis of the development of the West that highlights environmental, ethnic, labor, and social history.

Wyman, Mark. *Hard Rock Epic: Western Miners and the Industrial Revolution, 1860–1910* (1979). Miners experiencing the dual frontiers of the West and the industrial revolution.

Where to Learn More

- **Little Bighorn Battlefield National Monument, Crow Agency, Montana.** The site of Custer's crushing defeat includes a monument to the Seventh Cavalry atop Last Stand Hill. A newly authorized Indian Memorial will include sacred texts, artifacts, and pictographs of the Plains Indians. www.nps.gov/libi/home.htm

- **National Museum of the American Indian, Smithsonian Institution, Washington DC.** This spectacular museum opened in 2004 and reflects the world view of Native Americans, with exhibits on spirituality and identity, performances of traditional dances, and important lecture series. www.nmai.si.edu

- **National Cowboy Hall of Fame, Oklahoma City, Oklahoma.** This large institution contains an outstanding collection of western art, displays of cowboy and Indian artifacts, and both kitschy exhibitions of the mythic Hollywood West and serious galleries depicting the often hard realities of the cattle industry. Its many public programs also successfully combine fun with learning. www.cowboyhalloffame.org/index2.html

- **Golden Spike National Historic Site, near Promontory, Utah.** The completion of the transcontinental railroad here in 1869 is reenacted from May to October, using reproductions of the original locomotives. Visitors can drive the route of the railroad, now a National Backway Byway through abandoned mining and railroad towns, from Promontory to Nevada. Virtual tour, history, and tourist links. www.nps./gov/gosp

Study Resources

For study resources for this chapter, go to www.myhistorylab.com and choose *The American Journey*. You will find a wealth of study and review material for this chapter, including pre- and post-tests, customized study plan, key term review flash cards, interactive map and document activities, and documents for analysis.

In the late nineteenth century, parades like this Republican one in Canton, Ohio, in 1896 were popular features of a participatory political culture dominated by political parties and intense partisanship.

Politics and Government 20
1877–1900

The largest political procession of the season in Fort Wayne, so far, was that of the Republicans Saturday night. They turned out in very large numbers and paraded on the principal streets preparatory to the speaking which came later at the Rifles' armory. The following were in line:

First Regiment Band

Railroad Men's Club

Soldiers' and Sons' Union Club

Tippecanoe Club

Chase Club

Lincoln Club

McKinley Club

Colored Drum Corps

Colored Republicans' Club

Republican Voters

The McKinley Club wore tin hats and the Tippecanoe club carried torches that spouted fire at intervals. One of the prettiest illuminations was the railroad lantern light of the Railroad Men's Republican club. The numerous lights of the colors used in the railway service make as pretty a sight as can be seen anywhere.

Most of the clubs were in fine uniforms and made a grand appearance. Numerous banners and transparencies announcing mottoes of the campaign were carried. One banner bore the words, "Cleveland's record—Glad Lincoln was shot—Pronounced the war a failure."

The great parade was viewed by thousands of people who thronged the streets all along the line of march.

The hall was crowded and the meeting was most enthusiastic. Music was furnished by the band and Emerson quartette of Huntington.... The quartette just took the cake. Anything more enjoyable and mirth-provoking than their glees rendered as they render them would be hard to find. After music by the quartette, which was enthusiastically encored, Dr. Stemen, the presiding officer, introduced the speaker of the evening, Hon. L.R. Stookey, of Warsaw, Ind. Mr. Stookey is a ready and rapid speaker. He paid a glowing tribute to the soldiers, and referred in scathing terms to Grover Cleveland's treatment of them and his insulting vetoes of pension bills. He spoke ... [of a law providing for election supervisors at the polls] and what we ask is that it shall apply without limitation north and south whenever there is an attempt or danger of attempt, to deny equal rights of all to cast their free ballot and have it counted as cast.

When he concluded the Emerson quartette gave another selection and responded to an encore. The audience then began to call loudly for "You," "You." Mr. A.J. You, our candidate for congress, was then introduced and made a stirring address. Mr. You has been speaking nearly every day and evening and is holding out first rate and proving himself one of the most popular candidates in the field.

He was repeatedly and enthusiastically cheered during his speech. Another selection by the quartette, and the house resounded with calls for "Brown," "Brown." Rev. W.H. Brown, for years the pastor of the A.M.E. church, of this city, took the platform and, though he protested that the hour was too late to permit another speech, made it clearly evident in the course of a twenty minute speech that the colored people of the country understand the situation and intend to stand by the party that broke the chains and gave freedom to the slave. The meeting then adjourned to music by the Glee club.

Source: *Fort Wayne* (Ind.) *Weekly Gazette*, October 20, 1892.

myhistorylab

Personal Journeys Online

- Susan B. Anthony, *Speech to the National American Woman Suffrage Association*, 1894. Asking Congress for political justice.

- Henry Vincent, *Marching through Iowa*, 1894. The journey of Kelly's "industrial army."

- William Jennings Bryan, 1896. Campaigning across America.

The Fort Wayne Gazette, a fiercely Republican newspaper, proudly reported on the activities of the local Republicans in Indiana during the political campaign in 1892. Their grand torchlight parade through the streets of Fort Wayne, the thronging and enthusiastic crowds, the lengthy and bombastic speeches all illustrate much about U.S. politics in the late nineteenth century. Parties mobilized ardently partisan voters into a politics of participation, which included political clubs, campaign festivities, and record-high turnouts on election day. The pageantry and hoopla made politics a major source of popular entertainment for Republicans and Democrats alike. But the extreme campaign rhetoric and outright misrepresentation of opponents—the Republican insistence that the Democratic presidential candidate, Grover Cleveland, had been pleased by the assassination of Abraham Lincoln matched a Democratic assertion that the "vile, wicked, evil, and odious" Republican candidate was "a bully toward the feeble and a truckler to the powerful"—indicated the intensity of partisan emotions. So did the military-style campaign, with uniformed marchers organized into companies, brigades, and divisions; with signs, slogans, and speeches referring to soldiers and the Civil War; with rallies held in armories. These campaign features also pointed to the enduring importance of the Civil War as a basis for partisan divisions and loyalties and marked electoral politics as a rough-and-tumble masculine business.

At the same time, contemporary issues did matter. The marchers' tin hats were an unmistakable and favorable reference to a controversial Republican tariff law that had so prohibitively taxed foreign tin plate that an American tin-plate-manufacturing industry emerged. Stookey's stump appeal for election supervisors to protect voters' rights at the polls similarly pointed to an important policy issue while hinting at the sometimes violent nature of elections, including the suppression of voters. It also emphasized that suffrage was often a contested issue.

The prominent role of Rev. Brown, the content of his speech, and the participation of the Colored Drum Corps and the Colored Republicans' Club in the parade show

CHRONOLOGY

1867	Patrons of Husbandry (the Grange) is founded.
1869	Massachusetts establishes the first state regulatory commission.
1873	Silver is demonetized in the "Crime of '73."
1874	Woman's Christian Temperance Union is organized.
1875	U.S. Supreme Court, in *Minor v. Happersett,* upholds denial of suffrage to women.
1876	Greenback Party runs presidential candidate.
1877	Rutherford B. Hayes becomes president after disputed election.
	Farmers' Alliance is founded.
	Supreme Court, in *Munn v. Illinois,* upholds state regulatory authority over private property.
1878	Bland-Allison Act requires the government to buy silver.
1880	James A. Garfield is elected president.
1881	Garfield is assassinated; Chester A. Arthur becomes president.
1883	Pendleton Civil Service Act is passed.
1884	Grover Cleveland is elected president.
1886	Supreme Court, in *Wabash v. Illinois,* rules that only the federal government, not the states, can regulate interstate commerce.
1887	Interstate Commerce Act is passed.
1888	Benjamin Harrison is elected president.
1890	Sherman Antitrust Act is passed.
	McKinley Tariff Act is passed.
	Sherman Silver Purchase Act is passed.
	National American Woman Suffrage Association is organized.
	Wyoming enters the Union as the first state with woman suffrage.
1892	People's Party is organized.
	Cleveland is elected to his second term as president.
1893	Depression begins.
	Sherman Silver Purchase Act is repealed.
1894	Coxey's Army marches to Washington.
	Pullman strike ends in violence.
1895	Supreme Court, in *Pollock v. Farmers' Loan and Trust Company,* invalidates the federal income tax.
	Supreme Court, in *United States v. E. C. Knight Company,* limits the Sherman Antitrust Law to commerce, excluding industrial monopolies.
1896	William Jennings Bryan is nominated for president by Democrats and Populists.
	William McKinley is elected president.
1900	Currency Act puts U.S. currency on the gold standard.

that partisan divisions in the United States overlapped with racial, religious, and other social divisions. Black voters, for instance, would "stand by the party that broke the chains and gave freedom to the slave." The journey to the polls, symbolized by the parade through Fort Wayne, invoked the most basic beliefs and values of Americans.

While the *Gazette* lavished praise on the Republican campaign and "our candidate" and ridiculed the opposition, its Democratic counterpart, the *Fort Wayne Sentinel*, extolled the success of the Democratic campaign, the enthusiasm of Democratic crowds, the integrity of Democratic candidates, and the despicable nature of the Republican Party. Such partisanship permeated journalism as well as nearly all aspects of public life, including government agencies, even those sworn to uphold the Constitution, such as Indiana's judiciary. As a crucial swing state, Indiana particularly experienced the influence of political organization and partisanship, but their presence and effects were felt throughout the United States.

These features of late-nineteenth-century politics would eventually be transformed in significant ways. But while they endured, they shaped not only campaigns and elections but also the form and role of government. Only a national crisis in the 1890s would finally cause some Americans to demand more of their political leaders and institutions.

The Structure and Style of Politics

Politics in the late nineteenth century was an absorbing activity. Campaigns and elections expressed social values as they determined who held the reins of government. Political parties dominated political life. They organized campaigns, controlled balloting, and held the unswerving loyalty of most of the electorate. While the major parties worked to maintain a sense of unity and tradition among their followers, third parties sought to activate those the major parties left unserved. Other Americans looked outside the electoral arena to achieve their political goals.

Campaigns and Elections

Political campaigns and elections generated remarkable public participation and enthusiasm. They constituted a major form of entertainment at a time when recreational opportunities were limited. Campaign pageantry absorbed communities large and small. In cities and towns across the nation, as in Fort Wayne, thousands of men in elaborate uniforms marched in massive torchlight parades to demonstrate partisan enthusiasm. Political picnics and camp meetings

served a comparable function in rural areas. Attending party meetings and conventions, listening to lengthy speeches appealing to group loyalties and local pride, gathering at the polls to watch the voting and the counting, celebrating victory and drowning the disappointment of defeat—all these provided social enjoyment and defined popular politics.

The excitement of political contests prompted the wife of Chief Justice Morrison Waite to write longingly on election day, 1876, "I should want to vote all day." But women, though they often identified with a political party, could not vote at all in national elections. Justice Waite himself had just a year earlier written the unanimous opinion of the Supreme Court (in *Minor v. Happersett*) that the Constitution did not confer suffrage on women. Men generally believed that weakness and sentimentality disqualified women from the fierce conflicts of the public realm.

Virtually all men participated in politics. In many states, even immigrants not yet citizens were eligible to vote and flocked to the polls. African Americans voted regularly in the North and irregularly in the South before being disfranchised at the end of the century. Overall, turnout was remarkably high, averaging nearly 80 percent of eligible voters in presidential elections between 1876 and 1900, a figure far greater than ever achieved thereafter (see Figure 20–1).

Political parties mobilized this huge electorate. They kept detailed records of voters, transported them to the polls, saw that they were registered where necessary, and sometimes even paid their poll taxes or naturalization fees to make them eligible. With legal regulations and public machinery for elections negligible, parties dominated the campaigns and elections. Until the 1890s, most states had no laws to ensure secrecy in voting, and balloting often took place in open rooms or on sidewalks. Election clerks and judges were not public officials but partisans chosen by the political parties.

Nor did public authorities issue official ballots. Instead voters used party tickets—strips of paper printed by the parties—listing only the names of the candidates of the party issuing them and varying in size and color. Casting a ballot thus revealed the voter's party allegiance. Tickets were distributed by paid party workers known as peddlers or hawkers, who stationed themselves near the polls, each trying to force his ticket on prospective voters. Contending hawkers contributed greatly to the election day chaos. Fighting and intimidation were so commonplace at the polls that one state supreme court ruled in 1887 that they were "acceptable" features of elections.

As the court recognized, the open and partisan aspects of the electoral process did not necessarily lead to election fraud, however much they shaped the nature of political participation. In these circumstances, campaigns and elections provided opportunities for men to demonstrate publicly their commitment to their party and its values, thereby reinforcing their partisan loyalties.

Nonvoting women, too, often exhibited their partisanship in this exciting political environment. Women wrote

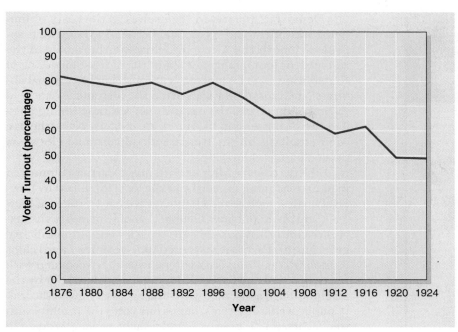

FIGURE 20–1   Voter Turnout in Presidential Elections, 1876–1924
The exciting partisan politics of the late nineteenth century produced very high voter turnouts, but as party competition declined and states enacted more restrictive voter regulations, popular participation in elections fell in the twentieth century.

partisan literature and gave campaign speeches; Anna Dickinson, one of the period's most popular orators, was hired by the Republican National Committee to campaign in the East and Midwest. Sometimes partisan women acted together with men; other times they worked through separate women's organizations. J. Ellen Foster established the Woman's National Republican Association in 1888 and built it into an organizing machine for the Republican Party with numerous state and local clubs. In these partisan groups women discussed and circulated party literature and devised plans to influence elections. Their partisanship was so deeply embedded that they remained loyal Republicans even when the party repudiated woman suffrage. "What discourages me about women," noted suffragist Susan B. Anthony, was that they care more for "[their] political party... than for [their] own political rights."

Partisan Politics

A remarkably close balance prevailed between the two major parties in the elections of this era. Democrats and Republicans had virtually the same level of electoral support, one reason they worked so hard to get out the vote (see Map 20–1). Control of the presidency and Congress shifted back and forth. Rarely did either party control both branches of government at once.

The party balance gave great influence to New York, New Jersey, Ohio, and Indiana, whose evenly divided voters controlled electoral votes that could swing an election either way. Both parties tended to nominate presidential and vice presidential candidates from those states to woo their voters. The parties also concentrated campaign funds and strategy on the swing states. Thus the Republican presidential candidate James Garfield of Ohio commented in 1880: "Nothing is wanting except an immediate and liberal supply of money for campaign expenses to make Indiana certain. With a victory there, the rest is easy." Garfield narrowly carried Indiana by 6,000 votes, and the nation by 9,000 out of 9.2 million cast. His victory was not the outcome of a contest over great issues but of carefully organized, tightly balanced parties mobilizing their supporters.

Party loyalty.   Interrelated regional, ethnic, religious, and local factors determined the party affiliations of most Americans. Economic issues, although important to the politics of the era, generally did not decide party ties. Farmers, for example, despite their many shared economic concerns, affiliated with both major parties. Like religious belief and ethnic identity, partisan loyalty was largely a cultural trait passed from parents to children, a situation that helps to explain the electoral stability of most communities.

Republicans were strongest in the North and Midwest, where they benefited from their party's role as the defender of the Union in the Civil War. "Republicanism in [Iowa] is not a logical conviction," reported one journalist in 1884; "it is a baleful fanaticism.... The war is still in progress in this region.... The women are worse than the men; they are intolerant, ferocious, implacable." But not all northerners voted for the Grand Old Party, or GOP. The Republican Party appealed primarily to old-stock Americans and other Protestants, including those of German and Scandinavian descent. African Americans, loyal to the party that had emancipated and enfranchised the slaves of the South, also supported the GOP where they could vote. Democrats were strongest in the South, where they stood as the defenders of the traditions of the region's white population. But Democrats also drew support in the urban Northeast, especially from Catholics and recent immigrants.

Party identities.   Each major party consisted of a complex coalition of groups with differing traditions and interests. One observer of the Democratic Party in California described it as "a sort of Democratic happy family, like we see in the prairie-dog villages, where owls, rattlesnakes, prairie dogs, and lizards all live in the same hole." This internal diversity often provoked conflict and threatened party stability. To hold its coalition together, each party identified itself

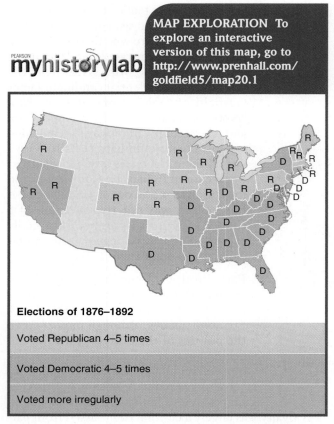

Elections of 1876–1892

Voted Republican 4–5 times

Voted Democratic 4–5 times

Voted more irregularly

MAP 20–1   The Two-Party Stalemate of the Late Nineteenth Century
Strong parties, staunch loyalties, and an evenly divided electorate made for exciting politics but often stalemated government in the late nineteenth century. Most states voted consistently for one of the major parties, leaving the few swing states like New York and Indiana the scenes of fierce partisan battles.

with a theme that appealed broadly to all its constituents, while suggesting that it was menaced by the members and objectives of the opposing party.

Republicans identified their party with nationalism and national unity and attacked the Democrats as an "alliance between the embittered South and the slums of the Northern cities." They combined a "bloody shirt" appeal to the memories of the Civil War with campaigns for immigration restriction and cultural uniformity. Seeing a threat to American society in efforts by Catholic immigrants to preserve their ethnic and cultural traditions, for example, Republican legislatures in several states in the 1880s and 1890s enacted laws regulating parochial schools, the use of foreign languages, and alcohol consumption. Similarly regarding Mormons as "subversive and treasonous" and engaged in "crime under the guise of religion," Republicans in both Congress and state legislatures enacted measures disfranchising them and otherwise restricting their civil rights.

Democrats portrayed themselves as the party of limited government and "personal liberties," a theme that appealed to both the racism of white southerners and the resentment immigrants felt about the nativist meddling of Republicans. The Democrats' commitment to personal liberties had limits. They supported the disfranchisement of African Americans, the exclusion of Chinese immigrants, and the dispossession of American Indians. Nevertheless, their emphasis on traditional individualism and localism proved popular.

The partisan politics of both major parties culminated in party machines, especially at the local level. Led by powerful bosses, such as the Democrat Richard Croker of New York and the Republican George Cox of Cincinnati, the machines controlled not only city politics but also municipal government. Party activists used well-organized ward clubs to mobilize working-class voters, who were rewarded with municipal jobs and baskets of food or coal doled out by the machine. Such assistance was often necessary, given the lack of public welfare systems, but to buy votes the machine also sold favors. Public contracts and franchises were peddled to businesses whose high bids covered kickbacks to the machine.

Third parties.   The partisan politics of the era left room for several third parties, organized around specific issues or groups. The **Prohibition Party** persistently championed the abolition of alcohol but also supported electoral reforms such as woman suffrage, economic reforms such as railroad regulation and income taxes, and social reforms including improved race relations. Some farmers and workers formed larger but shorter-lived third parties, charging that Republicans and Democrats had failed to respond to economic problems caused by industrialization or, worse still, had deliberately promoted powerful business interests at the expense of ordinary Americans. The **Greenback Party** of the 1870s denounced "the infamous financial legislation which takes all from the many to enrich the few." Its policies of labor reform and currency inflation (to stimulate and democratize the economy) attracted supporters from Maine to Texas. Other significant third parties included the Anti-Monopoly Party, the Union Labor Party, and, most important, the People's or **Populist Party** of the 1890s. Although third parties often won temporary success at the local or regional level, they never permanently displaced the major parties or undermined traditional voter allegiances.

Associational Politics

Much political activity was neither partisan nor electoral. Associations of like-minded citizens, operating as pressure groups, played an increasingly important role in late-nineteenth-century politics. These organizations worked to achieve public policies beneficial to their members. Farmers organized many such groups, most notably the Patrons of Husbandry, known familiarly as the Grange (see Chapter 17).

The Grange rejected partisanship but not politics. This sympathetic cartoon shows a Granger trying to warn Americans blindly absorbed in partisan politics of the dangers of onrushing industrialization.

Established in 1867, with both women and men eligible for membership, the Grange had 22,000 local lodges and nearly a million members by 1875. Its campaign for public regulation of the rates charged by railroads and grain elevators helped convince midwestern states to pass the so-called **Granger laws.** Labor organizations often pursued ambitious political agendas as well. Adopting nonpartisan tactics, the New Jersey Federation of Trades and Labor Unions drafted bills to require improved working conditions, testified before legislative committees, and marshaled delegations of workers to lobby for the measures.

Industrialists also formed pressure groups. Organizations such as the American Iron and Steel Association and the American Protective Tariff League lobbied Congress for high tariff laws and made campaign contributions to friendly politicians of both parties. At the state level business groups used their political clout to block the reform efforts of farmers and workers, sometimes in the legislatures but otherwise in the courts. Declaring that "lawmakers are too frequently influenced by public clamor and agitation for the cure of so-called social wrongs," the Illinois Manufacturers' Association in 1895 persuaded the Illinois Supreme Court to overturn a law establishing the eight-hour day for working women and girls.

A small group of conservative reformers known derisively as **Mugwumps** (the term derives from the Algonquian word for "chief") devoted most of their effort to campaigning for honest and efficient government through civil service reform. They organized the National Civil Service Reform League to publicize their plans, lobby Congress and state legislatures, and endorse sympathetic candidates. Other pressure groups focused on cultural politics. The rabidly anti-Catholic American Protective Association, for example, agitated for laws restricting immigration, taxing church property, and inspecting Catholic religious institutions.

Christian lobbyists committed their political energies to demanding laws imposing their view of personal moral behavior. The National Bureau of Reforms described itself as "the channel by which the swift protests, petitions, and letters of the people can be brought to bear in the interest of righteousness upon the lawmakers, both of the nation and the states." It campaigned for laws requiring Sabbath observance (no entertainment, work, or travel on Sundays) and Bible reading in schools, restricting divorce on scriptural grounds, and prohibiting gambling and other "sinful" activities. The greatest success for such Christian lobbyists was the Comstock Law, passed by Congress in 1873, which outlawed the possession or sale of "obscene" materials, including any contraceptive information or devices. Directly affecting the lives of many Americans, the Comstock Law clearly revealed the importance of this type of political activism.

Women as activists.   Women also sought power and influence through associational politics. Susan B. Anthony and others formed groups to lobby Congress and state legislatures for constitutional amendments extending the right to vote to women. The leading organizations merged in 1890 as the **National American Woman Suffrage Association.** Despite the opposition of male politicians of both major parties, suffragists had succeeded by the mid-1890s in gaining full woman suffrage in four western states, Wyoming, Colorado, Idaho, and Utah, and partial suffrage (the right to vote in school elections) in several other states, east and west.

Other women shaped public issues through social service organizations. Although the belief that women belonged in the domestic sphere limited their involvement in electoral politics, it furnished a basis for political action focused on welfare and moral reform. With petition campaigns, demonstrations, and lobbying, women's social service organizations sought to remedy poverty and disease, improve education and recreation, and provide day nurseries for the children of workingwomen. The Illinois Woman's Alliance—organized in 1888 by suffragists, women assemblies of the Knights of Labor, and middle-class women's clubs—investigated the conditions of women and children in workshops and factories and campaigned successfully for protective labor legislation and compulsory school-attendance laws. The Woman's Municipal League, organized in New York City in 1894, described itself as a "political club" concerned with "education, sanitation, public health, and police and fire protection."

Women also combined domesticity and politics in the temperance movement. Alcoholism, widespread in U.S. society, was regarded as a major cause of crime, wife abuse, and

In the 1880s many Americans feared that corporate power had too much influence in government and was endangering popular liberty. The question, as posed by this cartoon, was "What are you going to do about it?"

In 1875, sound money advocates in Congress enacted a deflationary law that withdrew some greenbacks from circulation and required that the remainder be convertible into gold after 1878. This action forced the money issue into electoral politics. Outraged inflationists organized the Greenback Party. They charged that the major parties had "failed to take the side of the people" and instead supported the "great moneyed institutions." The Greenbackers polled more than a million votes in 1878 and elected 14 members of Congress, nearly gaining the balance of power in the House. As the depression faded, however, so did interest in the greenback issue, and the party soon withered.

The silver issue.   Inflationists then turned to the silver issue, which would prove more enduring and disruptive. Historically, the United States had been on a bimetallic standard, using both gold and silver as the basis of its currency. But after the 1840s, the market price of silver rose above the currency value assigned to it by the government. Silver miners and owners began to sell the metal for commercial use rather than to the government for coinage, and little silver money circulated. In 1873, Congress passed a law "demonetizing" silver, thereby making gold the only standard for U.S. currency. Gold-standard supporters hoped that the law would promote international trade by aligning U.S. financial policy with that of Great Britain, which insisted on gold-based currency. But they also wanted to prevent new silver discoveries in the American West from expanding the money supply.

Despite the sometimes arcane and difficult nature of the money question, millions of Americans adopted positions on it and defended them with religious ferocity.

Creditors, especially bankers, as well as conservative economists and many business leaders favored limiting the money supply. They called this a **sound money** policy and insisted that it would ensure economic stability, maintain property values, and retain investor confidence. Farmers and other debtors complained that this deflationary monetary policy would depress already low crop prices, drive debtors further into debt, and restrict economic opportunities. They favored expanding the money supply to match the country's growing population and economy. They expected this inflationary policy to raise prices, stimulate the economy, reduce debt burdens, and increase opportunities.

The conservative leadership of both major parties supported the sound money policy, but their rank-and-file membership, especially in the West and the South, included many inflationists. As a result, the parties avoided confronting each other on the money issue.

The conflict between advocates of sound money and inflation centered on the use of paper money, or "greenbacks," and silver coinage. The greenback controversy had its roots in the Civil War. To meet its expenses during the war, the federal government issued $450 million in greenbacks, paper money backed only by the credit of the United States, not by gold or silver, the traditional basis of currency. After the war, creditors demanded that the greenbacks be withdrawn from circulation. Debtors and other Americans caught up in the postwar depression favored retaining the greenbacks and even expanding their use.

Indeed, silver production soon boomed, flooding the commercial market and dropping the value of the metal. Dismayed miners wanted the Treasury Department to purchase their surplus silver on the old terms and demanded a return to the bimetallic system. More important, the rural debtor groups seeking currency inflation joined in this demand, seeing renewed silver coinage as a means to reverse the long deflationary trend in the economy. Many passionately denounced the "Crime of '73" as a conspiracy of eastern bankers and foreign interests to control the money system to the detriment of ordinary Americans.

Again, both major parties equivocated. Eastern conservatives of both parties denounced silver; southerners and westerners demanded **free silver,** meaning unlimited silver coinage. One New York Democrat complained that western and southern members of his party were "mad as wild Texas steers on this silver dollar business. As we pass each other in the streets they seem to sneer, and hiss through their teeth the words 'gold bug,' and look as if they would like to spit upon [us]." By 1878, a bipartisan coalition succeeded in passing the Bland-Allison Act. This compromise measure required the government to buy and coin at least $2 million of silver a month. However, the government never exceeded the minimum, and the law had little inflationary effect. Republican President Arthur and Democratic President Cleveland recommended repealing the Bland-Allison Act, but the parties avoided the silver issue in their national platforms, fearing its divisive effect.

After hard times hit rural regions in the late 1880s, inflationists secured passage of the Sherman Silver Purchase Act of 1890. The Treasury now had to buy a larger volume of silver and pay for it with treasury notes redeemable in either gold or silver. But this, too, produced little inflation, because the government did not coin the silver it purchased, redeemed the notes only with gold, and, as western silver production increased further, had to spend less and less to buy the stipulated amount of silver. Debtors of both parties remained convinced that the government favored the "classes rather than the masses." Gold-standard advocates (again, of both parties) were even less happy with the law and planned to repeal it at their first opportunity. The division between the two groups was deep and bitter.

The Crisis of the 1890s

In the 1890s, social, economic, and political pressures created a crisis for both the political system and the government. A third-party political challenge generated by agricultural discontent disrupted traditional party politics. A devastating depression spawned social misery and labor violence. Changing public attitudes led to new demands on the government and a realignment of parties and voters. These developments, in turn, set the stage for important political, economic, and social changes in the new century.

Farmers Protest Inequities

The agricultural depression that engulfed the Great Plains and the South in the late 1880s brought misery and despair to millions of rural Americans. Falling crop prices and rising debt overwhelmed many people already exhausted from overwork and alarmed by the new corporate order. "At the age of 52 years, after a long life of toil, economy, and self-denial, I find myself and family virtual paupers," lamented one Kansan. His family's farm, rather than being "a house of refuge for our declining years, by a few turns of the monopolistic crank has been rendered valueless." To a large extent, the farmers' plight stemmed from bad weather and international over-production of farm products. Seeking relief, however, the farmers naturally focused on the inequities of railroad discrimination, tariff favoritism, a restrictive financial system, and apparently indifferent political parties.

Credit inequities.   Angry farmers particularly singled out the systems of money and credit that worked so completely against agricultural interests. Government rules for national banks directed credit into the urbanized North and East at the expense of the rural South and West and prohibited loans on farm property and real estate. As a result, farmers had to turn to other sources of credit and pay higher interest rates. In the West, farmers borrowed from mortgage companies to buy land and machinery, but declining crop prices made it difficult for them to pay their debts, and mortgage foreclosures then crushed the hopes of many. In the South, the credit shortage interacted with the practices of cotton marketing and retail trade to create the sharecropping system, which trapped more and more farmers, black and white, in a vicious pattern of exploitation. Moreover, the government's policies of monetary deflation worsened the debt burden for all farmers.

Freight rates and tariffs.   Farmers protested other features of the nation's economic system as well. Railroad freight rates were two or three times higher in the West and South than in the North and East. The near-monopolistic control of grain elevators and cotton brokerages in rural areas left farmers feeling exploited. Protective tariffs on agricultural machinery and other manufactured goods further raised their costs. The failure of political parties and the government to devise effective regulatory and antitrust measures or to correct the inequities in the currency, credit, and tariff laws capped the farmers' anger. By the 1890s, many were convinced that the nation's economic and political institutions were aligned against them.

Farmers organize.   In response, farmers turned to the **Farmers' Alliance,** the era's greatest popular movement of protest and reform. Originating in Texas, the Southern Farmers' Alliance spread throughout the South and across the Great Plains to the Pacific coast. African American farmers organized the Colored Farmers' Alliance. The Northwestern Farmers' Alliance reached westward and northward from Illinois to Nebraska and Minnesota. In combination, these groups constituted a massive grassroots movement committed to economic and political reform.

The Farmers' Alliance restricted membership to men and women of the "producing class" and urged them to stand "against the encroachments of monopolies and in opposition to the growing corruption of wealth and power." At first, the Alliance organized farmers' cooperatives to market crops and purchase supplies. Although some co-ops worked well, most soon failed because of the opposition of established business interests. Railroads suppressed Alliance grain elevators by refusing to handle their wheat. In Leflore County, Mississippi, when members of the Colored Farmers' Alliance shifted their trade to an Alliance store, local merchants provoked a conflict in which state troops killed 25 black farmers, including the local leaders of the Colored Alliance.

The Alliance also developed ingenious proposals to remedy rural credit and currency problems. In the South, the Alliance pushed the subtreasury system, which called on the government to warehouse farmers' cotton and advance them credit based on its value (see Chapter 17). In the West, the Alliance proposed a system of federal loans to farmers, using land as security. This land-loan scheme, like the subtreasury system, was a political expression of greenbackism; it would have expanded the money supply while providing immediate relief to distressed farmers. These proposals were immensely popular among farmers, but the major parties and Congress rejected them. The Alliance also took up earlier calls for free silver, government control of railroads, and banking reform, again to no avail. Denouncing the indifference of the major parties and the institutions of government, William A. Peffer, the influential editor of the Alliance newspaper the *Kansas Farmer,* declared that the "time has come for action. The people will not consent to wait longer.... The future is full of retribution for delinquents."

The People's Party

In the West, discontented agrarians organized independent third parties to achieve reforms the major parties had ignored. State-level third parties appeared in the elections of 1890 under many names. All eventually adopted the labels "People's" or "Populist," which were first used by a Kansas party formed by members of the Farmers' Alliance, the Knights of Labor, the Grange, and the old Greenback Party. The new party's campaign, marked by grim determination and fierce rhetoric, set the model for Populist politics and introduced many of the movement's leaders. These people, women as well as men, were earnest organizers and powerful orators. One was *Kansas Farmer* editor Peffer. Others included "Sockless Jerry" Simpson, Annie Diggs, and Mary E. Lease.

When hostile business and political leaders attacked the Populist program as socialistic, Lease retorted, "You may call me an anarchist, a socialist, or a communist. I care not, but I hold to the theory that if one man has not enough to eat three times a day and another has $25,000,000, that last man has something that belongs to the first." Lease spoke as clearly against the colonial status experienced by the South and West: "The great common people of this country are slaves, and monopoly is the master. The West and South are bound and prostrate before the manufacturing East."

The Populist parties proved remarkably successful. They gained control of the legislatures of Kansas and Nebraska and won congressional elections in Kansas, Nebraska, and Minnesota. Their victories came at the expense of the Republicans, who had traditionally controlled politics in these states, and contributed to a massive defeat of the GOP in the 1890 midterm elections. Thereafter, Populists won further victories throughout the West. In the mountain states,

A PARTY OF PATCHES.
Grand Balloon Ascension—Cincinnati, May 20th, 1891

Established interests ridiculed the Populists unmercifully. This hostile cartoon depicts the People's Party as an odd assortment of radical dissidents committed to a "Platform of Lunacy."

where their support came more from miners than from farmers, they won governorships in Colorado and Montana. On the Pacific coast, angry farmers found allies among urban workers in Seattle, Tacoma, Portland, and San Francisco, where organized labor had campaigned for reform since the 1880s. The Populists elected a governor in Washington, congressmen in California, and legislators in all three states. Even in the Southwest, where territorial status limited political activity, Populist parties emerged. In Oklahoma, the party drew support from homesteaders and tenant farmers; in Arizona, from miners and railroad workers; in New Mexico, from small stockraisers and poor Hispanics.

With their new political power, farmers enacted reform legislation in many western states. New laws regulated banks and railroads and protected debtors by capping interest rates and restricting mortgage foreclosures. Others protected unions and mandated improved workplace conditions. Still others made the political system more democratic. Populists were instrumental, for example, in winning woman suffrage in Colorado and Idaho, although the united opposition of Democrats and Republicans blocked their efforts to win it in other states.

In the South, the angry farmers did not initially form third parties but instead attempted to seize control of the dominant Democratic Party by forcing its candidates to pledge support to the Alliance platform. The rural southern electorate then swept these "Alliance Democrats" into office. But most of these Democrats then repudiated their Alliance pledges and remained loyal to their party and its traditional opposition to governmental activism. Betrayed again by the political system, disgruntled Alliance members began organizing their own Populist parties, but they faced obstacles that western farmers did not. A successful challenge to the entrenched Democrats would require the political cooperation of both white and black farmers, but that would expose Populists to demagogic attacks from Democrats for undermining white supremacy, frightening away potential white supporters. The *Baton Rouge Advocate,* for example, warned its readers that the Populists were "the most dangerous and insidious foe of white supremacy."

Some Southern Populists, black and white, did appeal for racial cooperation in political if not social action. In Texas, John B. Rayner, the "silver tongued orator of the colored race," spoke to racially mixed audiences across the state and helped shape the Texas Populist platform calling for "equal justice and protection under the law to all citizens without reference to race, color, or nationality." In Georgia, the Populist leader Tom Watson supported a biracial party organization and counseled white people to accept black people as partners in their common crusade. "You are kept apart," Watson told black and white southerners, "that you may be separately fleeced of your earnings. You are made to hate each other because upon that hatred is rested the keystone of the arch of financial despotism which enslaves you both."

But steeped in racism, most white southerners recoiled from the prospect of interracial unity. And for their part, most black people remained loyal to the Republican Party for its role in abolishing slavery and for the few patronage crumbs the party still threw their way. Moreover, primarily tenants and farm laborers, their interests were not identical to those of white landowning farmers who formed the core of the Populist Party. Unwilling or unable to mobilize black voters and largely unsuccessful in dislodging white voters from the Democratic Party, Populists in the South achieved but limited political success, making significant inroads only in the legislatures of Texas, Alabama, and Georgia, and sending Tom Watson to Congress.

National action.　Populists soon realized that successful reform would require national action. They met in Omaha, Nebraska, on July 4, 1892, to organize a national party and nominated former Greenbacker James B. Weaver for president. The party platform, known as the **Omaha Platform,** rejected the laissez-faire policies of the old parties: "We believe that the powers of government, in other words, of the people, should be expanded...to the end that oppression, injustice, and poverty shall eventually cease in the land." It demanded government ownership of the railroads and the telegraph and telephone systems, a national currency issued by the government rather than by private banks, the subtreasury system, free silver, a graduated income tax, and the redistribution to settlers of land held by railroads and spec-

ulative corporations. Accompanying resolutions endorsed the popular election of senators, the secret ballot, and other electoral reforms to make government more democratic and responsive to popular wishes. When the platform was adopted, "cheers and yells," one reporter wrote, "rose like a tornado from four thousand throats and raged without cessation for 34 minutes, during which women shrieked and wept, men embraced and kissed their neighbors...in the ecstasy of their delirium."

The Populists left Omaha to begin an energetic campaign. Weaver toured the western states and with Mary Lease invaded the Democratic stronghold of the South where some Populists tried to mobilize black voters. Southern Democrats, however, used violence and fraud to intimidate Populist voters and cheat Populist candidates out of office. Some local Populist leaders were murdered, and Weaver was driven from the South. One Democrat confessed that Alabama's Populist gubernatorial candidate "carried the state, but was swindled out of his victory... with unblushing trickery and corruption." Southern Democrats also appealed effectively to white supremacy, undermining the Populist effort to build a biracial reform coalition.

Elsewhere, too, Populists met disappointment. Midwestern farmers unfamiliar with Alliance ideas and organization ignored Populist appeals and stood by their traditional political allegiances. So did most eastern working-class voters, who learned little of the Populist program beyond its demand for inflation, which they feared would worsen their own conditions.

The Populists lost the election but showed impressive support. They garnered more than a million votes, carried several western states, and won hundreds of state offices throughout the West and in pockets of the South. Populist leaders immediately began working to expand their support, to the alarm of both southern Democrats and northern Republicans.

The Challenge of the Depression

The emergence of a significant third-party movement was but one of many developments that combined by the mid-1890s to produce a national political crisis. A harsh and lengthy depression began in 1893, cruelly worsening conditions not only for farmers but for most other Americans. Labor unrest and violence engulfed the nation, reflecting workers' distress but frightening more comfortable Americans. The persistent failure of the major parties to respond to serious problems contributed mightily to the growing popular discontent. Together these developments constituted an important challenge to America's new industrial society and government.

Although the Populists lost in 1892, the election nonetheless reflected the nation's spreading dissatisfaction. Voters decisively rejected President Harrison and the incumbent Republicans in Congress, putting the Democrats in

FROM THEN TO NOW

Political Parties

Few things in contemporary American politics present a sharper contrast to the nineteenth century than the role of political parties. In the late nineteenth century, parties dominated both politics and government, commanding the allegiance of Americans, controlling the selection of candidates, mobilizing voters, providing ballots, running elections, staffing government positions. Today, parties do practically none of these things.

This transformation began at the end of the nineteenth century. Extreme partisanship alienated increasing numbers of voters and prompted states to assert control over elections and parties. Civil service reform steadily reduced party influence in government. So did the evolution of special-interest lobbying groups and the growing reliance in the twentieth century on independent regulatory commissions, rather than partisan legislative committees, to make and implement policies. The introduction and spread of primary elections stripped parties of their control over nominations. Individual candidates now rely more on personal organizations than the party apparatus to manage campaigns and communicate directly to voters through the mass media rather than through party workers. Campaign finance reform laws and the rise of political action committees (PACs) have reduced party control over the funding and direction of campaigns. Finally, declining numbers of Americans identify with a particular party, with nearly half the electorate in favor of making all elections nonpartisan or even of abolishing parties. Fewer and fewer Americans bother to vote, and those who do are much more likely than before to split their ticket, voting for candidates of different parties for different offices. This often results in divided government—with the Congress controlled by one party and the presidency by the other, producing a stalemate that increases public cynicism about parties.

Partisanship asserts its influence in government offices in this 1881 cartoon for civil service reform.

Of course, parties endure and retain some importance. Election laws favor the two established parties, public funds subsidize party activities, Congress and state legislatures continue to rely on party divisions to organize their leadership and committee structures, and party discipline still influences the way legislators vote. But while such institutional factors guarantee the continuation of the two-party system, the parties themselves no longer enjoy the influence they had in the nineteenth century.

■ What are the advantages and the drawbacks of the historical decline of party influence in American political life?

The loss of party control over government personnel.

PEARSON
myhistorylab

From Then to Now Online

20-1 *Leaving the Party.* American labor song.

20-2 J. S. Clarkson, *In Defense of Politicians and Parties,* 1891. A leading Republican defends partisan politics and the spoils system.

control of Congress and Grover Cleveland back in the White House. But the conservative Cleveland was almost oblivious to the mounting demand for reform. He delivered an inaugural address championing laissez-faire and rejecting government action to solve social or economic problems.

Cleveland's resolve was immediately tested when the economy collapsed in the spring of 1893. Railroad overexpansion, a weak banking system, tight credit, and plunging agricultural prices all contributed to the disaster. So too did a depression in Europe, which reduced American export markets and prompted British investors to sell their American investments for gold. Hundreds of banks closed, and thousands of businesses, including the nation's major railroads, went bankrupt. By winter, 20 percent of the labor force was unemployed, and the jobless scavenged for food in a country that had no public unemployment or welfare programs. "Never within memory," said one New York minister, "have so many people literally starved to death as in the past few months."

Churches, local charity societies, and labor unions tried to provide relief but were overwhelmed. Most state governments offered little relief beyond encouraging private charity to the homeless. In Kansas, however, the Populist governor insisted that traditional laissez-faire policies were inadequate: "It is the duty of government to protect the weak, because the strong are able to protect themselves." (See American Views, A Populist Views American Government.) Cleveland disagreed and showed little sympathy for the struggling. The functions of the government, he said, "do not include the support of the people."

Appeals for federal action. If Cleveland and Congress had no idea how the federal government might respond to the depression, other Americans did. Jacob Coxey, a Populist businessman from Ohio, proposed a government public-works program for the unemployed to be financed with paper money. This plan would improve the nation's infrastructure, create jobs for the unemployed, and provide an inflationary stimulus to counteract the depression's deflationary effects. In short, Coxey advocated positive government action to combat the depression. Elements of his plan would be adopted for mitigating economic downturns in the twentieth century; in 1894, it was too untraditional for Congress to consider.

Coxey organized a march of the unemployed to Washington as "a petition with boots on" to support his ideas. **Coxey's Army** of the unemployed, as the excited press dubbed it, marched through the industrial towns of Ohio and Pennsylvania and into Maryland, attracting attention and support. Other armies formed in eastern cities from Boston to Baltimore and set out for the capital. Some of the largest armies organized in the western cities of Denver, San Francisco, and Seattle. Three hundred men in an army from Oakland elected as their commander Anna Smith, who promised to "land my men on the steps of the Capitol at Washington." "I'm not afraid of anything," Smith explained. "I have a woman's heart and a woman's sympathy, and these lead me to do what I have done for these men, even though it may not be just what a woman is expected to do."

Lewis Fry, the organizer of the Los Angeles army, declared: "If the government has a right to make us die in time of war, we have the right to demand of her the right to live in time of peace." Fry's 500 marchers captured a train to cross the Southwest and were feted and fed by townspeople from Tucson to El Paso. When the Southern Pacific uncoupled the train's locomotive and left the marchers stranded without food or water in West Texas, the governor of Texas threatened to hold the railroad responsible for murder "by torture and starvation." Texas citizens quickly raised funds to speed the army on to St. Louis. From there it marched to Washington on foot.

The sympathy and assistance with which Americans greeted these industrial armies reflected more than anxiety over the depression and unemployment. As one economist noted, what distinguished the Populists and Coxeyites from earlier reformers was their appeal for federal action. Their substantial public support suggested a deep dissatisfaction with the failure of the government to respond to social and economic needs.

Nonetheless, the government acted to suppress Coxey. When he reached Washington with 600 marchers, police and soldiers arrested him and his aides, beat sympathetic bystanders in a crowd of 20,000, and herded the marchers into detention camps. Unlike the lobbyists for business and finance, Coxey was not permitted to reach Congress to deliver his statement urging the government to assist "the poor and oppressed."

Protecting big business. The depression also provoked labor turmoil. In 1894, there were some 1,400 industrial strikes, involving nearly 700,000 workers, the largest number of strikers in any year in the nineteenth century. Cleveland had no response except to call for law and order. One result was the government's violent suppression of the Pullman strike (see Chapter 18).

In a series of decisions in 1895, the Supreme Court strengthened the bonds between business and government. First, it upheld the use of a court-ordered injunction to break the Pullman strike. As a result, injunctions became a major weapon for courts and corporations against labor unions, until Congress finally limited their use in 1932. Next, in *United States v. E. C. Knight Company,* the Court gutted the Sherman Antitrust Act by ruling that manufacturing, as opposed to commerce, was beyond the reach of federal regulation. Finally, the Court invalidated an income tax that agrarian Democrats and Populists had maneuvered through Congress. The conservative Court rejected the reform as an "assault upon capital." A dissenting justice noted that the decision gave vested interests "a power and influence" dangerous to

Jacob Coxey's "Army" of the unemployed marches to Washington, D.C., in 1894. Many such "industrial armies" were organized during the depressed 1890s, revealing dissatisfaction with traditional politics and limited government.

the majority of Americans. Not until 1913, and then only with an amendment to the Constitution, would it be possible to adopt an equitable system of taxation.

Surveying these developments, farmers and workers increasingly concluded that the government protected powerful interests while ignoring the plight of ordinary Americans. Certainly the callous treatment shown workers contrasted sharply with Cleveland's concern for bankers as he managed the government's monetary policy in the depression. Cleveland blamed the economic collapse on the Sherman Silver Purchase Act, which he regarded as detrimental to business confidence and a threat to the nation's gold reserve. He persuaded Congress in 1893 to repeal the law, enraging southern and western members of his own party. These Silver Democrats condemned Cleveland for betraying the public good to "the corporate interests."

Cleveland's policy failed to end the depression. By 1894, the Treasury began borrowing money from Wall Street to bolster the gold reserve. These transactions benefited a syndicate of bankers headed by J. P. Morgan. It seemed to critics that an indifferent Cleveland was helping rich bankers profit from the nation's economic agony. "A set of vampires headed by a financial trust has control of our destiny," cried one rural newspaper.

The Battle of the Standards and the Election of 1896

The government's unpopular actions, coupled with the unrelenting depression, alienated workers and farmers from the Cleveland administration and the Democratic Party. In the off-year elections of 1894, the Democrats suffered the greatest loss of congressional seats in American history. Populists increased their vote by 42 percent, making especially significant gains in the South. In North Carolina, for example, they gained control of the legislature and promptly enacted important electoral, economic, and educational reforms long blocked by the Democrats. But the real beneficiaries of the popular hatred of Cleveland and his policies were the Republicans. Denouncing Cleveland's "utter imbecility," they gained solid control of Congress as well as state governments across the North and West. All three parties began to plan for the presidential election of 1896.

As hard times persisted, the silver issue came to overshadow all others. Some Populist leaders, hoping to broaden the party's appeal, began to emphasize silver rather than the more radical but divisive planks of the Omaha Platform. Many southern and western Democrats, who had traditionally favored silver inflation, also decided to stress the issue, both to undercut the Populists and to distance themselves and their party from the despised Cleveland. They held rallies and conventions across the South and West, distributed silver literature, and argued that free silver would finally end the depression.

McKinley and the Republicans.   William McKinley, governor of Ohio and author of the McKinley Tariff Act of 1890, emerged as the front-runner of a crowd of hopeful Republican presidential candidates. His candidacy benefited particularly from the financial backing and political management of Mark Hanna, a wealthy Ohio industrialist. Hanna thought that McKinley's passion for high tariffs as the key to revived prosperity would appeal to workers as well as to industry and business. As governor, McKinley had reached out to workers by supporting pro-labor legislation and by avoiding the anti-Catholic positions that alienated immigrants from the Republican Party. Nonetheless, he shared Hanna's conviction that government should actively promote business in-

William Jennings Bryan in 1896. A powerful orator of great human sympathies, Bryan was adored by his followers as "the majestic man who was hurling defiance in the teeth of the money power." Nominated three times for the presidency by the Democrats, he was never elected.

terests; he was not Hanna's puppet, as opponents sometimes claimed.

The Republicans nominated McKinley on the first ballot at their 1896 convention. Their platform called for high tariffs but also endorsed the gold standard, placating eastern delegates but prompting several western Silver Republicans to withdraw from the party.

Bryan and the Silverites.   When the Democratic convention met, embattled supporters of the gold standard soon learned that the silver crusade had made them a minority in the party. With a fervor that conservatives likened to "scenes of the French Revolution," the Silver Democrats revolutionized their party. They adopted a platform repudiating Cleveland and his policies and endorsing free silver, the income tax, and tighter regulation of trusts and railroads. A magnificent speech supporting this platform by William Jennings Bryan helped convince the delegates to nominate him for president. Bryan was only 36 years old, but he had already served in Congress, edited an important newspaper, and gained renown for his oratorical skills and popular sympathies.

Holding their convention last, the Populists faced a terrible dilemma. The Democratic nomination of Bryan on a silver platform undercut their hopes of attracting disappointed reformers from the major parties. Bryan, moreover, had already worked closely with Nebraska Populists, who now urged the party to endorse him rather than split the silver vote and ensure the victory of McKinley and the gold standard. Other Populists argued that fusing—joining with the Democrats—would cost the Populists their separate identity and subordinate their larger political principles to the issue of free silver. After anguished discussion, the Populists nominated Bryan for president but named a separate vice presidential candidate, Tom Watson of Georgia, in an effort to maintain their identity. They hoped the Democrats would reciprocate by replacing their nominee with Watson, but the Democrats ignored the overture. The Populists' strength was in the South and West, regions that Bryan would control anyway. They could offer him little help in the battle for the Midwest and East, what Bryan called "the enemy's country."

Money and oratory.   The campaign was intense and dramatic, with each side demonizing the other. Eastern financial and business interests contributed millions of dollars to Hanna's campaign for McKinley. Standard Oil alone provided $250,000, about the same amount as the Democrats' total national expenses. Hanna used these funds to organize an unprecedented campaign. Shifting the emphasis from parades to information, Republicans issued 250 million campaign documents in a dozen languages, warning of economic disaster should Bryan be elected and the bimetallic standard be restored, but promising that McKinley's election would finally end the depression. Republicans were aided by a na-

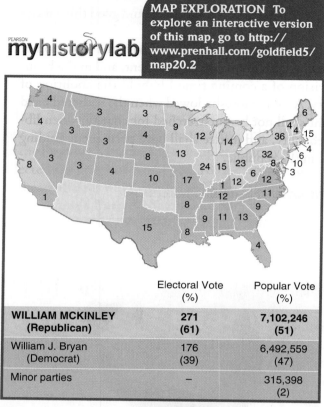

MAP EXPLORATION To explore an interactive version of this map, go to http:// www.prenhall.com/goldfield5/ map20.2

PEARSON
myhistorylab

	Electoral Vote (%)	Popular Vote (%)
WILLIAM MCKINLEY (Republican)	**271 (61)**	**7,102,246 (51)**
William J. Bryan (Democrat)	176 (39)	6,492,559 (47)
Minor parties	–	315,398 (2)

MAP 20–2   The Election of 1896
William Jennings Bryan carried most of the rural South and West, but his free silver campaign had little appeal to more urban and industrial regions, which swung strongly to Republican candidate William McKinley.

publicans a reputation as the party of prosperity and industrial progress, firmly establishing them in power for years to come. By contrast, the Democratic Party receded into an ineffectual sectional minority dominated by southern conservatives, despite Bryan's liberal views.

The People's Party simply dissolved. Demoralized by fusion with the Democrats, who had earlier violently repressed them, many southern Populists dropped out of politics. The Democrats' disfranchisement laws, directed at discontented poor white southerners as well as poor black southerners, further undermined the Populists in the South. In the West, the silver tide of 1896 carried many Populists into office, but with their party collapsing, they had no hope of reelection. By 1898, the Populist Party had virtually disappeared. Its reform legacy, however, proved more enduring. The issues it raised would continue to shape state and national politics.

McKinley plunged into his presidency. Unlike his predecessors, he had a definite, if limited, program, consisting of tariff protection, sound money, and overseas expansion. He worked actively to see it through Congress and to shape public opinion, thereby helping establish the model of the mod-

ern presidency. He had promised prosperity, and it returned, although not because of the record high tariff his party enacted in 1897 or the Currency Act of 1900, which firmly established the gold standard. Prosperity returned, instead, because of reviving markets and a monetary inflation that resulted from the discovery of vast new deposits of gold in Alaska, Australia, and South Africa. The silverites had recognized that an expanding industrial economy required an expanding money supply. Ironically, the new inflation was greater than the inflation that would have resulted from free silver. With the return of prosperity and the decline of social tensions, McKinley easily won reelection in 1900, defeating Bryan a second time.

Conclusion

In late-nineteenth-century America, politics and government often seemed at cross-purposes. Political contests were exciting events, absorbing public attention, attracting high voter turnout, and often raising issues of symbolic or substantive importance. Closely balanced political parties commanded the zealous support of their constituents and wielded power and influence. The institutions of government, by contrast, were limited in size, scope, and responsibility. A weakened presidency and an inefficient Congress, hampered by a restrictive judiciary, were often unable to resolve the very issues that were so dramatically raised in the political arena. The persistent disputes over tariff and monetary policy illustrate this impasse. But the issue that most reflected it was civil service reform. The patronage system provided the lifeblood of politics but also disrupted government business.

Localism, laissez-faire, and other traditional principles that shaped both politics and government were becoming increasingly inappropriate for America's industrializing society. New challenges were emerging that state and local governments could not effectively solve on their own. The national nature of the railroad network, for example, finally brought the federal government into the regulatory arena, however imperfectly, with the Interstate Commerce Act of 1887. Both the depression of the 1890s and the popular discontent articulated most clearly by the Populist rejection of laissez-faire underscored the need for change and discredited the limited government of the Cleveland administration.

By the end of the decade, the political system had changed. The Republicans had emerged as the dominant party, ending the two-party stalemate of previous decades. Campaign hoopla in local communities had given way to information-based campaigns directed by and through national organizations. A new, activist presidency was emerging. And the disruptive currency issue faded with the hard times that had brought it forth. Still greater changes were on the horizon. The depression and its terrible social and economic consequences undermined traditional ideas about the responsibilities of government and increased public support for activist policies. The stage was set for the Progressive Era.

Review Questions

1. What social and institutional factors shaped the disorderly nature of elections in the late nineteenth century? How did they operate in U.S. politics?

2. What social and institutional factors determined the role of government? How and why did the role of government change during this period?

3. What factors determined the party affiliation of American voters? Why did so many third parties develop during this era?

4. How might the planks of the Omaha Platform have helped solve farmers' troubles?

5. What factors shaped the conduct and outcome of the election of 1896? How did that contest differ from earlier elections?

Key Terms

Coxey's Army (p. 569)

Farmers' Alliance (p. 565)

Free silver (p. 564)

Granger laws (p. 557)

Greenback Party (p. 556)

Interstate Commerce Act (p. 563)

Interstate Commerce Commission (ICC) (p. 563)

Laissez-faire (p. 558)

Mugwumps (p. 557)

National American Woman Suffrage Association (p. 557)

Omaha Platform (p. 567)

Pendleton Civil Service Act (p. 560)

Populist Party (p. 556)

Prohibition Party (p. 556)

Sherman Antitrust Act (p. 563)

Sound money (p. 564)

Recommended Reading

Cherny, Robert W. *American Politics in the Gilded Age* (1997). An excellent brief analysis, emphasizing the importance of parties in both elections and public policy.

Foster, Gaines M. *Moral Reconstruction: Christian Lobbyists and the Federal Legislation of Morality, 1865-1920* (2002). A suggestive study of the efforts of Christian lobbyists to expand government authority over personal behavior.

Keller, Morton. *Affairs of State: Public Life in Late Nineteenth Century America* (1977). A detailed and fascinating account of the changing dimensions of government and politics.

McMath, Robert C., Jr. *American Populism: A Social History, 1877–1898* (1993). The best modern history of Populism; balanced and readable.

Summers, Mark. *Party Games: Getting, Keeping, and Using Power in Gilded Age Politics* (2004). A provocative account of the way partisan politicians (mis)shaped politics and public policy.

Where to Learn More

- **Rest Cottage, Evanston, Illinois.**   Frances Willard's home, from which she directed the Woman's Christian Temperance Union, is carefully preserved as a museum. The Willard Memorial Library contains more memorabilia and papers of Willard and the WCTU. www.wctu.org/house.html

- **President Benjamin Harrison's Home, Indianapolis, Indiana.**   President Harrison's brick Italianate mansion, completed in 1875, has been completely restored with the family's furniture and keepsakes. The former third-floor ballroom serves as a museum with exhibits of many artifacts of the Harrisons' public and private lives. www.presidentbenjaminharrison.org

- **Susan B. Anthony House National Historic Landmark, Rochester, New York.**   This modest house was the home of the prominent suffragist and contains Anthony's original furnishings and personal photographs. www.susanbanthonyhouse.org/main.html

- **Rutherford B. Hayes Presidential Center, Fremont, Ohio.**   This complex contains President Hayes's home, office, and extensive grounds together with an excellent library and museum holding valuable collections of manuscripts, artifacts, and photographs illustrating his personal interests and political career. www.rbhayes.org

Study Resources

For study resources for this chapter, go to www.myhistorylab.com and choose *The American Journey*. You will find a wealth of study and review material for this chapter, including pre- and post-tests, customized study plan, key term review flash cards, interactive map and document activities, and documents for analysis.

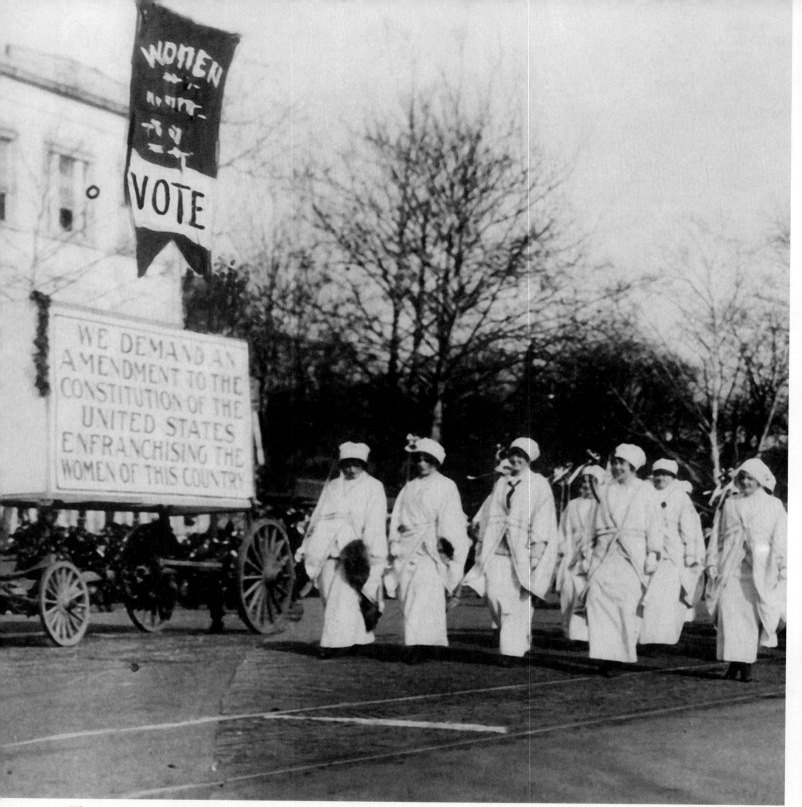

The great woman suffrage parade leaves Capitol Hill and heads for the White House, March 3, 1913. Dramatic tactics and careful organizing like those that marked this parade helped secure reform in the Progressive Era.

The Progressive Era 1900–1917

21

Five thousand women, marching in the woman suffrage pageant yesterday, practically fought their way foot by foot up Pennsylvania avenue, through a surging mass of humanity that completely defied the Washington police, swamped the marchers, and broke their procession into little companies. The women, trudging stoutly along under great difficulties, were able to complete their march only when troops of cavalry from Fort Myer were rushed into Washington to take charge of Pennsylvania avenue. No inauguration has ever produced such scenes, which in many instances amounted to little less than riots....

The parade in itself, in spite of the delays, was a great success....As a spectacle the pageant was entrancing. Beautiful women, posing in classic robes, passed in a bewildering array, presenting an irresistible appeal to the artistic, and completely captivating the hundred thousand spectators....

Miss Margaret Foley, bearing aloft a large "Votes for Women" flag, and Mrs. G. Farquhar, carrying an American flag, led the procession....After the float reading, "We Demand an Amendment to the United States Constitution Enfranchising the Women of This Country," came a body of ushers clad in light blue capes....Two large floats...represented the countries in which women are working for equal rights, followed by a large body of women on foot dressed in street clothes, who bore the banners and pennants of scores of suffrage associations throughout the world....The Homemakers...were dressed in long purple robes over their street clothes. Following them came a float, "In Patriotic Service,"...and

579

traditional partisan politics, reformers adopted new political techniques, including lobbying and demonstrating, as nonpartisan pressure groups. Reform work begun at the local and state levels—where the suffrage movement had already met some success—inexorably moved to the national level as the federal government expanded its authority and became the focus of political interest. Finally, this suffrage demonstration reveals the exceptional diversity of the progressive movement, for the women were marching, in part, against Woodrow Wilson, who had campaigned for the presidency as a progressive.

However, woman suffrage did not define progressivism. Indeed, in a sense, there was no "progressive movement," for progressivism had no unifying organization, central leadership, or consensus on objectives. Instead, it represented the coalescing of different and sometimes even contradictory movements that sought changes in the nation's social, economic, and political life. But reformers did share certain convictions. They believed that industrialization and urbanization had produced serious social disorders, from city slums to corporate abuses. They believed that new ideas and methods were required to correct these problems. In particular, they rejected the ideology of individualism in favor of broader concepts of social responsibility, and they sought to achieve social order through organization and efficiency. Finally, most progressives believed that government itself, as the organized agent of public responsibility, should address social and economic problems.

Other Americans resisted the progressives' plans. The interaction among the reformers and the conflict with their opponents made the two decades before World War I a period of remarkable ferment and excitement. The progressives' achievements, and their failures, profoundly shaped America.

The Ferment of Reform

The diversity of progressivism reflected the diverse impulses of reform. Reformers responded to the tensions of industrialization and urbanization by formulating programs according to their own interests and priorities. Clergy and professors provided new ideas to guide remedial action. Journalists exposed corporate excesses and government corruption and stirred public demand for reform. Business leaders sought to curtail disorder through efficiency and regulation, while industrial workers struggled to improve the horrible conditions in which they worked and lived. Women organized to protect their families and homes from new threats and even to push beyond domestic issues. Nearly every movement for change encountered fierce opposition. But in raising new issues and proposing new ideas, progressives helped America grapple with the problems of industrial society. (See Overview, Major Progressive Organizations and Groups.)

The Context of Reform: Industrial and Urban Tensions

The origins of progressivism lay in the crises of the new urban-industrial order that emerged in the late nineteenth century. The severe depression and mass suffering of the 1890s, the labor violence and industrial armies, the political challenges of Populism and an obviously ineffective government shattered the complacency many middle-class Americans had felt about their nation and made them aware of social and economic inequities that rural and working-class families had long recognized. Many Americans began to question the validity of social Darwinism and the laissez-faire policies that had justified unregulated industrial growth. They began to reconsider the responsibilities of government and, indeed, of themselves for social order and betterment.

By 1900, returning prosperity had eased the threat of major social violence, but the underlying problems intensified. Big business, which had disrupted traditional economic relationships in the late nineteenth century, suddenly became bigger in a series of mergers between 1897 and 1903, resulting in huge new business combinations. The formation in 1901 of the United States Steel Corporation, the world's largest firm, symbolized this development. Such gigantic corporations threatened to squeeze opportunities for small firms and workers, dominate markets, and raise social tensions. They also inspired calls for public control.

Industrial growth affected factory workers most directly. Working conditions were difficult and often dangerous. Most workers still toiled nine to ten hours a day; steelworkers and textile employees worked 12-hour shifts. Wages were minimal; an economist in 1905 calculated that 60 percent of all adult male breadwinners made less than a living wage. Family survival, then, often required women and children to work, often in the lowest paid, most exploited positions. Southern cotton mills employed children as young as 7; coal mines paid 12-year-old slate pickers 39 cents for a ten-hour day. Poor ventilation, dangerous fumes, open machinery, and the absence of safety programs threatened not only workers' health but their lives as well. Such conditions were gruesomely illustrated in 1911, when a fire killed 146 workers, most of them young women, trapped inside the factory of the Triangle Shirtwaist Company in New York because management had locked the exits. The fire chief found "skeletons bending over sewing machines." The United States had the highest rate of industrial accidents in the world. Half a million workers were injured and 30,000 killed at work each year. These terrible conditions cried out for reform.

OVERVIEW

Major Progressive Organizations and Groups

Group	Activity
Social Gospel movement	Urged churches and individuals to apply Christian ethics to social and economic problems
Muckrakers	Exposed business abuses, public corruption, and social evils through investigative journalism
Settlement House movement	Attempted through social work and public advocacy to improve living and working conditions in urban immigrant communities
National Consumers' League (1898)	Monitored businesses to ensure decent working conditions and safe consumer products
Women's Trade Union League (1903)	United workingwomen and their middle-class allies to promote unionization and social reform
National Child Labor Committee (1904)	Campaigned against child labor
Country Life movement	Attempted to modernize rural social and economic conditions according to urban-industrial standards
National American Woman Suffrage Association	Led the movement to give women the right to vote
Municipal reformers	Sought to change the activities and structure of urban government to promote efficiency and control
Conservationists	Favored efficient management and regulation of natural resources rather than uncontrolled development or preservation

Other Americans saw additional social problems in the continuing flood of immigrants who were transforming America's cities. From 1900 to 1917, more than 14 million immigrants entered the United States. Most of the arrivals were so-called new immigrants from southern and eastern Europe, rather than the British, Irish, Germans, and Scandinavians who had arrived earlier. Several hundred thousand Japanese also arrived, primarily in California, as did increasing numbers of Mexicans. Crowding into urban slums, immigrants overwhelmed municipal sanitation, education, and fire protection services. One Russian described his new life as "all filth and sadness."

Many native-born Americans associated the immigrants with rampant urban crime and disease and with city bosses and government corruption. Ethnic prejudices abounded. In 1902 Woodrow Wilson, then president of Princeton University, declared that Italian and Polish immigrants had "neither skill nor energy, nor any initiative or quick intelligence." Americans of the "Old Stock" often considered the predominantly Catholic and Jewish newcomers a threat to social stability and cultural identity and so demanded programs to reform either the urban environment or the immigrants themselves.

Church and Campus

Many groups, drawing from different traditions and inspirations, responded to these economic and social issues. Reform-minded Protestant ministers were especially influential, creating the **Social Gospel movement,** which sought to introduce religious ethics into industrial relations and appealed to churches to meet their social responsibilities. Washington Gladden, a Congregational minister in Columbus, Ohio, was one of the earliest Social Gospelers. Shocked in 1884 by a bloody strike crushed by wealthy members of his own congregation, Gladden began a ministry to working-class neighborhoods that most churches ignored. He endorsed unions and workers' rights and proposed replacing a cruelly competitive wage system with profit sharing.

A more profound exponent of the Social Gospel was Walter Rauschenbusch, a Baptist minister who had served impoverished immigrants in New York's slums. In his book *Christianity and the Social Crisis* (1907), he argued that Christians should support social reform to alleviate poverty, slums, and labor exploitation. He attacked low wages for transforming workers "into lean, sallow, hopeless, stupid, and vicious young people, simply to enable some group of

Overcome with grief, families of the victims of the Triangle Shirtwaist fire later received from the factory owners $75 for each life lost. Still mourning, family members asked, "Justice, what justice?"

stockholders to earn 10 percent." Such ideas were popularized by Charles Sheldon, a Kansas minister, whose book *In His Steps* sold 23 million copies and called on Americans to act in their daily lives as they believed Jesus Christ would in the same circumstances.

The Social Gospel was part of an emerging liberal movement in American religion. Scholars associated with this movement discredited the literal accuracy of the Bible and emphasized instead its general moral and ethical lessons. As modernists, they abandoned theological dogmatism for a greater tolerance of other faiths and became more interested in social problems. Liberal Protestantism had its Jewish and Catholic counterparts in Reform Judaism and liberal Catholicism, but the Social Gospel movement flowered mainly among Episcopalians, Congregationalists, and Methodists. It climaxed in 1908 in the formation of the Federal Council of Churches of Christ in America. The council, representing 33 religious groups, adopted a program that endorsed welfare and regulatory legislation to achieve social justice. By linking reform with religion (as "applied Christianity," in the words of Washington Gladden), the Social Gospel movement gave progressivism a powerful moral drive that affected much of American life.

The Social Gospel movement provided an ethical justification for government intervention to improve the social order. Scholars in the social sciences also gradually helped turn public attitudes in favor of reform by challenging the laissez-faire views of the social Darwinists and traditional academics. In *Applied Sociology* (1906), Lester Ward called for social progress through rational planning and government intervention rather than through unrestrained and unpredictable competition. Economists rejected laissez-faire principles in favor of state action to accomplish social evolution. Industrialization, declared economist Richard T. Ely, "has brought to the front a vast number of social problems whose solution is impossible without the united efforts of church, state, and science."

Muckrakers

Journalists also spread reform ideas by developing a new form of investigative reporting known as **muckraking.** Technological innovations had recently made possible the mass circulation of magazines, and editors competed to attract an expanding urban readership. Samuel S. McClure sent his reporters to uncover political and corporate corruption for *McClure's Magazine.* Sensational exposés sold magazines, and soon *Cosmopolitan, Everybody's,* and other journals began publishing investigations of business abuses, dangerous working conditions, and the miseries of slum life.

Muckraking articles aroused indignant public demands for reform. Lincoln Steffens detailed the corrupt links between "respectable" businessmen and crooked urban politicians in a series of articles called "The Shame of the Cities." Ida Tarbell revealed John D. Rockefeller's sordid construction of Standard Oil. Muckraking novels also appeared. *The Octopus* (1901), by Frank Norris, dramatized the Southern Pacific Railroad's stranglehold on California's farmers, and *The Jungle* (1906), by Upton Sinclair, exposed the nauseating conditions in Chicago's meatpacking industry. Surveying the work of such muckrakers in 1906, one newspaper declared, "The public conscience has been awakened and wrong-doers have been stricken with fear. But henceforth the work of exposing evil must be transformed into a steady-going, constructive effort to prevent it."

The Gospel of Efficiency

Many progressive leaders believed that efficiency and expertise could control or resolve the disorder of industrial society. President Theodore Roosevelt praised the "gospel of efficiency." Like many other progressives, he admired the success of corporations in applying management techniques to guide economic growth. Drawing from science and technology as well as from the model of the corporation, many progressives attempted to manage or direct change efficiently. They used scientific methods to collect extensive data and relied on experts for analysis and recommendations. "Scientific management," a concept often used interchangeably with "sound business management," seemed the key to eliminating waste and inefficiency in government, society, and industry. Rural reformers thought that "scientific agriculture" could bring prosperity to the impoverished southern countryside; urban reformers believed that improvements in medical science and the professionalization of physicians through uniform state-licensing standards could eradicate the cities' wretched health problems.

Business leaders especially advocated efficiency, order, and organization. Industrialists were drawn to the ideas of Frederick Taylor, a proponent of scientific management, for cutting factory labor costs. Taylor proposed to increase worker efficiency through imposed work routines, speedups, and mechanization. Workers, Taylor insisted, should "do what they are told promptly and without asking questions.... It is absolutely necessary for every man in our organization to become one of a train of gear wheels." By assigning workers simple and repetitive tasks on machines, Taylorization made their skills expendable and enabled managers to control the production, pace of work, and hiring and firing of personnel. Stripped of their influence and poorly paid, factory workers shared little of the wealth generated by industrial expansion and scientific management. When labor complained, one business leader declared that unions failed "to appreciate the progressivism of the age."

Sophisticated managers of big business saw some forms of government intervention as another way to promote order and efficiency. In particular, they favored regulations that could bring about safer and more stable conditions in society and the economy. Government regulations, they reasoned, could reassure potential consumers, open markets, mandate working conditions that smaller competitors could not provide, or impose systematic procedures that competitive pressures would otherwise undercut.

Labor Demands Its Rights

Industrial workers with different objectives also hastened the ferment of reform. Workers resisted the new rules of efficiency experts and called for improved wages and working conditions and reduced work hours. They and their middle-class sympathizers sought to achieve some of these goals through state intervention, demanding laws to compensate workers injured on the job, curb child labor, and regulate the employment of women. Sometimes they succeeded. After the Triangle Shirtwaist fire, for example, urban politicians with working-class constituencies created the New York State Factory Commission and enacted dozens of laws dealing with fire hazards, machine safety, and wages and hours for women.

Workers also organized unions to improve their lot. The American Federation of Labor (AFL) claimed 4 million members by 1920, recruiting mainly skilled workers, particularly native-born white males. New unions organized the factories and sweatshops where most immigrants and women worked. Despite strong employer resistance, the International Ladies Garment Workers Union (1900) and the Amalgamated Clothing Workers (1914) or-

ganized the garment trades, developed programs for social and economic reforms, and led their members—mostly young Jewish and Italian women—in spectacular strikes. The "Uprising of the 20,000," a 1909 strike in New York City, included months of massive rallies, determined picketing, and police repression. One observer marveled at the women strikers' "emotional endurance, fearlessness, and entire willingness to face danger and suffering."

A still more radical union tried to organize miners, lumberjacks, and Mexican and Japanese farm workers in the West, black dockworkers in the South, and immigrant factory hands in New England. Founded in 1905, the Industrial Workers of the World (IWW), whose members were known as **"Wobblies,"** used sit-down strikes, sit-ins, and mass rallies, tactics adopted by other industrial unions in the 1930s and the civil rights movement in the 1960s. "Respectable people" considered the Wobblies violent revolutionaries, but most of the violence was committed against IWW members. Private employers and public officials used every method, legal and illegal, to destroy the Wobblies, but broader labor unrest nonetheless stimulated the reform impulse.

Extending the Woman's Sphere

Women reformers and their organizations played a key role in progressivism. Women responded not merely to the human suffering caused by industrialization and urbanization but also to related changes in their own status and role. By the early twentieth century, more women than before were working outside the home—in the factories, mills, and sweatshops of the industrial economy and as clerks in stores and offices. In 1910, more than one-fourth of all workers

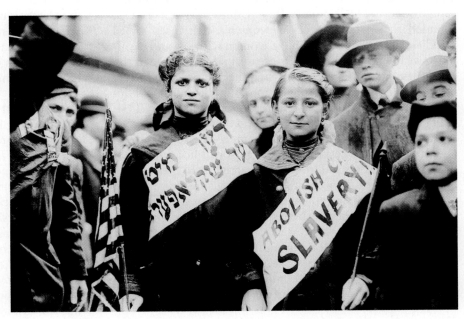

The campaign against child labor attracted passionate support from many Americans. Here two girls, wearing "Abolish Child Slavery" banners in Yiddish and English, participate in a labor parade in New York City on May 1, 1909.

were women, increasing numbers of them married. Their importance in the workforce and participation in unions and strikes challenged assumptions that woman's "natural" role was to be a submissive housewife. Shrinking family size, labor-saving household equipment, and changing social expectations enabled middle-class women to find more time and opportunities to pursue activities outside the home. Better educated than previous generations, they also acquired interests, information, skills, and confidence relevant to a larger public setting.

The women's clubs that had begun multiplying in the late nineteenth century became seed-beds of progressive ideas in the early twentieth century. Often founded for cultural purposes, women's clubs soon adopted programs for social reform and gave their members a route to public influence. In 1914, an officer of the General Federation of Women's Clubs proudly declared that every cause for social reform had "received a helpful hand from the clubwomen."

Women also joined or created other organizations that pushed beyond the limits of traditional domesticity. "Woman's place is in the home," observed one progressive, but "no longer is the home encompassed by four walls." By threatening healthy and happy homes, urban problems required that women become "social housekeepers" in the community. The National Congress of Mothers, organized in 1897, worried about crime and disease and championed kindergartens, foster-home programs, juvenile courts, and compulsory school attendance.

Led by the crusading Florence Kelley, the National Consumers' League, founded in 1898, tried to protect both women wage earners and middle-class housewives by monitoring stores and factories to ensure decent working conditions and safe products. The Women's Trade Union League (WTUL, founded in 1903) united working women and their self-styled middle-class "allies" to unionize women workers and eliminate sweatshop conditions. Its greatest success came in the 1909 garment workers' strike, when the allies assisted strikers with relief funds, bail money, food supplies, and a public-relations campaign. This cooperation, declared one WTUL official, demonstrated the "sisterhood of women."

Although most progressive women stressed women's special duties and responsibilities as social housekeepers, others began to demand women's equal rights. In 1914, for example, critics of New York's policy of dismissing women teachers who married formed a group called the Feminist Alliance and demanded "the removal of all social, political, economic and other discriminations which are based upon sex, and the award of all rights and duties in all fields on the basis of individual capacity alone." With these new organizations and ideas, women gave important impetus and direction to the reform sentiments of the early twentieth century.

Transatlantic Influences

A major source of America's progressive impulse lay outside its borders. European nations were already grappling with many of the problems that stemmed from industrialization and urbanization, and they provided guidance, examples, and possible solutions. Progressive reformers soon learned that America's political, economic, and social structures made it necessary to modify, adapt, or even abandon these imported ideas, but their influence was obvious.

University study in Europe taught Americans the limits of their traditional laissez-faire attitudes and the possibilities of state action. Trained in Germany, the economist Richard T. Ely returned to academic posts in America to teach that government "is the agency through which we must work." International influences were especially strong in the Social Gospel movement, symbolized by William T. Stead, a British social evangelist, whose idea of a "Civic Church" (a partnership of churches and reformers) captured great attention in the United States. Stead himself went to Chicago to promote "a broad and clear social programme," and his book *If Christ Came to Chicago* helped inspire Sheldon's *In His Steps*. Muckrakers not only exposed American problems but looked for foreign solutions. *McClure's* sent Ray Stannard Baker to Europe in 1900 "to see why Germany is making such progress"; *Everybody's* sent Charles E. Russell around the world in 1905 to describe the social advances in Europe and New Zealand. (See Global Perspectives, The New Zealand Way.)

Institutional connections also linked progressives with European reformers. The American Association for Labor Legislation, for example, was formed in 1905 as an offshoot of the International Association for Labor Legislation, founded in 1900 by French, Belgian, and German social economists. By 1912, American consumer activists, trade unionists, factory inspectors, and feminists regularly participated in international conferences on labor legislation, child welfare, social insurance, and housing reform and returned home with new ideas and strategies. State governments organized commissions to analyze European policies and agencies for lessons that might be applicable in the United States.

Socialism

The growing influence of socialist ideas also promoted the spirit of progressivism. Socialism never attracted a large following in the United States, but its criticism of the industrial economy gained increasing attention in the early twentieth century. American socialists condemned social and economic inequities, criticized limited government, and demanded public ownership of railroads, utilities, and communications. They also campaigned for tax reforms, better housing, factory inspections, and recreational facilities for all.

Muckrakers like Lincoln Steffens and Upton Sinclair were committed socialists, as were some Social Gospel ministers and labor leaders, but the most prominent socialist was the dynamic and engaging Eugene V. Debs. An Indiana labor leader who had converted to socialism while imprisoned for his role in the 1894 Pullman strike, Debs had evangelical energy and a generous spirit. He decried what he saw

Global Perspectives

The New Zealand Way

In its very name, the Progressive Era seems characteristically American, but its major developments were actually part of a worldwide phenomenon in which the peoples of many different nations promoted significant reforms, especially through the expansion of government responsibility and power. While Europeans provided an important range of reform ideas and models for Americans, it was often New Zealand, described by one muckraker as the "practical utopia of the South Seas," that "blazed the world's way" in social and economic reforms.

Small, rural, sparsely populated, only slightly industrialized, and still a colony of Great Britain, New Zealand might seem an unlikely candidate to lead progressive reform, but one American minister predicted in 1900 that "we fool Americans will go on for fifty or seventy-five years before we…undertake what they have already achieved in New Zealand." New Zealanders were less driven by a desire to correct the evils of industrialization and urbanization—poverty, sweatshops, slums, labor exploitation, social conflict—than by a determination to prevent their emergence in the first

place. As the charismatic Liberal leader Richard Seddon declared, "If we deal with [these problems] now, the curse of the older countries will never come to New Zealand."

With the election of a Liberal government in 1891, New Zealand launched two decades of reform. It began the serious regulation of working conditions in 1891. In 1894 the General Assembly mandated regular factory inspections and established maximum hours, first for women and then for men, and prohibited child labor in factories. Other laws in the 1890s established minimum wages for women. The Industrial Conciliation and Arbitration Act of 1894 both encouraged unionization and required compulsory arbitration to deal with industrial disputes and assure social peace and progress. A model system of workers' compensation was established in 1901.

New Zealand also pioneered in political and social reform. In 1893 it became the first country to establish woman suffrage in national elections. With one member of the parliament reasoning that "it is the duty of the State to make proper provision for the

aged," New Zealand initiated old age pensions in 1898. Early in the twentieth century it expanded state-funded, rather than contributory, pensions to cover widows with children, injured miners, and other groups. Beginning in 1905, it developed public housing programs, providing first rental housing for low-income families and then government loans for the purchase of homes. The Public Health Act of 1900 initiated a series of laws expanding government responsibility for proper sanitation, safe water, vaccinations, and the regulation of food and drugs.

New Zealand reformers urged the United States to follow the "New Zealand Way" and adopt these and other reforms, and many American progressives did look to that small country for guidance. "If a British colony dares to lead," noted one progressive journalist, "surely it is not visionary to expect our Republic to fall in line."

■ What economic, social, and political factors might explain why progressive reform emerged more slowly and less completely in the United States than in New Zealand?

---

as the dehumanization produced by industrial capitalism and hoped for an egalitarian society where everyone would have the opportunity "to develop the best there is in him for his own good as well as the good of society." Even a critical journalist concluded: "There was more of goodness in him than bubbled up in any other American."

In 1901, Debs helped organize the Socialist Party of America; thereafter, he worked tirelessly to attract followers to a vision of socialism deeply rooted in American political

and religious traditions. In the next decade, the party won many local elections, especially in Wisconsin and New York, where it drew support from German and Russian immigrants, and in Oklahoma, where it attracted poor tenant farmers.

Most progressives considered socialist ideas too drastic. Nevertheless, socialists contributed importantly to the reform ferment, not only by providing support for reform initiatives but often also by prompting progressives to push for changes to undercut increasingly attractive radical alternatives.

their findings, Veiller drafted a new housing code limiting the size of tenements and requiring toilet facilities, ventilation, and fire protection. In 1901, the New York Tenement House Law became a model for other cities. To promote uniform building codes throughout the nation, the tireless Veiller founded the National Housing Association in 1910.

Protective Legislation for Women and Children

While settlement workers initially undertook private efforts to improve society, many reformers eventually concluded that only government intervention could achieve social justice. As Veiller insisted, it was "unquestionably the duty of the state" to enforce justice in the face of "greed on the part of those who desire to secure for themselves an undue profit."

The maiming and killing of children in industrial accidents made it "inevitable," Addams said, "that efforts to secure a child labor law should be our first venture into the field of state legislation." The National Child Labor Committee, organized in 1904, led the campaign to curtail child labor (see Figure 21–1). Reformers documented the problem with extensive investigations and also benefited from the public outrage stirred by socialist John Spargo's muckraking book *The Bitter Cry of the Children* (1906). In 1900, most states had no minimum working age; by 1914, every state but one had such a law. Effective regulation, however, required national action, for many state laws were weak or poorly enforced.

Stiff resistance came from manufacturers who used child labor, conservatives who opposed government action as an intrusion into family life, and some poor parents who needed their children's income. But finally, Congress in 1912 estab-

lished the Children's Bureau to investigate the welfare of children. Julia Lathrop, from Hull House, directed the bureau, the first government agency headed and staffed almost entirely by women. Lathrop and the bureau lobbied Congress and in 1916 saw the passage of the Keating-Owen Act, prohibiting the interstate shipment of goods manufactured by children. The law was weaker than the ones in many states and did not cover most child workers. Even so, the Supreme Court declared the measure unconstitutional.

Social reformers also lobbied for laws regulating the wages, hours, and working conditions of women and succeeded in having states from New York to Oregon pass maximum-hours legislation. After the Supreme Court upheld such laws in *Muller v. Oregon* (1908), 39 states enacted new or stronger laws on women's maximum hours between 1909 and 1917. Fewer states established minimum wages for women. In 1912, Massachusetts created a commission to recommend such wages, and within a year, eight midwestern and western states authorized wage commissions to set binding rates. But few other states followed these examples.

Protective legislation for women posed a troubling issue for reformers. In California, for example, middle-class clubwomen favored protective legislation on the grounds of women's presumed weakness. They wanted to preserve "California's potential motherhood." More radical progressives, as in the socialist-led Women's Trade Union League of Los Angeles, supported such legislation to help secure economic independence and equality in the labor market for women, increase the economic strength of the working class, and serve as a precedent for laws improving conditions for all workers.

Progressive Era lawmakers adopted the first viewpoint. They limited protective legislation to measures reflecting the belief that women needed paternalist protection, even by excluding them from certain occupations. Laws establishing a minimum wage for women, moreover, usually set a wage level below subsistence rates. Rather than assuring women's economic independence, then, protective legislation in practice reinforced women's subordinate place in the labor force.

Protective legislation for male workers scarcely existed. Both lawmakers and judges rebuffed demands for the protection of all workers while approving reforms that endorsed inequality. Only in very dangerous industries did male workers gain much protection, due primarily to the relentless efforts of labor unions. The Western Federation of Miners persuaded several states that the extraordinary occupational hazards of mining—cave-ins, explosions, poisonous gasses, silicosis and other diseases—required laws regulating hours and conditions of work.

Social justice reformers forged the beginnings of the welfare state in further legislation. Prompted by both humanitarian and paternalistic urgings, many states began in 1910 to provide "mothers' pensions" to indigent widows with dependent children. Twenty-one states, led by Wisconsin in 1911, enacted workers' compensation programs, ending the custom of holding workers themselves liable for injuries on the job.

FIGURE 21–1   Child Labor, 1870–1930
Nearly 2 million children worked in factories and fields in 1900, twice as many as in 1870. Progressives' efforts to curtail child labor through laws for compulsory education and a minimum working age encountered resistance, and change came slowly.

Data source: U.S. Bureau of the Census.

Compared to the social insurance programs in western Europe, however, these were feeble responses to the social consequences of industrialization. Proposals for health insurance, unemployment insurance, and old-age pension programs went nowhere. Business groups and other conservative interests curbed the movement toward state responsibility for social welfare.

Reshaping Public Education

Concerns about child labor overlapped with increasing attention to the public schools. The rapid influx of immigrants, as well as the demands of the new corporate workplace, generated interest in education not only as a means of advancement but also as a tool for assimilation and the training of future workers. Middle-class women supported public school reforms. In 1900, for example, women's clubs in North Carolina launched a program to improve school buildings, increase teachers' salaries, and broaden the curriculum. School administrators also pushed for changes, both to upgrade their own profession and to expand their public influence. And some intellectuals predicted that schools themselves could promote social progress and reform. The philosopher John Dewey sketched his plans for progressive education in *The School and Society* (1899).

The famous photographer Lewis Hine used his camera to document child labor. The eleven-year-old boys at this North Carolina textile mill in 1908 earned sixty cents a day.

Between 1880 and 1920, compulsory school attendance laws, kindergartens, age-graded elementary schools, professional training for teachers, vocational education, parent-teacher associations, and school nurses became standard elements in American education. School reformers believed these measures to be both educationally sound and important for countering slum environments. As Jacob Riis contended, the kindergartner would "rediscover...the natural feelings that the tenement had smothered." Others supported the kindergarten as "the earliest opportunity to catch the little Russian, the little Italian, the little German, Pole, Syrian, and the rest and begin to make good American citizens of them." Further socialization came through vocational courses intended to instill discipline in poor students and prepare them to become productive adults.

Public education in the South lagged behind the North. Northern philanthropy and southern reformers brought some improvements after 1900, as per capita expenditures for education doubled, school terms were extended, and high schools spread across the region. But the South frittered away its limited resources on a segregated educational system that shortchanged both races. Black southerners particularly suffered, for the new programs increased the disparity in funding for white and black schools. South Carolina spent 12 times as much per white pupil as per black pupil. Booker T. Washington complained in 1906 that the educational reforms meant "almost nothing so far as the Negro schools are concerned." As a northern critic observed, "To devise a school system which shall save the whites and not the blacks is a task of such delicacy that a few surviving reactionaries are willing to let both perish together."

Racism also underlay important changes in the schooling of Native Americans. The earlier belief that education would promote equality and facilitate assimilation gave way to a conviction that Indians were inferior and fit merely for manual labor. Educators now rejected the notion of a common school education for Indian children in favor of manual training that would enable Indians to fill menial jobs and whites to "turn their attention to more intellectual employments." Educators also renounced the practice of integrating Indian children into previously all-white classrooms, a policy begun in 1891. The superintendent of the Chilocco, Oklahoma, school believed that the new commitment to practical vocational education "solved the Indian problem," but critics noted that limiting Indian children to a rudimentary and segregated education merely doomed them to the margins of American society.

Challenging Gender Restrictions

Most progressives held fairly conservative, moralistic views about sexuality and gender roles. Margaret Sanger, however, radically challenged conventional ideas about the social role of women. Despite great opposition, she initiated the modern birth control movement. A public-health nurse and an IWW organizer, she soon made the struggle for reproductive rights her personal crusade. Sanger saw in New York's immigrant neighborhoods the plight of poor women worn out from repeated pregnancies or injured or dead from self-induced knitting-needle abortions. Despite federal and state laws against contraceptives, Sanger began promoting birth control as a way to avert such tragedies. In 1914, Sanger published a magazine, *Woman Rebel,* in which she argued that "a woman's body belongs to herself alone. It does not belong to the United States of America or any other government on the face of the earth." Prohibiting contraceptives meant "enforced motherhood," Sanger declared. "Women cannot be on an equal footing with men until they have full and complete control over their reproductive function."

Sanger's crusade attracted support from many women's and labor groups, but it also infuriated those who regarded birth control as a threat to the family and morality. Indicted for distributing information about contraception, Sanger fled to Europe. Other women took up the cause, forming the National Birth Control League in 1915 to campaign for the repeal of laws restricting access to contraceptive information and devices. They had little immediate success, but their cause would triumph in later generations.

Reforming Country Life

Although most progressives focused on the city, others sought to reform rural life, both to modernize its social and economic conditions and to integrate it more fully into the larger society. They worked to improve rural health and sanitation, to replace inefficient one-room schools with modern consolidated ones under professional control, and to extend new roads and communication services into the countryside. To further these goals, President Theodore Roosevelt created the Country Life Commission in 1908. The country lifers had a broad program for social and economic change, involving expanded government functions, activist government agencies staffed by experts, and the professionalization of rural social services.

Agricultural scientists, government officials, and many business interests also sought to promote efficient, scientific, and commercial agriculture. A key innovation was the county-agent system: The U.S. Department of Agriculture and business groups placed an agent in each county to teach farmers new techniques and to encourage changes in the rural social values that had previously spawned the Populist radicalism that most progressives decried. Farmers, it was hoped, would acquire materialistic values and learn "economy, order, . . . patriotism, and a score of other wholesome lessons," as one progressive put it in 1910. The Smith-Lever Act (1914) provided federal subsidies for county agents throughout the country.

Few farmers, however, welcomed these efforts. As one Illinois county agent said in 1915, "Farmers, as a whole, resent exceedingly those forces which are at work with missionary intent trying to uplift them." School consolidation meant the loss of community control of education; good roads would raise taxes and chiefly benefit urban business interests. Besides, most farmers believed that their problems stemmed, not from rural life, but from industrial society and its nefarious trusts, banks, and middlemen. Rural Americans did not want their lives revolutionized.

Even so, rural people were drawn into the larger urban-industrial society during the Progressive Era. Government agencies, agricultural colleges, and railroads and banks steadily tied farmers to urban markets. Telephones and rural free delivery of mail lessened countryside isolation but quickened the spread of city values. Improved roads and the coming of the automobile eliminated many rural villages and linked farm families directly with towns and cities. Consolidated schools wiped out the social center of rural neighborhoods and carried children out of their communities, eventually encouraging an ever-growing migration to the city.

Moral Crusades and Social Control

Moral reform movements, although often appearing misguided or unduly coercive today, generally reflected the progressive hope to protect people in a debilitating environment. In practice, however, these efforts to shape society tended toward social control. Morerover, these efforts often meshed with the restrictive attitudes that conservative Americans held about race, religion, immigration, and morality. The result was widespread attempts to restrict certain groups and control behavior.

Controlling immigrants.   Many Americans wanted to limit immigration for racist reasons. Nativist agitation in California prompted the federal government to secure restrictions on Japanese immigration in 1907. Californians, including local progressives, also hoped to curtail the migration of Mexicans. A Stanford University researcher condemned Mexicans as an "undesirable class," and in 1916 the Los Angeles County supervisors urged the federal government to deport Mexican immigrants.

Nationally, public debate focused on restricting the flow of new immigrants from southern and eastern Europe. Some labor leaders believed that immigration held down wages and impeded unionization; many sociologists thought it created serious social problems; other Americans disliked the newcomers on religious, cultural, or ethnic grounds. Many backed their prejudice with a distorted interpretation of Darwinism, labeling the Slavic and Mediterranean peoples "inferior races." As early as 1894, nativists had organized the Immigration Restriction League, which lobbied for a literacy test for admission, sure that it would "bear most heavily upon the Italians, Russians, Poles, Hungarians, Greeks, and Asiatics, and very lightly or not at all upon English-speaking immigrants or Germans, Scandinavians, and French." Congress enacted a literacy law in 1917.

Other nativists demanded the "Americanization" of immigrants already in the country. The Daughters of the American Revolution sought to inculcate loyalty, patriotism, and conservative values. Settlement workers and Social Gospelers promoted a gentler kind of Americanization through English classes and home mission campaigns, but they too attempted to transfer their own values to the newcomers. The most prominent advocate of Americanization was a stereotypical progressive, Frances Kellor. She studied social work at the University of Chicago, worked in New York settlement houses, wrote a muckraking exposé of employment agencies that exploited women, and became director of the New York Bureau of Immigration. In 1915, she helped organize the National Americanization Committee and increasingly emphasized destroying immigrants' old-country ties and imposing an American culture.

Prohibition.   Closely linked to progressives' worries about immigrants was their campaign for **prohibition.** This movement engaged many of the progressives' basic impulses. Social workers saw liquor as a cause of crime, poverty, and family violence; employers blamed it for causing industrial accidents and inefficiency; Social Gospel ministers condemned the "spirit born of hell" because it impaired moral judgment and behavior. But also important was native-born Americans' fear of new immigrants—"the dangerous classes, who are readily dominated by the saloon." Many immigrants, in fact, viewed liquor and the neighborhood saloon as vital parts of daily life, and so prohibition became a focus of nativist hostility, cultural conflict, and Americanization pressures. In the South, racism also figured prominently. Alexander McKelway, the southern secretary for the National Child Labor Committee, endorsed prohibition as a way to maintain social order and white supremacy. McKelway himself drank, but he helped organize the North Carolina Anti-Saloon League to deny alcohol to African Americans, whom he considered naturally "criminal and degenerate."

Protestant fundamentalists also stoutly supported prohibition, working through the Anti-Saloon League, founded in 1893. Their nativism and antiurban bias surfaced in demands for prohibition to prevent the nation's cities from lapsing into "raging mania, disorder, and anarchy." With most urban Catholics and Jews opposing prohibition—the Central Conference of American Rabbis denounced it as "born of fanaticism"—the Anti-Saloon League justified imposing its reform on city populations against their will: "Our nation can only be saved by turning the pure stream of country sentiment...to flush out the cesspools of cities and so save civilization from pollution."

With these varied motivations, prohibitionists campaigned for local and state laws against the manufacture and sale of alcohol. Beginning in 1907, they proved increasingly successful, especially in the South, Midwest, and Far West. By 1917, 26 states had prohibition laws. Congress then approved the **Eighteenth Amendment,** which made prohibition the law of the land by 1920.

Less controversial were drives to control or prohibit narcotics and cigarettes. Patent (over-the-counter) medicines commonly contained opium, heroin, and cocaine (popularly used for hay fever), and physicians known as "dope doctors" openly dispensed drugs to paying customers. Fears that addiction was spreading in "the fallen and lower classes"—and particularly among black people and immigrants—prompted Congress in 1914 to pass the Harrison Act, prohibiting the distribution and use of narcotics for other than medicinal purposes. The Anti-Cigarette League of America, organized in 1899 and having 300,000 members by 1901, led the charge against cigarettes. Aided by educators and physicians worried about the effect of cigarette smoking on mental and physical health and by business leaders concerned with industrial productivity and efficiency, these activists were encouraged when national organizations of Baptists, Methodists, and Presbyterians all condemned smoking in 1909. They persuaded many states to prohibit the manufacture, sale, or use of cigarettes, but such restrictive laws were rarely enforced and often repealed within a few years.

Suppressing prostitution.   Reformers also sought to suppress the "social evil" of prostitution. Like crowded slums, sweatshops, and child labor, the "vice districts" where prostitution flourished were seen as part of the exploitation and disorder in the industrial cities. Women's low wages as factory workers and domestic servants explained some of the problem, as a muckraking article entitled "The Daughters of the Poor" pointed out. But nativism spurred public concern, as when New York officials insisted that most prostitutes and brothel owners, some of whom "have been

The Flanner House, a black settlement house in Indianapolis, provided the black community with many essential services, including health care. In addition to this baby clinic, pictured in 1918, it established a tuberculosis clinic at a time when the city's public hospitals refused to treat black citizens afflicted with the disease.

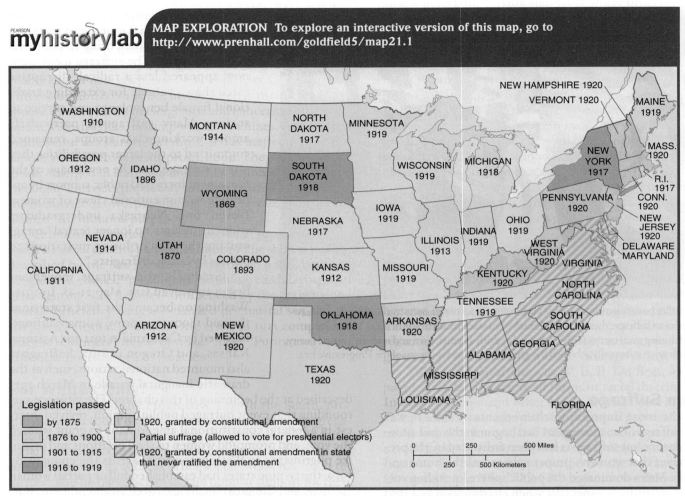

Legislation passed

- by 1875
- 1876 to 1900
- 1901 to 1915
- 1916 to 1919
- 1920, granted by constitutional amendment
- Partial suffrage (allowed to vote for presidential electors)
- 1920, granted by constitutional amendment in state that never ratified the amendment

MAP 21–1   Woman Suffrage in the United States before the Ratification of the Nineteenth Amendment
Beginning with Wyoming in 1869, woman suffrage slowly gained acceptance in the West, but women in the South and much of the
East got the ballot only when the Nineteenth Amendment was ratified in 1920.

These reforms weakened the influence of political parties. Their decreasing ability to mobilize voters was reflected
in a steady decline in voter participation, from 79 percent in
1896 to 49 percent in 1920 (see Figure 20–1). These developments had ominous implications, for parties and voting had
traditionally linked ordinary Americans to their government. As parties slowly contracted, nonpartisan organizations and pressure groups, promoting narrower objectives,
gained influence. Thus the National Association of Manufacturers (1895) and the United States Chamber of Commerce (1912) lobbied for business interests; the National
Farmers Union (1902), for commercial agriculture; the
American Federation of Teachers (1916), for professional
educators. Many of these special-interest groups represented
the same middle- or upper-class interests that had led the attack on parties. Their organized lobbying would steadily
give them greater influence over government and contribute
to the declining popular belief in the value of voting or participation in politics.

Disfranchisement more obviously undermined American democracy. In the South, Democrats—progressive and
conservative alike—eliminated not only black voters but also
many poor white voters from the electorate through poll
taxes, literacy tests, and other restrictions. Republicans in
the North adopted educational or literacy tests in ten states,
enacted strict registration laws, and gradually abolished the
right of aliens to vote. These restrictions reflected both the
progressives' anti-immigrant prejudices and their obsessions
with social control and with purifying politics and "improving" the electorate. Such electoral reforms reduced the political power of ethnic and working-class Americans, often
stripping them of their political rights and means of influence.

Municipal Reform
Antiparty attitudes also affected progressives' efforts to reform municipal government, which they regarded as inefficient and corrupt, at least partly because of the power of urban
political machines. Muckrakers had exposed crooked alliances

between city bosses and business leaders that resulted in wasteful or inadequate municipal services. In some cities, urban reformers attempted to break these alliances and improve conditions for those suffering most from municipal misrule. For example, in Toledo, Ohio, Samuel "Golden Rule" Jones won enough working-class votes to be elected mayor four times despite the hostility of both major parties. Serving from 1897 to 1904, Jones opened public playgrounds and kindergartens, established the eight-hour day for city workers, and improved public services. Influenced by the Social Gospel, he also provided free lodging for the homeless and gave his own salary to the poor. Other reforming mayors fought municipal corruption, limited the political influence of corporations, and championed public ownership of utilities.

More elitist progressives attempted to change the structure of urban government by replacing ward elections, which could be controlled by the neighborhood-based city machine, with at-large elections. To win citywide elections required greater resources and therefore helped swell middle-class influence at the expense of the working class. So did nonpartisan elections, which reformers introduced to weaken party loyalties.

Urban reformers developed two other structural innovations: the city commission and the city manager. Both attempted to institutionalize efficient, businesslike government staffed by professional administrators. By 1920, hundreds of cities had adopted one of the new plans, which business groups often promoted. In Des Moines, for example, the president of the Commercial Club declared that "the professional politician must be ousted and in his place capable businessmen chosen to conduct the affairs of the city." Again, then, reform often shifted political power from ethnic and working-class voters, represented however imperfectly by partisan elections, to smaller groups with greater resources.

Progressive State Government

Progressives also reshaped state government. Some tried to democratize the legislative process, regarding the legislature—the most important branch of state government in the nineteenth century—as ineffective and even corrupt, dominated by party bosses and corporate influences. The Missouri legislature reportedly "enacted such laws as the corporations paid for, and such others as were necessary to fool the people." Populists had first raised such charges in the 1890s and proposed two novel solutions. The **initiative** enabled reformers to propose legislation directly to the electorate, bypassing an unresponsive legislature; the **referendum** permitted voters to approve or reject legislative measures. South Dakota Populists established the first system of "direct legislation" in 1898, and progressives adopted these innovations in 20 other states between 1902 and 1915.

Conservative opponents and procedural difficulties, however, often blocked these reforms or turned them against progressives. In the state of Washington in 1914, an initiative to establish an eight-hour workday was defeated by an electorate alarmed by conservative propaganda, and organized labor had to fight seven referendum measures, such as an antipicketing law, that business interests had promoted.

Other innovations also expanded the popular role in state government. The **Seventeenth Amendment,** ratified in 1913, provided for the election of U.S. senators directly by popular vote instead of by state legislatures. Beginning with Oregon in 1908, ten states adopted the **recall,** enabling voters to remove unsatisfactory public officials from office.

As state legislatures and party machines were curbed, dynamic governors such as Robert La Follette in Wisconsin, Charles Evans Hughes in New York, and Hiram Johnson in California pushed progressive programs into law. Elected governor in 1900, "Fighting Bob" La Follette turned Wisconsin into "the laboratory of democracy." Overcoming fierce opposition from "stalwart" Republicans, La Follette established direct primaries, railroad regulation, the first state income tax, workers' compensation, and other important measures before being elected to the U.S. Senate in 1906. La Follette also stressed efficiency and expertise. The Legislative Reference Bureau that he created to advise on public policy was staffed by university professors. He used regulatory commissions to oversee railroads, banks, and other interests. Most states followed suit, and expert commissions became an important feature of state government, gradually gaining authority at the expense of elected local officials.

"Experts" were presumed to be disinterested and therefore committed to the general welfare. In practice, however, regulators were subject to pressures from competing interest groups, and some commissions became captives of the very industries they were supposed to control. This irony was matched by the contradiction between the expansion of democracy through the initiative and referendum and the increasing reliance on nonelected professional experts to set and implement public policy. Such inconsistencies emphasize the complex mixture of ideas, objectives, and groups that were reshaping politics and government.

Theodore Roosevelt and the Progressive Presidency

When an anarchist assassinated William McKinley in 1901, Theodore Roosevelt entered the White House, and the progressive movement gained its most prominent leader. The son of a wealthy New York family, Roosevelt had pursued a career in Republican politics, serving as a New York legislator, U.S. civil service commissioner, and assistant secretary of the navy. After his exploits in the Spanish-American War (see chapter 22), he was elected governor of New York in 1898 and vice president in 1900. His public life was matched by an active private life, in which he both wrote works of history and obsessively pursued what he called the "strenuous life":

MAP EXPLORATION To explore an interactive version of this map, go to
http://www.prenhall.com/goldfield5/map21.2

MAP 21–2   The Growth of Federal Reserves, Including Leading National Parks and National Forests
Rapid exploitation of the West prompted demands to preserve its spectacular scenery and protect its remaining forests. In 1872 Yellowstone became the first National Park, and the National Forest system began in the 1890s. Conservation became increasingly important during the Progressive Era but often provoked Western hostility.

Supreme Court ordered the dissolution of the Northern Securities Company. Ultimately, Roosevelt brought 44 antitrust suits against business combinations, but except for a few like Standard Oil, he avoided the giant firms. Many of the cases had inconclusive outcomes, but Roosevelt was more interested in establishing a regulatory role for government than in breaking up big businesses.

Elected president in his own right in 1904 over the colorless and conservative Democratic candidate, Judge Alton B. Parker, Roosevelt responded to the growing popular demand for reform by pushing further toward a regulatory government. He proposed legislation "to work out methods of controlling the big corporations without paralyzing

the energies of the business community." In 1906, Congress passed the Hepburn Act, the Pure Food and Drug Act, and the Meat Inspection Act. All three were compromises between reformers seeking serious government control of the industries involved and political defenders and lobbyists of the industries themselves.

The Hepburn Act authorized the Interstate Commerce Commission to set maximum railroad rates. Although a weaker law than many progressives had wanted, it marked the first time the federal government gained the power to set rules for a private enterprise. The two other laws aimed at consumer protection in food and drugs. In part, this legislation reflected public demand, but many business leaders also supported government regulation, convinced that it would expand their markets by certifying the quality of their products and drive their smaller competitors out of business. Thus the laws extended government supervision and regulation over business to protect the public health and safety, but they also served some corporate purposes.

Despite the compromises and weaknesses in the three laws, TR contended that they marked "a noteworthy advance in the policy of securing federal supervision and control over corporations." In 1907 and 1908, he pushed for an eight-hour workday, stock market regulation, and inheritance and income taxes. Republican conservatives in Congress blocked such reforms, and tensions increased between the progressive and conservative wings of the party. Old Guard Republicans thought Roosevelt had extended government powers dangerously, but in fact his accomplishments had been relatively modest because of his need to compromise in Congress. As La Follette noted, Roosevelt's "cannonading filled the air with noise and smoke, which confused and obscured the line of action, but, when the battle cloud drifted by and the quiet was restored, it was always a matter of surprise that so little had really been accomplished."

Taft and the Insurgents

TR handpicked his successor as president: a loyal lieutenant, William Howard Taft. Taft had been a federal judge, governor-general of the Philippines, and secretary of war. Later he would serve as chief justice of the United States. But if Roosevelt thought that Taft would be a successful president, continuing his policies and holding the Republican Party together, he was wrong. Taft's election in 1908, over Democrat William Jennings Bryan in his third presidential campaign, led to a Republican political disaster.

Taft did preside over important progressive achievements. His administration pursued a more active and successful antitrust program than Roosevelt's. He supported the Mann-Elkins Act (1910), which extended the ICC's jurisdiction to telephone and telegraph companies. Taft set aside more public forest lands and oil reserves than Roosevelt had. He also supported a constitutional amendment authorizing an income tax, which went into effect in 1913 under the **Sixteenth Amendment.** One of the most important accomplishments of the Progressive Era, the income tax would provide the means for the government to expand its activities and responsibilities.

Nevertheless, Taft soon alienated progressives and floundered into a political morass. His problems were twofold. First, the Republicans were divided. Midwestern reform Republicans, led by La Follette, clashed with conservative Republicans, led by Senator Nelson Aldrich of Rhode Island. Second, Taft was politically inept. Even his wife complained of his "unfortunate shortcoming of not knowing much and of caring less about the way the game of politics is played." He was unable to mediate between the two Republican factions, and the party split apart.

Reformers wanted to restrict the power of the speaker of the House, "Uncle Joe" Cannon, a reactionary who systematically blocked progressive measures and loudly declared, "I am goddamned tired of listening to all this babble of reform." After seeming to promise support, Taft backed down when conservatives threatened to defeat important legislation. The insurgents in Congress eventually restricted the speaker's powers, but they never forgave what they saw as Taft's betrayal. The tariff also alienated progressives from Taft. He had campaigned in 1908 for a lower tariff to curb inflation—and to the approval of midwestern Republicans. But when they introduced tariff reform legislation, the president failed to support them, and Aldrich's Senate committee added 847 amendments, many of which raised tariff rates. Taft justified his inaction as avoiding presidential interference with congressional business, but this position clashed with TR's example and the reformers' expectations. Progressives concluded that Taft had sided with the Old Guard against real change.

This perception solidified when Taft stumbled into a controversy over conservation. Gifford Pinchot had become embroiled in a complex struggle with Richard Ballinger, Taft's secretary of the interior. Ballinger, who was closely tied to western mining and lumbering interests, favored private development of public lands. When Pinchot challenged Ballinger's role in a questionable sale of public coal lands in Alaska to a J. P. Morgan syndicate, Taft upheld Ballinger and fired Pinchot. Progressives concluded that Taft had repudiated Roosevelt's conservation policies.

The Progressives determined to replace Taft, whom they now saw as an obstacle to reform. In 1911, the National Progressive League organized to champion La Follette for the Republican nomination in 1912. Roosevelt rejected an appeal for support, convinced that a challenge to the incumbent president was both doomed and divisive. Besides, his own position was closer to Taft's than to what he called "the La Follette type of fool radicalism." But Taft's political blunders increasingly angered Roosevelt. Condemning Taft as "disloyal to our past friendship," TR began to campaign for the Republican nomination himself. In 13 state primaries, he won 278 delegates, to only 46 for Taft. But most states did not then have primaries; as a result, Taft was able to dominate the Republican convention and win renomination. Roosevelt's forces formed a third party—the Progressive Party—and nominated the former president. The Republican split almost guaranteed victory for the Democratic nominee, Woodrow Wilson.

Woodrow Wilson and Progressive Reform

The pressures for reform called forth many new leaders. The one who would preside over progressivism's culmination, and ultimately its collapse, was Woodrow Wilson. Elected president in 1912 and 1916, he mediated among differing progres-

A portrait of Woodrow Wilson by Edward Charles Tarbell. A strong president, Wilson led Congress to enact sweeping and significant legislation.

quarreled during Taft's administration, Democrats pushed progressive remedies and achieved major victories in the state and congressional elections of 1910. To improve the party's chances in 1912, Bryan announced that he would step aside. The Democratic spotlight shifted to the governor of New Jersey, Woodrow Wilson.

Wilson combined public eloquence with a cold personality; he balanced a self-righteousness that led to stubborn inflexibility with an intense ambition that permitted the most expedient compromises. Wilson first entered public life as a conservative, steeped in the limited-government traditions of his native South. As president of Princeton University, beginning in 1902, he became a prominent representative of middle-class respectability and conservative causes. In 1910, New Jersey's Democratic bosses selected him for governor to head off the progressives, but once in office, Wilson championed popular reforms and immediately began to campaign as a progressive for the party's 1912 presidential nomination.

Wilson's progressivism differed from that of Roosevelt in 1912. TR emphasized a strong government to promote economic and social order. He defended big business as inevitable and healthy provided that government control ensured that it would benefit the entire nation. Roosevelt called this program the **New Nationalism,** reflecting his belief in a powerful state and a national interest. He also supported demands for social welfare, including workers' compensation and the abolition of child labor.

Wilson was horrified by Roosevelt's vision. His **New Freedom** program rejected what he called TR's "regulated monopoly." Wilson wanted "regulated competition," with the goverment's role limited to breaking up monopolies through antitrust action and preventing artificial barriers like tariffs from blocking free enterprise. Wilson opposed social welfare legislation as paternalistic, reaching beyond the proper scope of the federal government, which he hoped to minimize. (This position, shot back the alarmed Roosevelt, meant the repeal of "every law for the promotion of social and industrial justice.")

Roosevelt's endorsement of social legislation attracted many women into political action. As Jane Addams observed, "their long concern for the human wreckage of industry has come to be considered politics." (See American Views, Jane

sive views to achieve a strong reform program, enlarge the power of the executive branch, and make the White House the center of national politics.

The Election of 1912

Despite the prominence of Roosevelt and La Follette, progressivism was not simply a Republican phenomenon. In Congress, southern Democrats more consistently supported reform measures than Republicans did, and the Democratic leader William Jennings Bryan surpassed Roosevelt as a persistent advocate of significant reform. As the Republicans

American Views

Jane Addams and the Progressive Party

Jane Addams, the founder of Hull House in Chicago, was active not merely in a range of social reform movements but also in nearly every facet of progressive politics. An ardent suffragist, Addams seconded the presidential nomination of Theodore Roosevelt at the founding convention of the Progressive Party in 1912, while a "Jane Addams Chorus" sang "Onward, Christian Soldiers" and "The Battle Hymn of the Republic." In this reminiscence from her second autobiography, Addams describes the convention and her part in the party's campaign that year.

■ Why did settlement workers like Addams see the Progressive Party as the climax to their struggle for social justice?

■ How did Addams's political interests fit into Roosevelt's program of the New Nationalism?

■ How does Addams's rhetoric reflect the moral impulses underlying much of progressive reform?

■ Why does Addams believe that women were attracted to the Progressive Party?

It was in August, 1912, that the Progressive Party was organized.

Suddenly, as if by magic, the city of Chicago became filled with men and women from every state in the Union who were evidently haunted by the same social compunctions and animated by like hopes; they revealed to each other mutual sympathies and memories. They urged methods which had already been tried in other countries, for righting old wrongs and for establishing standards in industry. For three days together they defined their purposes and harmonized their wills into gigantic cooperation....

They believed that the program of social legislation placed before the country by the Progressive Party was of great significance to the average voter quite irrespective of the party which might finally claim his allegiance.

The platform, in the hope that the political organization of the nation might never again get so far away from the life of the people, advocated equal suffrage, direct primaries, the initiative and referendum.... In spite of our belief in our leader [Theodore Roosevelt], I was there, and I think the same was true of many others, because the platform expressed the social hopes so long ignored by the politicians; although we appreciated to the full our good fortune in securing on their behalf the magnetic personality of the distinguished candidate. Perhaps we felt so keenly the uplifting sense of comradeship with old friends and coworkers not only because we had all realized how inadequate we were in small groups but because the very sentiments of compassion and desire for social justice were futile unless they could at last find ex-

pression as an integral part of...government. At any rate, it was evident that measures of industrial amelioration and demands for social justice, so long discussed by small groups, were at last thrust into the stern arena of political action....

The Progressive Convention has been described many times, and perhaps never quite adequately. It was a curious moment of release from inhibitions, and it did not seem in the least strange that reticent men and women should speak aloud of their religious and social beliefs, confident that they would be understood.

The women who identified themselves with the Progressive Convention inevitably experienced moments of heart searching and compunction. It is hard to understand it now, after we have possessed the ballot for a decade and have come to deem it a virtue "to enter politics," but at the moment we felt it necessary to give to the public our reasons for thus identifying ourselves with a political party. We said that when a great party pledges itself to the protection of children, to the care of the aged, to the relief of overworked girls, to the safeguarding of burdened men, it is inevitable that it should appeal to women and should seek to draw upon the great reservoir of their moral energy so long undesired and unutilized in practical politics; that one is the corollary of the other; a program of human welfare, the necessity for women's participation.

The real interest in the measures advocated in the party platform came however during the campaign itself when it was possible to place them before many groups throughout the country. Sometimes the planks in our platform were sharply challenged, but more often regarded with approval and occasionally with enthusiasm. I recall a meeting in Leadville, Colorado, made up altogether of miners who were much surprised to find that politics had anything to do with such affairs. They had always supposed that hours of labor were matters to be fought for and not voted upon. It was very exhilarating to talk to them, and it seemed to me that I had never before realized how slow we had been to place the definite interests of the workingmen in such shape that they could be voted upon. As a campaign speaker I was sent from town to town in both Dakotas, in Iowa, Nebraska, Oklahoma, Colorado, Kansas, and Missouri. The comrade-

ship which a like-minded group always affords, combined with the heartiness of western good will, kept my spirits at high tide in spite of the fatigue of incessant speaking....

The campaign renewed one's convictions that if the community as a whole were better informed as to the ethical implications of industrial wrongs whole areas of life could be saved from becoming brutalized or from sinking into hard indifference....At moments we believed that we were witnessing a new pioneering of the human spirit, that we were in all humility inaugurating an exploration into the moral resources of our fellow citizens.

Source: Jane Addams, *The Second Twenty Years at Hull-House* (New York: Macmillan, 1930).

Addams and the Progressive Party.) The Progressive Party also endorsed woman suffrage, accepted women as convention delegates, and pledged to give women equal representation on party committees. The *New York Times* exaggerated in claiming that the 1912 campaign had become "feminized," but certainly women activists welcomed the opportunity of participating "in party affairs before the vote is won" and thereby "answering forcibly many of the objections to the vote" for women.

Despite his personal popularity, however, TR was unable to add progressive Democrats to the Republicans who followed him into the Progressive Party, and thus was doomed to defeat. Other reform voters embraced the Socialist candidate, Eugene V. Debs, who captured 900,000 votes—6 percent of the total. Taft played little role in the campaign. "I might as well give up as far as being a candidate," he lamented. "There are so many people in the country who don't like me."

Wilson won an easy electoral college victory, though he received only 42 percent of the popular vote and fewer popular votes than Bryan had won in any of his three campaigns (see Map 21–3). Roosevelt came in second, Taft third. The Democrats also gained control of Congress, giving Wilson the opportunity to enact his New Freedom program.

Implementing the New Freedom

As president, Wilson built on Roosevelt's precedent to strengthen executive authority. He proposed a full legislative program and worked forcefully to secure its approval. He held regular conferences with Democratic leaders and had a private telephone line installed between the Capitol and the White House to keep tabs on congressional actions. When necessary, he appealed to the public for support, ruth-

lessly used patronage, or compromised with conservatives. With such methods and a solid Democratic majority, Wilson gained approval of important laws.

Wilson turned first to the traditional Democratic goal of reducing the high protective tariff, the symbol of special privileges for industry. He forced through the **Underwood-Simmons Tariff Act** of 1913, the first substantial reduction in duties since before the Civil War. The act also levied the first income tax under the recently ratified Sixteenth Amendment. Conservatives condemned the "revolutionary" tax, but it was designed simply to compensate for lower tariff rates. The top tax rate paid by the wealthiest was a mere 7 percent.

Wilson next reformed the nation's banking and currency system, which was inadequate for a modernizing economy. A panic in 1907 and a subsequent congressional investigation had dramatized the need for a more flexible and decentralized financial system. Wilson skillfully maneuvered a compromise measure through Congress, balancing the demands of agrarian progressives for government control with the bankers' desires for private control. The **Federal Reserve Act** of 1913 created 12 regional Federal Reserve banks that, although privately controlled, were to be supervised by the Federal Reserve Board, appointed by the president. The law also provided for a flexible national currency and improved access to credit. Serious problems remained, but the new system promoted the progressive goals of order and efficiency and fulfilled Wilson's New Freedom principle of introducing limited government regulation while preserving private business control.

Wilson's third objective was new legislation to break up monopolies. Initially, he supported the Clayton antitrust bill, which prohibited unfair trade practices and sharply restricted holding companies. But when business leaders and other progressives strenuously objected, Wilson reversed himself.

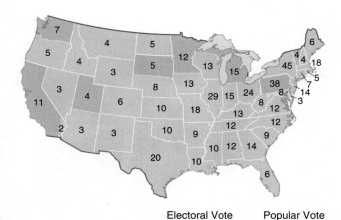

	Electoral Vote (%)	Popular Vote (%)
WOODROW WILSON (Democrat)	**435** **(82)**	**6,296,547** **(42)**
Theodore Roosevelt (Progressive)	88 (17)	4,118,571 (27)
William Taft (Republican)	8 (1)	3,486,720 (23)
Eugene Debs (Socialist)	–	900,672 (6)

MAP 21-3   The Election of 1912
The split within the Republican Party enabled Woodrow Wilson to carry most states and become president even though he won only a minority of the popular vote.

Opting for continuous federal regulation rather than for the dissolution of trusts, Wilson endorsed the creation of the **Federal Trade Commission (FTC)** to oversee business activity and prevent illegal restrictions on competition.

The Federal Trade Commission Act of 1914 dismayed many of Wilson's early supporters because it embraced the New Nationalism's emphasis on positive regulation. Roosevelt's 1912 platform had proposed a federal trade commission; Wilson now accepted what he had earlier denounced as a partnership between trusts and the government that the trusts would dominate. Indeed, Wilson's conservative appointments to the FTC ensured that the agency would not seriously interfere with business, and by the 1920s, the FTC had become virtually a junior partner of the business community.

The fate of the Clayton antitrust bill after Wilson withdrew his support reflected his new attitude toward big business. Congressional conservatives gutted the bill with crippling amendments before permitting it to become law in 1914. As one senator complained, "When the Clayton bill was first written, it was a raging lion with a mouth full of teeth. It has degenerated to a tabby cat with soft gums, a plaintive mew, and an anemic appearance. It is a sort of legislative apology to the trusts, delivered hat in hand, and accompanied by assurances that no discourtesy is intended."

These measures indicate the limited nature of Wilson's vision of reform. In fact, he now announced that no further reforms were necessary—astonishing many progressives whose objectives had been completely ignored. Wilson refused to support woman suffrage and helped kill legislation abolishing child labor and expanding credits to farmers. Race relations provided a flagrant instance of Wilson's indifference to issues of social justice. Raised in the South, he believed in segregation and backed the southern Democrats in his cabinet when they introduced formal segregation within the government itself. Government offices, shops, restrooms, and restaurants were all segregated; employees who complained were fired. Federal officials in the South discharged black employees. One Georgia official promised that there would be no more government jobs for African Americans: "A Negro's place is in the cornfield."

The Expansion of Reform

Wilson had won in 1912 only because the Republicans had split. By 1916, Roosevelt had returned to the GOP, and Wilson realized that he had to attract some of TR's former followers. Wilson therefore abandoned his opposition to social and economic reforms and promoted measures he had previously condemned. But he had also grown in the White House and now recognized that some problems could be resolved only by positive federal action.

To assist farmers, Wilson in 1916 convinced Congress to pass the Federal Farm Loan Act. This law, which Wilson himself had earlier rejected twice, provided farmers with federally financed long-term agricultural credits. The Warehouse Act of 1916 improved short-term agricultural credit. The Highway Act of 1916 provided funds to construct and improve rural roads through the adoption of the dollar-matching principle by which the federal government would expand its power over state activities in the twentieth century.

Wilson and the Democratic Congress also reached out to labor. Wilson signed the Keating-Owen Act prohibiting the interstate shipment of products made by child labor. In 1902, Wilson had denounced Roosevelt's intervention in the coal strike, but in 1916 he broke a labor-management impasse and averted a railroad strike by helping pass the Adamson Act establishing an eight-hour day for railroad workers. Wilson also pushed the Kern-McGillicuddy Act, which achieved the progressive goal of a workers' compensation system for federal employees. Together, these laws marked an important advance toward government regulation of the labor market.

Wilson also promoted activist government when he nominated Louis Brandeis to the Supreme Court. Known as "the people's lawyer," Brandeis had successfully defended protective labor legislation before the conservative judiciary. The nomination outraged conservatives, including William Howard Taft and the American Bar Association. Brandeis was the first Jew nominated to the court, and anti-Semitism motivated some of his opponents. Wilson overcame a vicious campaign against Brandeis and secured his confirmation.

FROM THEN TO NOW

The Environmental Movement

Many of the issues that concern environmentalists today were first raised by the conservationists and preservationists of the Progressive Era. Led by Theodore Roosevelt, conservationists favored the planned and regulated management of America's natural resources for the public benefit. In contrast, preservationists—like John Muir, who founded the Sierra Club in 1892—sought to protect wilderness from any development whatsoever. Opposing both were those who championed the uncontrolled development of public lands.

Decades later, public concern over polluted rivers, oil spills, and urban smog gave birth to the environmental movement, which drew on the legacy of both the conservation and preservation movements but had wider interests and broader support than either. Beginning in the 1970s, Congress passed laws to protect endangered species, reduce pollution, limit the use of pesticides, and control hazardous waste. The Environmental Protection Agency became the largest federal regulatory agency.

Again, however, as during the Progressive Era, efforts to protect the environment encountered opposition from proponents of unrestricted development, especially in the West. In the Sagebrush Rebellion in the 1980s, some Westerners condemned "outside" federal regulation and tried to seize control of public lands for private exploitation. One oil company dismissed catastrophic oil spills as merely "Mother Earth letting some oil come out." And four Republican presidents from the West—Californians Richard Nixon and Ronald Reagan and Texans George Bush and George W. Bush, all closely tied to oil and real estate interests—sought in varying degrees to curtail environmental policies, agencies, and budgets, even to deny the existence of global warming, and to oppose environmental protection as inconsistent with economic growth. This repudiation of Theodore Roosevelt's conservationism reflected the shift of the party's base to the sunbelt. As one presidential adviser said, "Conservation is not in the Republican ethic."

Congress, the courts, and the public, however, generally resisted efforts to weaken environmental policy. Debate is sure to continue over the cost and effectiveness of specific policies, but Americans are increasingly inclined to stand with Theodore Roosevelt and John Muir in looking to the federal government for effective action to resolve environmental problems.

■ How do differing economic and political attitudes underlie the conflicting stances of Americans toward environmental issues?

Former Vice President Al Gore won the Nobel Peace Prize for helping direct attention to the dangers of global warming.

Theodore Roosevelt and John Muir, here on a 1903 camping trip in Yosemite, championed public responsibility for the nation's scenic and other natural resources.

myhistorylab
PEARSON

From Then to Now Online

21-1 Gifford Pinchot, *The Fight for Conservation,* 1910. The man who coined the tern "conservation" defends the movement it describes.

21-2 George L. Knapp, *The Other Side of Conservation,* 1910. A publicist for the opponents of conservation attacks the movement.

By these actions, Wilson brought progressivism to a culmination of sorts and consolidated reformers behind him for a second term. Less than a decade earlier, Wilson the private citizen had assailed government regulation and social legislation; by 1916, he had guided an unprecedented expansion of federal power. His own transformation symbolized the development of progressivism.

Conclusion

In the early twentieth century, progressive reformers responded to the tensions of industrial and urban development by moving to change society and government. Rejecting the earlier emphasis on individualism and laissez-faire, they organized to promote social change and an interventionist state. Programs and laws to protect women, children, and injured workers testified to their compassion; the creation of new agencies and political techniques indicated their interest in order and efficiency; campaigns to end corruption, whether perceived in urban political machines, corporate influence, drunkeness, or "inferior" immigrants, illustrated their self-assured vision of the public good.

Progressivism had its ironies and paradoxes. It called for democratic reforms—and did achieve woman suffrage, direct legislation, and popular election of senators—but helped disfranchise black southerners and northern immigrants. It advocated social justice but often enforced social control. It demanded responsive government but helped create bureaucracies largely removed from popular control. It endorsed the regulation of business in the public interest but forged regulatory laws and commissions that tended to aid business. Some of these seeming contradictions reflected the persistence of traditional attitudes and the need to accommodate conservative opponents; others revealed the progressives' own limitations in vision, concern, or nerve.

Nonetheless, both the successes and the failures of progressivism revealed that the nature of politics and government had changed significantly. Americans had come to accept that government action could resolve social and economic problems, and the role and power of government expanded accordingly. The emergence of an activist presidency, capable of developing programs, mobilizing public opinion, directing Congress, and taking forceful action, epitomized this key development.

These important features would be crucial when the nation fought World War I, which brought new challenges and dangers to the United States. The Great War would expose many of the limitations of progressivism and the naiveté of the progressives' optimism.

Review Questions

1. How and why did the presidency change during the Progressive Era?

2. How did the progressive concern for efficiency affect social reform efforts, public education, government administration, and rural life?

3. How and why did the relationship between business and government change during this time?

4. Why did social reform and social control often intermingle in the Progressive Era? Can such objectives be separate?

5. What factors, old and new, stimulated the reform movements of progressivism?

6. How did the role of women change during the Progressive Era? How did the changes affect progressivism?

7. Why did the demand for woman suffrage provoke such determined support and such bitter opposition, as illustrated by the 1913 parade and riot in Washington, DC?

Key Terms

Australian ballot (p. 595)
Bureau of Reclamation (p. 599)
Conservation (p. 599)
Eighteenth Amendment (p. 593)
Federal Reserve Act (p. 604)
Federal Trade Commission (p. 605)
Fundamentalists (p. 588)
Initiative (p. 597)

Muckraking (p. 584)
New Freedom (p. 602)
New Nationalism (p. 602)
Niagara Movement (p. 594)
Nineteenth Amendment (p. 595)
Preservation (p. 599)
Progressive Era (p. 581)
Prohibition (p. 593)

Recall (p. 597)
Referendum (p. 597)
Seventeenth Amendment (p. 597)
Sixteenth Amendment (p. 601)
Social Gospel Movement (p. 583)
Underwood-Simmons Tariff Act (p. 604)
Wobblies (p. 585)

Recommended Reading

Addams, Jane. *Twenty Years at Hull House* (1910). Jane Addams's own classic story of settlement work.

Baker, Jean H. *Votes for Women* (2002). A valuable collection of essays illuminating themes, activities, and leaders of the woman suffrage movement.

Diner, Steven J. *A Very Different Age: Americans of the Progressive Era* (1998). An engaging survey of the era, stressing social history.

Flanagan, Maureen. *America Reformed: Progressives and Progressivisms* (2007). A valuable new study examining key progressive ideas and how they were implemented in public policy.

Gould, Lewis L. *The Presidency of Theodore Roosevelt* (1991). A balanced and comprehensive account of TR's presidency.

Wiebe, Robert. *The Search for Order, 1877–1920* (1967). A masterful essay that emphasizes the organizational thrust of middle-class progressives.

Where to Learn More

- **John Muir National Historic Site, Martinez, California.**   The architecture and furnishings of this 17-room house reflect the interests of John Muir, the writer and naturalist who founded the Sierra Club and led the preservationists in the Progressive Era. www.nps.gov/jomu

- **Sewall-Belmont House National Historic Site, Washington, DC.**   Headquarters of the National Woman's Party, this 200-year-old house on Capitol Hill has memorabilia of the woman suffrage movement, including posters, flags, and photographs of the early marches, and an extensive feminist library focused on the struggle for equal suffrage. Beginning in 1923 Alice Paul campaigned from this building for the Equal Rights Amendment. http://www.sewallbelmont.org

- **Hull House, Chicago, Illinois.**   This pioneering settlement house is now a museum on the campus of the University of Illinois, Chicago. www.uic.edu/jaddams/hull/hull_house.html

- **Lower East Side Tenement Museum, New York City, New York.**   A six-story tenement building containing 22 apartments, this museum vividly illustrates the congested and unhealthy living conditions of urban immigrants from the 1870s to the early twentieth century. See www.tenement.org for a virtual tour.

Study Resources

PEARSON
myhistorylab

For study resources for this chapter, go to www.myhistorylab.com and choose *The American Journey*. You will find a wealth of study and review material for this chapter, including pre- and post-tests, customized study plan, key term review flash cards, interactive map and document activities, and documents for analysis.

A jubilant Uncle Sam celebrates victory in the Spanish-American War and anticipates the building of an American empire.

Creating an Empire 22
1865–1917

Havana, Cuba October 1901

When the Spanish-American war was declared the United States . . . assumed a position as protector of the interests of Cuba. It became responsible for the welfare of the people, politically, mentally, and morally. The mere fact of freeing the island from Spanish rule has not ended the care which this country should give. . . . The effect will be to uplift the people, gaining their permanent friendship and support and greatly increasing our own commerce. At present there are two million people requiring clothing and food, for but a small proportion of the necessaries of life are raised on the island. It is folly to grow food crops when sugar and tobacco produce such rich revenues in comparison. The United States should supply the Cubans with their breadstuffs, even wine, fruit, and vegetables, and should clothe the people. . . . The money received for their crops will be turned over in a great measure in buying supplies from the United States. . . .

Naturally the manufacturers of the United States should have precedence in furnishing machinery, locomotives, cars, and rails, materials for buildings and bridges, and the wide diversity of other supplies required, as well as fuel for their furnaces. With the present financial and commercial uncertainty at an end the people of the island will . . . come into the American market as customers for products of many kinds.

The meeting of the Constitutional Convention on November 5th will be an event in Cuban history of the greatest importance, and much will depend upon the

611

action and outcome of this convention as to our future control of the island. . . . I considered it unwise to interfere, and I have made it a settled policy to permit the Cubans to manage every part of their constitution-making. This has been due to my desire to prevent any possible charge of crimination being brought against the United States in the direction of their constitutional affairs. . . .

There is no distrust of the United States on the part of the Cubans, and I know of no widespread antipathy to this country, its people, or its institutions. There are, of course, a handful of malcontents, as there must be in every country. . . .

I could not well conceive how the Cubans could be otherwise than grateful to the United States for its efforts in their behalf. . . . In the brief time since the occupation of the island by American troops the island has been completely rehabilitated—agriculturally, commercially, financially, educationally, and governmentally. This improvement has been so rapid and so apparent that no Cuban could mistake it. To doubt in the face of these facts that their liberators were not still their faithful friends would be impossible.

Major-General Leonard Wood, "The Future of Cuba," *The Independent* 54 (January 23, 1902): 193–194; idem, "The Cuban Convention," *The Independent* 52 (November 1, 1900): 265–266.

myhistorylab

Personal Journeys Online

- ■ Josiah Strong, *Our Country*, 1885. An appeal for Anglo-Saxon imperialism by an American minister.

- ■ Charles Denby, *Shall We Keep the Philippines?*, 1898. An argument for an economic empire by an American diplomat.

- ■ Vincent F. Howard, *Imperialism*, 1900. A poem denouncing the imperialist journey.

General Leonard Wood's reports on Cuba, then under his control as military governor, captured the complex mixture of attitudes and motives that underlay the journey of the United States from a developing nation to a world power. Plans for economic expansion, a belief in national mission, a sense of responsibility to help others, scarcely hidden religious impulses and racist convictions—all combined in an uneasy mixture of self-interest and idealism.

Wood himself had taken a symbolic journey in American expansionism. His earlier career had been on the American southwestern frontier with the troops chasing the Apache under Geronimo, but in 1898 he and Theodore Roosevelt organized the Rough Riders cavalry to participate in the Spanish-American War in Cuba. As Wood wrote on a transport ship headed for that Spanish colony: "[T]his is the first great expedition our country has sent overseas and marks the commencement of a new era in our relations with the world." Upon Spain's surrender, Cuba came under United States military occupation, and Wood was appointed military governor of the island.

Wood's support for the war was reflected in his activities as a colonial administrator. Convinced of the superiority of American institutions, he favored their expansion.

The United States had a responsibility, he believed, to uplift those less able. But expansion would promote American interests as well. Thus, Wood brought improved sanitation, schools, and transportation to Cuba, but he instituted these reforms through an authoritarian government and regarded Cubans as backward and incapable of self-government. And at the same time, he expected that American business interests would "naturally" be the beneficiaries of his reorganization of Cuban life. Thus, Wood combined changes that satisfied paternalistic or humanitarian instincts with attempts to incorporate Cuba into America's new commercial empire, fulfilling the traditional colonial role of providing raw materials and serving as a market for American products and capital.

The tension between what a friend of his called the "righteous" and the "selfish" aspects of expanding American influence lay beneath the surface in Wood's reports. His claim that he was not interfering with Cuba's constitutional convention was disingenuous, for he had already undertaken to limit those who could participate as voters or delegates and was even then devising means to restrict the convention's autonomy. And in his repeated insistence that the Cubans were grateful for the intervention of "their faithful friends," the Americans, Wood obviously protested too much: Cubans, as well as Filipinos, Puerto Ricans, and others, rarely perceived American motives or American actions as positively as did Wood and other proponents of American expansion. Victory in the Spanish-American War had provided the United States with an extensive empire, status as a world power, and opportunities and problems that would long shape U.S. foreign policy.

CHRONOLOGY

1861–1869	Seward serves as secretary of state.
1867	United States purchases Alaska from Russia.
1870	Annexation of the Dominican Republic is rejected.
1879	France conquers Algeria.
1881	Naval Advisory Board is created.
1882	Great Britain occupies Egypt.
1887	United States gains naval rights to Pearl Harbor.
1890	Alfred Thayer Mahan publishes *The Influence of Sea Power upon History*.
1893	Harrison signs but Cleveland rejects a treaty for the annexation of Hawaii.
1893–1897	Depression increases interest in economic expansion abroad.
1894–1895	Sino-Japanese War is fought.
1895	United States intervenes in Great Britain–Venezuelan boundary dispute.
	Cuban insurrection against Spain begins.
1896	William McKinley is elected president on an imperialist platform.
1898	Spanish-American War is fought.
	Hawaii is annexed.
	Anti-Imperialist League is organized.
	Treaty of Paris is signed.
1899–1902	Filipino-American War is fought.
1899	Open Door note is issued.
1900	Boxer Rebellion against foreign influence breaks out in China.
1901	Theodore Roosevelt becomes president.
1903	Platt Amendment restricts Cuban autonomy.
	Panama "revolution" is abetted by the United States.
1904	United States acquires the Panama Canal Zone.
	Roosevelt Corollary is announced.
1904–1905	Russo-Japanese War is fought.
1905	Treaty of Portsmouth ends the Russo-Japanese War through U.S. mediation.
1906–1909	United States occupies Cuba.
1907–1908	Gentlemen's Agreement restricts Japanese immigration.
1909	United States intervenes in Nicaragua.
1912–1933	United States occupies Nicaragua.
1914	Panama Canal opens.
1914–1917	United States intervenes in Mexico.
1915–1934	United States occupies Haiti.
1916–1924	United States occupies the Dominican Republic.
1917	Puerto Ricans are granted U.S. citizenship.
1917–1922	United States occupies Cuba.

The Roots of Imperialism

The United States had a long-established tradition of expansion across the continent. Through purchase, negotiation, or conquest, the vast Louisiana Territory, Florida, Texas, New Mexico, California, and Oregon had become U.S. territory. Indeed, by the 1890s, Republican Senator Henry Cabot Lodge of Massachusetts boasted that Americans had "a record of conquest, colonization, and territorial expansion unequalled by any people in the nineteenth century." Lodge now urged the country to build an overseas empire, emulating the European model of **imperialism** based on the acquisition and exploitation of colonial possessions. Other Americans favored a less formal empire, in which United States interests and influence would be ensured through extensive trade and investments rather than through military occupation. Still others advocated a cultural expansionism in which the nation exported its ideals and institutions. All such expansionists could draw from many sources to support their plans. Some cited political, religious, and racial ideas; some were concerned about national security and power; others pointed to economic trends at home and abroad (see Overview, Rationales for Imperialism).

Ideological and Religious Arguments

Scholars, authors, politicians, and religious leaders provided interlocking ideological arguments for the new imperialism. Some intellectuals, for example, invoked social Darwinism, maintaining that the United States should engage in a competitive struggle for wealth and power with other nations. "The survival of the fittest," declared one writer, was "the law of nations as well as a law of nature." As European nations expanded into Asia and Africa in the 1880s and 1890s, seeking colonies, markets, and raw materials, these advocates argued, the United States had to adopt similar policies to ensure national success.

Related to social Darwinism was a pervasive belief in racial inequality and in the superiority of people of English, or Anglo-Saxon, descent. To many Americans, the industrial progress, military strength, and political development of England and the United States were proof of an Anglo-Saxon superiority that carried with it a responsibility to extend the blessings of their rule to less able people. John Fiske, a philosopher and historian, popularized these ideas in his oft-repeated lecture "Manifest Destiny." "The work which the English race began when it colonized North America," Fiske declaimed, "is destined to go on until every land on the earth's surface that is not already the seat of an old civilization shall become English in its language, in its religion, in its political habits and traditions, and to a predominant extent in the blood of its people." As a popular expression put it, colonialism was the "white man's burden," carrying with it a duty to aid and uplift other peoples. Such attitudes led some expansionists to favor imposing American ideas and practices on other cultures regardless of their own values and customs.

The political scientist John W. Burgess, for example, concluded that Anglo-Saxons "must have a colonial policy" and "righteously assume sovereignty" over "incompetent" or "barbaric races" in other lands.

Reflecting this aggressiveness, as well as Darwinian anxieties, some Americans endorsed expansion as consistent with their ideals of masculinity. Forceful expansion would be a manly course, relying upon and building strength and honor among American males. Men who confronted the challenges of empire would thereby improve their ability to compete in the international arena. "Pride of race, courage, manliness," predicted one enthusiast, would be both the causes and the consequences of an assertive foreign policy.

American missionaries also promoted expansionist sentiment. Hoping to evangelize the world, American religious groups increased the number of Protestant foreign missions sixfold from 1870 to 1900. Women in particular organized foreign missionary societies and served in the missions. Missionaries publicized their activities throughout the United States, generating interest in foreign developments and support for what one writer called the "imperialism of righteousness." Abroad they pursued a religious transformation that often resembled a cultural conversion, for they promoted trade, developed business interests, and encouraged westernization through technology and education as well as religion. Sometimes, as in the Hawaiian Islands, American missionaries even promoted annexation by the United States.

Indeed, the American religious press endlessly repeated the themes of national destiny, racial superiority, and religious zeal. The Reverend J. H. Barrows in early 1898 lectured on the "Christian conquest of Asia," suggesting that American Christianity and commerce would cross the Pacific to fulfill "the manifest destiny of the Christian Republic." Missionaries contributed to the imperial impulse by describing their work, as Barrows did, in terms of the conquest of enemy territory. Thus, while missionaries were motivated by what they considered to be idealism and often brought real benefits to other lands, especially in education and health, religious sentiments reinforced the ideology of American expansion.

Strategic Concerns

Other expansionists were motivated by strategic concerns, shaped by what they saw as the forces of history and geography. America's location in the Western Hemisphere, its coastlines on two oceans, and the ambitions and activities of other nations, particularly Germany and Britain, convinced some Americans that the United States had to develop new policies to protect and promote its national security and interests. Alfred Thayer Mahan, a naval officer and president of the Naval War College, emphasized the importance of a strong navy for national greatness in his book *The Influence of Sea Power upon History*. To complement the navy, Mahan proposed that the United States build a canal across the isthmus of Panama to link its coasts, acquire naval bases in the

OVERVIEW

Rationales for Imperialism

Category	Beliefs
Racism and Social Darwinism	The conviction that Anglo-Saxons were racially superior and should dominate other peoples, either to ensure national success, establish international stability, or benefit the "inferior" races by imposing American ideas and institutions on them
Righteousness	The conviction that Christianity, and a supporting American culture, should be aggressively spread among the benighted peoples of other lands
Mahanism	The conviction, following the ideas advanced by Alfred Thayer Mahan, that U.S. security required a strong navy and economic and territorial expansion
Economics	A variety of arguments holding that American prosperity depended on acquiring access to foreign markets, raw materials, and investment opportunities

Caribbean and the Pacific to protect the canal, and annex Hawaii and other Pacific islands to promote trade and service the fleet. The United States must "cast aside the policy of isolation which befitted her infancy," Mahan declared, and "begin to look outward."

Mahanism found a receptive audience. President Benjamin Harrison declared in 1891 that "as to naval stations and points of influence, we must look forward to a departure from the too conservative opinions which have been held heretofore." Still more vocal advocates of Mahan's program were a group of nationalistic Republicans, predominantly from the Northeast. They included politicians like Henry Cabot Lodge and Theodore Roosevelt, journalists like Whitelaw Reid and Albert Shaw, and diplomats and lawyers like John Hay and Elihu Root.

Conscious of European colonialism, these men favored imperial expansion, as Shaw wrote, "for the sake of our destiny, our dignity, our influence, and our usefulness." Roosevelt promoted Mahan's ideas when he became assistant secretary of the navy in 1897, but he was even more militaristic. Praising "the most valuable of all qualities, the soldierly virtues," Roosevelt declared in 1897: "No triumph of peace is quite so great as the supreme triumphs of war." One British observer concluded on the eve of the Spanish-American War that Mahan's influence had served "as oil to the flame of 'colonial expansion' everywhere leaping into life" (see American Views, An Imperialist Views the World).

Even so, Mahan was not solely responsible for the large-navy policy popular among imperialists. Its origins went back to 1881, when Congress established the Naval Advisory Board, which successfully lobbied for larger naval appropriations. An extensive program to replace the navy's obsolete wooden ships with modern cruisers and battleships was well under way by 1890, when Mahan's book appeared. The United States soon possessed the formidable navy the expansionists wanted. This larger navy, in turn, demanded strategic bases and coaling stations. One writer indicated the circular nature of this development by noting in 1893 that Manifest Destiny now meant "the acquisition of such territory, far and near," as would secure "to our navy facilities desirable for the operations of a great naval power."

Economic Designs

One reason for the widespread support for a larger navy was its use to expand and protect America's international trade. Nearly all Americans favored economic expansion through foreign trade. Such a policy promised national prosperity: more markets for manufacturers and farmers, greater profits for merchants and bankers, more jobs for workers. Far fewer favored the acquisition of colonies that was characteristic of European imperialism. (See Global Perspectives, European Colonial Imperialism.) Commercial as opposed to colonial goals were the primary objective. As one diplomat declared in 1890, the nation was more interested in the "annexation of trade" than in the annexation of territory.

The United States had long aggressively fostered American trade, especially in Latin America and East Asia. As early as 1844, the United States had negotiated a trade treaty with China, and ten years later a squadron under Commodore Matthew Perry had forced the Japanese to open their ports to American products. In the late nineteenth century, the dramatic expansion of the economy caused many Americans to favor more government action to open foreign markets to American exports. Alabama Senator John Morgan had the cotton and textiles produced in the New South in mind when he warned in 1882: "Our home market is not equal to the demands of our producing and manufacturing classes and to the capital which is seeking employment.... We must either enlarge the field of our traffic, or stop the business of manufacturing just where it is." More ominous, a naval officer trying to open Korea to U.S. products declared in 1878, "At least one-third of our mechanical and agricultural products are now in excess of our wants, and we must *export* these products or *deport* the people who are creating them."

Emily Hartwell, an American missionary, and her Chinese converts ("Bible Women") in the Foochow Mission in 1902. American missionaries wanted to spread the Gospel abroad but inevitably spread American influence as well. Hartwell used the ethnocentric and militant rhetoric of the imperialism of righteousness in appealing to Americans for money and prayers for her "picket duty on the very outskirts of the army of the Lord."

Exports, especially of manufactured goods, which grew ninefold between 1865 and 1900, did increase greatly in the late nineteenth century. Still, periodic depressions fed the fears of overproduction. The massive unemployment and social unrest that accompanied these economic crises also provided social and political arguments for economic relief through foreign trade.

In the depression of the 1890s, with the secretary of state seeing "symptoms of revolution" in the Pullman strike and Coxey's Army of unemployed workers (see Chapter 20), the interest in foreign trade became obsessive. More systematic government efforts to promote trade seemed necessary, a conclusion strengthened by new threats to existing American markets. In that tumultuous decade, European nations raised tariff barriers against American products, and Japan and the European imperial powers began to restrict commercial opportunities in the areas of China that they controlled. Many American leaders decided that the United States had to adopt decisive new policies or face economic catastrophe.

First Steps

Despite the growing ideological, strategic, and economic arguments for imperialism, the government only fitfully interested itself in foreign affairs before the mid-1890s. It did not pursue a policy of isolationism from international affairs, for the nation maintained normal diplomatic and trade ties and at times vigorously intervened in Latin America and East Asia. But in general the government deferred to the initiative of private interests, reacted haphazardly to outside events,

and did little to create a professional foreign service. In a few bold if inconsistent steps, however, the United States moved to expand its influence.

Seward and Blaine

Two secretaries of state, William H. Seward, secretary under Presidents Abraham Lincoln and Andrew Johnson (1861–1869), and James G. Blaine, secretary under Presidents James Garfield and Benjamin Harrison (1881, 1889–1892), laid the foundation for a larger and more aggressive U.S. role in world affairs. Seward possessed an elaborate imperial vision, based on his understanding of commercial opportunities, strategic necessities, and national destiny. His interest in opening East Asia to American commerce and establishing American hegemony over the Caribbean anticipated the subsequent course of American expansion. Seward purchased Alaska from Russia in 1867, approved the navy's occupation of the Midway Islands in the Pacific, pushed American trade on a reluctant Japan, and repeatedly tried to acquire Caribbean naval bases (see Map 22–1). His policy of expansion, however, as one observer noted, "went somewhat too far and too fast for the public," and many of his plans fizzled. Congressional opposition frustrated his efforts to obtain Haiti and the Dominican Republic and to purchase the Danish West Indies; Colombia blocked his attempt to gain construction rights for a canal across the isthmus of Panama.

Blaine was an equally vigorous, if inconsistent, advocate of expansion. He worked to extend what he called America's "commercial empire" in the Pacific. And he sought to ensure U.S. sovereignty over any canal in Panama, insisting that it be "a purely American waterway to be treated as part of our own coastline." In an effort to induce Latin American nations to import manufactured products from the United States rather than Europe, Blaine proposed a customs union to reduce trade barriers, expecting it to strengthen U.S. control of hemispheric markets. Wary of economic subordination to the colossus of the north, however, the Latin American nations rejected Blaine's plan but did agree to establish what eventually came to be known as the **Pan American Union.** Based in Washington, it helped to promote hemispheric understanding and cooperation.

If U.S. officials were increasingly assertive toward Latin America and Asia, however, they remained little involved in Europe (one secretary of state declared in 1885 that he had no interest in European affairs, which he regarded "with impatience and contempt"). They were wholly indifferent to Africa, which the European powers were then carving up into colonies. In short, despite some important precedents

American Views

An Imperialist Views the World

Theodore Roosevelt, Henry Cabot Lodge, Alfred Thayer Mahan, and other influential imperialists frequently corresponded with one another, expressing their views forcefully if not always in depth. The following excerpts are from Roosevelt's private letters to Lodge and Mahan in 1897, while he was assistant secretary of the navy and before the Spanish-American War.

- In what ways does Roosevelt reflect the influence of Mahan?
- What is Roosevelt's view of war?
- How does Roosevelt view European nations?
- How does he view the independence of other nations in the Western Hemisphere?

I suppose that I need not tell you that as regards Hawaii I take your views absolutely, as indeed I do on foreign policy generally. If I had my way we would annex those islands tomorrow. If that is impossible I would establish a protectorate over them. I believe we should build the Nicaraguan canal at once, and in the meantime that we should build a dozen new battleships, half of them on the Pacific Coast; and these battleships should have a large coal capacity and a consequent increased radius of action....I think President Cleveland's action [in rejecting the annexation of Hawaii] was a colossal crime, and we should be guilty of aiding him after the fact if we do not reverse what he did. I earnestly hope we can make the President [McKinley] look at things our way. Last Saturday night Lodge pressed his views upon him with all his strength.

I agree with all you say as to what will be the result if we fail to take Hawaii. It will show that we either have lost, or else wholly lack, the masterful instinct which alone can make a race great. I feel so deeply about it I hardly dare express myself in full. The terrible part is to see that it is the men of education who take the lead in trying to make us prove traitors to our race.

I fully realize the importance of the Pacific coast....But there are big problems in the West Indies also. Until we definitely turn Spain out of those islands (and if I had my way that would be done tomorrow), we will always be menaced by trouble there. We should acquire the Danish Islands [in the West Indies], and by turning Spain out should serve notice that no strong European power, and especially not Germany, should be allowed to gain a foothold by supplanting some weak European power. I do not fear England; Canada is a hostage for her good behavior.

I wish we had a perfectly consistent foreign policy, and that this policy was that every European power should be driven out of America, and every foot of American soil, including the nearest islands in both the Pacific and the Atlantic, should be in the hands of independent American states, and so far as possible in the possession of the United States or under its protection.

To speak with a frankness which our timid friends would call brutal, I would regard a war with Spain from two standpoints: first, the advisability on the grounds both of humanity and self-interest of interfering on behalf of the Cubans, and of taking one more step toward the complete freeing of America from European dominion; second, the benefit done our people by giving them something to think of which isn't material gain, and especially the benefit done our military forces by trying both the Navy and the Army in actual practice. I should be very sorry not to see us make the experiment of trying to land, and therefore feed and clothe, an expeditionary force [on Cuba], if only for the sake of learning from our own blunders. I should hope that the force would have some fighting to do. It would be a great lesson, and we would profit much by it.

I wish there was a chance that the [U.S. battleship] Maine was going to be used against some foreign power; by preference Germany—but I am not particular, and I'd take even Spain if nothing better offered.

Source: Reprinted by permission of the publisher from *The Letters of Theodore Roosevelt*, Vol. I 1868–1898, selected and edited by Elting E. Morison (Cambridge, MA: Harvard University Press, 1951)

COASTING.
The old horse was too slow for Uncle Sam.

As other imperial powers look on, the United States abandons its traditional principles to rush headlong into world affairs. Uncle Sam would not always find it a smooth ride.

powers." Most Democrats believed that "the mission of our nation is to build up and make a greater country out of what we have, instead of annexing islands." The Hawaiian episode of 1893 thus foreshadowed the arguments over imperialism at the end of the century and emphasized the policy differences between Democrats and the increasingly expansionist Republicans.

Chile and Venezuela

American reactions to developments in other countries in the 1890s also reflected an increasingly assertive national policy and excitable public opinion. In 1891, American sailors on shore leave in Chile became involved in a drunken brawl that left two of them dead, 17 injured, and dozens in jail. Encouraged by a combative navy, President Harrison threatened military retaliation against Chile, provoking an outburst of bellicose nationalism in the United States. Harrison relented only when Chile apologized and paid an indemnity.

A few years later, the United States again threatened war over a minor issue but against a more formidable opponent. Although opposed to annexing Hawaii, President Cleveland adopted an increasingly aggressive policy in Latin America. In 1895, he intervened in a boundary dispute between Great Britain and Venezuela over British Guiana. Cleveland was motivated not only by the long-standing U.S. goal of challenging Britain for Latin American markets but also by ever

more expansive notions of the Monroe Doctrine and the authority of the United States. Secretary of State Richard Olney sent Britain a blunt note (a "twenty-inch gun," Cleveland called it) demanding arbitration of the disputed territory and stoutly asserting American supremacy in the Western Hemisphere. Cleveland urged Congress to establish a commission to determine the boundary and enforce its decision by war if necessary. The astonished British ambassador reported an "extraordinary state of excitement into which the Congress of the United States and the whole country were thrown by the warlike Message . . . a condition of mind which can only be described as hysterical." As war fever swept the United States, Britain agreed to arbitration, recognizing the limited nature of the issue that so convulsed Anglo-American relations.

Cleveland's assertion of U.S. hemispheric dominance angered Latin Americans, and their fears deepened when the United States decided arbitration terms with Britain without consulting Venezuela, which protested before bowing to American pressure. The United States had intervened less to protect Venezuela from the British bully than to advance its own hegemony. The further significance of the Venezuelan crisis, Captain Mahan noted, lay in its "awakening of our countrymen to the fact that we must come out of our isolation . . . and take our share in the turmoil of the world."

The Spanish-American War

The forces pushing the United States toward imperialism and international power came to a head in the Spanish-American War. Cuba's quest for independence from the oppressive colonial control of Spain activated Americans' long-standing interest in the island. Many sympathized with the Cuban rebels' yearning for freedom, others worried that disorder in Cuba threatened their own economic and political interests, and some thought that intervention would increase the influence of the United States in the Caribbean and along key Pacific routes to Asian markets. But few foresaw that the war that finally erupted in 1898 would dramatically change U.S. relationships with the rest of the world and give the United States a colonial empire.

The Cuban Revolution

The last major European colony in Latin America, Cuba held an economic potential that attracted American business interests and a strategic significance for any Central American canal. In the late nineteenth century, American investors expanded their economic influence in Cuba, while Cubans themselves rebelled repeatedly but unsuccessfully against increasingly harsh Spanish rule. Cuban discontent erupted again in 1895, when the Cuban patriot José Martí launched another revolt.

The rebellion was a classic guerrilla war, with the rebels controlling the countryside and the Spanish army the towns and cities. American economic interests were seriously affected, for both Cubans and Spaniards destroyed American property and disrupted American trade. The Cleveland administration, motivated as much by a desire to protect American property and establish a safe environment for further investments as by a concern for Cuban rights, urged Spain to adopt reforms. But the brutality with which Spain attempted to suppress the revolt promoted American sympathy for the Cuban insurgents. Determined to cut the rebels off from their peasant supporters, the Spanish herded most civilians into "reconcentration camps," where tens of thousands died of starvation and disease.

American sympathy was further aroused by the sensationalist **yellow press.** To attract readers and boost advertising revenues, the popular press of the day adopted bold headlines, fevered editorials, and real or exaggerated stories of violence, sex, and corruption. A circulation war between William Randolph Hearst's *New York Journal* and Joseph Pulitzer's *New York World* helped stimulate interest in Cuban war. "Blood on the roadsides, blood on the fields, blood on the doorsteps, blood, blood, blood! The old, the young, the weak, the crippled—all are butchered without mercy," the *World* feverishly reported of Cuba. "Is there no nation wise enough, brave enough to aid this blood-smitten land?" Failure to intervene to protect the innocent from Spanish lust and cruelty, insisted the yellow journalists, would be dishonorable and cowardly.

The nation's religious press, partly because it reflected the prejudice of many Protestants against Catholic Spain, also advocated American intervention. One religious newspaper endorsed an American war against Spain as God's instrument for attacking "that system of iniquity, the papacy." Another promised that if war came, "every Methodist preacher will be a recruiting officer" for the military. The *Catholic Herald* of New York sarcastically referred to the "bloodthirsty preachers" of the Protestant churches, but such preachers undeniably influenced American opinion against Spain.

As the Cuban rebellion dragged on, more and more Americans advocated intervention to stop the carnage, protect U.S. investments, or uphold various principles. Expansionists like Roosevelt and Lodge clamored for intervention, but so did their opponents. Populists, for example, sympathized with a people seeking independence from colonial rule and petitioned Congress to support the crusade for Cuban freedom; conservative Democrats hoped that the excitement of intervention and war "might do much towards directing the minds of the people from imaginary ills, the relief of which is erroneously supposed to be reached by 'Free Silver.'" In the election of 1896, both major parties endorsed Cuban independence.

Growing Tensions

In his 1897 inaugural address, President William McKinley outlined an expansionist program ranging from further enlargement of the navy to the annexation of Hawaii and the construction of a Central American canal in Nicaragua, but his administration soon focused on Cuba. McKinley's principal complaint was that chronic disorder in Cuba disrupted American investments and agitated public opinion. Personally opposed to military intervention, McKinley first used diplomacy to press Spain to adopt reforms that would settle the rebellion. Following his instructions, the U.S. minister to Spain warned the Spanish government that if it did not quickly establish peace, the United States would take whatever steps it "should deem necessary to procure this result." In late 1897, Spain modified its brutal military tactics and offered limited autonomy to Cuba. But Cubans insisted on complete independence, a demand that Spain refused to grant.

Relations between the United States and Spain deteriorated. In early 1898, the *New York Journal* published a private letter from a Spanish diplomat that mocked McKinley as "weak and a bidder for the admiration of the crowd." (The *Journal* called the letter "the worst insult to the United States in its history.") McKinley found more troubling the letter's intimation that Spain was not negotiating in good faith. Only days later, on February 15, 1898, the U.S. battleship *Maine* blew up in Havana harbor, killing 260 men. The Spanish were not responsible for the tragedy, which a modern naval inquiry has attributed to an internal accident. But many Americans agreed with Theodore Roosevelt, the assistant secretary of the navy, who called it "an act of dirty treachery on the part of the Spaniards" and told McKinley that only war was "compatible with our national honor." Others demanded war, in the words of an Illinois politician, "if we would uphold our manhood." Thus understandings of appropriate male conduct also influenced decisions as to how the nation should act.

Popular anger was inflamed, but the sinking of the *Maine* by itself did not bring war, though it did restrict McKinley's options and pressure him to be more assertive toward Spain. One newspaper expressed its hope to see "any signs, however faint, of manhood in the White House." Other pressures soon began to build on the president. Increasingly, business interests favored war as less disruptive than a volatile peace that threatened their investments. Senator Lodge reported a consensus "that this situation must end. We cannot go on indefinitely with this strain, this suspense, and this uncertainty, this tottering upon the verge of war. It is killing to business." Further, McKinley feared that a moderate policy would endanger Republican congressional candidates. Again Senator Lodge, although hesitant to suggest "war for political reasons," nevertheless advised McKinley, "If the war in Cuba drags on through the summer with nothing done, we shall go down in the greatest [election] defeat ever known."

At the end of March 1898 (when the French ambassador in Washington reported that "a sort of bellicose fury has seized the American nation"), McKinley sent Spain an ultimatum. He demanded an armistice in Cuba, an end to the reconcentration policy, and the acceptance of American arbitration, which implied Cuban independence. Desperately, it time to call all missionaries home and have them work on our own people."

Other Americans also denounced the war. The Anti-Imperialist League revived, citing the war as proof of the corrosive influence of imperialism on the nation's morals and principles. Women figured prominently in mass meetings and lobbying efforts to have the troops returned, their moral stature further undercutting the rationale for colonial wars. By 1902, the realities of imperial policy—including American casualties far exceeding those of the Spanish-American War—disillusioned most of those who had clamored to save Cuba.

By that time, however, the American military had largely suppressed the rebellion, and the United States had established a colonial government headed by an American governor general appointed by the president. Filipino involvement in the government was limited on educational and religious grounds. Compared to the brutal war policies, U.S. colonial rule was relatively benign, though paternalistic. William Howard Taft, the first governor general, launched a program that brought the islands new schools and roads, a public health system, and an economy tied closely to both the United States and a small Filipino elite. Independence would take nearly half a century.

China and the Open Door

America's determined involvement in the Philippines reflected its preoccupation with China. By the mid-1890s, other powers threatened prospects for American commercial expansion in China. Japan, after defeating China in 1895, annexed Formosa (Taiwan) and secured economic privileges in the mainland province of Fukien (Fujian); the major European powers then competed aggressively to claim other areas of China as their own **spheres of influence.** In Manchuria, Russia won control of Port Arthur (Lüshun) and the right to construct a railway. Germany obtained a 99-year lease on another Chinese port and mining and railroad privileges on the Shantung (Shandong) Peninsula. The British wrung special concessions in Kowloon, opposite Hong Kong, and in other Chinese provinces, as well as a port facing the Russians in Manchuria. France gained a lease on ports and exclusive commercial privileges in southern China.

These developments alarmed the American business community. It was confident that, given an equal opportunity, the United States would prevail in international trade because of its efficient production and marketing systems. But the creation of exclusive spheres of influence limited the opportunity to compete. In early 1898, business leaders organized the Committee on American Interests in China to lobby Washington to promote American trade in the shrinking Chinese market. The committee persuaded the nation's chambers of commerce to petition the McKinley administration to act. This campaign influenced McKinley's interest in acquiring the Philippines, but the Philippines, in the words of Mark Hanna, were only a "foothold";

China was the real target. The State Department soon reported that, given overproduction for the home market, "the United States has important interests at stake in the partition of commercial facilities in regions which are likely to offer developing markets for its goods. Nowhere is this consideration of more interest than in its relation to the Chinese Empire."

In 1899, the government moved to advance those interests. Without consulting the Chinese, Secretary of State John Hay asked the imperial powers to maintain an **Open Door** for the commercial and financial activities of all nations within their Chinese spheres of influence. Privately, Hay had already approved a plan to seize a Chinese port for the United States, if necessary to join in the partition of China, but equal opportunity for trade and investment would serve American interests far better. It would avoid the expense of military occupation, avert further domestic criticism of U.S. imperialism, and guarantee a wider sphere for American business.

The other nations replied evasively, except for Russia, which rejected the Open Door concept. In 1900, an antiforeign Chinese nationalist movement known as the Boxers laid siege to the diplomatic quarter in Beijing. The defeat of the Boxer Rebellion by a multinational military force, to which the United States contributed troops, again raised the

A FAIR FIELD AND NO FAVOR.
UNCLE SAM: "I'm out for commerce, not conquest."

The United States usually preferred the "annexation of trade" to the annexation of territory. The Open Door policy promised to advance American commercial expansion, but Uncle Sam had to restrain other imperialists with colonial objectives.

prospect of a division of China among the colonial powers. Hay sent a second Open Door note, reaffirming "the principle of equal and impartial trade" and respect for China's territorial integrity.

Despite Hay's notes, China remained a tempting arena for imperial schemes. But the Open Door became a cardinal doctrine of American foreign policy in the twentieth century, a means by which the United States sought to dominate foreign markets. The United States promoted an informal or economic empire, as opposed to the traditional territorial colonial empire identified with European powers. Henceforth, American economic interests expected the U.S. government to oppose any developments that threatened to close other nations' economies to American penetration and to advance "private enterprise" abroad.

Rivalry with Japan and Russia

At the turn of the twentieth century, both the Japanese and the Russians were more deeply involved in East Asia than was the United States. Japan and Russia expressed little support for the Open Door, which they correctly saw as favoring American interests over their own. But in pursuing their ambitions in China, the two countries came into conflict with each other. Alarmed at the threat of Russian expansion in Manchuria and Korea, Japan in 1904 attacked the Russian fleet at Port Arthur and defeated the Russian army in Manchuria.

American sympathies in the Russo-Japanese War lay with Japan, for the Russians were attempting to close Manchuria to foreign trade. President Theodore Roosevelt privately complained that a reluctant American public opinion meant that "we cannot fight to keep Manchuria open." He welcomed the Japanese attack in the belief that "Japan is playing our game." But he soon began to fear that an overwhelming Japanese victory would threaten American interests as much as Russian expansionism did, so he skillfully mediated an end to the war. In the Treaty of Portsmouth in 1905, Japan won control of Russia's sphere of influence in Manchuria, half the Russian island of Sakhalin, and recognition of its domination of Korea.

The treaty marked Japan's emergence as a great power, but, ironically, it worsened relations with the United States. Anti-American riots broke out in Tokyo. The Japanese people blamed Roosevelt for obstructing further Japanese gains and blocking a Russian indemnity that would have helped Japan pay for the war. Tensions were further aggravated by San Francisco's decision in 1906 to segregate Asian and white schoolchildren. Japan regarded this as a racist insult, and Roosevelt worried that "the infernal fools in California" would provoke war. Finally, he persuaded the city to rescind the school order in exchange for his limiting Japanese immigration, which lay at the heart of California's hostility. Under the **Gentlemen's Agreement,** worked out through a series of diplomatic notes in 1907 and 1908, Japan agreed to deny passports to workers trying to come to the United States, and the United States promised not to prohibit Japanese immigration overtly or completely.

The United States and Japan entered into other agreements aimed at calming their mutual suspicions in East Asia but failed to mend the deteriorating relationship. The Taft-Katsura Agreement (1905), the Root-Takahira Agreement (1908), and the Lansing-Ishii Agreement (1917) seemed to trade grudging American acceptance of Japan's special interests in Manchuria and control of Korea for Japanese promises to respect American rule in the Philippines and maintain the Open Door in China. But these agreements were vague, if not contradictory, and produced discord rather than harmony between the two countries.

Increasingly, Japan began to exclude American trade from its territories in East Asia and to press for further control over China. Elihu Root, Roosevelt's secretary of state, insisted that the Open Door and American access had to be maintained but asserted also that the United States did not want to be "a protagonist in a controversy in China with Russia and Japan or with either of them." The problem was that the United States could not sustain the Open Door without becoming a protagonist in China. This paradox, and the unwillingness to commit military force, would plague American foreign policy in Asia for decades.

Imperial Power: The United States and Latin America, 1899–1917

In Latin America, where no major powers directly challenged American objectives as Japan and Russia did in Asia, the United States was more successful in exercising imperial power (see Map 22–3). In the two decades after the Spanish-American War, the United States intervened militarily in Latin America no fewer than 20 times to promote its own strategic and economic interests (see Overview, U.S. Interventions in Latin America, 1891–1933). Policymakers believed that these goals required restricting the influence of European nations in the region, building an isthmian canal under U.S. control, and establishing the order thought necessary for American trade and investments to expand. Intervention at times achieved these goals, but it often ignored the wishes and interests of Latin Americans, provoked resistance and disorder, and aroused lasting ill will.

U.S. Rule in Puerto Rico

Well before 1898, expansionists like James G. Blaine had advocated acquiring Puerto Rico because of its strategic location in the Caribbean. During the Spanish-American War, Roosevelt urged Washington, "Do not make peace until we get" Puerto Rico. Military invasion and the Treaty of Paris brought the island under American control, with mixed consequences. A military government improved transportation and sanitation and developed public health and education.

sense of national rectitude and mission. Generous humanitarian impulses vied with ugly racist prejudices as Americans sought both to help other peoples and to direct them toward U.S. concepts of religion, sanitation, capitalist development, and public institutions. American motives ranged from ensuring national security and competing with European colonial powers to the conviction that the United States had to expand its economic interests abroad. But if imperialism, both informal and at times colonial, brought Americans greater wealth and power, it also increased tensions in Asia and contributed to anti-American hostility and revolutionary ferment in Latin America. It also entangled the United States in the Great Power rivalries that would ultimately result in two world wars.

Review Questions

1. After the Spanish-American War, General Leonard Wood asserted that Cubans believed that their American "liberators" were "still their faithful friends." Why might Cubans not have agreed with Wood?

2. What factors, old and new, shaped American foreign policy in the late nineteenth century? How were they interrelated?

3. How were individual politicians and diplomats able to affect America's foreign policy? How were they constrained by governmental institutions, private groups, and public opinion?

4. To what extent was the United States' emergence as an imperial power a break from, as opposed to a culmination of, its earlier policies and national development?

5. How effective were U.S. interventions in Latin America? What were the objectives and consequences?

6. In what ways did the policies of other nations shape the development of American foreign policy?

Key Terms

Dollar diplomacy (p. 632)

Gentlemen's Agreement (p. 627)

Imperialism (p. 614)

Mahanism (p. 615)

Open Door (p. 626)

Pan American Union (p. 616)

Platt Amendment (p. 629)

Roosevelt Corollary (p. 632)

Spheres of Influence (p. 626)

Teller Amendment (p. 622)

Yellow press (p. 621)

Recommended Reading

Beisner, Robert L. *From the Old Diplomacy to the New, 1865–1900,* 2d ed. (1986). An excellent analysis of historiographical issues.

Hoganson, Kristin L. *Fighting for American Manhood: How Gender Politics Provoked the Spanish-American and Philippine-American Wars* (1998). An innovative and provocative book showing how gender concerns influenced U.S. foreign policy.

LaFeber, Walter. *The American Search for Opportunity, 1865–1913* (1993). A fascinating study documenting the disruptive international consequences of America's rise to world power.

LaFeber, Walter. *The New Empire: An Interpretation of American Expansion, 1860–1898* (1963). An influential study that emphasizes economic factors in American foreign policy.

Perez, Louis A., Jr. *The War of 1898: The United States and Cuba in History and Historiography* (1998). A brief book that emphasizes how relations between Cuba and the United States shaped the war and its meaning.

Pletcher, David. *The Diplomacy of Trade and Investment: American Economic Expansion in the Hemisphere, 1865–1900* (1998). Stresses the complex but inconsistent and unsystematic nature of American economic expansion.

Where to Learn More

■ **Mission Houses, Honolulu, Hawaii.** Built between 1821 and 1841, these buildings were homes and shops of missionaries sent to Hawaii by the American Board of Commissioners for Foreign Missions. Their exhibits include furnishings and memorabilia of a group important in developing American ties with Hawaii. www.missionhouses.org

■ **Funston Memorial Home, Iola, Kansas.** Operated as a museum by the Kansas State Historical Society, this is the boyhood home of General Frederick Funston, prominent in the Spanish-American War and the Filipino-American War. For a virtual tour, together with military information, political cartoons, Roosevelt correspondence, and Funston links, see http://skyways.lib.ks.us/museums/funston

■ **James G. Blaine House, Augusta, Maine.** The Executive Mansion of Maine's governor since 1919, this house was formerly Blaine's home and still contains his study and furnishings from the time he served as secretary of state and U.S. senator. http://www.blainehouse.org

Study Resources

PEARSON
myhistorylab™

For study resources for this chapter, go to www.myhistorylab.com and choose *The American Journey*. You will find a wealth of study and review material for this chapter, including pre- and post-tests, customized study plan, key term review flash cards, interactive map and document activities, and documents for analysis.

SEND THE EAGLE'S ANSWER
MORE SHIPS
UNITED STATES SHIPPING BOARD   EMERGENCY FLEET CORPORATION

In World War I, mobilization of the home front was basic to military success. Government posters exhorted Americans to increase industrial and agricultural production, buy war bonds, and suppress dissent.

America and the Great War 23
1914–1920

The present German submarine warfare against commerce is a warfare against mankind. . . . It is a war against all nations. . . . Each nation must decide for itself how it will meet it. . . . There is one choice we cannot make, we are incapable of making: we will not choose the path of submission and suffer the most sacred rights of our nation and our people to be ignored or violated. . . . The world must be made safe for democracy. Its peace must be planted upon the tested foundations of political liberty.

Excerpted from President Woodrow Wilson's Request for Declaration of War, April 2, 1917.

Woodrow Wilson Presidential Library

If it is important for us to speak and vote our convictions in matters of internal policy, though we may unfortunately be in disagreement with the President, it is infinitely more important for us to speak and vote our convictions when the question is one of peace or war, certain to involve the lives and fortunes of many of our people and, it may be, the destiny of all of them and of the civilized world as well.

Mr. President, many of my colleagues on both sides of this floor have from day to day offered for publication in the *Record* messages and letters received from their constituents. I have received some 15,000 letters and telegrams [and] 9 out of 10 are an unqualified endorsement of my course in opposing war with Germany. . . .

The poor, sir, who are the ones called upon to rot in the trenches, have no organized power, have no press to voice their will upon the questions of peace or war; but, oh, Mr. President, at some time they will be heard.

The failure to treat the belligerent nations of Europe alike … is wholly accountable for our present dilemma. We should not seek to hide our blunder behind the smoke of battle to inflame the mind of our people by half truths into a frenzy of war in order that they may never appreciate the real cause of it until it is too late. I do not believe that our national honor is served by such a course.

Excerpts from Wisconsin Senator Robert M. La Follette's three-hour speech opposing the war, April 4, 1917—Congressional Record—Senate, April 4, 1917, 224–225.

PEARSON
myhistorylab

Personal Journeys Online

- Jane Addams, *Peace and Bread in Time of War*, 1922. Describing the transition of President Wilson from an advocate of peace to one of war.

- Letter from former president Theodore Roosevelt to Sir Edward Grey, 1915. Promoting American preparedness and support of the Allies.

Escorted by the U.S. cavalry on the evening of April 2, 1917, Woodrow Wilson drove through a misty rain eerily illuminated by searchlights down Pennsylvania Avenue to Capitol Hill to deliver his war address. Throughout the day the Emergency Peace Federation had frantically lobbied Congress, but sentiment in both houses was growing for war. Tension inside and outside the Capitol was palpable. Pro-war Senator Henry Cabot Lodge even punched a protesting pacifist, and mounted police with drawn sabers held back silent crowds as Wilson asked Congress to declare war on Germany, a war, Senator La Follette insisted, that had "no popular support." Even Wilson conceded that the war he requested would sow death, misery, and reaction throughout the nation but also threatened "the firm hand of repression" against disloyalty—anticipating battles at home as well as abroad. When Wilson promised to make the world "safe for democracy," many members of Congress, waving small American flags, broke into cheers, and Senator Lodge personally congratulated Wilson.

Although widely recognized for his oratorical talents, Senator La Follette proved unable to sway the forces for war in Congress. Indeed, his speech aroused such anger in the Senate chamber that he was handed a noose as he exited the room. Both the Senate and the House unanimously supported Wilson's request and the United States entered the war on April 6. Denounced in the press, Senator La Follette and his family were ostracized for his antiwar views, providing a sobering indication of the treatment Americans would face who dared to oppose the war against Germany.

Two years later on July 10, 1919, Wilson made the same journey down Pennsylvania Avenue to Capitol Hill. This time he rode in brilliant sunshine through cheering crowds and flag-decorated streets. He asked the Senate to ratify a peace treaty that most Americans favored and that he promised would prevent future wars. But Wilson's reception in the Senate was chilly; some even refused to stand when he entered the room and many others received the address in silence. Senator Lodge scarcely concealed his hatred of the president or his opposition to the treaty. The hostility in the room apparently affected the president who spoke without his usual eloquence. During the fierce

CHRONOLOGY

1914	World War I begins in Europe.
	President Woodrow Wilson declares U.S. neutrality.
1915	Germany begins submarine warfare.
	Lusitania is sunk.
	Woman's Peace Party is organized.
1916	Sussex Pledge is issued.
	Preparedness legislation is enacted.
	Woodrow Wilson is reelected president.
1917	The February Revolution ends tsarist regime in Russia.
	Germany resumes unrestricted submarine warfare.
	The United States declares war on Germany.
	Selective Service Act establishes the military draft.
	Espionage Act is passed.
	Committee on Public Information, War Industries Board, Food Administration, and other mobilization agencies are established.
	American Expeditionary Force arrives in France.
	East St. Louis race riot erupts.
	Bolshevik Revolution occurs in Russia.
1918	Wilson announces his Fourteen Points.
	Sedition Act is passed.
	Eugene Debs is imprisoned.
	The United States intervenes militarily in Russia.
	Armistice ends World War I.
1919	Paris Peace Conference is held.
	Steel, coal, and other strikes occur.
	Red Scare breaks out.
	Prohibition amendment is adopted.
	Wilson suffers a massive stroke.
1920	Palmer Raids round up radicals.
	League of Nations is defeated in the U.S. Senate.
	Woman suffrage amendment is ratified.
	U.S. troops are withdrawn from Russia.
	Warren Harding is elected president.
1921	United States signs a separate peace treaty with Germany.

political struggle over the treaty that followed, Wilson suffered an incapacitating stroke. The Senate ultimately rejected the treaty and Wilson's peace.

Between these two presidential appearances, Americans experienced the horrors of the Great War, confronting and overcoming challenges but also sacrificing some of their national ideals and aspirations. The war declaration came after a long period in which Americans tried to balance their desires for neutrality and peace with their ambitions for wealth, their sympathies for other countries, and their perceptions of America's security and world role. Not only was the war the United States' first major military conflict on foreign soil, but it also changed American life.

Many of the changes, from increased efficiency to Americanization, reflected prewar progressivism, and the war years did promote some reforms. But the war also diverted reform energies into new channels, subordinated generous impulses to attitudes that were more coercive and strengthened the conservative opposition to reform. The results were often reactionary and contributed to a postwar mood that not only curtailed further reform but also helped defeat the peace treaty upon which so much had been gambled.

Waging Neutrality

Few Americans were prepared for the Great War that erupted in Europe in August 1914, but fewer still foresaw that their own nation might become involved in it. With near unanimity, they supported neutrality. But American attitudes, decisions, and actions, both public and private, undercut neutrality, and the policies of governments in Berlin, London, and Washington drew the United States into the war.

The Origins of Conflict

There had been plenty of warning. Since the 1870s, the competing imperial ambitions of the European powers had led to economic rivalries, military expansion, diplomatic maneuvering, and international tensions. A complex system of alliances divided the continent into two opposing blocs. In central Europe, the expansionist Germany of Kaiser Wilhelm II allied itself with the multinational Austro-Hungarian Empire. Confronting them, Great Britain and France entered into alliances with tsarist Russia. A succession of crises threatened this precarious balance of power, and in May 1914, an American diplomat reported anxiously, "There is too much hatred, too many jealousies." He predicted "an awful cataclysm."

The cataclysm began a month later. On June 28, a Serbian terrorist assassinated Archduke Franz Ferdinand, the heir to the Austro-Hungarian throne, in Sarajevo. With Germany's support, Austria declared war on Serbia on July 28. Russia then mobilized its army against Austria to aid Serbia, its Slavic client state. To assist Austria, Germany declared war on Russia and then on Russia's ally, France. Hoping for a quick victory, Germany struck at France through neutral Belgium; in response, Britain declared war on Germany on August 4. Soon Turkey and Bulgaria joined Germany and Austria to form the **Central Powers.** The **Allies**—Britain, France, and Russia—were joined by Italy and Japan. Britain drew on its empire for resources, using troops from India, Canada, Australia, New Zealand, and South Africa. The war had become a global conflict, waged not only in Europe but also in Africa, the Middle East, and East Asia.

Mass slaughter enveloped Europe as huge armies battled to a stalemate. The British and French faced the Germans along a line of trenches stretching across France and Belgium from the English Channel to Switzerland. Little movement occurred despite great efforts and terrible casualties from artillery, machine guns, and poison gas. The British once suffered 300,000 casualties in an offensive that gained only a few square miles before being pushed back. Machine gunners went into shock at the carnage they inflicted. In the trenches, soldiers suffered in the cold and mud, surrounded by decaying bodies and human waste, enduring lice, rats, and nightmares, and dying from disease and exhaustion. The belligerents subordinated their economies, politics, and cultures to military demands. The Great War, said one German soldier, had become "the grave of nations."

American Attitudes

Although the United States had also competed for markets, colonies, and influence, few Americans had expected this calamity. Most believed that the United States had no vital interest in the war and would not become involved. "Our isolated position and freedom from entangling alliances," noted the *Literary Digest,* "inspire our press with the cheering assurance that we are in no peril of being drawn into the European quarrel." President Wilson issued a proclamation of neutrality and urged Americans to be "neutral in fact as well as in name . . . impartial in thought as well as in action."

However, neither the American people nor their president stayed strictly neutral. German Americans often sympathized with Germany, and many Irish Americans hoped for a British defeat that would free Ireland from British rule. But most Americans sympathized with the Allies. Ethnic, cultural, and economic ties bound most Americans to the British and French. Politically, too, most Americans felt a greater affinity for the democratic Western Allies—tsarist Russia repelled them—than for Germany's more authoritarian government and society. And whereas Britain and the United States had enjoyed a rapprochement since 1895, Germany had repeatedly appeared as a potential rival. Many Americans considered it a militaristic nation, particularly after it violated Belgium's neutrality.

Wilson himself admired Britain's culture and government and distrusted Germany's imperial ambitions. Like other influential Americans, Wilson believed that a German victory would threaten America's economic, political, and perhaps even strategic interests. "England is fighting our fight," he said privately. Secretary of State William Jennings Bryan was genuinely neutral, but most officials favored the Allies. Robert Lansing, counselor of the State Department; Walter Hines Page, the ambassador to England; and Colonel Edward House, Wilson's closest adviser on foreign affairs—all assisted British diplomats, undercut official U.S. protests against British violations of American neutrality, and encouraged Wilson's suspicions of Germany. Early in the war, House wrote to Page, "I cannot see how there can be any serious trouble between England and America, with all of us feeling as we do." House and Lansing assured the Allies privately that "we considered their cause our cause."

British propaganda bolstered American sympathies. British writers, artists, and lecturers depicted the Allies as fighting for civilization against a brutal Germany that mutilated nuns and babies. Although German troops, like most other soldiers, did commit outrages, they were not guilty of the systematic barbarity claimed by Allied propagandists. Britain, however, shaped America's view of the conflict. It cut the only German cable to the United States and censored war news to suit itself. German propaganda directed at American opinion proved so ineffectual that the German ambassador concluded it might as well be abandoned.

Sympathy for the Allies, however, did not mean that Americans favored intervention. The British ambassador complained that it was "useless" to expect any "practical" advantage from the Americans' sympathy, for they had no intention of joining the conflict. Indeed, few Americans doubted that neutrality was the appropriate course and peace the proper goal. The carnage in France solidified their convictions. Wilson was determined to pursue peace as long as his view of national interests allowed.

The Economy of War

Economic issues soon threatened American neutrality. International law permitted neutral nations to sell or ship war matériel to belligerents, and with the economy mired in a recession when the war began, many Americans looked to war orders to spur economic recovery. But the British navy prevented trade with the Central Powers. Only the Allies could buy American goods. Their orders for steel, explosives, uniforms, wheat, and other products, however, pulled the country out of the recession. One journalist rejoiced that "war, for Europe, is meaning devastation and death; for America a bumper crop of new millionaires and a hectic hastening of prosperity revival."

Other Americans worried that this one-sided war trade undermined genuine neutrality. Congress even considered an embargo on munitions. But few Americans supported the idea. One financial journal declared of the Allied war trade: "We need it for the profits which it yields." Whatever its justification, however, the war trade strengthened U.S. ties with the Allies and embittered Germany. As the German ambassador noted, American industry was "actually delivering goods only to the enemies of Germany."

A second economic issue complicated matters. To finance their war purchases, the Allies borrowed from American bankers. Initially, Secretary of State Bryan persuaded Wilson to prohibit loans to the belligerents as "inconsistent with the true spirit of neutrality." But as the importance of the war orders to both the Allies and the American economy became clear, Wilson ended the ban. Secretary of the Treasury William McAdoo argued that it would be "disastrous" not to finance the Allies' purchases, on which "our prosperity is dependent." By April 1917, American loans to the Allies exceeded $2 billion, nearly a hundred times the amount lent to Germany. These financial ties, like the war trade they underwrote, linked the United States to the Allies and convinced Germany that American neutrality was only a formality.

The Diplomacy of Neutrality

The same imbalance characterized American diplomacy. Wilson insisted on American neutral rights but acquiesced in British violations of those rights, while sternly refusing to yield on German actions. Wilson argued that while British violations of international law cost Americans property, markets, and time, German violations cost lives. As the *Boston Globe* noted, the British were "a gang of thieves" and the Ger-

mans "a gang of murderers. On the whole, we prefer the thieves, but only as the lesser of two evils."

When the war began, the United States asked belligerents to respect the 1909 **Declaration of London** on neutral rights. Germany agreed to do so; the British refused. Instead, skirting or violating established procedures, Britain blockaded Germany, mined the North Sea, and forced neutral ships into British ports to search their cargoes and confiscate material deemed useful to the German war effort. These British actions infringed U.S. trading rights. Wilson branded Britain's blockade illegal and unwarranted, but by October he had conceded many of America's neutral rights in order to avoid conflict with Britain. This concession reflected both Wilson's English sympathies and the profitable war trade with the Allies. He was also convinced that the Allied cause was vital to America's interests.

The British then prohibited food and other products that Germany had imported during peacetime, thereby interfering further with neutral shipping. Even the British admitted that these steps had no legal justification, and one American official complained privately, "England is playing a . . . high game, violating international law every day." But when the Wilson administration finally protested, it undermined its own position by noting that "imperative necessity" might justify a violation of international law. This statement virtually authorized the British to violate American rights. In January 1915, Wilson yielded further by observing that "no very important questions of principle" were involved in the Anglo-American quarrels over ship seizures and that they could be resolved after the war.

Submarine warfare.   This policy tied the United States to the British war effort and provoked a German response. With its army stalemated on land and its navy no match for Britain's, Germany decided in February 1915 to use its submarines against Allied shipping in a war zone around the British Isles. Neutral ships risked being sunk by mistake, partly because British ships illegally flew neutral flags. Germany maintained that the blockade and the acquiescence of neutral countries in British violations of international law made submarine warfare necessary.

Submarines could not readily follow traditional rules of naval warfare. These rules had been drawn up for surface ships and required them to identify enemy merchant ships and ensure the safety of passengers before attacking. But small and fragile submarines depended on surprise attacks. They could not surface without risking attack, and they were too small to rescue victims of their sinkings. Yet Wilson refused to see the same "imperative necessity" in German tactics that he found in British tactics, and he warned that he would hold Germany responsible for any loss of U.S. lives or property.

In May 1915, a German submarine sank a British passenger liner, the *Lusitania*. It had been carrying arms, and the German embassy had warned Americans against traveling on the ship, but the loss of life—1,198 people, including 128

Americans—caused Americans to condemn Germany. "To speak of technicalities and the rules of war, in the face of such wholesale murder on the high seas, is a waste of time," trumpeted one magazine. Yet only six of a thousand editors surveyed called for war, and even the combative Theodore Roosevelt estimated that 98 percent of Americans still opposed war. Wilson saw that he had to "carry out the double wish of our people, to maintain a firm front in respect of what we demand of Germany and yet do nothing that might by any possibility involve us in the war."

This was a difficult stance. Wilson demanded that Germany abandon its submarine campaign. His language was so harsh that Bryan resigned, warning that by requiring more of Germany than of Britain, the president violated neutrality and threatened to draw the nation into war. Bryan protested Britain's use of American passengers as shields to protect contraband cargo. "This country cannot be neutral and unneutral at the same time," he declared and proposed prohibiting Americans from traveling on belligerent ships. His proposal gained support in the South and West and was introduced as a resolution in both the Senate and the House in February 1916.

Wilson moved to defeat the resolutions, insisting that they impinged on presidential control of foreign policy and on America's neutral rights. In truth, the resolutions abandoned no vital national interest and offered to prevent another provocative incident. Moreover, neither law nor tradition gave Americans the right to travel safely on belligerent ships. Wilson's assertion of such a right committed him to a policy that could only lead to conflict. Of the nation's "double wish," then, Wilson placed more priority on confronting what he saw as a German threat than on meeting the popular desire for peace.

Arguments over submarine warfare climaxed in April 1916. A German submarine torpedoed the French ship *Sussex*, injuring four Americans. Wilson threatened to break diplomatic relations if Germany did not abandon unrestricted submarine warfare against all merchant vessels, enemy as well as neutral. This threat implied war. Germany promised not to sink merchant ships without warning but made its **Sussex Pledge** contingent on the United States' requiring Britain also to adhere to "the rules of international law universally recognized before the war." Wilson's diplomatic victory, then, was hollow. Peace for America would depend on the British adopting a course they had already rejected. As Wilson saw it, however, "any little German lieutenant can put us into the war at any time by some calculated outrage." Wilson's diplomacy had left the nation's future at the mercy of others.

The Battle over Preparedness

The threat of war sparked a debate over military policy. Theodore Roosevelt and a handful of other politicians, mostly northeastern Republicans convinced that Allied victory was in the national interest, advocated what they called **preparedness,** a program to expand the armed forces and establish universal military training. Conservative business groups also joined the agitation. The National Security League, consisting of eastern bankers and industrialists, combined demands for preparedness with attacks on progressive reforms.

But most Americans, certain that their nation would not join the bloody madness, opposed expensive military preparations. Many supported the peace movement. Leading feminists, such as Jane Addams, Charlotte Perkins Gilman, and Carrie Chapman Catt, formed the Woman's Peace Party in 1915, and other organizations, such as the American League to Limit Armaments, also campaigned against preparedness. William Jennings Bryan condemned preparedness as a program for turning the nation into "a vast armory with skull and crossbones above the door." Most opponents agreed that military spending would undermine domestic reform and raise taxes while enriching arms merchants and financiers.

Wilson also opposed preparedness initially, but he reversed his position when the submarine crisis with Germany intensified. He also began to champion military expansion lest Republicans accuse him in the 1916 election of neglecting national defense. In early 1916, he made a speaking tour to generate public support for enlarging the armed forces. Continuing opposition to preparedness, especially in the South and West, forced Wilson to drop his proposal for a national reserve force. Nevertheless, the National Defense Act and the Naval Construction Act increased the strength of the army and authorized a naval construction program. Draped in the flag, Wilson marched at the head of a huge preparedness parade in Washington to celebrate the military program.

The Election of 1916

Wilson's preparedness plans stripped the Republicans of one issue in 1916, and his renewed support of progressive reforms (see Chapter 21) helped to hold Bryan Democrats in line. Wilson continued his balancing act in the campaign itself, at first stressing Americanism and preparedness but then emphasizing peace. The slogan "He Kept Us Out of War" appealed to the popular desire for peace, and the Democratic campaign became one long peace rally. Wilson disliked the peace emphasis but exploited its political appeal. He warned, "The certain prospect of the success of the Republican party is that we shall be drawn, in one form or another, into the embroilments of the European war."

The Republicans were divided. They had hoped to regain their progressive members after Roosevelt urged the Progressive Party to follow him back into the GOP. But many joined the Democratic camp instead, including several Progressive Party leaders, who endorsed Wilson for having enacted the party's demands of 1912. Roosevelt's frenzied interventionism had alienated many midwestern Republicans opposed to preparedness and cost him any chance of gaining the nomination for himself. Instead, the GOP nominated Charles Evans Hughes, a Supreme Court justice and

A preparedness parade winds its way through Mobile, Alabama, on July 4, 1916. By 1916, President Wilson, invoking the spirit of patriotism, had given his support to the preparedness program of military expansion.

University of South Alabama Achives.

former New York governor. The platform denounced Wilson's "shifty expedients" in foreign policy and promised "strict and honest neutrality." Unfortunately for Hughes, Roosevelt's attacks on Wilson for not pursuing a war policy persuaded many voters that the GOP was a war party. The link with Roosevelt kept Hughes from exploiting qualms about Wilson's own lack of neutrality. "If Hughes is defeated," wrote one observer, "he has Roosevelt to thank for it."

The election was the closest in decades (see Map 23–1). When California narrowly went for Wilson, it decided the contest. The results reflected sectional differences, with the South and West voting for Wilson and most of the Northeast and Midwest for Hughes. The desire for peace, all observers concluded, had determined the election.

Descent into War

Still, Wilson knew that war loomed, and he made a last effort to avert it. In 1915 and 1916, he had tried to mediate the European conflict, using Colonel House as a secret intermediary. Now he again appealed for an end to hostilities. In January 1917, he sketched out the terms of what he called a "peace without victory." Anything else, he warned, would only lead to another war. The new world order should be based on national equality and **self-determination**, arms reductions, freedom of the seas, and an international organ-

ization to ensure peace. It was a distinctly American vision.

Neither the Allies nor the Central Powers were interested. Each side had sacrificed too much to settle for anything short of outright victory. Germany wanted to annex territory in eastern Europe, Belgium, and France and to take over Belgian and French colonies in Africa; Austria sought Balkan territory. The Allies wanted to destroy German military and commercial power, weaken the Austro-Hungarian Empire, take Germany's colonies in Africa, and supplant Turkish influence in the Middle East. One British leader denounced Wilson as "the quintessence of a prig" for suggesting that after three years of "this terrible effort," the two sides should accept American principles rather than their own national objectives. Wilson's initiative failed.

To break the deadlock, Germany resumed unrestricted submarine warfare. This decision seemed necessary to the Germans: By 1917, nearly 700 German civilians were dying each day because of the British blockade, far more than the daily toll of British soldiers in the trenches. German generals believed that even if the United States declared war, it could do little more in the short run to injure Germany than it was already doing. German submarines, they hoped, would end the war by cutting the Allies off from U.S. supplies before the United States could send an army to Europe. On January 31, Germany announced its decision to unleash its submarines in a broad war zone.

Wilson commits to war. Wilson was now virtually committed to a war many Americans opposed. He broke diplomatic relations with Germany and asked Congress to arm American merchant vessels. When the Senate refused, Wilson invoked an antipiracy law of 1819 and armed the ships anyway. Although no American ships had yet been sunk, he also ordered the naval gun crews to fire at submarines on sight. The secretary of the navy warned Wilson that these actions violated international law and were a step toward war; Wilson called his policy "armed neutrality." Huge rallies across America demanded peace.

Several developments soon shifted public opinion. On March 1, Wilson released an intercepted message from the German foreign minister, Arthur Zimmermann, to the German minister in Mexico. It proposed that in the event of war between the United States and Germany, Mexico should ally itself with Germany; in exchange, Mexico would recover its "lost territory in Texas, New Mexico, and Arizona." The Zimmermann note produced a wave of hostility toward Germany

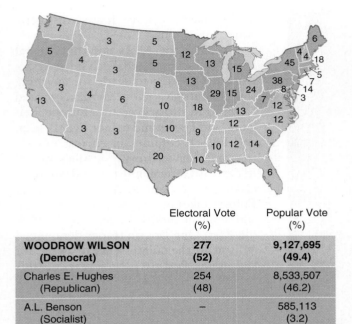

	Electoral Vote (%)	Popular Vote (%)
WOODROW WILSON (Democrat)	**277 (52)**	**9,127,695 (49.4)**
Charles E. Hughes (Republican)	254 (48)	8,533,507 (46.2)
A.L. Benson (Socialist)	–	585,113 (3.2)
Other parties (Socialist Labor, Prohibition)	–	233,909 (1.3)

MAP 23–1   The Election of 1916
Woodrow Wilson won reelection in 1916, despite a reunified Republican Party, by sweeping the South and West on campaign appeals to peace and progressive reform.

and increased support for intervention in the war, especially in the Southwest, which had opposed involvement. In addition, the Russian revolution overthrowing the tsarist regime now made Russia "a fit partner" for the United States, according to Wilson. When submarines sank four American freighters in mid-March, anti-German feeling broadened.

On April 2, 1917, Wilson delivered his war message, declaring that neutrality was no longer possible, given Germany's submarine "warfare against mankind." To build support for joining a war that most people had long regarded with revulsion and as alien to American interests, Wilson set forth the nation's war goals as simple and noble. The United States would not fight for conquest or domination but for "the ultimate peace of the world and for the liberation of its peoples." Interventionists were delighted with the decision for war but often distanced themselves from any goal other than promoting national interests. Some progressives who had opposed involvement were won over by Wilson's appeal to idealism.

But others in Congress opposed any involvement in the war. In addition to Senator Robert La Follette's opposition, Senator George Norris of Nebraska condemned the economic motives for American belligerency, crying out, "We are going to war upon the command of gold." Ridiculing Wilson's advocacy of war as a means to promote democracy, House Democratic leader Claude Kitchin of North Carolina

insisted that the American people opposed war and unsuccessfully urged holding a popular referendum on the question.

After vigorous debate, the Senate passed the war resolution 82 to 6 and the House 373 to 50. On April 6, 1917, the United States officially entered the Great War—what Kitchin predicted would be "one vast drama of horrors and blood, one boundless stage upon which will play all the evil spirits of earth and hell."

Waging War in America

Mobilizing for military intervention was a massive undertaking. "It is not an army that we must shape and train for war," announced President Wilson; "it is a Nation." The government reorganized the economy to emphasize centralized management, developed policies to control public opinion and suppress dissent, and transformed the role of government itself. Mobilization often built on the progressives' moralism and sense of mission and their efforts to resolve social and economic problems by government intervention. In other respects, however, the war experience undercut progressive achievements and withered the spirits of reformers. People on the home front, like the soldiers in Europe, would participate in the Great War in many different ways; all would find their lives changed.

Managing the War Economy

Surveying the nation's economy in May 1917, Secretary of War Newton Baker echoed Wilson. War no longer involved merely soldiers and weapons, he said. "It is the conflict of smokestacks now, the combat of the driving wheel and the engine." To harness those factories and machines for the war, federal and state governments developed a complex structure of agencies and controls for every sector of the economy, from industry and agriculture to transportation and labor (see Overview, Major Government Wartime Agencies). Supervised by the Council of National Defense, these agencies shifted resources to war-related enterprises, increased production of goods and services, and improved transportation and distribution.

Organizing industry.   The most important agency was the **War Industries Board (WIB),** established in July 1917 to set industrial priorities, coordinate military purchasing, and supervise business. Led by financier Bernard Baruch, the WIB exercised unprecedented power over industry by setting prices, allocating scarce materials, and standardizing products and procedures to boost efficiency. The number of sizes and styles of plows was reduced by 80 percent; the number of colors of typewriter ribbon dropped from 150 to 5. The WIB even specified how many trunks traveling salesmen could carry and how many stops elevators could make. Yet Baruch was not an industrial dictator; he aimed at business-government integration. The WIB promoted major business interests, helped suspend antitrust laws, and guar-

Major Government Wartime Agencies

Agency	Purpose
War Industries Board	Reorganized industry to maximize wartime production
Railroad Administration	Modernized and operated the nation's railroads
Food Administration	Increased agricultural production, supervised food distribution and farm labor
National War Labor Board	Resolved labor-management disputes, improved labor conditions, and recognized union rights as means to promote production and efficiency
Committee on Public Information	Managed propaganda to build public support for the war effort

anteed huge corporate profits. So many business leaders became involved in the WIB that there was a popular outcry against business infiltration of the government, and one corporate executive admitted, "We are all making more money out of this war than the average human being ought to." Some progressives began to see the dangers, and business leaders the advantages, of government economic intervention.

The Railroad Administration also linked business ambitions to the war economy. Under William McAdoo, it operated the nation's railroads as a unified system to move supplies and troops efficiently. Centralized management eliminated competition, permitted improvements in equipment, and brought great profits to the owners but higher prices to the general public. The progressive Republican Senator Hiram Johnson of California protested that the Railroad Administration was "outrageously generous to the railroads and shamefully unjust to the people."

Ensuring food supplies. Equally effective and far more popular was the Food Administration, headed by Herbert Hoover. Hoover had organized relief supplies for war-torn Belgium and now controlled the production and distribution of food for the United States and its allies. He persuaded millions of Americans to accept meatless and wheatless days, so that the Food Administration could feed military and foreign consumers. Half a million women went door to door to secure food-conservation pledges from housewives. City residents planted victory gardens in parks and vacant lots, and President Wilson even pastured sheep on the White House lawn.

Hoover also worked closely with agricultural processors and distributors, ensuring profits in exchange for cooperation. Farmers profited from the war, too. To encourage production, Hoover established high prices for commodities, and agricultural income rose by 30 percent. State and federal governments provided commercial farmers with sufficient farm labor despite the military draft and competition from high-wage war industries. The Food Administration organized the Woman's Land Army to work in the fields.

Most states formed units of the Boys' Working Reserve for agricultural labor. Many southern and western states required "loafers" and "slackers" to work in agriculture. Agribusinesses in the Southwest persuaded the federal government to permit them to import Mexicans to work under government supervision and be housed in special camps.

Overseeing labor relations. The National War Labor Board supervised labor relations. In exchange for labor's cooperation, this agency guaranteed the rights of unions to organize and bargain collectively. With such support, unions sharply increased their membership. The labor board also encouraged improved working conditions, higher wages, and shorter hours. War contracts stipulated an eight-hour day, and by the end of the war, nearly half the nation's workers had achieved the 48-hour week. Wages rose, too, but often only as fast as inflation. These improvements limited labor disputes during the war, and Secretary of War Baker praised labor as "more willing to keep in step than capital." But when such unions as the Industrial Workers of the World did not keep in step, the government suppressed them.

Although these and other government regulatory agencies were dismantled when the war ended, their activities reinforced many long-standing trends in the American economy, from the consolidation of business to the commercialization of agriculture and the organization of labor. They also set a precedent for governmental activism that would prove valuable during the crises of the 1930s and 1940s.

Women and Minorities:
New Opportunities, Old Inequities

Women and war work. The reorganization of the economy also had significant social consequences, especially for women and African Americans. In response to labor shortages, public officials and private employers exhorted women to join the work force—"For Every Fighter a Woman Worker"—urged one poster. Women now took jobs previously closed to them. Besides farm work, they built airplanes, the nation's professed idealistic war goals. The campaign also established unfortunate precedents for the future.

Congress rushed to stifle antiwar sentiment. The **Espionage Act** provided heavy fines and up to 20 years in prison for obstructing the war effort, a vague phrase but "omnipotently comprehensive," warned an Idaho senator who opposed the law. In fact, the Espionage Act became a weapon to crush dissent and criticism. Eventually, Congress passed the still more sweeping **Sedition Act of 1918,** which provided severe penalties for speaking or writing against the draft, bond sales, and war production and for criticizing government personnel or policies. Congress emphasized the law's inclusive nature by rejecting a proposed amendment stipulating that "nothing in this act shall be construed as limiting the liberty or impairing the right of any individual to publish or speak what is true, with good motives, and for justifiable ends." Senator Hiram Johnson lamented, "It is war. But, good God, . . . when did it become war upon the American people?"

Postmaster General Albert Burleson banned antiwar or radical newspapers and magazines from the mail, suppressing literature so indiscriminately that one observer said he "didn't know socialism from rheumatism." Even more zealous in attacking radicals and presumed subversives was the reactionary attorney general, Thomas Gregory, who made little distinction between traitors and pacifists, war critics, and radicals. Eugene Debs was sentenced to ten years in prison for a "treasonous" speech in which he declared it "extremely dangerous to exercise the right of free speech in a country fighting to make democracy safe in the world." By war's end, a third of the Socialist Party's national leadership was in prison, leaving the party in a shambles. Other notable radicals imprisoned included Ricardo Flores Magon, a Mexican American labor organizer who was sentenced to 20 years for publishing antiwar material in his Los Angeles Spanish-language newspaper, *Regeneración.*

Gregory also enlisted the help of private vigilantes, including the several hundred thousand members of the reactionary American Protective League, which sought to purge radicals and reformers from the nation's economic and political life. They wiretapped telephones, intercepted private mail, burglarized union offices, broke up German-language newspapers, harassed immigrants, and staged mass raids, seizing thousands of people who they claimed were not doing enough for the war effort.

State and local authorities also suppressed what they saw as antiwar, radical, or pro-German activities. They established 184,000 investigative and enforcement agencies, known as councils of defense or public-safety committees. They encouraged Americans to spy on one another, required people to buy Liberty Bonds, and prohibited teaching German in schools or using the language in religious services and telephone conversations. Indeed, suppression of all things German reached extremes. Germanic names of towns, streets, and people were changed; sauerkraut became liberty

"Beat Back the Hun," a poster to induce Americans to buy Liberty Bonds, demonizes the enemy in a raw, emotional appeal. Liberty bond drives raised the immense sum of $23 billion.

cabbage, and the hamburger the liberty sandwich. In Tulsa, a member of the council of defense killed someone for making allegedly pro-German remarks. The council declared its approval, and community leaders applauded the killer's patriotism. A midwestern official of the Council of National Defense noted, "All over this part of the country men are being tarred and feathered and some are being lynched. . . . These cases do not get into the newspapers nor is an effort ever made to punish the individuals concerned."

Members of the business community exploited the hysteria to promote their own interests at the expense of farmers, workers, and reformers. As one Wisconsin farmer complained, businessmen "now under the guise of patriotism are trying to ram down the farmers' throats things they hardly dared before." On the Great Plains from Texas to North Dakota, the business target was the Nonpartisan League, a radical farm group demanding state control or ownership of banks, grain elevators, and flour mills. Although the League supported the war, oversubscribed bond drives, and had George Creel affirm its loyalty, conservatives depicted it as seditious to block its advocacy of political and economic reforms, including the confiscation of large fortunes to pay for the war. Minnesota's public-safety commission condemned members of the Nonpartisan League as traitors and proposed a "firing squad working overtime" to deal with them. Nebraska's council of defense barred League meetings. Public officials and self-styled patriots broke up the League's meetings and whipped and jailed its leaders.

In the West, business interests targeted labor organizations, especially the Industrial Workers of the World. In Arizona, for example, the Phelps-Dodge Company broke a mine strike in 1917 by depicting the Wobblie miners as bent on war-related sabotage. A vigilante mob, armed and paid by the mining company, seized 1,200 strikers, many of them Wobblies and one-third of them Mexican Americans, and herded them into the desert without food or water. Federal investigators found no evidence of sedition among the miners and reported that the company and its thugs had been inspired, not by "patriotism," but by "ordinary strike-breaking motives." Corporate management was merely "raising the false cry of 'disloyalty'" to suppress workers' complaints.

Nonetheless, the government itself assisted the business campaign. It used the army to break loggers' support for the IWW in the Pacific Northwest, and it raided IWW halls across the country in September 1917. The conviction of nearly 200 Wobblies on charges of sedition in three mass trials in Illinois, California, and Kansas crippled the nation's largest industrial union.

In the end, the government was primarily responsible for the war hysteria. It encouraged suspicion and conflict through inflammatory propaganda, repressive laws, and violation of basic civil rights, by supporting extremists who used the war for their own purposes, and by tolerating mob violence against German Americans. This ugly mood would infect the postwar world.

Waging War and Peace Abroad

While mobilizing the home front, the Wilson administration undertook an impressive military effort to help the Allies defeat the Central Powers. Wilson also struggled to secure international acceptance for his plans for a just and permanent peace.

The War to End All Wars

When the United States entered the war, the Allied position was dire. The losses from three years of trench warfare had sapped military strength and civilian morale. French soldiers mutinied and refused to continue an assault that had cost 120,000 casualties in five days; the German submarine campaign was devastating the British. On the eastern front, the Russian army had collapsed, and the Russian government had gradually disintegrated after the overthrow of the tsarist regime.

What the Allies needed, said French Marshal Joseph Joffre in April 1917, was simple: "We want men, men, men." In May, Congress passed the **Selective Service Act of 1917,** establishing conscription. More than 24 million men eventually registered for the draft, and nearly 3 million entered the army when their numbers were drawn in a national lottery. Almost 2 million more men volunteered, as did more than 13,000 women, who served in the navy and marines. Nearly one-fifth of America's soldiers were foreign-born (Europeans spoke of the "American Foreign Legion"); 367,000 were black. Many Native Americans served with distinction as well; in recognition, Indian veterans were made citizens in 1919, a status extended to all Indians five years later.

Civilians were transformed into soldiers in hastily organized training camps, operated according to progressive principles. Prohibition prevailed in the camps; the poorly educated and largely working-class recruits were taught personal hygiene; worries about sin and inefficiency produced massive campaigns against venereal disease; and immigrants were taught English and American history. Some units were ethnically segregated: At Camp Gordon, Georgia, Italians and Slavs had separate units, with their own officers.

Racial segregation was more rigid, not only in training camps and military units but in assignments as well. The navy assigned black sailors to menial positions, and the army similarly used black soldiers primarily as gravediggers and laborers. But one black combat division was created, and four black regiments fought under French command. France decorated three of these units with its highest citations for valor. White American officers urged the French not to praise black troops, treat black officers as equals, or permit fraternization. But white racism could not diminish the extraordinary record of one of the most famous of the black units in France—the 369th Infantry Regiment, also known as the "Harlem Hellfighters." The 369th spent 191 days in combat and was the first Allied unit to reach the Rhine.

Women were recruited as noncombatant personnel, such as clerks, translators, and switchboard operators, thereby enabling more men to be assigned to combat duty. The navy awarded them equal rank with males performing the same tasks, and they were eligible after the war for veterans benefits. The army was a different story. Although they served in uniform and under military discipline, women had no formal military status, were ineligible for benefits, and often had their skills and contributions devalued. On the eve of a major battle in France, Merle Egan in the U.S. Army Signal Corps, feverishly training soldiers to operate switchboards to help coordinate the massive military buildup, found that some of the men resented taking instructions from a woman. But "when I reminded them that any soldier could carry a gun but the safety of a whole division might depend on the switchboard one of them was operating, I had no more trouble."

AEF helped defeat another German advance, at Rheims. The influx of American troops had tipped the balance toward Allied victory. By July 18, the German chancellor later acknowledged, "even the most optimistic among us knew that all was lost. The history of the world was played out in three days."

The Russian front.   In July, Wilson also agreed to commit 15,000 American troops to intervene in Russia. Russia's provisional government had collapsed when the radical **Bolshevik** faction of the communist movement had seized power in November 1917. Under V. I. Lenin, the Bolsheviks signed an armistice with Germany in early 1918, which freed German troops for the summer offensive in France. The Allied interventions were initially designed to reopen the eastern front and later to help overthrow the Bolshevik government.

Lenin's call for the destruction of capitalism and imperialism alarmed the Allied leaders. One Wilson adviser urged the "eradication" of the Russian government. Soon, American and British troops were fighting Russians in an effort to influence Russia's internal affairs. U.S. forces remained in Russia even after Germany surrendered in 1918. They did not leave until 1920. These military interventions failed, but they contributed to Russian distrust of the West.

The Western front.   The Allies were more successful on the western front. Having stopped the German offensive in July, they launched their own advance. The decisive battle began in late September when an American army over 1 million strong attacked German trenches in the Argonne Forest. Many Americans were still inexperienced; some had been drafted only in July and had spent more time traveling than training. Nevertheless, they advanced steadily, despite attacks with poison gas and heavy artillery. Lieutenant Maury Maverick (later a Texas congressman) described the shelling: "We were simply in a big black spot with streaks of screaming red and yellow, with roaring giants in the sky tearing and whirling and roaring." An exploding shell terrified him: "There is a great swishing scream, a smash-bang, and it seems to tear everything loose from you. The intensity of it simply enters your heart and brain, and tears every nerve to pieces."

The battle for the Argonne raged for weeks. A German general reported that his exhausted soldiers faced Americans who "were fresh, eager for fighting, and brave." But he found their sheer numbers most impressive. Eventually, this massive assault overwhelmed the Germans. Despite severe casualties, the AEF had helped the British and French to defeat the enemy. (See American Views, Letter from Albert Smith, October 15, 1918.) With its allies surrendering, its own army in retreat, and revolution breaking out among the war-weary residents of its major cities, Germany asked for peace. On November 11, 1918, an armistice ended the Great War. More than 115,000 Americans were among the 8 million soldiers and 7 million civilians dead.

The Fourteen Points

The armistice was only a step toward final peace. President Wilson had already enunciated America's war objectives on January 8, 1918, in a speech outlining what became known as the Fourteen Points. In his 1917 war message, Wilson had advocated a more democratic world system, and this new speech spelled out how to achieve it. But Wilson also had a political purpose. The Bolsheviks had published the Allies' secret treaties dividing up the expected economic and territorial spoils of the war. Lenin had called for an immediate peace based on the liberation of all colonies, self-determination for all peoples, and the rejection of annexations and punitive indemnities. Wilson's Fourteen Points reassured the American and Allied peoples that they were fighting for more than imperialist gains and offered an alternative to what he called Lenin's "crude formula" for peace.

Eight of Wilson's points proposed creating new nations, shifting old borders, or ensuring self-determination for peoples previously subject to the Austrian, German, or Russian empire. The point about Russia would haunt Wilson after the Allied interventions there began, for it called on all nations to evacuate Russian territory and permit Russia "an unhampered and unembarrassed opportunity for the independent determination of her own political development" under "institutions of her own choosing." Another five points invoked principles to guide international relations: freedom of the seas, open diplomacy instead of secret treaties, reduction of armaments, free trade, and the fair settlement of colonial claims. Wilson's fourteenth and most important point proposed a league of nations to carry out these ideals and ensure international stability.

Wilson and the German government had these principles in mind when negotiating the armistice. The Allies, however, had never explicitly accepted the Fourteen Points, and framing a final peace treaty would be difficult. While Wilson favored a settlement that would promote international stability and economic expansion, he recognized that the Allies sought "to get everything out of Germany that they can." Indeed, after their human and economic sacrifices, Britain and France wanted tangible compensation, not pious principles.

Convinced of the righteousness of his cause, Wilson decided to attend the peace conference in Paris, although no president had ever gone to Europe while in office. But Wilson weakened his position before he even set sail. First, he urged voters to support Democratic candidates in the November 1918 elections to indicate approval of his peace plan. But the electorate, responding primarily to domestic problems like inflation, gave the Republicans control of both houses of Congress. This meant that any treaty would have to be approved by Senate Republicans angry that Wilson had tried to use war and peace for partisan purposes. Second, Wilson refused to consult with Senate Republicans on plans for the peace conference and failed to name important Republicans to the Paris delegation. It was going to be Wilson's treaty, and Republicans would feel no responsibility to approve it.

American soldiers advancing through smoke and shattered trees of the Argonne Forest in October 1918. The Great War was a conflict of relentless attrition, marked by the horrors of poison gas, artillery bombardment, pandemic disease, and what one American called the "unburied dead."

U.S. Army Signal Corps. National Archives III-SC 94980.

The Paris Peace Conference

The peace conference opened on January 18, 1919. Meeting at the Palace of Versailles, the delegations were dominated by the principal Allied leaders: Wilson of the United States, David Lloyd George of Britain, Georges Clemenceau of France, and Vittorio Orlando of Italy. The Central Powers and Bolshevik Russia were excluded. The treaty would be one-sided except to the extent that Wilson could insist on the liberal terms of the Fourteen Points against French and British intransigence. As Clemenceau remarked, "God gave us the Ten Commandments and we broke them. Mr. Wilson has given us the Fourteen Points. We shall see." Wilson himself had broken two of the Fourteen Points before the conference began. He had acquiesced in Britain's rejection of freedom of the seas. And he had sent U.S. troops to intervene in Russia in violation of its right to self-determination.

For months, the conference debated Wilson's other goals and the Allies' demands for compensation and security. Lloyd George later commented, with reference to the self-righteous Wilson and the assertive Clemenceau, "I think I did as well as might be expected, seated as I was between Jesus Christ and Napoleon Bonaparte." Under protest, Germany signed the **Treaty of Versailles** on June 28, 1919. Its terms were far more severe than Wilson had proposed or Germany had anticipated. Germany had to accept sole responsibility for starting the war, a stipulation that all Germans bitterly resented. It was required to pay huge reparations to the Allies,

give up land to France, Poland, Belgium, and Denmark, cede its colonies, limit its army and navy to small self-defense forces, destroy military bases, and promise not to manufacture or purchase armaments.

Wilson gained some acceptance of self-determination. As the German, Austro-Hungarian, Turkish, and Russian empires had collapsed at the end of the war, nationalist groups had proclaimed their independence. On one hand, the peace settlement formally recognized these new nation-states: Poland, Finland, Estonia, Latvia, and Lithuania in eastern Europe and Austria, Hungary, Czechoslovakia, and Yugoslavia in central Europe (see Map 23–3). On the other hand, France, Italy, Romania, and Japan all annexed territory regardless of the wishes of the inhabitants. Germans were placed under Polish control in Silesia and Czech control in Bohemia. Austria was not allowed to merge with Germany. And the conference sanctioned colonialism by establishing a trusteeship system that enabled France, Britain, and Japan to take over German colonies and Turkish territory.

The Allied leaders endorsed the changes in eastern Europe in part because the new states there were anticommunist and would constitute a barrier against Bolshevism. Indeed, the Allies at Versailles were preoccupied with Bolshevik Russia, which one of Wilson's aides called the "black cloud of the east, threatening to overwhelm and swallow up the world." Communist movements in early 1919 in Germany, Austria, and Hungary caused the Allies to fear that "the Russian idea was still rising in power," and they hoped to isolate and weaken Bolshevik Russia. Allied armies were in Russia during the peace conference, and Wilson and the other leaders agreed to provide further aid to fight the Bolsheviks. This hostility to Russia, like the punitive terms for Germany and the concessions to imperial interests, boded ill for a stable and just postwar order. (see Global Perspectives, War and Revolution: The Bolsheviks and the International Community.)

But Wilson hoped that the final section of the Versailles treaty would resolve the flaws of the agreement by establishing his great international organization to preserve peace: the **League of Nations.** The Covenant, or constitution, of the League was built into the treaty. Its crucial feature, Article Ten, bound the member nations to guarantee each other's independence—a provision that was Wilson's concept of collective security. "At least," he told an aide, "we are saving the Covenant, and that instrument will work wonders, bring the blessing of peace, and then when the war psychosis has abated, it will not be difficult to settle all disputes

American Views

Letter from Albert Smith, October 15, 1918

Ultimately numbering over 2 million men, the American troops sent to Europe were organized as the American Expeditionary Forces (AEF) under the command of General Pershing. By August 1918, Pershing had enough troops to form the American First Army, which fought on its own front. In this letter to his brother, Albert Smith describes the largest campaign of the American forces—the Meuse-Argonnne campaign—which proved both decisive and costly for the Allies.

In the struggle, the AEF cooperated with an African American unit under French command, and the campaign produced one of the greatest heroes of World War I: Private Alvin York of Pall Mall, Tennessee, who would receive the Medal of Honor and promotion to sergeant for personally killing 20 Germans and destroying 35 German machine guns.

Smith's letter glowingly refers to the heroic actions of American doughboys—both white and black. More-over, even as he discourages his own brother from joining the war, he also takes great pride in his own role on the front lines.

- What does Smith's letter illustrate about the impact of total war on soldiers and civilians?
- How does Smith suggest both his confidence about defeating the Germans and his war weariness?
- How did Smith adapt to the new tools of war, especially the use of gas and machine guns?

France
Oct, 15, 1918
Mr. Mcgregor Smith
Cookeville, Tenn.

Dear "Greg";

I received a letter from you a few weeks ago but have not had time to answer for we have been exceedingly busy. We are speedy clearing France of the Huns and making Europe safe for you Kids to come over next spring. This will be the most peaceable country in the world in about sixty days. You just think that you want to come over here we wont need you. I wanted to come over pretty badly and was happy as a lark the day we left New York but that will be nothing to the state of my feeling when I start back to the states. If the Statue of liberty ever sees me again it will have to about face and come down south to find me after she sees me pass going into the harbor at New York on my way home. This is the wettest muddiest country I ever saw, it has been raining steadily for seven weeks. I stepped in a mud hole the other night and went up to my waist in mud and didnt get to change clothes and in fact I haven't changed yet. I haven't changed for over two month and haven't even had my clothes off for that length of time. I have not had a bath for six weeks and none in sight for I haven't the slightest idea of using what little drinking water I get in my canteen for batheing purposes. I shave as often as possible for the beard on my face keeps my Gas mask from being effective and the germans use quite a bit of gas. Gas and machine gun is their only effective weapons. I have been on every front in France. You cant imagine how torn up this country really is. Every where there are wire entanglements and trenches and dug outs. Even out of the war zone there are entanglements and dugouts to protect the civilians from air raids. . . . The hardest fight we were in was in the Argenne [Argonne] Forest. Our batteries were the one that destroyed the machine gun nest at Montfaucon. I was at the Forward observation post the night the barrage was laid during the big drive of the last few weeks. The barrage that night was the heaviest one ever laid in France. I saw every bit of it and saw the infantry go over the top. That certainly was a night that I will always remember. Our doughboy are the greatest men in the world, they certainly have "Fritz" bluffed. During Aug. When we were in a drive against mount Sac [Montsec] the strongest fortified hill in France we supported a regiment of Negro infantry and when they went over the top and up the hill they were saying to them germans "take yo hats off white folks no Kazerade to late now." They sure did slaughter the Huns. The southern boys are certainly hard fighters. The third Tenn. Infantry is the hardest fighting regiment over here. I understand that they have been cited by the British for bravery. At Cambrai they were the Americans that advanced thru the heart of the city and cleared the place of machine guns.

Don't worry about coming over here stay in school that is your service to your country. I am in good health and ready to come home after the war but not before, I will do my bit here. I was appointed for the officers, training camp this month for the third time but refused it, I will go later on in the year I want to stay on the front as long as the war lasts. Be good and study HARD have a good time and write often,

Love to all,

Albert
Corp. Albert P. Smith
Hq. Co. 115 F.A. American Expdt. France

Source: www.historychannel.com/letters/albert_smith.html

that baffle us now." Sailing home, he mused, "Well, it is finished, and, as no one is satisfied, it makes me hope we have made a just peace; but it is all on the lap of the gods."

Waging Peace at Home

Wilson was determined to defeat the opposition to the peace treaty. But many Americans were engaged in their own struggles with the new conditions of a nation suddenly at peace but riven by economic, social, and political conflict. Wilson's battle for the League of Nations would fail tragically. The other conflicts would rage until the election of 1920 restored a normalcy of sorts.

Battle over the League

Most Americans favored the Versailles treaty. A survey of 1,400 newspapers found fewer than 200 opposed. Thirty-three governors and 32 state legislatures endorsed the League of Nations. But when Wilson called for the Senate to accept "the moral leadership . . . and confidence of the world" by ratifying the treaty, he met resistance. Some Republicans wanted to prevent the Democrats from campaigning in 1920 as the party responsible for a victorious war and a glorious peace. But most Republican opponents of the treaty raised serious questions, often reflecting national traditions in foreign relations. Nearly all Democrats favored the treaty, but they were a minority; some Republicans would have to be converted for the treaty to be approved.

Progressive Republican senators, such as Robert La Follette and Hiram Johnson, led one group of opponents. Called the **Irreconcilables,** they opposed participation in the League of Nations, which they saw as designed to perpetuate the power of imperialist countries. Article Ten, they feared, would require the United States to help suppress rebellions in Ireland against British rule or to enforce disputed European borders. Johnson declared, "I am opposed to American boys policing Europe and quelling riots in every new nation's backyard." Most of the Irreconcilables gave priority to restoring civil liberties and progressive reform at home.

A larger group of opponents had reservations about the treaty's provisions. These **Reservationists** were led by Henry Cabot Lodge, the chair of the Senate Foreign Relations Committee. They regarded Article Ten as eroding congressional authority to declare war. They also fretted that the League might interfere with domestic questions, such as immigration laws. Lodge held public hearings on the treaty to rouse and focus opposition. German Americans resented the war-guilt clause; Italian and Polish Americans complained that the

With the defeat of Germany, Americans wanted their soldiers home. And although many returning African-American soldiers were denied celebratory homecomings and would face discrimination and hostility, their role in World War I brought fresh confidence and respect to the African-American community. Few units stirred the patriotism and pride as did the valiant 369th Infantry Regiment, decorated by the French government for heroism and "gallantry under fire." Here African-American friends and families turn out to welcome home the "Men of Bronze," as they were also called.

MAP EXPLORATION To explore an interactive version of this map, go to
http://www.prenhall.com/goldfield5/map23.3

Legend:
- Austria-Hungary, 1914
- Germany, 1914
- Areas lost by Germany in 1919
- Areas lost by Bulgaria
- Areas lost by Russia
- Areas lost by the Ottoman Empire

MAP 23–3 Europe and the Middle East after the Treaty of Versailles
World War I and the Treaty of Versailles rearranged the borders of Europe and the Middle East. Germany, Russia, and the Austrian and Turkish empires all lost land, and new nations were recognized, but the principle of self-determination was only imperfectly observed.

Global Perspectives

War and Revolution: The Bolsheviks and the International Community

An uneasy amalgam of distinctive nationalities, the Russian Empire at the start of World War I covered vast territories and included 178 million people. A poor, agrarian country, Russia suffered from autocratic tsarist rule. Long-standing economic problems and political aspirations, especially among land-starved peasants, combined to make Russia a cauldron of tensions inflamed by its involvement in the Great War. The Russian army reflected the discontent that plagued the empire; 400,000 soldiers were killed during the first six months of war, and thereafter desertion became a significant problem.

Food shortages provoked protests among peasants and workers—all challenging tsarist rule. Uprisings in February 1917 immobilized Petrograd, the capital, and persuaded the military to mutiny. The February Revolution ended the Romanov dynasty and brought to power a Provisional Government dominated by liberal reformers. Despite recognition and financial aid from its Allies—the United States, France, and Britain—the new government was politically vulnerable and unable to solve the country's pressing problems.

As frustrations mounted, support for the Bolshevik faction of the Communist Party grew. The Bolsheviks envisioned a world without classes or war—a vision that appealed to a war-weary society with a disintegrating economy. In October 1917, the Provisional Government collapsed and the Bolsheviks came to power.

Promising peace, land, and workers' control, the Bolsheviks were led by V. I. Lenin, a lawyer who had worked for a socialist revolution in Russia since the turn of the century. On March 3, 1918, Russia and Germany signed the Treaty of Brest-Litovsk, an armistice that cost Russia significant territory. But Lenin defended the treaty because Germany still occupied large parts of Russia and the counterrevolutionary, or "White," forces were gathering momentum.

The Allies decried both the Bolshevik revolution and the separate peace with Germany, which enabled Germany to strengthen its forces on the western front. Russia's withdrawal from the war emboldened the "Whites," the opponents of the Bolshevik "Reds," and encouraged the Allies to assist them with financial support and troops. But the Allied invasions of Russia were failures, serving only to convince Lenin that the Allies were imperialists bent on overthrowing the world's only socialist state. In the tumultuous postwar period, Lenin's call for workers to overthrow their governments, European and American leaders believed, fed the postwar labor unrest that wracked industrialized nations. Woodrow Wilson fumed that the "poison" of Bolshevism was "running through the veins of the world." Wilson feared that returning African American troops would serve as the "greatest medium in conveying bolshevism to America," but other policymakers targeted aliens, immigrants, and labor activists, culminating in the "Red Scare."

The fears stirred by the Bolshevik Revolution, however, did not provoke similar governmental extremism in either Great Britain or France, both of which would recognize the Soviet Union by 1924. But America, as the British ambassador noted, was singularly "frightened" of the revolution, and the United States would withhold recognition until 1933.

■ What was the impact of the Bolshevik revolution on the war and peace? How did the Allies respond to the Bolsheviks who came to power in Russia in 1917?

---

treaty did not satisfy the territorial ambitions of Italy and Poland; Irish Americans condemned the treaty's failure to give self-determination to Ireland. Many progressives criticized the treaty's compromises on self-determination, reparations, and colonies. Linking these failures with Wilson's domestic policies, one former supporter concluded; "The administration has become reactionary, and deserves no support from any of us."

Lodge's opposition was shaped by both partisanship and deep personal hostility. "I never expected to hate anyone in politics with the hatred I feel toward Wilson," Lodge confessed. Wilson reciprocated, and when Lodge proposed reservations or amendments to the treaty, Wilson refused to compromise. He proposed "a direct frontal attack" on his opponents. If they wanted war, he said, he would "give them a belly full." In early September 1919, Wilson set out across the country to win popular support for the League. In three weeks, he traveled 8,000 miles and delivered 37 speeches.

In poor health following a bout with influenza, Wilson collapsed in Pueblo, Colorado. Confused and in tears, he mumbled to his secretary, "I seem to have gone to pieces." Taken back to Washington, Wilson on October 2 suffered a massive stroke that paralyzed his left side and left him psychologically unstable and temporarily blind. Wilson's physician and his wife, Edith Galt Wilson, kept the nature of his illness secret from the public, Congress, and even the vice president and cabinet. Rumors circulated that Edith Wilson was running the administration, but she was not. Instead, it was immobilized.

By February 1920, Wilson had partially recovered, but he remained suspicious and quarrelsome. Bryan and other Democratic leaders urged him to accept Lodge's reservations to gain ratification of the treaty. Wilson refused. Isolated and inflexible, he ordered Democratic senators to vote with the Irreconcilables against the treaty as amended by Lodge. On March 19, 1920, the Senate killed the treaty.

Economic Readjustment and Social Conflict

The League was not the only casualty of the struggle to conclude the war. Grave problems shook the United States in 1919 and early 1920. An influenza epidemic had erupted in Europe in 1918 among the massed armies. It now hit the United States, killing perhaps 700,000 Americans, far more than had died in combat. Frightened officials closed public facilities and banned public meetings in futile attempts to stop the contagion.

Meanwhile, the Wilson administration had no plans for an orderly reconversion of the wartime economy, and chaos ensued. The government canceled war contracts and dissolved the regulatory agencies. Noting that "the war spirit of cooperation and sacrifice" had disappeared with the Armistice, Bernard Baruch decided to "turn industry absolutely free" and abolished the War Industries Board as of January 1, 1919. Other agencies followed in such haste that turmoil engulfed the economy.

The government also demobilized the armed forces. The army discharged 600,000 soldiers still in training camps; the navy brought AEF soldiers home from France so fast that it had to expand the troopship fleet to four times its peak size during the war. With no planning or assistance, veterans were hustled back into civilian life. There they competed for scarce jobs with workers recently discharged from the war industries.

As unemployment mounted, the removal of wartime price controls brought runaway inflation. The cost of food, clothing, and other necessities more than doubled over prewar rates. The return of the soldiers caused a serious housing shortage, and rents skyrocketed. Democratic leaders urged Wilson to devote less time to the League of Nations and more to the cost of living and the tensions it unleashed. Farmers also suffered from economic readjustments. Net farm income declined by 65 percent between 1919 and 1921. Farmers who had borrowed money for machinery and land to expand production for the war effort were left impoverished and embittered.

Postwar battles: gender and race.   Women also lost their wartime economic advances. Returning soldiers took away their jobs. Male trade unionists insisted that women go back to being housewives. One New York union maintained that "the same patriotism which induced women to enter industry during the war should induce them to vacate their positions after the war." At times, male workers struck to force employers to fire women and barred women from unions in jobs where union membership was required for employment. "During the war they called us heroines," one woman complained, "but they throw us on the scrapheap now." Indeed, state legislatures passed laws prohibiting women from working in many of the occupations they had successfully filled during the war. By 1919, half of the women newly employed in heavy industry during the war were gone; by 1920, women constituted a smaller proportion of the workforce than they had in 1910.

The postwar readjustments also left African Americans disappointed. During the war, they had agreed with W. E. B. Du Bois to "forget our special grievances and close our ranks shoulder to shoulder with our own white fellow citizens." Participation in the war effort, they had hoped, might be rewarded by better treatment thereafter. Now, the meagerness of their reward became clear.

Housing shortages and job competition interacted with racism in 1919 to produce race riots in 26 towns and cities, resulting in at least 120 deaths. In Chicago, 38 people were killed and more than 500 injured in a five-day riot that began when white thugs stoned to death a black youth swimming too near "their" beach. White rioters then fired a machine gun from a truck hurtling through black neighborhoods. But black residents fought back, no longer willing, the *Chicago Defender* reported, "to move along the line of least resistance as did their sires." The new militancy reflected both their experiences in the military and in industry and their exposure to propaganda about freedom and democracy. Racial conflict was part of a postwar battle between Americans hoping to preserve the new social relations fostered by the war effort and those wanting to restore prewar patterns of power and control. In recognition of both the persistence of white racism and the changed attitudes among African Americans, Du Bois revised his prewar stance, affirming, "We return. We return from fighting. We return fighting."

Fighting for industrial democracy.   Even more pervasive discontents roiled as America adjusted to the postwar world. More than 4 million angry workers launched a wave of 3,600 strikes in 1919. They were reacting not only to the soaring cost of living, which undermined the value of their wages, but also to employers' efforts to reassert their authority and destroy the legitimacy labor had won by its participation in the war effort. The abolition of government controls on industry enabled employers not only to raise prices but also to rescind their recognition of unions and reimpose objectionable working conditions. Employers also protected their rising profits by insisting that wages remain fixed. In response, strikers demanded higher wages, better conditions, and recognition of unions and the right of collective bargaining.

The greatest strike involved the American Federation of Labor's attempt to organize steelworkers, who endured dangerous conditions and 12-hour shifts. When the steel companies refused to recognize the union or even discuss issues, 365,000 workers went out on strike in September 1919. Strikers in Pennsylvania pointed out that they had worked "cheerfully, without strikes or trouble of any kind" during the war to "make the world safe for democracy" and that they now sought "industrial democracy." Employers hired thugs to beat the strikers, used strikebreakers to take their jobs, and exploited ethnic and racial divisions. To undercut support for the workers, management portrayed the strikers as disruptive radicals influenced by Bolshevism. After four months, the strike failed.

Employers used the same tactic to defeat striking coal miners, whose wages had fallen behind the cost of living. Refusing to negotiate with the United Mine Workers, coal operators claimed that Russian Bolsheviks had financed the strike to destroy the American economy. Attorney General Mitchell Palmer secured an injunction against the strike under the authority of wartime legislation. Because the government no longer controlled coal prices or enforced protective labor rules, miners complained bitterly that the war had ended for corporations but not for workers.

Two municipal strikes in 1919 also alarmed the public when their opponents depicted them as revolutionary attacks on the social order. In Seattle, the Central Labor Council called a general strike to support 35,000 shipyard workers striking for higher wages and shorter hours. When 60,000 more workers from 110 local unions also walked out, the city ground to a halt. The strikers behaved peacefully and protected public health and safety by operating garbage and fire trucks and providing food, water, and electricity. Nevertheless, Seattle's mayor, business leaders, and newspapers attacked them as Bolsheviks and anarchists. Threatened with military intervention, the labor council called off the strike, but not before it had caused a public backlash against unions across the nation.

Postwar labor unrest met determined suppression. Here, mounted police attack steelworkers in Pittsburgh in 1919. The strikers were seeking union recognition and an end to twelve-hour days.

In Boston, the police commissioner fired police officers for trying to organize a union to improve their inadequate pay. In response, the police went on strike. As in Seattle, Boston newspapers, politicians, and business leaders attributed the strike to Bolshevism, and Wilson denounced the strike as "a crime against civilization." Massachusetts Governor Calvin Coolidge mobilized the National Guard and gained nationwide acclaim when he stated, "There is no right to strike against the public safety by anybody, anywhere, anytime." The entire police force was fired; many of their replacements were war veterans.

The Red Scare

The strikes contributed to an anti-Bolshevik hysteria that swept the country in 1919. The **Red Scare** reflected fears that the Bolshevik revolution in Russia might spread to the United States. Steeped in the antiradical propaganda of the war years, many Americans were appalled by Russian Bolshevism, described by the *Saturday Evening Post* as a "compound of slaughter, confiscation, anarchy, and universal disorder." Their alarm grew in 1919 when Russia established the Third International to foster revolution abroad, and a few American socialists formed the American Communist Party. But the Red Scare also reflected the willingness of antiunion employers, ambitious politicians, sensational journalists, zealous veterans, and racists to exploit the panic to advance their own purposes.

Fed by misleading reports about Russian Bolshevism and its influence in the United States, the Red Scare reached panic levels by mid-1919. Bombs mailed anonymously to several prominent people on May Day seemed proof enough that a Bolshevik conspiracy threatened America. The Justice Department, Congress, and patriotic organizations like

At the peak of the Red Scare, few major newspapers questioned the wholesale assault on civil liberties and instead placed fears of Bolshevism above rights of individuals, especially workers, immigrants, and radicals. In this 1919 cartoon, the *Philadelphia Inquirer*, using the American flag as a protective cover, registers its support for the exile of radical immigrants and ideas.

In November 1919, Palmer and Hoover began raiding groups suspected of subversion. A month later, they deported 249 alien radicals, including the anarchist Emma Goldman, to Russia. Rabid patriots endorsed such actions. One minister favored deporting radicals "in ships of stone with sails of lead, with the wrath of God for a breeze and with hell for their first port." In January 1920, Palmer and Hoover rounded up more than 4,000 suspected radicals in 33 cities. Often without warrants, they broke into union halls, club rooms, and private homes, assaulting and arresting everyone in sight. People were jailed without access to lawyers; some were beaten into signing false confessions. In Lynn, Massachusetts, 39 people meeting to organize a bakery were arrested for holding a revolutionary caucus. The *Washington Post* declared, "There is no time to waste on hairsplitting over infringement of liberty."

Other Americans began to recoil from the excesses and illegal acts. Assistant Secretary of Labor Louis Post stopped further deportations by demonstrating that most of the arrested were "working men of good character, who are not anarchists or revolutionists, nor politically or otherwise dangerous in any sense." They had been arrested, he said, "for nothing more dangerous than affiliating with friends of their own race, country, and language." Support for the Red Scare withered. Palmer's attempt to inflame public emotion backfired. When his predictions of a violent attempt to overthrow the government on May 1, 1920, came to naught, most Americans realized that no menace had ever existed. They agreed with the *Rocky Mountain News:* "We can never get to work if we keep jumping sideways in fear of the bewhiskered Bolshevik." But if the Red Scare faded in mid-1920, the hostility to immigrants, organized labor, and dissent it reflected would endure for a decade.

The Election of 1920

The Democratic coalition that Wilson had cobbled together on the issues of progressivism and peace came apart after the war. Workers resented the administration's hostility to the postwar strikes. Ethnic groups brutalized by the Americanization of the war years blamed Wilson for the war or condemned his peace settlement. Farmers grumbled about wartime price controls and postwar falling prices. Wartime taxes and the social and economic turmoil of 1919–1920 alienated the middle class. Americans were weary of great crusades and social sacrifices; in the words of Kansas journalist William Allen White, they were

the American Legion joined with business groups to suppress radicalism, real and imagined. The government continued to enforce the repressive laws against Wobblies, socialists, and other dissenters; a Minnesota senator warned that the nation was more imperiled than during the war itself. Indeed, Wilson and Attorney General Mitchell Palmer called for more stringent laws and refused to release political prisoners jailed during the war. State governments harassed and arrested hundreds.

Palmer created a new agency, headed by J. Edgar Hoover, to suppress radicals and impose conformity. Its war on radicalism became the chief focus of the Justice Department. As an ambitious and ruthless bureaucrat, Hoover had participated in the government's assault on aliens and radicals during the war. Now he collected files on labor leaders and other "radical agitators" from Senator Robert La Follette to Jane Addams, issued misleading reports on communist influence in labor strikes and race riots, and contacted all major newspapers "to acquaint people like you with the real menace of evil-thinking, which is the foundation of the Red Movement."

"tired of issues, sick at heart of ideals, and weary of being noble." They yearned for what the Republican presidential candidate, Warren Harding of Ohio, called "normalcy."

The Republican ticket in 1920 symbolized the reassurance of simpler times. Harding was a genial politician who devoted more time to golf and poker than to public policy. An Old Guard conservative, he had stayed with the GOP when Theodore Roosevelt led the progressives out in 1912. His running mate, Calvin Coolidge, governor of Massachusetts, owed his nomination to his handling of the Boston police strike.

Wilson called the election of 1920 "a great and solemn referendum" on the League of Nations, but such lofty appeals fell flat. Harding was ambiguous about the League, and the Democratic national platform endorsed it but expressed a willingness to accept amendments or reservations. The Democratic nominees, James Cox, former governor of Ohio, and the young Franklin D. Roosevelt, Wilson's assistant secretary of the navy, favored the League, but it was not a decisive issue in the campaign.

Harding won in a landslide reflecting the nation's dissatisfaction with Wilson and the Democratic Party. "The Democrats are inconceivably unpopular," wrote Walter Lippmann, a prominent journalist. Harding received 16 million popular votes to Cox's 9 million. Running for president from his prison cell, Socialist Eugene Debs polled nearly a million votes. Not even his closest backers considered Harding qualified for the White House, but, as Lippmann said, the nation's "public spirit was exhausted" after the war years. The election of 1920 was "the final twitch" of America's "war mind."

Conclusion

The Great War disrupted the United States and much of the rest of the world. The initial American policy of neutrality yielded to sentimental and substantive links with the Allies and the pressure of German submarine warfare. Despite popular opposition, America joined the conflict when its leaders concluded that national interests demanded it. Using both military and diplomatic power, Woodrow Wilson sought to bring about a more stable and prosperous world order, with an expanded role for the United States. But the Treaty of Versailles only partly fulfilled his hopes, and the Senate refused to ratify the treaty and its League of Nations. The postwar world order would be unstable and dangerous.

Participation in the war, moreover, had changed the U.S. government, economy, and society. Some of these changes, including the centralization of the economy and an expansion of the regulatory role of the federal government, were already under way; some offered opportunities to implement progressive principles or reforms. Woman suffrage and prohibition gained decisive support because of the war spirit. But other consequences of the war betrayed both progressive impulses and the democratic principles the war was allegedly fought to promote. The suppression of civil liberties, manipulation of human emotions, repression of radicals and minorities, and exploitation of national crises by narrow interests helped disillusion the public. The repercussions of the Great War would linger for years, at home and abroad.

Review Questions

1. Why did Senator Robert La Follette oppose the war against Germany? How did many Americans regard the war and possible U.S. intervention?

2. What were the major arguments for and against U.S. entry into the Great War? What position do you find most persuasive? Why?

3. How and why did the United States shape public opinion in World War I? What were the consequences, positive and negative, of the propaganda of the Committee on Public Information, the Food Administration, and other government agencies?

4. How did the war affect women and minorities?

5. Evaluate the role of Woodrow Wilson at the Paris Peace Conference. What obstacles did he face? How successful was he in shaping the settlement?

6. Discuss the arguments for and against American ratification of the Treaty of Versailles.

Key Terms

Allies (p. 640)

Bolshevik (p. 652)

Central Powers (p. 640)

Committee on Public Information (CPI) (p. 647)

Declaration of London (p. 641)

Espionage Act (p. 648)

Irreconcilables (p. 655)

League of Nations (p. 653)

Liberty Bonds (p. 647)

Preparedness (p. 642)

Red Scare (p. 659)

Reservationists (p. 655)

Sedition Act of 1918 (p. 648)

Selective Service Act of 1917 (p. 649)

Self-determination (p. 643)

Sussex Pledge (p. 642)

Treaty of Versailles (p. 653)

War Industries Board (WIB) (p. 644)

Recommended Reading

Clements, Kendrick A. *The Presidency of Woodrow Wilson* (1992). The best single volume on the Wilson presidency.

Ferrell, Robert H. *Woodrow Wilson and World War I, 1917–1921* (1985). A useful synthesis that emphasizes diplomatic issues.

Kennedy, David M. *Over Here: The First World War and American Society* (1980). Thorough and illuminating discussion of the impact of World War I on American society.

Murray, Robert K. *The Red Scare: A Study in National Hysteria, 1919–1920* (1955). An important early study that retains much value.

Schaffer, Ronald. *America in the Great War: The Rise of the War Welfare State* (1991). An effective and provocative summary that illuminates the expanding role of government.

Zieger, Robert H. *America's Great War: World War I and the American Experience* (2000). A masterful account of the diplomatic, military, and domestic aspects of the war.

Where to Learn More

- **National Infantry Museum, Fort Benning, Georgia.** This sprawling collection of weapons, uniforms, and equipment includes exhibits on World War I. www.benningmwr.com/index.cfm

- **General John J. Pershing Boyhood Home, Laclede, Missouri.** Maintained by the Missouri State Park Board, Pershing's restored nineteenth-century home exhibits some of his personal belongings and papers. www.mostateparks.com/pershingsite.htm

- **Sgt. Alvin C. York Homeplace and State Historic Site, Pall Mall, Tennessee.** The home of America's greatest military hero of World War I contains fascinating artifacts, including York's letters written in the trenches. www.alvincyork.org

- **Wisconsin Veterans Museum, Madison, Wisconsin.** The most stunning museum of its size in the United States, this large building combines impressive collections of artifacts ranging from uniforms to tanks, with substantive exhibits and video programs based on remarkable historical research. It both documents and explains the participation of Wisconsin soldiers in the nation's wars, including the Spanish-American War and World War I. http://museum.dva.state.wi.us

Study Resources

For study resources for this chapter, go to www.myhistorylab.com and choose *The American Journey*. You will find a wealth of study and review material for this chapter, including pre- and post-tests, customized study plan, key term review flash cards, interactive map and document activities, and documents for analysis.

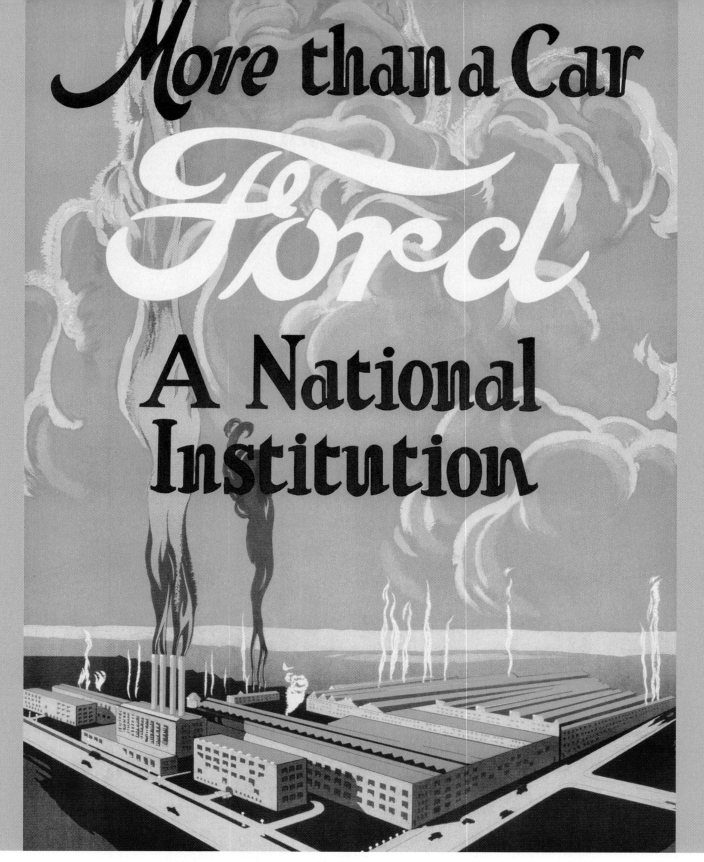

This image celebrates not only the centrality of the automobile but the mammoth size of the Ford enterprise and Henry Ford's vision of mass production in modern American society.

Toward a Modern America
The 1920s

24

Happy times were here again. American industry, adopting Henry Ford's policy of mass production and low prices, was making it possible for everybody to have his share of everything. The newspapers, the statesmen, the economists, all agreed that American ingenuity had solved the age-old problem of poverty. There could never be another depression....

The war had done something to Henry, it had taught him a new way to deal with his fellow men....He became more abrupt in his manner, more harsh in his speech. "Gratitude?" he would say. "There's no gratitude in business. Men work for money."...From now on he was a business man, and held a tight rein on everything. This industry was his, he had made it himself, and what he wanted of the men he hired was that they should do exactly as he told them....

Every worker had to be strained to the uttermost limit, every one had to be giving the last ounce of energy he had in his carcass....They were tired when they started in the morning, and when they quit they were grey and staggering with fatigue, they were empty shells out of which the last drop of juice had been squeezed....

Henry Ford was now getting close to his two million cars a year goal....From the moment the ore was taken out of the ship at the River Rouge plant [in Detroit], through all the processes turning it into steel and shaping it into automobile parts with a hundred-ton press, and putting five thousand parts together into a car which rolled off the assembly line under its own power—all those processes were completed in less than a day and a half!

Some forty-five thousand different machines were now used in the making of Ford cars, in sixty establishments scattered over the United States….Henry Ford was remaking the roads of America, and in the end he would remake the roads of the world—and line them all with filling stations and hot-dog stands of the American pattern.

Upton Sinclair, *The Flivver King: A Story of Ford-America* (Chicago: Charles H. Kerr, 1999).

myhistorylab

Personal Journeys Online

- ▪ Chicago Daily Tribune, "Capt. Charles Lindbergh, Lone U.S. Flyer, Wings Way from New York to Paris in 33 Hours 29 Minutes," 1927. Photographic essay of Lindbergh's accomplishment.

- ▪ Elsie Johnson McDougald, "The Double Task: The Struggle of Negro Women for Sex and Race Emancipation," 1925. Article attacks racial stereotypes and discusses the diversity among African American women in New York City.

Upton Sinclair, one of America's most famous muckraking journalists, won his greatest recognition with the 1906 publication of his novel *The Jungle*, which graphically depicted the wretched conditions endured by Chicago's immigrant meatpacking workers. In *The Flivver King*, Sinclair again demonstrates his extraordinary ability to weave together a dramatic and historical account of industrial America, as embodied in the rise of the automobile industry and the revolutionizing vision of Henry Ford, the entrepreneur who captured the American mind and symbolized modern America to the world.

"Machinery," proclaimed Henry Ford, "is the new Messiah." Others in the 1920s thought that Ford, too, deserved homage. "Just as in Rome one goes to the Vatican and endeavours to get audience of the Pope," noted a British observer, "so in Detroit one goes to the Ford Works and endeavours to see Henry Ford." Ford had in-troduced the assembly line at his automobile factory on the eve of World War I, and by 1925 it was turning out a Model T car every ten seconds. The term "mass production" originated in Henry Ford's 1926 description of the system of flow-production techniques popularly called "Fordism." The system symbolized the nation's booming economy: in the 1920s, Europeans used the word *Fordize* as a synonym for *Americanize*. Ford coupled machines and technology with managerial innovations. He established the five-dollar day, twice the prevailing wage in Detroit's auto industry, and slashed the workweek from 48 to 40 hours. These changes, Ford argued, would reduce the costs of labor turnover and boost consumer purchasing power, leading to further profits from mass production.

The assembly line, however, alienated workers, and even Ford himself conceded that the repetitive operations on the line were "so monotonous that it scarcely seems

CHRONOLOGY

1915	Ku Klux Klan is founded anew.
1919	Volstead Act is passed.
1920	Urban population exceeds rural population for the first time.
	Warren Harding is elected president.
	Prohibition takes effect.
	First commercial radio show is broadcast.
	Sinclair Lewis publishes *Main Street*.
1921	Sheppard-Towner Maternity and Infancy Act is passed.
	Washington Naval Conference limits naval armaments.
1922	Fordney-McCumber Act raises tariff rates.
	Sinclair Lewis publishes *Babbitt*.
	Country Club Plaza in Kansas City opens.
1923	Harding dies; Calvin Coolidge becomes president.
1924	National Origins Act sharply curtails immigration.
	Coolidge is elected president.
1925	Scopes trial is held in Dayton, Tennessee.
	F. Scott Fitzgerald publishes *The Great Gatsby*.
1927	Charles A. Lindbergh flies solo across the Atlantic.
1928	Kellogg-Briand Pact is signed.
	Herbert Hoover is elected president.
1929	Ernest Hemingway publishes *A Farewell to Arms*.

possible that any man would care to continue long at the same job." Ford first tried to adapt his mostly immigrant workers to these conditions through an Americanization program. His Education Department taught classes in English, sobriety, obedience, and industrial efficiency to the unskilled laborers entering the factory. After the course, they participated in a symbolic pageant: They climbed into a huge "melting pot," 15 feet across and 7 feet deep. After Ford managers stirred the pot with ten-foot ladles, the workers emerged wearing new clothes and waving American flags—new Americans made for the factory. When the labor market became more favorable to management in the early 1920s, Ford abolished the Education Department and relied on discipline to control workers, determined, as Sinclair observed, to keep "a tight rein on everything." To maximize profits and increase efficiency, Ford even prohibited talking, whistling, sitting, or smoking on the job. Wearing fixed expressions—"Fordization of the face"—workers could communicate only without moving their lips in the "Ford whisper." In keeping with the actions of other employers, Ford also joined the assault on labor organization, banning unions altogether and enlisting the aid of spies and informants to guard against their formation.

But even greater control and higher profits did not satisfy Henry Ford, for, like the 1920s itself, he remained conflicted about the progress he championed—the changes he saw and had helped facilitate. The automobile not only represented the new consumer culture, but it also forever transformed America and Americans—highways, filling stations, and hamburger stands sprang up across the nation, and the car even altered the dating practices of young Americans, alarming some parents and community leaders about what they feared as "bedrooms on wheels." Cars and cigarettes were among the most intensively advertised goods in the 1920s, and for some they

signaled rebellion and freedom. Women in short skirts and the rise of the Jazz Age all contributed to what Ford saw as the evils of the new America. Launching a crusade against the new direction America was headed, Ford decided, according to Sinclair, that "what America needed was to be led back to its past." Embracing nativism and Protestantism, Ford, an ardent anti-Semite, targeted Jewish Americans in his diatribes, blaming them for radicalism and labor organization, and he singled out the "International Jew" for allegedly controlling the international financial community.

Henry Ford and Fordism reflected the complexity of the 1920s. Economic growth and technological innovation were paired with social conflict as traditions were destroyed, values were displaced, and new people were incorporated into a society increasingly industrialized, urbanized, and dominated by big business. Industrial production and national wealth soared, buoyed by new techniques and markets for consumer goods. Business values pervaded society, and government promoted business interests.

But not all Americans prospered. Many workers were unemployed, and the wages of still more were stagnant or falling. Farmers endured grim conditions and worse prospects. Social change brought pleasure to some and deep concern to others. City factories like the Ford Works attracted workers from the countryside, increasing urbanization; rapid suburbanization opened other horizons. Leisure activities flourished, and new mass media promoted modern ideas and stylish products. Workers would have to achieve personal satisfaction through consumption and not production. But such experiences often proved unsettling, and some Americans sought reassurance by imposing their cultural or religious values on everyone around them. The tumultuous decade thus had many unresolved issues, much like the complex personality of Henry Ford himself. And Ford so dominated the age that when college students were asked to rank the greatest people of all time, Ford came in third, behind Christ and Napoleon.

The Economy That Roared

Following a severe postwar depression in 1920 and 1921, the American economy boomed through the remainder of the decade. Gross domestic product soared nearly 40 percent; output per worker-hour, or productivity, rose 72 percent in manufacturing; average per capita income increased by a third. Although the prosperity was not evenly distributed and some sectors of the economy were deeply troubled, most Americans welcomed the industrial expansion and business principles of the New Era.

Boom Industries

Many factors spurred the economic expansion of the 1920s. The huge wartime and postwar profits provided investment capital that enabled business to mechanize. Mass production spread quickly in American industry; machine-made standardized parts and the assembly line increased efficiency and production. Businesses steadily adopted the scientific management principles of Frederick W. Taylor (see Chapter 21). These highly touted systems, though often involving little more than an assembly-line speed-up, also boosted effi-

ciency. The nation more than doubled its capacity to generate electricity during the decade, further bolstering the economy. In factories, electric motors cut costs and improved manufacturing; in homes, electricity spurred demand for new products. Henry Ford was right: Mass production and consumption went hand in hand. Although not one in ten farm families had access to electric power, most other families did by 1929, and many bought electric sewing machines, vacuum cleaners, washing machines, and other labor-saving appliances.

The automobile industry drove the economy. Its productivity increased constantly, and sales rose from about 1.9 million vehicles in 1920 to nearly 5 million by 1929, when 26 million vehicles were on the road (see Figure 24–1). The automobile industry also employed one of every 14 manufacturing workers and stimulated other industries, from steel to rubber and glass. It created a huge new market for the petroleum industry and fostered oil drilling in Oklahoma, Texas, and Louisiana. It launched new businesses, from service stations (over 120,000 by 1929) to garages. It also encouraged the construction industry, a mainstay of the 1920s economy. Large increases in road building and residential housing, prompted by growing automobile ownership and migration to cities and suburbs, provided construction jobs, markets for lumber and other building materials, and profits.

New industries also sprang up. The aviation industry grew rapidly during the 1920s, with government support. The U.S. Post Office subsidized commercial air service by providing air mail contracts to private carriers. Congress then

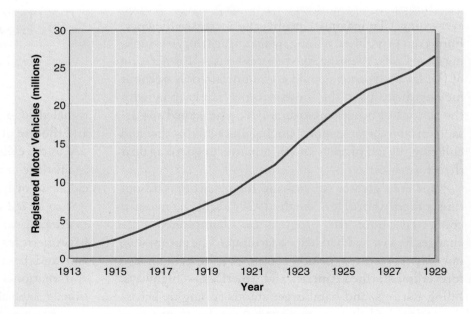

FIGURE 24–1 Registered Motor Vehicles, 1913–1929
The rapid adoption of automobiles shaped the 1920s, stimulating demand for steel and gasoline, encouraging the use of credit, facilitating urbanization, promoting tourism, and suggesting new cultural horizons.

Data Source: U.S. Bureau of Public Roads

authorized commercial passenger service over the mail routes, with regular traffic opening in 1927 between Boston and New York. By 1930, more than 100 airlines crisscrossed America.

The Great War also stimulated the chemical industry. The government confiscated chemical patents from German firms that had dominated the field and transferred them to U.S. companies like DuPont. With this advantage, DuPont in the 1920s became one of the nation's largest industrial firms, a chemical empire producing plastics, finishes, dyes, and organic chemicals. It developed products for the commercial market: enamel for household appliances and automobile finishes, gasoline additives to eliminate engine knocks (many workers died from producing what the *New York World* called "loony gas"), rayon for women's clothing, cellophane to package consumer goods. Led by such successes, the chemical industry became a $4 billion giant employing 300,000 workers by 1929.

The new radio and motion picture industries also flourished. Commercial broadcasting began with a single station in 1920. By 1927, there were 732 stations, and Congress created the Federal Radio Commission to prevent wave-band interference. The rationale for this agency, which was reorganized as the Federal Communications Commission (FCC) in 1934, was that the airwaves belong to the American people and not to private interests. Nevertheless, corporations quickly dominated the new industry. Westinghouse, RCA, and General Electric began opening strings of stations in the early 1920s. Large corporations also ultimately controlled radio manufacturing. Factory-made crystal radio sets became available in 1920, and some 5 million sets were sold by mid-decade. But corporate pressure and patent control eliminated more than 90 percent of the 750 manufacturers by 1927.

The motion-picture industry became one of the nation's five largest businesses, with 20,000 movie theaters selling 100 million tickets a week. Hollywood studios were huge factories, hiring directors, writers, camera crews, and actors to produce films on an assembly-line basis. While Americans watched Charlie Chaplin showcase his comedic genius in such films as *The Gold Rush* (1925), corporations like Paramount were integrating production with distribution and exhibition to maximize control and profit and eliminate independent producers and theaters. The advent of talking movies later in the decade brought still greater profits and power to the major studios, which alone could afford the increased engineering and production costs.

Corporate Consolidation

A wave of corporate mergers, rivaling the one at the turn of the century, swept over the 1920s economy. Great corporations swallowed up thousands of small firms. Particularly significant was the spread of **oligopoly**—the control of an entire industry by a few giant firms. The number of automobile manufacturers dropped from 108 to 44, while only three companies—Ford, General Motors, and Chrysler—produced 83 percent of the nation's cars. Their large-scale, integrated operations eliminated competition from small firms. In the electric light and power industry, nearly 4,000 local utility companies were merged into a dozen holding companies. Mergers also expanded oligopolistic control over other industries. By 1929, the nation's 200 largest corporations controlled nearly half of all nonbanking corporate wealth.

Oligopolies also dominated finance and marketing. Big banks extended their control through mergers and by opening branches. By 1929, a mere 1 percent of the nation's banks controlled half its banking resources. In marketing, national chain stores, such as A&P and Woolworth's, displaced local retailers. With 15,000 grocery stores and an elaborate distribution system, A&P could buy and sell goods for less than the corner grocer.

The corporate consolidation of the 1920s provoked little public fear or opposition. Independent retailers campaigned for local zoning regulations and laws to restrict chain stores, but for the most part, Americans accepted the idea that size brought efficiency and productivity.

Open Shops and Welfare Capitalism

Business also launched a vigorous assault on labor. In 1921, the National Association of Manufacturers organized an **open-shop** campaign to break union-shop contracts, which required all employees to be union members. Denouncing collective bargaining as un-American, businesses described the open shop, in which union membership was not required and usually prohibited, as the "American plan." They forced workers to sign so-called **yellow-dog contracts** that bound them to reject unions to keep their jobs. Business also used boycotts to force employers into a uniform antiunion front. Bethlehem Steel, for example, refused to sell steel to companies employing union labor. Where unions existed, corporations tried to crush them, using spies or hiring strikebreakers.

Some companies advocated a paternalistic system called **welfare capitalism** as an alternative to unions. Eastman Kodak, General Motors, U.S. Steel, and other firms provided medical services, insurance programs, pension plans, and vacations for their workers and established employee social clubs and sports teams. These policies were designed to undercut labor unions and persuade workers to rely on the corporation. Home-financing plans, for instance, increased workers' dependence on the company, and stock ownership plans inculcated business values among employees. Welfare capitalism, however, covered scarcely 5 percent of the workforce and often benefited only skilled workers already tied to the company through seniority. Moreover, it was directed primarily at men. General Electric, for example, dismissed women workers when they married. Women rarely built up enough seniority to obtain vacations and pensions.

Corporations in the 1920s also promoted company unions, management-sponsored substitutes for labor unions. But company unions were usually forbidden to handle wage and hour issues. Their function was to implement company policies and undermine real unionism. General Electric's

An Assembly Line
of the
Ford Motor Company

Ford Motor Company's assembly line at the River Rouge plant in Detroit. The increasing mechanization of work, linked to managerial and marketing innovations, boosted productivity in the 1920s and brought consumer goods within the reach of far more Americans than before.

State Historical Society of Wisconsin.

management reported that through the company union, "we have been able to educate and secure sympathy and support from a large body of employees who, under the old arrangement of bargaining with [AFL] craft unions, could not have been reached."

Partly because of these pressures, membership in labor unions fell from 5.1 million in 1920 to 3.6 million in 1929. But unions also contributed to their own decline. Conservative union leaders neglected ethnic and black workers in mass-production industries. Nor did they try to organize women, by 1930 nearly one-fourth of all workers. And they failed to respond effectively to other changes in the labor market. The growing numbers of white-collar workers regarded themselves as middle class and beyond the scope of union action.

With increasing mechanization and weak labor unions, workers suffered from job insecurity and stagnant wages. Mechanization, *Fortune* concluded, meant that "from the purely productive point of view, a part of the human race is already obsolete." Unemployment reached 12 percent in 1921 and remained a persistent concern of many working-class Americans during the decade. And despite claims to the contrary, hours were long: The average workweek in manufacturing remained more than 50 hours.

The promise of business to pay high wages proved hollow. Real wages (purchasing power) did improve, but most of the improvement came before 1923 and reflected falling prices more than rising wages. After 1923, American wages stabilized. Henry Ford made no general wage hike after 1919, although his workers would have needed an increase of 65 percent to recover the buying power they had enjoyed in 1914. Indeed, in 1928, Ford lowered wage rates. U.S. Steel also

reduced weekly wages, even while its profits almost doubled between 1923 and 1929. The failure to raise wages when productivity was increasing threatened the nation's long-term prosperity. In short, rising national income largely reflected salaries and dividends, not wages.

Some workers fared worse than others. Unskilled workers, especially southern and eastern Europeans, black migrants from the rural South, and Mexican immigrants, saw their already low wages decline relative to those of skilled workers. Southern workers earned much less than northerners, even in the same industry, and women were paid much less than men even for the same jobs. Male furniture assemblers, for example, earned 56 cents an hour; females only 32 cents. Overall, the gap between rich and poor widened during the decade (see Figure 24–2). By 1929, fully 71 percent of American families earned less than what the U.S. Bureau of Labor Statistics regarded as necessary for a decent living standard. The maldistribution of income meant that eventually Americans would be unable to purchase the products they made.

Consumer credit, rare before the 1920s, expanded during the decade. Credit offered temporary relief by permitting consumers to buy goods on time. General Motors introduced consumer credit on a national basis to create a mass market for expensive automobiles. By 1927, two-thirds of automobiles were purchased on the installment plan. By 1929, providing consumer credit had become the nation's tenth-largest business. Nevertheless, installment loans did not in the long run raise the purchasing power of an income; they simply added interest charges to the price of products.

Sick Industries

Despite the general appearance of prosperity, several "sick" industries dragged on the economy. Coal mining, textile and garment manufacturing, and railroads suffered from excess capacity (too many mines and factories), shrinking demand, low returns, and management-labor conflicts. For example, U.S. coal mines had a capacity of a billion tons, but scarcely half of that amount was needed because of increasing use of oil, natural gas, and hydroelectricity. Using company police, strikebreakers, and injunctions, mine operators broke the United Mine Workers and slashed wages by up to one-third. Unemployment in the industry approached 30 percent; by 1928, a reporter found "thousands of women and children literally starving to death" in Appalachia and the remaining miners held in "industrial slavery."

Similarly, the textile industry coped with overcapacity and declining demand by shifting operations from New En-

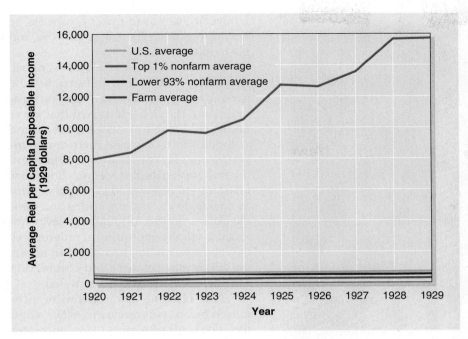

FIGURE 24–2   Growing Income Inequality in the 1920s
Despite the aura of prosperity in the 1920s, the vast majority of Americans received little or no increase in their real income. Farm families dragged the average down further, while the wealthiest Americans doubled their own incomes.

Data Source: Charles Holt, "Who Benefited from the Prosperity of the Twenties?" *Explorations in Economic History,* 14 (1977).

gland to the cheap-labor South, employing girls and young women for 56-hour weeks at 18 cents an hour. Textile companies, aided by local authorities, suppressed strikes in Tennessee and North Carolina. Ella May Wiggins sang of the worries in the mills:

> How it grieves the heart of a mother,
> You every one must know.
> For we can't buy for our children,
> Our wages are too low.

Wiggins was murdered by company thugs, leaving behind five small children. The textile industry, despite substandard wages and repressive policies, remained barely profitable.

American agriculture never recovered from the 1921 depression. In 1919, gross farm income amounted to 16 percent of the national income; by 1929, it had dropped to half that. Agricultural problems did not derive from inefficiency or low productivity. Mechanization (especially more tractors) and improved fertilizers and pesticides helped to produce crop surpluses. But surpluses and shrinking demand forced down prices. After the war, foreign markets dried up, and domestic demand for cotton slackened. Moreover, farmers' wartime expansion left them heavily mortgaged in the 1920s. Small farmers, unable to compete with larger, better-capitalized farmers, suffered most. Many lost their land and became tenants or farm hands. By 1930, only 57 percent of

American farmers owned the land they worked, the lowest percentage ever.

Racial discrimination worsened conditions for black and Hispanic tenants, sharecroppers, and farm workers. In the South, African American sharecroppers trapped in grinding poverty endured segregation, disfranchisement, and violence. Mexican immigrants and Hispanic Americans labored as migrant farm workers in the Southwest and California. Exploited by the contract-labor system pervasive in large-scale agriculture, they suffered from poor wages, miserable living conditions, and racism that created, in the words of one investigation, "a vicious circle" from which "few can escape through their own efforts."

By the end of the 1920s, the average per capita income for people on the nation's farms was only one-fourth that of Americans off the farm. "Widespread agricultural disaster," warned one Iowa newspaper, was producing "a highly dangerous situation." Like textile workers in New England and the Piedmont and coal miners in Appalachia, rural Americans suffered in the 1920s.

The Business of Government

The Republican surge in national politics also shaped the economy. In the 1920 election, the Republican slogan was "Less government in business, more business in government." By 1924, Calvin Coolidge, the decade's second Republican president, proclaimed, "This is a business country...and it wants a business government." Under such direction, the federal government advanced business interests at the expense of other objectives.

Republican Ascendancy

Republicans in 1920 had retained control of Congress and put Warren Harding in the White House. Harding was neither capable nor bright. One critic described a Harding speech as "an army of pompous phrases moving over the landscape in search of an idea." But he had a genial touch that contrasted favorably with Wilson. He pardoned Eugene Debs, whom Wilson had refused to release from prison, and he spoke out against racial violence. He also helped shape the modern presidency by supporting the Budget and Accounting Act of 1921, which gave the president authority over the budget and created the Budget Bureau and the General Accounting Office. Moreover, Harding recognized his own limitations and promised to appoint "the best minds" to his cabinet. Some of his appointees were highly accomplished,

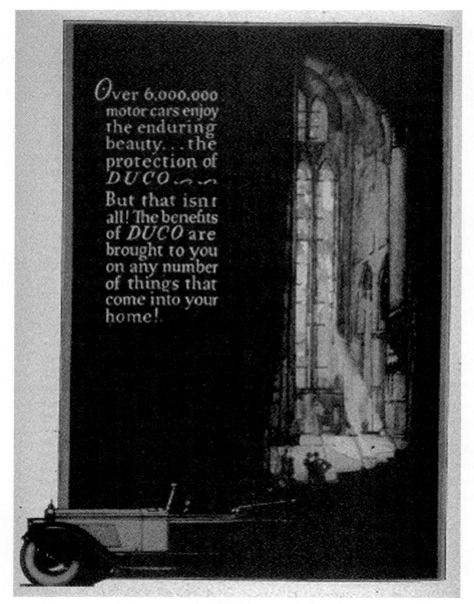

Over 6,000,000 motor cars enjoy the enduring beauty... the protection of DUCO. But that isn't all! The benefits of DUCO are brought to you on any number of things that come into your home!

DuPont became one of the nation's largest industrial corporations in the 1920s by developing new consumer products and marketing them aggressively. This advertisement for Duco automobile finishes blends images of a cathedral and an auto showroom, placing consumerism in a favorable light.

Hoover's goal was to foster prosperity by making business efficient, responsive, and profitable.

Andrew Mellon had a narrower goal. A wealthy banker and industrialist, he pressed Congress to reduce taxes on businesses and the rich. He argued that lower taxes would enable wealthy individuals and corporations to increase their capital investments, thereby creating new jobs and general prosperity. But Mellon's hope that favoring the rich would cause prosperity to trickle down to the working and middle classes proved ill-founded. Nevertheless, despite the opposition of progressives in Congress, Mellon succeeded in lowering maximum tax rates and eliminating wartime excess-profits taxes in 1921.

The Harding administration promoted business interests in other ways, too. The tariff of 1922 raised import rates to protect industry from foreign competition. High new duties on foreign aluminum, for instance, permitted manufacturers—including Mellon's own Alcoa Aluminum—to raise prices by 40 percent. But high tariffs made it difficult for European nations to earn the dollars to repay their war debts to the United States. High rates also impeded American farm exports and raised consumer prices.

The Harding administration aided the business campaign against unions. Attorney General Harry Daugherty secured an injunction against a railroad strike in 1922 and promised to "use the power of the government to prevent the labor unions of the country from destroying the open shop."

The Republicans also curtailed government regulation. By appointing advocates of big business to the Federal Trade Commission and the Federal Reserve Board, among others, Harding made government the collaborator rather than the regulator of business. Progressive Republican Senator George Norris of Nebraska condemned the new appointments, angrily asking, "If trusts, combinations, and big business are to run the government, why not permit them to do it directly rather than through this expensive machinery which was originally honestly established for the protection of the people of the country against monopoly?"

Finally, Harding reshaped the Supreme Court into a still more aggressive champion of business. He named the conservative William Howard Taft as chief justice and matched him with three other justices. All were, as one of them pro-

and two of them, Secretary of Commerce Herbert Hoover and Secretary of the Treasury Andrew Mellon, shaped economic policy throughout the 1920s.

A self-described progressive dedicated to efficiency, Hoover made the Commerce Department the government's most dynamic office. He cemented its ties with the leading sectors of the economy, expanded its collection and distribution of industrial information, pushed to exploit foreign resources and markets, and encouraged innovation. Thanks to his spreading influence, he was often called the secretary of commerce and "assistant secretary of everything else."

claimed, sympathetic to business leaders "beset and bedeviled with vexatious statutes, prying commissions, and government intermeddling of all sorts." The Court struck down much of the government economic regulation adopted during the Progressive Era, invalidated restraints on child labor and a minimum wage law for women, and approved restrictions on labor unions.

Government Corruption

The green light that Harding Republicans extended to private interests led to corruption and scandals. Harding appointed many friends and cronies who saw public service as an opportunity for graft. Attorney General Daugherty's associates in the Justice Department took bribes in exchange for pardons and government jobs. The head of the Veterans Bureau went to prison for cheating disabled veterans of $200 million. Albert Fall, the secretary of the interior, leased petroleum reserves set aside by progressive conservationists to oil companies in exchange for cash, bonds, and cattle for his New Mexico ranch. Exposed for his role in the Teapot Dome scandal, named after a Wyoming oil reserve, Fall became the first cabinet officer in history to go to jail. Daugherty escaped a similar fate by destroying records and invoking the Fifth Amendment.

Harding was appalled by the scandals. "My God, this is a hell of a job!" he told William Allen White. "I have no trouble with my enemies.... But my damned friends, ... they're the ones that keep me walking the floor nights!" Harding died shortly thereafter, probably of a heart attack.

Coolidge Prosperity

On August 3, 1923, Vice President Calvin Coolidge was sworn in as president by his father while visiting his birthplace in rural Vermont, thereby reaffirming his association with traditional values. This image reassured Americans troubled by the Harding scandals. Coolidge's calm appearance hid a furious temper and a mean spirit. Coolidge supported business with ideological conviction. He opposed the activist presidency of the Progressive Era, cultivating instead a deliberate inactivity calculated to lower expectations of government. He endorsed Secretary of the Treasury Mellon's ongoing efforts to reverse the progressive tax policies of the Wilson years and backed Secretary of Commerce Hoover's persistent efforts on behalf of the business community (although he privately sneered at Hoover as the "Wonder Boy").

Like Harding, Coolidge installed business supporters in the regulatory agencies. To chair the Federal Trade Commission he appointed an attorney who had condemned the agency as "an instrument of oppression and disturbance and injury instead of help to business." Under this leadership, the FTC described its new goal as "helping business to help itself," which meant approving trade associations and agreements to suppress competition. This attitude, endorsed by the Supreme Court, aided the mergers that occurred after 1925. The *Wall Street Journal* crowed, "Never before, here or anywhere else, has a government been so completely fused with business."

And Coolidge confined the government's role to helping business. When Congress tried to raise farm prices, Coolidge vetoed the measure as "preposterous" special-interest legislation. One economist said that Coolidge's vetoes revealed "a stubborn determination to do nothing," but they revealed more. For on the same day that Coolidge vetoed assistance to farmers, he raised by 50 percent the tariff on pig iron, thereby increasing manufacturers' profits and farmers' costs for tools. Government action was acceptable for business but not for nonbusiness interests.

"Coolidge prosperity" determined the 1924 election. The Democrats, hopelessly divided, took 103 ballots to nominate the colorless, conservative Wall Street lawyer John W. Davis. A more interesting opponent for Coolidge was Robert La Follette, nominated by discontented farm and labor organizations that formed a new Progressive Party. La Follette campaigned against "the power of private monopoly over the political and economic life of the American people." The Progressive platform demanded government ownership of railroads and utilities, farm assistance, and collective bargaining. The Republicans, backed by immense contributions from business, denounced La Follette as an agent of Bolshevism. The choice, Republicans insisted, was "Coolidge or Chaos." Thus instructed, Americans chose Coolidge, though barely half the electorate bothered to vote.

The Fate of Reform

But progressive reform was not completely dead. Even Harding proposed social welfare measures, and, during the 1921 depression, he convened a conference on unemployment and helped spark voluntary relief. A small group in Congress, led by La Follette and George Norris, attacked Mellon's regressive tax policies and supported measures regulating agricultural processors, protecting workers' rights, and maintaining public ownership of a hydroelectric dam at Muscle Shoals, Alabama, that conservative Republicans wanted to privatize. Yet the reformers' successes were few and often temporary.

The fate of women's groups illustrates the difficulties reformers faced in the 1920s. At first, the adoption of woman suffrage prompted politicians to champion women's reform issues. In 1920, both major parties endorsed many of the goals of the new **League of Women Voters.** Within a year, many states had granted women the right to serve on juries, several enacted equal-pay laws, and Wisconsin adopted an equal-rights law. Congress passed the **Sheppard-Towner Maternity and Infancy Act,** the first federal social-welfare law, in 1921. It provided federal funds for infant and maternity care, precisely the type of protective legislation that the suffragists had described as women's special interest. Women also ran for political office and by 1922 there were fifteen women mayors of small towns throughout the nation.

But thereafter women reformers gained little. As it became clear that women did not vote as a bloc but according to their varying social and economic backgrounds, Congress lost interest in women's issues. In 1929, Congress killed the Sheppard-Towner Act. Nor could reformers gain ratification of a child-labor amendment after the Supreme Court invalidated laws regulating child labor. Conservatives attacked women reformers as "Bolsheviks."

Disagreements and shifting interests also limited the success of women reformers. Led by the National Woman's Party, some feminists campaigned for an Equal Rights Amendment, whereas other reformers feared that it would nullify the progressive laws that protected working women. Such reform organizations as the Consumers' League lost their energy and focus. The General Federation of Women's Clubs, always relatively conservative, promoted home economics and the use of electrical appliances. Indeed, many younger women rejected the public reform focus of progressive feminists. The *Magazine of Business* even maintained that women valued the vacuum cleaner more than the vote. By 1927, the president of the Women's Trade Union League called the decade "hideous in the public life of our people and in the noisy flaunting of cheap hopes and cheaper materialism."

Cities and Suburbs

The 1920 census was the first to report that more Americans lived in urban than in rural areas. The trend toward urbanization accelerated in the 1920s as millions of Americans fled the depressed countryside for the booming cities. This massive population movement interacted with technological innovations to reshape cities, build suburbs, and transform urban life (see Map 24–1).

Expanding Cities

Urbanization affected every region of the country. In absolute terms, the older industrial cities of the Northeast and upper Midwest grew the most, attracting migrants from the

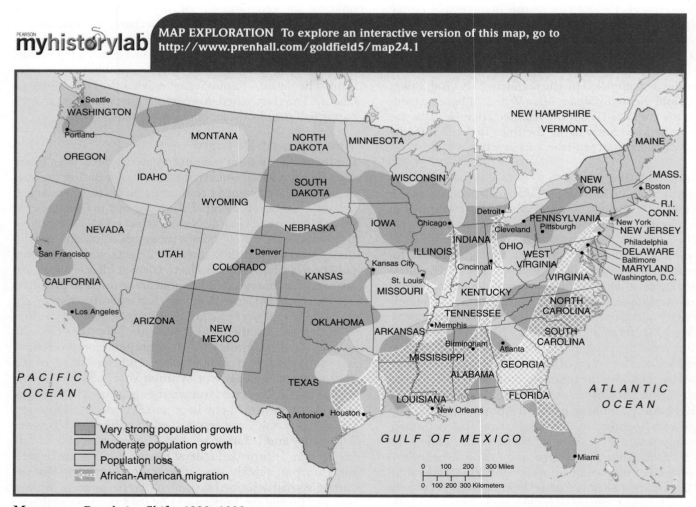

MAP 24–1　Population Shifts, 1920–1930
Rural Americans fled to the cities during the 1920s, escaping a declining agricultural economy to search for new opportunities. African Americans in particular left the rural South for eastern and midwestern cities, but the urban population also jumped in the West and in the South itself.

rural South and distressed Appalachia. New York remained the nation's foremost metropolis. All the other major cities also grew—none more spectacularly than Detroit, which now had 1.6 million people. The "Motor City" thrived on the booming automobile industry and related industries like glass manufacturing. Old trees and wide lawns gave way to multi-lane highways as apartment houses and parking lots obliterated old Detroit.

Rural southerners also headed for southern cities. In fact, the South was the nation's most rapidly urbanizing region. Migrants from the countryside poured into Atlanta, Birmingham, Memphis, and Houston. Little more than jungle before 1914, Miami became the fastest growing city in the United States during the 1920s—"the Magic City." Not all southerners welcomed urban growth and the values it represented. The novelist Thomas Wolfe cautioned against boosters in Asheville, North Carolina, "who shout 'Progress Progress Progress'—when what they mean is more Ford automobiles, more Rotary Clubs, more Baptist Ladies Social unions.... We are not necessarily four times as civilized as our grandfathers because we go four times as fast in automobiles, because our buildings are four times as tall."

In the West, Denver, Portland, and Seattle (each a regional economic hub) and several California cities grew rapidly. Los Angeles grew by 115 percent and by 1930 was the nation's fifth-largest city, with over 1.2 million people. Although it was the center of California's agricultural wealth and the motion-picture industry and one of the world's busiest ports, Los Angeles was also linked to the automobile industry. The southern California oil fields and the demand for gasoline made it the nation's leading refining center.

The population surge transformed the urban landscape. As land values soared, developers built skyscrapers, giving Cleveland, Kansas City, San Francisco, and many other cities modern skylines. By the end of the decade, American cities had nearly 400 skyscrapers taller than 20 stories.

The Great Black Migration

A significant feature of the rural-to-urban movement was the **Great Migration** of African Americans from the South. Like other migrants, they were responding chiefly to economic factors. Southern segregation and violence made migration attractive, but job opportunities made it possible. Prosperity created jobs, and with the decline in European immigration, black workers filled the positions previously given to new immigrants. Though generally the lowest paid and least secure jobs, they were better than sharecropping in the rural South. Black men worked as unskilled or semiskilled laborers; black women became domestics in white homes. The migrants often found adjustment to their new environment difficult. Southern rural black culture clashed with industrial work rhythms and discipline and with urban living. Still, more than 1.5 million African Americans moved to northern cities in the 1920s.

There black ghettos usually developed, more because of prejudice than the wishes of the migrants. Although African Americans, like European immigrants, often wanted to live together to sustain their culture, racist restrictions meant that segregation, not congregation, most shaped their urban community. With thousands of newcomers limited to certain neighborhoods, housing shortages developed. Rapacious landlords charged ever-increasing rents for ever-declining housing. Rents doubled in New York's Harlem during the decade. Racism exacerbated urban poverty; black workers earned less than working-class white workers but had to spend 50 percent more for housing. High rents and low wages forced black families to share inferior and unsanitary housing that threatened their health and safety. In Pittsburgh, only 20 percent of black houses had bathtubs, and only 50 percent had indoor toilets; in another city, an observer wrote that "the State would not allow cows to live in some of these apartments used by colored people."

However, the Great Migration also increased African Americans' racial consciousness, autonomy, and power. In 1928, for instance, black Chicagoans, using the ballot denied to African Americans in the South, elected the first black man to Congress since the turn of the century. Mutual-aid societies and fraternal orders proliferated. Churches were particularly influential. A reporter in 1926 counted 140 black churches in a 150-block area of Harlem. Most of these were "storefront churches" where "cotton-field preachers" provided an emotional and fundamentalist religion familiar to migrants from the rural South.

Another organization also appealed to poor black ghetto dwellers. The Universal Negro Improvement Association (UNIA), organized by Marcus Garvey, a Jamaican immigrant to New York, rejected the NAACP's goal of integration. A black nationalist espousing racial pride, Garvey exhorted black people to migrate to Africa to build a "free, redeemed, and mighty nation." In the meantime, he urged them to support black businesses. UNIA organized many enterprises, including groceries, restaurants, laundries, a printing plant, and the Black Star Steamship Line, intended as a commercial link between the United States, the West Indies, and Africa. UNIA attracted half a million members, the first black mass movement in American history. When Garvey was convicted of mail fraud and deported, however, the movement collapsed.

Racial pride also found expression in the **Harlem Renaissance,** an outpouring of literature, painting, sculpture, and music. Inspired by African American culture and black urban life, writers and artists created works of power and poignancy. The poetry of Langston Hughes reflected the rhythm and mood of jazz and the blues. When a white patron complained that his writing was not "primitive" enough, Hughes responded, "I did not feel the rhythms of the primitive surging through me, and so I could not live and write as though I did. I was Chicago and Kansas City and Broadway and Harlem. And I was not what she wanted me to be." Other

Zora Neale Hurston, folklorist, anthropologist, and novelist, wrote with wit and verve about the African-American South she so closely studied. Part of the dynamic community known as the Harlem Renaissance, Hurston won recognition in 1925 for her short story "Spunk." Her collective work, especially her later novel, *Their Eyes Were Watching God,* both reflected and advanced the creative pulse of what one black intellectual regarded as the first opportunity for African Americans to realize "group expression and self-determination."

leading authors of the Harlem Renaissance who asserted their independence included Claude McKay, who wrote of the black working class in *Home to Harlem* (1928), Zora Neale Hurston, James Weldon Johnson, and Dorothy West.

Barrios

Hispanic migrants also entered the nation's cities in the 1920s, creating their own communities, or barrios. Fifty thousand Puerto Ricans settled in New York, mostly in East ("Spanish") Harlem, where they found low-paying jobs. Far more migrants arrived from Mexico. Although many worked as migrant farm laborers, they often lived in cities in the off-season. Others permanently joined the expanding urban economy in industrial and construction jobs. The barrios, with their own businesses, churches, and cultural organizations, created a sense of permanency.

These communities enabled the newcomers to preserve their cultural values and build social institutions, such as *mutualistas* (mutual aid societies), that helped them obtain credit, housing, and healthcare. But the barrios also reflected the hostility that Hispanics encountered in American cities.

The number of Mexicans in Los Angeles tripled during the 1920s to nearly 100,000, but segregation confined them to East Los Angeles. Other areas of the city, such as El Segundo and Lynwood, boasted of being "restricted to the white race" and having "no Negroes or Mexicans." Los Angeles maintained separate schools for Mexicans, and a social worker reported that "America has repulsed the Mexican immigrant in every step he has taken" toward integration. As new migrants streamed in, conditions in the barrios deteriorated, for few cities provided adequate public services for them. Denver's barrio was described in 1924 as an area "both God and Denver had forgotten," with "no paving, no sidewalks, no sewers."

Some Hispanics fought discrimination. La Orden de Hijos de America ("The Order of the Sons of America"), organized in San Antonio in 1921, campaigned against inequities in schools and the jury system. In 1929, it helped launch the larger League of United Latin American Citizens (LULAC), which would help advance civil rights for all Americans.

The Road to Suburbia

As fast as the cities mushroomed in the 1920s, the suburbs grew twice as fast. Park Ridge outside Chicago, Inglewood outside Los Angeles, Shaker Heights outside Cleveland, and many others expanded by 400 percent. New suburbs arose across the country. Fourteen hundred new subdivisions appeared in Los Angeles County during the 1920s; two-thirds of the new municipal incorporations in Illinois and Michigan were suburbs of Chicago, St. Louis, or Detroit. Some suburbs, such as Highland Park, where Henry Ford built his factory near Detroit, and Fairfield, Alabama, were industrial, but most were havens for the middle and upper classes.

Automobiles created the modern suburb. Nineteenth-century suburbs were small and linear, stretching along the street railway system. The new developments were sprawling and dispersed, for the automobile enabled people to live in formerly remote areas. A single-family house surrounded by a lawn became the social ideal, a pastoral escape from the overcrowded and dangerous city. Many suburbs excluded African Americans, Hispanics, Jews, and working-class people. Shaker Heights, for instance, limited land sales to white buyers and required expensive building materials and professional architects. Suburbanites of more modest means found homes in such places as Westwood, outside Chicago, the "World's Largest Bungalow Development."

Suburbanization and the automobile brought other changes. The government provided federal money to states to build highways, and by the end of the decade, road construction was the largest single item in the national budget. Autos and suburbs also stimulated the growth of new industries. In 1922, J. C. Nichols opened the Country Club Plaza, the first suburban shopping center, in Kansas City; it provided free off-street parking. Department stores and other large retailers began leaving the urban cores for the suburbs, where both parking and more affluent customers were waiting. Drive-in restaurants began with Royce Hailey's Pig Stand in Dallas in 1921. That same year, the first fast-food franchise and the work and play of the whole nation." A less complacent observer calculated that in 1925, nearly 50 percent more was spent "to educate consumers in what they may or may not want to buy" than on education from grade school through university.

Advertisers exhorted consumers via newspapers, billboards, streetcar signs, junk mail, radio, movies, and even skywriting. They sought to create a single market where everyone, regardless of region and ethnicity, consumed brand-name products. Advertisers attempted to stimulate new wants by ridiculing previous models or tastes as obsolete, acclaiming the convenience of a new brand, or linking the latest fashion with status or sex appeal. "If I wear a certain brand of underwear," observed one critic, "I have the satisfaction of knowing that my fellow-men not so fortunately clad are undoubtedly fouled swine."

The home became a focus of consumerism. Middle- and upper-class women purchased mass-produced household appliances, such as electric irons, toasters, vacuum cleaners, washing machines, and refrigerators. Working-class women bought packaged food, ready-made clothing, and other consumer goods to lighten their workload. Advertisers attempted to redefine the housewife's role as primarily that of a consumer, purchasing goods for her family. To promote sales of clothing and cosmetics, advertising depicted women as concerned with fashion, beauty, and sex appeal. It thus contributed to the declining interest in the larger social issues that the earlier women's movement had raised.

A shifting labor market also promoted mass consumption. The increasing number of white-collar workers had more time and money for leisure and consumption. Factory workers, whose jobs often provided little challenge, less satisfaction, and no prospect for advancement, found in consumption not only material rewards but, thanks to advertisers' claims, some self-respect and fulfillment as stylish and attractive people worthy of attention. Women clerical workers, the fastest growing occupational group, found in the purchase of clothes and cosmetics a sign of social status and an antidote to workplace monotony.

Under the stimulus of advertising, consumption increasingly displaced the traditional virtues of thrift, prudence, and avoidance of debt. Installment buying became common. By 1928, fully 85 percent of furniture, 80 percent of radios, and 75 percent of washing machines were bought on credit. But with personal debt rising more than twice as fast as incomes, even aggressive advertising and the extension of credit could not indefinitely prolong the illusion of a healthy economy.

Making tortillas—the staple of the Mexican diet—these Mexican American women used stone mortars in the 1920s to grind the corn by hand at the El Sol del Mayo tortilla plant in East Los Angeles. Spurned by Anglo society, Mexican Americans found support, jobs, and community in the barrios where they lived and worked. The barrios also enabled some Mexican Americans, like plant owner Maria Zuevedo, to become small business owners. They provided products and services that satisfied the traditional cultural values of the Mexican community.

chain, White Castle, appeared, with its standardized menu and building, serving hamburgers "by the sack" to Americans in record numbers. Enjoying remarkable success, owners Walt Anderson and Billy Ingram described their volume of sales in one year: "Picture a line of buns, laid side by side, one hundred and sixty-three miles long, forty-one truckloads of hamburger, weighing two tons each, two carloads of onions, three carloads of pickles, ninety-six-hundred five gallon urns of coffee and you have an idea of the output of the White Castle System for the year 1925."

Mass Culture in the Jazz Age

The White Castle chain symbolized a new society and culture. Urbanization and the automobile joined with new systems of distributing, marketing, and communications to mold a mass culture of standardized experiences and interests. Not all Americans participated equally in the new culture, however, and some attacked it.

Advertising the Consumer Society

Advertising and its focus on increasing consumption shaped the new society. President Coolidge considered advertising "the most potent influence in adopting and changing the habits and modes of life, affecting what we eat, what we wear,

Leisure and Entertainment

During the 1920s, Americans also spent more on recreation and leisure, important features of the new mass society. Millions of people packed into movie theaters whose ornate style symbolized their social importance. In Chicago, the Uptown boasted a 4,000-seat theater, an infirmary, a nursery, and a restaurant; its turreted façade soared eight stories. Inside was a four-story lobby with twin marble staircases,

The soup for men who eat to win!

MEN with the success-habit eat wisely and well, both. They enjoy Campbell's Tomato Soup regularly and they get from it a sparkle and zest, which tell in the day's work. All of the rich, tonic goodness. All of the famous tomato healthfulness. 12 cents a can.

Advertisements for brand-name products, like this 1929 ad for Campbell's tomato soup, often tried to link simple consumption with larger issues of personal success and achievement.

crystal chandeliers, and an orchestra to entertain people waiting to enter. "It is beyond human dreams of loveliness," exclaimed one ad, "achieving that overpowering sense of tremendous size and exquisite beauty."

Movies helped to spread common values and to set national trends in dress, language, and behavior. Studios made films to attract the largest audiences and fit prevailing stereotypes. Cecil B. De Mille titillated audiences while reinforcing conventional standards with religious epics like *The Ten Commandments* (1923) and *The King of Kings* (1927). Set in ancient times, such movies depicted both sinful pleasures and the eventual triumph of moral order. One Hollywood executive called for "passionate but pure" films that would give "the public all the sex it wants with compensating values for all those church and women groups."

Radio also helped to mold popular culture. The first radio network, the National Broadcasting Company (NBC), was formed in 1926. Soon it was charging $10,000 to broadcast a commercial to a national market. Networks provided standardized entertainment, personalities, and news to Americans across the nation. Radio incorporated listeners

into a national society. Rural residents, in particular, welcomed the "talking furniture" for giving them access to the speeches, sermons, and business information available to city dwellers.

The phonograph, another popular source of entertainment, allowed families to listen to music of their choice in their own homes. The phonograph business boomed. Manufacturers turned out more than 2 million phonographs and 100 million records annually. Record companies promoted dance crazes, such as the Charleston, and developed regional markets for country, or "hillbilly," music in the South and West, as well as a "race market" for blues and jazz among the growing urban population, black and white. The popularity of the trumpet player Louis Armstrong and other jazz greats gave the decade its nickname, the **Jazz Age.**

Jazz derived from African American musical traditions. The Great Migration spread it from New Orleans and Kansas City to cities throughout the nation. Its improvisational and rhythmic characteristics differed sharply from older and more formal music and were often condemned by people who feared that jazz would undermine conventional restraints on behavior. A group in Cincinnati, arguing that the music would implant "jazz emotions" in babies, won an injunction against its performance near hospitals. Middle-class black Chicagoans frowned on jazz and favored "the better class of music." But the symphony conductor Leopold Stokowski defended jazz as the music of modern America: "Jazz has come to stay because it is an expression of the times, of the breathless, energetic, superactive times in which we are living; it is useless to fight against it." (See Global Perspectives, The International Journey of Jazz.)

Professional sports also became more commercialized. Millions of Americans, attracted by the popularity of such celebrities as Babe Ruth of the New York Yankees, crowded into baseball parks to follow major league teams. Ruth treated himself as a commercial commodity, hiring an agent, endorsing Cadillacs and alligator shoes, and defending a salary in 1932 that dwarfed that of President Hoover by declaring, "I had a better year than he did."

Large crowds turned out to watch boxers Jack Dempsey and Gene Tunney pummel each other; those who could not get tickets listened to radio announcers describe each blow. College football attracted frenzied followers among people with no interest in higher education. Universities built huge stadiums—Ohio State's had 64,000 seats. By 1929, the Carnegie Commission noted that the commercialization of college sports had "overshadowed the intellectual life for which the university is assumed to exist."

Other crazes, from flagpole sitting to miniature golf, also highlighted the spread of popular culture and its emphasis on leisure. Another celebrity who captured popular fascination was the aviator Charles Lindbergh, who flew alone across the Atlantic in 1927. In the *Spirit of St. Louis,* a tiny airplane built on a shoestring budget and nearly outweighed by the

Violinist Carroll Dickerson, at the Sunset Café in 1922, led one of the jazz bands that flourished in Chicago's many clubs, pointing up the central role of African Americans in the Jazz Age. *Variety* magazine dubbed Chicago the "hottest café town" in the United States, but the Illinois Vigilance Association despaired that "in Chicago alone" it had "traced the fall of 1,000 girls to jazz music" in just two years.

massive amount of fuel it had to carry, Lindbergh fought bad weather and fatigue for 34 hours before landing to a hero's welcome in Paris. Named its first "Man of the Year" by *Time,* one of the new mass-circulation magazines, Lindbergh won adulation and awards from Americans who still valued the image of individualism.

The New Morality

The promotion of consumption and immediate gratification weakened traditional self-restraint and fed a desire for personal fulfillment. The failure of wartime sacrifices to achieve promised glories deepened Americans' growing disenchantment with traditional values. The social dislocations of the war years and growing urbanization accelerated moral and social change. Sexual pleasure became an increasingly open objective. Popularization of Sigmund Freud's ideas weakened prescriptions for sexual restraint; the growing availability of birth-control information enabled women to enjoy sex with less fear of pregnancy; and movie stars like Clara Bow, known as "the It Girl," and Rudolph Valentino, flaunted sexuality to mass audiences. Traditionalists worried as divorce rates, cigarette consumption, and hemlines went up while respect for parents, elders, and clergy went down. A sociological study of Muncie, Indiana—the nation's "Middletown"—found that "religious life as represented by the churches is less pervasive than a generation ago."

Young people seemed to embody the new morality. Rejecting conventional standards, they embraced the era's frenzied dances, bootleg liquor, smoking, more revealing clothing, and sexual experimentation. They welcomed the freedom from parental control that the automobile afforded. The "flapper"—a frivolous young woman with short hair and a skimpy skirt who danced, smoked, and drank in oblivious self-absorption—was a major obsession in countless articles bearing such titles as "These Wild Young People" and "The Uprising of the Young." Few people were more alarmed than the president of the University of Florida. "The low-cut gowns, the rolled hose and short skirts are born of the Devil," he cried, "and are carrying the present and future generations to chaos and destruction." But feminists also condemned this symbol of changing standards. "It is sickening," Charlotte Perkins Gilman wrote in 1923, "to see so many of the newly freed abusing that freedom in mere imitation of masculine vice and weakness."

But the new morality was neither as new nor as widespread as its advocates and critics believed. Signs of change had appeared before the Great War in the popularity of new clothing fashions, social values, and public amusements among working-class and ethnic groups. And if it now became fashionable for the middle class to adopt such attitudes and practices, most Americans still adhered to traditional beliefs and values. Legislators in Utah and Virginia, for example, proposed laws requiring hemlines within 3 inches of the ankle and necklines within 3 inches of the throat. The city council in Oshkosh, Wisconsin, passed a law prohibiting partners from "looking into each other's eyes while dancing." Moreover, as Gilman's comment suggests, the new morality offered only a limited freedom. It certainly did not promote social equality for women, who remained subject to traditional double standards, with marriage and divorce laws, property rights, and employment opportunities biased against them.

The Searching Twenties

Many writers rejected what they considered the materialism, conformity, and provincialism of mass culture. Their criticism made the postwar decade one of the most creative periods in American literature. The brutality and hypocrisy of the war stimulated the critics' disillusionment and alienation. What Gertrude Stein called the Lost Generation considered, in the words of F. Scott Fitzgerald, "all Gods dead, all wars fought, all faiths in man shaken." Ernest Hemingway, wounded as a Red Cross volunteer during the war, rejected idealism in his novel *A Farewell to Arms* (1929), declaring that he no longer saw any meaning in "the words sacred, glorious, and sacrifice."

Novelists also turned their attention to American society. In *The Great Gatsby* (1925), Fitzgerald traced the self-deceptions

Global Perspectives

The International Journey of Jazz

A central part of American culture in the 1920s, jazz expanded its global reach in the decade known for mass production and mass consumerism. Just as Henry Ford sold his Model T cars abroad, jazz musicians took their distinctively American form of music south to Latin America and east to England, France, the Soviet Union, and China.

Jazz caught the imagination of the world. For many at home and abroad, the jarring spontaneity of jazz signaled a new age. It was, according to George Gershwin, the result of "energy stored up in America." For the composer John Alden Carpenter, it represented "the first art innovation originating in America to be accepted seriously in Europe." A German critic could not have agreed more, exclaiming, "Jazz is the expression of a Kultur epoch....Jazz is a musical revelation, a religion, a philosophy of the world, just like Expressionism and Impressionism."

Jazz also had its detractors—both in the United States and abroad. At home, one of the principal architects of mass production, Henry Ford, labeled jazz "musical slush" that encouraged the youth to imitate the "drivel of morons." A noted French poet called jazz "a triumph of barbaric folly," and an English observer worried that jazz—the "aboriginal music of the Negro"—might threaten American music.

Still, the enthusiasm for jazz was so strong that white jazz musicians claimed credit for its origins—at least until the 1930s, when the historical role of African Americans in creating jazz was more fully acknowledged in the United States and Europe. Black musicians had given Europe its first taste of jazz during World War I with James Reese Europe's 369th Division Band. Throughout the 1920s, other African American bands and performers traveled abroad, spreading the international message of jazz while escaping the racism of their home country. Sam Wooding's orchestra toured Europe and the Soviet Union; Herb Flemming's band, the Red Devils, and Benny Peyton's band along with remarkable performers like Josephine Baker dazzled audiences with dance and music in Buenos Aires, Paris, and London.

Jazz underscored to America and the world that an important part of the American heritage derived from an African—not European—heritage. But as the popularity of jazz grew internationally, the music no longer belonged exclusively to Americans, or even African Americans. Other countries appropriated the music and shaped it on their own terms. Still, the origins of jazz—this movement that captured the world's attention—belonged to black musicians who regarded jazz as a special expression of the African American community.

■ **How did the influence of jazz affect America domestically and internationally?**

---

of the wealthy. Sinclair Lewis ridiculed middle-class society and its narrow business culture in *Babbitt* (1922), whose title character provided a new word applied to the smug and shallow. In 1930, Lewis became the first American to win the Nobel Prize in literature.

Other writers condemned the mediocrity and intolerance of mass society. The critic Harold Stearns edited *Civilization in the United States* (1922), a book of essays. Its depiction of a repressive society sunk in hypocrisy, conformity, and materialism prompted his departure for Paris, where he lived, like Hemingway and Fitzgerald, as an expatriate, alienated from America. H. L. Mencken made his *American Mercury* the leading magazine of cultural dissenters. Conventional and conservative himself, Mencken heaped vitriol on the "puritans," "peasants," and "prehensile morons" he saw everywhere in American life.

When President Coolidge declined an invitation to exhibit American paintings in Paris by declaring that there were none, he seemed to confirm for the critics the boorishness of American society. But many of the critics were as self-absorbed as their targets. When the old progressive muckraker Upton Sinclair complained that he found nothing "constructive" in Mencken's voluminous writings, Mencken was delighted. "Uplift," he retorted, "has damn nigh ruined the country." Fitzgerald claimed to have "no interest in politics at all." Such attitudes dovetailed with the society they condemned.

Culture Wars

Despite the blossoming of mass culture and society in the 1920s, conflicts divided social groups. Some of these struggles involved reactions against the new currents in American life, including technological and scientific innovations, urban growth, and materialism. But movements to restrict immigration, enforce prohibition, prohibit the teaching of evolution, and even sustain the Ku Klux Klan did not have simple origins, motives, or consequences. The forces underlying the culture wars of the 1920s would surface repeatedly in the future (see Overview, Issues in the Culture Wars of the 1920s).

Nativism and Immigration Restriction

For years, many Americans, from racists to reformers, had campaigned to restrict immigration. In 1917, Congress required immigrants to pass a literacy test. But renewed immigration after the war revived the anti-immigration movement, and the propaganda of the war and the Red Scare years generated public support for more restriction. Depicting immigrants as radicals, racial inferiors, religious subversives, or criminals, nativists clamored for congressional action. The Emergency Quota Act of 1921 reduced immigration by about two-thirds and established quotas for nationalities on the basis of their numbers in the United States in 1910. Restrictionists, however, demanded more stringent action, especially against the largely Catholic and Jewish immigrants from southern and eastern Europe. Coolidge himself urged that America "be kept American," by which he meant white, Anglo-Saxon, and Protestant.

Congress adopted this racist rationale in the **National Origins Act of 1924,** which proclaimed its objective to be the maintenance of the "racial preponderance" of "the basic strain of our population." This law restricted immigration quotas to 2 percent of the foreign-born population of each nationality as recorded in the 1890 census, which was taken before the mass immigration from southern and eastern Europe. Another provision, effective in 1929, restricted total annual immigration to 150,000, with quotas that nearly eliminated southern and eastern Europeans. The law also completely excluded Japanese immigrants.

Other actions targeted Japanese residents in America. California, Oregon, Washington, Arizona, and other western states prohibited them from owning or leasing land, and in 1922, the Supreme Court ruled that, as nonwhites, they could never become naturalized citizens. A Japanese newspaper in Los Angeles criticized such actions as be-

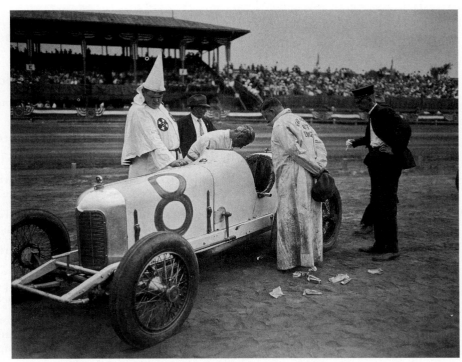

To entertain families and friends, the KKK held "Klan Day at the Races," pictured here at Denver's Overland Park Race Track.

traying America's own ideals. Dispirited by the prejudice of the decade, Japanese residents hoped for fulfillment through their children, the **Nisei,** who were American citizens by birth.

Ironically, the Philippines, as a U.S. territory, was not subject to the National Origins Act, and Filipino immigration increased ninefold during the 1920s. Most Filipino newcomers became farm laborers, especially in California, or worked in Alaskan fisheries. Similarly, because the law did not apply to immigrants from the Western Hemisphere, Mexican immigration also grew. Nativists lobbied to exclude Mexicans, but agribusiness interests in the Southwest blocked any restrictions on low-cost migrant labor.

The Ku Klux Klan

Nativism was also reflected in the popularity of the revived Ku Klux Klan, the goal of which, according to its leader, was to protect "the interest of those whose forefathers established the nation." Founded in Georgia in 1915 and modeled on its Reconstruction predecessor, the new Klan was a national, not only a southern, movement and claimed several million members by the mid-1920s. Admitting only native-born white Protestants, the Klan embodied the fears of a traditional culture threatened by social change. Ironically, its rapid spread owed much to modern business and promotional techniques as hundreds of professional recruiters raked in hefty commissions selling Klan memberships to those hoping to defend their way of life.

OVERVIEW

Issues in the Culture Wars of the 1920s

Issue	Proponent view	Opponent view
The new morality	Promotes greater personal freedom and opportunities for fulfillment	Promotes moral collapse
Evolutionism	A scientific advance linked to notions of progress	A threat to religious belief
Jazz	Modern and vital	Unsettling, irregular, vulgar, and primitive
Immigration	A source of national strength from ethnic and racial diversity	A threat to the status and authority of old-stock white Protestants
Great Migration	A chance for African Americans to find new economic opportunities and gain autonomy and pride	A threat to traditional white privilege, control, and status
Prohibition	Promotes social and family stability and reduces crime	Restricts personal liberty and increases crime
Fundamentalism	An admirable adherence to traditional religious faith and biblical injunctions	A superstitious creed given to intolerant interference in social and political affairs
Ku Klux Klan	An organization promoting community responsibility, patriotism, and traditional social, moral, and religious values	A group of religious and racial bigots given to violent vigilantism and fostering moral and public corruption
Mass culture	Increases popular participation in national culture; provides entertainment	Promotes conformity, materialism, mediocrity, spectacle, and relaxation
Consumerism	Promotes material progress and higher living standards	Promotes waste, sterility, and self-indulgence

In part, the Klan was a fraternal order, providing entertainment, assistance, and community for its members. Its picnics, parades, charity drives, and other social and family-oriented activities—perhaps a half-million women joined the Women of the Ku Klux Klan—sharply distinguished the organization from both the small, secretive Klan of the nineteenth century and the still smaller, extremist Klan of the later twentieth century. Regarding themselves as reformers, Klan members supported immigration restriction and Prohibition.

But the Klan also exploited racial, ethnic, and religious prejudices and campaigned against many social groups and what it called "alien creeds." It attacked African Americans in the South, Mexicans in Texas, Japanese in California, and Catholics and Jews everywhere. A twisted religious impulse ran through much of the Klan's organization and activities. It hired itinerant Protestant ministers to spread its message, erected altars and flaming crosses at its meetings, and sang Klan lyrics to the tunes of well-known hymns. One Klan leader maintained that "the Klan stood for the same things as the Church, but we did the things the Church wouldn't do." This included publishing anti-Catholic newspapers, boycotting Catholic and Jewish businesses, and lobbying for laws against parochial schools and for compulsory Bible reading in the public schools. The Klan also resorted to violence. In

1921, for example, a Methodist minister who belonged to the Klan murdered a Catholic priest on his own doorstep, and other Klansmen burned down Catholic churches. The leader of the Oregon Klan insisted that "the only way to cure a Catholic is to kill him."

To the Klan, Catholics and Jews symbolized not merely subversive religions but also the ethnic diversity and swelling urban population that challenged traditional Protestant culture. To protect that culture, the Klan attempted to censor or disrupt "indecent" entertainment, assaulted those it accused of adultery, and terrorized doctors who performed abortions.

While the Klan's appeal seemed rooted in the declining countryside, it also attracted urban residents. Chicago had the largest Klan organization in the nation, with 50,000 members, and Houston, Dallas, Portland, Indianapolis, Denver, and the satellite communities ringing Los Angeles were also Klan strongholds. Urban Klansmen were largely lower or lower middle class, many recently arrived from the country and retaining its attitudes; others were long-term urban residents who feared being marginalized by social changes, especially by competition from immigrants and new ideas.

The Klan also ventured into politics, with some success. But eventually it encountered resistance. In the North, Catholic workers disrupted Klan parades. In the South, too, Klan excesses provoked a backlash. After the Klan in Dallas

Evangelist Aimee Semple McPherson delivering her "Foursquare Gospel" that offered all sinners salvation.

flogged 68 people in a "whipping meadow" along the Trinity River in 1922, respect turned to outrage. Newspapers demanded that the Klan disband, district attorneys began to prosecute Klan thugs, and in 1924 Klan candidates were defeated by a ticket headed by Miriam "Ma" Ferguson, whose gubernatorial campaign called for anti-Klan laws and for the loss of tax exemptions for churches used for Klan meetings. Elsewhere the Klan was stung by revelations of criminal behavior and corruption by Klan leaders, who had been making fortunes pocketing membership fees and selling regalia to followers. The Klan crusade to purify society had bred corruption and conflict everywhere. By 1930, the Klan had nearly collapsed.

Prohibition and Crime

Like the Klan, Prohibition both reflected and provoked social tensions in the 1920s. Reformers had long believed that prohibiting the sale of alcohol would improve social conditions, reduce crime and family instability, increase economic efficiency, and purify politics. They rejoiced in 1920 when the Eighteenth Amendment, prohibiting the manufacture, sale, or transportation of alcoholic beverages, took effect. Congress then passed the **Volstead Act,** which defined the forbidden liquors and established the Prohibition Bureau to enforce the law. But many social groups, especially in urban ethnic communities, opposed Prohibition, and the govern-

ment could not enforce the law where public opinion did not endorse it.

Evasion was easy. By permitting alcohol for medicinal, sacramental, and industrial purposes, the Volstead Act gave doctors, priests, and druggists a huge loophole through which to satisfy their friends' needs. Hearing that the use of sacramental wines had increased by 800,000 gallons under Prohibition, one Protestant leader complained that "not more than one-quarter of this is sacramental—the rest is sacrilegious." City-dwellers made "bathtub gin," and rural people distilled "moonshine." Scofflaws frequented the speakeasies that replaced saloons or bought liquor from bootleggers and rumrunners, who imported it from Canada, Cuba, or Mexico. The limited resources of the Prohibition Bureau often allowed bootleggers to operate openly. Dozens met publicly in a Seattle hotel in 1922 and adopted "fair prices" for liquor and a code of ethics "to keep liquor runners within the limits of approved business methods."

The ethics and business methods of bootleggers soon shocked Americans, however. The huge profits encouraged organized crime, which had previously concentrated on gambling and prostitution, to develop elaborate liquor-distribution networks. Operating outside the law, crime "families" used violence to enforce contracts, suppress competition, and attack rivals. In Chicago, Al Capone's army of nearly a thousand gangsters killed hundreds. Using the profits from bootlegging and new tools like the automobile and the submachine gun, organized crime corrupted city governments and police forces.

Gradually, even many "drys"—people who had initially favored Prohibition—dropped their support, horrified by the boost the amendment gave organized crime and worried about the general disrespect for law that it promoted. A 1926 poll found that four-fifths of Americans wanted to repeal or modify Prohibition. Yet it remained in force because it was entangled in party politics and social conflict. Many rural Protestant Americans saw Prohibition as a symbolic cultural issue. As the comedian Will Rogers said, "Mississippi will vote dry and drink wet as long as it can stagger to the polls." Prohibition represented the ability of rural Protestants to control the newcomers in the expanding cities. Democrats called for repeal in their 1928 and 1932 platforms, and in 1933, 36 states ratified an amendment repealing what Herbert Hoover had called a "noble experiment."

Old-Time Religion and the Scopes Trial

Religion provided another fulcrum for traditionalists attempting to stem cultural change. Protestant fundamentalism, which emphasized the infallibility of the Bible, including the creation story, emerged at the turn of the century as a conservative reaction to religious modernism and the social changes brought by the mass immigration of Catholics and Jews, the growing influence of science and technology, and the secularization of public education. But the fundamentalist crusade to reshape America became formidable only

American Views

Evangelism and the Search for Salvation

Aimee Semple McPherson defied traditional roles for women in becoming one of the most famous evangelical leaders in the United States. Traveling in her "Gospel Car," she crisscrossed the nation reminding her followers that "Jesus Is Coming Soon" and advising them to "Get Ready." In 1923, she opened the Angelus Temple in Los Angeles—a white-domed building large enough for 5,000 followers of what McPherson called the "Foursquare Gospel." A lighted rotating cross on top of the dome could be seen from fifty miles away—a beacon for those who journeyed to her center of "spiritual energy." A charismatic orator, McPherson embraced the theatrics of Hollywood to stir her crowds and raised vast sums of money, or "love gifts," to finance the Temple and its activities. Playing upon the phrase shareholder, McPherson sold doll-house chairs for $25 each, enabling purchasers to be "chair-holders" in the Temple. Though tainted by a mysterious disappearance in 1926, she remained extraordinarily popular, attracting crowds of thousands who sought salvation during times of change and uncertainty. McPherson died in 1944 from an accidental overdose of sleeping pills.

In this excerpt from one of her autobiographies, McPherson describes the growth of the Angelus Temple and her pioneering use of radio to advance her "success in soul winning."

- Why was Aimee Semple McPherson so popular in the 1920s?

- What does her success suggest about the role of religion in American life?

- How do you think evangelicals like McPherson might have viewed the cult of business that also characterized the decade?

From the days the doors opened on January 1, 1923, a mighty spiritual revival surged into Angelus Temple with ever-increasing power and fervor. Eight thousand converts knelt at the altars in the first six months and fifteen hundred believers were immersed in the baptistry. Hundreds were healed and baptized with the Holy Spirit. One thousand young people convenanted together to serve as the Angelus Temple Foursquare Crusaders. And as the weeks and months passed, new outreaches commenced.

In February, the Prayer Tower opened, where prayer has not ceased as men gather in two-hour shifts during the night and women pray during the day, bringing God thousands of requests which come by mail, telephone, and telegraph from all over the world.

Then came the challenge of the radio!…My soul was thrilled with the possibilities this media offered for the spread of gospel. We secured time on a radio station and began broadcasting a few services. But the thought persisted that if Angelus Temple had her own radio station we could broadcast almost all of the meetings!

And God provided through the love gifts of his people for the radio station. In February 1924, KFSG—Kall Four Square Gospel—went on the air, broadcasting the glorious song, "Give the winds a mighty voice, Jesus saves!"…Time and time again converted gamblers, dope addicts, bootleggers, and white-slavery victims rose from knees to send thrilling testimonies out over radio station KFSG as well as to the Temple audience.…For three years I stayed close by Angelus Temple, preaching and teaching many times a week, conducting a daily "Sunshine Hour" broadcast, writing, editing, publishing, and praying for the sick.…The revival swept on and out. Branch churches sprang up in cities and towns. [And the Foursquare gospel] message has become well known around the world.

Source: *Aimee Semple McPherson: The Story of My Life* (Waco, TX: Word Books, 1973).

in the 1920s. Evangelists like Billy Sunday and Aimee Semple McPherson attracted thousands to their revivals across America. Striking and dramatic, McPherson conducted massive faith-healing ceremonies as she promoted her "Foursquare Gospel." (See American Views, Evangelism and the Search for Salvation.)

Fundamentalist groups, colleges, and publications sprang up throughout the nation, especially in the South. The anti-Catholic sentiment exploited by the Klan was but one consequence of fundamentalism's insistence on strict biblical Christianity. A second was the assault on Darwin's theory of evolution, which contradicted literal interpretations of biblical Creation. The Southern Baptist Convention condemned "every theory, evolutionary or other, which teaches that man originated or came by way of lower animal ancestry." Fundamentalist legislators tried to prevent the teaching of evolution in public schools in at least 20 states. In 1923, Oklahoma banned textbooks based on Darwinian theory, and Florida's legislature denounced teaching evolution as "subversive." In 1925, Tennessee forbade teaching any idea contrary to the biblical account of human origins.

Social or political conservatism, however, was not an inherent part of old-time religion. The most prominent antievolution politician, William Jennings Bryan, continued to campaign for political, social, and economic reforms. Never endorsing the Klan, he served on the American Committee on the Rights of Religious Minorities and condemned anti-Semitism and anti-Catholicism. Bryan feared that Darwinism promoted political and economic conservatism. The survival of the fittest, he complained, elevated force and brutality, ignored spiritual values and democracy, and discouraged altruism and reform. How could a person fight for social justice "unless he believes in the triumph of right?"

The controversy over evolution came to a head when the American Civil Liberties Union (ACLU) responded to Tennessee's violation of the constitutional separation of church and state by offering to defend any teacher who tested the antievolution law. John Scopes, a high school biology teacher in Dayton, Tennessee, did so and was arrested. The Scopes trial attracted national attention after Bryan agreed to assist the prosecution and Clarence Darrow, a famous Chicago lawyer and prominent atheist, volunteered to defend Scopes.

Millions of Americans tuned their radios to hear the first trial ever broadcast. The judge, a fundamentalist, sat under a sign urging people to "Read Your Bible Daily." He ruled that scientists could not testify in support of evolution: Because they were not present at the Creation, their testimony would be "hearsay." But he did allow Darrow to put Bryan on the stand as an expert on the Bible. Bryan insisted on the literal truth of every story in the Bible, allowing Darrow to ridicule his ideas and force him to concede that some biblical passages had to be construed symbolically. Though the local jury took only eight minutes to convict Scopes, fundamentalists suffered public ridicule from reporters, including H. L. Mencken, who sneered at the "hillbillies" and "yokels" of Dayton.

But fundamentalism was hardly destroyed, and antievolutionists continued their campaign. New organizations, such as the Bryan Bible League, lobbied for state laws and an antievolution amendment to the Constitution. Three more states forbade teaching evolution, but by 1929 the movement had faltered. Even so, fundamentalism retained religious influence and would again challenge science and modernism in American life (see From Then to Now, The Culture Wars).

Through the historical figures of William Jennings Bryan and Clarence Darrow, the Scopes Trial symbolized the cultural battles of the twenties. And when Darrow (standing) interrogated Bryan on the accuracy of the Bible, the *New York Times* called the exchange the "most amazing courtroom scene in Anglo-American history."

A New Era in the World?

Abroad and at home, Americans in the 1920s sought peace and economic order. Rejection of the Treaty of Versailles and the League of Nations did not foreshadow isolationism. Indeed, in the 1920s, the United States became more deeply involved in international matters than ever before in peacetime. This involvement both produced important successes and sowed the seeds for serious future problems.

War Debts and Economic Expansion

The United States was the world's dominant economic power in the 1920s, changed by the Great War from a debtor to a creditor nation. The loans the United States had made to its allies during the war troubled the nation's relations with Europe throughout the decade. American insistence on repayment angered Europeans, who saw the money as a U.S. contribution to the joint war effort against Germany. Moreover, high American tariffs blocked Europeans from exporting goods to the United States and earning dollars to repay their debts. Eventually, the United States readjusted the terms for repayment, and American bankers extended large loans to Germany, which used the money to pay reparations to Britain and France, whose governments then used the same money to repay the United States. This unstable system depended on a continuous flow of money from the United States.

America's global economic role expanded in other ways as well. Exports, especially of manufactured goods, soared; by 1929, the United States was the world's largest exporter, responsible for one-sixth of all exports. American investment abroad more than doubled between 1919 and 1930. To expand their markets and avoid foreign tariffs, many U.S. companies became **multinational corporations,** establishing branches or subsidiaries abroad. Ford built assembly plants in England, Japan, Turkey, and Canada. International Telephone and Telegraph owned two dozen factories in Europe and employed more overseas workers than any other U.S. corporation.

Other companies gained control of foreign supply sources. American oil companies invested in foreign oil fields, especially in Latin America, where they controlled more than half of Venezuelan production. The United Fruit Company developed such huge operations in Central America that it often dominated national economies. In Costa Rica, the company had a larger budget than the national government.

Europeans and Latin Americans alike worried about this economic invasion; even Secretary of Commerce Herbert Hoover expressed concerns. Multinationals, he warned, might eventually take markets from American manufacturers and jobs from American workers. Business leaders, however, dismissed such reservations.

Hoover's concerns, moreover, did not prevent him from promoting economic expansion abroad. The government worked to open doors for American businesses in foreign countries, helping them to secure access to trade, investment opportunities, and raw materials. Hoover's Bureau of Foreign Commerce opened 50 offices around the world to boost American business. Hoover also pressed the British to give U.S. corporations access to rubber production in the British colony of Malaya. Secretary of State Charles Evans Hughes negotiated access to Iraqi oil fields for U.S. oil companies. The government also authorized bankers and manufacturers to form combinations, exempt from antitrust laws, to exploit foreign markets.

Rejecting War

Although government officials cooperated with business leaders to promote American strategic and economic interests, they had little desire to use force abroad. Popular reaction against the Great War, strengthened by a strong peace movement, constrained policymakers. Having repudiated collective security as embodied in the League of Nations, the United States nonetheless sought to minimize international conflict and promote its national security. In particular, the State Department sought to restrict the buildup of armaments among nations.

At the invitation of President Harding, delegations from nine nations met in Washington at the Washington Naval Conference in 1921 to discuss disarmament. The conference drafted a treaty to reduce battleship tonnage and suspend the building of new ships for a decade. The terms virtually froze the existing balance of naval power, with the first rank assigned to Britain and the United States, followed by Japan and then France and Italy. Japan and the United States also agreed not to fortify their possessions in the Pacific any further and to respect the Open Door in East Asia. Public opinion welcomed the treaty; the U.S. Senate ratified it with only one dissenting vote, and the 1924 Republican platform hailed it as "the greatest peace document ever drawn."

The United States made a more dramatic gesture in 1928, when it helped draft the **Kellogg-Briand Pact.** Signed by 64 nations, the treaty renounced aggression and outlawed war. Without provisions for enforcement, however, it was little more than symbolic. The Senate reserved the right of self-defense, repudiated any responsibility for enforcing the treaty, and maintained U.S. claims under the Monroe Doctrine. These limitations on the treaty, Senator Hiram Johnson noted, "have made its nothingness complete."

Managing the Hemisphere

Senate insistence on the authority of the Monroe Doctrine reflected the U.S. claim to a predominant role in Latin America. The United States continued to dominate the hemisphere to promote its own interests. It exerted its influence through investments, control of the Panama Canal, invocation of the Monroe Doctrine, and, when necessary, military intervention.

In response to American public opinion, the peace movement, and Latin American nationalism, the United States retreated from the extreme gunboat diplomacy of the Progressive Era, withdrawing troops from the Dominican Republic and Nicaragua. Secretary of State Hughes assured Latin Americans that "we covet no territory; we seek no conquest; the liberty we cherish for ourselves we desire for others; and we accept no rights for ourselves that we do not accord to others." But Haiti remained under U.S. occupation throughout the decade, American troops stayed in Cuba and Panama, and the United States directed the financial policies of other Latin American countries. Moreover, it sent the marines into Honduras in 1924 and back to Nicaragua in 1926. Such interventions could establish only temporary stability while provoking further Latin American hostility. "We are hated and despised," said one American businessman in Nicaragua. "This feeling has been created by employing American marines to hunt down and kill Nicaraguans in their own country."

Latin American resentment led to a resolution at the 1928 Inter-America Conference denying the right of any nation "to intervene in the internal affairs of another." The U.S. delegation rejected the measure, but the anger of Latin Americans prompted the Hoover administration to rescind support for the Roosevelt Corollary (see chapter 22), and J. Reuben Clark, chief legal officer of the State Department, drafted the Clark Memorandum. Not published until 1930, this document stated that the Roosevelt Corollary was not a legitimate extension of the Monroe Doctrine and thereby helped prepare the way for the so-called Good Neighbor Policy toward Latin America. Still, the United States did not pledge nonintervention and retained the means, both military and economic, to dominate the hemisphere.

Herbert Hoover and the Final Triumph of the New Era

As the national economy steamed ahead in 1928, the Republicans chose as their presidential candidate Herbert Hoover, a man who symbolized the policies of prosperity and the New Era. Hoover was not a politician—he had never been elected to office—but a successful administrator who championed rational and efficient economic development. A cooperative government, he believed, should promote business interests and encourage corporations to form trade associations to ensure stability and profitability. It should not regulate economic activities. Hoover's stiff managerial image was softened by his humanitarian record and his roots in rural Iowa.

The Democrats, by contrast, chose a candidate who evoked the cultural conflicts of the 1920s. Alfred E. Smith, a four-term governor of New York, was a Catholic, an opponent of Prohibition, and a Tammany politician tied to the immigrant constituency of New York City. He had failed to gain the presidential nomination in 1924, when the party split over prohibition and the Klan, but in 1928 he won the dubious honor of running against Hoover. His nomination plunged the nation into the cultural strife that had divided the Democrats in 1924. Rural fundamentalism, anti-Catholicism, Prohibition, and nativism were crucial factors in the campaign. The fundamentalist assault was unrelenting. Billy

Sunday attacked Smith and the Democrats as "the forces of hell," and a Baptist minister in Oklahoma City warned his congregation, "If you vote for Al Smith, you're voting against Christ and you'll all be damned."

But Hoover was, in certain ways, the more progressive candidate. Sympathetic to labor, sensitive to women's issues, hostile to racial segregation, and favorable to the League of Nations, Hoover had always distanced himself from what he called "the reactionary group in the Republican party." By contrast, despite supporting factory reform and state welfare legislation to benefit his urban working-class constituents, Smith was essentially conservative and as parochial as his most rural adversaries. He responded to a question about the needs of the states west of the Mississippi by asking, "What states *are* west of the Mississippi?"

Although many Americans voted against Smith because of his social background, the same characteristics attracted others. Millions of urban and ethnic voters, previously Republican or politically uninvolved, voted for Smith and laid the basis for the new Democratic coalition that would emerge in the 1930s. In 1928, however, with the nation still enjoying the economic prosperity so closely associated with Hoover and the Republicans, the Democrats were routed (see Map 24–2).

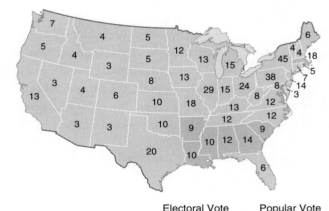

	Electoral Vote (%)	Popular Vote (%)
HERBERT HOOVER (Republican)	**444** **(82)**	**21,391,993** **(58)**
Alfred E. Smith (Democrat)	87 (17)	15,016,169 (41)
Norman Thomas (Socialist)	–	267,835 (1)
Other parties (Socialist Labor, Prohibition)	–	62,890 (–)

MAP 24–2   The Election of 1928
The cultural conflicts of the 1920s shaped the 1928 election. Al Smith carried the largest cities, but Herbert Hoover swept most of the rest of the nation, even attracting much of the usually Democratic South.

FROM THEN TO NOW

The Culture Wars

Cultural conflict raged through American society in the 1920s. Nativists demanded immigration restrictions; the Ku Klux Klan played on fears of racial, ethnic, and religious minorities; prohibitionists grappled with the minions of Demon Rum; and Protestant fundamentalists campaigned to prohibit the teaching of evolution in public schools.

Beginning in the 1960s, fueled as before by challenges to traditional values and beliefs—African American demands for civil rights, opposition to the Vietnam War, the women's rights movement and women's growing presence in the workplace, a new wave of immigration (dominated this time by Asians and Latin Americans), the gay rights movement—cultural conflict flared again and continues to burn.

Pro-choice and anti-abortion protesters square off at the pro choice "March for Women's Lives" in the Washington, D.C. Mall in April 2004.

The central battleground of today's culture wars, however, is women's rights, and especially abortion rights. Ever since the Supreme Court ruled in *Roe v. Wade* in 1973 that women had a right to an abortion, opponents have sought to curtail or abolish that right in the name of family values. Antiabortion protests became increasingly violent in the 1980s and 1990s. Although the Supreme Court has upheld *Roe v. Wade* and laws restraining demonstrations at abortion clinics, it has also upheld state laws imposing limits on abortion rights. In 2007, moreover, the Supreme Court reversed its earlier ruling by banning late-term abortions and specifically excluding a woman's health as a factor for consideration.

Gay rights is another battleground in the culture wars. Religious conservatives, again in the name of family values, have sought to counter efforts to extend civil rights protections to gays and lesbians. Same-sex marriage has produced a volatile struggle, igniting public debate and provoking protest and legal challenges.

According to one popular analysis, the antagonists in today's culture wars are, on one side, those who find authority in religious traditions, and, on the other, those who find authority in society and human reason. The war is not over and cultural conflict, motivated by deeply rooted convictions, is likely to remain a persistent undercurrent in American life.

■ What do these cultural conflicts reveal about American society?

PEARSON
myhistorylab

From Then to Now Online

Denouncing the Massachusetts ruling legalizing same-sex marriage, chanting protesters in California invoke "family values" to reaffirm their belief in heterosexual-only unions.

24-1 **"White Sheets in Washington, D.C.," 1925.** Photograph of 40,000 Ku Klux Klan members marching down Pennsylvania Avenue.

24-2 New York Times, **"Great Crowd Hears Aimee McPherson," 1926.** Mass congregation of 7,500 followers turn out to hear McPherson's "Four Square Gospel."

24-3 Los Angeles Times, **"California Supreme Court Overturns Gay Marriage Ban," 2008.** Article discussing the state court decision upholding the legality of same-sex marriage.

In his campaign, Hoover boasted that Republican policies could bring America to "the final triumph over poverty." But 1928 would be the Republicans' final triumph for a long time. The vaunted prosperity of the 1920s was ending, and the country faced a future dark with poverty.

Conclusion

The New Era of the 1920s changed America. Technological and managerial innovations produced giant leaps in productivity, new patterns of labor, a growing concentration of corporate power, and high corporate profits. Government policies, from protective tariffs and regressive taxation to the relaxation of regulatory laws, reflected and reinforced the triumphs of the business elite over traditional cautions and concerns.

The decade's economic developments, in turn, stimulated social change, drawing millions of Americans from the countryside to the cities, creating an urban nation, and fostering a new ethic of materialism, consumerism, and leisure and a new mass culture based on the automobile, radio, the movies, and advertising. This social transformation swept up many Americans but left others unsettled by the erosion of traditional practices and values. The concerns of traditionalists found expression in campaigns for prohibition and against immigration, the revival of the Ku Klux Klan, and the rise of religious fundamentalism. Intellectuals denounced the materialism and conformity they saw in the new social order and fashioned new artistic and literary trends.

But the impact of the decade's trends was uneven. Mechanization increased the productivity of some workers but cost others their jobs; people poured into the cities while others left for the suburbs; Prohibition, intended to stabilize society, instead produced conflict, crime, and corruption; government policies advanced some economic interests but injured others. Even the notion of a "mass" culture obscured the degree to which millions of Americans were left out of the New Era. With no disposable income and little access to electricity, rural Americans scarcely participated in the joys of consumerism; racial and ethnic minorities were often isolated in ghettos and barrios; and many workers faced declining opportunities. Most ominous was the uneven prosperity undergirding the New Era. Although living standards rose for many Americans and the rich expanded their share of the national wealth, more than 40 percent of the population earned less than $1,500 a year and fell below the established poverty level. The unequal distribution of wealth and income made the economy unstable and vulnerable to a disastrous collapse.

Review Questions

1. How did the automobile industry affect the nation's economy and society in the 1920s? In the excerpt from *The Flivver King,* how does Upton Sinclair illustrate the tension between workers and technology even as they both served Henry Ford's vision of mass production and mass consumerism?

2. What factors characterized the boom industries of the 1920s? The sick industries? How accurate is it to label the 1920s the decade of prosperity?

3. What were the underlying issues in the election of 1924? Of 1928? What role did politics play in the public life of the 1920s?

4. What were the chief points of conflict in the culture wars of the 1920s? What were the underlying issues in these clashes? Why were they so hard to compromise?

5. In what ways did the World War experience shape developments in the 1920s?

6. What were the chief features of American involvement in world affairs in the 1920s? To what extent did that involvement constitute a new role for the United States?

Key Terms

Great Migration (p. 675)

Harlem Renaissance (p. 675)

Jazz Age (p. 678)

Kellogg-Briand Pact (p. 686)

League of Women Voters (p. 673)

Multinational corporations (p. 686)

National Origins Act of 1924 (p. 681)

Nisei (p. 681)

Oligopoly (p. 669)

Open shop (p. 669)

Sheppard-Towner Maternity and Infancy Act (p. 673)

Volstead Act (p. 683)

Welfare capitalism (p. 669)

Yellow-dog contracts (p. 669)

Recommended Reading

Braeman, John, Robert Bremner, and David Brody, eds. *Change and Continuity in Twentieth Century America: The 1920s* (1968). Stimulating essays that cover important features of economic, social, and political history.

Dumenil, Lynn. *The Modern Temper: American Culture and Society in the 1920s* (1995). A complex account of cultural clashes and tensions during the 1920s.

Flink, James J. *The Car Culture* (1975). The fascinating history of the automobile and its social impact.

Hawley, Ellis W. *The Great War and the Search for a Modern Order* (1979). A valuable survey emphasizing economic and organizational changes.

Where to Learn More

- **F. Scott and Zelda Fitzgerald Museum, Montgomery, Alabama.**   The novelist and his wife lived a short while in this house in her hometown. www.alabamatravel.org/central/szfm.html

- **Herbert Hoover National Historic Site, West Branch, Iowa.**   Visitors may tour Hoover's birthplace cottage, presidential library, and museum. www.hoover.archives.gov

- **Henry Ford Museum and Greenfield Village, Dearborn, Michigan.**   Among many fascinating exhibits, "The Automobile in American Life" superbly demonstrates the importance of the automobile in American social history. www.hfmgv.org

- **Warren G. Harding House, Marion, Ohio.**   Harding's home from 1891 to 1921 is now a museum with period furnishings. www.ohiohistory.org/places/harding

- **Calvin Coolidge Homestead, Plymouth, Vermont.** Operated by the Vermont Division of Historic Sites, the homestead preserves the exact interiors and furnishings from when Coolidge took the presidential oath of office there in 1923. www.calvin-coolidge.org/pages/homestead and www.dhca.state.vt.us./HistoricSites/sites.htm

Study Resources

PEARSON
myhistorylab™

For study resources for this chapter, go to www.myhistorylab.com and choose *The American Journey*. You will find a wealth of study and review material for this chapter, including pre- and post-tests, customized study plan, key term review flash cards, interactive map and document activities, and documents for analysis.

and high winds hit the plains in 1932, crops failed, and nothing was left to hold the soil. Dust storms blew away millions of tons of topsoil, despoiling the land and darkening the sky a thousand miles away. Families abandoned their farms in droves. Many of these poor "Okies" headed for California, their plight captured in John Steinbeck's novel, *The Grapes of Wrath* (1939).

In 1935, Roosevelt established the Resettlement Administration to focus on land reform and help poor farmers. Under Rexford Tugwell, this agency initiated soil erosion projects and attempted to resettle impoverished farmers on better land, but the problem exceeded its resources. Congress moved to save the land, if not its people, by creating the Soil Conservation Service in 1935.

Expanding Relief

If reform gained priority in the Second New Deal, relief remained critical. With millions still unemployed, Roosevelt pushed through Congress in 1935 the Emergency Relief Appropriation Act, authorizing $5 billion—at the time the largest single appropriation in American history—for emergency public employment. Roosevelt created the Works Progress Administration (WPA) under Hopkins, who set up work relief programs to assist the unemployed and boost the economy. Before its end in 1943, the WPA gave jobs to 9 million people (more than a fifth of the labor force) and spent nearly $12 billion. Three-fourths of its expenditures went on construction projects that could employ manual labor: The WPA built 125,000 schools, post offices, and hospitals; 8,000 parks; nearly 100,000 bridges; and enough roads and sewer systems to circle the earth 30 times. The WPA laid much of the basic infrastructure on which the nation still relies.

The WPA also developed work projects for unemployed writers, artists, musicians, and actors. "Why not?" said FDR. "They are human beings. They have to live." The Federal Writers' Project put authors to work preparing state guidebooks, writing historical pamphlets, and recording the memories of ex-slaves. The Federal Art Project hired artists to teach art in night schools, prepare exhibits at museums, and paint murals on post office walls. The Federal Theatre Project organized theatrical productions and drama companies that in four years played to 30 million Americans. The Federal Music Project hired musicians to collect and perform folk songs. These WPA programs allowed people to use their talents while surviving the depression, increased popular access to cultural performances, and established a precedent for federal support of the arts. "What has happened and in such a short time is almost incredible," said one reviewer. "From a government completely apathetic to art, we suddenly have a government very art conscious."

The National Youth Administration (NYA), another WPA agency, gave part-time jobs to students, enabling 2 million high school and college students to stay in school, learn skills, and do productive work. At the University of Nebraska, NYA students built an observatory; at Duke University, law student Richard M. Nixon earned 35 cents an hour doing research in the library. Lyndon Johnson, a Texas NYA official, believed that "if the Roosevelt administration had never done another thing, it would have been justified by the work of this great institution for salvaging youth."

The Roosevelt Coalition and the Election of 1936

The 1936 election gave Americans an opportunity to judge FDR and the New Deal. Conservatives alarmed at the expansion of government, business people angered by regulation and labor legislation, and wealthy Americans furious with tax reform decried the New Deal. But they were a minority. Even the presidential candidate they supported, Republican Governor Alf Landon of Kansas, endorsed much of the New Deal, criticizing merely the inefficiency and cost of some of its programs. The New Deal's earlier critics on the left had also lost most of their following. The reforms of 1935 had undercut their arguments, and the assassination of Huey Long in the same year had removed their ablest politician. They formed the Union Party and nominated William Lemke for the presidency, but they were no longer a threat.

The programs and politicians of the New Deal had created an invincible coalition behind Roosevelt. Despite ambivalence about large-scale government intervention, the New Deal's agricultural programs reinforced the traditional Democratic allegiance of white southerners while attracting many western farmers. Labor legislation clinched the active support of the nation's workers; Sidney Hillman of the Amalgamated Clothing Workers promised that his union would campaign for FDR "to see to it that we hold onto the gains labor has won." Middle-class voters, whose homes had been saved and whose hopes had been raised, also joined the Roosevelt coalition.

So did urban ethnic groups, who had benefited from welfare programs and appreciated the unprecedented recognition Roosevelt's administration gave them. FDR named the first Italian American to the federal judiciary, for example, and appointed five times as many Catholics and Jews to government positions as the three Republican presidents had during the 1920s. African Americans voted overwhelmingly Democratic for the first time. Women, too, were an important part of the Roosevelt coalition, and Eleanor often attracted their support as much as Franklin did. As one campaigner said to a roaring crowd in 1936, "Many women in this country when they vote for Franklin D. Roosevelt will also be thinking with a choke in the throat of Eleanor Roosevelt!"

This political realignment produced a landslide. Roosevelt polled 61 percent of the popular vote and the largest electoral vote margin ever recorded, 523 to 8. Landon even lost Kansas, his own state, and Lemke received fewer than 900,000 votes. Democrats also won huge majorities in Congress. Roosevelt's political coalition reflected a mandate for

Eleanor Roosevelt campaigns with FDR in Fremont, Nebraska, in 1935. A visible activist for social and economic reform, she was also politically important in building the powerful Roosevelt coalition. "Previously," said the journalist Ruby Black, "a President's wife acted as if she didn't know that a political party existed."

from employers and their allies and required workers to organize, strike, and become politically active. Their achievement was remarkable.

The Second New Deal helped. By guaranteeing labor's rights to organize and bargain collectively, the Wagner Act sparked a wave of labor activism. But if the government ultimately protected union rights, the unions themselves had to form locals, recruit members, and demonstrate influence in the workplace.

At first, those tasks overwhelmed the American Federation of Labor (AFL). Its reliance on craft-based unions and reluctance to organize immigrant, black, and women workers left it unprepared for the rush of industrial workers seeking unionization. More progressive labor leaders saw that industry-wide unions were more appropriate for unskilled workers in mass-production industries. Forming the Committee for Industrial Organization (CIO) within the AFL, they campaigned to unionize workers in the steel, auto, and rubber industries, all notoriously hostile to unions. AFL leaders insisted that the CIO disband and then in 1937 expelled its unions. The militants reorganized as the separate **Congress of Industrial Organizations.** (In 1955, the two groups merged as the AFL-CIO.)

The split roused the AFL to increase its own organizing activities, but it was primarily the new CIO that put labor on the march. It inspired workers previously neglected by organized labor. The CIO's interracial union campaign in the Birmingham steel mills, said one organizer, was "like a second coming of Christ" for black workers, who welcomed the union as a chance for social recognition as well as economic opportunity. The CIO also employed new and aggressive tactics, particularly the sit-down strike, in which workers, rather than picketing outside the factory, simply sat inside the plant, thereby blocking both production and the use of strikebreakers. Conservatives were outraged, but Upton Sinclair said, "For seventy-five years big business has been sitting down on the American people, and now I am delighted to see the process reversed."

The CIO won major victories despite bitter opposition from industry and its allies. The issue was not wages but labor's right to organize and bargain with management. Sit-down strikes paralyzed General Motors in 1937 after it refused to recognize the United Auto Workers. GM tried to force the strikers out of its Flint, Michigan, plants by turning off the heat, using police and tear gas, threatening strikers' families, and obtaining court orders to clear the plant by

himself and the New Deal; it would enable the Democrats to dominate national elections for three decades.

The New Deal and American Life

The landslide of 1936 revealed the impact of the New Deal on Americans. Industrial workers mobilized to secure their rights, women and minorities gained increased, if still limited, opportunities to participate in American society, and southerners and westerners benefited from government programs they turned to their own advantage. Government programs changed daily life, and ordinary people often helped shape the new policies.

Labor on the March

The labor revival in the 1930s reflected both workers' determination and government support. Workers wanted to improve their wages and benefits as well as to gain union recognition and union contracts that would allow them to limit arbitrary managerial authority and achieve some control over the workplace. This larger goal provoked opposition assimilation by reducing Indian landholding and attacking Indian culture. Appointed commissioner of Indian affairs in 1933, John Collier prohibited interference with Native American religious or cultural life, directed the Bureau of Indian Affairs to employ more Native Americans, and prevented Indian schools from suppressing native languages and traditions.

Collier also persuaded Congress to pass the Indian Reorganization Act of 1934, often called the Indians' New Deal. The act guaranteed religious freedom, reestablished tribal self-government, and halted the sale of tribal lands. It also provided funds to expand Indian landholdings, support Indian students, and establish tribal businesses. But social and economic problems persisted on the isolated reservations, and white missionaries and business interests attacked Collier's reforms as atheistic and communistic. And not all Native Americans supported Collier's reforms, asserting that he, too, stereotyped Indians and their culture, and labeling his efforts as "back-to-the-blanket" policies designed to make Native American cultures historical commodities. Collier himself was disappointed by Congress's refusal to fund his more radical economic programs, acknowledging by the end of the decade that much more needed to be done for Native Americans. (See American Views, The Commissioner of the Bureau of Indian Affairs on the New Deal for Native Americans.)

Hispanic Americans received less assistance from the New Deal. Relief programs aided many Hispanics in California and the Southwest but ignored those who were not citizens. Moreover, local administrators often discriminated against Hispanics, especially by providing higher relief payments to Anglos. Finally, by excluding agricultural workers, neither the Social Security Act nor the Wagner Act gave Mexican Americans much protection or hope. Farm workers remained largely unorganized, exploited, and at the mercy of agribusinesses.

The New Deal: North, South, East, and West

"We are going to make a country," President Roosevelt declared, "in which no one is left out." And with that statement, along with his belief that the federal government must take the lead in building a new "economic constitutional order," FDR ensured that his New Deal programs and policies fanned out throughout the nation, bolstering the stock market and banking in New York, constructing public housing for poor white and African American families in most major cities, and building schools, roads, and bridges in every region of the United States. Ironically, the New Deal also offered special benefits to the South, which was traditionally averse to government activism, and to the West, which considered itself the land of rugged individualism.

The New Deal in the South.   The New Deal's agricultural program boosted farm prices and income more in the South than any other region. By controlling cotton produc-

tion, it also promoted diversification; its subsidies financed mechanization. The resulting modernization helped replace an archaic sharecropping system with an emergent agribusiness. The rural poor were displaced, but the South's agricultural economy advanced.

The New Deal also improved southern cities. FERA and WPA built urban sewer systems, airports, bridges, roads, and harbor facilities. Whereas northern cities had already constructed such facilities themselves—and were still paying off the debts these had incurred—the federal government largely paid for such modernization in the South, giving its cities an economic advantage.

Federal grants were supposed to be awarded to states in proportion to their own expenditures, but while southern politicians welcomed New Deal funds—"I'm gonna grab all I can for the state of Texas," said Governor Lee O'Daniel—they refused to contribute their share of the costs. Nationally, the federal proportion of FERA expenditures was 62 percent; in the South, it was usually 90 percent and never lower than 73 percent. Virginia officials refused to provide even 10 percent, declaring, "It takes people a long time to starve." Some southern cities and counties refused to contribute anything to relief, and Memphis spent less on relief—only 0.1 percent of its budget—than on maintaining public golf courses.

Federal money enabled southern communities to balance their budgets, preach fiscal orthodoxy, and maintain traditional claims of limited government. Federal officials complained about the South's "parasitic" behavior in accepting aid but not responsibility, and even southerners acknowledged the hypocrisy of the region's invocation of state's rights. "We recognize state boundaries when called on to give," noted the *Houston Press,* "but forget them when Uncle Sam is doing the giving."

The federal government had a particularly powerful impact on the South with the **Tennessee Valley Authority (TVA),** launched in 1933 (see Map 25–3). Coordinating activities across seven states, the TVA built dams to control floods and generate hydroelectric power, produced fertilizer, fostered agricultural and forestry development, encouraged conservation, improved navigation, and modernized school and health systems. Private utility companies denounced the TVA as socialistic, but most southerners supported it. Its major drawback was environmental damage that only became apparent later. Over a vast area of the South, it provided electricity for the first time.

The New Deal further expanded access to electricity by establishing the Rural Electrification Administration (REA) in 1935. Private companies had refused to extend power lines into the countryside because it was not profitable, consigning 90 percent of the nation's farms to drudgery and darkness. The REA revolutionized farm life by sponsoring rural nonprofit electric cooperatives. By 1941, 35 percent of American farms had electricity; by 1950, 78 percent. By providing electric power to light and heat homes and barns, pump

MAP 25–3   The Tennessee Valley Authority
By building dams and hydroelectric power plants, the TVA controlled flooding and soil erosion and generated electricity that did much to modernize a large region of the Upper South.

water, and run refrigerators, washing machines, and radios, one Arkansas newspaper concluded, the REA had made "a reality" of what had been only a "utopian dream."

The New Deal in the West.   The New Deal also changed the West. Westerners received the most federal money per capita in welfare, relief projects, and loans. Like southerners, they accepted federal aid and clamored for more. Utah, which received the most federal relief funds per capita, was the nation's "prize 'gimme state,'" said one FERA official. Western farmers and cattle raisers were saved by federal payments, and even refugees from the Dust Bowl depended on relief assistance and medical care in federal camps.

The Bureau of Reclamation, established in 1902, emerged as one of the most important government agencies in the West. It built huge dams to control the western river systems and promote large-scale development. The Hoover Dam on the Colorado River between Nevada and Arizona, completed in 1935; the Grand Coulee Dam on the Columbia River in Washington, finished in 1941; and other giant projects prevented flooding, produced cheap hydroelectric power, and created reservoirs and canal systems to bring water to farms and cities. By furnishing capital and expertise, the government subsidized and stimulated western economic development, particularly the growth of agribusiness.

Westerners welcomed such assistance but rarely shared the federal goals of rational resource management. Instead, they often wanted to continue to exploit the land and re-

sented federal supervision as colonial control. In practice, however, the government worked in partnership with the West's agribusinesses and timber and petroleum industries.

The New Deal and Public Activism

Despite Hoover's fear that government responsibility would discourage local initiative, the 1930s witnessed an upsurge in activism. New Deal programs, in fact, often encouraged or empowered groups to shape public policy. Moreover, because the administration worried about centralization, some federal agencies fostered what New Dealers called "grassroots democracy." The AAA set up committees that ultimately included more than 100,000 people to implement agricultural policy and held referendums on crop controls; local advisory committees guided the various federal arts projects; federal management of the West's public grasslands mandated cooperation with associations of livestock raisers.

At times, local administration of national programs enabled groups to exploit federal policy for their own advantage. Wealthy planters shaped AAA practices at the expense of poor tenant farmers; local control of TVA projects excluded black people. But federal programs often allowed previously unrepresented groups to contest traditionally dominant interests. By requiring that public housing projects be initiated locally, for example, New Deal programs prompted labor unions, religious and civic groups, neighborhood associations, and civil rights groups to form associations to overcome the hostility of

On November 9, 1938, Nazi Germany launched an attack on Jews, destroying their businesses and burning their synagogues. This street scene in Berlin shows the shattered windows of Jewish businesses. Nazi leader Joseph Goebbels recorded the event, known as Kristallnacht, in his diary: "Yesterday: Berlin. There, all proceeded fantastically. One fire after another. It is good that way.…100 dead. But no German property damaged."

by 1939 to create an authoritarian government. Meanwhile, Hitler implemented his plan of conquest: He remilitarized the Rhineland in 1936, and in 1938 he annexed Austria.

The aggressive actions of Germany and Italy failed to eclipse U.S. fears of becoming involved in another European war. Congress passed Neutrality Acts designed to continue America's trade with its world partners but prohibit the president from taking sides in the mounting European crisis. The first act, passed in 1935, prohibited Americans from traveling to a war zone, banned loans to belligerent nations, and instituted an embargo on armaments to belligerents. In 1936 Congress extended the legislation for another year and then in 1937 made the neutrality prohibitions permanent, with the addition of a "cash-and-carry" provision that required belligerent nations to pay for American goods in advance of shipment. President Roosevelt reluctantly signed the bill into law, but continued to work to heighten public awareness of the dangers of Nazism.

Appeasement and more neutrality.   After annexing Austria, Hitler pushed again in 1938 when he demanded the Sudetenland from Czechoslovakia. The French and the British refused to stand up to Hitler, following instead a policy of appeasement. Meeting in Munich in September 1938, the leaders of England and France abandoned their security obligations to the Czechs, yielding the Sudetenland to Hitler in exchange for a weak promise of no more annexations.

In America, too, the sentiment was for peace at all costs, and isolationism permeated the halls of Congress. Indeed, Hitler himself did not regard the United States as a threat to his expansionist plans: "America," he said in 1939, "is not dangerous to us." Hitler held FDR in low esteem and denounced America as a racially mixed nation of intellectual inferiors. "Transport a German to Kiev," Hitler declared, "and he remains a perfect German. But transplant him to Miami, and you make a degenerate out of him—in other words, an American."

Isolationism compounded by anti-Semitism and by the divisions between the leaders of the American Jewish community combined to ensure that the United States would not become a haven for Jews suffering under Nazi brutality. News of Nazi atrocities against Austrian Jews in 1938 shocked the American press, and Hitler's violent pogrom, known as *Kristallnacht* ("Night of the Broken Glass"), conducted against Jews throughout Germany in November 1938, added fresh proof of Nazi cruelty. Although the United States recalled its ambassador from Berlin to protest the pogrom (in response, Germany recalled its ambassador from Washington), it did not alter its restrictive immigration-quota system, the 1924 National Origins Act, to provide refuge for German Jews. Unchallenged, Hitler pressed on with his campaign of persecution and terror against those he termed "inferior races" and "anti-socials," herding Jews, Slavs, homosexuals, and the handicapped into concentration camps. As early as 1933, Hitler established the first concentration camp at Dachau, and by 1939, camps in Germany held over 25,000 people.

As Europe edged closer to war, the relationship between the United States and Japan, periodically tense in the twentieth century, became more strained. Japan resented U.S. economic interests in East Asia and was offended by the policy of excluding Japanese immigrants. The United States regarded Japan's desires for empire as threatening but also needed Japan as a trading partner, especially in the economically depressed 1930s. Consequently, in September 1931, when Japan seized Manchuria, the United States did little more than denounce the action. Again in 1937, after Japanese troops attacked Chinese forces north of Beijing and outright war began between Japan and China, the United States merely condemned the action. That same year, President Roosevelt denounced "the epidemic of world lawlessness," indicting the aggressiveness of Italy, Germany, and Japan and calling for a "quarantine" of aggressors, but he continued his policy of refusing to risk war with Japan.

Edging Toward Involvement

After the Munich agreement, President Roosevelt moved away from domestic reform toward preparedness for war, fearful that conflict in Europe was unavoidable and determined to revise the neutrality laws. In his State of the Union address in January 1939, FDR explained that America's neutrality laws might "actually give aid to an aggressor and deny it to the victim." By the fall of that year, he had won support for eliminating the prohibition on arms sales and adding armaments to the list of cash-and-carry items—a revision that would enable the United States to provide important assistance to Britain and France in the winter of 1939–1940. Hitler's defiance of the Munich agreement in Czechoslovakia, overrunning Prague by March 1939, merely anticipated his next move toward Poland and also convinced the British and the French that war was imminent.

Conclusion

The Great Depression and the New Deal mark a major divide in American history. The depression cast doubt on the traditional practices, policies, and attitudes that underlay not only the nation's economy but also its social and political institutions and relationships. The New Deal brought only partial economic recovery. However, its economic policies, from banking and securities regulation to unemployment compensation, farm price supports, and minimum wages, created barriers against another depression. The gradual adoption of compensatory spending policies expanded the government's role in the economy. Responding to the failures of private organizations and state and local governments, the federal government assumed the obligation to provide social welfare. The New Deal established pensions for the elderly, aid for dependent mothers and children and the blind, public housing for the poor, and public health services. Although these programs were limited in scope and access, they helped establish a responsible government. "Better the occasional faults of a Government that lives in a spirit of charity," Roosevelt warned, "than the constant omission of a Government frozen in the ice of its own indifference."

Roosevelt also expanded the role of the presidency. As his White House took the initiative for defining public policy, drafting legislation, lobbying Congress, and communicating with the nation, it became the model for all subsequent presidents. Not only was the president's power increased, but Roosevelt made the federal government, rather than state or local governments, the focus of public interest and expectations. Under Hoover, one secretary had handled all the White House mail; under FDR, a staff of 50 was overwhelmed.

Roosevelt and the New Deal also revitalized the Democratic Party, drawing minorities, industrial workers, and previously uninvolved citizens into a coalition with white southerners. The tensions in so broad-based a coalition sometimes prevented effective public policies, but the coalition made the Democrats the dominant national party.

Political constraints explain some of the New Deal's failures. Conservative southern Democrats and northern Republicans limited its efforts to curtail racial discrimination or protect the rural and urban poor. But Roosevelt and other New Dealers were often constrained by their own vision, refusing to consider the massive deficit spending necessary to end the depression or not recognizing the need to end gender discrimination. But if the New Deal did not bring the revolution its conservative critics claimed—it did not redistribute wealth or income—it did change American life.

By the end of the 1930s, as international relations deteriorated, FDR was already considering a shift, as he later said, from Dr. New Deal to Dr. Win-the-War. Reluctant to move beyond public opinion that did not want war and limited by neutrality legislation, FDR cautiously led the nation toward war—this time against an enemy far more threatening than the Great Depression. Ironically, only then would President Roosevelt end the depression that had ravaged the nation for nearly a decade.

Review Questions

1. Why did President Hoover's emphasis on voluntarism fail to resolve the problems of the Great Depression in the United States?

2. Describe the relief programs of the New Deal. What were they designed to accomplish? What were their achievements and their limitations?

3. What were the major criticisms of the early New Deal? How accurate were those charges?

4. How did the policies of the New Deal shape the constituency and the prospects of the Democratic Party in the 1930s?

5. Describe the conflict between management and labor in the 1930s. What were the major issues and motivations? How did the two sides differ in resources and tactics, and how and why did these factors change over time?

6. How did the role of the federal government change in the 1930s? What factors were responsible for the changes?

Key Terms

Bonus Army (p. 704)

Congress of Industrial Organizations (CIO) (p. 713)

Fascist government (p. 719)

Federal Deposit Insurance Corporation (FDIC) (p. 705)

Fireside chat (p. 705)

Great Depression (p. 697)

Hoovervilles (p. 698)

New Deal (p. 695)

Securities and Exchange Commission (SEC) (p. 705)

Tennessee Valley Authority (TVA) (p. 716)

Recommended Reading

Conkin, Paul. *The New Deal,* 3rd ed. (1992). A brief and insightful critique of FDR's programs.

Fraser, Steve, and Gary Gerstle, eds. *The Rise and Fall of the New Deal Order, 1930–1980* (1989). A valuable collection of essays that surveys the New Deal and explores its legacy.

Kennedy, David. *Freedom from Fear: The American People in Depression and War* (1999). The most recent and comprehensive survey of the period.

Leuchtenburg, William. *Franklin D. Roosevelt and the New Deal, 1932–1940* (1963). The best single-volume study of FDR's policies during his first two terms as president.

Where to Learn More

- **Center for New Deal Studies, Roosevelt University, Chicago, Illinois.**   The center contains political memorabilia, photographs, papers, and taped interviews dealing with Franklin D. Roosevelt and the New Deal; it also sponsors an annual lecture series about the Roosevelt legacy. www.roosevelt.edu/newdeal/

- **Franklin D. Roosevelt Home and Presidential Library, Hyde Park, New York.**   The Roosevelt home, furnished with family heirlooms, and the spacious grounds, where FDR is buried, personalize the president and provide insights into his career. The nearby library has displays and exhibitions about Roosevelt's presidency, and the Eleanor Roosevelt Wing is dedicated to her career. www.fdrlibrary.marist.edu

- **Eleanor Roosevelt National Historic Site, Hyde Park, New York.**   These two cottages, where Eleanor Roosevelt worked and, after 1945, lived, contain her furniture and memorabilia. Visitors can also watch a film biography of ER and tour the grounds of this retreat where she entertained personal friends and world leaders. www.nps.gov/elro.

- **New Deal Network.**   A valuable guide to the study of the Great Depression and the New Deal with a rich collection of photographs and documents. www.newdeal.feri.org

Study Resources

For study resources for this chapter, go to www.myhistorylab.com and choose *The American Journey*. You will find a wealth of study and review material for this chapter, including pre- and post-tests, customized study plan, key term review flash cards, interactive map and document activities, and documents for analysis.

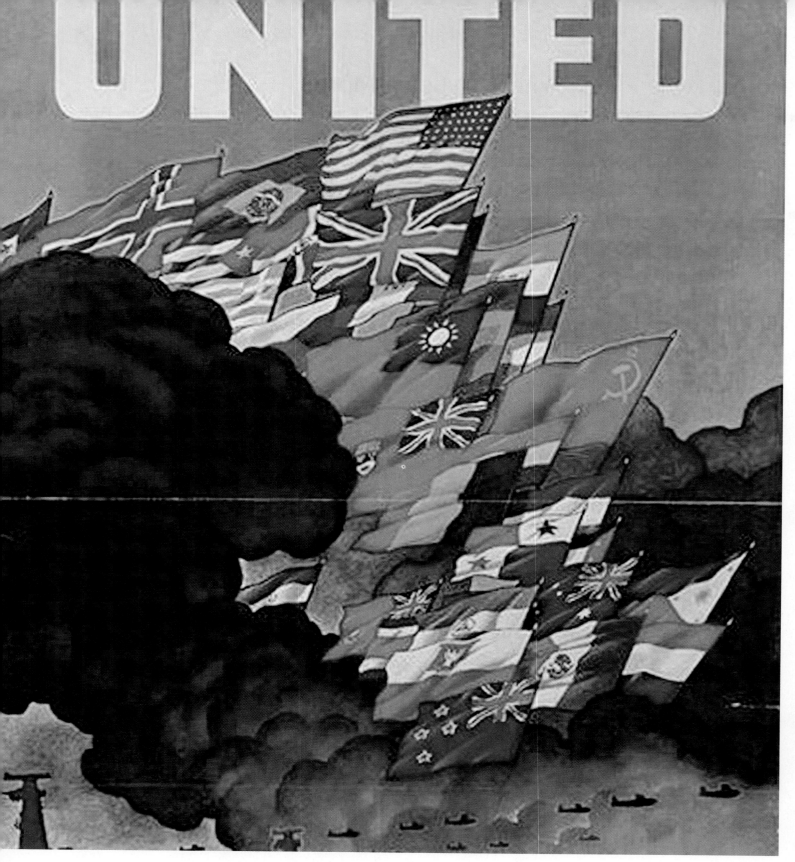

The United States fought Germany and Japan as part of an alliance known as the United Nations. This government poster shows the flags of the many nations advancing together, the Stars and Stripes, the Union Jack of Great Britain, and the hammer and sickle of the Soviet Union in the most prominent positions.

World War II 1939–1945 26

December, 1942

The scene [under the stadium] at The University of Chicago would have been confusing to an outsider, if he could have eluded the security guards and gained admittance. He would have seen only what appeared to be a crude pile of black bricks and wooden timbers....

Finally, the day came when we were ready to run the experiment. We gathered on a balcony about 10 feet above the floor of the large room in which the structure had been erected. Beneath us was a young scientist, George Weil, whose duty it was to handle the last control rod that was holding the reaction in check....

Finally, it was time to remove the control rods. Slowly, Weil started to withdraw the main control rod. On the balcony, we watched the indicators which measured the neutron count and told us how rapidly the disintegration of the uranium atoms under their neutron bombardment was proceeding.

At 11:35 A.M., the counters were clicking rapidly. Then, with a loud clap, the automatic control rods slammed home. The safety point had been set too low.

It seemed a good time to eat lunch. During lunch everyone was thinking about the experiment but nobody talked much about it.

At 2:30, Weil pulled out the control rod in a series of measured adjustments. Shortly after, the intensity shown by the indicators began to rise at a slow but ever-increasing rate. At this moment we knew that the self-sustaining [nuclear] reaction was under way.

The event was not spectacular, no fuses burned, no lights flashed. But to us it meant that release of atomic energy on a large scale would be only a matter of time.

Enrico Fermi, in *The First Reactor* (Washington, DC: U.S. Department of Energy, 1982).

PEARSON myhistorylab

Personal Journeys Online

■ Patricia Cain Koehler, *Oregon Historical Quarterly* (Fall 1990). Helping to build aircraft carriers during World War II.

■ Leon Overstreet in S. L. Sanger, *Working on the Bomb: An Oral History of World War II Hanford* (1995). A construction worker remembers the Manhattan Project.

■ Bill Mauldin, in Studs Terkel, *The Good War* (1985). The famous cartoonist explains the origins of his characters Willie and Joe, the typical WWII G.I.s.

Enrico Fermi was describing the first controlled nuclear chain reaction—the critical experiment from which atomic weapons and atomic power would soon develop. Fermi had emigrated to escape the growing political repression of Fascist Italy. In 1938, he had received the Nobel Prize in physics. While in Stockholm, Sweden, to accept the prize, he and his family put secret plans into action and went to the United States rather than return to Italy. In 1942, after the United States joined the ongoing global conflict of World War II, Fermi was put in charge of nuclear fission research at the University of Chicago and played a leading role in efforts to develop an atomic bomb. The following year found Fermi, other atomic scientists, and their families at Los Alamos, a science city that the government built hurriedly on a high plateau in northern New Mexico, where isolation was supposed to ensure secrecy and help the United States win the race with Nazi Germany to develop atomic weapons.

The instant city was a cross between a cheap subdivision and an army camp for deeply engaged but eccentric scientists. "I always pitied our Army doctors for their thankless job," Enrico's wife, Laura Fermi, later wrote: "They had prepared for the emergencies of the battlefields, and they were faced instead with a high-strung bunch of men, women, and children…high-strung because we were too many of a kind, too close to one another, and we were all crackpots." Scientists spent their days designing a bomb that would change world politics and returned to dinners cooked on wood-burning stoves.

The Fermis were not the only family to give Los Alamos a multinational flavor. Laura remembered that it was "all one big family and all one big accent….Everybody in science was there, both from the United States and from almost all European countries." British and Canadians worked alongside U.S. scientists. So did refugees from Europe, their presence making Los Alamos the most distinguished assemblage of physicists in the world (Laura Fermi later wrote about them in the book *Illustrious Immigrants*). Niels Bohr had fled Denmark to escape the Nazis. Edward Teller was a Hungarian who had studied in Germany. Hans Bethe had left Germany, and Stanislaus Ulam was the only member of his family to survive the Nazi conquest of Poland. Absent were scientists from the Soviet Union, which was bearing the worst of the fighting against Germany but was carefully excluded from the secret of the atomic bomb.

The internationalism of Los Alamos mirrored the larger war effort. Japan's attack on Pearl Harbor in December 1941 thrust the United States into a war that spanned the globe. America's allies against Japan in the Pacific and East Asia included Great Britain, Australia, and China. In Europe, its allies against Nazi Germany and Fascist Italy included Great Britain, the Soviet Union, and

more than 20 other nations. The scientists racing to perfect the atomic bomb knew that victory was far from certain. Germany and Japan had piled one conquest on another since the late 1930s, and they continued to seize new territories in 1942. Allied defeat in a few key battles could have resulted in a standoff or an Axis victory. A new weapon might end the war more quickly or make the difference between victory and defeat.

The war's domestic impacts were as profound as its international consequences. The race to build an atomic bomb was only one part of a vast effort to harness the resources of the United States to the war effort. The war highlighted racial inequalities, gave women new opportunities, and fostered growth in the South and West. By devastating the nation's commercial rivals, compelling workers to retrain and factories to modernize, World War II left the United States dominant in the world economy. It also increased the size and scope of the federal government and built an alliance among the armed forces, big business, and science that helped shape postwar America.

The Dilemmas of Neutrality

Americans in the 1930s wanted no part of another overseas war. According to a 1937 Gallup Poll, 70 percent thought that it had been a mistake for the United States to fight in 1917. Despite two years of German victories and a decade of Japanese aggression against China, opinion polls in the fall of 1941 showed that a majority of voters still hoped to avoid war. President Roosevelt's challenge was to lead the United States toward rearmament and support for Great Britain and China without alarming a reluctant public.

The Roots of War

The roots of World War II can be found in the aftereffects of World War I. The peace settlement created a set of small new nations in eastern Europe that were vulnerable to aggression by their much larger neighbors, Germany and the Soviet Union (more formally, the Union of Soviet Socialist Republics, or USSR). Italy and Japan thought that the Treaty of Versailles had not recognized their stature as world powers. Many Germans were convinced that Germany had been betrayed rather than defeated in 1918. In the 1930s, economic crisis undermined an already shaky political order. Unemployment rose in every country, and the level of international trade dropped by two-thirds. Economic hardship and political instability fueled the rise of right-wing dictatorships that offered territorial expansion by military conquest as the way redress old rivalries, dominate trade, and gain access to raw materials.

CHRONOLOGY

1931	Japan invades Manchuria.
1933	Hitler takes power in Germany.
1935	Congress passes first of three neutrality acts.
	Italy invades Ethiopia.
1936	Germany and Italy form the Rome-Berlin Axis.
	Civil war erupts in Spain.
1937	Japan invades China.
1938	Germany absorbs Austria.
	Munich agreement between Germany, Britain, and France.
1939	Germany and the Soviet Union sign a non-aggression pact.
	Germany absorbs Czechoslovakia.
	Germany invades Poland; Great Britain and France declare war on Germany.
1940	Germany conquers Denmark, Norway, Belgium, the Netherlands, and France.
	Japan, Germany, and Italy sign the Tripartite Pact.
	Germany bombs England in the Battle of Britain.
	The United States begins to draft men into the armed forces.
	Franklin Roosevelt wins an unprecedented third term.
1941	The United States begins a lend-lease program to make military equipment available to Great Britain and later the Soviet Union.
	The Fair Employment Practices Committee is established.
	Germany invades the Soviet Union.
	Roosevelt and Churchill issue the Atlantic Charter.
	Japan attacks U.S. military bases in Hawaii.
1942	American forces in the Philippines surrender to Japan.

	President Roosevelt authorizes the removal and internment of Japanese Americans living in four western states.
	Naval battles in the Coral Sea and off the island of Midway blunt Japanese expansion. U.S. forces land in North Africa.
	Soviet forces encircle a German army at Stalingrad.
	The first sustained and controlled nuclear chain reaction takes place at the University of Chicago.
1943	U.S. and British forces invade Italy, which makes terms with the Allies.
	Race conflict erupts in riots in Detroit, New York, and Los Angeles.
	The landing of Marines on Tarawa initiates the island-hopping strategy.
	U.S. war production peaks.
	Roosevelt, Churchill, and Stalin confer at Tehran.
1944	Allied forces land in Normandy.
	The U.S. Navy destroys Japanese sea power in the battles of the Philippine Sea and Leyte Gulf.
	The Battle of the Bulge is the last tactical setback for the Allies.
1945	Roosevelt, Stalin, and Churchill meet at Yalta to plan the postwar world.
	The United States takes the Pacific islands of Iwo Jima and Okinawa.
	Franklin Roosevelt dies; Harry S. Truman becomes president.
	Germany surrenders to the United States, Great Britain, and the Soviet Union.
	The United Nations is organized at an international meeting in San Francisco.
	Potsdam Conference.
	Japan surrenders after the detonation of atomic bombs over Hiroshima and Nagasaki.

Japanese internal propaganda in the 1930s stressed the need to rebuild Japan's greatness. Japanese nationalists believed that the United States, Britain, and France had treated Japan unfairly after World War I, despite its participation against Germany. They believed that Japan should expel the French, British, Dutch, and Americans from Asia and create a **Greater East Asia Co-Prosperity Sphere,** in which Japan gave the orders and other Asian peoples complied. Seizing the Chinese province of Manchuria to expand an East Asian empire that already included Korea and Taiwan emboldened Japan's military in 1931. A full-scale invasion of China followed in 1937. Japan took many of the key cities and killed tens of thousands of civilians in the "rape of Nanking,"

but failed to dislodge the government of Jiang Jieshi (Chiang Kai-shek) and settled into a war of attrition.

Italian aggression embroiled Africa and the Mediterranean. The Fascist dictator Benito Mussolini had sent arms and troops to aid General Francisco Franco's right-wing rebels in Spain. The three-year civil war, which ended with Franco's victory in 1939, became a bloody testing ground for new German military tactics and German and Italian ambitions against democratic Europe.

In Germany, Adolf Hitler mixed the desire to reassert national pride and power after the defeat of World War I with an ideology of racial hatred. Coming to power by constitutional means in 1933, Hitler quickly consolidated his grip by destroying opposition parties and made himself the German Führer, or absolute leader. Proclaiming the start of a thousand-year Reich ("empire"), he combined the historic German interest in eastward expansion with a long tradition of racialist thought about German superiority. In the Nazi scheme, Germany and other northern European nations ranked above the Slavs of eastern Europe, who were to be pushed aside to provide more territory for a growing German population.

Special targets of Nazi hatred were the Jews, who were prominent in German business and professional life but soon faced persecution aimed at driving them from the country. In 1935, the Nuremberg Laws denied civil rights to Jews and the campaign against them intensified. On November 9, 1938, in vicious attacks across Germany that became known as *Kristallnacht* ("Night of the Broken Glass"), Nazi thugs rounded up, beat, and murdered Jews, smashed property, and burned synagogues. The Nazi government began expropriating Jewish property and excluded Jews from most employment.

Germany and Italy formed the Rome-Berlin Axis in October 1936 and the Tripartite Pact with Japan in 1940, leading to the term **Axis Powers** to describe the aggressor nations. Political dissidents in all three nations had already been suppressed. Mussolini boasted of burying the "putrid corpse of liberty." Politicians in Japan feared assassination if they spoke against the army, and the Thought Police intimidated the public. Hitler's Germany, however, was the most repressive. The Nazi concentration camp began as a device for political terrorism, where socialists and other dissidents and "antisocials"—homosexuals and beggars—could be separated from "pure" Germans. In the camps, the inmates were overworked and abused. Hitler decreed that opponents should disappear into "night and fog." Soon the systematic discrimination and concentration camps would evolve into massive forced-labor camps and then into hellish extermination camps.

Hitler's War in Europe

After annexing Austria through a coup and seizing and slicing up Czechoslovakia, Germany demonstrated the worthlessness of the Munich agreement by invading Poland on September 1, 1939. Britain and France, Poland's allies, declared war on Germany but could not stop the German war machine. Western journalists covering the three-week conquest of Poland coined the term *Blitzkrieg,* or "lightning war," to describe the German tactics. Armored divisions with tanks and motorized infantry punched holes in defensive positions and raced forward 30 or 40 miles per day. Dive

bombers blasted defenses. Portable radios coordinated the tanks, trucks, and motorcycles. Ground forces with horse-drawn artillery and supply wagons encircled the stunned defenders.

Hitler's greatest advantage was the ability to attack when and where he chose. From September 1939 to October 1941, Germany marched from victory to victory (see Map 26–1). Striking from a central position against scattered enemies, Hitler chose the targets and timing of each new front: eastward to smash Poland in September 1939; northward to conquer Denmark and Norway in April and May 1940; westward to defeat the Netherlands, Belgium, and France in May and June 1940, an attack that Italy also joined; southward into the Balkans, enlisting Hungary, Romania, and Bulgaria as allies and conquering Yugoslavia and Greece in April and May 1941. Hitler also launched the Battle of Britain in the second half of 1940. German planes bombarded Britain mercilessly, in an unsuccessful effort to pound the British into submission.

Hitler gambled once too often in June 1941. Having failed to knock Britain out of the war, he invaded the Soviet Union. The attack caught the Red Army off guard. Germany and the USSR had signed a nonagression pact in 1939, and the Soviets had helped to dismember Poland. The Soviet dictator Joseph Stalin had disregarded warnings of a German buildup as a British attempt to goad him into war with Germany. Hitler hoped that smashing the USSR and seizing its vast resources would make Germany invincible. From June until December 1941, more than 4 million Germans, Italians, Hungarians, and Romanians pushed through Belarus, Ukraine, and western Russia. They encircled and captured entire Soviet armies. Before desperate Soviet counterattacks

The raspy-voiced Adolf Hitler had a remarkable ability to stir the German people. He and his inner circle made skillful use of propaganda, exploiting German resentment over the country's defeat in World War I and, with carefully staged mass rallies, such as this event in 1938, inspiring an emotional conviction of national greatness.

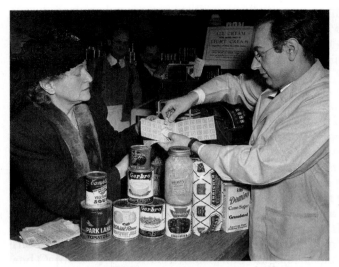

During the course of World War II, the government limited the consumption of a number of products to reserve supplies of products for the war effort and to prevent demand from pushing up the prices of scarce consumer goods. Shoppers like this woman at a grocery store counter used ration stamps to obtain their share of controlled products.

found that no one had shown up for their Sunday matinee concert. "Where is Pearl Harbor?" Maxine Andrews asked the theater's doorman.

War changed the lives of most Americans. Millions of men and women served in the armed forces, and millions more worked in defense factories. In order to keep track of this staggering level of activity, the number of civilian employees of the federal government quadrupled to 3.8 million, a much greater increase than during the New Deal. Meanwhile, youngsters saved tin foil, collected scrap metal, and followed the freedom-fighting stories of Wonder Woman in the comics. College science students might be recruited to work at scientific espionage against the Nazis. The breadth of involvement in the war effort gave Americans a common purpose that softened the divisions of region, class, and national origin while calling attention to continuing inequalities of race.

Organizing the Economy

The need to fight a global war brought a huge expansion of the federal government. Congress authorized the president to reorganize existing government departments and create new agencies. The War Manpower Commission allocated workers among vital industries and the military. The War Production Board invested $17 billion for new factories and managed $181 billion in war-supply contracts, favoring existing corporations because they had experience in large-scale production.

The Office of Price Administration (OPA) fought inflation with price controls and rationing that began with tires, sugar, and coffee and eventually included meat, butter, gaso-

line, and shoes. "Use it up, wear it out, make it do or do without" was the OPA's slogan. Consumers used ration cards and ration stamps to obtain scarce products. With gasoline scarce, horse-drawn delivery wagons made a comeback, while dads sometimes took over junior's bicycle for commuting to work.

By slowing price increases, the OPA helped convince Americans to buy the war bonds that financed half the war spending. Americans also felt the bite of the first payroll deductions for income taxes as the government secured a steady flow of revenues and soaked up some of the high wages that would have pushed inflation. In total, the federal budget in 1945 was $98 billion, eleven times as large as in 1939, and the national debt had increased more than sixfold.

Industry had reluctantly begun to convert from consumer goods to defense production in 1940 and 1941. By the time of the attack on Pearl Harbor, 25 percent of the national economy was devoted to military needs. Although corporations hated to give up the market for consumer goods, the last passenger car for the duration of the war rolled off the assembly line in February 1942. Existing factories retooled to make war equipment, and huge new facilities turned out thousands of planes and ships. Baltimore, Atlanta, Fort Worth, Los Angeles, and Seattle became centers for aircraft production. New Orleans, Portland, Oregon, and the San Francisco Bay area were shipbuilding centers.

The United States applied mass-production technology to aircraft production at a time when Japan was building warplanes one at a time and Germany in small batches. The most spectacular example was the new Ford plant at Willow Run, Michigan, designed to adapt assembly-line approaches to manufacturing B-24 bombers. Where the typical automobile had 15,000 parts, a B-24 had 1,550,000. The assembly line itself was more than a mile long, starting with four separate tracks that gradually merged into one. By 1943, the plant was delivering ten planes a day. American aircraft workers were twice as productive as their German counterparts and four times more productive than Japanese.

Most defense contracts went to such established industrial states as Michigan, New York, and Ohio, but the relative impact was greatest in the South and West, where the war marked the takeoff of what Americans would later call the Sunbelt (see Map 26–4). Washington, DC, teemed with staff officers, stenographers, and other office workers who helped to coordinate the war effort. Local leaders in cities from Charlotte to Fort Worth to Phoenix saw the war as an economic opportunity and campaigned for defense factories and military bases. Albuquerque, New Mexico, more than doubled in population during the 1940s. War-boom cities, such as San Diego (up 92 percent in population in the 1940s) and Mobile (up 68 percent), bustled with activity and hummed with tension. Factories operated three shifts, movies ran around the clock, and workers filled the streets after midnight.

The hordes of war workers found housing scarce. Workers in Seattle's shipyards and Boeing plants scrounged for

MAP EXPLORATION To explore an interactive version of this map, go to http://www.prenhall.com/goldfield5/map26.4

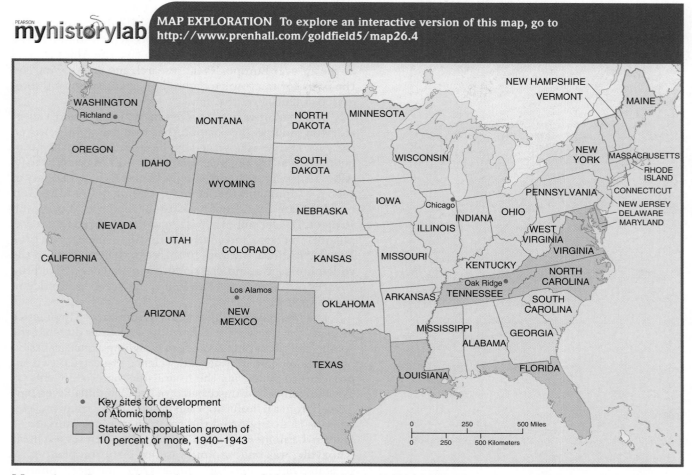

MAP 26–4   **States with Population Growth of 10 Percent or More, 1940–1943**
The conversion of U.S. industry to defense production and the headlong expansion of the armed forces pulled Americans to coastal states and cities and to the South, where the mild climate allowed year-round military training.

living space in offices, tents, chicken coops, and rooming houses where "hot beds" rented in shifts. The situation was similar in small towns like Seneca, Illinois, home to a company that normally made river barges. Between June 1942 and June 1945, it built 157 specialized ships to land tanks in amphibious assaults. Thousands of new workers flocked to Seneca. They lined up three deep at the bars with their Friday paychecks. Residents would sometimes find a stranger rolled up in a blanket on their front porch.

The output of America's war industries was staggering (see Figure 26–1). One historian estimates that 40 percent of the world's military production was coming from the United States by 1944. Equally impressive is the 30 percent increase in the productivity of U.S. workers between 1939 and 1945. Surging farm income pulled agriculture out of its long slump. Organized labor offered a no-strike pledge for the duration, assuring that no one could accuse unions of undermining the war effort but limiting the economic gains of some workers and damping the militancy of the CIO. Nev-

ertheless, overall per capita income doubled, and the poorest quarter of Americans made up some of the ground lost during the Great Depression.

The Enlistment of Science

The war reached into scientific laboratories as well as shops and factories. "There wasn't a physicist able to breathe who wasn't doing war work," remembered Professor Philip Morrison. At the center of the scientific enterprise was Vannevar Bush, former dean at the Massachusetts Institute of Technology. As head of the newly established Office of Scientific Research and Development, Bush guided spending to develop new drugs such as antibiotics, blood-transfusion procedures, weapons systems, radar, sonar, and dozens of other military technologies. The scale of research and development dwarfed previous scientific work and set the pattern of massive postwar federal support for science.

The most costly scientific effort was the development of radar, or radio detection and ranging devices. Building on

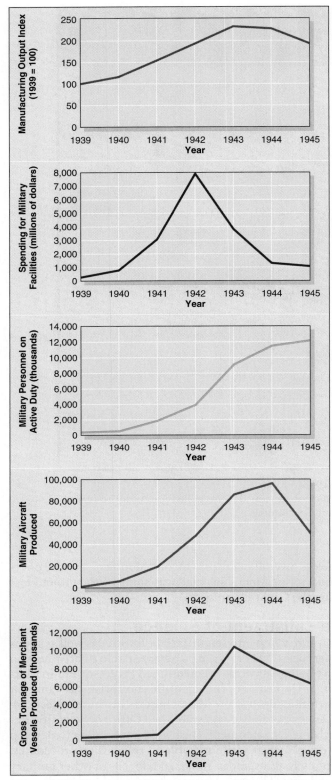

FIGURE 26–1   Making War: The United States Mobilizes, 1939–1945
The U.S. economic mobilization for World War II reached its peak in 1943, the year in which the Allies prepared for the offensives against Germany and Japan that they hoped would end the war. The number of men and women in uniform continued to grow until 1945.

British research on microwaves, the United States put $3 billion into the Radiation Laboratory at MIT. Increasingly compact and sophisticated radar systems helped to defeat the German and Japanese navies and to give the Allies control of the air over Europe. Radar research and engineering laid the basis for microwave technology, transistors, and integrated circuits after the war.

In the summer of 1945, *Time* magazine planned a cover story on radar as the weapon that won the war. However, the *Time* story was upstaged by the atomic bomb, the product of the war's other great scientific effort. As early as 1939, Albert Einstein had written to FDR about the possibility of such a weapon and the danger of falling behind the Germans. In late 1941, Roosevelt established the **Manhattan Project.** By December 2, 1942, scientists proved that it was possible to create and control a sustained nuclear reaction. Because Enrico Fermi was in charge of the experiment, the coded message about the scientific discovery evoked the voyages of Columbus: "The Italian navigator has landed in the new world."

The Manhattan Project moved from theory to practice in 1943. The physicist J. Robert Oppenheimer directed the young scientists at Los Alamos in designing a nuclear-fission bomb. Engineers in other new science cities tried two approaches to producing the fissionable material. Richland, Washington, on the dusty banks of the Columbia River, burgeoned from a handful of peach farmers into a sprawling metropolis that supported the creation of plutonium at the Hanford Engineer Works. Oak Ridge, Tennessee, near Knoxville, was built around gaseous-diffusion plants that separated rare and vital uranium-235 from the more common uranium-238. The two sites were chosen because of the proximity to hydroelectric power from new federal dams on the Columbia and Tennessee rivers, showing continuity from the New Deal to the war effort.

The Manhattan Project ushered in the age of atomic energy. Plutonium from Hanford fueled the first bomb tested at the Trinity site in New Mexico on July 16, 1945. The explosion astonished even the physicists; Oppenheimer quoted from Hindu scriptures in trying to comprehend the results: "Now I am become Death, destroyer of worlds."

Men and Women in the Military
World War II required a more than thirtyfold expansion of the U.S. armed forces from their 1939 level of 334,000 soldiers, sailors, and Marines. By 1945, 8.3 million men and women were on active duty in the army and army air forces and 3.4 million in the navy and Marine Corps, totals exceeded only by the Soviet Union. The military establishment was four times larger than in World War I. Once in the military, sailors and GIs served an average of 33 months. In total, some 350,000 women and more than 16 million men served in the armed forces; 292,000 died in battle, 100,000 survived prisoner-of-war camps, and 671,000 returned wounded.

Most of the Americans in uniform served in support jobs that kept the war machine going. They repaired airplanes and built runways, tracked supplies, and counted coffins. The poet John Ciardi wrote out commendations for valor. Bill Mauldin drew cartoons for the Army newspaper *Stars and Stripes*. As was true in wars throughout history, it was loyalty to the men in their own unit that kept fighting men steady. "The only thing that kept you going was your faith in your buddies," recalled a Marine from the Pacific theater. "You couldn't let 'em down. It was stronger than flag and country."

Native Americans in the military.   Twenty-five thousand American Indians served in the armed forces. Most were in racially integrated units, and Harvey Natcheez, of the Ute tribe, was the first American to reach the center of conquered Berlin. Because the Navajo were one of the few tribes that had not been studied by German anthropologists, the Army Signal Corps decided that their language would be unknown to the Axis armies. Roughly 400 members of the tribe were "code-talkers" who served in Marine radio combat-communication teams in the Pacific theater, transmitting vital information in Navajo.

African Americans in the military.   Approximately 1 million African Americans served in the armed forces during World War II. African American leaders had pressed for a provision in the Selective Service Act to bar discrimination "against any person on account of race or color." But as it had since the Civil War, the army organized black soldiers in segregated units and often assigned them to the menial jobs, such as construction work, and excluded them from combat until manpower shortages forced changes in policy.

The average black soldier encountered discrimination on and off the base. Towns adjacent to army posts were sometimes open to white soldiers but off-limits to blacks. At some southern bases, German prisoners of war watched movies from the first rows along with white GIs while African American soldiers watched from the back. Private Charles Wilson wrote President Roosevelt that Davis-Monthan Army Air Force Base in Tucson was color-coded: Barracks for African Americans were coated with black tar paper, and those for white soldiers sported white paint. Military courts were quick to judge and harshly punish black GIs. It took racially based riots at army bases in North Carolina and Georgia to open up equal (although segregated) access to base recreation facilities.

Despite the obstacles, all-black units, such as the 761st Tank Battalion and the 99th Pursuit Squadron, earned distinguished records. More broadly, the war experience helped to invigorate postwar efforts to achieve equal rights, as had also been true after World War I.

Women in the military.   The nation had a different—but also mixed—reaction to the women who joined the armed forces as army and navy nurses and as members of the WACS (Women's Army Corps), WAVES (Navy), SPARS (Coast Guard), and Marine Corps Women's Reserve. The armed services tried not to change established gender roles. Military officials told Congress that women in uniform could free men for combat. Many of the women hammered at typewriters, worked switchboards, inventoried supplies. Others, however, worked close to combat zones as photographers, code analysts, weather forecasters, radio operators, and nurses. WAC officers battled the tendency of the popular press to call females in the service "girls" rather than "women" or "soldiers" yet emphasized that military service promoted "poise and charm."

The greatest departure from expected roles was the work of the 1,074 members of the Women's Airforce Service Pilots (WASPS), a civilian auxiliary of the Army Air Forces. Many of the WASPS had learned to fly as civilians. From 1942 to 1944, they ferried military aircraft across the country, towed targets for antiaircraft practice, and tested new planes. Caro Bayley, from Springfield, Ohio, lied about her height so that she could pilot B-25s and later flew hazardous runs to test new radar systems. Nevertheless, WASPS were not allowed to carry male passengers, and the group was dissolved when the supply of male pilots caught up with demand.

The Home Front

The war inexorably penetrated everyday life. Residents in war-production cities had to cope with throngs of new workers. Especially in 1941 and 1942, many were unattached

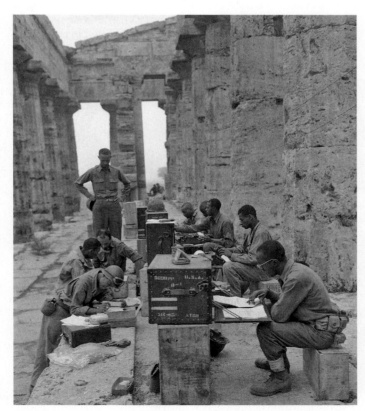

African Americans served in the military large numbers during World War II. Here a signals company has set up operations in the ruins of an ancient temple in southern Italy.

males—young men waiting for their draft call and older men without their families. They elbowed long-term residents in stores, snatched seats on the streetcars, and filled restaurants and theaters. Military and defense officials worried about sexually transmitted diseases and pressured cities to shut down their vice districts. At the same time, college officials scrambled to fill their classrooms, especially after the draft age dropped to 18 in 1942. Many colleges and universities responded to federal requests with special training programs for future officers and engineering and technical training for military personnel.

Families in Wartime

Many Americans put their lives on fast forward. Men and women often decided to beat the clock with instant matrimony. Couples who had postponed marriage because of the depression could afford to marry as the economy picked up. War intensified casual romances and heightened the appeal of marriage as an anchor in troubled times. Jewelers worried about running out of wedding rings. Altogether, the war years brought 1.2 million "extra" marriages, compared to the rate for the period 1920–1939.

The war's impact on families was gradual. The draft started with single men, then called up married men without children, and finally tapped fathers in 1943. Left at home were millions of "service wives," whose compensation from the government was $50 per month. Women who followed their husbands to stateside military posts and war factories often met cold welcomes from local residents. Harriet Arnow crafted a sensitive exploration of isolation from friends and family in her novel *The Dollmaker,* about a Kentucky farm woman who accompanied her husband to a Detroit war plant.

The war had mixed effects on children. "Latchkey children" of working mothers often had to fend for themselves, but middle-class kids whose mothers stayed home could treat the war as an interminable scout project, with salvage drives and campaigns to sell war bonds. In the rural Midwest children picked milkweed pods to stuff life jackets; in coastal communities, they participated in blackout drills. Seattle high schools set aside one class period a day for the High School Victory Corps, training boys as messengers for air-raid wardens, while girls knitted sweaters and learned first aid. Between the end of the school day and suppertime, children listened as Captain Midnight, Jack Armstrong, and Hop Harrigan ("America's ace of the airways") fought the Nazis and Japanese on the radio.

Learning About the War

The federal government tried to keep civilians of all ages committed to the war. It encouraged scrap drives and backyard victory gardens and created colorful posters to warn against espionage, inspire women to join the effort, and promote rationing and car-pooling. The government also managed news about the fighting. Censors screened soldiers' letters. Early in the war, they blocked publication of most photographs of war casualties, although magazines such as *Life* were full of strong and haunting images. Worried about flagging commitment, censors later authorized photographs of enemy atrocities to motivate the public.

Government officials had a harder time controlling Hollywood. The Office of War Information wanted propaganda in feature films, but not so heavy-handed that it drove viewers from theaters. Officials told movie directors to tone down car chases because screeching tires implied wasted rubber. War films revealed the nation's racial attitudes, often drawing distinctions between "good" and "bad" Germans but uniformly portraying Japanese as subhuman and repulsive. The most successful films dramatized the courage of the Allies. *Mrs. Miniver* (1942) showed the British transcending class differences in their battle with the Nazis. *So Proudly We Hail* (1943) celebrated the heroism of military nurses in the Philippines.

Women in the Workforce

As draft calls took men off the assembly line, women changed the composition of the industrial workforce. The war gave them new job opportunities that were embodied in the image of Rosie the Riveter. Women made up one-quarter of West

As millions of men entered the armed forces, millions of women went to work. By 1943, federal agencies were actively recruiting women workers. Those who took production-line jobs in shipyards and aircraft factories, such as the woman shown here, received the greatest attention.

The U.S. government developed the image of Rosie the Riveter to encourage women to take war production jobs. This 1942 poster shows a woman worker with the polka-dot bandanna associated with Rosie, and it equates the bandanna with the hats worn by WACS, WAVEs, and other women in the armed services.

Coast shipyard workers and nearly half of Dallas and Seattle aircraft workers. Most women in the shipyards were clerks and general helpers. The acute shortage of welders and other skilled workers, however, opened thousands of lucrative journeyman positions to them. Aircraft companies, which compounded the labor shortage by stubborn "whites only" hiring, developed new power tools and production techniques to accommodate the smaller average size of women workers, increasing efficiency for everyone on the production line.

By July 1944, 19 million women held paid jobs, up 6 million in four years. Women's share of government jobs increased from 19 to 38 percent; they typed and filed in offices, but they also wrote propaganda for the Office of War Information and analyzed intelligence data for the office of Strategic Service. Women's share of manufacturing jobs rose from 22 to 33 percent, many of them as W.O.W.s or Woman Ordnance Workers. Mirroring the sequence in which the military draft took men, employers recruited single women before turning to married women in 1943 and 1944. The federal government assisted female entry into the labor force by funding daycare programs that served 600,000 children. Some women worked out of patriotism. Many others, however, needed to support their families and already had years of experience in the workforce. As one of the workers recalled of herself and a friend, "We both had to work, we both had children, so we became welders, and if I might say so, damn good ones."

Americans did not know how to respond to the growing numbers of working women. The country needed their labor, but many worried that their employment would undermine families. Employment recruitment posters showed strong, handsome women with rolled-up sleeves and wrenches in hand, but *Life* magazine reassured readers that women in factories could retain their sex appeal. Men and women commonly assumed that women would want to return to the home after victory.

Ethnic Minorities in the War Effort

Mexican American workers made special contributions to the war effort. As defense factories and the military absorbed workers, western farms and railroads faced an acute shortage of workers. In the 1930s, western states had tried to deport Mexican nationals who were competing for scarce jobs. In 1942, however, the United States and Mexico negotiated the *bracero* program, under which the Mexican government recruited workers to come to the United States on six-to-twelve month contracts. More than 200,000 Mexicans worked on U.S. farms under the program, and more than 100,000 worked for western railroads. Although *bracero* workers still faced discrimination, the U.S. government tried to improve working conditions because it wanted to keep public opinion in Latin America favorable to the Allied cause.

The war was a powerful force for the assimilation of Native Americans. Forty thousand moved to off-reservation jobs; they were a key labor force for military supply depots throughout the West. The average cash income of Indian households tripled during the war. Many stayed in cities at its end. The experience of the war accelerated the fight for full civil rights. Congress had made Indians citizens in 1924, in part to recognize their contributions in World War I, but several states continued to deny them the vote. Activists organized the National Congress of American Indians in 1944 and began the efforts that led the U.S. Supreme Court in 1948 to require states to grant voting rights.

African Americans, too, found economic advancement through war jobs. Early in the mobilization, labor leader A. Philip Randolph of the Brotherhood of Sleeping Car Porters worked with Walter White of the NAACP to plan a "Negro March on Washington" to protest racial discrimination by the federal government. To head off a major embarrassment, Roosevelt issued Executive Order 8802 in June 1941, barring racial discrimination in defense contracts and creating the **Fair Employment Practices Committee** (FEPC); the order coined a phrase that reverberated powerfully through the coming decades: "No discrimination on grounds of race, color, creed, or national origin."

MAP 26–6   World War II in the Pacific, 1942–1945
The Allied strategy against Japan was to cut off Japan's southern conquests by retaking the central Pacific islands, the Philippines, and Burma and then to strike at the Japanese home islands. Submarine warfare and massive air attacks from November 1944 to August 1945 crippled Japan's capacity to wage war. The detonation of atomic bombs over Hiroshima and Nagasaki then forced surrender on August 15, 1945.

MacArthur used a version of the bypass strategy in the Solomon Islands and New Guinea, leapfrogging past Japanese strong points. The invasion of the Philippines repeated the approach by landing on Leyte, in the middle of the island chain. The Philippine campaign also destroyed the last offensive capacity of the Japanese fleet. In the Battle of Leyte Gulf, the U.S. Navy sank four Japanese battleships, four carriers, and ten cruisers. The Japanese home islands were left with no defensive screen against an expected invasion.

During 1943 and 1944, the United States also savaged the Japanese economy. Submarines choked off food, oil, and raw materials bound for Japan and island bases. By 1945, im-

ports to Japan were one-eighth of the 1940 level. Heavy bombing of Japan began in early 1944, using the new long-range B-29. Japan's dense wooden cities were more vulnerable than their German counterparts, and Japanese air defenses were much weaker. A fire-bomb raid on Tokyo on the night of March 9, 1945, killed 124,000 people and left 1 million homeless; it was perhaps the single biggest mass killing of all time. Overall, conventional bombing destroyed 42 percent of Japan's industrial capacity. By the time the United States captured the islands of Iwo Jima and Okinawa in fierce fighting (April–June 1945) and neared the Japanese home islands, Japan's position was hopeless.

Searching for Peace

At the beginning of 1945, the Allies sensed victory. Conferring from February 4 to 11 in the Ukrainian town of Yalta, Roosevelt, Stalin, and Churchill planned for the postwar world. The most important American goal was to enlist the Soviet Union in finishing off the Pacific war. Americans hoped that a Soviet attack on Manchuria would tie down enough Japanese troops to reduce U.S. casualties in invading Japan. Stalin repeated his intent to declare war on Japan within three months of victory in Europe, in return for a free hand in Manchuria.

In Europe, the Allies had decided in 1944 to divide Germany and Austria into French, British, American, and Soviet occupation zones and to share control of Berlin. The Red Army already controlled Bulgaria, Romania, and Hungary, countries that had helped the Germans; Soviet officials were installing sympathetic regimes there. Soviet armies also controlled Poland. The most that Roosevelt could coax from Stalin was a vague pledge to allow participation of non-communists in coalition governments in eastern Europe. Stalin also agreed to join a new international organization, the United Nations (UN), whose foundations were laid at a conference in San Francisco in the spring of 1945. The new organization was intended to correct the mistakes of World War I, when the United States had stayed aloof from the League of Nations and had relied on international treaties without mechanisms of enforcement. American leaders wanted the UN to provide a framework through which the United States could coordinate collective security against potential aggressors while retaining its own military strength as the primary means to preserve the peace.

Conservative critics later charged that the western powers "gave away" eastern Europe at the **Yalta Conference**. In fact, the Soviet Union gained little that it did not already control. In East Asia as well, the Soviets could seize the territories the agreement granted them. Roosevelt may have overestimated his ability to charm Stalin, but the Yalta talks could not undo the results of four years of fighting by the Soviet Army.

Truman and Potsdam.

On April 12, two months after Yalta, Roosevelt died of a cerebral hemorrhage. Harry Truman, the new president, was a shrewd politician, but his experience was limited; Roosevelt had not even told him about the Manhattan Project. Deeply distrustful of the Soviets, Truman first ventured into personal international diplomacy in July 1945 at a British-Soviet-American conference at Potsdam, near Berlin. Most of the sessions debated the future of Germany. The leaders endorsed the expulsion of ethnic Germans from eastern Europe and moved the borders of Poland 100 miles west into historically German territory. Truman also made it clear that the United States expected to dominate the occupation of Japan. Its goal was to democratize the Japanese political system and reintroduce Japan into the international community, a policy that succeeded. The **Potsdam Declaration** on July 26 summarized U.S. policy and gave Japan an opening for surrender. However, the declaration failed to guarantee that Emperor Hirohito would not be tried as a war criminal. The Japanese response was so cautious that Americans read it as rejection.

The atomic bomb.

Secretary of State James Byrnes now urged Truman to use the new atomic bomb, tested just weeks earlier. Japan's ferocious defense of Okinawa had confirmed American fears that the Japanese would fight to the death. Thousands of suicide missions by kamikaze pilots who tried to crash their planes into U.S. warships seemed additional proof of Japanese fanaticism. Prominent Americans were wondering if unconditional surrender was worth another six or nine months of bitter fighting. In contrast, using the bomb to end the conflict quickly would ensure that the United States could occupy Japan without Soviet participation, and the bomb might intimidate Stalin (see Overview, The Decision to Use the Atomic Bomb). In short, a decision not to use atomic weapons was never a serious alternative in the summer of 1945.

The ruins of Hiroshima in the aftermath of the atomic bomb. Atomic bombs, dropped first on Hiroshima and then on Nagasaki in August 1945, instantly destroyed most of each city. Now one airplane could wreak the kind of devastation that massive fire-bombing raids had inflicted on cities such as Hamburg and Tokyo, adding new terror to the idea of total war.

Facing Soviet intransigence over eastern Europe, Truman decided that the United States should "take the lead in running the world in the way the world ought to be run." One technique was economic pressure. The State Department "mislaid" a Soviet request for redevelopment loans. The United States and Britain objected to Soviet plans to take industrial equipment and raw materials from the western occupation zones in Germany, compensation that the Soviets thought they had been promised.

The United States also tried to involve the Soviet Union and eastern Europe in new international organizations. The Senate approved American membership in the newly organized United Nations (UN) with only two opposing votes, a sharp contrast to its rejection of the League of Nations in 1920. The Washington-based **International Monetary Fund (IMF)** and the **World Bank** were designed to revive international trade. The IMF stabilized national currencies against the short-term pressures of international trade. The World Bank drew on the resources of member nations to make economic development loans to governments for such projects as new dams or agricultural modernization. These organizations ensured that the reviving world economy would revolve around the industrial and technological power of the United States, and they continue to dictate the economic policy of many developing nations into the twenty-first century.

In 1946, the United States presented a plan in the United Nations to control atomic energy. Bernard Baruch suggested that an international agency should oversee all uranium production and research on atomic explosives. The Baruch plan emphasized enforcement and inspections that would have opened the Soviet nuclear effort to American interference, an unacceptable prospect for a nation trying to catch up with the United States by building its own atomic bombs. On-site inspection would remain a problem in arms-control negotiations for the next half-century.

While UN delegates debated the future of atomic energy, American leaders were becoming convinced of Soviet aggressiveness. In February 1946, George Kennan, a senior American diplomat in Moscow, sent a "long telegram" to the State Department. He depicted a Soviet Union driven by expansionist Communist ideology. The Soviets, he argued, would constantly probe for weaknesses in the capitalist world. The best response was firm resistance to protect the Western heartlands.

The British encouraged the same tough stand. Lacking the strength to shape Europe on its own, Great Britain repeatedly nudged the United States to block Soviet influence. Speaking at Westminster College in Missouri in March 1946, Winston Churchill warned that the Soviet Union had dropped an "iron curtain" across the middle of Europe and urged a firm Western response.

Churchill's speech matched the mood in official Washington. Truman's foreign-policy advisers shared the belief in an aggressive Soviet Union, and the president himself saw the world as a series of either-or choices. Administration leaders did not fear an immediate Soviet military threat to the United States, for they knew that World War II had exhausted the Soviet Union. But they knew that the Soviets were strong enough to brush aside the U.S. occupation forces in Germany. Added to military apprehension were worries about political and economic competition. Communist parties in war-ravaged Europe and Japan were exploiting discontent. In Asia and Africa, the allegiance of nationalists who were fighting for independence from European powers remained in doubt. America's leaders worried that much of the Eastern Hemisphere might fall under Soviet control.

Were Truman and his advisers right about Soviet intentions? The evidence is mixed. In their determination to avoid another Munich, Truman and his foreign-policy circle ignored examples of Soviet caution and conciliation. The Soviets withdrew troops from Manchuria in northern China and acquiesced in America's control of defeated Japan. They allowed a neutral but democratic government in Finland and technically free elections in Hungary and Czechoslovakia (although it was clear that Communists would do well there). They demobilized much of their huge army and reduced their forces in eastern Europe.

However, the Soviet regime also acted to justify American fears. The Soviet Union could not resist exerting influence in the Middle East. It pressured Turkey to give it partial control of the exit from the Black Sea. It retained troops in northern Iran until warned out by the United States. The Soviets were ruthless in support of Communist control in Eastern Europe in 1946 and 1947; they aided a Communist takeover in Bulgaria, backed a coup in Romania, and undermined the last non-Communist political opposition in Poland. U.S. policymakers read these Soviet actions as a rerun of Nazi aggression and determined not to let a new totalitarian threat undermine Western power.

The Truman Doctrine and the Marshall Plan

Whatever restraint the Soviet Union showed was too late or too little. Early in 1947, Truman and his advisers acted decisively. The British could no longer afford to back the Greek government that was fighting a civil war against Communists, and U.S. officials feared that a Communist takeover in Greece would threaten the stability of Italy, France, and the Middle East. Truman coupled his case for intervention in Greece with an appeal for aid to neighboring Turkey, which lived under the shadow of the Soviet Union. On March 12, he told Congress that the United States faced a "fateful hour" and requested $400 million to fight Communism in Greece and Turkey and secure the free world. Congress agreed, and the United States became the dominant power in the eastern Mediterranean.

Framing the specific request was a sweeping declaration that became known as the **Truman Doctrine.** The president pledged to use U.S. economic power to help free nations everywhere resist internal subversion or aggression. "It must be the policy of the United States," he said, "to support free peoples who are resisting attempted subjugation by armed minorities or by outside pressures.... I believe that our help should be primarily through economic and financial aid, which is essential to economic stability and orderly political processes."

Meanwhile, Europe was sliding toward chaos. Germany was close to famine after the bitter winter of 1946–1947. Western European nations were bankrupt and unable to import raw materials for their factories. Overstressed medical systems could no longer control tuberculosis and other diseases. Communist parties had gained in Italy, France, and Germany. Winston Churchill, again sounding the alarm, described Europe as "a rubble-heap, a charnel house, a breeding ground of pestilence and hate."

The U.S. government responded with unprecedented economic aid. Secretary of State George C. Marshall announced the European Recovery Plan on June 5, 1947. What the press quickly dubbed the **Marshall Plan** committed the United States to help rebuild Europe. The United States invited Soviet and eastern European participation, but under terms that would have reduced Moscow's control over its satellite economies. The Soviets refused, fearing that the United States wanted to undermine its influence, and instead organized their eastern European satellites in their own association for Mutual Economic Assistance, or Comecon, in 1949. In western Europe, the Marshall Plan was a success. Aid totaled $13.5 billion over four years. It met many of Europe's economic needs and quieted class conflict. The Marshall Plan expanded American influence through cooperative efforts. Because Europeans spent much of the aid on U.S. goods and machinery, and because economic recovery promised markets for U.S. products, business and labor both supported it. In effect, the Marshall Plan created an "empire by invitation," in which Americans and Europeans jointly planned Europe's recovery.

The Americans also micromanaged European politics. In Italy, for example, the U.S. forced the middle-of-the-road Christian Democrats to kick the Italian Communist party out of its governing coalition in return for economic aid. In 1948, Marshall warned the Italians that aid would vanish if they voted Communists into power. The State Department recruited Italian American organizations to pressure relatives in Italy and was relieved when the Christians Democrats won.

U.S. policy in Japan followed the pattern set in Europe. As supreme commander of the Allied Powers, General Douglas MacArthur acted as Japan's postwar dictator. He tried to change the values of the old war-prone Japan through social reform, democratization, and demilitarization. At the end of 1947, however, the United States decided that democracy and pacifism could go too far. Policymakers were fearful of economic collapse and political chaos, just as in Europe. The "reverse course" in occupation policy aimed to make Japan an economic magnet for other nations in East Asia, pulling them toward the American orbit and away from the Soviet Union. MacArthur reluctantly accepted the new policy of "economic crank-up" by preserving Japan's corporate giants and encouraging American investment. At American insistence, the new Japan accepted American bases and created its own "self-defense force" (with no capacity for overseas aggression).

George Kennan summed up the new American policies in the magazine *Foreign Affairs* in July 1947. Writing anonymously as "X," Kennan argued that the Soviet leaders were committed to a long-term strategy of expanding Communism. The proper posture of the United States, he said, should be an equally patient commitment to "firm and vigilant **containment** of Russian expansive tendencies." Kennan warned that the emerging Cold War would be a long conflict, with no quick fixes.

Soviet Reactions

The bold American moves in the first half of 1947 put the Soviet Union on the defensive. In response, Soviet leaders orchestrated strenuous opposition to the Marshall Plan by French and Italian Communists. East of the Iron Curtain, Hungarian Communists expelled other political parties from a coalition government. Bulgarian Communists shot opposition leaders. Romania, Bulgaria, and Hungary signed defense pacts with the Soviet Union.

In early 1948, the Soviets targeted Czechoslovakia. For three years, a neutral coalition government there on the model of Finland had balanced trade with the West with a foreign policy friendly to the Soviet Union. In February 1948, while Russian forces assembled on the Czech border, local Communists took advantage of political bumbling by other members of the governing coalition. Taking control through a technically legal process, they pushed aside Czechoslovakia's democratic leadership and turned the nation into a dictatorship and Soviet satellite within a week.

The climax of the Soviet reaction came in divided Berlin, located 110 miles inside the Soviet Union's East German occupation zone. The city was divided into four sectors: one controlled by the Soviets and three by the United States, Britain, and France. On June 4, 1948, Soviet troops blockaded surface traffic into Berlin, cutting off the U.S., British, and French sectors. The immediate Soviet aim was to block Western plans to merge their three German occupation zones into an independent federal republic (West Germany). Rather than abandon 2.5 million Berliners or shoot their way through, the Western nations responded to the **Berlin blockade** by airlifting supplies to the city. Stalin decided not to intercept the flights. After 11 months, the Soviets abandoned the blockade, making the Berlin airlift a triumph of American resolve.

American Rearmament

The coup in Czechoslovakia and the Berlin blockade shocked American leaders and backfired on the Soviets. The economic assistance strategy of 1947 now looked inadequate. Congress responded in 1948 by reinstating the military draft and increasing defense spending. Much of the money bought new warplanes, as thrifty congressmen decided that air power was the easiest way for the United States to project its military power abroad.

The United States had already begun to modernize and centralize its national security apparatus, creating the institutions that would run foreign policy in the second half of the century. The National Security Act of July 1947 created the **Central Intelligence Agency** (CIA) and the **National Security Council** (NSC). The CIA handled intelligence gathering and covert operations. The NSC assembled top diplomatic and military advisers in one committee. In 1949, legislation also created the Department of Defense to oversee the army, navy, and air force (independent from the army since 1947). The civilian secretary of defense soon began to exercise influence on foreign policy equal to that of the secretary of state. The new post of chairman of the joint chiefs of staff was supposed to coordinate the rival branches of the military.

In April 1949, ten European nations, the United States, and Canada signed the North Atlantic Treaty as a mutual defense pact. American commitments to the **North Atlantic Treaty Organization (NATO)** included military aid and the deployment of U.S. troops in western Europe. As Republican Senator Robert Taft warned in the ratification debate, NATO was the sort of "entangling alliance" that the United States had avoided for 160 years. It was also the insurance policy that western Europeans required if they were to accept the dangers as well as the benefits of a revived West Germany, which was economically and militarily necessary for a strong Europe. In short, NATO was a sort of marriage contract between Europe and the previously standoffish United States. After 1955, its counterpart would be the **Warsaw Pact** for mutual defense among the Soviet Union and its European satellites (see Map 27–2).

Two years later, the United States signed similar but less comprehensive agreements in the western Pacific: the ANZUS Pact with Australia and New Zealand and a new treaty with the Philippines. The alliances reassured Pacific allies that were nervously watching the United States negotiate a unilateral peace treaty with Japan (ignoring the Soviet Union). The United States overcame opposition from nations Japan had attacked in World War II by promising to assist their defense and maintaining military bases in Japan. Taken to-

gether, peacetime rearmament and mutual defense pacts amounted to a revolution in American foreign policy.

Cold War and Hot War

The first phase of the Cold War reached a crisis in the autumn of 1949. The two previous years had seen an uneasy equilibrium in which American success in southern and western Europe and the standoff over Berlin (the blockade ended in May 1949) balanced the consolidation of Soviet power in eastern Europe. Now, suddenly, two key events seemed to tilt the world balance against the United States and its allies. In September, Truman announced that the Soviet Union had tested its own atomic bomb. A month later, the Communists under Mao Zedong (Mao Tse-tung) took power in China. The following summer, civil war in Korea sucked the United States into a fierce war with Communist North Korea and China. While Americans studied maps that showed communism spreading across Europe and Asia, their government accelerated a 40-year arms race with the Soviet Union.

Berlin was still a devastated city in 1948. When the Soviet Union closed off ground access to the British, French, and American occupation zones, the city became a symbol of the West's Cold War resolve. Allied aircraft lifted in food, fuel, and other essentials for West Berliners for nearly a year until the Soviets ended the blockade.

MAP EXPLORATION To explore an interactive version of this map, go to
http://www.prenhall.com/goldfield5/map27.2

MAP 27–2   Cold War in Europe
In the late 1940s and 1950s, the Cold War split Europe into rigidly divided western and eastern blocs. Members of NATO allied with the United States to oppose Soviet expansion. The Soviet Union directed the military and foreign policies of members of the Warsaw Pact.

The Nuclear Shadow

Experts in Washington had known that the Soviets were working on an A-bomb, but the news dismayed the average citizen. As newspapers and magazines scared their readers with artists' renditions of the effects of an atomic bomb on New York or Chicago, the shock tilted U.S. nuclear policy toward military uses. In 1946, advocates of civilian control had won a small victory when Congress established the Atomic Energy Commission (AEC). The AEC tried to balance research on atomic power with continued testing of new weapons. Now Truman told the AEC to double the output of fissionable uranium and plutonium for "conventional" nuclear weapons.

A more momentous decision soon followed. Truman decided in January 1950 to authorize work on the "super" bomb—the thermonuclear fusion weapon that would become the hydrogen bomb (H-bomb). The debate over the "super" pitted a cautious scientific advisory committee and J. Robert Oppenheimer against powerful political figures and a handful of scientists who believed, correctly, that the for investigation had indeed been Communists or interested in Communism, usually in the 1930s and early 1940s. Most saw it as a way to increase social justice, and they sometimes excused the failures of Communism in the Soviet Union. Unlike the handful of real spies, however, they were targeted not for actions but for ideas. The investigations and loyalty programs were efforts to ensure that Americans kept any left-wing ideas to themselves.

Conclusion

In the face of confrontation over Berlin, fighting in Korea, and growing numbers of nuclear weapons, the Cold War stayed cool because each side achieved its essential goals. The Soviet Union controlled eastern Europe, while the United States built increasingly strong ties with the NATO nations and Japan. Although the result was a stalemate, it nevertheless absorbed huge shares of Soviet and American resources and conditioned the thinking of an entire generation.

The shift from prewar isolationism to postwar internationalism was one of the most important changes in the nation's history. To many of its advocates, internationalism represented a commitment to spread political democracy to other nations. As the 1950s and 1960s would show, the results often contradicted the ideal when the United States forcibly imposed its will on other peoples. Even as the results overseas fell short of the ideal, however, the new internationalism highlighted and helped change domestic racial attitudes.

The Truman years saw the implementation of a national security policy that dominated the next half-century. The armed forces were strong but subordinate to the civilian administration through the National Security Council and Department of Defense. The expansion of the close alliance between scientific research and defense needs that had begun with World War II augmented the national defense capacity. The United States led an international system of collective security based on mutual defense treaties, contributing financial assistance and sophisticated weapons while its allies helped to provide the military manpower.

These same years also brought increasing stability within the nation. The economic chaos of 1946 faded quickly. By identifying liberalism at home with anti-Communism abroad, Truman's efforts to define a vital center helped protect the New Deal. Americans in the early 1950s could be confident that New Deal and Fair Deal programs to expand economic opportunity and increase economic security were permanent, if incomplete, setting the stage for new social activism in the 1960s. If the Republicans had won in 1948, they might have dismantled the New Deal. By 1952, both presidential candidates affirmed the consensus that placed economic opportunity at the center of the national agenda. The suburban housing boom seemed to turn the dream of prosperity into reality for millions of families.

Despite the turmoil and injustice of the second Red Scare and deep worries about nuclear war, the United States emerged from the Truman years remarkably prosperous. It was also more secure from international threats than many nervous Americans appreciated. The years from 1946 to 1952 set the themes for a generation that believed that the United States could do whatever it set its mind to: end poverty, land an astronaut on the moon, thwart Communist revolutions in other countries. There was a direct line from Harry Truman's 1947 declaration that the United States would defend freedom around the world to John Kennedy's 1961 promise that the nation would bear any burden necessary to protect free nations from Communism. As the world moved slowly toward greater stability in the 1950s, Americans were ready for a decade of confidence.

Review Questions

1. As described in the opening of the chapter, what housing choices were available after World War II? How did these choices reshape American cities? How did the postwar readjustment create a suburban society?

2. What were the key differences between Harry Truman and congressional Republicans about the legacy of the New Deal? Why did regulating labor unions become a central domestic issue in the late 1940s? Why did Truman manage to win the presidential election of 1948 despite starting as an underdog?

3. How did the postwar years expand opportunity for veterans and members of the working class? How did they limit opportunities for women? How did they begin to challenge racial inequities in American society?

4. What foreign policy priorities did United States set after 1945? To what extent did the United States achieve its most basic objectives? How did mutual mistrust fuel and deepen the Cold War?

5. How did the Cold War change character in 1949 and 1950? What were key actions by the Soviet Union and China, and how did the United States respond? What was the effect of the chaotic fighting in Korea on U.S. domestic politics and diplomacy?

6. What factors motivated an increasingly frantic fear of domestic subversion in the late 1940s and early 1950s? Who were the key actors in the second Red Scare? What was its long-term impact on American society?

7. How did the continuation and expansion of the nation's global commitments after 1945 affect life in the United States?

Key Terms

Berlin blockade (p. 771)

Central Intelligence Agency (p. 771)

Cold War (p. 760)

Containment (p. 771)

Council of Economic Advisers (p. 762)

Dixiecrats (p. 766)

GI Bill of Rights (p. 763)

House Committee on Un-American Activities (HUAC) (p. 779)

International Monetary Fund (IMF) (p. 770)

Korean War (p. 777)

Levittown (p. 763)

Marshall Plan (p. 771)

McCarthyism (p. 791)

National Security Council (p. 772)

National Security Council Paper 68 (NSC-68) (p. 774)

North Atlantic Treaty Organization (NATO) (p. 772)

Redlining (p. 764)

Taft-Hartley Act (p. 762)

Truman Doctrine (p. 770)

Warsaw Pact (p. 772)

World Bank (p. 770)

Recommended Reading

Boyer, Paul. *By the Bomb's Early Light: American Thought and Culture at the Dawn of the Atomic Age* (1985). Examines the mixture of hopes and fears with which Americans greeted the arrival of the atomic age, giving detailed attention to popular culture as well as national policy.

Fried, Richard. *The Russians Are Coming! The Russians Are Coming! Propaganda and Patriotism in Cold War America* (1998). Explores how the Cold War shaped everyday life.

Goulden, Joseph C. *The Best Years, 1945–1950* (1976). A very readable portrayal of the ways in which Americans adjusted to the postwar years, drawing heavily on contemporary magazine accounts.

Leffler, Melvyn. *A Preponderance of Power: National Security, the Truman Administration, and the Cold War* (1992). Provides a balanced interpretation of responsibility for the Cold War in a detailed but readable account of American policy.

McCullough, David. *Truman* (1992). A readable and sympathetic biography of the thirty-third president.

Navasky, Victor. *Naming Names* (1980). The impact of HUAC on Hollywood and the entertainment industry, told by a strong opponent of the committee.

Rampersad, Arnold. *Jackie Robinson* (1997). Presents Jackie Robinson as a pioneer of racial integration on and off the ballfield.

Stueck, William. *Rethinking the Korean War: A New Diplomatic and Strategic History* (2002). An up-to-date analysis of the global impact of the war in Korea.

Where to Learn More

■ **Harry S Truman National Historical Site, Library, and Museum, Independence, Missouri.** The museum has exhibits on Truman's political career and U.S. history during his administration. Also in Independence is the Harry S Truman Courtroom and Office, with exhibits on his early career. www.nps.gov/hstr

■ **General Douglas MacArthur Memorial, Norfolk, Virginia.** The MacArthur Memorial in downtown Norfolk commemorates the career of a key figure in shaping the postwar world. www.macarthurmemorial.org

■ **United Nations Headquarters, New York, New York.** A tour of the United Nations complex in New York is a reminder of the new organizations for international cooperation that emerged from World War II. www.un.org

Study Resources

For study resources for this chapter, go to www.myhistorylab.com and choose *The American Journey*. You will find a wealth of study and review material for this chapter, including pre- and post-tests, customized study plan, key term review flash cards, interactive map and document activities, and documents for analysis.

On August 28, 1963, Rev. Martin Luther King, Jr. delivered his famous "I have a dream" speech to the March on Washington for Jobs and Freedom. The address was a climactic moment in the civil rights movement, encapsulating the optimism of decades of struggle, but the March on Washington also papered over emerging divisions that would become apparent later in the 1960s.

The Confident Years 28
1953–1964

The first day I was able to enter Central High School [in Little Rock, Arkansas, September 23, 1957], what I felt inside was terrible, wrenching, awful fear. On the car radio I could hear that there was a mob. I knew what a mob meant and I knew that the sounds that came from the crowd were very angry. So we entered the side of the building, very, very fast. Even as we entered there were people running after us, people tripping other people. There has never been in my life any stark terror or any fear akin to that. I'd only been in the school a couple of hours and by that time it was apparent that the mob was just overrunning the school. Policemen were throwing down their badges and the mob was getting past the wooden sawhorses because the police would no longer fight their own in order to protect us. So we were all called into the principal's office, and there was great fear that we would not get out of this building. We were trapped. And I thought, Okay, so I'm going to die here, in school. . . . Even the adults, the school officials, were panicked, feeling like there was no protection. . . . [A] gentleman, who I believed to be the police chief, said . . . "I'll get them out." And we were taken to the basement of this place. And we were put into two cars, grayish blue Fords. And the man instructed the drivers, he said, "Once you start driving, do not stop." And he told us to put our heads down. This guy revved up his engine and he came up out of the bowels of this building, and as he came up, I could just see hands reaching across this car, I could hear the yelling, I could see guns, and he was told not to stop. "If you hit somebody, you keep rolling, 'cause the kids are dead." And he did just that, and he didn't hit anybody, but he certainly was forceful and aggressive in the way he exited this driveway, because people tried to stop him and he didn't stop. He dropped me off at home. And I remember saying, "Thank you for the ride," and I should've said, "Thank you for my life."

Melba Patillo Beals, in Henry Hampton and Steve Frayer, eds., *Voices of Freedom: An Oral History of the Civil Rights Movement from the 1950s through the 1980s* (New York: Bantam, 1990).

myhistorylab

Personal Journeys Online

- Diane Nash, Interview in Mathew Allman, *The New Negro*, 1961. The civil rights sit-in movement in Nashville in 1960.

- Suzette Miller, in Staughton Lynd, *Nonviolence in America*, 1966. Grass roots civil rights efforts in Mississippi in 1961.

Melba Pattillo was one of the nine African American students who entered previously all-white Central High in the fall of 1957. Her enrollment in the high school, where she managed to last through a year of harassment and hostility, was a symbolic step in the journey toward greater racial equality in U.S. society. School integration in Little Rock implemented the U.S. Supreme Court decision in the case of *Brown v. Board of Education* in 1954, which declared that racially segregated schools violated the mandate that all citizens receive equal protection of the law. The violence with which some white residents of Little Rock responded, and the courage of the students, marked one of the key episodes in the civil rights revolution that spanned roughly a decade from the *Brown* decision to the Voting Rights Act of 1965.

The struggle for full civil rights for all Americans was rooted in national ideals, but it was also shaped by the continuing tensions of the Cold War. President Dwight Eisenhower acted against his own inclinations and sent federal troops to keep the peace in Little Rock in part because he worried about public opinion in other nations. As the United States and the Soviet Union maneuvered for influence in Africa and Asia, domestic events sometimes loomed large in foreign relations. Few Americans questioned the rightness or necessity of contesting the Cold War—or of America's ultimate triumph. This consensus gave U.S. policy an overarching goal of containment but also narrowed American options by casting issues at home and abroad in terms of the U.S.-Soviet rivalry.

Melba Pattillo's life after Little Rock also reveals something about the increasing economic opportunities available to most Americans. She graduated from San Francisco State University, earned a master's degree from Columbia University, and worked as a television reporter and writer. San Francisco State was part of the great expansion of higher education that helped millions of Americans move into middle-class jobs and neighborhoods. The prosperous years from 1953 to 1964 spread the economic promise of the 1940s across American society. Young couples could afford large families and new houses. Labor unions grew conservative because cooperation with big business offered immediate gains for their members.

Despite challenges at home and abroad, Americans were fundamentally confident during the decade after the Korean War. They expected corporations to use scientific research to craft new products for eager customers and medical researchers to conquer diseases. When the USSR challenged U.S. preeminence and launched the first artificial space satellite in 1957, Americans responded with shock followed by redoubled efforts to regain what they considered their rightful world leadership in science and technology.

A Decade of Affluence

Americans in the 1950s believed in the basic strength of the United States. Television's *General Electric Theater* was third in the ratings in 1956–1957. Every week, its host, Ronald Reagan, a popular Hollywood lead from the late 1930s, stated, "At General Electric, progress is our most important product." It made sense to his viewers. Large, technologically sophisticated corporations were introducing new marvels: Orlon sweaters and Saran Wrap, long-playing records, and Polaroid cameras. As long as the United States defended free enterprise, Reagan told audiences on national speaking tours, the sky was the limit.

CHRONOLOGY

1953	CIA-backed coup returns Shah Reza Pahlevi to power in Iran.
	Soviet Union detonates hydrogen bomb.
1954	Vietnamese defeat the French; Geneva conference divides Vietnam.
	United States and allies form SEATO.
	Supreme Court decides *Brown v. Board of Education of Topeka*.
	CIA overthrows the government of Guatemala.
	China provokes a crisis over Quemoy and Matsu.
1955	Salk polio vaccine is announced.
	Black citizens boycott Montgomery, Alabama, bus system.
	Soviet Union forms the Warsaw Pact.
	AFL and CIO merge.
1956	Interstate Highway Act is passed.
	Soviets repress Hungarian revolt.
	Israel, France, and Britain invade Egypt.
1957	U.S. Army maintains law and order in Little Rock after violent resistence to integration of Central High School.
	Soviet Union launches *Sputnik*, world's first artificial satellite.
1958	United States and Soviet Union voluntarily suspend nuclear tests.
1959	Fidel Castro takes power in Cuba.
	Nikita Khrushchev visits the United States.
1960	U-2 spy plane shot down over Russia.
	Sit-in movement begins in Greensboro, North Carolina.

1961	Bay of Pigs invasion fails.
	Kennedy establishes the Peace Corps.
	Vienna summit fails.
	Freedom rides are held in the Deep South.
	Berlin crisis leads to construction of the Berlin Wall.
1962	John Glenn orbits the earth.
	Cuban missile crisis brings the world to the brink of nuclear war.
	Michael Harrington publishes *The Other America*.
1963	Civil rights demonstrations rend Birmingham.
	Civil rights activists march in Washington.
	Betty Friedan publishes *The Feminine Mystique*.
	Limited Test Ban Treaty is signed.
	Ngo Dinh Diem is assassinated in South Vietnam.
	President Kennedy is assassinated.
1964	Civil Rights Act is passed.
	Freedom Summer is organized in Mississippi.
	Office of Economic Opportunity is created.
	Gulf of Tonkin Resolution is passed.
	Wilderness Act marks new direction in environmental policy.
1965	Medical Care Act establishes Medicare and Medicaid.
	Elementary and Secondary Education Act extends direct federal aid to local schools.
	Selma-Montgomery march climaxes era of nonviolent civil rights demonstrations.
	Voting Rights Act suspends literacy tests for voting.

Many Americans valued free enterprise and family life as part of the anti-Communist crusade. Social and intellectual conformity ensured a united front. Congress established Loyalty Day in 1955. National leaders argued that strong families were bulwarks against Communism and that churchgoing inoculated people against subversive ideas. Under the lingering cloud of McCarthyism, the range of political ideas that influenced government policy was narrower than in the 1930s and 1940s. Nevertheless, critics began to voice the discontents that exploded in the 1960s and 1970s.

What's Good for General Motors

Dwight Eisenhower presided over the prosperity of the 1950s. Both Democrats and Republicans had courted him as a presidential candidate in 1948. Four years later, he picked the Republicans because he wanted to make sure that the party remained committed to NATO and collective security in Europe rather than retreat into isolationism. He easily defeated the Democratic candidate, Adlai Stevenson, the moderately liberal governor of Illinois. Stevenson was a thoughtful politician, a witty campaigner, and a favorite in academic circles. He also carried Truman's negative legacy of domestic policy confrontation, the hated war in Korea, and the "loss" of China, and he had no chance of winning.

Eisenhower and the politics of the middle.   Over the next eight years, Eisenhower claimed the political middle for Republicans. Publicists tried a variety of labels for his domestic views: "progressive moderation," "New Republicanism," "dynamic conservatism." Satisfied with postwar America, Eisenhower accepted much of the New Deal but saw little need for further reform. In a 1959 poll, liberals considered him a fellow liberal and conservatives thought him a conservative. Eisenhower's first secretary of defense, "Engine Charlie" Wilson, had headed General Motors. At his Senate confirmation hearing, he proclaimed, "For years, I thought what was good for the country was good for General Motors and vice versa." Wilson's statement captured a central theme of the 1950s. Not since the 1920s had Americans been so excited about the benefits of big business. When *Fortune* magazine began in 1957 to publish an annual list of the 500 largest U.S. corporations, it tapped a national fascination with America's productive capacity.

The new prosperity.   The economy in the 1950s gave Americans much to like. Between 1950 and 1964, output grew by a solid 3.2 percent per year. Automobile production, on which dozens of other industries depended, neared 8 million vehicles per year in the mid-1950s. Less than 1 percent of new car sales were imports, and people avidly awaited each year's new models from Detroit, pondering their preferences for a gull-winged Chevrolet or a fantastically finned DeSoto.

American workers in the 1950s had more disposable income than ever before. Their productivity, or output per worker, increased steadily. Average compensation per hour of work rose faster than consumer prices in nine of eleven years

from 1953 to 1964. Rising productivity made it easy for corporations to share gains with large labor unions. The steel and auto industries set the pace with contracts that gave their workers a middle-class way of life. In turn, labor leaders lost interest in making radical changes in American society. In 1955, the older and politically more conservative American Federation of Labor absorbed the younger Congress of Industrial Organizations. The new AFL-CIO positioned itself as a partner in prosperity and foe of Communism at home and abroad.

For members of minority groups with regular industrial and government jobs, the 1950s were also economically rewarding. Detroit, Dayton, Oakland, and other industrial cities offered them factory jobs at wages that could support a family. Black people worked through the Urban League, the National Association of Colored Women, and other race-oriented groups to secure fair-employment laws and jobs with large corporations. Many Puerto Rican migrants to New York found steady work in the Brooklyn Navy Yard. Mexican American families in San Antonio benefited from maintenance jobs at the city's military bases. Steady employment allowed black people and Latinos to build strong community institutions and vibrant neighborhood business districts.

However, there were never enough family-wage jobs for all of the African American and Latino workers who continued to move to northern and western cities. Many Mexican Americans were still migrant farm laborers and workers in nonunionized sweatshops. Minority workers were usually the first to suffer from the erosion of some industrial jobs and the shift of other jobs to new suburban factories that were isolated from minority neighborhoods. Black unemployment crept upward to twice the white rate, laying the seeds of frustration that would burst forth in the 1960s.

Native Americans faced equally daunting prospects. To cut costs and accelerate assimilation, Congress pushed the policy of termination between 1954 and 1962. The government sold tribal land and assets, distributed the proceeds among tribal members, and terminated its treaty relationship with the tribe. Applied to such tribes as the Klamaths in Oregon and the Menominees in Wisconsin, termination gave thousands of Indians one-time cash payments but cut them adrift from the security of tribal organizations. The Bureau of Indian Affairs encouraged Indians to move to large cities, but jobs were often unavailable. The new urban populations would nourish growing militancy among Native Americans in the 1960s and 1970s.

Reshaping Urban America

If Eisenhower's administration opted for the status quo on many issues, it nevertheless reshaped U.S. cities around an agenda of economic development. In 1954, Congress transformed the public housing program into urban renewal. Cities used federal funds to replace low-rent businesses and run-down housing on the fringes of their downtowns with new hospitals, civic centers, sports arenas, office towers,

Daly City, south of San Francisco, typified the mass-produced suburbs that housed the growing postwar middle class. It was the inspiration for the satirical song, "Little Boxes."

and luxury apartments. Urban renewal temporarily revitalized older cities in the Northeast and Midwest that were already feeling the competition of the fast-growing South and West. *Fortune* in 1956 concluded that some of the largest cities were the best run—Cincinnati, New York, Philadelphia, Detroit, Milwaukee.

Only a decade later, the same cities would top the list of urban crisis spots, in part because of accumulating social costs from urban renewal. The bulldozers often leveled minority neighborhoods in the name of downtown expansion. Urban renewal displaced Puerto Ricans in New York, African Americans in Atlanta and Norfolk, Mexican Americans in Denver. Los Angeles demolished the seedy Victorian mansions of Bunker Hill, just northwest of downtown, for a music center and bank towers. A mile to the north was Chavez Ravine, whose Mexican American population lived in substandard housing but maintained a lively community. When conservative opposition blocked plans for public housing, the residents were evicted, and Dodger Stadium was built. Here as elsewhere, urban showplaces rose at the expense of minority groups.

The Eisenhower administration also revolutionized American transportation. Americans had long dreamed of something better than two-lane highways that routed motorists through the stop-and-go traffic of cities and trapped them behind creeping trucks. By the early 1950s, they were fed up with roads designed for Model A Fords: They wanted to enjoy their new V-8 engines and the 50 million new cars sold between 1946 and 1955. The solution was the **Federal Highway Act of 1956,** creating a national system of interstate and defense highways. The legislation wrapped a program to build 41,000 miles of freeways in the language of the

Cold War. The roads would be wide and strong enough for trucks hauling military hardware; they were also supposed to make it easy to evacuate cities in case of a Soviet attack.

Although the first interstate opened in Kansas in 1956, most of the mileage came into use in the 1960s and 1970s. Interstates halved the time of city-to-city travel. They were good for General Motors, the steel industry, and the concrete industry, requiring the construction equivalent of 60 Panama Canals. The highways promoted long-distance trucking at the expense of railroads. They also wiped out hundreds of homes per mile when they plunged through large cities. As with urban renewal, the bulldozers most often plowed through African American or Latino neighborhoods, where land was cheap and white politicians could ignore protests. Some cities, such as Miami, used the highways as barriers between white and black neighborhoods.

Interstates accelerated suburbanization. The beltways or perimeter highways that began to ring most large cities made it easier and more profitable to develop new subdivisions and factory sites than to reinvest in city centers. Federal grants for sewers and other basic facilities further cut suburban costs. Continuing the pattern of the late 1940s, suburban growth added a million new single-family houses per year.

Comfort on Credit

Prosperity transformed spending habits. The 1930s had taught Americans to avoid debt. The 1950s taught them to buy on credit. Families financed their new houses with 90 percent Federal Housing Administration (FHA) mortgages and 100 percent Veterans Administration (VA) mortgages. They filled the rooms by signing installment contracts at furniture and appliance stores and charging the drapes and carpeting on department-store credit cards. The value of consumer debt, excluding home mortgages, tripled from 1952 to 1964.

New forms of marketing facilitated credit-based consumerism. The first large-scale suburban shopping center was Northgate in Seattle, which assembled all the elements of the full-grown mall—small stores facing an interior corridor between anchor department stores and surrounded by parking. By the end of the decade, developers were building malls with 1 million square feet of shopping floor. At the start of the 1970s, the universal credit card (Visa, MasterCard) made shopping even easier.

Surrounding the new malls were the servants and symbols of America's car culture. Where cities of the early twentieth century had been built around public transportation—streetcars and subways—those of the 1950s depended on prion *The Adventures of Ozzie and Harriet* (1952–1966), *Father Knows Best* (1954–1962), and *Leave It to Beaver* (1957–1962) were white, polite, and happy. The Nelsons, Andersons, and Cleavers bore northern European names and lived in single-family houses with friendly neighbors. Thousands of school-aged baby boomers wondered why their families didn't have good times like the families on the picture tube.

Stay-at-home moms and working women.   The 1950s extended the stay-at-home trend of the postwar years. Women gave up some of their earlier educational gains. Their share of new college degrees and professional jobs fell. Despite millions of new electrical appliances, the time spent on housework increased. Magazines proclaimed that proper families maintained distinct roles for dad and mom, and mom was urged to find fulfillment in a well-scrubbed house and children. While television programming helped limit women's roles by power of example, TV actresses assured readers that they were housewives first and career women second.

In fact, far from allowing women to stay home as housewives, family prosperity in the 1950s often depended on their earnings. The number of employed women reached new highs. By 1960, nearly 35 percent of all women held jobs, including 7.5 million mothers with children under 17 (see Figure 28–2). The pressures of young marriages, large families, and economic needs interacted to erode some of the assumptions behind the idealized family and laid the groundwork for dramatic social changes in the 1960s and 1970s.

Inventing Teenagers

Teenagers in the 1950s joined adults as consumers of movies, clothes, and automobiles. Advertisers tapped and expanded the growing youth market by promoting a distinct "youth culture," an idea that became omnipresent in the 1960s and 1970s. While psychologists pontificated on the special problems of adolescence, many cities matched their high schools to the social status of their students: college-prep curricula for middle-class neighborhoods, vocational and technical schools for future factory workers, and separate schools or tracks for African Americans and Latinos. "Maturity" in middle-class high schools meant self-confidence and leadership; at vocational schools, it meant neatness and respect for authority. In effect, the schools trained some children to be doctors and officers and others to be mechanics and enlisted men.

All teenagers shared rock-and-roll, a new music of the mid-1950s that adapted black urban rhythm-and-blues for a white mass market. Rhythm-and-blues was the hard-edged and electrified offspring of tra-

ditional blues and gospel music. In turn, rock music augmented its black roots by drawing vitality from poor white southerners familiar with country and western music (Buddy Holly, Elvis Presley), Hispanics (Richie Valens), and, in the 1960s, the British working class (the Beatles). Record producers played up the association between rock music and youthful rebellion. The 1955 movie *Blackboard Jungle* depicted juvenile delinquency to the music of Bill Haley's "Rock Around the Clock." Elvis Presley's meteoric career, launched in 1956 with "Heartbreak Hotel," depended both on his skill at blending country music with rhythm-and-blues and the sexual suggestiveness of his stage act. The music allowed black performers like Chuck Berry and Ray Charles to "cross over" to mainstream pop music.

Technological changes helped rock split off from adult pop music. Portable phonographs and 45-rpm records let kids listen to rock-and-roll in their own rooms. Car radios and transistor radios (first marketed around 1956) let disc jockeys reach teenagers outside the home. The result was separate music for young listeners and separate advertising for teenage consumers, the roots of the teenage mall culture of the next generation.

The raucous sounds and rebellious lyrics of early rock and roll gave adult authorities even more reason to emphasize social conformity. Schools, churches, and elected officials responded with dress codes, campaigns against sinful comic books, and worry about juvenile delinquency. Young people responded by crowding movie theaters for *Rebel Without a Cause*

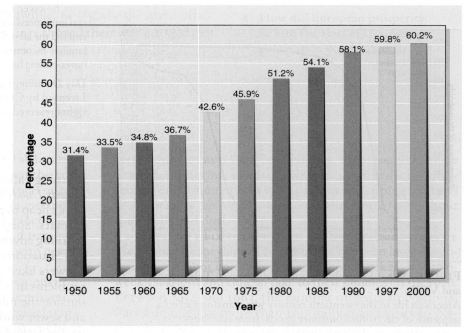

FIGURE 28–2   Working Women as a Percentage of All Women, 1950–2000
The proportion of American women who are part of the labor force (working or looking for work) has increased steadily since 1950, with the fastest increase between 1965 and 1985.

(1955), in which James Dean played an anguished teenager in stifling suburbia. Outside the realm of mass entertainment, the Beats were coming together in San Francisco, where novelists like Jack Kerouac, poets like Gary Snyder, artists, and musicians drifted in and out of the City Lights bookstore. They attracted national attention in 1955 when Allen Ginsberg first chanted his poem "Howl," with its blistering attack on stifling materialism.

Turning to Religion

Leaders from Dwight Eisenhower to FBI Director J. Edgar Hoover advocated churchgoing as an antidote for Communism. Regular church attendance grew from 48 percent of the population in 1940 to 63 percent in 1960. Moviegoers flocked to biblical epics: *The Robe* (1953), *The Ten Commandments* (1956), and *Ben-Hur* (1959). *Newsweek* talked about the "vast resurgence of Protestantism," and *Time* claimed that "everybody knows that church life is booming in the U.S."

In his first years as a star, Elvis Presley brought new energy to the world of popular music. Frank Driggs/Archive Photos

The situation was more complex. Growing church membership looked impressive at first, but the total barely kept pace with population growth. In some ways, the so-called return to religion was new. Congress created new connections between religion and government when it added "under God" to the Pledge of Allegiance in 1954 and required currency to bear the phrase "In God We Trust" in 1955.

Radio and television preachers added a new dimension to religious life. Bishop Fulton J. Sheen brought vigorous anti-Communism and Catholic doctrine to millions of TV viewers who would never have entered a Catholic church. Norman Vincent Peale blended popular psychology with Protestantism, presenting Jesus Christ as "the greatest expert on human nature who ever lived." His book *The Power of Positive Thinking* (1952) sold millions of copies.

Another strand in the religious revival was found in the revitalized evangelical and fundamentalist churches. During the 1950s, the theologically and socially conservative Southern Baptists passed the Methodists as the largest Protestant denomination. The evangelist Billy Graham continued the grand American tradition of the mass revival meeting. In auditoriums and stadiums, he preached personal salvation in words that everyone could understand. Graham was a pioneer in the resurgence of evangelical Christianity that gradually shifted the tone of American religious life by stressing an individual approach to belief and social issues. "Before we can solve the economic, philosophical, and political problems in the world," he said, "pride, greed, lust, and sin are going to have to be erased."

African American churches were community institutions as well as religious organizations. With limited options for enjoying their success, the black middle class joined prestigious churches. Black congregations in northern cities swelled in the postwar years. Prestigious black churches thrived and often supported extensive social service programs. In southern cities, churches were centers for community pride and training grounds for the emerging civil rights movement.

Other important changes to come in American religion had their roots in the 1950s and early 1960s. Boundaries between many Protestant denominations blurred as church leaders emphasized national unity, paving the way for the ecumenical movement and denominational mergers. Supreme Court decisions sowed the seeds for later political activism among evangelical Christians. In *Engel v. Vitale* (1962), the Court ruled that public schools could not require children to start the school day with group prayer. *Abington Township v. Schempp* (1963) prohibited devotional Bible reading in the schools. Such decisions alarmed many evangelicals; within two decades, school prayer would be a central issue in national politics.

The Gospel of Prosperity

Writers and intellectuals often marveled at the prosperity of Eisenhower's America. For scholars and journalists who had grown up during the Great Depression, the lack of economic hardship was the big story. William H. Whyte, Jr., searched American corporations for the changing character

American Views

Two Presidents Assess the Implications of the Cold War

In speeches two days apart in January 1961, outgoing President Dwight Eisenhower and incoming President John Kennedy offered contrasting interpretations of America's Cold War crusade. Eisenhower spoke with concern about the effects of defense spending on American society. Kennedy promised an unlimited commitment of resources to achieve national goals.

- Why did Kennedy define the American mission to the world so broadly?
- What changes in the 1950s led Eisenhower to warn about the dangers of pursuing that mission?
- Do the selections show basic agreement or disagreement about the goals of national policy?

Dwight D. Eisenhower
Farewell Address, January 18, 1961

Our military organization today bears little relation to that known by any of my predecessors in peacetime.... This conjunction of an immense military establishment and a large arms industry is new in the American experience. The total influence—economic, political, even spiritual—is felt in every city, every State house, every office of the federal government. We recognize the imperative need for this development. Yet we must not fail to comprehend its grave implications....

In the councils of government, we must guard against the acquisition of unwarranted influence, whether sought or unsought, by the military-industrial complex. The potential for the disastrous rise of misplaced power exists and will persist. We must never let the weight of this combination endanger our liberties or democratic processes. We should take nothing for granted. Only an alert and knowledgeable citizenry can compel the proper meshing of the huge industrial and military machinery of defense with our peaceful methods and goals.

John F. Kennedy
Inaugural Address, January 20, 1961

Let the word go forth from this time and place, to friend and foe alike, that the torch has been passed to a new generation of Americans—born in this century, tempered by war, disciplined by a hard and bitter peace, proud of our ancient heritage—and unwilling to witness or permit the slow undoing of those human rights to which this nation has always been committed, and to which we are committed today at home and around the world.

Let every nation know, whether it wishes us well or ill, that we shall pay any price, bear any burden, meet any hardship, support any friends, oppose any foe to assure the survival and the success of liberty.

---

a hero from World War II, he tempered ruthless ambition with respect for public service. His forthright campaigning allayed voter concern about his Roman Catholicism. Nixon had wider experience and was a shrewd tactician, but he was also self-righteous and awkward. Eisenhower had wanted to drop Nixon as vice president in 1956 and gave him only lukewarm support in 1960—when a reporter asked Eisenhower to cite important decisions to which Nixon had contributed, Ike replied, "Give me a week and I might think of one."

Television was crucial to the outcome. The campaign featured the first televised presidential debates. In the first session, Nixon actually gave better replies, but his nervousness and a bad makeup job turned off millions of viewers, who admired Kennedy's energy. Nixon never overcame the setback, but the race was tight, with tiny margins in crucial states giving Kennedy the victory. His televised inauguration was the perfect setting for an impassioned plea for national unity: "My fellow Americans," he challenged, "ask not what your country can do for you—ask what you can do for your country."

Kennedy brought dash to the White House. His beautiful and refined wife, Jackie, made sure to seat artists and writers next to diplomats and businessmen at White House dinners. Kennedy's staff and large family played touch football, not golf. No president had shown such verve since Teddy Roosevelt. People began to talk about Kennedy's "charisma," his ability to lead by sheer force of personality. In fact, the image of a fit, vigorous man concealed the reality that he was

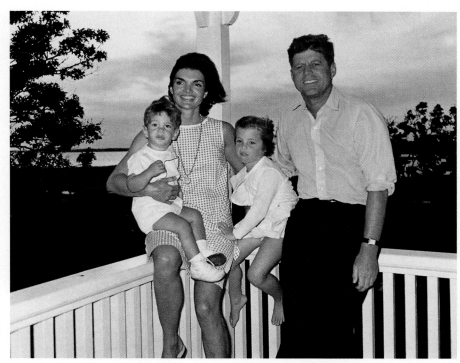

For many Americans in the early 1960s, John and Jacqueline Kennedy and their two children represented the ideal family, although the carefully posed pictures with happy smiles concealed the president's severe health problems and deep rifts in the marriage.

battling severe physical ailments that demanded constant medical attention and often left him with debilitating pain.

Behind the glamorous façade, Kennedy remained a puzzle. One day, Kennedy could propose the Peace Corps, which gave thousands of idealistic young Americans a chance to help developing nations; another day, he could approve plots to assassinate Fidel Castro. Visitors who expected a shallow glad-hander were astonished to meet a sharp, hard-working man who was eager to learn about the world. One savvy diplomat commented, "I have never heard of a president who wanted to know so much."

Kennedy's Mistakes

Kennedy and Khrushchev perpetuated similar problems. Talking tough to satisfy their more militant countrymen, they repeatedly pushed each other into a corner, continuing the problems of mutual misunderstanding that had marked the 1950s. When Khrushchev promised, in January 1961, to support "wars of national liberation," he was really fending off Chinese criticism. But Kennedy overreacted in his first State of the Union address by asking for more military spending.

Three months later, Kennedy fed Soviet fears of American aggressiveness by sponsoring an invasion of Cuba. At the start of 1959, Fidel Castro had toppled the corrupt dictator Fulgencio Batista, who had made Havana infamous for Mafia-run gambling and prostitution. Castro then national-

ized American investments, and thousands of Cubans fled to the United States.

When 1,400 anti-Castro Cubans landed at Cuba's **Bay of Pigs** on April 17, 1961, they were following a plan prepared by the Eisenhower administration. The CIA had trained and armed the invaders and convinced Kennedy that the landing would trigger spontaneous uprisings. But when Kennedy refused to commit U.S. armed forces to support them, Cuban forces captured the attackers.

Kennedy followed the Bay of Pigs debacle with a hasty and ill-thought-out summit meeting with Khrushchev in Vienna in June. Poorly prepared and nearly incapacitated by agonizing back pain, Kennedy made little headway. Khrushchev saw no need to bargain and subjected him to intimidating tirades. "He just beat the hell out of me," Kennedy told a reporter. Coming after Kennedy's refusal to salvage the Bay of Pigs by military intervention, the meeting left the Soviets with the impression that the president was weak and dangerously erratic.

To exploit Kennedy's perceived vulnerability, the Soviet Union renewed tension over Berlin, deep within East Germany. The divided city served as an escape route from Communism for hundreds of thousands of East Germans. Khrushchev now threatened to transfer the Soviet sector in Berlin to East Germany, which had no treaty obligations to France, Britain, or the United States. If the West had to deal directly with East Germany for access to Berlin, it would have to recognize a permanently divided Germany. Kennedy sounded the alarm: He doubled draft calls, called up reservists, and warned families to build fallout shelters. Boise, Idaho, families paid $100 for a share in a community shelter with its own power plant and hospital. Outside New York, Art Carlson and his son Claude put up a prefabricated steel shelter in four hours; Sears planned to sell the same model for $700.

Rather than confront the United States directly, however, the Soviets and East Germans on August 13, 1961, built a wall around the western sectors of Berlin while leaving the access route to West Germany open. The **Berlin Wall** thus isolated East Germany without challenging the Western allies in West Berlin itself. In private, Kennedy accepted the wall as a clever way to stabilize a dangerous situation: "A wall," he said, "is a hell of a lot better than a war." Tensions remained high for months as the two sides tested each other's resolve. Berlin remained a point of East-West tension until East German Communism collapsed in 1989 and Berliners tore down the hated wall.

Getting into Vietnam

U.S. involvement in Vietnam, located in Southeast Asia on the southern border of China, dated to 1949–1950. After World War II ended, France had fought to maintain its colonial rule there against rebels who combined Communist ideology with fervor for national independence under the leadership of Ho Chi Minh. Although the United States supported independence of most other European colonies, the triumph of Mao Zedong in China and the Korean War caused policymakers to see Vietnam as another Cold War conflict. The United States picked up three-quarters of the costs. Nevertheless, the French military position collapsed in 1954 after Vietnamese forces overran the French stronghold at Dien Bien Phu. The French had enough, and President Eisenhower was unwilling to join another Asian war. A Geneva peace conference "temporarily" divided Vietnam into a Communist north and a non-Communist south and scheduled elections for a single Vietnamese government.

The United States then replaced France as the supporter of the pro-Western Vietnamese in the south. Washington's client was Ngo Dinh Diem, an anti-Communist from South Vietnam's Roman Catholic elite. U.S. officials encouraged Diem to put off the elections and backed his efforts to construct an independent South Vietnam. Ho meanwhile consolidated the northern half as a communist state that claimed to be the legitimate government for all Vietnam. The United States further reinforced containment in Asia by bringing Thailand, the Philippines, Pakistan, Australia, New Zealand, Britain, and France together in the **Southeast Asia Treaty Organization (SEATO)** in 1954 (see Map 28–3).

Another indirect consequence of the Vienna summit was the growing U.S. entanglement in South Vietnam, where Kennedy saw a chance to take a firm stand and reassert America's commitment to containment. In the countryside, Communist insurgents known as the **Viet Cong** were gaining strength. The anti-Communist leader, Diem, controlled the cities with the help of a large army and a Vietnamese elite that had worked with the French. The United States stepped up its supply of weapons and sent advisers, including members of one of Kennedy's military innovations, the Army Special Forces Group (Green Berets).

MAP 28–3   SEATO and Other East Asian Countries with Ties to the United States
In East Asia and the western Pacific, the United States in the 1950s constructed a series of alliances to resist Soviet and Chinese Communist influence.

U.S. aid did not work. Despite overoptimistic reports and the help of 16,000 U.S. troops, Diem's government by 1963 was losing the loyalty—the "hearts and minds"—of many South Vietnamese. North Vietnamese support for the Viet Cong canceled the effect of U.S. assistance. Diem courted a second civil war by violently crushing opposition from Vietnamese Buddhists. Kennedy's administration tacitly approved a coup on November 1 that killed Diem and his brother and installed an ineffective military junta.

Missile Crisis: A Line Drawn in the Waves

The escalating tensions of 1961 in Southeast Asia, the Caribbean, and Germany were a prelude to the crisis that came closest to triggering a nuclear war. In the summer of 1962, congressional Republicans had hounded Kennedy about the Soviet military presence in Cuba. On October 15, reconnaissance photos revealed Soviets at work on launching sites from which nuclear missiles could hit the United States. Top officials spent five exhausting and increasingly desperate days sorting through the options. Doing nothing was never considered: The missiles would be a political disaster and a threat to national security. A full-scale invasion of Cuba was not feasible on short notice, and "surgical" air strikes were technically impossible. Either sort of military operation would kill hundreds of Soviet personnel and force Moscow to react. Secretary of Defense Robert McNamara suggested demanding removal of the missiles and declaring a naval "quarantine" against the arrival of further offensive weapons. A blockade would buy time for diplomacy.

Kennedy imposed the blockade in a terrifying speech on Monday, October 22. He emphasized the "deceptive" deployment of the Russian missiles and raised the specter of nuclear war. Americans would have been even more afraid had they known that some of the missiles were operational and that Soviets in Cuba were authorized to use them in self-defense. While Khrushchev hesitated, Soviet ships circled outside the quarantine line. On Friday, Khrushchev offered to withdraw the missiles in return for a U.S. pledge not to invade Cuba. On Saturday, a second communication nearly dashed this hopeful opening by raising a new complaint about U.S. missiles on the territory of NATO allies. The letter was the result of pressure by Kremlin hard-liners and Khrushchev's own wavering. Kennedy decided to accept the first letter and ignore the second. The United States pledged not to invade Cuba and secretly promised to remove obsolete Jupiter missiles from Turkey. Khrushchev accepted these terms on Sunday, October 28.

Why did Khrushchev risk the Cuban gamble? One reason was to protect Castro as a symbol of Soviet commitment to anti-Western regimes in the developing world. Americans hated the Castro government out of proportion to its geopolitical importance, but they rightly feared that Cuba would try to export revolution throughout Latin America. Kennedy had tried to preempt Castroism in 1961 by launching the **Alliance for Progress,** an economic-development program for Latin America that tied aid to social reform. However, the United States had also orchestrated the Bay of Pigs invasion and funded a CIA campaign to sabotage Cuba. High U.S. officials were not contemplating a full-scale invasion, but Castro and Khrushchev had reason to fear the worst.

Khrushchev also hoped to redress the strategic balance. As Kennedy discovered on taking office, the United States actually led the world in the deployment of strategic missiles. Intermediate-range rockets gave the USSR a nuclear club over western Europe, but in October 1962, the Soviet Union had fewer than 50 ICBMs to aim at the United States and China. The United States was creating a defensive triad of 1,000 land-based Minuteman missiles, 500 long-range bombers, and 600 Polaris missiles on nuclear submarines targeted on the USSR. The strategic imbalance had sustained NATO during the Berlin confrontation, but 40 launchers in Cuba with two warheads each would have doubled the Soviet capacity to strike at the United States.

Soviet missiles in Cuba thus flouted the Monroe Doctrine and posed a real military threat. Kennedy and Khrushchev had also backed each other into untenable positions. In September, Kennedy had warned that the United States could not tolerate Soviet offensive weapons in Cuba, never dreaming that they were already there. Had Khrushchev acted openly (as the United States had done when it placed missiles in Turkey), the United States would have been hard pressed to object under international law. By acting in secret and breaking previous promises, the Soviets outsmarted themselves. When the missiles were discovered, Kennedy had to act.

In the end, both sides were cautious. Khrushchev backed down rather than fight. Kennedy fended off hawkish advisers who wanted to destroy Castro. The world had trembled, but neither nation wanted war over "the missiles of October."

Science and Foreign Affairs

The two superpowers competed through science as well as diplomacy. When Kennedy took office, the United States was still playing catch-up in space technology. A Russian, Yuri Gagarin, was the first human to orbit the earth, on April 12, 1961. American John Glenn did not match Gagarin's feat until February 1962. Kennedy committed the United States to placing a U.S. astronaut on the moon by 1970. The decision narrowed a multifaceted scientific and military program to a massive engineering project that favored the economic capacity of the United States.

The Soviet Union and the United States were also fencing about nuclear weapons testing. After the three-year moratorium, both resumed tests in 1961–1962. The United States started with underground tests to minimize fallout, but then followed with atmospheric detonations. Renewed testing let the Russians show off huge hydrogen bombs with yields of 20 and 30 megatons—roughly 1,000 times the power of the bombs dropped on Japan. Both nations worked on multiple-targetable warheads, antiballistic missiles, and other innovations that might destabilize the balance of terror.

After the missile crisis showed his toughness, however, Kennedy had enough political maneuvering room to respond to pressure from liberal Democrats and groups like Women Strike for Peace and the Committee for a Sane Nuclear Policy by giving priority to disarmament. In July 1963, the United States, Britain, and the USSR signed the **Limited Test Ban Treaty,** which outlawed nuclear testing in the atmosphere, in outer space, and under water, and invited other nations to join in. A more comprehensive treaty was impossible because the Soviet Union refused the on-site inspections the United States deemed necessary to distinguish underground tests from earthquakes. France and China, the other nuclear powers, refused to sign, and the treaty did not halt weapons development, but it was the most positive achievement of Kennedy's foreign policy and a step toward later disarmament treaties.

Righteousness like a Mighty Stream: The Struggle for Civil Rights

Supreme Court decisions are based on abstract principles, but they involve real people. One was Linda Brown of Topeka, Kansas, a third-grader whose parents were fed up with sending her past an all-white public school to attend an all-black school a mile away. The Browns volunteered to help the NAACP challenge Topeka's school segregation by trying to enroll Linda in their neighborhood school, beginning a legal case that reached the Supreme Court. On May 17, 1954, the Court decided ***Brown v. Board of Education of Topeka***, opening a new civil rights era. Led by the persuasive power of the new chief justice, Earl Warren, the Court unanimously reversed the 1896 case of *Plessy v. Ferguson* by ruling that sending black children to "separate but equal" schools denied them equal treatment under the Constitution. When Linda Brown's father heard the news, his eyes filled with tears, and he said, "Thanks be to God."

The *Brown* decision made the growing effort to secure equal legal treatment for African Americans an inescapable challenge to American society. The first phase of the civil rights struggle built from the Supreme Court's decision in 1954 to a vast gathering at the Lincoln Memorial in 1963. In between, African Americans chipped away at the racial segregation of schools, universities, and public facilities with marches, boycotts, sit-ins, and lawsuits, forcing segregated communities to choose between integration and violent defiance. In the two years following the 1963 March on Washington, the federal government passed landmark legislation.

Getting to the Supreme Court

The *Brown* decision climaxed a 25-year campaign to reenlist the federal courts on the side of equal rights (see Overview, Civil Rights: The Struggle for Racial Equality). The work began in the 1930s when Charles Hamilton Houston, dean of Howard University's law school, trained a corps of civil rights lawyers. Working on behalf of the NAACP, he hoped to erode *Plessy* by suits focused on interstate travel and professional graduate schools (the least defensible segregated institutions, because states seldom provided alternatives). In 1938, Houston's student Thurgood Marshall, a future Supreme Court justice, took over the NAACP job. He and other NAACP lawyers such as Constance Baker Motley risked personal danger crisscrossing the South to file civil rights lawsuits wherever a local case emerged. In 1949, Motley was the first black lawyer to argue a case in a Mississippi courtroom since Reconstruction.

Efforts in the 1940s and early 1950s, often fueled by the experience of World War II soldiers, had important successes. In *Smith v. Allwright* (1944), the Supreme Court invalidated the all-white primary, a decision that led to increased black voter registration in many southern communities. With new political power, and often with the cooperation of relatively progressive white leaders, blacks fought for specific improvements, such as equal pay for teachers or the hiring of black police officers.

The *Brown* case combined lawsuits from Delaware, Virginia, South Carolina, the District of Columbia, and Kansas. In each instance, students and families braved community pressure to demand equal access to a basic public service. Chief Justice Earl Warren brought a divided Court to unanimous agreement. Viewing public education as central for the equal opportunity that lay at the heart of American values, the Court weighed the consequences of segregated school systems and concluded that separate meant unequal. The reasoning fit the temper of a nation that was proud of making prosperity accessible to all.

Brown also built on efforts by Mexican Americans in the Southwest to assert their rights of citizenship. After World War II, Latino organizations such as the League of United Latin American Citizens battled

Elizabeth Eckford, one of the first black students to attend Central High in Little Rock, Arkansas, in 1957, enters the school amid taunts from white students and bystanders.

Civil Rights: The Struggle for Racial Equality

Area of Concern	Key Actions	Results
Public school integration	Federal court cases	*Brown v. Board of Education of Topeka* (1954) Enforcement by presidential action, Little Rock (1957)
		Follow-up court decisions, including mandatory busing programs
Equal access to public facilities	Montgomery bus boycott (1955)	Civil Rights Act of 1964
	Lunch counter sit-ins (1960)	
	Freedom rides (1961)	
	Birmingham demonstrations (1963)	
	March on Washington (1963)	
Equitable voter registration	Voter registration drives, including Mississippi Summer Project (1964) Demonstrations and marches, including Selma to Montgomery march (1965)	Voting Rights Act of 1965

job discrimination and ethnic segregation. In 1946, Mexican American parents sued five Orange County, California school districts that systematically placed their children in separate schools. In the resulting case of *Mendez v. Westminster,* federal courts prohibited segregation of Mexican American children in California schools as a violation of the equal protection clause of the Fourteenth Amendment. Eight years later, the Supreme Court forbade Texas from excluding Mexican Americans from juries. These cases provided precedents for the Court's decision in *Brown* and subsequent civil rights cases.

Deliberate Speed

Racial segregation by law was largely a southern problem, the legacy of Jim Crow laws (see Chapter 17). The civil rights movement therefore focused first on the South, allowing Americans elsewhere to think of racial injustice as a regional issue.

Southern responses to *Brown* revealed regional differences. Few southern communities desegregated schools voluntarily, for to do so undermined the entrenched principle of a dual society. Their reluctance was bolstered in 1955 when the Supreme Court allowed segregated states to carry out the 1954 decision "with all deliberate speed" rather than immediately. The phrase recognized that the courts had limited powers to enforce broad decisions and allowed communities to find reasons for delay; Thurgood Marshall later commented, "I've finally figured out what 'all deliberate speed' means. It means slow."

The following year, 101 southern congressmen and senators issued the **Southern Manifesto,** which asserted that the Court decision was unconstitutional. President Eisenhower privately deplored the desegregation decision, which violated his sense of states' rights and upset Republican attempts to gain southern votes; he called both those who resisted the decision and those who wanted to enforce it "extremists." At the same time, many in Washington knew that racial discrimination offered, in the worlds of Dean Acheson, "the most effective kind of ammunition" for Soviet propaganda.

Eisenhower's distaste for racial integration left the Justice Department on the sidelines. Courageous parents and students had to knock on schoolhouse doors, often carrying court orders. Responses varied: school districts in border states, such as Maryland, Kentucky, and Oklahoma, desegregated relatively peacefully; farther south, African American children often met taunts and violence.

The first crisis came in Little Rock, Arkansas, in September 1957. The city school board admitted nine African Americans, including Melba Pattillo, to Central High, while segregrationist groups, such as the White Citizens Council, stirred up white fears. Claiming he feared violence, Governor Orval Faubus surrounded Central High with the National Guard and turned the new students away. Under intense national pressure, Faubus withdrew the Guard. The black students entered the school, but a howling mob forced the police to sneak them out after two hours. Fuming at the governor's defiance of federal authority, Eisenhower reluctantly nationalized the National Guard and sent in the 101st Airborne Division to keep order. Eight of the students endured a year of harassment in the hallways of Central.

Virginians in 1958–1959 tried avoidance rather than confrontation. Massive resistance was a state policy that required local school districts to close rather than accept black

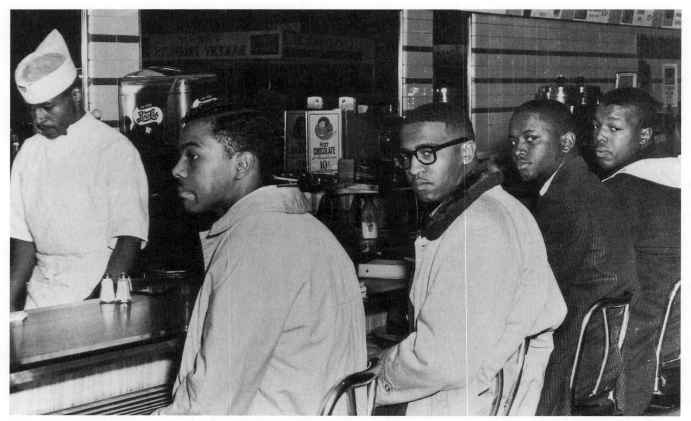

Students from North Carolina A&T, an all-black college, began the lunch-counter sit-in movement in February 1960. Here four students sit patiently in the Greensboro Woolworth's without being served. Participants wore their best clothes and suffered politely through days of verbal and sometimes physical abuse.

students. When court orders to admit 19 black students triggered the shutdown of four high schools and three junior highs in Norfolk, white parents tried to compensate with private academies and tutoring, but it was soon apparent that a modern community could not dismantle public education. Norfolk's leaders realized that no large business was going to locate in a city whose claim to fame was the "lost class of '59," and Virginia's elite privately welcomed federal court decisions that got them off the hook by striking down their own law.

Change came slowly to state universities. Border states desegregated colleges and professional schools with few incidents. Again, the story was different in the lower South. In 1956, the University of Alabama admitted Autherine Lucy under court order but then expelled her before she could attend classes. In September 1962, James Meredith tried to enter the University of Mississippi, igniting a riot that the state refused to control. Because the governor directly defied the federal courts and broke promises to the administration, President Kennedy sent in the army. A year later, Governor George Wallace of Alabama grabbed headlines by "standing in the schoolhouse door" to prevent integration of the University of Alabama, gaining a national

prominence that culminated in a third-party candidacy for president in 1968.

The breakthrough in school integration did not come until the end of the 1960s, when the courts rejected further delays, and federal authorities threatened to cut off education funds. As late as 1968, only 6 percent of African American children in the South attended integrated schools. By 1973, the figure was 90 percent. Attention thereafter shifted to northern communities, whose schools were segregated, not by law, but by the divisions between white and black neighborhoods and between white suburbs and multiracial central cities, a situation known as *de facto* segregation.

Public Accommodations

The civil rights movement also sought to integrate public accommodations. Most southern states separated the races in bus terminals and movie theaters. They required black riders to take rear seats on buses. They labeled separate restrooms and drinking fountains for "colored" users. Hotels denied rooms to black people, and restaurants refused them service.

The struggle to end segregated facilities started in Montgomery, Alabama. On December 1, 1955, Rosa Parks, a seamstress who worked at a downtown department store, refused to give up her bus seat to a white passenger and was arrested. Parks acted spontaneously, but she was part of a network of civil rights activists who wanted to challenge segregated buses and was the secretary of the Montgomery NAACP. As news of her action spread, the community institutions that enriched southern black life went into action. The Women's Political Council, a group of college-trained black women, initiated a mass boycott of the privately owned bus company. Alabama State College professor Jo Ann Robinson worked through the night to mimeograph 52,500 flyers and enlisted students to spread them through the city. Martin Luther King, Jr., a 26-year-old pastor, led the boycott. He galvanized a mass meeting with a speech that quoted the biblical prophet Amos: "We are determined here in Montgomery to work and fight until justice runs down like water, and righteousness like a mighty stream."

Montgomery's African Americans organized their boycott in the face of white outrage. A car pool substituted for the buses despite police harassment. As the boycott survived months of pressure, the national media began to pay attention. After nearly a year, the Supreme Court agreed that the bus segregation law was unconstitutional.

Victory in Montgomery depended on steadfast African American involvement. Leaders included Ralph Abernathy, other black preachers, and faculty members from Alabama State College. Participants cut across the class lines that had divided black southerners. Success also revealed the discrepancy between white attitudes in the Deep South and national opinion. For white southerners, segregation was a local concern best defined as a legal or constitutional matter. For other Americans, it was increasingly an issue of the South's deviation from national moral norms.

The Montgomery boycott won a local victory and made King famous, but it did not propel immediate change. King formed the **Southern Christian Leadership Conference (SCLC)** and sparred with the NAACP about community-based versus court-based civil rights tactics, but four African American college students in Greensboro, North Carolina, started the next phase of the struggle. On February 1, 1960, they put on jackets and ties and sat down at the segregated lunch counter in Woolworth's, waiting through the day without being served. Their patient courage brought more demonstrators; within two days, 85 students packed the store. Nonviolent sit-ins spread throughout the South.

The sit-ins had both immediate and long-range effects. In such comparatively sophisticated border cities as Nashville, Tennessee, sit-ins integrated lunch counters. Elsewhere, they precipitated white violence and mass arrests. Like soldiers on a battlefield, nervous participants in sit-ins and demonstrations drew strength from one another. "If you don't have courage," said one young woman in Albany, Georgia, "you can borrow it." King welcomed nonviolent confrontation. SCLC leader Ella Baker, one of the movement's most important figures, helped the students form a new organization, the **Student Nonviolent Coordinating Committee (SNCC)**.

The year 1961 brought "freedom rides" to test the segregation of interstate bus terminals. The idea came from James Farmer of the **Congress of Racial Equality (CORE)**, who copied a little-remembered 1947 Journey of Reconciliation that had tested the integration of interstate trains. Two buses carrying black and white passengers met only minor problems in Virginia, the Carolinas, and Georgia, but Alabamians burned one of the buses and attacked the riders in Birmingham, where they beat demonstrators senseless and clubbed a Justice Department observer. The governor and police refused to protect the freedom riders. The riders traveled into Mississippi under National Guard protection but were arrested at the Jackson bus terminal. Despite Attorney General Robert Kennedy's call for a cooling-off period, freedom rides continued through the summer. The rides proved that African Americans were in charge of their own civil rights revolution.

The March on Washington, 1963

John Kennedy was a tepid supporter of the civil rights movement and entered office with no civil rights agenda. Since entering politics in Massachusetts, he had been strong on rhetoric and symbolic gestures but weak on follow through. He appointed segregationist judges to mollify southern congressmen and would have preferred that African Americans stop disturbing the fragile Democratic Party coalition. As Eisenhower did at Little Rock, Kennedy intervened at the University of Mississippi in 1962 because of a state challenge to federal authority, not to further racial justice.

In the face of the slow federal response, the SCLC concentrated for 1963 on rigidly segregated Birmingham. April began with sit-ins and marches that aimed to integrate lunch counters, restrooms, and stores and secure open hiring for some clerical jobs. Birmingham's commissioner of public safety, Bull Connor, used fire hoses to blast demonstrators against buildings and roll children down the streets. When demonstrators fought back, his men chased them with dogs. Continued marches brought the arrest of hundreds of children. King's "Letter from Birmingham City Jail" stated the case for protest: "We have not made a single gain in civil rights without determined legal and nonviolent pressure.... Freedom is never voluntarily given by the oppressor; it must be demanded by the oppressed."

The Birmingham demonstrations were inconclusive. White leaders accepted minimal demands on May 10 but delayed enforcing them. Antiblack violence continued, including a bomb that killed four children in a Birmingham church. Meanwhile, the events in Alabama had forced President Kennedy to board the freedom train with an eloquent June 11 speech and to send a civil rights bill to Congress. "Are we to say... that this is the land of the free, except for Negroes, that we have no second-class citizens, except Negroes...? Now the time has come for the nation to fulfill its promise."

On August 28, 1963, a rally in Washington transformed African American civil rights into a national cause. A quarter of a million people, black and white, marched to the Lincoln Memorial. The day gave Martin Luther King, Jr., a national pulpit. His call for progress toward Christian and American goals had immense appeal. Television cut away from afternoon programs for his "I Have a Dream" speech.

The March on Washington demonstrated the mass appeal of civil rights and its identification with national values. It also papered over growing tensions within the civil rights movement. In the mid-1960s a growing militancy split the civil rights effort and moved younger African Americans, as well as Latinos and Native Americans, to emphasize their own distinct identities within American society.

Religious Belief and Civil Rights

Although *Brown* and other civil rights court decisions drew on the secular Constitution, much of the success of the southern civil rights movement came from grassroots Christianity. A century earlier, the abolitionist crusade had drawn much of its power from evangelistic revival movements. Now in the 1950s and 1960s, black southerners drew on prophetic Christianity to forge and act on a vision of a just society. Religious conviction and solidarity provide courage in the face of opposition.

At the same time, most white Christians understood that segregation contradicted the message of the Bible. The two largest religious groups in the South, the Presbyterian Church of the United States and the Southern Baptist Convention, took public stands in favor of desegregation in the mid-1950s. Revival leader Billy Graham shared a pulpit with Martin Luther King, Jr., in 1957 and insisted against local laws that his revival services be integrated. The opponents of civil rights thus lacked the moral support of the South's most fundamental cultural institutions.

In this context, it was no accident that black churches were organizing centers for civil rights work. King named his organization the Southern Christian Leadership Conference with clear intent and purpose. His famous speech in Washington drew on religious imagery and ended: "Free at last! Free at last! Thank God almighty, we are free at last!"

"Let Us Continue"

The two years that followed King's speech mingled despair and accomplishment. The optimism of the March on Washington shattered with the assassination of John Kennedy in November 1963. In 1964 and 1965, however, President Lyndon Johnson pushed through Kennedy's legislative agenda and much more in a burst of government activism unmatched since the 1930s. Federal legislation brought victory to the first phase of the civil rights revolution, launched the **War on Poverty,** expanded health insurance and aid to education, and opened an era of environmental protection.

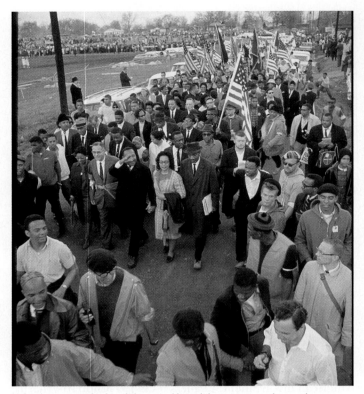

After being attacked and dispersed by Alabama state police as they attempted a fifty-three mile march from Selma to Montgomery, Alabama, civil rights demonstrators regrouped. Under the glare of national press coverage, Alabama authorities let the march proceed. Here the leaders—including Martin Luther King, Jr., Coretta Scott King, Hosea Williams, Bayard Rustin, and Ralph Bunche—enter Montgomery.

Dallas, 1963

In November 1963, President Kennedy visited Texas to raise money and patch up feuds among Texas Democrats. On November 22, the president's motorcade took him near the Texas School Book Depository building in Dallas, where Lee Harvey Oswald had stationed himself at a window on the sixth floor. When Kennedy's open car swung into the sights of his rifle, Oswald fired three shots that wounded Texas Governor John Connally and killed the president. As doctors vainly treated the president in a hospital emergency room, Dallas police arrested Oswald. Vice President Lyndon Johnson took the oath of office as president on Air Force One while the blood-spattered Jacqueline Kennedy looked on. Two days later, as Oswald was being led from one jail cell to another, Jack Ruby, a Texas nightclub owner, killed him with a handgun in full view of TV cameras.

Lee Oswald was a 24-year-old misfit. He had served in the Marines and worked maintaining U-2 spy planes before defecting to the Soviet Union, which he found to be less than a workers' paradise. He returned to the United States after three years with a Russian wife and a fervent commitment to Fidel Castro's Cuban revolution. It was later learned that he had tried to shoot a right-wing general in 1963. He visited the Soviet and Cuban embassies in Mexico City in September trying to drum up a job, but neither country thought him worth hiring.

Some Americans believe there is more to the story. Why? One possibility is the expectation that important events should have great causes. Oswald seems too insignificant to be responsible on his own for the murder of a charismatic president. The sketchy job done by the Warren Commission, appointed to investigate the assassination, also bred doubts. The commission hurried to complete its work before the 1964 election. It also sought to assure Americans that Kennedy had not been killed as part of a Communist plot. The Warren Commission calmed fears in the short run but left loose ends that have fueled conspiracy theories.

All of the theories remain unproved. Until they are, logic holds that the simplest explanation is usually the best. Oswald was a social misfit with a grievance against U.S. society. Ruby was an impulsive man who told his brother on his deathbed that he thought he had done the country a favor. Like Presidents Garfield and McKinley before him, Kennedy died at the hands of one unbalanced man acting alone.

War on Poverty

Five days after the assassination, Lyndon Johnson claimed Kennedy's progressive aura for his new administration. "Let us continue," he told the nation, promising to implement Kennedy's policies. In fact, Johnson was vastly different from Kennedy. He was a professional politician who had reached the top through Texas politics and congressional infighting. As Senate majority leader during the 1950s, he had built a web of political obligations and friendships. Johnson's presence on the ticket in 1960 had helped to elect Kennedy by attracting southern voters, but the Kennedy entourage loathed him. He lacked Kennedy's polish and easy relations with the eastern elite. He knew little about foreign affairs but was a master of domestic politics. Johnson's upbringing in rural Texas shaped a man who was endlessly ambitious, ruthless, and often personally crude, but also deeply committed to social equity. He had entered public life with the New Deal in the 1930s and believed in its principles. Johnson, not Kennedy, was the true heir of Franklin Roosevelt. African American writer Ralph Ellison called him "the greatest American president for the poor and for the Negroes."

Johnson inherited a domestic agenda that the Kennedy administration had defined but not enacted. Kennedy's New Frontier had met the same fate as Truman's Fair Deal. Initiatives in education, medical insurance, tax reform, and urban affairs had stalled or been gutted by conservatives in Congress.

Kennedy's farthest-reaching initiative was rooted in the acknowledgment that poverty was a persistent U.S. problem. Michael Harrington's study *The Other America* became an unexpected bestseller. As poverty captured public attention, Kennedy's economic advisers devised a community action program that emphasized education and job training, a national service corps, and a youth conservation corps. They prepared a package of proposals to submit to Congress in 1964 that focused on social programs intended to alter behaviors that were thought to be passed from generation to generation, thus following the American tendency to attribute poverty to the personal failings of the poor.

Johnson made Kennedy's antipoverty package his own. Adopting Cold War rhetoric, he declared "unconditional war on poverty." The core of Johnson's program was the **Office of Economic Opportunity (OEO).** Established under the direction of Kennedy's brother-in-law R. Sargent Shriver in 1964, the OEO operated the Job Corps for school dropouts, the Neighborhood Youth Corps for unemployed teenagers, the Head Start program to prepare poor children for school, and VISTA (Volunteers in Service to America), a domestic Peace Corps. OEO's biggest effort went to Community Action Agencies. By 1968, more than 500 such agencies provided health and educational services. Despite flaws, the War on Poverty improved life for millions of Americans.

Civil Rights, 1964–1965

Johnson's passionate commitment to economic betterment accompanied a commitment to civil rights. In Johnson's view,

"President Lyndon Johnson was a crafty and sometimes ruthless politician, but he also had a deep personal commitment to solving problems of poverty and inequality in American society."

segregation not only deprived African Americans of access to opportunity but also distracted white southerners from their own poverty and underdevelopment. As he complained in a speech in New Orleans, southern leaders ignored the region's economic needs in favor of racial rabble-rousing.

One solution was the **Civil Rights Act of 1964,** which Kennedy had introduced but which Johnson got enacted. The law prohibited segregation in public accommodations, such as hotels, restaurants, gas stations, theaters, and parks, and outlawed employment discrimination on federally assisted projects. It also created the Equal Employment Opportunity Commission (EEOC) and included gender in the list of categories protected against discrimination, a provision whose consequences were scarcely suspected in 1964.

Even as Congress was debating the 1964 law, **Freedom Summer** moved political power to the top of the civil rights agenda. Organized by SNCC, the Mississippi Summer Freedom Project was a voter-registration drive that sent white and black volunteers to the small towns and back roads of Mississippi. The target was a political system that used rigged literacy tests and intimidation to keep black southerners from voting. In Mississippi in 1964, only 7 percent of eligible black citizens were registered voters. Local black activists had laid the groundwork for a registration effort with years of courageous effort through the NAACP and voter leagues. Now an increasingly militant SNCC took the lead. The explicit goal was to increase the number of African American voters. The tacit intention was to attract national attention by putting middle-class white college students in the line of fire. Freedom Summer gained 1,600 new voters and taught 2,000 children in SNCC-run Freedom Schools at the cost of beatings, bombings, church arson, and the murder of three project workers.

Another outgrowth of the SNCC effort was the Mississippi Freedom Democratic Party (MFDP), a biracial coalition that bypassed Mississippi's all-white Democratic Party, followed state party rules, and sent its own delegates to the 1964 Democratic convention. To preserve party harmony, President Johnson refused to expel the "regular" Mississippi Democrats and offered instead to seat two MFDP delegates and enforce party rules for 1968. The MFDP walked out, seething with anger. Fannie Lou Hamer, a MFDP delegate who had already suffered in the struggle for voting rights, remembered, "We learned the hard way that even though we had all the law and all the righteousness on our side—that white man is not going to give up his power to us. We have to build our own power."

Freedom Summer and political realities both focused national attention on voter registration. Lyndon Johnson and Martin Luther King, Jr., agreed on the need for federal voting legislation when King visited the president in December 1964 after winning the Nobel Peace Prize. For King, power at the ballot box would help black southerners to take control of their own communities. For Johnson, voting reform would fulfill the promise of American democracy. It would also benefit the Democratic Party by replacing with black voters the white southerners who were drifting toward the anti-integration Republicans.

The target for King and the SCLC was Dallas County, Alabama, where only 2 percent of eligible black residents were registered, compared with 70 percent of white residents. Peaceful demonstrations started in January 1965. By early February, jails in the county seat of Selma held 2,600 black people whose offense was marching to the courthouse to demand the vote. The campaign climaxed with a march from Selma to the state capital of Montgomery. SNCC leader John Lewis remembered, "I don't know what we expected. I think maybe we thought we'd be arrested and jailed, or maybe they wouldn't do anything to us. I had a little knapsack on my shoulder with an apple, a toothbrush, toothpaste, and two books in it: a history of America and a book by [Christian theologian] Thomas Merton."

On Sunday, March 7,500 marchers crossed the bridge over the Alabama River, to meet a sea of state troopers. The troopers gave them two minutes to disperse and then attacked on foot and horseback "as if they were mowing a big field." The attack drove the demonstrators back in bloody confusion while television cameras rolled.

As violence continued, Johnson addressed a joint session of Congress to demand a voting-rights law: "Our mission is at once the oldest and the most basic of this country: to right wrong, to do justice, to serve man." He ended with the refrain of the civil rights movement: "We shall overcome." By opening the political process to previously excluded citizens, the Voting Rights Act was as revolutionary and far-reaching as the Nineteenth Amendment, which guaranteed women the right to vote, and the Labor Relations Act of 1935, which recognized labor unions as the equals of corporations.

Johnson signed the **Voting Rights Act** on August 6, 1965. The law outlawed literacy tests and provided for federal voting registrars in states where registration or turnout in 1964 was less than 50 percent of the eligible population. It applied initially in seven southern states. Black registration in these states jumped from 27 percent to 55 percent within the first year. In 1975, Congress extended coverage to Hispanic voters in the Southwest. The Act required new moderation from white leaders, who had to satisfy black voters, and it opened the way for black and Latino candidates to win positions at every level of state and local government. In the long run, the Voting Rights Act climaxed the battle for civil rights and shifted attention to the continuing problems of economic opportunity and inequality.

War, Peace, and the Landslide of 1964

Lyndon Johnson was the peace candidate in 1964. Johnson had maintained Kennedy's commitment to South Vietnam. On the advice of such Kennedy holdovers as Defense Secretary Robert McNamara, he stepped up commando raids and naval shelling of North Vietnam, on the assumption that North Vietnam controlled the Viet Cong. On August 2, North Vietnamese torpedo boats attacked the U.S. destroyer *Maddox* in the Gulf of Tonkin while it was eavesdropping on North Vietnamese military signals. Two days later, the *Maddox* and the *C. Turner Joy* reported another torpedo at-

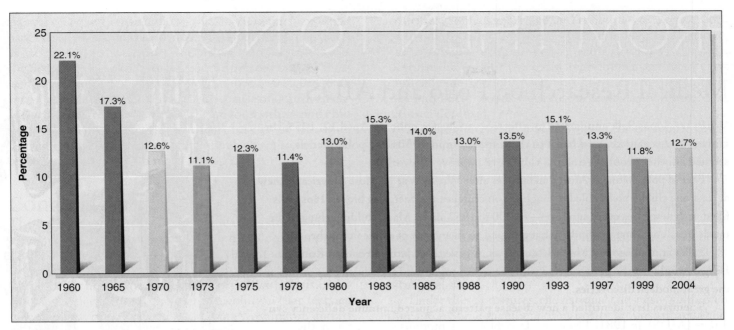

FIGURE 28–4 Poverty Rate, 1960–2004

With the improvement of federal health insurance, assistance for the elderly, and antipoverty programs, the proportion of Americans living in poverty dropped dramatically in the later 1960s. It began to inch upward again in the 1980s, when the priorities of the federal government shifted.

Data Source: *Statistical Abstract of the United States.*

tack (probably false sonar readings). Johnson ordered a bombing raid in reprisal and asked Congress to authorize "all necessary measures" to protect U.S. forces and stop further aggression. Congress passed the **Gulf of Tonkin Resolution** with only two nay votes, effectively authorizing the president to wage undeclared war.

Johnson's militancy paled beside that of his Republican opponent. Senator Barry Goldwater of Arizona represented the new right wing of the Republican Party, which was drawing strength from the South and West. Goldwater wanted minimal government interference in free enterprise and aggressive confrontation with Communism. Campaign literature accurately described him as "a choice, not an echo." He declared that "extremism in the defense of liberty is no vice," raising visions of vigilantes and mobs. Goldwater's campaign made Johnson look moderate. Johnson pledged not "to send American boys nine or ten thousand miles from home to do what Asian boys ought to be doing for themselves" while Goldwater proposed an all-out war.

The election was a landslide. Johnson's 61 percent of the popular vote was the greatest margin ever recorded in a presidential election. Democrats racked up two-to-one majorities in Congress. For the first time in decades, liberal Democrats could enact their domestic program without begging votes from conservative southerners or Republicans, and Johnson could achieve his goal of a **Great Society** based on freedom and opportunity for all.

The result was a series of measures that Johnson pushed through Congress before the Vietnam War eroded his polit-

ical standing and distracted national attention. The National Endowment for the Arts and the National Endowment for the Humanities seemed uncontroversial at the time but would later become the focus of liberal and conservative struggles over the character of American life. The Wilderness Act (1964), which preserved 9.1 million acres from development, would prove another political battlefield in the face of economic pressures in the next century.

The goal of increasing opportunity for all Americans stirred the president most deeply. As he told a July 1965 news conference, "When I was young, poverty was so common that we didn't know it had a name. An education was something that you had to fight for.... It is now my opportunity to help every child get an education, to help every Negro and every American citizen have an equal opportunity, to have every family get a decent home, and to help bring healing to the sick and dignity to the old." The Elementary and Secondary Education Act was the first general federal aid program for public schools, allocating $1.3 billion for textbooks and special education. The Higher Education Act funded low-interest student loans and university research facilities. The Medical Care Act created **Medicare,** federally funded health insurance for the elderly, and **Medicaid,** which helped states offer medical care to the poor. The Appalachian Regional Development Act funded economic development in the depressed mountain counties of 12 states from Georgia to New York and proved a long-run success.

It is sometimes said that the United States declared war on poverty and lost. In fact, the nation came closer to winning nomination night. Mixed in were the Yippies (the term supposedly stood for Youth International Party, but the idea of hippies making yippie! came first and the word later). The Yippies planned to attract young people to Chicago with the promise of street theater, media events, and confrontation that would puncture the pretensions of the power structure. To the extent they had a program, it was to use the youth culture to attract converts to radical politics.

The volatile mix was ready for a spark. On August 28, the same night that Democratic delegates were nominating Humphrey, tensions exploded in a police riot. Protesters and Yippies had congregated in Grant Park, across Michigan Avenue from downtown hotels. Undisciplined police waded into the crowds with clubs and tear gas. Young people fought back with rocks and bottles. Television caught the hours of violence that ended when the National Guard separated police from demonstrators. On the convention floor, Senator Abraham Ribicoff of Connecticut decried "Gestapo tactics" on the streets of Chicago. Mayor Daley shouted back obscenities. For Humphrey, the convention was a catastrophe, alienating liberal Democrats and associating Democrats with disorder in the public mind.

The election was closer than Humphrey had any right to hope (see Map 29–2). Many Americans who liked Wallace's message were unwilling to vote for a radical third party. Nixon appealed to the white middle class and claimed that he had a secret plan to end the war. He also used increasing fears about crime and street violence as a "wedge issue" to split worried white voters from the Democrats. Humphrey picked up strength in October after he separated himself from Johnson's war policy. Election day gave Wallace 13.5 percent of the popular vote, Humphrey 42.7 percent of the popular vote and 191 electoral votes, and Nixon 43.4 percent of the popular vote and 301 electoral votes.

The Wallace candidacy was a glimpse of the future. The national media saw Wallace in terms of bigotry and a backlash against civil rights, getting only part of the story. Many of Wallace's northern backers were unhappy with both parties. Liberal on economic issues but conservative on family and social issues, many of these working-class voters evolved into "Reagan Democrats" by the 1980s. In the South, Wallace was a transitional choice for conservative voters who would eventually transfer their allegiance from the Democratic to the Republican Party.

Nixon, Watergate, and the Crisis of the Early 1970s

The new president was an unlikely politician, ill at ease in public and consumed by a sense of inferiority. A product of small-town California, he felt rejected by the eastern elite. After losing a 1962 race for governor of California, he announced that he was quitting politics and that the press would no longer have Dick Nixon "to kick around." In 1968, he skill-

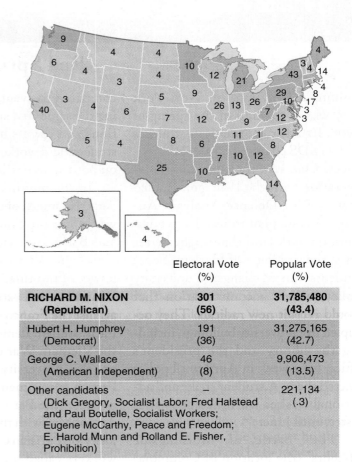

	Electoral Vote (%)	Popular Vote (%)
RICHARD M. NIXON (Republican)	**301 (56)**	**31,785,480 (43.4)**
Hubert H. Humphrey (Democrat)	191 (36)	31,275,165 (42.7)
George C. Wallace (American Independent)	46 (8)	9,906,473 (13.5)
Other candidates (Dick Gregory, Socialist Labor; Fred Halstead and Paul Boutelle, Socialist Workers; Eugene McCarthy, Peace and Freedom; E. Harold Munn and Rolland E. Fisher, Prohibition)	–	221,134 (.3)

MAP 29–2 The Election of 1968
Richard Nixon won the presidency with the help of George Wallace, the American Independent Party candidate. Wallace won several southern states, offering an alternative to white southerners unhappy with the Democratic Party but not yet prepared to vote Republican. He also drew northern working-class votes away from Hubert Humphrey and thus helped Nixon to take several midwestern states.

fully sold a "new Nixon" to the media. Seven years later, the press was his undoing as it uncovered the Watergate scandal.

Nixon's painful public presence and dishonesty have tended to obscure his administration's accomplishments. He reduced tensions in the Cold War. He reluctantly upgraded civil rights enforcement, set goals for minority hiring by federal contractors, and presided over impressive environmental legislation.

Getting Out of Vietnam, 1969–1975

After 1968, things got worse in Southeast Asia before they got better. Nixon had no secret plan to end the war. Opposition intensified with the revelation that U.S. soldiers in March 1968 had slaughtered hundreds of men, women, and children in the South Vietnamese village of My Lai after failing to find any Viet Cong. This crime accentuated the dehumanizing power of war and showed how far the United States was straying from its ideals. William Calley, who had been in immediate command, eventually served ten years in military prison. Protests at home culminated in 1969 with the Vietnam Moratorium on October 15, when 2 million protesters joined rallies across the country.

Disaffection also mounted in Vietnam. Racial tensions sapped morale on the front lines. Troops lost discipline, took drugs, and hunkered down waiting for their tours of duty to end, and the high command had to adapt its code of justice to keep an army on the job.

Nixon and Vice President Spiro Agnew responded by trying to isolate the antiwar opposition, but Nixon also reduced the role of U.S. ground forces. He claimed that his policies represented "the great silent majority of my fellow Americans." Agnew blamed bad morale on journalists and intellectuals—on "nattering nabobs of negativism" and "an effete corps of impudent snobs." The administration arranged for a "spontaneous" attack by construction workers on antiwar protesters in New York. The hard-hat counterattack was a cynically manipulated symbol, but Nixon and Agnew tapped genuine anger about failure in Asia and rapid change in U.S. society.

The New Left had already split into factions. Many activists continued to focus on peace work, draft resistance, and other efforts to link radical and liberal agendas. About a hundred angry SDS members, however, declared themselves the Weather Underground in 1969, taking their name from a Bob Dylan lyric ("You don't need a weatherman to know which way the wind blows"). They tried to disrupt Chicago and Washington with window-smashing "days of rage." Three Weatherpeople accidentally blew themselves up with a homemade bomb in New York in 1970. Others robbed a Boston bank to get money for the revolution. Still others bombed a University of Wisconsin building and killed a student.

"Vietnamization" and the secret war against Cambodia.
Nixon's secretary of defense, Melvin Laird, responded to the antiwar sentiment with "Vietnamization," withdrawing U.S. troops as fast as possible without undermining the South Vietnamese government. In July 1969, the president announced the **Nixon Doctrine.** The United States would help other countries fight their wars with weapons and money but not with soldiers. The policy substituted machines for men. Americans rearmed and enlarged the South Vietnamese army and surreptitiously bombed Communist bases in neutral Cambodia.

The secret war against Cambodia culminated on April 30, 1970, with an invasion. The aim was to smash Viet Cong and North Vietnamese bases to allow time to rebuild the South Vietnamese army. Americans who had hoped that the war was fading away were outraged. Students shut down hundreds of colleges. At Kent State University in Ohio, the National Guard was called in to maintain order. Taunts, tossed bottles, and the recent record of violence put them on edge. On May 4, one unit fired on a group of young people and killed four of them. At Jackson State University in Mississippi, two students were killed when troops fired on their dormitory.

Stalemate and cease-fire.   The Cambodian "incursion" extended the military stalemate in Vietnam to U.S. policy. Beginning in December 1969, a new lottery system for determining the order of draft calls by birthdate let two-thirds of young men know they would not be drafted. In December 1970, Congress repealed the Gulf of Tonkin Resolution and prohibited the use of U.S. ground troops outside South Vietnam. Cambodia, however, was already devastated. The U.S. invasion had destabilized its government and opened the way for the bloodthirsty Khmer Rouge, who killed millions of Cambodians in the name of a working-class revolution. Vietnamization continued; only 90,000 U.S. ground troops were still in Vietnam by early 1972. A final air offensive in December smashed Hanoi into rubble and helped to force four and a half years of peace talks to a conclusion.

The cease-fire began on January 27, 1973. It confirmed U.S. withdrawal from Vietnam. North Vietnamese and Viet Cong forces would remain in control of the territory they occupied in South Vietnam, but they were not to be reinforced or substantially reequipped. The United States promised not to increase its military aid to South Vietnam. There were no solid guarantees for the South Vietnamese government. Immediately after coming to terms with North Vietnam, Nixon suspended the draft in favor of an all-volunteer military.

In 1975, South Vietnam collapsed. Only the U.S. presence had kept its political, ethnic, and religious factions together. For the first two years after the Paris agreement, North Vietnam quietly rebuilt its military capacity. In the spring of 1975, it opened an offensive, and South Vietnamese morale evaporated. Resistance crumbled so rapidly that the United States had to evacuate its embassy in Saigon by helicopter while frantic Vietnamese tried to join the flight.

Nixon and the Wider World

To his credit, Richard Nixon took U.S. foreign policy in new directions even while he was struggling to escape from Vietnam and Cambodia. Like Dwight Eisenhower before him, Nixon's reputation as an anti-Communist allowed him to improve relations with China and the Soviet Union. Indeed, he hoped to distract the American people from frustration in Southeast Asia with accomplishments elsewhere.

Nixon and Henry Kissinger, his national security adviser (and later secretary of state), shared what they considered a realistic view of foreign affairs. For both men, foreign policy was not about crusades or moral stands. It was about the balance of world economic and military power and securing the most advantageous agreements, alliances, and military positions. In particular, they hoped to trade improved relations with China and the Soviet Union for help in settling the Vietnam War.

Since 1950, the United States had acted as if China did not exist, refusing economic relations and insisting that the that the purpose was to clear the decks so that the nation could think about the future rather than the past. He also offered clemency to thousands of draft resisters.

Ford's administration presided over the collapse of South Vietnam in 1975, but elsewhere in the world, *détente* continued. U.S. diplomats joined the Soviet Union and 30 other European nations in the capital of Finland to sign the **Helsinki Accords.** The agreements called for increased commerce between the Eastern and Western blocs and for human-rights guarantees. They also legitimized the national boundaries that had been set in eastern Europe in 1945.

At home, the federal government did little new during Ford's two and a half years in office. The economy slid into recession, unemployment climbed above 10 percent, inflation diminished the value of savings and wages. Ford beat back Ronald Reagan for the Republican presidential nomination, but he was clearly vulnerable.

His Democratic opponent was a political enigma. James Earl Carter, Jr., had been a navy officer, a farmer, and the governor of Georgia. He was one of several new-style politicians who transformed southern politics in the 1970s. Carter and the others left race-baiting behind to talk like modern New Dealers, emphasizing that whites and blacks both needed better schools and economic growth. He appealed to Democrats as someone who could reassemble LBJ's political coalition and return the South to the Democratic Party. In his successful campaign, Carter presented himself as an alternative to party hacks and Washington insiders (see Map 29–3).

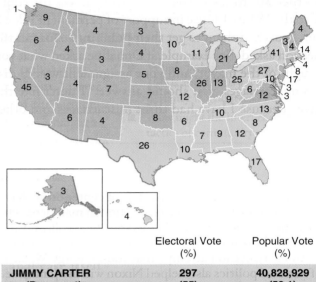

	Electoral Vote (%)	Popular Vote (%)
JIMMY CARTER (Democrat)	**297 (55)**	**40,828,929 (50.1)**
Gerald R. Ford (Republican)	240 (45)	39,148,940 (47.9)
Ronald Reagan	1	–
Other candidates (McCarthy, Independent; Libertarian)	–	1,575,459 (2.1)

Map 29–3   The Election of 1976
Georgian Jimmy Carter ran in 1976 as an outsider to Washington politics. He capitalized on a reputation as a progressive governor and on the Watergate scandal, which had damaged the Republican Party.

Jimmy Carter: Idealism and Frustration in the White House

Johnson and Nixon had both thought of themselves as outsiders even after nearly 30 years in national politics. Carter was the real thing, a stranger to the national policy establishment that revolves around Washington think tanks and New York law firms. As an outsider, Carter had one great advantage: freedom from the narrow mindset of experts who talk only to each other. However, he lacked both the knowledge of key political players and the experience to resolve legislative gridlock.

The new president's personal background compounded his problems. Intellectuals found this devout Baptist hard to fathom. Labor leaders and political bosses did not know what to make of a farmer from the deep South. The national press was baffled. It was only after his presidency, when Americans took a clear look at Carter's moral character, that they decided they liked what they saw.

Even had he been the most skilled of politicians, however, Carter took office with little room to maneuver. Watergate bequeathed him a powerful and self-satisfied Congress and a combative press. OPEC oil producers, Islamic fundamentalists, and Soviet generals followed their own agendas. The American people themselves were fractionalized and quarrelsome, uneasy with the new advocacy of equality for women, uncertain as a nation whether they

shared the same values and goals. Carter's attempt to govern like a preacher, with appeals to moral principles, did more to reveal divisions than establish common ground.

Carter, Energy, and the Economy

Carter was refreshingly low-key. After his inauguration, he walked from the Capitol to the White House, as Jefferson had. He preferred sweaters to tuxedos and signed official documents "Jimmy." He tended to tell the public what he thought rather than what pollsters said the people wanted to hear.

Carter's approach to politics reflected his training as an engineer. He was analytical, logical, and given to breaking a problem into its component parts. He was better at working with details than at defining broad goals. He filled his cabinet with experts rather than with political operators. He failed to understand the importance of personalities and was uncomfortable with compromise. He did not seem to understand the basic rules of Washington politics. For example, he and his cabinet officers developed policies and made appointments without consulting key congressional committee chairs.

The biggest domestic problem remained the economy, which slid into another recession in 1978. Another jump in oil prices helped make 1979 and 1980 the worst years for inflation in the postwar era. Interest rates surged past 20 percent as the Federal Reserve tried to reduce inflation by squeezing business and consumer credit. Carter himself was a fiscal conservative whose impulse was to cut federal spending. This course worsened unemployment and alienated liberal Democrats, who wanted to revive the Great Society.

Carter simultaneously proposed a comprehensive energy policy. He asked Americans to make energy conservation the moral equivalent of war—to accept individual sacrifices for the common good. Congress created the Department of Energy but refused to raise taxes on oil and natural gas to reduce consumption. However, the Energy Policy and Conservation Act (1978) did encourage alternative energy sources to replace foreign petroleum. Big oil companies poured billions of dollars into western Colorado to squeeze a petroleum substitute from shale. Solar energy research prospered.

However, antinuclear activism blocked one obvious alternative to fossil fuels. The antinuclear movement had started with concern about the ability of the Atomic Energy Commission to monitor the safety of nuclear-power plants and about the disposal of spent fuel rods. In the late 1970s, activists staged sit-ins at the construction sites of nuclear plants. A near-meltdown at the Three Mile Island nuclear plant in Pennsylvania in March 1979 stalemated efforts to expand nuclear-power capacity. Utilities were soon worrying about the cost of shutting down and dismantling their old nuclear plants rather than trying to build new ones.

When the OPEC price hikes undermined the inflation-fighting effort in the summer of 1979, Carter told the nation that a "moral and spiritual crisis" demanded a rebirth of the American spirit. The public did not know whether he had preached a sermon or given them marching orders. A cabinet reshuffle a few days later was supposed to show that he was firmly in charge. Instead, the media painted the president as inconsistent and incompetent.

Carter's problems were both personal and structural. In effect, opinion leaders had decided by 1979 that he was not capable of leading the nation and then interpreted every action as confirming that belief. There was also the practical problem of trying to hold the loyalty of Democratic liberals while attracting middle-of-the-road voters.

Closed Factories and Failed Farms

Ford and Carter both faced massive problems of economic transition that undercut their efforts to devise effective government programs. Here is how novelist John Updike described the fictional city of Brewer, Pennsylvania, at the start of the 1970s:

> Railroads and coal made Brewer. Everywhere in this city…structures speak of expended energy. Great shapely stacks that have not issued smoke for half a century.... The old textile plants given over to discount clothing outlets teeming with a gimcrack cheer of banners FACTORY FAIR and slogans Where a Dollar Is Still a Dollar.... All

this had been cast up in the last century by what now seem giants, in an explosion of iron and brick still preserved intact in this city where the sole new buildings are funeral parlors and government offices.

Updike's Brewer was like dozens of specialized industrial cities that fell behind a changing economic world in the 1970s and 1980s. Industrial decay stalked such "gritty cities" as Allentown, Pennsylvania; Trenton, New Jersey; and Gary, Indiana. Communities whose workers had made products in high volume for a mass market found that technological revolutions made them obsolete. When radial tires replaced bias-ply tires, Akron rubber workers paid the price. Merchants who replaced mechanical cash registers with electronic models left Dayton with block after block of outmoded factories. Asian steelmakers undercut the aging mills of Pittsburgh and Birmingham. Critics renamed the old manufacturing region of the Northeast and Middle West the Rustbelt in honor of its abandoned factories.

Stories of **deindustrialization** were similar in small cities like Springfield, Ohio, and large cities like Cleveland. Springfield lost 10,000 manufacturing jobs and 4,000 people during the 1970s, suffered unemployment of 17 percent, and needed $30 million in public subsidies to keep its largest factory going in 1982. Cleveland had built a century of prosperity on oil refining, steel, and metalworking; the metropolitan area had grown from 1.3 million in 1940 to 2.1 million in 1970. In the 1970s, however, it lost 165,000 people. As high-paying jobs in unionized industries disappeared, sagging income undermined small businesses and neighborhoods. Falling tax revenue brought the city to the verge of bankruptcy in 1978; bankers forced public service cuts and tax increases, which meant further job losses.

Outmoded facilities and foreign competition undermined the competitiveness of much of the nation's heavy manufacturing in the 1970s and 1980s. Many older factories were closed and abandoned, lending the name Rustbelt to the old industrial heartland.

Plant closures were only one facet of business efforts to increase productivity by substituting machinery for employees. Between 1947 and 1977, American steelmakers doubled output while cutting their workforce from 600,000 to 400,000. High interest rates and a strong dollar made U.S. exports too expensive and foreign imports cheap, forcing American manufacturers to cut costs or perish.

Despite the despairing headlines, some older industries and their workers found new roles in the sink-or-swim environment of technological and international competition. Buffalo, New York, lost much of its steel industry but retained smaller and more flexible factories making diverse products. The auto industry went through a similar cycle of crisis and response. Prosperity in the 1950s had led automobile executives to believe that they knew how to manipulate U.S. consumers. Booming imports of well-made Toyotas and Hondas and customer demand for smaller cars destroyed their complacency in the fuel-short 1970s. In response, Ford, Chrysler, and finally General Motors tried to remake themselves on the Japanese model as lean and flexible manufacturers. They cast off old plants, workers, and executives, started over, often in new locations, and forced Japanese companies to shift production to U.S. localities and workers.

Parallel to the decline of heavy industry was the continuing transformation of American agriculture from small family enterprises to corporate agribusinesses. Agriculture was a national success story in the aggregate, but one accompanied by many human and environmental costs. The early 1970s brought an unexpected boom in farming. Crop failures and food shortages around the world in 1972 and 1973 expanded markets and pushed up prices for U.S. farm products. For a few years, agriculture looked like the best way for the United States to offset the high cost of imported oil. But the boom was over by the 1980s, when global commodity prices slumped. Farmers found themselves with debts they could not cover. Farm bankruptcies in Iowa reached levels unseen since the 1930s, and rock stars staged "Farm Aid" concerts to raise money to fend off foreclosures.

The boom of the 1970s was thus a brief interruption in the long-term transformation of U.S. agriculture. The number of farms slid from 4 million in 1960 to 2.4 million in 1980 and 1.9 million in 2000. Many farmers sold out willingly, glad to escape from drudgery and financial insecurity. Others could not compete in an agricultural system that favored large-scale production by demanding large amounts of capital for equipment and fertilizer. By 2000, fewer than 2 percent of American workers made their living from farming.

Building a Cooperative World

Despite troubles on the home front, Carter's first two years brought foreign-policy successes that reflected a new vision of a multilateral world. As a relative newcomer to international politics, Carter was willing to work with African, Asian, and Latin American nations on a basis of mutual respect. Carter appointed Andrew Young—an African American from Georgia with long experience in the civil rights movement—

Egyptian President Anwar al-Sadat, U.S. President Jimmy Carter, and Israeli Prime Minister Menachem Begin share a symbolic handshake after the signing of a peace treaty between Egypt and Israel on August 26, 1979. The treaty codified the historic agreement that the leaders had hammered out at Camp David, Maryland, in September 1978.

as ambassador to the United Nations, where he worked effectively to build bridges to third-world nations. Carter convinced the Senate in 1978 to approve treaties to transfer control of the Panama Canal to Panama by 2000, removing a sore point in relations with Latin America.

Carter's moral convictions were responsible for a new concern with human rights around the globe. He criticized the Soviet Union for prohibiting free speech and denying its citizens the right to emigrate, angering Soviet leaders, who did not expect the human rights clauses of the Helsinki Accords to be taken seriously. Carter was also willing to criticize some (but not all) American allies. He withheld economic aid from South Africa, Guatemala, Chile, and Nicaragua, which had long records of human rights abuses. In Nicaragua, the change in policy helped left-wing Sandinista rebels topple the Somoza dictatorship.

The triumph of the new foreign policy was the **Camp David Agreement** between Egypt and Israel. Carter risked his reputation and credibility in September 1978 to bring Egyptian President Anwar al-Sadat and Israeli Prime Minister Menachem Begin together at Camp David, the presidential retreat. He refused to admit failure and dissuaded the two leaders from walking out. A formal treaty was signed in Washing-

The Iran hostage crisis reflected intense anti-American feelings in Iran and provoked an equally bitter anti-Iranian reaction in the United States. Fifty-two of the more than 60 U.S. embassy employees first seized were held for 444 days, giving the United States a painful lesson about the limits on its ability to influence events around the world.

ton on March 26, 1979. The pact normalized relations between Israel and its most powerful neighbor and led to Israel's withdrawal from the Sinai Peninsula. It was a vital prelude to further progress toward Arab-Israeli peace in the mid-1990s.

New Crises Abroad

The Cold War was a noxious weed that détente trimmed but did not uproot. In the last two years of Carter's administration, it sprang back to life around the globe and smothered the promise of a new foreign policy. The Soviets ignored the human-rights provisions of the Helsinki Accords. Soviet advisers or Cuban troops intervened in African civil wars. At home, Cold Warriors who had never accepted détente found it easier to attack Carter than Nixon.

The failure of SALT II.   Carter inherited negotiations for SALT II—a strategic arms-limitation treaty that would have reduced both the U.S. and Soviet nuclear arsenals—from the Ford administration. SALT II met stiff resistance in the Senate. Opponents claimed it would create a "window of vulnerability" in the 1980s that would invite the Soviets to launch a nuclear first strike. Carter tried to counter criticism by stepping up defense spending, starting a buildup that would accelerate under Ronald Reagan.

Hopes for SALT II vanished on December 24, 1979, when Soviet troops entered Afghanistan, a technically neutral Muslim nation on the southern border of the Soviet Union. A pro-Soviet government had fallen into factional strife, while tribespeople, unhappy with modernization, were mounting increasing resistance. One of the factions invited intervention by the Soviets, who quickly installed a client government. The situation resembled the U.S. involvement in South Vietnam. Similar, too, was the inability of Soviet forces to suppress the Afghan guerrillas, who had American weapons and controlled the mountains. In the end, it took the Soviets a decade to find a way out.

The Iranian Hostage Crisis.   The final blow to Carter's foreign policy came in Iran. Since 1953, the United States had strongly backed Iran's monarch, Shah Reza Pahlevi. The shah modernized Iran's economy, but his feared secret police jailed and tortured political opponents. U.S. aid and oil revenues helped him build a large army, but the Iranian middle class despised his authoritarianism, and Muslim fundamentalists opposed the Westernizing influence of modernization. A revolution toppled the shah at the start of 1979.

The upheaval installed a nominally democratic government, but the Ayatollah Ruhollah Khomeini, a Muslim cleric who hated the United States, exercised real power. Throughout 1979, Iran grew increasingly anti-American. After the United States allowed the exiled shah to seek medical treatment in New York, a mob stormed the U.S. embassy in Tehran on November 4, 1979, and took more than 60 Americans hostage. They demanded that Carter surrender the shah. Television brought pictures of blindfolded hostages and anti-American mobs burning effigies of Uncle Sam and wrapping American flags around garbage. The administration tried economic pressure and diplomacy, but Khomeini had no desire for accommodation. When Iran announced in April 1980 that the hostages would remain in the hands of the militants rather than be transferred to the government, Carter ordered an airborne rescue. Even a perfectly managed effort would have been difficult. The hostages were held in the heart of a city of 4 million hostile Iranians, hundreds of miles from the nearest aircraft carrier and thousands of miles from U.S. bases. Hampered by lack of coordination among the military services, the attempt turned into a fiasco that added to the national embarrassment and a feeling of powerlessness. The United States and Iran finally reached agreement on the eve of the 1980 election. The hostages gained their freedom after 444 days, at the moment Ronald Reagan took office as the new president.

The hostage crisis consumed Jimmy Carter the way that Vietnam had consumed Lyndon Johnson. It gripped the public and stalemated other issues. For weeks, Carter limited public appearances to statements in the White House Rose Garden. The public blamed him for problems literally beyond his control, for failing to use military force, and then for using it and failing. Carter's tragedy was that "his" Iranian crisis was the fruit of policies hatched by the Eisenhower administration and pursued by every president since then, all of whom had overlooked the shah's despotic government because of his firm anti-Communism.

After 30 years in which the United States had viewed the entire world as a Cold War battlefield, Carter was willing to accept the developing world on its own terms. His human-rights efforts showed that evangelical religious convictions could be tied to progressive aims. He wanted to avoid supporting oppressive regimes, but the past was too burdensome. Iranian rage at past policies of the sort Carter hoped to change destroyed his ability to direct a new course. After he left office, his continuing work for peace and humanitarian efforts would earn him the Nobel Peace Prize in 2002.

Conclusion

In the mid-1970s, Americans encountered real limits to national capacity. From 1945 to 1973, they had enjoyed remarkable prosperity. That ended in 1974. Long lines at gas stations showed that prosperity was fragile. Cities and regions felt the costs of obsolete industries. Environmental damage caused many Americans to reconsider the goal of economic expansion.

The nation also had to recognize that it could not run the world. American withdrawal from Vietnam in 1973 and the collapse of the South Vietnamese government in 1975 were defeats; the United States ended up with little to show for a long and painful war. SALT I stabilized the arms race, but it also recognized that the Soviet Union was an equal. The American nuclear arsenal might help deter a third world war, but it could not prevent the seizure of hostages in Iran.

These challenges came amid deep economic and social changes in the United States. The ways Americans made their livings and the range of opportunities they faced were in flux. The nation finished the 1970s more egalitarian than it had been in the early 1960s but also more divided. More citizens had the opportunity to advance economically and to seek political power, but there were deepening fissures between social liberals and cultural conservatives, old and new views about roles for women, rich and poor, whites and blacks. In 1961, John Kennedy had called on his fellow citizens to "bear any burden, pay any price" to defend freedom. By 1980, the nation had neither the economic capacity to pay any price nor the unity to agree on what burdens it should bear.

Review Questions

1. Why did the United States fail to achieve its objectives in Vietnam? What factors limited President Johnson's freedom of action there? How did the Tet Offensive affect U.S. policy? How did antiwar protests in the United States influence national policy?

2. How did racial relations change between 1965 and 1970? What were the relationships between the civil rights movement and minority separatism? What were the similarities and differences between African American, Latino, and Native American activism?

3. In what ways was 1968 a pivotal year for U.S. politics and society? How was it influenced by global events?

4. What were the implications of *détente?* Why did the Cold War reappear in the late 1970s? How and why did U.S. influence over the rest of the world change during the 1970s?

5. How did Richard Nixon's political strategy respond to the growth of the South and West? How did it respond to the shift of population from central cities to suburbs?

6. How did the backgrounds of Presidents Johnson, Nixon, and Carter shape their successes and failures as national leaders?

7. What political and constitutional issues were at stake in the Watergate scandal? How did it change American politics?

8. Why was the space race important for the United States? How did it strengthen the alliance between American science, government, and industry?

Key Terms

American Indian Movement (AIM) (p. 832)

Baker v. Carr (p. 833)

Black Panthers (p. 831)

Black Power (p. 830)

Camp David Agreement (p. 846)

Counterculture (p. 825)

Deindustrialization (p. 845)

Détente (p. 838)

Environmental Protection Agency (EPA) (p. 840)

Free Speech Movement (FSM) (p. 825)

Helsinki Accords (p. 844)

Model Cities Program (p. 825)

Nation of Islam (p. 830)

New Federalism (p. 838)

Nixon Doctrine (p. 837)

Organization of Petroleum Exporting Countries (Opec) (p. 838)

Pentagon Papers (p. 841)

Search and destroy (p. 821)

Selective Service System (p. 823)

Stonewall Rebellion (p. 829)

Strategic Arms Limitation Treaty (SALT) (p. 838)

Students for a Democratic Society (SDS) (p. 824)

Swann v. Charlotte-Mecklenburg Board of Education (p. 833)

Watergate (p. 840)

Recommended Reading

Appy, Christian. *Patriots: The Vietnam War Remembered from All Sides* (2003). Summarizes interviews with American and Vietnamese officials and veterans.

Caute, David. *Year of the Barricades* (1988). Tour the events of 1968 on both sides of the Atlantic.

Emerson, Gloria. *Winners and Losers* (1976). The impact of the war in Vietnam on American society is told through the stories of individuals changed by the war.

Farber, David. *Chicago '68* (1988); *Medium Cool* (1969), directed by Haskell Wexler. Farber's book contrasts the perspectives and language of city officials and protesters.

Wexler's film captures the tension of Chicago in the hot summer through the eyes of a reporter.

Halberstam, David. *October 1964* (1994). Halberstam uses the baseball season of 1964 and the World Series between the St. Louis Cardinals and New York Yankees to encapsulate the impact of changing racial relations on American society.

Karnow, Stanley. *Vietnam: A History* (1983). This comprehensive history of American involvement in Vietnam details the collapse of French rule and early U.S. relations with Vietnam.

Where to Learn More

■ **Lyndon B. Johnson National Historical Park, Johnson City, Texas.** Johnson's ranch, southwest of Austin, gives visitors a feeling for the open landscape in which Johnson spent his early years. www.nps.gov/lypo

■ **Vietnam Veterans Memorial, Washington, DC.** A simple wall engraved with the names of the nation's Vietnam War dead is testimony to one of the nation's most divisive wars. www.nps.gov/vive

■ **Richard Nixon Library and Birthplace, Yorba Linda, California.** Exhibits trace Nixon's political career and related world events with a sympathetic interpretation. www.nixonfoundation.org/index.shtml

■ **Titan Missile Museum, Green Valley, Arizona.** The Green Valley complex near Tucson held 18 Titan missiles. They were deactivated after SALT I, and the complex is now open to visitors. www.pimaair.org/titan_01.htm.

Study Resources

For study resources for this chapter, go to www.myhistorylab.com and choose *The American Journey*. You will find a wealth of study and review material for this chapter, including pre- and post-tests, customized study plan, key term review flash cards, interactive map and document activities, and documents for analysis.

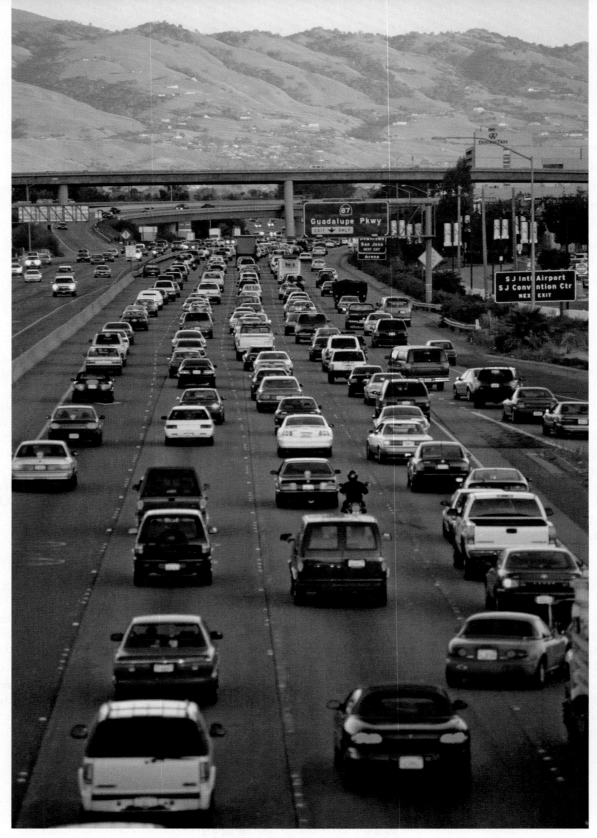

Freeway traffic near San Jose, California reflects the development of the Silicon Valley electronics industry, the ongoing suburban trend, and the continued shift of population and economic activity to the Sunbelt region of the West and South.

The Reagan Revolution and a Changing World

1981–1992

30

The Khmer Rouge marched into the city [Phnom Penh, the capital of Cambodia], dressed in black. Young Khmer Rouge [Marxist revolutionary] soldiers, eight or ten years old, were dragging their rifles, which were taller than them. The whole city, more than two million people was forced out of their homes into the streets. My family walked until we reached Mao Tse-Tung Boulevard, the main boulevard in Phnom Penh. All the population of the city was gathered there. The Khmer Rouge were telling everyone to leave the city.

Although my two middle children were safe in France, my oldest and youngest daughters were close be-side me. Parika was only seven. Mealy, who was nineteen, carried her infant son. I kept my children huddled together. As soon as a parent let go, a child would be lost in the huge crowd. And the Khmer Rouge kept ordering everybody, "You must go forward." They shot their guns in the air. Even during the middle of the night the procession was endless. The Khmer Rouge kept shooting and we kept moving forward.

Recently I saw the movie *Doctor Zhivago*, about the Russian Revolution. If you compare that to what happened in Phnom Penh, the movie is only on a very small scale. Even *Killing Fields* only gives you part of the idea of decided to reverse the growth of federal government responsibilities that had marked both Republican and Democratic administrations since the 1930s. By the 1990s, the center of U.S. politics had shifted substantially to the right, and even a liberal Democrat like Bill Clinton would sound like an Eisenhower Republican.

The backdrop to the political changes were massive readjustments in the American economy that began in the 1970s with the decline of heavy industry and then continued to shift employment from factory jobs to service jobs in the 1980s (Celia Noup's small shop was part of the service economy). The ideology of unregulated markets celebrated economic success and made "yuppies," or young urban professionals, the center of media attention; some of the yuppies probably grabbed a donut on their way to catch a flight from Los Angeles to New York to help close a deal. But behind the lifestyle stories was a troubling reality: a widening gap between the rich and poor. The result by 1992 was a nation that was much more secure in the world than it had been in 1980, but also more divided against itself.

Reagan's Domestic Revolution

Political change began in 1980, when Ronald Reagan and running his mate, George H.W. Bush, rode American discontent to a decisive victory in the presidential election (see Map 30–1). Building on a conservative critique of American policies and developing issues that Jimmy Carter had placed on the national agenda, Reagan presided over revolutionary changes in U.S. government and policies. He was a "Teflon president" who managed to take credit for successes but avoid blame for problems, and he rolled to a landslide reelection in 1984 and set the stage for George Bush's victory in 1988. The consequences of his two terms included an altered role for government, powerful but selective economic growth, and a shift of domestic politics away from bread-and-butter issues toward moral or lifestyle concerns.

An unresolved question is whether Ronald Reagan planned an economic revolution or simply presided over changes initiated by others. Most memoirs by White House insiders suggest the latter; so do journalists who titled books about the Reagan administration *Sleepwalking through History, The Acting President,* and *The Role of a Lifetime.* Even if Reagan was acting out a role scripted by others, however, his policies moved forward, and he was a hit at the polling places. Americans, worried about inflation at home and declining power abroad, elected Reagan by voting *against* Jimmy Carter in 1980, but they enthusiastically voted *for* Reagan in 1984.

Reagan's Majority

Ronald Reagan reinvented himself several times on his unusual journey to the White House. A product of small-town

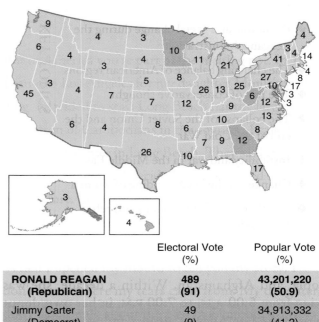

	Electoral Vote (%)	Popular Vote (%)
RONALD REAGAN (Republican)	**489 (91)**	**43,201,220 (50.9)**
Jimmy Carter (Democrat)	49 (9)	34,913,332 (41.2)
John B. Anderson (Independent)	–	5,581,379 (6.6)
Other candidates (Libertarian)	–	921,299 (1.1)

Map 30–1   The Election of 1980
Ronald Reagan won in a landslide in 1980. Independent candidate John Anderson took more votes from Jimmy Carter than from Reagan, but Reagan's personal magnetism was a powerful political force. His victory confirmed the shift of the South to the Republican Party.

Illinois, he succeeded in Hollywood in the late 1930s as a romantic lead actor while adopting the liberal politics common at the time. After World War II, he moved rapidly to the political right as a spokesman for big business. For several years, he traveled the country under the sponsorship of the General Electric Company, giving a standard speech that extolled the virtues of free enterprise. He entered politics with a rousing conservative speech at the 1964 Republican convention and then accepted the invitation of wealthy California Republicans to run for governor in 1966. In two terms in that office, he offered little formal leadership but spoke for a state and then a nation that were drifting toward more conservative values and expectations.

With a common touch that made him a favorite for a sizable segment of the public, Reagan tapped into the nostalgia for a simpler America. Although he was 69 when elected, his status as a movie and television personality made him seem up-to-date. His Hollywood background made it easy for him to use popular films to make his points. He once threatened to veto legislation by challenging Congress with Clint Eastwood's "Make my day." Many blockbuster movies reinforced two of Reagan's messages. One was the importance of direct

Ronald Reagan and his wife, Nancy, celebrate Reagan's inauguration as president.

confrontation with bad guys, ranging from terrorists (*Die Hard*) to drug dealers (*Lethal Weapon*). The second was the incompetence of government bureaucracies, whose elitist mistakes could only be set right by tough individuals like the movie heroes Dirty Harry Callahan and John Rambo.

Some of Reagan's most articulate support came from anti-Communist stalwarts of both parties, who feared that the United States was losing influence in the world. Despite Jimmy Carter's tough actions in 1979 and 1980 and increased defense spending, such conservatives had not trusted him to do enough. The inability to free the hostages in Iran grated. The Panama Canal and SALT II treaties seemed to give away American power. Soviet military buildup, charged the critics, was creating a "window of vulnerability," a dangerous period when the Soviet Union might threaten the United States with a first strike by nuclear weapons.

Other Reagan voters directed their anger at government bureaucracies. Wealthy entrepreneurs from the fast-growing South and West believed that Nixon-era federal offices, such as the Environmental Protection Agency and the Occupational Safety and Health Administration, were choking their businesses in red tape. Many of these critics had amassed new fortunes in oil, real estate, and retailing and hated the taxes that funded social programs.

Christian conservatives worried that social activists were using the federal courts to alter traditional values. Jimmy Carter, a member of the Southern Baptist church, had won a clear majority among white evangelical voters in 1976, but Reagan's contrasting position on school prayer and abortion gave him the edge in 1980 and made him the overwhelming preference of conservative Christian voters in 1984.

In many ways, the two groups were mismatched. Christian moralists had little in common with the high-rolling hedonists and Hollywood tycoons with whom Reagan rubbed shoulders. But they shared a deep distrust of the federal establishment.

Foreign policy activists and opponents of big government would have been unable to elect Reagan without disaffected blue-collar and middle-class voters who deserted the Democrats. Reagan's campaign hammered on the question "Are you better off than you were four years ago?" Democrats faced a special dilemma with the deepening tension between working-class white voters and black voters. They needed both groups to win but found white blue-collar voters deeply alienated by affirmative action and busing for school integration. When pollsters read white Detroiters a statement from Robert Kennedy that called on Americans to recognize special obligations to black citizens who had endured racial discrimination, responses were vehement: "I can't go along with that!" "That's bull!" The same sorts of voters worried about inflation and blamed their difficulties on runaway government spending.

A further Democratic challenge was Ronald Reagan's personal appeal. The new president won over many Americans by surviving a 1981 assassination attempt in fine spirits. Reagan's popularity compounded the Democrats' inability to excite younger voters. The mid-1980s consistently showed that roughly two-thirds of people in their twenties and early thirties were choosing the Republicans as the party of energy and new ideas, leaving the Democrats to the middle-aged and elderly.

In the election of 1984, Democrats sealed their fate by nominating Walter Mondale, who had been vice president under Carter. Mondale was earnest, honest, and dull. Reagan ran on the theme "It's Morning in America," with the message that a new age of pride and prosperity had begun. Mondale assumed that Americans cared enough about the exploding federal deficit that Reagan's defense spending had produced to accept an across-the-board tax increase. With the economy growing and inflation now in check, most voters did not want Mondale to remind them of long-range financial realities, and Reagan won reelection with 98 percent of the electoral votes. His election confirmed that the American public found conservative ideas increasingly attractive.

The New Conservatism

Reagan's approach to public policy drew on conservative intellectuals who offered a coherent critique of the New Deal–New Frontier approach to U.S. government. Some of the leading figures were journalists and academics who had embraced the ideas of the "vital center" a generation earlier (see Chapter 27). Now they feared that the antiwar movement had undermined the anti-Communist stance and that social changes were corrupting mainstream values. *Commentary* magazine became a platform for these combative neoconservative arguments. *The Public Interest* was a new magazine for conservative or skeptical academic writers.

Downsizing the Great Society.   Worries about big government permeated the critique of domestic policy. Edward

As the movie character John Rambo, actor Sylvester Stallone in the early 1980s gave voice to American frustrations with the country's place in the world. The Rambo movies clearly distinguished the good guys from the bad guys and suggested that stronger determination could have brought victory in Vietnam.

page to outspoken versions of neoconservatism. Politicians such as Congressman Jack Kemp built support for specific steps to cut economic regulation and encourage business enterprise.

The common themes of the conservative critique were simple: Free markets work better than government programs; government intervention does more harm than good; government assistance saps the initiative of the poor. In 1964, three-quarters of Americans had trusted Washington "to do what is right." By 1980, three-quarters were convinced that the federal government wasted tax money. The neoconservatives offered the details to support Reagan's own summary: "Government is not the solution to our problems; government is the problem." The cumulative effect of the neoconservative arguments was to trash the word "liberal" and convince many Americans that labor unions and minorities were "special interests" but that oil tycoons, defense contractors, and other members of Reagan's coalition were not.

The conservative cause found support in new "think tanks" and political lobbying organizations. Many conservatives were convinced that university faculty members were hopelessly liberal. In response, wealthy businesspeople funded alternative organizations, such as the Manhattan Institute, the Heritage Foundation, and the American Enterprise Institute, where conservative analysts could develop policy proposals and opinion pieces for newspapers. The result was to shift the terms of political discussion substantially in a conservative direction between 1975 and 1990.

Conservative political savvy. Conservatives promoted their ideology with new political tactics. Targeted mailings raised funds and mobilized voters with emotional appeals while bypassing the mass media, with their supposed preference for mainstream or liberal policies. Conservative organizers also knew how to use radio call-in shows to spread their message. Such appeals contrasted with the Democrats's reliance on more traditional ways to get out the vote through personal contacts and labor unions. Through the 1980s, Democrats repeatedly found themselves blindsided by creative Republican campaign tactics.

Reaganomics: Deficits and Deregulation

The heart of the 1980s revolution was the **Economic Recovery and Tax Act of 1981 (ERTA),** which reduced personal income tax rates by 25 percent over three years. The explicit goal was to stimulate business activity by lowering taxes overall and slashing rates for the rich. Cutting the government's

Banfield's radical ideas about the failures of the Great Society set the tone of the neoconservative analysis. In *The Unheavenly City* (1968), he questioned the basic idea of public solutions for social problems. He argued that inequality is based on human character and rooted in the basic structure of society; government action can only solve problems that require better engineering, such as pollution control, better highways, or the delivery of explosives to military targets. Government's job, said Banfield, was to preserve public order, not to right wrongs or encourage unrealistic expectations.

Other conservative writers elaborated Banfield's ideas. The most influential was Charles Murray, whose 1984 book, *Losing Ground,* tried to do for neoconservative domestic policy what Michael Harrington's *The Other America* had done for liberal policy. Murray's basic argument was simple: Welfare assistance hurt more than it helped, by encouraging dependency and discouraging individual efforts at self-improvement. Despite massive antipoverty and welfare efforts since 1965, he contended, poverty, minority unemployment, and deviant behavior had increased rather than decreased. The blame, he said, must lie in the welfare programs themselves. Scholars have shown that Murray's book distorts the evidence and makes flawed arguments, but it had a major impact on political debates.

Free market utopians. Another strand of conservative argument came from free market utopians. After years of stagflation, Americans were eager to hear that unleashing free markets would trigger renewed prosperity. The *Wall Street Journal* evolved from a narrow business newspaper into a national conservative forum by devoting its editorial total income by $747 billion over five years, ERTA meant less money for federal programs and more money in the hands of consumers and investors to stimulate economic growth.

Reagan's first budget director, David Stockman, later revealed a second goal. ERTA would lock in deficits by "pulling the revenue plug." Because defense spending and Social Security were untouchable, Congress would find it impossible to create and fund new programs without cutting old ones. Compared with spending patterns in effect in 1980, the Reagan administration also shifted $70 billion per year from domestic to military programs. The first year's tax reductions were accompanied by cuts of $40 billion in federal aid to mass transit, school lunches, and similar programs. If Americans still wanted social programs, they could enact them at the local or state level, but Washington would no longer pay.

The second part of the economic agenda was to free capitalists from government regulations, in the hope of increasing business innovation and efficiency. The **deregulation** revolution built on a head start from the 1970s. A federal antitrust case had split the unified Bell System of AT&T and its subsidiaries into seven regional telephone companies and opened long-distance service to competition. Congress also deregulated air travel in 1978. During the first 40 years of commercial air service, the Federal Aviation Administration had matched airlines and routes (treating air service like a public utility); deregulation now allowed air carriers to start and stop service at will, resulting in cheaper and more frequent air service for major hubs and poorer and more expensive service for small cities. Economists tend to be satisfied that the net gains have outweighed the costs.

Environmental regulation and federal lands.   Corporate America used the Reagan administration to attack environmental legislation as "strangulation by regulation." Reagan's new budgets sliced funding for the Environmental Protection Agency. Vice President Bush headed the White House Task Force on Regulatory Relief, which delayed or blocked regulations on hazardous wastes, automobile emissions, and exposure of workers to chemicals on the job.

Most attention, however, went to the controversial appointment of a Colorado lawyer, James Watt, as secretary of the interior. Watt had long worked to open up federal lands in the West to more intensive development. He was sympathetic to a western movement known as the **Sagebrush Rebellion,** which wanted the vast federal land holdings in the West transferred to the states for less environmental protection and more rapid economic use. He once blamed air pollution on natural emissions from trees and compared environmentalists to Nazis and Bolsheviks. Federal resource agencies sold trees to timber companies at a loss to the Treasury, expanded offshore oil drilling, and expedited exploration for minerals.

Deregulation of the banking industry.   The early 1980s also transformed American financial markets. Savings and loans had traditionally been conservative financial institutions that funneled individual savings into safe home mortgages. Under new rules, they began to compete for deposits by offering high interest rates and reinvesting the money in much riskier commercial real estate. By 1990, the result was a financial crisis in which bad loans destroyed hundreds of S&Ls, especially in the Southwest. American taxpayers were left to bail out depositors to the tune of hundreds of billions of dollars to prevent a collapse of the nation's financial and credit system.

With the deregulation of financial markets, corporate consolidations and mergers flourished. Corporate raiders raised money with "junk bonds"—high-interest, high-risk securities—and snapped up profitable and cash-rich companies that could be milked of profits and assets. The merger mania channeled capital into paper transactions rather than investments in new equipment and products. Another effect was to damage the economies of small and middle-sized communities by transferring control of local companies to outside managers.

In the short term, the national economy boomed in the mid-1980s. Deregulated credit, tax cuts, and massive deficit spending on defense fueled exuberant growth. The decade as a whole brought nearly 20 million new jobs, especially for professional and managerial workers, office support staff, salespeople, and workers providing personal services. Inflation dipped to 3 percent per year. The stock market mirrored the overall prosperity; the Dow Jones average of blue-chip industrial stock prices more than tripled from August 1982 to August 1987.

Crisis for Organized Labor

The flip side of the economic boom was another round in the Republican offensive against labor unions. Reagan set the tone when he fired more than 11,000 members of the Professional Air Traffic Controllers Organization for violating a no-strike clause in their hiring agreements. He claimed to be enforcing the letter of the law, but the message to organized labor was clear. For many years, corporations had hesitated to hire permanent replacements for striking workers. With Reagan's example, large companies, such as Hormel and Phelps-Dodge, chose that option, undercutting the strike as an effective union strategy. During the Reagan administration, the National Labor Relations Board and other federal agencies also weakened collective bargaining by their interpretation of labor-management regulations.

Decline of union membership and blue-collar jobs. Organized labor counted a million fewer members at the end of Reagan's administration in 1989 than in 1964, even though the number of employed Americans had nearly doubled. Many unions that had been the mainstays of the labor movement in the Roosevelt and Truman years found themselves in trouble, saddled with leaders who were unable to cope with the restructuring of the economy. As union membership declined and unions struggled to cope with the

The working-class family depicted on the television show *Roseanne* offered viewers a glimpse of the problems facing many Americans in an era of economic change marked by deindustrialization and the rise of service jobs.

changing economy, corporations seized the opportunity to demand wage rollbacks and concessions on working conditions as trade-offs for continued employment, squeezing workers in one plant and then using the settlement to pressure another. Workers in the 1970s and 1980s faced the threat that employers might move a factory to a new site elsewhere in the United States or overseas. Or a company might sell out to a new owner, who could close a plant and reopen without a union contract. One 16-year-old described the changes in the grocery chain where her father had worked for 26 years: "They're letting people go with no feelings for how long they've worked there, just lay 'em off. It's sad. He should be getting benefits after all these years and all the sacrifices he's made. Now they're almost ready to lay him off without a word."

Another cause for shrinking union membership was the overall decline of blue-collar jobs, from 36 percent of the American workforce in 1960 to roughly 25 percent at the end of the 1990s. Unionization of white-collar workers made up only part of the loss from manufacturing. Unions were most successful in recruiting government workers, such as police officers, teachers, and bus drivers. By the late 1980s, the American Federation of State, County, and Municipal Employees had twice the membership of the United Steel Workers. In the private sector, however, many white-collar jobs were in small firms that were difficult to organize.

Impact of economic restructuring.   Popular culture's best take on the problems of blue-collar America was the television situation comedy *Roseanne* (1988–1997). Living in an in-

dustrial satellite of Chicago, Roseanne and Dan Conner struggle to raise a family on the income from a series of jobs as small business owner, assembly-line worker, waitress, skilled laborer. The lifelong unionized factory job is a thing of the past as the shifting economy makes it hard to accumulate savings and stay ahead of the financial crises of normal life, let alone keep kids in college. A telling statistic about the problems of the real equivalents of the Conners was the increase in personal bankruptcy filings from roughly 300,000 per year in the early 1980s to 1,200,000 per year by the later 1990s.

In the 1950s and 1960s, increasing productivity, expanding markets for U.S. goods, and strong labor unions had made it possible for factory workers to enter the middle class. In an era of deindustrialization, however, companies replaced blue-collar workers with machinery or shifted production to nonunion plants. The corporate merger mania of the 1980s added to instability when takeover specialists loaded old companies with new debt, triggering efforts to cut labor costs, sell off plants, or raid pension funds for cash to pay the interest. Manufacturing employment in the 1980s declined by nearly 2 million jobs, with the expansion of high-tech manufacturing concealing much higher losses in traditional industries. In sum, while corporate merger specialists steered their BMWs along the fast lane to success, displaced mill hands drove battered pickups along potholed roads to nowhere.

An Acquisitive Society

The new prosperity fueled lavish living by the wealthy and a fascination with the "lifestyles of the rich and famous." The television show of the same name, which premiered in 1984, offered its viewers glimpses of "champagne wishes" and "caviar dreams" as lived by entertainment stars and business tycoons. Prime-time soap operas flourished, bringing to the small screen stories of intrigue among the rich folks of fast-growing Texas in *Dallas* (1978–1991), Colorado in *Dynasty* (1981–1989), and California in *Knots Landing* (1979–1993). With a few exceptions, even the "middle class" in television sitcoms enjoyed lives available only to the top 20 percent of Americans.

The national media in the early 1980s discovered yuppies, or young urban professionals, who were both a marketing category and a symbol of social change. These upwardly mobile professionals supposedly defined themselves by elitist consumerism. Middle-line retailers like Sears had clothed Americans for decades and furnished their homes. With the help of catalog shopping, status-seeking consumers now flocked to such upscale retailers as Neiman-Marcus and Bloomingdale's. Yuppie as a marketing category meanwhile

"*They're museum quality!*"

This 1993 cartoon contrasting a yuppie couple and a family dressed as hippies makes two points. While highlighting the rapid changes in American styles and tastes from the 1970s to the 1990s, it also satirizes the supposed yuppie tendency to value everything as a commodity or "collectible."

© The New Yorker Collection from CartoonBank.com/CORBIS

New movements in popular music reacted to the acquisitive 1980s. Punk rock pared rock-and-roll to its basics, lashing out at the emptiness of 1970s disco sound. Punk music influenced grunge bands such as Nirvana, which expressed alienation from consumerism. Hip-hop originated among African Americans and Latinos in New York, soon adding the angry and often violent lyrics of rap. Rap during the 1980s was about personal power and sex, but it also dealt with social inequities and deprivation and tapped some of the same anger and frustration that had motivated black power advocates in the 1960s. When it crossed into mainstream entertainment, it retained a hard-edged "attitude" that undercut any sense of complacency about an inclusive American society.

Mass Media and Fragmented Culture

On June 1, 1980, CNN Cable News Network gave television viewers their first chance to watch news coverage 24 hours a day. Newscasters Bernard Shaw and Mary Alice Williams brought instant information to an initial audience of 1.7 million subscribers; a decade later, CNN had hundreds of millions of viewers in more than 75 countries. Business executives in Zurich, college students in Nairobi, and farmers in Omaha all tuned in to the version of world events pulled together in CNN's Atlanta headquarters. CNN made a global reputation with live reporting on the pro-democracy protests of Chinese students in Beijing in 1989. When American bombs began to fall on Baghdad in January 1991, White House officials watched CNN to find out how their war was going.

Fourteen months after CNN went on the air, another new cable channel, MTV: Music Television, started broadcasting. By the time it reached the key New York and Los Angeles markets in January 1983, MTV's round-the-clock programming of music videos had created a new form of popular art and advertising. With its own programming aimed at viewers aged 18 to 34, MTV inspired Nickelodeon for kids and VH-1 for baby boomers.

CNN, MTV, and the rest of cable television reflected both the fragmentation of American society in the 1980s and 1990s and the increasing dependence on instant communication. As late as 1980, ordinary Americans had few choices for learning about their nation and world: virtually identical newscasts on NBC, CBS, and ABC and similar stories in *Time* and *Newsweek* helped to create a common understanding. Fifteen years later, they had learned to surf through dozens of cable channels in search of specialized programs and were

spawned variations, such as "buppie" for black urban professional. It was difficult for most Americans to feel much sympathy for the family in a *New York Times* profile in 1987 who had difficulty making ends meet on $600,000 a year.

Far richer than even such atypical yuppies were wheeler-dealers who made themselves into media stars of finance capitalism. The autobiography of Lee Iacocca, who had helped revive the fortunes of the Chrysler Corporation, was a bestseller in 1984, portraying the corporate executive as hero. *Forbes* magazine began to publish an annual list of the nation's 400 richest people. Long before his television show, real-estate developer Donald Trump made himself a celebrity with a well-publicized personal life and a stream of projects crowned with his name: office tower, hotel, casino. Before he admitted to violating the law against profiting from insider information, the corporate-merger expert Ivan Boesky had told a business-school audience, "Greed is all right. You shouldn't feel guilty," epitomizing an era of big business takeovers driven by paper profits rather than underlying economic fundamentals. In his bestselling novel *The Bonfire of the Vanities* (1987), Tom Wolfe depicted a New York where the art dealers and stockbrokers of glitzy Manhattan meet the poor of the devastated South Bronx only through an automobile accident, to their mutual incomprehension and ruin.

economy because of poor education, drug abuse, or sheer laziness. In fact, talk of an underclass was a way to avoid confronting the realities of limited economic opportunity. Most of the nation's millions of poor people lived in households with employed adults. In 1992, fully 18 percent of all full-time jobs did not pay enough to lift a family of four out of poverty, a jump of 50 percent over the proportion of underpaid jobs in 1981. One of the biggest barriers to better employment was not a disinterest in work, but rather the isolation of many job seekers in poverty neighborhoods without access to suburban jobs or the informal social networks that are the best way to find good employment.

The wage gap and the feminization of poverty.   Nor could most women, even those working full-time, expect to earn as much as men. In the 1960s and 1970s, the average working woman earned just 60 percent of the earnings of the average man (see Figure 30–2). Only part of the wage gap could be explained by measurable factors, such as education or experience. The gap narrowed in the 1980s and 1990s, with women's earnings rising to 75 percent of men's by 2003. About half of the change was the result of bad news—the decline of earnings among men as high-wage factory jobs disappeared. The other half was the positive result of better-educated younger women finding better jobs. Indeed, women earned 57 percent of the four-year college degrees awarded in 2002 (up from 38 percent in 1960) and 47 percent of first professional degrees (up from 3 percent).

Nevertheless, the low earning capacity of women with limited educations meant that women were far more likely than men to be poor. Women constituted nearly two-thirds of poor adults at the end of the 1980s. Only 6 percent of married-couple households were below poverty level, but 32 percent of households headed by a woman without a husband present were poor. The feminization of poverty and American reliance on private support for child rearing also meant that children had a higher chance of living in poverty than adults and that poor American children were worse off than their peers in other advanced nations.

Homelessness in America.   Falling below even the working poor were growing numbers of homeless Americans. Large cities have always had transient laborers, derelict alcoholics, and voluntarily homeless hobos. In the 1980s, several factors made homelessness more visible and pressing. A new approach to the treatment of the mentally ill reduced

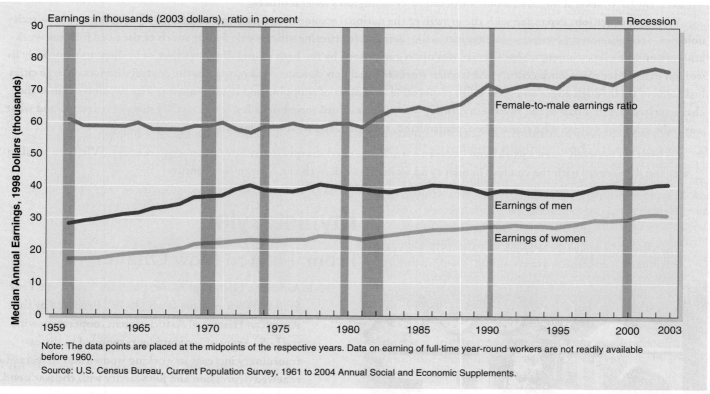

Note: The data points are placed at the midpoints of the respective years. Data on earning of full-time year-round workers are not readily available before 1960.

Source: U.S. Census Bureau, Current Population Survey, 1961 to 2004 Annual Social and Economic Supplements.

FIGURE 30–2   Comparison of Men's and Women's Earnings, 1960–2003
U.S. Census data show that the median earnings of women who worked full time and year round compared to those of men. Since the 1960s, the gap between women and men has narrowed. One reason is better pay for jobs traditionally held by women, but another has been the declining earning power of men without college educations. Nevertheless, the gender gap in earning power remains an important economic issue.

the population of mental hospitals from 540,000 in 1960 to only 140,000 in 1980. Deinstitutionalized patients were supposed to receive community-based treatment, but many ended up on the streets and in overnight shelters. New forms of self-destructive drug abuse, such as crack addiction, joined alcoholism. A boom in downtown real estate destroyed old skid-row districts with their bars, missions, and dollar-a-night hotels.

These factors tripled the number of permanently homeless people during the early and middle 1980s, from 200,000 to somewhere between 500,000 and 700,000. Twice or three times that many may have been homeless for part of a given year. For every person in a shelter on a given night, two people were sleeping on sidewalks, in parks, in cars, and in abandoned buildings. Because homeless people made middle-class Americans uncomfortable, it was reassuring to assume they were outsiders attracted by local conditions, such as tolerant attitudes (as some claimed in Seattle) or mild climate (as some claimed in Phoenix). In fact, few of the down-and-out have the resources to move from town to town. Bag ladies, panhandlers, working people, and yuppies were all parts of the same communities, neighbors in the broadest sense.

Consolidating the Revolution: George Bush

In 1988 George H. W. Bush, Reagan's vice president for eight years, won the presidential election with 56 percent of the popular vote and 40 out of 50 states. Bush's view of national and world politics reflected a background in which personal connections counted. He was raised as part of the New England elite, built an oil business in Texas, and then held a series of high-level federal appointments. As someone who had survived 20 years of bureaucratic infighting, his watchword was prudence. Using a comparison from baseball, Bush described himself as the sort of guy who would play the averages and "bunt 'em over" rather than go for the big inning.

Michael Dukakis, the Democratic nominee in 1988, was a dry-as-dust, by-the-numbers manager who offered the American people "competence." The Bush campaign director, Lee Atwater, looked for hot-button issues that could fit onto a three-by-five card. He found that Dukakis as governor of Massachusetts had delayed cleanup of Boston Harbor, favored gun control, and vetoed a bill requiring schoolchildren to recite the Pledge of Allegiance (arguing

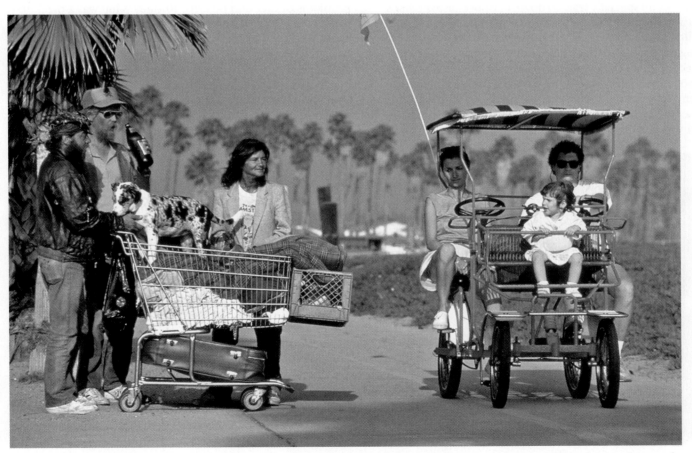

An affluent family pedals past a group of homeless people in Santa Barbara, California. In the 1980s a combination of rising housing prices and the closing of most mental hospitals pushed increasing numbers of Americans onto the streets. Estimates of the number of homeless Americans in the late 1980s ranged from 300,000 to 3 million, depending on the definition of homelessness and the political goals of the estimator.

correctly that it would be overturned in the courts). Even more damaging, Massachusetts officials had allowed a murderer named Willie Horton a weekend furlough from prison, during which he committed a brutal rape. Pro-Bush advertisements tapped into real worries among the voters—fear of crime, racial tension (Horton was black), eroding social values. George Bush, despite his background in prep schools and country clubs, came out looking tough as nails, while the Democrats looked inept.

The ads locked Bush into a rhetorical war on crime and drugs that was his major domestic policy. Americans had good cause to be worried about public safety, but most were generally unaware that the likelihood of becoming the target of a violent crime had leveled off and would continue to fall in the 1990s or that crime was far worse in minority communities than elsewhere, in part due to gang- and drug-related activities.

The Bush administration stepped up the fight against illegal drugs, and the federal drug-control budget tripled. In the early 1980s, a quarter of federal prison inmates were in jail for drug offenses. Longer sentences, mandatory jail time, and tougher parole terms for drug crimes pushed the proportion over 50 percent by 1990. The United States tried to stop the flow of cocaine by blockading its borders with airplanes, sea patrols, and specially trained dogs at airport customs lines. Casual and middle-class use of cocaine and marijuana began to decline in the mid-1980s. Drug use and drug sales were increasingly a problem of poor and minority neighborhoods.

George Bush believed that Americans wanted government to leave them alone. He ignored a flood of new ideas from entrepreneurial conservatives, such as HUD Secretary Jack Kemp. The major legislation from the Bush administration was a transportation bill that shifted federal priorities from highway building toward mass transit and the **Americans with Disabilities Act** (1990) to prevent discrimination against people with physical handicaps. In the areas of crime and healthcare, however, Bush's lack of leadership left continuing problems.

The same attitude produced weak economic policies. The national debt had amounted to 50 percent of personal savings in 1980 but swelled to 125 percent by 1990. The massive budget deficits of the 1980s combined with growing trade deficits to turn the United States from an international creditor to a debtor nation. When Reagan took office, foreigners owed the United States and its citizens the equivalent of $2,500 for every American family. When Bush took office, the United States had used up its foreign assets and become the world's biggest debtor, with liabilities that averaged $7,000 per family. After pledging no new taxes in his campaign, Bush backed into a tax increase in 1990. A strong leader might have justified the taxes to the nation, but voters found it hard to forget the president's waffling and attempts to downplay the importance of his decision.

The most conspicuous domestic event of the Bush administration—the "Rodney King riot" of April 1992 in Los Angeles—was a reminder of the nation's inattention to the problems of race and poverty. Rodney King was a black motorist who had been savagely clubbed and kicked by police officers while being arrested after a car chase on March 3, 1991. A nearby resident captured the beating on videotape from his apartment. Within two days, the tape was playing and replaying on national television. The grainy pictures shocked the nation and confirmed African Americans' worst fears about biased police behavior. Early the next year, the four officers stood trial for unjustified use of force before a suburban jury. The televised trial and the unexpected verdict of not guilty on April 29 stirred deep anger that escalated into four days of rioting.

The disorder revealed multiple tensions among ethnic groups and was far more complex than the Watts outbreak of 1965 (see Chapter 29). African Americans from south-central Los Angeles participated, but so did Central American and Mexican immigrants in adjacent districts, who accounted for about one-third of the 12,000 arrests. The disorder spread south to Long Beach and north to the edge of upscale neighborhoods in Westwood and Beverly Hills. Rioters assaulted the downtown police headquarters, city hall, and the *Los Angeles Times* building. As in 1965, some targets were white passers-by and symbols of white authority. But members of competing minority groups were also victims as angry black people targeted hundreds of Korean-owned and Vietnamese-owned shops as symbols of economic discrimina-

After a jury acquitted the police officers involved in the beating of motorist Rodney King in April 1992, much of Los Angeles erupted in rioting that left much smoldering buildings and revealed deep racial and economic tensions.

tion. Four days of disorder left 58 people dead, mostly African Americans and Latinos.

The Second (Short) Cold War

Ronald Reagan entered office determined to reassert U.S. leadership in world affairs and not to lose the Cold War. He considered the Soviet Union not a coequal nation with legitimate world interests but an "evil empire," like something from the *Star Wars* movies. After the era of détente, global tensions had started to mount in the late 1970s. They were soon higher than they had been since the 1960s. But by the end of Reagan's two terms, unexpected changes were rapidly bringing the Cold War to an end, and George Bush faced a radically new set of foreign policy issues.

Confronting the Soviet Union

Who renewed the Cold War after Nixon's diplomacy of *détente* and Carter's early efforts at negotiation? The Soviets had pursued military expansion in the 1970s, triggering the fear that they might stage a nuclear Pearl Harbor. The Soviet Union in 1980 was supporting Marxist regimes in civil wars in Angola, Ethiopia, Nicaragua, and especially Afghanistan, where its 1980 intervention led to a decade of costly and futile military occupation. Were these actions parts of a careful plan? Or did they result from the Cold War inertia of a rudderless nation that reacted to situations one at a time? Given the aging Soviet leadership and the economic weaknesses revealed in the late 1980s, it makes more sense to see the Soviets as muddling along rather than executing a well-planned global strategy.

On the American side, Reagan's readiness to confront "the focus of evil in the modern world" reflected the views of many conservative supporters that the Soviet Union was a monolithic and ideologically motivated foe bent on world conquest. In hindsight, some Reaganites claim that the administration's foreign policy and massive increases in defense spending were part of a deliberate and coordinated scheme to check a Soviet offensive and bankrupt the Soviet Union by pushing it into a new arms race. It is just as likely, however, that the administration's defense and foreign policy initiatives were a set of discrete but effective decisions.

The Reagan administration reemphasized central Europe as the focus of superpower rivalry, just as it had been in the 1950s and early 1960s. To counter improved Soviet armaments, the United States began to place cruise missiles and mid-range Pershing II missiles in Europe in 1983. NATO governments approved the action, but it frightened millions of their citizens. By the mid-1980s, many Europeans saw the United States as the dangerous and aggressive force in world affairs and the Soviet Union as the voice of moderation—international attitudes that continue to this day.

The controversy over new missiles was part of new thinking about nuclear strategy. Multiple warheads on U.S. missiles already allowed Washington to target 25,000 separate places in the Soviet Union. National Security Directive D-13 (1981) set forth a new doctrine that it might be possible to fight and win a nuclear war despite its enormous costs. A reactivated civil defense program also suggested that the United States was serious about nuclear war. All Americans needed for survival, said one administration official, were "enough shovels" to dig fallout shelters.

Escalation of the nuclear arms race reinvigorated the antiwar and antinuclear movement in the United States as well as Europe. Drawing on the experience of the antiwar movement, the nuclear-freeze campaign caught the imagination of many Americans in 1981 and 1982. It sought to halt the manufacture and deployment of new atomic weapons by the great powers. The movement gained urgency when distinguished scientists argued that the smoke and dust thrown up by an atomic war would devastate the ecology of the entire globe by triggering "nuclear winter." Nearly a million people turned out for a nuclear-freeze rally in New York in 1982. Hundreds of local communities endorsed the freeze or took the symbolic step of declaring themselves nuclear-free zones.

In response, Reagan announced the **Strategic Defense Initiative (SDI),** or Star Wars program, in 1983. SDI was to deploy new defenses that could intercept and destroy ballistic missiles as they rose from the ground and arced through space. Ideas included superlasers, killer satellites, and clouds of projectiles to rip missiles to shreds before they neared their targets. All of the technologies were untested; some existed only in the imagination. Few scientists thought that SDI could work. Many arms control experts thought that defensive systems were dangerous and destabilizing, because strong defenses suggested that a nation might be willing to risk a nuclear exchange. Nevertheless, President Reagan found SDI appealing, for it offered a way around the balance of terror.

Risky Business: Foreign Policy Adventures

The same administration that sometimes seemed reckless in its grand strategy also took risks to assert U.S. influence in global trouble spots to block or roll back Soviet influence. Reagan asserted America's right to intervene anywhere in the world to support local groups fighting against Marxist governments. The assumption underlying this assertion, which later became known as the **Reagan Doctrine,** was that Soviet-influenced governments in Asia, Africa, and Latin America needed to be eliminated if the United States was to win the Cold War.

Nevertheless, Reagan kept the United States out of a major war and backed off in the face of serious trouble. Foreign interventions were designed to achieve symbolic victories rather than change the global balance of power. The exception was the Caribbean and Central America, the "backyard" where the United States had always claimed an overriding interest and where left-wing action infuriated Reagan's conservative supporters.

On October 25, 1983, for example, U.S. troops invaded the small independent Caribbean island of Grenada. A left-leaning government had invited Cuban help in building an airfield, which the United States feared would turn into a Cuban military base. Two thousand American troops overcame Cuban soldiers thinly disguised as construction workers, "rescued" American medical students, and put a more sympathetic and locally popular government in power.

Intervention and covert activities in Central America. The Reagan administration attributed political turmoil in Central America to Soviet influence and to arms and agitators from Soviet-backed Cuba. Between 1980 and 1983, the United States sent more military aid to conservative governments and groups in Central America than it had during the previous 30 years. Indeed, Central America became the focus of a secret foreign policy operated by the CIA and then by National Security Council (NSC) staff, since a Democratic Congress was not convinced of the danger. The CIA and the NSC engaged not just in espionage but in direct covert operations. The chief target was Nicaragua, the Central American country where leftist Sandinista rebels had overthrown the Somoza dictatorship in 1979. Reagan and his people were determined to prevent Nicaragua from becoming "another Cuba," especially when Sandinistas helped left-wing insurgents in neighboring El Salvador. In the early 1980s, Reagan approved CIA plans to arm and organize approximately 10,500 so-called Contras, from the remnants of Somoza's national guard. From bases in Honduras, the Contras harassed the Sandinistas with sabotage and raids. Reagan called the Contras "freedom fighters," listened to stories of their exploits, and hunched over maps to follow their operations in detail. Meanwhile, Americans with different views aided refugees from the war zones of Central America through the church-based sanctuary movement ("sanctuary" could imply both legal economic assistance and direct defiance of efforts to deport refugees).

The Reagan administration bent the law to support its covert effort to overthrow the Sandinista regime. An unsympathetic Congress blocked U.S. funding for the Contras. In response, CIA director William Casey directed Lieutenant Colonel Oliver North of the National Security Council staff to illegally organize aid from private donors. The arms pipeline operated until a supply plane was shot down in 1986. The Contras failed as a military effort, but the civil war and international pressure persuaded the Sandinistas to allow free elections that led to a democratic, centrist government.

The war against drugs.   The American war against drugs was simultaneously shaping U.S. policy in the Caribbean and straining relations with Latin America. The United States pressured Colombia and Peru to uproot coca plants grown by poor farmers. As president, George Bush parlayed the war on drugs into war on Panama during his first year in office, extending the American tradition of ousting uncooperative governments around the Caribbean. General Manuel Noriega, the Panamanian strongman, had once been on the CIA payroll. He had since turned to international drug sales in defiance of United States antismuggling efforts. On December 20, 1989, American troops invaded Panama, hunted down Noriega, and brought him back to stand trial in the United States on drug-trafficking charges. A handful of Americans and thousands of Panamanians died, many of them civilians caught in the crossfire.

Intervention in the Middle East.   If the results of intervention in Nicaraugua and Panama were mixed, intervention in the Middle East was a failure. In 1982 Israel invaded Lebanon, a small nation to its north, to clear Palestinian guerrillas from its borders and set up a friendly Lebanese government. The Israeli army bogged down in a civil war between Christian Arabs and Muslims. Reagan sent U.S. Marines to preserve the semblance of a Lebanese state and provide a face-saving exit for Israel. Although the Marines arrived in Beirut to interpose themselves between Israeli tanks and the Lebanese, they remained on an ill-defined "presence mission" that angered Arabs and motivated terrorist actions against Israel and the United States by Islamic radicals. In October 1983, a terrorist car bomb killed 241 Marines in their barracks. The remainder were soon gone, confirming the Syrian observation that Americans were "short of breath" when it came to Middle East politics. The debacle in Lebanon undermined U.S.-backed peace initiatives in the Middle East. Continuing terrorist acts such as taking Americans hostage, bombing cruise ships, and sabotaging airliners were aimed at inhibiting U.S. support of Israel.

The Iran-Contra Affair.   Even less effective were the Reagan administration's secret efforts to sell weapons to Iran in return for Iranian help in securing the release of Americans held hostage by pro-Iranian Islamic radicals in Lebanon. The United States in 1985 joined Israel in selling 500 antitank missiles to Iran, then embroiled in a long, bitter war with Iraq. The deal followed stern public pronouncements that the United States would never negotiate with terrorists and considered Iran's religious leaders to be backers of international terrorism. It also violated the official trade embargo against Iran, which had been in place since the U.S. embassy seizure in 1979. In May 1986, National Security adviser Robert McFarlane flew to Iran for more arms-for-hostages talks, carrying a chocolate cake and a Bible autographed by Reagan to present to the Iranian leader Ayatollah Khomeini. The pro-Iranian radicals released several hostages, but others were soon taken. When the deals came to light in 1986 and congressional hearings were held in the summer of 1987, Americans were startled to learn that Colonel North had funneled millions of dollars from the arms sales to the Nicaraguan Contras in a double evasion of the law.

As had been true with Watergate, the Iran-Contra affair was a two-sided scandal. First was the blatant misjudgment of operating a secret, bumbling, and unlawful foreign policy that depended on international arms dealers and ousted Nicaraguan military officers. Second was a concerted effort to cover up the illegal and unconstitutional actions. North shredded relevant documents and lied to Congress. In his final report in 1994, Special Prosecutor Lawrence Walsh found that President Reagan and Vice President Bush were aware of much of what had gone on and had participated in efforts to withhold information and mislead Congress.

U.S. policy in Asia.   American policy in Asia was a refreshing contrast with practices in Central America and the Middle East. In the Philippines, American diplomats helped push corrupt President Ferdinand Marcos out and opened the way for a popular uprising to put Corazon Aquino in office. Secretary of State George Shultz made sure that the United States supported popular democracy while reassuring the Philippine military. In South Korea, the United States similarly helped ease out an unpopular dictator by firmly supporting democratic elections that brought in a more popular but still pro-American government.

Embracing *Perestroika*

Thaw in the Cold War started in Moscow as Soviet leaders sought to salvage a system under severe economic stress. Mikhail Gorbachev became general secretary of the Communist Party in 1985, when the Soviet Union was trapped in the sixth year of its failed attempt to control Afghanistan. Gorbachev was the picture of vigor compared to his three elderly predecessors. A master of public relations who charmed western Europe's leaders and public, he was also a modernizer in a long Russian tradition that stretched back to Tsar Peter the Great in the eighteenth century. Gorbachev startled Soviet citizens by urging *glasnost,* or political openness, with free discussion of issues and relaxation of controls on the press. He followed by setting the goal of *perestroika,* or restructuring of the painfully bureaucratic Soviet economy that was falling behind capitalist nations. His hope was that market-oriented reforms would help the Soviet Union keep up with the United States.

Gorbachev decided that he needed to reduce the crushing burden of Soviet defense spending if the Soviet Union was to have any chance of modernizing. During Reagan's second term, the Soviets offered one concession after another in a drive for arms control. They agreed to cut the number of land-based strategic weapons in half. They gave up their demand for an end to SDI research. In negotiations on conventional forces in Europe, they accepted bigger cuts for the Warsaw Pact nations than for NATO. They even agreed to on-site inspections to control chemical weapons.

Reagan had the vision (or audacity) to embrace the new Soviet position. He cast off decades of belief in the dangers of Soviet Communism and took Gorbachev seriously. One of his reasons for SDI had been his personal belief that the abolition of nuclear weapons was better than fine-tuning the balance of terror. Now he was willing to forget his own rhetoric. He frightened his own staff when he met with Gorbachev in the summer of 1986 and accepted the principle of deep cuts in strategic forces. Reagan explained that when he railed against the evil empire, he had been talking about Brezhnev and the bad old days; Gorbachev and *glasnost* were different.

In the end, Reagan negotiated the **Intermediate Nuclear Force Agreement (INF)** over the strong objections of the CIA and the Defense Department. INF was the first true nuclear-disarmament treaty (see Overview, Controlling Nuclear Weapons: Four Decades of Effort). Previous agreements had only slowed the growth of nuclear weapons; they were "speed limits" for the arms race. The new pact matched Soviet SS-20s with U.S. cruise missiles as an entire class of weapons that would be destroyed, with on-site inspections for verification.

Crisis and Democracy in Eastern Europe

President Bush loved to run the world by Rolodex. When someone's name came up at a formal dinner, he was likely to grab a phone and call the person. When Congress was heading in the wrong direction, he started dialing senators and representatives. When a crisis threatened world peace, he would start chatting with presidents and prime ministers. He viewed diplomacy as a series of conversations and friendships among leaders, not the reconciliation of differing national interests.

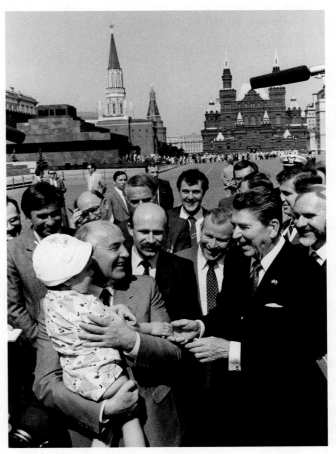

Mikhail Gorbachev, holding the child, hosted a summit meeting with President Reagan in Moscow in May 1988. Their smiles ignored the lack of progress toward disarmament beyond the Intermediate Nuclear Force Agreement of the previous year.

OVERVIEW

Controlling Nuclear Weapons: Four Decades of Effort

Limiting the testing of nuclear weapons	Limited Test Ban Treaty (1963)	Banned nuclear testing in the atmosphere, ocean, and outer space.
	Comprehensive Test	Banned all nuclear tests, including underground tests.
	Ban Treaty (1996)	Rejected by U.S. Senate in 1999.
Halting the spread of nuclear weapons	Nuclear Non-Proliferation Treaty (1968)	Pledged five recognized nuclear nations (United States, Soviet Union, Britain, France, China) to pursue disarmament in good faith, and 140 other nations not to acquire nuclear weapons.
	Strategic Arms Limitation Treaty (SALT I, 1972)	Limited the number of nuclear-armed missiles and bombers maintained by the United States and Soviet Union. Closely associated with U.S.-Soviet agreement to limit deployment of antiballistic missile systems to one site each.
	Strategic Arms Limitation Treaty (SALT II, 1979)	Further limited the number of nuclear-armed missiles and bombers. Not ratified but followed by Carter and Reagan administrations.
Reducing the number of nuclear weapons	Intermediate Nuclear Force Agreement (1987)	Required the United States to eliminate 846 nuclear armed cruise missiles, and the Soviet Union to eliminate 1,846 SS-20 missiles.
	Strategic Arms Reduction Treaty (START I, 1991)	By July 1999, led to reductions of approximately 2,750 nuclear warheads by the United States and 3,725 warheads by the nations of the former USSR.
	Strategic Arms Reduction Treaty (START II, 1993)	Set further cuts in nuclear arsenals. Ratified by Russia in April 2000. Russia withdrew in 2002 after the U.S. abandoned the Anti-Ballistic Missile Treaty.
	Strategic Offensive Reductions (2002)	Russia and the United States each agree to deploy no more than 1,700–2,200 strategic nuclear warheads.

Data Source: Arms Control Association.

As a believer in personal diplomacy, George Bush based much of his foreign policy on his changing attitudes toward Mikhail Gorbachev. He started lukewarm, talking tough to please the Republican right wing. Bush feared that Gorbachev, by instituting reforms that challenged the entrenched Communist Party leaders, was being imprudent: one of the worst things he could say about another leader. Before 1989 was over, however, the president had decided that Gorbachev was OK. For the next two years, the United States pushed the prodemocratic transformation of eastern Europe while being careful not to gloat in public or damage Gorbachev's position at home. Bush tried not to push the Soviet Union too hard and infuriate Russian hard-liners. "I don't want to do something that would inadvertently set back the progress," Bush said. Later asked whether the United States had a new foe after the end of the Cold War, Bush answered without hesitation, "The enemy is unpredictability. The enemy is instability."

The end of Communist regimes in Eastern Europe. The people of eastern Europe overcame both U.S. and Soviet caution. Gorbachev had urged his eastern European allies to emulate *perestroika* to free their economies from stifling controls and proclaimed what his Foreign Ministry called the "Sinatra doctrine," alluding to the ballad "My Way" popularized by Frank Sinatra. Each Communist nation could "do it its way" without fearing the Soviet tanks that had crushed change in Hungary in 1956 and Czechoslovakia in 1968. Instead of careful economic liberalization, the Warsaw Pact system collapsed. Poland held free elections in June 1989,

Hungary adopted a democratic constitution in October, and prodemocracy demonstrations then forced out Communist leaders in other eastern European countries. When East Germans began to flee westward through Hungary, the East German regime bowed to mounting pressure and opened the Berlin Wall on November 9. By the end of 1989, there were new democratic or non-Communist governments in Czechoslovakia, Romania, Bulgaria, and East Germany. These largely peaceful revolutions destroyed the military and economic agreements that had harnessed the satellites to the Soviet economy (the Warsaw Pact and Comecon). The Soviet Union swallowed hard, accepted the loss of its satellites, and slowly withdrew its army from eastern Europe.

German reunification and the dissolution of the Soviet Union.   Events in Europe left German reunification as a point of possible conflict. Soviet policy since 1945 had sought to prevent the reemergence of a strong, united Germany that might again threaten its neighbors. West German Chancellor Helmut Kohl removed one obstacle when he reassured Poland and Russia that Germany would seek no changes in the boundaries drawn after World War II. By July 1990, the United States and the Soviet Union had agreed that a reunited Germany would belong to NATO. The decision satisfied France and Britain that a stronger Germany would still be under the influence of the Western allies. In October, the two Germanies completed their political unification, although it would be years before their mismatched economies functioned as one. Reunification was the last step in the diplomatic legacy of World War II.

The final act in the transformation of the Soviet Union began with a failed coup against Mikhail Gorbachev in August 1991. The Soviet Union had held free elections in 1989. Now Gorbachev scheduled a vote on a new constitution that would decrease the power of the central government. Old-line Communist bureaucrats who feared the change arrested Gorbachev in his vacation house and tried to take over the government apparatus in Moscow. They turned out to be bumblers and drunks who had not secured military support and even failed to take over radio and television stations. Boris Yeltsin, president of the Russian Republic, organized the resistance. Muscovites flocked to support Yeltsin and

defied tank crews in front of the Russian parliament building. Within three days, the plotters themselves were under arrest.

The coup hastened the fragmentation of the Soviet Union. Before the month was out, the Soviet parliament banned the Communist Party. Gorbachev soon resigned. Previously suppressed nationalist feelings caused all 15 component republics of the Soviet Union to declare their independence. The superpower Union of Soviet Socialist Republics ceased to exist. Russia remained the largest and strongest of the new states, followed by Ukraine and Kazakhstan.

The wall that divided East from West Berlin from 1962 to 1989 was a hated symbol of the Cold War. When the Communist government of East Germany collapsed in November 1989, jubilant Berliners celebrated the opening of the wall and the reuniting of the divided city.

The end of the Cold War leaves the historical assessment of the last half-century of U.S. foreign policy open to debate. Analysts agree that the relentless pressure of American defense spending helped bankrupt and undermine the Soviet Union. It is an open question whether this defense spending also weakened the U.S. economy and America's ability to compete in the world marketplace. Some scholars see the demise of the Soviet empire as ultimate justification for 40 years of Cold War. Dissenters argue the opposite— that the collapse of European Communism shows that American leaders had magnified its threat. Before we can choose among these views, we need to wait for scholars to explore Russian archives and develop a fuller history of Soviet Cold War policy to place alongside our understanding of U.S. policy (see Overview, Why Did the Cold War End?).

The Persian Gulf War

On August 2, 1990, President Saddam Hussein of Iraq seized the small neighboring oil-rich country of Kuwait. The quick conquest gave Iraq control of 20 percent of the world's oil production and reserves. President Bush demanded unconditional withdrawal, enlisted European and Arab allies in an anti-Iraq coalition, and persuaded Saudi Arabia to accept substantial U.S. forces to protect it against Iraqi invasion. Within weeks, the Saudis were host to tens of thousands of U.S. soldiers and hundreds of aircraft.

The background for Iraq's invasion was a simmering dispute over border oil fields and islands in the Persian Gulf. Iraq was a dictatorship that had just emerged from an immensely costly eight-year war with Iran. Saddam Hussein had depended on help from the United States and Arab nations in this war, but Iraq was now economically exhausted. Kuwait was a small, rich nation whose ruling dynasty enjoyed few friends but plenty of oil royalties. The U.S. State Department had signaled earlier in 1990 that it might support some concessions by Kuwait in its dispute with Iraq. Saddam Hussein read the signal as an open invitation to do what he wanted; having been favored in the past by the United States, he probably expected denunciations but no military response.

The Iraqis gave George Bush a golden opportunity to assert America's world influence. The Bush administration was concerned that Iraq might target oil-rich Saudi Arabia. The importance of Middle Eastern oil helped to enlist France and Britain as military allies and to secure billions of dollars from Germany and Japan. Iraq had antagonized nearly all its neighbors. The collapse of Soviet power and Gorbachev's interest in cooperating with the United States meant that the Soviets would not interfere with U.S. plans.

Bush and his advisers offered a series of justifications for U.S. actions. First, and most basic, were the desire to punish armed aggression and the presumed need to protect Iraq's other neighbors. In fact, there was scant evidence of Iraqi preparations against Saudi Arabia. The buildup of U.S. air power plus effective economic sanctions would have accomplished both protection and punishment. Sanctions and diplomatic pressure might also have brought withdrawal from most or all of Kuwait. However, additional American objectives— to destroy Iraq's capacity to create nuclear weapons and to topple Saddam's regime—would require direct military action.

The Persian Gulf itself offered an equally golden opportunity to the U.S. and allied armed forces. Here were no tangled jungles, invisible guerrillas, or civilians caught in a civil war. The terrain was open and nearly uninhabited. The enemy had committed regular forces to traditional battle in open land outside Iraq's cities, where the superiority of American equipment and training would be telling. Indeed, the United States could try out the tactics of armored maneuver and close land-air cooperation that the Pentagon had devised to protect Germany against Soviet invasion.

Bush probably decided on war in October, eventually increasing the number of American troops in Saudi Arabia to 580,000. The United States stepped up diplomatic pressure by securing a series of increasingly tough United Nations resolutions that culminated in November 1990 with Security Council Resolution 678, authorizing "all necessary means" to liberate Kuwait. The president convinced Congress to

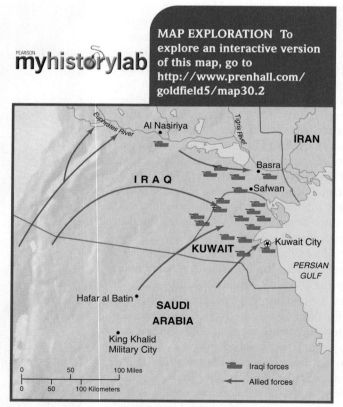

MAP 30–2   The Persian Gulf War
Ground operations against Iraq in the Persian Gulf War followed six weeks of aerial bombardment. The ground attack, which met quick success, was a multinational effort by the United States, Britain, France, Saudi Arabia, and other Arab nations threatened by an aggressive Iraq. The war freed Kuwait from Iraqi occupation but stopped before forcing a change in Iraq's government.

OVERVIEW

Why Did the Cold War End?

Commentators have offered a number of explanations for the rapid failure of the USSR and the collapse of Soviet power at the end of the 1980s. All of these factors made contributions to the complex unraveling of the Cold War.

Economic exhaustion:	The United States in the late 1970s embarked on a great modernization and expansion of its military forces. The USSR exhausted its economy and revealed its technical backwardness by trying to keep pace. Gorbachev's policy of *perestroika* was an attempt to reduce the bureaucratic inertia of the economy.
Failure of leadership:	The Soviet Union in the 1970s and early 1980s was governed by unimaginative bureaucrats. A closed elite that thought only of preserving their privileges and authority could not adapt to a changing world. The policy of *glasnost* was an effort to encourage new ideas.
Intervention in Afghanistan:	The disastrous intervention in Afghanistan revealed the limits of Soviet military power. It alienated the large Muslim population of the USSR and brought disillusionment with the incompetence of Soviet leaders.
Triumph of democratic ideas:	As political discussion became more free, the appeal of democratic ideas took on its own momentum, especially in eastern European satellite nations such as East Germany, Czechoslovakia, and Poland.
Power of nationalism:	The collapse of the Soviet empire was triggered by the resurgence of national sentiments throughout the Soviet empire. National sentiments fueled the breakaway of the eastern European satellite nations such as Hungary, Romania, and Poland. Nationalism also broke up the USSR itself as 14 smaller socialist republics declared independence from the Russian-dominated Union.

agree to military action under the umbrella of the UN. The United States ignored compromise plans floated by France and last-minute concessions from Iraq.

War began one day after the UN's January 15 deadline for Iraqi withdrawal from Kuwait. **Operation Desert Storm** opened with massive air attacks on command centers, transportation facilities, and Iraqi forward positions. The air war destroyed 40 to 50 percent of Iraqi tanks and artillery by late February. The attacks also seriously hurt Iraqi civilians by disrupting utilities and food supplies.

Americans found the **Persian Gulf War** fascinating. They bought millions of Middle East maps to follow the conflict. They watched CNN's live transmission of Baghdad under bombardment. They read about Stealth fighter bombers that were invisible to radar and about precision-guided missiles (although most of the damage came from traditional bombing and low-tech A-10 antitank aircraft).

The 40-day rain of bombs was the prelude to a ground attack (see Map 30–2). Despite Saddam Hussein's threats that the coalition faced the "mother of all battles," the Iraqi military made the land war easy. They concentrated their forces near the Persian Gulf in Kuwait because they expected an amphibious landing near Kuwait City and a direct strike north along the coast. Instead, the allies moved 235,000 U.S., French, and British soldiers far into the interior. On February 24, 1991, these forces swept into Iraq in a great arc. Americans, Saudis, Syrians, and Egyptians advanced directly to liberate Kuwait. A cease-fire came 100 hours after the start of the ground war.

The Iraqis had been driven out of Kuwait, but the relatively slow advance of the left wing failed to prevent many of the Iraqi troops from escaping. Allied forces suffered only 240 deaths in action, compared to perhaps 100,000 for the Iraqis.

Bush directed Desert Storm with the "Vietnam syndrome" in mind, believing that Americans were willing to accept war only if it involved overwhelming U.S. force and ended quickly. The United States hoped to replace Saddam Hussein without disrupting Iraqi society. Instead, the 100-hour war incited armed rebellions against Saddam in southern Iraq by Shiites, a group within the Muslim religion whose adherents comprise a majority in Iraq, and in the north by the ethnically distinct Kurds. Because Bush and his advisers were unwilling to get embroiled in a civil war or commit the United States to occupy all of Iraq, they stood by while Saddam crushed the uprisings. In one sense, the United States won the war but not the peace. Saddam Hussein became a hero to many in the Islamic world simply by remaining in power. In another sense, Bush had accomplished exactly what he wanted: the restoration of the status quo. In 2002, however, President George W. Bush (his son, elected in 2000), made a change in the Iraqi regime a centerpiece of U.S. foreign policy.

Growth in the Sunbelt

The rise in military and defense spending from the late 1970s through the early 1990s and the Persian Gulf War was one of the most powerful sources of growth in the **Sunbelt,** the southern and western regions of the United States. Americans had discovered this "new" region in the 1970s. Kevin Phillips's book *The Emerging Republican Majority* (1969) first popularized the term "Sunbelt." Phillips pointed out that people and economic activity had been flowing southward and westward since World War II, shifting the balance of power away from the Northeast. Sections of the South and West, historically controlled from the northeastern industrial core, have developed as independent centers of economic change.

The Sunbelt was a region of conservative voting habits where Republicans solidified their status as a majority party, a process continuing to the present. In the 1990s, the region's economic power was reflected in a conservative tone in both the Republican and Democratic parties and in the prominence of southern political leaders. Indeed, the career of George Bush, who got his start in New England but gained his greatest success as a new Texan, epitomized the political trend (see Map 30–3).

The rise of the Sunbelt, which is anchored by Florida, Texas, and California, reflected the leading economic trends of the 1970s and 1980s, including military spending, immigra-

tion from Asia and Latin America, and recreation and retirement spending. Corporations liked the business climate of the South, which had weak labor laws, low taxes, and generally low costs of living and doing business.

New factories dotted the southern landscape, often in smaller towns rather than cities. General Motors closed factories in Flint, Michigan, but invested in a new Saturn plant in Spring Hill, Tennessee. In contrast to troubled industrial cities in the Northeast and Midwest, cities like Orlando, Charlotte, Atlanta, Dallas, and Phoenix enjoyed headlong prosperity. Houston, with sprawling growth, business spinoffs from NASA, and purring air-conditioners epitomized the booming metropolitan areas of the South and West. It was "the place that scholars flock to for the purpose of seeing what modern civilization has wrought."

The Defense Economy
The Vietnam buildup and reinvestment in the military during the Carter (1977–1981) and Reagan (1981–1989) adminis-

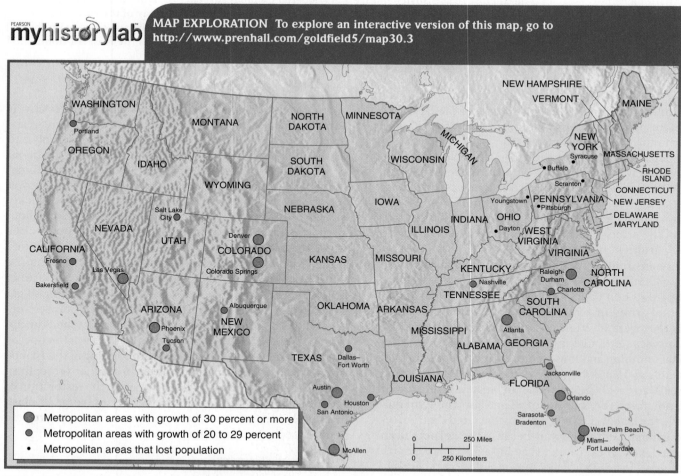

MAP EXPLORATION To explore an interactive version of this map, go to http://www.prenhall.com/goldfield5/map30.3

● Metropolitan areas with growth of 30 percent or more
● Metropolitan areas with growth of 20 to 29 percent
• Metropolitan areas that lost population

MAP 30–3 **Fast-Growing and Shrinking Metropolitan Areas, 1990–2000**
In the 1990s, boom cities were found in the Southeast, the Southwest, and on the West Coast. In contrast, the large metropolitan areas that lost population were all in Ohio, New York, or Pennsylvania, the area hardest hit by the decline of jobs in established manufacturing industries.

Global Perspectives

Disney in Tokyo and Paris

Tokyo Disneyland opened in 1983 as the first Disney theme park outside the United States. Designed by Walt Disney Imagineering, it copied California's original Disneyland and Florida's Walt Disney World. It includes the classic Disneyland features of Adventureland, Westernland, Tomorrowland, and Fantasyland (complete with a Cinderella Castle that looks just like its Florida counterpart).

Tokyo Disney was been enormously successful from the start. It has consistently attracted huge crowds. For many years was the most popular theme park in the world, and developers have added Tokyo DisneySea to keep visitors coming back.

If Japanese immediately took to Tokyo Disneyland, Europeans were much less excited by the Euro Disney Resort that opened east of Paris in 1992. Critics complained about the strict rules for workers. Intellectuals criticized the invasion of American popular culture into the heart of Europe. It took several years, and new attractions like De la Terre à la Lune (Space Mountain), to bring in enough visitors to put the project in the black.

The contrasting experiences demonstrate the close affinities between American and Japanese pop culture. Japanese monster movies of the 1950s, including Godzilla, King of Monsters, and his various opponents, earned money in both Japan and the United States. The huge Japanese animation, or anime, industry that developed after World War II drew on Disney cartoon style. It developed into an economic powerhouse of comic books, TV series, video games, and spinoff toys that made fortunes for Sony, Nintendo, and other companies. Pokemon, which began as a children's game for handheld computers, grew into a marketing phenomenon that made the cover of *Time* magazine.

This exchange of entertainment and consumer products has been part of the increasingly close engagement between the economies of the United States and East Asia. Its roots lie in the democratic revival of Japan after World War II and in the opening of political relations between the United States and the People's Republic of China in the 1970s. It has grown into a huge field of investment and exchange of everything from sneakers to steel, comic book artists to centerfielders.

■ **What are some reasons for the contrasting ways that Japan and France have responded to Disney theme resorts?**

---

trations fueled the growth of the Sunbelt. Over the 40 years from the Korean conflict to the Persian Gulf War, the United States made itself the mightiest military power ever known. Military bases and defense contractors remolded the economic landscape, as mild winters and clear skies for training and operations helped the South and West attract more than 75 percent of military payrolls.

Big cities and small depended on defense spending. Southern California thrived on more than 500,000 jobs in the aircraft industry. Lockheed's huge Burbank plant drew thousands of families to the new suburbs of the San Fernando Valley; McDonnell-Douglas shaped the area around Los Angeles International Airport. Twelve thousand smaller firms and a third of the area's jobs depended on defense spending. A thousand miles away, visitors to Colorado Springs could drive past sprawling Fort Carson and visit the new Air Force Academy, opened in 1958. Sunk deep from view was the North American Air Defense Command headquarters beneath Cheyenne Mountain west of the city.

Defense spending underwrote the expansion of American science and technology. Nearly one-third of all engineers worked on military projects. Large universities, such as MIT, the University of Michigan, the California Institute of Technology, and Stanford, were leading defense contractors. The modern electronics business started in New York, Boston, and the San Francisco Bay area with research and development for military uses, such as guided-missile controls. California's Silicon Valley grew with military sales long before it turned to consumer markets. The space component of the aerospace industry was equally reliant on the defense economy, with NASA spending justified by competition with the Soviet Union. NASA's centers were scattered across the South: launch facilities at the Kennedy Space Center in Cape Canaveral, Florida; research labs at Huntsville, Alabama; and Houston's Manned Spacecraft Center as the control center for space exploration.

Americans from Around the World

Few Americans anticipated the effects of the **Immigration and Nationality Act of 1965,** which transformed the ethnic mix of the United States and helped to stimulate the Sunbelt boom. The new law initiated a change in the composition of the American people by abolishing the national quota system in effect since 1924. Quotas had favored immigrants from western Europe and limited those from other parts of the world. The old law's racial bias contradicted the self-proclaimed role of the United States as a defender of freedom, and immigration reform was part of the propaganda battle of the Cold War. The new law gave preference to family reunification and welcomed immigrants from all nations equally. The United States also accepted refugees from Communism outside the annual limits.

Immigration reform opened the doors to Mediterranean Europe, Latin America, and Asia. Legal migration to the United States surged from 1.1 million in 1960–1964 to nearly 4 million for 1990–1994. Nonlegal immigrants may have doubled the total number of newcomers in the 1970s and early 1980s. Not since World War I had the United States absorbed so many new residents. By the early 1990s, legal immigration accounted for 37 percent of all U.S. population growth, compared with 10 percent before 1965. Meanwhile, over 2 million nonlegal immigrants had taken advantage of the Immigration Reform and Control Act of 1986 to legalize their presence in the United States.

Immigration changed the nation's ethnic mix. Members of officially defined ethnic and racial minorities accounted for 25 percent of Americans in 1990 and 30 percent in 2000 (see Table 30.1). Roughly 28 million Americans had been born in other countries according to the 2000 census, or 10.4 percent of the population. This was lower than the high of 14.7 percent in 1910 but a great increase from the low of 4.7 percent in 1970. One-third of the foreign born were from Latin America and one-fourth were from Asia.

The largest single group of new Americans came from Mexico. The long border has facilitated easy movement from south to north. Especially in the border states of Texas, New Mexico, Arizona, and California, permanent immigrants have mingled with tourists, family members on visits, temporary workers, and other workers without legal permission to enter the United States. Mexican Americans were the largest minority group in many southwestern and western states in the later twentieth century. They were transforming neighborhoods in Chicago and other midwestern cities and changing everything from politics to the Catholic Church.

The East Coast has especially welcomed migrants from the West Indies and Central America. Many Puerto Ricans, who hold U.S. citizenship, came to Philadelphia and New York in the 1950s and 1960s. The 110th Street subway station in East Harlem marked the center of *El Barrio de Nueva York* for the city's 600,000 Puerto Ricans. Other countries sending large numbers of immigrants include Haiti, the Dominican Republic, Guatemala, Honduras, Nicaragua, El Salvador, and Jamaica. Cuban refugees from Castro's regime concentrated in Miami and in major cities such as Chicago and New York.

Another great immigration has occurred eastward across the Pacific. Chinese, Filipinos, Koreans, Samoans, and other Asians and Pacific Islanders constituted only 6 percent of newcomers to the United States in 1965 but nearly half of all arrivals in 1990. The number of ethnic Chinese in the United States jumped from a quarter of a million in 1965 to 1,645,000 in 1990. Immigrants from Taiwan, Hong Kong, and the People's Republic created new Chinatowns in Houston and San Diego and crowded into the historic Chinatowns of New York and San Francisco.

The most publicized Asian immigrants were refugees from Indochina after the Communist victory in 1975. The first arrivals tended to be highly educated professionals who had worked with the Americans. Another 750,000 Vietnamese, Laotians, and Cambodians arrived after 1976 by way of refugee camps in Thailand, as did Celia Noup. Most settled on the West Coast. The San Francisco Bay area, for example, had more than a dozen Vietnamese-language newspapers, magazines, and cable television programs.

In addition to southeast Asians, political conflicts and upheavals sent other waves of immigrants to the United States. Many Iranians fled the religious regime that took power in their country in the late 1970s, at the same time that Ethiopians were fleeing a nation shattered by drought, civil war, and doctrinaire Marxism. To escape repression in the Soviet Union, Jews and conservative Christians came to the United States in the 1980s, and the collapse of Communism in the Soviet Union opened the door for more Russians, Ukrainians, Romanians, and other eastern Europeans.

Recent immigrants have found both economic possibilities and problems. On the negative side, legal and illegal immigration has added to the number of nonunion workers. By one estimate, two-thirds of the workers in the Los Angeles garment trade were undocumented immigrants. Most worked for small, nonunion firms in basements and storefronts, without health insurance or pensions. But a positive

Table 30–1
Major Racial and Ethnic Minorities in the United States

	1960 Population (in millions)	Percentage of total	2000 Population (in millions)	Percentage of total
American Indians	0.5	0.3	2.5	0.9
Asians and Pacific Islanders	1.1	0.6	10.6	3.7
African Americans	18.9	10.5	34.7	12.3
Hispanics	not available		35.3	12.5

contrast was the abundance of opportunities for talent and ambition in the expanding economy of the mid-1980s and 1990s. The 130,000 Vietnamese immigrants of 1975 now have an average income above the national figure. Asians and Pacific islanders by 2000 constituted 22 percent of the students in California's public universities. Like earlier European immigrants, many newcomers have opened groceries, restaurants, and other businesses that serve their own group before expanding into larger markets. Juan Fernandez found it easier to set up a successful car repair shop in Gary, Indiana, than in Guadalajara, Mexico, because his fellow immigrants preferred a Spanish-speaking mechanic. Asian-born business owners filled retail vacuums in central city neighborhoods abandoned by chain stores. One Korean told a typical story: "A friend of mine came over with his family. He invested a few dollars in a vegetable stand in downtown Manhattan. He and his sons got up early, went to the market early. He took some of his earnings and invested in a candy store. Then he bought two more vegetable and fruit stands. Their kids work hard too and they make a lot of money."

Old Gateways and New

The new immigration from Asia, Latin America, and the Caribbean had its most striking effects in coastal and border cities. New York again became a great mixing bowl of the U.S. population. By 1990, some 28 percent of the population of New York City was foreign-born, compared to 42 percent at the height of European immigration in 1910. ZIP code 11373 in northern Queens was reportedly the most diverse neighborhood in the world.

Just as important was the transformation of southern and western cities into gateways for immigrants from Latin America and Asia. Los Angeles emerged as "the new Ellis Island" that rivaled New York's historic role in receiving immigrants. As *Time* magazine put it in 1983, the arrival of more than 2 million immigrants in greater Los Angeles altered "the collective beat and bop of L.A." In 1960, a mere 1 percent of the Los Angeles County population was Asian and 11 percent was Hispanic. By 2000, the figures for the area's population of 9.5 million were 12 percent Asian and 45 percent Hispanic. The sprawling neighborhoods of East Los Angeles make up the second-largest Mexican city in the world. New ethnic communities appeared in Los Angeles suburbs: Iranians in Beverly Hills, Chinese in Monterey Park, Japanese in Gardena, Thais in Hollywood, Samoans in Carson, Cambodians in Lakewood. One hundred languages are spoken among students entering Los Angeles schools.

New York and Los Angeles are world cities as well as immigrant destinations. Like London and Tokyo, they are capitals of world trade and finance, with international banks and headquarters of multinational corporations. They have the country's greatest concentrations of international lawyers, accounting firms, and business consultants. The deregulation of international finance and the explosive spread of instant electronic communication in the 1980s confirmed their importance as global decision centers (see Table 30–2).

Similar factors have turned Miami into an economic capital of the Caribbean. A quarter-million Cuban businessmen, white-collar workers, and their families moved to the United States between 1959 and 1962 to escape Castro's socialist government. New "freedom flights" carried 150,000 additional Cubans to the United States from 1966 to 1973, and a third round added 125,000 in 1980. Most of the newcomers stayed in South Florida. By the late 1970s Cubans owned about one-

---

Table 30–2

Global Cities

Ranked by Population in 2005 (population in millions)		Ranked as Economic Decision Centers
Tokyo, Japan	35.2	1. London
Cuidad de Mexico	19.4	2. New York
New York	18.7	3. Hong Kong
Sao Paulo, Brazil	18.3	4. Paris
Mumbai, India	18.2	5. Tokyo
Delhi, India	15.0	6. Singapore
Shanghai, China	14.5	7. Chicago
Kolkata, India	14.3	8. Milan
Jakarta, Indonesia	13.2	9. Los Angeles
Buenos Aires, Argentina	12.6	10. Toronto
Dhaka, Bangladesh	12.4	11. Madrid
Los Angeles	12.3	12. Amsterdam

Sources: UN Department of Economic and Social Affairs/Population Division, *World Urbanization Prospects: The 2005 Revision*; Peter J. Taylor and Robert Lang, "U.S. Cities in the 'World City Network," The Brookings Institution, February 2005.

We beg of you, in the name of God, to do justice and love mercy in the administration of your office. We ask that "extended voluntary departure" be granted to refugees from Central America and that current deportation proceedings against these victims be stopped.

Until such time, we will not cease to extend the sanctuary of the church. Obedience to God requires this of us all.

Sources: Gary E. McCuen, ed., *The Religious Right* (Hudson, WI, G. E. McCuen, 1989); Ann Crittenden, *Sanctuary* (New York, Weidenfeld & Nicolson, 1988).

Conclusion

Americans entered the 1980s searching for stability. The 1970s had brought unexpected and uncomfortable change. Soviet actions in Asia and Africa seemed to be destabilizing the world. The memory of defeat in Vietnam left a bitter taste, and hostages in Tehran seemed to signal the end to U.S. global postwar dominance. Energy crises, inflation, and boarded-up factories eroded purchasing power and undermined confidence in the future. Traditional values seemed under siege. Ronald Reagan's presidential campaign played to these insecurities by promising to revitalize the older ways of life and restore the United States to its former influence.

Taken as a whole, the years from 1981 through 1992 brought transformations that redirected the course of American life. Because many changes were associated with national policy choices, it is fair to call this the era of the Reagan revolution. The astonishing collapse of the Soviet Union ended 40 years of Cold War. New political leadership in Washington reversed the 50-year expansion of federal government programs to deal with economic and social inequities. Prosperity alternated with recessions that shifted the balance between regions. The stock market rode a roller coaster, familiar corporate names vanished, and the national media made temporary heroes of business tycoons. Economic inequality increased after narrowing for a generation at the same time

that more and more leaders proclaimed that unregulated markets could best meet social needs. Middle-class Latinos and African Americans made substantial gains, while many other minority Americans sank deeper into poverty.

At the same time, it is important to recognize that every revolution has its precursors. Intellectuals have been clarifying the justifications for Reagan administration actions since the 1960s. The Reagan-Bush years extended changes that began in the 1970s, particularly the conservative economic policies and military buildup of the troubled Carter administration. In retrospect, the growing weakness of the USSR should also have been apparent in the same decade, had not the United States been blinded by its fear of Communist power. Intervention in the Persian Gulf amplified U.S. policies that had been in place since the CIA intervened in Iran in 1953. The outbreak of violence in Los Angeles after the Rodney King verdict showed that race relations were as tense as they had been in the 1960s.

In 1992, the United States stood as the undisputed world power. Its economy was poised for a surge of growth at the same time that rivals such as Japan were mired in economic crisis. It was the leader in scientific research and the development of new technologies. Its military capacities far surpassed those of any rival and seemed to offer a free hand in shaping the world—capacities that would be tested and utilized in the new century.

Review Questions

1. Is it accurate to talk about a Reagan Revolution in U.S. politics? Did Reagan's presidency change the economic environment for workers and business corporations? How did economic changes in the 1980s affect the prospects of the richest and poorest Americans?

2. How did American ideas about the proper role of government change during the 1980s? What were the basis of these changes?

3. What caused the breakup of the Soviet Union and the end of the Cold War? Did U.S. foreign policy under Reagan and Bush contribute significantly to the withdrawal of Soviet power from eastern Europe? Did the collapse of the USSR show the strength of the United States and its allies or the weakness of Soviet Communism?

4. How did the United States use military force during the Reagan and Bush administrations? Did military actions achieve the expected goals?

5. What were some of the important economic trends that shifted American growth toward the Sunbelt (South and West)? How has immigration from other nations affected the different American regions?

6. What changes in family roles and sexual behavior became divisive political issues? How have churches responded to cultural changes? What are some of the ways in which churches and religious leaders have tried to influence political decisions?

7. How did U.S. military involvement in southeast Asia in the 1960s continue to affect American society for decades to come?

Key Terms

Acquired immune deficiency syndrome (AIDS) (p. 877)

Americans with Disabilities Act (p. 864)

Deregulation (p. 857)

Economic Recovery and Tax Act of 1981 (ERTA) (p. 856)

Glasnost (p. 887)

Immigration and Nationality Act of 1965 (p. 873)

Intermediate Nuclear Force Agreement (INF) (p. 867)

Operation Desert Storm (p. 871)

Persian Gulf War (p. 871)

Perestroika (p. 867)

Reagan Doctrine (p. 865)

Roe v. Wade (p. 877)

Sagebrush Rebellion (p. 857)

Strategic Defense Initiative (SDI) (p. 865)

Sunbelt (p. 871)

Recommended Reading

Anderson, Elijah. *Streetwise: Race, Class, and Change in an Urban Community* (1990). A deeply troubling portrait of the culture of the streets in the Philadelphia ghetto during the 1980s.

Beschloss, Michael, and Strobe Talbott. *At the Highest Levels* (1993). A dramatic narrative of the last years of the Cold War, based on detailed interviews with American and Soviet participants.

Coutin, Susan Bibler. *The Culture of Protest: Religious Activism and the U.S. Sanctuary Movement* (1993). Examining foreign policy from the grassroots, sympathetically portrays the meanings that participants in the sanctuary movement gave their actions.

Edsall, Thomas Byrne, and Mary D. Edsall. *Chain Reaction: The Impact of Race, Rights, and Taxes on American Politics* (1991). Argues that the Democratic Party has systematically alienated its working-class supporters.

Fitzgerald, Frances. *Way Out There in the Blue: Reagan, Star Wars, and the End of the Cold War* (2000). A detailed analysis of the technical weaknesses and political appeal of strategic missile defense.

Liebow, Elliot. *Tell Them Who I Am: The Lives of Homeless Women* (1993). A sensitive depiction of street people and bag ladies as complex individuals coping with personal problems and economic crisis.

Phillips, Kevin. *Boiling Point: Democrats, Republicans, and the Decline of Middle-Class Prosperity* (1992). Expresses the belief that the economic policies of the Reagan and Bush administrations systematically harmed working- and middle-class families.

Rubin, Lillian. *Families on the Fault Line: America's Working Class Speaks about the Family, the Economy, Race, and Ethnicity* (1994). Interviews with American families about their efforts to cope with economic and social change.

Wills, Garry. *Reagan's America: Innocents at Home* (1987). A biography critical of Reagan's ideas but insightful about his personality.

Where To Learn More

■ **Ronald Reagan Boyhood Home, Dixon, Illinois.** The home where Reagan lived from 1920 to 1923 tells relatively little about Reagan himself but a great deal about the small-town context that shaped his ideas. www.ronaldreaganhome.com

■ **The Intermediate Nuclear Force Agreement (INF).** The full-text document of the INF agreement between the United States and the Soviet Union, the first true nuclear-disarmament treaty. http://www.state.gov/www/global/arms/treaties/inf1.html

■ **The Gulf War.** See video clips from the Canadian Broadcasting Corporation that provide a running narrative of the military crisis and war. http:archives.cbc.ca/war_conflict/1991_gulf_war/.

Study Resources

PEARSON

myhistorylab

For study resources for this chapter, go to www.myhistorylab.com and choose *The American Journey*. You will find a wealth of study and review material for this chapter, including pre- and post-tests, customized study plan, key term review flash cards, interactive map and document activities, and documents for analysis.

The terrorist attack on the World Trade Center on September 11, 2001, brought a spontaneous outpouring of efforts to assist the victims. The collapse of the World Trade Center towers killed hundreds of emergency workers. This New York City firefighter looks toward the collapsing buildings where many of his co-workers perished.

Complacency, Crisis, and Global Reengagement 31
1993–2008

I'm a firefighter for the FDNY [Fire Department New York]. I had gotten off the night before....My friend woke me up early that morning to borrow my car to take his sick cat to the vet....I was up so I went to my local bagel store for my coffee and paper...when I heard a lady scream a plane had hit the Trade Center....I thought since it was a beautiful day that perhaps a Cessna with the pilot having a heart attack had accidentally done this....I ran home to put the TV on....as soon as I saw what damage was done I knew this wasn't any Cessna....my god people were jumping...phone rang it was a fellow from my station and he hadn't turned his TV on yet....I screamed to him to turn his #*#* TV on....

When the second plane hit...I said goodbye and told him I was going in....I jumped in my car and was off to the races....the highway was closed...but open for us.

... I had the gas pedal to the floor as I headed toward the city looking out my window I see both towers burning...when I hear a rumble and see the south tower #2 fall....I have to get my gear so I pull off the highway going down the on ramp...arriving at the firehouse everyone's in shock and we know we gotta get there

885

The Election of 1992: A New Generation

Every 15 to 20 years, a new group of voters and leaders comes to power, driven by the desire to fix the mess that the previous generation left behind. The men and women who came of age during World War II learned to accept the need to struggle and the expectation of success. Their attitudes shaped the Cold War, dynamic conservatism, the New Frontier, and foreign policy under Johnson and Nixon. The conservative agenda for Ronald Reagan's and George H. W. Bush's administrations arose from the disillusion and crises of the late 1960s and 1970s, shaping leaders who believed that the answer was to turn the nation's social and economic problems over to the market while asserting America's influence and power around the world.

The mid-1990s brought another generation into the political arena. The members of "Generation X" came of voting age with deep worries about the foreclosing of opportunities. They worried that previous administrations had ignored growing economic divisions and let the competitive position of the United States deteriorate. The range of suggested solutions differed widely—individual moral reform, a stronger labor movement, leaner competition in world markets—but the generational concern was clear.

This generational change made 1992 one of the most volatile national elections in decades. A baby boomer and successful governor of Arkansas who was not widely known nationally, Democrat Bill Clinton decided that George H.W. Bush was vulnerable when more senior Democrats opted to pass on the contest. His campaign for the nomination overcame minimal name recognition, accusations of womanizing, and his use of a student deferment to avoid military service in Vietnam. Clinton made sure that the Democrats fielded a full baby boomer (and southern) ticket by choosing as his running mate the equally youthful Tennessean Albert Gore, Jr., who had served in the Senate for two terms and was widely known for his book on the environment, *Earth in the Balance.*

Bush, the last politician of the World War II generation to gain the White House, won renomination by beating back the archconservative Patrick Buchanan, who claimed that the last 12 years had been a long betrayal of true conservatism. The Republican National Convention in Houston showed how important cultural issues had become to the Republican Party. The party platform conformed to the beliefs of the Christian right. Buchanan delivered a startling speech that called for right-thinking Americans to crusade against unbelievers. Buchanan's divisive comments were a reminder of the multiple ways that religious belief was reshaping U.S. politics.

The wild card was the Texas billionaire Ross Perot, whose independent campaign started with an appearance on a television talk show. Perot loved flip charts, distanced himself from professional politicians, and claimed to talk sense to the American people. He also tried to occupy the political center, appealing to the middle of the middle-class—small business owners, middle managers, and professionals who had approved of Reagan's antigovernment rhetoric but distrusted his corporate cronies. In May, Perot outscored both Bush and Clinton in opinion polls, but his behavior became increasingly erratic. He withdrew from the race and then reentered after floating stories that he was the target of dark conspiracies.

Bush campaigned as a foreign policy expert. He expected voters to reward him for the end of the Cold War, but he ignored anxieties about the nation's direction at home. His popularity had surged immediately after the Persian Gulf War, only to fall rapidly as the country became mired in a recession. In fact, voters in November 1992 ranked the economy first as an issue, the federal budget deficit second, health care third, and foreign policy eighth. Clinton hammered away at economic concerns, appealing to swing voters, such as suburban independents and blue-collar Reagan Democrats. He presented himself as the leader of new, pragmatic, and livelier Democrats. He put on sunglasses and played the saxophone on a late-night talk show. His campaign theme song came from Fleetwood Mac, a favorite rock group of thirty-something Americans: "Don't stop thinking about tomorrow.... Yesterday's gone. Yesterday's gone."

Election day gave the Clinton-Gore ticket 43 percent of the popular vote, Bush 38 percent, and Perot 19 percent. Clinton held the Democratic core of northern and midwestern industrial states and loosened the Republican hold on the South and West (see Map 31–1). Millions who voted for Perot were casting a protest vote for "none of the above" and against "politics as usual" rather than hoping for an actual

Despite personal flaws, Bill Clinton was enormously effective as a political campaigner.

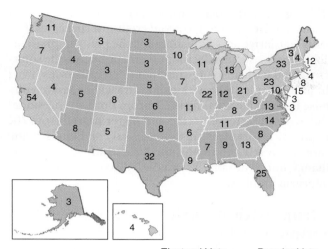

	Electoral Vote (%)	Popular Vote (%)
BILL CLINTON **(Democrat)**	**370** **(69)**	**43,728,275** **(43.2)**
George Bush (Republican)	168 (31)	38,167,416 (37.7)
H. Ross Perot (United We Stand, America)	–	19,237,247 (19.0)

MAP 31–1   The Election of 1992
Bill Clinton defeated George H. W. Bush in 1992 by reviving the Democratic Party in the industrial Northeast and enlisting new Democratic voters in the western states, where he appealed both to Hispanic immigrants and to people associated with fast-growing high-tech industries. He won reelection in 1996 with the same pattern of support. However, the coalition was an unstable combination of "Old Democrats," associated with older industries and labor unions, and "New Democrats," favoring economic change, free trade, and globalization.

Perot victory. Clinton ran best among voters over 65, who remembered FDR and Harry Truman, and voters under 30.

Policing the World

Although Clinton was much more interested in domestic policies, he inherited a confused expectation that the United States could use its military and economic power to keep the world on an even keel and counter ethnic hatred without incurring serious risks to itself. During the administration's first years, U.S. diplomats helped broker an Israel-PLO accord that gave Palestinians self-government in Gaza and the West Bank, only to watch extremists on both sides undermine the accords and plunge Israel into a near–civil war by 2002. The United States in 1994 used diplomatic pressure to persuade North Korea to suspend building nuclear weapons, temporarily calming a potentially explosive trouble spot. The world also benefitted from a gradual reduction of nuclear arsenals and from a 1996 treaty to ban the testing of nuclear weapons.

Elsewhere in the world, Clinton used military power with caution. Given the national distaste for overseas entanglements, he responded far more effectively than critics expected. He inherited a U.S. military presence in Somalia (in northeastern Africa) because of a post-election decision by President Bush; he withdrew U.S. forces when their humanitarian mission of guarding food relief to starving Somalis was overshadowed by the need to take sides in a civil war. Clinton intervened decisively in Haiti to restore an elected president.

Bosnia and Kosovo.   Clinton reluctantly committed the United States to a multinational effort to end the bloody civil war in ethnically and religiously divided Bosnia in 1995. In the early 1990s, the former Communist nation of Yugoslavia, in southeastern Europe, fragmented into five independent nations: Slovenia, Macedonia, Croatia, Bosnia, and Yugoslavia (the name retained by the predominantly Serbian nation with its capital at Belgrade). Bosnia, divided both ethnically and religiously between Christians and Muslims, erupted in bitter civil war. Christian Serbs, supported by Belgrade, engaged in massacres and deportations of Muslim Bosnians with the goal of creating "ethnically clean" Serbian districts. Too late to stop most bloodshed, NATO troops after 1995 enforced a brittle peace accord and a division of territory into Bosnian and Serb sectors under a shaky federated government.

The U.S. military revisited the same part of Europe in 1999, when the United States and Britain led NATO's intervention in Kosovo. The overwhelming majority of people in this Yugoslav province were ethnic Albanians who had chafed under the control of the Serb-controlled Yugoslav government. When a Kosovar independence movement began a rebellion, Yugoslav president Slobodan Milosevic responded with brutal repression that threatened to drive over 1 million ethnic Albanians out of the province. To protect the Kosovars, NATO in March 1999 began a bombing campaign that targeted Yugoslav military bases and forces in Kosovo. In June, Yugoslavia agreed to withdraw its troops and make way for a multinational NATO peacekeeping force with 50,000 troops from Britain, France, Germany, Italy, the Netherlands, and the United States, marking a measured success for U.S. policy.

The reinvention of NATO.   To satisfy Russia, the peacekeeping force that entered Kosovo in June was technically a U.S. operation, but it was a reinvented NATO that negotiated with Yugoslavia. Fifty years earlier, the North Atlantic Treaty Organization had been created for three purposes. The first was to unite non-Communist nations of western Europe in an alliance against the Soviet Union. The second was to formally commit the United States and Canada to the defense of western Europe by placing substantial U.S. military forces in Europe. The third was to establish a framework that would make the rearmament of West Germany acceptable to other European nations. For the next 40 years—until the collapse of eastern European Communism—NATO coordinated western European defense planning and remained a foundation stone of United States foreign policy.

The new NATO is a product of the new Europe of the 1990s. A key step was expansion into the former Soviet sphere in eastern Europe. In 1999, NATO formally admitted Poland, Hungary, and the Czech Republic over the objections of Russia. Three years later, NATO agreed to give Russia a formal role in discussions about a number of its policy decisions, further eroding the barriers of the Cold War, and it added another seven nations of eastern Europe in 2004.

Clinton's Neoliberalism   Domestic policy attracted Clinton's greatest interest, and his first term can be divided into two parts. In 1993–1994, he worked with a slim Democratic majority in Congress to modernize the U.S. economy, taking advantage of an economic upturn that lasted for most of the decade. In 1995 and 1996, however, he faced solid Republican majorities, the result of an unanticipated Republican tide in the November 1994 elections.

The heart of Clinton's agenda was an effort to make the United States economy more equitable domestically and more competitive internationally. These goals marked Clinton as a **neoliberal** who envisioned a partnership between a leaner government and a dynamic private sector. Steps to "reinvent" government cut federal employment below Reagan administration levels. A new tax bill reversed some of the inequities of the 1980s by increasing taxes on the weathiest 1.2 percent of households. An improved college student-aid program spread benefits to more students by allowing direct federal loans. In early 1993, Clinton pushed through the Family and Medical Leave Act, which provided up to 12 weeks of unpaid leave for workers with newborns or family emergencies and had been vetoed twice by George H.W. Bush.

Clinton's biggest setback was the failure of comprehensive healthcare legislation. The goals seemed simple at first: containment of healthcare costs and extension of basic medical insurance from 83 percent of Americans under age 65 to 100 percent. In the abstract, voters agreed that something needed to be done. So did individuals like the 25-year-old photographer's assistant who found herself facing cancer surgery without savings or health insurance: "I work full-time, and because it's a very small business, we don't get any benefits.... It just devastated everybody financially. And that shouldn't happen. That's the American dream that's lost."

Clinton appointed his wife, Hillary Rodham Clinton, to head the healthcare task force. Many found this an inappropriate role for a first lady. The plan that emerged from the White House ran to 1,342 pages of complex regulations, with something for everyone to dislike. Senior citizens worried about limits on Medicare spending. Insurance companies did not want more regulations. Businesses did not want the costs of insuring their workers. Taxpayers liked the idea of wider medical insurance coverage but not the idea of paying for it through higher taxes or rationing of medical services. Thus the reform effort went nowhere.

If Reagan avoided blame for mistakes, Clinton in his first two years in office seemed to avoid credit for successes. Despite his legislative accomplishments, the press emphasized his difficulty in reaching decisions. Perhaps because he sometimes started with absolute statements and positions, what might in another leader have looked like a willingness to compromise looked like waffling in Clinton. Both the president and his wife attracted extreme and bitter hatred from the far right, of a sort previously reserved for Franklin and Eleanor Roosevelt and the Kennedy family. Indeed, Hillary Rodham Clinton became a symbol of discomfiting changes in American families.

Contract with America and the Election of 1996

Conservative political ideology and personal animosity against the Clintons were both part of the background for an extraordinary off-year election in 1994, in which voters defeated dozens of incumbents and gave Republicans control of Congress. For most of 1995, the new speaker of the House, Newt Gingrich of Georgia, dominated political headlines as he pushed the **Contract with America,** the official Republican campaign platform for the 1994 elections, which called for a revolutionary reduction in federal responsibilities.

Clinton lay low and let the new Congress attack environmental protections, propose cuts in federal benefits for the elderly, and try to slice the capital-gains tax to help the rich. As Congress and president battled over the budget, congressional Republicans refused to authorize interim spending and forced the federal government to shut down for more than three weeks between November 1995 and January 1996. Gingrich was the clear loser in public opinion, both for the shutdowns and for his ideas. Democrats painted Gingrich and his congressional allies as a radical fringe who wanted to gut Medicare and Medicaid, undermine education, punish legal immigrants, and sell off national parks—core values and programs that most Americans wanted to protect.

After the budget confrontations, 1996 brought a series of measures to reward work—a centrist position acceptable to most Americans. The minimum wage increased. Congress made pension programs easier for employers to create and made health insurance portable when workers changed jobs. After tough negotiations, Clinton signed bipartisan legislation to "end welfare as we know it." **Temporary Assistance to Needy Families (TANF)** replaced Aid to Families with Dependent Children (AFDC). TANF had strict requirements that aid recipients by seeking work or be enrolled in schooling, and it set a time limit on assistance. By 2001, the number of public-assistance recipients had declined 58 percent from its 1994 high, but there are doubts that many of the former recipients have found jobs adequate to support their families.

Clinton's reelection in 1996 was a virtual replay of 1992. His opponent, Robert Dole, represented the World War II generation of politicians. The Republican Party was uncertain whether to stress free markets or morality. The party tried to paper over its uneasy mix of traditional probusiness and socially moderate country-club Republicans, radical proponents of unregulated markets, and religious conservatives increasingly active in politics. Evangelicals dominated many state parties, but they made many traditional party regulars uncomfortable and carried few statewide elections. The Republicans thus displayed many of the internal fractures that characterized U.S. society as a whole.

Because the nation was prosperous and at peace, and because Clinton had claimed the political center and sounded like Dwight Eisenhower, the results were never in doubt. Clinton became the first Democratic president to be elected to a second term since Franklin Roosevelt. The Clinton-Gore ticket took 70 percent of the electoral votes and 49 percent of the popular vote (versus 41 percent for Dole and 9 percent for a recycled Ross Perot). Clinton easily won the Northeast, the industrial Midwest, and the Far West; Hispanic voters alienated by anti-immigrant rhetoric from the Republicans helped Clinton also take the usually Republican states of Florida and Arizona.

The election confirmed that voters liked the pragmatic center. They were cautious about the radical free-market advocates on the extreme right, showing little interest in having Republicans actually put the Contract with America into practice. They were equally unimpressed by liberal advocates of extensive entitlements on the European model. What voters wanted was to continue the reduction of the federal role in domestic affairs that had begun in the 1980s without damaging social insurance programs.

The Dangers of Everyday Life

Part of the background for the sometimes vicious politics of mid-decade was a sense of individual insecurity and fear of violence that coexisted with an economy that was booming in some sectors but still leaving many Americans behind.

Random violence and domestic terrorism.   One after another, headlines and news flashes proclaimed terrifying random acts of violence. The greatest losses of life came in Waco, Texas, and in Oklahoma City. On April 19, 1993, federal agents raided the fortified compound of the Branch Davidian cult outside Waco after a 51-day siege. The raid triggered a fire, probably set from inside, that killed more than 80 people. On the second anniversary of the Waco raid, Timothy McVeigh packed a rented truck with explosive materials and detonated it in front of the federal office building in downtown Oklahoma City, presumably as revenge against what he considered an oppressive government. The blast collapsed the entire front of the nine-story building and killed 169 people.

In April 1999, two high school students in Littleton, Colorado, took rifles and pipe bombs into Columbine High School to kill 12 classmates, a teacher, and themselves; schools in Arkansas and Oregon experienced similar terror from gun-wielding students. A national manhunt in 1997 captured Ted Kaczynski, the so-called Unabomber, who since 1978 had

Search and rescue worker Anthony Fernandez and rescue dog Aspen pause during the search through the ruins of the Oklahoma City federal building after its bombing by domestic terrorists in 1995.

mailed more than a dozen bombs to college professors and airlines as protest against an industrialized economy.

Gun control.   Workplace assassins, schoolroom murders, and domestic terrorism invigorated efforts to monitor access to firearms. The Brady Handgun Violence Prevention Act, passed in 1994, took its name from James Brady, President Reagan's first press secretary, who was seriously injured in the 1981 attempt to kill the president. The act set up a waiting period and background checks for purchases of firearms from retailers, pawnshops, and licensed firearm dealers. Congress also debated detailed restrictions on certain types of weapons, such as assault rifles and particularly lethal types of ammunition. Police forces and urban residents tended to favor such laws, while rural representatives opposed them.

Gun control was political dynamite, for Americans have drastically differing understandings of the Second Amendment, which states: "A well regulated militia, being necessary to the security of a free State, the right of the people to keep and bear arms, shall not be infringed." The powerful National

Rifle Association, the major lobby for gun owners and manufacturers, now argued that the amendment establishes an absolute individual right. Federal courts for many decades interpreted the Second Amendment to apply to the possession of weapons in connection with citizen service in a government-organized militia. In June 2008, however, the Supreme Court in *District of Columbia v. Heller* struck down Washington, D.C.'s absolute ban on the ownership or possession of handguns. The majority in the 5-4 decision argued that the Second Amendment implied an individual right to own firearms. However, it left most state and federal firearms laws intact by allowing restrictions on individual categories of weapons and regulations on acquisition and use that fall short of prohibitions.

Crime and the war on drugs.   Conservatives, including many gun-ownership absolutists, put their faith in strict law enforcement as the best route to public security. The 1990s saw numerous states adopt "three-strike" measures that drastically increased penalties for individuals convicted of a third crime. One result was an explosive growth of the prison industry. Mandatory minimum sentencing caused Louisiana's prison population to grow by 50 percent between 1994 and 2001. Mississippi legislation that severely restricted the possibility of parole caused an even greater jump in the state's prison population from 10,700 in 1994 to 37,700 in 2001. States diverted funds from education and healthcare to build and staff more prisons. The number of people serving sentences of a year or longer in state and federal prisons grew from 316,000 in 1980 to 740,000 in 1990 and 1,422,000 in 2004, with another 714,000 being held for shorter periods in local jails. By 2007, one in every 99.1 adults was behind bars.

The war on drugs, begun in the 1980s, was the biggest contributor to the prison boom. As the drug war dragged on through the 1990s, the federal government poured billions of dollars into efforts to stop illegal drugs from crossing the Mexican border or from landing by boat or airplane. The United States intervened in South American nations that produced cocaine, particularly Peru and Colombia, aiding local military efforts to uproot crops and battle drug lords. Meanwhile, aggressive enforcement of domestic laws against drug possession or sales filled U.S. prison cells. The antidrug campaign fell most heavily on minorities. Connecticut, for example, required mandatory sentences for selling or possessing drugs within two-thirds of a mile of a school, daycare center, or public housing project. Because these criteria encompassed nearly all the neighborhoods in Hartford and New Haven with large minority populations, minority offenders arrested on drug charges were nine times more likely than white offenders to end up in jail.

In fact, crime fell steadily for a decade after reaching a peak in 1991. The rate of violent crime (murder, rape, robbery, aggravated assault) fell by 33 percent from 1991 to 2000, including a 36 percent drop in the number of murders. The rate of major property crimes (burglary, larceny-theft, and motor vehicle theft) fell by 30 percent over the same period. Easing fears combined with escalating costs to cause some states to rethink the reliance on prison terms. California voters adopted a measure that provides for treatment rather than prison for many drug offenders. A handful of states adopted measures legalizing marijuana for medical use. Other states, ranging from Mississippi to Connecticut to North Dakota, softened some of their sentencing laws.

Debating the death penalty.   Governor George Ryan of Illinois was elected in 1998 as a conservative Republican. In January 2003, this small-town businessman emptied death row in the Illinois prison system by commuting the death sentences of 167 convicted murderers to prison terms of life or less. He asserted that his review of individual cases had led him to doubt the justice of the death-penalty system as a whole, which he said is "haunted by the demons of error—error in determining guilt and error in determining who among the guilty deserves to die." Ryan's extraordinary action reflected a wider uncertainty about the fair application of capital punishment that came from cases in which the new technique of DNA testing showed mistaken convictions, revelations about incompetent defense attorneys, and evidence of malfeasance by prosecuting attorneys in withholding evidence that might have exonerated defendants accused of murder.

Specific discussion of flaws in the application of the death penalty reveals basic disagreements about the best approach to public order. Thirty-eight of the 50 states impose the death penalty, although sixteen states have not carried out an execution since 1976. The majority of Americans have accepted capital punishment as a flawed but necessary defense for society. In the presidential campaign of 2000, George W. Bush cited the record number of executions that had taken place in Texas while he was governor as evidence of his toughness against crime. He was confident, he said, that "everybody who has been put to death has been guilty of the crime charged."

In contrast, a passionate minority thinks that capital punishment is a tool so bent and blunted as to be worse than useless. They point out that the deterrent effect of capital punishment is weak at best; murder rates are often higher in death-penalty states than in similar states without the penalty. They note that African Americans and Latinos receive the death penalty far more often than whites charged with the same crimes. The nation's Roman Catholic bishops in 1999 joined with the National Council of Synagogues to condemn the death penalty as contrary to teachings about the sanctity of human life. In *Atkins v. Virginia* (2002), the Supreme Court forbade the execution of mentally retarded persons. In 2005, a divided Court in *Roper v. Simmons* prohibited the execution of anyone who committed the crime for which sentenced while younger than 18. The debate about capital punishment exemplifies the fault lines that divide

Americans as they try to balance the demands of justice and public order.

Morality and Partisanship

If the economy was the fundamental news of the later 1990s, Bill Clinton's personal life was the hot news. In 1998 and 1999, the United States was riveted by revelations about the president's sex life, doubts about his integrity, and debates about his fitness for high office. Years of rumors, innuendos, and lawsuits culminated in 1999 in the nation's second presidential impeachment trial. To his enemies, Clinton's behavior seemed one more example of disregard for law and morality, while his supporters found the entire issue to be nothing but partisan politics.

The president's problems began in 1994 with the appointment of a special prosecutor to investigate possible fraud in the **Whitewater** development, an Arkansas land promotion in which Bill and Hillary Clinton had invested in the 1980s. The probe by Kenneth Starr, the independent counsel, however, expanded into a wide-ranging investigation that encompassed the firing of the White House travel-office staff early in 1993, the suicide of White House aide Vincent Foster, and the sexual behavior of the president. Meanwhile, Paula Jones had brought a lawsuit claiming sexual harassment by then-governor Clinton while she was a state worker in Arkansas. The investigation of Whitewater brought convictions of several friends and former associates of the Clintons, but no evidence pointing decisively at either Bill or Hillary Clinton.

The legal landscape changed in January 1998, with allegations about an affair between the president and Monica Lewinsky, a former White House intern. Lewinsky admitted to the relationship privately and then to Starr's staff after the president had denied it in a sworn deposition for the Paula Jones case. This opened Clinton to charges of perjury and obstruction of justice. Although a federal judge dismissed Jones's suit in April, the continued unfolding of the Lewinsky affair treated the nation to a barrage of personal details about Bill Clinton and to semantic debates over what exactly constituted "having sex." The affair certainly revealed deep flaws in Clinton's character and showed his willingness to shade the truth. Newspaper editorials, radio talk shows, and politicians debated whether such flaws were relevant to his ability to perform his constitutional duties.

In the fall of 1998, the Republican leaders who controlled Congress decided that Clinton's statements and misstatements justified initiating the process of impeachment. In December, the majority on the House Judiciary Committee recommended four articles of impeachment, or specific charges against the president, to the House of Representatives. By a partisan vote, the full House approved two of the charges and forwarded them to the Senate. The formal trial of the charges by the Senate began in January 1999 and ended on February 12. Moderate Republicans joined Democrats, thereby ensuring that the Senate would fall far short of the two-thirds majority required for conviction and removal from office. Article 1, charging that the president had perjured himself, failed by a vote of 45 to 55. Article 2, charging that he had obstructed justice, failed by a vote of 50 to 50.

Why did Congressional Republicans pursue impeachment to the bitter end? It was clear by the end of 1998 that a majority of Americans strongly disapproved of Clinton's conduct but did not think that his personal behavior merited removal from office (see Overview, Presidential Impeachment). The 1998 election, which reduced the Republican majority in the House and resulted in the resignation of Newt Gingrich, confirmed the opinion polls. At the same time, 25 to 30 percent of Americans remained convinced that Clinton was a disgrace whose presence in the White House demeaned the nation. It was not so much that they disliked his policies, which were often quite conservative, but that they felt that his personal flaws and sins made him unfit to lead and represent the nation and deprived him of the moral authority necessary to inspire its people. In other words, although anti-Clinton people were a powerful force within the Republican Party and impeachment was certainly motivated by politics, it was also another battle in America's continuing culture wars.

A New Economy?

Within months of the impeachment trial, Americans had a new worry. In the closing months of 1999, many people stocked up on canned food and kerosene, powdered milk, ammunition, and cash. They were preparing to survive, not foreign invasion or natural disaster, but rather the possible collapse of the global computer network. Europeans called the problem the "millennium bug," Americans the "Y2K" problem (for Year 2000). In the early years of computers, memory space was precious, causing programmers to designate dates with only the last two digits of the year (thus, "82" for 1982). In the mid-1990s, many realized that such programs might treat the year 2000 as 1900, or might choke in electronic confusion, throwing information systems into chaos. While a small army of programmers worked to rewrite and repair the software, the media offered a steady diet of dire stories that urged preparations—just in case.

In fact, almost nothing happened. The software patches worked. Americans on the evening of December 31, 1999, could watch the progression of millennium celebrations and fireworks from Singapore to Rome and then to London as midnight swept westward across the globe. Since civilization did not collapse in Asia and Europe, North Americans could greet midnight with a sigh of relief.

In larger perspective, the Y2K worries illustrate how much the American economy had changed in the preceding decade, and how mysterious the changes seemed. More than ever, it was a global economy. And, unlike any time in the

OVERVIEW

Presidential Impeachment

Andrew Johnson, 1868	Charges:	Failure to comply with Tenure of Office Act requiring congressional approval to fire cabinet members.
	Political Lineup:	Radical Republicans against Johnson; Democrats and moderate Republicans for him.
	Actions:	Tried and acquitted by Senate.
	Underlying Issues:	Johnson's opposition to Republican plans for reconstruction of southern states after the Civil War.
Richard Nixon, 1974	Charges:	Obstruction of justice in Watergate investigation, abuse of power of federal agencies for political purposes, refusal to recognize congressional subpoena.
	Political Lineup:	Democrats and many Republicans against Nixon.
	Actions:	Charges approved by House committee; Nixon resigned before action by the full House of Representatives.
	Underlying Issues:	Nixon's construction of a secret government and his efforts to undermine integrity of national elections.
Bill Clinton, 1999	Charges:	Perjury and obstruction of justice in the investigation of sexual-misconduct allegations by Paula Jones.
	Political Lineup:	Conservative Republicans against Clinton; Democrats and some moderate Republicans for him.
	Actions:	Tried and acquitted by Senate.
	Underlying Issues:	Republican frustration with Clinton's ability to block their agenda; deep concern about Clinton's character and moral fitness for presidency.

past, it was an economy that depended on electronic computing to manage and transmit vast quantities of data. The impact of the electronic revolution was still being absorbed into the structures and routines of everyday life as Americans put Y2K behind them and looked to a new century.

The Prosperous 1990s

From 1992 through 2000, Americans enjoyed nine years of continuous economic expansion. Unemployment dropped from 7.2 percent in 1992 to 4.0 percent at the start of 2000 as American businesses created more than 12 million new jobs. Key states like California rebounded from economic recession with new growth driven by high-tech industries, entertainment, and foreign trade. The stock market soared during the nineties; rising demand for shares in established blue-chip companies and new **Internet** firms swelled the value of individual portfolios, retirement accounts, and pension funds. The rate of home ownership rose after declining for 15 years. Prosperity also trickled down to Americans at the bottom of the economic ladder. The proportion of Americans in poverty dropped to 12 percent in 1999, and the gap between rich and poor began to narrow (slightly) for the first time in two decades.

The economic boom was great news for the federal budget. Tight spending and rising personal income turned perennial deficits into surpluses for 1998, 1999, and 2000. Reduced borrowing by the U.S. Treasury resulted in low interest rates, which further fueled corporate expansion and consumer spending. Both political parties anticipated a growing surplus for the next decade and debated whether to offer massive tax cuts, buy down the national debt, or shore up Social Security and Medicare. In 1997, Clinton signed a deficit-reduction bill that seemed to promise fiscal stability.

Behind the statistics were substantial gains in the efficiency of the U.S. economy. International rivals, especially Japan, experienced severe economic slumps in the mid-1990s. In the United States, in contrast, by the end of the decade the productivity of manufacturing workers was increasing more than 4 percent per year, the highest rate in a generation. Part of the gain was the payoff from the painful business restructuring and downsizing of the 1970s and 1980s. Another cause was improvements in efficiency from the full incorporation of personal computers and electronic communication into everyday life and business practice.

It remains to be seen whether the growth of the 1990s marked the beginning of a new wave of sustained economic expansion like earlier waves triggered by technological innovation. Until now, such waves have followed 50-year cycles that begin with a 30-year period of rapid expansion followed by two decades of consolidation and slow growth. From 1945 to 1974, for example, the automobile and aerospace industries helped Europe, Japan, and the United States enjoy an era of sustained growth that was followed by two decades of painful economic readjustment and problems. In the later 1990s, fast-growing information-based industries such as electronic communications, software, biotechnology, and medicine may have jump-started another era of prosperity, although many individual technology companies failed in 2001 and 2002; the dotcom bust dragged down the stock market for several years.

The Service Economy

At the beginning of the twenty-first century, the United States was an economy of services. As fewer Americans drove tractors and toiled on assembly lines, more became service workers. The service sector includes everyone not directly involved in producing and processing physical products. Service workers range from lawyers to hair stylists, from police officers who write traffic tickets to theater employees who sell movie tickets. In 1965, services already accounted for more than half of American jobs. By the end of the 1990s, their share rose to more than 75 percent.

Service work varies greatly. At the bottom of the scale are minimum-wage jobs held mostly by women, immigrants, and the young, such as cleaning people, childcare workers, hospital orderlies, and fast-food workers. These positions offer little in terms of advancement, job security, or benefits. In contrast, many of the best new jobs are in information industries. Teaching, research, advertising, mass communications, and professional consulting depend on producing and manipulating information. All of these fields have grown. They add to national wealth by creating and applying new ideas rather than by supplying standardized products and services.

The information economy flourishes in large cities with libraries, universities, research hospitals, advertising agencies, and corporate headquarters. New York's bankers and stockbrokers made Manhattan an island of prosperity in the 1980s. Pittsburgh, with major universities and corporate headquarters, made the transition to the information economy even while its steel industry failed. A good benchmark of a brain-powered economy is whether more than a quarter of the adults (people aged 25 or over) have finished college. The District of Columbia, with its high-priced lawyers and lobbyists, ranked first in 2005, with 47 percent. Next were Connecticut and Massachusetts (37 percent), followed closely by Maryland, New Jersey, and Colorado.

The rise of the service economy had political consequences. Rapid expansion

of jobs in state and local government triggered popular revolts against state taxes that started in 1978 with passage of California's Proposition 13, which limited property taxes, and continued into the 1990s. Another growth industry was healthcare. Spending on medical and health services amounted to 15 percent of the gross domestic product in 2000, up from 5 percent in 1960. The need to share this huge expense fairly was the motivation for Medicare and Medicaid in the 1960s and the search for a national health insurance program in the 1990s and beyond.

The High-Tech Sector

The epitome of the "sunrise" economy was electronics, which grew hand-in-glove with the defense budget. The first computers in the 1940s were derived in part from wartime code-breaking efforts. In the 1950s, IBM got half its revenues from air defense computers and guidance systems for B-52 bombers. "It was the Cold War that helped IBM make itself the king of the computer business," commented the company's president, Thomas J. Watson. Employment in computer manufacturing rose in the mid-1960s with the expansion of mainframe computing. Large machines from IBM, Honeywell, NCR, and other established corporations required substantial support facilities and staff and were used largely by universities, government agencies, and corporations. In the 1970s, new companies began to build smaller, specialized machines for such purposes as word processing. One cluster of firms sprang up outside Boston around Route 128, benefitting from proximity to MIT and other Boston-area universities. California's **Silicon Valley,** north of San Jose, took off with corporate spinoffs and civilian applications of military technologies and benefitted from proximity to Stanford University.

Seattle in the 1980s and 1990s prospered from the globalizing economy and the rise of the information industries. Only old-timers noticed the disappearance of fish canneries and lumber mills. Taking their place were Boeing, which fueled an international travel revolution; Microsoft, which made Seattle a high-tech capital; and the many foreign companies that used Seattle's port for access to the U.S. market.

American Views

Relief Work in Africa

In the early twenty-first century, thousands of Americans work in other countries for relief and reconstruction organizations such as the Peace Corps, CARE, and Mercy Corps, and thousands more do similar work under the sponsorship of religious groups. In 2003, Peggy Senger Parsons, an evangelical Quaker minister and trauma counselor from "far off Planet America" spent several months in the small African nation of Burundi, trying to help residents develop strategies for dealing with the impacts of civil war and endemic criminal violence. Here are some excerpts from her blog.

- What does Peggy Parsons's experience suggest about the spread of American culture around the world?

- How does the level of personal safety in a nation such as Burundi compare to that in the United States?

- What questions does Parsons's experience raise about the challenges of building peace and democracy in troubled and divided nations?

- How might religiously based work in other countries differ from efforts sponsored by the U.S. government, such as with the Peace Corps? How might it be the same?

We function in Swahili and French, mine bad and hers good....I have been in the company of four children who have been giving me language and cultural tutorials, which I exchanged for introducing them to the Beatles.

Pavement is a subjective concept in Burundi. Traffic is extremely real. We fly in a zig zag pattern through cars, trucks, bicycles, and lots of little children. If you notice a lack of angels in America, it is because they are all in Burundi keeping the babies from being killed on the road....And in four days I am totally immune to the sight of guys with automatic weapons. My host says that he cannot tell a rebel from a Burundi soldier and sometimes neither can they.

We have a night watchman...we live in a walled compound and he is there to keep us safe. His only weapon is a whistle. The children tell me that if there is trouble he whistles, and all the nearby watchmen whistle and then come running to help. Then I met Gadi the moneychanger. He walks around with rolls of money as big as softballs in every pocket and he does not carry a gun. He has a quiet gentle confidence that reminds me of every wiseguy I ever met in Chicago. I do not know what happens if you jump a moneychanger—but it must be bad enough that nobody tries. Some things are very familiar.

My traumatology students are amazing. They have come from great distances and at great sacrifice to study with me....Many of the terms I need to use have no equivalent. I have learned the face that my translator makes when I give her a hard one. She signals for me to stop, and the students confer and when a consensus is reached about a newly coined phrase someone shouts *Voila!* And we have a new psychological term. My students were interviewed on Burundi National Radio. The reporter came on the second day to do a quick filler piece and stayed all afternoon and then asked to join the class. He carries a huge reel-to-reel recorder. The voices of these students went out to 22 million listeners this morning in Burundi, Congo, Rwanda, and Tanzania. They were fabulous explaining the effects of trauma and how they themselves had been helped in the class. On Friday my class thanked me for telling them the truth and for bringing them the best of myself. They compared me to a Jonah "who did not run away but ran towards her call," can't get better pay than that.

I was not prepared for the fact that my trauma class students would be such recent victims [many bearing fresh wounds from beatings or torture]. Thursday there was a bit of shooting outside of the teaching compound.

I had to be told what it was—a "thump" and then a "tat, tat, tat." But it was quiet after that and we resume. After a long morning of brain physiology and learning about the left brain functions, my translator said, "Peggy have mercy on them—they say they need to sing." And so they did, all Christian music. I taught them "We Shall Overcome" and told them about Dr. King and we marched around the room singing that "I do believe, deep in my heart, that Burundi will have peace one day."

Tourism and travel.   In the 1960s, "jet set" referred to a handful of the idle rich who could treat the world as their playground. Forty years later, nearly everyone was part of the jet set. In 2000, Americans made 27 million visits to other countries in addition to 34 million visits to Canada and Mexico, an 80 percent increase in just the 1990s. At the same time, the United States received 25 million visitors from Canada and Mexico and 26 million from other nations. California, Florida, New York, Hawaii, and Nevada were the top destinations. The number of foreign students studying in the United States passed the half-million mark in 2000. Meanwhile, American college students with the necessary financial resources had come to expect a semester or year abroad as part of their studies.

In addition to temporary visitors, 4 million Americans lived and worked abroad in 2000. Some had retired to Mexico or Spain. Some were military personnel or worked for the State Department. Many more worked for multinational corporations, represented nonprofit organizations, or served as medical and religious missionaries (see American Views, Relief Work in Africa). Americans might supervise the mass production of American brands in Asian factories. They might also work building houses or coordinating relief aid in Afghanistan, counseling victims of genocide in Burundi, or assisting city planners in Tadzhikistan.

Broadening Democracy

Closely related to the changes in the American economy were the changing composition of the American people and the continued emergence of new participants in U.S. government. Bill Clinton's first cabinet, in which three women and four minority men balanced seven white men, recognized the makeup of the American population and marked the maturing of minorities and women as distinct political constituencies. The first cabinet appointed by George W. Bush in 2001 included four minority men and four women, one of whom was Asian American. In both administrations, the new prominence of women and minorities in the national government followed years of growing success in cities and states.

Americans in 2000

The federal census for the year 2000 found 281,400,000 Americans in the 50 states, District of Columbia, and Puerto Rico (and probably 2–3 million more residents were not counted).

The increase from 1990 was 13.2 percent, or 32,700,000. It was the largest ten-year population increase in U.S. history, evidence of the nation's prosperity and its attractiveness for immigrants. More than 12 percent of Americans had been born in other countries, the highest share since 1920 (Table 31–1). One third of all Americans lived in four states: California, Texas, New York, and Florida. These were the key prizes in presidential elections. Their regulations and consumer preferences conditioned national markets for products ranging from automobiles to textbooks.

The West grew the fastest. The super boom states were Nevada (66 percent growth), Arizona (40 percent), Colorado (31 percent), Utah (30 percent), and Idaho (29 percent). Fast growth implies young populations, and the states with the lowest average ages were all western: Utah, Alaska, Idaho, and Texas. The Southwest and South also had the fastest growing metropolitan areas. Las

Protests against the WTO have united environmentalists and labor unions, interests that are often in opposition over domestic issues.

Working 24/7 in Bangalore

Bangalore is a beautiful city in the highlands of southern India. Its cool climate attracted retired British officials in the days of the British Empire, leaving a legacy of Victorian parks and wide boulevards. After India achieved independence in 1947, the new government made Bangalore a center for scientific research, leaving a legacy of four universities, dozens of technical schools, and a home-grown high-tech industry. In the 1990s, U.S. electronics companies began to establish branches and subsidiaries to take advantage of the concentration of talent, creating a new suburban landscape of technology parks and gated residential neighborhoods with a strong resemblance to Silicon Valley.

The logical extension came in the twenty-first century. Computers and telephone lines have brought Bangalore, Delhi, and other Indian cities into instant contact with American businesses and consumers. Enough U.S. companies have outsourced their customer-service operations to India to become a comic-strip joke.

The development is a logical extension of the global economy. India represents the world's second-largest concentration of English speakers after the United States. Its high-quality educational system produces a million college graduates a year. Many of them are glad to work for U.S. companies at pay that is cheap by U.S. standards but good by comparison with other opportunities in India.

Any kind of routine customer service can be outsourced—telephone catalog sales, billing and debt collection, credit card marketing, help lines for Internet providers, technical support for computer manufacturers. Tens of thousands of simple income tax returns are now processed in India each year. An American accountant scans in a customer's tax information, an Indian accountant logs on and fills out the return, the American accountant prints it out for signature.

The magic of electronics and the 12-hour time differential allow Indians to do specialized work while Americans sleep. Hospitals can transit MRIs to be read in India and get the results the next morning. Publishers can send files to be formatted and proofread while authors and editors sleep. Software companies can transmit code to be debugged overnight.

There is both a light side and a serious side to this 24/7 economy. It is amusing to learn that Indian workers practice American accents and take "phone names" that sound American; CBS reported that one young woman named Sangita becomes "Julia" because Julia Roberts is her favorite actress. But it is also important to understand that distance scarcely matters when an economy's important products take the form of information, and that information flows back and forth across the oceans linking the United States to the world in ways not seen in earlier centuries.

■ In twenty-first century, is the English language the most important asset of the American economy?

Vegas topped them all with an increase of 83 percent. Among large metro areas with over 500,000 people in 2000, all 20 of the fastest growing of were in the West and Southeast.

In contrast, parts of the American midlands grew slowly. Rural counties continued to empty out in Appalachia and across the Great Plains as fewer and fewer Americans were needed for mining and farming or for the small towns associated with those industries. No state lost population, but North Dakota and West Virginia had ten-year gains of only 1 percent.

Another important trend was increasing ethnic and racial diversity (Table 31–2). Hispanics were the fastest growing group in the U.S. population. Indeed, the number of Hispanics in 2000 (35.2 million) surprised many officials and matched the number of African Americans. Although immigrants concentrated in the coastal and border states, Hispanics and Asian Americans were also spreading into interior states. Asians and Hispanics who had been in the United States for some time showed substantial economic success. Non-Hispanic whites are now a minority in California at 47 percent, in the District of Columbia, in Hawaii, and in New Mexico.

The changing ethnicity of the American people promises to be increasingly apparent in coming decades. Immigrants tend to be young adults who are likely to form families, and birth rates have been high among Hispanics and Asian Amer-

Table 31–1
Immigrants 1991–2005, by Continent and by Twenty Most Important Countries of Origin

Total	14,083,000
North America	5,657,000
Mexico	3,127,000
Dominican Republic	469,000
El Salvador	359,000
Cuba	300,000
Haiti	270,000
Jamaica	250,000
Canada	227,000
Guatemala	183,000
Asia	4,557,000
Philippines	773,000
India	729,000
China	708,000
Vietnam	576,000
Korea	267,000
Pakistan	191,000
Iran	167,000
Europe	2,067,000
Poland	234,000
Ukraine	232,000
Russia	218,000
United Kingdom	214,000
South America	912,000
Colombia	225,000
Africa	697,000
Oceania	76,000

Source: *Statistical Abstract of the United States.*

Table 31–2
States with Highest Proportions of Minority Residents in 2000 (percentage of total population)

Hispanic	
New Mexico	42%
California	32%
Texas	32%
Arizona	25%
Nevada	20%
Asian and Pacific Islander	
Hawaii	51%
California	11%
Washington	6%
New Jersey	6%
New York	6%
Black	
Mississippi	36%
Louisiana	33%
South Carolina	30%
Georgia	29%
Maryland	28%
American Indian	
Alaska	16%
New Mexico	10%
South Dakota	8%
Oklahoma	8%
Montana	6%

icans. The result is a sort of multiethnic baby boom. In 1972, at the peak of the post–World War II baby boom, 80 percent of elementary and high school students were non-Hispanic whites. By 1999 the figure was 63 percent and falling. Over the coming decades, the effects of ethnic change will be apparent not only in schools but also in the workplace, popular culture, and politics.

Women from the Grassroots to Congress

The increasing prominence of women and family issues in national politics was a steady, quiet revolution that bore fruit in the 1990s, when the number of women in Congress more than doubled. In 1981, President Reagan appointed Arizona judge Sandra Day O'Connor to be the first woman on the United States Supreme Court. In 1984, Walter Mondale chose New York Congresswoman Geraldine Ferraro as his vice presidential candidate. In 1993 Clinton appointed the second woman to the Supreme Court, U.S. Appeals Court judge Ruth Bader Ginsburg. Clinton appointee Janet Reno was the first woman to serve as attorney general, and Madeleine K. Albright the first to serve as secretary of state. George W. Bush continued to break new ground by naming Condoleezza Rice as his national security advisor in 2001 and as secretary of state in 2005.

Political gains for women at the national level reflected their growing importance in grassroots politics. The spreading suburbs of postwar America were "frontiers" that required concerted action to solve immediate needs like adequate schools and decent parks. Because pursuit of such community services was often viewed as "woman's work" (in contrast to the "man's work" of economic development), postwar metropolitan areas offered numerous opportunities for women to engage in volunteer civic work, learn political skills, and run for local office. Moreover, new cities and suburbs had fewer established political institutions, such as political machines and strong parties; their politics were open to energetic women. The entry of more women into politics is a bipartisan affair. Important support and training grounds are the League of Women Voters, which does nonpartisan studies of basic issues, and the National Women's Political Caucus, designed to support women candidates of both parties. Most women in contemporary politics have been more liberal than men—a difference that political scientists attribute to women's interest in the practical problems of schools, neighborhoods, and two-earner families. But women's grassroots mobilization, especially through evangelical churches, has also strengthened groups committed to conservative social values.

Regional differences have affected women's political gains. The West has long been the part of the country most open to women in state and local government and in business. Several western states granted voting rights to women before the adoption of the Nineteenth Amendment. More recently, Westerners have been more willing than voters in the East or South to choose women as mayors of major cities and as members of state legislatures. Many of the skills learned from politics were also useful as women played a growing role in professional and managerial occupations (see Map 31–2).

In 1991, the nomination of Judge Clarence Thomas, an African American, to the U.S. Supreme Court ensured that everyone knew that the terms of U.S. politics were changing. Because of his conservative positions on social and civil rights issues, Thomas was a controversial nominee. Controversy deepened when law professor Anita Hill accused Thomas of harassing her sexually while she served on his staff at the Equal Employment Opportunity Commission. The accusations led to riveting hearings before a U.S. Sen-

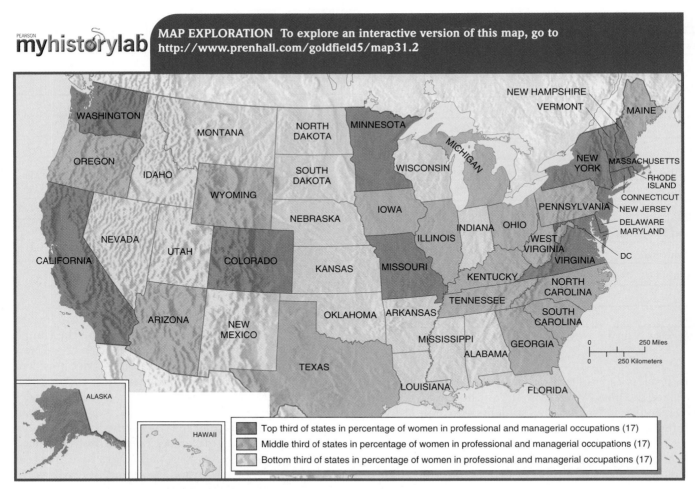

MAP EXPLORATION To explore an interactive version of this map, go to http://www.prenhall.com/goldfield5/map31.2

Top third of states in percentage of women in professional and managerial occupations (17)

Middle third of states in percentage of women in professional and managerial occupations (17)

Bottom third of states in percentage of women in professional and managerial occupations (17)

MAP 31–2   Women in Professional and Managerial Occupations, 2001
Some parts of the nation are more inviting to women-owned businesses than are others. The western and Great Lakes states, with histories of innovative politics, stand out as supportive of business opportunities for women.

Bureau of Labor Statistics, 2003. Compiled by Institute for Women's Policy Research.

ate committee. Critics tried to discredit Hill with vicious attacks on her character, and the committee failed to call witnesses who could have supported her claims. The public was left with Hill's plausible but unproved allegations and Thomas's equally vigorous but unproved denials. The Senate confirmed Thomas to the Supreme Court. Partisans on each side continued to believe the version that best suited their preconceptions and agendas.

Whatever the merits of her charges, Hill's badgering by skeptical senators angered millions of women. In the shadow of the hearings, women made impressive gains in the 1992 election, which pushed women's share of seats in the 50 state legislatures above 20 percent. The number of women in the U.S. Senate jumped from two to seven (and grew further to eleven Democrats and five Republicans in 2007). Bill Clinton appointed women to 37 percent of the 500 or so high-level jobs in the White House and federal departments. That is far higher than Jimmy Carter's 15 percent or Lyndon Johnson's 4 percent, and also above George W. Bush's 26 percent of initial appointments (see Figure 31–1). The number of women serving as federal judges grew from 48 in 1981 to more than 200 — roughly a quarter of the total.

Women have influenced national politics as voters as well as candidates and cabinet members. Since the 1980s, voting patterns have shown a gender gap. Women in the 1990s identified with the Democratic Party and voted for its candidates at a higher rate than men. The reasons include concerns about the effect of government spending cuts and interest in measures to support families rather than in conservative rhetoric. This gender gap has helped keep Democrats competitive and dampened the nation's conservative swing on social issues.

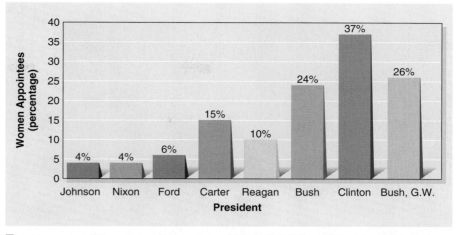

FIGURE 31–1   Women as a Percentage of Initial High-Level Presidential Appointments: Lyndon Johnson to George W. Bush
By the 1990s, Americans were willing to accept women in positions that would have been reserved for men only in earlier decades, such as attorney general, secretary of state, and national security advisor.

Minorities at the Ballot Box

The changing makeup of the American populace also helped black and Latino candidates for public office to increased success. After the racial violence of the 1960s, many black people turned to local politics to gain control of their own communities. The first black mayor of a major twentieth-century city was Carl Stokes in Cleveland in 1967. The 1973 election brought victories for Tom Bradley in Los Angeles, Maynard Jackson in Atlanta, and Coleman Young in Detroit. By 1983, three of the nation's four largest cities had black mayors. In 1989, Virginia made Douglas Wilder the first black governor in any state since Reconstruction.

The election of a minority mayor was sometimes more important for its symbolism than for the transfer of real power. Efforts to restructure the basis of city council elections, however, struck directly at the balance of power. Most mid-sized cities stopped electing city councils by wards or districts during the first half of the twentieth century. Voting at large shifted power away from geographically concentrated ethnic groups. It favored business interests that claimed to speak for the city as a whole but could assign most of the costs of economic growth to older and poorer neighborhoods.

In the 1970s, minority leaders and community activists realized that a return to district voting could convert neighborhood segregation from a liability to a political resource. As amended in 1975, the federal Voting Rights Act allowed minorities to use the federal courts to challenge at-large voting systems that diluted the impact of their votes. Blacks and Mexican Americans used the act to reestablish city council districts in the late 1970s and early 1980s in city after city across the South and Southwest.

The political rebalancing meant that local leaders faced strong pressures to ensure equitable distribution of the benefits and burdens of growth. Newly empowered minorities began to press for a fair share of an expanding economic pie. In San Antonio and Denver, for example, young Hispanic politicians brought new ideas into city government in the 1980s. Henry Cisneros of San Antonio defeated a representative of the downtown establishment in 1981, and in Denver, Federico Peña ousted a 16-year incumbent with the help of an army of volunteers. Both men ran on platforms of planned growth and later served in Clinton's cabinet. Progressive African American mayors in other cities included Dennis Archer in Detroit and Andrew Young in Atlanta, leaders who won on positive platforms of growth and equity and who mended fences with business leaders. Meanwhile, Washington state elected a Chinese American as governor, and Hawaii elected Japanese American, native Hawaiian, and Filipino American governors.

As leadership opportunities for African Americans have increased in recent decades, they have gained positions of influence in a growing range of activities. In the field of foreign policy, for example, President George W. Bush choose Colin Powell as secretary of state and Condoleezza Rice as national security advisor. Here Powell (second from left) and Rice (right) observe a White House meeting between Bush and United Nations Secretary General Kofi Annan.

At the national level, minorities gradually increased their representation in Congress. Ben Nighthorse Campbell of Colorado, a Cheyenne, brought a Native American voice to the U.S. Senate in 1992. The number of African Americans in the House of Representatives topped 40 after 1992, with the help of districts drawn to concentrate black voters. Even after a series of Supreme Court cases invalidated districts drawn with race as the "predominant factor," however, African Americans held most of their gains, while the number of Latino members of Congress rose to 26 by 2007 (see Figure 31–2).

In struggling for political influence, recent immigrants have added new panethnic identities to their national identities. In the nineteenth century, English-speaking Americans looked at European immigrants from widely separated regions and backgrounds and saw "Italians" or "Jews." In turn, newcomers found economic and political strength by making common cause across their differences, molding identities as ethnic groups within the U.S. context. Newer immigrants have gone through a parallel process. Hispanic activists revived the term "Chicano" to bridge the gap between recent Mexican immigrants and Latinos whose families had settled in the Southwest before the American conquest in 1848. Great gaps of experience and culture separated Chinese, Koreans, Filipinos, and Vietnamese, but they gained political recognition and influence if they dealt with other Americans as "Asians." Native Americans have similarly downplayed tribal differences in efforts to secure better opportunities for Indians as a group.

Rights and Opportunities

The increasing presence of Latinos and African Americans in public life highlighted a set of troublesome questions about the proper balance between equal rights and equal opportunities. Was government justified in seeking to equalize outcomes as well as starting points? More broadly, was the United States to be a unitary society in which everyone assimilated to a single culture and adhered to a single set of formal and informal rules, or might it be a plural society in which different groups accepted different goals and behaviors? The debates at the end of the twentieth century replayed many of the questions that European immigration raised at the century's beginning.

Illegal Immigration and Bilingual Education   One issue is the economic impact of illegal immigration. Advocates of tight borders assert that illegal immigrants take jobs away from legal residents and eat up public assistance. Many studies, however, find that illegal immigrants fill jobs that nobody else wants. Over the long run, high employment levels among immigrants mean that their tax contributions through sales taxes and Social Security taxes and payroll deductions more than pay for their use of welfare, food stamps, and unemployment benefits, which illegal immigrants are often afraid to claim for fear of calling attention to themselves. Nevertheless, high immigration can strain local government budgets even if it benefits the nation as a whole. Partly for this reason, 60 percent of California voters approved **Proposition 187** in 1994, cutting off access to state-funded public education and healthcare for illegal immigrants.

A symbolic issue was the degree to which American institutions should accommodate non–English speakers. Referendums in Alaska (1996) and Utah (2000) raised to 26 the number of states that declared English their official language. The measures ranged from general statements to specific prohibitions on printing forms and ballots in multiple languages. California voters in 1998 banned bilingual public education, a system under which children whose first language was Spanish or another "immigrant" tongue were taught for several years in that language before shifting to English-language classrooms. Advocates of bilingual education claimed that it eased the transition into American society, but opponents said that it blocked immigrant children from fully assimilating into American life.

The issue of illegal immigration simmered in the 1990s, but exploded in the new century. As the total of undocumented immigrants reached 11 to 12 million by best estimates, many

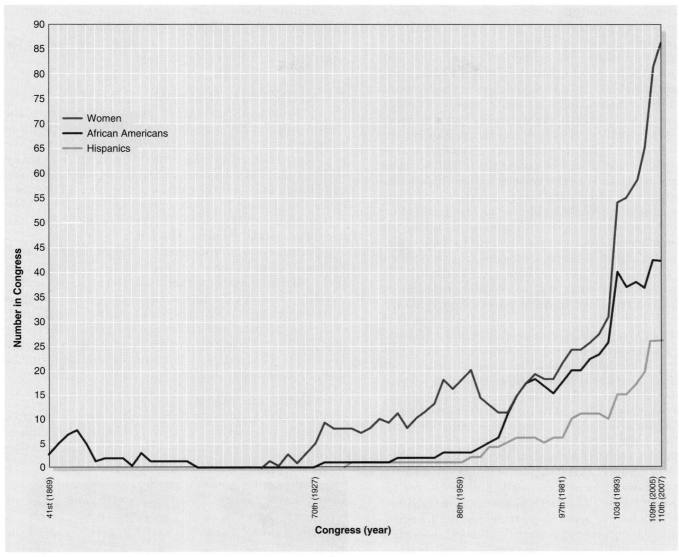

FIGURE 31–2   Minorities and Women in Congress, 1869–2005
The number of African Americans, Hispanics, and women serving in the House of Representatives and Senate increased rapidly in the 1980s and early 1990s and more slowly in the middle 1990s. The increases reflected changing attitudes, the impact of the Voting Rights Act, and decades of political activism at the grassroots.

Americans became increasingly concerned about a porous southern border. Unlike early eras of concern about immigration that had usually coincided with economic downturns, the new immigration worries came in an era of economic prosperity. In 2007, the president and leaders in both political parties were blindsided when a carefully constructed compromise over immigration policy failed because of public outcry over provisions that many voters interpreted as amnesty for rule-breaking.

Affirmative Action   An equally divisive issue was a set of policies that originated in the 1960s as **affirmative action,** a phrase that first appeared in executive orders issued by Presidents Kennedy and Johnson. The initial goal was to re-

quire businesses that received federal contracts to "take affirmative action to ensure that applicants are employed, and that employees are treated during employment without regard for their race, creed, color, or national origin." By the 1970s, many states and cities had adopted similar policies for hiring their own employees and choosing contractors and extended affirmative action to women as well as minorities. Colleges and universities used affirmative-action policies in recruiting faculty and admitting students.

As these efforts spread, the initial goal of nondiscrimination evolved into expectations and requirements for active ("affirmative") efforts to achieve greater diversity among employees, students, or contractors. Government agencies began to set aside a small percentage of contracts for woman-owned or minority-owned firms. Cities actively worked to hire more minority police officers and firefighters. Colleges made special efforts to attract minority students. The landmark court case about affirmative action was **University of California v. Bakke** (1978). Alan Bakke was an unsuccessful applicant to the medical school at the University of California at Davis. He argued that the university had improperly set aside 16 of 100 places in its entering class for minority students, thereby engaging in reverse discrimination against white applicants. In a narrow decision, the U.S. Supreme Court ordered Bakke admitted because the only basis for his rejection had been race. At the same time, the Court stated that race or ethnicity could legally be one of several factors considered in college and university admissions as long as a specific number of places were not reserved for minorities.

In 1996, California voters took grassroots action, approving a ballot measure to eliminate state-sponsored affirmative action. One effect was to prohibit state-funded colleges and universities from using race or ethnicity as a factor in deciding which applicants to admit. In the same year, the Supreme Court let stand a lower-court ruling in *Hopwood v. Texas,* which had forbidden the University of Texas to consider race in admission decisions. The number of black freshmen in the University of Texas dropped by half in 1997 and the number of blacks and Hispanics among first-year law students by two-thirds. The results were similar at the University of California at Berkeley, where the number of blacks among entering law students dropped from twenty to one.

Affirmative action has come under such close scrutiny and attack because it is a lightning rod for disagreements about the character of American society. The problem is that the goal of diversity seems to conflict with the fundamental American value of individual opportunity. In opinion polls, a majority of Americans reject the idea that past injustice and unequal opportunity can justify special consideration for all members of a group. Instead, they believe that individual merit and qualifications should be the sole basis for getting into school or getting a job, and that such factors as SAT scores and civil service exams can measure such qualifications. Others argue that the merit system is severely flawed, that students from poor families lack the advantages at home and at school that give upper-middle-class and wealthy students a head start for success. Affirmative action, they argue, helps to level the field. Nevertheless, many minorities worry that affirmative action undermines their success by suggesting that they received jobs or contracts by racial preference rather than merit.

In 2003, the Supreme Court affirmed the basic principle of affirmative action in two cases involving admission to the University of Michigan. Aided by supporting statements filed by major corporations and by members of the U.S. military, the Court found that promoting ethnic and racial diversity among students constitutes a compelling state interest, and it approved narrowly tailored affirmative-action programs that weigh race and ethnicity along with other admissions criteria on an individual basis. But four years later, a differ-

ent majority on the Court rejected public school plans in Seattle and Lexington, Kentucky, that took race into account in deciding how to match students and schools, leaving the larger issue for further court cases.

Edging into a New Century

On the evening of November 7, 2000, CBS-TV made the kind of mistake that journalists dread. Relying on questions put to a sample of voters after they cast their ballots in the presidential contest between Albert Gore, Jr., and George W. Bush, the CBS newsroom first projected that Gore would win Florida and likely the election, then reversed itself and called the election for Bush, only to find that it would be days or even weeks before the votes in several pivotal states, including Florida, could be certified.

The miscue was reminiscent of the premature *Chicago Tribune* headline in November 1948 that proclaimed "Dewey Beats Truman" when the actual results were the reverse. The inability to predict the outcome in 2000 was an indication of the degree to which Americans were split down the middle in their political preferences and their visions for the future. The United States entered the twenty-first century both divided and balanced, with extremes of opinion revolving around a center of basic goals and values.

The 2000 Election

On November 8, 2000, the day after their national election, Americans woke up to the news that neither Republican George W. Bush nor Democrat Albert Gore, Jr., had a major-

In November 2002, Linda Sanchez (left) and Loretta Sanchez celebrate Linda's election to Congress from Los Angeles County. Loretta had won a Congressional seat from Orange County in 1996, and Linda's victory made them the first sisters to serve simultaneously in the House of Representatives.

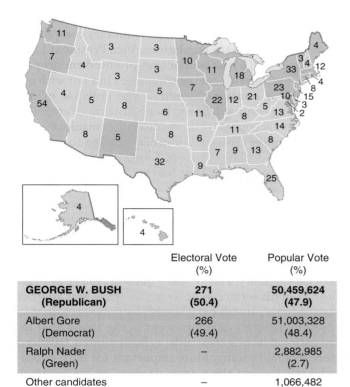

	Electoral Vote (%)	Popular Vote (%)
GEORGE W. BUSH (Republican)	**271** **(50.4)**	**50,459,624** **(47.9)**
Albert Gore (Democrat)	266 (49.4)	51,003,328 (48.4)
Ralph Nader (Green)	–	2,882,985 (2.7)
Other candidates	–	1,066,482 (1.0)

Map 31–3   The Election of 2000
In the nation's closest presidential election, Democrat Al Gore was most successful in the Northeast and Far West, while George W. Bush swept the South and won most of the Great Plains states. Green Party candidate Ralph Nader took most of his votes from Gore, and, in an ironic twist, helped to swing the election to Bush.

ity of votes in the electoral college. For the next five weeks, they woke every day to the same news. Although Gore held a lead in the popular vote (about 340,000 votes out of more than 100 million cast), both candidates needed a majority in Florida to win its electoral votes and the White House. After protracted protests about voting irregularities and malfunctioning voting equipment, politically divided Floridians engaged in an on-again off-again recount in key counties. The U.S. Supreme Court finally preempted the state process and ordered a halt to recounting on December 12 by the politically charged margin of 5 to 4. The result was to make Bush the winner in Florida by a few hundred votes and the winner nationwide by 271 electoral votes to 267 (see Map 31–3).

The heart of the controversy involved how to read Florida's punchcard ballots. Americans learned a new word, *chad,* for the little paper ovals that get punched out. How should election officials count dangling chads that were partially detached? What should they do with ballots where the chad was dimpled but not punched through? Until the Supreme Court put an end to the discussion, teams of officials struggled through recounts. Both parties put their own spin on the process. Republicans framed the issue as "following the

rules," while Democrats framed it as "making every vote count." It is difficult to know who "really" won Florida. There is good evidence that African American voters, who strongly favored Gore, were turned away in disproportionate numbers because of technical challenges to their registration. In one county, a ballot with a particularly poor design probably caused several thousand mistaken votes for a minor candidate rather than Gore. But recounts by teams of newspaper reporters came to different conclusions about who might have won, depending on what criteria were used to accept or reject disputed punchcard ballots. In the aftermath, each side could claim to have won, but the Supreme Court ruling and Bush's inauguration made the point irrelevant.

The outcome of the election showed a nation that was paradoxically divided around a strong center. The votes showed basic differences between the parties. Gore appealed especially to residents of large cities, to women, to African Americans, and to families struggling to make it economically. Bush appealed to people from small towns, to men, and to members of households that had benefitted the most from the prosperity of the Clinton era. These were divisions that had marked the two parties since the 1930s, and their persistence was a reminder of the nation's diversity of opinions and values. The nation also divided regionally, with Gore strong in the Northeast, upper Middle West, and Pacific Coast, Bush in the South, Ohio Valley, Great Plains, and Rocky Mountain states.

At the same time, both Bush, governor of Texas and son of President George H. W. Bush (1989–93), and Gore, vice president for the previous eight years, targeted their campaigns at middle Americans. Each offered to cut taxes, downsize the federal government, and protect Social Security, differing in the details rather than the broad goals. In trying to claim the political middle, they reflected the successful political message of the Clinton administration. Voters also shaved the Republican control of Congress to razor-thin margins, further undermining any chance of radical change in either a conservative or a liberal direction. To those on the political left and right who had hoped for new directions for the nation, it looked like a formula for paralysis; for the majority of Americans, it looked like stability.

Reaganomics Revisited

Despite the message of stability, the Bush administration took the Republican return to executive power as an opportunity to tilt domestic policy abruptly to the right. In effect, the new administration decided it had a mandate for change and acted boldly to implement its goals. Following the example of Ronald Reagan, Bush made massive tax cuts the centerpiece of his first months in office. By starting with proposals for ten-year cuts so large that two generations of federal programs were threatened, Bush and congressional Republicans forced the Democrats to "compromise" on reductions far higher than the economy could probably support. The resulting cuts to income taxes and estate taxes were projected to total $1,350 billion over the decade, with one-third of the benefits going to families earning more than

Firefighters work in the rubble of one of the World Trade Center towers soon after its destruction on September 11, 2001.

administration had ignored its recommendations to reorganize federal homeland security. The problem, however, had been to connect broad concerns to specific threats. After September 11, there were reports of information-gathering failures by the FBI and CIA, to be investigated by a commission appointed by President Bush at the end of 2002. However, it is always enormously difficult to separate and correlate key points in the vast flood of information that flows through law-enforcement and intelligence agencies. Experts call this the problem of discerning real "signals" in the "noise" of information. It is much easier to read the warnings after an event has occurred than to pick out the essential data before the unexpected happens—something as true about the attack on Pearl Harbor, for example, as about the attack of 9–11.

Security and Conflict

On September 12, President George W. Bush called the Pentagon and World Trade Center attacks "acts of war." Three days later, Congress passed a Joint Resolution that gave the president sweeping powers "to use all necessary and appropriate force against those nations, organizations, or persons

he determines planned, authorized, committed, or aided the terrorist attacks that occurred on September 11, 2001." Only one member voted against the resolution—the same level of agreement that the nation showed after December 7, 1941.

The government response in the United States was a hodge-podge of security measures and arrests. Air travelers found endless lines and stringent new screening procedures, watched over by army reservists called to duty by the president. Federal agents detained more than 1,000 terrorist suspects, mostly men from the Middle East, releasing some but holding hundreds without charges, evidence, or legal counsel. President Bush also declared that "enemy combatants" could be tried by special military tribunals, although domestic and international protest caused the administration to agree to more legal safeguards than originally planned. Congress passed the **PATRIOT Act** (Providing Appropriate Tools Required to Intercept and Obstruct Terrorists) in late October, which gave federal authorities substantial new capacity to conduct criminal investigations, in most provisions for the next three to five years. These included the power to request "roving" wiretaps of individuals rather than single telephones, obtain nationwide search warrants, tap information in computerized records, and detain foreigners without filing charges for up to a week. These measures raised a number of concerns about the protection of civil liberties, as noted by the several dozen members of Congress who voted against the act. The law would be renewed in 2006 with a few added provisions to protect basic constitutional and political rights.

In November 2002, Congress approved a massive reorganization of the federal government to improve security at home. The new Department of Homeland Security includes the Immigration and Naturalization Service, Customs Service, Coast Guard, Secret Service, federal airport security workers, bioterrorism experts, and many others. With 170,000 employees, it is the second-largest federal agency, after the Defense Department. In 2004 Congress adopted a package of reforms to improve intelligence gathering and analysis, creating the position of director of national intelligence to oversee the CIA and report directly to the president.

In contrast to the suppression of dissent during World War I or the internment of Japanese Americans during World War II, Americans in 2001 and 2002 were careful on the home front. The leaders and supporters of the War on Terror reacted to dissenting voices, particularly those from a pacifist tradition, with caustic remarks rather than repression. Censorship consisted of careful management of the news and stonewalling of requests under the Freedom of Information Act rather than direct censorship of speech and the press. Violations of civil liberties have affected individuals rather than entire groups. President Bush made an important gesture soon after September 11 by appearing at a mosque and arguing against blanket condemnation of Muslims. Ethnic profiling has resulted in heightened suspicion and surveillance of Muslims, selective enforcement of immigration laws on visitors from 20 Muslim nations, and detention of several hundred U.S. residents of Middle Eastern origin, rather than incarceration of entire ethnic groups.

In the months after 9-11, the military response overseas focused on Afghanistan, where the ruling Taliban regime was harboring Bin-Laden. Afghanistan had been wracked by civil war since the invasion by the Soviet Union in 1979. The Taliban, who came to power after the Soviet withdrawal and civil war, were politically and socially repressive rulers with few international friends. U.S. bombing attacks on Taliban forces began in early October 2001, and internal opposition groups in Afghanistan threw the Taliban out of power by December. Bin-Laden, however, escaped with the aid of mountainous terrain and the confusion of war. The United States and NATO allies were left with an uncertain commitment to rebuild a stable Afghanistan, which remained an active war zone where resurgent Taliban activity in 2007 and 2008 threatened previous gains. The Al-Qaeda network and sympathetic groups remained active around the world with bombings in places as distant as Indonesia and Kenya.

Iraq and Conflicts in the Middle East

Even while the United States was intervening in Afghanistan, the administration was extending its attention to other nations that supported or condoned anti-American terrorists or had the potential to produce chemical, biological, or nuclear weapons of mass destruction. George Bush named North Korea, Iran, and Iraq as an "axis of evil" for these reasons, and then focused on Iraq. After the Gulf War, Iraq had grudgingly accepted a United Nations requirement that it eliminate such weapons, but gradually made UN inspections impossible. This resistance caused Bush to make the overthrow of Iraq's ruthless dictator, Saddam Hussein, the center of foreign policy. In effect, he declared one small, possibly dangerous nation to be the greatest menace the United States faced. In the meantime, North Korea created a further crisis by actively pursuing its atomic weapons program with the threat of additional war. However, it did enter into talks with China, Japan, Russia, South Korea, and the United States and agreed in 2007 to suspend its nuclear weapons program under international supervision and took initial steps toward compliance in 2008—an example of the potential of persistent and patient diplomacy.

In addition to the direct fallout from the Persian Gulf War, the background to the deep-seated tensions in the Middle East included U.S. support of Israel amidst the deterioration of relations between Israel and the Arab Palestinians in territories occupied by Israel since 1967. The United States has consistently backed Israel since the 1960s. The cornerstones of U.S. policy have been the full endorsement of Israel's right to exist with secure borders and agreement on the right of Palestinians to a national state—in effect, a policy of coexistence. The United States helped to broker an Israel-Egypt peace agreement in 1977 and agreements pointing toward an independent Palestinian state in the 1990s. But hardline Israeli governments have repeatedly taken advantage of U.S. support from the 1980s in Lebanon (see Chapter 30) to the present.

In 2001–2002, the United States watched from the sidelines as the Israeli-Palestinian agreements for transition to a Palestinian state fell apart. Palestinian extremists and suicide bombers and an Israeli government that favored military responses locked each other into a downward spiral that turned into civil war. As a result, many Arabs identify the United States as an enemy of Arab nations and peoples. Israel's decision in 2005 to withdraw from the Gaza Strip and transfer authority there to the Palestinian government was a step toward resolution that unfortunately led to radical takeover there in 2007-08. The deep and long unsolvable Israel-Palestinian conflict helps to explain anti-American terrorism among Arabs, and sometimes other Muslims.

In the spring and summer of 2002, the administration escalated threats of unilateral intervention to change the Iraqi regime and began preparations for a second war in the Persian Gulf region. On October 10, Congress authorized preemptive military action against Iraq. However, international pressure from unenthusiastic allies and from other Arab nations persuaded Bush to put diplomacy ahead of war and devote two months to making his case at the United Nations. On November 8, the UN Security Council unanimously adopted a compromise resolution that gave Iraq three and a half months to allow full and open inspections before military action might be considered. In the following months, UN inspectors searched Iraqi military sites while the United States built up forces in the Middle East in preparation for war. On March 17, 2003, Bush suspended further diplomatic efforts, and on March 19 a full scale U.S.-British invasion of Iraq began (see Map 31–4).

The war to overthrow Saddam Hussein was a success as a large-scale military operation. Heavy bombing disrupted the communications and command systems for Iraq's armed forces, while the technological superiority of the U.S. armed forces overwhelmed them. Coalition forces encountered pockets of resistance from Iraqi army units, but the battles failed to stop the steady push northward from the Persian Gulf. U.S. troops took control of Baghdad without the door-to-door fighting that many had feared. On May 1, 2003, President Bush declared "mission accomplished"—that U.S. and British forces now controlled Iraq and major combat operations in Iraq were over.

Peace proved far more difficult than war. Reconstruction of damaged bridges, roads, water systems, and electrical systems took far longer than expected and many basic services were still fragile or nonexistent four years after the U.S. invasion. Meanwhile, American troops and relief workers were the continuing targets of car bombs, booby-trapped highways, mortar attacks, and similar guerrilla

MAP 31–4   Beginning in 2001, the United States engaged in major and continuous military operations in western Asia. Operation Enduring Freedom in late 2001 deposed the Taliban regime in Afghanistan and installed a democratic government in Kabul and vicinity, although the mountainous southeastern border of Afghanistan remained insecure into 2005. The United States, Britain, and other coalition allies invaded Iraq in March, 2003 and defeated the regular Iraqi military in less than a month. However, guerilla insurgency and terrorism continued to challenge the U.S. presence.

resistance. By July 2008, more than 4,100 U.S. soldiers had died in Iraq, over 90 percent of them after the president declared victory.

By 2007, a consensus had emerged among both critics of the war and realistic supporters that the United States had overthrown Saddam without any clear plan for next steps. Because of decisions by Secretary of Defense Donald Rumsfeld, the occupation force was inadequate in size from the start—a deficiency that a "surge" of additional U.S. forces in 2007 could not fully remedy. U.S. officials dismantled the Iraqi army and police, putting 650,000 unemployed but armed men onto the streets. The decision to shut down state industries and purge members of Saddam's political party from low-level government jobs like schoolteachers created massive unemployment. The result was the decimation of

Iraq's middle class, a collapse of living standards, and the creation of roughly two million refugees who fled Iraq's new chaos for neighboring nations.

The aftermath of the war also created political problems for George Bush. A systematic search found no active production facilities or stockpiles for chemical, nuclear, or biological weapons of mass destruction. In October 2004, the final report of the U.S. bomb hunters concluded that Saddam has disbanded his chemical and nuclear weapons efforts after 1991, refuting one of the basic justifications for the war. The continuing necessity to mobilize National Guard and reserve units met heavy criticism. The need to keep an occupying army in Iraq stretched the military close the breaking point at exactly the same time that the Taliban showed renewed strength in Afghanistan.

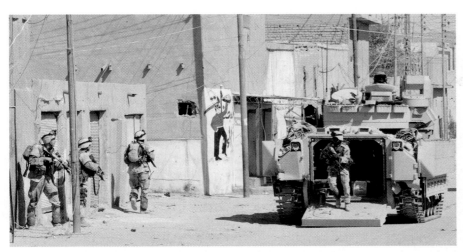

After the defeat of the Iraqi army in 2003, U.S. forces faced continuing challenges and casualties from a stubborn resistance from anti-American insurgents.

2004 and After

Wars past and present were the pivotal issue in the 2004 election. George W. Bush argued for staying the course with the same administration. Democratic candidate John Kerry had a liberal voting record as a Massachusetts senator and decorations for meritorious service in Vietnam, but central to the Republican campaign were attacks on the veracity of his war record. A wild card was the issue of same-sex marriage. Courts in Massachusetts and politicians in Oregon and San Francisco decided that legal marriage could not be denied to same-sex couples. Their actions mobilized religious and cultural conservatives and led to successful ballot measures banning same-sex marriage in 11 states.

Bush won a solid although not overwhelming victory that helped Republicans extend their lead in Congress. Commentators liked to talk about a nation divided on issues of morality between Democratic "blue states" and Republican "red states" (colors drawn from television maps of election results). In fact, many states remained closely divided and only three shifted from one party to the other (New Hampshire to Kerry, and Iowa and New Mexico to Bush). Pundits also claimed that Bush used the issue of "moral values," including opposition to same-sex marriage, to mobilize voters, but he did not do any better among regular church-goers in 2004 than in 2000.

After the election, Bush reaffirmed his commitment to a U.S. presence in Iraq, where a deeply divided nation held elections for a new government early in 2005. Kurds from northern Iraq and Shiite Muslims from southern Iraq voted in large numbers and formed a coalition govern-ment. Participation was much lower among Sunni Muslims in central Iraq, who had benefitted most from Saddam Hussein's regime and who were the heart of continued guerrilla resistance to the United States occupation forces. The same divisions were evident in October when Iraqis approved a new constitution that met Shiite and Kurdish desires for greater autonomy but left many Sunnis dissatis-fied. Those tensions played into the hands of militants who kept the level of violence among Iraqis high. In mid-2007, Congress concluded that the new Iraqi government had failed to meet most of the benchmarks that would have indicated progress toward normalcy in that devastated country, al-though progress was shown in 2008. Mean-while, U.S. coalition allies such as Britain were quietly packing and leaving Iraq to its American conquerors.

As the nation worried about the open-ended commit-ment in Iraq, it received a devastating reminder of vulnera-bility. At the end of August 2005, hurricane Katrina devastated the Gulf Coast. It first seemed to spare New Orleans, much of which lies below sea level, but its backlash breached levees that protected the city. Much of the city and its surround-ings flooded. Tens of thousands of residents who had not evacuated found themselves trapped in homes or huddled in the Superdome. The slowness and inadequacy of the emer-gency response raised serious doubts about the effectiveness of the Department of Homeland Security and its Federal Emergency Management Agency and revealed the deep fault

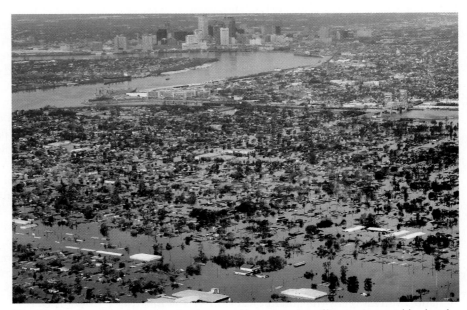

The flooding from Hurricane Katrina devastated huge expanses of low income neighborhoods in New Orleans.

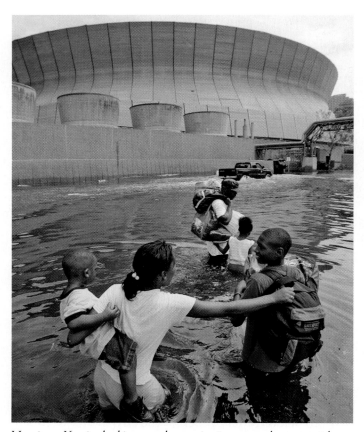

Hurricane Katrina had its most devastating impact on the poor neighborhoods of New Orleans, where many residents lacked the ability to evacuate. Instead, thousands of families had to make their way to temporary shelter in the Superdome and other makeshift refuges.

lines that still separate the poor from the larger society—exacerbated in New Orleans by the fact that most of the poor residents were African American. Two years after the disaster, only 60 percent of the city's pre-Katrina residents had stayed or returned, and large sections of the city had seen only sporadic rebuilding. Behind the growing discussion about whether and how to rebuild New Orleans on its vulnerable site was a larger problem of continuing inequality.

Iraq and Katrina combined to deal Republicans a blow in the 2006 Congressional elections, in which Democrats regained effective control of Congress for the first time in 12 years. The results reflected the reality that the red state/blue state division of 2000 and 2004 had been poised on a knife's edge, ready to tilt toward one party or the other. Through 2007, as candidates of both parties jockeyed for presidential nominations, important domestic issues like immigration policy, health insurance, and the future of social security remained unresolved. Federal courts began to cautiously consider the basic issues of civil liberties raised by the PATRIOT Act and, even more, by the unilateral actions of the Bush administration in claiming free rein to deal with persons suspected as terrorists. And there was no clear consensus in

Congress or the nation about the best steps in Iraq—whether a quick exit or a long-term U.S. occupation would do more damage to Iraq itself, to the U.S. military, and to U.S. standing in the world.

In September 2008, Americans faced a presidential election campaign with two improbable candidates. The Republicans nominated John McCain, an Arizona senator who had been a prisoner of war during the Vietnam War and who cultivated a reputation as a maverick. Nevertheless, he outlasted more mainstream candidates to win his party's nomination. Democrats had a hard-fought contest between Hillary Rodham Clinton, who hoped to be the first woman nominated for President by a major party, and Barack Obama, an Illinois senator who became the first African American nominee. Whatever the outcome of the election in November, Obama's nomination was a milestone in the long, often painful history of race relations in America.

Conclusion

If there was a dominant theme that ran through the changes and challenges of the 1990s and early 2000s, it was interconnection. The Internet, e-mail, and cell phones brought instant communication. The national economy was more and more deeply engaged with the rest of the world through trade, investment, travel, and immigration. Corporate mismanagement affected far more people than before because of pensions and savings invested in the stock market.

The nation's growing diversity—closely connected to its internationalized economy—was reflected in the political gains of African Americans and Hispanics, as well as women. The same diversity fueled battles over affirmative action and language politics. It underlay the effort to increase security against terrorism without endangering the civil liberties of Muslim Americans.

Despite what some might have wished, Americans also found that they could not always isolate the nation from the problems and conflicts that wracked much of the rest of the world. The Clinton administration joined international peacekeeping efforts in Bosnia and Kosovo. The Bush administration chose to ignore several international agreements, but still sought the cover of United Nations approval for action against Iraq (although it largely disregarded international opinion in its pursuit of the war).

Beyond its growing military commitments, the United States in the first years of the twenty-first century was deeply connected to the world. Travel, work and study abroad—and foreign tourists, workers, and students in the United States—improved American understanding of other nations. But the ease and volume of travel and trade also brought problems and fears. Many Americans had long worried that the United States was being flooded by illegal immigrants, and the revelation that some of the 9-11 terrorists had learned to fly in U.S. training schools compounded fears of a porous border. A ballooning national debt and fast-growing trade deficits reduced the

FROM THEN TO NOW

America's Mission to the World

U.S. President George W. Bush delivers his inauguration speech January, 2005.

On April 2, 1917, President Woodrow Wilson addressed Congress and asked for a declaration of war against Germany. Germany's decision to engage in unrestricted submarine warfare had made than nation the enemy of international law and morality

Wilson argued the need for the United States to protect its citizens, but he also proclaimed a crusade to make "the world safe for democracy." Wilson's idealism echoed repeatedly through the twentieth century—in Franklin Roosevelt's proclamation of the Four Freedoms, in John Kennedy's claim that Americans would "bear any burden" in the defense of liberty, in Jimmy Carter's emphasis on advancing human rights in other nations.

But the clearest echo came in January 2005, in the second inaugural address of George W. Bush. Like Wilson, Bush proclaimed that the United States has a mission and destiny to actively and tirelessly extend democracy throughout the world. "It is the policy of the United States to seek and support the growth of democratic movements and institutions in every nation and culture, with the ultimate goal of ending tyranny in our world. America's influence is considerable and we will use it confidently."

■ In what circumstances might a sense of mission enhance the effectiveness of U.S. foreign policy? When might it create problems?

myhistorylab
PEARSON

From Then to Now Online

31-1 Senator Henry Cabot Lodge, *Speech in Washington, D.C.*, 1919. Cabot Lodge sets forth his opposition to U.S. membership in League of Nations.

31-2 John F. Kennedy, *Inaugural Address*, 1961. Kennedy on national mission to the World.

31-3 Jimmy Carter, *Commencement Speech at Notre Dame University*, 1977. Carter talks about human rights and foreign policy.

President Woodrow Wilson called on Congress to formalize a state of war between the revolution that had overthrown the Czar in Russia and also promised "a firm band of stern repression" against any disloyalty at home—a prelude to substantial curtailment of free speech in the United States for the duration of the war.

and with the advice and consent of the Senate, shall appoint ambassadors, other public ministers and consuls, judges of the Supreme Court, and all other officers of the United States, whose appointments are not herein otherwise provided for, and which shall be established by law; but the Congress may by law vest the appointment of such inferior officers, as they think proper, in the President alone, in the courts of laws, or in the heads of departments.

3. The President shall have power to fill up all vacancies that may happen during the recess of the Senate, by granting commissions which shall expire at the end of their next session.

Section 3. He shall from time to time give to the Congress information of the state of the Union, and recommend to their consideration such measures as he shall judge necessary and expedient; he may, on extraordinary occasions, convene both Houses, or either of them, and in case of disagreement between them with respect to the time of adjournment, he may adjourn them to such time as he shall think proper; he shall receive ambassadors and other public ministers; he shall take care that the laws be faithfully executed, and shall commission all the officers of the United States.

Section 4. The President, Vice President, and all civil officers of the United States, shall be removed from office on impeachment for, and conviction of, treason, bribery, or other high crimes and misdemeanors.

Article III

Section 1. The judicial power of the United States shall be vested in one Supreme Court, and in such inferior courts as the Congress may from time to time ordain and establish. The judges, both of the Supreme and inferior courts, shall hold their offices during good behavior, and shall, at stated times, receive for their services, a compensation, which shall not be diminished during their continuance in office.

Section 2. 1. The judicial power shall extend to all cases, in law and equity, arising under this Constitution, the laws of the United States, and treaties made, or which shall be made, under their authority;—to all cases of admiralty and maritime jurisdiction;—to controversies to which the United States shall be a party;[7]—to controversies between two or more States;—between a State and citizens of another State;—between citizens of different States;—between citizens of the same State claiming lands under grants of different States, and between a State, or the citizens thereof, and foreign States, citizens or subjects.

2. In all cases affecting ambassadors, other public ministers and consuls, and those in which a State shall be party, the Supreme Court shall have original jurisdiction. In all the other cases before mentioned, the Supreme Court shall have appellate jurisdiction, both as to law and fact, with such exceptions, and under such regulations as the Congress shall make.

3. The trial of all crimes, except in cases of impeachment, shall be by jury; and such trial shall be held in the State where the said crimes shall have been committed; but when not committed within any State, the trial shall be such place or places as the congress may by law have directed.

Section 3. 1. Treason against the United States shall consist only in levying war against them, or in adhering to their enemies, giving them aid and comfort. No person shall be convicted of treason unless on the testimony of two witnesses to the same overt act, or on confession in open court.

2. The Congress shall have power to declare the punishment of treason, but no attainder of treason shall work corruption of blood, or forfeiture except during the life of the person attained.

Article IV

Section 1. Full faith and credit shall be given in each State to the public acts, records, and judicial proceedings of every other State. And the Congress may by general laws prescribe the manner in which such acts, records and proceedings shall be proved, and the effect thereof.

Section 2. 1. The citizens of each State shall be entitled to all privileges and immunities of citizens in the several States.[8]

2. A person charged in any State with treason, felony, or other crime, who shall flee from justice, and be found in another State, shall on demand of the executive authority of the State from which he fled, be delivered up to be removed to the State having jurisdiction of the crime.

3. No person held to service or labor in one State under the laws thereof, escaping into another, shall, in consequence of any law or regulation therein, be discharged from such service or labor, but shall be delivered up on claim of the party to whom such service or labor may be due.[9]

Section 3. 1. New States may be admitted by the Congress into this Union; but no new State shall be formed or erected within the jurisdiction of any other State, nor any State be formed by the junction of two or more States, or parts of States, without the consent of the legislatures of the States concerned as well as of the Congress.

2. The Congress shall have power to dispose of and make all needful rules and regulations respecting the territory or other property belonging to the United States; and nothing in this Constitution shall be so construed as to prejudice any claims of the United States, or of any particular State.

Section 4. The United States shall guarantee to every State in this Union a republican form of government, and shall

---

[7]See the Eleventh Amendment.

[8]See the Fourteenth Amendment, Sec.1.
[9]See the Thirteenth Amendment.

protect each of them against invasion; and on application of the legislature, or of the executive (when the legislature cannot be convened) against domestic violence.

Article V

The Congress, whenever two thirds of both Houses shall deem it necessary, shall propose amendments to this Constitution, or, on the application of the legislatures of two thirds of the several States, shall call a convention for proposing amendments, which in either case shall be valid to all intents and purposes, as part of this Constitution, when ratified by the legislatures of three fourths of the several States, or by conventions in three fourths thereof, as the one or the other mode of ratification may be proposed by the Congress; Provided that no amendment which may be made prior to the year one thousand eight hundred and eight shall in any manner affect the first and fourth clauses in the ninth section of the first article; and that no State, without its consent, shall be deprived of its equal suffrage in the Senate.

Article VI

1. All debts contracted and engagements entered into, before the adoption of this Constitution, shall be as valid against the United States under this Constitution, as under the Confederation.[10]

2. This Constitution, and the laws of the United States which shall be made in pursuance thereof; and all treaties made, or which shall be made, under the authority of the United States, shall be the supreme law of the land; and the judges in every State shall be bound thereby, any thing in the Constitution or laws of any State to the contrary notwithstanding.

3. The senators and representatives before mentioned, and the members of the several State legislatures, and all executive and judicial officers, both of the United States and of the several States, shall be bound by oath or affirmation to support this Constitution; but no religious test shall ever be required as a qualification to any office or public trust under the United States.

Article VII

The ratification of the conventions of nine States shall be sufficient for the establishment of this Constitution between the States so ratifying the same.

Done in Convention by the unanimous consent of the States present the seventeenth day of September in the year of our Lord one thousand seven hundred and eighty-seven, and of the independence of the United States of America the twelfth. In witness whereof we have hereunto subscribed our names.

[Signatories' names omitted]

---

[10]See the Fourteenth Amendment, Sec.4.

Articles in addition to, and amendment of, the Constitution of the United States of America, proposed by Congress, and ratified by the legislatures of the several States, pursuant to the fifth article of the original Constitution.

Amendment I

[First ten amendments ratified December 15, 1791]
Congress shall make no law respecting an establishment of religion, or prohibiting the free exercise thereof; or abridging the freedom of speech, or of the press; or the right of the people peaceably to assemble, and to petition the government for a redress of grievances.

Amendment II

A well regulated militia, being necessary to the security of a free State, the right of the people to keep and bear arms, shall not be infringed.

Amendment III

No soldier shall, in time of peace be quartered in any house, without the consent of the owner, nor in time of war, but in a manner to be prescribed by law.

Amendment IV

The right of the people to be secure in their persons, houses, papers, and effects, against unreasonable searches and seizures, shall not be violated, and no warrants shall issue, but upon probable cause, supported by oath or affirmation, and particularly describing the place to be searched, and the persons or things to be seized.

Amendment V

No person shall be held to answer for a capital or otherwise infamous crime, unless on a presentment or indictment of a grand jury, except in cases arising in the land or naval forces, or in the militia, when in actual service in time of war or public danger; nor shall any person be subject for the same offense to be twice put in jeopardy of life or limb; nor shall be compelled in any criminal case to be a witness against himself, nor be deprived of life, liberty, or property, without due process of law; nor shall private property be taken for public use, without just compensation.

Amendment VI

In all criminal prosecutions, the accused shall enjoy the right to a speedy and public trial, by an impartial jury of the State and district wherein the crime shall have been committed, which district shall have been previously ascertained by law, and to be informed of the nature and cause of the accusation; to be confronted with the witnesses against him; to have compulsory process for obtaining witnesses in his favor, and to have the assistance of counsel for his defense.

Amendment VII

In suits at common law, where the value in controversy shall exceed twenty dollars, the right of trial by jury shall be preserved, and no fact tried by a jury shall be otherwise reexamined in any court of the United States, than according to the rules of the common law.

Amendment VIII

Excessive bail shall not be required, nor excessive fines imposed, nor cruel and unusual punishments inflicted.

Amendment IX

The enumeration in the Constitution of certain rights shall not be construed to deny or disparage others retained by the people.

Amendment X

The powers not delegated to the United States by the Constitution, nor prohibited by it to the States, are reserved to the States respectively, or to the people.

Amendment XI [January 8, 1798]

The judicial power of the United States shall not be construed to extend to any suit in law or equity, commended or prosecuted against one of the United States by citizens of another State, or by citizens or subjects of any foreign State.

Amendment XII [September 25, 1804]

The electors shall meet in their respective States, and vote by ballot for President and Vice President, one of whom, at least, shall not be an inhabitant of the same State with themselves; they shall name in their ballots the person voted for as President, and in distinct ballots, the person voted for as Vice President, and they shall make distinct lists of all persons voted for as President and of all persons voted for as Vice President, and of the number of votes for each, which lists they shall sign and certify, and transmit sealed to the seat of the government of the United States, directed to the President of the Senate;—The President of the Senate shall, in the presence of the Senate and House of Representatives, open all the certificates and the votes shall then be counted;—The person having the greatest number of votes for President, shall be the President, if such number be a majority of the whole number of electors appointed; and if no person have such majority, then from the persons having the highest numbers not exceeding three on the list of those voted for as President, the House of Representatives shall choose immediately, by ballot, the President. But in choosing the President, the votes shall be taken by States, the representation from each State having one vote; a quorum for this purpose shall consist of a member or members from two thirds of the States, and a majority of all the States shall be necessary to a choice. And if the House of Representatives shall not choose a Pres-

ident whenever the right of choice shall devolve upon them, before the fourth day of March next following, then the Vice President shall act as President, as in the case of the death or other constitutional disability of the President. The person having the greatest number of votes as Vice President shall be the Vice President, if such number be a majority of the whole number of electors appointed, and if no person have a majority, then from the two highest numbers on the list, the Senate shall choose the Vice President; a quorum for the purpose shall consist of two thirds of the whole number of Senators, and a majority of the whole number shall be necessary to a choice. But no person constitutionally ineligible to the office of President shall be eligible to that of Vice President of the United States.

Amendment XIII [December 18, 1865]

Section 1. Neither slavery nor involuntary servitude, except as a punishment for crime whereof the party shall have been duly convicted, shall exist within the United States, or any place subject to their jurisdiction.

Section 2. Congress shall have power to enforce this article by appropriate legislation.

Amendment XIV [July 28, 1868]

Section 1. All persons born or naturalized in the United States, and subject to the jurisdiction thereof, are citizens of the United States and of the State wherein they reside. No State shall make or enforce any law which shall abridge the privileges or immunities of citizens of the United States; nor shall any State deprive any person of life, liberty, or property, without due process of law; nor deny to any person within its jurisdiction the equal protection of the laws.

Section 2. Representatives shall be apportioned among the several States according to their respective numbers, counting the whole number of persons in each State, excluding Indians not taxed. But when the right to vote at any election for the choice of electors for President and Vice President of the United States, representatives in Congress, the executive and judicial officers of a State, or the members of the legislature thereof, is denied to any of the male inhabitants of such State, being twenty-one years of age, and citizens of the United States, or in any way abridged, except for participating in rebellion, or other crime, the basis of representation there shall be reduced in the proportion which the number of such male citizens shall bear to the whole number of male citizens twenty-one years of age in such State.

Section 3. No person shall be a senator or representative in Congress, or elector of President and Vice President, or hold any office, civil or military, under the United States, or under any State, who having previously taken an oath, as a member of Congress, or as an officer of the United States, or as a member of any State legislature, or as an executive or judicial officer of any State, to support the Constitution of the United States, shall have engaged in insurrection or rebellion against the same, or given aid or comfort to the enemies thereof. But Congress may by a vote of two thirds of each House, remove such disability.

Section 4. The validity of the public debt of the United States, authorized by law, including debts incurred for payment of pensions and bounties for services in suppressing insurrection or rebellion; shall not be questioned. But neither the United States nor any State shall assume or pay any debt or obligation incurred in aid of insurrection or rebellion against the United States, or any claim for the loss or emancipation of any slave; but all such debts, obligations, and claims shall be held illegal and void.

Section 5. The Congress shall have the power to enforce, by appropriate legislation, the provisions of this article.

Amendment XV [March 30, 1870]
Section 1. The right of citizens of the United States to vote shall not be denied or abridged by the United States or by any State on account of race, color, or previous condition of servitude.

Section 2. The Congress shall have power to enforce this article by appropriate legislation.

Amendment XVI [February 25, 1913]
The Congress shall have power to lay and collect taxes on incomes, from whatever source derived, without apportionment among the several States, and without regard to any census or enumeration.

Amendment XVII [May 31, 1913]
The Senate of the United States shall be composed of two senators from each State, elected by the people thereof, for six years; and each senator shall have one vote. The electors in each State shall have the qualifications requisite for electors of the most numerous branch of the State legislature.

When vacancies happen in the representation of any State in the Senate, the executive authority of such State shall issue writs of election to fill such vacancies: Provided, That the legislature of any State may empower the executive thereof to make temporary appointments until the people fill the vacancies by election as the legislature may direct.

This amendment shall not be so construed as to affect the election or term of any senator chosen before it becomes valid as part of the Constitution.

Amendment XVIII[11] [January 29, 1919]
After one year from the ratification of this article, the manufacture, sale, or transportation of intoxicating liquors within, the importation thereof into, or the exportation thereof from the United States and all territory subject to the jurisdiction thereof for beverage purposes is thereby prohibited.

The Congress and the several States shall have concurrent power to enforce this article by appropriate legislation.

This article shall be inoperative unless it shall have been ratified as an amendment to the Constitution by the legislatures of the several States, as provided in the constitution, within seven years from the date of the submission hereof to the States by Congress.

Amendment XIX [August 26, 1920]
The right of citizens of the United States to vote shall not be denied or abridged by the United States or by any State on account of sex.

Congress shall have the power to enforce this article by appropriate legislation.

Amendment XX [January 23, 1933]
Section 1. The terms of the President and Vice President shall end at noon on the 20th day of January and the terms of Senators and Representatives at noon on the 3d day of January, of the years in which such terms would have ended if this article had not been ratified; and the terms of their successors shall then begin.

Section 2. The Congress shall assemble at least once in every year, and such meeting shall begin at noon on the 3d day of January, unless they shall by law appoint a different day.

Section 3. If, at the time fixed for the beginning of the term of President, the President-elect shall have died, the Vice President-elect shall become President. If a President shall not have been chosen before the time fixed for the beginning of his term, or if the President-elect shall have failed to qualify, then the Vice President-elect shall act as President until a President shall have qualified; and the Congress may by law provide for the case wherein neither a President-elect nor a Vice President-elect shall have qualified, declaring who shall then act as President, or the manner in which one who is to act shall be selected, and such person shall act accordingly until a President or Vice President shall have qualified.

Section 4. The Congress may by law provide for the case of the death of any of the persons from whom, the House of

---

[11]Repealed by the Twenty-first Amendment.

Representatives may choose a President whenever the right of choice shall have devolved upon them, and for the case of the death of any of the persons from whom the Senate may choose a Vice President whenever the right of choice shall have devolved upon them.

Section 5. Sections 1 and 2 shall take effect on the 15th day of October following the ratification of this article.

Section 6. This article shall be inoperative unless it shall have been ratified as an amendment to the Constitution by the legislatures of three-fourths of the several States within seven years from the date of its submission.

Amendment XXI [December 5, 1933]

Section 1. The Eighteenth Article of amendment to the Constitution of the United States is hereby repealed.

Section 2. The transportation or importation into any State, Territory, or possession of the United States for delivery or use therein of intoxicating liquors in violation of the laws thereof, is hereby prohibited.

Section 3. This article shall be inoperative unless it shall have been ratified as an amendment to the Constitution by conventions in the several States, as provided in the Constitution, within seven years from the date of the submission thereof to the States by the Congress.

Amendment XXII [March 1, 1951]

No person shall be elected to the office of the President more than twice, and no person who has held the office of President, or acted as President, for more than two years of a term to which some other person was elected President shall be elected to the office of the President more than once.

But this article shall not apply to any person holding the office of President when this article was proposed by the Congress, and shall not prevent any person who may be holding the office of President, or acting as President, during the term within which this article becomes operative from holding the office of President or acting as President during the remainder of such term.

This article shall be inoperative unless it shall have been ratified as an amendment to the Constitution by the legislatures of three-fourths of the several States within seven years from the date of its submission to the States by the Congress.

Amendment XXIII [March 29, 1961]

Section 1. The District constituting the seat of Government of the United States shall appoint in such manner as the Congress may direct.

A number of electors of President and Vice President equal to the whole number of Senators and Representatives in Congress to which the District would be entitled if it were a State, but in no event more than the least populous State; they shall be in addition to those appointed by the States, but they shall be considered, for the purposes of the election of President and Vice President, to be electors appointed by a State; and they shall meet in the District and perform such duties as provided by the twelfth article of amendment.

Section 2. The Congress shall have power to enforce this article by appropriate legislation.

Amendment XXIV [January 23, 1964]

Section 1. The right of citizens of the United States to vote in any primary or other election for President or Vice President, for electors for President or Vice President, or for Senator or Representative in Congress, shall not be denied or abridged by the United States or any State by reason of failure to pay any poll tax or other tax.

Section 2. The Congress shall have power to enforce this article by appropriate legislation.

Amendment XXV [February 10, 1967]

Section 1. In case of the removal of the President from office or of his death or resignation, the Vice President shall become President.

Section 2. Whenever there is a vacancy in the office of the Vice President, the President shall nominate a Vice President who shall take office upon confirmation by a majority of both Houses of Congress.

Section 3. Whenever the President transmits to the President pro tempore of the Senate and the Speaker of the House of Representatives his written declaration that he is unable to discharge the powers and duties of his office, and until he transmits to them a written declaration to the contrary, such powers and duties shall be discharged by the Vice President as Acting President.

Section 4. Whenever the Vice President and a majority of either the principal officers of the executive departments or of such other body as Congress may by law provide, transmit to the President pro tempore of the Senate and the Speaker of the House of Representatives their written declaration that the President is unable to discharge the powers and duties of his office, the Vice President shall immediately assume the powers and duties of the office as Acting President.

Thereafter, when the President transmits to the President pro tempore of the Senate and the Speaker of the House of Representatives his written declaration that no inability exists, he shall resume the powers and duties of his office unless the Vice President and a majority of either the principal officers of the executive departments or of such other body as Congress may by law provide, transmit within four days to the President pro tempore of the Senate and the Speaker of the House of Representatives their written declaration that the President is unable to discharge the powers and duties of his office. Thereupon Congress shall decide the issue, assembling within forty-eight hours for that purpose if not in session. If the Congress, within twenty-one days after receipt of the latter written declaration, or, if Congress is not in session, within twenty-one days after Congress is required to assemble, determines by two-thirds vote of both Houses that the President is unable to discharge the powers and duties of his office, the Vice President shall continue to discharge the same as Acting President; otherwise, the President shall resume the powers and duties of his office.

Amendment XXVI *[June 30, 1971]*

Section 1. The right of citizens of the United States who are eighteen years of age or older to vote shall not be denied or abridged by the United States or by any State on account of age.

Section 2. The Congress shall have power to enforce this article by appropriate legislation.

Amendment XXVII[12] *[May 7, 1992]*

No law, varying the compensation for services of the Senators and Representatives, shall take effect until an election of Representatives shall have intervened.

---

[12]James Madison proposed this amendment in 1789 together with the ten amendments that were adopted as the Bill of Rights, but it failed to win ratification at the time. Congress, however, had set no deadline for its ratification, and over the years—particularly in the 1980s and 1990s—many states voted to add it to the Constitution. With the ratification of Michigan in 1992 it passed the threshold of 3/4ths of the states required for adoption, but because the process took more than 200 years, its validity remains in doubt.

PRESIDENTIAL ELECTIONS

Year	Number of States	Candidates	Party	Popular Vote*	Electoral Vote†	Percentage of Popular Vote
1789	11	GEORGE WASHINGTON	No party designations		69	
		John Adams			34	
		Other Candidates			35	
1792	15	GEORGE WASHINGTON	No party designations		132	
		John Adams			77	
		George Clinton			50	
		Other Candidates			5	
1796	16	JOHN ADAMS	Federalist		71	
		Thomas Jefferson	Democratic-Republican		68	
		Thomas Pinckney	Federalist		59	
		Aaron Burr	Democratic-Republican		30	
		Other Candidates			48	
1800	16	THOMAS JEFFERSON	Democratic-Republican		73	
		Aaron Burr	Democratic-Republican		73	
		John Adams	Federalist		65	
		Charles C. Pinckney	Federalist		64	
		John Jay	Federalist		1	
1804	17	THOMAS JEFFERSON	Democratic-Republican		162	
		Charles C. Pinckney	Federalist		14	
1808	17	JAMES MADISON	Democratic-Republican		122	
		Charles C. Pinckney	Federalist		47	
		George Clinton	Democratic-Republican		6	
1812	18	JAMES MADISON	Democratic-Republican		128	
		DeWitt Clinton	Federalist		89	
1816	19	JAMES MONROE	Democratic-Republican		183	
		Rufus King	Federalist		34	
1820	24	JAMES MONROE	Democratic-Republican		231	
		John Quincy Adams	Independent-Republican		1	
1824	24	JOHN QUINCY ADAMS	Democratic-Republican	108,740	84	30.5
		Andrew Jackson	Democratic-Republican	153,544	99	43.1
		William H. Crawford	Democratic-Republican	46,618	41	13.1
		Henry Clay	Democratic-Republican	47,136	37	13.2
1828	24	ANDREW JACKSON	Democrat	647,286	178	56.0
		John Quincy Adams	National Republican	508,064	83	44.0
1832	24	ANDREW JACKSON	Democrat	687,502	219	55.0
		Henry Clay	National Republican	530,189	49	42.4
		William Wirt	Anti-Masonic	33,108	7	2.6
		John Floyd			11	
1836	26	MARTIN VAN BUREN	Democrat	765,483	170	50.9
		William H. Harrison	Whig		73	
		Hugh L. White	Whig		26	
		Daniel Webster	Whig	739,795	14	49.1
		W. P. Mangum	Whig		11	

* Percentage of popular vote given for any election year may not total 100 percent because candidates receiving less than 1 percent of the popular vote have been omitted.
† Prior to the passage of the Twelfth Amendment in 1904, the electoral college voted for two presidential candidates; the runner-up became Vice-President. Data from Historical Statistics of the United States, Colonial Times to 1957 (1961), pp. 682–683, and The World Almanac.

PRESIDENTIAL ELECTIONS (CONTINUED)

Year	Number of States	Candidates	Party	Popular Vote	Electoral Vote	Percentage of Popular Vote
1840	26	WILLIAM H. HARRISON	Whig	1,274,624	234	53.1
		Martin Van Buren	Democrat	1,127,781	60	46.9
1844	26	JAMES K. POLK	Democrat	1,338,464	170	49.6
		Henry Clay	Whig	1,300,097	105	48.1
		James G. Birney	Liberty	62,300		2.3
1848	30	ZACHARY TAYLOR	Whig	1,360,967	163	47.4
		Lewis Cass	Democrat	1,222,342	127	42.5
		Martin Van Buren	Free Soil	291,263		10.1
1852	31	FRANKLIN PIERCE	Democrat	1,601,117	254	50.9
		Winfield Scott	Whig	1,385,453	42	44.1
		John P. Hale	Free Soil	155,825		5.0
1856	31	JAMES BUCHANAN	Democrat	1,832,955	174	45.3
		John C. Frémont	Republican	1,339,932	114	33.1
		Millard Fillmore	American ("Know Nothing")	871,731	8	21.6
1860	33	ABRAHAM LINCOLN	Republican	1,865,593	180	39.8
		Stephen A. Douglas	Democrat	1,382,713	12	29.5
		John C. Breckinridge	Democrat	848,356	72	18.1
		John Bell	Constitutional Union	592,906	39	12.6
1864	36	ABRAHAM LINCOLN	Republican	2,206,938	212	55.0
		George B. McClellan	Democrat	1,803,787	21	45.0
1868	37	ULYSSES S. GRANT	Republican	3,013,421	214	52.7
		Horatio Seymour	Democrat	2,706,829	80	47.3
1872	37	ULYSSES S. GRANT	Republican	3,596,745	286	55.6
		Horace Greeley	Democrat	2,843,446	*	43.9
1876	38	RUTHERFORD B. HAYES	Republican	4,036,572	185	48.0
		Samuel J. Tilden	Democrat	4,284,020	184	51.0
1880	38	JAMES A. GARFIELD	Republican	4,453,295	214	48.5
		Winfield S. Hancock	Democrat	4,414,082	155	48.1
		James B. Weaver	Greenback-Labor	308,578		3.4
1884	38	GROVER CLEVELAND	Democrat	4,879,507	219	48.5
		James G. Blaine	Republican	4,850,293	182	48.2
		Benjamin F. Butler	Greenback-Labor	175,370		1.8
		John P. St. John	Prohibition	150,369		1.5
1888	38	BENJAMIN HARRISON	Republican	5,447,129	233	47.9
		Grover Cleveland	Democrat	5,537,857	168	48.6
		Clinton B. Fisk	Prohibition	249,506		2.2
		Anson J. Streeter	Union Labor	146,935		1.3
1892	44	GROVER CLEVELAND	Democrat	5,555,426	277	46.1
		Benjamin Harrison	Republican	5,182,690	145	43.0
		James B. Weaver	People's	1,029,846	22	8.5
		John Bidwell	Prohibition	264,133		2.2
1896	45	WILLIAM McKINLEY	Republican	7,102,246	271	51.1
		William J. Bryan	Democrat	6,492,559	176	47.7

*Because of the death of Greeley, Democratic electors scattered their votes.

PRESIDENTIAL ELECTIONS (CONTINUED)

Year	Number of States	Candidates	Party	Popular Vote	Electoral Vote	Percentage of Popular Vote
1900	45	WILLIAM McKINLEY	Republican	7,218,491	292	51.7
		William J. Bryan	Democrat; Populist	6,356,734	155	45.5
		John C. Woolley	Prohibition	208,914		1.5
1904	45	THEODORE ROOSEVELT	Republican	7,628,461	336	57.4
		Alton B. Parker	Democrat	5,084,223	140	37.6
		Eugene V. Debs	Socialist	402,283		3.0
		Silas C. Swallow	Prohibition	258,536		1.9
1908	46	WILLIAM H. TAFT	Republican	7,675,320	321	51.6
		William J. Bryan	Democrat	6,412,294	162	43.1
		Eugene V. Debs	Socialist	420,793		2.8
		Eugene W. Chafin	Prohibition	253,840		1.7
1912	48	WOODROW WILSON	Democrat	6,296,547	435	41.9
		Theodore Roosevelt	Progressive	4,118,571	88	27.4
		William H. Taft	Republican	3,486,720	8	23.2
		Eugene V. Debs	Socialist	900,672		6.0
		Eugene W. Chafin	Prohibition	206,275		1.4
1916	48	WOODROW WILSON	Democrat	9,127,695	277	49.4
		Charles E. Hughes	Republican	8,533,507	254	46.2
		A. L. Benson	Socialist	585,113		3.2
		J. Frank Hanly	Prohibition	220,506		1.2
1920	48	WARREN G. HARDING	Republican	16,143,407	404	60.4
		James M. Cox	Democrat	9,130,328	127	34.2
		Eugene V. Debs	Socialist	919,799		3.4
		P. P. Christensen	Farmer-Labor	265,411		1.0
1924	48	CALVIN COOLIDGE	Republican	15,718,211	382	54.0
		John W. Davis	Democrat	8,385,283	136	28.8
		Robert M. La Follette	Progressive	4,831,289	13	16.6
1928	48	HERBERT C. HOOVER	Republican	21,391,993	444	58.2
		Alfred E. Smith	Democrat	15,016,169	87	40.9
1932	48	FRANKLIN D. ROOSEVELT	Democrat	22,809,638	472	57.4
		Herbert C. Hoover	Republican	15,758,901	59	39.7
		Norman Thomas	Socialist	881,951		2.2
1936	48	FRANKLIN D. ROOSEVELT	Democrat	27,752,869	523	60.8
		Alfred M. Landon	Republican	16,674,665	8	36.5
		William Lemke	Union	882,479		1.9
1940	48	FRANKLIN D. ROOSEVELT	Democrat	27,307,819	449	54.8
		Wendell L. Willkie	Republican	22,321,018	82	44.8
1944	48	FRANKLIN D. ROOSEVELT	Democrat	25,606,585	432	53.5
		Thomas E. Dewey	Republican	22,014,745	99	46.0
1948	48	HARRY S. TRUMAN	Democrat	24,105,812	303	49.5
		Thomas E. Dewey	Republican	21,970,065	189	45.1
		J. Strom Thurmond	States' Rights	1,169,063	39	2.4
		Henry A. Wallace	Progressive	1,157,172		2.4
1952	48	DWIGHT D. EISENHOWER	Republican	33,936,234	442	55.1
		Adlai E. Stevenson	Democrat	27,314,992	89	44.4

PRESIDENTIAL ELECTIONS (CONTINUED)

Year	Number of States	Candidates	Party	Popular Vote	Electoral Vote	Percentage of Popular Vote
1956	48	DWIGHT D. EISENHOWER	Republican	35,590,472	457*	57.6
		Adlai E. Stevenson	Democrat	26,022,752	73	42.1
1960	50	JOHN F. KENNEDY	Democrat	34,227,096	303†	49.9
		Richard M. Nixon	Republican	34,108,546	219	49.6
1964	50	LYNDON B. JOHNSON	Democrat	42,676,220	486	61.3
		Barry M. Goldwater	Republican	26,860,314	52	38.5
1968	50	RICHARD M. NIXON	Republican	31,785,480	301	43.4
		Hubert H. Humphrey	Democrat	31,275,165	191	42.7
		George C. Wallace	American Independent	9,906,473	46	13.5
1972	50	RICHARD M. NIXON‡	Republican	47,165,234	520**	60.6
		George S. McGovern	Democrat	29,168,110	17	37.5
1976	50	JIMMY CARTER	Democrat	40,828,929	297***	50.1
		Gerald R. Ford	Republican	39,148,940	240	47.9
		Eugene McCarthy	Independent	739,256		
1980	50	RONALD REAGAN	Republican	43,201,220	489	50.9
		Jimmy Carter	Democrat	34,913,332	49	41.2
		John B. Anderson	Independent	5,581,379		
1984	50	RONALD REAGAN	Republican	53,428,357	525	59.0
		Walter F. Mondale	Democrat	36,930,923	13	41.0
1988	50	GEORGE H. W. BUSH	Republican	48,901,046	426****	53.4
		Michael Dukakis	Democrat	41,809,030	111	45.6
1992	50	BILL CLINTON	Democrat	43,728,275	370	43.2
		George Bush	Republican	38,167,416	168	37.7
		H. Ross Perot	United We Stand, America	19,237,247		19.0
1996	50	BILL CLINTON	Democrat	45,590,703	379	49.0
		Robert Dole	Republican	37,816,307	159	41.0
		H. Ross Perot	Reform	7,866,284		8.0
2000	50	GEORGE W. BUSH	Republican	50,459,624	271	47.9
		Albert Gore, Jr.	Democrat	51,003,328	266	49.4
		Ralph Nader	Green	2,882,985		2.7

*Walter B. Jones received 1 electoral vote.
† Harry F. Byrd received 15 electoral votes.
‡ Resigned August 9, 1974: Vice President Gerald R. Ford became President.
** John Hospers received 1 electoral vote.
*** Ronald Reagan received 1 electoral vote.
**** Lloyd Bentsen received 1 electoral vote.

DEMOGRAPHICS OF THE UNITED STATES

POPULATION GROWTH

Year	Population	Percent Increase
1630	4,600	
1640	26,600	478.3
1650	50,400	90.8
1660	75,100	49.0
1670	111,900	49.0
1680	151,500	35.4
1690	210,400	38.9
1700	250,900	19.2
1710	331,700	32.2
1720	466,200	40.5
1730	629,400	35.0
1740	905,600	43.9
1750	1,170,800	29.3
1760	1,593,600	36.1
1770	2,148,100	34.8
1780	2,780,400	29.4
1790	3,929,214	41.3
1800	5,308,483	35.1
1810	7,239,881	36.4
1820	9,638,453	33.1
1830	12,866,020	33.5
1840	17,069,453	32.7
1850	23,191,876	35.9
1860	31,443,321	35.6
1870	39,818,449	26.6
1880	50,155,783	26.0
1890	62,947,714	25.5
1900	75,994,575	20.7
1910	91,972,266	21.0
1920	105,710,620	14.9
1930	122,775,046	16.1
1940	131,669,275	7.2
1950	151,325,798	14.5
1960	179,323,175	18.5
1970	203,302,031	13.4
1980	226,542,199	11.4
1990	248,718,301	9.8
2000	281,421,906	13.1

Source: Historical Statistics of the United States (1975); Statistical Abstract by the United States (2001).
Note: Figures for 1630–1780 include British colonies within limits of present United States only; Native American population included only in 1930 and thereafter. Figures before 1790 are estimates.

WORK FORCE

Year	Total Number Workers (1000s)	Farmers as % of Total	Women as % of Total	% Workers in Unions
1810	2,330	84	(NA)	(NA)
1840	5,660	75	(NA)	(NA)
1860	11,110	53	(NA)	(NA)
1870	12,506	53	15	(NA)
1880	17,392	52	15	(NA)
1890	23,318	43	17	(NA)
1900	29,073	40	18	3
1910	38,167	31	21	6
1920	41,614	26	21	12
1930	48,830	22	22	7
1940	53,011	17	24	27
1950	59,643	12	28	25
1960	69,877	8	32	26
1970	82,049	4	37	25
1980	106,940	3	43	23
1990	125,840	3	45	16
2000	140,863	2	47	12

Source: Historical Statistics of the United States (1975); Statistical Abstract of the United States (2001).

VITAL STATISTICS
(IN THOUSANDS)

Year	Births	Deaths	Marriages	Divorces
1800	55	(NA)	(NA)	(NA)
1810	54.3	(NA)	(NA)	(NA)
1820	55.2	(NA)	(NA)	(NA)
1830	51.4	(NA)	(NA)	(NA)
1840	51.8	(NA)	(NA)	(NA)
1850	43.3	(NA)	(NA)	(NA)
1860	44.3	(NA)	(NA)	(NA)
1870	38.3	(NA)	9.6 (1867)	0.3 (1867)
1880	39.8	(NA)	9.1 (1875)	0.3 (1875)
1890	31.5	(NA)	9.0	0.5
1900	32.3	17.2	9.3	0.7
1910	30.1	14.7	10.3	0.9
1920	27.7	13.0	12.0	1.6
1930	21.3	11.3	9.2	1.6
1940	19.4	10.8	12.1	2.0
1950	24.1	9.6	11.1	2.6
1960	23.7	9.5	8.5	2.2
1970	18.4	9.5	10.6	3.5
1980	15.9	8.8	10.6	5.2
1990	16.7	8.6	9.8	4.7
1997	14.6	8.6	8.9	4.3

Source: Historical Statistics of the United States (1975); Statistical Abstract of the United States (1999).

POPULATIONS BY RACIAL GROUPS AND HISPANIC ORIGINS (IN THOUSANDS)

Year	White	Black	Indian	Asian/Pacific Islander	Other Race*	Hispanic Origin**
1790	3,172	757	(NA)	(NA)	(NA)	(NA)
1800	4,306	1,002	(NA)	(NA)	(NA)	(NA)
1820	7,867	1,772	(NA)	(NA)	(NA)	(NA)
1840	14,196	2,874	(NA)	(NA)	(NA)	(NA)
1860	26,923	4,442	(NA)	(NA)	(NA)	(NA)
1880	43,403	6,581	(NA)	(NA)	(NA)	(NA)
1900	66,809	8,834	(NA)	(NA)	(NA)	(NA)
1910	81,732	9,828	(NA)	(NA)	(NA)	(NA)
1920	94,821	10,463	(NA)	(NA)	(NA)	(NA)
1930	110,287	11,891	(NA)	(NA)	(NA)	(NA)
1940	118,215	12,866	(NA)	(NA)	(NA)	(NA)
1950	134,942	15,042	(NA)	(NA)	(NA)	(NA)
1960	158,832	18,872	(NA)	(NA)	(NA)	(NA)
1970	178,098	22,581	(NA)	(NA)	(NA)	(NA)
1980	194,713	26,683	1,420	3,500	6,758	14,609
1990	208,727	30,511	1,959	7,273	9,805	22,354
2000	211,461	34,658	2,476	10,642	22,185	35,603

Source: U.S. Bureau of the Census, U.S. Census of Population: 1940, vol. II, part 1, and vol. IV, part 1; 1950, vol. II, part 1; 1960, vol. I, part 1; 1970, vol. I, part B; and Current Population Reports, P25-1095 and P25-1104; Statistical Abstract of the United States (2001).
* Other or multiple race as self-identified.
** Hispanic population may be of any race.

THE ECONOMY AND FEDERAL SPENDING

Year	Gross National Product (GNP) (in billions)	Foreign Trade (in millions)			Federal Budget (in billions)	Federal Surplus/Deficit (in billions)	Federal Debt (in billions)
		Exports	Imports	Balance of Trade			
1790	(NA)	$ 20	$ 23	$ −3	$ 0.004	$ +0.00015	$ 0.076
1800	(NA)	71	91	−20	0.011	+0.0006	0.083
1810	(NA)	67	85	−18	0.008	+0.0012	0.053
1820	(NA)	70	74	−4	0.018	−0.0004	0.091
1830	(NA)	74	71	+3	0.015	+0.100	0.049
1840	(NA)	132	107	+25	0.024	−0.005	0.004
1850	(NA)	152	178	−26	0.040	+0.004	0.064
1860	(NA)	400	362	−38	0.063	−0.01	0.065
1870	$ 7.4	451	462	−11	0.310	+0.10	2.4
1880	11.2	853	761	+92	0.268	+0.07	2.1
1890	13.1	910	823	+87	0.318	+0.09	1.2
1900	18.7	1,499	930	+569	0.521	+0.05	1.2
1910	35.3	1,919	1,646	+273	0.694	−0.02	1.1
1920	91.5	8,664	5,784	+2,880	6.357	+0.3	24.3
1930	90.7	4,013	3,500	+513	3.320	+0.7	16.3
1940	100.0	4,030	7,433	−3,403	9.6	−2.7	43.0
1950	286.5	10,816	9,125	+1,691	43.1	−2.2	257.4
1960	506.5	19,600	15,046	+4,556	92.2	+0.3	286.3
1970	992.7	42,700	40,189	+2,511	195.6	−2.8	371.0
1980	2,631.7	220,783	244,871	+24,088	590.9	−73.8	907.7
1990	5,524.5	394,030	494,042	−101,012	1,251.8	−220.5	3,233.3
2000	9,958.7	1,068,397	1,438,086	−369,689	1,788.8	+236.4	5,629.0

Source: U.S. Office of Management and Budget, Budget of the United States Government, annual; Statistical Abstract of the United States (2001).

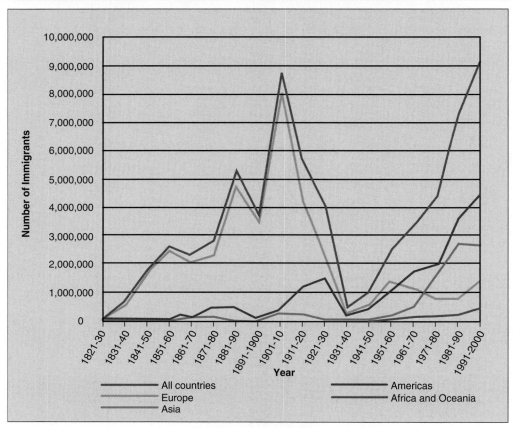

IMMIGRATION TO THE UNITED STATES
SINCE 1820 (BY DECADE)

Source: Statistical Yearbook of the Immigration and Naturalization Service, 2001.

GLOSSARY

Abolitionist movement   A radical antislavery crusade committed to the immediate end of slavery that emerged in the three decades before the Civil War.

Act for Religious Toleration   The first law in America to call for freedom of worship for all Christians. It was enacted in Maryland in 1649 to quell disputes between Catholics and Protestants, but it failed to bring peace.

Actual representation   The practice whereby elected representatives normally reside in their districts and are directly responsive to local interests.

Affirmative Action   A set of policies to open opportunities in business and education for members of minority groups and women by allowing race and sex to be factors included in decisions to hire, award contracts, or admit students to higher education programs.

Age of Enlightenment   Major intellectual movement occurring in western Europe in the late seventeenth and early eighteenth centuries. Inspired by recent scientific advances, thinkers emphasized the role of human reason in understanding the world and directing its events. Their ideas placed less emphasis on God's role in ordering worldly affairs.

Agricultural Wheel   One of several farmer organizations that emerged in the South during the 1880s. It sought federal legislation to deal with credit and currency issues.

AIDS (Acquired immune deficiency syndrome)   A complex of deadly pathologies resulting from infection with the human immunodeficiency virus (HIV).

Alamo   Franciscan mission at San Antonio, Texas, that was the site in 1836 of a siege and massacre of Texans by Mexican troops.

Albany Plan of Union   Plan put forward in 1754 by Massachusetts Governor William Shirley, Benjamin Franklin, and other colonial leaders, calling for an intercolonial union to manage defense and Indian affairs. The plan was rejected by participants at the Albany Congress.

Albany Regency   Popular name after 1820 for the state political machine in New York headed by Martin Van Buren.

Alien and Sedition Acts   Collective name given to four acts passed by Congress in 1798 that curtailed freedom of speech and the liberty of foreigners resident in the United States.

Alien Friends Act   Law passed by Congress in 1798 authorizing the president during peacetime to expel aliens suspected of subversive activities; one of the **Alien and Sedition Acts.**

Alliance for Progress   Program of economic aid to Latin America during the Kennedy administration.

Allies   In World War I, Britain, France, Russia, and other belligerent nations fighting against the **Central Powers** but not including the United States, which insisted upon being merely an associated nation. In World War II, the Allies fighting the **Axis Powers** included the United States as well as the Soviet Union, Great Britain, France, China, and other nations.

American Anti-Slavery Society   The first national organization of abolitionists, founded in 1833.

American Colonization Society   Organization, founded in 1817 by antislavery reformers, that called for gradual emancipation and the removal of freed blacks to Africa.

American Federation of Labor (AFL)   Union formed in 1886 that organized skilled workers along craft lines and emphasized a few workplace issues rather than a broad social program.

American Female Moral Reform Society   Organization founded in 1839 by female reformers that established homes of refuge for prostitutes and petitioned for state laws that would criminalize adultery and the seduction of women.

American Indian Movement (AIM)   Group of Native American political activists who used confrontations with the federal government to publicize their case for Indian rights.

American Liberty League   Business group organized to sway popular opinion against the **New Deal.**

American Revenue Act   See **Sugar Act.**

Americans with Disabilities Act   Legislation in 1992 that banned discrimination against physically handicapped persons in employment, transportation, and public accommodations.

American System   The program of government subsidies favored by Henry Clay and his followers to promote American economic growth and protect domestic manufacturers from foreign competition.

American system of manufacturing   A technique of production pioneered in the United States in the first half of the nineteenth century that relied on precision manufacturing with the use of interchangeable parts.

American Temperance Society   National organization established in 1826 by evangelical Protestants that campaigned for total abstinence from alcohol and was successful in sharply lowering per capita consumption of alcohol.

Anarchist   A person who believes that all government interferes with individual liberty and should be abolished by whatever means.

Anglican   Of or belonging to the Church of England, a Protestant denomination.

Anglo–American Accords   Series of agreements reached in the British–American Convention of 1818 that fixed the western boundary between the United States and Canada at the 49th parallel, allowed for the joint occupation of the Oregon Country, and restored to Americans fishing rights off Newfoundland.

Anglo-Saxon   Broadly, a person of English descent.

Annapolis Convention   Conference of state delegates at Annapolis, Maryland, that issued a call in September 1786 for a convention to meet at Philadelphia in May 1787 to consider fundamental changes to the **Articles of Confederation.**

Antifederalist   An opponent of the **Constitution** in the debate over its ratification.

Anti-Masons   Third party formed in 1827 in opposition to the presumed power and influence of the Masonic order.

Appeal to the Colored Citizens of the World   Pamphlet published in 1829 by David, a Boston free black, calling for slaves to rise up in rebellion.

Archaic Period   The period roughly between 8000 and 1500 B.C., during which time Native Americans adapted to a changed continental climate, developed larger communities, and, in several regions, adopted agriculture.

Articles of Confederation   Written document setting up the loose confederation of states that comprised the first national government of the United States from 1781 to 1788.

Atlanta Compromise   Booker T. Washington's policy accepting segregation and **disfranchisement** for African Americans in exchange for white assistance in education and job training.

Atlantic Charter   Statement of common principles and war aims developed by President Franklin Roosevelt and British Prime Minister Winston Churchill at a meeting in August 1941.

Australian ballot   Secret voting and the use of official ballots rather than party tickets.

Axis Powers   The opponents of the United States and its allies in World War II. The Rome–Berlin Axis was formed between Germany and Italy in 1936 and included Japan after 1940.

Aztecs   A warrior people who dominated the Valley of Mexico from about 1100 until their conquest in 1519–21 by Spanish soldiers led by Hernán Cortés.

Bacon's Rebellion   Violent conflict in Virginia (1675–1676), beginning with settler attacks on Indians but culminating in a rebellion led by Nathaniel Bacon against Virginia's government.

Baker v. Carr   U.S. Supreme Court decision in 1962 that allowed federal courts to review the apportionment of state legislative districts and established the principle that such districts should have roughly equal populations ("one person, one vote").

Bank War   The political struggle between President Andrew Jackson and the supporters of the **Second Bank of the United States.**

Battles of Lexington and Concord   The first two battles of the American Revolution which resulted in a total of 273 British soldiers dead, wounded, and missing and nearly 100 Americans dead, wounded, and missing.

Battle of the Atlantic   The long struggle between German submarines and the British and U.S. navies in the North Atlantic from 1940 to 1943.

Bay of Pigs   Site in Cuba of an unsuccessful landing by fourteen hundred anti-Castro Cuban refugees in April 1961.

Beaver Wars   Series of bloody conflicts, occurring between 1640s and 1680s, during which the Iroquois fought the French and their Indian allies for control of the fur trade in eastern North America and the Great Lakes region.

Benevolent empire   Network of reform associations affiliated with Protestant churches in the early nineteenth century dedicated to the restoration of moral order.

Berlin blockade   Three-hundred-day Soviet blockade of land access to United States, British, and French occupation zones in Berlin, 1948–1949.

Berlin Wall   Wall erected by East Germany in 1961 and torn down in 1989 that isolated West Berlin from the surrounding areas in Communist-controlled East Berlin and East Germany.

Bill of Rights   A written summary of inalienable rights and liberties.

Black codes   Laws passed by states and municipalities denying many rights of citizenship to free blacks before the Civil War. Also, during the **Reconstruction era,** laws passed by newly elected southern state legislatures to control black labor, mobility, and employment.

Black Hawk's War   Short 1832 war in which federal troops and Illinois militia units defeated the Sauk and Fox Indians led by Black Hawk.

Black Panthers   Political and social movement among black Americans, founded in Oakland, California, in 1966 and emphasizing black economic and political power.

Black Power   Philosophy emerging after 1965 that real economic and political gains for African-Americans could come only through self-help, **self-determination,** and organizing for direct political influence. Latinos and Native Americans developed their own versions as Brown Power and Red Power, respectively.

"Bleeding Kansas"   Violence between pro- and antislavery forces in Kansas Territory after the passage of the **Kansas-Nebraska Act** in 1854.

Blitzkrieg   German war tactic in World War II ("lightning war") involving the concentration of air and armored firepower to punch and exploit holes in opposing defensive lines.

Bolshevik   Member of the communist movement in Russia that established the Soviet government after the 1917 Russian Revolution; hence, by extension, any radical or disruptive person or movement seeking to transform economic and political relationships.

Bonus Army   A group of unemployed veterans who demonstrated in Washington for the payment of service bonuses, only to be dispersed violently by the U.S. Army in 1932.

Bosnia   A nation in southeast Europe that split off from Yugoslavia and became the site of bitter civil war and religious war, requiring NATO and U.S. intervention in the 1990s.

Boston Massacre   After months of increasing friction between townspeople and the British troops stationed in the city, on March 5, 1770, British troops fired on American civilians in Boston.

Boston Tea Party   Incident that occurred on December 16, 1773, in which Bostonians, disguised as Indians, destroyed £9,000 worth of tea belonging to the British East India Company in order to prevent payment of the duty on it.

British Constitution   The principles, procedures, and precedents that governed the operation of the British government. These could be found in no single written document; Parliament and the king made the Constitution by their actions.

Brook Farm   A utopian community and experimental farm established in 1841 near Boston.

Brown v. Board of Education of Topeka   Supreme Court decision in 1954 that declared that "separate but equal" schools for children of different races violated the **Constitution.**

Bureau of Reclamation   Federal agency established in 1902 providing public funds for irrigation projects in arid regions; played a major role in the development of the West by constructing dams, reservoirs, and irrigation systems, especially beginning in the 1930s.

Cahokia   Located near modern St. Louis, this was one of the largest urban centers created by Mississippian peoples, containing perhaps 30,000 residents in 1250.

Californios   Persons of Spanish descent living in California.

Camp David Agreement   Agreement to reduce points of conflict between Israel and Egypt, hammered out in 1977 with the help of U.S. President Jimmy Carter.

carpetbaggers   Pejorative term to describe Northern transplants to the South, many of whom were Union soldiers who stayed in the South after the war.

Central Intelligence Agency (CIA)   Agency that coordinates the gathering and evaluation of military and economic information on other nations, established in 1947.

Central Powers   Germany and its World War I allies Austria, Turkey, and Bulgaria.

Chain migration   Process common to many immigrant groups whereby one family member brings over other family members, who in turn bring other relatives and friends and occasionally entire villages.

Charles River Bridge v. Warren Bridge   Supreme Court decision of 1837 that promoted economic competition by ruling that the broader rights of the community took precedence over any presumed right of monopoly granted in a corporate charter.

Cherokee War   Conflict (1759–1761) on the southern frontier between the Cherokee Indians and colonists from Virginia southward. It caused South Carolina to request the aid of British troops and resulted in the surrender of more Indian land to white colonists.

Chesapeake **Incident**   Attack in 1807 by the British ship *Leopard* on the American ship *Chesapeake* in American territorial waters that nearly provoked an Anglo-American war.

Chisholm Trail   The route followed by Texas cattle raisers driving their herds north to markets at Kansas railheads.

Church of Jesus Christ of Latter-day Saints   *See* **Mormon Church.**

Civil Rights Act of 1866   Law that defined national citizenship and specified the civil rights to which all national citizens were entitled.

Civil Rights Act of 1875   Law that prohibited racial discrimination in jury selection, public transportation, and public accommodations; declared unconstitutional by the U.S. Supreme Court in 1883.

Civil Rights Act of 1964   Federal legislation that outlawed discrimination in public accommodations and employment on the basis of race, skin color, sex, religion, or national origin.

Claims club   A group of local settlers on the nineteenth-century frontier who banded together to prevent the price of their land claims from being bid up by outsiders at public land auctions.

Coercive Acts   Legislation passed by Parliament in 1774; included the Boston Port Act, the Massachusetts Government Act, the Administration of Justice Act, and the **Quartering Act** of 1774.

Cold War   The political and economic confrontation between the Soviet Union and the United States that dominated world affairs from 1946 to 1989.

Collective bargaining   Representatives of a union negotiating with management on behalf of all members.

Colored Farmers' Alliance   An organization of southern black farmers formed in Texas in 1886 in response to the **Southern Farmers' Alliance,** which did not accept black people as members.

Columbian exchange   The transatlantic exchange of plants, animals, and diseases that occurred after the first European contact with the Americas.

Committees of correspondence   Committees formed in Massachusetts and other colonies in the pre-Revolutionary period to keep Americans informed about British measures that would affect the colonies.

Committee of Safety   Any of the extralegal committees that directed the Revolutionary movement and carried on the functions of government at the local level in the period between the breakdown of royal authority and the establishment of regular governments under the new state constitutions. Some Committees of Safety continued to function throughout the Revolutionary War.

Committee on Public Information (CPI)   Government agency during World War I that sought to shape public opinion in support of the war effort through newspapers, pamphlets, speeches, films, and other media.

Communism   A social structure based on the common ownership of property.

Compromise of 1850   The four-step compromise which admitted California as a free state, allowed the residents of the New Mexico and Utah territories to decide the slavery issue for themselves, ended the slave trade in the District of Columbia, and passed a new fugitive slave law to enforce the constitutional provision stating that a slave escaping into a free state shall be delivered back to the owner.

Compromise of 1877   The Congressional settling of the 1876 election which installed Republican Rutherford B. Hayes in the White House and gave Democrats control of all state governments in the South.

Conciliatory Proposition   Plan proposed by Lord North and adopted by the House of Commons in February 1775 whereby Parliament would "forbear" taxation of Americans in colonies whose assemblies imposed taxes considered satisfactory by the British government. The Continental Congress rejected this plan on July 31, 1775.

Confederate States of America   Nation proclaimed in Montgomery, Alabama, in February 1861 after the seven states of the Lower South seceded from the United States.

Confiscation Act of 1862   Second confiscation law passed by Congress, ordering the seizure of land from disloyal Southerners and the emancipation of their slaves.

Congressional Reconstruction   Name given to the period 1867–1870 when the Republican-dominated Congress controlled **Reconstruction Era** policy. It is sometimes known as Radical Reconstruction, after the radical faction in the **Republican party.**

Congress of Industrial Organizations   An alliance of industrial unions that spurred the 1930s organizational drive among the mass-production industries.

Congress of Racial Equality (CORE)   Civil rights group formed in 1942 and committed to nonviolent civil disobedience, such as the 1961 "freedom rides."

Conservation   The efficient management and use of natural resources, such as forests, grasslands, and rivers, as opposed to **preservation** or uncontrolled exploitation.

Constitutional Convention   Convention that met in Philadelphia in 1787 and drafted the **Constitution of the United States.**

Constitutional Union party   National party formed in 1860, mainly by former **Whigs,** that emphasized allegiance to the Union and strict enforcement of all national legislation.

Constitution of the United States   The written document providing for a new central government of the United States, drawn up at the **Constitutional Convention** in 1787 and ratified by the states in 1788.

Containment   The policy of resisting further expansion of the Soviet bloc through diplomacy and, if necessary, military action, developed in 1947–48.

Continental Army   The regular or professional army authorized by the Second Continental Congress and commanded by General George Washington during the Revolutionary War. Better training and longer service distinguished its soldiers from the state militiamen.

Continental Association   Agreement, adopted by the **First Continental Congress** in 1774 in response to the **Coercive Acts,** to cut off trade with Britain until the objectionable measures were repealed. Local committees were established to enforce the provisions of the association.

Contract theory of government   The belief that government is established by human beings to protect certain rights—such as life, liberty, and property—that are theirs by natural, divinely sanctioned law and that when government protects these rights, people are obligated to obey it. But when government violates its part of the bargain (or contract) between the rulers and the ruled, the people are no longer required to obey it and may establish a new government that will do a better job of protecting them. Elements of this theory date back to the ancient Greeks; John Locke used it in his *Second Treatise on Government* (1682), and Thomas Jefferson gave it memorable expression in the Declaration of Independence, where it provides the rationale for renouncing allegiance to King George III.

Contract with America   Platform on which many Republican candidates ran for Congress in 1994. Associated with House Speaker Newt Gingrich, it proposed a sweeping reduction in the role and activities of the federal government.

Copperheads   A term Republicans applied to Northern war dissenters and those suspected of aiding the Confederate cause during the Civil War.

Council of Economic Advisers   Board of three professional economists established in 1946 to advise the president on economic policy.

Counterculture   Various alternatives to mainstream values and behaviors that became popular in the 1960s, including experimentation with psychedelic drugs, communal living, a return to the land, Asian religions, and experimental art.

Country (Real Whig) ideology   Strain of thought first appearing in England in the late seventeenth century in response to the growth of governmental power and a national debt. Main ideas stressed the threat to personal liberty posed by a standing army and high taxes and emphasized the need for property holders to retain the right to consent to taxation.

Coureur de bois   French for "woods runner," an independent fur trader in New France.

covenant   A formal agreement or contract.

Coxey's Army   A protest march of unemployed workers, led by Populist businessman Jacob Coxey, demanding inflation and a public works program during the depression of the 1890s.

Cult of domesticity   The belief that women, by virtue of their sex, should stay home as the moral guardians of family life.

culture areas   Geographical regions inhabited by peoples who share similar basic patterns of subsistence and social organization.

Currency Act   Law passed by Parliament in 1764 to prevent the colonies from issuing **legal tender** paper money, which often depreciated.

Dartmouth College v. Woodward   Supreme Court decision of 1819 that prohibited states from interfering with the privileges granted to a private corporation.

Dawes Act   An 1887 law terminating tribal ownership of land and allotting some parcels of land to individual Indians with the remainder opened for white settlement.

D-Day   June 6, 1944, the day of the first paratroop drops and amphibious landings on the coast of Normandy, France, in the first stage of **Operation OVERLORD** during World War II.

Declaration of Independence   The document by which the Second Continental Congress announced and justified its decision (reached July 2, 1776) to renounce the colonies' allegiance to the British government. Drafted mainly by Thomas Jefferson and adopted by Congress on July 4, the declaration's indictment of the king provides a remarkably full catalog of the colonists' grievances, and Jefferson's eloquent and inspiring statement of the **contract theory of government** makes the document one of the world's great state papers.

Declaration of London   Statement drafted by an international conference in 1909 to clarify international law and specify the rights of neutral nations.

Declaration of Rights and Grievances   Resolves, adopted by the **Stamp Act Congress** at New York in 1765, asserting that the **Stamp Act** and other taxes imposed on the colonists without their consent, given through their colonial legislatures, were unconstitutional.

Declaration of Sentiments   The resolutions passed at the **Seneca Falls Convention** in 1848 calling for full female equality, including the right to vote.

Declaration of the Causes and Necessity of Taking Up Arms   Document, written mainly by John Dickinson of Pennsylvania and adopted on July 6, 1775, by which the Second Continental Congress justified its armed resistance against British measures.

Declaratory Act   Law passed in 1766 to accompany repeal of the **Stamp Act** that stated that Parliament had the authority to legislate for the colonies "in all cases whatsoever." Whether "legislate" meant tax was not clear to Americans.

Deindustrialization   The process of economic change involving the disappearance of outmoded industries and the transfer of factories to new low-wage locations, with devastating effects in the Northeast and Middle West, especially in the 1970s and 1980s.

Deism   Religious orientation that rejects divine revelation and holds that the workings of nature alone reveal God's design for the universe.

Democratic Party   Political party formed in the 1820s under the leadership of Andrew Jackson; favored states' rights and a limited role for the federal government, especially in economic affairs.

Denmark Vesey's Conspiracy   The most carefully devised slave revolt, named after its leader, a free black in Charleston. The rebels planned to seize control of Charleston in 1822 and escape to freedom in Haiti, a free black republic, but they were betrayed by other slaves, and seventy-five conspirators were executed.

Deregulation   Reduction or removal of government regulations and encouragement of direct competition in many important industries and economic sectors.

Disfranchisement   The use of legal means to bar individuals or groups from voting.

Dollar diplomacy   The U.S. policy of using private investment in other nations to promote American diplomatic goals and business interests.

Dominion of New England   James II's failed plan of 1686 to combine eight northern colonies into a single large province, to be governed by a royal appointee (Sir Edmund Andros) with an appointed council but no elective assembly. The plan ended with James's ouster from the English throne and rebellion in Massachusetts against Andros's rule.

***Dred Scott* decision**   Supreme Court ruling, in a lawsuit brought by Dred Scott, a slave demanding his freedom based on his residence in a free state and a free territory with his master, that slaves could not be U.S. citizens and that Congress had no jurisdiction over slavery in the territories.

Eastern Front   The area of military operations in World War II located east of Germany in eastern Europe and the Soviet Union.

Economic Recovery and Tax Act of 1981 (ERTA)   A major revision of the federal income tax system.

Eighteenth Amendment   Constitutional revision, ratified in 1919 and repealed in 1933, that prohibited the manufacture or sale of alcohol in the United States.

Emancipation Proclamation   Decree announced by President Abraham Lincoln in September 1862 and formally issued on January 1, 1863, freeing slaves in all Confederate states still in rebellion.

Embargo Act of 1807   Act passed by Congress in 1807 prohibiting American ships from leaving for any foreign port.

Empresario   An agent who received a land grant from the Spanish or Mexican government in return for organizing settlements.

Encomienda   In the Spanish colonies, the grant to a Spanish settler of a certain number of Indian subjects, who would pay him tribute in goods and labor.

Enumerated products   Items produced in the colonies and enumerated in acts of Parliament that could be legally shipped from the colony of origin only to specified locations, usually England and other destinations within the British empire.

Environmental Protection Agency (EPA)   Federal agency created in 1970 to oversee environmental monitoring and cleanup programs.

Era of Good Feelings   The period from 1817 to 1823 in which the disappearance of the **Federalists** enabled the **Republicans** to govern in a spirit of seemingly nonpartisan harmony.

Espionage Act of 1917   Law whose vague prohibition against obstructing the nation's war effort was used to crush dissent and criticism during World War I.

Fair Employment Practice Committee (FEPC)   Federal agency established in 1941 to curb racial discrimination in war production jobs and government employment.

Farmers' Alliance   A broad mass movement in the rural South and West during the late nineteenth century, encompassing several organizations and demanding economic and political reforms; helped create the **Populist party**.

Fascist   Subscribing to a philosophy of governmental dictatorship that merges the interests of the state, armed forces, and big business; associated with the dictatorship of Italian leader Benito Mussolini between 1922 and 1943 and also often applied to Nazi Germany.

Federal Deposit Insurance Corporation (FDIC)   Government agency that guarantees bank deposits, thereby protecting both depositors and banks.

Federal Highway Act of 1956   Measure that provided federal funding to build a nationwide system of interstate and defense highways.

Federalism   The sharing of powers between the national government and the states.

Federalist   A supporter of the **Constitution** who favored its ratification.

Federal Reserve Act   The 1913 law that revised banking and currency by extending limited government regulation through the creation of the Federal Reserve System.

Federal Trade Commission (FTC)   Government agency established in 1914 to provide regulatory oversight of business activity.

Field Order No. 15   Order by General William T. Sherman in January 1865 to set aside abandoned land along the southern Atlantic coast for forty-acre grants to freedmen; rescinded by President Andrew Johnson later that year.

Fifteenth Amendment   Passed by Congress in 1869, guaranteed the right of American men to vote, regardless of race.

Fireside chats   Speeches broadcast nationally over the radio in which President Franklin Roosevelt explained complex issues and programs in plain language, as though his listeners were gathered around the fireside with him.

First Continental Congress   Meeting of delegates from most of the colonies held in 1774 in response to the **Coercive Acts.** The Congress endorsed the **Suffolk Resolves,** adopted the **Declaration of Rights and Grievances,** and agreed to establish the **Continental Association** to put economic pressure on Britain to repeal its objectionable measures. The Congress also wrote addresses to the king, the people of Britain, and the American people.

Fletcher v. Peck   Supreme Court decision of 1810 that overturned a state law by ruling that it violated a legal contract.

Fort Sumter   Begun in the late 1820s to protect Charleston, South Carolina, it became the center of national attention in April 1861 when President Lincoln attempted to provision federal troops at the fort, triggering a hostile response from on-shore Confederate forces, opening the Civil War.

Fourierist communities   Short-live utopian communities in the 1840s based on the ideas of economic cooperation and self-sufficiency popularized by the Frenchman Charles Fourier.

Fourteenth Amendment   Constitutional amendment passed by Congress in April 1866 incorporating some of the features of the **Civil Rights Act of 1866.** It prohibited states from violating the civil rights of its citizens and offered states the choice of allowing black people to vote or losing representation in Congress.

Frame of Government   William Penn's 1682 plan for the government of Pennsylvania, which created a relatively weak legislature and strong executive. It also contained a provision for religious freedom.

Franco-American Accord of 1800   Settlement reached with France that brought an end to the **Quasi-War** and released the United States from its 1778 alliance with France.

Freedmen's Bureau   Agency established by Congress in March 1865 to provide social, educational, and economic services, advice, and protection to former slaves and destitute whites; lasted seven years.

Freedom Summer   Voter registration effort in rural Mississippi organized by black and white civil rights workers in 1964.

Free silver   Philosophy that the government should expand the money supply by purchasing and coining all the silver offered to it.

Free Speech Movement (FSM)   Student movement at the University of California, Berkeley, formed in 1964 to protest limitations on political activities on campus.

French and Indian War   The last of the Anglo-French colonial wars (1754–1763) and the first in which fighting began in North America. The war (which merged with the European conflict known as the Seven Years' War) ended with France's defeat and loss of its North American empire.

Fugitive Slave Act   Law, part of the Compromise of 1850, that required that authorities in the North to assist southern slave catchers and return runaway slaves to their owners.

Fundamental Constitutions of Carolina   A complex plan for organizing the colony of Carolina, drafted in 1669 by Anthony Ashley Cooper and John Locke. Its provisions included a scheme for creating a hierarchy of nobles who would own vast amounts of land and wield political power; below them would be a class of freedmen and slaves. The provisions were never implemented by the Carolina colonists.

Fundamentalists   Religious conservatives who believe in the literal accuracy and divine inspiration of the Bible; the name derives from an influential series of pamphlets, *The Fundamentals* (1909–1914).

Gabriel Prosser's Rebellion   Slave revolt that failed when Gabriel Prosser, a slave preacher and blacksmith, organized a thousand slaves for an attack on Richmond, Virginia, in 1800. A thunderstorm upset the timing of the attack, and a slave informer alerted the whites. Prosser and twenty-five of his followers were executed.

Gag rule   Procedural rule passed in the House of Representatives that prevented discussion of antislavery petitions from 1836 to 1844.

Gang system   The organization and supervision of slave field hands into working teams on southern plantations.

General Union for Promoting the Observance of the Christian Sabbath   See **Sabbatarian movement.**

Gentlemen's Agreement   A diplomatic agreement in 1907 between Japan and the United States curtailing but not abolishing Japanese immigration.

Ghent, Treaty of   Treaty signed in December 1814 between the United States and Britain that ended the **War of 1812.**

GI Bill of Rights   Legislation in June 1944 that eased the return of veterans into American society by providing educational and employment benefits.

Gibbons v. Ogden   Supreme Court decision of 1824 involving coastal commerce that overturned a steamboat monopoly granted by the state of New York on the grounds that only Congress had the authority to regulate interstate commerce.

Gilded Age   Term applied to late-nineteenth-century America that refers to the shallow display and worship of wealth characteristic of the period.

Glasnost   Russian for "openness," applied to Mikhail Gorbachev's encouragement of new ideas and easing of political repression in the Soviet Union.

Glorious Revolution   Bloodless revolt that occurred in England in 1688 when parliamentary leaders invited William of Orange, a Protestant, to assume the English throne and James II fled to France. James's ouster was prompted by fears that the birth of his son would establish a Catholic dynasty in England.

Gospel of Wealth   Thesis that hard work and perseverance lead to wealth, implying that poverty is a character flaw.

Grandfather clause   Rule that required potential voters to demonstrate that their grandfathers had been eligible to vote; used in some southern states after 1890 to limit the black electorate, as most black men's grandfathers had been slaves.

Grand Settlement of 1701   Separate peace treaties negotiated by Iroquois diplomats at Montreal and Albany that marked the beginning of Iroquois neutrality in conflicts between the French and the British in North America.

Grange   The National Grange of the Patrons of Husbandry, a national organization of farm owners formed after the Civil War.

Granger laws   State laws enacted in the Midwest in the 1870s that regulated rates charged by railroads, grain elevator operators, and other middlemen.

Great Awakening   Tremendous religious revival in colonial America. Sparked by the tour of the English evangelical minister George Whitefield, the Awakening struck first in the Middle Colonies and New England in the 1740s and eventually spread to the southern colonies by the 1760s.

Great Compromise   Plan proposed by Roger Sherman of Connecticut at the 1787 **Constitutional Convention** for creating a national bicameral legislature in which all states would be equally represented in the Senate and proportionally represented in the House.

Great Depression   The nation's worst economic crisis, extending throughout the 1930s, producing unprecedented bank failures, unemployment, and industrial and agricultural collapse and prompting an expanded role for the federal government.

Great League of Peace and Power   Spiritual union of five Iroquois nations that aimed to maintain peace among them and unite them to fight against common enemies.

Great Migration   The mass movement of African Americans from the rural South to the urban North, spurred especially by new job opportunities during World War I and the 1920s.

Great Society   Theme of Lyndon Johnson's administration, focusing on poverty, education, and civil rights.

Great Uprising   Unsuccessful railroad strike of 1877 to protest wage cuts and the use of federal troops against strikers; the first nationwide work stoppage in American history.

Greenback party   A third party of the 1870s and 1880s that garnered temporary support by advocating currency inflation to expand the economy and assist debtors.

Greenville, Treaty of   Treaty of 1795 in which Native Americans in the Old Northwest were forced to cede most of the present state of Ohio to the United States.

Halfway Covenant   Plan adopted in 1662 by New England clergy to deal with the problem of declining church membership. It allowed adults who had been baptized because their parents were church members but who had not yet experienced conversion to have their own children baptized. Without the Halfway Covenant, these third-generation children would remain unbaptized until their parents experienced conversion.

Harlem Renaissance   A new African-American cultural awareness that flourished in literature, art, and music in the 1920s.

headright system   A system of land distribution during early colonial era that granted settlers 50 acres for themselves and another 50 for each "head" (or person) they brought to the colony.

Helsinki Accords   Agreement in 1975 among NATO and Warsaw Pact members that recognized European national boundaries as set after World War II and included guarantees of human rights.

Holocaust   The systematic murder of millions of European Jews and others deemed undesirable by Nazi Germany.

Homestead Act   Law passed by Congress in May 1862 providing homesteaders (mainly in the West) with 160 acres of free land in exchange for improving the land (as by cultivating it and erecting a house) within five years of the grant.

Hooverville   Shantytown, sarcastically named after President Hoover, in which unemployed and homeless people lived in makeshift shacks, tents, and boxes. Hoovervilles cropped up in many cities in 1930 and 1931.

Horatio Alger Stories   A series of best-selling tales about young rags-to-riches heroes first published in 1867 stressing the importance of neat clothes, cleanliness, thrift, and hard work. The books also highlighted the importance of chance in getting ahead and the responsibility of those better off to serve as positive role models.

horizontal integration   The merger of competitors in the same industry.

House of Burgesses   The legislature of colonial Virginia. First organized in 1619, it was the first institution of representative government in the English colonies.

Hull House   Chicago **settlement house** that became part of a broader neighborhood revitalization project led by Jane Addams.

Immigration and Nationality Act of 1965   Federal legislation that replaced the national quota system for immigration with overall limits of 170,000 immigrants per year from the Eastern Hemisphere and 120,000 per year from the Western Hemisphere.

Imperialism   The policy and practice of exploiting nations and peoples for the benefit of an imperial power either directly through military occupation and colonial rule or indirectly through economic domination of resources and markets.

Impressment   The British policy of forcibly enlisting American sailors into the British navy.

Indentured servant   An individual—usually male but occasionally female—who contracted to serve a master for a period of four to seven years in return for payment of the servant's passage to America. Indentured servitude was the primary labor system in the Chesapeake colonies for most of the seventeenth century.

Independent Treasury System   Fiscal arrangement first instituted by President Martin Van Buren in which the federal government kept its money in regional vaults ("pet banks") and transacted its business entirely in hard money.

Indian Removal Act   Legislation passed by Congress in 1830 that provided funds for removing and resettling eastern Indians in the West. It granted the president the authority to use force if necessary.

Initiative   Procedure by which citizens can introduce a subject for legislation, usually through a petition signed by a specific number of voters.

Intermediate Nuclear Force Agreement (INF)   Disarmament agreement between the United States and the Soviet Union under which an entire class of missiles would be removed and destroyed and on-site inspections would be permitted for verification.

International Monetary Fund (IMF)   International organization established in 1945 to assist nations in maintaining stable currencies.

Internet   The system of interconnected computers and servers that allows the exchange of e-mail, posting of web sites, and other means of instant communication.

Interstate and Defense Highways   Federal legislation in 1956 committed the federal government to finance more than 40,000 miles of new limited access freeways to criss-cross the United States.

Interstate Commerce Act   The 1887 law that expanded federal power over business by prohibiting pooling and discriminatory rates by railroads and establishing the first federal regulatory agency, the **Interstate Commerce Commission.**

Interstate Commerce Commission (ICC)   The first federal regulatory agency, established in 1887 to oversee railroad practices.

Intolerable Acts   American term for the **Coercive Acts** and the **Quebec Act.**

Iroquois League   The union of five Indian nations (Mohawks, Oneidas, Onondagas, Cayugas, and Senecas) formed around 1450, also known as the League of Five Nations. Essentially a religious organization, its purpose was to maintain peace among the five nations and unite them to fight against other enemies. After the Tuscarora War (1713–1715), the Tuscaroras joined the league, thereafter known as the League of Six Nations.

Irreconcilables   Group of U.S. senators adamantly opposed to ratification of the **Treaty of Versailles** after World War I.

Jacksonian Democrats   *See* **Democratic Party.**

Jay's Treaty   Treaty with Britain negotiated in 1794 in which the United States made major concessions to avert a war over the British seizure of American ships.

Jazz Age   The 1920s, so called for the popular music of the day as a symbol of the many changes taking place in the mass culture.

Jeffersonian Republicans   *See* **Republican Party (Jeffersonian).**

Jim Crow laws   Segregation laws that became widespread in the South during the 1890s, named for a minstrel show character portrayed satirically by white actors in blackface.

John Brown's Raid   New England abolitionist John Brown's ill-fated attempt to free Virginia's slaves with a raid on the federal arsenal at Harpers Ferry, Virginia, in 1859.

Joint-stock company   Business enterprise in which a group of stockholders pooled their money to engage in trade or to fund colonizing expeditions. Joint-stock companies participated in the founding of the Virginia, Plymouth, and Massachusetts Bay colonies.

Judicial review   A power implied in the **Constitution** that gives federal courts the right to review and determine the constitutionality of acts passed by Congress and state legislatures.

Judiciary Act of 1789   Act of Congress that implemented the judiciary clause of the **Constitution** by establishing the Supreme Court and a system of lower federal courts.

Kansas-Nebraska Act   Law passed in 1854 creating the Kansas and Nebraska Territories but leaving the question of slavery open to residents, thereby repealing the **Missouri Compromise.**

Kellogg-Briand Pact   1928 international treaty that denounced aggression and war but lacked provisions for enforcement.

King George's War   The third Anglo-French war in North America (1744–1748), part of the European conflict known as the War of the Austrian Succession. During the North American fighting, New Englanders captured the French fortress of Louisbourg, only to have it returned to France after the peace negotiations.

King Philip's War   Conflict in New England (1675–1676) between Wampanoags, Narragansetts, and other Indian peoples against English settlers; sparked by English encroachments on native lands.

King William's War   The first Anglo-French conflict in North America (1689–1697), the American phase of Europe's War of the League of Augsburg. Ended in negotiated peace that reestablished the balance of power.

Knights of Labor   Labor union that included skilled and unskilled workers irrespective of race or gender; founded in 1869, peaked in the 1880s, and declined when its advocacy of the eight-hour workday led to violent strikes in 1886.

Know-Nothing Party   Anti-immigrant party formed from the wreckage of the **Whig Party** and some disaffected northern Democrats in 1854.

Kosovo   Province of Yugoslavia, in southeast Europe, where the U.S. and NATO intervened militarily in 1999 to protect ethnic Albanians from expulsion by Yugoslavia.

Ku Klux Klan   Perhaps the most prominent of the vigilante groups that terrorized black people in the South during **Reconstruction Era,** founded by Confederate veterans in 1866.

Laissez-faire   The doctrine that government should not intervene in the economy, especially through regulation.

Lancaster, Treaty of   Negotiation in 1744 whereby Iroquois chiefs sold Virginia land speculators the right to trade at the Forks of the Ohio. Although the Iroquois had not intended this to include the right to settle in the Ohio Country, the Virginians assumed that it did. Ohio Valley Indians considered this treaty a great grievance against both the English and the Iroquois.

Land Grant College Act   Law passed by Congress in July 1862 awarding proceeds from the sale of public lands to the states for the establishment of agricultural and mechanical (later engineering) colleges. Also known as the Morrill Act, after its sponsor, Congressman Justin Morrill of Vermont.

Land Ordinance of 1785   Act passed by Congress under the **Articles of Confederation** that created the grid system of surveys by which all subsequent public land was made available for sale.

League of Nations   International organization created by the **Versailles Treaty** after World War I to ensure world stability.

League of Women Voters   Group formed in 1920 from the National American Woman Suffrage Association to encourage informed voting and social reforms.

Lecompton Constitution   Proslavery draft written in 1857 by Kansas territorial delegates elected under questionable circumstances; it was rejected by two governors, supported by President Buchanan, and decisively defeated by Congress.

Legal tender   An attribute of money that results from legislation declaring it to be, as in the case of modern United States currency, "legal tender for all debts public and private." Creditors must therefore accept it at face value.

Lend-Lease   Program begun in 1941 through which the U.S. transferred military equipment to Britain and other World War II allies.

Liberal Republicans   Members of a reform movement within the **Republican Party** in 1872 that promoted measures to reduce government influence in the economy and restore control of southern governments to local white elites.

Liberty Bonds   Interest-bearing certificates sold by the U.S. government to finance the American World War I effort.

Liberty Party   The first antislavery political party, formed in 1840.

Lincoln-Douglas debates   Series of debates in the 1858 Illinois senatorial campaign during which Democrat Stephen A. Douglas and Republican Abraham Lincoln staked out their differing opinions on the issue of slavery in the territories.

Little Bighorn, Battle of the   Battle in which Colonel George A. Custer and the Seventh Cavalry were defeated by the Sioux and Cheyennes under Sitting Bull and Crazy Horse in Montana in 1876.

Lost Cause   The phrase many white Southerners applied to their Civil War defeat. They viewed the war as a noble cause but only a temporary setback in the South's ultimate vindication.

Lynching   Execution, usually by a mob, without trial.

Mahanism   The ideas advanced by Alfred Thayer Mahan, stressing U.S. naval, economic, and territorial expansion.

Manhattan Project   The effort, using the code name Manhattan Engineer District, to develop an atomic bomb under the management of the U.S. Army Corps of Engineers during World War II.

Manifest Destiny   Doctrine, first expressed in 1845, that the expansion of white Americans across the continent was inevitable and ordained by God.

Marbury v. Madison   Supreme Court decision of 1803 that created the precedent of judicial review by ruling as unconstitutional part of the **Judiciary Act of 1789.**

Massive retaliation   Popular name for the military doctrine adopted in the 1950s, whereby the U.S. promised to respond to any attack on itself or its allies with massive force, including nuclear weapons.

McCarthyism   Anticommunist attitudes and actions associated with Senator Joe McCarthy in the early 1950s, including smear tactics and innuendo.

McCulloch v. Maryland   Supreme Court decision of 1819 upholding the constitutionality of the Second Bank of the United States and the exercise of federal powers within a state.

Medicaid   Supplementary medical insurance for the poor, financed through the federal government; program created in 1965.

Medicare   Basic medical insurance for the elderly, financed through the federal government; program created in 1965.

Mercantilism   Economic system whereby the government intervenes in the economy for the purpose of increasing national wealth. Mercantilists advocated possession of colonies as places where the mother country could acquire raw materials not available at home.

Middle Passage   The voyage between West Africa and the New World slave colonies.

Minute Men   Special companies of militia formed in Massachusetts and elsewhere beginning in late 1744. These units were composed of men who were to be ready to assemble with their arms at a minute's notice.

Missouri Compromise   Sectional compromise in Congress in 1820 that admitted Missouri to the Union as a slave state and Maine as a free state and prohibited slavery in the **Louisiana Purchase** territory above 36°30′ north latitude.

Model Cities Program   Effort to target federal funds to upgrade public services and economic opportunity in specifically defined urban neighborhoods between 1966 and 1974.

Molly Maguires   Secret labor organization of mostly Irish miners in the Pennsylvania anthracite coal region in the decade after the Civil War. Named after a woman who led a massive protest against landlords in Ireland in the 1840s, the Maguires carried out selective murders of coal company officials until an infiltrator exposed the group in 1877 and its leaders were arrested, tried, and executed.

Monroe Doctrine   Declaration by President James Monroe in 1823 that the Western Hemisphere was to be closed off to further European colonization and that the United States would not interfere in the internal affairs of European nations.

Mormon Church (Church of Jesus Christ of Latter-day Saints)   Church founded in 1830 by Joseph Smith and based on the revelations in a sacred book he called the Book of Mormon.

Muckraking   Journalism exposing economic, social, and political evils, so named by Theodore Roosevelt for its "raking the muck" of American society.

Mugwumps   Elitist and conservative reformers who favored **sound money** and limited government and opposed tariffs and the **spoils system.**

Multinational corporation   Firm with direct investments, branches, factories, and offices in a number of countries.

National Aeronautics and Space Administration (NASA)   Federal agency created in 1958 to manage American space flights and exploration.

National American Woman Suffrage Association   The organization, formed in 1890, that coordinated the ultimately successful campaign to achieve women's right to vote.

Nationalists   Group of leaders in the 1780s who spearheaded the drive to replace the **Articles of Confederation** with a stronger central government.

National Origins Act   A 1924 law sharply restricting immigration on the basis of immigrants' national origins and discriminating against southern and eastern Europeans and Asians.

National Security Council (NSC)   The formal policymaking body for national defense and foreign relations, created in 1947 and consisting of the president, the secretary of defense, the secretary of state, and others appointed by the president.

National Security Council Paper 68 (NSC-68)   Policy statement that committed the United States to a military approach to the **Cold War.**

National War Labor Board   Government agency that supervised labor relations during World War I, guaranteeing union rights in exchange for industrial stability.

Nation of Islam   Religious movement among black Americans that emphasizes self-sufficiency, self-help, and separation from white society.

Nativist/Nativism   Favoring the interests and culture of native-born inhabitants over those of immigrants.

Nat Turner's Rebellion   Uprising of slaves in Southampton County, Virginia, in the summer of 1831 led by Nat Turner that resulted in the death of fifty-five whites.

Natural rights   Political philosophy that maintains that individuals have an inherent right, found in nature and preceding any government or written law, to life and liberty.

Neoconservative   Advocate of or participant in the revitalized conservative politics of the 1980s and 1990s, calling for a strong government role in defense and foreign policy and a limited role in social and economic policy.

Neoliberal   Advocate of or participant in the effort to reshape the **Democratic party** for the 1990s around a policy emphasizing economic growth and competitiveness in the world economy.

New Deal   The economic and political policies of the Roosevelt administration in the 1930s.

New Federalism   President Richard Nixon's policy to shift responsibilities for government programs from the federal level to the states.

New Freedom   Woodrow Wilson's 1912 program for limited government intervention in the economy to restore competition by curtailing the restrictive influences of trusts and protective tariffs, thereby providing opportunities for individual achievement.

New Frontier   John F. Kennedy's domestic and foreign policy initiatives, designed to reinvigorate a sense of national purpose and energy.

New Harmony   Short-lived utopian community established in Indiana in 1825, based on the socialist ideas of Robert Owen, a wealthy Scottish manufacturer.

New Jersey Plan   Proposal of the New Jersey delegation at the 1787 **Constitutional Convention** for a strengthened national government in which all states would have equal representation in a **unicameral legislature.**

New Lights   People who experienced conversion during the revivals of the **Great Awakening.**

New Nationalism   Theodore Roosevelt's 1912 program calling for a strong national government to foster, regulate, and protect business, industry, workers, and consumers.

New Orleans, Battle of   Decisive American **War of 1812** victory over British troops in January 1815 that ended any British hopes of gaining control of the lower Mississippi River Valley.

New York Draft Riot   A mostly Irish-immigrant protest against conscription in New York City in July 1863 that escalated into class and racial warfare that had to be quelled by federal troops.

Niagara Movement   African-American group organized in 1905 to promote racial integration, civil and political rights, and equal access to economic opportunity.

Nineteenth Amendment   Constitutional revision that in 1920 established women citizens' right to vote.

Nisei   U.S. citizens born of immigrant Japanese parents.

Nixon Doctrine   In July, 1969, President Nixon described a new American policy toward Asia, in which the U.S. would honor treaty commitments but would gradually disengage and expect Asian nations to handle military defense on their own.

Nonimportation Movement   A tactical means of putting economic pressure on Britain by refusing to buy its exports to the colonies. Initiated in response to the taxes imposed by the **Sugar** and **Stamp Acts,** it was used again against the **Townshend duties** and the **Coercive Acts.** The nonimportation movement popularized resistance to British measures and deepened the commitment of many ordinary people to a larger American community.

Nonintercourse Act   Law passed by Congress in 1809 that prohibited American trade with Britain and France.

North American Free Trade Agreement (NAFTA)   Agreement reached in 1993 by Canada, Mexico, and the United States to substantially reduce barriers to trade.

Northwest Ordinance of 1787   Legislation passed by Congress under the **Articles of Confederation** that prohibited slavery in the Northwest Territories and provided the model for the incorporation of future territories into the Union as coequal states.

Nullification   A constitutional doctrine holding that a state has a legal right to declare a national law null and void within its borders.

Nullification crisis   Sectional crisis in the early 1830s in which a **states' rights** party in South Carolina attempted to nullify federal law.

Office of Economic Opportunity (OEO)   Federal agency that coordinated many programs of the **War on Poverty** between 1964 and 1975.

Oligopoly   An industry, such as steel making or automobile manufacturing, that is controlled by a few large companies.

Olive Branch Petition   Petition, written largely by John Dickinson and adopted by the Second Continental Congress on July 5, 1775, as a last effort of peace that avowed America's loyalty to George III and requested that he protect them from further aggressions. Congress continued military preparations, and the king never responded to the petition.

Omaha Platform   The 1892 platform of the **Populist party** repudiating laissez-faire and demanding economic and political reforms to aid distressed farmers and workers.

Oneida Community   Utopian community established in upstate New York in 1848 by John Humphrey Noyes and his followers.

Open Door   American policy of seeking equal trade and investment opportunities in foreign nations or regions.

Open shop   Factory or business employing workers whether or not they are union members; in practice, such a business usually refuses to hire union members and follows antiunion policies.

Operation Desert Storm   Code name for the successful offensive against Iraq by the United States and its allies in the Persian Gulf War (1991).

Operation OVERLORD   U.S. and British invasion of France in June 1944 during World War II.

Oregon Trail   Overland trail of more than two thousand miles that carried American settlers from the Midwest to new settlements in Oregon, California, and Utah.

Organization of Petroleum Exporting Countries (OPEC)   Cartel of oil-producing nations in Asia, Africa, and Latin America that gained substantial power over the world economy in the mid- to late 1970s by controlling the production and price of oil.

Ostend Manifesto   Message sent by U.S. envoys to President Pierce from Ostend, Belgium, in 1854, stating that the United States had a "divine right" to wrest Cuba from Spain.

Pan American Union   International organization originally established as the Commercial Bureau of American Republics by Secretary of State James Blaine's first Pan-American Conference in 1889 to promote cooperation among nations of the Western Hemisphere through commercial and diplomatic negotiations.

Panic of 1857   Banking crisis that caused a credit crunch in the North; it was less severe in the South, where high cotton prices spurred a quick recovery.

Pan-Indian resistance movement   Movement calling for the political and cultural unification of Indian tribes in the late eighteenth and early nineteenth centuries.

Patriot Act   Federal legislation adopted in 2001, in response to the terrorist attacks of September 11, intended to facilitate anti-terror actions by federal law enforcement and intelligence agencies.

Peace of Paris   Treaties signed in 1783 by Great Britain, the United States, France, Spain, and the Netherlands that ended the Revolutionary War. First in a preliminary agreement and then in the final treaty with the United States, Britain recognized the independence of the United States, agreed that the Mississippi River would be its western boundary, and permitted it to fish in some Canadian waters. Prewar debts owed by the inhabitants of one country to those of the other were to remain collectible, and Congress was to urge the states to return property confiscated from Loyalists. British troops were to evacuate United States territory without removing slaves or other property. In a separate agreement, Britain relinquished its claim to East and West Florida to Spain.

Pendleton Civil Service Act   A law of 1883 that reformed the **spoils system** by prohibiting government workers from making political contributions and creating the Civil Service Commission to oversee their appointment on the basis of merit rather than politics.

Pentagon Papers   Classified Defense Department documents on the history of the United States' involvement in Vietnam, prepared in 1968 and leaked to the press in 1971.

People's Party   *See* **Populist Party.**

Pequot War   Conflict between English settlers (who had Narragansett and Mohegan allies) and Pequot Indians over control of land and trade in eastern Connecticut. The Pequots were nearly destroyed in a set of bloody confrontations, including a deadly English attack on a Mystic River village in May 1637.

Perestroika   Russian for "restructuring," applied to Mikhail Gorbachev's efforts to make the Soviet economic and political systems more modern, flexible, and innovative.

Persian Gulf War   War (1991) between Iraq and a U. S. led coalition that followed Iraq's invasion of Kuwait and resulted in the expulsion of Iraqi forces from that country.

Pietists   Protestants who stress a religion of the heart and the spirit of Christian living.

Pilgrims   Settlers of Plymouth Colony, who viewed themselves as spiritual wanderers.

Pinckney's Treaty   Treaty with Spain in 1795 in which Spain recognized the 31st parallel as the boundary between the United States and Spanish Florida and opened the Mississippi River through the port of New Orleans to American shipping.

Platt Amendment   A stipulation the United States had inserted into the Cuban constitution in 1901 restricting Cuban autonomy and authorizing U.S. intervention and naval bases.

Plattsburg, Battle of   American naval victory on Lake Champlain in September 1814 in the **War of 1812** that thwarted a British invasion from Canada.

Pogroms   Government-directed attacks against Jewish citizens, property, and villages in tsarist Russia beginning in the 1880s; a primary reason for Russian Jewish migration to the United States.

Poll tax   A tax imposed on voters as a requirement for voting. Most southern states imposed poll taxes after 1900 as a way to disfranchise black people; the measures also restricted the white vote.

Pontiac's Rebellion   Indian uprising (1763–1766) led by Pontiac of the Ottawas and Neolin of the Delawares. Fearful of their fate at the hands of the British after the French had been driven out of North America, the Indian nations of the Ohio River Valley and the Great Lakes area united to oust the British from the Ohio-Mississippi Valley. They failed and were forced to make peace in 1766.

Popular Sovereignty   A solution to the slavery crisis suggested by Michigan senator Lewis Cass by which territorial residents, not Congress, would decide slavery's fate.

Populist Party   A major third party of the 1890s, also known as the **People's Party.** Formed on the basis of the **Southern Farmers' Alliance** and other reform organizations, it mounted electoral challenges against the Democrats in the South and the Republicans in the West.

Potsdam Declaration   Statement issued by the United States during a meeting of U.S. President Harry Truman, British Prime Minister Winston Churchill, and Soviet Premier Joseph Stalin held at Potsdam, near Berlin, in July 1945 to plan the defeat of Japan and the future of eastern Europe and Germany. In it, the United States declared its intention to democratize the Japanese political system and reintroduce Japan into the international community and gave Japan an opening for surrender.

Predestination   The belief that God decided at the moment of Creation which humans would achieve salvation.

Preparedness   Military buildup in preparation for possible U.S. participation in World War I.

Preservation   Protecting forests, land, and other features of the natural environment from development or destruction, often for aesthetic appreciation.

Proclamation Line   Boundary, decreed as part of the **Proclamation of 1763,** that limited British settlements to the eastern side of the Appalachian Mountains, thereby threatening colonial expansionists and causing resentment. It proved unenforceable.

Proclamation of 1763   Royal proclamation setting the boundary known as the **Proclamation Line.**

Progressive Era   The period of the twentieth century before World War I when many groups sought to reshape the nation's government and society in response to the pressures of industrialization and urbanization.

Prohibition   A ban on the production, sale, and consumption of liquor, achieved temporarily through state laws and the Eighteenth Amendment.

Prohibition Party   A venerable third party still in existence that has persistently campaigned for the abolition of alcohol but has also introduced many important reform ideas into American politics.

Proposition 187   California legislation adopted by popular vote in California in 1994, which cuts off state-funded health and education benefits to undocumented or illegal immigrants.

Proprietary colony   A colony created when the English monarch granted a huge tract of land to an individual or group of individuals, who became "lords proprietor." Many lords proprietor had distinct social visions for their colonies, but these plans were hardly ever implemented. Examples of proprietary colonies are Maryland, Carolina, New York (after it was seized from the Dutch), and Pennsylvania.

Pueblo Revolt Rebellion in 1680 of Pueblo Indians in New Mexico against their Spanish overlords, sparked by religious conflict and excessive Spanish demands for tribute.

Puritan An individual who believed that Queen Elizabeth's reforms of the Church of England had not gone far enough in improving the church, particularly in ensuring that church members were among the saved. Puritans led the settlement of Massachusetts Bay Colony.

Put-in-Bay, Battle of American naval victory on Lake Erie in September 1813 in the **War of 1812** that denied the British strategic control over the Great Lakes.

Putting-out system System of manufacturing in which merchants furnished households with raw materials for processing by family members.

Quakers Members of the Society of Friends, a radical religious group that arose in the mid-seventeenth century. Quakers rejected formal theology and an educated ministry, focusing instead on the importance of the "Inner Light," or Holy Spirit that dwelt within them. Quakers were important in the founding of Pennsylvania.

Quartering Acts Acts of Parliament requiring colonial legislatures to provide supplies and quarters for the troops stationed in America. Americans considered this taxation in disguise and objected. None of these acts passed during the pre-Revolutionary controversy required that soldiers be quartered in an occupied house without the owner's consent.

Quasi-War Undeclared naval war of 1797 to 1800 between the United States and France.

Quebec Act Law passed by Parliament in 1774 that provided an appointed government for Canada, enlarged the boundaries of Quebec southward to the Ohio River, and confirmed the privileges of the Catholic Church. Alarmed Americans termed this act and the **Coercive Acts** the **Intolerable Acts.**

Queen Anne's War American phase (1702–1713) of Europe's War of the Spanish Succession. At its conclusion, England gained Nova Scotia.

Radical Republicans A shifting group of Republican congressmen, usually a substantial minority, who favored the abolition of slavery from the beginning of the Civil War and later advocated harsh treatment of the defeated South.

Reagan Doctrine The policy assumption that Soviet-influenced governments in Asia, Africa, and Latin America needed to be eliminated if the United States was to win the Cold War.

Recall The process of removing an official from office by popular vote, usually after using petitions to call for such a vote.

Reconquista The long struggle (ending in 1492) during which Spanish Christians reconquered the Iberian peninsula from Muslim occupiers, who first invaded in the eighth century.

Reconstruction Era The era (1865–1877) when the resolution of two major issues—the status of the former slaves and the terms of the Confederate states' readmission into the Union—dominated political debate.

Redeemers Southern Democrats who wrested control of governments in the former Confederacy, often through electoral fraud and violence, from Republicans beginning in 1870.

Redemptioners Similar to **indentured servants,** except that redemptioners signed labor contracts in America rather than in Europe, as indentured servants did. Shipmasters sold redemptioners into servitude to recoup the cost of their passage if they could not pay the fare upon their arrival.

Red Scare Post–World War I public hysteria over **Bolshevik** influence in the United States directed against labor activism, radical dissenters, and some ethnic groups.

Referendum Submission of a law, proposed or already in effect, to a direct popular vote for approval or rejection.

Reformation Sixteenth-century movement to reform the Catholic Church that ultimately led to the founding of new Protestant Christian religious groups.

Regulators Vigilante groups active in the 1760s and 1770s in the western parts of North and South Carolina. The South Carolina Regulators attempted to rid the area of outlaws; the North Carolina Regulators sought to protect themselves against excessively high taxes and court costs. In both cases, westerners lacked sufficient representation in the legislature to obtain immediate redress of their grievances. The South Carolina government eventually made concessions; the North Carolina government suppressed its Regulator movement by force.

Repartimiento In the Spanish colonies, the assignment of Indian workers to labor on public works projects.

Republicanism A complex, changing body of ideas, values, and assumptions, closely related to **country ideology,** that influenced American political behavior during the eighteenth and nineteenth centuries. Derived from the political ideas of classical antiquity, Renaissance Europe, and early modern England, republicanism held that self-government by the citizens of a country, or their representatives, provided a more reliable foundation for the good society and individual freedom than rule by kings. The benefits of monarchy depended on the variable abilities of monarchs; the character of republican government depended on the virtue of the people. Republicanism therefore helped give the American Revolution a moral dimension. But the nature of republican virtue and the conditions favorable to it became sources of debate that influenced the writing of the state and federal constitutions as well as the development of political parties.

Republican Party Party that emerged in the 1850s in the aftermath of the bitter controversy over the **Kansas-Nebraska Act,** consisting of former **Whigs,** some northern Democrats, and many **Know-Nothings.**

Republican Party (Jeffersonian) Party headed by Thomas Jefferson that formed in opposition to the financial and diplomatic policies of the **Federalist Party;** favored limiting the powers of the national government and placing the interests of farmers and planters over those of financial and commercial groups; supported the cause of the French Revolution.

Rescate Procedure by which Spanish colonists would pay ransom to free Indians captured by rival natives. The rescued Indians then became workers in Spanish households.

Reservationists Group of U.S. senators favoring approval of the **Treaty of Versailles,** the peace agreement after World War I, after amending it to incorporate their reservations.

Rhode Island system During the industrialization of the early nineteenth century, the recruitment of entire families for employment in a factory.

Roe v. Wade U.S. Supreme Court decision in 1973 that disallowed state laws prohibiting abortion during the first three months (trimester) of pregnancy and established guidelines for abortion in the second and third trimesters.

Roosevelt Corollary President Theodore Roosevelt's policy asserting U.S. authority to intervene in the affairs of Latin American nations; an expansion of the **Monroe Doctrine.**

Rush–Bagot Agreement Treaty of 1817 between the United States and Britain that effectively demilitarized the Great Lakes by sharply limiting the number of ships each power could station on them.

Sabbatarian movement Reform organization founded in 1828 by Congregationalist and Presbyterian ministers that lobbied for an end to the delivery of mail on Sundays and other Sabbath violations.

"Sack of Lawrence" Vandalism and arson committed by a group of proslavery men in Lawrence, the free-state capital of Kansas Territory.

Sagebrush Rebellion Political movement in the western states in the early 1980s that called for easing of regulations on the economic use of federal lands and the transfer of some or all of those lands to state ownership.

SALT Strategic Arms Limitation Treaty signed in 1972 by the United States and the Soviet Union to slow the nuclear arms race.

Sand Creek Massacre The near annihilation in 1864 of Black Kettle's Cheyenne band by Colorado troops under Colonel John Chivington's orders to "kill and scalp all, big and little."

San Jacinto, Battle of   Battle fought in eastern Texas on April 21, 1836, in which Texas troops under General Sam Houston overwhelmed a Mexican army and forced its commander, General Antonio López de Santa Anna, to recognize the independence of Texas.

San Lorenzo, Treaty of   *See* **Pinckney's Treaty.**

Santa Fe Trial   Overland trial across the southern Plains from St. Louis to New Mexico that funneled American traders and goods to Spanish-speaking settlements in the Southwest.

Scalawags   Southern whites, mainly small landowning farmers and well-off merchants and planters, who supported the southern **Republican Party** during **Reconstruction** for diverse reasons; a disparaging term.

Search and destroy   U.S. military tactic in South Vietnam, using small detachments to locate enemy units and then massive air, artillery, and ground forces to destroy them.

Second Bank of the United States   A national bank chartered by Congress in 1816 with extensive regulatory powers over currency and credit.

Second Continental Congress   An assemblage of delegates from all the colonies that convened in May 1775 after the outbreak of fighting in Massachusetts between British and American forces. It became the national government that eventually declared independence and conducted the Revolutionary War.

Second Great Awakening   Series of religious revivals in the first half of the nineteenth century characterized by great emotionalism in large public meetings.

Second party system   The national two-party competition between **Democrats** and **Whigs** from the 1830s through the early 1850s.

Second Treaty of Fort Laramie   The treaty acknowledging U.S. defeat in the Great Sioux War in 1868 and supposedly guaranteeing the Sioux perpetual land and hunting rights in South Dakota, Wyoming, and Montana.

Securities and Exchange Commission (SEC)   Federal agency with authority to regulate trading practices in stocks and bonds.

Sedition Act of 1918   Broad law restricting criticism of America's involvement in World War I or its government, flag, military, taxes, or officials.

Segregation   A system of racial control that separated the races, initially by custom but increasingly by law during and after **Reconstruction.**

Selective Service Act of 1917   The law establishing the military draft for World War I.

Selective Service System   Federal agency that coordinated military conscription before and during the Vietnam War.

Self-determination   The right of a people or nation to decide on its own political allegiance or form of government without external influence.

Seneca Falls Convention   The first convention for women's equality in legal rights, held in upstate New York in 1848. *See also* **Declaration of Sentiments.**

Separatist   Member of an offshoot branch of Puritanism. Separatists believed that the Church of England was too corrupt to be reformed and hence were convinced that they must "separate" from it to save their souls. Separatists helped found Plymouth Colony.

Settlement house   A multipurpose structure in a poor neighborhood that offered social welfare, educational, and homemaking services to the poor or immigrants; usually under private auspices and directed by middle-class women.

Seventeenth Amendment   Constitutional change that in 1913 established the direct popular election of U.S. senators.

Shakers   The followers of Mother Ann Lee, who preached a religion of strict celibacy and communal living.

Sharecropping   Labor system that evolved during and after **Reconstruction** whereby landowners furnished laborers with a house, farm animals, and tools and advanced credit in exchange for a share of the laborers' crop.

Shays's Rebellion   An armed movement of debt-ridden farmers in western Massachusetts in the winter of 1786–1787. The rebellion shut down courts and created a crisis atmosphere, strengthening the case of **nationalists** that a stronger central government was needed to maintain civil order in the states.

Sheppard-Towner Maternity and Infancy Act of 1921   The first federal social welfare law; funded infant and maternity health care programs in local hospitals. Social Gospel movement: An effort by leading Protestants to apply religious ethics to industrial conditions and thereby alleviate poverty, slums, and labor exploitation.

Sherman Antitrust Act   The first federal antitrust measure, passed in 1890; sought to promote economic competition by prohibiting business combinations in restraint of trade or commerce.

Silicon Valley   The region of California between San Jose and San Francisco that holds the nation's greatest concentration of electronics firms.

Sixteenth Amendment   Constitutional revision that in 1913 authorized a federal income tax.

***Slaughterhouse* cases**   Group of cases resulting in one sweeping decision by the U.S. Supreme Court in 1873 that contradicted the intent of the **Fourteenth Amendment** by decreeing that most citizenship rights remained under state, not federal, control.

Slave codes   Sometimes known as "black codes." A series of laws passed mainly in the southern colonies in the late seventeenth and early eighteenth centuries to define the status of slaves and codify the denial of basic civil rights to them. Also, after American independence and before the Civil War, state laws in the South defining slaves as property and specifying the legal powers of masters over slaves.

Slave Power   A key concept in abolitionist and northern antislavery propaganda that depicted southern slaveholders as the driving force in a political conspiracy to promote slavery at the expense of white liberties.

Social Darwinism   The application of Charles Darwin's theory of biological evolution to society, holding that the fittest and the wealthiest survive, the weak and the poor perish, and government action is unable to alter this "natural" and beneficial process.

Socialism   A social order based on government ownership of industry and worker control over corporations as a way to prevent worker exploitation.

Solid South   The one-party (Democratic) political system that dominated the South from the 1890s to the 1950s.

Songhai empire   A powerful West African state that flourished between 1450 and 1591, when it fell to a Moroccan invasion.

Sons of Liberty   Secret organizations in the colonies formed to oppose the **Stamp Act.** From 1765 until independence, they spoke, wrote, and demonstrated against British measures. Their actions often intimidated stamp distributors and British supporters in the colonies.

Sound money   Misleading slogan that referred to a conservative policy of restricting the money supply and adhering to the gold standard.

Southeast Asia Treaty Organization (SEATO)   Mutual defense alliance signed in 1954 by the United States, Britain, France, Thailand, Pakistan, the Philippines, Australia, and New Zealand.

Southern Christian Leadership Conference (SCLC)   Black civil rights organization founded in 1957 by Martin Luther King, Jr., and other clergy.

Southern Farmers' Alliance   The largest of several organizations that formed in the post-Reconstruction South to advance the interests of beleaguered small farmers.

Southern Homestead Act   Largely unsuccessful law passed in 1866 that gave black people preferential access to public lands in five southern states.

Southern Manifesto   A document signed by 101 members of Congress from southern states in 1956 that argued that the Supreme Court's decision in ***Brown v. Board of Education of Topeka*** itself contradicted the **Constitution.**

Southwest Ordinance of 1790   Legislation passed by Congress that set up a government with no prohibition on slavery in U.S. territory south of the Ohio River.

Specie Circular   Proclamation issued by President Andrew Jackson in 1836 stipulating that only gold or silver could be used as payment for public land.

Sphere of influence   A region dominated and controlled by an outside power.

Spoils system   The awarding of government jobs to party loyalists.

Stamp Act   Law passed by Parliament in 1765 to raise revenue in America by requiring taxed, stamped paper for legal documents, publications, and playing cards. Americans opposed it as "taxation without representation" and prevented its enforcement. Parliament repealed it a year after its enactment.

Stamp Act Congress   October 1765 meeting of delegates sent by nine colonies, held in New York City, that adopted the **Declaration of Rights and Grievances** and petitioned against the **Stamp Act.**

States' rights   Favoring the rights of individual states over rights claimed by the national government.

Stonewall Rebellion   On June 27, 1969, patrons fought back when police raided the gay Stonewall Inn in New York; the name refers to that event and to the increase in militancy by gay Americans that it symbolizes.

Stono Rebellion   Uprising in 1739 of South Carolina slaves against whites; inspired in part by Spanish officials' promise of freedom for American slaves who escaped to Florida.

Strategic Defense Initiative (SDI)   President Reagan's program, announced in 1983, to defend the United States against nuclear missile attack with untested weapons systems and sophisticated technologies; also known as "Star Wars."

Student Nonviolent Coordinating Committee (SNCC)   Black civil rights organization founded in 1960 and drawing heavily on younger activists and college students.

Students for a Democratic Society (SDS)   The leading student organization of the New Left of the early and mid-1960s.

Subtreasury plan   A program promoted by the **Southern Farmers' Alliance** in response to low cotton prices and tight credit. Farmers would store their crop in a warehouse (or "subtreasury") until prices rose, in the meantime borrowing up to 80 percent of the value of the stored crops from the government at a low interest rate.

Suffolk Resolves   Militant resolves adopted in September 1774 in response to the **Coercive Acts** by representatives from the towns in Suffolk County, Massachusetts, including Boston. They termed the **Coercive Acts** unconstitutional, advised the people to arm, and called for economic sanctions against Britain. The **First Continental Congress** endorsed these resolves.

Suffrage   The right to vote in a political election.

Sugar Act   Law passed in 1764 to raise revenue in the American colonies. It lowered the duty from 6 pence to 3 pence per gallon on foreign molasses imported into the colonies and increased the restrictions on colonial commerce.

Sunbelt   The states of the American South and Southwest.

***Sussex* Pledge**   Germany's pledge during World War I not to sink merchant ships without warning, on the condition that Britain also observe recognized rules of international law.

Swann v. Charlotte-Mecklenburg Board of Education   U.S. Supreme Court decision in 1971 that upheld cross-city busing to achieve the racial integration of public schools.

Sweatshops   Small, poorly ventilated shops or apartments crammed with workers, often family members, who pieced together garments.

Taft-Hartley Act   Federal legislation of 1947 that substantially limited the tools available to labor unions in labor–management disputes.

Tammany Hall   New York City's **Democratic party** organization, dating from well before the Civil War, that evolved into a powerful political machine after 1860, using patronage and bribes to maintain control of the city administration.

Taos Revolt   Uprising of Pueblo Indians in New Mexico that broke out in January 1847 over the imposition of American rule during the Mexican War; the revolt was crushed within a few weeks.

Tariff Act of 1789   Apart from a few selected industries, this first tariff passed by Congress was intended primarily to raise revenue and not protect American manufacturers from foreign competition.

Tariff Act of 1798   Law placing a duty of 5 percent on most imported goods, designed primarily to generate revenue and not to protect American goods from foreign competition.

Tea Act of 1773   Act of Parliament that permitted the East India Company to sell tea through agents in America without paying the duty customarily collected in Britain, thus reducing the retail price. Americans, who saw the act as an attempt to induce them to pay the Townshend duty still imposed in the colonies, resisted this act through the **Boston Tea Party** and other measures.

Tejano   A person of Spanish or Mexican descent born in Texas.

Teller Amendment   A congressional resolution adopted in 1898 renouncing any American intention to annex Cuba.

Temperance   Reform movement originating in the 1820s that sought to eliminate the consumption of alcohol.

Temporary Assistance for Needy Families (TANF)   Federal program created in 1996 to replace earlier welfare programs to aid families and children; it involves explicit work requirements for receiving aid and places a time limit on benefits.

Tenement   Four- to six-story residential dwelling, once common in New York and certain other cities, built on a tiny lot without regard to providing ventilation or light.

Tennessee Valley Authority (TVA)   Federal regional planning agency established to promote **conservation,** produce electric power, and encourage economic development in seven southern states.

Tenure of Office Act   Passed by the Republican controlled Congress in 1867 to limit presidential interference with its policies, the Act prohibited the president from removing certain officeholders without the Senate's consent. President Andrew Johnson, angered at which he believed as an unconstitutional attack on presidential authority, deliberately violated the act by firing Secretary of War Edwin M. Stanton. The House responded by approving articles of impeachment against a president for the first time in American history.

Thirteenth Amendment   Constitutional amendment ratified in 1865 that freed all slaves throughout the United States.

Tonnage Act of 1789   Duty levied on the tonnage of incoming ships to U.S. ports; tax was higher on foreign-owned ships to favor American shippers.

Tordesillas, Treaty of   Treaty negotiated by the pope in 1494 to resolve the territorial claims of Spain and Portugal. It drew a north–south line approximately 1,100 miles west of the Cape Verde Islands, granting all lands west of the line to Spain and all lands east of the line to Portugal. This limited Portugal's New World empire to Brazil but confirmed its claims in Africa and Asia.

Tories   A derisive term applied to loyalists in America who supported the king and Parliament just before and during the American Revolution. The term derived from late-seventeenth-century English politics when the Tory party supported the Duke of York's succession to the throne as James II. Later the Tory party favored the Church of England and the crown over dissenting denominations and Parliament.

Townshend Duty Act   Act of Parliament, passed in 1767, imposing duties on colonial tea, lead, paint, paper, and glass. Designed to take advantage of the supposed American distinction between internal and external taxes, the Townshend duties were to help support government in America. The act prompted a successful colonial nonimportation movement.

Trail of Tears   The forced march in 1838 of the Cherokee Indians from their homelands in Georgia to the Indian Territory in the West; thousands of Cherokees died along the way.

Transcendentalism   A philosophical and literary movement centered on an idealistic belief in the divinity of individuals and nature.

Trans-Continental Treaty of 1819   Treaty between the United States and Spain in which Spain ceded Florida to the United States, surrendered all claims to the Pacific Northwest, and agreed to a boundary between the Louisiana Purchase territory and the Spanish Southwest.

Transportation revolution   Dramatic improvements in transportation that stimulated economic growth after 1815 by expanding the range of travel and reducing the time and cost of moving goods and people.

Truman Doctrine   President Harry Truman's statement in 1947 that the United States should assist other nations that were facing external pressure or internal revolution; an important step in the escalation of the **Cold War.**

Underground Railroad   Support system set up by antislavery groups in the Upper South and the North to assist fugitive slaves in escaping the South.

Underwood-Simmons Tariff Act   The 1913 reform law that lowered tariff rates and levied the first regular federal income tax.

Unicameral legislature   A legislative body composed of a single house.

Union League   A **Republican party** organization in northern cities that became an important organizing device among freedmen in southern cities after 1865.

United States v. Cruikshank   Supreme Court ruling of 1876 that overturned the convictions of some of those responsible for the Colfax Massacre, ruling that the Enforcement Act applied only to violations of black rights by states, not individuals.

University of California v. Bakke   U.S. Supreme Court case in 1978 that allowed race to be used as one of several factors in college and university admission decisions but made rigid quotas unacceptable.

Valley Forge   Area of Pennsylvania approximately 20 miles northwest of Philadelphia where General George Washington's continental troops were quartered from December 1777 to June 1778 while British forces occupied Philadelphia during the Revolutionary War. Approximately 2,500 men, about a quarter of those encamped there, died of hardship and disease.

Versailles, Treaty of   The treaty ending World War I and creating the **League of Nations.**

vertical integration   The consolidation of numerous production functions, from the extraction of the raw materials to the distribution and marketing of the finished products, under the direction of one firm.

Viet Cong   Communist rebels in South Vietnam who fought the pro-American government established in South Vietnam in 1954.

Virginia Plan   Proposal of the Virginia delegation at the 1787 **Constitution Convention** calling for a national legislature in which the states would be represented according to population. The national legislature would have the explicit power to veto or overrule laws passed by state legislatures.

Virtual representation   The notion, current in eighteenth-century England, that parliamentary members represented the interests of the nation as a whole, not those of the particular district that elected them.

Volstead Act   The 1920 law defining the liquor forbidden under the Eighteenth Amendment and giving enforcement responsibilities to the Prohibition Bureau of the Department of the Treasury.

Voting Rights Act   Legislation in 1965 that overturned a variety of practices by which states systematically denied voter registration to minorities.

Waltham system   During the industrialization of the early nineteenth century, the recruitment of unmarried young women for employment in factories.

War Hawks   Members of Congress, predominantly from the South and West, who aggressively pushed for a war against Britain after their election in 1810.

War Industries Board (WIB)   The federal agency that reorganized industry for maximum efficiency and productivity during World War I.

War of 1812   War fought between the United States and Britain from June 1812 to January 1815 largely over British restrictions on American shipping.

War on Poverty   Set of programs introduced by Lyndon Johnson between 1963 and 1966 designed to break the cycle of poverty by providing funds for job training, community development, nutrition, and supplementary education.

Watergate   A complex scandal involving attempts to cover up illegal actions taken by administration officials and leading to the resignation of President Richard Nixon in 1974.

Webster–Ashburton Treaty   Treaty signed by the United States and Britain in 1842 that settled a boundary dispute between Maine and Canada and provided for closer cooperation in suppressing the African slave trade.

Welfare capitalism   A paternalistic system of labor relations emphasizing management responsibility for employee well-being. While providing some limited benefits, its function was primarily to forestall the formation of unions or public intervention.

Whig party   Political party, formed in the mid-1830s in opposition to the **Jacksonian Democrats,** that favored a strong role for the national government in promoting economic growth.

Whigs   The name used by advocates of colonial resistance to British measures during the 1760s and 1770s. The Whig party in England unsuccessfully attempted to exclude the Catholic Duke of York from succession to the throne as James II; victorious in the **Glorious Revolution,** the Whigs later stood for religious toleration and the supremacy of Parliament over the crown.

Whiskey Rebellion   Armed uprising in 1794 by farmers in western Pennsylvania who attempted to prevent the collection of the excise tax on whiskey.

Whitewater   Arkansas real estate development in which Bill and Hillary Clinton were investors; several fraud convictions resulted from investigations into Whitewater, but evidence was not found that the Clintons were involved in wrong-doing.

Wide Awakes   Group of red-shirted, black-caped young men who paraded through city streets in the North extolling the virtues of the **Republican party** during the 1860 presidential election campaign.

Wilmot Proviso   The amendment offered by Pennsylvania Democrat David Wilmot in 1846 which stipulated that "as an express and fundamental condition to the acquisition of any territory from the Republic of Mexico . . . neither slavery nor involuntary servitude shall ever exist in any part of said territory."

Wobblies   Popular name for the members of the Industrial Workers of the World (IWW).

Woman's Christian Temperance Union (WCTU)   National organization formed after the Civil War dedicated to prohibiting the sale and distribution of alcohol.

Workingmen's movement   Associations of urban workers who began campaigning in the 1820s for free public education and a ten-hour workday.

World Trade Organization   International organization that sets standards and practices for global trade, and the focus of international protests over world economic policy in the late 1990s.

World Wide Web   Since 1991, the Web has expanded the use of the Internet by allowing organizations and companies to create web sites that place political and commercial information only a few clicks away from wired consumers.

Wounded Knee Massacre   The U.S. Army's brutal winter massacre in 1890 of at least two hundred Sioux men, women, and children as part of the government's assault on the tribe's Ghost Dance religion.

Writs of assistance   Documents issued by a court of law that gave British officials in America the power to search for smuggled goods wherever they wished. The legality of these writs became an important cause of controversy in Massachusetts in 1761 and 1762.

XYZ Affair   Diplomatic incident in 1798 in which Americans were outraged by the demand of the French for a bribe as a condition for negotiating with American diplomats.

Yalta Conference   Meeting of U.S. President Franklin Roosevelt, British Prime Minister Winston Churchill, and Soviet Premier Joseph Stalin held in February 1945 to plan the final stages of World War II and postwar arrangements.

Yellow-dog contracts   Employment agreements binding workers not to join a union.

Yellow press   A deliberately sensational journalism of scandal and exposure designed to attract an urban mass audience and increase advertising revenues.

BIBLIOGRAPHY

Chapter 1
Native American Cultures
Bragdon, Kathleen J. *Native People of Southern New England, 1500–1650* (1996).

Clendinnen, Inga. *Aztecs: An Interpretation* (1991).

Fagan, Brian M. *Ancient North America: The Archaeology of a Continent,* 4th ed. (2005).

Milner, George. *The Cahokia Chiefdom: The Archaeology of a Mississippian Society* (1998).

Rouse, Irving. *The Tainos: Rise and Decline of the People Who Greeted Columbus* (1992).

West African Society
Bohannan, Paul, and Philip Curtin. *Africa and Africans,* 3rd ed. (1988).

Iliffe, John. *Africans: The History of a Continent* (1995).

Reader, John. *Africa: A Biography of the Continent* (1998).

Europe in the Age of Discovery
Canny, Nicholas. *Making Ireland British, 1580–1650* (2000).

Cantor, Norman F. *In the Wake of the Plague: The Black Death and the World It Made* (2001).

Cipolla, Carlo M. *Guns, Sails, and Empire: Technological Innovation and the Early Phases of European Expansion, 1400–1700* (1965).

Lewis, Bernard. *Cultures in Conflict: Christians, Muslims, and Jews in the Age of Discovery* (1995).

Marty, Martin. *Martin Luther: A Penguin Life* (2004).

McDermott, James. *Martin Frobisher: Elizabethan Privateer* (2001).

Scammell, G. V. *The First Imperial Age: European Overseas Expansion, c. 1400–1715* (1989).

Conquest and Colonization
Andrews, Kenneth R. *Trade, Plunder, and Settlement: Maritime Enterprise and the Genesis of the British Empire, 1480–1630* (1984).

Crosby, Alfred W., Jr. *Ecological Imperialism: The Biological Expansion of Europe, 900–1900* (1986).

De Las Casas, Bartolomé. *Short Account of the Destruction of the Indies* (several editions).

Eccles, W. J. *France in America,* rev. ed. (1990).

Elliott, J. H. *Empires of the Atlantic World: Britain and Spain in America 1492–1830* (2006).

Hudson, Charles. *Knights of Spain, Warriors of the Sun: Hernando de Soto and the South's Ancient Chiefdoms* (1997).

Kamen, Henry. *Empire: How Spain Became a World Power, 1492–1763* (2003).

Kupperman, Karen Ordahl. *Roanoke: The Abandoned Colony* (1984).

Seed, Patricia. *Ceremonies of Possession in Europe's Conquest of the New World 1492–1640* (1995).

Weber, David J. *Bárbaros: Spaniards and Their Savages in the Age of Enlightenment* (2006).

Chapter 2
New France
Choquette, Leslie. *Frenchmen into Peasants: Modernity and Tradition in the Peopling of French Canada* (1997).

Eccles, W. J. *Essays on New France* (1987).

Moogk, Peter. *La Nouvelle France: The Making of French Canada—A Cultural History* (2000).

New Netherland
Israel, Jonathan. *The Dutch Republic: Its Rise, Greatness, and Fall, 1477–1806* (1995).

Price, J. L. *The Dutch Republic in the Seventeenth Century* (1998).

Shorto, Russell. *The Island at the Center of the World: The Epic Story of Dutch Manhattan, the Forgotten Colony That Shaped America* (2004).

Chesapeake Society
Horn, James. *A Land As God Made It: Jamestown and the Birth of America* (2005).

Krugler, John. *English and Catholic: The Lords Baltimore in the Seventeenth Century* (2004).

Kupperman, Karen Ordahl. *The Jamestown Project* (2007).

Townsend, Camilla. *Pocahontas and the Powhatan Dilemma* (2004).

New England
Bremer, Francis J. *John Winthrop: America's Forgotten Founding Father* (2003).

Cave, Alfred. *The Pequot War* (1996).

Morgan, Edmund S. *Puritan Dilemma: The Story of John Winthrop* (1958).

Philbrick, Nathaniel. *Mayflower: A Story of Courage, Community, and War* (2006).

Ulrich, Laurel Thatcher. *Good Wives: Image and Reality in the Lives of Women in Northern New England, 1650–1750* (1982).

The West Indies
Beckles, Hilary. *White Servitude and Black Slavery in Barbados, 1627–1715* (1989).

Gragg, Larry. *Englishmen Transplanted: The English Colonization of Barbados, 1627–1660* (2003).

Mintz, Sidney. *Sweetness and Power: The Place of Sugar in Modern History* (1985).

The Restoration Colonies

Dunn, Richard S., and Mary Maples Dunn, eds. *The World of William Penn* (1986).

Goodfriend, Joyce D. *Before the Melting Pot: Society and Culture in Colonial New York City, 1664–1730* (1992).

Levy, Barry. *Quakers and the American Family: British Settlement in the Delaware Valley* (1988).

Merwick, Donna. *Death of a Notary: Conquest and Change in Colonial New York* (1999).

Weir, Robert. *Colonial South Carolina: A History* (1983).

Chapter 3
Indians and Europeans

Anderson, Virginia. *Creatures of Empire: How Domestic Animals Transformed Early America* (2004).

Calloway, Colin. *New Worlds for All: Indians, Europeans, and the Remaking of Early America* (1997).

Cronon, William. *Changes in the Land: Indians, Colonists, and the Ecology of New England* (1983).

Drake, James. *King Philip's War: Civil War in New England, 1675–1676* (2000).

Gallay, Alan. *The Indian Slave Trade: The Rise of the English Empire in the American South, 1670–1717* (2003).

Greer, Allan. *Mohawk Saint: Catherine Tekakwitha and the Jesuits* (2004).

Knaut, Andrew L. *The Pueblo Revolt of 1680: Conquest and Resistance in Seventeenth-Century New Mexico* (1995).

Kupperman, Karen. *Indians and English: Facing Off in Early America* (2000).

Merrell, James H. *Into the American Woods: Negotiators on the Pennsylvania Frontier* (1999).

Merwick, Donna. *The Shame and the Sorrow: Dutch-Amerindian Encounters in New Netherland* (2006).

Silverman, David. *Faith and Boundaries: Colonists, Christianity, and Community among the Wampanoag Indians of Martha's Vineyard, 1600–1871* (2005).

Steele, Ian K. *Warpaths: Invasions of North America* (1994).

Washburn, Wilcomb E. *The Governor and the Rebel: A History of Bacon's Rebellion in Virginia* (1957).

White, Richard. *The Middle Ground: Indians, Empires, and Republics in the Great Lakes Region, 1650–1815* (1991).

Africans in America

Breen, T. H., and Stephen Innes. *"Myne Owne Ground": Race and Freedom on Virginia's Eastern Shore, 1640–1676* (1980).

Davis, David Brion. *Inhuman Bondage: The Rise and Fall of Slavery in the New World* (2006).

Jordan, Winthrop. *White over Black: American Attitudes toward the Negro, 1550–1812* (1968).

Lepore, Jill. *New York Burning: Liberty, Slavery, and Conspiracy in Eighteenth-Century Manhattan* (2005).

Littlefield, Daniel. *Rice and Slaves: Ethnicity and the Slave Trade in Colonial South Carolina* (1981).

Morgan, Philip. *Slave Counterpoint: Black Culture in the Eighteenth-Century Chesapeake & Lowcountry* (1998).

Mullin, Michael. *Africa in America: Slave Acculturation and Resistance in the American South and the British Caribbean, 1736–1831* (1994).

Parent, Anthony S. *Foul Means: The Formation of a Slave Society in Virginia, 1660-1740* (2006).

Wood, Betty. *The Origins of American Slavery: Freedom and Bondage in the English Colonies* (1997).

Labor Systems and European Immigration

Bailyn, Bernard. *The Peopling of British North America: An Introduction* (1986).

Bailyn, Bernard. *Voyagers to the West: A Passage in the Peopling of America on the Eve of the Revolution* (1986).

Baseler, Marilyn. *"Asylum for Mankind": America 1607–1800* (1998).

DeWolfe, Barbara, ed. *Discoveries of America: Personal Accounts of British Emigrants to America in the Revolutionary Era* (1997).

Ekirch, A. Roger. *Bound for America: The Transportation of British Convicts to the Colonies, 1718–1775* (1987).

Griffin, Patrick. *The People with No Name: Ireland's Ulster Scots, America's Scots Irish, and the Creation of a British Atlantic World, 1689–1764* (2001).

Innes, Stephen, ed. *Work and Labor in Early America* (1988).

Otterness, Philip. *Becoming German: The 1709 Palatine Migration to New York* (2004).

Roeber, A. G. *Palatines, Liberty, and Property: German Lutherans in Colonial British America* (1993).

Salinger, Sharon V. *"To Serve Well and Faithfully": Labor and Indentured Servants in Pennsylvania, 1682–1800* (1987).

Wokeck, Marianne. *Trade in Strangers: The Beginnings of Mass Migration to North America* (1999).

Chapter 4
Colonial Economic Development

McCusker, John and Kenneth Morgan, eds. *The Early Modern Atlantic Economy* (2001).

Steele, Ian K. *The English Atlantic, 1675–1740: An Exploration of Communication and Community* (1986).

Walton, Gary M., and James F. Shepherd. *The Economic Rise of Early America* (1979).

Waterhouse, Richard. *A New World Gentry: The Making of a Merchant and Planter Class in South Carolina, 1670–1770* (1989).

Religion, Society, and Culture in Early America

Bonomi, Patricia. *Under the Cope of Heaven: Religion, Society, and Politics in Colonial America* (1986).

Boyer, Paul, and Stephen Nissenbaum. *Salem Possessed: The Social Origins of Witchcraft* (1974).

Butler, Jon. *Becoming America: The Revolution before 1776* (2000).

Chaplin, Joyce. *The First Scientific American: Benjamin Franklin and the Pursuit of Genius* (2006).

Dayton, Cornelia Hughes. *Women before the Bar: Gender, Law, & Society in Connecticut, 1639–1789* (1995).

Hall, Gwendolyn Midlo. *Africans in Colonial Louisiana: The Development of Afro-Creole Culture in the Eighteenth Century* (1992).

Herndon, Ruth. *Unwelcome Americans: Living on the Margin in Early New England* (2001).

Isaac, Rhys. *The Transformation of Virginia, 1740–1790* (1982).

May, Henry. *The Enlightenment in America* (1976).

Norton, Mary Beth. *In the Devil's Snare: The Salem Witchcraft Crisis of 1692* (2002).

Colonial and Imperial Politics

Bailyn, Bernard. *The Origins of American Politics* (1968).

Brewer, John. *The Sinews of Power: War, Money, and the English State, 1688–1783* (1989).

Bushman, Richard. *King and People in Provincial Massachusetts* (1985).

Lovejoy, David S. *The Glorious Revolution in America, 1660–1692* (1972).

McConville, Brendan. *The King's Three Faces: The Rise and Fall of Royal America, 1688–1776* (2006).

Morgan, Edmund S. *Inventing the People: The Rise of Popular Sovereignty in England and America* (1988).

Nash, Gary B. *The Urban Crucible: The Northern Seaports and the Origins of the American Revolution,* abr. ed. (1986).

Shannon, Timothy. *Indians and Colonists at the Crossroads of Empire: The Albany Congress of 1754* (1999).

The Expansion of Empires

Barr, Juliana. *Peace Came in the Form of a Woman: Indians and Spaniards in the Texas Borderlands* (2007).

Bond, Bradley, ed. *French Colonial Louisiana and the Atlantic World* (2005).

DuVal, Kathleen. *The Native Ground: Indians and Colonists in the Heart of the Continent* (2006).

Hinderaker, Eric, and Peter Mancall. *At the Edge of Empire: The Backcountry in British North America* (2003).

Hofstra, Warren. *The Planting of New Virginia: Settlement and Landscape in the Shenandoah Valley* (2004).

Richter, Daniel. *Ordeal of the Longhouse: The Peoples of the Iroquois League in the Era of European Colonization* (1992).

Usner, Daniel H., Jr. *Indians, Settlers, and Slaves in a Frontier Exchange Economy: The Lower Mississippi Valley before 1783* (1992).

Weber, David J. *The Spanish Frontier in North America* (1992).

Imperial Warfare

Black, Jeremy. *Britain as a Military Power, 1688–1815* (1999).

Calloway, Colin. *The Scratch of a Pen: 1763 and the Transformation of America* (2006).

Jennings, Francis. *Empire of Fortune: Crowns, Colonies, and Tribes in the Seven Years' War in America* (1988).

Merritt, Jane. *At the Crossroads: Indians and Empires on a Mid-Atlantic Frontier, 1700–1763* (2003).

Steele, Ian K. *Betrayals: Fort William Henry and the "Massacre"* (1990).

Titus, James. *The Old Dominion at War: Society, Politics, and Warfare in Late Colonial Virginia* (1991).

Chapter 5
Imperial Reorganization

Alden, John R. *John Stuart and the Southern Colonial Frontier: A Study of Indian Relations, War, Trade, and Land Problems in the Southern Wilderness, 1754–1775* (1944, 1966).

Alexander, John K. *Samuel Adams: America's Revolutionary Politician* (2002).

Anderson, Fred. *Crucible of War: The Seven Years' War and the Fate of Empire in British North America, 1754–1766* (2000).

Barrow, Thomas C. *Trade and Empire: The British Customs Service in Colonial America, 1660–1775* (1967).

Bonwick, Colin. *The American Revolution* (1991).

Brooke, John. *King George III* (1972).

Cashin, Edward J. *William Bartram and the American Revolution on the Southern Frontier* (2000).

Dowd, Gregory. *War Under Heaven: Pontiac, the Indian Nations, and the British Empire* (2002).

Hatley, Tom. *The Dividing Paths: Cherokees and South Carolinians through the Era of Revolution* (1993).

Langford, Paul. *A Polite and Commercial People: England, 1727–1783* (1989).

Oliphant, John. *Peace and War on the Anglo-Cherokee Frontier, 1756–63* (2001).

Richter, Daniel. *Facing East from Indian Country: A Native History of Early America* (2001).

Shy, John. *Toward Lexington: The Role of the British Army in the Coming of the American Revolution* (1965).

Snapp, J. Russell. *John Stuart and the Struggle for Empire on the Southern Frontier* (1996).

Weber, David J. *The Spanish Frontier in North America* (1992).

White, Richard. *The Middle Ground: Indians, Empires, and Republics in the Great Lakes Region, 1650–1815* (1991).

American Reactions

Breen, Timothy H. *The Marketplace of Revolution: How Consumer Politics Shaped American Independence* (2004).

Brown, Richard D. *Revolutionary Politics in Massachusetts: The Boston Committee of Correspondence and the Towns, 1772–1774* (1970).

Brown, Richard M. *The South Carolina Regulators* (1963).

Calhoon, Robert M. *Dominion and Liberty: Ideology in the Anglo-American World, 1660–1801* (1994).

Countryman, Edward. *A People in Revolution: The American Revolution and Political Society in New York, 1760–1790* (1981).

Egnal, Marc. *A Mighty Empire: The Origins of the American Revolution* (1988).

Ekirch, Robert A. *"Poor Carolina": Politics and Society in Colonial North Carolina, 1729–1776* (1981).

Greene, Jack P. *Negotiated Authorities: Essays in Colonial Political and Constitutional History* (1994).

Chapter 8
Washington's America
Aron, Stephen. *How the West Was Lost: The Transformation of Kentucky from Daniel Boone to Henry Clay* (1996).

Cayton, Andrew R. L. *Frontier Republic: Ideology and Politics in the Ohio Country, 1780–1825 (1989).*

Harvey, Tamara, and Greg O'Brien, eds. *George Washington's South* (2004).

McColley, Robert. *Slavery and Jeffersonian Virginia* (1964).

Nash, Gary B. *Forging Freedom: The Formation of Philadelphia's Black Community, 1720–1840* (1988).

Newman, Simon P. *Parades and the Politics of the American Street* (1997).

Smith, Billy G. The *"Lower Sort": Philadelphia's Laboring People, 1750–1800* (1990).

Ulrich, Laurel Thatcher. *A Midwife's Tale: The Life of Martha Ballard, Based on Her Diary 1785–1812* (1990).

Wallace, Anthony F. C. *The Death and Rebirth of the Seneca* (1970).

White, Richard. *The Middle Ground: Indians, Empires, and Republics in the Great Lakes Region, 1650-1815* (1991).

Wood, Betty. *Women's Work, Men's Work: The Informal Slave Economies of Lowcountry Georgia* (1995).

Forging a New Government
Chernow, Ron. *Alexander Hamilton* (2004).

Cunliffe, Marcus. *George Washington: Man and Monument* (1958).

Ketcham, Ralph. *Presidents above Party: The First American Presidency, 1789–1829* (1984).

Kohn, Richard H. *Eagle and Sword: The Federalists and the Creation of the Military Establishment in America, 1783–1802* (1975).

Phelps, Glenn A. *George Washington and American Constitutionalism* (1993).

Ellis, Joseph J. *Founding Brothers: The Revolutionary Generation* (2000).

The Emergence of Parties
Appleby, Joyce. *Capitalism and a New Social Order: The Republican Vision of the 1790s* (1984).

Buel, Richard Jr., *Securing the Revolution: Ideology in American Politics, 1789–1815* (1972).

Branson, Susan. *Those Fiery Frenchified Dames: Women and Political Culture in Early National Philadelphia* (2001).

Cunningham, Noble E., Jr. *The Jeffersonian Republicans: The Formation of Party Organization, 1789–1801* (1957).

De Conde, Alexander. *Entangling Alliance: Politics and Diplomacy under George Washington* (1958).

Slaughter, Thomas P. *The Whiskey Rebellion: Frontier Epilogue to the American Revolution* (1986).

Young, Alfred F. *The Democratic Republicans of New York: The Origins, 1763–1797* (1967).

The Last Federalist Administration
Dauer, Manning. *The Adams Federalists* (1953).

Ferling, John E. *Adams vs. Jefferson: The Tumultuous Election of 1800* (2004).

Kurtz, Stephen G. *The Presidency of John Adams: The Collapse of Federalism, 1795–1800* (1957).

Sharp, Roger. *American Politics in the Early Republic: The New Nation in Crisis* (1993).

Smith, James M. *Freedom's Fetters: The Alien and Sedition Laws and American Civil Liberties,* rev. ed. (1966).

Stinchcombe, William. *The XYZ Affair* (1980).

Chapter 9
Jefferson's Presidency
Ackerman, Bruce. *The Failure of the Founding Fathers: Jefferson, Madison, and the Rise of Presidential Democracy* (2005).

Ambrose, Stephen. *Undaunted Courage: Meriwether Lewis, Thomas Jefferson, and the Opening of the American West* (1996).

Banning, Lance. *The Jeffersonian Persuasion: Evolution of a Party Ideology* (1978).

Ben-Atar, Doron S. *The Origins of Jeffersonian Commercial Policy and Diplomacy* (1993).

Dunn, Susan. *Jefferson's Second Revolution: The Election Crisis of 1800 and the Triumph of Republicanism* (2004).

Fischer, David Hackett. *The Revolution of American Conservatism: The Federalist Party in the Era of Jeffersonian Democracy* (1965).

Kennon, Donald R., ed. *A Republic for the Ages: The United States Capitol and the Political Culture of the Early Republic* (1999).

Kukla, Jon. *A Wilderness So Immense: The Louisiana Purchase and the Destiny of America* (2003).

McDonald, Forrest. *The Presidency of Thomas Jefferson* (1976).

Shankman, Andrew. *Crucible of American Democracy: The Struggle to Fuse Egalitarianism and Capitalism in Jeffersonian Pennsylvania* (2004).

Smelser, Marshall. *The Democratic Republic, 1801–1815* (1968)

Young, James Sterling. *The Washington Community, 1800–1828* (1966).

Madison and the Coming of War
Brown, Roger H. *The Republic in Peril* (1964).

Dowd, Gregory Evans. *A Spirited Resistance: The North American Indian Struggle for Unity, 1745–1815* (1992).

Edmunds, R. David. *The Shawnee Prophet* (1983) and *Tecumseh and the Quest for Indian Leadership* (1984).

Owsley, Frank Lawrence, Jr., and Gene H. Smith. *Filibusters and Expansionists: Jeffersonian Manifest Destiny* (1997).

Perkins, Bradford. *Prologue to War: England and the United States, 1805–1812* (1961).

Rutland, Robert A. *Madison's Alternatives: The Jeffersonian Republicans and the Coming of War* (1975).

The War of 1812
Banner, James M. *To the Hartford Convention: The Federalists and the Origins of Party Politics in the Early Republic, 1789–1815* (1967).

Gribbin, William. *The Churches Militant: The War of 1812 and American Religion* (1973).

Horsman, Reginald. *The War of 1812* (1969).

Stagg, J. C. A. *Mr. Madison's War: Politics, Diplomacy, and Warfare in the Early Republic, 1783–1830* (1983).

Watts, Steven. *The Republic Reborn: War and the Making of Liberal America* (1987).

The Era of Good Feelings
Bemis, Samuel Flagg. *John Quincy Adams and the Foundations of American Foreign Policy* (1949).

Cunningham, Noble E., Jr. *The Presidency of James Monroe* (1996).

Livermore, Shaw. *The Twilight of Federalism: The Disintegration of the Federalist Party, 1815–1830* (1962).

May, Ernest R. *The Making of the Monroe Doctrine* (1975).

White, G. Edward. *The Marshall Court and Cultural Change, 1815–1835* (1991).

The Breakdown of Unity
Forbes, Robert Pierce. *The Missouri Compromise and its Aftermath: Slavery and the Meaning of America* (2007).

Rothbard, Murray N. *The Panic of 1819: Reactions and Policies* (1962).

Chapter 10
The Egalitarian Impulse
Butler, Jon. *Awash in a Sea of Faith: Christianizing the American People* (1990).

Hargreaves, Mary W. M. *The Presidency of John Quincy Adams* (1985).

Hatch, Nathan O. *The Democratization of American Christianity* (1989).

Peterson, Merrill D., ed. *Democracy, Liberty, and Property: The State Constitutional Conventions of the 1820s* (1966).

Tocqueville, Alexis de. *Democracy in America,* ed. Phillips Bradley, 2 vols. (1845).

Williamson, Chilton. *American Suffrage from Property to Democracy, 1760–1860* (1960).

Jackson's Presidency
Cole, Donald B. *The Presidency of Andrew Jackson* (1993).

Ellis, Richard E. *The Union at Risk: Jacksonian Democracy, States' Rights, and the Nullification Crisis* (1987).

Freehling, William W. *Prelude to Civil War: The Nullification Controversy in South Carolina, 1816–1836* (1966).

Magliocca, Gerald N. *Andrew Jackson and the Constitution: The Rise and Fall of Generational Regimes* (2007).

Perdue, Theda. *The Cherokee Nation and the Trial of Tears* (2007).

Rogin, Michael Paul. *Fathers and Children: Andrew Jackson and the Subjugation of the American Indian* (1975).

Schlesenger, Arthur, Jr. *The Age of Jackson* (1945).

Wallace, Anthony F. C. *The Long, Bitter Trail: Andrew Jackson and the Indians* (1993).

Ward, John William. *Andrew Jackson: Symbol for an Age* (1955).

Van Buren and Hard Times
McFaul, John M. *The Politics of Jacksonian Finance* (1972).

McGrane, Reginald Charles. *The Panic of 1837* (1924).

Sharp, Roger. *The Jacksonians versus the Banks: Politics in the States after the Panic of 1837* (1970).

Temin, Peter. *The Jacksonian Economy* (1969).

Wilson, Major L. *The Presidency of Martin Van Buren* (1984).

The Rise of the Whig Party
Ashworth, John. *"Agrarians" and "Aristocrats": Party Political Ideology in the United States, 1837–1846* (1983).

Howe, Daniel Walker. *The Political Culture of the American Whigs* (1979).

Kohl, Lawrence Frederick. *The Politics of Individualism: Parties and the American Character in the Jacksonian Era* (1989).

McCormick, Richard P. *The Second American Party System* (1966).

Peterson, Merrill. *The Great Triumvirate: Webster, Clay, and Calhoun* (1987).

The Whigs in Power
Brock, William R. *Parties and Political Conscience* (1979).

Holt, Michael F. *The Rise and Fall of the American Whig Party* (1999).

Merk, Frederick. *Slavery and the Annexation of Texas* (1972).

Peterson, Norma Louis. *The Presidencies of William Henry Harrison and John Tyler* (1990).

Remini, Robert V. *Henry Clay: Statesman for the Union* (1991).

Chapter 11
The Lower South
Bowman, Shearer. *Masters and Lords: Mid-19th Century U.S. Planters and Prussian Junkers* (1993).

Fogel, Robert W., and Stanley Engerman. *Time on the Cross: The Economics of American Negro Slavery* (1974).

Ford, Lacy K., Jr. *Origins of Southern Radicalism: The South Carolina Upcountry, 1800–1860* (1988).

Lockley, Timothy J. *Lines in the Sand: Race and Class in Lowcountry Georgia, 1750–1860* (2001).

McCurry, Stephanie. *Masters of Small Worlds* (1995).

Morris, Christopher. *Becoming Southern: The Evolution of a Way of Life, Warren County and Vicksburg, Mississippi, 1770–1860* (1995).

Rothman, Adam. *Slave Country: American Expansion and the Origins of the Deep South* (2005).

Scarborough, William Kauffman. *Masters of the Big House: Elite Slaveholder's of are Mid-Nineteenth-Century South* (2003).

Thornton, J. Mills, III. *Politics and Power in a Slave Society* (1978).

Vlach, John Michael. *The Planter's Prospect: Privilege and Slaves in Plantation Paintings* (2002).

Wright, Gavin. *The Political Economy of the Cotton South* (1978).

The Upper South
Allmendinger, David F. *Ruffin: Family and Reform in the Old South* (1990).

Bailey, Fred Arthur. *Class and Tennessee's Confederate Generation* (1987).

Crofts, David W. *Old Southampton: Politics and Society in a Virginia County, 1834–1869* (1992)

Dunn, Susan. *Dominion of Memories: Jefferson, Madison, and the Decline of Virginia* (2007).

Fields, Barbara J. *Slavery and Freedom on the Middle Ground: Maryland during the Nineteenth Century* (1985).

McKenzie, Robert Tracey. *One South or Many? Plantation Belt and Upcountry in Civil War Era Tennessee* (1994).

Tadman, Michael. *Speculators and Slaves: Masters, Traders, and Slaves in the Old South* (1989).

Slave Life and Culture

Blassingame, John W. *The Slave Community: Plantation Life in the Antebellum South* (1972).

Camp, Stephanie M. H. *Closer to Freedom: Enslaved Women and Everyday Resistance in the Plantation South* (2004).

Dew, Charles B. *Bond of Iron: Master and Slave at Buffalo Forge* (1994).

Gates, Henry Louis, Jr., ed. *The Bondwoman's Narrative* (2002).

Gutman, Herbert G. *The Black Family in Slavery and Freedom, 1750–1925* (1974).

Kaye, Anthony E. *Joining Places: Slave Neighborhoods in the Old South* (2007).

Kolchin, Peter. *Unfree Labor: American Slavery and Russian Serfdom* (1987).

McLaurin, Melton A. *Celia, a Slave* (1991).

Penningroth, Dylan. *The Claims of Kinfolk: African American Property and Community in the Nineteenth-Century South* (2003).

Starobin, Robert. *Industrial Slavery in the Old South* (1970).

Wade, Richard C. *Slavery in the Cities* (1964).

Free Society

Berlin, Ira. *Slaves without Masters: The Free Negro in the Antebellum South* (1974).

Bolton, Charles C. *Poor Whites of the Antebellum South* (1994).

Bynum, Victoria E. *Unruly Women: The Politics of Social and Sexual Control in the Old South* (1992).

Cecil-Fronsman, Bill. *Common Whites: Class and Culture in Antebellum North Carolina* (1992).

Fox-Genovese, Elizabeth. *Within the Plantation Household: Black and White Women of the Old South* (1988).

Harris, J. William. *Plain Folk and Gentry in a Slave Society* (1985).

Owsley, Frank. *Plain Folk in the South* (1949).

The Proslavery Argument

Bailey, David L. *Shadow on the Church: Southwestern Evangelical Religion and the Issue of Slavery, 1783–1860* (1985).

Fredrickson, George M. *The Black Image in the White Mind* (1971).

Genovese, Eugene D., and Fox-Genovese, Elizabeth. *The Mind of the Master Class: History and Faith in the Southern Slaveholders' Worldview* (2005).

Jenkins, W. S. *Pro-Slavery Thought in the Old South* (1935).

Mathews, Donald G. *Religion in the Old South* (1977).

McKivigan, John R., and Mitchell Snay, eds. *Religion and the Antebellum Debate over Slavery* (1998).

Snay, Mitchell. *Gospel of Disunion: Religion and Separatism in the Antebellum South* (1993).

Chapter 12
Industrial Change and Urbanization

Anbinder, Tyler. *Five Points* (2001).

Bernstein, Peter L. *Wedding of the Waters: The Erie Canal and the Making of a Great Nation* (2005).

Blumin, Stuart M. *The Emergence of the Middle Class: Social Experience in the American City, 1760–1900* (1989).

Bushman, Richard L. *The Refinement of America: Persons, Houses, Cities* (1992).

Cochran, Thomas C. *Frontiers of Change: Early Industrialization in America* (1981).

Dublin, Thomas. *Women at Work: The Transformation of Work and Community in Lowell, Massachusetts, 1826–1860* (1979).

Handlin, Oscar. *Boston's Immigrants: A Study of Acculturation*, rev. ed. (1959).

Horowitz, Morton J. *The Transformation of American Law, 1790–1860* (1977).

Johnson, Paul E. *A Shopkeeper's Millennium: Society and Revivals in Rochester, New York, 1815–1837* (1978).

Laurie, Bruce. *Artisans into Workers: Labor in Nineteenth-Century America* (1989).

Pessen, Edward. *Riches, Class, and Power before the Civil War* (1973).

Roediger, David. *The Wages of Whiteness: Race and the Making of the American Working Class* (1991).

Ryan, Mary. *Cradle of the Middle Class: The Family in Oneida County, New York, 1790–1865* (1981).

Stansel, Christine. *City of Women: Sex and Class in New York, 1789–1860* (1986).

Steinberg, Theodore. *Nature Incorporated: Industrialization and the Waters of New England* (1991).

Wade, Richard C. *The Urban Frontier* (1964).

Wilentz, Sean. *Chants Democratic: New York City and the Rise of the American Working Class, 1790–1865* (1984).

Reform and Moral Order

Burin, Eric. *Slavery and the Peculiar Solution: A History of the American Colonization Society* (2005).

Cott, Nancy F. *The Bonds of Womanhood: "Woman's Sphere" in New England, 1780–1835* (1977).

Cross, Whitney R. *The Burned-Over District: The Social and Intellectual History of Enthusiastic Religion in Western New York, 1800–1850* (1950).

Epstein, Barbara Leslie. *The Politics of Domesticity: Women, Evangelicalism, and Temperance in Nineteenth-Century America* (1981).

Foster, Charles I. *An Errand of Mercy: The Evangelical United Front* (1960).

Ginzberg, Lori D. *Women and the Work of Benevolence: Morality, Politics, and Class in the 19th-Century United States* (1990).

Hanley, Mark Y. *Beyond a Christian Commonwealth: The Protestant Quarrel with the American Republic, 1830–1860* (1994).

Horowitz, Helen L. *Rereading Sex: Battles over Sexual Knowledge and Suppression in Nineteenth-Century America* (2002).

Smith-Rosenberg, Carroll. *Religion and the Rise of the American City* (1971).

Rorabaugh, W. J. *The Alcoholic Republic* (1979).

Walters, Ronald A. *American Reformers, 1815–1860* (1978).

Winn, Kenneth H. *Exiles in a Land of Liberty: Mormons in America, 1830–1846* (1989).

Wosh, Peter J. *Spreading the Word: The Bible Business in Nineteenth-Century America* (1994).

Institutions and Social Improvement

Capper, Charles, and Conrad Edick Wright, eds. *Transient and Permanent: The Transcendentalist Movement and Its Contexts* (1999).

Grob, Gerald N. *Mental Institutions in America: Social Policy to 1875* (1973).

Guarneri, Carl J. *The Utopian Alternative: Fourierism in Nineteenth-Century America* (1991).

Hirsh, Adam Jay. *The Rise of the Penitentiary* (1992).

Kaestle, Carl F. *Pillars of the Republic: Common Schools and American Society, 1780–1860* (1983).

Katz, Michael B. *In the Shadow of the Poorhouse: A Social History of Welfare in America* (1986).

Rothman, David. *The Discovery of the Asylum: Social Order and Disorder in the New Republic* (1971).

Abolitionism and Women's Rights

Basch, Norma. *In the Eyes of the Law: Women, Marriage, and Property in Nineteenth-Century New York* (1982).

Cutter, Barbara. *Domestic Devils, Battlefield Angels: The Radicalism of American Womanhood 1830–1865* (2003).

Hewitt, Nancy A. *Women's Activism and Social Change: Rochester, New York, 1822–1872* (1984).

Isenberg, Nancy. *Sex and Citizenship in Antebellum America* (1998).

Jeffrey, Julie Roy. *The Great Silent Army of Abolitionism: Ordinary Women in the Antislavery Movement* (1998).

Litwack, Leon F. *North of Slavery: The Negro in the Free States, 1790–1860* (1961).

Lumpkin, Katharine Du Pre. *The Emancipation of Angelina Grimké* (1974).

McKivigan, John R. *The War against Proslavery Religion: Abolitionism and the Northern Churches, 1830–1865* (1984).

Newman, Richard S. *The Transformation of American Abolitionism: Fighting Slavery in the Early Republic* (2002).

Rael, Patrick. *Black Identity and Black Protest in the Antebellum North* (2002).

Richards, Leonard L. *The Slave Power: The Free North and Southern Domination, 1780–1860* (2000).

Ripley, C. Peter, Finkenbine, Roy E., Hembree, Michael E., and Yacovone, Donald., eds. *Witness for Freedom: African-American Voices on Race, Slavery, and Emancipation* (1993).

Salerno, Beth A., *Sister Societies: Women's Antislavery Organizations in Antebellum America* (2005).

Chapter 13
The Agricultural Frontier

Cashin, Joan E. *A Family Venture: Men and Women on the Southern Frontier* (1991).

Faragher, John Mack. *Sugar Creek: Life on the Illinois Prairie* (1986).

Hudson, John C. *Making the Corn Belt: A Geographical History of Middle-Western Agriculture* (1994).

Moore, John Hebron. *The Emergence of the Cotton Kingdom in the Old Southwest: Mississippi, 1770–1860* (1987).

Rohrbough, Malcolm J. *The Trans-Appalachian Frontier: People, Societies, and Institutions, 1775–1850* (1978).

Stoll, Steven. *Larding the Lean Earth: Soil and Society in Nineteenth-Century America* (2002).

The Frontier of the Plains Indians

Clark, Malcolm, Jr. *Eden Seekers: The Settlement of Oregon, 1810–1862* (1981).

Goetzmann, William H. *Exploration and Empire: The Explorer and Scientist in the Winning of the American West* (1966).

Jeffrey, Julie R. *Frontier Women: The Trans-Mississippi West, 1840–1880* (1979).

Moore, John H., ed. *The Political Economy of the North American Indians* (1993).

Unruh, John. *The Plains Across: The Overland Emigrations and the Trans-Mississippi West, 1840–1860* (1979).

Utley, Robert M. *A Life Wild and Perilous: Mountain Men and the Paths to the Pacific* (1997).

West, Elliott. *The Way to the West: Essays on the Central Plains* (1995).

White, Richard. *The Roots of Dependency: Subsistence, Environment, and Social Change Among the Choctaws, Pawnees, and Navajos* (1983).

The Mexican Borderlands

Acuña, Rudolfo. *Occupied America: A History of Chicanos* (1988).

Anderson, Gary Clayton. *The Conquest of Texas: Ethnic Cleansing in the Promised Land* (2005).

Arrington, Leonard J. *Great Basin Kingdom: An Economic History of the Latter-Day Saints, 1830–1900,* New ed. (2005).

Gonzales, Manuel G. *Mexicanos: A History of Mexicans in the United States* (1999).

Lack, Paul D. *The Texas Revolutionary Experience: A Political and Social History, 1835–1836* (1992).

Lecompte, Janet. *Pueblo, Hardscabble, Greenhorn: The Upper Arkansas, 1832–1856* (1978).

Phillips, George Harwood. *Indians and Intruders in Central California, 1769–1849* (1993).

Roberts, Randy, and James L. Olsen, *A Line in the Sand: The Alamo in Blood and Memory* (2001).

Tijerina, Andres. *Tejanos and Texas under the Mexican Flag, 1821–1836* (1994).

Topping, Gary, ed. *Utah Historians and the Reconstruction of Western History* (2003).

Weber, David J. *The Mexican Frontier, 1821–1846: The American Southwest under Mexico* (1982).

Politics, Expansion, and War

Griswold del Castillo, Richard. *The Treaty of Guadalupe Hidalgo: A Legacy of Conflict* (1990).

Eisenhower, John S. D. *So Far from God: The U.S. War with Mexico* (1989).

Foos, Paul W. *A Short, Offhand, Killing Affair: Soldiers and Social Conflict during the Mexican-American War* (2002).

Henderson, Timothy J. *A Glorious Defeat: Mexico and its War with the United States* (2007).

Hietala, Thomas R. *Manifest Design: American Aggrandizement in Late Jacksonian America* (1985).

Horsman, Reginald. *Race and Manifest Destiny: The Origins of American Racial Anglo-Saxonism* (1981).

Johannsen, Robert W. *To the Halls of Montezuma: The Mexican War in the American Imagination* (1985).

Merle, Frederic. *Manifest Destiny and Mission in American History* (1963).

Sellers, Charles G. *James K. Polk: Continentalist, 1843–1846* (1966).

Silbey, Joel H. *Storm over Texas: The Annexation Controversy and the Road to Civil War* (2005).

Chapter 14
Slavery in the Territories

Berwanger, Eugene H. *The Frontier against Slavery: Western Anti-Negro Prejudice and the Slavery Extension Controversy* (1967).

Hamilton, Holman. *Prologue to Conflict: The Crisis and Compromise of 1850* (1966).

Hedrick, Joan D. *Harriet Beecher Stowe: A Life* (1993).

Johnson, Susan Lee. *Roaring Camp: The Social World of the California Gold Rush* (2000).

Morrison, Michael E. *Slavery and the American West: The Eclipse of Manifest Destiny and the Coming of the Civil War* (1997).

Peterson, Merrill. *The Great Triumvirate: Webster, Clay, and Calhoun* (1987).

Quarles, Benjamin. *Black Abolitionists* (1969).

Rohrbough, Malcolm J. *Days of Gold: The California Gold Rush and the American Nation* (1997).

Political Realignment

Anbinder, Tyler. *Nativism and Slavery: The Northern Know-Nothings and the Politics of the 1850s* (1992).

Carwardine, Richard J. *Evangelicals and Politics in Antebellum America* (1993).

Cooper, William J., Jr. *The South and the Politics of Slavery, 1828–1856* (1978).

Fehrenbacher, Don E. *Slavery, Law, and Politics: The Dred Scott Case in Historical Perspective* (1981).

Foner, Eric. *Free Soil, Free Labor, Free Men: The Ideology of the Republican Party before the Civil War* (1970).

Gienapp, William E. *The Origins of the Republican Party, 1852-1856* (1987).

Holt, Michael F. *The Fate of their Country: Politicians, Slavery Extension, and the Coming of the Civil War* (2004).

Howe, Daniel Walker. "The Evangelical Movement and Political Culture in the North during the Second Party System," *Journal of American History*, 77 (March 1991): 1216–1239.

Johannsen, Robert W., ed. *The Lincoln-Douglas Debates of 1858* (1965).

Long, Kathryn Teresa. *The Revival of 1857–58: Interpreting an American Religious Awakening* (1998).

Rawley, James A. *Race and Politics: "Bleeding Kansas" and the Coming of the Civil War* (1969).

SenGupta, Ganja. *For God and Mammon: Evangelicals and Entrepreneurs, Masters and Slaves in Territorial Kansas, 1854–1860* (1996).

von Frank, Albert J. *The Trials of Anthony Burns: Freedom and Slavery in Emerson's Boston* (1998).

Wolff, Gerald W. *The Kansas-Nebraska Bill: Party, Section, and the Coming of the Civil War* (1977).

The Road to Disunion

Banks, Russell. *Cloudsplitter* (1997).

Barney, William L. *The Road to Secession: A New Perspective on the Old South* (1972).

Current, Richard N. *Lincoln and the First Shot* (1963).

Dew, Charles B. *Apostles of Disunion: Southern Secession Commissioners and the Causes of the Civil War* (2001).

Helper, Hinton Rowan. *The Impending Crisis of the South: How to Meet It* (1857).

Johnson, Michael P., and James L. Roark, eds. *No Chariot Let Down: Charleston's Free People of Color on the Eve of the Civil War* (1984).

Levine, Bruce. *Half Slave and Half Free: The Roots of Civil War* (2005).

McCardell, John. *The Idea of a Southern Nation: Southern Nationalists and Southern Nationalism, 1830–1860* (1979).

Snay, Michael. *Gospel of Disunion: Religion and Separatism in the Antebellum South* (1993).

Thornton, J. Mills. *Politics and Power in a Slave Society: Alabama, 1800-1860* (1978).

Walther, Eric H. *The Fire-Eaters* (1992).

Chapter 15
Mobilization, North and South

Cooper, William J. *Jefferson Davis: American* (2000).

Davis, William C. *"A Government of Our Own": The Making of the Confederacy* (1994).

Donald, David. *Lincoln* (1995).

Grant, Ulysses S. *Personal Memoirs of U.S. Grant* (1885, 1996).

Royster, Charles. *The Destructive War: William Tecumseh Sherman, Stonewall Jackson, and the Americans* (1991).

Schultz, Jane E. *Women at the Front: Hospital Workers in Civil War America* (2004).

Thomas, Emory M. *Robert E. Lee: A Biography* (1995).

Watkins, Sam R. *"Co. Aytch": A Confederate Memoir of the Civil War* (1882; 2003).

The Early War, 1861–1862

Bierce, Ambrose. *Civil War Stories* (1909; 1994).

Cooling, Benjamin Franklin. *Forts Henry and Donelson: The Key to the Confederate Heartland* (1988).

Daniel, Larry J. *Shiloh: The Battle That Changed the Civil War* (1997).

Fellman, Michael. *Inside War: The Guerrilla Conflict in Missouri during the Civil War* (1989).

Linderman, Gerald F. *Embattled Courage: The Experience of Combat in the American Civil War* (1989).

McPherson, James M. *What They Fought For, 1861–1865* (1994).

Robertson, James I. *Stonewall Jackson: The Man, the Soldier, the Legend* (1997).

Turning Points, 1862–1863

Berlin, Ira, et al., eds. *Freedom: A Documentary History of Emancipation, 1861–1867*, Ser. 1, Vol. 1: *The Destruction of Slavery* (1985).

Josephy, Alvin M., Jr. *The Civil War in the American West* (1993).

McFeely, William S. *Grant: A Biography* (1981).

Quarles, Benjamin. *The Negro in the Civil War* (1953).

Reardon, Carol. *Pickett's Charge in History and Memory* (1997).

Sears, Stephen W. *Landscape Turned Red: The Battle of Antietam* (1983).

Shaara, Michael. *The Killer Angels: A Novel* (1974).

Smith, David Paul. *Frontier Defense in the Civil War: Texas' Rangers and Rebels* (1992).

Striner, Richard, *Father Abraham: Lincoln's Relentless Struggle to End Slavery* (2006).

Wills, Garry. *Lincoln at Gettysburg: The Words That Remade America* (1992).

War Transforms the North

Baker, Kevin. *Paradise Alley: A Novel* (2002)

Mitchell, Reid. *The Vacant Chair: The Northern Soldier Leaves Home* (1993).

Neely, Mark E., Jr. *The Fate of Liberty: Abraham Lincoln and Civil Liberties* (1991).

Pryor, Elizabeth B. *Clara Barton: Professional Angel* (1987).

Richardson, Heather Cox. *The Greatest Nation of the Earth: Republican Economic Policies during the Civil War* (1997).

The Confederacy Disintegrates

Ash, Stephen V. *When the Yankees Came: Conflict and Chaos in the Occupied South, 1861–1865* (1995).

Campbell, Edward D. C., Jr., and Kym S. Rice, eds. *A Woman's War: Southern Women, Civil War, and the Confederate Legacy* (1996).

Clinton, Catherine, and Nina Silber, eds. *Divided Houses: Gender and the Civil War* (1992).

Durden, Robert F. *The Gray and the Black: The Confederate Debate on Emancipation* (1972).

Edwards, Laura. *Scarlett Doesn't Live Here Anymore: Southern Women in the Civil War Era* (2000).

Faust, Drew Gilpin. *Mothers of Invention: Women of the Slaveholding South in the American Civil War* (1996).

Frazier, Charles. *Cold Mountain* (1997).

Grimsley, Mark. *The Hard Hand of War: Union Policy Toward Southern Civilians, 1861–1865* (1995).

Woodward, C. Vann, ed. *Mary Chesnut's Civil War* (1981).

The Union Prevails

Beringer, Richard E., Herman Hattaway, Archer Jones, and William N. Still, Jr. *Why the South Lost the Civil War* (1986).

Glatthaar, Joseph T. *The March to the Sea and Beyond* (1985).

Rubin, Anne Sarah. *A Shattered Nation: The Rise and Fall of the Confederacy, 1861–1868* (2005).

Chapter 16
White Southerners and the Ghosts of the Confederacy

Blight, David W. *Race and Reunion: The Civil War in American Memory* (2001).

Edwards, Laura F. *Gendered Strife and Confusion: The Political Culture of Reconstruction* (1997).

Goldfield, David, *Still Fighting the Civil War: The American South and Southern History* (2002).

More Than Freedom: Black African-American Aspirations in 1865

Berlin, Ira, et al. *Freedom: A Documentary History of Emancipation, 1861–1867. The Wartime Genesis of Free Labor: The Lower South* (1990).

Cimbala, Paul A., and Randall M. Miller, eds. *The Freedmen's Bureau and Reconstruction: A Reconsideration* (1999).

Fitzgerald, Michael W. *The Union League Movement in the Deep South: Politics and Agricultural Change during Reconstruction* (1989).

Gutman, Herbert G. *The Black Family in Slavery and Freedom, 1750–1925* (1976).

Hahn, Steven. *A Nation under Our Feet: Black Political Struggles in the Rural South from Slavery to the Great Migration* (2003).

Jaynes, Gerald. *Branches without Roots: The Genesis of the Black Working Class in the American South, 1862–1882* (1986).

Jones, Jacqueline. *Labor of Love, Labor of Sorrow: Black Women, Work, and the Family from Slavery to the Present* (1985).

Kolchin, Peter. *Unfree Labor: American Slavery and Russian Serfdom* (1990).

Rabinowitz, Howard N. *Race Relations in the Urban South, 1865–1890* (1978).

Rabinowitz, Howard N., ed. *Southern Black Leaders of the Reconstruction Era* (1982).

Stowell, David W. *Rebuilding Zion: The Religious Reconstruction of the South, 1863–1877* (1998).

Thornbrough, Emma Lou., ed. *Black Reconstructionists* (1972).

Williamson, Joel. *After Slavery: The Negro in South Carolina during Reconstruction, 1861–1877* (1965).

Federal Reconstruction, 1865–1870

Benedict, Michael Les. *A Compromise of Principle: Congressional Republicans and Reconstruction, 1863–1869* (1974).

Harris, William C. *With Charity for All: Lincoln and the Restoration of the Union* (1997).

McFeely, William S. *Grant: A Biography* (1981).

Moneyhon, Carl H. *Republicanism in Reconstruction Texas* (1980).

Perman, Michael. *Reunion without Compromise: The South and Reconstruction, 1865–1868* (1973).

Rose, Willie Lee. *Rehearsal for Reconstruction: The Port Royal Experiment* (1964).

Summers, Mark W. *Railroads, Reconstruction, and the Gospel of Prosperity: Aid Under the Radical Republicans, 1865–1877* (1984).

Trefousse, Hans. *The Radical Republicans: Lincoln's Vanguard for Racial Justice* (1969).

Counter-Reconstruction, 1870–1874

Blum, Edward J. *Reforging the White Republic: Race, Religion, and American Nationalism, 1865–1898* (2005).

Current, Richard N. *Those Terrible Carpetbaggers: A Reinterpretation* (1988).

Hogue, James. *Uncivil War: Five New Orleans Street Battles and the Rise and Fall of Radical Reconstruction* (2006).

Perman, Michael. *The Road to Redemption: Southern Politics, 1869–1879* (1984).

Rable, George C. *But There Was No Peace: The Role of Violence in the Politics of Reconstruction* (1984).

Trelease, Allen W. *White Terror: The Ku Klux Klan Conspiracy and Southern Reconstruction* (1971).

Redemption, 1874–1877

Campbell, Randolph B. *Grass-Roots Reconstruction in Texas, 1865–1880* (1997).

Lemann, Nicholas. *Redemption: The Last Battle of the Civil War* (2006).

Richardson, Heather Cox. *The Death of Reconstruction: Race, Labor, and Politics in the Post–Civil War North, 1865–1901* (2001).

Woodward, C. Vann. *Reunion and Reaction: The Compromise of 1877 and the End of Reconstruction* (1951).

The Failed Promise of Reconstruction

Franklin, John Hope. *Reconstruction after the Civil War* (1961).

Ransom, Roger L., and Richard Sutch. *One Kind of Freedom: The Economic Consequences of Emancipation* (1977).

Richardson, Heather Cox. *West from Appomattox: The Reconstruction of America after the Civil War* (2007).

Stampp, Kenneth M. *The Era of Reconstruction, 1865–1877* (1965).

Chapter 17
The Newness of the New South

Billings, Dwight B. Jr. *Planters and the Making of a "New South"* (1979).

Burton, Orville Vernon. *In My Father's House Are Many Mansions: Family and Community in Edgefield County, South Carolina* (1985).

Carlton, David L. *Mill and Town in South Carolina, 1880–1920* (1980).

Clark, Thomas D. *Pills, Petticoats, and Plows: The Southern Country Store* (1944).

Davis, Harold E. *Henry Grady's New South: Atlanta, a Brave and Beautiful City* (1990).

Doyle, Don H. *New Men, New Cities, New South: Atlanta, Nashville, Charleston, Mobile, 1860–1910* (1990).

Durden, Robert F. *The Dukes of Durham, 1865–1929* (1975).

Eller, Ronald D. *Miners, Millhands, and Mountaineers: Industrialization of the Appalachian South, 1880–1920* (1982).

Hall, Jacqueline Dowd, et al. *Like a Family: The Making of a Southern Cotton Mill World* (1987).

Hearden, Patrick J. *Independence and Empire: The New South's Cotton Mill Campaign, 1865–1901* (1982).

Horwitz, Tony, *Confederates in the Attic: Dispatches from the Unfinished Civil War* (1998).

Lewis, W. David, *Sloss Furnaces and the Rise of the Birmingham District: An Industrial Epic* (1994).

Russell, James M. *Atlanta, 1847–1890: City Building in the Old South and the New* (1988).

Tilley, Nannie M. *The R. J. Reynolds Tobacco Company* (1985).

Wright, Gavin, *Old South, New South: Revolutions in the Southern Economy since the Civil War* (1986).

The Southern Agrarian Revolt

Barnes, Donna. *Farmers in Rebellion: The Rise and Fall of the Southern Farmers' Alliance and People's Party in Texas* (1987).

Barr, Alwyn. *Reconstruction to Reform: Texas Politics, 1876–1906* (1971).

Daniel, Pete. *Breaking the Land: The Transformation of Cotton, Tobacco and Rice Cultures since 1880* (1985).

Hahn, Steven. *The Roots of Southern Populism: The Transformation of the Georgia Upcountry, 1850–1890* (1983).

McMath, Robert, Jr. *The Populist Vanguard: A History of the Southern Farmers' Alliance* (1975).

Minnix, Kathleen. *Laughter in the Amen Corner: The Life of Evangelist Sam Jones* (1993).

Newby, I. A. *Plain Folk in the New South: Social Change and Cultural Persistence, 1880–1915* (1989).

Ownby, Ted. *Subduing Satan: Religion, Recreation, and Manhood in the Rural South, 1865–1920* (1990).

Ransom, Roger, and Richard Sutch. *One Kind of Freedom: The Economic Consequences of Emancipation* (1977).

Wallenstein, Peter. *From Slave South to New South: Public Policy in Nineteenth-Century Georgia* (1987).

Webb, Samuel L. *Two-Party Politics in the One-Party South: Alabama's Hill Country, 1874–1920* (1997).

Wiener, Jonathan. *Social Origins of the New South: Alabama, 1860–1885* (1978).

Woodman, Harold D. *King Cotton and His Retainers: Financing and Marketing the Cotton Crop of the South, 1800–1925* (1968).

Woodward, C. Vann. *Tom Watson: Agrarian Rebel* (1938).

Women in the New South

Bernhard, Virginia, et al., eds. *Southern Women: Histories and Identities* (1992).

Enstam, Elizabeth York. *Women and the Creation of Urban Life: Dallas, Texas, 1843–1920* (1998).

Friedman, Jean E. *The Enclosed Garden: Women and Community in the Evangelical South, 1830–1900* (1985).

Gilmore, Glenda Elizabeth. *Gender and Jim Crow: Women and the Politics of White Supremacy in North Carolina, 1896–1920* (1996).

Green, Elna C. *Southern Strategies: Southern Women and the Woman Suffrage Question* (1997).

Higginbotham, Evelyn Brooks. *Righteous Discontent: The Women's Movement in the Black Baptist Church, 1880–1920* (1993).

Hunter, Tera W. *To 'Joy My Freedom: Southern Black Women's Lives and Labors after the Civil War* (1997).

Lumpkin, Katharine DuPre. *The Making of a Southerner* (1947).

McArthur, Judith N. *Creating the New Woman: The Rise of Southern Women's Progressive Culture in Texas, 1893–1918* (1998).

McDowell, John P. *The Social Gospel in the South: The Woman's Home Mission Movement in the Methodist Episcopal Church, South, 1886–1939* (1982).

Scott, Anne Firor. *The Southern Lady: From Pedestal to Politics, 1830–1930* (1970).

Sims, Anastatia. *The Power of Femininity in the New South: Women's Organizations and Politics in North Carolina, 1880–1930* (1997).

Terrell, Mary Church. *A Colored Woman in a White World* (1980).

Thomas, Mary Martha. *The New Woman in Alabama: Social Reforms and Suffrage, 1890–1920* (1992).

Turner, Elizabeth Hayes. *Women, Culture, and Community: Religion and Reform in Galveston, 1880–1920* (1997).

Wheeler, Marjorie Spruill. *New Women of the New South: The Leaders of the Woman Suffrage Movement in the Southern States* (1993).

Settling the Race Issue

Ayers, Edward L. *Vengeance and Justice: Crime and Punishment in the Nineteenth-Century American South* (1984).

Beatty, Bess. *A Revolution Gone Backwards: The Black Response to National Politics, 1876–1896* (1987).

Blum, Edward J. *Reforging the White Republic: Race, Religion, and American Nationalism, 1865–1898* (2005).

Brundage, W. Fitzhugh. *Lynching in the New South: Georgia and Virginia, 1880–1930* (1993).

Cell, John W. *The Highest Stage of White Supremacy: The Origins of Segregation in South Africa and the American South* (1982).

Clayton, Bruce. *The Savage Ideal: Intolerance and Intellectual Leadership in the South, 1890–1914* (1972).

Dailey, Jane. *Before Jim Crow: The Politics of Race in Postemancipation Virginia* (2000).

Greenwood, Janette Thomas. *Bittersweet Legacy: The Black and White "Better Classes" in Charlotte, 1850–1910* (1994).

Hale, Grace Elizabeth. *Making Whiteness: The Culture of Segregation in the South, 1890–1940* (1998).

Harlan, Louis R. *Booker T. Washington: The Making of a Black Leader, 1856–1901* (1972).

Kantrowitz, Stephen. *Ben Tillman and the Reconstruction of White Supremacy* (2000).

Kenzer, Robert C. *Enterprising Southerners: Black Economic Success in North Carolina, 1865–1915* (1997).

Kousser, J. Morgan, *The Shaping of Southern Politics: Suffrage Restriction and the Establishment of the One-Party South, 1880–1910* (1974).

Letwin, Daniel. *The Challenge of Interracial Unionism: Alabama Coal Miners, 1878–1921* (1998).

Litwack, Leon F. *Trouble in Mind: Black Southerners in the Age of Jim Crow* (1998).

Lofgren, Charles A. *The "Plessy" Case: A Legal-Historical Interpretation* (1987).

Meier, August. *Negro Thought in America, 1880–1915: Racial Ideologies in the Age of Booker T. Washington* (1963).

Prather, H. Leon. *We Have Taken a City: The Wilmington Racial Massacre and Coup of 1898* (1989).

Silber, Nina. *The Romance of Reunion: Northerners and the South* (1993).

Tolnay, Stewart E., and E. M. Beck. *A Festival of Violence: An Analysis of Southern Lynchings, 1882–1930* (1995).

Weare, Walter B. *Black Business in the New South: A Social History of the North Carolina Mutual Life Insurance Company* (1973).

Woodward, C. Vann. *The Strange Career of Jim Crow* (1955).

Chapter 18
New Industry

Bazerman, Charles. *The Languages of Edison's Light* (1999).

Bellamy, Edward. *Looking Backward* (1888).

Benson, Susan Porter. *Counter Cultures: Saleswomen, Managers, and Customers in American Department Stores, 1890–1940* (1986).

Boris, Eileen. *Home to Work: Motherhood and the Politics of Industrial Homework in the United States* (1994).

Buder, Stanley. *Pullman: An Experiment in Industrial Order and Community Planning, 1880–1930* (1967).

Chernow, Ron. *Titan: The Life of John D. Rockefeller, Sr.* (1998).

Davies, Marjorie. *Woman's Place Is at the Typewriter, 1870–1930* (1982).

Dye, Nancy Schrom. *As Equals and as Sisters: Feminism, the Labor Movement, and the Women's Trade Union League of New York* (1981).

Gilfoyle, Timothy J. *City of Eros: New York City, Prostitution, and the Commercialization of Sex, 1790–1920* (1992).

Gutman, Herbert. *Work, Culture, and Society in Industrializing America* (1976).

Katzman, David M. *Seven Days a Week: Women and Domestic Service in Industrializing America* (1978).

Kaufman, Stuart. *Samuel Gompers and the Origins of the American Federation of Labor, 1848–1896* (1973).

Kessler-Harris, Alice. *Out to Work: A History of Wage-Earning Women in the United States* (1982).

Lane, James B. *Jacob A. Riis and the American City* (1974).

Montgomery, David. *The Fall of the House of Labor: The Workplace, the State, and American Labor Activism, 1865–1925* (1987).

Morris, Charles R. *Tycoons: How Andrew Carnegie, John D. Rockefeller, and J.P. Morgan Invented the American Supereconomy* (2005).

Salvatore, Nick. *Eugene V. Debs: Citizen and Socialist* (1982).

Sinclair, Upton. *The Jungle* (1906).

Stromquist, Shelton. *A Generation of Boomers: The Pattern of Railroad Labor Conflict in Nineteenth-Century America* (1987).

Tentler, Leslie Woodcock. *Wage-Earning Women: Industrial Work and Family Life, 1900–1930* (1979).

New Immigrants

Blanck, Dag. *Becoming Swedish-American: The Construction of an Ethnic Identity in the Augustana Synod, 1860–1917* (1997).

Cahan, Abraham. *The Rise of David Levinsky* (1917).

Camarillo, Albert. *Chicanos in a Changing Society: From Mexican Pueblos to American Barrios in Santa Barbara and Southern California, 1848–1930* (1979).

Chen, Yong. *Chinese San Francisco, 1850–1943: A Trans-Pacific Community* (2000).

Clark, Dennis. *The Irish in Philadelphia: Ten Generations of Urban Experience* (1973).

Daniels, Roger. *Not Like Us: Immigrants and Minorities in America, 1890–1924* (1997).

Daniels, Roger. *Guarding the Golden Door: American Immigration Policy and Immigrants since 1882* (2004).

Diner, Hasia. *Erin's Daughters in America* (1983).

Gabaccia, Donna. *From Sicily to Elizabeth Street: Housing and Social Change among Italian Immigrants, 1880–1930* (1984).

Glenn, Evelyn Nakano. *Issei, Nisei, War Bride: Three Generations of Japanese American Women in Domestic Service* (1986).

Howe, Irving. *World of Our Fathers* (1976).

Ignatiev, Noel. *How the Irish Became White* (1995).

Jacobson, Matthew Frye. *Whiteness of a Different Color: European Immigrants and the Alchemy of Race* (1998).

Jacobson, Matthew Frye. *Barbarian Virtues: The United States Encounters Foreign Peoples at Home and Abroad, 1876–1917* (2000).

Kessner, Thomas. *The Golden Door: Italian and Jewish Immigrant Mobility in New York City, 1880–1915* (1977).

Kraut, Alan M. *The Huddled Masses: The Immigrant in American Society, 1880–1921* (1982).

Kusmer, Kenneth. *A Ghetto Takes Shape: Black Cleveland, 1870–1930* (1976).

Lerda, Valeria Gennaro, ed. *From "Melting Pot" to Multiculturalism: The Evolution of Ethnic Relations in the United States and Canada* (1990).

Modell, John. *The Economics and Politics of Racial Accommodation: The Japanese of Los Angeles, 1900–1942* (1977).

Roediger, David R. *The Wages of Whiteness: Race and the Making of the American Working Class* (rev. ed. 1999).

Reimers, David M. *Other Immigrants: The Global Origins of the American People* (2004).

Smith, Betty. *A Tree Grows in Brooklyn* (1943).

Stewart, Kenneth L., and Arnoldo De Leon. *Not Room Enough: Mexicans, Anglos, and Socio-Economic Change in Texas, 1850–1900* (1993).

Wong, K. Scott, and Sucheng Chan, eds. *Claiming America: Constructing Chinese American Identities during the Exclusion Era* (1998).

Yezierska, Anzia. *Bread Givers: A Novel: A Struggle between a Father of the Old World and a Daughter of the New* (1925; new ed. 1975).

New Cities

Barth, Gunther. *Instant Cities: Urbanization and the Rise of San Francisco and Denver* (1975).

Barth, Gunther. *City People: The Rise of Modern City Culture in Nineteenth-Century America* (1982).

Beckert, Sven. *The Monied Metropolis: New York City and the Consolidation of the American Bourgeoisie, 1850–1896* (2001).

Bluestone, Daniel. *Constructing Chicago* (1991).

Bolotin, Norman and Christine Laing. *The World's Columbian Exposition: The Chicago World's Fair of 1893* (1992).

Burrows, Edwin G., and Mike Wallace. *Gotham: A History of New York City to 1898* (1998).

Couvares, Francis G. *The Remaking of Pittsburgh: Class and Culture in an Industrializing City, 1877–1919* (1984).

Deutsch, Sarah. *Women and the City: Gender, Space, and Power in Boston, 1870–1940* (2000).

Fishman, Robert. *Bourgeois Utopias: The Rise and Fall of Suburbia* (1987).

Foy, Jessica, and Thomas J. Schlereth, eds. *American Home Life, 1880–1930: A Social History of Spaces and Services* (1991).

Hayden, Dolores. *Building Suburbia: Green Fields and Urban Growth, 1820–2000* (2004).

Hood, Clifton. *722 Miles: The Building of the Subways and How They Transformed New York* (1993).

Jackson, Kenneth T. *Crabgrass Frontier: The Suburbanization of the United States* (1985).

Kasson, John F. *Amusing the Millions: Coney Island at the Turn of the Century* (1978).

Peiss, Kathy. *Cheap Amusements: Working Women and Leisure in Turn-of-the-Century New York* (1986).

Platt, Harold L. *The Electric City: Energy and the Growth of the Chicago Area, 1880–1930* (1991).

Rosenzweig, Roy. *Eight Hours for What We Will: Workers and Leisure in an Industrial City, 1870–1920* (1983).

Sklar, Kathryn Kish. *Catharine Beecher: A Study of Domesticity* (1973).

Warner, Sam Bass, Jr. *Streetcar Suburbs: The Process of Growth in Boston, 1870–1900* (1962).

Wright, Gwendolyn. *Moralism and the Model Home: Domestic Architecture and Cultural Conflict in Chicago, 1873–1913* (1980).

Chapter 19
General Studies

Armitage, Susan, and Elizabeth Jameson, eds. *The Women's West* (1987).

Butler, Anne M. *Daughters of Joy, Sisters of Misery: Prostitutes in the American West* (1985).

Cronon, William. *Nature's Metropolis: Chicago and the Great West* (1991).

Hine, Robert V. *Community on the American Frontier: Separate But Not Alone* (1980).

Jameson, Elizabeth, and Susan Armitage, eds. *Writing the Range: Race, Class, and Culture in the Women's West* (1997).

Jeffrey, Julie Roy. *Frontier Women* (1998).

Limerick, Patricia Nelson. *The Legacy of Conquest* (1987).

Milner, Clyde A., Carol A. O'Connor, and Martha A. Sandweiss, eds. *The Oxford History of the American West* (1994).

Pascoe, Peggy. *Relations of Rescue: The Search for Female Moral Authority in the American West* (1990).

Riley, Glenda. *A Place to Grow: Women in the American West* (1992).

Robbins, William G. *Colony and Empire: The Capitalist Transformation of the American West* (1994).

West, Elliott. *The Way to the West* (1995).

Worster, Donald. *Rivers of Empire: Water, Aridity, and the Growth of the American West* (1985).

Native Americans

Adams, David W. *Education for Extinction: American Indians and the Boarding School Experience* (1995).

Hoxie, Frederick E. *A Final Promise: The Campaign to Assimilate the Indians, 1880–1920* (2001).

Hutton, Paul. *Phil Sheridan and His Army* (1985).

Iverson, Peter. *Diné: A History of the Navajos* (2002).

Josephy, Alvin M., Jr. *The Nez Percé Indians and the Opening of the Northwest* (1965).

Larson, Robert W. *Red Cloud: Warrior-Statesman of the Lakota Sioux* (1997).

McDonnell, Janet. *The Dispossession of the American Indian* (1991).

Ostler, Jeffrey. *The Plains Sioux and U.S. Colonialism from Lewis and Clark to Wounded Knee* (2004).

Price, Catherine. *The Oglala People, 1841–1879* (1996).

Utley, Robert M. *The Lance and the Shield: The Life and Times of Sitting Bull* (1994).

West, Elliott. *The Contested Plains: Indians, Goldseekers, and the Rush to Colorado* (1998).

Wishart, David. *An Unspeakable Sadness: The Dispossession of the Nebraska Indians* (1994).

Wooster, Robert. *The Military and United States Indian Policy, 1865–1903* (1988).

The Mining Bonanza

Aiken, Katherine G. *Idaho's Bunker Hill: The Rise and Fall of a Great Mining Company* (2005).

Emmons, David. *The Butte Irish: Class and Ethnicity in an American Mining Town* (1989).

James, Ronald, and Elizabeth Raymond, eds. *Comstock Women: The Making of a Mining Community* (1998).

Lingenfelter, Richard. *The Hardrock Miners: A History of the Mining Labor Movement in the American West, 1863–1893* (1974).

Marks, Paula M. *Precious Dust: The American Gold Rush Era* (1994).

Paul, Rodman W. *Mining Frontiers of the Far West, 1848–1880* (1963).

Peterson, Richard H. *The Bonanza Kings: The Social Origins and Business Behavior of Western Mining Entrepreneurs* (1977).

Petrik, Paula. *No Step Backward: Women and Family on the Rocky Mountain Mining Frontier, Helena, Montana* (1987).

Rohrbough, Malcolm. *Aspen: The History of a Silver-Mining Town* (2000).

Smith, Duane A. *Mining America: The Industry and the Environment* (1987).

West, Elliott. *The Saloon on the Rocky Mountain Mining Frontier* (1979).

Zhu, Liping. *A Chinaman's Chance: The Chinese on the Rocky Mountain Mining Frontier* (1997).

The Cattle Kingdom

Atherton, Lewis. *The Cattle Kings* (1961).

Carlson, Paul. *The Cowboy Way* (2000).

Dale, Edward. *The Range Cattle Industry* (1969).

Dary, David. *Cowboy Culture* (1981).

Durham, Philip, and Everett L. Jones. *The Negro Cowboys* (1965).

Dykstra, Robert. *The Cattle Towns* (1968).

Gressley, Gene M. *Bankers and Cattlemen* (1966).

Haywood, C. Robert. *Victorian West: Class and Culture in Kansas Cattle Towns* (1991).

Igler, David. *Industrial Cowboys: Miller & Lux and the Transformation of the Far West* (2001).

Miner, H. Craig. *Wichita: The Early Years, 1865–1880* (1982).

Skaggs, Jimmy M. *The Cattle Trailing Industry* (1973).

Walker, Don D. *Clio's Cowboys* (1981).

The Expansion of Agriculture

Bogue, Allan G. *Money at Interest: The Farm Mortgage on the Middle Border* (1955).

Fite, Gilbert. *The Farmers' Frontier, 1865–1900* (1966).

Garceau, Dee. *The Important Things of Life: Women, Work, and Family in Sweetwater County, Wyoming* (1997).

Handy-Marchello, Barbara. *Women of the Northern Plains: Gender and Settlement on the Homestead Frontier* (2005).

Isern, Thomas. *Bull Threshers and Bindlestiffs: Harvesting and Threshing on the North American Plains* (1990).

Miner, H. Craig. *West of Wichita: Settling the High Plains of Kansas, 1865–1890* (1986).

Nelsen, Jane Taylor, ed. *Prairie Populist: The Memoirs of Luna Kellie* (1992).

Painter, Nell. *Exodusters: Black Migration to Kansas after Reconstruction* (1976).

Pisani, Donald J. *Water, Land, and Law in the West* (1996).

Shannon, Fred A. *The Farmer's Last Frontier: Agriculture, 1860–1897* (1945).

Ethnic and Cultural Frontiers

Camarillo, Albert. *Chicanos in a Changing Society* (1979).

Chan, Sucheng. *This Bittersweet Soil: The Chinese in California Agriculture* (1986).

Deutsch, Sarah. *No Separate Refuge: Culture, Class, and Gender on an Anglo-Hispanic Frontier in the American Southwest* (1987).

Garcia, Mario T. *Desert Immigrants: The Mexicans of El Paso, 1880–1920* (1981).

Gjerde, Jon. *From Peasants to Farmers: The Migration from Balestrand, Norway, to the Upper Midwest* (1985).

McQuillan, D. Aidan. *Prevailing over Time: Ethnic Adjustment on the Kansas Prairies, 1875–1925* (1990).

Takaki, Ronald. *Strangers from a Different Shore: A History of Asian Americans* (1989).

Chapter 20
The Structure and Style of Politics

Argersinger, Peter H. *Structure, Process, and Party* (1992).

Baker, Paula. *The Moral Frameworks of Public Life: Gender, Politics, and the State in Rural New York* (1991).

Bordin, Ruth. *Frances Willard: A Biography* (1986).

Edwards, Rebecca. *Angels in the Machinery: Gender in American Party Politics* (1997).

Gallman, J. Matthew. *America's Joan of Arc: The Life of Anna Elizabeth Dickinson* (2006).

Goldberg, Michael. *An Army of Women: Gender and Politics in Gilded Age Kansas* (1997).

Gustafson, Melanie Susan. *Women and the Republican Party* (2001).

Keyssar, Alexander. *The Right to Vote: The Contested History of Democracy in the United States* (2000).

Kleppner, Paul. *The Third Electoral System, 1853–1892* (1979).

McCormick, Richard L. *The Party Period and Public Policy* (1986).

McGerr, Michael. *The Decline of Popular Politics: The American North, 1865–1928* (1988).

Mead, Rebecca J. *How the Vote Was Won: Woman Suffrage in the Western United States* (2004).

Schneirov, Richard. *Labor and Urban Politics* (1998).

Shafer, Byron, and Anthony Badger. *Contesting Democracy* (2001).

Silbey, Joel. *The American Political Nation, 1838–1893* (1991).

The Limits of Government

Aron, Cindy. *Ladies and Gentlemen of the Civil Service: Middle-Class Workers in Victorian America* (1987).

Brock, William R. *Investigation and Responsibility: Public Responsibility in the United States, 1865–1900* (1984).

Calhoun, Charles W. *The Republican Party and the Southern Question, 1869–1900* (2006).

Campbell, Ballard C. *Representative Democracy: Public Policy and Midwestern Legislatures in the Late Nineteenth Century* (1980).

Hoogenboom, Ari. *Rutherford B. Hayes: Warrior and President* (1996).

Sklar, Kathryn Kish. *Florence Kelley and the Nation's Work: The Rise of Women's Political Culture* (1995).

Skowronek, Stephen. *Building a New American State: The Expansion of National Administrative Capacities* (1982).

Thompson, Margaret S. *The "Spider Web": Congress and Lobbying* (1985).

White, Leonard D. *The Republican Era* (1958).

Public Policies and National Elections

Hoogenboom, Ari. *Outlawing the Spoils: A History of the Civil Service Movement, 1865–1883* (rev. ed., 1982).

Marcus, Robert D. *Grand Old Party: Political Structure in the Gilded Age, 1880–1896* (1971).

Morgan, H. Wayne. *From Hayes to McKinley* (1969).

Reitano, Joanne. *The Tariff Question in the Gilded Age: The Great Debate of 1888* (1995).

Ritter, Gretchen. *Goldbugs and Greenbacks: The Antimonopoly Tradition and the Politics of Finance* (1997).

Socolofsky, Homer E., and Allan B. Spetter. *The Presidency of Benjamin Harrison* (1987).

Sproat, John. *The Best Men: Liberal Reformers in the Gilded Age* (1968).

Summers, Mark. *Rum, Romanism, and Rebellion: The Making of a President, 1884* (2000).

The Crisis of the 1890s

Argersinger, Peter H. *The Limits of Agrarian Radicalism* (1995).

Cantrell, Gregg. *Feeding the Wolf: John B. Rayner and the Politics of Race* (2001).

Glad, Paul. *McKinley, Bryan, and the People* (1964).

Goodwyn, Lawrence. *The Populist Moment* (1978).

Kazin, Michael. *A Godly Hero: The Life of William Jennings Bryan* (2006).

Kousser, J. Morgan. *The Shaping of Southern Politics* (1974).

Larson, Robert W. *Populism in the Mountain West* (1986).

McSeveney, Samuel. *The Politics of Depression* (1972).

Miller, Worth Robert. *Oklahoma Populism* (1987).

Ostler, Jeffrey. *Prairie Populism* (1993).

Postel, Charles. *The Populist Vision* (2007).

Ross, William G. *A Muted Fury: Populists, Progressives, and Labor Unions Confront the Courts* (1994).

Schneirov, Richard, Shelton Stromquist, and Nick Salvatore. *The Pullman Strike and the Crisis of the 1890s* (1999).

Schwantes, Carlos A. *Coxey's Army: An American Odyssey* (1985).

Shaw, Barton. *The Wool-Hat Boys: Georgia's Populist Party* (1984).

Welch, Richard. *The Presidencies of Grover Cleveland* (1988).

Chapter 21
The Ferment of Reform

Blair, Karen. *The Clubwoman as Feminist: True Womanhood Redefined, 1868–1914* (1980).

Brown, Victoria Bissell. *The Education of Jane Addams* (2003).

Chesler, Ellen. *Woman of Valor: The Life of Margaret Sanger* (1992).

Cohen, Nancy. *The Reconstruction of American Liberalism, 1865–1914* (2002).

Coleman, Peter. *Progressivism and the World of Reform* (1987).

Cott, Nancy. *The Grounding of Modern Feminism* (1987).

Curtis, Susan. *A Consuming Faith: The Social Gospel and Modern American Culture* (1991).

Danbom, David B. *"The World of Hope": Progressives and the Struggle for an Ethical Public Life* (1987).

Dubofsky, Melvyn. *We Shall Be All: A History of the Industrial Workers of the World* (1969).

Flanagan, Maureen. *Seeing with Their Hearts: Chicago Women and the Vision of the Good City* (2002).

Marsden, George. *Fundamentalism and American Culture* (1980).

McArthur, Judith N. *Creating the New Woman: The Rise of Southern Women's Progressive Culture in Texas* (1998).

McGerr, Michael. *A Fierce Discontent: The Rise and Fall of the Progressive Movement in America* (2003).

Peiss, Kathy. *Cheap Amusements: Working Women and Leisure in Turn-of-the-Century New York* (1986).

Rodgers, Daniel. *Atlantic Crossings: Social Politics in a Progressive Age* (1998).

Salvatore, Nick. *Eugene V. Debs: Citizen and Socialist* (1982).

Shore, Elliott. *Talkin' Socialism: J. A. Wayland and the Role of the Press in American Radicalism* (1988).

Sklar, Kathryn Kish. *Florence Kelley and the Nation's Work* (1995).

Wheeler, Margaret Spruill. *New Women of the New South* (1993).

Reforming Society

Barron, Hal S. *Mixed Harvest: The Second Great Transformation in the Rural North* (1997).

Boyer, Paul. *Urban Masses and Moral Order in America* (1978).

Carson, Mina. *Settlement Folk: Social Thought and the American Settlement Movement* (1990).

Crocker, Ruth H. *Social Work and Social Order* (1992).

Danbom, David. *The Resisted Revolution: Urban America and the Industrialization of Agriculture* (1979).

Davis, Allen F. *American Heroine: The Life and Legend of Jane Addams* (1973).

Davis, Allen F. *Spearheads of Reform: The Social Settlements and the Progressive Movement* (1968).

Derickson, Alan. *Workers' Health, Workers' Democracy* (1988).

Deverell, William, and Tom Sitton. *California Progressivism Revisited* (1994).

Dorsett, Lyle. *Billy Sunday and the Redemption of Urban America* (1991).

Dye, Nancy S. *As Equals and as Sisters: Feminism, the Labor Movement, and the Women's Trade Union League of New York* (1980).

Frankel, Noralee, and Nancy S. Dye. *Gender, Class, Race, and Reform in the Progressive Era* (1991).

Gorn, Elliott. *Mother Jones: The Most Dangerous Woman in America* (2001).

Hamm, Richard. *Shaping the Eighteenth Amendment* (1995).

Ladd-Taylor, Molly. *Mother-Work: Women, Child Welfare, and the State, 1890–1930* (1994).

Lindenmeyer, Kriste. *A Right to Childhood: The U.S. Children's Bureau and Child Welfare* (1997).

Link, William A. *The Paradox of Southern Progressivism* (1992).

Lubove, Roy. *The Progressives and the Slums* (1962).

Muncy, Robyn. *Creating a Female Dominion in American Reform, 1890–1935* (1991).

Nelson, Daniel. *Frederick W. Taylor and the Rise of Scientific Management* (1980).

Payne, Elizabeth Anne. *Reform, Labor, and Feminism: Margaret Dreier Robins and the Women's Trade Union League* (1988).

Southern, David. *The Progressive Era and Race: Reaction and Reform* (2005).

Tate, Cassandra. *Cigarette Wars: The Triumph of "The Little White Slaver"* (1999).

Timberlake, James. *Prohibition and the Progressive Movement* (1963).

Willrich, Michael. *City of Courts: Socializing Justice in Progressive Era Chicago* (2003).

Reforming Politics and Government

Allswang, John M. *The Initiative and Referendum in California* (2000).

Buenker, John D. *Urban Liberalism and Progressive Reform* (1973).

DuBois, Ellen Carol. *Harriot Stanton Blatch and the Winning of Woman Suffrage* (1997).

Goebel, Thomas. *A Government by the People: Direct Democracy in America* (2002).

Graham, Sara Hunter. *Woman Suffrage and the New Democracy* (1996).

Grantham, Dewey. *Southern Progressivism* (1983).

Gustafson, Melanie S. *Women and the Republican Party* (2001).

Johnston, Robert D. *The Radical Middle Class: Populist Democracy and the Question of Capitalism in Progressive Era Portland, Oregon* (2003).

Kousser, J. Morgan. *The Shaping of Southern Politics* (1974).

McCormick, Richard L. *From Realignment to Reform: Political Change in New York State, 1893–1910* (1983).

McGerr, Michael E. *The Decline of Popular Politics* (1986).

Mead, Rebecca J. *How the Vote Was Won: Woman Suffrage in the Western United States* (2004).

Pegram, Thomas. *Partisans and Progressives* (1992).

Reynolds, John F. *Testing Democracy: Electoral Behavior and Progressive Reform in New Jersey* (1988).

Schiesl, Martin. *The Politics of Efficiency: Municipal Administration and Reform in America* (1977).

Thelen, David P. *The New Citizenship: Origins of Progressivism in Wisconsin* (1972).

Unger, Nancy. *Fighting Bob La Follette: The Righteous Reformer* (2000).

Wright, James E. *The Progressive Yankees: Republican Reformers in New Hampshire* (1987).

Theodore Roosevelt and the Progressive Presidency

Blum, John M. *The Republican Roosevelt* (1954).

Brands, H. W. *T.R.: The Last Romantic* (1997).

Burton, David. *The Learned Presidency: Theodore Roosevelt, William Howard Taft, Woodrow Wilson* (1988).

Dalton, Kathleen. *Theodore Roosevelt: A Strenuous Life* (2002).

Hays, Samuel P. *Conservation and the Gospel of Efficiency: The Progressive Conservation Movement* (1962).

Keller, Morton. *Regulating a New Economy* (1990).

Kolko, Gabriel. *The Triumph of Conservatism* (1963).

Morris, Edmund. *Theodore Rex* (2002).

Rauchway, Eric. *Murdering McKinley: The Making of Theodore Roosevelt's America* (2003).

Righter, Robert. *The Battle over Hetch Hetchy* (2005).

Sanders, Elizabeth. *Roots of Reform: Farmers, Workers, and the American State* (1999).

Sklar, Martin. *The Corporate Reconstruction of American Capitalism* (1988).

Woodrow Wilson and Progressive Reform

Blum, John M. *Woodrow Wilson and the Politics of Morality* (1956).

Clements, Kendrick A. *The Presidency of Woodrow Wilson* (1992).

Cooper, John Milton, Jr. *The Warrior and the Priest: Woodrow Wilson and Theodore Roosevelt* (1983).

Gould, Lewis L. *Reform and Regulation: American Politics from Roosevelt to Wilson* (1996).

Hecksher, August. *Woodrow Wilson* (1991).

Link, Arthur. *Woodrow Wilson and the Progressive Era* (1954).

Livingston, James. *Origins of the Federal Reserve System* (1986).

Sarasohn, David. *The Party of Reform: Democrats in the Progressive Era* (1989).

Thompson, John A. *Woodrow Wilson* (2002).

Urofsky, Melvin. *Louis D. Brandeis and the Progressive Tradition* (1981).

Chapter 22
The Roots of Imperialism

Anderson, David L. *Imperialism and Idealism: American Diplomats in China, 1861–1898* (1985).

Anderson, Stuart. *Race and Rapprochement: Anglo-Saxonism and Anglo-American Relations, 1895–1904* (1981).

Crapol, Edward P. *James G. Blaine: Architect of Empire* (2000).

Hearden, Patrick J. *Independence and Empire: The New South's Cotton Mill Campaign, 1865–1901* (1982).

Hill, Patricia R. *The World Their Household: The American Woman's Foreign Mission Movement and Cultural Transformation, 1870–1920* (1985).

Hunt, Michael H. *Ideology and U.S. Foreign Policy* (1987).

Hunter, Jane. *The Gospel of Gentility: American Women Missionaries in Turn-of-the-Century China* (1984).

Jacobson, Matthew Frye. *Barbarian Virtues: The United States Encounters Foreign Peoples at Home and Abroad* (2000).

Paolino, Ernest. *The Foundations of the American Empire: William Henry Seward and U.S. Foreign Policy* (1973).

Plesur, Milton. *America's Outward Thrust: Approaches to Foreign Affairs, 1865–1890* (1971).

Rosenberg, Emily S. *Spreading the American Dream: American Economic and Cultural Expansion, 1890–1945* (1982).

Shulman, Mark R. *Navalism and the Emergence of American Seapower, 1882–1893* (1995).

Widenor, William. *Henry Cabot Lodge and the Search for an American Foreign Policy* (1980).

Williams, William A. *The Roots of the Modern American Empire* (1969).

The Spanish-American War

Challener, Richard. *Admirals, Generals, and American Foreign Policy, 1889–1914* (1973).

Cosmas, Graham A. *An Army for Empire: The United States Army and the Spanish-American War* (1971).

Dobson, John. *Reticent Expansionism: The Foreign Policy of William McKinley* (1988).

Gatewood, Willard B. Jr. *Black Americans and the White Man's Burden, 1898–1903* (1975).

Gould, Lewis L. *The Spanish-American War and President McKinley* (1982).

Healy, David F. *U.S. Expansionism: The Imperialist Urge in the 1890s* (1970).

Linderman, Gerald. *The Mirror of War: American Society and the Spanish-American War* (1974).

McCartney, Paul T. *Power and Progress: American National Identity, the War of 1898, and the Rise of American Imperialism* (2006).

Milton, Joyce. *The Yellow Journalists* (1989).

Morgan, H. Wayne. *America's Road to Empire: The War with Spain and Overseas Expansion* (1965).

Offner, John. *An Unwanted War: The Diplomacy of the United States and Spain Over Cuba* (1992).

Schoonover, Thomas. *Uncle Sam's War of 1898 and the Origins of Globalization* (2003).

Trask, David R. *The War with Spain in 1898* (1981).

Anti-Imperialism

Beisner, Robert L. *Twelve against Empire: The Anti-Imperialists, 1898–1900* (1968).

Osborne, Thomas J. *"Empire Can Wait": American Opposition to Hawaiian Annexation, 1893–1898* (1981).

Schirmer, Daniel B. *Republic or Empire: American Resistance to the Philippine War* (1972).

Tompkins, E. Berkeley. *Anti-Imperialism in the United States: The Great Debate, 1890–1920* (1970).

Imperial Ambitions: The United States and East Asia, 1899–1917

Cohen, Warren I. *America's Response to China* (1989).

Gates, John M. *Schoolbooks and Krags: The United States Army in the Philippines* (1973).

Hunt, Michael H. *The Making of a Special Relationship: The U.S. and China to 1914* (1983).

Iriye, Akira. *Pacific Estrangement: Japanese and American Expansion, 1897–1911* (1972).

Kramer, Paul A. *The Blood of Government: Race, Empire, the United States, and the Philippines* (2006).

Linn, Brian. *The Philippine War, 1899–1902* (2000).

McCormick, Thomas. *China Market: America's Quest for Informal Empire* (1967).

Miller, Stuart. *"Benevolent Assimilation": The American Conquest of the Philippines, 1899–1903* (1982).

Pletcher, David M. *The Diplomacy of Involvement: American Economic Expansion across the Pacific, 1784–1900* (2001).

Welch, Richard E. *Response to Imperialism: The United States and the Philippine-American War* (1979).

Imperial Power: The United States and Latin America, 1899–1917

Beale, Howard K. *Theodore Roosevelt and the Rise of America to World Power* (1956).

Benjamin, Jules. *Hegemony and Development: The United States and Cuba, 1890–1934* (1977).

Calder, Bruce. *The Impact of Intervention: The Dominican Republic during the U.S. Occupation of 1916 to 1924* (1984).

Carr, Raymond. *Puerto Rico: A Colonial Experiment* (1984).

Carrion, Arturo Morales. *Puerto Rico* (1983).

Cooper, John M., Jr. *The Warrior and the Priest: Woodrow Wilson and Theodore Roosevelt* (1983).

Eisenhower, John. *The United States and the Mexican Revolution, 1913–1917* (1993).

Healy, David F. *Drive to Hegemony: The United States in the Caribbean, 1898–1917* (1988).

Hitchman, James. *Leonard Wood and Cuban Independence, 1898–1902* (1971).

LaFeber, Walter. *Inevitable Revolutions: The United States in Central America* (1993).

LaFeber, Walter. *The Panama Canal* (1990).

Langley, Lester. *The Banana Wars: An Inner History of the American Empire, 1900–1934* (1983).

McCullough, David. *The Path between the Seas: The Creation of the Panama Canal* (1977).

Millett, Allan R. *The Politics of Intervention: The Military Occupation of Cuba, 1906–1909* (1968).

Perez, Louis A., Jr. *Cuba under the Platt Amendment, 1902–1934* (1986).

Chapter 23
General Studies

Chambers, John Whiteclay II. *The Tyranny of Change* (1992).

Clayton, James D., and Anne Sharp Wells. *America and the Great War, 1914–1920* (1998).

Cooper, John M., Jr. *Pivotal Decades: The United States, 1900–1920* (1990).

Gilbert, Martin. *The First World War: A Complete History* (1994).

Hawley, Ellis W. *The Great War and the Search for a Modern Order* (1992).

Lyons, Michael J. *World War I: A Short History* (1994).

Wynn, Neil. *From Progressivism to Prosperity: World War I and American Society* (1986).

Diplomacy of Neutrality, War, and Peace

Ambrosius, Lloyd. *Woodrow Wilson and the American Diplomatic Tradition* (1987).

Bailey, Thomas A., and Paul B. Ryan. *The Lusitania Disaster* (1975).

Burk, Kathleen. *Britain, America, and the Sinews of War* (1985).

Coogan, John. *The End of Neutrality* (1981).

Cooper, John M., Jr. *Breaking the Heart of the World: Woodrow Wilson and the Fight for the League of Nations* (2001).

Foglesong, David S. *America's Secret War against Bolshevism: United States Intervention in the Russian Civil War, 1917–1920* (1995).

Gardner, Lloyd. *Safe for Democracy: The Anglo-American Response to Revolution, 1913–1923* (1984).

Gregory, Ross. *The Origins of American Intervention in the First World War* (1971).

Kaufman, Burton I. *Efficiency and Expansion: Foreign Trade Organization in the Wilson Administration* (1974).

Knock, Thomas J. *To End All Wars: Woodrow Wilson and the Creation of the League of Nations* (1992).

Levin, N. Gordon, Jr. *Woodrow Wilson and World Politics: America's Response to War and Revolution* (1968).

Levine, Lawrence W. *Defender of the Faith: William Jennings Bryan, the Last Decade* (1965).

May, Ernest R. *The World War and American Isolation, 1914–1917* (1966).

McFadden, David W. *Alternative Paths: Soviets and Americans, 1917–1920* (1993).

Stone, Ralph A. *The Irreconcilables* (1970).

Thompson, John A. *Woodrow Wilson* (2002).

Walworth, Arthur. *Wilson and the Peacemakers* (1986).

The Military

Barbeau, A. E., and Florette Henri. *The Unknown Soldiers: Black American Troops in World War I* (1974).

Bristow, Nancy. *Making Men Moral: Social Engineering during the Great War* (1996).

Chambers, John Whiteclay II. *To Raise an Army* (1987).

Coffman, Edward M. *The Hilt of the Sword: The Career of Peyton C. March* (1966).

Mead, Gary. *Doughboys: America and the First World War* (2000).

Patton, Gerald W. *War and Race: The Black Officer in the American Military* (1981).

Stallings, Laurence. *The Doughboys: The Story of the AEF, 1917–1918* (1963).

Trask, David. *The AEF and Coalition Warmaking, 1917–1918* (1993).

Vandiver, Frank E. *Black Jack: The Life and Times of John J. Pershing* (1977).

Zeiger, Susan. *In Uncle Sam's Service: Women Workers with the American Expeditionary Force, 1917–1919* (1999).

Wartime Economy and Society

Breen, William J. *Uncle Sam at Home: Civilian Mobilization, Wartime Federalism, and the Council of National Defense, 1917–1919* (1984).

Britten, Thomas. *American Indians in World War I: At Home and at War* (1997).

Brown, Carrie. *Rosie's Mom: Forgotten Women Workers of the First World War* (2002).

Connor, Valerie. *The National War Labor Board* (1983).

Cuff, Robert D. *The War Industries Board: Business-Government Relations during World War I* (1973).

Danbom, David. *The Resisted Revolution: Urban America and the Industrialization of Agriculture* (1979).

DeBauche, Leslie M. *Reel Patriotism: The Movies and World War I* (1997).

Greenwald, Maurine Weiner. *Women, War, and Work: The Impact of World War I on Women Workers in the United States* (1980).

Haydu, Jeffrey. *Making American Industries Safe for Democracy* (1997).

Henri, Florette. *Black Migration: The Movement North, 1900–1920* (1975).

Koistinen, Paul. *Mobilizing for Modern War: The Political Economy of American Warfare, 1865–1919* (1997).

Luebke, Frederick C. *Bonds of Loyalty: German-Americans and World War I* (1974).

McCartin, Joseph A. *Labor's Great War: The Struggle for Industrial Democracy and the Origins of Modern American Labor Relations, 1912–1921* (1997).

Rudwick, Elliot M. *Race Riot at East St. Louis, July 2, 1917* (1964).

Thompson, John A. *Reformers and War: American Progressive Publicists and the First World War* (1987).

Vaughn, Stephen L. *Holding Fast the Inner Lines: Democracy, Nationalism, and the Committee on Public Information* (1980).

Wartime Dissent and Repression

Early, Frances R. *A World without War: How U.S. Feminists and Pacifists Resisted World War I* (1997).

Gibbs, Christopher. *The Great Silent Majority: Missouri's Resistance to World War I* (1989).

Kennedy, Kathleen. *Disloyal Mothers and Scurrilous Citizens: Women and Subversion during World War I* (1999).

Morlan, Robert. *Political Prairie Fire: The Nonpartisan League, 1915–1922* (1955).

Peterson, H. C., and Gilbert Fite. *Opponents of War, 1917–1918* (1957).

Preston, William, Jr. *Aliens and Dissenters: Federal Suppression of Radicals, 1903–1933* (1963).

Weinstein, James. *The Decline of Socialism in America* (1967).

Postwar Conflict

Brody, David. *Labor in Crisis: The Steel Strike of 1919* (1965).

Coben, Stanley A. *A. Mitchell Palmer, Politician* (1963).

Ellsworth, Scott. *Death in a Promised Land: The Tulsa Race Riot of 1921* (1992).

Frank, Dana. *Purchasing Power: Consumer Organizing, Gender, and the Seattle Labor Movement. 1919–1929* (1994).

Noggle, Burl. *Into the Twenties: The United States from Armistice to Normalcy* (1974).

Theoharis, Athan, and John Stuart Cox. *The Boss: J. Edgar Hoover and the Great American Inquisition* (1988).

Tuttle, William M., Jr. *Race Riot: Chicago in the Red Summer of 1919* (1970).

Chapter 24
General Studies

Hicks, John D. *Republican Ascendancy, 1921–1933* (1960).

Leuchtenberg, William. *The Perils of Prosperity* (1958).

Parrish, Michael E. *Anxious Decades: America in Prosperity and Depression, 1920–1941* (1992).

Perrett, Geoffrey. *America in the Twenties* (1982).

Economic Developments

Argersinger, Jo Ann E. *Making the Amalgamated: Gender, Ethnicity, and Class in the Baltimore Clothing Industry* (1999).

Bernstein, Irving L. *The Lean Years: A History of the American Worker, 1920–1933* (1960).

Flink, James J. *The Automobile Age* (1988).

Kessler-Harris, Alice. *Out to Work: A History of Wage-Earning Women* (1982).

Marchand, Roland. *Creating the Corporate Soul: The Rise of Public Relations and Corporate Imagery in American Big Business* (1998).

Meyer, Stephen III. *The Five Dollar Day: Labor Management and Social Control in the Ford Motor Company* (1981).

Smulyan, Susan. *Selling Radio: The Commercialization of American Broadcasting, 1920–1934* (1994).

Strasser, Susan. *Satisfaction Guaranteed: The Making of the American Mass Market* (1989).

Zahavi, Gerald. *Workers, Managers, and Welfare Capitalism* (1988).

Politics and Government

Burner, David. *Herbert Hoover: A Public Life* (1979).

Clements, Kendrick A. *Hoover, Conservation, and Consumerism: Engineering the Good Life* (2000).

Craig, Douglas B. *After Wilson: The Struggle for the Democratic Party* (1992).

Hawley, Ellis W., ed. *Herbert Hoover as Secretary of Commerce* (1981).

LaFeber, Walter. *Inevitable Revolutions: The United States in Central America* (1984).

Lichtman, Allan J. *Prejudice and the Old Politics: The Presidential Election of 1928* (1979).

Lowitt, Richard. *George W. Norris: The Persistence of a Progressive* (1971).

McCoy, Donald R. *Calvin Coolidge* (1967).

Murray, Robert. *The Politics of Normalcy* (1973).

Perry, Elisabeth Israels. *Belle Moskowitz: Feminine Politics & The Exercise of Power in the Age of Alfred E. Smith* (1987).

Schulzinger, Robert D. *The Making of the Diplomatic Mind* (1975).

Trani, Eugene P., and David L. Wilson. *The Presidency of Warren G. Harding* (1977).

Wilson, Joan Hoff. *American Business and Foreign Policy, 1920–1933* (1968).

Wilson, Joan Hoff. *Herbert Hoover: Forgotten Progressive* (1975).

Cities and Suburbs

Deutsch, Sarah. *No Separate Refuge: Culture, Class, and Gender on an Anglo-Hispanic Frontier in the American Southwest* (1987).

Garcia, Juan. *Mexicans in the Midwest, 1900–1932* (1996).

Goldfield, David. *Cotton Fields and Skyscrapers* (1982).

Gottlieb, Peter. *Making Their Own Way: Southern Blacks' Migration to Pittsburgh, 1916–30* (1987).

Hogan, David Gerard. *Selling 'em by the Sack: White Castle and the Creation of American Food* (1997).

Jackson, Kenneth T. *Crabgrass Frontier: The Suburbanization of the United States* (1985).

Lewis, Earl. *In Their Own Interests: Race, Class, and Power in Twentieth-Century Norfolk, Virginia* (1991).

Osofsky, Gilbert. *Harlem: The Making of a Ghetto* (1968).

Romo, Ricardo. *East Los Angeles: History of a Barrio* (1983).

Teaford, John C. *Cities of the Heartland* (1993).

Worley, William. *J. C. Nichols and the Shaping of Kansas City* (1990).

Society and Culture

Alexander, Charles C. *The Ku Klux Klan in the Southwest* (1965).

Blee, Kathleen M. *Women and the Klan: Racism and Gender in the 1920s* (1991).

Clark, Norman. *Deliver Us from Evil: An Interpretation of American Prohibition* (1976).

Coben, Stanley. *Rebellion against Victorianism* (1991).

Cott, Nancy F. *The Grounding of American Feminism* (1987).

Ewen, Stuart. *Captains of Consciousness: Advertising and the Social Roots of the Consumer Culture* (1976).

Fass, Paula. *The Damned and the Beautiful: American Youth in the 1920s* (1977).

Flanagan, Maureen A. *Seeing With Their Hearts: Chicago Women and the Vision of the Good City, 1871–1933* (2002).

Hobson, Fred. *Mencken: A Life* (1994).

Huggins, Nathan. *Harlem Renaissance* (1971).

Jackson, Kenneth T. *The Ku Klux Klan in the City* (1967).

Jacobson, Matthew Frye. *Whiteness of a Different Color: European Immigrants and the Alchemy of Race* (1998).

Laird, Pamela Walker. *Advertising Progress: American Business and the Rise of Consumer Marketing* (1998).

Latham, Angela J. *Posing a Threat: Flappers, Chorus Girls, and Other Brazen Performers of the American 1920s* (2000).

Lawrence, Bruce B. *Defenders of God: The Fundamentalist Revolt against the Modern Age* (1989).

Levine, Lawrence W. *Defender of the Faith: William Jennings Bryan, the Last Decade, 1915–1925* (1965).

Lewis, David L. *When Harlem Was in Vogue* (1981).

Maclean, Nancy. *Behind the Mask of Chivalry: The Making of the Second Ku Klux Klan* (1994).

May, Lary. *Screening Out the Past: The Birth of Mass Culture and the Motion Picture Industry* (1980).

Moore, Leonard. *Citizen Klansmen: The Ku Klux Klan in Indiana* (1991).

Muncy, Robyn. *Creating a Female Dominion in American Reform* (1991).

Ogren, Kathy H. *The Jazz Revolution: Twenties America and the Meaning of Jazz* (1989).

Payne, Elizabeth A. *Reform, Labor, and Feminism: Margaret Dreier Robins and the Women's Trade Union League* (1988).

Pegram, Thomas R. *Battling Demon Rum: The Struggle for a Dry America, 1800–1933* (1998).

Rader, Benjamin G. *American Sports: From the Age of Folk Games to the Age of Spectators* (1983).

Sklar, Robert. *Movie-Made America: A Cultural History of American Movies* (1994).

Stein, Judith. *The World of Marcus Garvey* (1986).

Wiggins, David. *Sport in America* (1995).

Chapter 25
Hard Times in Hooverville

Bernstein, Michael. *The Great Depression* (1987).

Blackwelder, Julia Kirk. *Women of the Depression: Caste and Culture in San Antonio* (1984).

Chafe, William H. *The American Woman, 1920–1970* (1972).

Galbraith, John Kenneth. *The Great Crash: 1929* (1989).

Garraty, John. *The Great Depression* (1986).

Kelley, Robin D. G. *Hammer and Hoe: Alabama Communists during the Great Depression* (1990).

Klein, Maury. *Rainbow's End: The Crash of 1929* (2001).

McElvaine, Robert. *The Great Depression: America, 1929–1941* (1984).

Mullins, William. *The Depression and the Urban West Coast, 1929–1933* (1991).

Reisler, Mark. *By the Sweat of Their Brow: Mexican Immigrant Labor in the United States* (1976).

Scharf, Lois. *To Work and to Wed: Female Employment, Feminism, and the Great Depression* (1980).

Shover, John. *Cornbelt Rebellion: The Farmers' Holiday Association* (1965).

Herbert Hoover and the Depression

Burner, David. *Herbert Hoover: A Public Life* (1979).

Daniels, Roger. *The Bonus March* (1971).

Fausold, Martin L. *The Presidency of Herbert C. Hoover* (1985).

Hamilton, David E. *From New Day to New Deal: American Farm Policy from Hoover to Roosevelt* (1991).

Lisio, Donald. *The President and Protest* (1974).

Romasco, Albert. *The Poverty of Abundance: Hoover, the Nation, the Depression* (1965).

Schwartz, Jordan A. *Interregnum of Despair* (1970).

Watkins, T. H. *The Hungry Years: A Narrative History of the Great Depression in America* (1999).

Wilson, Joan Hoff. *Herbert Hoover: Forgotten Progressive* (1975).

Launching the New Deal

Badger, Anthony J. *The New Deal: The Depression Years, 1933–1940* (1989).

Bernstein, Irving. *Turbulent Years: A History of the American Worker, 1933–1941* (1970).

Blackorby, Edward C. *Prairie Rebel: William Lemke* (1963).

Brinkley, Alan. *Voices of Protest: Huey Long, Father Coughlin, and the Great Depression* (1982).

Conrad, David. *The Forgotten Farmers: The Story of the Sharecroppers in the New Deal* (1965).

Freidel, Frank. *Franklin D. Roosevelt: A Rendezvous with Destiny* (1990).

Grubbs, Donald H. *Cry from the Cotton: The Southern Tenant Farmers Union and the New Deal* (1971).

Hawley, Ellis. *The New Deal and the Problem of Monopoly* (1966).

Leuchtenburg, William. *The FDR Years* (1995).

Ribuffo, Leo P. *The Old Christian Right: The Protestant Far Right from the Great Depression to the Cold War* (1983).

Romasco, Albert. *The Politics of Recovery: Roosevelt's New Deal* (1983).

Saloutos, Theodore. *The American Farmer and the New Deal* (1982).

Williams, T. Harry. *Huey Long* (1969).

Consolidating the New Deal

Allswang, John. *The New Deal and American Politics* (1978).

Andersen, Kristi. *The Creation of a Democratic Majority* (1979).

Berkowitz, Edward D. *America's Welfare State* (1991).

Biles, Roger. *A New Deal for the American People* (1991).

Gamm, Gerald. *The Making of New Deal Democrats* (1989).

Gordon, Colin. *New Deals: Business, Labor, and Politics in America* (1994).

McCoy, Donald R. *Landon of Kansas* (1966).

McJimsey, George. *Harry Hopkins* (1987).

The New Deal and American Life

Argersinger, Jo Ann E. *Toward a New Deal in Baltimore: People and Government in the Great Depression* (1988).

Barnard, John. *Walter Reuther and the Rise of the Auto Workers* (1983).

Biles, Roger. *The South and the New Deal* (1994).

Cohen, Lisabeth. *Making a New Deal: Industrial Workers in Chicago* (1990).

Faue, Elizabeth. *Community of Suffering and Struggle: Women, Men, and the Labor Movement in Minneapolis* (1991).

Fine, Sidney. *Sitdown: The General Motors Strike of 1936–1937* (1969).

Fraser, Steven. *Labor Will Rule: Sidney Hillman and the Rise of American Labor* (1991).

Gregory, James. *American Exodus: The Dust Bowl Migration and Okie Culture in California* (1989).

Gutierrez, David G. *Walls and Mirrors: Mexican Americans, Mexican Immigrants, and the Politics of Ethnicity* (1995).

Kelly, Laurence C. *The Assault on Assimilation: John Collier and the Origins of Indian Policy Reform* (1983).

Lichtenstein, Nelson. *The Most Dangerous Man in Detroit: Walter Reuther and the Fate of American Labor* (1995).

Lowitt, Richard. *The New Deal and the West* (1984).

Mink, Gwendolyn. *The Wages of Motherhood: Inequality in the Welfare State, 1917–1942* (1995).

Sitkoff, Harvard. *A New Deal for Blacks* (1978).

Smith, Douglas L. *The New Deal in the Urban South* (1988).

Stock, Catherine. *Main Street in Crisis: The Great Depression and the Old Middle Class on the Northern Plains* (1992).

Taylor, Graham. *The New Deal and American Indian Tribalism* (1980).

Ware, Susan. *Beyond Suffrage: Women in the New Deal* (1981).

Ware, Susan. *Holding Their Own: American Women in the 1930s* (1982).

Worster, Donald. *Dust Bowl* (1979).

Worster, Donald. *Rivers of Empire* (1985).

Zieger, Robert. *The CIO, 1935–1955* (1995).

Zieger, Robert. *John L. Lewis* (1988).

Ebbing of the New Deal

Brinkley, Alan. *The End of Reform: New Deal Liberalism in Recession and War* (1995).

Cole, Wayne. *Roosevelt and the Isolationists, 1932–1945* (1983).

Dallek, Robert. *Franklin Delano Roosevelt and American Foreign Policy, 1932–1945* (1979).

Davis, Kenneth S. *FDR: Into the Storm, 1937–1940* (1993).

Heinrichs, Waldo. *Threshold of War: Franklin D. Roosevelt and American Entry into World War II* (1988).

Leff, Mark. *The Limits of Symbolic Reform: The New Deal and Taxation* (1984).

Lipstadt, Deborah E. *Beyond Belief: The American Press and the Coming of the Holocaust, 1933–1945* (1986).

Mettler, Suzanne. *Dividing Citizens: Gender and Federalism in New Deal Public Works* (1998).

Patterson, James T. *Congressional Conservatism and the New Deal* (1967).

Patterson, James T. *The New Deal and the States* (1969).

Storrs, Landon R. Y. *Civilizing Capitalism: The National Consumers' League, Women's Activism, and Labor Standards in the New Deal Era* (2000).

Chapter 26
The Politics of War

Dallek, Robert. *Franklin D. Roosevelt and American Foreign Policy, 1932–1945* (1979).

Doenecke, Justus D. *Storm on the Horizon: The Challenge to American Intervention, 1939–1941* (2000).

Iriye, Akira. *Power and Culture: The Japanese-American War, 1941–1945* (1981).

Kimball, Warren. *The Juggler: Franklin Roosevelt as Wartime Statesman* (1991).

Reynolds, David. *From Munich to Pearl Harbor: Roosevelt, America, and the Origins of the Second World War* (2001).

Schneider, James. *Should America Go to War? The Debate over Foreign Policy in Chicago, 1939–1941* (1989).

Military Operations

Beevor, Anthony. *Stalingrad* (1998).

Chappell, John D. *Before the Bomb: How Americans Approached the Pacific War* (1997).

Keegan, John. *Six Armies in Normandy; From D-Day to the Liberation of Paris* (1982).

Morrison, Samuel Eliot. *The Two-Ocean War: A Short History of the United States Navy in the Second World War* (1963).

Prange, Gordon. *At Dawn We Slept: The Untold Story of Pearl Harbor* (1981).

Spector, Ronald H. *Eagle against the Sun: The American War with Japan* (1985).

Syrett, David. *The Defeat of the German U-Boats: The Battle of the Atlantic* (1994).

Tuchman, Barbara W. *Stillwell and the American Experience in China, 1911–1945* (1970).

Weinberg, Gerhard. *A World at Arms: A Global History of World War II* (1994).

The Experience of War

Ambrose, Stephen. *Citizen Soldiers: The U.S. Army from the Normandy Beaches to the Bulge to the Surrender of Germany, June 7, 1944–May 7, 1945* (1997).

Cameron, Craig M. *American Samurai: Myth, Imagination, and the Conduct of Battle in the First Marine Division, 1941–1951* (1994).

Doubler, Michael. *Closing with the Enemy: How GIs Fought the War in Europe, 1944–1945* (1994).

Fussell, Paul. *Wartime: Understanding and Behavior in the Second World War* (1989).

Leinbaugh, Harold P., and John D. Campbell. *The Men of Company K: The Autobiography of a World War II Rifle Company* (1985).

Manchester, William. *Goodbye Darkness: A Memoir of the Pacific War* (1980).

Moore, Christopher Paul. *Fighting for America: Black Soldiers—the Unsung Heroes of World War II* (2005).

Schrijvers, Peter. *The Crash of Ruin: American Combat Soldiers in Europe during World War II* (1996).

Sledge, E. B. *With the Old Breed at Peleliu and Okinawa* (1981).

Mobilizing the Home Front

Blum, John M. *V Was for Victory: Politics and American Culture during World War II* (1976).

Dew, Stephen. *The Queen City at War: Charlotte, North Carolina during World War II* (2001).

Doherty, Thomas. *Projections of War: Hollywood, American Culture, and World War II* (1994).

Goodwin, Doris Kearns. *No Ordinary Time: Franklin and Eleanor Roosevelt, the Home Front in World War II* (1994).

Johnson, Marilynn. *The Second Gold Rush* (1993).

Koppes, Clayton, and Gregory Black. *Hollywood Goes to War* (1987).

Lichtenstein, Nelson. *Labor's War at Home: The CIO in World War II* (1983).

Nash, Gerald. *The American West Transformed: The Impact of the Second World War* (1985).

Newton, Wesley P. *Montgomery in the Good War: Portrait of a Southern City, 1939–1946* (2000).

O'Neill, William L. *A Democracy at War: America's Fight at Home and Abroad in World War II* (1993).

Polenberg, Richard. *War and Society: The United States, 1941–1945* (1972).

Rhodes, Richard. *The Making of the Atomic Bomb* (1986).

Vatter, Harold. *The U.S. Economy in World War II* (1985).

Women and the War Effort

Anderson, Karen. *Wartime Women: Sex Roles, Family Relations, and the Status of Women during World War II* (1981).

Campbell, D'Ann. *Women at War with America: Private Lives in a Patriotic Era* (1984).

Hartmann, Susan. *The Home Front and Beyond: American Women in the 1940s* (1982).

Kesselman, Amy. *Fleeting Opportunities: Women in Portland and Vancouver Shipyards during World War II and Reconversion* (1990).

Litoff, Judy Barrett. *We're in This War Too: World War II Letters of American Women in Uniform* (1994).

Racial Attitudes and U.S. Policy

Daniels, Roger. *Concentration Camps U.S.A.: Japanese Americans and World War II* (1971).

Dower, John. *War without Mercy: Race and Power in the Pacific War* (1986).

Capeci, Dominic J., Jr. *Race Relations in Wartime Detroit: The Sojourner Truth Controversy of 1942* (1984).

Pagán, Jose Obregón. *Murder at Sleepy Lagoon: Zoot Suits, Race and Riot in Wartime Los Alamos* (2004).

Wyman, David S. *The Abandonment of the Jews: America and the Holocaust, 1941–1945* (1984).

Chapter 27
Foreign and Military Policy

Behrman, Greg. *The Most Noble Adventure: The Marshall Plan and the Time When America Helped Save Europe* (2007).

Beisner, Robert. *Dean Acheson: A Life in the Cold War* (2006).

Gaddis, John L. *The United States and the Cold War* (1992).

Herken, Greg *The Winning Weapon: The Atomic Bomb in the Cold War, 1945–1950* (1980).

Hogan, Michael. *Cross of Iron: Harry S Truman and the Origins of the National Security State, 1945–1954* (1998).

Hogan, Michael. *The Marshall Plan* (1987).

Lawrence, Mark. *Assuming the Burden: Europe and the American Commitment to War in Vietnam* (2005).

Le Feber, Walter. *America, Russia, and the Cold War* (1985).

May, Ernest R. ed. *American Cold War Strategy: Interpreting NSC-68* (1993).

Offner, Arnold. *Another Such Victory: President Truman and the Cold War* (2002).

Paterson, Thomas G. *On Every Front: The Making of the Cold War* (1979).

Rhodes, Richard. *Dark Sun: The Making of the Hydrogen Bomb* (1995).

Schaller, Michael. *The American Occupation of Japan* (1985).

York, Herbert F. *The Advisors: Oppenheimer, Teller and the Super* (1976).

Zubok, Vladislav, and Constantine Pleshkanov. *Inside the Kremlin's Cold War: From Stalin to Khrushchev* (1996).

Korean War

Cumings, Bruce. *The Origins of the Korean War* (1981, 1990).

Foot, Rosemary. *The Wrong War: American Policy and the Dimensions of the Korean Conflict, 1950–1953* (1985).

James, D. Clayton. *Refighting the Last War: Command and Crisis in Korea, 1950–1953* (1992).

Kaufman, Burton I. *The Korean War: Challenges in Crisis, Credibility, and Command* (1986).

Stueck, William. *The Korean War: An International History* (1995).

Society and Politics at Home

Gillon, Steven. *Politics and Vision: The ADA and American Liberalism* (1987).

Goldman, Eric F. *The Crucial Decade and After: America, 1945–1960* (1960).

Hamby, Alonzo. *A Man of the People: A Life of Harry Truman* (1995).

Kelly, Barbara M. *Expanding the American Dream: Building and Rebuilding Levittown* (1993).

Lubell, Samuel. *The Future of American Politics* (1952).

McCoy, Donald R., and Richard Ruetten. *Quest and Response: Minority Rights and the Truman Administration* (1973).

Meyerowitz, Joanne, ed. *Not June Cleaver: Women and Gender in Postwar America* (1994).

Patterson, James. *Mr. Republican: A Biography of Robert A. Taft* (1972).

Randall, Gregory. *America's Original G.I. Town: Park Forest, Illinois* (2000).

Rosswurm, Steven. *The CIO's Left-Led Unions* (1992)

White, Graham, and John Maze. *Henry A. Wallace: His Search for a New World Order* (1995).

Wright, Gwendolyn. *Building the Dream: A Social History of Housing in America* (1981).

Red Scare

Caute, David. *The Great Fear* (1978).

Fried, Richard. *Nightmare in Red: The McCarthy Era in Perspective* (1990).

Griffith, Robert. *The Politics of Fear: Joseph R. McCarthy and the Senate* (1970).

Klehr, Harvey, and John Earl Haynes. *Verona: Decoding Soviet Espionage in America* (1999).

Kutler, Stanley. *The American Inquisition* (1982).

Schrecker, Ellen. *Many Are the Crimes: McCarthyism in America* (1998).

Sibley, Katherine. *Red Spies in America: Stolen Secrets and the Dawn of the Cold War* (2004).

Theoharis, Athan, and John Stuart Cox. *The Boss: J. Edgar Hoover and the Great American Inquisition* (1988).

White, G. Edward. *Alger Hiss's Looking-Glass Wars: The Covert Life of a Soviet Spy* (2004).

Whitfield, Stephen. *The Culture of the Cold War* (1996).

Chapter 28
The Eisenhower Presidency

Ambrose, Stephen E. *Ike's Spies: Eisenhower and the Espionage Establishment* (1981).

Bowie, Robert, and Richard Immerman. *Waging Peace: How Eisenhower Shaped an Enduring Cold War Strategy* (1998).

Brands, H. W. *Cold Warriors: Eisenhower's Generation and American Foreign Policy* (1988).

Divine, Robert. *Eisenhower and the Cold War* (1981).

Dudziak, Mary. *Cold War Civil Rights: Race and the Image of American Democracy* (2000).

Greenstein, Fred. *The Hidden-Hand Presidency: Eisenhower as Leader* (1982).

Hixson, Walter. *Parting the Curtain: Propaganda, Culture and the Cold War* (1997).

Pach, Chester. *The Presidency of Dwight David Eisenhower* (1991).

Plummer, Brenda Gayle. *A Rising Wind: Black Americans and U.S. Foreign Affairs, 1935–1960* (1996).

Science, Politics, and Society

Divine, Robert. *The Sputnik Challenge* (1993).

Grossman, Andrew. *Neither Dead nor Red: Civil Defense and American Political Development during the Early Cold War* (2001).

Kleidman, Robert. *Organizing for Peace: Neutrality, the Test Ban, and the Freeze* (1993).

McDougall, Walter. *The Heavens and the Earth: A Political History of the Space Age* (1985).

McEnaney, Laura. *Civil Defense Begins at Home: Militarization Meets Everyday Life in the Fifties* (2000).

Olshansky, David. *Polio: An American Story* (2005).

Rhodes, Richard. *Arsenal of Folly: The Making of the Nuclear Arms Race* (2007).

Smith, Jane. *Patenting the Sun* (1990).

Titus, M. Costandina. *Bombs in the Backyard: Atomic Testing and American Politics* (1986).

Winkler, Allan. *Life under a Cloud: American Anxiety about the Atom* (1993).

The Politics of Growth

Abbott, Carl. *The New Urban America: Growth and Politics in Sunbelt Cities* (1986).

Cohen, Lizabeth. *A Consumers' Republic: The Politics of Mass Consumption in Postwar America* (2003).

Jackson, Kenneth. *The Crabgrass Frontier* (1985).

McQuaid, Kim. *Uneasy Partners: Big Business in American Politics, 1945–1990* (1993).

O'Neill, William L. *American High: The Years of Confidence, 1945–1960* (1986).

Rose, Mark. *Interstate: Express Highway Politics* (1990).

Sugrue, Thomas. *The Origins of the Urban Crisis: Race and Inequality in Postwar Detroit* (1996)

Teaford, Jon. *The Rough Road to Renaissance: Urban Revitalization in America* (1990).

Family Life and Culture

Altshuler, Glenn. *All Shook Up: How Rock 'n' Roll Changed America* (2003).

Altschuler, Glenn, and David Grossvogel. *Changing Channels: America in "TV Guide"* (1992).

Dierenfeld, Bruce. *The Battle over School Prayer: How Engle v. Vitale Changed America* (2007).

Doherty, Thomas. *Cold War, Cool Medium: Television, McCarthyism, and American Culture* (2003)

Horowitz, Daniel. *Vance Packard and American Social Criticism* (1994).

Jamison, Andrew, and Ron Eyerman. *Seeds of the Sixties* (1994).

Kaledin, Eugenia. *Mothers and More: American Women in the 1950s* (1984).

May, Elaine Tyler. *Homeward Bound: American Families in the Cold War Era* (1988).

Rupp, Leila, and Verta Taylor. *Survival in the Doldrums: The American Women's Rights Movement, 1945 to the 1960s* (1987).

Weiss, Jessica. *To Have and To Hold: Marriage, the Baby Boom, and Social Change* (2000).

Whyte, William. *The Organization Man* (1956).

The Early 1960s

Beschloss, Michael. *The Crisis Years: Kennedy and Khrushchev, 1960–1963* (1991).

Dallek, Robert. *An Unfinished Life: John F. Kennedy, 1917–1963* (2003).

Freedman, Lawrence. *Kennedy's Wars: Berlin, Cuba, Laos, and Vietnam* (2001).

Giglio, James. *The Presidency of John F. Kennedy* (1991).

Goldberg, Robert Alan. *Barry Goldwater* (1995).

Hoffman, Elizabeth Cobbs. *All You Need Is Love: The Peace Corps and the Spirit of the 1960s* (1998).

Kearns, Doris. *Lyndon Johnson and the American Dream* (1976).

Logeval, Fredrik. *Choosing War: The Last Chance for Peace and the Escalation of War in Vietnam* (1999).

Moise, Edward. *Tonkin Gulf and the Escalation of the Vietnam War* (1996).

Patterson, James T. *America's Struggle against Poverty, 1900–1985* (1986).

Stern, Mark. *Calculating Visions: Kennedy, Johnson, and Civil Rights* (1992).

Wyden, Peter. *Bay of Pigs: The Untold Story* (1979).

Struggles for Equal Rights

Acuña, Rodolfo. *Occupied America: A History of Chicanos* (1988).

Arsenault, Raymond. *Freedom Riders: 1961 and the Struggle for Racial Justice* (2006).

Branch, Taylor. *Parting the Waters: America in the King Years, 1954–1963* (1988).

Burner, Eric. *And Gently He Shall Lead Them: Robert Parris Moses and Civil Rights in Mississippi* (1994).

Chafe, William. *Civilities and Civil Rights: Greensboro, North Carolina, and the Black Struggle* (1980).

Dittmer, John. *Local People: A History of the Mississippi Movement* (1994).

Egerton, John. *Speak Now against the Day: The Generation before the Civil Rights Movement in the South* (1994).

Garrow, David. *Bearing the Cross: Martin Luther King Jr. and the Southern Christian Leadership Conference* (1986).

Goldman, Roger, and David Gallen. *Thurgood Marshall: Justice for All* (1993).

Halberstam, David. *The Children* (1998).

Hogan, Wesley. *Many Minds, One Heart, SNCC's Dream for a New America* (2007).

Huckaby, Elizabeth. *Crisis at Central High: Little Rock, 1957–1958* (1980).

Kirk, John. *Redefining the Color Line: Black Activism in Little Rock, 1940–1970* (2002).

Klarman, Michael. *From Jim Crow to Civil Rights: The Supreme Court and the Struggle for Racial Equality* (2004).

Kluger, Richard. *Simple Justice: The History of Brown v. Board of Education* (1976).

Marsh, Charles. *God's Long Summer: Stories of Faith and Civil Rights* (1998).

McWhurter, Diane. *Carry Me Home: Birmingham, Alabama: The Climactic Battle of the Civil Rights Revolution* (2000).

Mills, Kay. *This Little Light of Mine: The Life of Fannie Lou Hamer* (1993).

Payne, Charles. *I've Got the Light of Freedom: The Organizing Tradition and the Mississippi Freedom Struggle* (1995).

Ramsky, Barbara. *Ella Baker and the Black Freedom Movement* (2005).

Sitkoff, Harvard. *The Struggle for Black Equality; 1954–1992* (1992).

Thornton, J. Mills III. *Dividing Line: Municipal Politics and the Struggle for Civil Rights in Montgomery, Birmingham and Selma* (2002).

Chapter 29
Overviews

McQuaid, Kim. *The Anxious Years: America in the Vietnam-Watergate Era* (1989).

Blum, John Morton. *Years of Discord: American Politics and Society, 1961–1974* (1991).

Farber, David, *The Age of Great Dreams* (1994).

War in Vietnam

Appy, Christian. *Working-Class War: American Combat Soldiers and Vietnam* (1993).

Auster, Albert, and Leonard Quart. *How the War Was Remembered: Hollywood and Vietnam* (1988).

Buzzanco, Robert. *Masters of War* (1996).

Fitzgerald, Frances. *Fire on the Lake* (1972).

Kimball, Jeffrey. *Nixon's Vietnam War* (1998).

Levy, David W. *The Debate over Vietnam* (1991).

Schulzinger, Robert. *A Time for War: The United States and Vietnam, 1941–1975* (1997).

Shawcross, William. *Sideshow: Kissinger, Nixon, and the Destruction of Cambodia* (1979).

Sheehan, Neil. *A Bright Shining Lie: John Paul Vann and America in Vietnam* (1988).

Van De Mark, Brian. *Into the Quagmire: Johnson and the Escalation of the Vietnam War* (1991).

Van Devanter, Lynda. *Home before Morning* (1984).

Wells, Tom. *The War Within: America's Battle over Vietnam* (1994).

Young, Marilyn. *The Vietnam Wars, 1945–1990* (1991).

The Revolt of the Young

Anderson, Terry. *The Movement and the Sixties* (1995).

Bates, Tom. *Rads: The 1970 Bombing of the Army Math Research Center at the University of Wisconsin and Its Aftermath* (1992).

Breines, Wini. *Community and Organization in the New Left, 1962–1968* (1982).

Evans, Sara. *Personal Politics: The Roots of Women's Liberation in the Civil Rights Movement and the New Left* (1979).

Foley, Michael. *Confronting the War Machine: Draft Resistance during the Vietnam War* (2003).

Gitlin, Todd. *The Sixties: Years of Hope, Days of Rage* (1987).

Lyons, Paul. *The People of This Generation: The Rise and Fall of the New Left in Philadelphia* (2003).

Miller, James. *"Democracy Is in the Streets": From Port Huron to the Siege of Chicago* (1987).

Perry, Charles. *The Haight-Ashbury* (1985).

Rorabaugh, William. *Berkeley at War* (1989).

Sale, Kirkpatrick. *SDS* (1973).

Minority Rights and Minority Separatism

Countryman, Matthew, *Up South: Civil Rights and Black Power in Philadelphia* (2005).

Duberman, Martin, *Stonewall* (1993).

Giddings, Paula, and Cornel West, *Regarding Malcolm X* (1994).

Joseph, Peniel. *Waiting 'Til the Midnight Hour: A Narrative History of Black Power in America* (2006).

Mathiesson, Peter. *In the Spirit of Crazy Horse* (1983).

Padilla, Felix. *Puerto Rican Chicago* (1987).

Smith, Paul Chait, and Robert Allen Warrior. *Like a Hurricane: The Indian Movement from Alcatraz to Wounded Knee* (1996).

Thomas, Piri. *Down These Mean Streets* (1967).

Van Deburg, William L. *New Day in Babylon: The Black Power Movement and American Culture, 1965–1975* (1993).

Foreign Policy in the 1970s

Bill, James A. *The Eagle and the Lion: The Tragedy of American-Iranian Relations* (1988).

Garthoff, Raymond. *Détente and Confrontation* (1985).

Isaacson, Walter. *Kissinger: A Biography* (1992).

Le Feber, Walter. *The Panama Canal: The Crisis in Historical Perspective* (1978).

Nelson, Keith. *The Making of Détente* (1995).

Quando, William B. *Camp David: Peacemaking and Politics* (1986).

Schulzinger, Robert. *Henry Kissinger: Doctor of Diplomacy* (1989).

Smith, Gaddis. *Morality, Reason, and Power* (1986).

Talbot, Strobe. *Endgame: The Inside Story of SALT II* (1979).

Watergate and Politics in the Nixon Years

Carter, Dan T. *The Politics of Rage: George Wallace, the Origins of the New Conservatism, and the Transformation of American Politics* (1996).

Flamm, Michael. *Law and Order: Street Crime, Civil Unrest, and the Crisis of Liberalism in the 1960s* (2005).

Hoff, Joan. *Nixon Reconsidered* (1994).

Kotlowski, Dean. *Nixon's Civil Rights: Politics, Principles, and Policy* (2002).

Kutler, Stanley. *The Wars of Watergate* (1990).

Olson, Keith. *Watergate: The Presidential Scandal That Shook America* (2003).

Schudson, Michael. *Watergate in American Memory: How We Remember, Forget, and Reconstruct the Past* (1992).

Small, Melvin. *The Presidency of Richard Nixon* (1999).

Jimmy Carter and His Presidency

Carter, Jimmy. *Keeping Faith: Memoirs of a President* (1982).

Farber, David. *Taken Hostage: The Iran Crisis and America's First Encounter with Radical Islam* (2004).

Hargrove, Erwin C. *Jimmy Carter as President: Leadership and the Politics of the Public Good* (1988).

Jones, Charles O. *The Trusteeship Presidency: Jimmy Carter and the United States Congress* (1988).

Kaufman, Burton I. *The Presidency of James Earl Carter, Jr.* (1993).

Miller, William Lee. *Yankee from Georgia: The Emergence of Jimmy Carter* (1978).

Environmental Politics

Gottlieb, Robert. *Forcing the Spring: The Transformation of the American Environmental Movement* (1993).

Hays, Samuel. *Beauty, Health, and Permanence: Environmental Politics in the United States, 1955–1985* (1987).

Rome, Adam. *The Bulldozer in the Countryside: Suburban Sprawl and the Rise of American Environmentalism* (2001).

Sale, Kirkpatrick. *The Green Revolution: The American Environmental Movement, 1962–1992* (1993).

Chapter 30
Economic Change: Opportunity and Inequality

Beam, Frank, and Gillian Stevens. *American's Newcomers and the Dynamics of Diversity* (2003).

Duneier, Mitchell. *Slim's Table: Race, Respectability, and Masculinity* (1992).

Ehrenreich, Barbara. *Fear of Falling: The Inner Life of the Middle Class* (1989).

Hacker, Andrew. *Two Nations: Black and White, Separate, Hostile, Unequal* (1992).

Levy, Frank. *The New Dollars and Dreams: American Incomes and Economic Change* (1998).

Markusen, Ann, et al. *The Rise of the Gunbelt: The Military Remapping of Industrial America* (1991).

Spain, Daphne, and Suzanne Bianchi. *Balancing Act: Motherhood, Marriage and Employment among American Women* (1996).

Stewart, James B. *Den of Thieves* (1991).

Wilson, William Julius. *The Truly Disadvantaged* (1967).

Zukin, Sharon. *Loft Living: Culture and Capital in Urban Change* (1982).

The New Conservatism

Bennett, William. *The De-Valuing of America: The Fight for Our Culture and Our Children* (1992).

Critchlow, Donald. *Phyllis Schlafly and Grassroots Conservatism: A Woman's Crusade* (2005).

Edwards, Lee. *The Conservative Revolution: The Movement That Remade America* (1999).

Ehrman, John. *The Rise of Neo-Conservative Intellectuals and Foreign Affairs, 1945–1994* (1995).

Hoeveler, J. David, Jr. *Watch on the Right: Conservative Intellectuals in the Reagan Era* (1991).

Katz, Michael. *The Undeserving Poor: From the War on Poverty to the War on Welfare* (1989).

Kintz, Linda. *Between Jesus and the Market: The Emotions That Matter in Right-Wing America* (1997).

Kristol, Irving. *Neoconservatism: The Autobiography of an Idea* (1995).

Lowi, Theodore J. *The End of the Republican Era* (1995).

Murray, Charles. *Losing Ground: American Social Policy, 1950–1980* (1984).

Politics, Society, and the Mass Media

Denisoff, R. Serge. *Inside MTV* (1988).

Flournoy, Don. *CNN World Report: Ted Turner's International News Coup* (1992).

Gitlin, Todd. *Watching Television* (1987).

Goodwin, Andrew. *Dancing in the Distraction Factory: Music Television and Popular Culture* (1992).

Mills, Nicolaus. *Culture in an Age of Money* (1990).

Military and Foreign Policy

Allin, Dana H. *Cold War Illusions: America, Europe, and Soviet Power, 1969–1989* (1998).

Cortright, David. *Peace Works: The Citizen's Role in Ending the Cold War* (1993).

Draper, Theodore. *A Very Thin Line* (1991).

Freedman, Lawrence, and Efraim Karsh. *The Gulf Conflict, 1990–1991: Diplomacy and the New World Order* (1993).

Friedberg, Aaron L. *In the Shadow of the Garrison State: America's Anti-Statism and the Cold War* (2000).

Gaddis, John L. *Now We Know: Rethinking Cold War History* (1997).

Graubard, Stephen. *Mr. Bush's War* (1992).

Hogan, Michael J., ed. *The End of the Cold War: Its Meaning and Implications* (1992).

Smith, Christian. *Resisting Reagan: The U.S. Central American Peace Movement* (1997).

Tucker, Robert W., and David C. Hendrickson. *The Imperial Temptation: The New World Order and America's Purposes* (1992).

Wirls, Daniel. *Buildup: The Politics of Defense in the Reagan Era* (1992).

Politics and Politicians in the 1980s

Anderson, Martin. *Revolution* (1989).

Berman, William. *America's Right Turn: From Nixon to Bush* (1994).

Clavel, Pierre, and Wim Wiewel, eds., *Harold Washington and the Neighborhoods* (1991).

Diggins, John. *Ronald Reagan: Fate, Freedom, and the Making of History* (2007).

Gallon, Steven M. *The Democrats' Dilemma: Walter F. Mondale and the Liberal Legacy* (1992).

Greene, John Robert. *The Presidency of George Bush* (2000).

Johnson, Haynes. *Sleepwalking through History: America in the Reagan Years* (1991).

Pemberton, William. *Exit with Honor: The Life and Presidency of Ronald Reagan* (1997).

Schaller, Michael. *Reckoning with Reagan: American and Its President in the 1980s* (1992).

Sloan, John W. *The Reagan Effect: Economics and Presidential Leadership* (1999).

Stockman, David. *The Triumph of Politics: How the Reagan Revolution Failed* (1986).

Chapter 31
The New Economy

Castells, Manuel. *The Internet Galaxy: Reflections on the Internet, Business, and Society* (2001).

Gilpin, Robert. *Global Political Economy* (2001).

Kidder, Tracy. *The Soul of a New Machine* (1981).

Micklethwait, John, and Adrian Wooldridge. *A Future Perfect: The Challenge and Hidden Promise of Globalization* (2000).

Markusen, Ann, Peter Hall, and Amy Glasmeier. *High-Tech America: The What, How, Why and When of the Sunrise Industries* (1986).

Moody, Kim. *Workers in a Lean World: Workers in the International Economy* (1997)

Sassen, Saskia. *The Global City* (1991).

Wallace, James, and Jim Erickson. *Hard Drive: Bill Gates and the Making of the Microsoft Empire* (1993).

Wresch, William. *Disconnected: Haves and Have-Nots in the Information Age* (1996).

Politics

Balz, Dan, and Ronald Brownstein. *Storming the Gates: Protest Politics and the Republican Revival* (1996).

Barber, Benjamin. *The Truth of Power: Intellectual Affairs in the Clinton White House* (2001).

Colburn, David, and Jeffrey Adler, eds. *African-American Mayors: Race, Politics and the American City* (2001).

Dionne, E. J., Jr. *Why Americans Hate Politics* (1991).

Gillman, Howard. *The Votes That Counted: How the Courts Decided the 2000 Presidential Election* (2001).

Maraniss, David. *First in His Class: The Biography of Bill Clinton* (1996).

Rae, Nicol, and Colton Campbell. *Impeaching Clinton: Partisan Strife on Capitol Hill* (2003).

Renshon, Stanley. *High Hopes: The Clinton Presidency and the Politics of Ambition* (1998).

Rozell, Mark, and Clyde Wilcox. *Second Coming: The New Christian Right in Virginia Politics* (1996).

Sunstein, Cass, and Richard Epstein. *The Vote: Bush, Gore, and the Supreme Court* (2001).

The Iraq War and Foreign Policy

Baker, James A., III, and Lee Hamilton. *The Iraq Study Group Report* (2006).

Holmes, Stephen. *The Matador's Cape: America's Reckless Response to Terror* (2007).

Keegan, John. *The Iraq War* (2004).

The 9/11 Commission Report: The Final Report of the National Commission on Terrorist Attacks upon the United States (2004).

Ricks, Thomas. *Fiasco: The American Military Adventure in Iraq* (2006).

Social Issues

Anderson, Terry. *The Pursuit of Fairness: A History of Affirmative Action* (2004).

Baldwin, Peter, *Disease and Democracy: The Industrial World Faces AIDS* (2005).

Bowen, William, and Derek Bok. *The Shape of the River: The Long-Term Consequences of Considering Race in College and University Admissions* (1998).

Cohen, Michael Lee. *The Twenty-Something American Dream* (1993).

Cornell, Saul. *A Well Regulated Militia: The Founding Fathers and the Origins of Gun Control in America* (2006).

Linenthal, Edward. *The Unfinished Bombing: Oklahoma City in American Memory* (2001).

Weiss, Michael J. *The Clustered World: How We Live, What We Buy, and What It Means about Who We Are* (2000).

The New American Landscape

Abbott, Carl. *Greater Portland: Urban Life and Landscape in the Pacific Northwest* (2001).

Blackford, Mansel. *Fragile Paradise: The Impact of Tourism on Maui* (2001).

Calthorpe, Peter, and William Fulton. *The Regional City* (2001).

Ford, Larry. *Metropolitan San Diego* (2004).

Riebsame, William, et al. *Atlas of the New West* (1997).

Rothman, Hal. *Neon Metropolis: How Las Vegas Started the Twenty-First Century* (2002).

Warner, Sam Bass, Jr. *Greater Boston: Adapting Regional Traditions to the Present* (2001).

CREDITS

CHAPTER 1 Copyright (c) The Granger Collection, New York / The Granger Collection, 1; The Granger Collection, New York, 4; Muench Photography, Inc., (c) David Muench, 7; Cahokia Mounds State Historic Site, 8; Art Resource, N.Y., Benin bronze plaque. National Museum of African Art, Smithsonian Institution, Washington, DC, U.S.A. Aldo Tutino, /Art Resource, NY, 9; The Granger Collection, 12; Getty Images/De Agostini Editore Picture Library, 13; Courtesy of the Library of Congress, 16; University of Minnesota, James Ford Bell Library, From the collections of the James Ford Bell Library, University of Minnesota, Minneapolis, Minnesota, 17; Picture Desk, Inc./Kobal Collection, The Art Archive/Biblioteca Nacional Madrid/Dagli Orti, 19; The Granger Collection, Algonquian Indian village of Pomeiooc (North Carolina): watercolor, c1585, by John White, 26; Canadian Government Travel Bureau, 25.

CHAPTER 2 The Granger Collection, New York, 28; From Samuel de Champlain, "Les Voyages," Paris, 1613. Illustration opp. pg. 232. Rare Books Division, The New York Public Library, Astor Lenox and Tilden Foundations. The New York Public Library/Art Resource, NY, 32; Ira Block/National Geographic Image Collection, 35; Library of Congress, 36; PhotoEdit Inc., 39; Plimoth Plantation. (c) Cary Wolinsky/Stock Boston, 42; Courtesy, American Antiquarian Society, 43; The Freake-Gibbs Painter (American, Active 1670), "David, Joanna, and Abigail Mason," 1670. Oil on canvas, 39 1/2 x 42 1/2 in.; Frame: 42 3/4 x 45 1/2 x 1 1/2 in. Fine Arts Museums of San Francisco, Gift of Mr. and Mrs. John D. Rockefeller 3rd to The Fine Arts Museums of San Francisco, 1979.7.3, 45; The Granger Collection, New York, 47; Carolina Art Association/Gibbes Museum of Art, Thomas Coram, "View of Mulberry Street, House and Street." Oil on paper, 10 x 17.6 cm. Gibbes Museum of Art/Carolina Art Association. 68.18.01, 50; The Pennsylvania Academy of the Fine Arts, Philadelphia. Gift of Mrs. Sarah Harrison (The Joseph Harrison, Jr. Collection), 52.

CHAPTER 3 The Bridgeman Art Library International, Archives Charmet, Musee des Arts d'Afrique et d'Oceanie, Paris, France, 56; Courtesy of the Library of Congress, 60; Ira Block/National Geographic Image Collection, 64; TLM Photo, 65; Royal Albert Memorial Museum, Exeter, Devon, UK/Bridgeman Art Library, 71; Peter Arnold, Inc., 72; The Granger Collection, New York, 73; Abby Aldrich Rockefeller Folk Art Museum, Colonial Williamsburg Foundation, VA, 74; The Saint Louis Art Museum, John Greenwood, American, 1727-1792, "Sea Captains Carousing in Surinam". Oil on bed ticking. 37 3/4 x 75 1/4 in. 95.9 x 191.2 cm. The Saint Louis Art Museum (Modern Art). Museum Purchase, 78; AP Wide World Photos, 78.

CHAPTER 4 Gansevoort Limner, Susanna Truax. Mattress ticking, 1730. The Granger Collection, New York, 84; Samuel Scott (c. 1702-1772) "Old East India Wharf at London Bridge" (CT2825). (C)Victoria & Albert Museum, London/Art Resource, NY, 90; Peter Cooper "The Southeast Prospect of the City of Philadelphia" ca. 1720. The Library Company of Philadelphia, 92; Paul Revere. ca. 1768-70. John Singleton Copley, U.S., 1738-1815. Oil on Canvas, 35 1/8 x 28 1/2 in. (88.9 x 72.3 cm.). Gift of Joseph W. Revere, William B. Revere and Edward H.R. Revere, 30.781. Courtesy, Museum of Fine Arts, Boston. Reproduced with permission. (c)1999 Museum of Fine Arts, Boston. All Rights Reserved., 93; Robert Feke(1707-1752) Portrait of Benjamin Franklin(1706-1790), c.1746. Oil on Canvas, 127 x 102 cm. Courtesy of the Harvard University Portrait Collection. Bequest of Dr. John Collins Warren, 1856., 95; Collection of The New-York Historical Society, 99; Getty Images, Inc – Liaison, 99; The Granger Collection, New York, 97; Library of Congress, 100; Copyright © North Wind/North Wind Picture Archives— All rights reserved., 105; Getty Images Inc. - Hulton Archive Photos, 109; Washington-Custis-Lee Collection, Washington and Lee University, Lexington, Virginia., 112; Benjamin West (1738-1820), "The Death of General Wolfe," 1770. Oil on canvas, 152.6 x 214.5 cm. Transfer from the Canadian War Memorials, 1921 (Gift of the 2nd Duke of Westminster, Eaton Hall, Cheshire, 1918). National Gallery of Canada, Ottawa, Ontario., 114.

CHAPTER 5 Courtesy of the Library of Congress, 116; The Granger Collection, New York, 122; Samuel Adams, about 1772, John Singleton Copley, American, 1738-1815, Oil on canvas, 125.73 x 100.33 cm (49 1/2 x 39 1/2 in.), Deposited by the City of Boston, L-R 30.76c, 125; The Granger Collection, 126; North Wind Picture Archives, 127; John Singleton Copley, Portrait of Mr. and Mrs. Thomas Mifflin. Philadelphia Museum of Art: Bequest of Mrs. Esther B. Wistar to the Historical Society of Pennsylvania in 1900 and acquired by the Philadelphia Museum of Art. Accession # EW 1999-45-1, Photograph (c) Museum of Fine Arts, Boston, 128; Library of Congress, 130; Courtesy of the Library of Congress, 133.

CHAPTER 6 National Museum of American History(Smithsonian),138; Peale, Charles Willson (1741-1827). (after): George Washington after the battle of Princeton, January 3, 1777. 1779. Oil on canvas, 234.5 x 155 cm. Inv.:MV 4560. Photo: Gerard Blot. Chateaux de Versailles et de Trianon, Versailles, France. Reunion des Musees Nationaux / Art Resource, NY, 145; The Granger Collection, 146; Library of Congress, 149; Courtesy of the Library of Congress, 151; Independence National Historical Park, 153; Courtesy of the Library of Congress, 159; The Granger Collection, New York, 160; John Trumbull (American 1756-1843), "The Surrender of Lord Cornwallis at Yorktown, 19 October 1781", 1787-c. 1828. Oil on canvas, 53.3 x 77.8 x 1.9 cm (21 x 30 5/8 x 3/4 in.)), 1832.4. Yale University Art Gallery /

Art Resource., NY, 162; Benjamin West, 1783 "American Commissioners of Preliminary Negotiations". Courtesy, Winterthur Museum, 163.

CHAPTER 7 Courtesy of the Library of Congress, 168; (c) Bettmann/CORBIS, 172; Getty Images Inc. - Hulton Archive Photos, 173; The Library Company of Philadelphia, 174; Getty Images Inc. - Hulton Archive Photos, 178; Courtesy of The Historical Society of Pennsylvania Collection, Atwater Kent Museum of Philadelphia, 180; The Granger Collection, New York, 181; Charles Allen Munn Collection, Fordham University Library, Bronx, NY, 187; Independence National Historical Park, 191; Corbis/Bettmann, 191; Colonial Williamsburg Foundation, Williamsburg, VAAbby Aldrich Rockefeller Folk Art Museum, Colonial Williamsburg Foundation, Williamsburg, VA, 192.

CHAPTER 8 Courtesy of the Library of Congress, 196; (c) Bettmann/CORBIS, 202; Collection of The New-York Historical Society, Negative number 28824c, 203; The Metropolitan Museum of Art, The Edward W. C. Arnold Collection of New York Prints. Bequest of Edward W. C. Arnold, 1954. (54.90.491) Photograph (c) 1986 The Metropolitan Museum of Art., 205; The Granger Collection, New York, 214; The Granger Collection, New York, 215; AP Wide World Photos, 215; Collection of The New-York Historical Society, Neg. #33995., 216; Collection of The New-York Historical Society, negative # 35609, 217.

CHAPTER 9 The Granger Collection, New York, 220; Jane Braddick Petticolas (1791-1852) "View of the West Front of Monticello and Garden" 1825, watercolor on paper, 13 5/8 x 18 1/18 inches. Edward Owen/Monticello/Thomas Jefferson Foundation, Inc., 225; (c) Walters Art Museum, Baltimore/Bridgeman Art Library, 226; Courtesy of the Library of Congress, 231; Courtesy of the Library of Congress, 232; Courtesy of the Library of Congress, 235; Corbis/Bettmann, 236; Picture Desk, Inc./Kobal Collection, 238; Corbis/Bettmann, 242; David R. Frazier Photolibrary, Inc., 242.

CHAPTER 10 John L. Krimmel, Painting, (1786-1821), Oil on Canvas, H. 16 3/8˝ x W. 25 5/8˝. (AN: 59.131) Courtesy, Winterthur Museum, "Election Day in Philadelphia" (1815) - DETAIL., 246; Collection of The New-York Historical Society, Negative # 26275, 253; First State Election in Detroit, Michigan, 1837, c. 1837. Thomas Mickell Burnham. Gift of Mrs. Samuel T. Carson. Photograph (c) 1991 The Detroit Institute of Arts, 254; Courtesy of the Library of Congress, 255; Corbis/Bettmann, 256; The Granger Collection, New York, 257; The Granger Collection, New York, 259; Courtesy of the Library of Congress, 263; The Cincinnati Historical Society, 268; [Photographer]/Agence France Presse/Getty Images, 268.

CHAPTER 11 The Granger Collection, New York, 272; Library of Congress, 277; "Returning from the Cotton Fields in South Carolina", ca. 1860, stereograph by Barbard, negative number 47843. (c) Collection of The New-York Historical Society., 279; AP Wide World Photos, 279; Collection of The New-York Historical Society, 281; Courtesy of the Library of Congress, 282; From the Collection of the Louisiana State Museum, 284; Abby Aldrich Rockefeller Folk Art Museum, Williamsburg, VA, 285; Library of Congress, 287; Smith College, Sophia Smith Collection, Northampton, Massachusetts, 289; James Cameron (1817-1882), "Colonel and Mrs. James A. Whiteside, Son Charles and Servants", oil on canvas; c. 1858-1859. Hunter Museum of Art, Chattanooga, Tennessee, Gift of Mr. and Mrs. Thomas B. Whiteside. Hunter Museum of American Art, Chattanooga, Tennessee, 291; The Granger Collection, New York, 294; Courtesy of the Library of Congress, 295.

CHAPTER 12 North Wind Picture Archives, 298; Collection of The New-York Historical Society, Negative # 34684, 304; American Textile History Museum, Lowell, Mass., 308; Courtesy of the Library of Congress, 309; (c) Stapleton Collection/CORBIS, 310; Family Group, Joesph H. Davis, American, 1811-1865, Graphite pencil and watercolor on paper, Sheet: 24.8 x 41 cm (9 3/4 x 16 1/8 in.), Museum of Fine Arts, Boston, Gift of Maxim Karolik for the proposed M. and M. Karolik Collection of American Watercolors, (c) 2003 Museum of Fine Arts, Boston, 313; Corbis/Bettmann, 315; The Granger Collection, 319; Library of Congress, 320; Library of Congress, 322; Fenimore Art Museum, Cooperstown, New York., 327; Library of Congress, 329; Courtesy of the Library of Congress, 329.

CHAPTER 13 The Old Print Shop Inc. Kenneth M. Newman, 338; Shirt, about 1860s, unknown Sioux artist Deer skin, hair, quills, feathers, paint Denver Art Museum Collection: Native Arts acquisition funds, 1947.235 (c) Photo by the Denver Art Museum. All Rights Reserved., 341; North Wind Picture Archives, 343; Alfred Jacob Miller, "The Interior of Fort Laramie," 1858-60. The Walters Art Museum, Baltimore, 345; CRIS BOURONCLE/Agence France Presse/Getty Images, 352.

CHAPTER 14 (R)New-York Historical Society, New York, USA / Bridgeman Art Library International, 358; Courtesy of Elliot Koeppel, www.malakoff.com, 364; Courtesy of the Library of Congress, 367; (c) Bettmann/CORBIS, 368; Library of Congress, 374; Abraham Lincoln Presidental Library & Museum (ALPLM), 377; Courtesy of the Library of Congress, 382; The Granger Collection, New York, 387.

CHAPTER 15 National Archives and Records Administration, 392; Boston Public Library / Rare Books Department - Courtesy of the Trustees, 403; Center of Military

History, U.S. Army, 405; Robert A. Sabo/Getty Images, 405; Theodor Kaufmann (American, b. 1814),"On to Liberty," 1867. Oil on canvas, 36˝ x 56˝ (91.4 x 142.2 cm). The Metropolitan Museum of Art, Gift of Erving and Joyce Wolf, 1982. (1982.443.3) Photograph (c) 1982 The Metropolitan Museum of Art, 408; Manuscripts, Archives and Rare Books Division, Schomberg Center for Research in Black Culture, The New York Public Library. Astor, Lenox and Tilden Foundations, 409; Picture Collection, The Branch Libraries, The New York Public Library. Astor, Lenox and Tilden Foundations., 410; Courtesy of the Library of Congress, 415; (c) Bettmann/CORBIS, 417; National Archives and Records Administration, 421; Courtesy of the Library of Congress, 424; Picture Collection, The Branch Libraries, The New York Public Library. Astor, Lenox and Tilden Foundations, 425; Picture Collection, The Branch Libraries, The New York Public Library. Astor, Lenox and Tilden Foundations., 427.

CHAPTER 16 Courtesy of the Library of Congress, 432; The Granger Collection, New York., 437; The Granger Collection, New York., 438; Austin History Center, Austin Public Library / PICA 05496, 440; Courtesy of the Library of Congress, 441; The Granger Collection, New York., 445; Courtesy of the Library of Congress, 448; General Research & Reference Division, Schomberg Center for Research in Black Culture, The New York Public Library. Astor, Lenox and Tilden Foundations, 449; Michael Elazier, Congressional Black Caucus, June 1999, 449; Courtesy of the Library of Congress, 451; Courtesy of the Library of Congress, 453; Courtesy of the Library of Congress, 455; Courtesy of the Library of Congress, 457.

CHAPTER 17 Courtesy of the Library of Congress, 464; T. E. Armitstead Collection, University of South Alabama Archives, 473; Valentine Museum/Richmond History Center, 475; Courtesy of the Library of Congress, 477; Courtesy of the Library of Congress, 480; The Granger Collection, New York, 481; The Ohio Historical Society, 482; North Carolina Mutual Life Insurance Company, 485; West Point Museum Collections, USMA, 486; AP Wide World Photos, 486; Courtesy of the Library of Congress, 488.

CHAPTER 18 Courtesy of the Library of Congress, 492; W. Louis Sonntag, Jr., "The Bowery at Night", watercolor, 1895. Copyright Museum of the City of New York. 32.275.2, 498; Ford Motor Company, 499; Courtesy of the Library of Congress, 501; Getty Images Inc. - Hulton Archive Photos, 503; 22 Baxter Street Court. The Jacob A. Riis Collection, Museum of the City of New York., 503; The Granger Collection, New York, 505; (c) Tetra images/Getty Images, 507; Courtesy of the Nebraska State Historical Society, 510; Courtesy of the Library of Congress, 511; Courtesy of The Bancroft Library. University of California, Berkeley, 513; Brown Brothers, 515; Culver Pictures, Inc., 520.

CHAPTER 19 The Granger Collection, New York, 524; Union Pacific Historical Collection, 528; Denver Public Library, Western History Collection, Call Number : B-115, 531; Western History Collections, University of Oklahoma Libraries. Phillips Collection 357, 532; Western History Collections, University of Oklahoma Libraries, 537; Chinese mining laborers, Idaho, 76-119.2/A, Idaho State Historical Society., 538; Courtesy of the Library of Congress, 539; Courtesy Photographic Archives, Palace of the Governors, Museum of New Mexico, Santa Fe, New Mexico / DCA Negative No.:22468, 542; Courtesy of the Nebraska State Historical Society, 545; (c) Bettmann/CORBIS All Rights Reserved, 546.

CHAPTER 20 Reproduced from the collections of the Ohio Historical Society Archives/Library, 550; The Granger Collection, New York, 557; Courtesy of the Library of Congress, 558; provided courtesy HarpWeek., LLC, 562; Courtesy of the Library of Congress, 564; Kansas State Historical Society, 566; (c) Stock Montage, 2004, 568; Courtesy of the Library of Congress, 570; Culver Pictures, 571; The Granger Collection, New York, 573.

CHAPTER 21 Brown Brothers, 578; Kheel Center, Cornell University, Ithaca, NY 14853-3901, 584; Courtesy of the Library of Congress, 585; Kheel Center, Cornell University, Ithaca, NY 14853-3901, 588; Courtesy of the Library of Congress, 591; Indiana Historical Society, A70, 593; Courtesy of the Library of Congress, 595; provided courtesy HarpWeek., LLC, 598; Courtesy of the Library of Congress, 602; Portrait #65, Courtesy of the Bancroft Library, University of California, Berkeley., 606; (c) JEWEL SAMAD/AFP/Getty Images, 606.

CHAPTER 22 The Granger Collection, New York, 610; Courtesy of the Library of Congress, 616; (c) Bettmann/CORBIS, 620; Courtesy of the Library of Congress, 623; Denver Public Library, Western History Collection, Call Number: RH-234, 624; Courtesy of the Library of Congress, 625; (c) Stock Montage, 2004, 626; provided courtesy HarpWeek., LLC, 630; provided courtesy HarpWeek., LLC, 631; AP Photo/John Moore, 631; The Granger Collection, New York, 632.

CHAPTER 23 Corbis/Bettmann, 636; University of South Alabama Archives, 643; Photograph courtesy of the Hagley Museum and Library, Wilmington, Delaware, 646; National Archives and Records Administration, 647; The Granger Collection, New York, 648; John Hay Library, Brown University, 650; Getty Images Inc. - Hulton Archive Photos, 653; National Archives and Records Administration, 655; The Granger Collection, New York, 660.

CHAPTER 24 (c) Swim Ink/CORBIS, 664; Wisconsin Historical Society/WHi-5020, 670; By Permission of DuPont Automotive, 672; Courtesy of the Library of Congress, 676; Security Pacific Collection / Los Angeles Public Library, 677; By permission of Campbell Soup Company, 678; Frank Driggs Collection, 679; The Denver Public Library, Western History Collection, The Harry M. Rhoads Photograph Collection, Call Number Rh-460, 681; AP Wide World Photos, 683; Getty Images, Inc., 685; (c) Stephen Boitano/Reuters/Corbis, 688; (c) David McNew/Getty Images, Inc., 688.

CHAPTER 25 Getty Images, Inc., 692; University of Washington Libraries, Special Collections, Lee 20102, 699; Courtesy of the Library of Congress, 701; Culver Pictures, Inc. / SuperStock, 702; Courtesy of the Library of Congress, 703; Corbis/Bettmann, 706; Corbis/Bettmann, 708; Courtesy of the Library of Congress, 709; The Denver Public Library, Western History Collection, The Harry M. Rhoads Photograph Collection, Call Number Rh-557, 711; Corbis/Bettmann, 713; Courtesy of the Library of Congress, 715; UPI/CORBIS-BETTMANN, 720.

CHAPTER 26 U.S. Air Force, 724; Bildarchiv PreuBischer Kulturbesitz, Berlin, 729; National Archives and Records Administration, 734; (c) Bettmann/CORBIS, 738; National Archives and Records Administration, 741; Poster Collection / Hoover Institution Archives, 742; Poster Collection / Hoover Institution Archives, 743; Reprinted with Permission of the Dallas Morning News, 744; Courtesy of the Library of Congress, 745; (c) Bettmann/CORBIS, 750; National Archives and Records Administration, 751; Getty Images, Inc – Liaison, 753; Corbis/Bettmann, 754; Peter Arnold, Inc., 754.

CHAPTER 27 Getty Images/Time Life Pictures, 758; RKO Radio Pictures/Hulton Archive, 762; Corbis/Bettmann, 764; The Granger Collection, New York, 765; AP Wide World Photos, 766; Charles Fenno Jacobs/Getty Images, Inc., 772; Getty Images Inc. - Hulton Archive Photos, 775; AP Wide World Photos, 775; National Archives and Records Administration, 776; Corbis/Bettmann, 782; (c) Bettmann/CORBIS, 783.

CHAPTER 28 AP Wide World Photos, 786; Photo Researchers, Inc., 791; "Day dreaming" by Constantin Alajalov. (c) 1959 SEPS: Liscened by Curtis Publishing Co., Indianapolis, IN. All rights reserved. www.curtispublishing.com, 793; Getty Images Inc. - Hulton Archive Photos, 795; Picture Desk, Inc./Kobal Collection, 796; Magnum Photos, Inc., 797; Ruth Sondak, 799; Cecil Stoughton, White House/John Fitzgerald Kennedy Library, Boston, 803; AP Wide World Photos, 806; News & Record Library/ John G. Moebes, 808; (c)1976, Matt Herron/Take Stock-Images of Change, 810; UPI/CORBIS-BETTMANN, 811; Copyright (WHO) World Health Organization, 814; Courtesy of Remote Medicine, 814.

CHAPTER 29 Jeffery Blankfort /Jeroboam, 818; Getty Images Inc. - Hulton Archive Photos, 824; Corbis/Bettmann, 825; Black Star, 826; AP Wide World Photos, 828; Corbis/Bettmann, 830; (c) Bettmann/CORBIS All Rights Reserved, 831; Walter P. Reuther Library, Wayne State University, 832; Agence France Presse/Getty Images, 833; Corbis/Bettmann, 834; Corbis/Bettmann, 839; Getty Images, Inc., 839; Black Star, 840; (c) Vince Streano / CORBIS All Rights Reserved, 845; (c) Wally McNamee/CORBIS, 846; SIPA Press, 847.

CHAPTER 30 Peter Arnold, Inc., 850; Corbis/Bettmann, 855; Photofest, 856; Corbis/Bettmann, 858; (c)The New Yorker Collection 2008 Koren from cartoonbank.com. All Rights Reserved., 859; National Archives and Records Administration, 861; Corbis/Bettmann, 861; P. F. Bentley/PFPIX.COM, 863; PhotoEdit Inc., 864; AP Wide World Photos, 867; Corbis/Sygma, 869; Black Star, 877; AP Wide World Photos, 880.

CHAPTER 31 James Natchway/VII (detail), 884; (c) IRA WYMAN/CORBIS SYGMA, 888; AP Wide World Photos, 891; Corbis Digital Stock, 895; Agence France Presse/Getty Images, 899; Stephen Jaffe Photography, 904; (c) Reuters/CORBIS, 906 AP Wide World Photos, 908; (c) DAEMMRICH BOB/CORBIS SYGMA, 909; AP Wide World Photos, 910; Getty Images, Inc., 913; AP Wide World Photos, 913; (c) Michael Ainsworth / Dallas Morning News / CORBIS All Rights Reserved, 914; Library of Congress, 915 .

INDEX

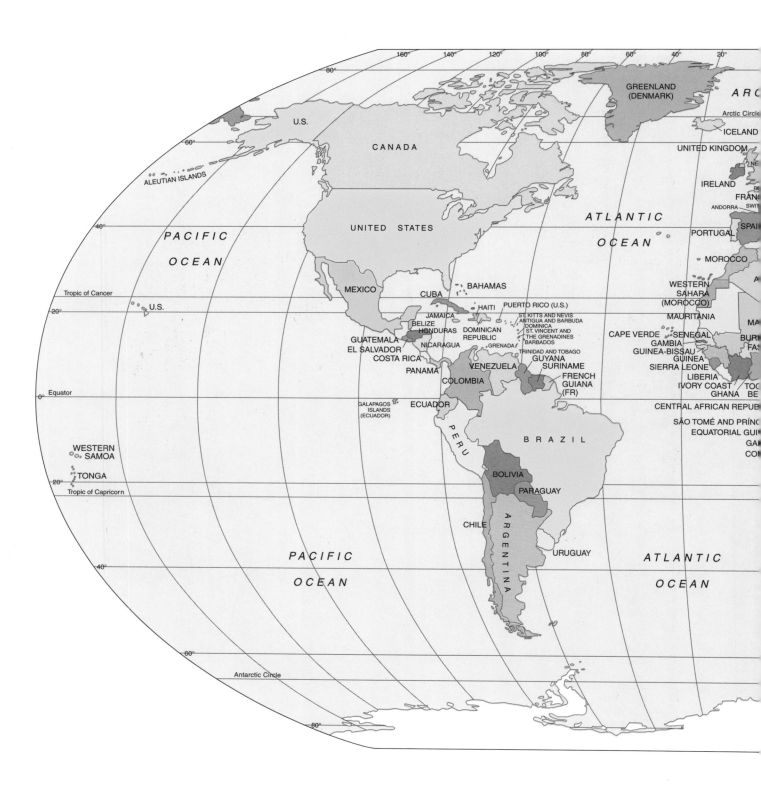